AMERICAN DEFENSE POLICY

SO-BJU-332

AMERICAN DEFENSE POLICY

Seventh Edition

Edited by

PETER L. HAYS, BRENDA J. VALLANCE, and ALAN R. VAN TASSEL

The Johns Hopkins University Press, Baltimore and London

© 1965, 1968, 1973, 1977, 1982, 1990, 1997 The Johns Hopkins University Press
All rights reserved. First edition 1965
Seventh edition 1997
Printed in the United States of America on acid-free paper
06 05 04 03 02 01 00 99 98 97   5 4 3 2 1

The Johns Hopkins University Press
2715 North Charles Street
Baltimore, Maryland 21218-4319
The Johns Hopkins Press Ltd., London

The views and conclusions expressed by military personnel in articles contained in this volume are those of the authors and not necessarily those of the USAF Academy, the Department of Defense, or any particular service thereof.

Library of Congress Cataloging-in Publication Data

American defense policy / edited by Peter L. Hays, Brenda J. Vallance,
and Alan R. Van Tassel.—7th ed.
p.   cm.
Includes bibliographical references and index.
ISBN 0-8018-5472-5 (hardcover: alk. paper).—ISBN 0-8018-5473-3 (paperback: alk. paper)
1. United States, Military policy. I. Hays, Peter L. II. Vallance, Brenda J. III. Van Tassel, Alan R.
UA23.A626   1997
355′.033073—dc20   96-26544
                                                          CIP

A catalog record for this book is available from the British Library.

TO COLONEL SAMUEL NELSON DREW

who gave his life in pursuit of peace and freedom—
values so treasured by Americans
and yet so elusive around the world

CONTENTS

FOREWORD

It is with great pleasure that I write the foreword to the seventh edition of *American Defense Policy*. More than thirty years ago, as the acting chairman of the Political Science Department at the United States Air Force Academy, I was "present at the creation" of the first edition of this textbook. In the early 1960s, the Air Force Academy had taken the lead among the country's undergraduate institutions by teaching defense policy to all cadets. However, we lacked textbooks specifically designed for this task. Thus in that first edition (1965) we sought to bring together in one volume the seminal articles in the nascent field of defense policy studies. That first edition met our needs at the academy well, and by filling a special niche it also contributed to the burgeoning growth in defense policy studies during the 1960s. Even today, I am very pleased with how well that first edition reads.

The five subsequent editions of *American Defense Policy*, published during the Cold War (1968, 1973, 1977, 1982, and 1990), built upon this foundation of excellence as each sought to reflect accurately the then-current state of U.S.–Soviet relations as well as to include the most important articles dealing with the major defense issues of the day. Many of these editions continued with the practice we had established in the first by reprinting seminal articles in the field, while others focused more on the hottest current defense issues. Those of us teaching or actually developing American defense policy during the "long twilight struggle" of the Cold War often turned to these volumes for information, inspiration, and guidance. I know of no other single textbook that consistently captured the essential nature of American defense processes and policies so completely and so well.

Now, for this first post–Cold War edition of *American Defense Policy*, the editors have chosen to build incrementally upon the previous editions by emphasizing two overarching themes: (1) the most important of the various models and paradigms designed to simplify and explain the defense policy processes of the Cold War era; and (2) the major issue areas that represent the most important security challenges for the United States in today's fundamentally restructured international security environment. This two-level incremental approach is highly appropriate; there is as much to be relearned and understood about how America formulated defense policy during the Cold War era as there is to be learned about today's security challenges. The seventh edition of *American Defense Policy* reemphasizes several of the classic pieces that examine how American defense policy is formulated and also includes many articles that deal with today's most important security issues. For the student, this approach highlights both the enduring aspects of the political process by which American defense policy is formulated and the possible application of this process to today's major security challenges.

Through this approach, the seventh edition of *American Defense Policy* provides a context and continuity too often lacking in defense policy textbooks. Unlike many recent books, this text does not assume that American defense policy for the post–Cold War era will be written anew on a blank slate or will deal with our new security challenges in completely novel ways. Instead of glossing over the Cold War, the editors use this critical period as a laboratory—they evaluate the utility of the major conceptual models from the Cold War in explaining the major defense policy outcomes of this era and point out the most helpful of these models. *American Defense Policy* not only presents these models to help the reader understand how defense policy was formulated during the Cold War but also uses them to create a foundation for examining today's most important security issues. I believe this is an appropriate focus for the study of defense policy: the continuing development and refinement of models and paradigms designed to explain the complex process of formulating American defense policy. While acknowledging that these models are far from complete, the editors also remind us that the study of American defense policy during the Cold War has already provided us with theoretical tools that remain useful even in today's changed security environment. Moreover, the editors' approach is highly appropriate from the perspective of organizational process and bureaucratic politics. Barring major changes to the current decision-making structure for American defense policy (and I do not at present envision any), our near-term security decisions will be made within the structure developed for the Cold War. Thus understanding how this structure operates remains critical even in the post–Cold War era. Indeed, a solid understanding of the theoretical context in which these processes operate would seem to be a prerequisite if we are to be most effective in allocating our limited defense resources to the daunting security challenges of the post–Cold War world.

In sum, I believe this book will help students better grasp and understand the complex processes involved in making American defense policy. It will help them draw important lessons from our experiences during the Cold War while also providing them with a glimpse of many of the more important security challenges to come. Maintaining America's security will require much hard work preparing the students who will make up our next generation of defense leadership for the new security challenges they will inevitably face.

To the cadets at the Air Force Academy and the other professionals who will use this book, I wish you Godspeed and wisdom in your preparation for these challenges.

BRENT SCOWCROFT
Lieutenant General, U.S. Air Force (Retired)
Bethesda, Maryland

PREFACE

The faculty at the United States Air Force Academy has been teaching courses in defense policy since 1958, three years after the first class of cadets entered the newest of America's military academies. Back then, U.S. defense policy was a new academic discipline, and there was no textbook that brought the growing literature together in one volume. Hence, this book was born in 1965 "to organize American defense policy into a coherent field of study."

Considerable progress has been made toward that goal during the past three decades, with *American Defense Policy* playing a role in the discipline's evolution. The six previous editions, published periodically throughout the Cold War, have been consulted by defense scholars, decision makers, and practitioners. They also have been used in a variety of undergraduate and graduate courses in political science, international relations, U.S. national security, and military affairs.

This, however, is the first post–Cold War edition, and as such it has been substantially revised. Gone, like the Cold War itself, is the previous emphasis on global ideological conflict and the containment and deterrence policies designed to deal with it. Underscored instead are the regional security challenges facing the United States and contemporary defense issues such as domestic missions for the armed forces, peacekeeping operations, the revolution in military affairs, and information warfare.

Increased emphasis also has been placed on the actors who influence American defense policy and the processes they use to do so. Unlike the policy shifts resulting from fundamental changes in the international and domestic environments, these aspects of American defense policy have remained essentially the same. The United States, in other words, continues to use Cold War institutions and procedures to devise its post–Cold War defense policies.

In addition to these content changes, *American Defense Policy* has returned to the popular "reader" format of the first five editions. Rather than original articles that summarize the relevant literature, the seventh edition is a compendium of published materials. Moreover, almost all of the readings are new to this text, and a number of essential government documents have been included, most in their entirety.

Although much about the seventh edition has changed, some things remain the same. In one form or another, *American Defense Policy* always has been organized along the lines of David Easton's political

system model, although this edition uses it more extensively and explicitly than the others. As it is used here, the model has eight main components— inputs, communications channels, conversion structures, outputs, lenses, and feedback within an international environment and a domestic environment—which are treated individually or collectively in the book's five sections.[1]

Part I provides some important introductory material and examines the context in which American defense policy is made. As the defense policy process model illustrates, the international and domestic environments provide inputs that are acted upon by the communications channels and conversion structures. Outputs also become inputs by feeding back into the system.

Part II, which introduces the actors with the greatest influence on American defense policy, corresponds with the model's communications channels and conversion structures. Communications channels are the means by which inputs are aggregated, organized, and represented to the conversion structures, while conversion structures are the makers and implementers of defense policy—namely, the institutions of government and their associated bureaucracies. Because these different actors view American defense policy through their own individual and organizational lenses, coalition building, bargaining, and compromise are necessary if outputs are to be produced and implemented. Agreement is made possible by shared images and rules of the game, both of which result largely from the actors' common strategic and political cultures.

Part III explores the formulation of American defense policy. The discussion here is organized around three topics: the major formal processes by which the communications channels and conversion structures interact; the way these processes operate when the elements in Parts I–III are brought together, as illustrated in case studies; and factors that affect the quality of defense decisions.

Part IV presents the most significant outputs of the post–Cold War era: the current national security and military strategies of the United States, its defense policies across the spectrum of armed conflict, and its policies regarding issues such as arms control, proliferation, and civil-military relations.

Part V examines the regional and technological challenges presented by the international and domestic environments. It also offers some predictions

Defense Policy Process Model

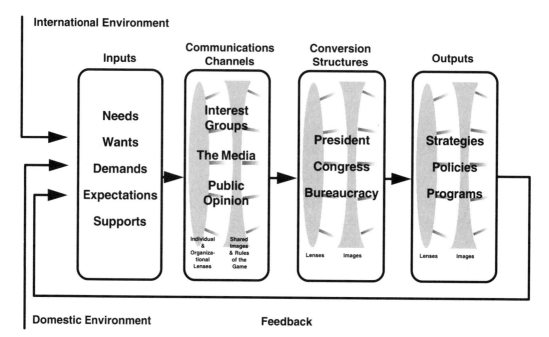

about the future of American defense policy and presents a summary of the book and its contents.

Like the book's format, our dedication to including the best possible readings in *American Defense Policy* has not changed. We began with an exhaustive literature search, from which more than fifty articles were selected, edited, and organized for presentation. Whenever possible, classic works were included. This was especially the case for Parts II and III, since the areas they cover have been least affected by the end of the Cold War. The best recent articles were used wherever the classics no longer pertain. We wrote brief introductions to each part and the opening and closing readings to frame and integrate the other materials.

Although defense policy has been deemphasized in favor of other foreign and domestic interests in recent years, it is still vital. The international system is still anarchic—that is, there is no sovereign authority above that of states—and war remains a persistent characteristic of international relations. States, therefore, must ultimately rely on themselves for their security and are obliged to recruit, train, equip, deploy, and use military forces to deter armed conflicts and, if deterrence fails, fight and win them. They must do so not just for today's threats but also for those they may encounter in the future.

Most of today's threats, however, do not seriously impinge on U.S. defense interests, and conflicts that would have compelled military intervention during the Cold War no longer do so. This means greater choice, and greater choice demands choosing wisely, especially in the face of limited resources and other

interests. The ability of the United States to make these decisions, however, has been hampered by the complexity of an emerging multipolar international system and the continuing uncertainty of the post–Cold War era, both of which increase the likelihood of misperception and miscalculation. This trend is further exacerbated by the indifference of many Americans to defense issues at a time when fewer of them have had military experience or appreciate what armed forces can and cannot do.

Still, defense policy remains too important to be left to political elites, especially unelected bureaucrats. If defense is a vital state interest and the state is to be popularly governed, then its citizens must understand defense policy making and have a voice in how much is spent on the military, what those dollars buy, and how its armed forces are used. In the words of the first edition's editors, "This book concerns a subject of commanding interest for all thoughtful citizens."

NOTE

1. The discussion and model that follow are largely adapted from Schuyler Foerster and Edward N. Wright, "The Twin Faces of Defense Policy: International and Domestic," in *American Defense Policy*, 6th ed., ed. Schuyler Foerster and Edward N. Wright (Baltimore: Johns Hopkins University Press, 1990), 10–14; and James M. Keagle, "Introduction and Framework," in *Bureaucratic Politics and National Security: Theory and Practice*, ed. David C. Kozak and James M. Keagle (Boulder, Colo.: Lynne Rienner Publishers, 1988), 17–23.

ACKNOWLEDGMENTS

Producing *American Defense Policy* has long been an important tradition in the Department of Political Science at the United States Air Force Academy. Many of the early editors have gone on to distinguished careers as Air Force officers, leading academics, and recognized American statesmen. We are privileged to take up this task for the newest edition of this unique text. We hope our efforts, to build on previous works yet reflect the reality of the new defense environment, continue the tradition of quality emphasized by earlier editors.

Creating a textbook of this magnitude is always a time-intensive and difficult job requiring the assistance of many people. Indeed, many people have contributed their time and energy to this effort, and we wish we could thank each and every one of them. The following is an effort to let at least some of them know how much we appreciate their help on this project.

First, our thanks to Lieutenants Julian Cheater and Jessica Nickodem, who took on the early task of searching through journals, periodicals, special studies, and books to find that seminal piece we just had to have but could not remember where we saw it. In their effort to meet our demands, they remained surprisingly enthusiastic and never lost their composure despite our often confusing directions.

We also are indebted to Lieutenants Mike Lyons and Jim Hackbarth, Captain Greg Rose, and especially Major John Buckley, all of whom waded through the task of obtaining copyright permissions; Lieutenants Allen Duckworth, Brian Gregory, Reid Rasmussen, and Jim Roy for their assistance in proofreading this volume; and Tom Terry and Judy Danielson for their administrative support. We are likewise grateful to Colonel Doug Murray, who guided our initial efforts and approved our overall "plan of attack," and Colonel Bill Berry and the entire Department of Political Science at the Air Force Academy. Colonel Berry provided the space, time, and encouragement we needed to tackle this job. Our department colleagues were gracious in working around our countless editing meetings and tolerated our frequent disappearances into closed-door "discussion" sessions.

We also have been guided by a kind and understanding editor in the person of Dr. Henry Tom at the Johns Hopkins University Press. We are grateful for his advice and patience, which we tried on a regular basis.

As always, we could not have made it through this process without the understanding and encouragement of our families. To Hillary, Justin, Emily, Molly, Peter, and Steven we send our deep thanks. And especially to Constance, Dena, and Don, thanks for being there and withstanding the ups and downs, the weekends and evenings spent reading and writing, and the times it seemed that this project would never end.

Finally, we dedicate this book to some very important people. To the men and women of the Air Force Academy, both officers and cadets, we hope this edition of *American Defense Policy* will enhance your professional development and your vision for tomorrow. Today, America faces many significant challenges. Those you must face, however, have clear implications for our freedom, the future of democracy, and the assurance of peace. Good luck in your future endeavors.

PART I

AN INTRODUCTION TO
AMERICAN DEFENSE POLICY

INTRODUCTION

ALAN R. VAN TASSEL

Part I of *American Defense Policy* provides some important introductory material and examines the context in which U.S. defense policy is made. The introductory material appears in the first two chapters. Chapter 1 explores the meaning of the term "American defense policy" and the traditional uses and limits of military power, while Chapter 2 examines how scholars, policy makers, and practitioners think about defense policy making. Chapter 3 of this section discusses the international and domestic environments affecting American defense policy today.

In the opening essay of Chapter 1, Peter Hays, Brenda Vallance, and Alan Van Tassel define American defense policy in four ways. First, American defense policy is obviously "a plan or course of action regarding the recruitment, training, organizing, equipping, deployment, and use of U.S. military forces." It is, in other words, an output of the American political system. That output, however, is just one part of a broader goal—national security. Second, as the military component of the U.S. national

security strategy, American defense policy refers to "protecting the United States, its citizens, and its interests through the threatened and actual use of military power." Third, American defense policy is a political process. As such, it can be viewed as a system containing inputs from the international and domestic environments, the means by which those inputs are communicated to policy makers and implementers, the policy makers and implementers themselves, and the outputs that result from their actions and that feed back into the system to create additional inputs (see the model below). Moreover, who the players are and how they interact with one another can affect the policies and programs produced. Fourth, American defense policy is "a field of study that combines international relations and American politics with elements of comparative politics, political philosophy, history, economics, law, psychology, and sociology."

The second essay of Chapter 1 examines the traditional uses and limits of military power. In "To What Ends Military Power?" Robert Art categorizes

Defense Policy Process Model: Environment, Inputs, and Feedback

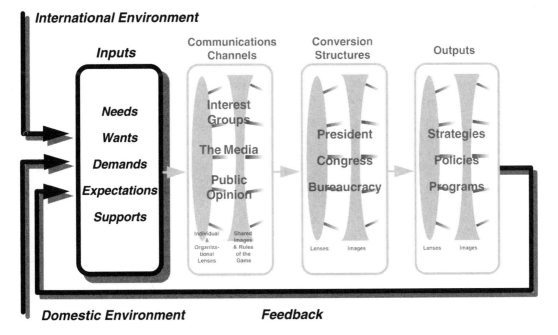

the uses as defense, deterrence, compellence, and "swaggering." Defense refers to using military power to stop or minimize the effects of an actual or planned attack, while deterrence means keeping adversaries from doing something they otherwise would have done. Art also equates defense with counterforce targeting (using armed force against other armed forces) and deterrence with countervalue targeting (threatening the use of armed force against an adversary's population or industry). Conversely, compellence is getting adversaries to do something they otherwise would not have done, while swaggering is "a residual category, the deployment of military power for purposes other than defense, deterrence, or compellence."

Despite its many uses, military force is but one instrument of national power. Thus while armed forces can help a state succeed politically and economically in its relations with other states, they cannot substitute for sound political and economic policies. "No matter how militarily powerful a nation is," Art writes, "force cannot achieve those things for which only political skill and economic industry are suited."

In the essays that follow, especially those in Chapter 3 and Parts IV and V, the following questions come to mind. Are Art's uses of military power still applicable today? How, for instance, do military operations other than war fit his typology? Moreover, should armed forces be used for contingencies such as operations other than war, or should they be reserved for more traditional military roles and missions? Are there fewer or more limitations on the use of force today? Have the political and economic aspects of power become more important, for example? Finally, what is the future of military force in the post–Cold War era? For his part, Art predicts that the military will remain a vital component of national security. "If the past be any guide to the future," he writes, "then military power will remain central to the course of international relations."

Of the numerous approaches to politics and defense policy, Chapter 2 examines the two taken by most American scholars, policy makers, and practitioners: the bureaucratic politics model and realism. As noted in Chapter 1 and illustrated by the model above, the basic assumption of the bureaucratic politics model is that individuals and organizations are the principal actors in defense policy making, and they view inputs to the defense policy process through their own perceptual lenses, thereby creating "competing interests." Policy making, therefore, requires coalition building, bargaining, and compromise, which take place through identifiable processes or "action channels." Agreement is made possible by shared images and general concordance regarding the rules of the game, both of which result largely from the actors' common strategic and political cultures. Moreover, the "pulling and hauling" between actors is not confined to the making of policy, that is, to "decision games." Rather, it affects policy implementation, or "action games," as well.

Allison and Halperin's discussion, "Bureaucratic Politics: A Paradigm," is a classic example of the literature on this subject. Graham Allison is the author of *Essence of Decision*, a groundbreaking examination of the Cuban Missile Crisis from three theoretical perspectives.[1] Morton Halperin is best known for *Bureaucratic Politics and Foreign Policy*.[2] In this reading, however, the authors combine two of Allison's perspectives into a single paradigm and illustrate it using a four-part strategy. It should be noted that this essay was written before the Congress, the media, and the public became major players in American defense policy and thus tends to neglect their roles. This issue is addressed in the subsequent literature and in this book. Still, Allison and Halperin's essay remains an excellent introduction to the bureaucratic politics model.

In contrast to Allison and Halperin, Robert Art, in "A Critique of Bureaucratic Politics," approaches politics and policy making from the realist perspective. As elaborated in Chapter 1, the realist paradigm assumes that states are the principal actors in international relations and can, for all intents and purposes, be considered unitary, rational actors. Thus in Art's view the bureaucratic politics model gives inadequate weight to the president's power, overstates the influence of organizational factors on individuals' decisions, is ambiguous and unreliable, and is not backed by empirical evidence.

Despite these shortcomings, Art admits his critique "does not constitute a good case against ever using a bureaucratic paradigm." Once the realist perspective has been considered, the bureaucratic politics model "may tell us some things that we would otherwise overlook," especially when it comes to budget and procurement decisions and the implementation of policy. Moreover, we should remind ourselves that every effort to describe, explain, and predict political phenomena has its detractors and that realism also has been criticized for lacking precision, predictive power, and empirical support. To that end, one might ask whether Art is holding the bureaucratic politics model to a higher standard than other political science theories.

Chapter 3 examines the context or environment in which defense policy is formulated, and it is here that we begin using the defense policy process model to organize the book's readings. As the model demonstrates, the international and domestic environments create inputs that are acted upon by the communications channels and conversion structures. Communications channels are the means by which inputs are aggregated, organized, and represented to the conversion structures, while conversion structures are the makers and implementers of policy. Outputs also become inputs by feeding back into the system.

As the Cold War drew to a close, there were numerous predictions about the future of the international environment. Owen Harries categorized these predictions into four models. The first is the interdependence-global village model. Its basic assumption is that: "the countries of the world are now so closely intermeshed, with such a density of transactions, that the old zero-sum games of power politics no longer apply. Conflict and competition will soon be replaced by harmony and complementarity. Instead of the separation that fostered ignorance and suspicion, there will be growing familiarity and understanding."[3] The second model, *Pax Democratica*, assumes that the number of democracies is growing and that democracies do not go to war with each other.[4] Therefore, the amount of world peace should increase and the number of interstate armed conflicts should diminish. The collective security model, on the other hand, portends that the United Nations finally will operate as envisioned by its founders.[5] Finally, the *Pax Americana* model predicts that the United States, as the sole remaining superpower, will "impose order on a recalcitrant world."[6] A fifth possibility, and the one Harries seems to advocate, is that the New World Order will be at least as disorderly as the Cold War world. It will be a "New World Disorder," to use Ted Galen Carpenter's phrase.[7]

Donald Snow's description of the contemporary international environment in "National Security in a World of Tiers" suggests that a combination of *Pax Democratica* and New World Disorder has emerged. According to Snow, the Cold War's three worlds—those of the industrialized democracies, communist states, and developing countries—have given way to a two-tier system, each with "a different set of governing rules and dynamics." The first tier consists of interdependent capitalist democracies, among which it is "essentially impossible" to conceive of war. "These countries," Snow writes, "have more in common than they have that divides them." The second tier, on the other hand, is composed of a diverse group of states that tend to be undemocratic, noncapitalistic, and "marked by instability and the potential or actuality of violence," including primordial nationalism, religious and ethnic strife, international violence, and the proliferation of weapons of mass destruction.

Most of the second tier's instability and violence, however, do not pose a threat to first tier security and will not compel member states to intervene militarily. The result of this situation will be what Snow calls an "interest–threat mismatch." Snow therefore predicts that "the United States will employ armed forces where it chooses to do so, not where it has to fight," and closes with some suggested guidelines for the use of military power in the post–Cold War era.

Despite the efforts of Snow and others, the nature of the international environment remains a controversial subject, and one that has obvious repercussions for U.S. defense policy. Also controversial is the proper balance between America's domestic and international agendas. In the final selection of Part I, Peter Peterson and James Sebenius argue for "the primacy of the domestic agenda." Although Peterson and Sebenius acknowledge that international security threats remain in the post–Cold War era, they contend that America's economic and social problems are even more pressing. Its economic problems include budget deficits, trade deficits, low savings and investment rates, and a decline in global competitiveness. Its social issues include inadequate public education, poverty, crime, and declining expectations for a better future. These domestic difficulties can, however, affect the nation's ability to defend itself. It is impossible, for instance, to buy sophisticated weapons if there are no funds to pay for them. Likewise, it is impossible to develop, manufacture, operate, and maintain sophisticated weapons without an educated populace.

Focusing too much on the domestic agenda today, however, would be as short-sighted as focusing too much on the international agenda during the Cold War. The United States is a global power with global interests in an interdependent world where the lines between international and domestic issues are increasingly blurred. In addition, threats to U.S. security interests continue to exist, as Peterson and Sebenius concede. Thus the United States must be prepared to protect its interests, perhaps in conjunction with other states, perhaps with armed force. To do otherwise is unconscionable and courts disaster.

NOTES

1. Graham T. Allison, *Essence of Decision: Explaining the Cuban Missile Crisis* (Boston: Little, Brown, 1971).

2. Morton H. Halperin, with the assistance of Priscilla Clapp and Arnold Kanter, *Bureaucratic Politics and Foreign Policy* (Washington, D.C.: Brookings Institution, 1974).

3. Owen Harries, "Defining the New World Order: An Impossibility," *Harper's Magazine* 282 (May 1991): 60.

4. Ibid.

5. Ibid., 61.

6. Ibid.

7. Ted Galen Carpenter, "The New World Disorder," *Foreign Policy* 84 (Fall 1991): 24–39.

CHAPTER 1

DEFINING AMERICAN
DEFENSE POLICY

WHAT IS AMERICAN DEFENSE POLICY?

PETER L. HAYS, BRENDA J. VALLANCE, AND ALAN R. VAN TASSEL

The best way to begin a discussion of American defense policy is to go straight to the heart of the matter: the term itself. A great deal of confusion can arise if one fails to recognize that this term has more than one meaning. The various meanings it can convey are illustrated in the following sentences. "I agree with the president's defense policy regarding Haiti." "American defense policy needs to be viewed more broadly and take factors such as economic competitiveness into consideration." "More Americans should be concerned with and involved in the defense policy making process." "All Air Force Academy cadets are required to study U.S. defense policy." What these sentences reveal is that defense policy can be viewed as a plan or course of action, a component of U.S. national security, a political process, and a field of study. The political process definition also introduces the model used to organize the readings in this book.

AMERICAN DEFENSE POLICY AS A PLAN OR COURSE OF ACTION

The meaning that defense policy first brings to mind is "a plan or course of action, as of a government, political party, or business, intended to influence and determine decisions, actions, and other matters."[1] Thus American defense policy can be seen as a plan or course of action regarding the recruitment, training, organizing, equipping, deployment, and use of U.S. military forces.

Examples of this definition cover the spectrum of armed conflict depicted in Figure 1. At one end of the spectrum is U.S. nuclear policy, including arms control and counterproliferation efforts. Representative of this aspect of American defense policy is the Defense Counterproliferation Initiative, which identifies a "range of possible government responses" to the proliferation and use of nuclear, chemical, and biological weapons of mass destruction (WMD). One of these responses may be to try to persuade state and nonstate actors that it is not in their interest to acquire WMD; another may be to deny state and nonstate actors access to the knowledge, technology, and materials required to build WMD. Still others may be to seek arms control agreements and confidence-building measures; deter the use of WMD through threats of retaliation; maintain a capability to destroy WMD during times of conflict; or create active and passive defenses against the use of WMD. Active defenses include antiballistic missile systems, while passive defenses include protective clothing and vaccines against chemical and biological agents.[2]

At the other end of the spectrum are military operations other than war, military assistance and humanitarian aid, for example. Military assistance "helps friends and allies deter and defend against aggression" through programs such as foreign military sales, foreign military financing, international military education and training, and military-to-military contacts.[3] U.S. armed forces provided humanitarian assistance to sixty countries during fiscal

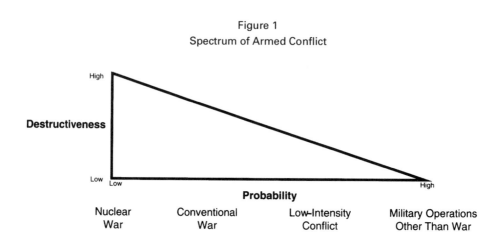

Figure 1
Spectrum of Armed Conflict

1994. This included the delivery of approximately 85,000 tons of supplies to Rwandan refugees, the former Yugoslavia, and the Kurds in northern Iraq.[4]

Between the two extremes are conventional war and low-intensity conflict. A recent example of conventional war is Operation Desert Shield/Desert Storm, during which the United States organized a thirty-eight-nation coalition to protect Saudi Arabia and expel Iraq from Kuwait. Although the opposing forces were the largest to face one another since the Korean War, Iraq was defeated after just forty-three days of fighting—which included a mere 100-hour air-land campaign—an accomplishment largely made possible by the coalition's air supremacy, technological superiority, and near monopoly on intelligence information.[5] Low-intensity conflict can be defined as "political-military confrontations between contending states or groups below conventional war and above the routine, peaceful competition among states."[6] Examples include insurgency operations by guerrilla forces and counterinsurgency operations against guerrilla forces.

Although American defense policy is *intended* to influence and determine decisions, actions, and other matters regarding U.S. military forces, it also can have unintended or unforeseen consequences, as is evident from some of the current concerns of American defense scholars, policy makers, and practitioners. What, for instance, has a decade of budget and manpower reductions done to America's ability to recruit quality soldiers, sailors, airmen, and marines? How do declining operations and maintenance budgets affect the military's ability to train realistically for a variety of contingencies? Should the U.S. military be organized so that the army, navy, air force, and Marine Corps each have their own air forces? What effect will nonlethal weapons like "sticky foams" that immobilize people have on the use of U.S. armed forces around the globe? As U.S. military members spend more time away from their homes and families, what will happen to morale? How will nontraditional roles and missions like peacekeeping operations affect America's combat readiness?

Our first definition of American defense policy applies to much of Parts IV and V of this book. Chapter 12 is about U.S. national military strategy; Chapters 13–16 examine American defense policies across the spectrum of armed conflict; Chapter 17 discusses U.S. civil–military relations; and Chapters 18 and 19 look forward to the future. Viewing American defense policy in this way, however, begs a fundamental question: what is the policy's objective? In attempting to answer this question, one encounters the term's second meaning: American defense policy is also a component of U.S. national security.

AMERICAN DEFENSE POLICY AS A COMPONENT OF U.S. NATIONAL SECURITY

The terms "American defense policy" and "U.S. national security" are often used interchangeably. They are not synonymous, however, and a distinction can and should be made between them. National security refers to protecting the United States, its citizens, and its interests through the threatened and actual use of power. Power is A's ability to get B to do something that B otherwise would not have done (compellence). It also is A's ability to stop B from doing something that B otherwise would have done (deterrence). The sources of national power are numerous. Among the tangible sources are geography, population, natural resources, industrial capacity, and military capability. Intangible sources include national character, morale, and leadership.[7] American defense policy is therefore but one component of U.S. national security. The military component in turn consists of numerous tangible and intangible elements, including the size and structure of a force, the quantity and quality of weapons, and the kind of strategy and tactics pursued.[8]

The other major components of U.S. national security are economic and political power. Economic power depends on a country's natural resources and industrial capacity. It is most commonly used to compel and deter through sanctions affecting international trade, international finance, and international monetary policy. Trade sanctions include embargoes, boycotts, tariffs, and a number of nontariff barriers, such as quotas and voluntary export restraints. Financial sanctions encompass foreign aid, foreign direct investment, the control of access to financial assets, and the payment or withholding of dues for international organizations such as the United Nations. International monetary policy has to do with the regulation of currency exchange rates to influence a variety of factors, including economic growth and the balance of trade.[9] Political power usually is exercised through diplomacy, which can be defined as "the formation and execution of foreign policy on all levels, the highest as well as the subordinate."[10] Diplomacy is conducted by representing interests, gathering and interpreting information, sending and receiving signals, negotiating agreements, and managing crises.[11]

The major components of U.S. national security are reflected in the Clinton administration's *National Security Strategy of Engagement and Enlargement,* which finds three broad goals emerging from the "new threats and new opportunities" of the post–Cold War era. The first is "to credibly sustain our security with military forces that are ready to fight"; the second is "to bolster America's economic revitalization"; and the third is "to promote democracy abroad."[12] The first half of the Clinton administration's national security strategy is presented in Chapter 12, the second half in Chapter 18.

It is also important to note that power is a complex concept, the components of national security are highly interrelated, and the components affect and are affected by both international and domestic factors. Power is complex because it is dynamic, subjective, relative, and situational. It is dynamic in that it changes over time. What is a significant source of power today may not be as important tomorrow.

Figure 2
Components of National Security

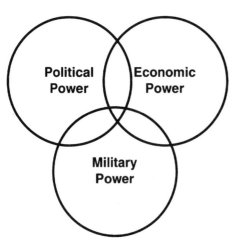

What is subjective is the perception of power in the eye of the beholder. That perception matters. If a country is considered powerful, it is unlikely to be attacked, even if the perception is incorrect. Power is assessed in relation to the actor against which it is directed. Iraq may be more powerful than Kuwait and Saudi Arabia, for example, but it is not as powerful as the United States. It is also assessed in relation to the situation in which it is being threatened or used. Although U.S. military power succeeded during World War II, it failed during the Vietnam War.[13]

As Figure 2 indicates, the political, economic, and military components of national security are highly interrelated. Diplomacy, for instance, is more likely to succeed if it is backed by a credible threat of economic sanctions or military force. These combinations of power often are referred to as coercive diplomacy. A threat is credible if the threatening party has both the power and the will to use that power. Economic and military power also are highly interrelated. It is difficult for a state to sustain a strong military if it does not have a strong economy. In many cases all three components of national security come into play. Currency exchange rates, for example, can affect political relations between states, the competitiveness of certain industries or economic sectors, and the cost of basing U.S. forces overseas. Likewise, foreign military sales can strengthen political ties between the states involved, provide economic profits for the weapons' manufacturers, and reduce the cost of domestic weapons purchases. These examples also indicate that the components of national security affect and are affected by both international and domestic factors. In other words, U.S. national security and American defense policy are "Janus-like" and face the international and domestic systems simultaneously.[14]

As our second definition suggests, national security involves the determination of national interests; the identification of threats to those interests; and the formulation and implementation of strategies, policies, and programs to reduce the identified threats. Although the primary objective of U.S. national security—which is to protect the United States, its citizens, and its interests—has not changed much since the founding of the Republic, the nation's interests, threats, and strategies have changed. These changes can be divided according to the periods in which they occurred: before the Cold War, during the Cold War, and after the Cold War.

Before the Cold War, U.S. security interests focused on protecting the lives, liberty, and property of American citizens from domestic threats.[15] Although the British and Spanish continued to threaten the United States during its first few decades of independence—witness the War of 1812—they no longer did so by the 1820s: "All factions in Britain seemed finally reconciled to the former colonies being independent. Spain no longer posed a threat. It had ceded to the United States Florida, the mouth of the Mississippi, and disputed territory to the west. Its American colonies had mostly become independent, and the British navy prevented any continental European power from helping Spain reconquer them."[16] Indian uprisings and regional disputes persisted, however, with the latter resulting in a bloody civil war. Thus the United States' security strategy was largely one of international isolationism. This strategy was made possible by weak neighbors to the north and south, oceans to the east and west, and the "free security" provided by the British navy.[17] It was reinforced by a strong desire not to become involved in Europe's conflicts and a fear of large standing armies. The former is illustrated by George Washington's Farewell Address, in which he declared that the "true policy" of the United States was to "steer clear of permanent alliances with any portion of the foreign world."[18] The latter resulted from British history and America's colonial experiences. Following the Puritan Revolution, Britain forbade a standing army during peacetime, and in their Declaration of Independence the American colonists listed numerous "injuries and usurpations" associated with the stationing and conduct of British troops. Consequently, both countries relied on the mobilization of citizen-soldiers during wartime and quickly demobilized their forces when peace returned.[19]

The Cold War brought a sea change in U.S. national security and American defense policy. The United States emerged from the Second World War a superpower with interests extending well beyond its borders. The Soviet Union also emerged a superpower and threatened U.S. interests around the globe, especially in Western Europe. Moreover, Soviet intercontinental ballistic missiles could destroy targets in the United States in less than thirty minutes. To overcome these threats, the United States adopted a strategy of containment and deterrence that included large standing nuclear and conventional forces, various peacetime alliances, and active intervention in the affairs of other nations.[20] The military component of U.S. national security clearly was elevated to the status of "high politics" during this period, while the political and economic components were considered "low politics."

The end of the Cold War brought another sea change to U.S. national security and American defense policy. Although the United States still has global interests, the threats are more difficult to identify, are less vital to U.S. security, and may neither demand nor deserve a military response. Thus the other components of U.S. national security have received increased emphasis. In fact, some analysts contend that the most significant threats to U.S. security are economic ones such as the national debt and trade deficits, social problems such as drug abuse and poor education, demographic problems such as overpopulation and migration, environmental concerns such as clear air and global warming, and resource concerns such as "energy security" and "food security."[21] As a result, there is no consensus yet on what America's post–Cold War security strategy ought to be. Many, for instance, disagree with the Clinton administration's call to "remain actively engaged in global affairs" and "promote the spread of democracy abroad."[22] There also is no consensus on when and how the military component of U.S. national security should be used.[23]

These debates are likely to continue for years to come. As they do, we should keep the following warnings in mind. First, if the definition of national security is too broad, it will lose its utility for political discourse. Or, as Joseph Romm put it, "If the term national security is not already meaningless there is serious risk that it is rapidly becoming so, as every problem the nation faces is characterized as a threat to its security."[24] Second, many national security issues are actually international, transnational, or global problems that require multinational solutions. Examples include many of the economic, social, demographic, environmental, and resource issues mentioned above. They also include a number of military security issues, such as nuclear nonproliferation. Third, if the military is used to solve nonmilitary problems, it may fail or create even greater problems. After the United States' stunning victory over Iraq in the Persian Gulf War, for instance, there were numerous calls for the military to become involved in "nontraditional" missions such as law enforcement, medical care, education, public works, and environmental cleanup. Opponents argue that these tasks are best left to civilian agencies and could reduce the military's combat readiness or lead to its overinvolvement in domestic politics.[25] Finally, we need to recognize that post–Cold War security issues will, for the foreseeable future, be examined and dealt with using structures and processes created during the Cold War. That point leads us to our third definition—American defense policy is a political process.

AMERICAN DEFENSE POLICY AS A POLITICAL PROCESS

In his oft-cited examination of the level-of-analysis problem, J. David Singer noted that "in any area of scholarly inquiry, there are always several ways in which the phenomena under study may be sorted and arranged for purposes of systematic analysis. Whether in the physical or social sciences, the observer may choose to focus upon the parts or upon the whole, upon the components or upon the system."[26] Thus far, we have focused on the state as a whole using the realist paradigm.[27] The realist paradigm makes two simplifying assumptions. First, it assumes that states are the principal actors in the international system. Although other actors exist, their effects generally can be ignored. Second, it assumes that states are unitary, rational actors. States are unitary in that their actions can be understood without examining the politics occurring within them; they are considered rational actors because they weigh the advantages and disadvantages of each possible option before selecting the one with the greatest net benefit.[28] Thus, as Figure 3 illustrates, states can be viewed as "black boxes" that determine their interests; identify threats to those interests; and select the best strategies, policies, and programs to address the identified threats. One need not look inside the state to understand its actions.

While the realist paradigm may be useful for some phenomena, such as crisis decision making and politics at the systemic level of analysis, its explanatory power is greatly diminished when it comes to more routine decisions and the politics occurring within states.[29] For the latter, a model like the one depicted in Figure 4 is more appropriate. The defense policy process model combines and modifies the political system model from the last edition of this text and another model presented in David Kozak and James Keagle's *Bureaucratic Politics and National Security*.[30] As such, the defense policy process model consists of inputs, communications channels, conversion structures, outputs, lenses, and feedback within an international environment and a domestic environment. Our description of the model's operation is drawn largely from the literature on bureaucratic politics, which arose in reaction to the realist paradigm and its assumptions.[31]

The defense policy process model begins with inputs. These consist of needs, wants, demands, expectations, and supports from three sources: the international environment, the domestic environment, and feedback from previous outputs. Most military threats to U.S. national security originate in the international environment, which can be described as anarchic. In other words, there is no sovereign power above that of states. Therefore conflict and war remain persistent features of international relations, and states must be prepared to deter them and, if deterrence fails, to fight and win. This is what Ken Waltz called the permissive cause of war. "With many sovereign states, with no system of law enforceable among them, with each state judging its grievances and ambitions according to the dictates of its own reason or desire—conflict, sometimes leading to war, is bound to occur."[32]

Figure 3
Realist Paradigm

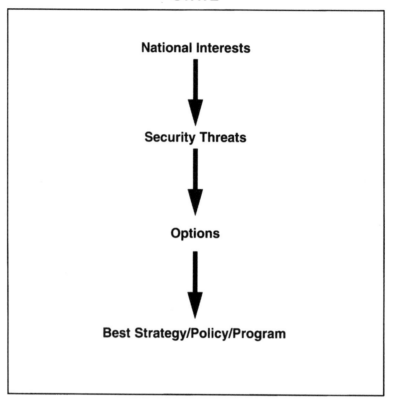

STATE

National Interests

Security Threats

Options

Best Strategy/Policy/Program

Although the anarchic nature of the international system is the permissive cause of conflict and war, the immediate causes occur at every level of analysis. States, for example, may disagree about the distribution of power in the international system; societies may hold conflicting values or pursue opposing ideologies; and individual leaders may interpret events differently.[33] A classic interstate explanation of war is the security dilemma, a term coined by John Herz:[34] "In an anarchic international system, State A may sincerely increase its level of defense spending only for defensive purposes and self-preservation, but it is rational for other states to assume the worst and impute aggressive intentions to State A. They therefore also increase their level of arms, leading State A to feel insecure and contemplate a further increase in military spending. Hence, by initially trying to enhance its own security, State A sets in motion a process that results ironically in its feeling less secure."[35] It was events like these that Thucydides blamed for the Peloponnesian War: "What made war inevitable was the growth of Athenian power and the fear which this caused in Sparta."[36]

While most military threats to U.S. security originate in the international environment, the domestic environment shapes America's responses to those

threats. A key component of the domestic environment is U.S. strategic culture—how Americans think about national security and defense. In addition to the isolationism and fear of large standing armies mentioned above, American strategic culture is marked by an emphasis on public opinion, a dissociation and depreciation of power and diplomacy, utopianism, a crusading spirit, and impatience. If democracy means the government is accountable to the people, then their opinions must play a role in the making of policy, including defense policy. Although the American public is involved in defense policy making, it believes that conflicts can and should be resolved without resorting to military force and that diplomacy should involve "open covenants, openly arrived at." To that end, Americans feel the U.S. example is one that should be emulated by others—a utopian "city on a hill," so to speak. Americans also believe the United States should only participate in "just wars" fought for self-defense or collective security. On those occasions when the United States must resort to arms, America's crusading spirit demands total victory. In addition, Americans are impatient and want a quick return to peace, which they feel is the norm in international relations.[37] U.S. strategic culture is a subset of America's political culture, which often is described using concepts like liberty, equality, democracy, civic duty, and individual responsibility.[38]

Domestic politics, including a variety of economic, social, and environmental issues, also can affect American defense policy. Although U.S. defense spending has declined by about 40 percent since the mid-1980s, it still exceeds $240 billion and therefore remains an inviting target for additional reductions. Those who want to spend defense dollars elsewhere often argue that the issues of concern to them also pertain to U.S. national security and are even more pressing than America's defense needs, in view of the current international environment. Among America's most pressing economic problems are its annual budget deficits, its national debt (which is in excess of $5 trillion), slow economic growth, continuing trade deficits, and low savings rates. Its social issues include poverty, crime, and shortfalls in the public education system. In addition, significant environmental problems exist in the forms of pollution, toxic waste, acid rain, and global warming. Because budgets are finite, tough choices have to be made between these and other public policy issues. To make these choices, however, the government needs to know how much defense spending is enough. Unfortunately, this question is extremely difficult to answer. In fact, a definitive answer can be found in only one place—on the field of battle.

Inputs also are created through feedback from previous outputs. As outputs are implemented, they are assessed to determine whether they should be continued, terminated, or modified. Overwhelm- ingly positive feedback creates needs, wants, demands, expectations, and supports to continue an output. Overwhelmingly negative feedback creates inputs to end a strategy, policy, or program. Mixed feedback falls somewhere between these extremes. A decision in any of these directions, however, results in additional inputs for the actors involved in the American defense policy process.

Unlike the realist paradigm, the defense policy process model assumes that individuals and organizations are the most important actors. More specifically, the president, the Congress, the bureaucracy, interests groups, the media, and public opinion are the principal actors in the American defense policy process. Interest groups, the media, and public opinion serve as communications channels—the second box in our model—and "provide for the aggregation, organization, and representation of needs, wants, demands, expectations, and supports" to the government institutions.[39] The president, the Congress, and the bureaucracy are conversion structures—the model's third box. They "receive the varied, and frequently conflicting, system inputs and convert them into decisions of government."[40]

Each of these actors has its own sources of power. The president, for instance, is commander in chief of the U.S. military, while the Congress declares war, raises and maintains armed forces, and makes rules and regulations for those forces. Bureaucratic organizations like the Department of Defense (DOD) provide information and analysis to decision makers and implement outputs. Information and money are the primary sources of interest group power and are

Figure 4
Defense Policy Process Model

International Environment

| Inputs | Communications Channels | Conversion Structures | Outputs |

Domestic Environment   **Feedback**

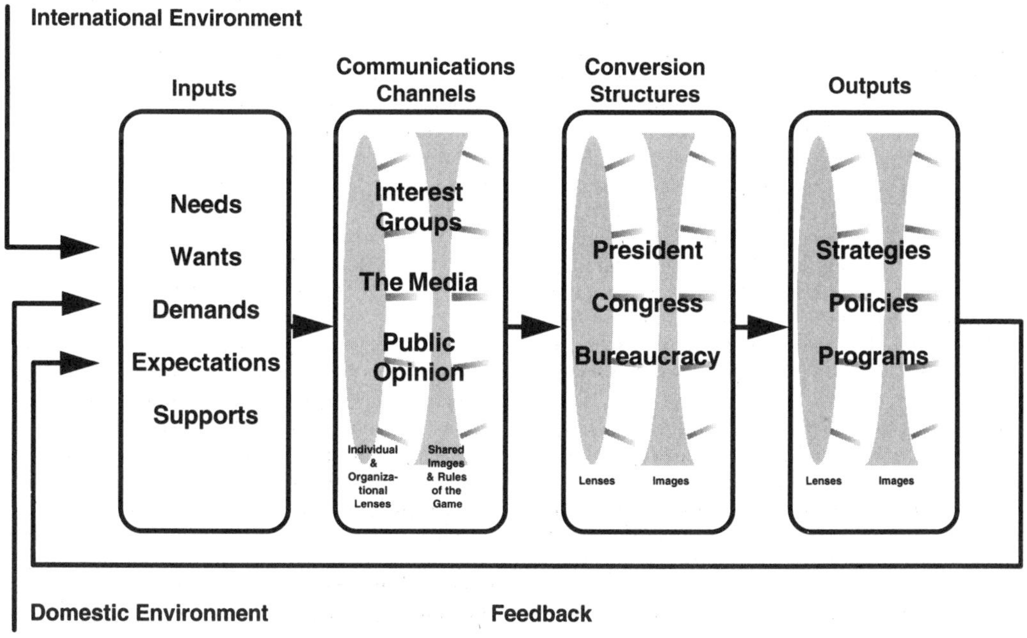

used to lobby the government and the American people. Information also is the media's most important asset, since the media largely determine what we see and how we see it. For its part, public opinion usually sets the broad parameters for American defense policy. In high-profile cases, however, it also can affect the specifics of a strategy, policy, or program, thereby reminding us that power is dynamic, subjective, relative, and situational—a fact that applies to individuals and organizations as well as states.

Along with their own sources of power, the individuals and organizations involved in the American defense policy process have their own preferences regarding ends and means. The president, for example, may want to use military forces to implement a peace agreement. The Congress may not be convinced that vital U.S. interests are at stake, however, and the DOD may want to give diplomacy and economic sanctions more time to work. Meanwhile, some interest groups may support the president and lobby for his plan, whereas others may consider the peace unjust and disagree with the ends as well as the means. The media's role includes reporting dissension within the government, while the public probably will remain skeptical about risking American lives in faraway places. Understanding American defense policy, therefore, requires a knowledge of not only who the actors are but also their points of view and why they hold those views. This divergence of opinion is represented by the concave lenses in each of the model's last three boxes.

Because there are numerous actors and each has its own powers and perspectives, converting inputs into outputs requires coalition building, bargaining, and compromise. These occur through a number of formal, informal, and ad hoc processes. The most important formal defense processes are defense budgeting, defense acquisition, and the interagency process. Defense budgeting and defense acquisition occur largely within the DOD, while the interagency process coordinates potential outputs across executive branch agencies. Achieving agreement among the actors is made easier by what Morton Halperin and Arnold Kanter called "widely shared values and images of international reality" and certain "rules of the game."[41] These images and rules are associated mainly with the actors' common strategic and political cultures and are represented by the convex lenses in each of the model's last three boxes. They also result from "the constitutional provisions, statutes, regulations, procedures, customs, traditions, etc. which organize the government and structure the process by which decisions are made and actions are undertaken."[42]

In addition to emphasizing individuals and organizations, the defense policy process model assumes that decision making is not rational since, more often than not, the actors fail to agree on interests and threats, examine every alternative, consider every advantage and disadvantage, and select optimal solutions. Rather, in most cases decision making is incremental, results in satisficing, and falls prey to a variety of psychological and sociological limitations. Decision making is incremental because political, economic, and military issues are highly complex. Thus small steps are taken to avoid mistakes that could lead to catastrophe, especially when the nation's security is at stake. Decision making also is incremental because it requires coalition building, bargaining, and compromise. Often small steps are the only ones on which the actors can agree.[43] Satisficing occurs when solutions are adopted because the actors can agree to them rather than searching for the single best solution.[44] As Roger Hilsman put it: "The test of a policy is not whether it is in fact the most rational means for achieving an agreed-upon objective or whether the objective is in the true national interest. The test of a policy is whether enough of the people and organizations having a stake in the policy and holding power agree to that policy."[45] Graham Allison and Morton Halperin were thinking along similar lines when they wrote that "the actions of a nation result not from an agreed upon calculus of strategic interests, but rather from pulling and hauling among individuals with differing perceptions and stakes."[46] Decision making also is affected by psychological and sociological limitations such as stress, groupthink, and misperception. Groupthink occurs "when the group members' striving for unanimity override their motivation to realistically appraise alternative courses of action."[47]

The end result of the defense policy process is outputs like the strategies, policies, and programs discussed earlier in this essay. The pulling and hauling that occurs along the way is not confined to policy making, however, since the actors' powers and perceptions do not end once a decision has been made. Rather, they continue with the implementation of policy. In fact, conflict and competition may grow even stronger, especially when outputs are vaguely stated and must be interpreted. Thus "particularism and parochialism are reborn, with resultant organizational twists to implementation that can take the actors in numerous directions."[48] Some may implement an output in both its letter and spirit, while others may try to limit its effects to the greatest extent possible. Once again, shared images and rules of the game help the various actors find common ground.

AMERICAN DEFENSE POLICY AS A FIELD OF STUDY

As the discussion thus far indicates, American defense policy is rooted in a number of academic disciplines. The most important are international relations and American politics. Others of some bearing are comparative politics and political philosophy—the other major subfields of political science—along with history, economics, law, psychology, and sociology.

Because U.S. defense policy is Janus-like and faces both the international and domestic systems simultaneously, it requires an understanding of international relations and American politics. International relations is concerned with the interaction of state and nonstate actors within an anarchic international system. Although states remain the most powerful actors in international relations, nonstate actors include intergovernmental organizations (IGOs), nongovernmental organizations (NGOs), multinational corporations (MNCs), and private individuals. Each can affect U.S. defense policy, as recent events have illustrated. Two prominent IGOs, the United Nations and the North Atlantic Treaty Organization, are involved in the conflict in Bosnia, as are NGOs such as the International Red Cross. More important, each of these organizations has its own agenda, which can conflict with U.S. interests and objectives. Likewise, MNCs are motivated by economic profit and may act contrary to government wishes. One recent example is an American firm's efforts to sell Iran crop-dusting aircraft that also could have been used to deliver chemical and biological weapons, possibly against U.S. and allied forces. Private individuals also can become involved in foreign and defense matters, sometimes without the government's full endorsement, as was the case when former President Jimmy Carter negotiated with Haitian and North Korean officials.

Although American defense policy is focused on threats from the international system, it is made and implemented by domestic actors and influenced by domestic politics. Thus an understanding of "the authoritative allocation of values" for the United States is essential to understanding U.S. defense policy.[49] American politics is concerned with government institutions and other actors that influence U.S. strategies, policies, and programs. It also examines the processes by which decisions are made and the outputs that emerge from them. Defense is but one form of public policy and must be balanced with other needs, wants, demands, and expectations.

While not as central as international relations and American politics, comparative politics and political theory make important contributions to the study of U.S. defense policy. The former helps us better understand U.S. defense policy by placing it in a comparative context.[50] The latter, unlike the other subfields of political science, focuses on normative rather than empirical questions. In other words, political philosophy is concerned with "what ought to be" versus "what is." Although good policy certainly must be grounded in empirical reality, political philosophy helps guide decision makers by providing them with a vision for the future. This is a central premise of E. H. Carr's The Twenty Years' Crisis: "Any sound political thought must be based on elements of both utopia [i.e., what ought to be] and reality [i.e., what is]. Where utopianism has become a hollow and intolerable sham, which serves merely as a disguise for the interests of the privileged, the realist performs an indispensable service in unmasking it. But pure realism can offer nothing but a naked struggle for power which makes any kind of international society impossible."[51]

Textbooks in the field demonstrate the importance of political science to understanding U.S. defense policy. They also suggest the significance of history, economics, and law. U.S. and world history shed light on the evolution of American defense policy. Like comparative politics, history provides a much-needed sense of perspective. As for economics, much of American defense policy is about budgeting and acquisition. Furthermore, the economics of defense has become increasingly important since the end of the Cold War and in the face of continuing U.S. budget deficits.[52] Likewise, American defense policy is affected by domestic and international law. U.S. law includes constitutional provisions regarding defense; legislation such as the annual defense authorization and appropriations acts; and executive orders, which have the force of law. International law includes a growing number of treaties and customs. Thus although the international system is anarchic, it is not chaotic. States create, and usually abide by, international law because it is in their interest to do so; it provides order and predictability within the international system, just as domestic law does within states.

Finally, because policies are decided and implemented by individuals, often working together in groups, some knowledge of psychology and sociology also is useful to the study of American defense policy. Pertinent psychological factors range from personality disorders to ego defense mechanisms to misperception. As one author put it: "The basic assumption at this level of analysis is that individuals do make a difference. It matters that Boris Yeltsin sits in the Kremlin instead of Josef Stalin; it makes a difference whether George Bush sits in the Oval Office instead of Jimmy Carter. It matters, presumably, because in most cases wars are precipitated by the decisions of individual leaders and their advisers."[53] Sociological or group-level factors include groupthink and bureaucratic politics. Decision making, therefore, is less rational than many believe it is or wish it to be.

In summary, American defense policy can be defined in four ways. First, it is a plan or course of action regarding the recruitment, training, organizing, equipping, deployment, and use of U.S. military forces. Second, it entails protecting the United States, its citizens, and its interests through the threatened and actual use of military power. Third, it is a political process that includes inputs, communications channels, conversion structures, outputs, lenses, and feedback within an international environment and a domestic environment. And fourth, it is a field of study that combines international relations and American politics with elements of comparative politics, political philosophy, history, economics, law, psychology, and sociology. In short, American defense policy is as interesting as it is complex.

NOTES

1. The American Heritage Dictionary, 2d college ed. (Boston: Houghton Mifflin, 1982), 959.

2. U.S. Department of Defense, *Annual Report to the President and the Congress* (Washington, D.C.: GPO, February 1995), 72–73.

3. Ibid., J-1.

4. Ibid., 23.

5. Anthony H. Cordesman, "Gulf War, 1991," in *International Military and Defense Encyclopedia,* vol. 3, ed. Trevor N. Dupuy (Washington, D.C.: Brassey's, 1993), 1110–16.

6. U.S. Department of Defense, *Department of Defense Dictionary of Military and Associated Terms* (Washington, D.C.: GPO, 23 March 1994), 222.

7. See, for instance, Hans J. Morgenthau, *Politics among Nations: The Struggle for Power and Peace,* 5th ed. (New York: Alfred A. Knopf, 1973), 112–49.

8. Ibid., 120–24.

9. For an excellent discussion of economic sanctions and their effectiveness, see David A. Baldwin, *Economic Statecraft* (Princeton, N.J.: Princeton University Press, 1985).

10. Morgenthau, *Politics among Nations,* 140.

11. Daniel S. Papp, *Contemporary International Relations: Frameworks for Understanding,* 3d ed. (New York: Macmillan, 1991), 503–5.

12. William J. Clinton, *A National Security Strategy of Engagement and Enlargement* (Washington, D.C.: GPO, February 1995), i.

13. Amos A. Jordon, William J. Taylor Jr., and Lawrence J. Korb, *American National Security: Policy and Process,* 4th ed. (Baltimore: Johns Hopkins University Press, 1993), 9.

14. Huntington, for example, observed that defense policy stands at the crossroads of two worlds: international politics and domestic politics. See Samuel P. Huntington, *The Common Defense: Strategic Programs in National Politics* (New York: Columbia University Press, 1961), 1.

15. This era generally is ignored in texts about U.S. national security and American defense policy. An excellent overview of this period can be found in Ernest R. May, "National Security in American History," in *Rethinking America's Security: Beyond Cold War to New World Order,* ed. Graham Allison and Gregory F. Treverton (New York: W. W. Norton, 1992), 94–114.

16. Ibid., 96.

17. The term "free security" was coined by historian C. Vann Woodward in "The Age of Reinterpretation," *American Historical Review* 66, no. 1 (1960): 1, 2–8.

18. George Washington, "Farewell Address," in *Two Centuries of U.S. Foreign Policy: The Documentary Record,* ed. Stephen J. Valone (Westport, Conn.: Praeger, 1995), 7.

19. Although the United States dabbled in imperialism during the late 1800s and early 1900s, militaristic mind-sets remained antithetical to basic American values, and real or potential military power seldom shaped American foreign policy in decisive ways.

20. In contrast to the pre–Cold War period, the Cold War saw volumes written about U.S. national security and American defense policy. An excellent starting point is Richard Smoke, *National Security and the Nuclear Dilemma: An Introduction to the American Experience in the Cold War,* 3d ed. (New York: McGraw-Hill, 1993).

21. See, for example, Joseph J. Romm, *Defining National Security: The Nonmilitary Aspects* (New York: Council on Foreign Relations Press, 1993). The Clinton administration's national security strategy is representative of this trend; it states that "not all security risks are military in nature. Transnational phenomena such as terrorism, narcotics trafficking, environmental degradation, rapid population growth, and refugee flows also have security implications for both present and long term American policy" (Clinton, *Strategy of Engagement,* 1).

22. Clinton, *Strategy of Engagement,* iii.

23. For an excellent introduction to U.S. national security and American defense policy in the post–Cold War era, see Donald M. Snow, *National Security: Defense Policy for a New International Order,* 3d ed. (New York: St. Martin's Press, 1995).

24. Romm, *Defining National Security,* 6–7.

25. This issue is discussed at length in Chapter 17, "Civil–Military Relations."

26. J. David Singer, "The Level-of-Analysis Problem in International Relations," in *International Politics and Foreign Policy: A Reader in Research and Theory,* ed. James Rosenau (New York: Free Press, 1969), 20.

27. Realism traces its roots to Thucydides' *History of the Peloponnesian War.* Its most prominent modern proponent is Hans Morgenthau, who discussed the approach's six principals in *Politics among Nations.*

28. An excellent discussion of realism and its assumptions can be found in Paul R. Viotti and Mark V. Kauppi, *International Relations Theory: Realism, Pluralism, Globalism,* 2d ed. (New York: Macmillan, 1993), 35–83. Also see James E. Dougherty and Robert L. Pfaltzgraff Jr., *Contending Theories of International Relations: A Comprehensive Survey,* 3d ed. (New York: HarperCollins, 1990), 81–135.

29. For a discussion of policy types and how they are handled differently by the actors involved, see Randall B. Ripley and Grace A. Franklin, *Congress, the Bureaucracy, and Public Policy,* 3d ed. (Homewood, Il.: Dorsey Press, 1984). Ripley and Franklin distinguish between three types of policy: crisis, strategic, and structural. Crises are "short-run responses to immediate problems that are perceived to be serious, that have burst on the policymakers with little or no warning, and that demand immediate action." Strategic policies are "designed to assert and implement the basic military and foreign policy stance of the United States." Structural policies are those primarily aimed at "procuring, deploying, and organizing personnel and material, presumably within the confines and guidelines of previously determined strategic decisions" (ibid., 26–27).

30. See Schuyler Foerster and Edward N. Wright, "The Twin Faces of Defense Policy: International and Domestic," in *American Defense Policy,* 6th ed., ed Schuyler Foerster and Edward N. Wright (Baltimore: Johns Hopkins University Press, 1990), 3–17; and James M. Keagle, "Introduction and Framework," in *Bureaucratic Politics and National Security: Theory and Practice,* ed. David C. Kozak and James M. Keagle (Boulder, Colo.: Lynne Rienner, 1988), 16–25.

31. The most important works in this literature include Graham Allison, *Essence of Decision: Explaining the Cuban Missile Crisis* (Boston: Little, Brown, 1971); I. M. Destler, *Presidents, Bureaucrats and Foreign Policy: The Politics of*

Organizational Reform (Princeton, N.J.: Princeton University Press, 1974); Morton H. Halperin with the assistance of Priscilla Clapp and Arnold Kanter, *Bureaucratic Politics and Foreign Policy* (Washington, D.C.: Brookings Institution, 1974); and Morton H. Halperin and Arnold Kanter, eds., *Readings in American Foreign Policy: A Bureaucratic Perspective* (Boston: Little, Brown, 1973). Much of the bureaucratic politics literature predates the Congress's resurgence and the growing importance of interest groups, the media, and public opinion and therefore discounts their effects on American foreign and defense policy. Later efforts began to include these actors, however. See, for example, Graham T. Allison and Peter Szanton, *Remaking Foreign Policy: The Organizational Connection* (New York: Basic Books, 1976).

32. Kenneth N. Waltz, *Man, the State and War* (New York: Columbia University Press, 1959), 159.

33. For a thorough examination of the many causes of war, see Greg Cashman, *What Causes War? An Introduction to Theories of International Conflict* (New York: Lexington Books, 1993). See also Seyom Brown, *The Causes and Prevention of War*, 2d ed. (New York: St. Martin's Press, 1994).

34. See John Herz, "Idealist Internationalism and the Security Dilemma, *World Politics* 5, no. 2 (1950): 157–80.

35. Viotti and Kauppi, *International Relations Theory*, 592–93.

36. Thucydides, *History of the Peloponnesian War,* trans. Rex Warner (New York: Penguin Books, 1988), 49.

37. Jordan, Taylor, and Korb, *American National Security*, 47–61.

38. See, for example, James Q. Wilson and John J. DiIulio Jr., *American Government*, 6th ed. (Lexington, Mass.: D.C. Heath, 1995), 80.

39. Foerster and Wright, "The Twin Faces of Defense Policy," 11.

40. Ibid., 12.

41. Morton H. Halperin and Arnold Kanter, "The Bureaucratic Perspective: A Preliminary Framework," in *Readings in American Foreign Policy,* 19.

42. Ibid.

43. On the concept on incrementalism, see Charles E. Lindblom, "The Science of 'Muddling Through,'" *Public Administration Review* 19, no. 2 (1959): 79–88.

44. The term "satisficing" was coined by Herbert Simon in *Administrative Behavior* (New York: Macmillan, 1959).

45. Roger Hilsman, *The Politics of Policy Making in Defense and Foreign Affairs: Conceptual Models and Bureaucratic Politics* (Englewood Cliffs, N.J.: Prentice-Hall, 1987), 65.

46. Graham T. Allison and Morton H. Halperin, "Bureaucratic Politics: A Paradigm and Some Policy Implications," in *Theory and Policy in International Relations*, ed. Raymond Tanter and Richard H. Ullman (Princeton, N.J.: Princeton University Press, 1972), 57.

47. Irving Janis, *Groupthink,* 2d ed. (Boston: Houghton Mifflin, 1982), 9.

48. Keagle, "Introduction and Framework," 22.

49. This is David Easton's classic definition of politics.

50. An excellent source that examines every region of the world and key states within each is Douglas J. Murray and Paul R. Viotti, ed., *The Defense Policies of Nations: A Comparative Study*, 3d ed. (Baltimore: Johns Hopkins University Press, 1994).

51. Quoted in Viotti and Kauppi, *International Relations Theory,* 43.

52. An excellent example of this literature is Ethan B. Kapstein, *The Political Economy of National Security: A Global Perspective* (Columbia: University of South Carolina Press, 1992).

53. Cashman, *What Causes War?* 37.

TO WHAT ENDS MILITARY POWER?

ROBERT J. ART

It is vital to think carefully and precisely about the uses and limits of military power. That is the purpose of this essay. It is intended as a backdrop for policy debates, not a prescription of specific policies. It consciously eschews elaborate detail on the requisite military forces for scenarios *a . . . n* and focuses instead on what military power has and has not done, can and cannot do. Every model of how the world works has policy implications. But not every policy is based on a clear view of how the world works. What, then, are the uses to which military power can be put? And what is the future of force?

WHAT ARE THE USES OF FORCE?

The goals that states pursue range widely and vary considerably from case to case. Military power is more useful for realizing some goals than others,

This essay has been edited and is reprinted from International Security 4 (Spring 1980): 3–35, *by permission of MIT Press.*

Table 1

The Purposes of Force

Type	Purpose	Mode	Targets	Characteristics
Defensive	Fend off attacks or reduce damage of an attack	Peaceful and physical	Primarily military; secondarily industrial	Defensive preparations can have dissuasion value; defensive preparations can look aggressive; first strikes can be taken for defense.
Deterrent	Prevent adversary from initiating an action	Peaceful	Primarily civilian; secondarily industrial; tertiary military	Threats of retaliation made so as not to have to be carried out; second strike preparations can be viewed as first-strike preparations.
Compellent	Get adversary to stop doing something or start doing something	Peaceful and physical	All three with no clear ranking	Easy to recognize but hard to achieve; compellent actions can be justified on defensive grounds.
Swaggering	Enhance prestige	Peaceful	None	Difficult to describe because of instrumental and irrational nature; swaggering can be threatening.

though it is generally considered of some use by most states for all of the goals that they hold. If we attempt, however, to be descriptively accurate, to enumerate all of the purposes for which states use force, we shall simply end up with a bewildering list. Descriptive accuracy is not a virtue per se for analysis. In fact, descriptive accuracy is generally bought at the cost of analytical utility. (A concept that is descriptively accurate is usually analytically useless.) Therefore, rather than compile an exhaustive list of such purposes, I have selected four categories that themselves analytically exhaust the functions that force can serve: defense, deterrence, compellence, and "swaggering" (Table 1).[1]

Not all four functions are necessarily well or equally served by a given military posture. In fact, usually only the great powers have the wherewithal to develop military forces that can serve more than two functions at once. Even then, this is achieved only vis-à-vis smaller powers, not vis-à-vis the other great ones. The measure of the capabilities of a state's military forces must be made relative to those of another state, not with reference to some absolute scale. A state that can compel another state can also defend against it and usually deter it. A state that can defend against another state cannot thereby automatically deter or compel it. A state can deter another state without having the ability to either defend against or compel it. A state that can swagger vis-à-vis another may or may not be able to perform any of the other three functions relative to it. Where feasible, defense is the goal that all states aim for first. If defense is not possible, deterrence is generally the next priority. Swaggering is the function most difficult to pin down analytically; deterrence, the one whose achievement is the most difficult to

demonstrate; compellence, the easiest to demonstrate but among the hardest to achieve. The following discussion develops these points more fully.

The *defensive* use of force is the deployment of military power so as to be able to do two things—to ward off an attack and to minimize damage to oneself if attacked. For defensive purposes, a state will direct its forces against those of a potential or actual attacker, but not against his unarmed population. For defensive purposes, a state can deploy its forces in place prior to an attack, use them after an attack has occurred to repel it, or strike first if it believes that an attack upon it is imminent or inevitable. The defensive use of force can thus involve both peaceful and physical employment and both repellent (second) strikes and offensive (first) strikes.[2] If a state strikes first when it believes an attack upon it is imminent, it is launching a preemptive blow. If it strikes first when it believes an attack is inevitable but not momentary, it is launching a preventive blow. Preemptive and preventive blows are undertaken when a state calculates, first, that others plan to attack it and, second, that to delay in striking offensively is against its interests. A state preempts in order to wrest the advantage of the first strike from an opponent. A state launches a preventive attack because it believes that others will attack it when the balance of forces turns in their favor and therefore attacks while the balance of forces is in its favor. In both cases it is better to strike first than to be struck first. The major distinction between preemption and prevention is the calculation about when an opponent's attack will occur. For preemption, it is a matter of hours, days, or even a few weeks at the most; for prevention, months or even a few years. In the case of preemption, the state has almost no control over the timing of its attack; in the case of prevention, the state can in a more leisurely way contemplate the timing of its attack. For both cases, it is the belief in the certainty of war that governs the offensive, defensive attack. For both cases, the maxim, "the best defense is a good offense," makes good sense.

The *deterrent* use of force is the deployment of military power so as to be able to prevent adversaries from doing something that one does not want them to do and that they might otherwise be tempted to do by threatening them with unacceptable punishment if they do it. Deterrence is thus the threat of retaliation. Its purpose is to prevent something undesirable from happening. The threat of punishment is directed at an adversary's population or industrial infrastructure. The effectiveness of the threat depends upon a state's ability to convince potential adversaries that it has both the will and power to punish them severely if they undertake the undesirable action in question. Deterrence therefore employs force peacefully. It is the threat to resort to force in order to punish that is the essence of deterrence. If the threat has to be carried out, deterrence by definition has failed. A deterrent threat is made precisely with the intent that it will not have to be carried out. Threats are made to prevent actions from being undertaken. If the threat has to be implemented, the action has already been undertaken. Hence deterrence can be judged successful only if the retaliatory threats have not been implemented.

Deterrence and defense are alike in that both are intended to protect the state or its closest allies from physical attacks. The purpose of both is dissuasion—persuading others *not* to undertake actions harmful to oneself. The defensive use of force dissuades by convincing adversaries that they cannot conquer one's military forces. The deterrent use of force dissuades by convincing adversaries that their population and territory will suffer terrible damage if they initiate the undesirable action. Defense dissuades by presenting an unvanquishable military force. Deterrence dissuades by presenting the certainty of retaliatory devastation.

Defense is possible without deterrence, and deterrence is possible without defense. A state can have the military wherewithal to repel an invasion without also being able to threaten devastation to the invader's population or territory. Similarly, a state can have the wherewithal credibly to threaten an adversary with such devastation and yet be unable to repel his invading force. Defense, therefore, does not necessarily buy deterrence, nor deterrence defense. A state that can defend itself from attack, moreover, will have little need to develop the wherewithal to deter. If physical attacks can be repelled or if the damage from them drastically minimized, the incentive to develop a retaliatory capability is low. A state that cannot defend itself, however, will try to develop an effective deterrent if that be possible. No state will leave its population and territory open to attack if it has the means to redress the situation. Whether a given state can defend or deter, or do both, vis-à-vis

another depends upon two factors: (1) the quantitative balance of forces between it and its adversary; and (2) the qualitative balance of forces, that is, whether the extant military technology favors the offense or the defense. These two factors are situation-specific and therefore require careful analysis of the case at hand.

The *compellent* use of force is the deployment of military power so as to be able either to stop adversaries from doing something that they have already undertaken or to get them to do something that they have not yet undertaken. Compellence, in Schelling's words, "involves initiating an action . . . that can cease, or become harmless, only if the opponent responds."[3] Compellence can employ force either physically or peacefully. A state can start actually harming another with physical destruction until the latter abides by the former's wishes. Or, a state can take actions against another that do not cause physical harm but that require the latter to pay some type of significant price until it changes its behavior. America's bombing of North Vietnam in early 1965 was an example of physical compellence; Tirpitz's building of a German fleet aimed against England's in the two decades before World War I, an example of peaceful compellence. In the first case, the United States started bombing North Vietnam in order to stop it from assisting the Vietcong forces in South Vietnam. In the latter case, Germany built a battlefleet that in an engagement threatened to cripple that of England in order to compel it to make a general political settlement advantageous to Germany. In both cases, one state initiated some type of action against another precisely so as to be able to stop it, to bargain it away for the appropriate response from the "put upon" state.

The distinction between compellence and deterrence is one between the active and passive use of force. The success of a deterrent threat is measured by its not having to be used. The success of a compellent action is measured by how closely and quickly the adversary conforms to one's stipulated wishes. In the case of successful deterrence, one is trying to demonstrate a negative, to show why something did not happen. It can never be clear whether one's actions were crucial to, or irrelevant to, why another state chose *not* to do something. In the case of successful compellence, the clear sequence of actions and reactions lends a compelling plausibility to the centrality of one's actions. Figure 1 illustrates the distinction. In successful compellence, state B can claim that its pressure deflected state A from its course of action. In successful deterrence, state B has no change in state A's behavior to point to, but instead must resort to claiming that its threats were responsible for the continuity in A's behavior. State A may have changed its behavior for reasons other than state B's compellent action. State A may have continued with its same behavior for reasons other than state B's deterrent threat. "Proving" the importance of B's influence on A for either case is not easy, but it is more plausible to claim that B influenced A when

Figure 1
Distinguishing Compellence and Deterrence

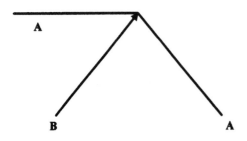

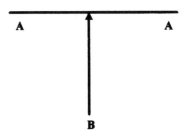

Compellence	**Deterrence**

Compellence

(1) A is doing something that B cannot tolerate

(2) B initiates action against A in order to get him to stop his intolerable actions

(3) A stops his intolerable actions and B stops his (or both cease simultaneously)

Deterrence

(1) A is presently not doing anything that B finds intolerable

(2) B tells A that if A changes his behavior and does something intolerable, B will punish him

(3) A continues not to do anything B finds intolerable

there is a change in A's behavior than when there is not. Explaining why something did not happen is more difficult than explaining why something did.

Compellence may be easier to demonstrate than deterrence, but it is harder to achieve. Schelling argues that compellent actions tend to be vaguer in their objectives than deterrent threats and for that reason more difficult to attain.[4] If adversaries have a hard time understanding what it is that one wishes them to do, their compliance with one's wishes is made more difficult. There is, however, no inherent reason why a compellent action must be vaguer than a deterrent threat with regard to how clearly the adversaries understand what is wanted from them. "Do not attack me" is not any clearer in its ultimate meaning than "stop attacking my friend." A state can be as confused or as clear about what it wishes to prevent as it can be about what it wishes to stop. The clarity, or lack of it, of the objectives of compellent actions and deterrent threats does not vary according to whether the given action is compellent or deterrent in nature, but rather according to a welter of particularities associated with the given action. Some objectives, for example, are inherently clearer and hence easier to perceive than others. Some statesmen communicate more clearly than others. Some states have more power to bring to bear for a given objective than others. It is the specifics of a given situation, not any intrinsic difference between compellence and deterrence, that determine the clarity with which an objective is perceived.

We must, therefore, look elsewhere for the reason as to why compellence is comparatively harder to achieve than deterrence. It lies not in what one asks another to do, but in *how* one asks. With deterrence, state B asks something of state A in this fashion: "do not take action X; for if you do, I will bash you over the head with this club." With compellence, state B asks something of state A in this fashion: "I am now going to bash you over the head with this club and will continue to do so until you do what I want." In the former case, state A can easily deny with great plausibility any intention of having planned to take action X. In the latter case, state A cannot deny either that it is engaged in a given course of action or that it is being subjected to pressure by state B. If they are to be successful, compellent actions require a state to alter its behavior in a manner quite visible to all in response to an equally visible forceful initiative taken by another state. In contrast to compellent actions, deterrent threats are both easier to appear to have ignored or easier to acquiesce to without great loss of face. In contrast to deterrent threats, compellent actions more directly engage the prestige and the passions of the put-upon state. Less prestige is lost in not doing something than in clearly altering behavior due to pressure from another. In the case of compellence, a state has publicly committed its prestige and resources to a given line of conduct that it is now asked to give up. This is not so for deterrence. Thus compellence is intrinsically harder to attain than deterrence, not because its objectives are vaguer, but because it demands more humiliation from the compelled state.

The fourth purpose to which military power can be put is the most difficult to be precise about.

Swaggering is in part a residual category, the deployment of military power for purposes other than defense, deterrence, or compellence. Force is not aimed directly at dissuading another state from attacking, at repelling attacks, nor at compelling it to do something specific. The objectives for swaggering are more diffuse, ill defined, and problematic than that. Swaggering almost always involves only the peaceful use of force and is expressed usually in one of two ways: displaying one's military might at military exercises and national demonstrations and buying or building the era's most prestigious weapons. The swagger use of force is the most egoistic: it aims to enhance the national pride of a people or to satisfy the personal ambitions of its ruler. A state or statesman swaggers in order to look and feel more powerful and important to be taken seriously by others in the councils of international decision making, to enhance the nation's image in the eyes of others. If its image is enhanced, the nation's defense, deterrent, and compellent capabilities may also be enhanced; but swaggering is not undertaken solely or even primarily for these specific purposes. Swaggering is pursued because it offers to bring prestige "on the cheap." Swaggering is pursued because of the fundamental yearning of states and statesmen for respect and prestige. Swaggering is more something to be enjoyed for itself than to be employed for a specific, consciously thought-out end.

And yet, the instrumental role of swaggering cannot be totally discounted because of the fundamental relation between force and foreign policy that obtains in an anarchic environment. Because there is a connection between the military might that a nation is thought to possess and the success that it achieves in attaining its objectives, the enhancement of a state's stature in the eyes of others can always be justified on *realpolitik* lines. If swaggering causes other states to take one's interests more seriously into account, then the general interests of the state will benefit. Even in its instrumental role, however, swaggering is undertaken less for any given end than for all ends. The swaggering function of military power is thus at one and the same time the most comprehensive and the most diffuse, the most versatile in its effects and the least focused in its immediate aims, the most instrumental in the long run and the least instrumental in the short run, easy to justify on hard-headed grounds and often undertaken on emotional grounds. Swaggering mixes the rational and irrational more than the other three functions of military power and, for that reason, remains both pervasive in international relations and elusive to describe.

Defense, deterrence, compellence, and swaggering—these are the four general purposes for which force can be employed. Discriminating among them analytically, however, is easier than applying them in practice. This is due to two factors. First, we need to know the motives behind an act in order to judge its purpose; but the problem is that motives cannot be readily inferred from actions because several motives can be served by the same action. But neither can one readily infer the motives of a state from what it publicly or officially proclaims them to be. Such statements should not necessarily be taken at face value because of the role that bluff and dissimulation play in statecraft. Such statements are also often concocted with domestic political, not foreign audiences in mind or else are deliberate exercises in studied ambiguity. Motives are important in order to interpret actions, but neither actions nor words always clearly delineate motives.

It is, moreover, especially difficult to distinguish defensive from compellent actions and deterrent from swaggering ones unless we know the reasons for which they were undertaken. Peaceful defensive preparations often look largely the same as peaceful compellent ones. Defensive attacks are nearly indistinguishable from compellent ones. Is he who attacks first the defender or the compeller? Deterrence and swaggering both involve the acquisition and display of an era's prestigious weapons. Are such weapons acquired to enhance prestige or to dissuade an attack?

Second, to make matters worse, consider the following example. Germany launched an attack upon France and Russia at the end of July 1914 and thereby began World War I. There are two schools of thought as to why Germany did this. One holds that its motives were aggressive—territorial aggrandizement, economic gain, and elevation to the status of a world empire. Another holds that its motives were preventive and hence defensive. It struck first because it feared encirclement, slow strangulation, and then inevitable attack by its two powerful neighbors, foes whom it felt were daily increasing their military might faster than it was. Germany struck while it had the chance to win.

It is not simple to decide which school is the more nearly correct because both can marshall evidence to build a powerful case. Assume for the moment, though, that the second is closer to the truth. There are then two possibilities to consider: (1) Germany launched an attack because it *was* the case that its foes were planning to attack it ultimately, and Germany had the evidence to prove it; or (2) Germany felt it had reasonable evidence of its foes' *intent* to attack it eventually, but in fact its evidence was wrong because it misperceived their intent from their actions. If the first was the case, then we must ask this question: how responsible was Germany's diplomacy in the fifteen years before 1914, aggressive and blundering as it was, in breeding hostility in its neighbors? Germany attacked in the knowledge that they would eventually have struck it, but if its fifteen-year diplomatic record was a significant factor in causing them to lay these plans, must we conclude that Germany in 1914 was merely acting defensively? Must we confine our judgment about the defensive or aggressive nature of the act to the month or even the year in which it occurred? If not, how many years back in history do we go in order to make a judgment? If the second was the case, then we must ask this question: if Germany attacked in the belief, mistakenly as it turns out, that it would be attacked, must we conclude that Germany was acting defensively? Must we confine our judgment about the defensive or aggressive nature of the act simply to Germany's beliefs about others' intent, without reference to their actual intent?

It is not easy to answer these questions. Fortunately, we do not have to. Asking them is enough because it illustrates that an assessment of the *legitimacy* of a state's motives in using force is integral to the task of determining what its motives are. One cannot, that is, specify motives without at the same time making judgments about their legitimacy. The root cause of this need lies in the nature of state action. In anarchy every state is a valid judge of the legitimacy of its goals because there is no supranational authority to enforce agreed-upon rules. Because of the lack of universal standards, we are forced to examine each case within its given context and to make individual judgments about the meaning of the particulars. When individual judgment is exercised, individuals may well differ. Definitive answers are more likely to be the exception rather than the rule.

Where does all of this leave us? Our four categories tell us what are the four possible purposes for which states can employ military power. The attributes of each alert us to the types of evidence for which to search. But because the context of an action is crucial in order to judge its ultimate purpose, these four categories cannot be applied mindlessly and ahistorically. Each state's purpose in using force in a given instance must fall into one of these four categories. We know a priori what the possibilities are. Which one it is, is an exercise in judgment, an exercise that depends as much upon the particulars of the given case as it does upon the general features of the given category.

WHAT ARE THE LIMITS ON THE USE OF FORCE?

There are inherent limits to what force can accomplish. Military power can be used to conquer the territory of another nation, but not to conquer the minds of its inhabitants. Military power is a necessary ingredient for political power but is no substitute for political support and political leadership. Military power can create the necessary political preconditions for an economy to prosper but cannot substitute for the industry of a people or for a sound trading and monetary policy.[5] First and foremost, a state uses its military power to check, deter, or defend against the forces of another nation. With greater difficulty it tries to compel others, but compellence, as we have seen, is difficult to achieve. Force can easily be used to maim and kill, but only with greater difficulty and with great expenditure of effort, to rule and pacify. Nuclear weapons can maim and kill more swiftly and with greater ease than can conventional weapons, but they do not thereby automatically enable one nation to rule or pacify another, nor to bring political harmony to its populace. The effectiveness with which military functions can be discharged does not translate directly into the effectiveness with which political functions can be performed. If that were the case, then military power alone would be sufficient to conduct a successful foreign policy. But that, clearly, is not the case. If one nation possesses a military edge over another, it is in a stronger bargaining position than it would otherwise be. But it still has to bargain, and it is here that diplomatic-political skills and economic resources come into play. In international relations, superior military strength means enhanced resources with which to bargain but does not guarantee outright control. As Kenneth Waltz has succinctly put it: "Inability to exercise *political* control over others does not indicate *military* weakness."[6]

Even for the greatest of nations, moreover, military power is always in short supply. Great powers have great ambition and consequently need to ration their military power among competing goals. Smaller powers have great needs and little wherewithal to satisfy them and consequently must carefully husband their military power for the most pressing needs. For the great and small alike, there are, in addition, always opportunity costs in the exercise of military power. Except in those situations in which a nation is fighting for its very existence, there are always good reasons for limiting the amount of force actually applied to achieve a given goal. Thus military power is a necessary ingredient for political and economic success in international relations, but not the *sole* ingredient. No matter how militarily powerful a nation is, force cannot achieve those things for which only political skill and economic industry are suited. In an anarchic world, it is better to be militarily strong than weak. But such strength alone, especially when there are other strong powers, is not a panacea.

WHAT IS THE FUTURE OF FORCE?

If the past be any guide to the future, then military power will remain central to the course of international relations. Those states that do not have the wherewithal to field large forces (for example, Denmark) or those that choose to field forces far smaller than their economies can bear (for example, Japan) will pay the price. Both will find themselves with less control over their own fate than would otherwise be the case. Those states that field powerful military forces will find themselves in greater control, but they will also find that their great military power can produce unintended effects and that such power is not a solution to all their problems. For both the strong and the weak, however, as long as anarchy obtains, force will remain the final arbiter to resolve the disputes that arise among them. As has always been the case, most disputes will be settled short of the physical use of force. But as long as the physical use of force remains a viable option, military power will vitally affect the manner in which all states in peacetime deal with one another.

The efficacy of force endures. It must. For in anarchy, force and politics are connected. By itself, military power guarantees neither survival nor prosperity. But it is almost always the essential ingredient for both. Because resort to force is the ultimate card of all states, the seriousness of a state's intentions is conveyed fundamentally by its having a credible military posture. Without it, a state's diplomacy generally lacks effectiveness. Force need not be physically used to be politically useful. Threats need not be overtly made to be communicated. The mere presence of a credible military option is often sufficient to make the point. It is the capability to resort to military force if all else fails that serves as the most effective brake against having to do so. Lurking behind the scenes, unstated but explicit, lies the military muscle that gives meaning to the posturings of the diplomats. Diplomacy is the striking of compromises by parties with differing perspectives and clashing interests. The ultimate ability of each to resort to force disciplines the diplomats. Precisely because each knows that all can come to blows if they do not strike compromises do the diplomats engage in the hard work necessary to construct them. There is truth to the old adage: "The best way to keep the peace is first to prepare for war."

NOTES

1. The term "compellence" was coined by Thomas C. Schelling in his *Arms and Influence* (New Haven, Conn.: Yale University Press, 1966). Part of my discussion of compellence and deterrence draws upon his as it appears in Chapter 2, 69–86, but, as will be made clear below, I disagree with some of his conclusions.

2. Military power can be used in one of two modes: "physically" and "peacefully." The physical use of force refers to its actual employment against an adversary, usually but not always in a mutual exchange of blows. The peaceful use of force refers either to an explicit threat to resort to force, or to the implicit threat to use it that is communicated simply by a state's having it available for use. The physical use of force means that one nation is literally engaged in harming, destroying, or crippling those possessions that another nation holds dear, including its military forces. The peaceful use of force is referred to as such because, while force is "used" in the sense that it is employed explicitly or implicitly for the assistance it is thought to render in achieving a given goal, it does not result in any physical destruction to another nation's valued possessions. There is obviously a gray area between these two modes of use—the one in which a nation prepares (that is, gears up or mobilizes or moves about) its military forces for use against another nation but has not yet committed them such that they are inflicting damage.

3. Schelling, *Arms and Influence,* 72.

4. Ibid., 72–73.

5. For a brilliant sketch of the role that American military power played in creating the political conditions conducive to economic and monetary expansion, see Robert Gilpin, *U.S. Power and the Multinationals* (New York: Basic Books, 1975), chap. 4.

6. Kenneth N. Waltz, "National Force, International Structure and the World Balance of Power," *Journal of International Affairs* 21 (1967). Reprinted in part in Robert Art and Robert Jervis, eds., *International Politics* (Boston: Little, Brown, 1973), 252.

CHAPTER 2

THINKING ABOUT
AMERICAN DEFENSE POLICY

BUREAUCRATIC POLITICS: A PARADIGM

GRAHAM T. ALLISON AND MORTON H. HALPERIN

Our purpose here is to outline a rough-cut framework for focusing primarily on the individuals within a government, and the interaction among them, as determinants of the actions of a government in international politics.[1] What a government does in any particular instance can be understood largely as a result of bargaining among players positioned hierarchically in the government. The bargaining follows regularized circuits. Both the bargaining and the results are importantly affected by a number of constraints, in particular, organizational processes and shared values.[2]

In contrast to the realist paradigm, this bureaucratic politics model sees no unitary actor but rather many actors as players—players who focus not on a single strategic issue but on many diverse intranational problems as well. Players choose in terms of no consistent set of strategic objectives, but rather according to various conceptions of national security, organizational, domestic, and personal interests. Players make governmental decisions not by a single rational choice, but by pulling and hauling. (This by no means implies that individual players are not acting rationally, given their interests.)[3]

The conception of national security policy as "political" result contradicts both public imagery and academic orthodoxy. Issues vital to national security are considered too important to be settled by political games. They must be "above" politics: to accuse someone of "playing politics with national security" is a most serious charge. Thus, memoirs typically handle the details of such bargaining with a velvet glove. For example, both Sorensen and Schlesinger present the efforts of the Executive Committee in the Cuban missile crisis essentially as rational deliberation among a unified group of equals.[4] What public expectation demands, the academic penchant for intellectual elegance reinforces. Internal politics is messy; moreover, according to prevailing doctrine, politicking lacks intellectual substance. It constitutes gossip for journalists, rather than a subject for serious investigation. Occasional memoirs, anecdotes in historical accounts, and several detailed case studies to the contrary, most of the foreign policy literature avoids bureaucratic politics.

The gap between academic literature and the experience of participants in government is nowhere wider than at this point. For those who participate in government, the terms of daily employment cannot be ignored: government leaders have competitive, not homogeneous interests; priorities and perceptions are shaped by positions; problems are much more varied than straightforward, strategic issues; the management of piecemeal streams of decisions is more important than steady state choices; making sure that the government does what is decided—and does not do what has not been directed—is more difficult than selecting the preferred solution.

This general orientation can be stated more sharply by formulation of the bureaucratic politics model as an "analytic paradigm" in the technical sense developed by Robert K. Merton for sociological analysis.[5] Systematic statement of basic assumptions and concepts will highlight the distinctive thrust of this style of analysis. In formulating the paradigm, wherever possible, we use words the way they are used in ordinary language. But the terms that constitute this paradigm are often given a more specific definition for purposes of clarity.

BASIC UNIT OF ANALYSIS

In thinking about problems of foreign affairs, what most participants and analysts are really interested in are *outcomes*—that is, selectively delimited states of the real world importantly affected by the actions of governments. Thus, for example, the problem of proliferation for most participants or analysts is: how many nations will have what nuclear capabilities at some point in the future.[6] Similarly, an explanation of the Cuban missile crisis must allow one to understand why at some point, Soviet missiles were no longer in Cuba. The United States was publicly committed not to invade Cuba, and all this had been accomplished without nuclear war. The selection of variables is made by the analyst or participant with reference to his perception of some problem or issue. When explaining, predicting, or planning, an analyst, at least implicitly, specifies some characteristics of the real world—an outcome—that focus his attention.

The basic unit of analysis of the approach developed here is *actions* of a government that we define

This essay has been edited and is reprinted from World Politics 24, *supplement (Spring 1972): 40–79, by permission of the Johns Hopkins University Press.*

as the various acts of officials of a government in exercises of governmental authority that can be perceived outside the government. According to this definition, a presidential announcement of a decision to bomb North Vietnam, the subsequent movement of an aircraft carrier into a position near North Vietnam, and the actual dropping of bombs are actions of a government. Whereas a secret paper sent from the secretary of defense to the president recommending bombing of North Vietnam or a private presidential decision to bomb North Vietnam are not actions of a government. It is an assumption of the approach developed here that in order to explain, predict, or plan outcomes it is necessary to identify the actions of particular governments that affect the outcome, to treat these actions separately (including how one nation's actions affect another) and in this way to treat the event in its entirety.

In explaining, predicting, or planning actions of a government, one must identify the *action channels*—that is, regularized sets of procedures for producing particular classes of actions. For example, one action channel for producing U.S. military intervention in another country includes a recommendation by the ambassador to that country, an assessment by the regional military commander, a recommendation by the Joint Chiefs of Staff, an assessment by the intelligence community of the consequences of intervention, recommendations by the secretaries of state and defense, a presidential decision to intervene, the transmittal of an order from the president through the secretary of defense and Joint Chiefs of Staff to the regional military commander, his determination of what troops to employ, the order from him to the commander of those troops, and the orders from that commander to the individuals who actually move into the country. The path from initiation to action frequently includes a number of *decisions,* that is, authoritative designations, internal to a government, of specific actions to be taken by specific officials. Thus a secret decision by the president to intervene, and the determination by the regional commander are both decisions, but a public announcement of either is an action of the government.

The action channel for major foreign policy decisions can be usefully divided into that portion that leads to decisions by senior players and that part that follows from those decisions. The latter is frequently referred to as "implementation," but we resist that terminology as too restrictive. Many elements of implementation stem from sources other than decisions by senior players. Thus, for example, the presence of U.S. troops in the Dominican Republic in 1965 stemmed from a decision by the president to send the marines to that country, but the actions of the 18,000 marines in the Dominican Republic (e.g., the precise positions that they occupied) followed from much lower-level decisions, as well as from other factors. Moreover, many actions of governments occur in the absence of any high-level decision. For example, in the earlier Dominican crisis

that led to the overthrow of Juan Bosch, Ambassador John B. Martin's offer to Bosch to send in the U.S. Marines was not preceded by any high-level decision to make that offer.[7] Actions may also be affected by decisions on other issues and by *policy,* that is, authoritative aspirations, internal to a government, about outcomes. For example, Martin's behavior was influenced by the U.S. *policy* of supporting democratic governments in Latin America. The actions of the marines, when they did intervene, were affected by prior budget decisions. For purposes of analysis we will identify the activity of players leading to decisions by senior players as *decision games,* activities leading to policy as *policy games,* and activities that follow from, or proceed in the absence of, decisions by senior players as *action games.*

Thus we have defined the following terms: outcomes, actions, action channels, decisions, policy, and decision games, policy games, and action games.

ORGANIZING CONCEPTS

The organizing concepts of this paradigm can be arranged as elements in the answers to three central questions: (1) Who plays? (2) What determines each player's stand? (3) How are players' stands aggregated to yield governmental decisions and actions?

WHO PLAYS? THAT IS, WHOSE INTERESTS AND BEHAVIOR HAVE AN IMPORTANT EFFECT ON THE GOVERNMENT'S DECISIONS AND ACTIONS?

In any government, there exists a circle of *senior players* in the national security policy game.[8] This circle includes the major political figures, the heads of the major national security organizations, including intelligence, the military and, for some purposes, the organization that manages budgetary allocations and the economy. Generally one of these players is the chief executive of the government. This player may have a disproportionate share of influence on major decisions. The president of the United States, for example, has a range of both interests and formal powers that set him apart from other players. Other individuals can enter this central circle, either on a more regular or a strictly ad hoc basis, because of their relation with the head of the government. Organizations and groups can for some purposes be treated as players, for example, when (1) the official papers that emerge from an organization can be summarized as coherent calculated moves of a unitary actor; (2) the actions of the head of an organization, whose goals are determined largely by that organization, can be treated as actions of the organization; and (3) the various behaviors of different individual members of an organization can be regarded as coherent strategies and tactics in a single plan.

Around the central circle of *senior players* there are various circles of *junior players.* In the United States actors in the wider governmental game ("congressional influentials," members of the press, spokesmen for important interest groups, especially the "bipartisan foreign policy establishment" in and out of Congress, and surrogates for each of these groups) can enter the game in a more or less regularized fashion. Other members of the Congress, the press, interest groups, and public form concentric circles around the central arena—circles that demarcate limits within which the game is played.

The mix of players will vary depending on the issue and the type of game. Action channels determine, in large part, which players enter what games, with what advantages and handicaps. Senior players will dominate in decision games. But in action games on the same issue quite junior players in the organization who are charged with carrying out the decision may play a major role.

WHAT DETERMINES EACH PLAYER'S STAND? WHAT DETERMINES THE PERCEPTIONS AND INTERESTS THAT LEAD TO A STAND?

Answers to the questions "What is the issue?" or "What must be done?" are colored by the position from which the question is considered.

A player is an individual in a *position*. One's perceptions and preferences stem both from one's individual characteristics (for example, attitudes shared with other members of the society and government and attitudes special to oneself) and from one's position.

The *interests* that affect players' desired results can be characterized under four headings: national security interests, organizational interests, domestic interests, and personal interests. Some elements of national security interests are widely accepted, such as the interest in the United States' avoiding foreign domination, and the belief that if the United States were to disarm unilaterally, other nations would use military force against it and its allies with very serious adverse consequences. But in most cases, reasonable men can disagree on how national security interests will be affected by a specific issue. Other interests can affect an individual's perception of the national security interest. Members of an organization, particularly career officials, come to believe that the health of their organization is vital to the national interest.[9] The health of the organization, in turn, is seen to depend on maintaining influence, fulfilling its mission, and securing the necessary capabilities. The latter two interests lead to concern for maintaining autonomy and organizational morale, protecting the organization's essence, maintaining or expanding roles and missions, and maintaining or increasing budgets. While many bureaucrats are unconcerned with domestic affairs and politics and do not ask themselves how a proposed change in policy or behavior would affect domestic political issues, some senior players will almost always be concerned about domestic implications. Finally a player's stand depends on his or her personal interests and conception of his or here role.

When an ostensible issue arises—for example, when a new weapons system is proposed—players will come to see quite different *faces of the issue*. For example, a proposal to withdraw American troops from Europe is to the army a threat to its budget and size; to the Budget Bureau a way to save money; to Treasury a balance of payments gain; to the State Department Bureau of European Affairs a threat to good relations with NATO; to the president's congressional adviser an opportunity to remove a major irritant in the president's relations with Capitol Hill. (Senior players, especially, tend to see several faces of the issue simultaneously.) Given the face of the issue that each player sees, that individual must calculate how the resolution of this issue may affect his or her interests. This defines one's *stakes* in the issue at hand. In the light of these stakes one then determines one's *stand* on the issue.

HOW ARE THE PLAYERS' STANDS AGGREGATED TO YIELD DECISIONS AND ACTIONS OF A GOVERNMENT?

We consider first how players' stands aggregate to produce policies and decisions by senior players; second, we consider how policies, decisions, and other factors produce governmental actions.

Policy and Decision Games

Sometimes an issue arises because players see something that they want to change, and move. Most often, however, the game is begun by the necessity that something be done, either in response to a *deadline* (e.g., the annual budget) or an event (external or domestic). When they become aware that a game has begun, players must determine their stand and then decide whether to play (if they have a choice) and if so, how hard. These decisions require a calculation (often implicit) about both resources and reputation. Resources are finite and fungible; they may consist, for example, of time and senior players' reputation with the president. Reputation depends on one's track record; thus players consider the probability of success as part of their stake.

Decision games do not proceed randomly, but rather according to fixed rules. Typically, issues are recognized and determined within an established channel for producing policies or decisions. Where a deadline or event initiates the game, that trigger influences the selection of the action channel. In most cases, however, there are several possible channels through which an issue could be resolved. Because action channels structure the game by preselecting the major players, determining the usual points of entrance into the game, and by distributing particular advantages for each game, players maneuver to get the issue into the channel that they believe is most likely to yield the desired result.

Each player's probability of success depends upon at least three elements: bargaining advantages, skill and will in using bargaining advantages, and other players' perceptions of the first two ingredients. Bargaining advantages stem from control of implementation, control over information that enables one to define the problem and identify the available options, persuasiveness with other players (including players outside the bureaucracy), and the ability to affect other players' objectives in other games, including domestic political games.

What emerges from the game is also importantly affected by constraints, in particular by the routines of organizations in supplying information and options, and by the shared values within the society and the bureaucracy.

The game consists of each player engaging in various maneuvers to achieve his or her desired results. Some players develop sophisticated plans, though most players seem to plan very little. All players can try to change other players' stands by arguments.

The resolution of an issue can be a policy, a decision, or the avoidance of a decision. Decisions may be very general or quite specific. In some cases, senior players will have no choice about who will carry out the action. But in other cases, the rules permit a choice of implementers. For example, negotiations with foreign governments are usually the domain of the foreign office; but they can be assigned to a special envoy of the head of government, or to the intelligence services. Bombing missions must be assigned to the military, but there may be a choice between services or within a service, for example, between the navy, Strategic Air Command, or Tactical Air Command. Monitoring functions may be assigned to an organization with an interest in the action, but with no capability to carry it out.

Action Games

The actions of a government that affect an outcome typically include a large number of distinct elements. For example, recent U.S. government actions that affect the spread of nuclear weapons include the State Department's efforts to gain adherence to the Non-Proliferation Treaty; presidential offers of guarantees to nonnuclear nations against nuclear blackmail; Atomic Energy Commission (AEC) tests of nuclear explosives for peaceful purposes (which provide a convenient shield for nonnuclear powers' development of nuclear devices); withdrawal of U.S. forces from the Far East (which may increase the concern of some Japanese or Indians about their national security); statements by the AEC about the great prospects for peaceful nuclear weapons (which are designed to influence AEC budgets); an AEC commissioner's argument, in the absence of any higher-level decision, to a Brazilian scientist about the great virtues of peaceful nuclear explosives; and the U.S. government's refusal to confirm or deny the reported presence of nuclear weapons aboard ships calling in foreign ports. As this list suggests, actions that affect outcomes may be importantly affected by policies about that outcome, by decision games about that outcome, and by decision games about other outcomes. Actions that affect outcomes may also be actions in the absence of higher-level decisions designed to affect an outcome,

maneuvers in decision games, or routine behavior of organizations.

To treat the actions of a government that affect an outcome, the analyst needs to separate out these various strands of action and provide explanations for each. Obviously most actions are an amalgam of several strands.

If the action is in fact a result of routine behavior of organizations, one needs to explain the organizational standard operating procedures (SOPs) that produced that behavior.[10] If the action is a maneuver in a decision or policy game, one needs to identify the game and explain why the maneuver was used. If the action was taken without a high-level decision, one must identify the circumstances that permitted the player that leeway and explain what led the player to take that step. If the action resulted from a policy or a decision game unrelated to the outcome being analyzed, one must identify the relevant decision or policy game and provide an explanation of the decision and the action that followed. Finally, if the action flows from a relevant decision game, one needs an explanation of that action game.

Action games, which follow from decision games, do not proceed at random. The decision that triggers the game and the rules of the game assign the action to a player and pick the action channel. However, there are likely to be several subchannels. Players will maneuver to get the issue into the channel they believe offers the best prospects for getting the desired result.

As in decision games, players' probabilities of success depend upon their power. In this case, bargaining advantages stem from formal authority, control over the resources necessary to carry out the action, responsibility for carrying out the action, control over information that enables one to determine the feasibility of the action and its consequences, control over information that enables senior players to determine whether the decision is being implemented, and persuasiveness with other players, particularly those responsible for implementation. Action is also affected by the constraints imposed by the standard operating procedures of large organizations.

In some cases, players responsible for implementing decisions will feel obligated to implement the spirit as well as the letter of the decision. Even in such cases, the action may differ from the action that the senior players thought would result from their decision. This is in part because actions are carried out by large organizations according to existing routines, in part because decisions do not usually include an explanation of what the action is intended to accomplish, and in part because when specifying details junior players may distort the action.

In most cases, players will feel that the decision leaves them considerable leeway in implementation. Players who supported the decision will maneuver to see it implemented. They may go beyond the spirit if not the letter of the decision. Those who opposed the decision, or who oppose the action, will maneuver to delay implementation, to limit implementation to the letter but not the spirit, or even to have the decision disobeyed.

The characterization of decision and action games captures the thrust of the bureaucratic politics approach. If problems of foreign policy arose as discrete issues, and decisions and actions were determined one game at a time, this account would suffice. But most "issues"—for example, Vietnam or the proliferation of nuclear weapons—emerge piecemeal over time, one lump in one contest, a second in another. Hundreds of issues compete for players' attention every day. Each player is forced to fix upon his or her issues for that day, deal with them on their own terms, and rush on to the next. Thus the character of the emerging issue and the pace at which the game is played converge to yield a collage of government decisions and actions. Choices by one player (e.g., to authorize action by his or her department, to make a speech, or to refrain from acquiring certain information), decisions and "foul-ups" (e.g., points that are not decided because they are not recognized, raised too late, or misunderstood) are pieces that, when stuck to the same canvas, constitute actions relevant to an outcome.

CONSTRAINTS

The factors highlighted in this model assume a ceteris paribus clause. Other features, treated here as constraints, bias the outcome of the bureaucratic politics game. For some classes of governmental behavior (e.g., the detail characteristics of the behavior of large organizations), these other factors may be more important than those emphasized by the bureaucratic politics model. Indeed, what is described here as an "organizational constraint" has been elaborated elsewhere by one of us as an alternative model.[11] The issue of topology, that is, what factors weigh most heavily for what classes of outcomes, is a central issue for further research.

ORGANIZATIONAL CONSTRAINTS

The game among players (and organizations considered as players) proceeds within a context. A large part of that context is the existing configuration of large organizations, their established programs and standard operating procedures for performing various functions. These organizational routines are especially important in determining (1) the information available to the central players, (2) the options that the senior players consider, and (3) the actual details of whatever is done by the government.

How does *information* about most national problems become available to members of a government? For example, how did the U.S. government become aware of the Soviet construction of missiles in Cuba in 1962? For the most part, information is collected and processed by large organizations. In the Cuban Missile Crisis, the existence of the Central Intelligence Agency and air force, with existing capabilities and processes, yielded a U-2 flight over Cuba according to a pattern that discovered the missiles in the second week of October.

The menu of *alternatives* defined by organizations in sufficient detail to be live options is severely limited in both number and character. The character of the alternatives available to a leader (i.e., the location of the set of alternatives in the universe of possible alternatives relevant to his or her objectives) differs significantly from the character of alternatives presented by a team of five disinterested experts. The difference is a function of the configuration of established organizations and their existing goals and procedures. Those alternatives that are built into existing organizational goals (e.g., incremental improvements in each military service's primary weapons system) will be adequate (i.e., compare favorably with the experts' list, though with less sensitivity to cost). However, alternatives that require coordination of several organizations (e.g., multiservice military operations or weapons systems) and alternatives in areas between organizations (e.g., weapons that are not represented by a major service component) are likely to be inadequate.

Action according to standard operating procedures and programs does not constitute far-sighted, flexible adaptation to "the issue" (as it is conceived by an analyst). Detail and nuance of actions by organizations are determined chiefly by organizational routines. Standard operating procedures constitute routines for dealing with standard situations. Routines allow large numbers of individuals on low organizational levels to deal with numerous situations day after day, without much thought. But this regularized capacity for adequate performance is purchased at the price of standardization. Specific instances, particularly critical instances that typically do not have "standard" characteristics, are often handled sluggishly or inappropriately. A program, that is, a complex cluster of standard operating procedures, is rarely tailored to the specific situation in which it is executed. Rather, the program is (at best) the most appropriate of programs in the existing repertoire. Since repertoires are developed by parochial organizations for standard scenarios that the organization has defined, the programs available for dealing with a particular situation are often ill suited to it.

SHARED ATTITUDES

Perceptions of issues or arguments about the national interest do not begin ab initio. Beneath the differences that fuel bureaucratic politics is a foundation of shared assumptions about basic values and facts. These underlying assumptions are reflected in various attitudes and images that are taken for granted by most players.

Shared attitudes and images provide common answers to such questions as Who are the actual or potential enemies of the United States? What are their intentions and capabilities? Who are our friends? What are their capabilities and intentions?

and What influences the behavior of other nations? Among the attitudes and the images that have recently prevailed in the U.S. bureaucracy are

- The United States should act to halt the spread of communism.

- Only force will deter the Chinese from aggression.

- The loss of American gold to foreign central banks is a threat to U.S. prosperity and should be avoided.

- The capability for assured destruction is necessary to deter the Soviet Union.

- European unification is desirable.

- Good relations with Japan are important to U.S. security interests.

Most participants accept these images. Their idea of the national interest is shaped by these attitudes, and their arguments are based on them. Most participants tend to interpret the actions of other nations to make them consistent with held images, rather than reexamining basic views. Even those in the bureaucracy who do not share some or all of these values and images are inclined to act and to argue as if they believed them. They do this because to do otherwise would make them suspect in the eyes of other members of the bureaucracy.

INTERACTION BETWEEN NATIONS

How does the behavior of one nation affect that of another?

Most analysts of international politics approach this question by applying a version of realism to the behavior of each nation. This approach leads them to treat the interaction between nations as if it resulted from a competition between two purposive individuals. Each nation's actions are seen to be an attempt to influence the actions of the other by affecting its strategic calculus. The behavior of each nation is explained as a reaction to the behavior of the other.

Consider how analysts who take this approach explain arms races. Nation A builds military forces for the purpose of influencing nation B. If it fears that nation B is stronger and hence may be tempted to attack or to exploit its military superiority, nation A will increase the size of its own forces. Nation B, observing this buildup, and fearful of the increased strength of nation A, in turn increases its own forces.

The bureaucratic politics model suggests an alternative answer to the question of how one nation's behavior affects the behavior of another. Explanation focuses primarily on processes internal to each nation. The actions of a nation result not from an agreed-upon calculus of strategic interests, but rather from pulling and hauling among individuals with differing perceptions and stakes. These arise not only from differing conceptions of national security interest but also from differing domestic, organ-izational, and personal interests. The influence of one nation's actions on another result from the actions' impact on the stands, or on the power of players in decision or action games in the other nation.

From this alternative perspective, the explanation of an "arms race" is to be found primarily within each nation—in particular in the process by which each one procures and deploys military forces. At any given time some players in nation A will take stands in favor of increasing defense expenditures and procuring particular weapons systems. The interests that lead them to these stands will be diverse. Career officers in the armed services, for example, will seek additional funds for forces controlled by their services. Other players' stands will be affected by their perceptions of how particular decisions will affect the influence of particular players. Actions by another nation will be interpreted by those seeking additional weapons to enhance their arguments and influence. These actions will affect decisions to increase defense spending if they affect senior players' perceptions of what is necessary for national security or of what is necessary to promote their other interests.

Analysis based on the realist paradigm can be relied on to predict the fact that a large increase in nation A's defense budget will produce an increase in nation B's defense spending. But the size of that increase and, even more importantly, the specific characteristics of weapons purchased with the increase are better explained or predicted by the bureaucratic politics model. In general, realism is more useful for explaining actions where national security interests dominate, where shared values lead to a consensus on what the national security requires, and where actions flow rather directly from decisions. The bureaucratic politics model is more useful where there are data on the interests of players and the rules of the game, where organizational and domestic interests predominate, or where one wishes to treat the details of action.

The bureaucratic politics model's emphasis on intranational processes stems not only from the fact that individuals within nations do the acting but also from the observation that the satisfaction of players' interests are to be found overwhelmingly at home. Political leaders of a nation rise and fall depending on whether they satisfy domestic needs. Individuals advance in the bureaucracy when they meet the standards set by political leaders or by career ladders. Organizations prosper or decline depending on domestic support in that bureaucracy and beyond it—but within the nation. These struggles are what preoccupy players in foreign-policy bureaucracies. Threats to interests from rival organizations, or competing political groups, are far more real than threats from abroad.

This is not to say that players do not have national security interests. No leader wants to see the nation attacked, and few desire to send their soldiers off to fight in distant wars. Some leaders are committed to a conception of world order. Some players have a wide range of interests beyond the borders of the nation. Even when players are concerned about national security interests, however, they are likely to see the battles as being won or lost mainly at home. This has become a truism of the Vietnam War, but it is true for other policies as well. For President Harry S Truman, the problem of the Marshall Plan was how to get Congress to establish the program and vote the funds, not how to get European governments to take the money or use it wisely. For President Dwight D. Eisenhower, the problem of arms control was how to get imaginative proposals from his associates. For planners in the Pentagon, the drive to get the forces necessary to defend the nation is stymied, not by foreign governments, but by rival services, the secretary of defense, and the president.

It is not that actions of other nations do not matter, but rather they matter if and when they influence domestic struggles. A player's efforts to accomplish his or her objectives—whether to advance domestic political interests, organizational interests, personal interests, or national security interests—are sometimes affected by what he or she and other players come to believe about the actions of other nations. A German chancellor whose domestic position depends upon his reputation for being able to get what the country needs from the United States will be concerned about American actions that lead his colleagues and opponents to conclude Washington no longer listens to him. An American secretary of defense or president who wishes to cut defense spending will see that his position requires Soviet actions that permit him to argue that the nation's security can be protected with reduced forces. A State Department official who believes his or her government's security requires European unification will fear that his or her efforts to get the United States to promote this cause could be undercut by Common Market trade policies, since these offer an opportunity for others to point to the adverse economic consequences of European unification. Since actions by other nations can affect the stands players take, and thereby affect decisions and actions, we must consider how actions of other nations enter into the process of decision bargaining and how they affect actions.

Many nations are doing many things at any given time. Not all of these foreign activities become relevant to decision or action games within a nation. Those that do are the actions reported by the nation's foreign office or intelligence organizations, or by senior players directly. Intelligence organizations are not perfect and neutral transmission belts. They notice what their images of the world lead them to think will be important to senior players. They report events and opinions according to established procedures and in ways designed to protect their own organizational interests. Senior players notice what may help them or their opponents and relate mainly to the former. If a new interpretation of another nation's actions comes to be accepted among senior players, some players will see new opportunities to seek decisions or actions. Others will see threats to ongoing actions or desired new ones. Still others will be unconcerned.

Reports of the actions of other nations will never be more than one of many influences on decisions and actions. However, when players are evenly divided, or new action suggests to many a substantial change in anticipated future actions, these reports of another nation's actions can be decisive. The Japanese attack on Pearl Harbor, to take an extreme example, affected the perceptions of many Americans about whether the national security required American forces to engage in war against Japan. The Soviet antiballistic missile (ABM) deployment may well have tipped the balance in the hard-fought American controversy over whether to deploy an ABM. President Lyndon Johnson's estimate of the effect of not deploying an American ABM system on his reelection prospects may have been substantially changed by the possibility that he could be charged with permitting an "ABM gap."[12]

When the actions of one nation are effective in changing the behavior of a second, the new action is rarely what was intended by any player in the first nation. Changes in stands will lead to desired changes in action, which in turn will produce desired changes in the action of another nation only: when a clear signal is sent, when someone in the other nation already wants to take the desired action and the action increases that player's influence. More often, the effects are marginal or unintended.

NOTES

1. This presentation of a bureaucratic politics approach to foreign policy builds upon previous works of both authors. Specifically, it takes as a point of departure Allison's "Conceptual Models and the Cuban Missile Crisis," *American Political Science Review* 63 (September 1970) and *Essence of Decision: Explaining the Cuban Missile Crisis* (Boston: Little, Brown, 1971); and Halperin's *Bureaucratic Politics and Foreign Policy* (Washington, D.C.: Brookings Institution, 1974). Here we focus on the further development of "Model III," recognizing that organizations can be included as players in the game of bureaucratic politics, treating the factors emphasized by an organizational process approach as constraints, developing the notion of shared attitudes, and introducing a distinction between "decision games" and "action games."

2. For a review of earlier proponents of the bureaucratic politics approach, see Allison, "Conceptual Models."

3. In order to highlight the distinctive characteristics of the bureaucratic politics model, we contrast it with the traditional approach. Our argument is not, however, that the approaches are exclusive alternatives. The relationship between these approaches is discussed in Allison, "Conceptual Models."

4. Arthur Schlesinger Jr., *A Thousand Days* (Boston: Houghton Mifflin, 1965); see Theodore C. Sorensen *Kennedy* (New York: Harper & Row, 1965).

5. Robert K. Merton, *Social Theory and Social Structures* (New York: 1957).

6. More specifically, the outcome might be defined in terms of a set of variables: (a) the number of states that have formally renounced nuclear weapons, (b) the number

of states that have announced intentions to acquire nuclear weapons, (c) the nuclear technology of various nations, (d) the number of states with a standby capability, (e) the number of states that have tested nuclear weapons, (f) the number of states that have nuclear stockpiles and the size of these stockpiles.

7. John B. Martin, *Overtaken by Events* (New York: Doubleday, 1966).

8. In the statement of this paradigm we focus primarily on issues of foreign policy that arise as matters of national security. Extension of the argument to other issue areas, for example, foreign trade, is straightforward.

9. For an elaboration of the discussion of organizational interests see Halperin "Why Bureaucrats Play Games," *Foreign Policy*, no. 2 (Spring 1971).

10. For an elaboration of the discussion of organizational routines, programs and SOPs, see Allison, "Conceptual Models."

11. See Allison's "Model II," "Conceptual Models." The discussion of organizational constraints draws heavily on that account.

12. On the ABM discussion see Morton Halperin, "The Decision to Deploy the ABM," *World Politics* 25 (October 1972).

A CRITIQUE OF BUREAUCRATIC POLITICS

ROBERT J. ART

Bureaucracies, we are told, have become central to the forging and welding of American foreign policy, but with consequences adverse to the substance of that policy. In the words of a past critic and present practitioner of American foreign policy: "The nightmare of the modern state is the hugeness of bureaucracy, and the problem is how to get coherence and design in it."[1] That bureaucracies are crucial to our foreign policy and that they can make life difficult for presidents are two propositions with which any analyst of American foreign policy could scarcely disagree. But what precisely do these propositions mean? Do they mean that bureaucracies largely determine our foreign policy through their ability to select the information presented to top political leaders and through the control they exert over the details of implementing policy? Do they mean that Congress has little effect on foreign policy because Congress as an institution plays a small role in formulating policy and virtually none in implementing it? Do they mean that the systemic perspective on international politics is of no use, or that presidential assumptions, perspectives, and decisions are not the controlling factors in our foreign policy? Do they mean that bureaucracies, if they are powerful, are equally powerful in all areas of foreign policy? Do these propositions mean that we must concentrate primarily on the mechanics of the foreign policy bureaucracy in order to understand or adduce the substance of policy? Must we look to the nuts and bolts of bureaucracy to explain the thrust of policy? Should we now adopt as the most fruitful method of analysis what is variously called "the governmental politics model," "the bureaucratic politics

paradigm," or "the bureaucratic perspective"? What, in short, are we now being told; and how does it differ from what we have known or assumed for a long time?[2]

THE FIRST WAVE—POLICY VIA POLITICS

What we have known for the last ten years has been a result of the "first wave" of theorists who applied a bureaucratic, but essentially a political perspective to foreign policy making. In the works of the early sixties of Roger Hilsman, Samuel Huntington, Richard Neustadt, and Warner Schilling,[3] we were given some crucial insights into the ways that process affects the content of policy—how the manner in which we make decisions influences the types of decisions that we do make. Five distinct propositions that bear on a bureaucratic perspective can be extracted from their works.[4] The first four propositions specify the internal structural conditions or constraints under which foreign policy is made in our system of government; the fifth derives the content of policy—the outcome of the process—from the first four constraints:

1. Political power (the ability to get someone to do something he or she would otherwise not do) is widely dispersed at the national governmental level. There is no sovereign power in Washington; rather there are a series of sovereign powers. No one figure has a monopoly of power; all the important ones possess a veto power. It is easier to block the policy initiatives of others than it is to get one's own initia-

This essay has been edited and is reprinted from Policy Sciences 4 (December 1973): 467–90, *by permission of Kluwer Academic Publishers.*

tives translated into action. In Neustadt's famous phrase, we have "separated institutions *sharing* powers."[5] Diffusion of power is thus the structural starting point from which actors and analysts must begin their respective tasks.

2. Within these institutions, which Schilling termed "quasi-sovereign powers,"[6] sit participants in the policy process with differing views on what they would like done on any given issue. The basis of their differences in view stems *partly* from their differences in position. With position comes responsibility, but different institutional positions bring with them a different cluster of responsibilities. Participants who have different roles to perform will see different issues as of consequence to them, but even when they do focus on the same issue, they will almost invariably emphasize different aspects of it. Participants can look at the same issue but see it differently. Differing institutional perspectives can thus partially account for differing policy stances.

3. Political leadership within or across these institutions is exercised primarily through persuasion, but that persuasion is dependent upon the skill with which figures make use of the limited power that their positions give them. With no figure having a monopoly of power and with the most important possessing a blocking power, the task of participants who want to get something done is to convince others that what they want is what others would or should do for their own interests.[7]

4. Foreign policy making is thus a political process of building consensus and support for a policy among those participants who have the power to affect the outcome and who often disagree over what they think the outcome should be. As Hilsman said in 1959, "The making of policy in government . . . is essentially a political process, even when it takes place entirely inside the government, screened from the voter's view, or even when it takes place entirely within one agency of the government."[8] The aspects of this process that make it political, then, are first, that there are divergences among participants over the ends and means of policy; second, that these participants can influence, though in varying degree, the choices that are made; and, third, that the forging of a policy consensus is achieved through the standard techniques of negotiation, bargaining, and compromise. In what probably remains the best analytical discussion of the foreign policy process, Schilling captures the essence of its political nature:

> The general character of conflict among such "powers" is in many respects comparable to the diplomatic struggle among contending nations. Each endeavors to isolate the other, to secure "allies" for itself, and to gain the favorable opinion of "neutrals"—activities of great importance given the dispersion of power among elite groups. Discussions between the contending parties are negotiatory rather than analytical in nature. The object is to persuade the opponent that his position is unreasonable (either by arguments designed to show that it will not really serve his interest or by appeals to other interests alleged to be both common and more important), or, failing that, to search for grounds on which a satisfactory settlement can be made. This may take the form of a direct compromise on the issue concerned (where the incentive to accommodate stems from the desire to avoid the costs of even winning a fight) or of a bargain reached by bringing into negotiation another issue in dispute and thereby permitting each (provided they evaluate the two issues disproportionately) to give up something of less value than that which it receives.[9]

5. The outcome or resultant of such a process is clear. The content of any particular policy reflects as much the necessities of the conditions in which it is forged—what is required to obtain agreement—as it does the substantive merits of that policy. How we go about making decisions does affect the kinds of decisions we make. Process influences content. Hilsman put it nicely:

> In a political process the relative power of these participating groups is as relevant to the final decisions as the cogency and wisdom of the arguments used in support of the policy adopted. Who advocates a particular policy may be as important as what he advocates. . . . The test of policy is not that it will most effectively accomplish an agreed-upon value but that a wider number of people decide to endorse it.[10]

These are important insights. They alert us to the effects of process on substance. They tell us that "organization is politics by other means." They remind us that we cannot look solely to the impact of other nations' actions on the United States in order to explain America's reactions to what they do to us. Above all, they impress upon us the political aspects of our foreign policy: that conflicts over goals and the means appropriate to attain them are reconciled in a domestic arena of bargaining, negotiation, compromise, and consensus building. In foreign policy, politics may "stop at the water's edge"; but there certainly is a lot of it before we reach the coastlines.

Notice, however, what these theorists have *not* told us about what characterizes this political process. First, they have not told us to ignore the effects that Congress has on foreign policy. To the contrary, they have emphasized Congress's reactive role to executive initiative, with the attendant stress on the lobbyist and anticipatory functions that it performs in the policy process. Huntington stresses Congress's lobbyist function in framing military policy: "The unwillingness of Congress to exercise a veto over strategic programs does not mean that Congress has no role in the formulation of those programs. . . . The most prominent congressional role is that of prodder or goad of the Administration on behalf of specific programs or activities. With the executive the decision-maker, Congress becomes the lobbyist."[11] Hilsman accentuates the anticipatory function and the general constraints that Congress puts on executive action:

Congress participates only fitfully in the actual formulation of foreign policy. . . . Yet it is equally clear that Congress—subtly and indirectly, but, nevertheless, effectively—sets the tone of many policies and limits on many others. . . . It seems obvious that Executive proposals are shaped by estimates of how Congress and individual congressmen will react, the mood of Congress, and the probability, circumstances, and possible means they may use in reprisal.[12]

Second, the first wave never said that the perspectives of participants, the stances they take on issues, and the resulting conflicts over policy stem *solely* from the institutional positions these participants occupy. To the contrary, what emerges from a close reading of their work is the crucial significance of the fundamental assumptions (what I appropriately think should be called "mind-sets") that participants bring to their jobs in determining their perspectives and subsequent stances. In characterizing the conflicts inherent in the foreign policy process, Schilling tells us something quite important:

There are two basic causes for policy conflict among government elites and . . . these conflicts lead to two different kinds of groupings among them. Many of these conflicts simply reflect the diversity of opinion Americans are likely to hold in the absence of sanctions to the contrary, regarding the state of the world and what America should do in it. *The groups that coalesce in support of one or another of these views appear, for the most part, to cut across formal institutional and organizational lines* (Congress, Executive, State, Defense).

In contrast, some policy conflicts are "institutionally grounded." These are differences that result from the peculiar responsibilities (with respect either to values or to skills) of various government institutions and organizations. Not sharing the same responsibilities (or, put the other way, not charged with the representation of the same values or skills), government organizations will necessarily bring divergent interests and approaches to common problems. When conflicts of this order occur, the lines of battle are more likely to conform to the boundaries of the organizations involved. These are also the more enduring of the two kinds of group conflict. Specific ideas about what to do in the world will change, and with them the ad hoc groupings that once espoused them. But divergent responsibilities are built into the structure of government. The allocation of responsibility may be changed, but the effect is usually to shift the location of battle rather than to bring it to an end.[13]

Allison's summary of Schilling's work accurately states that the budgetary process is characterized in part by "participants whose policy differences stem from *both intellectual and institutional differences.*"[14] Organizational role (or institutional responsibility) is a component of a participant's outlook, but often only a component and often not even the overriding one.

Third, and integrally related to the second point, the first-wave theorists have not emphasized the nature of the policy process over the images that participants have of the international environment when they assess the relative weights of each on the substance of policy. To the contrary, the images are primary, the process secondary, though not inconsequential, in the framing of policy. In prefacing his analysis of the politics of the fiscal 1950 defense budget, an area where one would expect the process to be more significant than the mind-sets,[15] Schilling cautions us thus: "The kind of defenses a budget provides will be *primarily a reflection of the kinds of ideas people have about the political-military world in which they are living.* . . . But the influence exercised on the content of the budget by the character of the political process, *while definitely subordinate,* is not insignificant."[16] If Schilling is representative of the first wave, then preexisting mind-sets tell us more about the direction and character of our foreign policy than the nature of the governmental political process in which it is forged.

Fourth, the first wave never told us that the resultant of the political process, the *compromised* nature of the policy that emerges from the pulling and hauling of the participants, was one unintended by many or most of them. To the contrary, the spirit, if not the substance of their work, is to assert the reverse: participants frame their actions with a view toward what is required to get a policy adopted. Initial positions are so framed, negotiations are undertaken, compromises are entered into precisely because participants are aware of what it takes to get a particular proposal accepted. In our system, the cost of consensus is compromise; but the participants know that before they begin their policy battles. Initial positions are taken with a view toward the negotiations and compromises that will be necessary in order to obtain agreement. What participants want and what they know they are likely to get are two different things. What they ask for will not always, nor perhaps even usually, reflect what they ideally would like or what they know they can get. The need to "anticipate" the probable reactions of others to one's initiatives requires that participants frame their positions with these "anticipated reactions" in mind. In a bargaining situation, never ask for what you know you can get; if you do so, you will not get it. This need to anticipate reactions and to get others to go along is what Hilsman meant when he said: "The test of a policy is that a wider number of people decide to endorse it." This is what Schilling meant when he said, "Discussions between contending parities are negotiatory rather than analytical in nature." This is what Huntington meant when he said, "In strategy, as elsewhere, meaningful policy requires both content and consensus. . . . Consensus is a cost to each participant in the policy-making process, but it is a prerequisite to any policy."[17] The point, then, is that the compromise that results from the pulling and hauling was deliberately intended by the participants. The *exact nature* of the compromise that results may be unintended or unforeseen, but not the *initial intent* to achieve some sort of a compromise.

Fifth and last, the first wave has not allowed us to neglect the influence of domestic politics on foreign policy—not the politics of executive legislative relations, not the politics of executive pulling and hauling, but the politics of getting elected, staying in office, and carrying constituents along in support of particular foreign policies. This theme emerges most conspicuously from Huntington's study of national security policy from 1945 through 1960: "If this book has any distinctive message, it is that military policy can only be understood as the responses of the government to conflicting pressures from its foreign and domestic environments. . . . Military policy cannot be separated from foreign policy, fiscal policy, and domestic policy. *It is part of the warp and woof of American politics.*"[18] In assessing the effects of domestic politics on military policy, Huntington's study stresses two general points: First, that major shifts in strategic policy by Administrations and major criticisms by the party out of power were as much partisan and political as they were reactions to external threats or refinements due to strategic analysis;[19] second, although the public's opinions only loosely constrained executive choice in framing military policy, nevertheless, these opinions affected executive action, not because of the nature of those opinions per se, but because elites were responsive to the images that they had in their heads of what the public wanted, demanded, or merely would tolerate.[20]

THE SECOND WAVE—POLICY VIA BUREAUCRATIC POLITICS

Why discuss the first-wave theorists in so much detail? Why quote copiously from their works? Why retread ground so familiar to all of us? The answer is simple: to build a record in order to determine whether the "second wave" is saying something different from the first and, if so, in what respects it differs. If the second-wave theorists are not merely rehashing in another guise the significant insights of the first wave, then we must compare what they are saying with what has been said before. Stating the latter, however, is easier than specifying the former. The second-wave theorists have engaged in considerable "waffling" (ambiguity and backtracking) on precisely those propositions that would merit calling their approach something new. If we are sufficiently severe about their waffling, we could conclude that the bureaucratic approach is in fact "old (but extremely) fine wine in new bottles." That is, unless we can tighten up their argument, the bureaucratic politics paradigm rapidly decays into the political process approach of the first wave. By tightening up

their central propositions, we can form a clear picture of what the bureaucratic approach *should* be and then determine its merits. Therefore, if a *bureaucratic* politics approach is to claim any distinctness, much less validity, it must at the least assert the following propositions:

Proposition One: Organizational position determines policy stance, or, "where you stand depends on where you sit."[21]

The first-wave theorists never specified under what precise circumstances or in which particular issue areas this proposition held, but because most of their work centered on national security policy and particularly on issues that had immediate budgetary implications (especially for the military services), by inference one could assume this proposition applied primarily to decisions having clear, immediate budgetary effects. Hence Allison asserts "for large classes of issues—e.g., budgets and procurement decisions—the stance of a particular player can be predicted with high reliability from information about his seat."[22] So far we have not gone too far—but the second wave has as yet not gone any further with this proposition, and they have, moreover, surrounded it with so many qualifiers and such ambiguity that its reliability (and hence predictive power) must be seriously questioned. Witness the following:

Each participant sits in a seat that confers separate responsibilities. Each man is committed to fulfilling his responsibilities *as he sees them.*[23]

Thus propensities and priorities stemming from position are sufficient to allow analysts to make reliable predictions about a player's stand *in many cases.* But these propensities are filtered through the baggage that players bring to positions. *Some knowledge of both the pressures and the baggage is thus required for sound predictions.*[24]

We believe that membership in the bureaucracy *substantially determines the participants' perceptions and goals.*[25]

Participants whose stands on issues can be predicted with high reliability from a knowledge of their organizational affiliation will be termed organizational participants and those for whom organizational membership is not a good predictor will be termed players. . . . *The higher the formal position occupied by the participant, the more likely it is that he will behave like a player.*[26]

Their [senior players'] perceptions of the national security interest are more likely to be dominated *by images shared with society, their own experiences, and their historical memories.*[27]

In any specific case it is difficult to predict the exact mix of interests which will determine the face of a national security issue seen by the participant, his stake in its resolution, and *his stand on it.*[28]

The left hand taketh away what the right hand giveth! If each man is "committed to fulfilling his responsibilities as he sees them," do different men who occupy the *same* seat over time see the responsibilities of the office in the same way? If not, then what is the relative weight of position in policy stance? How constraining are the top positions in our governmental bureaucracy for the roles that senior participants who fill these positions choose to play? If "senior players" are the most powerful participants in the policy process, but if their stances on issues are not correlated with their organizational affiliations, then of what use is the first proposition for analysis and prediction? If one cannot specify stance from position for these players in most issue areas, then why bother with their *bureaucratic* position? If "shared images" (or mind-sets) are far more important for determining the policy stance of senior players, then again why disaggregate them by *bureaucratic* position? If senior officials actually *share* mind-sets, then how do the mechanics of pulling and hauling explain the thrust of our foreign policy; or, better yet, do we in fact *have* pulling and hauling?[29] If one cannot specify in what issue areas other than budgetary and procurement decisions stance correlates highly with position, instead merely stating that this works "in many cases," then why claim something for a paradigm that one's own analysis does not bear out? By asking these questions of the position-perception proposition, we begin to see in microcosm one of the central difficulties with the bureaucratic politics paradigm: we must qualify it with so many amendments before it begins to work that when it does, we may not be left with a bureaucratic paradigm but may in reality be using another one quite different.

Proposition Two: In foreign policy, governmental decision and actions do not represent the intent of any one figure, but are rather the unintended resultant of bargaining, pulling, and hauling among the principal participants.

Allison puts the case this way:

The decisions and actions of governments are intranational political *resultants*: resultants in the sense that what happens is not chosen as a solution to a problem but rather results from compromise, conflict and confusion of officials with diverse interests and unequal influence; *political* in the sense that the activity from which decisions and actions emerge is best characterized as bargaining along regularized channels among individual members of the government.

The sum of behavior of representatives of a government relevant to an issue is rarely intended by any individual or group. Rather, in the typical case, separate individuals with different intentions contribute pieces to a resultant (italics added).

Equally often however, different groups pulling in different directions produce a result, or better a restraint . . . distinct from what any person or group intended.

If a nation performed an action, that action was the *resultant* of bargaining among individuals and groups within the government.[30]

In one fundamental sense this proposition is descriptive of what goes on in our governmental machinery.

No analyst could deny that there is pulling, hauling, and bargaining by the principal participants involved in a given issue. As the first wave told us, in a system of government where power is dispersed, all have "to give a little to get a little."[31] But in another fundamental sense, proposition two begs the issue because it does not specify for us *how much difference all the pulling and hauling and bargaining actually make;* or, to put the matter more carefully, under what circumstances and in what issue areas does all the commotion make a significant difference? If, for example, the resultant of governmental mechanics was a decision to buy three nuclear-powered aircraft carriers instead of two conventionally powered ones initially intended, is this to be considered a resultant significantly different from that which anyone intended? In short, if there is pulling, hauling, and bargaining (and there often is), what are the precise effects on the decisions made and the actions taken?

To ask the question this way is not to nitpick, but rather to raise the central question about bureaucratic politics paradigm: in foreign policy formulation (the act of making a choice), how much does the pulling, hauling, and bargaining below the president affect presidential choice? How much does he have to give in order to get? If there is no direction or control from the top, then obviously a bureaucratic paradigm is essential for analyzing the foreign policy process; then, decisions are truly the resultants of governmental mechanics. But if there is central control from the top, then how much of a difference do the mechanics make? How far do they deflect presidential decisions from presidential intent? Are the mechanics only marginally important, or do they cause significant deflection? When do presidential perspectives override bureaucrats' preferences, or do they at all?[32]

The second-wave theorists have not ignored the role the president plays, but they have not helped us answer the deflection question. They appear to want to have their cake (assert the resultant effect of the bureaucratic perspective) and yet eat it too (acknowledge the president's signal importance in foreign policy formulation). Again,

Action . . . [is] a resultant of political bargaining among a number of independent players, *the President being* only a "superpower" among many lesser but considerable powers.[33]

The details of the action are therefore not chosen by any individual (and are rarely identical with what any of the players would have chosen if he had confronted the issue as a matter of simple, detached choice). *Nevertheless, resultants can be roughly consistent with some group's preference in the context of the political game.*[34]

Where an outcome was for the most part the triumph of an individual (e.g., the President) or group (e.g., the President's men or a cabal) *this model attempts to specify the details of the game that made the victory possible.*[35]

The President stands at the center of the foreign policy process in the United States. *His role and influence over decisions are qualitatively different than those of any other participants.* In any foreign policy decision widely perceived at the time to be important, the President will be a principal if not the principal figure determining the general direction of actions.[36]

As the ABM decision illustrates, *the President is qualitatively different—not simply a very powerful player among less powerful players.*[37]

The diplomatic and defense spheres yield our man [the president] *authority for binding judgments on behalf of the whole government.* Although he rarely gets unquestioning obedience and often pays a price, *his personal choices are authoritative,* for he himself is heir to royal prerogatives.[38]

The bureaucratic paradigm will explain a great deal about foreign policy formulation if we assume that presidential preferences do not significantly constrain senior executive players in what they can do. But the paradigm will explain very little if we accept the amendments about the presidency that the second wave has made to proposition two. When we accept the amendments, moreover, we are forced by inference to adopt two corollaries that bring into doubt the usefulness of proposition two:

Corollary One: When senior executive players are split on their policy stances, the president, by virtue of the division, has considerable leeway to choose that which he wishes to do, or that which he thinks he ought to do, or that which he reasons he must do.

Corollary Two: When senior executive players are split on their policy stances, the president, to the extent that he reasons he must take account of bureaucrats' pressures, will respond to those demands that he thinks will damage him politically if he does not respond.

Corollary one reminds us of the old divide-and-conquer adage. If we press it to its extreme, then we might very well conclude that it is the very divisions that arise in the executive branch that preserve presidential flexibility in foreign policy. Corollary two reminds us that we must not lose sight of the forest by concentrating on the quirks of each and every tree: the preferences of senior players per se are not what count, but rather presidential estimation of who outside the executive branch, which members of Congress, for example, will back these players. A close look at proposition two thus forces us away from the nuts and bolts of executive wrangling to the truisms of American government. It is presidential anticipation of congressional and public response that causes him to heed those bureaucrats' demands he chooses to accede to. By reminding us of the power that presidents derive from executive decisions, corollary one makes us dubious of the *resultant* aspects of proposition two. By reminding us of the president's need to anticipate the congressional reactions that stem from the sharing of powers, corollary two makes us dubious of the *unintended* aspect of proposition two. Each requires that we focus on what Neustadt ten years ago told us was crucial to presidential power—the choices that presidents make.

Both force us to concentrate on the conscious act of presidential choice and thereby refresh our memory about presidential predominance in foreign policy. Where, then, are we? What shall we conclude from proposition two: presidential preferences and decisions are (check one) —always, —usually, —often, —sometimes, —not usually, —rarely, —not at all, decisive in the foreign policy choices we make?

If this were not enough, let us open one more can of worms about proposition two, one that forces us to look at the perceived external constraints, not the internal mechanics of government. How often and over what issues do participants disagree in their policy stances? Does it ever happen that participants are unanimously opposed to Presidential preferences? How often and over what issues do participants *not* disagree over the thrust of action to be taken? These queries raise again the significance of mind-sets in foreign policy formulation. If shared images dominate senior players' outlooks and if they are truly *shared,* then what is the merit in asserting that governmental actions are the resultants of pulling, hauling, and bargaining? If organizational responsibilities do not pull players apart and if the images they share draw them together, then are we not talking about what Allison calls the nation-state as a "unitary purposive actor"?[39] In this case, governmental action does not represent the intent of any one figure but the intent of most, if not all. Finally, have not the cases of shared mind-sets occurred on precisely the pivotal decisions of American foreign policy since 1945? And if that be so, why not spend time on the mind-sets of the senior players rather than on the mechanics of their position in order to explain the thrust of our foreign policy? Thus, if both of these criticisms are valid—that presidents have predominated in our postwar foreign policy and that similar or shared mind-sets have characterized decisions on pivotal issues—then the result is to give much more weight to the nation-state-as-unitary-actor view than the bureaucratic paradigm would lead us to believe.

Proposition Three: Organizational routine, standard operating procedures, and vested interests can affect the presidential implementation of policy much more than they can its formulating.

The first two propositions are aimed at showing how bureaucratic politics affect the formulation of policy, but they apply there the least. Where the bureaucratic paradigm finds its forte is with the implementation of policy. As Allison puts it:

Making sure that the government does what is decided is more difficult than selecting the preferred solution.

Detail and nuance of actions by organizations are determined chiefly by organizational routines, not government leaders' directions.

A considerable gap separates what leaders choose . . . and what organizations implement.[40]

Practitioners agree with parts of this proposition and with the distinction between policy formulation and policy implementation. The most recent expression of agreement is by Henry Kissinger: "Making foreign policy is easy; what is difficult is its coordination and implementation. . . . [t]he outsider believes a Presidential order is consistently followed out. Nonsense. I have to spend considerable time seeing that it is carried out and in the spirit the President intended."[41]

That making decisions is easier for presidents than getting them implemented is no accident. Presidents have been ingenious at developing sources of information outside of bureaucratic channels and hence have reduced their dependence on standard information operating procedures. The deference that Congress and the public have given to presidential lead in foreign affairs in the postwar era accounts for the predominance of presidential perspectives and preferences. The primacy and immediacy of foreign policy since 1945 have turned all presidents into activists in the realm of foreign policy, even if they have wished otherwise, with the consequent presidential attention and energy directed to these matters. Almost all of our presidents, moreover, have come into office with clear and fixed ideas on what they wished to do, or not wished to do, in foreign policy. With the necessary information, political deference, will and determination, presidents have been able to make decisions tailored to their own desires. But when presidents and their personal staffs have had to implement these decisions, necessity has forced them to delegate. The limits of their collective physical capabilities and of the time they can devote to any single issue require that presidents rely largely on existing bureaucratic machinery in order to implement the decisions they make. When the organizational machinery is engaged, then the standard operating procedures begin to take their toll. Presidential monitoring and oversight of bureaucratic motion can mitigate, if not remedy, the distorting effects of bureaucratic momentum; but the opportunity costs of too much time spent on any one issue can be quite high due to the pressure of other issues that require resolution. Unless presidents carefully follow up the decisions they make, there is *some* slippage between presidential intent and organizational output.

Where, then, does this proposition leave us? If presidential intent can be subverted by bureaucratic implementation, then what difference does the initial decision make? If bureaucracies determine the "detail and nuance" of policy, then does not the bureaucratic paradigm work even if its validity with respect to policy formulation is close to nil? Does acceptance of proposition three nullify the criticisms of propositions one and two? What we make of proposition three hangs heavily on how we answer three additional questions. First, how important are the initial acts of presidential choice? Second, how much slippage is there between intent and output? Third, how detrimental is the slippage to the success of policy?

Unfortunately, these questions are not easy to answer in the abstract. The answers, especially to the last two, depend largely on the particular circumstances attendant to the decision at issue. There are, however, three general points to be made that put the significance of proposition three into its proper perspective. First, the initial act of choice is crucial, no matter how the choice is implemented. As Alexander George remarks: "the fact that any Presidential decision has to be effectively implemented cannot be used to down-grade the importance of choices which the President makes."[42] Analytically, there are two types of choices—to do something, or not to do something. In cases where the president decides not to do something—not to intervene some place with military force, not to buy new bombers, not to conclude an alliance, not to negotiate an arms control agreement, not to recognize a country, not to extend foreign aid to some nation—implementing the decision is irrelevant to its success. In acts of negative choice, presidential decisions obviate the need to implement them. The case is not so sharp with acts of positive choice, but even here the choices themselves are nevertheless critical. We may wish to know, for example, how organizational interests affected the air war and ground strategy in Vietnam,[43] but we still would want to know why we had an air war over North Vietnam and American combat troops in South Vietnam, that is, why we intervened in the first place. We may wish to know how standard operating procedures influenced the way our troops were deployed in the Dominican Republic in 1965, but we would not want to forget why we put them there in the first place.[44] We may wish to know how MacArthur made life difficult for Truman in the Korean War, but we would still wish to know why MacArthur was there leading troops in the first place.[45] We may be interested in why we chose to blockade Cuba in October of 1962 instead of launching an air strike in order to get Soviet missiles out of Cuba, but we would not want to ignore the reasons why Kennedy decided that we had to get the missiles out in the first place.[46] To state the matter in this fashion is to show the critical importance of presidential decisions to do something. The details of implementation will, of course, influence the likelihood of success of a policy; but they become operative only after an act of positive choice. And while slippage can affect success, it cannot explain why the policy was launched. The "detail and nuance" of actions by organizations cannot be used to denigrate the signal importance of the act of presidential choice.

Second, the slippage between presidential intent and organizational output is greatest on those issues that presidents consider least important and smallest on those that they deem most important. This point is a logical consequence of proposition three: organizational procedures can cause slippage, but they do not automatically or mechanistically do so. Whether they do so depends on the president's degree of determination *not* to permit them to do so. Slippage is inversely correlated with a presidential commitment to make his decision stick. Allison himself confirms this inverse correlation in his study of presidential control of the Cuban missile crisis blockade:

Thus the governmental leaders had both the capability and the incentive to reach out beyond the traditional limits of their control. Maps in the "Situation Room" in the basement of the White House tracked the movement of all Soviet ships. The members of the Ex. Com. knew each of the ships by name and argued extensively about which should be stopped first, at what point, and how. Sorenson records, "The President's personal direction of the quarantine's operation . . . his determination not to let needless incidents or reckless subordinates escalate so dangerous and delicate a crisis beyond control. *Thus, for the first time in U.S. military history, local commanders received repeated orders about the details of their military operations.*[47]

Nor is this an isolated case. Lyndon Johnson's personal conduct of the air war over North Vietnam and Richard Nixon's personal conduct of negotiations to "end" the war are but two recent examples. Therefore, not only do the pivotal issues find their way up to the president for resolution; but once he deems them to be so, the president finds ways to reach down into the bureaucracy so as to ensure that his intent will be realized. This requires considerable time and effort, and presidents are thereby forced to be selective.[48] Thus on issues the president deems pivotal, the bureaucratic paradigm will alert us to the exertions that a president must go through in order to get the executive bureaucracies to give them what he wants; but it will err if it tells us that presidents do not get substantially what they want. The paradigm will account for the effort required, but it will not predict the result of that effort.

Third, slippage is not equally detrimental on all types of policy issues.[49] For one type of decision, all that matters to the president is that the positive choice be made. The details of implementation are not of consequence from his perspective, and slippage is irrelevant. For example, for Lyndon Johnson in 1967, what mattered was that a decision be made to deploy *an* ABM system, never mind the details of what kind of system. He cared most about avoiding an "ABM gap" in the 1968 election and about getting arms control talks started with the Soviet Union. From his vantage point almost any kind of initial ABM deployment served his purposes. What mattered least to him (and most to McNamara) were the details—whether the ABM would be designed as thick or thin, whether it would appear to be directed against the Chinese or the Russians, what contractor would build it, which service would "own" it.[50] For another type of decision, one where slippage can hurt it, it will, unless presidential commitment is there. If it is, then, as we saw above, the slippage is least likely to occur. Finally, for a third type of issue, slippage may be desirable from the president's perspective; or, perhaps a clearer way to put it is that the president wants to communicate ambiguity over what decision has been made, not only to his subordinates, but to foreigners. The multilateral force

(MLF) is a good case in point. Kennedy and Johnson gave enough of a commitment to enable the bureaucratic partisans to go "hunting," but not so much of a commitment that they could not discount it if it proved a disaster. Their intent was to see whether the Europeans would buy the idea of an MLF. The ambiguity over what it would look like and how fully the president was committed served presidential purposes of testing European reactions and of killing it (as Johnson did) if they proved too hostile.[51]

The thrust of the above three points is not to deny that slippage between presidential intent and executive output can result from the mediating impact of organizational procedures. Such slippage does occur, sometimes even on issues presidents deem vital. The above points, however, do tell us, first, that the slippage is neither as automatic nor always as crucial as the second wave would have us believe; second, that the probability of slippage is lowest on those issues presidents fully commit themselves to and wholly invest their prestige in; and third, therefore, that when the detail and the nuance of action are critical in implementing a decision presidents deem vital, more often that not "the directions of government leaders," not organizational routine, will determine them. Presidents are not omnipotent, but neither, then, are they impotent. No president can control everything, but that does not mean he cannot control a great many things. His capacity to get what he wants from his executive subordinates should not be underestimated. The constraints he works under should not blind us to the constraints he can and does make them work under. In short, the gap is not always, nor even usually, considerable between "what leaders choose and organizations implement." Precisely because the size of the gap is correlated with the degree of presidential commitment, presidential intent becomes all the more significant. It is the key variable for determining the degree of applicability of the bureaucratic paradigm. Thus, a close look at what the paradigm says about policy implementation drives us inexorably back to policy formulation—to the act of presidential choice, to the area where the paradigm works weakly, if at all.

CONCLUSION

More questions have obviously been raised in this essay than can be answered here.[52] But enough has been said to raise severe doubts about the merits of the bureaucratic paradigm as an approach for analyzing American foreign policy. These doubts point the way to two fundamental weaknesses of the paradigm: first, it undervalues the influence (or weight) of both generational mind-sets and domestic politics on the manner in which top decision makers approach foreign policy; second, it is too sloppy, vague, and imprecise as constituted at present to make its use worthwhile. Both of these weaknesses boil down to one central complaint: too many constraints of a nonbureaucratic nature must be set before the paradigm works, and more often than not, once we set the constraints, the paradigm will account for very little, if anything. That complaint, however, does not constitute a good case against ever using a bureaucratic paradigm. Rather it is an argument for keeping the proper perspective. Once we have specified the external and internal constraints—once we have adopted the systemic perspective—the paradigm may tell us some things that we would otherwise overlook. But we need the systemic perspective in order to avoid the opposite dangers that an uncritical acceptance of the paradigm would bring—looking for things that are not there and seeing things that we should overlook.

NOTES

1. Henry A. Kissinger, quoted in I. M. Destler, *Presidents, Bureaucrats, and Foreign Policy* (Princeton, N.J.: Princeton University Press, 1972), 3.

2. The best statements on what the "second wave" thinks the bureaucratic policies paradigm is and on what we should expect from it can be found in the following works: Graham T. Allison, *Essence of Decision: Explaining the Cuban Missile Crisis* (Boston: Little, Brown, 1971), esp. chaps. 5 and 6; Graham T. Allison and Morton H. Halperin, "Bureaucratic Politics: A Paradigm and Some Policy Implications," *World Politics* 24 (Spring 1972): 40–80, Supplement; Raymond Tanter and Richard H. Ullman, eds., *Theory and Policy in International Relations* (Princeton, N.J.: Princeton University Press, 1972); Morton H. Halperin, *Bureaucratic Politics and Foreign Policy* (Washington, D.C.: Brookings Institution, 1974); Morton H. Halperin and Arnold Kanter, "The Bureaucratic Perspective: A Preliminary Framework," in *Readings in American Foreign Policy,* ed. Halperin and Kanter (Boston: Little, Brown, 1973), 1–42; Richard E. Neustadt, *Alliance Politics* (New York: Columbia University Press, 1970), esp. chaps. 5 and 6; Morton H. Halperin, "The Decision to Deploy the ABM: Bureaucratic and Domestic Politics in the Johnson Administration," *World Politics,* 25 (October 1972): 62–96; and Morton H. Halperin, "Why Bureaucrats Play Games," *Foreign Policy,* no. 2 (Spring 1971).

3. See Richard E. Neustadt, *Presidential Power: The Politics of Leadership* (New York: John Wiley 1960); Warner R. Schilling, "The Politics of National Defense: Fiscal 1950," in *Strategy, Politics and Defense Budgets,* ed. Warner R. Schilling, Paul T. Hammond, and Glenn H. Snyder (New York: Columbia University Press, 1962), 1–267; Samuel P. Huntington, *The Common Defense: Strategic Programs in National Politics* (New York: Columbia University Press, 1961); Roger Hilsman, "The Foreign-Policy Consensus: An Interim Report," *Journal of Conflict Resolution* 3 (December 1959): 361–82 and his *To Move a Nation* (Garden City, N.Y.: Doubleday, 1967), esp. 1, 2, and 10.

4. In Chapter 5 of *Essence of Decision,* Allison has carefully cataloged the insights of these scholars. The list that follows does not parallel Allison's but rather reflects my estimation of what we should select from the "first wave" in order to be better able to analyze and evaluate the contribution of the "second wave." Why I have selected these five and not others will become clear shortly.

5. Neustadt, *Presidential Power,* 33.

6. Schilling, "The Politics of National Defense," 22.

7. A paraphrase of Neustadt, *Presidential Power,* 34.

8. Hilsman, "The Foreign-Policy Consensus," 365.

9. See pp. 5–27 of Schilling's "The Politics of National Defense." The quotation comes from p. 22.

10. "The Foreign-Policy Consensus," 365 and 364.

11. Huntington, *The Common Defense,* 135.

12. Hilsman, "The Foreign-Policy Consensus," 369. See also his "Congressional-Executive Relations and the Foreign Policy Consensus," *American Political Science Review* 52 (September 1958): 725–44.

13. Schilling, "The Politics of National Defense," 21–22 (italics added).

14. Allison, *Essence of Decision,* 154–55 (italics added).

15. I shall discuss why this should be so later.

16. Schilling, "The Politics of National Defense," 15 (italics added).

17. Huntington, *The Common Defense,* 167.

18. Ibid., x–xi (italics added).

19. Ibid., chap. 4.

20. Ibid., 251.

21. Attributed to Don K. Price; quoted in Allison, *Essence of Decision,* 176.

22. Ibid., 176.

23. Ibid., 148 (italics added).

24. Ibid., 167 (italics added).

25. Halperin and Kanter, "The Bureaucratic Perspective," 3.

26. Ibid., 9–10 (italics added).

27. Ibid., 16 (italics added).

28. Ibid., 15 (italics added).

29. I shall amplify this point below, for it is crucial in assessing the merits of the "realist paradigm" vs. the bureaucratic politics paradigm.

30. Allison, *Essence of Decision,* 162, 175, 145, and 173.

31. A phrase attributed to former Speaker of the House of Representatives, Sam Rayburn.

32. In his "The Politics of National Defense," Schilling, for example, found that Truman had to give very little. He details marvelously the bargaining among the chiefs and between them and Secretary of Defense James V. Forrestal and the extensive maneuvers Forrestal went through in order to get the chiefs something above the $15 billion figure that Truman had set for the services. Schilling concludes thus (p. 199):

Finally, the day for which Forrestal had been seven months in preparation arrived. On December 9 he and Webb [Director of the Budget Bureau] met with the President at the White House, together with the Chiefs, the service Secretaries, Gruenther, Webb and Souers. With maps and charts the military briefed Truman on the difference between what they could accomplish with a $14.4 billion budget and a $16.9 billion budget. The President listened. When the presentation was over he thanked them and then announced that the ceiling still stood.

Forrestal's defeat on December 9 was complete and final. "In the person of Harry Truman," he concluded, "I have seen the most rocklike example of civilian control that the world has ever witnessed."

33. Allison, *Essence of Decision,* 162 (italics added).

34. Ibid., 175 (italics added).

35. Ibid., 173 (italics added).

36. Halperin and Kanter, "The Bureaucratic Perspective," 6 and 7 (italics added).

37. Halperin, "The Decision to Deploy the ABM," 91.

38. Neustadt, "White House and Whitehall," *Public Interest,* no. 2 (1966): 50–69; reprinted in Halperin and Kanter, *Readings in American Foreign Policy,* 40 (italics added).

39. Allison, *Essence of Decision,* chap. 1.

40. Ibid., 146, 89, 93.

41. Quoted in John P. Leacacos, "Kissinger's Apparat," and I. M. Destler, "Can One Man Do?" both in *Foreign Policy* 5 (Winter 1971–72): 5 and 2.

42. "The Case for Multiple Advocacy in Making Foreign Policy," *American Political Science Review* 66 (September 1972): 792.

43. See Robert Gallucci, "U.S. Military Policy in Vietnam: A View from the Bureaucratic Perspective" (Ph.D. diss., Brandeis University, 1973).1

44. See Abraham F. Lowenthal, *The Dominican Intervention* (Cambridge, Mass.: Harvard University Press, 1972).

45. See Neustadt, *Presidential Power,* chaps. 2 and 6.

46. Allison, *Essence of Decision,* chaps. 2, 4, and 6.

47. Ibid., 128 (italics added).

48. See I. M. Destler's *Presidents, Bureaucrats, and Foreign Policy* for a prescription of how a president can increase the range of issues on which he can make his will felt, especially Chapter 9.

49. I have not been able to devise suitable analytical categories, by policy issue, for which slippage is more or less important and have therefore resorted to listing the three possible cases. Someone else should try to do so.

50. Halperin, "The Decision to Deploy the ABM."

51. See John Steinbrunner, *The Cybernetic Theory of Decision: New Dimensions of Political Analysis* (Princeton, N.J.: Princeton University Press, 1974); also Philip Geyelin, *LBJ and The World* (New York: Praeger, 1966), chap. 7.

52. My forthcoming monograph will treat these questions and others more fully in an attempt to specify more precisely where the paradigm works, where it does not, and why it does and does not work.

CHAPTER 3

THE CONTEXT OF
AMERICAN DEFENSE POLICY

NATIONAL SECURITY IN A WORLD OF TIERS

DONALD M. SNOW

It is now reasonably clear what the general nature of the international system that is succeeding the Cold War system will be. We lack general agreement on the terminology with which to describe the new arrangements. For lack of a better set of terms, I will refer to it as a "world of tiers."

TIERS AND THE SECURITY EQUATION: A FIRST BRUSH

The basic idea is simple: as the post–Cold War world evolves, the international system is clearly divided into two distinct groups (or tiers) of states. The first tier, composed basically of the membership of the Organization of Economic Cooperation and Development (OECD), represents the most prosperous countries in the world. The second tier, representing the rest of humankind (about six-sevenths of the world's population, according to Max Singer and the late Aaron Wildavksy), is composed of those countries materially and politically less prosperous and content.

This division suggests that the system consists of two separate components, each with a different set of governing rules and dynamics such that no single set of descriptions can encompass them both. Rather, each has its own distinct set of relationships and problems. The national security equation, in turn, will largely be the result of where the two tiers intersect.

THE FIRST TIER

The defining characteristic of the countries of the first tier is their political and economic similarity: all have democratic political systems (although the form of democracy is not uniform), and they all share a commitment to market-driven capitalist economics. Moreover, they are all part of the interlocking global international economy in which the distinctly national basis of economic activity is decreasingly possible.

These countries thus have much more in common than they have that divides them. The central relationship among them is probably most dramatically symbolized by the ongoing concert of summit meetings between their leaders, such as the Group of Seven (G-7) biannual meetings. Certainly they are not in accord on all matters. They disagree, for instance, on the terms of trade among themselves and on the amount and pace of assistance that should be given to rehabilitate Russia and other parts of the former Soviet Union.

Their disagreements are, however, marginal, not central. The leadership has progressed into the third industrial revolution that has globalized economic activity; their economic differences can hardly deteriorate except beyond the peripheries of the central relationship. Cultural differences may create a different view on democratic politics (say American versus Japanese variants), but the core common commitment remains the same among the most consequential members of the international system.

This commonality leads to a striking, if intuitively obvious, national security consequence: *it is essentially impossible to think of war among any of the members of the first tier.* Singer and Wildavsky, indeed, refer to the first tier as the "zone of peace." This means that among the most technologically advanced countries—those with the prospects of raising the most sophisticated and formidable threats—there is basically no national security problem.

Why is this so? For one thing, it has become an accepted tenet that modern political democracies do not go to war with one another: free people do not willingly choose to attack other free people. At the same time, there is little reason for any of the countries of the first tier to fight; the economic and political ideological differences that marked the Cold War have simply disappeared.

Because the countries of the first tier comprise the heart of the international system, this also means the absence of conflicts that could basically threaten the viability of the system as a whole, as did the confrontation between the United States–led North Atlantic Treaty Organization coalition and the Soviet-led Warsaw Pact. Rather than being divided, the first tier stands together. Our principal disagreements arise over how to deal with the problems of the second tier and with instances where the prob-

This essay has been edited and is excerpted from Donald M. Snow, National Security: Defense Policy for a New International Order, *3d ed. (New York: St. Martin's Press, 1995), 11–17 and 312–27. Copyright © 1995. Reprinted by permission of St. Martin's Press, Inc.*

lems of the second tier offer the prospects of disruption within the general tranquillity of the first tier.

THE SECOND TIER

The basic tranquillity and unity of the first tier stands in stark contrast to the roughly six-sevenths of the world's population that comprises the second tier. Roughly speaking, the second tier is made up of most of what used to be called the Third World—the developing countries of Africa, Asia, and Latin America—and the majority of the former Second (or communist/socialist) World, although the status of some formerly communist countries is in question. For instance, it is possible that several of the formerly communist Eastern and Central European countries such as Poland or Hungary will join the first tier, while countries such as Albania or Bulgaria will almost certainly join the second tier.

The most obvious characteristic of the second tier is its diversity. What distinguishes the second tier from the first is that its countries lack either or both a commitment to, or attainment of, political democracy or advanced market capitalism, defined as entrance into the high-technology revolution. Those countries that most closely resemble the first tier approximate it on one dimension or the other. The so-called Four Tigers of East Asia (Republic of Korea, Hong Kong, Taiwan, and Singapore) have economies that look much akin to those of the first tier, but they have not evolved the politically democratic forms of the first tier. In the former Second World, a number of states (Poland and the Baltic states, for example) have made political progress, but still lag behind economically.

Second-tier states differ from one another on both the political and economic dimensions. There are very wealthy second-tier states—the oil-rich states of the Middle East come to mind—that have highly undemocratic political systems, and there are extremely poor countries such as Bangladesh and Mali. Similarly, India is the world's largest democracy, but various forms of despotism are the rule in many areas.

Although there are exceptions, the second tier is marked by instability and the potential or actuality of violence that is quite absent in the first tier. Some of this instability is a concomitant of the developmental process itself, as economic and political forces adjust to modernization. At the same time, what Samuel Huntington has called democracy's "third wave" has spawned a form of revived, exclusionary nationalism that is tearing apart nation-states and is forcing a redrawing of political maps in many places.

The instability and violence has both internal and international roots. Domestically, the post–Cold War world has watched in increasing horror a surge of national self-assertion by ethnic and national groups within states seeking power at the expense of other groups. Primordial nationalism—an attachment to ethnic and other roots not overcome by socialization into a broader national identity—has torn the fabric

of states as diverse as Yugoslavia, Iraq, a number of the successor states of the Soviet Union (such as Armenia, Azerbaijan, and Georgia), and much of Africa (Somalia, Sudan, Mozambique, Rwanda, and Angola, for example).

The worst of these conflicts involve countries divided on religious or ethnic grounds, where attempts to suppress differences in the past have failed and where the hints of freedom have been expressed not in a desire for inclusionary democracy but in a mean and spiteful exclusionary self-determination that pits neighbors against one another in frenzies of hatred and violence with incredible passion. The communal bloodletting in Bosnia is the most visible instance of this for most Americans; it is, unfortunately, by no means rare.

International violence may also increase in the second tier. Regional conflicts—disagreements between neighboring countries in geographic regions—have long festered in places such as the Asian subcontinent and Southeast Asia. During the Cold War, a certain control was imposed by the superpowers, which generally supported opposite sides (the Soviets aiding India, the United States helping Pakistan, for instance) in regional conflicts. Motivated by a desire to avoid being drawn physically into shooting conflicts with escalatory potential, the superpowers sought to contain those conflicts within reasonable bounds that did not risk direct confrontation.

As the Soviet Union dissolved and its successor Russia retreated from this competition, so too did the United States; consequently, many of the constraints have disappeared as well. These conflicts are now enlivened by the introduction of weapons of mass destruction—notably nuclear, biological, or chemical (NBC) munitions—and ballistic missile means of delivery that potentially raise the stakes and deadliness of already volatile situations.

Three of the world's largest and most important states—China, India, and the former Soviet Union—reside in the second tier, and each has some or all of these problems. China continues its economic miracle as one of the world's most vibrant economies, but within a system of political repressiveness that the *New York Times* called "market Leninism" in 1993. China's future raises questions of inevitable demands for political liberalization and the possibility of political breakup at the peripheries—for instance, in Tibet.

India, the world's second most populous country after China, faces severe challenges. Internally, the possibility of secessionary demands that could break apart the Indian state are clear and compelling. These are especially evident in the northern states such as Kashmir, but they could occur in the south (the Tamil region, for instance) as well. India is also locked in a long international conflict with Pakistan that is made more tense by the mutual possession—or near possession—of nuclear weapons.

The breakup of the former Soviet Union has also unleashed violence and instability with two bases. First, Soviet policy consciously encouraged the migration of national groups across the boundaries of the internal republics (states) that are now independent nation-states. Most notably, over 25 million ethnic Russians live outside Russia and are potentially subject to repression that Russia is unlikely to ignore. Second, Stalinist policy drew arbitrary boundaries between the republics that now manifest themselves in international violence. The most obvious case in point is the Armenian-Azerbaijani conflict over the Armenian enclave of Nagorno-Karabakh within Azerbaijan and the Azeri enclave of Nakichevan within Armenia. These conflicts are especially lively in those parts of the former Soviet Union where Islam and Christianity collide—a general source of problems in those parts of the world where it occurs.

FIRST TIER–SECOND TIER INTERSECTION AND THE NATIONAL SECURITY PROBLEM

Violence and instability in the second tier is not a new phenomenon; both internal and international wars were waged regularly throughout the Cold War period. Three factors, however, have raised second-tier conflict to a position on the national security agenda that it formerly did not occupy.

The first and most obvious factor is that second-tier violence is the *major, even sole,* source of violence in the system. If one is to see where the general tranquillity is being upset, it is in the second tier. Second, the mechanisms that used to serve to moderate that violence have largely disappeared. The superpowers have reduced their commitments in most second-tier areas, and most of the regions lack regional organizations that can readily restore or enforce the peace.

Third, and possibly most importantly, second-tier violence is much more public than it used to be, courtesy of global television outlets such as Cable News Network (CNN) and the Independent Television Network (ITN). Violence and its accompanying atrocities and gore are an everyday part of television news, impossible to ignore. The visual images that television produces are far more evocative than written accounts of violence: it is one thing to read that 100 civilians were killed in fighting somewhere; it is quite another to see the maimed bodies, live and in color.

Television may, in an indirect and largely unintended way, be setting the national security agenda. People see an atrocity and are horrified by it. The result is clamor for redress, the "do-something syndrome." Would the United States have come to the aid of the Iraqi Kurds huddled on Turkish mountainsides had CNN not publicized their suffering? Would there have been such a public outpouring had televised pictures not shown us Somali starvation? Would we have been so embarrassed by our apparent impotence had the siege of Sarajevo not been a nightly reality? Slaughter of innocents and acts of barbarity are nothing new; unrelenting coverage of them is.

Because of the general peace in the first tier, the way we think about national security changes. We no longer need to devote considerable resources to preventing a general war that could threaten to destroy the system, as we once did. The violence and instability to be dealt with now is at the periphery of the central system defined as the first tier. The traditional military base of national security now lies at the intersection of the first and second tiers.

What should be our attitude toward violence in the second tier? To begin answering that question requires confronting two realities about the pattern. First, it is difficult—maybe impossible—to think of any conflict in the second tier that has the escalatory potential to engulf the entire system in general war—that is, World War III or its equivalent. Probably the worst case that one can conjure is a general war on the Asian subcontinent between India and Pakistan that escalated to nuclear exchange. Such a prospect would be gruesome and awful, and the literal fallout would pose a health hazard for those downwind. Such a war would *not,* however, necessarily draw in the major countries, except possibly as mediaries to end the violence. Although it can only be viewed as a hypothesis, there is no conflict that can occur in the second tier that would compel first-tier (including American) involvement. We can, quite literally, ignore such conflicts and, by any objective manner, be hardly worse off.

This leads to the second reality: *with the possible exception of areas where there are large amounts of petroleum, first-tier (including American) important interests are nowhere threatened by second-tier military conflict.* The traditional use of military force has been grounded in so-called vital interests, conditions a state would not willingly tolerate and that it would use armed force to prevent. A European continent forcibly communized represented a vital threat to the United States; a militantly anti-American, nuclear-armed Mexico would also.

With the exception of the Persian Gulf, from which the oil necessary to satisfy first-tier petroleum addiction comes, there are no equivalents in the second tier. When one combines this realization with the assertion that none of these conflicts threatens the central system, the calculation of national security also must change.

First, the changed conditions mean that, at least for the foreseeable future, the United States will employ armed forces *where it chooses to do so, not where it has to fight.* A realpolitik analysis will not send us to war in any but the most unforeseen situations. Unforeseen things do, of course, happen, and one must be prepared for uncertainty. Who would have thought in early 1990, for example, that we would mount a huge military expedition against Iraq? The offshoot of the "optional use of force" is not that we do not need force, but that the calculation of when we may use it is different.

This leads to a second conditioning observation: the way we view national security will be increasingly nontraditional. Responses to events in places such as

Iraq and Somalia suggested to many (most notably, United Nations Secretary-General Boutros Boutros-Ghali) a new category of occasions to use force. Called "humanitarian vital interests," this category calls for employing force—probably under U.N. auspices—in situations where the atrocious behavior of states against their own people or other states violates basic humanitarian standards. This idea had broad currency as the vestiges of the Cold War dissipated; the souring of the most glowing application of the principle in Somalia has cooled the ardor. The idea is unlikely to go away, however.

Other nontraditional roles will also likely emerge. One way in which second-tier states can affect the first tier is through the promotion of terrorism or the production of narcotics. These kinds of acts do not threaten the first tier, but they are annoyances with which we may decide to deal. At the same time, it has become fashionable to think of so-called transnational issues such as environmental degradation and the population explosion in something like national security terms.

NATIONAL SECURITY IN A WORLD OF TIERS

In structural terms, the major difference between the Cold War system and that of the present is the disappearance of the old Second World and the adversarial relationship between the First and Second Worlds that was its principal dynamic and the driver of the national security system. Indeed, one reason to redesignate the system into two tiers is to remove the ordinal gap created by having to go directly from the first to the third worlds. That the notion of ordinality and, thus, implicit rank remains is an unavoidable limitation of language; zones of peace and turmoil, despite the absence of overt ordinality, still retain the core value (peace is better than turmoil).

The disappearance of the Second World has more impact on the national security structure than on any other aspect of the dynamics of the international system. The reason, simply enough, is that the East–West confrontation, while both political and military in nature, was basically a military competition; if one side or the other fell perilously vulnerable on the military dimension, nothing else was of great consequence.

It is because of this centrality that thinking about national security is more affected in the new order than thinking about other issues such as economic development or the environment. Lifting the veil of East–West confrontation allows clarification of other issues; development, for instance, can now be argued on its own merits, shorn of Marxist–market or anticommunist–communist political arguments. Lifting the Cold War veil from the national security structure leaves a decidedly intellectually naked emperor; there is very little intellectual structure left.

How does the end of the Cold War affect the remaining structures? It can be argued that it simply clarifies relations that were blurred by the Cold War obsession. The countries of the first tier, for instance, have been growing more alike for well over a decade. Now that the Cold War has disappeared, we simply have the time to concentrate on the implications of that similarity. The dynamics of the second tier also are different from what they were during the Cold War, but only to the extent that existing differences are no longer caught up in the chess game between East and West. There was conflict and instability within and among second tier states then, and there still is now. The perspective through which we view those problems is different, however, and we have yet to come entirely to grips with what that new perspective means in national security terms.

NATIONAL SECURITY IN THE FIRST TIER

The relations among the states of the first tier remain in a state of basic tranquillity. The key word here is *remain*. The national security problem of opposing Soviet communism and its expansion was part of the glue that bound together the countries that composed the first tier; the transformation of Japan and Germany into market democracies was largely motivated in terms of geopolitics, for instance. However, as time has passed and the countries of the first tier have become more economically and politically similar, their common bonds have come to transcend the military competition. We no longer need the negative glue of common opposition to remain in harmony.

Some argue that this is too optimistic an assessment, that the collapse of the common enemy will allow us to turn upon one another and to invigorate old differences suppressed in the name of a united front before the enemy. Thus, for instance, Japan no longer needs the United States to form a shield against Soviet expansionism in the Far East, and it can now act more independently—specifically, in terms of the economic competition between the two. Similarly, the European members of the North Atlantic Treaty Organization (NATO) no longer need American protection from the Red Army; differences about questions such as terms of trade can now become more prominent, driving wedges between first-tier states.

All of this may indeed, be true, but the central point is that the countries of the first tier have become so much more alike that disputes among them are disagreements between friends that may cause occasional acrimony but do not threaten the basic friendship. Japan and the United States, for instance, have too much involvement in one another's economies for either to take action that would threaten the other, and the same is largely true of Europe and the United States. To project "the coming war with Japan" (the title of a sensational book about likely trade wars) is to miss the point.

The standard rejoinder to this kind of optimism is to go back to the period leading to World War I, when it was widely argued that the economies of

Europe were so interdependent that general war was impossible. That analogy, however, is flawed: the governments of that time were not uniformly democratic, and the narrower horizons of people then allowed a demonization of other peoples that is quite unlikely today. To suggest that the popularly elected government of Japan could make the case to its citizens to go to war with the "demon Americans, the white hordes" (or vice versa) is absolutely fanciful.

The countries of the first tier share four basic characteristics with overwhelming national security implications. First, there is a general structure of peace among them that is likely to endure. Second, there is general agreement among them about the kind of overall international system and national security environment they prefer. Third, their economic superiority to the second-tier nations extends to military might; the first-tier has the bulk of the political, economic, *and* military power in the international system. Fourth, the natural leader of the first tier is the United States, and the rest of the first tier will turn to it for leadership whenever such leadership is forthcoming (which it will not necessarily always be).

In a sense, none of these characteristics is new; only the environment in which they are pursued is different. The countries of the first tier have been at peace with one another since 1945; they have generally preferred a peaceful world and have looked to American leadership. The only thing different is that Soviet power made the superiority of Western military power arguable during the Cold War.

The general peace, to repeat, has two basic elements. The first is the existence of the shared values of political democracy and the capitalist, market economics among first tier members. The second is economic interdependence among the members. Each of these characteristics reinforces the general pacificity among them. Political democracies do not engage in physical violence with one another, because free people do not choose to initiate war, especially with other peoples who share their basic political values. Interdependence adds to this general predilection in two ways. It promotes greater interchange among the economic elite, who get to know one another and thus become impervious to appeals based in their differences. It also makes war more difficult because of mutual dependence on one another for production.

The result is to create a condition within the first tier roughly analogous to that in eighteenth-century Europe, where the elites of the major countries shared a common ideology and freely circulated among the capitals of Europe that effectively comprised the international system. The series of economic summits (G-7) in which the major economic powers engage likewise provides an ongoing forum for interchange. The successful conclusion of the Uruguay Round of the General Agreement on Tariffs Trade shows that problems can be overcome through patience and compromise, and the emergence of truly international corporations—especially the so-called stateless corporations—provides a circulation of economic elites similar to that in the eighteenth century.

The bottom line is that there are no significant national security problems among members of the first tier. Time, effort, and resources do not need to be devoted to military preparations to deter or defend against military attacks from other first-tier states. Since these states, by virtue of their superior technological bases, possess the greatest military power, the result is a situation where there are no military threats that threaten the integrity of the international order that the first tier dominates.

This simple difference is the greatest contrast between the current order and the Cold War system. That system was necessarily obsessed with avoiding a nuclear confrontation between the major protagonists, and there is simply no analogous problem in the current environment.

This revelation does not mean that the millennium is upon us. The eighteenth-century analogy may be instructive: it was the emergence of diverse political ideologies spawned by the American and French revolutions that reintroduced divergent political ideology to the European continent and divided states along political lines worth fighting over. It is not apparent what parallel division might create the same effect in the contemporary world, but it would be foolhardy not to admit the possibility.

The second shared characteristic of first-tier nations is their general preference for an orderly, peaceful world. Expanding the pacific nature of First World relations to the second tier via expansion of the ring of market democracies is a shared preference, even if it is recognized that such a process will be difficult and, in some cases, impossible. It is, nonetheless, a preference both because a peaceful world would be one where first-tier states would not be drawn into second-tier conflict and where the climate for expanding the global economy more broadly would be enhanced.

There is nothing Pollyannish in this preference, and the first tier is under no illusions about the prospects. Faced with very certain breaches in worldwide tranquillity, this preference suggests that collective efforts to enforce the peace are preferred to unilateral efforts. This tendency arises both from the recognition that there are more disturbances of the peace than any one, or handful, of states, can deal with, and their general agreement on the world they prefer.

There will, nevertheless, remain special circumstances in which individual first-tier states will feel the need to act individually in pursuit of their particular interests. A general breakdown in the Philippines, for instance, would evoke a particularly strong American response. The Russians, although not admitted members of the first tier, have already demonstrated in Georgia that they will take a strong hand in unrest in the former Soviet Union, and former colonial rulers will be more prone to act where they once held power and authority.

The third characteristic of the first tier is their preponderance of military power. The source of this strength is not numbers: only about one-seventh of the people on earth, according to Singer and Wildavsky, live in the zone of peace. Rather, the source of preponderance lies in technological superiority that allows smaller but more sophisticated military forces to overwhelm and defeat much larger but less sophisticated forces. This advantage holds even when second-tier forces possess some of the advanced weaponry associated with the first tier because of differences in training and competence.

This advantage is reinforced because most of the first-tier militaries have practice in coordinating the application of military force as members of NATO. While NATO is an organization with a questionable future due to the disappearance of its enemy, it has allowed the militaries of the major powers to learn how to deal with one another in detailed ways. This coordination, for example, contributed to the ability of the British and French to interact with the United States in Operation Desert Storm (despite the fact that France is not technically a member of the military command of NATO).

This military advantage is not without limitations. There have been, and will continue to be, situations where there will not be consensus that even a coordinated effort will bring about a favorable outcome. Bosnia is the obvious example. As well, the major self-limitation for all first-tier states will be public opinion, which generally opposes the application of military force except in very measured ways or where overwhelming interests are clearly involved—neither of which characteristics are clearly present in most second-tier conflicts.

Fourth and finally, there is general, if in some cases grudgingly admitted, agreement that the United State must provide the significant leadership in first-tier security matters. This is so partly because of its status as the remaining superpower, which includes the fact that it is the only country that still retains global military reach. It also reflects the fact that the Americans retain more military punch than other first-tier states.

The American leadership role is bounded. The rest of the first tier may look to the United States to lead, but it increasingly does so through the United Nations. The United States is in a push-and-shove match with the United Nations about the relations between the world body and its most powerful member. The issue is basically about leadership: is the United Nations the vehicle for carrying out first-tier wishes, or does the United Nations set the agenda? President Clinton's September 1993 entreaty that

the United Nations must learn to say no in some cases of possible actions before the United States says yes defines that relationship. The ongoing debate about the creation of a permanent U.N. force creates a continuing debate. Resolution of this critical question of leadership is made more difficult because the United States has yet to articulate a coherent set of policies and strategies for dealing with second-tier unrest.

NATIONAL SECURITY IN THE SECOND TIER

The tranquillity within the first tier is clearly not matched in the second tier, the locus of almost all of the world's instability and unrest. Much of the violence in the second tier can be traced back to the pattern of decolonization that began after World War II. States unprepared by their colonial masters for political independence inherited situations of great poverty, imperfect political boundaries, and a host of other conditions that would have made stable governance difficult for the best prepared. For those lacking the skills and experience of self-rule, the task was overwhelming. The last spate of decolonization is currently at work in the successor states of the Soviet Union and, sadly enough, the same pattern is emerging.

It oversimplifies matters to talk of a single second tier. Rather, we can identify four characteristics that make up the national security problem of the second tier, noting its differential application in specific regions. The first characteristic is, indeed, that very lack of uniformity: some parts of the second tier are more unstable than others. Next, the second tier lacks a set of common values that would enable it to approach the first tier in any monolithic sense. Third, the splintered nature of the second tier leads to a preference to view military matters in terms of collective defense rather than collective security, which has great import for the United Nations. Finally, the military capabilities of the second tier limit the kind and extent of goals that can be pursued by military means.

The pattern of instability in various regions of the second tier is depicted by conflict type in Table 1. As the table shows, the potential for internal conflict resides in all regions, although it is most prevalent in specific subregions, sub-Saharan Africa, notably central Africa, has shown the most internal violence, and places such as Zaire are almost certain to experience this form of violence in the future. Latin American internal violence is mostly found in Central America and the poorest regions of the Caribbean such as

Table 1

Instability in the Second Tier

Form	Africa	Latin America	Middle East	Asia	Second World
Internal	X	X	X	X	X
Regional			X	X	X

Haiti. There is potential for internal unrest in Iraq and the most politically backward of the oil-rich states such as Saudi Arabia. South and Southeast Asia have simmering internal problems, and the Balkans and the southern successor states to the Soviet Union show considerable violence potential. Major regional conflicts are concentrated in the Persian Gulf, South and Southeast Asia, and in Korea.

One striking note is that the potential for violence is least pronounced in those parts of the second tier that are closest to joining the first tier. In the past decade or so, large-scale democratization has occurred in South America that, while still in its infancy, has nonetheless stabilized politics on the continent. Regional conflict between the two major South American states, Brazil and Argentina, seems considerably more unlikely than it did ten years ago. The Pacific Rim countries, with the exception of divided Korea, have likewise achieved considerable tranquillity.

This diversity is also manifested in the absence of common bonds between and among second-tier regions. There is a common cry and appeal for developmental assistance from the first tier, but it is largely drowned out by particularism and attempts to gain special status. There is some commonality on aspirations to attainment of first-tier status, but on specific attributes of first-tier characteristics such as human rights, there is less than accord, as was clearly manifest in the 1993 U.N. Conference on Human Rights and Development. At that conference, mostly authoritarian second-tier regimes tried, without success, to argue that the meaning of human rights was cultural rather than universal, largely a way to cover up what are human rights abuses by Western standards. The inability to articulate common values and thereby present a united front compromises any leverage the second tier has with the first.

The third characteristic is that the second tier will likely look increasingly toward individual, rather than collective, solutions to their problems. The collective security, multilateral approach to problem solving evolving in the first tier will likely be unmatched in the second tier, for the simple reason that collective efforts will be organized *against* second-tier states, including possible intervention in internal conflicts that entails violation of the state sovereignty of select second-tier states. Since there will be far fewer cases where individual first-tier states will act unilaterally in second-tier conflicts, the best strategy for noninterference is to avoid the principle of collective action. This preference will make second-tier interaction with the United Nations more adversarial than it has been in the past.

Fourth and finally, the absence of advanced military capability will limit the kinds of military involvement of second-tier states. While those states possessing nuclear, biological, and chemical capabilities are a partial exception, this has three direct consequences. The first is that internal wars are likely to continue to be fought in the manner of low-intensity conflicts, for the simple reason that

insurgents will have little alternative and that governments will be militarily incapable of anything but counterinsurgency. The second is that regional conflicts will also be self-limited in terms of ambition by the absence of physical capacity for greater ambition. The possible exceptions to this rule are South Asia (India and Pakistan) and the Persian Gulf (Iran and Iraq).

NATIONAL SECURITY AT THE INTERSECTION OF THE TIERS

For the countries of the first tier generally, and for the United States specifically, the implications of this analysis for national security are clear. Shorn of the old Cold War rivalry, the national security problem now moves to the intersection between the first and second tiers (including parts of the old Second World that became part of the second tier). The reason is equally clear: the occasions for employing military force are in the second tier, not the first.

Once again, there is nothing terribly new about this scenario. Since World War II, the United States has been involved in a series of military activities which, with the exception of the Berlin Airlift of 1948, have been in areas that are part of the second tier: Korea, Quemoy and Matsu (islands off the Chinese coast that are part of Taiwan), the Dominican Republic, Vietnam, Lebanon, Grenada, Iran, Panama, and Iraq, to name the most prominent.

The common thread in all but the most recent of these involvements was the Cold War confrontation. Communist North Korea invaded anticommunist South Korea, communist China threatened the Republic of China, communists were purportedly posed to take over the Dominican Republic and later Grenada, and the Republic of Vietnam was menaced by the communist North Vietnamese.

The Cold War provided criteria to guide possible involvement that are absent in the wake of communism's effective disappearance. Instead, we can begin to think about where we will likely become involved by asking a series of four questions, the answers to which we will then try to convert into possible priorities in the final section of this essay. The first question is: What is the nature of the first tier–second tier relationship? Do we care what happens in large parts of the second tier? The second has to do with connecting interests and threats: how do we resolve the interest-threat mismatch? The third is a matter of first tier/American role in the second tier: how much do we wish to impose? Finally, there is the question of self-limitation: how much involvement will democratic publics allow?

The kind of relationship the first tier has to the second is likely to depend on situation-specific circumstances. The question, in essence, is what—if any—basis for involvement in the second tier exists in the absence of a Cold War motivation. For former colonial powers, the answer may be residual interests in former colonies: economic investments or colonial settler populations that need protection in the event of hostilities, for instance. Geographic proximity may also provide motivation in some cases.

These kinds of motivations will not activate American concern except in limited ways: the United States might feel the need for involvement should the New People's Army be on the verge of taking over power in the Philippines, and it has historically shown an interest in quelling anti-American unrest in Central America and in protecting American access to vital petroleum reserves, as in the Persian Gulf.

But what of involvement where those criteria are not met? It is difficult to imagine any overwhelming sense of kindredness or traditional American interest that would involve the United States in internal violence and atrocity on the African continent. As noted, we have ignored very brutal, atrocious wars in places like Angola, Mozambique, Burundi, Rwanda, and the Sudan within the last few years; the same is true of the Asian subcontinent. At the same time, the United States became involved in the longest war in its history in Vietnam, where no discernible American interests existed, and it threw its military might into the fray in Somalia. The answer to the question, "Do we care?" appears to be, "Sometimes."

The second question returns the discussion to the matter of national interests and the interest–threat mismatch. In traditional terms, the situation can be restated: the threats in the new environment are not particularly interesting, and American interests are not particularly threatened by the pattern of second-tier instability and violence. A traditional analysis would suggest that the United States would hardly ever involve itself physically in the violent affairs of most of the second tier.

There are two polar responses to the mismatch. One is simply to acknowledge it, argue that the mismatch is irreconcilable, and conclude that the United States has little business getting involved in internal wars and regional conflicts where demonstrable American vital interests are not affected adversely by worst outcomes. This position is the classic realist argument. Had it been applied, for instance, to Somalia, the United States would have stayed home; the only demonstrable American interests in the Horn of Africa are access to the Suez Canal and as a staging area to move into the Persian Gulf. The level of those interests is questionable, and it is unclear how any outcome in Somalia would affect those interests adversely.

The other polar response is to realign interests to match the threat. The mechanism for doing so is to expand those situations deemed of national vital interest. The specific instrument is the adoption of humanitarian vital interests to justify intervention in the internal affairs of states that act atrociously toward their populations. The accompanying precept of this expansion of interest is to adopt the notion of universal sovereignty, thereby making it both an interest and an obligation to aid the beleaguered. This has become the position of the idealists; their agency of choice to carry out the mission is the United Nations. Accepting this rationale provides the justification for involvement in Somalia and future analogous situations.

This debate about interests turns the traditional realist-idealist debate on its head. In the Cold War, realists were more likely to advocate the use of American force out of geopolitical necessity: countering communist expansion was the definition of vitality of interest. Idealists, on the other hand, generally counselled the husbanding of force, preferring nonmilitary solutions and downplaying the vital importance of unfavorable worst case outcomes. The debate over what to do about the Sandinistas in Nicaragua during the early 1980s captures this traditional debate nicely: the possibility of a hostile Marxist regime in Central America aroused realists to call for action to overthrow the Sandinistas, while idealists argued that vital interests were not involved and that force was thus not justified.

In the post–Cold War system, positions on the use of force are nearly reversed. The realist analysis suggests a very limited role for American force in the world, because traditional vital interests are generally unaffected by second-tier violence. The idealist position embraces the expansion of what constitutes a vital interest and thus concludes that the use of American force is justified in nontraditional situations. Thus, idealists favor a more expanded use of force than do realists.

The third question has to do with the kind of role that the United States and other first-tier states will acquire in dealing with second-tier problems. Recognizing that there are more candidate situations for involvement—particularly if involvement in internal wars is part of the list—than there are available resources, the question has two parts.

The first part is the extent of involvement. Is the first tier to intervene only in select cases and for the limited objectives of peacekeeping as outlined by Boutros-Ghali? Or is the purpose to impose an order wherever violence and atrocity occur, and to act as a collective hegemon over the second tier? The latter is clearly a much more involved, expensive, and demanding task and leads to the second part of the question. Who will do the work? If either goal is to be pursued, American leadership will have to be evident, but it is also clear that the United States cannot physically lead in all instances for reasons of resources and will. That being the case, what mechanisms will exist for choosing those who will lead specific missions? Assuming that something like the lead country concept would be in place, who will choose the leader?

This topic leads to the fourth question, which is about the extent to which first-tier publics will support military actions in the second tier. The concern arises because the chief military limitation on democratic states of the first tier is public support. This is nothing new: Carl von Clausewitz articulated the "holy trinity" of linkage between the government, the army, and the people over a century and a half ago: If any element in the trinity fails to support the use of military force, it will likely fail.

This problem is not only American, because the first-tier countries that possess the military might to intervene into the second tier are all democracies. A corollary to the proposition that democracies do not initiate wars against other democracies is that democracies do not accept casualties—body bags coming home—unless there is some compelling justification that will often be difficult to make and sustain, especially if involvement becomes lengthy. The afterglow of Vietnam makes Americans particularly sensitive to this charge; depending on the eventual outcome, Somalia may provide a parallel caution for the future.

THE FOGGY FUTURE

Predicting the future is always much more treacherous than describing the past because, as I pointed out in an earlier book, *The Shape of the Future,* the past has happened and the future has not. The future always entails occurrences that we are unable to predict—factors unforeseen and, in some cases, unforeseeable. The problem is particularly acute when the change in conditions is fundamental and the search for analogies proves difficult, as is clearly the case today.

The American national security apparatus is in the midst of a crisis about its future role and mission. Its predicament approaches the state of a dilemma. The professional community is, on the whole, conservative and realist in its orientation. It does not view lightly the idea of putting young American lives at risk unless there is some demonstrable threat to American interests. The dilemma is that the apparatus also faces severe reductions in resources that can only be staunched by embracing uses of force that contradict its own basic realist precepts. The strained attempt of the professional officer corps to find a way to embrace support for the United Nations—an institution it has reflexively rejected for decades—captures the agony involved.

The early post–Cold War experience does not provide much guidance as to where and when the United States should use force in the future. The contrast between systemic reaction in Somalia and inaction in Bosnia provides little positive direction; if anything, images of the residents of Sarajevo suffering a second snowy winter under siege bred cynicism about the system's reactions.

With this conceptual uncertainty in mind, the best we can do is to suggest some guidelines for the United States in choosing when and where to apply force in the second tier. To this end, nine influences will be identified and presented, in no particular order of importance, on the assumption that some will be more important than others. The first three address the question of our level of awareness of situations. The next two concern what the United States is being asked to undertake. The last four influences reflect National Security Advisor Anthony Lake's four rules on using force and suggest the

Table 2

Involvement Factors

What we know:
1. Level of atrocity
2. Amount of publicity
3. Recognition factor

What we are asked to do:
4. Burden sharing/leadership
5. Time commitment

Prospects of success:
6. Interests involved
7. Efficacy of force
8. Cost
9. End game

likelihood of success. For clarity's sake, the factors are summarized in Table 2.

The first factor is the level of atrocity and horror of a given situation. As a general rule, the greater the horror and atrocity involved, the more likely some form of international action will be contemplated. In the two post–Cold War situations in which the United States became involved, Operation Provide Comfort for the Kurds and Operation Restore Hope in Somalia, the term "genocide" was prominently mentioned. Kurdish fears (warranted or not) of genocidal attacks by Iraqi forces caused them to flee; genocidal levels of death predicted in Somalia from starvation similarly partly motivated intervention. By contrast, in Bosnia, there have been occasional accusations of genocide in isolated occasions, but all three principal parties have been accused of the practice at one time or another.

Genocide represents a level of atrocity that could reasonably activate international efforts, including an American component, especially if such acts were committed by a country signatory to the U.N. Convention on Genocide (which includes most countries). Operationalizing genocide is, however, never easy in individual cases, and it leaves open the question of what actions short of genocide should create international intervention.

A second and corollary factor is the level of publicity received by instances of second-tier violence. This factor suggests the strong role of global television, which has the option of publicizing instances of great suffering and atrocity or ignoring them. In some cases, global television has been effectively prevented from covering the gory details of ethnic and other violence, as in the Sudan. There is also, as mentioned earlier, the possibility that the viewing public will eventually become desensitized to carnage, to the point that television pictures will not activate the "do something syndrome." In addition, the effect of moderate levels of coverage—as in Burundi in 1993 or in Azerbaijan and Armenia—on world opinion is still an open question.

A third factor, influenced by the first two, is the average American's low degree of recognition of distant places and the people involved. The well-chronicled American lack of interest and knowledge about foreign affairs is especially great in matters dealing with the countries of the second tier, and it will be hard to gain widespread public support for sending forces to places and/or over issues of which the average citizen has never heard. Stimulating sufficient public interest—especially where threats are not particularly compelling—will require a good deal of citizen education, a process in which the global media will play a major role.

The next two factors on the list deal with what the American people, through their armed forces, are being asked to do in specific situations. Who will authorize and participate in the actions? The United States has shown willingness to act unilaterally where its interests are clearly engaged or where it simply feels that it must. We would, for instance, have conducted Operation Desert Storm on our own had others not volunteered, and the same was true of early efforts in Somalia.

Burden sharing, however, will be a hallmark of American willingness in the future, especially if the roster of actions expands. Spreading the lead country role widely will be necessary for the American people, who instinctively shrink from being designated the world's "globocop." Moreover, it remains to be seen how long the "honeymoon" between American military forces and the United Nations will last. If the U.N. bureaucracy insists on an aggressive, inclusive presence wherever violence breaks out—that is, if it fails to learn to say no, in President Clinton's terms—that relationship will likely sour. At the same time, the active campaign to attach American forces directly to U.N. control will create an anti-U.N. backlash.

The fifth factor is the duration of the operations. It is virtually an axiom in democratic societies that they tolerate best military actions that are quick, decisive, and generally as bloodless as possible. Lengthy involvements are tolerated only when the aims are so overwhelmingly important as to justify greater sacrifice, an idea elaborated in Snow and Drew, *From Lexington to Desert Storm*. Second-tier actions will hardly ever meet this criterion. Recent evidence of this truism is found in Somalia: the first time in was short, decisive, bloodless, and overwhelmingly popular. When the Americans returned for an apparently open-ended stay, the public debate quickly turned to a congressional–White House debate on setting a time limit to get the troops out and forced their withdrawal.

The last four factors, borrowed with acknowledgment from Lake, address the likelihood of achieving goals to which the American people can subscribe. Item six raises the question of what American interests are involved. This is important both as a guiding criterion and as the basis for rationalizing action to the American people. The statement of what American interests are engaged in some unfavorable outcome are, in effect, a statement of why the country is asking some Americans to sacrifice, up to and including their lives.

This will, in my view, be a principal bone of contention that will end up limiting American participation in the second tier. Those favoring broad involvement argue that the forces are, after all, well-paid professionals who volunteered to be placed in harm's way: they go wherever they are sent. Those hastening caution retort that those professionals are also the sons and daughters of voters who will take out their displeasure on officials who put their children in physical danger for less than truly vital reasons. The interventionist argument is better cocktail party talk than good politics.

The seventh item turns on whether the insertion of American forces can actually do any good. Despite the high combat effectiveness of American forces, the answer is not always obvious. A number of the potential roles will be in peace imposition, and it is not at all clear that military force can solve those situations. Inaction in the primary contemporary situation where peace imposition might have been contemplated, Bosnia, suggests recognition of the possibility that applying American force might not be efficacious in all circumstances.

The eighth factor is cost and its acceptability. If potential engagements are short and decisive, cost is less likely to be a problem. But if commitments become extensive and individual involvements are extended, then cost—including the sacrifices entailed in other areas—will have to become part of the calculation.

Finally, there is the necessity of finding a way to end commitment—the endgame. The United Nations record is not encouraging here: peacekeeping missions develop a life of their own and, in places such as Cyprus, become solutions of their own. The United States, upon returning to Somalia, was faced with the question of how to know when its purpose had been accomplished and it was time to go home. Setting and implementing an arbitrary date for withdrawal answered the second part of that question, but not the first. Involvements are likely to be inversely attractive to their open-endedness.

All these issues are in a state of flux, forcing us to think about national security in very different ways than we did only a few years ago. The future is foggy because it is so unlike the recent past and because we have been unable to find satisfactory parallels in history to guide us.

The very real difference between the contemporary setting and the Cold War is defined by the kinds of questions that are swirling in the public policy debate about national security, some of which have been represented in this essay. If someone had proposed as little as six or seven years ago that the primary national security questions we would face today would deal with how the first tier would engage with the second tier, the response would have been a blank stare of noncomprehension. But that is, indeed, the nature of defense policy for the new international order.

THE PRIMACY OF THE DOMESTIC AGENDA

PETER G. PETERSON
With JAMES K. SEBENIUS

The legislative mandate of the National Security Council (NSC) on its creation in 1947 was to serve as a forum for integrating "domestic, foreign, and military policies relating to the national security." First articulated in the early 1950s, the NSC's working definition of our national security is as appropriate now as then: "*to preserve the United States as a free nation with our fundamental institutions and values intact.*" This goal implied a combination of military, political, and economic objectives. These were explicit in the early years of the NSC, when issues such as America's role in rebuilding the shattered economies of Europe and Japan were routinely discussed as priorities on a par with the creation of the North Atlantic Treaty Organization, the U.S.–Japan security agreement, and other Cold War military matters. Moreover, the concept of national security has historically encompassed domestic threats, such as armed insurrections, as well as foreign considerations.

In practice, however, national security policy in the 1970s and 1980s came to mean *foreign* policy in general and *military* policy in particular. Rarely, if ever, were domestic economic challenges seriously considered to be a significant part of the national security agenda. When I joined the government in the early 1970s, "high politics," to Henry Kissinger and its other masters, meant the metaphysics of multiple independently targetable reentry vehicles and other more seductive issues of managing the superpower balance of terror. By contrast, as the president's assistant for international economic affairs focused on trade, productivity, and the dollar, I was consigned to the realm of "low politics." Indeed, Kissinger once chided me about being preoccupied with "minor commercial affairs." I retorted with surprise that he was being uncharacteristically redundant; in his worldview, were there any *other* sorts of commercial affairs? (In fairness, the problem was not just that the military-strategic experts ceased to be very interested in industry and commerce. It is also that the economic experts ceased to be very interested in geopolitics and history.)

In the postwar period, whenever "economics" clashed directly with military "security policy," the United States instinctively opted to give precedence to the latter. Economic factors often heavily entered, constrained, or even dictated the foreign policy "choices" of other, then less affluent countries, whose military security costs we often paid. Now

something similar is happening to us; our own economic constraints are beginning to influence, if not dictate, America's relations with others. For some time, it has been clear that U.S. national security interests *must* include the development of policies that will increase our economic strength and domestic stability. Now, I believe a new definition of national security that recalls the vision of 1947—and augments it with more forceful economic and domestic policy components—is urgently needed. Indeed, I suspect that no foreign challenge of the 1990s will affect America's security as much as what we do, or fail to do, at home on a range of economic and social issues. We should not forget Eisenhower's admonition not to "undermine from within that which we are seeking to protect from without." In this spirit, I will advance the following proposition:

After four decades of the cold war, failure to make progress on a "domestic agenda" now threatens America's long-term national security more than the external military threats that have traditionally preoccupied security and foreign policy. While the world remains a dangerous place requiring us to maintain military strength, our failure to invest in productive capacity, research and development (R & D), and infrastructure; the crisis in American education; the exploding underclass, and other domestic problems may have greater *direct* impact on "the United States as a free society with its fundamental institutions and values intact" than the threats from abroad, such as the possibility of Soviet nuclear attack, which have traditionally preoccupied the national security community. Moreover, continued failure to address these domestic priorities may entail a progressive loss both of political will and economic capacity to take actions abroad that promote our real national security interests.

CHANGING THREATS TO U.S. NATIONAL SECURITY

No one can dispute the fact that the postwar world has been a dangerous one for the United States. With Soviet nuclear weapons and military adventurism (especially through proxies), North Korean and Chinese aggression, assorted menacing regional conflicts, an expanding nuclear club, terrorism, and so on, "eternal vigilance" has been a

This article has been edited and is reprinted from Rethinking America's Security: Beyond Cold War to New World Order, *ed. Graham Allison and Gregory F. Treverton (New York: W. W. Norton & Co., 1992), 57–93, by permission of W. W. Norton & Company, Inc. Copyright © 1992 by The American Assembly.*

military necessity. Iraq's malevolence and military capacities sound a current warning against complacency, or neoisolationism. Yet the world is changing. One need not belabor the importance of the powerful East–West thaw and the spread of democracy to conclude that some of the "old threats" have diminished.

Beyond the now-defunct Warsaw Pact, consider China as a specific example of a receding threat. Quaint as it may sound today, much of our Southeast Asian defense policy was formulated with a keen remembrance of "hordes of Chinese" pouring across the Yalu River. Indeed, even in the late 1960s, as a private citizen member of the president's Arms Control Advisory Board, I vividly remember presentations by the Joint Chiefs of Staff about the threat of a Chinese nuclear first strike against us. China was an unambiguous and dangerous enemy and was a key part of discussions about the Southeast Asian "conceptual balance of power" vis-à-vis the Soviet Union during the Vietnam War.

As just this single example illustrates, traditional external threats to our security are changing and require reassessment. Yet it is not just the geographic sources of the threats that are changing: it is their nature. Today, the threats are far more likely to be from regional aggressors like Saddam Hussein, contagious conflict arising from ethnic/religious problems, or nuclear proliferation in Third World countries. All these threats of conflict require very different responses than those for which we have traditionally prepared. In this essay, however, I am concerned with emerging security threats of a still different character. In particular, largely self-inflicted *economic* weaknesses now indirectly threaten our national security. After sketching these economic factors in the context of the proposition stated above (the primacy of the domestic agenda in our national security), I will then consider "domestic threats."

ECONOMIC WEAKNESS AS A NATIONAL SECURITY THREAT

Despite the euphoria over America's success in the war in Iraq, the 1990s will be a decade of new and increasing tensions for the United States between international needs and economic constraints. These constraints are caused by budget deficits, balance-of-payments deficits, growing foreign debts, debt-service costs, paltry levels of investment, anemic productivity growth, a loss of technological leadership in key cutting-edge industries, and a general decline in our global competitiveness. The awkward but enduring fact is that, taken together, the claims of our various national interests and global obligations will far outrun our available resources to sustain or defend them. As the full implications of being the world's largest debtor dawn on us *and* on the rest of the world, the gap between our interests and our capacities will become larger, more obvious, and more painful. As Eisenhower sought to teach us, military and economic security over time depend on each other; countries that lose control of their economic destinies lose control over their foreign policies.

New Resource Constraints

Apart from the anomaly of Uncle Sam brandishing a saber toward Iraq in one hand while rattling a tin cup in the other, we have already seen the effects of chronic budget stringency on foreign policy interests: State Department allocations (even to maintain embassies and consulates abroad) dropping and under further siege, administration proposals for massive cuts in foreign aid (except to Egypt and Israel), 10 percent real cuts in all our international budgets, our virtual inability to offer meaningful financial support to a newly democratic but fragile Philippine government (a meager $50 million at a time Corazon Aquino appeared before a joint session of Congress), our financial paralysis in the face of enormous Eastern European changes (the president's embarrassing offer of $25 million at the time of his visit to Hungary), as well as our inability to make essential investments in economic growth and social harmony in our own hemisphere. Just as cutting back on subway and infrastructure maintenance during its 1970s fiscal crisis ended up costing New York vastly greater sums to later repair the damage, the costs to the United States of its increasing inability to respond constructively to changing opportunities and threats abroad will become dramatically higher. The United States faces constraints on policy that are unprecedented for a great power. Spreading slowly like a silent progressive disease, the long-term effects are both cumulative and debilitating.

One could well argue, for example, that Mexico presents a veritable cauldron of potential threats that could easily become immense national security problems for the United States. Political, social, demographic, economic, and financial trends combine to make an "explosion" south of our border at least as likely as the detonation of a nuclear bomb. If Mexico fails to grow economically in step with its population—which before long will grow to twice its current size—Mexico's problems will become our problems. Some sixty million *more* Mexicans, many unemployed and just across our effectively open border, for example, could rapidly become our immigration problem.

If we were thinking in a "zero-base" mode, this set of conditions might easily place Mexico—as well as other Latin American countries—near the top of the external threats and opportunities that we face in terms of our national security. Beyond the valuable, though partial, step of a Mexican free trade agreement, this kind of thinking might easily lead to compelling proposals for comprehensive and bold programs to include further debt restructuring or relief, immigration reform, investment flows, economic development programs, as well as a major, coordinated attack on drug problems. Though I believe that most observers sense the importance of such initiatives, there seems to be a conspiracy of silence. Even at the cost of ignoring a major developing threat to our national security, virtually everyone avoids the issue since proponents of such initiatives are soon confronted with the awkward question: *where will the money come from?*

Before the decade of the 1990s is out, I predict a surge of domestic budgetary pressures to bring home costly U.S. troops from Europe, Korea, and from far-flung bases and ships. Ideally, this fiscal necessity may present major opportunities for enhanced security at lower economic cost, but there is a far less desirable likelihood that we take these steps as a result of fiscal crisis and in an atmosphere of severe trade tension. Keep in mind that these pressures to cut our military commitments will likely intensify just as the United States is desperately striving to increase its share of world exports and to further reduce its current account deficit. Undoubtedly, the Japanese and Europeans—who, especially after Iraq, will increasingly be seen by resentful Americans as the affluent beneficiaries of long-time military free rides—will also be straining to retain their trade positions. As the General Agreement on Tariffs and Trade's late 1990 deadlock warns us anew, competitive attempts to win global share could give way to an "antagonistic mercantilism." These economic conflicts will put serious strains on the cohesiveness of our military and political alliances. Truly acrimonious debates over allied burden sharing that turn into fundamental questioning of collective purposes are already becoming an unwelcome feature of the foreign policy landscape. It will be very difficult to keep trade wars limited to trade issues alone.

If we get our own budgetary house in order and begin attempting to increase our exports further, we will need to exert strenuous diplomatic efforts to induce other countries simultaneously to adopt complementary economic policies that expand world trade. (The alternative of deep global recession or depression would also "solve" our trade and current account problems; recall that we had a trade surplus every year during the 1930s.) But such coordination will be exceedingly difficult to sustain in an atmosphere strained by foreign policy disagreements.

New Vulnerabilities

Moreover, there are specific risks inherent in our passive decisions to run huge deficits and to rely on foreign investors to fund them. Though it is unlikely to occur in a brazen form, a decision by investors or central bankers to cease buying additional dollars—for economic *or* political reasons—would put us in deep trouble. We have generally downplayed such possibilities, often pointing to our potential leverage over Japan, a generally unflagging purchaser of dollars. After all, almost 40 percent of Japanese exports have come to our markets in recent years. Yet if we took serious protectionist measures aimed at the Japanese, they could threaten powerful retaliation by ceasing to fund our deficits. This could cause a dollar plunge, an interest rate surge, and a deep recession along with a host of other unpleasant consequences.

Such an action by the Japanese or others could parallel a dramatic 1956 foreign policy incident. Shortly before the U.S. elections that year, the British surprised the United States by spearheading, in tandem with the French and the Israelis, an invasion of Suez, responding to nationalization of the canal by Gamal Abdel Nasser. Opposing this "risky, imperialistic" gambit, the United States forced the invading armies to withdraw by threatening to dump the pound sterling and cut off British access to international credit—measures that could have caused a steep devaluation of the pound and highly unpopular gasoline rationing. (And remember, we were alliance partners and "special *friends*" of the British.)

Monetary historian Susan Strange has examined some of the consequences of Britain's unprecedented growth in foreign debt. She observed that "by the time of the 1967 devaluation Britain had become, in effect, the ward of the other developed countries of the non-Communist world. They constituted a creditors' club exercising the same watchful concern over the British economy that the Aid Consortia exercised over those of India, Indonesia, or Turkey."

"Given the stream of postwar balance of payments crises to which Britain has been subjected," noted British financial expert Michael Stewart, "I am amazed at the insouciance with which the United States has quietly amassed such an astronomical foreign debt." In my view, our passivity has become pathological. Perhaps Stewart should not be so amazed. The painful lessons of great debtorhood were hard for the British to perceive. Susan Strange eerily noted that "at a time when the British had amassed by far the largest government foreign debt per head of population of any country in the world . . . comment in Britain . . . tended to stop short at expressing regret for the necessity to borrow so heavily, and hope that the loans may soon be repaid, so that the 'crushing burden' of debt may be lifted from British shoulders." Most Britons, however, did not seem too sensitive to the "crushing burden"—either on their pockets or on their consciences. Their regret seemed a trifle perfunctory, their concern superficial, and their appreciation of the scale and urgency with which the creditors required repayment very vague indeed. Economic reality, however, soon translated into harsh wage freezes and incomes policies as well as unpleasant constraints on public expenditures—much as has been the case with developing-country debtors in recent years trying to work their way out from under staggering debt loads. These domestic economic costs for Britain, of course, only added to the foreign policy vulnerabilities so painfully illustrated earlier by the 1956 Suez crisis.

The United States, of course, is not postwar Great Britain. Among many differences, our debts are in our own currency. Indeed, Charles de Gaulle used to lament the "extravagant privilege" accorded the United States from our reserve currency status—our ability to repay borrowings from foreign lenders in our own currency. This special position allowed us to avoid taxation to pay for the Vietnam War and permitted our recent defense buildup, entitlement increases, and tax cuts to occur without a surge in interest rates. (Arguably, the capacity to have both guns and butter resulted in increased inflation that ultimately led to the breakdown of the international monetary system.)

Further, should the Japanese (or other major buyers or holders of dollars or dollars-denominated assets) seek to exert direct foreign policy leverage on the United States today as a result of their new-found creditor position, they would simultaneously inflict grave costs on *themselves* from the resulting dollar plunge, huge foreign exchange losses, the likelihood that their exports would be sharply curtailed, the risk of global recession, and worse. But nowhere is it written that countries, in emotional political spasms, will not act in ways that prove to be counterproductive. And though governments and central banks tend toward relatively measured action, the herd mentality and psychological panics may sweep the private investing community, adding to underlying volatilities and dangers. In sum, worldwide economic risks are sharply increased by the predicament in which we now find ourselves. Ironically, with the possibilities of lethal economic and financial actions, reactions, and counterreactions, we now face an economic version of MAD, or *Mutually Assured Destruction*, with which we have uneasily lived in the military "security" realm.[1]

Yet there is a broader point here. It is not so much the threat of a creditor strike per se. Instead, continued U.S. economic weakness will cause a subtle but very real worldwide shift of *political* perceptions. Perhaps ironically, in a world that is increasingly multipolar and complex, the need for collective action puts an increasing premium on the capacity for effective leadership. As the Gulf War coalition underlined, the United States is virtually the only candidate for such a role. Yet our capacity to exert leadership may be undermined to the extent that increasing domestic and economic failures cause us to be taken less seriously. An extreme but instructive analogy, of course, is the effect of domestic failure in the Soviet Union on the reality and perception of Soviet influence. Despite the surge, perhaps temporary, in worldwide admiration for U.S. military capacities generated by the Persian Gulf War, perceptions of relative U.S. economic decline could well mark a psychological turning point in others' perception of our long-term ability to back allies and oppose enemies, of our vulnerability, and of our unreliability. And since perceptions can govern actions, I believe that we would see our "friends" take more independent stances, our enemies act with less restraint, and, generally, our presence, stature, and security diminished.

DIRECT DOMESTIC THREATS TO NATIONAL SECURITY

When I survey the changing postwar sources of threats to our national security, I certainly do not see external threats as having vanished. Rather, I am struck by the emergence of a series of powerful domestically generated trends that increasingly seem to pose direct and indirect threats to our fundamental institutions and values. The first of these trends—economic weakness and relative decline—may *indirectly* constrain essential actions abroad and increase our vulnerabilities. I will now turn briefly to some domestic trends, which, if unchecked, may progressively and *directly* threaten the basic character of our society's institutions and values. Not surprisingly, these include education, poverty, the underclass, and economic expectations.

Education

One-quarter of school-age children can neither read nor write at a satisfactory level. Since 1985 every fourth student in high school has failed to earn a diploma and has dropped out. *Every year,* 2 million Americans leave school without having learned to read and write. The 1985 White House Commission headed by John A. Young, chief executive of Hewlett-Packard, concluded that this is particularly bad news, because the highest dropout rate—from 40 to 45 percent—is found among blacks and Hispanics, the fastest growing segments of the population. "It is clear that the competitiveness of American industry is threatened when many young workers lack the basic skills for productive work," he says. We have the largest number of functional illiterates in the world—nearly one in five American workers falls into this tragic category. Indeed, it is almost incredible that we, unlike the Japanese, fail to *act* as if we believed in the intimate connection between an educated society and a competitive one. "If a hostile foreign power had attempted to give America the bad education that it has today," the National Commission on excellence in Education has warned, "we would have viewed it as an act of war."

Poverty and the Underclass

Almost a fourth of all children younger than six, and about half of all black children younger than six, live beneath the official poverty line. In urban areas, infant mortality rates rival those in traditionally agrarian, less developed countries. Overall, some 31.5 million Americans live below the official poverty line. Minorities are particularly affected: more than 30 percent of blacks and 26 percent of Hispanics earn less than this amount. Many of them are working at full-time jobs; about 7 million Americans do not earn enough from their jobs to escape poverty.

Not *coincidentally,* the United States leads the world in crime. Explanations abound: the symbiosis of poverty and poor education, the drug catastrophe, racism, guns. Since 1975, more American citizens have met their deaths through firearms than the U.S. military lost in World War II. Partly in response, some 3.7 million Americans, constituting nearly 2 percent of the adult population, are under continual supervision by prison or police authorities. The number of prisoners in federal and state penitentiaries has almost *tripled*, from 250,000 in 1975 to 710,000 in 1989. (Japan has 50,000.) Incredibly, the average black male child today is more likely to go to prison than to college. Beyond crime, our litigious society (about two-thirds of all the lawyers in the world practice in the United States with their number growing at about four times the rate of population growth) and the related insurance costs have now added significantly to our uncompetitiveness. (The cost of our tort system was estimated at 2.6 percent of gross national product [GNP] in 1987, over three times higher than the next highest industrial country.)

Expectations

From the mid-1970s through 1986, the median income of young males without some college education plummeted by 35 percent in real terms. For those who do not finish high school, the corresponding decline is an incredible 42 percent in real terms. Since approximately half of young Americans do not ever attend college at all, this downward mobility is pervasive and deeply disturbing. More generally, as Senator Daniel Patrick Moynihan of New York has noted, the wages of production and nonsupervisory workers, after Social Security taxes and adjustment for inflation, are *lower today than the week that Eisenhower left the presidency.* After a careful study of income and wealth accumulation trends, Frank Levy and Richard Michel concluded that it is highly unlikely that Americans born in or since the 1950s will *ever* achieve the same level of real household net worth currently held by now-retiring Americans born in the 1930s.

"Our country used to have dreams," said journalist John Chancellor recently. "We dreamed of independence, and we got it. We dreamed of becoming a continental power, and we became it. Our immigrants dreamed of a different life in prosperity, and they created it. We dreamed of the moon landing and carried it out. But where are our dreams now?" Without hope of improvement, without dreams of a better life for our children, what kind of society will we have? Can a stable center hold in the face of such unprecedented income gaps? Will citizens at the bottom exercise their civic and political responsibilities when their basic economic security is threatened? Will our freedoms as well as our fundamental values and institutions—that is to say, our national security—remain intact?

I know of no more perceptive spokesperson on these questions than Daniel Yankelovich, public opinion researcher and social commentator, whose words bear repeating:

This situation is a formula for social and political instability.

The history of this century shows that there is no more potent negative political force than downward mobility. If the American Dream becomes a mockery for tens of millions of vigorous young Americans who, it should be remembered, represent mainstream American youth, not just inner city minorities, the nation can expect rising levels of violence, crime, drug addiction, rioting, sabotage, and social instability. The surge of racial tension between young whites and blacks is already an expression of it. We will be lucky if this is the worst of it.

Let me summarize: the world is still a dangerous place that requires us to maintain military strength. Yet failure to make progress on a domestic economic and social agenda now threatens America's long-term national security more than the traditional preoccupations of security and foreign policy such as the menace of Soviet nuclear bombs or conventional attacks on our territory or vital interests. To put this proposition a bit more concretely, suppose we were now deciding where to spend, say, an *additional* trillion dollars to enhance our national security, broadly construed. Faced with this decision, would not these domestic economic and social agendas have a strong claim to primacy over additional efforts to mitigate traditional external threats?

IMPLICATIONS

I have urged that the concept of "national security" be interpreted broadly to mean the preservation of the United States as a free society with its fundamental institutions and values intact. If this characterization is accepted, then my proposition implies that there is a strong *national security* case for the primacy of the domestic economic and social agendas as I have described them above.

This proposition argues that if those who have been traditionally concerned with our foreign policy and national security are to have maximum effect, they should broaden their focus. Separating "foreign" from "domestic" policies is increasingly untenable. And as these policies are more effectively integrated, the primacy of the domestic agenda in our national security becomes evident. Though not among the most-traveled paths in the conventional world of "national security," this agenda can no longer be treated as incidental to our "real" security policy; it should now move to center stage. In this regard, what should be some of the special responsibilities of those in the traditional world of security policy, who have often been especially farsighted, enlightened, and sophisticated in their outlooks?

First, members of the foreign policy "establishment" must look afresh at subjects that have traditionally been outside their purview. The security links to intensely domestic topics must not be overlooked. National security demands a focus well beyond things "foreign" and "military." (In this same vein, those in our society who have up to now focused on things overtly economic and fiscal must broaden their angle of view to include national security concerns.)

Second, foreign policy specialists tend to be very comfortable with the notion of necessary *trade-offs* within the national security spectrum (as between MX missiles and submarines for example, or even between foreign aid that contributes to security versus a direct military presence or military aid). In line with my first point above, I would urge that this same logic and style of analysis be extended from traditional national security concerns to encompass the larger agenda that I have outlined above. For instance, is our real national security better served by an additional $10 billion spent on selected aircraft systems or on the programs that the Committee on Economic Development (CED) deems essential to attack the problems of our children? True generalists are needed to begin making, in a nonpolemical way, the kinds of trade-offs that bear on *all* aspects of our national security.

Third, and more broadly, we must create an *overall*, balanced plan to achieve our wider national security goals. Such an "integrated national security budget" should combine both foreign and domestic priorities. It must lay out the true financial and intellectual requirements for military security, as well as economic security/competitiveness (including education, the underclass, infrastructure, research and development, productivity-enhancing investment, etc.). It must include a realistic plan to pay for the associated costs (e.g., spending cuts, tax increases, etc.). Incidentally, security specialists trained in cost-benefit analyses are well-equipped to assess the cost effectiveness of domestic programs such as prenatal care and Headstart. Moreover, along with an integrated national security budget should come serious consideration of the *institutional changes* that would foster its formulation and execution. Should a revamped and broadened NSC be set up that includes members concerned with competitiveness and productivity, such as the Commerce Department and the Office of Management and Budget? What institutional changes may be needed in the structure and operation of the associated congressional committees? These are the kinds of questions that need to be asked—and answered.

Fourth, to this substantive agenda must be added a *moral* dimension. For years, national security and foreign policy goals have attracted domestic support not only from naked self-interest, but also from a sense of equity and compassion. The response to the plight of the Kurds is but one recent example of this theme in U.S. foreign policy. One humanizing element of our foreign policy has always been to narrow the gap between the haves and the have-nots. As we strive to develop the concept of a new *world* order, can we permit the *domestic* equivalent of this gap to continue to widen? Can we succeed in the world economy, let alone as a democracy, with such internal disparities and discords? In my view, as we seek to forge a domestic consensus, it must be within the context of a larger moral purpose—a familiar element for those who have contributed to and relied on the consensus "beyond the waters' edge."

NOTE

1. Less dramatic than our "debt mountain," but, over time more troubling in some ways, is the gradual but significant decline in America's technological leadership.

PART II

THE ACTORS WHO INFLUENCE AMERICAN DEFENSE POLICY

INTRODUCTION

ALAN R. VAN TASSEL

Power within the United States is highly fragmented, and this is no less true for American defense policy, where numerous communications channels and conversion structures play a role. Communications channels are the means by which inputs are aggregated, organized, and represented to the conversion structures, while conversion structures are the makers and implementers of policy (see the model below). Knowing who these actors are and how they influence U.S. defense policy is vital to a full appreciation of this important subject. To that end, Part II of *American Defense Policy* examines the president and the Congress (Chapter 4); the Office of the Secretary of Defense and the military services (Chapter 5); the intelligence community (Chapter 6); and interest groups, the media, and public opinion (Chapter 7).

Richard Neustadt's "The President's Power to Persuade" sets the stage for Part II by reminding us that American political power is shared by the national and state governments, the branches within the national government, the organizations within those branches, and the government and its citizens.

Thus the president is not as powerful as many think he is or wish he was. Rather, the president is one of many actors, albeit a central one, in a complex process where his most important power is his ability to persuade others, often through bargaining and compromise. This thesis is illustrated using an in-depth discussion of Truman's efforts to push the Marshall Plan through the Congress in the early years following World War II.

Neustadt notes, for instance, that the executive and legislative branches are "separated institutions sharing power." Thus the Constitution designates the president commander in chief, but grants Congress the right to declare war, raise and support armed forces, and make rules for the regulation of those forces. Although the president has been and remains the dominant partner in foreign and defense policy due to a variety of extra-Constitutional factors—including the executive branch's hierarchical structure, ability to act quickly and discreetly, and access to information and analysis—Congress has expanded its role during the past three decades, as James Lindsay points out in "Congress and Defense Policy."

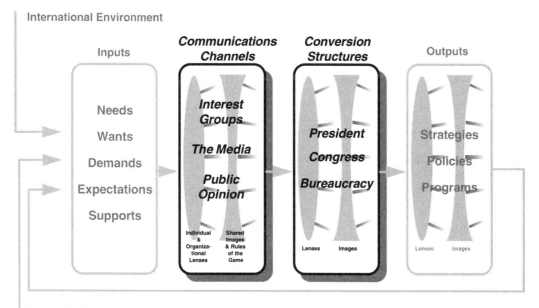

Defense Policy Process Model: Communications Channels and Conversion Structures

During the 1960s congressional defense policy was an "inside game," in which the central actors were senior members of the defense committees and saw themselves as the military's advocates on Capitol Hill.[1] By the 1980s, however, it had become an "outside game," with numerous players who were much more likely to challenge the administration's defense policies and programs. An early example is the 1973 War Powers Act, which requires that the president consult with the Congress whenever possible before troops are introduced into hostilities or situations where hostilities are imminent; report to the Congress within forty-eight hours if troops are used in such situations; and terminate the use of force within sixty days unless the Congress declares war, extends the time frame by law, or is physically unable to meet due to an armed attack upon the United States.

This increase in congressional activism is due to three factors, according to Lindsay. First, an expanded authorization process gave more members of Congress more opportunities to become involved in defense policy. Second, events like the Vietnam War and Watergate destroyed the bipartisan consensus that had existed since World War II and brought the executive branch's competence and veracity into question, thereby providing members of Congress with an incentive to act. And third, the legislative reforms of the 1970s "democratized" the Congress and gave its members greater freedom to challenge not only the executive branch but also their own leadership. Although these changes made American defense policy more representative of the Congress and the people who elect it, it also slowed the legislative process and increased micromanagement of the executive bureaucracy.

Recognizing that "Congress today has an influence over foreign policy unprecedented in the history of the Republic," Linda Jamison recommends in "Executive–Legislative Relations after the Cold War" that the Congress focus on "the large strategic questions facing the country" and that the president "negotiate rather than dictate policy on these larger questions." "The time has come to reinforce the explicit and appropriate functions and strengths that each branch brings to the policy-making process," Jamison writes. "It is time to move beyond the argument over who controls foreign affairs and into determining the nation's course for the next century."

Doing so will be difficult for several reasons, however. First of all, Jamison notes that there is no consensus among the major actors concerning the United States' role in the post–Cold War world. Moreover, the "invitation to struggle" that has long defined executive–legislative relations has been "reinvigorated" by the end of the Cold War. Thus getting the president and the Congress to cooperate will be difficult. Finally, most Americans, including their elected representatives, are focused on domestic policy issues but ignore the growing interdependence that exists between domestic and international interests.

In addition to the president and the Congress, Neustadt notes that "the executive establishment consists of separated institutions sharing powers." The Department of Defense (DOD), for instance, has its own sources of influence, including a fiscal 1996 budget of more than $240 billion; over 3.2 million employees, including an active duty force of almost 1.5 million; and the information and expertise the president and others need to make informed decisions. Moreover, the DOD views the world through its own set of individual and organizational lenses and is loyal to actors other than the president, including itself, the congressional defense committees, and various defense interest groups.

The Defense Department is headed by the secretary of defense, who is the president's principal defense adviser and has a number of responsibilities as discussed by former Secretary of Defense James Schlesinger in "The Office of the Secretary of Defense." They include establishing political guidance for the military, developing military strategy, formulating defense budgets, and "overall administration and coordination" of the department. The Office of the Secretary of Defense (OSD) is the secretary's immediate staff and assists him through a hierarchy of undersecretaries, assistant secretaries, and lower-ranking officials organized along regional and functional lines (Figure 1).

The DOD consists of more than the secretary of defense and OSD, however. It also includes the military departments and the armed services within them, the Joint Chiefs of Staff (JCS) and the Joint Staff, the unified combatant commands, and various other defense agencies and field activities (Figure 2). Moreover, each of these organizations has power and interests of its own, leading Schlesinger to write that "much of the secretary's time is devoted to gathering support for the department's activities." "Although the responsibilities are very imposing," Schlesinger continues, "they are not matched by the powers of the office." As is the case with the president, "the office provides the secretary simply with a license to persuade outside parties. Even within the [Pentagon], quite frequently, it is only a license to persuade."

Carl Builder illustrates the power and interests of the armed services in "Service Identities and Behavior." He argues that (1) institutions, like individuals, have personalities that affect their behavior; (2) the armed services are the most powerful institutions in American defense policy; and (3) knowing the services' personalities allows us to "understand much that has happened and much that will happen in the American military and national security arenas." After examining the five "faces" of the navy, air force, and army personalities, Builder concludes that "despite the logical wrappings of defense planning, there is considerable evidence that the qualities of the U.S. military forces are determined more by cultural and institutional preferences for certain kinds of military forces than by the 'threat.'" His discussion raises the following questions: Have the service personalities changed with the end of the

Figure 1

Office of the Secretary of Defense

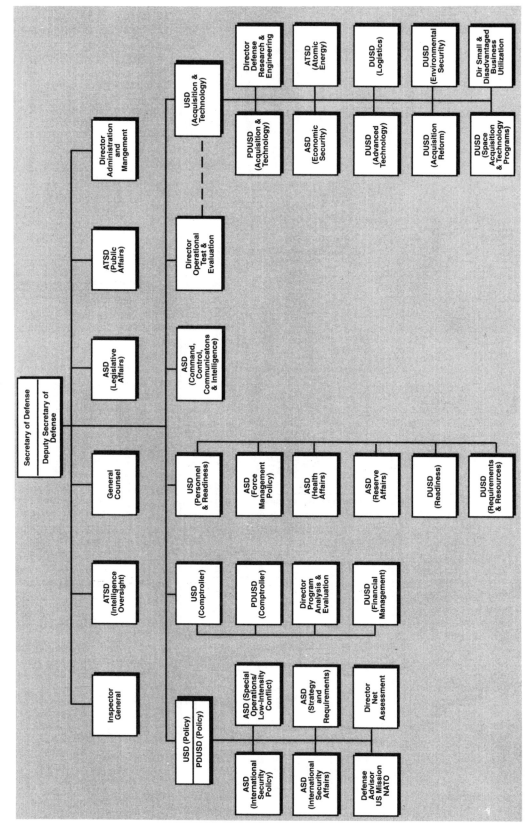

Figure 2
Department of Defense

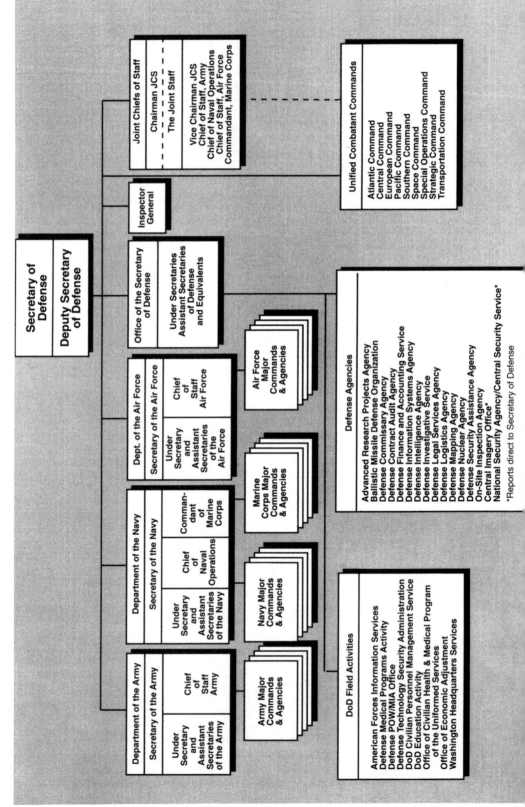

Cold War? If not, why not? What needs to be done to affect change? What form should that change take?

One major attempt to change the services' "cultural and institutional preferences" is the 1986 Goldwater-Nichols Defense Reorganization Act, the subject of Vincent Davis's "Defense Reorganization and National Security." By increasing the JCS chairman's power, requiring that officers serve in joint assignments before they can attain the rank of general or admiral, and giving the unified combatant commanders greater control over their forces, Goldwater-Nichols is breaking down barriers between the services and promoting greater "jointness" or teamwork. Although institutional cultures are slow to change and interservice rivalry still exists, gone are the days when JCS advice was often little more than a compromise among individual service positions and promising officers avoided assignments to the Joint Staff (Figure 3), fearing that being associated with another branch's policies and programs would prove to be detrimental at promotion time.

Thus the military services, unified combatant commands, and JCS currently are organized as follows. The military departments are separate entities with their own secretaries and service chiefs (Figure 4). They are responsible to the secretary of defense, and their mission is to organize, train, and equip forces for use by the unified combatant commands (Figure 5). The unified combatant commanders are responsible to the president and the secretary of defense, otherwise known as the National Command Authority, and the chain of command runs from the president to the secretary of defense to the unified commands. Although the chairman of the JCS transmits orders from the National Command Authority to the unified commanders, he is not formally part of the operational chain of command.

The final component of the executive bureaucracy to be considered here is the intelligence community—the dozen or so agencies involved in the collection, analysis, and dissemination of intelligence information. As Paula Scalingi points out in "U.S. Intelligence in an Age of Uncertainty," the community is at a watershed and must be restructured and reoriented to reflect the realities of the post–Cold War world. Budgeting pressures demand that the intelligence community be consolidated, cooperate more among its components, and be better managed overall, while the new international environment requires that greater attention be paid to the proliferation of weapons of mass destruction, political and economic developments in the former Soviet Union, the strategic nuclear threat, instability in Eastern Europe, potential areas of regional conflict, and arms control monitoring and support. Successfully making these adjustments, Scalingi contends, will require greater flexibility and more long-range planning than currently exists within the intelligence community. They are essential, however, given the number, complexity, and ambiguity of today's threats to U.S. security interests.

In "Glasnost for the CIA," David McCurdy argues that "the U.S. intelligence community needs a new defining mission" and suggests that it correspond with the Clinton administration's three national security objectives. The first is "revitalizing U.S. economic strength and competitiveness." Here, McCurdy agrees with Paula Scalingi that counterespionage and the collection of detailed economic data should continue, but economic espionage should not become an intelligence mission. "Economic espionage could undermine relations among the major trading partners, making political cooperation and free trade agreements less likely and setting the stage for a return to confrontation in the West," McCurdy writes. The second national security objective is "promoting democracy abroad." If, as many contend, democracies do not go to war with one another, it would be in America's interest to increase their numbers around the world. Deciding how this is best accomplished, however, will require detailed information about the countries in question. The third Clinton administration objective is to maintain "a strong defense posture." Again, intelligence is central to this effort, but it must be adapted to a world where peacekeeping, faster and more precise weapons, and coalition warfare are becoming more common. Moreover, these changes should occur with greater *glasnost* between intelligence agencies and the academic and business communities and between the United States and other countries.

"Preparing for the 21st Century," by the Commission on the Roles and Capabilities of the U.S. Intelligence Community, makes many of the same points that Scalingi and McCurdy make. It also recommends numerous reforms in issue areas ranging from the need to maintain an intelligence capability to accountability and oversight. Especially noteworthy is the commission's recommendation that "the President or his designee disclose the total amount of money appropriated for intelligence activities during the current fiscal year and the total amount being requested for the next fiscal year." These figures are currently classified. As the commission put it, intelligence agencies "are institutions within a democracy, responsible to the president, the Congress, and, ultimately, the people. Where accountability can be strengthened without damaging national security, . . . it should be."

Finally, power in American politics is shared by the government and the governed, especially as the latter are represented by communications channels such as interest groups, the media, and public opinion. Interest groups are "organization[s] of people sharing a common interest or goal that [seek] to influence the making of public policy."[2] They also are inherent to democracy, as James Madison noted in "Federalist 10" when he wrote that "liberty is to faction what air is to fire."[3] Thus there are thousands of interest groups covering virtually every aspect of American domestic and foreign policy. In "The Business of Defense," Gordon Adams describes how defense industries influence American defense policy

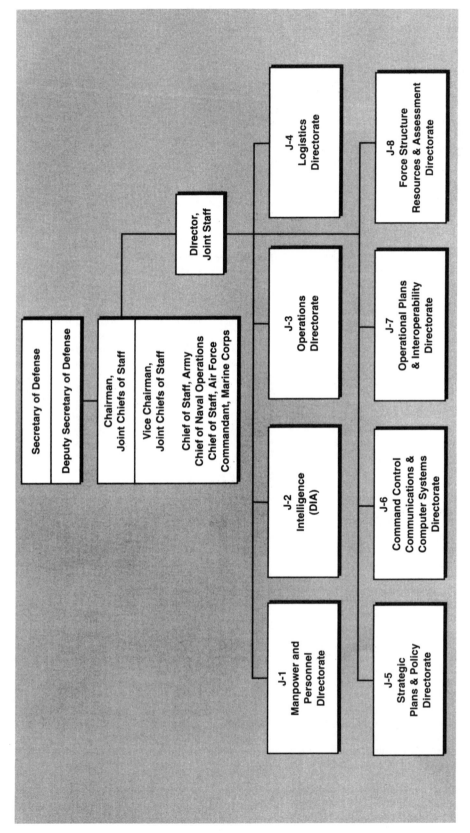

Figure 3
Joint Chiefs of Staff

Figure 4
Military Departments

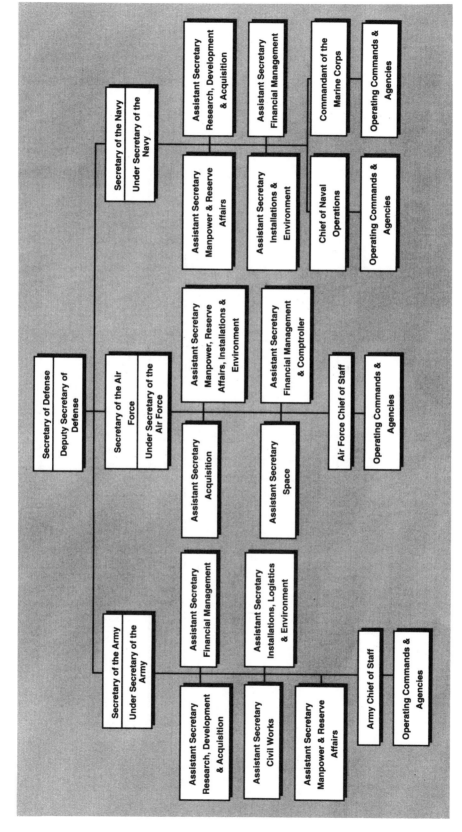

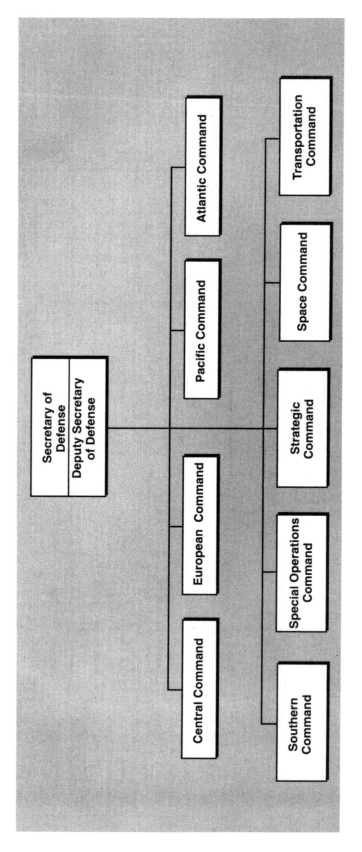

Figure 5
Unified Combatant Commands

and illustrates the process using a parable involving "General Electronics International" and the "Sting-Ray" missile. By using a fictitious case, Adams describes virtually every major tactic used by defense lobbyists. Especially important is Adams's discussion of "iron triangles" consisting of interest groups, executive branch agencies, and key congressional committees with "common values, interests, and perceptions."

Like interest groups, the media can be very powerful, given their large audiences and significant resources. This is especially true in the age of cable television and direct broadcast satellites; witness, for example, CNN's live coverage of the Persian Gulf War and the media's influence on U.S. military intervention in Somalia. In "Soldiers and Scribblers: A Common Mission," Richard Halloran examines the often bitter relationship between the military and the media by summarizing "the questions asked, complaints made, and allegations charged by military officers" and reporting his "replies based on three years of meetings with military people, seven years of covering the armed forces, and thirty years of experience in journalism." Halloran's credibility on this issue is enhanced by his service as an army enlisted man and officer before becoming an accomplished military correspondent.

Finally, public opinion can be defined as "the collected attitudes of citizens on a given issue or question."[4] Although the public tends to be poorly informed, frequently changes its mind, and often is ambivalent, it also provides broad guidelines for policy makers. Moreover, public support is necessary to the success of any significant defense policy or program. Thus Catherine Kelleher examines recent opinion about the military in "Presidents, Polls, and the Use of Force." The bottom line, according to Kelleher, is that Americans feel "there still is a need for a strong but reduced defense as insurance against uncertainty." However, "the use of military force is to be the exception in American foreign policy, it is rarely to be unilateral, and it is to involve limited goals and limited means."

NOTES

1. The defense committees are the Senate Armed Services Committee, the House National Security Committee, and their associated subcommittees in the Senate and House Appropriations Committees. The House National Security Committee was called the House Armed Services Committee until the 104th Congress.

2. James Q. Wilson and John J. DiIulio Jr., *American Government*, 6th ed. (Lexington, Mass.: D. C. Heath, 1995), A50.

3. Alexander Hamilton, James Madison, and John Jay, *The Federalist Papers* (New York: Mentor, 1961), 78.

4. Kenneth Janda, Jeffrey M. Berry, and Jerry Goldman, *The Challenge of Democracy: Government in America* (Boston: Houghton Mifflin, 1987), A31.

CHAPTER 4

THE PRESIDENT AND THE CONGRESS

THE PRESIDENT'S POWER TO PERSUADE

RICHARD E. NEUSTADT

The limits on command suggest the structure of our government. The Constitutional Convention of 1787 is supposed to have created a government of "separated powers." It did nothing of the sort. Rather, it created a government of separated institutions *sharing* powers.[1] "I am part of the legislative process," Eisenhower often said in 1959 as a reminder of his veto.[2] Congress, the dispenser of authority and funds, is no less part of the administrative process. Federalism adds another set of separated institutions. The Bill of Rights adds others. Many public purposes can only be achieved by voluntary acts of private institutions; the press, for one, in Douglass Cater's phrase, is a "fourth branch of government."[3] And with the coming of alliances abroad, the separate institutions of a London, or a Bonn, share in the making of American public policy.[4]

The separateness of institutions and the sharing of authority prescribe the terms on which a president persuades. When one shares authority with another, but does not gain or lose his job upon the other's whim, his willingness to act upon the urging of the other turns on whether he conceives the action right for him. The essence of a president's persuasive task is to convince such men that what the White House wants of them is what they ought to do for their sake and on their authority. (Sex matters not at all; for *man* read *woman*.)

Persuasive power, thus defined, amounts to more than charm or reasoned argument. These have their uses for a president, but these are not the whole of his resources. For the individuals he would induce to do what he wants done on their own responsibility will need or fear some acts by him on his responsibility. If they share his authority, he has some share in theirs. Presidential "powers" may be inconclusive when a president commands but always remain relevant as he persuades. The status and authority inherent in his office reinforce his logic and his charm.

Status adds something to persuasiveness; authority adds still more. In Walter Bagehot's charming phrase "no man can *argue* on his knees." Although there is no kneeling in this country, few men—and exceedingly few cabinet officers—are immune to the impulse to say "yes" to the president of the United States. It grows harder to say "no" when they are seated in his Oval Office at the White House, or in his study on the second floor, where almost tangibly he partakes of the aura of his physical surroundings.

A President's authority and status give him great advantages in dealing with the men he would persuade. Each "power" is a vantage point for him in the degree that other men have use for his authority. From the veto to appointments, from publicity to budgeting, and so on down a long list, the White House now controls the most encompassing array of vantage points in the American political system. With hardly an exception, those who share in governing this country are aware that at some time, in some degree, the doing of *their* jobs, the furthering of *their* ambitions, may depend upon the president of the United States. Their need for presidential action, or their fear of it, is bound to be recurrent if not actually continuous. Their need or fear is his advantage.

A president's advantages are greater than mere listing of his "powers" might suggest. Those with whom he deals must deal with him until the last day of his term. Because they have continuing relationships with him, his future, while it lasts, supports his present influence. Even though there is no need or fear of him today, what he could do tomorrow may supply today's advantage. Continuing relationships may convert any "power," any aspect of his status, into vantage points in almost any case. When he induces other people to do what he wants done, a president can trade on their dependence now and later.

The president's advantages are checked by the advantages of others. Continuing relationships will pull in both directions. These are relationships of mutual dependence. A president depends upon the persons whom he would persuade; he has to reckon with his need or fear of them. They too will possess status, or authority, or both, else they would be of little use to him. Their vantage points confront his own; their power tempers his. Persuasion is a two-way street.

This essay has been edited and is excerpted from Richard E. Neustadt, Presidential Power and Modern Presidents: The Politics of Leadership from Roosevelt to Reagan *(New York: The Free Press, 1990), 29–49, by permission of Simon & Schuster, Inc. Copyright © 1990 by Richard E. Neustadt*

The power to persuade is the power to bargain. Status and authority yield bargaining advantages. But in a government of "separated institutions sharing powers," they yield them to all sides. With the array of vantage points at his disposal, a president may be far more persuasive than his logic or his charm could make him. But outcomes are not guaranteed by his advantages. There remain the counter pressures those whom he would influence can bring to bear on him from vantage points at their disposal. Command has limited utility; persuasion becomes give-and-take. It is well that the White House holds the vantage points it does. In such a business any president may need them all—and more.

POWER AND THE EXECUTIVE BRANCH

This view of power as akin to bargaining is one we commonly accept in the sphere of congressional relations. Every textbook states and every legislative session demonstrates that save in times like the extraordinary Hundred Days of 1933—times virtually ruled out by definition at midcentury—a president will often be unable to obtain congressional action on his terms or even to halt action he opposes. The reverse is equally accepted: Congress often is frustrated by the president. Their formal powers are so intertwined that neither will accomplish very much, for very long, without the acquiescence of the other. By the same token, though, what one demands the other can resist. The stage is set for that great game, much like collective bargaining, in which each seeks to profit from the other's needs and fears. It is a game played catch-as-catch-can, case by case. And everybody knows the game, observers and participants alike.

The concept of real power as a give-and-take is equally familiar when applied to presidential influence outside the formal structure of the federal government. Influence becomes still more a matter of give-and-take when presidents attempt to deal with allied governments. In only one sphere is the concept unfamiliar: the sphere of executive relations. Perhaps because of civics textbooks and teaching in our schools, Americans instinctively resist the view that power in this sphere resembles power in all others. Even Washington reporters, White House aides, and members of Congress are not immune to the illusion that administrative agencies comprise a single structure, "the" executive branch, where presidential word is law, or ought to be. Yet when a president seeks something from executive officials his persuasiveness is subject to the same sorts of limitations as in the case of members of Congress or governors, or national committeemen, or private citizens, or foreign governments. It is plain that here as elsewhere influence derives from bargaining advantages; power is a give-and-take.

Like our governmental structure as a whole, the executive establishment consists of separated institutions sharing powers. The president heads one of these; cabinet officers, agency administrators, and military commanders head others. Below the departmental level, virtually independent bureau chiefs head many more. Federal operations spill across dividing lines on organization charts; almost every policy entangles many agencies; almost every program calls for interagency collaboration. Everything somehow involves the president. But operating agencies owe their existence least of all to one another—and only in some part to him. Each has a separate statutory base; each has its statutes to administer; each deals with a different set of subcommittees at the Capitol. Each has its own peculiar set of clients, friends, and enemies outside the formal government. Each has a different set of specialized careerists inside its own bailiwick. Our Constitution gives the president the "take-care" clause and the appointive power. Our statutes give him central budgeting and a degree of personnel control. All agency administrators are responsible to him. But they also are responsible to Congress, to their clients, to their staffs, and to themselves. In short, they have five masters. Only after all of those do they owe any loyalty to each other.

"The members of the cabinet," Charles G. Dawes used to remark, "are a president's natural enemies." Dawes had been Harding's budget director, Coolidge's vice president, and Hoover's ambassador to London; he also had been General Pershing's chief assistant for supply in World War I. The words are highly colored, but Dawes knew whereof he spoke. The men who have to serve so many masters cannot help but be somewhat the "enemy" of any one of them. By the same token, any master wanting service is in some degree the "enemy" of such a servant. A president is likely to want loyal support but not to relish trouble on his doorstep. Yet the more his cabinet members cleave to him, the more they may need help from him in fending off the wrath of rival masters. Help, though, is synonymous with trouble. Many a cabinet officer, with loyalty ill rewarded by his lights and help withheld, has come to view the White House as innately hostile to department heads. Dawes's dictum can be turned around.

Executive officials are not equally advantaged in their dealings with a president. Nor are the same officials equally advantaged all the time. Not every officeholder can resist the president with effective counterpressure. The vantage points conferred upon officials by their own authority and status vary enormously. The variance is heightened by particulars of time and circumstance. When officials have no powers in their own right, or depend upon the president for status, their counterpressure may be limited indeed. White House aides, who fit both categories, are among the most responsive men of all, and for good reason. As a director of the budget once remarked to me, "Thank God I'm here and not across the street. If the president doesn't call me, I've got plenty I can do right here and plenty coming up to me, by rights, to justify my calling him. But those poor fellows over there, if the boss doesn't call them, doesn't ask them to do something, what *can* they do but sit?" Authority and status so conditional are frail reliances in resisting a president's own wants. Within the White House precincts, lifted eyebrows may suffice to set an aide in motion; command, coercion, even charm aside. But even in the White House a president does not monopolize effective power. Even there persuasion is akin to bargaining. A former Roosevelt aide once wrote of cabinet officers:

Half of a President's suggestions, which theoretically carry the weight of orders, can be safely forgotten by a Cabinet member. And if the President asks about a suggestion a second time, he can be told that it is being investigated. If he asks a third time, a wise Cabinet officer will give him at least part of what he suggests. But only occasionally, except about the most important matters, do Presidents ever get around to asking three times.[5]

The rule applies to staff as well as to the cabinet, and certainly has been applied *by* staff.

Some aides will have more vantage points than a selective memory. Any aide who demonstrates to others that he has the president's consistent confidence and a consistent part in presidential business will acquire so much business on his own account that he becomes in some sense independent of his chief. Nothing in the Constitution keeps a well-placed aide from converting status into power of his own, usable in some degree even against the president.

The more an officeholder's status and his powers stem from sources independent of the president, the stronger will be his potential pressure on the president. Department heads in general have more bargaining power than do most members of the White House staff; but bureau chiefs may have still more, and specialists at upper levels of established career services may have almost unlimited reserves of the enormous power which consists of sitting still. As Franklin Roosevelt once remarked:

The Treasury is so large and far-flung and ingrained in its practices that I find it almost impossible to get the action and results I want—even with Henry [Morgenthau] there. But the Treasury is not to be compared with the State Department. You should go through the experience of trying to get any changes in the thinking, policy, and action of the career diplomats and then you'd know what a real problem was. But the Treasury and the State Department put together are nothing compared with the Na-a-vy. The admirals are really something to cope with—and I should know. To change anything in the Na-a-vy is like punching a feather bed. You punch it with your right and you punch it with your left until you are finally exhausted, and then you find the damn bed just as it was before you started punching.[6]

In the right circumstances, of course, a president can have his way with any of these people. But one needs to recognize that as between a president and his "subordinates," no less than others on whom he depends, real power is reciprocal and varies markedly with organization, subject matter, personality, and situation. The mere fact that persuasion is di-rected at executive officials signifies no necessary easing of his way. Any new member of Congress of the administration's party, especially if narrowly elected, may turn out more amenable (though less useful) to the president than any seasoned bureau chief "downtown." *The probabilities of power do not derive from the literary theory of the Constitution.*

PERSUASION AND SELF-INTEREST

There is a widely held belief in the United States that were it not for folly or for knavery, a reasonable president would need no power other than the logic of his argument. But faulty reasoning and bad intentions do not cause all quarrels with presidents. The best of reasoning and of intent cannot compose them all. For in the first place, what the president wants will rarely seem a trifle to the people he wants it from. And in the second place, they will be bound to judge it by the standard of their own responsibilities, not his. However logical his argument according to his lights, their judgment may not bring them to his view.

Those who share in governing this country frequently appear to act as though they were in business for themselves. So, in a real though not entire sense, they are and have to be. There is no reason to suppose that men of large but differing responsibilities will see all things through the same glasses. On the contrary, it is to be expected that their views of what ought to be done and what they then should do will vary with the differing perspectives their particular responsibilities evoke. Since their duties are not vested in a "team" or a "collegium" but in themselves, as individuals, one must expect that they will see things for themselves. Moreover, when they are responsible to many masters and when an event or policy turns loyalty against loyalty—a day-by-day occurrence in the nature of the case—one must assume that those who have the duties to perform will choose the terms of reconciliation. This is the essence of their personal responsibility. When their own duties pull in opposite directions, who else but they can choose what they will do?

Outside the executive branch the situation is the same, except that loyalty to the president may often matter *less.* There is no need to spell out the comparison with governors, steel company executives, trade union leaders, and the like. And when one comes to members of Congress who can do nothing for themselves (or their constituents) save as they are elected, term by term, in districts and through party structures differing from those on which a president depends, the case is very clear. An able Eisenhower aide with long congressional experience remarked to me in 1958: "The people on the Hill don't do what they might *like* to do, they do what they think they *have* to do in their own interest as *they* see it." This states the case precisely.

The essence of a president's persuasive task, with members of Congress and everybody else, is to induce them to believe that what he wants of them is what their own appraisal of their own responsibilities requires them to do in their interest, not his. Because men may differ in their views on public policy, because differences in outlook stem from differences in duty—duty to one's office, one's constituents, oneself—that task is bound to be more like collective bargaining than like a reasoned argument among philosopher kings. Overtly or implicitly, hard bargaining has characterized all illustrations offered up to now. This is the reason why: persuasion deals in the coin of self-interest with men who have some freedom to reject what they find counterfeit.

POWER AND BARGAINING

A president draws influence from bargaining advantages. But does he always need them? Suppose such sharp divergences are lacking, suppose most players of the governmental game see policy objectives much alike, then can he not rely on logic (or on charm) to get him what he wants? The answer is that even then most outcomes turn on bargaining. The reason for this answer is a simple one: most who share in governing have interests of their own beyond the realm of policy objectives. The sponsorship of policy, the form it takes, the conduct of it, and the credit for it separate their interest from the president's despite agreement on the end in view. In political government the means can matter quite as much as ends; they often matter more. And there are always differences of interest in the means.

Let me introduce a case: the European Recovery Program of 1948, the so-called Marshall Plan. This is perhaps the greatest exercise in policy agreement since the end of World War II. When the then secretary of state, George Catlett Marshall, spoke at the Harvard commencement in June 1947, he launched one of the most creative, most imaginative ventures in the history of American foreign relations. What makes this policy most notable for present purposes, however, is that it became effective upon action by the Eightieth Congress, at the behest of Harry Truman, in the election year 1948.[7]

Eight months before Marshall spoke at Harvard, the Democrats had lost control of both houses of Congress for the first time in fourteen years. Truman, whom the secretary represented, had just finished his second troubled year as president-by-succession. Truman was regarded with so little warmth in his own party that in 1946 he had been urged not to participate in the congressional campaign. At the opening of Congress in January 1947, Senator Robert A. Taft, "Mr. Republican," had somewhat the attitude of a president-elect. This was a vision widely shared in Washington, with Truman relegated thereby to the role of caretaker-on-term. Moreover, within just two weeks of Marshall's commencement address, Truman was to veto two prized accomplishments of Taft's congressional majority: the Taft-Hartley Act and tax reduction.[8] Yet scarcely ten months later the Marshall Plan was under way on terms to satisfy its sponsors, its authorization completed, its first-year funds in sight, its administering agency in being: all managed by as thorough a display of executive–congressional cooperation as any we have seen since the Second World War. For any president at any time this would have been a great accomplishment. In years before midcentury it would have been enough to make the future reputation of his term. And for a Truman, at this time, enactment of the Marshall Plan appears almost miraculous.

How was the miracle accomplished? How did a president so situated bring it off? In answer, the first thing to note is that he did not do it by himself. Truman had help of a sort no less extraordinary than the outcome. Although each stands for something more complex, the names of Marshall, Vandenberg, Patterson, Bevin, and Stalin tell the story of that help.

In 1947, two years after V-J Day, General Marshall was something more than secretary of state. He was a man venerated by the president as "the greatest living American," literally an embodiment of Truman's ideals. He was honored at the Pentagon as an architect of victory. He was thoroughly respected by Secretary of the Navy James V. Forrestal, who that year became the first secretary of defense. On Capitol Hill, Marshall had an enormous fund of respect stemming from his war record as army chief of staff, and in the country generally no officer had come out of the war with a higher reputation for judgment, intellect, and probity. Besides, as secretary of state, he had behind him the first generation of matured foreign service officers produced by the reforms of the 1920s, and mingled with them, in the departmental service, were some of the ablest of the men drawn by the war from private life to Washington. In terms both of staff talent and staff use, Marshall's years began a State Department "golden age" that lasted until the era of McCarthy. Moreover, as his undersecretary, Marshall had, successively, Dean Acheson and Robert Lovett, men who commanded the respect of the professionals and the regard of members of Congress. (Acheson had been brilliantly successful at congressional relations as assistant secretary in the war and postwar years.) Finally, as a special undersecretary Marshall had Will Clayton, a man highly regarded, for good reason, at both ends of Pennsylvania Avenue.

Taken together, these are exceptional resources for a secretary of state. In the circumstances, they were quite as necessary as they obviously are relevant. The Marshall Plan was launched by a lame-duck administration "scheduled" to leave office in eighteen months. Marshall's program faced a congressional leadership traditionally isolationist and currently intent upon economy. European aid was viewed with envy by a Pentagon distressed and virtually disarmed through budget cuts, and by domestic agencies intent on enlarged welfare programs. It was not viewed with liking by a Treasury intent on budget surpluses. The plan had need of every asset that could be extracted from the personal position of its nominal author and from the skills of his assistants.

Without the equally remarkable position of the senior senator from Michigan, Arthur H. Vandenberg, it is hard to see how Marshall's assets could have been enough. Vandenberg was chairman of the Senate Foreign Relations Committee. Actually, he was much more than that. Twenty years a senator, he was the senior member of his party in the chamber. Assiduously cultivated by FDR and Truman, he was a chief Republican proponent of bipartisanship in foreign policy and consciously conceived himself its living symbol to his party, to the country, and abroad. Moreover, by informal but entirely operative agreement with his colleague Taft, Vandenberg held the acknowledged lead among Senate Republicans in the whole field of international affairs. This acknowledgment meant more in 1947 than it might have meant at any other time. With confidence in the advent of a Republican administration two years hence, most of the gentlemen were in a mood to be responsive and responsible. The war was over, Roosevelt dead, Truman a caretaker, theirs the trust. That the senator from Michigan saw matters in this light his diaries make clear.[9] And this was not the outlook from the Senate side alone; the attitudes of House Republicans associated with the Herter Committee and its tours abroad suggest the same mood of responsibility. Vandenberg was not the only source of help on Capitol Hill. But relatively speaking his position there was as exceptional as Marshall's was downtown.

Help of another sort was furnished by a group of dedicated private citizens who organized one of the most effective instruments for public information seen since the Second World War: the Committee for the Marshall Plan, headed by the eminent Republicans whom FDR in 1940 had brought to the Department of War: Henry L. Stimson as honorary chairman and Robert P. Patterson as active spokesman. The remarkable array of bankers, lawyers, trade unionists, and editors, who had drawn together in defense of "internationalism" before Pearl Harbor and had joined their talents in the war itself, combined again to spark the work of this committee. Their efforts generated a great deal of vocal public support to buttress Marshall's arguments, and Vandenberg's, in Congress.

But before public support could be rallied, there had to be a purpose tangible enough, concrete enough, to provide a rallying ground. At Harvard, Marshall had voiced an idea in general terms. That this was turned into a hard program susceptible of presentation and support is due, in major part, to Ernest Bevin, the British foreign secretary. He well deserves the credit he has sometimes been assigned as, in effect, coauthor of the Marshall Plan. For Bevin seized on Marshall's Harvard speech and organized a European response with promptness and concreteness beyond the State Department's expectations. What had been virtually a trial balloon to test reactions on both sides of the Atlantic was hailed in London as an invitation to the Europeans to send Washington a bill of particulars. This they promptly organized to do, and the American administration then organized in turn for its reception without further argument internally about the pros and cons of issuing the "invitation" in the first place. But for Bevin there might have been trouble from the secretary of the treasury and others besides.[10]

If Bevin's help was useful at that early stage, Stalin's was vital from first to last. In a mood of self-deprecation Truman once remarked that without Moscow's "crazy" moves "we would never have had our foreign policy . . . we never could have got a thing from Congress."[11] George Kennan, among others, had deplored the anti-Soviet overtone of the case made for the Marshall Plan in Congress and the country, but there is no doubt that this clinched the argument for many segments of American opinion. There also is no doubt that Moscow made the crucial contributions to the case.

By 1947 events, far more than governmental prescience or open action, had given a variety of publics an impression of inimical Soviet intentions (and of Europe's weakness) and a growing urge to "do something about it." Three months before Marshall spoke at Harvard, Greek-Turkish aid and promulgation of the Truman Doctrine had seemed rather to crystallize than to create a public mood and a congressional response. The Marshall planners, be it said, were poorly placed to capitalize on that mood, nor had the secretary wished to do so. Their object, indeed, was to cut across it, striking at the cause of European weakness rather than at Soviet aggressiveness, per se. A strong economy in Western Europe called, ideally, for restorative measures of continental scope. American assistance proffered in an anti-Soviet context would have been contradictory in theory and unacceptable in fact to several of the governments that Washington was anxious to assist. As Marshall, himself, saw it, the logic of his purpose forbade him to play his strongest congressional card. The Russians then proceeded to play it for him. When the Europeans met in Paris, Molotov walked out. After the Czechs had shown continued interest in American aid, a communist coup overthrew their government while Soviet forces stood along their borders within easy reach of Prague. Molotov transformed the Marshall Plan's initial presentation; Czechoslovakia assured its final passage, which followed by a month the takeover in Prague.

Such was the help accorded Truman in obtaining action on the Marshall Plan. Considering his politically straitened circumstances he scarcely could have done with less. Conceivably some part of Moscow's contribution might have been dispensable, but not Marshall's or Vandenberg's or Bevin's or Patterson's or that of the great many other men whose work is represented by their names in my account. Their aid was not extended to the president for his own sake. He was not favored in this fashion just because they liked him personally or were spellbound by his intellect or charm. They might have been as helpful had all held him in disdain, which some of them certainly did. The Londoners who seized the ball, Vandenberg and Taft and the congressional majority, Marshall and his planners, the officials of other agencies who actively supported them or "went along," the host of influential private citizens who rallied to the cause— all these played the parts they did because they thought they had to, in their interest, given their responsibilities, not Truman's. Yet they hardly would have found it in their interest to collaborate with one another or with him had he not furnished them precisely what they needed from the White House. Truman could not do without their help, but he could not have had it without unremitting effort on his part.

The crucial thing to note about this case is that despite compatibility of views on public policy, Truman got no help he did not pay for (except Stalin's). Bevin scarcely could have seized on Marshall's words had Marshall not been plainly backed by Truman. Marshall's interest would not have comported with the exploitation of his prestige by a president who undercut him openly or subtly or even inadvertently at any point. Vandenberg, presumably, could not have backed proposals by a White House that begrudged him deference and access gratifying to his fellow partisans (and satisfying to himself). Prominent Republicans in private life would not have found it easy to promote a cause identified with Truman's claims on 1948—and neither would the prominent New Dealers then engaged in searching for a substitute.

Truman paid the price required for their services. So far as the record shows, the White House did not falter once in firm support for Marshall and the Marshall Plan. Truman backed his secretary's gamble on an invitation to all Europe. He made the plan his own in a well-timed address to the Canadians. He lost no opportunity to widen the involvements of his own official family in the cause. Averell Harriman, the secretary of commerce; Julius Krug, the secretary of the interior; Edwin Nourse, the Economic Council chairman; James Webb, the director of the budget—all were made responsible for studies and reports contributing directly to the legislative presentation. Thus these men were committed in advance. Besides, the president continually emphasized to everyone in reach that he did not have doubts, did not desire complications, and would foreclose all he could. Reportedly his emphasis was felt at the Treasury, with good effect. And Truman was at special pains to smooth the way for Vandenberg. The senator insisted on "no politics" from the administration side; there was none. He thought a survey of American resources and capacity essential; he got it in the Krug and Harriman reports. Vandenberg expected advance consultation; he received it, step by step, in frequent meetings with the president and weekly conferences with Marshall. He asked for an effective liaison between Congress and agencies concerned; Lovett and others gave him what he wanted. When the senator decided on the need to change financing and administrative features of the legislation, Truman disregarded Budget Bureau grumbling and ac-

quiesced with grace. When, finally, Vandenberg desired a Republican to head the new administering agency, his candidate, Paul Hoffman, was appointed despite the president's own preference for another. In all these ways Truman employed the sparse advantages his "powers" and his status then accorded him to gain the sort of help he had to have.

Truman helped himself in still another way. Traditionally and practically, no one was placed as well as he to call public attention to the task of Congress (and its Republican leadership). Throughout the fall and winter of 1947 and on into the spring of 1948, he made repeated use of presidential "powers" to remind the country that congressional action was required. Messages, speeches, and an extra session were employed to make the point. Here, too, he drew advantage from his place. However, in his circumstances, Truman's public advocacy might have hurt, not helped, had his words seemed directed toward the forthcoming election. Truman gained advantage for his program only as his own endorsement of it stayed on the right side of that fine line between the "caretaker" in office and the would-be candidate. In public statements dealing with the Marshall Plan he seems to have risked blurring this distinction only once, when he called Congress into session in November 1947 asking both for interim aid to Europe and for peacetime price controls. The second request linked the then inflation with the current Congress (and with Taft), becoming a first step toward one of Truman's major themes in 1948. By calling for both measures at the extra session he could have been accused—and was—of mixing home-front politics with foreign aid. In the event no harm was done the European program (or his politics). But in advance a number of his own advisers feared that such a double call would jeopardize the Marshall Plan. Their fears are testimony to the narrowness of his advantage in employing his own "powers" for its benefit.[12]

POWER AND PRESIDENTIAL "CHOICE"

Had Truman lacked the personal advantages his "powers" and his status gave him, or if he had been maladroit in using them, there probably would not have been a massive European aid program in 1948. Something of the sort, perhaps quite different in its emphasis, would almost certainly have come to pass before the end of 1949. Some American response to European weakness and to Soviet expansion was as certain as such things can be. But in 1948 temptations to await a Taft plan or a Dewey plan might well have caused at least a year's postponement of response had the outgoing administration bungled its congressional or public or allied or executive relations. Quite aside from the specific virtues of their plan. Truman and his helpers gained that year, at least, in timing the American response. As European time was measured then, this was a precious gain. The president's own share in this accomplishment was vital. He made his contribution by exploiting his advantages. Truman, in effect, lent Marshall and the rest the perquisites and status of his office. In return they lent him their prestige and their own influence. The transfer multiplied his influence despite his limited authority in form and lack of strength politically. Without the wherewithal to make this bargain, Truman could not have contributed to European aid.

Bargaining advantages convey no guarantees. Influence remains a two-way street. In the fortunate instance of the Marshall Plan, what Truman needed was actually in the hands of men who were prepared to "trade" with him. He personally could deliver what they wanted in return. Marshall, Vandenberg, Harriman, and the others, possessed the prestige, energy, associations, staffs essential to the legislative effort. Truman himself had a sufficient hold on presidential messages and speeches, on budget policy, on high-level appointments, and on his own time and temper to carry through all aspects of his necessary part. But it takes two to make a bargain. It takes those who have prestige to lend it on whatever terms. Suppose that Marshall had declined the secretaryship of state in January 1947; Truman might not have found a substitute so well equipped to furnish what he needed in the months ahead. Or suppose that Vandenberg had fallen victim to a cancer two years before he actually did; Senator Wiley of Wisconsin would not have seemed to Taft a man with whom the world need be divided. Or suppose that the secretary of the treasury had been possessed of stature, force, and charm commensurate with that of his successor in Eisenhower's time, the redoubtable George M. Humphrey. And what if Truman then had seemed to the Republicans what he turned out to be in 1948, a formidable candidate for president? It is unlikely that a single one of these "supposes" would have changed the final outcome; two or three, however, might have altered it entirely. Truman was not guaranteed more power than his "powers" just because he had continuing relationships with cabinet secretaries and with senior senators. Here, as everywhere, the outcome was conditional on who they were and what he was and how each viewed events, and on their actual performance in response.

Granting that persuasion has no guarantee attached, how can a president reduce the risks of failing to persuade? How can he maximize his prospects for effectiveness by minimizing chances that his power will elude him? The Marshall Plan suggests an answer: He guards his power prospects in the course of making choices. Marshall himself, and Forrestal and Harriman, and others of the sort held office on the president's appointment. Vandenberg had vast symbolic value partly because FDR and Truman had done everything they could, since 1944, to build him up. The Treasury Department and the Budget Bureau—which together might have jeopardized the plans these others made—were headed by officials whose prestige depended wholly on their jobs. What Truman needed from those "givers" he received, in part, because of his past choice of men and measures. What they received in turn were actions taken

or withheld by him, himself. The things they needed from him mostly involved his own conduct where his current choices ruled. The president's own actions in the past had cleared the way for current bargaining. His actions in the present were his trading stock. Behind each action lay a personal choice, and these together comprised his control over the give-and-take that gained him what he wanted. In the degree that Truman, personally, affected the advantages he drew from his relationships with other men in government, his power was protected by his choices.

By "choice" I mean no more than what is commonly referred to as "decision": a president's own act of doing or not doing. Decision is so often indecisive, and indecision is so frequently conclusive, that *choice* becomes the preferable term. "Choice" has its share of undesired connotations. In common usage it implies a black-and-white alternative. Presidential choices are rarely of that character. It also may imply that the alternatives are set before the choice maker by someone else. A president is often left to figure out his options for himself.

If presidents could count upon past choices to enhance their current influence, as Truman's choice of men had done for him, persuasion would pose fewer difficulties than it does. But presidents can count on no such thing. Depending on the circumstances, prior choices can be as embarrassing as they were helpful in the instance of the Marshall Plan. Assuming that past choices have protected influence, not harmed it, present choices still may be inadequate. If presidents could count on their own conduct to provide them enough bargaining advantages, as Truman's conduct did where Vandenberg and Marshall were concerned, effective bargaining might be much easier to manage than it often is. Yet in practice, if not theory, many of *their* crucial choices never were the president's to make. Decisions that are legally in others' hands, or delegated past recall, have an unhappy way of proving just the trading stock most needed when the White House wants to trade. One reason why Truman was consistently influential in the instance of the Marshall Plan is that the Marshall Plan directly involved Congress. In congressional relations there are some things that no one but the president can do. His chance to choose is higher when a message must be sent, or a nomination submitted, or a bill signed into law, than when the sphere of action is confined to the executive, where all decisive tasks may have been delegated past recall.

But adequate or not, a president's own choices are the only means in his own hands of guarding his own prospects for effective influence. He can draw power from continuing relationships in the degree that he can capitalize upon the needs of others for the presidency's status and authority. He helps himself to do so, though, by nothing save ability to recognize the preconditions and the chance advantages and to proceed accordingly in the course of the choice making that comes his way. To ask how he can guard prospective influence is thus to raise a further question: what helps him guard his power stakes in his own acts of choice?

NOTES

1. The reader will want to keep in mind the distinction between two senses in which the word *power* is employed. When I have used the word (or its plural) to refer to formal constitutional, statutory, or customary authority, it is either qualified by the adjective "formal" or placed in quotation marks as "power(s)." Where I have used it in the sense of effective influence on the conduct of others, it appears without quotation marks (and always in the singular). Where clarity and convenience permit, *authority* is substituted for "power" in the first sense and *influence* for power in the second.

2. See, for example, his press conference of 22 July 1959, as reported in the *New York Times*, 23 July 1959.

3. See Douglass Cater, *The Fourth Branch of Government* (Boston: Houghton Mifflin, 1959).

4. For distinctions drawn throughout between power and powers see note 1.

5. Jonathan Daniels, *Frontier on the Potomac* (New York: Macmillan, 1946), 31–32.

6. As reported in Marriner S. Eccles, *Beckoning Frontiers* (New York: Knopf, 1951), 336.

7. In drawing together these observations on the Marshall Plan, I have relied on the record of personal participation by Joseph M. Jones, *The Fifteen Weeks* (New York: Viking, 1955), esp. 89–256; the study by Harry Bayard Price, *The Marshall Plan and Its Meaning* (Ithaca, N.Y.: Cornell University Press, 1955), esp. 1–86; Harry S Truman, *Memoirs,* vol. 2, *Years of Trial and Hope* (Garden City, N.Y.: Doubleday, Time, 1956), chaps. 7–9; Arthur H. Vandenberg Jr., ed., *The Private Papers of Senator Vandenberg* (Boston: Houghton Mifflin, 1952), esp. 373 ff.; and notes of my own made at the time.

8. Secretary Marshall's speech, formally suggesting what became known as the Marshall Plan, was made at Harvard on 5 June 1947. On 20 June the president vetoed the Taft-Hartley Act; his veto was overridden three days later. On 16 June he vetoed the first of two tax reduction bills (HR 1) passed at the first session of the Eightieth Congress; the second of these (HR 3950), a replacement for the other, he also disapproved on 18 July. In both instances his veto was narrowly sustained.

9. *Private Papers of Senator Vandenberg,* 378–79, 446.

10. The initial reluctance of Secretary of the Treasury John Snyder to support large-scale spending overseas became a matter of public knowledge on 25 June 1947. At a press conference on that day, he interpreted Marshall's Harvard speech as a call on Europeans to help themselves, by themselves. At another press conference the same day, Marshall for his own part had indicated that the United States would consider helping programs on which Europeans agreed. The next day, Truman held a press conference and was asked the inevitable question. He replied, "General Marshall and I are in complete agreement." When pressed further, Truman remarked sharply, "The secretary of the treasury and the secretary of state and the President are in complete agreement." Thus the president cut Snyder off, but had programming gathered less momentum overseas, no doubt he would have been heard from again as time passed and opportunity offered.

The foregoing quotations are from the stenographic transcript of the presidential press conference, 26 June 1947, on file in the Truman Library at Independence, Missouri.

11. A remark made in December 1955, three years after he left office, but not unrepresentative of views he expressed, on occasion, while he was president.

12. This might also be taken as testimony to the political timidity of officials in the State Department and the Budget Bureau where that fear seems to have been strongest. However, conversations at the time with White House aides incline me to believe that there, too, interjection of the price issue was thought a gamble and a risk. For further comment see my "Congress and the Fair Deal: A Legislative Balance Sheet," *Public Policy* 5 (1954):362–64.

CONGRESS AND DEFENSE POLICY

JAMES M. LINDSAY

In the 1960s Congress generally made few changes to Department of Defense (DOD) requests. It routinely disposed of defense authorization and appropriations bills with little debate and few floor amendments. By 1986, however, extensive changes in budget line items, lengthy floor debates, and a blizzard of floor amendments had become the norm for DOD bills. Why did congressional activity on defense policy change so dramatically during those twenty-five years?

The changes in congressional decision making on defense policy were due to three main causes. First,

This essay has been edited and is reprinted from Armed Forces and Society 13 (Spring 1987): 371–401, *by permission of Transaction Publishers. Copyright © 1987; all rights reserved.*

because of the ascent of the annual authorization process, legislators were afforded increasing *opportunities* to intervene in defense issues. Second, the political volatility of defense policy affected congressional decision making. In the early 1970s and again in the 1980s the politicization of defense policy expanded legislators' *incentives* to address defense issues. Third, the congressional reforms of the 1970s eroded the institutional constraints on the behavior of congressional members, giving lawmakers greater *freedom* to participate in the defense debate.

As a result of these changes, congressional decision making on defense policy has undergone distinctive modes since 1961, when the current system of annual line-item authorizations and appropriations first began. In the 1960s, congressional decision making was an "inside game." The most senior members, and especially the chairs, of the House and Senate defense committees—the Armed Services committees and the Defense Appropriations subcommittees—dominated Congress's handling of defense policy. In the 1970s, the congressional reform movement dispersed power on Capitol Hill and strengthened the subcommittee system within the Armed Services committees. This produced a decentralized variant of the inside game, in which more committee members participated in decision making, but the defense committees continued to dominate the defense debate. In the 1980s, however, an "outside game" emerged. Congressional defense committees remain the major players, but their parent chambers circumscribed their freedom of action.

With the emergence of the outside game, the congressional defense debate in the 1980s became more representative of members' views than in previous decades. In turn, Congress was more willing to address major issues in the defense budget. Yet these developments came at the price of a more protracted budgetary process, the erosion of the committee system, and an increase in micromanagement. As more legislators have joined the defense debate, Congress has failed to pass appropriations bills before the start of the fiscal year and committees regularly duplicate one another's work. Nor has the increase in congressional activity been solely in the direction of greater policy oversight—much activity has involved micromanagement of the defense budget.

OVERVIEW OF CONGRESS AND DEFENSE POLICY

By virtually any empirical indicator, congressional involvement in the policy process has grown sharply over the last several decades. This is especially true in defense policy. Congress has become much more likely to alter DOD line-item requests, to demand justifications for DOD programs, and to mandate that the Pentagon undertake specific actions. These changes are true not only for the defense committees, which have direct legislative responsibility for defense matters, but also for the average member of Congress.

One aspect of the exploding congressional intervention in defense policy is the defense committees' shift since 1961 to more detailed reviews of DOD requests. The number of pages in the Armed Services committees' and Defense Appropriations subcommittees' annual reports on the defense budget sketches a rough picture of this shift. Between 1961 and 1969, the reports issued by the four defense committees averaged a total of 231 pages. During the 1970s this figure rose to 829 pages; and between 1980 and 1985 the total number in the four reports averaged 1,186 pages.[1] The increased length of the hearings held by the defense committees paints a similar portrait. For example, between 1961 and 1969 the hearings held by the Senate Committee on Armed Services (SASC) on the defense authorization bill averaged 1,098 pages.[2] By comparison, the SASC's hearings on the fiscal year 1986 defense authorization bill ran to 4,759 pages.

Floor debates on DOD authorization bills have also greatly expanded, as Table 1 illustrates (debates on DOD appropriations bills are not included because the use of continuing resolutions in recent years makes comparisons across decades misleading). During the 1960s, floor activity was low in both chambers. Floor debate rose sharply in 1969, stimulated largely by congressional disillusionment over the Vietnam War; it dropped off in the mid-1970s. In the 1980s, however, floor activity again soared. The growth in the Senate floor debate is especially striking—during the fiscal 1985 and 1986 debates, the Senate averaged slightly more than one amendment per senator—since it has only one-fourth as many members as the House.

As a result of the growth both of committee and floor activity, Congress is more likely than ever to alter defense budget details. In 1969 Congress made 180 changes to the defense authorization bill and 650 to the appropriations bill. In 1975 these figures were 222 and 1,032, respectively. In 1985, however, Congress made 1,145 adjustments in the authorization bill and 2,156 in the appropriations bill (representing more than a sixfold and a threefold increase, respectively, in changes to the defense authorization and appropriations bills). There has been a similar jump in congressional directions to the DOD. In 1969 Congress requested 36 reports from the Pentagon, directed 18 other actions, and changed 64 provisions in the law. By comparison, in 1985 Congress requested 676 reports (an increase of 1,778%), mandated 184 other directions (922%), and made 227 changes in the law (255%). Overall, congressional directions rose by nearly 1,000 percent between 1969 and 1985.[3]

One major reason for the growth of congressional intervention in defense policy, and particularly the increased activity of the defense committees, has been the growth of the annual authorization process. Before 1961 the Armed Services committees provided lump-sum authorizations for most DOD programs. Typically, this authorization was no more specific than "The Secretary of the Air Force may procure guided missiles and 24,000 serviceable air-

Table 1

Characteristics of House and Senate Debate on the Annual Defense
Authorization Bill, 1961–1985

Calendar Year	House		Senate	
	Days of Debate	Amendments	Days of Debate	Amendments
1961	1	2	1	0
1962	1	7	1	0
1963	2	2	1	2
1964	1	10	1	1
1965	1	0	1	0
1966	1	1	1	0
1967	1	5	1	0
1968	1	7	3	8
1969	3	21	37	34
1970	3	23	28	31
1971	3	21	13	30
1972	2	14	8	15
1973	2	14	9	50
1974	2	11	8	35
1975	3	15	6	28
1976	2	12	4	18
1977	3	16	2	6
1978	2	19	2	18
1979	3	33	3	11
1980	4	26	3	24
1981	7	49	3	17
1982	7	78	7	58
1983	8	64	13	68
1984	6	52	10	108
1985	9	140	9	108
1986	10	116	7	83
Average:				
1961–69	1	6	5 (1)[a]	5 (1)[a]
1970–79	3	20	8	24
1980–86	7	75	7	67

Source: The figures for the House are drawn from an examination of the
authorization debates in the *Congressional Record* between 1961 and
1985. The chief clerk of the Senate Committee on Armed Services
provided the figures for the Senate.
[a]These numbers reflect the Senate averages for the 1960s if the 1969
ABM debate is excluded.

craft."[4] Except for the military construction account—which constituted roughly 3 percent of the
budget—the committees did not examine DOD
budget requests on a line-item basis. As a result, "the
annual authorization of specific line items was in
essence provided through appropriations acts."[5]

Annual authorizations were initiated with the
passage in 1959 of the Russell amendment. Named
after Senator Richard Russell (Democrat of Georgia), the SASC chair, it stipulated that after 1960 all
appropriations for the procurement of aircraft,
missiles, and naval vessels had to be preceded by
specific annual authorizations. Since that time, Con-

gress, at the urging of the Armed Services committees, gradually has extended the annual line-item
authorization requirement to virtually the entire defense budget.[6]

The growth of the annual authorization process
in part reflects the Armed Services committees' efforts to gain power and status vis-à-vis the Defense
Appropriations subcommittees. In the 1950s the latter were the preeminent congressional actors involved in defense policy, while in the DOD "the
Armed Services Committees [were] often regarded
with a kind of gracious toleration that border[ed] on
contempt."[7] This disparity in power and status

stemmed from the differences in how authorizations and appropriations were handled. The lump-sum authorizations the Armed Services committees approved generally were expansive enough to leave DOD's plans unfettered. The Pentagon was more solicitous of the Defense Appropriations subcommittees, however, because they had the power to alter individual line items.

Not surprisingly, the House and Senate Armed Services committees pushed for annual line-item authorizations to regain their legislative influence. Even in the 1980s, when both committees had secured their status as major players, they still sought to limit the influence of the Defense Appropriations subcommittees. A major factor in the decision to push for extending annual authorizations to Operations and Maintenance and Other Procurement accounts in the 1980s was the view that "if the Defense Subcommittees continued to have a free hand in these accounts, then it would be they, not the Armed Services Committees, that would then determine the state of readiness of the forces."[8]

The Armed Services committees also have fought to extend the authorization process "to reduce the area of discretionary power of the Office of the Secretary of Defense . . . and to strengthen legislative control of programs."[9] The committees traditionally have been skeptical of the Office of the Secretary of Defense (OSD), instead, favoring the views of the individual services. By extending annual line-item authorizations, the Armed Services committees have been able to keep the OSD under close scrutiny and also have been provided opportunities to solicit the advice of the professional military.

The rise of the authorization process has stimulated the Defense Appropriations subcommittees to increase their scrutiny of the defense budget. In part, this increased activity has been automatic. Under House and Senate rules, appropriations cannot exceed authorizations, so the funding cuts in the authorization cycle necessitate cuts by the Defense Appropriations subcommittees. In addition, the process also has given the subcommittees an incentive to take a more activist role on defense policy. If they only ratified authorization decisions, then the Armed Services committees would become the major congressional actors on defense issues.

The emergence of annual line-item authorizations has produced a twin-track decision-making process. As the authorization and appropriations cycles have come more and more to cover the same terrain, Congress has had to make decisions on defense requests twice each year. Although the degree of coordination and conflict between these two tracks has varied over the years, their growth has expanded the opportunities for congressional intervention in defense policy.

THE 1960s: THE INSIDE GAME

The senior members of the defense committees—and especially the chairs—were the major congressional actors on defense policy during the 1960s. By virtue of congressional rules, these chairs had the power to create subcommittees, set committee agendas, choose committee staff, and manage defense bills on the floor. Moreover, congressional norms held that junior members would see their role as an apprenticeship and defer to committee leaders. These rules and norms produced an inside game in Congress, a closed decision-making style with relatively few participants. As a result, the senior members of the defense committees generally could command the support of Congress for their positions on defense matters.

The power of the committee chair was most obvious in the House Committee on Armed Services (HASC): Carl Vinson (Democrat of Georgia) and his successor, L. Mendel Rivers (Democrat of South Carolina), ran the committees as their personal baronies.[10] Both hearings and markups of the annual defense authorization bills were done in full committee, where Vinson and Rivers dominated deliberations. There were four standing subcommittees, but they lacked formal jurisdictions and simply were numbered one through four. Vinson and Rivers also frequently created special (temporary) subcommittees. Many of these, however, were formed to investigate a specific problem (for example, the Pueblo incident) and did not have the power to write legislation. Moreover, House rules gave the committee head great discretion in assigning legislation to subcommittees, and both chairs often used this power to promote or bury legislation. As a result, "the Armed Services subcommittees were little more than useful devices for implementing the legislative will of the Chairman."[11]

The House Appropriations Defense Subcommittee (HADS) operated in a less autocratic fashion. Being a subcommittee itself, there were no subcommittee slots to control, and George Mahon (Democrat of Texas)—the chair throughout the 1960s—was less heavy-handed than his counterpart on the HASC.[12] Still, Mahon and the most-senior members dominated deliberations. The subcommittee was small (generally, eleven members), and there was little turnover; of the five ranking Democrats on the subcommittee in 1961, four still sat on it in 1969. By tradition, congressional members were appointed to the HADS only after they had served several terms in the House and on other appropriations subcommittees and had demonstrated strong prodefense views.

The Senate defense committees, like their House counterparts, were run from the top down. The norms of apprenticeship and deference to the committee chair were strong, and the chair possessed a wide range of formal powers to direct the committee's operations.[13] In the case of the SASC, the full committee marked up all defense legislation; none of the subcommittees had standing responsibility for any element of the authorization bill or any major aspect of defense policy. For example, from 1961 to 1966 the SASC's subcommittees were on

Preparedness Investigation, the Central Intelligence Agency, National Stockpile and Naval Petroleum Reserves, and Officer Grade Limitations. Although the Preparedness Investigation subcommittee was active in the early 1960s, it did not write legislation.

None of the defense committees made extensive changes to DOD budget requests in the 1960s. In general, members of these committees saw their task as the military's advocate on Capitol Hill. As Rivers explained the HASC's role, "You must remember this is the most important committee in this Congress. This is the only voice, official voice, the military has in the House of Representatives."[14] Often the defense committees supported positions of the services that were against the administration, as in the case of the RS-70 manned strategic bomber. Further, for most of the 1960s the committees faced few objections on the floor to their decisions.

The degree of coordination between the defense committees, however, differed markedly in both chambers. In the House the two defense committees worked in isolation from one another. There was no membership overlap (HADS members generally had no other committee assignments), and HADS members generally did not read HASC's hearings or reports.[15] In the Senate, however, Russell chaired both defense committees from 1963 to 1968 and several other senators sat on both committees. Moreover, the Senate Appropriations Defense Subcommittee (SADS) had three ex officio members from SASC with voting rights at the subcommittee level (although not in the full appropriations committee). This "interlocking directorate" in the Senate gave the twin authorization-appropriations process an informal coordinating mechanism.

The House and Senate defense committees also had different experiences in managing their legislation on the floor. The powerful House Rules Committee enabled the defense committees to obtain rules that restricted debate, making it virtually impossible to amend defense legislation unless the defense committees approved. The Senate lacked an analog to the House Rules Committee. As a result, the 1969 debate over the ABM system lasted thirty-seven days in the Senate but only three in the House. Even with this difference, none of the four defense committees lost a floor fight during the 1960s on any amendments to the annual authorization and appropriations bills.[16]

THE 1970s: THE DECENTRALIZED INSIDE GAME

The major change in congressional decision making on defense issues in the 1970s was the rise of the subcommittee system within the Armed Services committees. Although it came at the expense of the power of the chair, the locus of influence remained within the defense committees. Noncommittee members became more interested in defense matters in the early 1970s, but their influence over defense legislation remained slight and indirect. The result was the emergence of a decentralized version of the inside game.

The dispersal of power within the Armed Services committees, part of a broader trend in Congress, reflected both internal and external pressures. Many legislators, especially in the House, chafed against the tremendous power of the chairs. They hoped not only to increase their say in policy making, but also to increase the potential for gaining political credit with constituents through committee work.[17] Their cause was aided by the arrival in the late sixties and early seventies of new, more individualistic legislators who were unwilling to enter into an apprenticeship while the more senior members managed the business of Congress. They were vocal in their criticisms of the concentration of power in the hands of senior representatives and senators.

The House adopted two sets of reforms in the 1970s that affected the HASC.[18] The Legislative Reorganization Act of 1970 (which also applied to the Senate) required committees to make public all recorded votes, placed limits on proxy voting, empowered a majority of committee members to call meetings, and encouraged committees to hold open hearings. The more important reforms, however, came in 1973, when the House Democratic Caucus adopted the Subcommittee Bill of Rights. These new rules stripped the committee chairs of their power to make subcommittee assignments. Committee members won the right to bid for subcommittee chairs, in the order of their committee seniority, as well as the right to at least one choice subcommittee assignment. The new rules also mandated that subcommittees have formal jurisdictions, adequate budgets, authorization to hold hearings, and a staff selected by the subcommittee chair.

Despite these changes, F. Edward Hebert (Democrat of Louisiana), who became HASC chair upon Rivers's death, continued to run the committee autocratically. He frequently violated procedural rules and opposed the mood in the House to trim defense spending. House Democrats had become less tolerant of imperious chairs, however; and in January 1975 the Democratic Caucus removed Hebert and two other committee chairs. The caucus chose Melvin Price (Democrat of Illinois), the next-ranking member of the HASC, as Hebert's successor. The selection of Price suggests that House Democrats were opposed more to Hebert's style and personality than to his defense views. Price also was pro-defense—he had repeatedly voted against amendments to cut defense spending—but he had a reputation for fairness.

Price accepted the reduced role of the committee chair and shared legislative responsibility with the subcommittee heads. He democratized committee procedures, assigned permanent staff to the subcommittee, and made legislative referrals automatic. Hearings and markups of the annual defense authorization bill were done in the subcommittees, and Price was less involved in subcommittee work than his two predecessors. He remained the most powerful member of the HASC, but "as a group, the [sub-committee] chairmen equalled the committee head in power."[19]

The Senate adopted several reforms in the seventies that encouraged committee decentralization.[20] The Legislative Reorganization Act of 1970 limited future senators to only one seat on the Senate's top four committees: Appropriations, Armed Services, Finance, and Foreign Relations. This enabled junior senators to sit on the most prestigious committees earlier in their careers. In 1975 the Senate increased the size of the legislative staff that junior senators could hire for their committee work. The Senate adopted its most important reforms two years later when it prohibited senators from chairing more than one subcommittee per committee—forcing Senators John Stennis (Democrat of Mississippi) and Howard Cannon (Democrat of Nevada) to surrender one SASC subcommittee chair each—and limited senators to three subcommittee seats per committee. The 1977 reforms also changed the procedures for selecting subcommittee assignments. Under the new rules each member picked one subcommittee seat before the next-ranking member chose. Previously, committee members chose all their subcommittee assignments within the committee, in order of their seniority, before the next-ranking member selected.

Informal changes, however, played the greatest role in the SASC decentralization, the most important coming with Senator Stennis's ascension to the committee chair.[21] Committee head from 1969 to 1980, Stennis was more predisposed than Russell to allow other senators to participate in committee business. In 1971, Stennis set up subcommittees on Research and Development (R&D) and on Tactical Air Power, also authorizing them to mark up those parts of the DOD budget. In addition, he created subcommittees to address other aspects of defense policy. Even when subcommittee chairs opposed committee decisions on the floor, such as when Research and Development Subcommittee Chair Senator Thomas McIntyre (Democrat of New Hampshire) waged several floor battles in the mid-1970s to kill nuclear counterforce programs, Stennis did not use his power to subvert the subcommittee structure. The arrival of new, more assertive senators to the SASC reinforced Stennis's willingness to give other committee members increased responsibility.

The growth of the subcommittee system was greater in the House than in the Senate because of the wide-ranging nature of the House's Subcommittee Bill of Rights. By 1979 the HASC's subcommittees marked up the entire annual defense authorization bill, and they had the right to schedule hearings on virtually any subject. Moreover, in the Ninety-Sixth Congress (1979–80), the HASC referred 99 percent of its legislation to the relevant subcommittee, as compared with 12 percent during the Ninety-First Congress (1969–71).[22] In contrast, the SASC continued to mark up the procurement account, except for requests for tactical aircraft, in the full committee. The SASC chair also retained the power to schedule

hearings and meetings, and the committee staff remained more centralized than in the House. Finally, the SASC's small size meant that most of its subcommittees included nearly half of the full committee's members.

The rise of the subcommittee system strengthened the ability of the Armed Services committees to intervene in defense policy. This new ability was enhanced by the increase in committee staff size—during the period 1970–78, the HASC's staff grew from thirty-seven to forty-five, while the SASC's rose from nineteen to thirty.[23] The increased floor debates in the early 1970s further stimulated the Armed Services committees. As Alton Frye argues, "Whatever instincts John Stennis may have had to energize the [Senate Armed Services] committee, they were undoubtedly reinforced by the fact that he inherited the chair at a moment when the committee, no less than the Pentagon itself, was beleaguered by critics."[24] To retain credibility in their parent chambers, the Armed Services committees (and the Defense Appropriations subcommittees as well) had to establish that they did not simply rubber-stamp DOD requests.

The rise in floor activity in the early 1970s was stimulated largely by congressional disillusionment with the Vietnam War. Legislators adopted a more critical posture toward defense programs (most evident in the case of the ABM) than was true for most of the 1960s. Revelations that several major weapons systems (in particular, the C-5 transport plane) had suffered enormous cost overruns fueled their skepticism. The heightened political volatility of defense issues also drew new committees into the defense debate. With the end of the war, however, congressional interest in defense issues tapered off.

Although the Armed Services committees had to be more sensitive to the likely floor reaction than in the 1960s, they retained their influence over defense policy. For the most part, congressional floor activity in the early 1970s focused on a small (albeit important) number of issues. Excluding committee and technical amendments, the House adopted only 8 percent (5 of 60) of those that sought to change the dollar amounts HASC had recommended for programs in the procurement and R&D accounts. This figure was higher in the Senate, standing at 19 percent (10 of 53), which reflects the less-restricted nature of debate in the upper chamber.

The congressional reforms of the 1970s did not have a major impact on the Defense Appropriations subcommittees. The major change in their operation—their increased scrutiny of the defense budget—was prompted by the expansion of the authorization process and the increase in floor activity. Further, like the Armed Services committees, the Defense Appropriations subcommittees generally defended their dollar recommendations for programs in the procurement and R&D accounts. The House adopted only 3 percent (1 of 32) of these amendments—excluding committee and technical ones—but the Senate passed 42 percent (11 of 26).

Members of the defense committees offered nine of the successful Senate amendments.

THE 1980s: THE OUTSIDE GAME

The major change in congressional decision making on defense policy in the 1980s was the emergence of the outside game. This new decision-making style merits the description *outside* in two ways. First, unlike the preceding decades, much of the congressional activity on defense now took place in the public arena and thus became highly visible. Second, much activity bypassed the traditional channels of power within the defense committees. The outside game owes its emergence to the rise of the authorization process, the growth of legislative "individualism," and the increased politicization of defense issues.

One key aspect of the outside game has been the explosion of floor activity in the House and Senate. As Table 1 shows, the average number of floor amendments the Senate considers on the annual defense authorization bill has nearly tripled since the 1970s; it has nearly quadrupled in the House. In practical terms, this means that senators typically debate nine amendments—and congressmen, ten— each day the authorization bill is on the respective floors.

The second aspect of the outside game has been the tremendous growth in congressional action off the floor.[25] On the one hand, there is much more activity by individual legislators. Whereas in the 1970s lawmakers like Senator William Proxmire (Democrat of Wisconsin) and Representative Les Aspin (Democrat of Wisconsin) were unique in their vocal criticisms of the Pentagon, today many legislators (both liberals and conservatives) emulate their tactics. On the other hand, activity on defense issues by groups of legislators has risen markedly. One bicameral example of this was the formation in 1981 of the Military Reform Caucus, a loosely organized, bipartisan coalition of legislators interested in broad changes in U.S. defense policy.

In the House, the most important group activity has centered around the Democratic Caucus. Several examples of the caucus's new assertiveness are noteworthy. First, following the congressional decision in May 1983 to approve flight-testing of the MX missile, the caucus forced the House Democratic leadership into uniform opposition to the production of MX. Congressmen who held leadership positions (or aspired to them) apparently believed their leadership futures depended upon their opposing the missile.[26] Second, in 1984 the caucus forced the HASC to accept dozens of special delegates to the House-Senate conference on the defense authorization bill to argue on behalf of one or two specific issues. The caucus insisted on these "bullet vote" conferees because it feared that the HASC's conferees would not defend controversial amendments that the House had added to the bill.[27]

Third, in January 1985 the caucus replaced Melvin Price as chair of the HASC with Les Aspin, the seventh-ranking Democrat on the committee, over the objections of the House leadership. Unlike Hebert's removal a decade earlier, the decision on Price's successor reflected ideological concerns. The caucus passed over five conservative Democrats to select Aspin because it wanted an HASC chair closer to the party's mainstream.[28] Subsequently, the caucus closely watched Aspin's chairmanship, registering displeasure over his handling of several defense issues.[29]

The House Democratic Caucus has no analog in the Senate, where activity has been more individualistic. For example, after Senator Charles Grassley (Republican of Iowa) made national headlines by exposing abuses in the Pentagon's pricing of spare parts, many senators rushed to find horror stories of their own.[30] Still others released their own suggested defense budgets.[31] This activity has not been limited to senators seeking to cut defense spending; several conservative senators publicly challenged the Reagan administration on a range of arms control and defense issues.

The outside game owes its rise in part to the expansion of the authorization process, which dramatically increased the opportunities members of Congress have to alter defense programs. More decisions mean more legislators are likely to find an issue important to themselves or their constituents. At the same time, the congressional reforms of the 1970s loosened the constraints on legislative behavior and ushered in legislative "individualism."[32] In the 1980s, lawmakers could debate defense issues with less fear of retribution by congressional and/or committee leaders.

These two changes have enabled legislators (both members and nonmembers of the defense committees) to apply reasons of "good policy" on defense issues. This was most evident in the 1980s battles over strategic weapons, in which congressmen and senators challenged both the defense committees and the president on a wide range of policy issues. Such floor challenges were rare in the 1960s (the ABM debate in the Senate being the primary exception). At the same time, junior members of the defense committees have become influential "players" on policy matters early in their careers. This achievement was next to impossible when the inside game was dominant in the 1960s.

The increase in opportunities and the decline in legislative constraints also have enabled more legislators to use defense requests for "pork barrel" purposes—a practice, of course, as old as the Republic. What is new, however, is the *extent* of pork barreling today. When the inside game reigned, legislators had to cultivate the support of the senior defense committee members for new funds and jobs for constituents.[33] This process was inherently time-consuming, and success was by no means guaranteed. Currently, however, the ability of defense committee leaders to control pork barreling has diminished.[34] Junior defense committee members have greater influence on marking up the authorization and appropriations bills. And other legislators now can use floor amendments to gain pork barrel benefits for constituents because, as Senator Sam Nunn (Democrat of Georgia) has pointed out, "Both the House and Senate tend to accept floor amendments rather than to take them on and defeat them."[35]

The third factor contributing to the burgeoning outside game has been the increased political volatility of defense policy, in part due to the increased partisanship on defense issues since Vietnam.[36] During the 1960s it was common to see congressional leaders from both parties united on major national security issues. Bipartisanship also characterized opposition to administration defense policies in the late 1960s and early 1970s. For example, a Democrat and a Republican led both the anti-ABM coalition (Senators Philip Hart, Democrat of Michigan, and John Sherman Cooper, Republican of Kentucky) and the antinuclear counterforce coalition (Senators Thomas McIntyre and Edward Brooke, Republican of Massachusetts). In contrast, the major defense debates in the 1980s essentially split along party lines.

The Reagan presidency fueled this partisanship by coupling sharp increases in defense spending with attempts to eliminate social programs. This spurred lengthy and acrimonious debates in Congress over both the composition of the defense budget and its relative share of federal expenditures. Finally, both defense and peace lobbies have grown tremendously in number, size, and strength. These groups have attempted to mobilize constituents to lobby legislators to vote for or against particular weapons programs.

The politicization of defense policy has expanded the electoral incentives for legislators to address defense issues. With the growth of peace and defense lobbies, there are now tangible electoral benefits—financial contributions and constituent support—for lawmakers who champion one defense cause or another. The prolonged congressional debates over the MX and the nuclear freeze attest to this. Conversely, there are potential electoral penalties for legislators who choose the "wrong" side of defense issues. The peace and defense lobbies alike have tried to defeat members of Congress who have opposed their political positions.

The political volatility of defense policy also has made defense issues fertile ground for lawmakers who seek to enhance their reputation and, in turn, their electability. The temptation to use defense issues for "political grandstanding" is especially great on the floor, where amendments targeting real or imagined ills in the Pentagon have become another means of campaigning. According to Senator Nunn, "There is much greater public relations value in a floor amendment—irrespective of its value—than there is in proceeding with responsible suggestions through the committee process."[37] Similarly, former Senator Gaylord Nelson (Democrat of Wisconsin)

notes that "the floor is being used as an instrument of political campaigning far more than it ever has before."[38]

The clearest example of this has been the controversy over the cost of spare parts for defense programs. When stories of overpricing first drew national media attention, congressional members rushed to expose other examples. Theodore Crackel writes, "It made little difference that the sum of all the spare parts and tool overcharges did not approach the roundoff error of major programs such as the B-1. The stories played well at home."[39] As a result, the Senate considered eleven amendments on DOD procurement policies and the House twenty-four during the debate on the fiscal 1986 defense authorization bill.

IMPLICATIONS OF THE OUTSIDE GAME

The emergence of the outside game in the 1980s has made decision making on defense issues more representative of the views in Congress than in previous decades. Although the defense committees remain the most influential players in the defense debate, their parent chambers have constrained legislators' freedom of maneuver. The outside game also has inflicted costs. Congress is unable to pass defense appropriations bills before the start of the year, committees increasingly duplicate one another's work, and congressional micromanagement of the defense budget has skyrocketed.

The outside game has made the defense debate on Capitol Hill more representative of members' views. The Armed Services committees continue to be more conservative than their parent bodies, and, thus, the outside game has aired views held by few members of the defense committees. Moreover, to the extent that Congress mirrors the attitudes of the American public, the debate in Congress has become more representative of the body politic. Both developments are important. After all, one of Congress's primary functions is to articulate the views of the American public.

The increased representativeness of the outside game has led Congress to debate a wider range of defense issues than was true in the 1960s or even the 1970s. In 1985 alone, Congress debated the MX, Midgetman, the Strategic Defense Initiative, antisatellite (ASAT) weapons, the advanced technology ("Stealth") bomber, chemical weapons, and procurement reform, among other issues. Of course, both conservatives and liberals criticized these debates, arguing that Congress endangered the U.S. defense posture (conservatives), failed to cancel dangerous weapons systems (liberals), and misunderstood the fundamental issues involved (both). These complaints notwithstanding, Congress has attempted to grapple with at least some major defense issues.

These floor debates have circumscribed the actions of the defense committees: in the congressional debate over the MX missile, the committee system was effectively abandoned.

The major avenues of congressional influence [on the MX] were almost entirely separate from committee and party structures. Although some of the principal actors served on committees and subcommittees relevant to defense and arms control issues . . . , the pressure brought to bear on the administration came not from the standing committees but from a bipartisan and ultimately bicameral group of Representatives and Senators who had different amounts of seniority on different committees.[40]

After the Scowcroft commission issued its report, the defense committees failed to sustain its recommendations on the number of MX missiles required. In 1985 Congress voted to limit the deployment of the MX to half what the commission advised, even though all four defense committees previously had supported full procurement.

Although the MX is an extreme example of how the power of the defense committees has been curbed, it is not unique. For example, the pressure to limit tests of ASAT, to protect the Stealth bomber, and to reform the defense procurement process all originated outside the defense committees. Moreover, these committees have been less able to protect their dollar recommendations for weapons programs. In the 1980s the House adopted twenty out of sixty-two amendments (32%) to the defense authorization bills (figures on defense appropriations amendments are not provided because of the use of continuing resolutions in several years). For its part, the Senate has adopted sixteen out of thirty-six authorization amendments (44%). In both chambers the absolute number of successful amendments was greater only six years into the eighties than for all of the seventies.

The increased success of floor amendments also has placed greater indirect constraints on the defense committees. Congressional decision making operates heavily on the principle of anticipated reactions. Michael West, an HASC staff member, writes, "The Hill is totally success-oriented in measuring power and influence. . . . Whatever else the committee and its staff accomplish, they must draw up legislation that will be approved. Defeats on the floor for whatever reason must be avoided like the plague."[41] Although it is impossible to measure the impact of anticipated reactions, it has unquestionably been greater than in previous decades. The defense committees' decisions face greater scrutiny on the floor currently than at any time since the early 1970s. And, unlike in the early 1970s, the committees cannot always override opposition; as a result, they have greater incentives to incorporate floor views into their recommendations.

The four House and Senate defense committees, however, remain the most powerful congressional actors on defense issues. The size of the defense budget precludes floor debate from addressing most of their decisions. Further, defense committee members still carry extra weight in congressional debates because many legislators see them as "experts" on defense policy. Nonetheless, the outside game has ended the hegemony of the defense committees.

At the same time, the emergence of the outside game has had its costs. Critics have pointed to three problems in particular: the inability of Congress to adhere to its budget schedule, the erosion of the committee system, and an increase in micromanagement. With respect to the first problem, from 1977 to 1986 Congress had not completed a defense appropriations bill before the start of the fiscal year (October 1). Moreover, Congress had to resort to omnibus continuing resolutions to fund the DOD in 1982, 1984, and 1985. Admittedly, Congress rarely passed defense appropriations bills before the start of the fiscal year even when the inside game dominated. Nonetheless, the legislative delay of the 1980s is noteworthy because it came after the passage of the Budget Control and Impoundment Act of 1974 added three months to Congress's deliberations on the federal budget.

These delays in the budgetary process have emerged because more members of Congress are making more decisions on a more politically volatile defense budget. The current budget process requires Congress to complete three budget cycles (budget resolution, authorizations, and appropriations) within nine months. There is no consensus in Congress, however, on the level of defense spending relative to total federal expenditures (resolution). The disagreement over budget targets pushes the other two cycles further back in the fiscal year. (For example, in 1986 both the HASC and the SASC waited until June to formally assemble their legislation because Congress could not agree on an overall budget figure for defense spending.) Thus, it is not too surprising that Congress consistently fails to pass an appropriations bill until after the fiscal year has begun.

The delay in passing DOD appropriations injects uncertainty into the Pentagon's planning, which increases the likelihood of wasteful spending. This delay also means that legislators spend much of their time simply on the defense *budget*—reducing the time available to consider other aspects of defense *policy*. Although continuing resolutions provide a way out of legislative impasses, they are not necessarily in the public interest. Senator Barry Goldwater (Republican of Arizona) has argued:

Continuing resolutions . . . prevent Senators and Representatives from holding a careful and deliberate review of spending plans. Last year [1984] was the worst example of this abuse. . . . The actual legal spending authority for the Department of Defense . . . was contained in a continuing resolution that was never debated on the floor of either the House or the Senate. . . . It was done at the last minute and no one had the opportunity to challenge the provisions of the bill on the floor.[42]

Finally, because the closing days of each legislative session place great pressure to pass an appropriations bill, some provisions become law that probably would not survive congressional scrutiny in other circumstances. For example, the fiscal 1986 Continuing Resolution contained $852 million to finance the construction and lease of commercial cargo vessels that could be used in wartime for military sea lift. The Armed Services committees, however, had not authorized it on the grounds that it was "pure pork barrel."[43]

That the committee system is eroding is evident in the proliferation of committees involved in defense policy. By 1986 ten committees in the Senate and eleven in the House had formal jurisdiction over some aspect of defense policy.[44] In addition, the political volatility of the defense budget often encourages committees with no direct jurisdiction to hold hearings on defense matters. The most important aspect of the eroding committee system, however, has been the increased overlapping of the Armed Services and Appropriations committees' functions. With the authorization process extended to virtually the entire defense budget, the two committees essentially duplicate each other's work.

This overlap has bred conflict between these committees. In recent years the Defense Appropriations subcommittees have appropriated funds for a wide range of programs that were either never authorized or authorized at much lower levels. This violates rules of both chambers. The problem first emerged in fiscal 1982 when the DOD received $500 million more than had been authorized. Lower in fiscal 1983 and fiscal 1984, appropriations add-ons jumped to $2.8 billion in fiscal 1985 and $6.5 billion in fiscal 1986.[45] The major reason for this increased conflict was the demise of the interlocking directorate between the SASC and SADS. Senators whose tenure began after 1970 cannot sit on both committees and the SADS ended the tradition of ex officio members in 1977.

Unlike a protracted budgetary process, some overlap in the work of congressional committees is beneficial. Committee duplication provides groups that cannot gain a hearing in congressional defense committees with alternative forums for their views. The knowledge that other committees may address defense issues also stimulates the defense committees to discharge their responsibilities to review defense policy. This happened in the spare-parts controversy: the House Energy and Commerce Committee played a leading role uncovering overcharges. Although this controversy undoubtedly involved political grandstanding, it encouraged the Armed Services committees to address the problem. Thus, in 1985, the SASC created a subcommittee on defense acquisition policy, and in 1986 the HASC established a panel to examine procurement reform.

The erosion of the committee system currently, however, goes beyond that needed to stimulate healthy committee competition. Committees devote substantial resources simply to protect or enlarge their turf. Senator John Tower (Republican of Texas), while chair of the SASC, complained, "Our committee spends a large portion of its time trying to fend off competition from other committees and monitoring what other committees are doing."[46] As an example, the Armed Services committees have been attempting to force the Defense Appropriations subcommittees to observe authorization ceilings. This legislative battle not only absorbed significant committee time and effort but dealt only tangentially with the quality of U.S. defense policy; the fight primarily involved prerogatives within Congress. At the same time, extensive legislative fragmentation undermines the very reason for having a committee system: the recognition that the complexities of government require specialization and delegation.

Finally, micromanagement is evident in the extensive congressional intervention into defense programs. Today Congress changes upward of 40 percent of defense budget line items. In addition, it orders a sizable array of reports and issues a wide variety of directives. Floor debates tend to receive the most criticism because many amendments address minor issues and therefore are easily subjected to ridicule. Yet the defense committees do the majority of micromanaging of the defense budget. They are the only congressional actors who have the opportunity to alter a broad range of line-item requests and to issue a variety of directives.

A fair degree of congressional intervention in the defense budget is both necessary and desirable. Congress's main vehicle for shaping policy is its control of the purse strings. If Congress were to forgo altering the budget, it would in effect abdicate its responsibility to oversee the DOD (recall the experience of the Armed Services committees in the 1950s). At the same time, congressional intervention into the defense budget is often needed to align defense spending with the budget resolution ceiling or to delay programs that have suffered cost overruns, test failures, or production delays. Finally, some cases of micromanagement undoubtedly are attempts to remedy the grievances of groups that have been harmed by DOD actions but which have no voice inside the defense establishment. Although these cases may involve issues peripheral to U.S. defense policy, they are nonetheless legitimate.

The degree of congressional intervention in recent years, however, exceeds that which can be justified on grounds of shaping policy, correcting management problems, or remedying grievances. Much of Congress's micromanagement has resulted from the growth of the authorization process. The Armed Services and Appropriations committees all have become more involved in budgetary minutiae to protect their influence over defense policy. The expansion of committee staff has aided this focus on details. At the same time, micromanagement has ballooned because of the increased willingness and ability of legislators to use defense requests to provide pork-barrel benefits to constituents.

Micromanagement frustrates DOD's ability to plan because so many line items are changed each year and the amount of change generally is unknown until after the fiscal year begins. Moreover, in many instances micromanagement protects programs that are unjustified either economically or militarily. Both consequences add to defense costs. The numerous line-item changes also tend to promote imbalanced acquisition programs: one program is often altered without due consideration of its effect on related programs. Finally, the need to justify every line item, coupled with the tremendous congressional demand for studies and reports, places enormous demands on the DOD staff and reinforces the DOD's tendency to focus on *resource* questions at the expense of *strategic planning.*[47]

Micromanagement does not, however, prevent Congress from discharging its responsibility for policy oversight: to evaluate whether the programs DOD requests meet U.S. military needs and are consistent with U.S. strategy. Complaints about congressional policy oversight long predate the spread of micromanagement.[48] These complaints often assume an idealized conception of policy oversight in which Congress reviews programs consistently and dispassionately. Yet it is difficult if not impossible to structure the decision-making process in Congress so that it both encourages orderly reviews of major policy issues and protects the right to air dissenting views.

Congress debated, however imperfectly, a range of major issues in the 1980s. Admittedly, it did not address all the issues the critics wished to see discussed (or in the way they wished to see them aired), frequently returned to the same issue time and again (for example, the MX), and often failed to anticipate problems. Still, Congress made greater attempts to grapple with major issues then than the talk of micromanagement suggests.

A balance sheet on the benefits and costs of the outside game inevitably depends upon one's views on Congress's proper role in defense policy and on the wisdom of the prevailing administration's policies. In making such judgments, however, it is important to recognize two things. For one, the inside game should not be idealized simply because it was more orderly than the outside game has been. The inside game had its own costs.[49] For another, for all its disorder, the outside game has meant a more equitable debate in Congress. In a political system that is built on representation, the importance of this development should not be underestimated.

NOTES

This research was assisted by an award from the Social Science Research Council of a MacArthur Foundation Fellowship in International Security; it was written while in residence at the Center for International Affairs and the Center for Science and International Affairs at Harvard University. Vincent Auger, Ivo Daalder, Aaron Friedberg, Stephen Flanagan, Elisa Harris, Larry Smith, Peter Trubowitz, and two anonymous referees provided valuable comments on earlier drafts. Responsibility for the final manuscript remains mine alone.

1. Figures derived from Robert J. Art, "Congress and the Defense Budget: Enhancing Policy Oversight," *Political Science Quarterly* 100 (Summer 1985): 232–33; and the annual reports of the Armed Services and Appropriations committees on the administration's defense budget request.

2. Figure derived from Edward J. Laurance, "The Changing Role of Congress in Defense Policy-Making," *Journal of Conflict Resolution* 20 (June 1976): 228.

3. Data provided by the Office of the Comptroller, Department of Defense.

4. Quoted in Herbert W. Stephens, "The Role of the Legislative Committees in the Appropriations Process: A Study Focused on the Armed Services Committees," *Western Political Quarterly* 24 (March 1971): 147.

5. Ibid.

6. For discussions of the rise of the authorization process see Art, "Congress and the Defense Budget," 228–31; Raymond H. Dawson, "Congressional Innovation and Intervention in Defense Policy: Legislative Authorization of Weapons Systems," *American Political Science Review* 55 (March 1962): 42–57; Senate Committee on Armed Services (SASC), *Defense Organization: The Need for Change*, 99th Cong., 1st sess., October 1985, 574–76; Louis Fisher, "Annual Authorizations: Durable Roadblocks to Biennial Budgeting," *Public Budgeting & Finance* 3 (Spring 1983): 23–40; John R. Gist, "The Impact of Annual Authorizations on Military Appropriations in the U.S. Congress," *Legislative Studies Quarterly* 6 (August 1981): 439–54; Bernard K. Gordon, "The Military Budget: Congressional Phase," *Journal of Politics* 23 (November 1961): 689–710; Edward A. Kolodziej, *The Uncommon Defense and Congress, 1945–1963* (Columbus: Ohio State University, 1966), 364–82; and Stephens, "Role of the Legislative Committees," 146–51.

7. Gordon, "The Military Budget," 692.

8. Art, "Congress and the Defense Budget," 229.

9. William A. Lucas and Raymond H. Dawson, *The Organizational Politics of Defense* (Pittsburgh, Pa.: International Studies Association, 1974), 120.

10. For an extended discussion of the HASC during the 1960s, see Eugene Armand Dunne Jr., *Variations in Committee Response to the House Reforms of the 1970s: A Study of the Armed Services and Banking Committees* (Ph.D. diss., Harvard University, 1985), chap. 2. See also "Armed Services Committees: Advocates or Overseers?" *Congressional Quarterly Weekly* (hereafter *CQW*), 25 March 1972, 633–37; John M. Collins, *U.S. Defense Planning* (Boulder, Colo.: Westview Press, 1982), 76–77; Michael Glennon, "Committee Has a History of Controversial Chairmen," *CQW*, 31 March 1984, 732; and "House Votes $21.3-Billion Defense Procurement Bill," *CQW*, 10 October 1969, 1950.

11. Dunne, *Variations in Committee Response*, 40.

12. "Defense Subcommittees: Profiles of Two Key Groups," *CQW*, 20 May 1972, 1143.

13. See Donald R. Matthews, *U.S. Senators and Their World* (Chapel Hill: University of North Carolina Press, 1960), 92–97; Norman J. Ornstein, Robert L. Peabody, and David W. Rohde, "The Changing Senate: From the 1950s to the 1970s," in *Congress Reconsidered*, ed. Lawrence C. Dodd and Bruce I. Oppenheimer (New York: Praeger, 1977), 6–8; and Randall B. Ripley, *Power in the Senate* (New York: St. Martin's Press, 1969), 90–92.

14. Quoted in Dunne, *Variations in Committee Response*, 49.

15. "Defense Subcommittees: Profiles of Two Key Groups," 1142.

16. Ibid., 1141; and "Armed Services Committees: Advocates or Overseers?" 675.

17. This pressure was acute in the HASC. See Craig Liske and Barry Rundquist, *The Politics of Weapons Procurement: The Role of Congress* (Denver, Colo.: University of Denver, 1974), 55.

18. See Christopher J. Deering and Steven S. Smith, "Majority Party Leadership in the New House Subcommittee System," in *Understanding Congressional Leadership,* ed. Frank H. Mackaman (Washington, D.C.: Congressional Quarterly Press, 1981), 264; Lawrence C. Dodd and Bruce I. Oppenheimer, "The House in Transition," in *Congress Reconsidered,* ed. Oppenheimer and Dodd, 29–31; David W. Rohde, "Committee Reform in the House of Representatives and the Subcommittee Bill of Rights," *The Annals* 411 (January 1974): 39–47; and Steven S. Smith and Christopher J. Deering, *Committees in Congress* (Washington, D.C.: Congressional Quarterly Press, 1984), 44–45.

19. Dunne, *Variations in Committee Response,* 309.

20. See Ornstein, Peabody, and Rohde, "The Changing Senate," 8–9; and Smith and Deering, *Committees in Congress,* 134–35.

21. Alton Frye praises Stennis as a "conservative innovator." See Frye, *A Responsible Congress: The Politics of National Security* (New York: McGraw-Hill, 1975), 101–4.

22. Smith and Deering, *Committees in Congress,* 134–35.

23. Michael J. Malbin, *Unelected Representatives: Congressional Staff and the Future of Representative Government* (New York: Basic Books, 1980), 254–55.

24. Frye, *A Responsible Congress,* 105.

25. See Brent Baker, "National Defense and the Congressional Role," *Naval War College Review* 35 (July–August 1982): 4–15.

26. See Pat Towell, "MX Gains Narrow House OK, but Further Battles Expected," *CQW,* 23 July 1983, 1483; and Pat Towell with Steven Pressman, "House Gives President Go-Ahead on MX," *CQW,* 30 March 1985, 565.

27. See Pat Towell, "Pentagon's Buying Practices: Battle Lines Drawn," *CQW,* 13 July 1985, 1369.

28. See "Price Faces Challenge for Armed Services Job," *CQW,* 22 December 1984, 3143–44; and Nadine Cohodas and Diane Granat, "House Seniority System Jolted; Price Dumped, Aspin Elected," *CQW,* 5 January 1985, 7–9.

29. See Andy Plattner, "To Les Aspin, MX Victory Brings Some Pain," *CQW,* 30 March 1985, 564; Fred Kaplan, "How Aspin Piloted Defense Bill," *Boston Sunday Globe,* 17 August 1986, A17, A20; and Mary McGrory, "Showdown with Aspin," *Boston Globe,* 13 September 1985, 13.

30. Theodore Crackel, "Pentagon Management Problems: Congress Shares the Blame," Heritage Foundation *Backgrounder,* no. 405, (January 1985): 3.

31. David Durenberger, *America's Defense: A Plan for the 1980s,* and *Neither Madmen nor Messiahs* (Minneapolis, Minn.: Piranha Press, 1984); Ernest F. Hollings, *Con-*

gressional Record, 10 February 1982, S670–S688; and Denny Smith and others, *Should We Exempt Defense from Economic Reality: The Need for a Defense Budget Freeze,* A Recommendation to the Senate and House Budget Committees and Republican Leadership, February 1985.

32. See Gregg Easterbrook, "What's Wrong with Congress?" *Atlantic,* December 1984, 57–84; Alan Ehrenhalt, "In the Senate of the '80s, Team Spirit Has Given Way to the Rule of Individuals," *CQW,* 4 September 1982, 2175–82; and Clifford Hardin, Kenneth A. Shepsle, and Barry R. Weingast, *Public Policy Excesses: Government by Congressional Subcommittee* (St. Louis, Mo.: Washington University, 1982).

33. For a firsthand account of this cultivation process by a then-junior member of the HASC, see G. William Whitehurst, *Diary of a Congressman* (Norfolk, Va.: Donning, 1983), 41–43, 64–65, 104.

34. See Crackel, "Congress Shares the Blame," 7.

35. *Congressional Record,* 1 October 1985, S12341.

36. For statistical documentation of this in the case of the Senate, see Peter Trubowitz, *Ideology, Party, and U.S. Foreign and Defense Policy: An Analysis of Senate Voting, 1947–1984* (Ph.D. diss., Massachusetts Institute of Technology, 1986).

37. *Congressional Record,* 1 October 1985, S12341.

38. Quoted in Ehrenhalt, "In the Senate of the '80s," 2176. See also Joseph M. Bessette, "Is Congress a Deliberative Institution?" in *The United States Congress,* ed. Dennis Hale (New Brunswick, N.J.: Transaction Books, 1983), 8–11.

39. Crackel, "Congress Shares the Blame," 3.

40. House Committee on Foreign Affairs, *Congress and Foreign Policy 1983* (Washington, D.C.: GPO, 1984), 86.

41. Michael A. West, "The Role of Congress in the Defense Budget Process—A Positive View," *Naval War College Review* 30 (May–June 1979): 89.

42. *Congressional Record,* 1 October 1985, S12339–S12340.

43. Michael Ganley, "New Congressional Dispute Sparked by FY86 DoD Appropriations Add-ons," *Armed Forces Journal International* (hereafter *AFJI*) 123 (May 1986): 13.

44. SASC, *Defense Organization,* 578–79.

45. See Michael Ganley, "House Armed Services Panel Fumes over 'Excess' FY86 Appropriations," *AFJI* 122 (April 1985): 10; Ganley, "FY86 DoD Appropriations Add-ons," 11, 13; and Michael Ganley, "Disputes over FY86 Appropriations Add-ons Ends in Funding Compromise," *AFJI* 123 (July 1986): 18–19.

46. Quoted in Easterbrook, "What's Wrong with Congress?" 59.

47. SASC, *Defense Organization,* 592.

48. See Art, "Congress and the Defense Budget," 237, 241.

49. For discussions of the costs of the inside game, see Gordon M. Adams, "Disarming the Military Subgovernment," *Harvard Journal on Legislation* 14 (April 1977): 462–64; and Frye, *A Responsible Congress,* 97–116.

EXECUTIVE–LEGISLATIVE RELATIONS AFTER THE COLD WAR

LINDA S. JAMISON

Writing amidst America's rebellion against England, Thomas Paine set forth his ideas for a new nation founded on the principles of liberty and individual freedom. "We have it in our power to begin the world all over again," he wrote triumphantly in *Common Sense* in January 1776. With the end of the Cold War, the country faces a similar new beginning and a fresh reappraisal of its place in the world.

It is useful to recall, however, the problems that faced the newly independent colonies and their struggle to form coherent relations among themselves and the wider world, culminating in the abandonment of the Articles of Confederation and the creation of the new Constitution and federal government. During this period of American history major debates raged about the conduct of foreign affairs among the framers of the U.S. Constitution. Today, with the passing of the strategy of containment as a central organizing principle between the executive and legislative branches of government on questions related to the international role of the United States, age-old questions of the purposes and conduct of U.S. foreign policy are returning. U.S. interests are shifting, and the process of redefining those interests in a changing world has only begun.

The character of the executive–legislative relationship on foreign affairs will be a critical determinant of the U.S. world role in the years ahead and of the credibility and effectiveness of U.S. foreign policy. An optimist might look at current circumstances and project a smooth relationship, noting the declining domestic political importance of foreign and defense policy and the dominance by one party of the House of Representatives, the Senate, and the White House. Pessimists will no doubt recall the frequency with which divided government has led to interbranch conflicts as well as the past failures of the executive to solicit congressional support for policy initiatives. It is not surprising therefore that in recent years the continued debate about whether Congress is an asset or a liability in foreign policy has assumed renewed importance.

This literature survey offers a review of these issues in light of the strategic environment of the 1990s. It begins with a review of the historical context and of the central themes that have dominated the debate about the power of the executive and the legislature in the conduct of the nation's foreign affairs throughout the life of the republic. It then turns to the current period and the debate about executive–legislative cooperation after the Cold War, in an era marked by global uncertainty and domestic apprehension. Recognizing that cooperation between the two branches is necessary and fundamental, and that both branches bring strengths and weaknesses to the foreign policy process, how should new leadership at both ends of Pennsylvania Avenue think about their common tasks? Can a consensus be built over foreign policy goals and objectives for a new era? Should the Congress play a diminished role in foreign policy? Might it play an enhanced role? If so, is the Congress institutionally prepared to enter into a meaningful dialogue over the role of the United States in the post–Cold War era? The term "foreign policy" is used here in the broadest possible sense, to encompass the full range of policies related to the geostrategic and international economic interests of the United States.

DIVIDED GOVERNMENT AND THE QUESTION OF PREEMINENCE

The question of who controls the nation's foreign policy is one that has often caused heated debate among Americans since the writing of the Constitution. Alexander Hamilton and James Madison, among others, argued vehemently over who had the inherent power to pursue foreign initiatives. Was the president intended to dominate foreign affairs or was Congress meant to be the preeminent body?

The noted constitutional scholar, Edward Corwin, popularized the description of divided power as "an invitation to struggle for the privilege of directing American foreign policy." He wrote that although the president proposes policy while the Congress is relegated to policy disposition, the president enjoys the upper hand despite constitutional division of authority.[1] Paraphrasing *The Federalist*, Corwin lists four reasons for presidential leverage: (1) unity of office—whereas the president operates as a single decision maker, Congress speaks with many voices; (2) secrecy and dispatch—the president conducts policy in private, away from public scrutiny, whereas Congress by nature is a very public institution; (3) superior sources of information—the president has access to information from the entire executive branch apparatus; (4) presidential availability—whereas Congress must meet formally and act as one body, the president has the flexibility to act without formal processes, increasing his ability to respond to rapidly changing events.[2]

This essay has been edited and is reprinted from The Washington Quarterly 16 (Spring 1993): 191–204, *by permission of* MIT Press.

Scholars have generally assumed that the Founders knew that the ambiguity of the Constitution would cause conflict between the branches, but that the curbs on the power of the executive were seen as necessary given their fear of the central, monarchical power that prevailed throughout Europe. Louis Henkin, for example, has recently argued that the constitutional division of power was "an article of faith" among the framers, inconclusively crafted without a fundamental principle to clarify its provisions.[3]

U.S. presidents have often exploited constitutional ambiguity to exercise precisely that unchecked executive power. They have tended to pursue foreign policy objectives abroad without the consent and, in many instances, without the prior knowledge of Congress. Indeed, with few exceptions, throughout the first 200 years of U.S. history, the balance of power in the foreign policy domain tipped decisively in favor of the executive.[4] This was clearest with regard to the making of war: "Over the course of U.S. history, the United States has been involved in more than 125 'undeclared wars' and other instances of violent conflict abroad conducted under presidential authority."[5] When George Washington unilaterally declared U.S. neutrality in the war between France and Britain in 1793 (prompted by political rather than military motives), he unknowingly sparked a debate that continues today. As one scholar notes, "Washington established the precedent that the president plays an active and assertive role in foreign policy and military affairs, and subsequent occupants of the White House followed suit."[6] Although Washington later went before Congress to explain his actions, the presidential practice of acting independently and without the prior, explicit authorization of Congress was set in motion. More recent examples include Franklin Roosevelt's initiatives during the early years of World War II and the 1990 deployment of U.S. troops in Saudi Arabia. Arguably, such actions were not clearly forbidden in a narrow legal sense, but they do reveal the propensity of presidents to exploit constitutional ambiguity in foreign affairs at the expense of involving and consulting the legislature.

The powers of Congress are clearly prescribed by the U.S. Constitution: to provide for the common defense, declare war, support and raise armies and a navy, and regulate commerce with other nations (paraphrase of Article I, Section 8). Arthur Schlesinger has argued that preeminence falls not to the executive but to the legislature: "The framers were unambiguous in their decisions. With the war-making predilections of absolute monarchs much in mind, they assigned the vital powers in international affairs to Congress."[7] Many scholars argue that the framers intended Congress to be the dominant political institution in foreign affairs by noting that Congress was assigned the most important powers. Within this context, of course, some powers are designated for the president. As one scholar describes the distribution of constitutional power, "Congress neither makes treaties nor appoints ambassadors. It leaves to the president the management of diplomatic relations with other countries and the conduct of authorized military operations."[8]

In recent decades Congress has become more active on foreign affairs. This was in part a Cold War–era phenomenon, as the Congress became a primary venue for defining and sustaining the containment strategy. But with the breakdown of executive–legislative trust during the 1960s and 1970s, as a result of the Vietnam War and the Watergate scandal, congressional activism had a different purpose—a desire to challenge presidential initiatives, primarily those involving the commitment of U.S. troops and other military resources. One manifestation of this has been the continuing debate about the War Powers Act, an issue that falls outside the purview of this survey.[9]

Congress has become more assertive in recent decades, actively seeking to sharpen its foreign policy differences with the president. Thus the presidency began to lose its stature as the unchallenged arbiter of foreign policy.

As Congress has become more determined to assert its role, it has likewise developed the expertise to sustain its voice. Throughout the 1970s and 1980s, many members began to travel to foreign countries, meet with dignitaries there, and scrutinize U.S. policy from a nonparochial vantage point.[10] They hired staff with expertise in international and strategic affairs. Congress also created a variety of support agencies, including the Congressional Research Service, the Congressional Budget Office, and the Office of Technology Assessment, to counter the executive advantage. The emergence of private, nonprofit policy research institutes, or think tanks, has provided members of Congress with further sources of information and forums in which to develop their opinions on matters of international significance.[11]

As the Cold War consensus began to weaken during the Vietnam era, Congress also came to reflect the divisions among an increasingly vocal American people on questions of the U.S. world role. Interest groups formed and began to lobby Congress and exert influence over U.S. conduct abroad. The combination of these and other developments has fundamentally altered the congressional role in policy formulation.[12]

As a result, Congress today has an influence over foreign policy unprecedented in the history of the Republic. Even during the final decades of the Cold War and in the context of a consensus to contain Soviet power and influence, Congress became less willing to acquiesce in the president's wishes. Looking to the future, it is doubtful that Congress will quickly relinquish its power in the foreign policy process. The control of U.S. foreign policy is unlikely to revert back to executive domination. Indeed, with the passing of the Cold War era, a growing congressional role in defining and pursuing U.S. interests globally can be anticipated.

THE END OF CONSENSUS?

There is a certain nostalgia today for the easy bipartisanship of the early Cold War years. It merits careful scrutiny.

Whether such absolute, unequivocal bipartisanship ever existed is an open question.[13] Yet Congress, from the end of World War II until almost the end of the Vietnam War, demonstrated very little opposition to presidential initiatives and likewise exerted very little independent leadership over identifying policy goals and objectives. But bipartisan unity of purpose was present between the branches and provided the United States with several early Cold War successes such as the Marshall Plan, the Truman Doctrine, the North Atlantic Treaty Organization (NATO), and the United Nations (UN) Charter.[14] Unity of purpose ultimately helped to end the Cold War as Congress and the president focused on a common enemy.[15] But the potential for nuclear war with the Soviet Union as well as containment of communism legitimized presidential dominance as well as congressional compliance in the conduct of foreign affairs.

Often, however, the Cold War years also revealed a healthy give and take between the two branches of government on the means to implement the basic containment strategy. This was increasingly so in the later decades of the Cold War but was also evident in the 1940s and 1950s. Such give-and-take is hardly synonymous with "unequivocal bipartisanship" and legislative acquiescence in executive initiative.

This dialogue is the essence of the executive-legislative balance struck by the authors of the Constitution. In the debate over who is preeminent in foreign policy, it is essential to recall that both branches of government have responsibilities, and neither can cede fully those obligations. Both branches of government must "accept not only the constitutional necessity, but also the policy worth of the contributions made by the other."[16] It is as important now as in all previous historical eras to strike a balance by encouraging debate between both branches over substantive differences, ultimately leading to the development of sound policy.[17]

In discussing the virtues of congressional engagement in the foreign policy process, former White House staffer Robert Pastor argues for a willingness among executive and congressional leaders to respect and facilitate the contributions of the other, so that there may be a complete policy engagement.[18] Brademas and his fellow authors, noting that Congress is institutionally ill equipped to control the day-to-day instruments of foreign policy such as dispatching diplomats, entering into negotiations, and managing daily U.S. operations abroad, argue that Congress is better suited than the executive to debate the larger issues of how the United States will develop sound policy and to what degree U.S. interests should be protected abroad.[19] Another observer, former Senator J. William Fulbright, has put it slightly differently:

Account [should be taken] of the essential congressional role in the authorization of military and major political commitments, and in advising broad policy directions, while leaving to the executive the necessary flexibility to conduct policy within the broad parameters approved by the legislature.[20]

The nature of executive–legislative relations has been fundamentally altered by the end of the Cold War, and there is currently no widespread agreement among the main political forces about the U.S. role in the postwar era. Absent a firmly based consensus over the goals and purposes of policy, political parties could begin to exploit different perceptions for short-term political advantage. This could translate into sustained dissensus when control of the two branches of government is again divided between political parties. But it may not await such a political event: the inherent distrust and constant friction between the two branches could rapidly turn divisive and obstructionist.

The task, then, for the president and Congress is twofold. First, policy makers must begin to collaborate in order to define the new directions for U.S. foreign policy by identifying the predominant organizing principles of the postwar era. Because the Soviet threat was so easily discernible by the public in general, these new principles must be grounded in American values and attitudes in order to sustain public support for new policy initiatives and justify the U.S. role in the world. Second, policy makers must begin to close the gap between domestic and foreign policy priorities. Global interdependence has made economic and political autonomy obsolete. A new era of executive–legislative cooperation must prevail in order to reformulate U.S. foreign policy. As one scholar has written, "It is time to consider in detail the consequences for American foreign policy of these profound changes. It is time to debate in earnest the very different paths the country might follow in a post–Cold War world."[21] As another observer has noted, the post–Cold War era "will be marked by power politics, national rivalries and ethnic tensions."[22]

Without a vigorous national debate laying out a set of new organizing principles of postwar policy, it will be extremely difficult to meet these challenges and to sustain public support, let alone provide the necessary conditions for bipartisan cooperation between the president and Congress. In *Mandate for Change*, the Progressive Policy Institute contends that "the American people need compelling reasons for supporting an active U.S. role in the world."[23] It is the responsibility of the president and Congress to articulate why U.S. engagement is necessary and how it will be carried out.

This will not be easy at a time when the interest of most Americans, and of the Clinton administration appears to be focused on domestic issues. Americans today are more economically distraught and politically discontent than at any time in the recent past; thus they have demanded that leaders pay more attention to domestic problems and less to international crises. The Clinton administration and Congress face the difficult challenge of fulfilling this mandate while also stewarding the international interests of the nation. One of their tasks is to convince the American public that a strong foreign policy is required and that it will be conducted in tandem with domestic priorities.

Both the executive and the legislature must also confront honestly the gap between a political rhetoric emphasizing the ascendancy of domestic over foreign priorities and the reality of a close intertwining of the two. Indeed, with the increasing blurring of the lines between international and domestic interests, there is no clear political choice between the two. This will not be easy because in the past domestic and international affairs were distinct and independent missions. This tradition of dualism is reflected in the national budget, the institutional order of the federal government, and the structure of congressional committee jurisdiction.[24] Such integration of domestic and international priorities at the political and policy levels is necessary not just to explain and predict the circumstances the United States faces, but also to build a stronger, more stable America.[25]

Such integration is advocated throughout current public policy research. Peter Tarnoff calls for a "comprehensive national strategy," which purposefully integrates domestic and foreign policy. He contends that national defense is "inextricably linked" to American education, technology, and economic growth and taxation.[26]

Noting that "foreign policy must help create American jobs, protect the American environment, assure American security and reflect American values," a Carnegie Endowment study argues that new objectives for U.S. policy have been advanced with the underlying assumption that foreign policy must help to cure some of America's ills.[27] The CSIS Strengthening of America Commission has also published recommendations for restoring the economic, education, and military infrastructure of the United States, and has noted the salience of these domestic steps for U.S. international interests and global leadership.[28]

The necessity of such integration is given further impetus by economic interdependence. Given the international economic context of the U.S. economy—and hence of U.S. prosperity and employment—the United States cannot afford a go-it-alone policy on economic affairs. But nor can it hope to dominate the international economy as it once did. The U.S. consumer's preference for foreign products, U.S. dependency on foreign investment to stimulate the business cycle, and vulnerability to international currency fluctuations, are only a few of the ways in which the United States has become an integral part of the global economic system. Economic and social stability have begun to replace military strength as a measure of national vitality among all nations. In fact, there was noteworthy agreement between George Bush and Bill Clinton during the 1992 election campaign that, in order to remain a global leader, the United States must maintain its domestic economic strength.

Indeed, there are very few domestic issues that do not have strong international implications, and likewise there are numerous transnational issues in which all nations have a stake. Environmental degradation, the proliferation of weapons of mass destruction, population control, migration, international narcotics trafficking, the spread of AIDS, and the deterioration of the human condition in the less developed world are circumstances affecting all corners of the globe. Neither political isolation nor policy bifurcation is an option for the United States.

Global circumstances have drastically changed with the end of the Cold War and the political and policy conditions that sustained bipartisan consensus are not applicable to the post-war era. The formulation of foreign policy must be grounded in broadly based principles that reflect domestic economic, political, and social concerns while providing practical solutions to new situations.

TOWARD A COOPERATIVE U.S. FOREIGN POLICY FOR THE 1990s

If the federal government is to meet the new international policy challenges of the post–Cold War era, institutional dissension caused by partisan competition and executive–legislative friction must give way to a new way of business. Policy flexibility must be the watchword of the 1990s in the foreign policy domain if the United States is to have any hope of securing its interests in the uncertain years ahead. One former policy maker, noting the historical tendency of the United States to make fixed "attachments," has argued that a changing world dictates policy flexibility, where practical solutions can be developed on principles of broadly based foreign policy objectives.[29]

Flexibility, however, will not be possible without interbranch cooperation. Reconfiguring post–Cold War objectives requires comprehension of the remarkable transformations in world affairs and demands an intense political dialogue that goes beyond the executive branch.[30]

Cooperation that is more than pro forma entails genuine partnership. As one observer notes, "Overcoming divided government, changing public opinion, building consensus, and establishing the nation's policy priorities call for leadership, accommodation, and compromise by Congress and the president."[31] The tasks of the executive in promoting such partnership are generally well understood–consultation, dialogue, and consensus-building with congressional leadership, the Congress more generally, and with the American people.[32]

But the role of the Congress in achieving such partnership is probably less well understood today. If Congress is to fulfill its obligations as a full partner in the foreign policy process, it must look beyond its recent role as a challenger of executive authority. The main strength of the Congress lies in the framers' intention that it be a deliberative body, close to the people, "enabling the voices of majorities to ring louder than the extremes."[33] Congress has a critical role to play as an innovator of policy and strategy, as a political tool for probing national interests in a changing world, defining the means to protect and advance those interests, and generating and sustaining the political will domestically in support of those means and ends.

Is Congress ready to play such a role? Might it cede the foreign policy agenda to the Clinton administration and focus instead on domestic issues? Even if it chooses to assert leadership on foreign policy issues, is it capable of doing so?

LESSONS FROM RECENT YEARS

The recent past offers some lessons for speculating about these questions. The extraordinary debate over whether the United States should commit troops to battle in the Persian Gulf offers a number of important insights. Not only did lawmakers rise to their constitutional challenge, but for the first time since World War II Congress directly confronted the difficult issues related to sending large numbers of troops into combat.[34] The level of political discourse that ensued was unprecedented in recent U.S. history, and it signaled to all Americans, and especially the president, that Congress was prepared to confront foreign policy questions with integrity, intelligence, and vigor.

The congressional debate of January 1991 also showed that Congress can overcome its own partisan divisions to act in the best interests of the country. Although Congress has found it difficult to back the president in matters of foreign policy in recent decades,[35] and despite the sharp political divisions evident in the floor debate, members were ready to stand united after the votes were tallied.[36] With the Gulf debate, the halls of Congress once again became the national forum for debate on the purposes and use of U.S. power.[37]

The debate also demonstrated the clear passing of the foreign policy agenda of the Cold War and the fact that Congress expects to be actively involved in defining U.S. strategy and policy in the post–Cold War era, especially given the passing of the Cold War–vintage consensus on strategy. President George Bush apparently recognized these matters, although only rather late in the lead-up to the beginning of actual armed conflict. As one observer has noted, "The President's tactical concession of the utility of such action may prove in the end to have strengthened the ability of future congresses to insist upon a similar involvement in the use of force in other crises."[38]

The Gulf war also highlighted the inherent foreign policy strengths and weaknesses of each branch. The massive military buildup in Saudi Arabia, the skillfully assembled military and diplomatic coalition, and the U.N. endorsement demonstrated the strength the president has acquired in rapidly responding to an overseas crisis and the capacity of that office to call upon the enormous resources of the executive branch. But when the president positioned the country for military conflict without prior congressional authorization, he also demonstrated the historical proclivity of the executive to act independently. Many lawmakers were appalled that the president would so carefully and consciously court international support for his course of action in the Gulf while ignoring congressional appeals for cooperation and unity at home.[39]

Congress, on the other hand, initially exhibited apprehension at becoming involved in the larger questions associated with going to war with Iraq. In fact, Congress was unable to act on the possibility of war in a timely fashion. Congress conducts business through formal, public actions, and many political as well as practical obstacles prevented lawmakers from earlier deliberation. The November 1990 elections delayed many opportunities for debate and congressional leaders postponed committee hearings until after election day. When the debate on the Gulf crisis finally took place in early January 1991, it demonstrated that Congress is able to set the broad outlines of sustainable policy that reflect public opinion and national objectives.

The Persian Gulf War was the first major post–Cold War challenge to U.S. policy. It demonstrated that specific U.S. interests are not as easily defined in the postwar era as they were during the Cold War, when U.S. military action reflected basic anticommunist strategy. Prior to the military intervention in the Gulf, precise political objectives were never fully agreed upon between the president, Congress, and the American people. U.S. military action seemed arbitrarily justified on the grounds that Iraq had violated international law and national sovereignty, threatened the world's oil supply, intimidated U.S. allies in the region, endangered the economic stability of the Middle East, abused international standards of human rights, and boasted of developing weapons of mass destruction.

Congress must take up where the Gulf debate left off. An undifferentiated foreign policy agenda awaits the nation's decision makers. War in the former Yugoslavia, continued instability in the former Soviet Union and Eastern Europe, and a host of regional tensions ranging from Somalia to Cambodia, although each quite different from the Persian Gulf conflict, represent further important challenges to U.S. policy. Congress must play its critical role in bridging the gaps in policy formulation while building public support. But is Congress institutionally prepared to lead this debate, ultimately fulfilling its role as a full partner in foreign policy making?

CONCLUSION

Issues related to the proper balance of executive and legislative authority in the conduct of the nation's foreign affairs have been reinvigorated by the end of the Cold War. Along with the Soviet threat, bipartisan consensus has disappeared as an organizing principle of policy. Congress appears more ready and able to exercise its full constitutional responsibilities in the foreign policy domain than at any time in the history of the republic. The emergence of new challenges in the 1990s requires of the United States a clearly defined international role, one that serves U.S. domestic interests but also exercises U.S. leadership in defense of the common good. These needs cannot be met without sustained political debate about U.S. interests and without the cultivation of political consensus, both between the executive and legislature, and in the body politic more generally. These goals will not be achieved, and the nation's world role as well as its own economy will suffer, unless Congress rises to the challenge.

The United States is on the verge of a national redefinition, one that requires institutional and political reevaluation. It is time to move beyond the argument over who controls foreign affairs and on to determining the nation's course for the next century. Congress must restore its capacity as a deliberative body on the larger strategic questions facing the country, and through honest and reasoned rhetorical exchange define the basic elements of a creative policy agenda. The president has indicated a willingness to cooperate with Congress and would be well advised to honor that commitment by being prepared to negotiate rather than dictate policy on these larger questions.

This literature survey has revealed the growing importance of the executive–legislative agenda in foreign affairs at this time. But it has also shown that these issues do not engage a broad cross section of scholarly investigators or policy makers, which reflects perhaps the dominance of domestic affairs in the national mind at this point. The literature adequately presents the larger questions of divided government and the foreign policy process, but it does not include a large body of detailed policy recommendations of the kind to be found in many other areas of current policy concern. Indeed, scholarly and practical inquiry must sharpen its focus on the inextricable links between the character of executive–legislative relations and U.S. foreign policy. Neither branch can hope to exert independent control over foreign policy. The time has come to reinforce the explicit and appropriate functions and strengths that each branch brings to the policy-making process.

NOTES

This essay reflects the opinions of the author and does not represent the views of the CSIS or its Office of Government Relations.

1. Edward S. Corwin, *The President: Office and Powers 1787–1957,* 4th rev. ed. (New York: New York University Press, 1957).

2. Ibid., 171.

3. Louis Henkin, "Foreign Affairs and the Constitution," *Foreign Affairs* 66 (Winter 1987/88): 285–289.

4. William C. Olson, "The U.S. Congress: An Independent Force in World Politics?" *International Affairs* 67, no. 3 (1991): 547.

5. Cecil V. Crabb Jr. and Pat M. Holt, *Invitation to Struggle: Congress, the President, and Foreign Policy,* 4th ed. (Washington, D.C.: Congressional Quarterly Press, 1992), 12.

6. Thomas E. Mann, "Making Foreign Policy: President and Congress," in *A Question of Balance: The President, the Congress, and Foreign Policy,* ed. Thomas E. Mann (Washington, D.C.: Brookings Institution, 1990), 6.

7. Arthur M. Schlesinger Jr., "The Legislative–Executive Balance in International Affairs: The Intentions of the Framers," *Washington Quarterly* 12 (Winter 1989): 100.

8. Mann, "Making Foreign Policy," 5.

9. For details on the continuing debate over the War Powers Resolution see Louis Fisher, *Constitutional Conflicts between Congress and the President,* 3d rev. ed. (Lawrence: University Press of Kansas, 1991); and John Lehman, *Making War: The 200-Year-Old Battle between the President and Congress over How America Goes to War* (New York: Charles Scribner's Sons, 1992).

10. Olson, "The U.S. Congress," 548.

11. James Allen Smith, *The Idea Brokers: Think Tanks and the Rise of the New Policy Elite* (New York: Free Press, 1991).

12. Olson, "The U.S. Congress."

13. Duane M. Oldfield and Aaron Wildavsky, "Reconsidering the Two Presidencies," *Society* 26 (July/August 1989): 56–57.

14. Jay Winik, "The Quest for Bipartisanship: A New Beginning for a New World Order," *Washington Quarterly* 14 (Autumn 1991), reprinted in Brad Roberts, ed., *U.S. Foreign Policy after the Cold War* (Cambridge, Mass.: MIT Press, 1992), 314.

15. Zbigniew Brzezinski, "The Cold War and Its Aftermath," *Foreign Affairs* 71 (Fall 1992): 31–49.

16. John Brademas and others, "Building a New Consensus: Congress and Foreign Policy," *SAIS Review* 9 (Summer–Fall 1989): 61–71.

17. Mann, "Making Foreign Policy," 34.

18. Robert A. Pastor, "Congress and U.S. Foreign Policy: Comparative Advantage or Disadvantage?" *Washington Quarterly* 14 (Autumn 1992), reprinted in Brad Roberts, ed., *U.S. Foreign Policy after the Cold War* (Cambridge, Mass.: MIT Press), 339.

19. Brademas and others, "Building a New Consensus."

20. William J. Fulbright, "The Legislator as Educator," *Foreign Affairs* 57 (Winter 1979): 726.

21. Charles William Maynes, "America without the Cold War," *Foreign Policy,* no. 78 (Spring 1990): 3.

22. James Schlesinger, "New Instabilities, New Priorities," *Foreign Policy,* no. 85 (Winter 1991–92): 3–24.

23. Progressive Policy Institute, *Mandate for Change,* ed. Will Marshall and Martin Schram (New York: Berkley, 1992), 290–91.

24. Irving Louis Horowitz, "Moral Theory and Policy Science: A New Look at the Gap between Foreign and Domestic Affairs," *Ethics and International Affairs* 6 (1992): 81–93.

25. Ibid., 81.

26. Peter Tarnoff, "An End to Foreign Policy," *Harvard International Review* 14 (Summer 1992).

27. Carnegie Endowment, National Commission on America and the New World, *Changing Our Ways* (Washington, D.C.: Carnegie Endowment for International Peace, 1992), 7.

28. Center for Strategic and International Studies, *The CSIS Strengthening of America Commission, First Report* (Washington, D.C.: CSIS, 1992).

29. Fulbright, "The Legislator as Educator."

30. Mann, "Making Foreign Policy."

31. James A. Thurber, "The Roots of Divided Democracy," in *Divided Democracy: Cooperation and Conflict between the Presidency and Congress,* ed., James A. Thurber (Washington, D.C.: Congressional Quarterly Press, 1991), 7.

32. Arthur M. Schlesinger Jr., *The Imperial Presidency* (Boston, Mass.: Houghton Mifflin, 1989).

33. Thomas E. Mann and Norman J. Ornstein, *The First Report of the Renewing Congress Project* (Washington, D.C.: American Enterprise Institute and Brookings Institution, 1992), 3.

34. Carroll J. Doherty, "Bush Is Given Authorization to Use Force against Iraq," *Congressional Quarterly* 49, no. 48 (1991): 65.

35. Olson, "The U.S. Congress," 551.

36. Richard Gephardt, *Congressional Record,* 10 January 1991.

37. See *Congressional Record,* 10–12 January 1991.

38. Olson, "The U.S. Congress," 559.

39. Pamela Fessler, "Bush Quiets His Critics on Hill by Sending Baker to Iraq," *Congressional Quarterly* 48, no. 48 (1990).

CHAPTER 5

OSD AND THE MILITARY SERVICES

THE OFFICE OF THE SECRETARY OF DEFENSE

JAMES SCHLESINGER

I have chosen to provide some ruminations on the Office of the Secretary of Defense and on how the defense organization looks from the standpoint of that office. As many people know, that office evokes strong passions in some quarters. So I ask the reader to put aside preconceptions, and be guided by those words from Isaiah which are, perhaps, too painfully familiar to many from the Johnson years: "Come now let us reason together."

My initial observation bears on the nature of American democracy. In the United States, power is more broadly diffused than it is in any other major military nation. That dispersion of power markedly affects the American military establishment. In all nations, to be sure, there inevitably is tension between the military establishment and the political authority. In the United States, however, that tension occurs at many points, and, thereby, is ultimately diluted. Indeed, such tensions are forged into a principle: the separation of powers.

In the United States power is widely dispersed, and all of these powers may come back to influence the operation of the Pentagon. There is, first of all, the White House. I refer here not to the commander in chief, but, rather, to the political operatives in the White House. There is the Congress, a steadily growing influence since the 1970s, whose overall role now transcends the historic functions of its duly appointed committees. The courts also play a role—recent rulings on gays in the military, for instance. In the United States, power is spread across the landscape. The system of checks and balances, fundamental as it may be to the American democracy, markedly detracts, not only from unity of command (save in periods of dire national emergency), but even from the possibility of coherent and consistent policy formation.

RESPONSIBILITIES VERSUS POWERS

The overall responsibility of the secretary of defense is to relate U.S. policy objectives, as established through the National Security Council (NSC) system, to the development, the sustaining, and the deployment of forces. That overall responsibility is broken down into specific tasks that are assigned to the secretary—tasks that I shall now outline. One should recognize, however, that there are no sharp lines—that all these tasks, to some extent, overlap. Broadly speaking, these tasks are divided into the categories of organizational, operational, and other responsibilities.

Foremost in the operational category is the development and articulation of strategy and the associated deployment of forces. In this connection, the secretary of defense, acting on behalf of the president, tends, along with the chairman, to be the principal advocate of force readiness. The services are far more uneven in their support for readiness. Whenever budget money is generous, the services can be enthusiastic about readiness. Yet, if the pursuit of readiness is going to interfere with procurement programs, readiness is likely to suffer in the service's budget submissions. Those in Washington, furthest from the deployed forces in the field, tend to be more partial to procurement. It is the secretary of defense who must weigh in to protect readiness money.

As part of his operational responsibilities, the secretary is primarily responsible for political and military affairs. In this role he becomes a major guardian of alliance relations. Those relations have become increasingly important as the gross military advantages of the United States have declined. In alliance relations, quite frequently the secretary of defense must play a larger role than does the secretary of state. One final point regarding the political–military responsibilities of the secretary (to which I will later return) is that the secretary of defense must establish the political framework—the context in which military operations are either prospectively or actually carried out.

Let me now turn from the operational to the organizational tasks. While several of the secretarial tasks can be described as critical, in terms of visibility and impact, budget formulation is second to none in importance. The budget is where it all comes together. It is the presumption (perhaps *hope* would be a better word) that the budget will reflect and carry forward the strategy that has been adopted.

This essay has been edited and is reprinted from Reorganizing America's Defense: Leadership in War and Peace, *ed. Robert J. Art, Vincent Davis, and Samuel P. Huntington (Washington, D.C.: Pergamon-Brassey's International Defense Publishers, 1985), 255–74, by permission of Pergamon-Brassey's, Inc.*

This requires unremitting effort and attention. Regrettably, the reality is frequently different from the expectation.

Broadly speaking, in allocating available resources, we are looking at trade-offs among three factors: force structure, readiness, and modernization. When budgets are rising, the question of allocation should not be too painful. When, however, budgets are shrinking, the problem of allocation becomes increasingly painful. Indeed, this can occur even with rising budgets, when aspirations are rising even more rapidly. The temptation will always be to skimp on readiness; it remains the secretary's responsibility to resist that temptation. More generally, the problem for the department is that modernization can readily encroach upon the resources required to maintain the force structure or, above all, to maintain the forces in an adequate readiness posture.

Beyond the problem of budget formulation, the secretary is responsible for overall administration and coordination of the Department of Defense (DOD). This includes some obligation for keeping the DOD a relatively harmonious whole. That, however, is easier said than done, for it cuts against the grain of some of his other responsibilities. Hard decisions tend to detract from harmony, particularly when there is overall budgetary pressure. Nobody in the Department of Defense, especially the navy and the air force, would wish a repetition of the explosion of 1949. As a consequence, many possible decisions, which would seem logically sound, will, nonetheless, be avoided, simply for the purpose of maintaining peace within the family. Bob McNamara was, perhaps, the most notable example of a secretary prepared primarily to follow his own logic, even at the cost of the internal harmony of the department. As a consequence, he may have pressed his luck too far. Nonetheless, it was McNamara himself who observed: "One can only slay so many dragons each day."

In the organizational area the secretary has a responsibility for personnel. This includes approval of proposed candidates for three or four stars. It also includes selection of prospective chiefs and major commanders, and the forwarding of such recommendations to the White House. In different administrations, the role of the secretary with respect to such promotions may vary considerably.

Finally, it should be noted that operational and organizational responsibilities are supposed to be tied together by the secretary through the issuance of the policy guidance. Once again, this may be more hope than reality: it is not certain that this occurs.

The secretary has *other* responsibilities. In a democracy, public relations is vastly important. Much of the secretary's time is devoted to gathering support for the department's activities. The secretary has overall responsibility for congressional relations, and congressional oversight has become increasingly detailed. Consequently, congressional relations now include the selling of the defense budget (call it proselytizing), the overseas deployment of various forces, the lobbying for specific weapons systems that have become controversial, or the sale of weapons systems to those allies who may not enjoy universal support on Capitol Hill. This was clearly the case in regard to the sale of the AWACS to the Saudis. Frequently, in such matters, the department will require White House or even presidential support.

The secretary is also responsible for both White House relations and executive branch relations. This includes maintaining support across the river, down through both the White House and the Office of Management and Budget (OMB), for the activities and financing of the department.

These matters are simply the broader and weightier responsibilities of the secretary. In addition, he is obliged to pay attention to all sorts of details. These include such diverse matters as the number of positive indications in urinalysis for the forces deployed in Europe, striptease dancers on the foredeck of nuclear submarines in Hampton Roads, the reception of black colonels in Latin America and how their services handled such reactions, or homosexuality among commanding officers on U.S. Navy ships. These issues are specific and apparently less a responsibility. Nonetheless, such issues are the ones that can be most painful in public relations. It is the little things that can kill.

Let me offer two comments, now that I have arrayed this long list of the secretary's responsibilities. First, although the responsibilities are very imposing, they are not matched by the powers of the office. Those powers are not awe inspiring. To some extent it is like the office of the president. The office provides the secretary simply with a *license to persuade* outside parties. Even within the building, quite frequently, it is only a license to persuade. The powers of the office, not particularly awesome in themselves, have become even less suited to the fulfillment of the department's mission, as America's gross advantages in international competition have declined. When all one had to do was to threaten massive retaliation, persuasion was relatively easy—most clearly with one's prospective opponent, but also with one's allies and even within the country. It is both ironical and worrisome that, as America's gross advantages have declined, checks and balances have steadily increased. For example, congressional oversight (or meddling) is not likely to recede.

The upshot is that the overall system that sustains the department of defense has been deteriorating. I am not here talking about budget support. I am speaking of the overall political system that sustains the department. In the past, the powers of the secretary of defense may have been adequate in relation to his responsibilities. The question at the present time is whether or not they continue to be adequate.

My second comment regarding a secretary's responsibilities is somewhat more diffuse. One ought not generalize about the very different men who have served as secretary. They have had their own, and rather different, preferences, and they have had rather different skills as well. Some were generally talented; some had specific talents; some had no talents at all. In the latter case, the Pentagon system must effectively compensate for the defects of the secretary.

More generally, the system should take advantage of the secretary's strengths and build around his weaknesses. For example, Melvin Laird was extraordinarily good at congressional relations. He was one of their own. Indeed, he could be sufficiently good on the Hill to build backfires against orders from the White House or from the national security advisor. In my opinion, Harold Brown was simply superb in those things for which he had an affinity: research and development, evaluation of technology and its role, procurement, weapon systems analysis, and budget formation (aside from the fact that Jimmy Carter gave him insufficient funds). Harold loved to attend to these specific and detailed responsibilities. In simple truth, with the resources that he was given, Harold Brown was probably without peer. However, on other matters, such as deployments, alliance relations, and so on, he did not have a similar feel.

Robert McNamara was extremely good in the overall construction of the department. Even those who decry McNamara must still, even today, pay tribute to the planning, programming, and budgeting system (PPBS). McNamara believed in and allowed logic to drive policy, to an extent that was admirable in a sense, but not entirely suited to this world. This was most clearly indicated in our relations with our European allies, when he generated long and, to some extent, unnecessary controversy over nuclear deterrence and alliance strategy. During the Vietnam years, some wag observed that McNamara was a great secretary of defense and a poor secretary of war. Perhaps there was some truth in that observation, but it points to a more general proposition: the inevitable variability of talent even in the most exceptional men. Perhaps the final point to be recognized is that the list of secretarial responsibilities is so imposing that no single individual can totally fulfill them all.

SALIENT ELEMENTS OF THE OFFICE

I turn now from a simple outline of the responsibilities to a deeper exploration of the office. Of such elements, the salient elements of the office. Of such elements, the first is *fixing strategy*. One example is the role of the secretary in determining doctrine and strategy for the use of nuclear weapons. Nuclear weapons have raised political control from the level of desirability to the level of necessity. Consequently, the secretary is obliged to establish nuclear strategy. Since the late fifties, all secretaries have done so. Prior to that it was Secretary John Foster Dulles who articulated strategy, in "massive retaliation" and, later, in the more selective employment of nuclear weapons "at times and in places of our own choosing." (The early years of the Eisenhower administration until Secretary Thomas Gates were not the high point for the office of secretary of defense. This reflected Eisenhower's own role and experience and the fact that he served, to a large extent, as his own secretary of defense.)

One way or another, any serious changes in nuclear doctrine—as opposed to a continuation of the existing routine—will have to come from the secretary of defense. It was McNamara who, after some flirtation with damage limiting, introduced mutual assured destruction (MAD). I myself moved sharply away from mutual assured destruction and emphasized selective strikes and city avoidance. In large degree this reflected my years at RAND. I had found mutual assured destruction politically and intellectually defective, particularly in its impact on alliance responsibilities, and dubious in terms of its morality.

Let me provide several cautionary notes. Perhaps I could start with a reminiscence regarding General Creighton Abrams, who, while sitting in my office one day, observed: "The secretary of defense is up there on the bridge, enjoying the splendid view of the horizon and his authority to give orders. So he's signaling, 'hard rudder left, hard rudder right'—and he thinks he's making some dramatic changes. What he forgets is that there are a lot of people down in the engine room who are simply getting seasick."

Some secretaries are simply not very good at the task of fixing strategy. When they are obliged to perform that role, the results can be unfortunate. I know of no cure for this problem, other than to leave existing doctrine in place. The major source of the difficulty is a lack of professionalism or a desire to placate domestic opinion. The least negative cost of such activities is strategic doctrine that is both unconvincing and amusing.

As part of the process of maintaining deterrence, the United States will elaborate a declaratory posture, normally enunciated by the secretary of defense. But some cautions are in order here. There are three, quite separate elements: the declaratory posture, the war plans, and the capabilities of the weapons systems. These three elements do not have to coincide. Indeed, there may be considerable inconsistency among them. For example, when Bob McNamara was talking about mutual assured destruction, one should recall that the overwhelming majority of our weapons was directed against Soviet military targets, not against urban centers. The war plans diverged quite markedly from our declaratory posture. Similar gaps may occur with regard to the capabilities of the weapons systems. There has been a great deal of talk about counterforce over the years, for example. This may be reflected both in our declaratory posture and in our targeting doctrine (war plans). Nonetheless, the weapons in the inventory may not be able to destroy the targets. Thus, even when a strategy is publicly enunciated by the secretary, one should be cautious about whether that strategy can, indeed, be implemented. Declaratory posture is intended to affect the attitudes of both potential foes and allies. Although it may make a public splash, it is not necessarily implementable.

One should always bear in mind that simple admonition in Clausewitz's *On War:* "In strategy then, everything is simple, but not, on that account, easy."

The second salient responsibility of the secretary is to establish the *political framework* within which the military must operate. This is, of course, closely related to the issue of strategy. National policy cannot be based on military considerations alone. For example, the strategy of arms control—to say nothing of detente—was not fully embraced even by the relatively enlightened military establishment of the 1970s. How much harder would it have been for, say, General Curtis LeMay to accept the political constraints embodied in the pursuit of arms control. The mutual acceptance of such limitations was simply too foreign to the Air Force thinking of the fifties and sixties. Nonetheless, it is simply a fact of life that the military, either in choosing weapons or in making war plans, must operate within the context of a political framework set from outside. It is only the national command authority, the president, and the secretary of defense, who can establish that political framework.

In the wake of Grenada, there was a lot of chatter—in *Wall Street Journal* editorials, for example—that finally we took responsibility for making decisions away from weak-kneed civilians and have given it back to the military men who can decide upon and carry out the right military actions. There is an eager belief in the efficacy of "letting military commanders do their own thing." Indeed, Secretary Caspar Weinberger has said "I would not dream of overruling a military commander." Whether or not he dreams about doing such a thing is immaterial, so long as he actually would do it when required.

Much of this is just some more misreading of the so-called lessons of Vietnam. Let me underscore a few things about the need for a suitable political framework. The indispensable first point is that there is no responsible and serious alternative to the careful creation of a political framework for the military. In matters of arms control this is, of course, axiomatic. It has also been implicit in all arrangements regarding nuclear release authority since the passage of the Atomic Energy Act. Such a political framework would apply to any use of nuclear weapons in time of war. This has been quite explicit, at least since the establishment of the various, Single Integrated Operational Plan (SIOP) options for the president. Since the priority of political decision is so obvious in the case of nuclear weapons, I pass on to other episodes that exemplify the need for an effective political framework to provide for nonnuclear military forces.

It is not too long since we in this country had the opportunity to observe and react to a Soviet experience in allowing the military to determine their own rules of engagement. I refer, of course, to the shooting down of the KAL jetliner. Within the Soviet system of air defense, that outcome was quite logical and almost inevitable. Nonetheless, the Soviet Union paid an enormously high political price for letting their military commanders do their own thing.

In this context, however, it is most important to consider our own reactions to the Soviets' allowing rules of engagement to be established on the basis of military considerations. I emphasize the KAL jetliner story because, here in the United States, the very people who have been most enthusiastic about getting rid of the civilian overlay and the political framework and letting military commanders do their own thing were the most critical of the Soviet Union for its inflexibility and brutality in this incident.

At the time that Vietnam fell in 1975, I am sure that some will recall how strong was the disposition among our military to re-engage one way or another in South Vietnam. Many had invested a substantial part of their lives in attempting to maintain the independence of South Vietnam and they felt, quite strongly: "We can't let those bastards get away with *this.*" The only problems with reengagement, however, were that, first, it was against the law and, second, speaking politically in the light of prior experience, the United States had no reason—at least in my judgment—to get on that tar baby once again. In that troubled period much of my own efforts were devoted to heading off the instinctive response of our people who wanted to help and had forgotten the clear dictates of the law. I cite this experience, once again, because it indicates so clearly that the political framework has to be set and maintained by the civilian leaders at the Pentagon.

In the Mayaguez incident, after the American captives had been released by the Cambodians, it was necessary to give a direct order to the commander in chief, Pacific Command (CINPAC) to abandon his goal of overrunning Cambodian defenses on Koh-Ta. Whenever U.S. forces are engaged, the instinctive reaction is not to seek the political objective, but, rather, a military victory. Indeed, the inculcated reaction is to destroy one's opponents' military forces. It was quite clear to me at the time that the purpose of the engagement of U.S. military forces was simply to extract our people from Cambodia, and to provide a lesson for the Cambodians and others. But that political objective was lost sight of by one of our military leaders as the engagement wore on. It is not my intention, retrospectively, to chide him for an oversight. Rather, it is my intention to point out that even in these lesser contests, it is indispensable that the political framework be established by civilian leaders.

I close on this point by observing that the Grenada incident should not be taken, as some in the press implied, as an indication of the ease and appropriateness of turning such matters over to the military. It is not a clear example that reverses the fundamental truths that I have outlined regarding the need for a political framework. Grenada was a case in which there was very little military opposition. In that case, the problem of dealing with one's allies was simply to cope with their reactions, not all of which can be said to be uniformly supportive. The simplicity and ease of the Grenada operation meant that the political constraints could be minimal. It does not vitiate the need for establishing coherence in a military operation through political guidelines. One should not conclude from the Grenadian example, that we could go back to a world that never existed, indeed, a world that exists only as the inverse of what was supposed to have happened in Vietnam.

Let me turn to my third salient element: how the secretary of defense influences the *military setting*. In this connection, I reiterate that the secretary of defense, backed up by the chairman and by the CINCs, must be the patron of readiness.

In a crisis, the secretary of defense should insist that the military professionals be responsible for setting military plans. There should be a rebuttable presumption in favor of the professionals, and they should be overruled *only* when there are clear political requirements to the contrary. The military should be responsible for the design and execution of the plan for dealing with the crisis. A wise secretary will keep that enormous host of aspiring field marshals—the logisticians, budgeteers, systems analysts, engineers, scientists, and the like, all those who want to have the fun of becoming a field marshal— well to the background in such a crisis.

One should realize, of course, that debilitating logrolling can also come from the outside—from civilians. Too much shaving of the military plans for political reasons quite frequently results in disaster. The Bay of Pigs is but one relatively recent example of this point. In order to make Ambassador Adlai Stevenson happy, essential air strikes were canceled. This may have spared the ambassador further bouts with his conscience, but the simple consequence was that any chance for the success of the Bay of Pigs operation was lost.

I would have thought that such an episode would remain a clear reminder to the political authorities that they should be extremely careful about canceling air strikes. Nonetheless, all that was forgotten during the Mayaguez episode. After the removal of the American captives from the island, the only leverage the United States had was the threat to inflict punishment on Cambodia if the regime failed to return the captives. Nonetheless, for some mysterious reason, during the twenty minutes in which the secretary of defense was driven from the Pentagon to the White House for dinner, the White House canceled the air strikes directed against Cambodia. After my arrival at the White House, I succeeded in getting the second and later strikes restored. Of course, the initial strike could not be belatedly restored. Only the restoration of the air strikes permitted the Mayaguez rescue operation to be successful.

William Y. Smith has told us that the military are the most reluctant to use force. I remind him that his initial statement, rapidly corrected, that the military were the least reluctant to use force, which I called a Freudian slip, was essentially correct. To be sure, the military are quite reluctant to have *recourse to force*. They are distinctly reluctant, for example, to put

fourteen hundred marines into Beirut, for they recognize that such a lodgment puts both the United States and the handful of marines into a position in which, as the Soviets used to say, the correlation of forces is adverse to us. Nonetheless, when the United States does decide to have recourse to force, the military are then most willing to use that force. Quite correctly, they are not inclined to shave the use of force for political purposes—particularly for domestic political purposes.

PROBLEMS IN BUDGET MAKING

Let me turn now to those salient responsibilities of the secretary of defense that fall outside of the operational area. It has always seemed to me that one of the most significant roles of the secretary is to establish incentives to which the services respond. Sometimes these incentives are established unwittingly, even haphazardly. Far better is it explicitly to face the issue of incentives, so that they can be consciously considered and consciously designed. Such decisions go far beyond the daily routine.

When McNamara introduced the PPBS within the Pentagon, he proceeded to use that system for a purpose not inherent in it. He determined precisely the force structure for the services. Yet, when he prescribed force structure, he created an overwhelming incentive for the services to drive up per-unit costs. Their goal, no doubt, was to get as much capability as one could into each force unit. Yet, by driving up per-unit costs, it moved us further along the road, later caricatured, of a military establishment ultimately consisting of one aircraft, one ship, and one tank. When the Army was told that it had sixteen divisions, it had an incentive to add support units to the divisions, to increase personnel and equipment. The budgetary incentives precluded the navy from saying that it could get one-and-a-half cheaper carriers for the price of one large carrier, or the air force from saying that it could, through economizing on tactical air wings, get two additional ones for the same budget total. The services feared that if they designed cheaper capabilities they would simply lose resources.

In my years at the bureau of the budget, I had pondered those pernicious effects on service incentives, and had advocated that resources, rather than force structure, be frozen. So, when I became secretary of defense, I attempted to cure the problem as I saw it. The services were informed, somewhat to their disbelief, that we were not going to determine force structure. It was the service responsibility, and opportunity, to extract as much as possible out of the prescribed resources. If the service could increase force structure, it would be protected. The secretary of defense, under those circumstances, had a direct obligation to protect service resources from the "enemy"; that is, from the office of management and budget, the Congress, and, perhaps, even from the systems analysis office.

In the services there was considerable skepticism. The army comptroller assured General Abrams that he should not trust any commitment that I made; intentionally or not, it was just a device to cut the army budget. General Abrams decided to accept the bureaucratic risk. I indicated that we freeze personnel at the 785,000 level. If he could field additional combat units from obsolete, redundant, or marginal support activities, he would have my steady support and protection. The arrangements with General Abrams, sometimes described in the army as the "golden handshake," became the basis for moving from thirteen to sixteen divisions.

Similar opportunities were created for the air force and the navy, notably those involving the lightweight fighter competition. George Brown, who had become a devotee of the F-15 while at systems command, never saw much attraction in cost-quantity tradeoffs with the F-16. His successor as air force chief of staff, General David Jones, did some shrewd bargaining along the lines of the "golden handshake." He said, in effect: "The price, sir, is four additional tactical airwings." It was the introduction of the F-16—at roughly half the cost of the F-15—that permitted the expansion to twenty-six wings. However, we were not equivalently successful with the navy. The navy took the F-18 (successor to the YF-17), which was intended to be a low-cost fighter like the F-16, and ran the cost above that of the F-14, seemingly chasing the costs of the B-1.

I, myself, believe it critical to proffer appropriate incentives to the services that are maintained over time. Failure of the services to accept the logic of cost-quantity tradeoffs should not be rewarded. That is, no doubt, a splendid principal, but it requires consistency over successive administrations, and it also requires the agreement of Congress. The services may be prepared to wait. In the long run, the navy did not suffer much for its failures regarding the lightweight fighter and other cost-effective tradeoffs, even though it had to wait several administrations. The army has had one notable experience that was similar. In 1974 the army was instructed to acquire a low altitude air defense system, cheaply, from overseas. The army chose the Roland. This decision went down rather badly with the managers of the army procurement system, something like the introduction of a foreign organ into the host body. The usual antibodies were produced, ultimately leading to the rejection of the foreign system. The army Americanized the system; it wasted an immense amount of money; and, finally, under a new secretary of defense, it got rid of the Roland in 1981.

Finally, let me turn to budget formulation, for it remains a preeminent responsibility of the secretary. There is a fundamental problem in budget making and it is getting worse. Of the discretionary resources of the U.S. Government, much goes to the Department of Defense. As everything other than entitlements payments, interest payments, and defense outlays diminish, that figure tends to rise. Given the distressing inflexibility of that number, and the nature of our decision-making processes, the support for Pentagon programs becomes inherently unstable. If one seeks to get the budget total down, there is now only one major source of discretionary spending: defense. That is the heart of the problem. The defense comptroller may decry the "midnight raids" of the Office of Management and Budget. For lack of alternatives, however, the OMB is driven to those midnight raids. Similarly, if Congress wishes to protect or increase social spending, there is only one serious source of funding.

Members of Congress increasingly learn more of the defects of Pentagon decision making. Themselves past masters at tactical maneuvering, they understand full well the anomalous character of many of the outcomes in the Pentagon. Members of Congress have learned a good deal about the vested interests within the department. They are familiar with the various establishments—the research and development establishment, the health establishment, the nuclear establishment, and so on—even before they get into the parochial interests of the individual services.

If one wishes significantly to improve the performance of congressional budget review, one must, at minimum, provide the Congress with serious and well-constructed material at the outset. I concede that the present system works quite poorly. That, too, is a reflection of checks and balances. There are too many field marshals on Capitol Hill and in the press, as well as in the Pentagon. The net result is the creation of side payments for almost everybody and a serious diminution in the defense capabilities in relation to what we spend. How can one run a rational program on this basis? I do not know; but I do know that the initial step in the cure must be the reestablishment of congressional trust. I can state that only as a principle. I do not know how to execute it.

SERVICE IDENTITIES AND BEHAVIOR

CARL H. BUILDER

This essay advances three simple arguments:

1. Institutions, while composed of many, ever-changing individuals, have distinct and enduring personalities of their own that govern much of their behavior.

2. The most powerful institutions in the American national security arena are the military services—the army, navy, and air force—not the Department of Defense or Congress or even their commander in chief, the president.

3. To understand the distinct and enduring personalities of the army, navy, and air force is to understand much that has happened and much that will happen in the American military and national security arenas.

To grasp these three arguments is to master the message of this discussion. While advancing these arguments is no great leap, making them credible and vivid, so they result in empathetic understanding and a reliable basis for action, is a much more extensive undertaking. And it is that larger undertaking, rather than the arguments themselves, that justifies the many words and pages that follow.

An empathetic understanding of the American military institutions, as personalities, requires spending time with them, wrestling with their problems, interests, and aspirations—or at least trying to stand in their shoes as they deal with these things. Perhaps nothing is more revealing about the problems, interests, and aspirations of the American military institutions than their approaches to military strategy, planning, and analysis. It is here, on these matters, that they write and therefore leave some durable, analyzable record of their thinking. And it is here that we can look for evidence of their personalities.

THE ROOTS OF AMERICAN MILITARY STRATEGIES

Most contemporary texts on military strategy treat the subject as an artful exercise in logic, one that can be mastered by careful study of its immutable principles. Yet anyone who tries to follow the current debates over the maritime strategies or those of the North Atlantic Treaty Organization (NATO), or the concepts of assured destruction or "Star Wars," must be struck by the great diversity of answers that seem to flow from, or are often justified by, those immutable principles of strategy.

The explanation, of course, is that strategies, and the concepts or conclusions that are drawn from them, come from much more than science or analysis or axioms. Their sources are deeply embedded in the interests of the people or institutions that advocate them. Though the words and arguments used to support or attack strategies and concepts may be referenced to classic strategic principles, the motivations toward or away from a strategic theory often lie hidden even from its proponent.

The roots of modern American military strategies lie buried in the country's three most powerful institutions: the army, navy, and air force. Though many people outside the military institutions, including academics and presidents, may propose military strategies and concepts, these can be implemented only if and when military institutions accept and pursue them. To understand the American military institutions, then—who they are and what they are about—is to understand almost everything of enduring significance in the national debates over military issues.

The roots of modern American military strategies can be unearthed by digging down into the institutional personalities of American military services, by looking at their history and behavior instead of the words they may use to mask or explain themselves. When those institutional personalities are compared, much of the unique behavior attributed to each of the services suddenly pops into focus. The evidence is not new, only newly perceived as a part of a larger and consistent pattern that fits the recognizable personality of a particular service. Everything observed here about the service personalities has been seen before—somewhere, by someone, perhaps by many, so often as to become an invisible part of the background to the national security arena. When the fragments are assembled into the patterns of a recognizable personality, then the behavior suddenly becomes coherent rather than chaotic or quixotic. Historical behavior can be explained; and future behavior can be predicted with greater confidence. The personality differences of the three American military services are profound, pervasive, and persistent.

Since these personalities are deeply embedded inside large military institutions, they will persist despite changes in administrations, the Department of

This essay has been edited and is excerpted from Carl H. Builder, The Masks of War: American Military Styles in Strategy and Analysis *(Baltimore: The Johns Hopkins University Press, 1989), 3–43, by permission of the Johns Hopkins University Press.*

Defense, the Joint Chiefs, and the joint or specified commands. They will even persist through the trauma of war. They affect how the services, in peacetime, perceive war and then plan and buy and train forces. To understand the American military styles is to understand what is going on and much of what is likely to happen in the national security arena—from Star Wars to the Persian Gulf.

THE TRADITIONAL VIEW OF MILITARY PLANNING

The traditional view of military planning presumes that military forces are acquired and deployed as the military means, alongside economic and diplomatic means, for the pursuit of political ends. For the United States, in peacetime, those political ends are generally assumed to be the promotion of international stability, prosperity, and security. Thus it follows that peacetime military forces can and should be derived as appropriate military means to ensure international political objectives in the face of perceived threats.

Of course, such logic is not so neatly applied. Military forces are the products of much more complex processes. Powerful people and institutions, and their combining or conflicting interests, intrude. Nevertheless, in any formal discussion of military planning, the semblance of the logic is assiduously maintained. The military planning catechism goes something like this:

- These are the agreed-upon national objectives.

- Those are threats to these objectives.

- To secure these objectives in the face of those threats, that is the adopted strategy.

- This is the set of military capabilities needed to underwrite that strategy.

- And thus the following military forces are required to provide this set of capabilities.

The elements are laid out in this way because it is a rational, logical approach to security problems, not because it is really how we arrive at military forces; it is how we explain them.[1]

Despite the logical wrappings of defense planning, there is considerable evidence that the qualities of the U.S. military forces are determined more by cultural and institutional preferences for certain kinds of military forces than by the "threat." There are many ways to interpret a threat; there are many ways to deal with any particular interpretation of a threat. There is, after all, an American style about military forces, just as there is about business and life. It is people, not threats, who argue for and against the acquisition and maintenance of specific military forces. The advocates for a particular kind of military instrument can hardly be faulted (at least in peacetime) if their interpretations of the threat— and the effectiveness of a particular military system to counter it—reflects the interests of their institutions and the importance of their chosen careers.

And, since these incentives derive more from human nature than ideology, we may reasonably assume that much the same is true for other military institutions.

Is the arcane logic of military planning then only a sham, a deliberately contrived cover to mask the parochial ambitions of the military services? It is no more a sham than the logic that most of us use to explain to friends the purchase of our new automobile. Or the logic that both sides to an *offensive* arms race may use to explain their *defensive* motives: "So central is the concept of defense to the security debate that it would now be surprising for an accretion of military power to be justified by anything other than defensive motives—a response to the apparently more offensive orientation of the potential adversary. As a result it is quite normal for two opponents each to claim defensiveness and to charge the other with offensiveness."[2]

Even if military forces are only partly driven by institutional and cultural preferences, it may still be useful to explore the implications of those preferential engines at the extreme: what if military forces were not what we pretend them to be—the military means to political ends—but were, instead, institutional ends in themselves that may or may not serve the larger interests of the nations that support them? If that hyperbole is entertained as an intellectual device for thinking about military forces, then the qualities of those forces are likely to be more important (and revealing) than their quantities. The size of forces may be determined by national allocations of resources—by the Congress or Politburo or Parliament—but the character of those forces—the types of weapons chosen—are typically decided or promoted by the military institutions.

If we understand the American military institutions and their interests not simply as faceless, mindless bureaucracies doing their "thing," but as unique characters or personalities, like ourselves, we can begin to see a rationality in what they are doing, and have been doing for so long. It is asserted here that such an understanding explains their behavior much better than all the elaborate logic and language that have been developed around the traditional descriptions of military planning.

INSTITUTIONS AS PERSONALITIES

Like all individuals and durable groups, the military services have acquired personalities of their own that are shaped by their experiences and that in turn shape their behavior. And like individuals, the service personalities are likely to be significantly marked by the circumstances attending their early formation and their most recent traumas.

But treating institutions as if they were individuals with a personality raises several troublesome issues. Even for individuals, personality sketches can be misdrawn; the discernment of personality remains an art, not a science. Institutions, made up of large numbers of individuals, are more than the sum of those complex human individuals;[3] and complexity alone would seem to increase the risks of misdrawing their personalities. On the other hand, one's access to information on an institution, its behavior and words, is likely to be much greater than that for any individual.

Nevertheless, the complexity of institutions when examined closely—approaching the resolution of its individual members—requires that sketches of their personalities be made from a distance and with a very broad brush. To emphasize the differences among the services, their positions or attitudes on some aspects take the form of caricatures, with all that the word implies about exaggeration and loss of detail. The complex has been made simple; the great diversity of views within each of the services has been transformed into a monolithic voice speaking for the service.[4] The purpose in these obvious distortions is not ridicule, but discernment—to bring that which has become so familiar as to be hidden from view back into focus in order to understand the past, present, and future behavior of the services.

Despite that purpose, many will still object: individual members of an institution that has been turned into a caricature will deny that the caricature speaks for their views or values or that it exhibits their own behavior or motivations. That is, they do not recognize themselves in the caricature of their institution; and they are, after all, loyal, mainstream members of that institution and ought to be able to find themselves in the caricature. The problem, of course, is attributing a "personality" to any body made up of individuals. The variance among individuals may be enormous, yet the institution may take on a distinctive personality. Few, perhaps none, of the individuals will have the same personality as the institution; but, collectively, they take on a recognizable personality. Thus to attribute a personality to a military service is not to say that any individual member—regardless of loyalty, longevity, or position— could be found with the views, values, behavior, or motivations attributed to that service. Arthur Hadley wrestled with the same difficulties in *The Straw Giant*: "Such broad generalizations are always open to challenge. . . . How can a service that includes carrier pilots and submariners have an integrated personality? How can one that includes missile engineers and fighter jocks? Yet they most certainly do, though there are important subsets of attitudes within each service."[5]

Personality characterizations are like analytical models: they cannot be perfect precisely because they are models. If they were perfect, they would not be models; they would be the modeled object itself. The utility of the model is not its perfection of the object but the capturing of essential or important features in something simpler than the object. The utility of personality characterizations of the services is not their accuracy or completeness but the capture of some important aspects of the service behavior in something far less complex than the service itself, something we can hold in our minds and easily manipulate to project future behavior.

Institutional personalities do not account for everything; they are not the only aspect that needs to be considered in understanding the debates of military issues. But they may be simultaneously one of the most useful and most neglected aspects deserving consideration. Their value is that they reveal or explain so much, yet take so little effort to grasp and remember.

Each of the services can suffer or in turn shine by comparison with its sisters on one or more facets of their personalities. Those most loyal to one of the services may take exception to (or pride in) the way their service has been portrayed here. But the proper tests for these comparisons is whether they capture recognizable differences among the services and are substantially correct in direction and color, even if not always in degree or detail. If they are to be useful for their purposes here, these comparisons must be compelling on the basis of what one already knows; their general truth must be self-evident, for they rely on recognition more than revelation.

Finally, the service comparisons have been limited to the army, navy, and air force. What about the Marine Corps and the Coast Guard? They certainly have distinctive, even colorful, institutional personalities. However, neither the Marine Corps nor the Coast Guard enters the defense planning arena as an independent institutional actor with a significant voice in the national approach to strategy or military force planning. This is partly because of their institutional subordination,[6] partly because of their relative size, and, perhaps, partly because of their own institutional personalities or styles.[7]

Characterizing institutions as personalities can be amusing (or painful), but that, of course, is not the reason for doing so here. Turning institutions into personalities is a way of converting something amorphous and hard to grasp into a vivid picture that can be easily recalled and recognized again. The extraordinary human ability to recognize human faces is well known. Having once seen a face, most of us are able to recognize it again, even though it has changed in expression, age, and context. Giving institutions a personality is a way of giving them a "face" that can be remembered, recalled, and applied in evaluating future behavior or circumstances. As with the police artist's sketch, it need not be photographic in its details; the essential features, even if exaggerated somewhat, are the keys to recognition.

DO THE MASKS EVER DROP?

Do the American military services ever drop their masks of war and admit to their institutional self-interests? Rarely, I think, and then only within earshot of their own family.

The first time I saw an open admission of self-interest by a military institution was in a 1982 White Paper on the British decision to modernize their submarine-launched ballistic missiles (SLBMs) by exchanging the Polaris missiles for the new Trident.[8] For Britain and the British defense establishment, this was a difficult and contentious decision. For the United States, the Trident program was simply another step in the continuing evolution of its submarine-launched ballistic missile force—from Polaris to Poseidon to Trident—which, in turn, was only a part of a broader program of modernization for the U.S. strategic forces. But the change from Polaris to Trident represented an enormous investment for the British, one that would both bulge their defense budget and cut into the budget slices for other forces and services.

The opposition in Britain to the Trident modernization was substantial; it found voice in both the public and various segments of the British armed forces. In the face of this opposition, the Ministry of Defense took pains to explain the need for modernizing the SLBMs in a White Paper. Most of the paper was devoted to the typical military planning arguments—Britain's strategic objectives, the threat to those objectives, the strategy being pursued, and so on. Perhaps the strongest possible argument for modernizing the SLBMs—that they were wearing out—was missing because the government had earlier been forced to admit that the old Polaris missiles were good for at least another ten years.

Then, toward the end of the paper, almost as an afterthought, was a remarkable argument that can be paraphrased as follows: "Besides, if we don't modernize the Polaris, we won't be able to continue to attract and retain the very best people for our strategic nuclear forces, and that is the place where we want our very best." That, I would submit, is a very real and important concern of institutions about their future. Whether or not it is considered a valid or appropriate argument for modernizing Britain's strategic nuclear forces or for spending billions of pounds sterling, it reflects the understandable concern of an institution that has been made responsible for those forces. It is not the concern that is remarkable; it is its explicit expression.

Central to most institutions and their future is the ability to attract and retain good people. When I told a colleague[9] about the British using that concern as an argument for modernizing their SLBM force, he recalled one of his experiences with the American Strategic Air Command (SAC).

In the mid-1960s, the air force wanted to replace its B-52 bombers with a bomber that would be recognized today as the B-1, only then it was called the AMSA—the advanced manned strategic aircraft. But it was not successful in convincing the administration or Congress of the need; and Secretary of Defense Robert McNamara was pushing the air force to accept a strategic bomber adapted from his controversial TFX program—the FB-111. It would be an understatement to say that none of the services was enthusiastic about the TFX or its variants; it simply was not their airplane; it was McNamara's child.

The then fathers of SAC, who at the time were also essentially the fathers of the air force, met in the SAC "board room" to decide what to do about the next bomber they wanted so badly for the institution, since they would probably never fly it. My colleague was a "strap hanger" in the back rows and shadows around the main conference table. It was unlikely that they would be able to get the bomber they wanted, the AMSA, for another ten years. But they could get the bomber they did not want—the small, short-legged FB-111—if they would go along with Secretary McNamara.

My colleague remembers what he thought to be a telling argument made during the deliberations that day. Someone pointed out that even though the FB-111 was not the right airplane for SAC, it did offer some glamour with its supersonic speed and therefore would attract young pilots into SAC. It was those young pilots SAC needed to ensure its institutional future now; the right bomber could come later. And that is pretty much what happened: SAC, as an institution, never loved the FB-111; but a new generation of SAC pilots teethed on it; and SAC finally did get the plane it wanted, the B-1.

If the institutional fathers ultimately make such fateful decisions about forces and weapons, how can they avoid looking out for the future of the institution that has been entrusted to them? The choices for war are seldom clear or unambiguous, despite all the military planning and analysis rhetoric; but the choices for the institution are almost always urgent and painfully apparent. And thus the masks of war cover what the institution must do.

FIVE FACES OF THE SERVICE PERSONALITIES

By comparing the services on five aspects, or "faces," I initially sketch here some basic outlines or features of the service personalities. I originally considered more than two dozen aspects in a search for attitudes, questions, behavior, and concerns that might distinguish the services from one another. Some differences, like uniforms and insignia, while substantial, did not appear to shed any light on service approaches to strategy or analysis. Others, like critical command progressions for officer advancement, seem to show only minor differences among the services. And still others, such as the differences in their public images (as portrayed, for example, in motion pictures), were rich in color but difficult to relate to service self-images and behavior toward strategy or analysis.[10]

The five faces used here for the initial sketches of the service personalities have been deliberately chosen to reveal differences rather than similarities among the services: (1) altars for worship, (2) concerns with self-measurement, (3) preoccupation with toys versus the arts, (4) degrees and extent of intraservice (or branch) distinctions, and (5) insecurities about service legitimacy and relevancy. Their order is one that seems naturally to unfold the distinctions in service identities or personalities. Each of these faces invites a fresh comparison of the three services, comparisons intended to draw out important differences among them, progressively capturing sufficient features to "recognize" the personality that seems to be lurking inside the institution.[11]

ALTARS FOR WORSHIP

What do the services revere most as a principle or cherish as an ideal? How do the services differ in the altars at which they choose to worship?[12] The question concerns the ideas or concepts that serve as inspirations and aspirations. For the knights of old, the altar might have been the code of chivalry. For the hippies or "flower children" of the 1960s, it might have been "love." Altars worshiped are revealing about how the worshipers see themselves and their values.

Tradition has always been an important part of military life, but the navy, much more than any of the other services, has cherished and clung to tradition. The U.S. Navy was born and bravely fought its way out from under the massive shadow of the British Royal Navy and its rich traditions. Some who served in the new navy had served (perhaps involuntarily) in the Royal Navy, and the extraordinary success of that navy, with its traditions, frequently served as an institutional model of professionalism for the U.S. Navy.[13] This reverence for tradition in the U.S. Navy has continued right to the present, not just in pomp or display, but in the navy's approach to almost every action from eating to fighting—from tooth to fang. In tradition, the navy finds a secure anchor for the institution against the dangers it must face. If in doubt, or if confronted with a changing environment, the navy looks to its traditions to keep it safe.

If tradition is the altar at which the navy worships, then one of the icons on that altar is the concept of independent command at sea, which, like the Holy Grail, is to be sought and honored by every true naval officer. The reference to religious concepts in describing the navy is not new: "As Secretary Stimson once remarked, the admirals were wrapped up in a 'peculiar psychology' in which 'Neptune was God, Mahan his prophet, and the United States Navy the only true Church.'"[14] Independent command of ships at sea is a unique, godlike responsibility unlike that afforded to commanding officers in the other services. Until the advent of telecommunications, a ship "over the horizon" was a world unto itself, with its captain absolutely responsible for every soul and consequence that fell under his command.

The idealization of independent command at sea is probably well captured by the exploits of Commodore Matthew Perry in opening up Japan to Western trade in the 1850s. Perry, halfway around the globe and months away from Washington, acted as presidential emissary, ambassador, commander in chief, secretary of state, and trade commissioner, all under the guns of his ships, as he threatened war and negotiated treaties with feudal Japan. The nearest examples of such autonomy and power being vested in military officers on land are the early expeditions to

the new world and the American West. On land, military officers were brought under scrutiny and supervision by means of the telegraph in the middle of the nineteenth century. But naval officers, once their ship was "hull down, over the horizon," remained beyond the pesky grasp of the telegraph. Until the advent of reliable, worldwide radio communications in the middle of this century, the responsibility and opportunity of the independent command at sea remained unique to naval officers. It is not surprising, therefore, to find the navy as the most disgruntled of the services over the encroachment of Washington into the details of its command and control.[15] The broad authority to engage and retaliate against provocations, granted to the Sixth Fleet commander during that fleet's maneuvers off the Libyan coast in spring 1986, comes close to the naval ideal of independent command at sea.

The air force could be said to worship at the altar of technology. The airplane was the instrument that gave birth to independent air forces; the airplane has, from its inception, been an expression of the miracles of technology. The very knowledge of how to fly came from technical devices and experiments, and fliers have been the major instigators and beneficiaries of technological advances in everything from structural materials to microelectronics.

If flight is a gift of technology, and if the expansion of technology poses the only limits on the freedoms of that gift, then it is to be expected that the fountain of technology will be worshiped by fliers and the air force. If the air force is to have a future of expanding horizons, it will come only from understanding, nurturing, and applying technology. There is a circle of faith here: if the air force fosters technology, then that inexhaustible fountain of technology will ensure an open-ended future for flight (in airplanes or spacecraft); that, in turn, will ensure the future of the air force. The critical element of this faith, of course, is the continued expansion of flight-related technologies, which is at least arguable as the air and space technologies mature.[16]

The altar at which the army worships is less apparent than the altars for the other two services. That may be because its ideals are more diffuse or variable or subtle. Several consistent themes surface, however, when the army talks about itself: They have to do with the depth of its roots in the citizenry,[17] its long and intimate history of service to the nation, and its utter devotion to country. For example:

Although each of our armed services is unique and different, the U.S. Army holds a special position of significance and trust. Its ranks come from the people, the country's roots, and it is closest to the people.[18]

Out of the Army's long and varied service to our nation, tested and tempered through 200 years of peace and war, have emerged certain fundamental roles, principles and precepts. . . . They constitute the Army's anchor in history, law and custom, suggesting the sources of its present strength and the trust and confidence of the nation in the essential role of the Army.[19]

[T]he Army ethic must strive to set the institution of the Army and its purpose in proper context—that of service to the larger institution of the nation, and fully responsive to the needs of its people.[20]

These ideas are sufficiently altruistic and patriotic that they could be ratified with little modification by any of the military services. What makes them unique to the army is that they really are important to the army as matters of belief and expression. They represent, at a level that is probably deep and difficult to express, who the army thinks it is and what it believes in. Of all the military services, the army is the most loyal servant and progeny of this nation, of its institutions and people.

If the army worships at an altar, the object worshiped is the country; and the means of worship are service.

Measuring Themselves

Each of the military services measures itself against some institutional standard of health:

It is a well-known fact that service Chiefs who advocate in their respective budgets 17 divisions, 27 tactical fighter wings, or 15 aircraft carriers are unlikely . . . to advocate less. Those who hope each year that they will, hope against impossible odds.[21]

For the military services, the size of their budgets—both absolutely and relative to those of the other services—is a measure of organization success.[22]

The question here is not how the services choose to measure themselves but how important those measurements are to them. How concerned or preoccupied are they with taking or meeting those measurements?

The navy has been the most consistently concerned of the three services about its size, which it measures first in the number of its capital ships and then, so they may be adequately backed up, in the numbers of other ships, by category, and, more recently, in the aggregate.[23] The navy's peacetime demand for capital ships has remained essentially unchanged since before World War I, even though the kind of capital ship has changed from dreadnought to battleship to carrier to supercarrier; the perceived enemy and geographical orientation of the navy have changed as many times. The navy demand for 100 submarines goes back before World War II, despite dramatic changes in submarines, their role, and the threat.[24] It would be difficult not to notice that the size and composition of the required fleet have been remarkably constant despite the changes wrought by several wars, the fall and rise of empires, dramatic technological advances, new enemies, and even an altered sense of national purpose.

The navy's concern about meeting these measurements is acute: Being one capital ship down is to be "a quart low," with ominous consequences if not corrected soon. Part of that concern is justified in the long lead times required to produce a capital ship

and in the impact of even one key ship on the rotation schedules for forward deployments. Quick to question its ability to "make do" when it is short a capital ship, the navy is equally quick to rebuff any questioning of the need for the forward deployments that drive its requirements. The navy is the hypochondriac of the services, constantly taking its own temperature or pulse, finding it inadequate, caught up in an anxiety largely of its own making.

The air force has, from time to time, argued strongly for its size in terms of the number of wings of bombers or fighters needed or desired.[25] But the air force appetite for newer and more technologically advanced aircraft, with their attendant higher cost, has tempered its demands when the choice came to more of the old or fewer of the new. For the air force, the aerodynamic performance and technological quality of its aircraft have always been a higher priority than the number. Thus in measuring itself the air force is likely to speak first of the kind or quality of its aircraft (speed, altitude, maneuverability, range, armament) and then the numbers.

Evidence for this emphasis on quality over quantity is easily observed: The air force does not lament the size of its bomber force so much as it does the age of its B-52s. It considers the necessity of fathers and sons flying the same bomber as a national disgrace. The trade of larger quantities of arguably less capable F-16s for F-15s was never attractive to the air force. Confronted with a mix of the new B-1 bomber and an even newer advanced technology bomber (the B-2), the air force favors more of the B-2s. The air force concern about self-measurement becomes acute only if its qualitative superiority is threatened. New aircraft developments by potential adversaries are of much greater concern if they reflect new flight envelopes than if they are being produced in large quantities. To be outnumbered may be tolerable, but to be outflown is not. The way to get the American flier's attention is to confront him with a superior machine; that has not happened very often or for very long in the relatively short history of aviation.

The army appears to be the most phlegmatic of the three services about measuring itself. Although division flags are one indication of its current status, the army has been accustomed to growing and shrinking with the nation's demands for its services. At least until recently, the army has consisted mostly of people, and over thirty of the last forty-five years, those people have been conscripted from the citizenry. To the extent that the army publicly expresses concern about its health, it is likely to be about the "end strength" (number of people) of its "active component" (not counting guard and reserve units). That is the salient measure of its readiness to fight or to expand, as may be demanded of it.[26]

Thus, when the army does talk about its size, it tends to be in terms of people, not equipment. The army may refer to the number of active divisions, to its state of modernization or readiness, as percentages of the whole, but the basic measure remains the number of people. And the army is accustomed to that number varying, depending upon the commitment of society and the government to defined causes.

Toys versus the Arts

How do the services differ in their devotion, possessiveness, or pride toward their equipment and skills? With what do people in military service tend to identify themselves? The things that attract and hold the attention of service professionals at the individual level provide an insight into the preoccupations of the service that go deeper than the assertions of the institution itself.

The air force is, by far, the most attached of the services to toys.[27] Air force pilots often identify themselves with an airplane: "I'm a 141 driver." "I flew buffs." Sometimes this identification goes right down to a particular model of an airplane: "I fly F-4Cs."[28] The pride of association is with a machine, even before the institution. One could speculate that, if the machines were, somehow, moved en masse to another institution, the loyalty would be to the airplanes (or missiles).

Air force pilots delight in showing visitors their toys. It is not hard to get an invitation to sit in the cockpit, to share its owner's excitement with the power and freedom of flight. The cockpit visitor will probably find it easier to engage the owner in a discussion of the difficulties and restrictions associated with weather and airspace in peacetime than the relationship of the man and machine to war. This is not to denigrate the great skill and courage of those who are prepared to fly and fight but simply to note that flying and flying machines are nearest to their hearts. The prospect of combat is not the essential draw; it is simply the justification for having and flying these splendid machines.[29]

The history of American airmen flying for foreign governments shows just how strong the draw has been. The Lafayette Escadrille, Chennault's Flying Tigers, the Eagle Squadron, the migration of fliers to the Royal Canadian Air Force in the early 1940s, all attest to the overriding love of flying and flying machines. When America did not possess the planes or the reasons to fly them, the pilots (or would-be pilots) followed the airplanes, even if that meant serving in other nations' military services and wars. To be sure, the pilots rationalized their extranational services sometimes in terms of helping with noble wartime causes, seldom just for money, but almost always, upon reflection, by their love of flight. They rejoined American units when that option became available, but flying came first.[30]

The navy is far less toy oriented, even though it has a more diverse set of toys to play with and a love for both ships and the sea. But the true lover of the sea and ships can be just as attracted to yachts or working at sea as to the modern fighting ship or the navy. Whereas the things the navy owns and operates are clearly a source of interest and pride for those who serve in them, navy personnel are more likely to associate themselves with the navy as an institution. This loyalty to institution appears to extend even to navy fliers:

> Whereas the Army aviators under General Billy Mitchell had continually agitated following World War I for a new aviation service separate from the Army, the Navy fliers had always been Navy officers first and aviators second.[31]

> These seagoing aviators, unlike their Army counterparts, had always had a stronger affection for their service than for their aviation units.[32]

Army people have historically taken greater pride in the basic skills of soldiering than in their equipment. Until the last few decades, the army was notorious for its reluctance to embrace new technologies or methods. The army took great pride in the marksmanship of the citizen soldier and clung to a marksman's rifle (the M-14) whereas the air force, as might be expected, quickly embraced the high-technology, volume-of-fire approach embodied in the Stoner AR-15 (later known as the M-16) rifle.

If one engages, say, an army artilleryman in conversation about his business, it is soon apparent that his pride is in the art of laying a battery of guns for accurate fire. The kind of gun—155-mm, 8-inch, or even a captured gun—is incidental; the power and satisfaction are in the knowledge and skills required to do something that is both important and general to warfare. Conversations with infantry and armored officers reveal a similar pride of skills—a thorough grounding in the basic arts of employing infantry or tanks effectively in battle.

Of late, however, the army seems to be moving toward the other services in an attachment to machines. The Abrams tank and the Bradley fighting vehicle have some of the color of institutional toys. That shift may be a necessary response to the technology changes now confronting the army, or it may be seen as a better way for the army to compete for budget slices in a toy-oriented defense program. In any event, there are signs the army is getting "hooked" on toys too.

Intraservice Distinctions

> For no service was intraservice competition ever equal in importance to competition among the services. The organizational and administrative ties which bind a service together preclude intraservice controversy from becoming as intense as interservice controversy.[33]

> Interservice cleavages ordinarily will dominate intraservice distinctions. . . . . Each of the services, however, is itself a complex organization composed of numerous subsidiary units and components. . . . Moreover, these differences are important to the members of each service. In particular, promotions to higher rank typically are reported (albeit unofficially) in terms of a variety of intraservice distinctions.[34]

All three services make intraservice distinctions among their people, particularly their officers, on the basis of their specialties or skills. They differ, however, in how these distinctions are made and used. Therefore, these distinctions are a useful clue to differences among the services on what they think is important and what they are about.

The navy is the most elaborate in its distinctions among, and the relative ranking of, its various components, branches, or activities. The implicit intraservice distinctions within the navy provide an extensive, fine-structured, hierarchical pecking order from top to bottom. At the pinnacle of this structure, since World War II, has been carrier-based fighter aviation.[35] At (or very near) the bottom is mine warfare. Submarine and surface warfare specialties, in that order, lie in between. But the distinctions go further. Among aviators, carrier (tail-hook) pilots are above land-based fliers. Within the tail-hookers, attack aviation is not so high as fighters, but above antisubmarine warfare aviation. Among submariners, attack submarines are, without any doubt, preferable over ballistic missile launchers. Nearer the bottom of the heap are amphibious warfare and land-based patrol (VP) aviation. The captain of a carrier with origins in fighter aviation clearly has credentials. The greater the diversity of experience, the better, but it cannot compensate for good bloodlines acquired somewhere in carrier aviation and surface warfare. Career devotion to the VP squadrons or the "boomers" (SSBNs) is deadly; similar devotion to carrier aviation or attack submarines is not.

It is apparent from this hierarchy that the distinctions are made on the basis of what the navy calls "platforms," the machines in which people serve, and their basing. These distinctions usually divide careers at their beginning; the blending (if any) usually comes at the 06 level (captain); in between, few cross over from one career (platform) path to another. The navy supports the notion that every new line officer is a potential candidate for the navy's top job, the chief of naval operations (CNO). Therefore, the hierarchy in career specializations can be associated with the experience relevant to the management of the total navy: The SSBNs are too isolated from the mainstream of naval operations; carrier aviation is at the heart. Curiously enough, despite these strong and important discriminations, naval officers see themselves, first, as naval officers, and only secondarily as specialists (e.g., as fighter pilots or submariners).[36]

The air force and army are quite similar in their intraservice distinctions, perhaps because the air force has been separate from the army for only forty-five years. Both have divided their officers into two groups that stand on different levels—in effect, a two-plateau or two-caste system of status. In the air force, the division is between pilots and all others. Whereas there has always been a healthy rivalry among pilots of different types of aircraft (not only among the categories of aircraft flown, but even down to models of the same category), pilots are collectively on a plateau quite far removed from all others, including flight crew members and ballistic missile officers.[37] Pilots are likely to identify them-

selves with a specific model of aircraft and to see themselves as pilots even more than as air force officers.

Although the ownership of the air force is clearly in the hands of pilots, the rivalry between fighter and bomber pilots still manifests itself in swings of ruling power. Currently, the air force is dominated by fighter pilots. Although the major commands tend to capture and put their marks upon officers throughout their careers, crossovers and mavericks are more evident in the air force than in the navy.

In the army, the basic division is between the traditional combat arms (e.g., infantry, artillery, and armor) and all others, who are seen in (and fully accept) support roles to the combat arms.[38] The branch distinctions are a source of pride and banter, but their effect upon promotion and power within the army is not so clear as it is with the navy and air force. Kanter argues that the army is the least differentiated of the services, noting: "It is perhaps symptomatic of the relatively low salience of intra-Army cleavages that, when Army officers are promoted to flag grade, they remove their branch insignia from their uniforms."[39]

Nevertheless, army officers are more likely to offer up their specialty when identifying themselves than are officers in either of the other two services. Whereas navy and air force officers, as authors, may be content to be identified by their service alone, army officers almost always append their specialty (e.g., artillery or infantry). This identifying probably has less to do with status than it does with pride or candor in the officer's qualifications. When army officers identify themselves with the army engineers, it is evident that they are saying much more about their background and qualifications than they are about their status in the army, since this branch is not one of the traditional combat arms.

Despite self-identification by branch within the army, the branches have a relationship not evident among the specialties in the other services. To a degree significantly beyond that exhibited by the navy and air force, the army branches acknowledge their interdependency and pay tribute to their siblings. Whereas the navy submariners and fliers and the air force pilots may privately think that they could get the job done largely on their own, the army branches of infantry, artillery, and armor each see themselves as inextricably dependent upon the branches if they are to wage war effectively. That dependency is longstanding, comfortable, and almost eagerly acknowledged. While each branch is proud of its unique skills and contribution, there is seldom any hint of dominance over, or independence from, the other branches.[40]

INSTITUTIONAL LEGITIMACY AND RELEVANCY

If institutional concerns about the legitimacy and relevancy of a military service were plotted as orthogonal vectors, the three services would be found widely separated at three of the four corners. Here, institutional legitimacy refers to the confidence of the service in its rightful independent status, and relevancy refers to the pertinence of its missions and capabilities. The substantial differences among the three services in their concerns about legitimacy and relevancy are important because they mark the behavior of the institutions in their approaches to strategy, analysis, and military planning.

The air force, as the newest of the three services and the one whose separation from the others had to be justified within living memories, has always been most sensitive to defending or guarding its legitimacy as an independent institution. The fight for autonomy by the air force was long and hard; and the victory was not total: the navy retained control of its aviation, and the army has periodically threatened encroachments. If aviation in support of naval operations is controlled by the navy, why should not aviation in support of ground operations be controlled by the army? If the air force is not a decisive and independent instrument of warfare, the reasons for having a separate service to wield aerospace power evaporate.

The doctrine and the decisiveness of strategic bombardment in future warfare were inextricably tied to the army air force case for autonomy. If strategic bombardment could not be decisive in warfare, and if victory could be obtained only by having an army actually meet and defeat the enemy on the battlefield, then it would be difficult to refute the case for maintaining the United States Army with the Army Air Corps (with its missions of close support of ground troops and interdiction of lines of communication) in order to support the majority of this nation's forces.[41]

Even though the air force has broadened its purview beyond strategic bombardment, particularly in the last half of its forty-five-year life, to include tactical air warfare, its legitimacy as an independent, autonomous institution still rests on the decisive and independent nature of the air war. Support of the ground troops and interdiction of the lines of communication may be the ultimate ends, but the means to those ends is success in waging the air war; and that is the true business of the air force.

At the same time, the air force is supremely confident about its relevance, about the decisiveness of airpower as an instrument of war, whether that instrument is wielded for strategic or tactical objectives. Indeed, the air force's arguments for its autonomy and legitimacy are rooted in the very same theory that provides its confidence about its relevancy and pertinence. With such vital institutional interests vested in a single theory, the institution can no longer question the validity of that theory:

Making all due allowances for the difficulties and the genuine accomplishments of our strategists, it should, nevertheless, be perfectly clear that every salient belief of prewar American air doctrine was either overthrown or drastically modified by the experience of war.[42]

The one great, determining factor which shaped the course of the Second [World] War was not, as is so often said and so generally believed, independent airpower. It was the mechanization of the ground battlefield with automatic transport, with the "tactical" airplane and above all with the tank. Airpower in its independent form was, in sober fact, relatively ineffective. It was the teaming of the internal combustion engine in the air and on the surface, in order to take the traditional objectives of surface warfare which, together with the remarkable development of electronic communications, really determined the history of the Second World War.[43]

Instead of making the common mistake of planning to fight the next war with weapons and techniques that had been effective in the last, the Air Corps planners were laying plans to conduct the next war using weapons and techniques that had been proven largely ineffective in the present war. The reason is quite obvious: the planners were not making detailed plans for fighting the next war but rather were planning for a force that could provide the justification for autonomy.[44]

In exactly the opposite corner is the navy. The navy is supremely confident of its legitimacy as an independent institution, but with the advent of long-range aviation, and again with nuclear weapons, its relevancy has come into question.

After 1945, U.S. naval power ceased to be something explainable in its own right and assessable in its own terms. . . .

Advocates of strategic airpower argued that World War II had proven decisively that there would never again be a war like it, and that armies and navies were now virtually obsolete. . . .

The Navy's position in this regard was by no means curious; in a unified Department of Defense, it saw grave threats to its institutional identity, and with some justification. The Navy had long viewed itself as possessed of a peculiar strategic mission and faced with peculiar strategic and technical problems beyond the ken of the other services. In the establishment of a higher central control lay risks that the Army and the Air Force would dominate both strategic planning and resource allocation, leaving the Navy in the perennial position of poor step-sister.[45]

The institutional navy has been buffeted by technology since the advent of steam power, through iron-cladding, rifled guns, airplanes, the atomic bomb, ballistic missiles, space surveillance, and anti-ship missiles. It was the airplane and atomic bomb, in the hands of the airpower enthusiasts, that brought the relevance of the navy explicitly into question. The threat posed by the airplane was ultimately coopted by transferring the capital ship mantle from the battleship to the carrier;[46] but the navy has dealt with the threat of nuclear weapons to its relevance by its dismissal of nuclear war as being much less likely than a protracted conventional war.[47] The ballistic missile was adapted to the submarine, but it has never been close to the heart of the navy, despite the envy of the air force and the affection of the arms control community.

The army has always been the most secure of the three services on both counts. Although the air force seriously challenged the relevancy and necessity of both the army and navy after World War II, the army was secure in the absolute necessity of its purpose and continued existence. The army could console itself in the view that modern warfare, as demonstrated in Korea, the Middle East, and Vietnam, was ultimately decided on the ground. There might be air campaigns and support from the sea, but in the end, someone had to take and hold the ground. To be sure, the army's size might be whittled down to a shadow because of new strategic theories, but the army had suffered drastic expansion and reduction before; its job was fundamental and remained, even if its popularity and support might vary over time and circumstances.

This army sense of security has been evident throughout the forty years of efforts to unify the U.S. armed services. If the navy has been the most resistant of the three services to accepting the constraints of unification and "jointness," the army has been cooperative to the point of taking the initiative, with the air force falling in between. A good example is provided by the army's pursuit of the air force in the evolution of the AirLand Battle doctrine. Though such joint planning is obviously appropriate, of the two services the army appears to be the more enthusiastic for the venture.

THE POWER OF IDENTITY

Of the American military services, the navy currently has the clearest sense of its identity and interests. Whether or not one admires the navy's identity or agrees with its interests, the clarity of its identity and interests in navy decision making is remarkable. The navy knows what it wants and knows its priorities. Even though the navy, like the other services, must deal with diverse interests within the institution, there is little doubt of, or challenge to, the exquisite and well-established hierarchy of those interests.[48] The salutory significance of this hierarchy is that everyone knows where one stands in the navy and what the navy priorities will be. Thus, the navy is less likely than the other services to have difficulty in making decisions, even painful decisions. The navy may resist cuts in its budgets, but if forced to take them, it immediately knows how and where to proceed for the interests of the navy. If higher authorities—outside the institutional navy—override the navy's decisions, then they have made a direct assault on the navy's sense of itself as an independent arm of the nation. More than once, such an insult has prompted the navy to respond with an insult of its own: resignation of its leadership.[49]

The navy may very well face tough times in the years to come, but it will not be burdened by a lack of clarity about who it is, what it is about, or what it wants to be. Those things are embodied in the clear vision the navy has of itself. There may be troubles lurking in the validity of the navy's vision, but not in any lack of clarity or confidence in how it sees itself. It will find its decisions easy to make, even though outsiders may criticize, dispute, or overturn them.

Why is that sense of self so clear in the navy and less so in the air force and army? And how, then, does any institution come to a clear sense of its identity and interests? Institutions are made up of people. Some people come early and easily to a sense of identity and purpose; others struggle to achieve that sense throughout their lives. And of those who do achieve it, some have realistic and constructive self-visions, whereas others do not. Still others develop a distorted sense of identity as a result of "heady" experiences.

Institutions display similar variety. The navy came early and easily to its sense of identity. The navy sees itself, first and foremost, as an institution. The air force identifies itself with flying and things that fly; the institution is secondary, it is a means to those things. A brave band of intrepid aviators, bonded primarily in the love of flight and flying machines, may have a clear sense of themselves, but it is not so much an institutional as it is an individual sense of self. And it is not focused so much on who they are as it is on what they want to do.

Of the three services, it appears that the army is currently suffering the most with its sense of identity and interests. Though many would point to the traumatizing effects of the debacle in Vietnam, I see a longer-term problem: the army's identity as the nation's "handyman" or loyal military servant is a fair characterization of most of its history. But something happened to the army in its passage through World War II that it liked; and it has not been able to free itself from the sweet memories of the army that liberated France and swept victoriously into Germany. That heady experience has marked the army with an image of itself that is distinctly different from that which it had before and, more important, from its experiences since.[50] Thus, the army finds itself dealing with something like a "split personality." Part of the army is trying to revert to its traditional, historical role; and part is hanging on to an image of the army at its finest year, the last year of World War II.

FUTURE BEHAVIOR

Because these sketches of the service identities are based on historical behavior, they do not necessarily portray how the services will behave in the future. There is evidence that all three services are changing:

- The submariners (or more generally, the nuclear power community) are rising relative to the aviators and surface warfare officers in the navy.

- The fighter pilots have superseded the bomber pilots in control of the air force.

- The army increasingly emphasizes high-cost toys.

But much more is constant. The personalities of the services, like those of individuals, are hard to change quickly or deliberately. They are the products of the culture and acculturation of hundreds of thousands of people, whose leadership requires decades of institutional experience, and whose behavior is continuously reinforced by social and professional incentives.[51] A strong, radical leader, such as Admiral Elmo Zumwalt, may disturb the identity of a service while in command, but reactionary, restoring forces are likely to form quickly and persist longer. Since people are more likely to associate themselves with an institution for positive rather than negative reasons, a large reservoir of restorative attitudes always maintains those values which originally attracted the institution's membership.

Many who choose a particular military institution and dedicate their lives to it make their choice because there is something about the service—who it is or what it is about—that appeals to them. They see something in that service attractive or admirable and make an implicit contract with that service to serve in exchange for the associative benefit they perceive.[52] If impending changes in their service then threaten that which they found attractive, they will exert a restoring or stabilizing pressure. With tens or hundreds of thousands of such implicit contracts outstanding, the potential for voluntarily changing the institution is very small. Significant, rapid change is almost certain to be imposed from the outside and vigorously resisted from the inside.

Thus, barring a catastrophe that decimates one or more of the services,[53] the unique service identities (whether they have been portrayed here correctly or not) are likely to persist for a very long time. Indeed, the service identities or personalities are likely to be one of the most stable aspects of the nation's future security prospects.

THE ENGINES FOR STABILITY

The engines for stability in institutions are visible when one looks not only at the whole but also at any level of detail, right down to the individuals who compose the institution. Like fractals, the pattern appears to be the same no matter what magnification one uses to examine it. Though the ballistic missile has never enjoyed the status of the airplane in the air force, the history of the MX missile illustrates the stability and persistence of eddies or side currents off the mainstream of the institution. In 1965 the blueprints for the last of the Minuteman missile series, the Minuteman III, were finished and being rolled up from the drawing boards. Fresh sheets of paper were then rolled out on those same boards, and the designers began to lay out the lines of the next missile—the follower to the Minuteman III. The missile that took shape there would be instantly recognized today, more than twenty years later: the MX, the Peacekeeper, in all of its essential features—a large, solid propellant, highly MIRVed, silo-based ICBM.

For the next twenty years, the air force tried vainly to bring that missile, under various program names, into the world. Each time it tried to go ahead with development of the new missile, Congress or the Department of Defense (DOD) or the White House would push it back up its birth canal. And each time the air force and its contractors went back to the drawing boards, made some changes (more in the basing, which they did not care about, than in the "bird," which was what they really coveted), and tried again a few years later. After twenty years of watching this natal pushing and shoving, any logical observer would be impelled to ask, "What is going on here? Do these people really want or need a new missile?" The arguments were about land-based missile basing and its vulnerability; but the shoving match looked as if it was about the missile itself.

After twenty years, and over considerable objection, a few of these missiles were allowed to enter the world, where they were put into the same cribs as the Minuteman missiles that had preceded them. One could reasonably infer this compromise: the air force got its new bird, with unexpressed hopes that it might be able to get more of them, while its opponents felt assured that they had firmly limited the size of that unwanted flock (or clutch).

But the troubling residual of this history was the source of the continuous, sustained pressure to develop a new ICBM. After the new ICBM was rejected the first time, why did the effort not stop there and then? The pressure to continue did not come from any urgent concern about the existing missiles wearing out and needing to be replaced; the life of the Minuteman missile was greater than expected. It did not come from an accepted need for a bigger missile, because the Scowcroft Commission immediately recommended the development of a smaller missile. Was it—one hesitates even to suggest—simply an example of Eisenhower's warning about the evils of the "military-industrial complex"?

This conjunction of an immense military establishment and a large arms industry is new in the American experience. The total influence—economic, political, even spiritual—is felt in every city, every State house, every office of the Federal government. We recognize the imperative need for this development. Yet we must not fail to comprehend its grave implications. *Our toil, resources and livelihood are all involved; so is the very structure of our society.*

In the councils of government, we must guard against the acquisition of unwarranted influence, whether sought or unsought, by the military-industrial complex. The potential for the disastrous rise of misplaced power exists and will persist.[54]

It would be easy to attribute the twenty-year sustained pressure for a new ICBM to the air force and its contractors in their pursuit of power and profit. But if one carefully watched and listened to the people who were most committed to the birth of a new ICBM, power and profit were not their motives. They argued effectively and ardently, in national security terms, about why America needed a new ICBM and what would happen if it did not develop one. If someone suggested that the country did not need a new ICBM, they could only shake their heads in disbelief. Such suggestions were either Soviet-inspired- or rooted in wishful thinking. They really believed (then and now) in what they were trying to do.

At some abstract level, perhaps power and greed came into play, as we sometimes suppose they do when nations choose to go to war. But those who are on the front lines are not there for those reasons. The ardent advocates of the new ICBM were committed to that cause because they could not be otherwise. They had devoted their professional lives to those machines. Their own personal worth and the worth of ICBMs had become intertwined in a way that could not be easily separated. To consider that development of new ICBMs might no longer be necessary or worthwhile was equivalent to considering whether they, themselves, were any longer necessary or worthwhile. And for their sense of personal worth, people will fight hard and long.

The fight over the MX was not a test between good and evil, right and wrong, or simply the predations of a military-industrial complex. Eisenhower had touched upon the very core of the problem in the words emphasized above: "Our toil, resources and livelihood are all involved; so is the very structure of our society." We have a society in which people identify themselves with their toils and thence with things. As with railroad firemen, their livelihood and self-worth are involved. Though the debates about the MX were carried out in the esoterica of the nuclear age—first strike, throw weight, window of vulnerability, deterrence, counterforce, and so on, they were really very much about people, what they have devoted their lives to, and the worth of their contribution to community, society, and country.

The engines for stability in the American military services are evident not only in the subinstitutional pressures to continue the development of a weapon, such as the ICBM, but in the institutional resistance to the introduction of new weapons, such as the cruise missile. Cruise missile technology and its implications for weaponry became widely recognized in the late 1970s, when the DOD instigated the serious development of modern cruise missiles in a joint navy–air force program, and when the potential of cruise missiles for good or evil was the subject of much public debate.

But the technology for modern cruise missiles had been lying fallow for more than ten years, ignored or dismissed by the services, because it offered little for, or even threatened, their institutional interests. The critical technology components of the modern cruise missile were small, efficient turbofan engines to propel them and terrain-following and matching radars to guide them at low altitude. Both these developments had been carried into the flight testing stage by the mid-1960s; their potential combination in cruise missiles of revolutionary capabilities were immediately evident to the few who were aware of the developments. They imagined such small missiles being built by the thousands, being carried by the dozens in airplanes, ships, trucks, and submarines, and capable of saturating any defenses against them by their sheer numbers.

Alas, those few visionaries had not reckoned with the affected institutions. The air force certainly had no love for a small, unmanned aerial torpedo flying hundreds of miles into enemy territory to attack the target—that was precisely the job of big, manned airplanes. When the cruise missile advocates suggested to the air force that the new missiles might be carried by big, manned airplanes to a safe point outside the enemy's defenses and then launched toward their targets, one SAC colonel reminded them that SAC was not about to abandon its intention to fly over the targets, open the bomb-bay doors, and watch the bombs fall until they detonated. The imagery of World War II was alive and well—twenty years later.

Nor did the prospect of such cruise missiles offer much to a navy dominated by carrier aviators, except as another potential threat to the carriers themselves. The attack submariners might have become advocates if the new missiles could be stuffed into a torpedo tube, if they had more of a voice in the navy, or if they had been aware of the technology; but all these things would have to wait for another ten years. The only advocates were the technologists and analysts; and they had little effect inside or outside the services. The cruise missile had no home in the technology laboratories that had been organized around airplanes and ballistic missiles. The cruise missile was neither an airplane nor a ballistic missile, so it was a technological orphan and therefore an institutional orphan.

Hence for the next ten years after their conception and the demonstration of their critical technologies, cruise missiles became back-burner developments for both the air force and navy. Then in the late 1970s, when the DOD was confronted with rising claims by the services for resources, the cruise missile surfaced again, this time as a cheaper alternative to some big ticket items, like the air force B-1 bomber. When the DOD set up a joint program office to coordinate the development of cruise missiles and put a naval officer in charge, things began to move much more quickly. Today, a decade later, modern cruise missiles are an accepted (if not universally loved) weapon carried by airplanes, ships, and submarines in the navy and air force. But if the DOD had not forced the issue upon those two services, cruise missiles might still be simmering slowly as experimental programs, being deferred by more urgent expenditures for new airplanes or another carrier and its entourage.

Thus the engines for stability within the American military institutions tend to continue those activities that have established a significant constituency within their ranks and at the same time tend to reject any new activities that might encroach upon those already established. The effect of those engines is sufficiently powerful and predictable as to be a good guide to institutional actions in the future on new and old issues.

NOTES

1. An excellent summary of this rational, logical approach to military planning is provided in Naval War College, Force Planning Faculty, ed., *Foundations of Force Planning: Concepts and Issues* (Newport, R.I.: Naval War College Press, 1986).

2. Lawrence Freedman, *Strategic Defense in the Nuclear Age,* International Institute for Strategic Studies, Adelphi Paper 224 (London: Autumn 1987), 3.

3. My colleague William Jones, who shares my interest in institutional analysis, has pointed out that institutions are also, in some respects, less than the sum of their human individuals. For example, institutional change requires considerable renegotiating of the roles of the institution's human components and since that usually requires a great deal of time, change can seldom occur at more than a glacial pace.

4. Of course, the service, as an institution, may itself limit the range of views that its members may safely express in dealing with "outsiders," reinforcing the appearance of a single voice.

5. Arthur T. Hadley, *The Straw Giant—Triumph and Failure: America's Armed Forces* (New York: Random House, 1986), 71–72.

6. The Marine Corps falls within the Department of the Navy and the Coast Guard within the Department of Transportation.

7. For example, the Marine Corps has enjoyed a reputation with Congress for its competency within a well-defined, if limited, role and for its relatively modest claims for resources. Thus, the marines have generally been bystanders in the almost continuous jostling and bumping of the army, navy, and air force over military strategy and resources. They appear to be protected from harm by Congress and seem quite comfortable with hand-me-down equipment developed by the other services, taking more pride in who they are than in what they own.

8. Ministry of Defense, *The Future United Kingdom Strategic Nuclear Deterrent Force,* Defense Open Government Document 80/23 (London: Her Majesty's Stationery Office, 15 July 1980).

9. Herbert G. Hoover, a RAND colleague with a distinguished career as an air force analyst.

10. Some other aspects considered were the differences among the services in how they program and budget and how they relate to one another and to the JCS. These could be interesting studies by themselves.

11. The most useful sources for differentiating among the services varied with the aspect being considered. Some aspects are treated extensively in the literature and have been cited accordingly. For other aspects that have not yet received attention in the literature, I have drawn upon my own experiences or conversations in suggesting the differences among the services. If my literature support is sparse, I welcome relevant citations, anecdotal support, and alternative interpretations, for this aspect of my research will never be completed.

12. This comparison was suggested by Rear Admiral James A. Winnefeld, U.S. Navy (ret.), who offered, as an example, a possible answer for the navy.

13. See, for example, Samuel P. Huntington, *The Soldier and the State* (Cambridge, Mass.: Harvard University Press, Belknap Press, 1957), 248–49.

14. Ibid., 303; the quotations are from Henry L. Stimson and McGeorge Bundy, *On Active Service in Peace and War* (New York: Harper Bros., 1947), 506.

15. Even as the navy discusses its maritime strategy, it reiterates its need for independence in command and control: "One of the truly unique aspects of naval warfare is its awesome complexity. . . . The complexity of the tasks makes it essential that we not attempt to micro-manage the war from Washington" (James D. Watkins, "The Real Reformers," *The Maritime Strategy* [Annapolis, Md.: U.S. Naval Institute, January 1986], 13).

16. One sign of a slowing in the expansion of the aeronautical technologies is the growing lifetimes of aircraft before obsolescence. The most successful (or ubiquitous) models of aircraft have always had useful lifetimes about equal to the time interval between Kittyhawk (1903) and the year of their design. That rule of thumb can be applied across more than eighty years of aviation during which airplane designs have generally succumbed to technological obsolescence. It can be applied equally well to the Curtiss Jenny, the Douglas DC-3, and the Boeing 707. The best military aircraft designs have had somewhat shorter useful lives but have followed the same trend. This continuing extension of useful lifetimes implies that technological obsolescence in aircraft is slowing. This slowing might be welcomed by those paying the bills for aircraft, but not by those devoted to designing and building new ones; they have to search harder for reasons—the threat or competition or technology—to replace the existing aircraft.

17. Evidence of the army's roots in the citizenry is to be found in its composition—over a third of the army's force structure (as measured in divisions) is vested in National Guard units.

18. Bruce Palmer Jr., *The 25-Year War: America's Military Role in Vietnam* (New York: Simon & Schuster, 1984), 209.

19. Bernard W. Rogers, *The Army,* Field Manual FM-100-1, 29 September 1978, i.

20. *The Army,* Field Manual FM-100-1, 14 August 1981, 24.

21. Robert J. Murray, "JCS Reform: A Defense of the Current System," *Naval War College Review* 38, no. 5 (1985): 25.

22. Arnold Kanter, *Defense Politics: A Budgetary Perspective* (Chicago: University of Chicago Press, 1979), 5.

23. See John F. Lehman Jr., "The 600-Ship Navy," *The Maritime Strategy* (Annapolis, Md.: U.S. Naval Institute, January 1986), 35–36.

24. The persistence of these goals for navy ships was pointed out to me in 1971 by Arthur Herrington, who served as the director, Naval Forces, in the Office of Assistant Secretary of Defense for Systems Analysis during the Johnson administration. For further evidence of this constancy, see Vincent Davis, *Post War Defense Policy and the U.S. Navy, 1943–1946* (Chapel Hill: University of North Carolina Press, 1966), 202. See also Samuel P. Huntington, "National Policy and the Transoceanic Navy," *U.S. Naval Institute Proceedings* 80, no. 5 (1954): 484.

25. The air force sought seventy groups after World War II, when it was dominated by strategic bombing enthu-

siasts. See Paul R. Schratz, "The Admiral's Revolt," *U.S. Naval Institute Proceedings* 112, no. 2 (1986): 70. More recently, under leadership dominated by the Tactical Air Command, the air force sought twenty-seven tactical fighter wings. See Murray, "JCS Reform."

26. My colleague William Jones notes that the army's focus on people is not surprising since combat success is traditionally measured in the taking and controlling of territory. With the technological age, the taking of territory may increasingly depend upon equipment and machines; but the controlling (secure occupation) of territory remains a task mostly for people—lots of them. Jones observes: "Pity the poor Soviet army planner trying to plan the conquest of China."

27. Several colleagues have objected to my use of the term "toys" instead of equipment, platforms, or weapons. They find the term pejorative, even insulting, given the destructiveness of these machines and the seriousness with which their operators treat them. Nevertheless, I have observed an excitement and enthusiasm over these machines best captured by possessing toys. To call them toys is not to say that their operators are children or that they will be used like toys; rather, it is an attempt to capture a particular relationship between a machine and its operator. Note that the relationship between a child and its toy is quite different from that, say, between a pet and its master or between workers and their tools.

28. Colonel Clifford R. Krieger (USAF) has pointed out to me that the association sometimes goes beyond the model designation, right down to the block: "Flying a Block 30 F-16C is more fun than just about anything else in the world" (from a letter to the author dated 19 September 1987).

29. General Jack Ryan, when he was chief of staff of the air force, promoted the slogan "The job of the Air Force is to fly and fight—and don't you ever forget it!" Yet the two were probably not equally attractive: to be told that you will fly but not fight is not the same as being told that you will fight but not fly.

30. There were not prominent instances of American volunteers for the British Army or Navy in World War II, although Americans in the French Foreign Legion in World War I were fairly numerous.

31. Davis, *Post War Defense Policy,* 120.

32. Ibid., 45.

33. Samuel P. Huntington, *The Common Defense: Strategic Programs in National Politics* (New York: Columbia University Press, 1961), 407.

34. Kanter, *Defense Politics,* 18.

35. The submariners are now increasingly challenging the naval aviators for the top of the hierarchy, probably because of the twenty-year ascendancy of the bright young officers who were handpicked by Admiral Hyman Rickover for the navy nuclear power training program.

36. Davis, *Post War Defense Policy,* 120.

37. See Kanter, *Defense Politics,* 108.

38. Aviation and air defense artillery are more recent additions to the combat arms; they probably do not fully share the higher status of the traditional branches.

39. Kanter, *Defense Politics,* 19. This may be definitional rather than symptomatic: The name "general" was originally intended to apply to those officers capable of commanding all the branches in a combined arms force. It is fitting, therefore, that they no longer associate themselves with a single branch but with all branches under their command.

40. This does not mean that the branches are free from rivalry. Like siblings, they frequently tease one another about their respective abilities and chores but not about their contribution to the army or its missions.

41. Perry McCoy Smith, *The Air Force Plans for Peace, 1943–1945* (Baltimore, Md.: Johns Hopkins University Press, 1970). 27.

42. William R. Emerson, "Operation Pointblank: A Tale of Bombers and Fighters," *Harmon Memorial Lectures in Military History,* no. 4 (Colorado Springs: United States Air Force Academy, 1962), 40; quoted by Smith, *The Air Force Plans for Peace,* 27.

43. Walter Millis, *Arms and Men: A Study in American Military History* (New York: G. P. Putnam, 1956), 283; quoted by Smith, *The Air Force Plans for Peace,* 35.

44. Smith, *The Air Force Plans for Peace,* 28. My colleague William Jones suggests that the old saw about the military "planning to fight the last war" is imprecise: They really plan to refight the last battle of their last victorious war.

45. James L. Lacy, *Within Bounds: The Navy in Postwar Security Policy,* Center for Navy Analyses CNA 05 83 1178, 28 July 1983, 2, 19, 60.

46. However, that transfer was effected only through the trauma of World War II and the disastrous losses of battleships to aircraft by all the major naval powers.

47. Not surprisingly, each service tends to focus on the kind of war that would make its own forces the principal player. By elevating the importance or likelihood of its particular brand of war, each service raises the stature of its own role, mission, and forces.

48. See the discussion under "Intraservice Distinctions."

49. The resignation of Navy Secretary James Webb in 1988 was triggered by a dispute, over, among other things, whether the navy could decide how to absorb budget cuts. The navy did not have difficulty in deciding the budget cuts it wanted to take; but it had great difficulty with that decision being taken out of its hands by political leaders. And this was not the first such dispute that has led to a navy resignation. Again, see Schratz, "The Admiral's Revolt."

50. E. B. Vandiver has cautioned me that two other important dislocations in the post–World War II era have influenced the army's historical perception of itself. First, the army enjoyed decisive victories in all its prior wars except the War of 1812, whereas the wars in Korea and Vietnam ended in stalemate and withdrawal, if not defeat. Second, since World War II, the army has maintained the largest peacetime force—in both absolute and relative terms—in its history. Both these experiences represent important breaks with the past for the army.

51. See Arthur T. Hadley, "The Split Military Psyche," *New York Times Magazine,* 13 July 1986, 26–33.

52. A navy wife confided to me that when she "joined" the navy, one of the attractions was the lifestyle of its most senior officers, particularly the large navy-furnished quarters staffed with enlisted personnel for household services. That prospect made the sacrifices demanded of junior officers and their families seem a little more bearable. But over

the space of twenty-five years, American societal attitudes changed to make that navy tradition intolerable. When her husband attained flag rank, they got the big home but not the servants to make full use of it. Her implicit contract with the navy was broken, and she was bitterly disappointed. If the change had not been imposed from the outside, she (and probably many others) would have resisted from inside the institution any efforts for change.

53. Perhaps the best modern example of a military institution being decimated and therefore able to build a new personality is the Wehrmacht. If the Japanese self-defense forces significantly rebuild themselves, they, too, may emerge with personalities distinct from those of the Imperial Army and Navy up to 1945.

54. President Dwight D. Eisenhower's farewell address on 17 January 1961; emphasis added.

DEFENSE REORGANIZATION AND NATIONAL SECURITY

VINCENT DAVIS

The Goldwater-Nichols Department of Defense Reorganization Act of 1986 dramatically punctuated almost a century of efforts to make the leadership, management, and use of American armed forces more cohesive and efficient. The primary approach was an increasing centralization of civilian authority, including the creation of the Office of the Secretary of Defense by the landmark National Security Act of 1947 and the further strengthening of the Office of the Secretary of Defense by the amendments of 1949, 1953, and 1958.

This centralization still left the traditional armed services in a divisive and contentious framework under the intentionally emaciated authority of a weakly centralized collectivity on the uniformed side of the defense establishment. This collectivity, also chartered by the National Security Act of 1947, was the Joint Chiefs of Staff (JCS) along with its chairman and associated joint-arena entities. To be in one of those joint assignments, or any assignment away from one's parent service while working in conjunction with other military personnel, was said to be a purple-suit job—because it meant belonging to none of the military services while in that capacity, and of course nobody wore a purple uniform as a member of any of the military services.

The Goldwater-Nichols Act was truly revolutionary. It meant dropping the other shoe, centralizing the uniformed side of the Pentagon in parallel with the civilian side, running the risk that this could lead to civil-military conflict instead of a smooth partnership between the secretary of defense and the JCS chairman immediately under him, but in any case suddenly making purple—the metaphor of the moment—the Pentagon's most fashionable color.

Goldwater-Nichols was unique in many other respects. For one thing, it was the only major defense reorganization that did not receive significant media coverage and that even as of late 1990 had received virtually no attention from the academic community of defense specialists. Still controversial mainly among senior military officers, broad agreement among all those interviewed for this discussion held that it was a good step in a proper direction, and that—even amid large-scale policy turbulence and rumors of war in Washington while the overall global scene was undergoing profound transformations—the four-year-old law was working better than anyone might have expected. Yet, there were some worrisome concerns.[1]

THE CHAIRMAN OF THE JOINT CHIEFS OF STAFF

Perhaps most important, Goldwater-Nichols successfully made the chairman of the Joint Chiefs of Staff, institutionally speaking, the most powerful military officer in the history of the United States. This was partly because the two persons thus far to hold the office under the terms of the law, Admiral William Crowe and General Colin Powell, each in his own way and in different historical circumstances, shrewdly determined to exercise the new range of authorities, responsibilities, and capacities assigned to the chairman. But it was also because of the provisions of the law itself.

The law made the JCS chairman the big boss of the entire joint system on the uniformed side of the defense establishment, a side that was previously weak and without an effective boss or patron or constituency. The chairman was located immediately under the secretary of defense, who in turn was directly under the president of the United States as commander in chief.

This essay has been edited and is reprinted from Annals, AAPSS *517 (September 1991): 157–73, by permission of Sage Publications, Inc.*

1. The law made the chairman the principal military adviser to the commander in chief and the National Security Council in the White House, by implication to such others as the commander in chief might stipulate, and to the secretary of defense at the Pentagon.

2. The chairman was to perform this role as an individual, no longer representing what had previously been called the collective judgment of the Joint Chiefs as a group. The chiefs, in effect, became merely a committee of advisers to him, and he was free to accept, reject, or modify that advice.

3. He would own and operate the Joint Staff, a group of several hundred officers drawn from the various services and previously working for the collective Joint Chiefs, although doing poor work and having no clear boss. The chairman's new powers included substantial forms of control over personnel management pertaining to officers assigned to the Joint Staff and other joint jobs before, during, and after those assignments.

4. Perhaps most important, officers in all the armed services were required to work in jobs designated as joint at certain stipulated periods in their careers in order to qualify for later promotion to star ranks.

5. The chairman for the first time was given a vice chairman to assist in his greatly enlarged duties, and at the four-star level at that.

6. The law also assigned him to become, in effect, the chief strategic thinker for the United States.

7. Finally, the law put him in charge of the joint unified and specified command system and in turn gave substantially new powers to the officers—known as the commanders in chief (CINCs)[2]—heading each of those eleven commands. Those entities, technically and collectively serving as the American armed forces for most of the time following World War II and headquartered at various places around the nation and the world, were previously neglected orphans under four-star CINCs with weak authority except insofar as they became captives of one of the traditional armed services.

Laws are not self-enforcing. One extremely fortuitous circumstance was that Admiral Crowe and General Powell were nearly perfect choices for their pioneering roles. First, both were true purple suiters in their visceral commitment to effective interservice cooperation and operational coordination. Second, both were diplomats in uniform, typically establishing friendly useful working relations with almost anybody regardless of status or views.

Third, both had a good mix of operational experience well removed from Washington combined with political-military staff experience in Washington. Without hands-on operational experience—both Crowe and Powell were criticized by a few unreconstructed old-timers who thought they were a little short in this area—they could never have gained the necessary legitimacy with the troops. Crowe's predecessor as JCS chairman, Army General John Vessey, aptly illustrated this kind of problem. Known as a "soldier's soldier" for whom time spent on Washington staffs or in school was a frustrating diversion, Vessey was sometimes overheard derisively snorting about an officer with extensive staff duty in air-conditioned offices but little time in the field: "Wonder how long it's been since that guy smelled the sweat of an infantryman?!" The academic variation was the professor who believed that nobody lacking years of rank-and-file classroom experience as a teacher-scholar should be a university president.

Without top political-military staff experience around Washington, a JCS chairman could not effectively operate in that ultimate arena of big-league political hardball. Lacking both high-level operational experience with deployed forces far away from Washington and high-level staff experience "inside the beltway," a chairman could not achieve and maintain credibility with the one person on whom his own effectiveness depended: the secretary of defense.

The drafters of Goldwater-Nichols performed an elaborate ritual dance in writing the law, carefully avoiding an explicit designation of the chairman as a commander—indeed, explicitly disavowing this in the way that military people understand the verb "command"—because this would have ruffled too many feathers and yet making the chairman a de facto commander in dealings with the joint unified and specified CINCs. But this understanding could quickly evaporate if a secretary of defense lost faith in a JCS chairman and decided to exercise his or her own fully legal command authority in a direct relationship with the CINCs.

A potential problem was having in the future a secretary like a McNamara, who disliked and distrusted senior military people and who could therefore ignore or sidetrack a chairman, no matter how able, in dealing directly with the CINCs. In this sense, it would have been preferable if the law had formally put the chairman in the chain of command under the secretary, so that the secretary would either have to work through him or fire him.

The accumulated precedents established over the first four years of Goldwater-Nichols caused the chairman to be perceived almost everywhere within the defense establishment and throughout Washington, if not also elsewhere around the world, as the United States' number-one military person with full command authority over operational forces. But, again, it would not have to be that way if a strong secretary of defense lacked faith in a chairman's capabilities. This illustrated several other major points, such as the critical importance of personal relationships when the top figures who must work with each other are very few in number.

The personal chemistry generally worked well during the first four years under Goldwater-Nichols. Chairman Crowe's first year was Secretary Caspar Weinberger's last year. Crowe was always totally respectful and dutiful toward Weinberger as toward all superiors and indeed toward subordinates as well, but some observers thought that a tiring Weinberger lacked the will to take on Crowe when the two of them disagreed—and Crowe picked his disagreements carefully. Observers perceived that Weinberger somehow felt intimidated by Crowe because the admiral possessed an array of talents that Weinberger had not seen in a predecessor and that he himself generally lacked: a Princeton Ph.D. to offset Weinberger's Harvard law degree, formidable intellectual capabilities aside from formal schooling, great writing skills, awesome speaking abilities, and a common-touch sense of humor endearing him to almost any audience.

Chairman Crowe's time under Defense Secretary Frank Carlucci provided the strongest foundations for Goldwater-Nichols in practice. Crowe once described Carlucci as "the ultimate pragmatist," and the secretary might have said the same about the admiral. Both men had high respect for each other, but neither was awestruck or intimidated. Each saw in the other a reflection of his own lofty ideals of public service, and each valued the great range of important jobs performed by the other at earlier career stages. They formed a nearly perfect team as the two top figures at the apex of the Pentagon, complementing each other in important ways, both secure in their sense of themselves so that they required no special ego deference, both totally dedicated to getting an important job done at a critical time in national history.

Chairman Crowe faced a difficult winter of 1989 at the start of the Bush administration when most of the top jobs on the civilian side of the Pentagon were vacant pending the outcome of the prolonged struggle over the nomination of Senator John Tower to succeed Carlucci as secretary of defense. It was a time when further implementation of Goldwater-Nichols and indeed many important dimensions of defense policy were necessarily held in abeyance. The admiral limped along as best he could, consolidating the chairman's role wherever this was possible and in some ways even pinch-hitting for a nonexistent secretary, but not moving much freight during a challenging time.

Newly approved Secretary of Defense Richard Cheney reported for duty in March 1989, fully impressed with the good job Chairman Crowe had done under some duress but needing time to learn the ropes himself. By the time General Powell succeeded to the JCS chairmanship on Crowe's retirement at the end of September, Cheney was largely on top of his job, while Powell needed little or no warm-up time. His still-recent duties as national security adviser in the White House put him abreast of most major policy issues, and he needed no additional guidance in learning the Pentagon or commanding forces. Every indication available to this writer in the fall of 1990 suggested that Cheney and Powell had formed an effective team at the top, reminiscent of the Carlucci-Crowe period.

One could imagine the systemic distortions and dangers that could have existed if a strong, willful secretary of defense such as McNamara, with his congenital distrust of all subordinates and inferiors, categories including just about everybody, from his perspective, had found himself paired with a weak JCS chairman such as—from another era—General George McClellan. In the other direction, distortions might have been even more severe if strong, willful individuals such as Generals Douglas MacArthur, George Patton, or Curtis LeMay, or Admirals Ernest King or Hyman Rickover, had served as JCS chairman while paired with a weak secretary of defense.

Goldwater-Nichols thereby put heavy pressure on the commander in chief in the White House to choose very carefully when appointing people as defense secretary and JCS chairman—in particular, to consider the prospects for effective teamwork between them. Adding a criterion, Admiral Crowe was also once overheard saying that "it could be a real disaster if somebody other than a true 'purple suiter' were ever picked as chairman."

COMPLEX ROLES AND RELATIONSHIPS

The widespread perception of the JCS chairman as the United States' number-one military officer with full command authority illustrated a second point. To the extent that he was in fact a commander, he was an operational commander. He was the only top officer in the Pentagon whose job description required him to be concerned about operational issues—everything pertaining to deployed forces—on a daily basis. This was an unremitting preoccupation for the chairmen serving during the first four years of Goldwater-Nichols, in part because American forces were extensively deployed, maneuvered, augmented, and used in intervention situations during that period.[3] For those who wondered whether the main role model for the chairman under the new law would be that of the war fighter or the staffy thinker, the former clearly predominated during the first four years. What kind of relationship might or should exist, how the labor should be divided, and what kinds of personalities would be ideal as between a secretary and a chairman during a prolonged period of quiescence on the defense scene were matters for conjecture.

The civilian service secretaries and uniformed chiefs, on the other hand, typically had been preoccupied with the somewhat more glamorous but also tedious tasks of deciding on future weapons systems developments and acquisitions. Goldwater-Nichols authorized the chairman also to get deeply into the acquisitions business, through his new vice chairman—more on this later—but several observers expressed concern that no one in the Pentagon would be looking at daily immediate operational matters if everybody including the chairman were preoccupied with the futuristic perspectives inherent in research and development, acquisition, and procurement.

A third key point illustrated by the widespread perception of the chairman as an operational commander was the role model he himself created. One of the great wrangles in drafting Title IV of Goldwater-Nichols was the attempt to set up a newly designated category known as joint specialty officer (JSO). The key Capitol Hill staffers wanted a small and exact number of precise qualifications for the JSO designation, which in turn would be a necessary requirement for promotion to general or admiral. "More congressional micromanagement," bellowed the critics. The separate services had a vested interest in making the number of qualifying jobs and schools as large and as easy as possible, so that no difficult new barriers would be created for top young officers rapidly climbing the career ladder toward star ranks. "The services wanted it to count as a JSO qualification if you ever rode in a carpool with somebody on the Joint Staff," said one source.

Chairman Crowe, in one of his first big decisions under Goldwater-Nichols, picked a compromise number between the small figure desired by Capitol Hill and the gross total preferred by the services. The important discovery, however, was that the number was irrelevant as soon as bright younger officers detected the shift in power toward the chairman and the overall joint arena, away from the services, noticing the chairman's role model as the boss, in an operational sense, for the entire defense establishment. Young officers were typically oriented toward war-fighter operations in any case. No problem existed—contrary to worries expressed on Capitol Hill—in attracting the best young officers to the most demanding joint jobs.

This created a generation gap between the old-timers at the two-star level and higher—most of these retiring in another few years—and those at lower levels. For example, the commandant of the Marine Corps and Admiral Rickover's successor as head of the navy's nuclear programs were a pair of four-star officers adamantly unenthusiastic about forcing any of their people to jump through a set of JSO so-called purple hoops. Yet those younger officers themselves were circumspectly but eagerly looking for a chance at the hoops anyway. It was clear by the end of fiscal 1990, especially since some of the best younger officers would soon be up for their second assignments in joint jobs, that the new joint mentality would quickly pervade the overall officer corps.

The law in addition brightened the new purple fashion by cutting service headquarters staffs an initial 15 percent in advance of further cuts expected for budget-driven reasons, thus helping to level the field between those groups and the Joint Staff. Several interviewees for this essay, adhering to a typical view that power in Washington was a fixed quantity, spoke in terms of a zero-sum game. Given that the chairman, his Joint Staff, the secretary of defense and his staff, and all other joint-arena people were the big "winners" in the "power sweepstakes" inherent in Goldwater-Nichols, the major "losers" were the separate service chiefs and their previously huge staffs. The only people within the separate services who perhaps gained an increment of bureaucratic clout under Goldwater-Nichols were the civilian service secretaries, largely because of their enhanced responsibilities in acquisition and procurement.

One question was whether the new mentality was an internalized belief in the necessity for jointness or merely career opportunism. A four-star true believer said, "Our system raises some 'purple' people, but it doesn't raise enough yet." The numerical quotas for the JSO contingent and related parts of the law represented techniques for generating adequately large quantities while other provisions sought to ensure high quality. Yet even naval officers, historically the most resistant to joint assignments or schools, proved able to read the writing in the bill. The Bureau of Naval Personnel was taking extra steps to ensure that the fast climbers among the younger officers would get required assignments to "good joint duty" so as to remain competitive for flag, or star-rank, promotions on schedule. Moreover, the ones to whom I talked were apparently true believers, wanting to be part of the new quality as well as the new quantity in jointness, internalizing the principles of the new thinking rather than cooperating in a cynical accommodation based on career opportunism. But they still took some paradoxical service pride in believing that the navy had the most to gain, because the navy never before had put its most effective people into the good joint jobs to sell the navy's case.

Every knowledgeable observer in the fall of 1990 seemed eager to remark on the extraordinarily high quality of work coming from the Joint Staff and other joint organizations and offices, given that the services were now assigning their best rather than their leftovers to those jobs. It was a startling reversal from the earlier times when the various joint groups cranked out dull and mostly useless drafts whereas the service staffs, with their monopoly on fast climbers, consistently produced the winning policy papers. Indeed, if there were a problem created by the new orientation, it might have been that too many bright youngsters were crowding into assignments carrying the JSO qualifications even though some of those situations were not especially rigorous. The problem, in short, was that some jobs were attracting more bright and gifted people than they could effectively use just because they carried the newly coveted designations, whereas more demanding jobs elsewhere were starved for talent.

A fourth point needed to be discussed in connection with the widespread perception that the JCS chairman was not only the senior American military officer on active duty—Goldwater-Nichols was quite explicit about this—but was also the operational commander of the armed forces—the law was equally explicit that this was not the case. The question was precisely what did he command, and the answer was the eleven CINCs of the joint unified and specified command system. He became their representative and spokesman, with all of his new powers, in exercising their new forms of participation in the budget, acquisition, and procurement processes. Each CINC in turn was free, under Goldwater-Nichols, to build his force however he thought best for any particular task requirement, without a tacit need to take along some preordained amount of component commander forces from each of the traditional armed services. Under the old system, each service had wanted to make sure it had a full opportunity to strut its stuff in any combat operations under the aegis of a CINC.

In addition, the new law made each CINC responsible for training and logistics down to the component level, which was another new form of power. In summary, the CINCs had been neglected orphans, expected to be ready and able to go to war on short notice but—aside from whatever they got by virtue of being captured by one of the traditional services—with little or no control over their capabilities. Goldwater-Nichols changed all that, dramatically empowering the CINCs themselves and their chairman back in Washington.

The new position of vice chairman of the Joint Chiefs was stipulated to be a four-star officer junior in rank only to the chairman within the entire defense establishment, from a service background other than the chairman's original service. The initial idea was that the chairman needed a senior deputy. Under the old system, there had been a provision for one or another of the chiefs to preside at JCS meetings on a rotational basis if the chairman were absent, and the chairman was also entitled to a three-star assistant and horse-holder.

Perhaps in keeping with the bureaucratic principle that work expands to the limits of those potentially available to do it, a movement gained strength following Goldwater-Nichols to give the new vice chairman a specific set of duties and responsibilities. This meant that the vice chairman had decreasing amounts of spare time to help with the chairman's overall range of duties and instead was increasingly focused on the acquisition and procurement dimensions of the chairman's new work. One key instrument for performing this role was the vice chairman's evolution as chairman of the Joint Requirements Oversight Council (JROC). The JROC was something like the JCS junior varsity, mainly including the vice chiefs of each of the services and assorted others. The function of the JROC was to assist the JCS chairman in making decisions and recommendations about which weapons systems and other military equipment needed to be developed, bought, modified, or canceled in order to meet the potential combat requirements of the CINCs.

The key functions and staff hierarchies pertaining to these matters remained embedded in the services. It was said that no CINC would really want to be driven to take over more of the roles in this category because this would require a major enlargement of the CINC's staff while diverting its attentions from its main focus on operations. But the Congress appeared to like the concept of one-stop shopping whereby it could handle virtually all of its business with the defense establishment by working through the paired secretary on the civilian side and the chairman on the uniformed side. It was a dramatically new approach, but it was part of the new ethos embodying Goldwater-Nichols. It was also conceivable that it could help in alleviating the age-old accountability problem.

THE SECRETARY OF DEFENSE AND REQUIRED REPORTS

Goldwater-Nichols focused primarily on dramatically strengthening the roles and powers of the JCS chairman and the CINCs but in the process also strengthened the secretary of defense by stipulating that almost all of the chairman's new powers were to be exercised ultimately through the secretary. The law also added new offices to the defense secretary's staff empire and made other provisions especially in the budget, acquisition, and procurement category that had the effect of strengthening the secretary.

Among the new mandates potentially strengthening the secretary's hand were new reporting requirements. As for most executive agencies, there was always a requirement for an annual report to the Congress by the secretary of defense. Over the Cold War years, this elaborately produced document came to be known as the "posture statement," describing, explaining, and justifying the military posture of the United States against stipulated threats. But Secretary Cheney from the time of his arrival apparently decided to save money by drastically cutting the size, quality of paper, and distribution list for this yearly document. The same decision applied to the annual booklet *Soviet Military Power* issued by the Defense Intelligence Agency on behalf of the defense secretary. Indeed, Cheney moved to make sharp cuts in the number, quality, and address lists for all the myriad documents produced by the Pentagon.

What these cuts failed to consider was the fundamental usefulness of the annual posture statement and a few of the other reports for an important array of audiences for the secretary of defense beyond the minimally prescribed number for members of Congress. People throughout the defense establishment itself, the think tanks, campus-based defense research specialists, and friendly parties in allied countries—not to mention parties in not-so-friendly governments who would get the reports in any case because they were not classified—needed these reports as authoritative baseline sources for their own projections and contributions to the overall national security effort. Cheney subsequently made some upward modification in his sharp reductions regarding these reports.

Goldwater-Nichols required a new annual National Security Strategy Report from the president. The first, drafted by a military officer on the National Security Council staff, appeared in January 1987, and the second on schedule a year later. The outgoing Reagan team declined to submit a National Security Strategy Report in January 1989 on the reasonable basis that new thoughts should originate with the new administration. The Bush team needed a year—at least—to get organized, publishing its first version in January 1990 in the attractive original format and, some thought, breaking new ground with innovative ideas about new realities after participation by all key White House thinkers including the president himself. Others saw it covering only minimum ground, similar to the annual posture statement, while even more eagerly promoting the White House's main positions of the past year—"more politics than strategy," as one person described it.

Finally, Goldwater-Nichols directed the JCS chairman every three years to submit to the secretary of defense a report recommending any changes needed in the assigned "roles and missions" of the armed forces in order "to achieve maximum effectiveness." Retiring Chairman William Crowe very quietly submitted the first of these documents in classified form as he was on his way out the door in 1989, giving successor Chairman Colin Powell a full three years and into a presumed second two-year term before the next such report was due. This first report amounted to a nifty installation of a time-delay fuse on the most explosive policy time bomb in the Pentagon.

The most recent previous occasion when "roles and missions" were formally discussed was in 1948 when Secretary of Defense James Forrestal took the Joint Chiefs first to Key West and then to Newport in an unsuccessful search for tranquil agreement. If there were ever a single subject guaranteed to arouse maximum controversy especially among the armed services themselves, it was the mere hint of a possible revision of assigned "roles and missions." Assigned "roles and missions" were so professionally sacred that their first articulations were probably enshrined with the bones of Emory Upton, A. T. Mahan, and Billy Mitchell.

CONCLUDING THOUGHTS AND SECOND THOUGHTS

While the sources for this analysis were uniformly persuaded that Goldwater-Nichols was a good and proper step, they communicated a variety of nagging anxieties. Some will be encapsulated in the following.

First, the Goldwater-Nichols Act was based on the assumed continuation of the same unhurried and relatively stable threat environment characterizing the Cold War era, calling for the same kind of incremental changes in American defense capabilities.

Furthermore, it presupposed the same kind of elaborate decision-making structures and processes, with careful considerations and slow reviews at various levels by interagency task forces. But that world and most that it contained had been profoundly altered as of the end of the 1980s. The Panama coup occurred on General Powell's first day in the JCS chairman's office—October 1, 1989. Should he have taken some kind of action prescribed by Goldwater-Nichols?

Secretary of Defense Weinberger regularly held huge decision-making meetings, usually every Monday. Secretary Carlucci cut this to about a dozen people monthly. Cheney further reduced the size and frequency, matching the trend toward far smaller and irregular meetings at the presidential level. Foreign policy—including crisis management—and arms control decisions from the outset of the Bush administration largely were made only by the president with five helpers: National Security Adviser (NSA) Brent Scowcroft, Secretary of State James Baker, and Baker's inner circle of Dennis Ross, Robert Zoellick, and Robert Kimmitt. NSA Scowcroft carefully included Cheney and the JCS chairman when defense policy was the agenda, but defense policy was defined as long-term force building and structuring programs at a time when Persian Gulf events pushed true long-term thinking ever farther into the background than usual.

Admiral Crowe and General Powell probably knew President Bush better on a personal basis than Secretary of Defense Cheney did, and those personal ties counted heavily in Bush administration decision making. The Bush administration also included the closest-ever tie between a president and a secretary of state. Whether Goldwater-Nichols can be consistently applicable and useful in the changing Washington and global environment is a question for conjecture—and for history.

The Goldwater-Nichols Act complemented White House directives in stunning successes toward one major goal: sharply reducing layers in the chain of command between the White House and deployed forces. Command and control had become by 1990 far more efficiently handled. But this very fact constituted a new barrier between the United States and its allies. The allied military commanders came to believe that the American command structure worked with such great fluid efficiency in the aftermath of reforms associated with Goldwater-Nichols that those allied chieftains wanted no more forty-year alliances with the United States along the lines of the North Atlantic Treaty Organization—only short-term, highly specific, limited-goal agreements. The reason: they could never expect to get the reassuring political guidance from their governments that American forces could now obtain quickly; thus the allied commanders feared being swept forward by American forces well beyond the political guidance in hand via the still-awkward and slow command and control arrangements used by their home governments. This explained, it was said, why no combined command system had yet been settled on by allied forces deployed in Saudi Arabia and the Persian Gulf areas as late as November 1, 1990.

Second, several expressed serious concern that the new concept of the joint specialty officer was successful in making JSO assignments but perhaps not in developing leaders. "True in-the-bones jointness does not result from joint staff assignments but must be gained in frequent and intensive joint training exercises and to some extent in PME [professional military education] schools . . . and this is why probable big budget cuts for training exercises and schooling could really hurt us," said one senior officer.

The basic critique was that purpling occurs far too late in an officer's career; by contrast, it should occur very early and probably often, in tactical exercises at low levels. One person mentioned my longstanding proposal to convert service academy curricula into five-year programs, with the first and fifth years in purple-suit environments. It was said that radical ideas of this kind were under consideration by several congressional committees.

Third and similarly, the sources for this essay lauded the efforts particularly by Representative Ike Skelton of the House Armed Services Committee to register significant improvements in the PME system. Some of these changes were reflected in Goldwater-Nichols requirements for the intermediate and senior war colleges to participate more effectively in the new emphasis on increasing the quality and quantity of purple-suit officers. But even those who applauded these changes expressed anxiety that other steps had not been carefully taken.

Some were concerned about the new emphasis on using civilian professors at the PME institutions, wondering if many of these might not turn out to be merely "retreaded military retirees" or, conversely, "immature whippersnapper civilians with their fresh doctoral diplomas but no exposure to 'the real world'—or an appreciation of professional military perspectives."

Even more interviewees were concerned that far too little was being done at the PME schools to assist in the task mandated by the 1986 law to develop new joint doctrine, especially tactical doctrine. "What [should be taught] if there is no doctrinal agreement on what joint forces should do under certain standardized circumstances?" asked one individual.

Fourth, concern was expressed about morale. The quality of young officers and enlisted personnel in all the services was probably better in 1990 by any measure than ever before, all largely agreed, and a national economic downturn—as serious as that would be for everybody—might improve the quality of military personnel even further. But projected budget cuts alongside the extraordinarily complicated new requirements for joint assignments—on top of all the old requirements—would make career management extremely difficult and thus threaten to produce serious morale problems.

Fifth, there was concern about congressional management of defense. Whatever the problems in

the American defense establishment, the primary leadership for change, for exploring new ideas and approaches, and for moving instead of standing still came very largely from Congress over the past decade and was continuing to come from Congress, rather than from the White House or other executive-branch figures. All sources consulted in the research for this analysis agreed on this point, taking an essentially laudatory and admiring look at Congress.

Offsetting this praise, however, was the observation that Congress could not seem to avoid the temptation to "micromanage." A bizarre mix of important and trivial requirements was often found nowadays not in the major bills with understandable labels but in "oddball clauses in reports and riders." The requirements were sometimes hints or threats of congressional action rather than anything more specific, but hints or threats that the Department of Defense felt compelled to take seriously.

Finally, the Department of Defense remembered all too well that it did not take seriously the appeals from Senator William Cohen and others to develop meaningful capabilities for low-intensity conflict potentially involving or including commando or guerrilla squads, underwater swimmers, and small parachute units for missions such as assistance for insurgency and counterinsurgency groups—depending on which side the United States happened to be on in a given situation—hostage rescue, and antiterrorist purposes. These kinds of groups, in the aggregate, came to be called Special Operations Forces.

When the Defense Department dragged its feet on these proposals for most of the first Reagan administration, Senator Cohen and those in agreement with him succeeded in getting an insertion into the Defense Authorization Act in the fall of 1986 that mandated first, a new board at the level of the National Security Council; second, a new assistant secretary of defense for special operations in the Pentagon; and third, a new unified command within the armed forces, headed by the commander in chief of the Special Operations Command.

The board at the National Security Council level was convened for the first time at the end of the Reagan administration, but inconclusively, and a new board was convened soon after the Bush administration took over. James Locher, the staff specialist who wrote the bill for the Senate Armed Services Committee, was named to be the first assistant secretary of defense for Special Operations Forces, low-intensity conflict, in the Pentagon. Overall, it was an unprecedented development, actually another major force program more like a new armed service than a unified command. The command was stood up— that is, it technically came into existence—somewhat like a new warship just after launching but not yet ready for commissioning or action. Choices were still being made between various possibilities for small arms and other equipment, training procedures, and other needs, but people debated whether stacks of paper resembled a cohesive doctrine.

One key conclusion reachable at this point was the likelihood of further unique innovations imposed on the American defense establishment by a Congress at least trying to lead when a White House was unable or unwilling to do so. If the White House itself should successfully assert new leadership, too, the result could be an American defense establishment not resembling anything familiar over the past century at least in terms of organizational formats, structures, and processes. One might even say that Goldwater-Nichols had already accomplished this much. Whether the ultimate bottom-line judgment will prove to be favorable or unfavorable could not yet be guessed.

NOTES

1. The following works, arranged in chronological order, contain substantiating details and further analyses of the history of American defense reorganizations, especially the more recent history leading up to the 1986 Goldwater-Nichols Act: Vincent Davis, "The Evolution of Central U.S. Defense Management," in *Reorganizing America's Defense: Leadership in War and Peace,* ed. Robert J. Art, Vincent Davis, and Samuel P. Huntington (Washington, D.C.: Pergamon-Brassey's, 1985), 149; Davis, "Organization and Management," in *American Defense Annual 1987–1988,* ed. Joseph Kruzel (Lexington, Mass.: D. C. Heath, 1987), 171; Carl H. Builder, *The Masks of War: American Military Styles in Strategy and Analysis* (Baltimore, Md.: Johns Hopkins University Press, 1989); C. Kenneth Allard, *Command, Control and the Common Defense* (New Haven, Conn.: Yale University Press, 1990); James A. Blackwell Jr., and Barry M. Blechman, eds., *Making Defense Reform Work* (Washington, D.C.: Brassey's, 1990).

2. The acronym CINC is pronounced "sink."

3. For example, see the *Economist,* 1 September 1990, 26: "Less than a year into his job, [Chairman of the Joint Chiefs Colin Powell] has deployed American troops six times—twice in Panama, once each in the Philippines, Liberia, El Salvador and now Saudi Arabia."

CHAPTER 6

THE INTELLIGENCE COMMUNITY

U.S. INTELLIGENCE IN AN AGE OF UNCERTAINTY

PAULA L. SCALINGI

U.S. intelligence, after more than forty years of evolution, is at a watershed. Created to counter the threats inherent in a bipolar world, today its mission is no longer relevant. The Union of Soviet Socialist Republics no longer exists. With the primary adversary gone, some national security experts are calling for draconian cuts in U.S. defense spending and for the United States to retreat from its international responsibilities. Among these voices are those who would substantially curtail the U.S. intelligence effort, even dismantle the Central Intelligence Agency (CIA). Most of the U.S. foreign policy establishment, however, with an eye to history, recognize that in an uncertain world a strong intelligence capability is a necessity. Thus it is a matter of determining how best to strengthen and refocus U.S. intelligence to meet the challenges of a new era. Indeed, the extraordinary and unexpected events of the early 1990s—including the conflict in the Persian Gulf, the abortive coup in the Soviet Union, and their respective reverberations—underscore the need for accurate, forward-looking intelligence.

Even before the demise of the USSR, the end of the Cold War, budgetary constraints, and new international uncertainties had reinvigorated long-standing congressional interest in strengthening the individual and collective output of the dozen or so entities that make up the intelligence community. There is currently an emerging consensus within the congressional committees that oversee intelligence that the community is not prepared to meet today's challenges. The House and Senate intelligence committees and the Senate Armed Services Committee made suggestions on reorganization and the need to improve community-wide management in their respective reports on their fiscal 1992 authorization bills.[1] The committees indicated that they intended to take an even more activist approach to reform in calendar year 1992.

Community members, for their part, have undertaken their own internal reviews of programs and resources and have already taken some modest steps. The future role, structure, and, ultimately, effectiveness of U.S. intelligence will depend on how well Congress, the executive branch, and the community cooperate in undertaking the necessary initiatives.

LOOKING FOR A NEW WORLD ORDER

What the international scene will look like in six months, a year, or five years from now is problematical. The post–World War II structure has been swept away and nearly three-quarters of a century of communist rule in the USSR ended. Even the best intelligence analysts know better than to try to predict with any certainty trends and outcomes beyond the immediate.

The major impetus behind the genesis of the intelligence community was the Soviet threat—namely, the threat from the USSR, its allies and friends, Communist regimes, and radical political organizations. With the exception of the CIA, which was created by legislation, the other major community organizations were created by executive directive to cope with requirements generated by the Cold War. Also, unlike the independent CIA, they function as part of a parent agency. (The Defense Intelligence Agency [DIA], the National Security Agency [NSA], and the organization that handles U.S. national technical means systems are technically part of the Department of Defense; the Federal Bureau of Investigation [FBI] is part of the Justice Department, and the State Department's intelligence component is the Bureau of Intelligence and Research. The Departments of Energy and the Treasury and the military services have their own intelligence components.) Successive U.S. administrations have tinkered with the structure and mission of these organizations, often for political reasons, but have never considered a major restructuring.[2]

The CIA, alone among the members of the community, has a comprehensive mission. Its all-source collection and analytical efforts have traditionally covered all regions of the world and functional areas. The Soviet threat, however, until very recently, was the primary target within this broad, international context. Thus CIA components tasked with covering, for example, Central America, the Middle East, or Africa tended to focus on Soviet machinations in those regions. Collection and analysis on technology transfer, emerging technologies, weapons development and monitoring, nonproliferation, and economic analysis were also skewed in that direction.

This essay has been edited and is reprinted from The Washington Quarterly 15 (Winter 1992): 147–56, *by permission of* MIT Press.

Not unexpectedly, many top and midlevel CIA managers have made their reputation as Soviet experts or spent a portion of their career dealing with Soviet-related concerns. For example, both the former deputy director of central intelligence, Richard Kerr, and his former director, Robert Gates, had been Soviet analysts.

For the other community members involved in strategic intelligence—the DIA and the NSA—the Soviet threat has been the paramount focus chiefly because of these agencies' defense orientation. In the area of tactical intelligence, emphasis until very recently was on intelligence support in the event of an East–West conflict.

Through the decades, the amount of funds Congress has pumped into intelligence programs has ebbed and flowed, influenced by the public perception of the relative coolness of U.S.–Soviet relations. The biggest intelligence buildup, however, occurred in the 1980s. As a result of the revolution in Iran and direct or indirect Soviet interventionism in Afghanistan, Poland, Central America, and Africa, there was a broad political consensus in the early Reagan years that intelligence needed to be strengthened with expanded covert action programs, personnel, and technical collection assets.

The community naturally greeted this new state of affairs with considerable enthusiasm, particularly the CIA, which had experienced personnel cuts and a diminished prestige during the Carter administration. The aura of optimism was best expressed by one top intelligence manager, who observed that in the "fat years" U.S. intelligence should move to "stack new officers like cordwood" to prepare for the inevitable belt-tightening in the post-Reagan era.

The result was an unprecedented, and at times uncoordinated, buildup of U.S. intelligence assets—collection and information-processing technologies, personnel, and infrastructure. Intelligence agencies hustled to hire and acquire and to secure more space to house their burgeoning resources. The DIA built a spacious flagship building at Bolling Air Force Base and immediately began lobbying to expand the facility. The CIA constructed a second behemoth building on its headquarters compound, ostensibly to consolidate its workforce, which was dispersed in leased buildings throughout the Washington area. The additional space proved woefully inadequate by the time the structure was completed in 1987. The CIA then leased an even greater number of buildings to handle the overflow and in summer 1991 designated two sites on which to construct large facilities.

In true bureaucratic fashion, the number and scope of intelligence requirements in the 1980s increased to accommodate the rapidly expanding workforce. Within the CIA's Directorate of Intelligence, an analyst tasked with covering a particular country or issue was soon sharing this responsibility with two or more analysts, each now handling a subset of the same account. In certain cases, a branch (the directorate's smallest organizational unit) of a few analysts tasked with a single topic mushroomed into a division several times its original size. Although some of this rapid growth was justified on the basis of new requirements, much of the increase was associated with the emphasis on Soviet and East–West issues. For example, in 1979 the directorate had two analysts specifically tasked with covering the North Atlantic Treaty Organization (NATO) and associated European security issues. By 1988 there were two separate divisions within the Office of European Analysis working on such issues, as well as dozens of analysts in the sprawling Office of Soviet Analysis and other analytical components.

Consequently, turf battles became the norm—between analysts on the same account, within divisions in the same office, and between competing offices. Analysts increasingly found themselves forced to coordinate their work with several components and their many counterparts in different parts of the directorate.

The agencies and organizations involved in defense intelligence also experienced unprecedented overall growth. The DIA, the NSA, and the military services substantially beefed up their collection and analytical capabilities.

By the late 1980s, the community was expanding its focus somewhat beyond the Soviet threat to meet new requirements. State-sponsored terrorism, high-profile espionage cases, and the international drug trade became major areas of concern, leading the director of central intelligence (DCI) to create centers for counterterrorism, counterintelligence, and counternarcotics. The implementation of the Treaty to Eliminate Intermediate-Range Nuclear Forces and anticipated follow-on treaties on conventional and strategic nuclear forces resulted in the expansion of the small arms-control intelligence staff, then part of the CIA's Directorate of Intelligence, into a community-wide body several times the original size and directly under the DCI.

CURRENT AND FUTURE REQUIREMENTS

The demands on the intelligence community today to isolate and assess pressing issues and predict future crises accurately are greater than ever before. The United States has had the luxury for half a century of knowing who its chief adversaries were. Now the world is experiencing one of its periodic eras of instability. The community in the 1990s must be able to cover a diverse array of regional and functional topics and have the personnel and technical resources, as well as management flexibility, necessary to fulfill this mission.

Today, the challenges facing the community are daunting. In the Middle East, the defeat of Iraq has left a power vacuum that its neighbors will move to fill. Third world countries continue to develop weapons of mass destruction with the help of armaments and technologies provided by industrialized nations. The components of the former Soviet empire face an uncertain future. Once again, in Europe and elsewhere, ethnic and nationalist rivalries are threatening to undermine the status quo. It is useful to remember that since the mid–nineteenth century, these forces have helped cause several major and lesser conflicts, including two world wars. As history has shown, the United States can ill afford to take an ad hoc approach to national security planning and act only when the crisis is upon it. Desert Shield/Desert Storm and the subsequent belated discovery of Baghdad's advanced nuclear weapons program are grim reminders of this fact.

Intelligence managers, spurred by budget cutbacks and congressional concerns over the direction of the community in a post–Cold War world, are reassessing and in some cases restructuring the way they do business. The CIA, the DIA, and the NSA have been reviewing their programs and requirements. For example, the CIA has reassigned a portion of its Soviet military and technical experts to other responsibilities and has been downsizing in other areas. The military services are consolidating and coordinating their collection and analytical operations. The Department of Defense (DOD) has adopted a plan that streamlines defense intelligence programs, promotes joint cooperation, and gives the Office of the Secretary of Defense greater coordination responsibilities.

Meanwhile, the congressional oversight committees are holding hearings and collecting data to better determine current and future intelligence needs. The committees have reacted positively to community efforts to strengthen intelligence but note that further initiatives are necessary. The committees also maintain that their own studies are in the early phase and that they intend to be ready to take more vigorous action if the community is reluctant to undertake the necessary steps.[3]

The committees have several areas under study that are of particular importance: creation of a director of national intelligence (DNI), the devising of charters for certain community organizations established by executive directive, consolidation of duplicative programs, identification of the key intelligence requirements for the 1990s, and follow-up on the lessons learned from Operation Desert Shield/Desert Storm.

REORGANIZATION ISSUES

Congressional interest in legislating changes in the leadership structure of the community and devising charters for individual agencies is not new but has fluctuated in concert with the perceived need to strengthen and reform intelligence.[4] This latest congressional push for restructuring and reorienting U.S. intelligence has stemmed, as noted previously, from budgetary constraints and the end of the Cold War. Other factors, however, have a role, including the continued fallout from the Iran-Contra investigation and the recognition that the intelligence community greatly needs consolidation, more cross-component cooperation, and overall better management.

Old ideas to rectify these shortcomings have been resurrected toward this end, including the creation of a cabinet-level director of national intelligence. The rationale is that the CIA has long ceased to be the dominant player in U.S. intelligence while defense intelligence has become a major participant, and that the DCI has no real time or interest in the community as a whole because of his other "hat" as head of the CIA. Critics argue that creating a DNI would only add another layer to the intelligence management structure and that without a power base an intelligence czar would be a toothless tiger.

Another idea is to strengthen the coordination and oversight responsibilities of the intelligence community staff, which has received strong criticism from both within and outside the community. Yet another recommendation is to create an assistant deputy of operations within the CIA to coordinate agency and DOD activities. The position would be filled by a top military officer recommended by the secretary of defense and appointed by the DCI.

KEY REQUIREMENTS

It is clear at this point that certain key issues dominating U.S. interests in the 1990s necessitate adjustments in the focus and scope of the analytical process and in human and technical collection.

Proliferation of Weapons of Mass Destruction. Already emerging as a key intelligence requirement for the 1990s, proliferation of nuclear, chemical, and biological weapons and ballistic missile delivery vehicles has become a top U.S. priority, especially in light of the collapse of the USSR and of the outcome of the United Nations inspections of Iraqi facilities. In the latter case, the failure of U.S. intelligence fully to gauge the magnitude of Baghdad's nuclear weapons program underscores the fact that the community must find ways to improve its collection and analysis in this area.

Political and Economic Developments Associated with the Former Soviet Empire. For the foreseeable future, these developments will remain a number-one intelligence priority. How the map of this vast region will ultimately be redrawn will determine international stability throughout the world, but especially in Europe.

The Strategic Nuclear Threat. Despite the end of the Cold War and the signing of the Strategic Arms Reduction Treaty (START) by the United States and the former Soviet government, the threat remains. Russia now has the lion's share of the USSR's strategic nuclear arsenal. Prior to the failed coup of August 1991, the Soviets had been modernizing their strategic nuclear forces, and it remains to be seen if this trend continues with Russia in the driver's seat. Whatever the case, the 30 to 35 percent force reductions mandated by the as-yet-unratified START treaty would still leave the United States vulnerable to nuclear attack.

Instability in Eastern Europe. Ethnic and nationalist antagonisms, unleashed by the collapse of Communist regimes in the region and the withdrawal of Soviet forces from the territory of the former Warsaw Pact members, have sparked civil war in Yugoslavia and have resurfaced in neighboring countries. Meanwhile, Germany continues to cope with the political and economic fallout from reunification. The impact of such forces on European Community (EC) cohesion and international stability overall must not be underestimated. Although progress toward European unity continues, movement will be slow, and economic problems, including growing unemployment and inflationary pressures, exacerbated by civil conflict, could derail or significantly set back further EC integration.

Potential Areas of Regional Conflict. Operation Desert Shield/Desert Storm starkly revealed the importance of intelligence contingency planning and the difficulty in assessing an adversary's intentions and predicting hostilities. U.S. intelligence needs to do significantly better in this area.

From the early years of its existence, the CIA in particular has periodically been taken to task for not providing adequate warning of impending crises. Unfortunately, Iraq has provided Congress and the media with yet another example of a perceived intelligence shortcoming. U.S. intelligence officials have publicly expressed satisfaction that the community indeed predicted that Saddam Hussein would invade Kuwait shortly before the invasion began and have blamed policy makers for not heeding mounting evidence of possible Iraqi military action. They also maintain that intelligence on Iraq's nuclear capability was good considering the paucity of information. The fact remains, however, that a primary responsibility of intelligence is to provide timely predictions of events that could affect U.S. security and warning of impending crisis or conflict.[5]

A way to improve the odds of timely forecasting of a conflict or crisis is to maintain constant vigilance over potential problem areas. Although the community already keeps watch on the world's trouble spots, it needs to have the capability to mobilize a coordinated response to support regional military operations when and where required (in effect, a movable regional joint intelligence center).

Such an approach would clearly place an additional burden on the intelligence community to create the kind of flexibility in analytical and collection operations that would allow the reassignment of personnel and technical assets to cover different and changing regional targets. It would also require improved dissemination and information-processing capabilities and the development of comprehensive data bases.

For personnel, this would mean training and maintaining language and area studies expertise in more than one country or region. This would be no easy feat, considering that the community currently lacks an adequate cadre of proficient linguists. To encourage the community to move aggressively on this problem, both the House and Senate intelligence committees have proposed initiatives in their respective reports on fiscal 1992 authorization legislation.

Arms-Control Monitoring and Support. In terms of support personnel and technical collection assets, monitoring the new conventional and strategic nuclear arms-control treaties will be a major drain on community resources. U.S. intelligence, by law, is required to monitor treaty compliance by other signatories. This includes all past and future agreements to which the United States is a party. Although the future direction of arms control has yet to emerge, it is likely that the United States will push to wrap up the multilateral chemical weapons agreement, to revitalize negotiations on defense and space systems, to move toward further limits on nuclear testing, and to initiate negotiations aimed at strengthening agreements on nonproliferation.

ECONOMIC ISSUES

In the last few years economic intelligence has been oversold as a major requirement both by top intelligence officials and the media. The traditional community focus on reporting international economic developments, emerging technologies, and technology transfer is an area in which U.S. intelligence has performed relatively well. More should be done, particularly on the latter two topics, and ongoing programs strengthened where possible.

The concept of economic intelligence, however, has lately expanded to mean something more than these traditional concerns. Although this "something" remains undefined, the idea is that the intelligence community should help policy makers and business interests make U.S. industry more competitive.[6]

Although this is an admirable goal, several factors militate against such a role for U.S. intelligence. Today, in an era of multinational corporations and international cooperation in research and development and operations, it is difficult to define what legally constitutes a U.S. company or a U.S. product. According to the former deputy director of central intelligence, Richard Kerr, U.S. intelligence has no role in industrial espionage or the collection and dissemination of corporate secrets. Other current and former top intelligence officials have also pointed out that there is a problem in determining what business enterprises the intelligence community should target and what entities, apart from the U.S. government, should receive such information.

Environmental intelligence is yet another area that has been emphasized as a key focus for the 1990s. U.S. intelligence routinely covers natural and man-made disasters and the politics of international environmental issues. Although environmental issues are an increasingly important concern, they are not a high priority compared with other more pressing intelligence requirements.

THE NEED FOR FLEXIBILITY

It should be kept in mind that the key issues noted previously are those that demand attention today. Within a matter of weeks, if not days, however, some of these requirements may have changed focus or new issues come to the fore. The community must constantly monitor intelligence requirements and should place greater emphasis on long-range predictions (i.e., a time frame beyond six months). Unlike the media, which focuses only on the event of the moment, the community must always be looking ahead. Unfortunately, U.S. intelligence has increasingly been paying lip service to its responsibility to predict while in reality withstanding pressures to lean forward and postulate possible outcomes or assign percentage values to the likelihood of future developments. The community routinely produces National Intelligence Estimates that policy makers and intelligence officials agree offer scenarios in terms of broad generalities. Today, the intelligence that "really sells downtown" (at the National Security Council and White House) is analysis that is directly tailored to the immediate concerns of top U.S. policy makers. Typescript memos, situation reports, and other forms of current intelligence, unlike long-range analysis, often elicit positive feedback from policy makers. Although the community's responsibility is to support such efforts, it must not become so caught up in the psychic rewards of current intelligence that its long-range analytical capability suffers.

The recommended emphasis on the key issues outlined above does not mean that the community should curtail its fulfillment of traditional intelligence responsibilities. It is rather a matter of judiciously reallocating shrinking resources to maintain and enhance capabilities to deal with ongoing requirements while building up analytical and, particularly, human collection resources. Considering the duplicative and overlapping programs within the community today, there appears to be ample room for creative restructuring and reorientation.

IS MORE BETTER?

In light of these suggestions, the intelligence agencies need to take a hard look at their analytical output and determine whether the quantity produced is justified. The number of reports, memorandums, and studies the community generates daily has dramatically increased in the last ten years, chiefly as a result of the great expansion of the analytical force and enhanced technical collection rather than the demands of consumers. In the mid-1980s, Robert Gates, then head of the CIA's Directorate of Intelligence, on a number of occasions publicly pointed to the jump in the number of longer analytical studies produced by the CIA as evidence of improvement in the quality of intelligence. Also, during this period, the number of pages of the *National Intelligence Daily,* the CIA's vehicle for current intelligence, doubled and a new special "in-brief" section provided abbreviated information on additional topics not deemed worthy of in-depth treatment. The idea was that any data of intelligence value should be duly noted, if only for the record.

Greater selectivity in choosing items for publication can free up shrinking analytical assets to focus on key areas. In addition, analysts covering low-priority accounts could handle two or more countries or functional issues.

INTELLIGENCE AND DESERT SHIELD/DESERT STORM

The war in the Persian Gulf has significantly influenced intelligence requirements for the 1990s as the Department of Defense and the intelligence community assess the successes and shortcomings of the U.S. intelligence effort. There appears to be an emerging consensus that close cooperation among tactical and strategic intelligence organizations is crucial in wartime. According to a preliminary DOD study on the conflict, there was an unprecedented level of such cooperation, but there were also areas where the effort fell short.[7] The report observes that a month after the Iraqi invasion the Pentagon established a Joint Intelligence Center (JIC) in Washington to provide coordinated defense intelligence to send to the military theater. A similar center was established in Saudi Arabia to provide on-the-spot support to the theater commander in chief. The report points out that overall the advanced level of operational cooperation among U.S. military services was not reflected in a similar "jointness" on the part of intelligence agencies. In particular, the report cites the need to develop "compatible intelligence and communications systems" to provide timely data. The report also underscores the need for better imagery reconnaissance systems to provide tactical intelligence support and better ways to disseminate imagery to tactical intelligence consumers. The report, in addition, calls for the development of a broad, all-weather search surveillance system to provide better intelligence to commanders in the field.[8]

The above shortcomings were first aired publicly by the U.S. central commander in chief, General Norman Schwarzkopf, in mid-June 1991. Schwarzkopf also pointed to battlefield damage assessment as "one of the major areas of confusion," claiming that the CIA and the DIA provided far more conservative estimates of damage to Iraqi forces by U.S. air operations and artillery than the Central Command.[9]

The general's charges were publicly countered by Kerr, who observed that the general's "complaints should be taken with a grain of salt," adding that intelligence support for the war was excellent and asking, "What more would you expect?"[10]

The DOD views, however, received a sympathetic audience on Capitol Hill, motivating the Senate Intelligence Committee and Senate Armed Services Committee to include in their reports on their fiscal 1992 authorization bills several recommendations and directives aimed at addressing the problem areas. For example, the committees mandated CIA participation in joint intelligence centers under DOD direction and recommended the creation of "a DOD imagery manager" to oversee and standardize all defense imagery systems.[11]

OUTLOOK

It is unclear at this time whether the current impetus toward intelligence restructuring and reorientation will result in meaningful initiatives by Congress or the intelligence community. Although there are compelling factors behind the revitalized interest in intelligence reform, equally weighty factors could block any real progress. Not unexpectedly, many current and former intelligence leaders see no need to go beyond limited fine-tuning of priorities and programs. Sentiment within Congress has yet to coalesce around any particular major new courses of action. The continued fallout from the demise of the Soviet empire and other pressing international issues will demand constant congressional monitoring. Moreover, domestic politics will be competing with international concerns for the attention of Congress and the executive branch.

Lastly, Congress will expect the new DCI to move vigorously to implement its recommendations and other initiatives and will be amenable to allowing sufficient time for a response. The DCI, more than any other single variable, will influence the future direction of U.S. intelligence. In the final analysis, the personality, goals, and vision of the new DCI will largely determine whether U.S. intelligence emerges stronger in the next administration or clings defensively to the status quo. Congress can recommend, direct, and legislate changes, but without a forward-looking individual to reshape the community for the future, U.S. intelligence will remain poorly prepared to meet the challenges of the 1990s and beyond.

NOTES

The views expressed in this paper are those of the author and do not necessarily reflect those of the House Permanent Select Committee on Intelligence or the U.S. government.

1. U.S. House of Representatives, Permanent Select Committee on Intelligence, *Report on the Intelligence Authorization Act, Fiscal Year 1992*, 15 May 1991; U.S. Senate, Select Committee on Intelligence, *Report on Authorizing Appropriations for Fiscal Year 1992 for Intelligence Activities of the U.S. Government*, 24 July 1991; U.S. Senate, Committee on Armed Services, *Report on the National Defense Authorization Act for Fiscal Years 1992 and 1993*, 19 July 1991. (The Senate Armed Services Committee has responsibility for defense intelligence matters. Thus it shares oversight responsibility with the Senate Select Committee on Intelligence. This distinct division of labor is not reflected in the House of Representatives, where the House Permanent Select Committee on Intelligence traditionally has had broad responsibility for intelligence oversight.)

2. For a synopsis of the history of intelligence reform, see Alfred B. Prado, *Intelligence Reform Issues* (Washington, D.C.: Congressional Research Service, updated 16 November 1990).

3. U.S. House, *Report on the Intelligence Authorization Act*; U.S. Senate, *Report on Authorizing Appropriations*.

4. Prado, *Intelligence Reform*, 1–2.

5. For a discussion of warning intelligence, see Art Hulnick, "The Intelligence Producer-Policy Consumer Linkage: A Theoretical Approach," *Intelligence and National Security* 1 (May 1986): 223–24; U.S. House, *Report on the Intelligence Authorization Act*, 17–18.

6. "The New Spy Wars," *U.S. News and World Report*, 3 June 1991, 22.

7. Department of Defense, *Conduct of the Persian Gulf Conflict: An Interim Report to Congress* (Washington, D.C.: Government Printing Office, July 1991), 14-1, 14-3.

8. Ibid., 14-3.

9. *New York Times*, 13 June 1991, A-1.

10. *Oregonian*, 16 July 1991.

11. U.S. Senate, *Report on Authorizing Appropriations*, 5–8; U.S. Senate, *Report on the National Defense Authorization Act*, 17–20.

GLASNOST FOR THE CIA

DAVE McCURDY

During the Cold War, the purpose of the U.S. intelligence community was clear. American intelligence was a spyglass focused on the Soviet Union, keeping track of Soviet military research and development and watching Soviet activities throughout the developing world. U.S. intelligence caught other things only in its peripheral vision. Now the Cold War is over. But its passing has hardly put an end to conflict, instability, or history.

COMING IN FROM THE COLD

A dozen world hot spots clamor for attention, from Bosnia to North Korea, from Angola to Armenia, from Cambodia to Somalia. New areas of dispute—religious, ethnic, and national rather than ideological—threaten to replace the U.S.—Soviet standoff as the engines of world instability. At the same time, the United States has undertaken the herculean task of shepherding Eastern Europe and Russia through divisive and incredibly expensive economic and political reforms. In short, the Cold War has bequeathed an uncertain legacy to the economically and socially exhausted West; and if anything, U.S. intelligence must now come to resemble a wide-angle lens, focusing equally on a host of different countries and issues. In a time of geopolitical uncertainty and sharp cutbacks in U.S. defense spending, the flexibility and foresight provided by good intelligence may be America's most important foreign policy and defense asset in coming years.

In this new era, many U.S. defense doctrines and institutions must be reformed—and no reforms are more important than those focusing on intelligence. While reforms in budgeting and organization are badly needed, thinking about U.S. intelligence requirements must begin with a fundamental reassessment of what the United States needs its intelligence services to do. What kind of information should they collect? To what uses will that information be put? We must redefine the nature of intelligence itself.

A major underlying theme of the following analysis is that the U.S. intelligence community needs a new defining mission, an overarching purpose like the Cold War's emphasis on containing Soviet expansion, that serves to focus and justify the community's efforts. Many short-run tasks, from peacekeeping to regional conflict, will demonstrate the importance of good intelligence. But in the long run, the leaders of U.S. intelligence will need a grander notion of what

they are about, a more sweeping definition of their job. Today, that defining mission can be the same one that justified the founding of the present intelligence community in 1947: to foresee and help prevent catastrophic attacks against the United States—that is, to avoid future Pearl Harbors, of whatever type.

During his 1992 campaign and the early weeks of his presidency, Bill Clinton articulated three organizing principles of U.S. foreign policy. These points provide a sound basis for crafting post–Cold War U.S. priorities abroad, and by extension for outlining U.S. intelligence needs. They include

- revitalizing U.S. economic strength and competitiveness,

- promoting democracy abroad, and

- maintaining a strong defense posture.

American intelligence capabilities must be geared, over the next decade, to serve these goals.

OPENING UP INTELLIGENCE

As intelligence has become more important, it has also become more challenging. There are many reasons for this, but three stand out. One is the advent of what might be called "the CNN era"—the near-instantaneous reporting of news and events from around the world, broadcast complete with pictures and instant analysis by reporters and media-contracted experts. Intelligence must now be more rapid and thorough than ever before to allow decision makers to respond speedily, and it must be accurate enough to allow public officials to correct the truncated, sound-bite version of events so often provided by television news. At the same time, the CNN era has broadened the American public's interest in foreign affairs; crises that in the past might have been ignored in Washington now receive daily news coverage, focusing public attention and ensuring that decisions will have to be taken—and that intelligence will be required.

The second challenge has to do with the blurring of lines between geopolitical categories. With U.S. political leaders now concerned with economic renewal and international trade, it is more and more difficult to separate economic policy from foreign and defense policy; because all of America's relationships with other major powers now involve elements

This essay has been edited and is reprinted from Foreign Affairs 73 *(January/February 1994): 125–40, by permission of* Foreign Affairs. *Copyright 1994 by the Council on Foreign Relations, Inc.*

of competition and of cooperation, it is perhaps more difficult to tell friend from foe. All of this makes it more difficult for the managers of U.S. intelligence agencies to know where to focus their resources, and there is a danger that U.S. intelligence activities could become so thinly spread among various crises and issues that the quality of analysis will suffer.

America's most basic challenge, however, relates to the way its intelligence services interact with other areas of society. Much of U.S. Cold War policy was aimed at promoting reform in the former Soviet Union, but ironically, what the U.S. intelligence community may need more than anything today is a little glasnost of its own. In many cases, the deepest reservoirs of expertise about developing countries lie in our academic and business communities. Even on the military front what is needed is in-depth analysis of a regime's intentions, not laundry lists of its weaponry. This is especially true of the former Soviet bloc, where hundreds of U.S. firms have established operations; their experiences and observations would provide a wealth of information to intelligence analysts. American analysts would benefit from more access to colleagues outside the community and more freedom to share their impressions with people on Capitol Hill and in academia, business, and international organizations. The intelligence agencies must make it possible for analysts to spend a great deal of time living in their regions of specialty, building a knowledge of the situation on the ground and making friends and acquaintances who will serve as long-term sources of information. This process will encourage analysts to cast a wider net and will help reinvigorate the image of the intelligence community among those other constituencies. One hopes, as a result, that there will be growth in the already abundant pride and professionalism within the community.

The more open the intelligence process is, moreover, the more useful it will be to its customers. A broader canvas of opinion will produce better analysis and will allow analysts, rather than bureaucrats, to work more closely with decision makers themselves. Openness will also address a persistent difficulty faced by intelligence analysts: the uneven attention given to intelligence by policy makers. Even the best intelligence is useless if policy makers ignore it. There is no permanent cure for this problem, but an executive branch official or legislator will be less likely to ignore a warning issued from someone he or she has known for years and has learned to be reliable and accurate.

INTELLIGENCE AND ECONOMIC STRENGTH

The Clinton administration's most important task, and the mandate on which it was elected, is to reinvigorate the U.S. domestic economy. Already the administration has proposed plans to reduce the federal deficit, invest in U.S. industries and workers, and reform the health care system.

Defense and foreign policy can play an important role in domestic economic renewal. U.S. security commitments can promote regional stability and the free flow of commerce and trade. Through forward-deployed military forces, the United States can defend key economic interests, such as Persian Gulf oil supplies, and nourish friendships and alliances abroad that provide leverage in trade negotiations.

Those missions require traditional military and political intelligence. But the broader connection between defense and foreign policy (and thus intelligence) and economic performance raises an important —and troubling—question: to what degree should existing U.S. intelligence capabilities be used for economic, as opposed to military or political, purposes? Should U.S. satellites and spies look for the designs of Japanese steel yards or the plans for a new German optical device rather than the next Russian bomber?

At stake in the answer to these questions, which R. James Woolsey Jr., former director of the Central Intelligence Agency (CIA), called "the hottest current topic in intelligence policy," may be not only the mission of U.S. intelligence services, but the whole tenor of international relations. If the world's major trading powers begin viewing each other with suspicion, hoarding economic breakthroughs like atomic secrets and monitoring each other like enemies, the world could easily slide into an economic version of the Cold War.

This issue is not at all theoretical. U.S. allies have long used intelligence services to spy on foreign firms for economic purposes, and Russia—with a vast intelligence apparatus and little idea what to do with it—may expand its decade-old program of industrial espionage. Public attention was focused on this issue in April 1993, with the disclosure that the CIA had warned U.S. defense firms of espionage directed at them by French intelligence.

Any effort to approach the problem of economic intelligence will face a variety of complications. The United States and its allies differ sharply on this issue. Many important U.S. trading partners in Europe and Asia have long viewed economic performance as a critical variable of national power and see nothing wrong with using their intelligence assets to enhance that performance. One German official reacted to the alleged French action by suggesting that "no self-respecting intelligence agency would not obtain information in this manner."

Increasing U.S. and allied reliance on dual-use equipment and other attempts to gain the most civilian economic benefits from military spending further blurs the distinction between civilian and military initiatives. It will become correspondingly difficult to distinguish between military and economic espionage. If a Russian spy is caught looking for secrets about the U.S. National Space Plane, for example, has he or she been caught conducting military or economic espionage? What if the spy is

French; is there such a thing as military espionage conducted against allies, as the Jonathan Pollard case suggested? In addition, the end of the Cold War has made it more difficult to tell adversaries from allies. Polls indicate that the American people now view Japan as a greater threat to national security than Russia. I do not agree, but that perception illustrates how difficult it will be to balance the competitive and cooperative elements of our major relationships in the years ahead.

The activities of multinational companies further cloud the picture. How is one to determine today to which country a particular business belongs? Many modern industrial giants have large operations in several, or even many, countries; which ones deserve U.S. protection? Would Washington protect from espionage all companies doing research in the United States—even Japanese ones? What if an American firm relocated its headquarters abroad but kept many manufacturing sites in the United States; would it still qualify for protection?

The definition of industrial espionage also remains vague. U.S. analysts routinely look at foreign economic trends and occasionally brief U.S. executives on this information; U.S. intelligence agencies provide support to U.S. officials attending various economic summits; and the CIA keeps track of other countries' attempts to steal U.S. industrial secrets. At what point does this activity reach a critical mass and deserve the title "industrial espionage"?

There may be some distinction between active and passive industrial espionage. Active measures would be those designed to acquire industrial secrets through spying, such as placing an agent in a U.S. defense firm and using him or her to steal the designs for new equipment. Passive steps would refer to the gathering of economic intelligence only indirectly—as part, for example, of a general national assessment or a specific operation designed to acquire political or military facts. Admittedly, while such a distinction may exist in theory, it would be hard to sustain, and especially to enforce, in practice.

What, then, should the U.S. position be on economic intelligence? Two policies seem clearly justified. One is counterintelligence. U.S. spy services must keep a careful watch on the industrial espionage conducted by other countries and warn U.S. firms that have been targeted. Defending U.S. economic secrets can reveal interesting facts itself: if a particular country is targeting a specific industry, that may indicate something about that country's economic priorities.

Second, U.S. intelligence services should continue gathering detailed economic data about dozens of other countries. U.S. officials use this information when making various economic and trade decisions. Economic intelligence will also continue to play a major role in country risk assessments, analyses of foreign military potential, and other political-military intelligence, thereby helping U.S. leaders avoid an economic Pearl Harbor in which our major trade competitors achieve a sudden breakthrough in economic policies or practices. And the intelligence community can share more open-source information with U.S. companies, including currently classified translations of unclassified foreign publications. But these activities will not be conducted for the purpose of acquiring trade secrets.

Finally, there is the ultimate question. Should the United States place its intelligence apparatus in the service of its businesses? In 1929 Secretary of State Henry Stimson decided to close his department's code-breaking agency; twenty years later, he explained his decision with the caustic remark that "gentlemen do not read each other's mail." Is our reluctance to engage in industrial espionage as anachronistic today as that sentiment had become by 1948?

I do not believe that it is. For one thing, there are the risks mentioned above: economic espionage could undermine relations among the major trading partners, making political cooperation and free trade agreements less likely and setting the stage for a return to confrontation in the West. The hope for a new concert of major powers united against aggression and tyranny would not long survive a round of economic warfare.

Even more fundamentally, however, the information gained through industrial espionage would have only a marginal impact on U.S. economic performance. Individual trade secrets are seldom profound enough to shape the activity of an entire economy. Most of the time, in fact, U.S. businesses know exactly what their competitors are doing and why it works; the "secrets" of Japanese automobiles or German optics did not remain hidden for long. Even the macroeconomic strategies of most major trade powers and their primary corporations are reasonably well known today. The problem for U.S. businesses is not so much a lack of information, but applying the tactics and techniques used by others to U.S. operations.

The world's major economic powers have little to gain and much to lose in industrial espionage. The United States might therefore consider leading an international effort to ban active industrial espionage. This ban would be an international treaty that could do for economic spying what the General Agreement on Tariffs and Trade aims to do for protectionism. The treaty might even actively encourage openness and the sharing of information, the better to promote scientific research, technological breakthroughs, and economic development.

Such a treaty will clearly take some persuasion and cajoling, as well as some hair-splitting definitions of what is and what is not permitted. But even an agreement that is not universal in application would be helpful in moving the major economic powers toward greater openness while providing a means of punishment if egregious violations are uncovered.

PROMOTING DEMOCRACY

President Clinton is also dedicated to the promotion of democracy abroad. The spread of democracy and free-market economies would clearly abet U.S. interests: democracies are less likely to go to war or undermine stability than authoritarian states. Especially in Eastern Europe and the former Soviet Union, the success of the democratic experiment is of vital importance to the United States.

Once again, rapid news reporting has complicated the U.S. task. Television pictures of human-rights abuses, either persistent violations or sudden outbursts such as the Tiananmen Square massacre, can inflame U.S. public opinion and mandate a U.S. response. The media played the decisive role in forcing U.S. involvement (such as it was, and is) in both the Somalia and Bosnia crises.

But the debate over human rights is seldom about ends; it is about means. The United States and many other nations would benefit from the evolution of a fully democratic China, for example, ruled by moderate and responsible elected officials answerable to their people. The question is how to bring about such an outcome.

In general, there are two schools of thought on this question. The "engagement" school contends that isolation nurtures tyranny and that opening up authoritarian states—trading with them, encouraging outside investment and communications—is the surest way to promote reform and, eventually, democracy. The "sanctions" school rejects these ideas. Authoritarian states are expert at using outside economic investment and trade to prop up their inherently inefficient regimes, this school insists. It contends that the best way to promote democracy is to isolate repressive regimes and impose sanctions until they carry out the desired democratic reforms.

In promoting human rights and democracy, therefore, our fundamental choice is whether to engage or to isolate, to encourage or to demand. In the past, the choice was often made for strategic or political reasons having little to do with democracy. China benefited from engagement, for example, because of its importance in the global balance of power, while Vietnam is left out of U.S. trade and diplomatic circles because of the POW/MIA issue.

Over time the strategic and political straitjacket that has bound U.S. policy on these issues may loosen. The United States may soon be left, then, to decide whether to promote democracy more on the merits of the case than on standards imposed by strategic or political concerns. Some observers will view this as a liberating process, but in fact it will impose new burdens on U.S. decision makers. Already President Clinton faces this question on China: what is the best strategy for achieving his stated goal of promoting human rights, democracy, and free markets? This process will be complicated by the fact that the sanctions-versus-engagement issue can only be resolved on the merits of each case.

In many cases, U.S. leaders will use their intelligence services to make these tough choices. They will ask about the political situation in undemocratic states, the prospects of the regimes there, and the likely effect of various U.S. policies. A perfect example today is U.S. policy toward China: reliable information on Chinese political prisoners, repression of dissent, use of prison labor, treatment of Tibetans, and related subjects such as missile sales will be absolutely indispensable to the formation of a sound U.S. policy. The same is true in Vietnam and many other cases.

Equally important will be the U.S. intelligence assessment of the status of reforms under way in countries that are attempting to make the transition to democracy and free markets, particularly within the former Soviet Union. If there is to be another coup in Moscow, for example, U.S. policy makers will want to know—and have some informed suggestions about how to help head it off—in advance. If two East European nations are about to go to war, Washington cannot help avoid the conflict if it is not aware of the risks. This sort of information will give warning of the most catastrophic possible attack of all, the most devastating replay of Pearl Harbor imaginable: a nuclear or conventional surprise attack from Russia, unthinkable today but conceivable again if the far right in Moscow comes to power.

OPERATIONAL INTELLIGENCE

Another broad issue facing the intelligence community is how to conduct operational military intelligence in support of America's second pillar of foreign policy: a strong defense posture. In regional wars such as the Persian Gulf War and a host of other military operations, the United States will continue to defend and promote its interests as it did during the Cold War. But the nature of both the military operations themselves and modern warfare have undergone a profound shift, and intelligence must evolve to accommodate this fact.

The advent of instant news reporting from around the globe poses its own challenges to operational intelligence. As in the Persian Gulf War, the U.S. military will need continuing battlefield reports to keep the media and public opinion satisfied. Rapid news reporting is often incorrect or exaggerated and at best provides only a snapshot of the real situation. It is the journalistic equivalent of a satellite photo, providing some basic, often misleading facts and very little in-depth information. Intelligence serves as a check on such clipped news reporting, rounding out the picture and giving leaders the information they need to offer a more balanced view of events. Accurate wartime intelligence can provide images of successful U.S. air strikes, interdictions at sea, or ground assaults.

All major U.S. military actions in the coming years will be multilateral enterprises. The United States will bring to such operations no commodity more valuable than its ability to collect information. Modern, broadly based, high-technology intelligence collection remains an area of unique U.S. competency, one that contributes disproportionately to the success of collective enterprises. In the Persian Gulf War, U.S. intelligence on the whereabouts of Iraqi combat forces, headquarters units, supply depots, and other assets provided the coalition with a devastating advantage on the battlefield. U.S. satellite imagery has also played a central role in marshaling international concern about the North Korean nuclear program.

But multilateralism will also pose new challenges for the U.S. intelligence community. Perhaps the two most pertinent questions are what information should be shared with allies, and how that sharing should be facilitated. The impulses of the community itself are not always helpful: in the North Korean case, former CIA Director Robert Gates had to overrule powerful objections and force the agency to share satellite photos with the International Atomic Energy Agency, and once he left his post CIA analysts promptly made a new attempt to undermine the policy. Promoting intelligence sharing among allies will also be an uphill battle as long as national defense procurement systems continue to downplay collaborative defense programs in such areas as command, control, and communications.

Leaders in the U.S. defense establishment and intelligence community should fight against both of these biases. The new emphasis on openness should extend not only to the U.S. government but also to the coalitions, alliances, and international organizations that will legitimize and support U.S. military action in the future. For the most part, the resulting international cooperation and solidarity will far outweigh the risk of leaking secrets about U.S. intelligence capabilities.

U.S. intelligence requirements are also profoundly affected by the growing prominence of peacekeeping and "peace enforcement" missions. U.S. military forces in the years ahead are likely to conduct far more operations like those in Somalia and Bosnia than that of the full-scale Persian Gulf War. Peacekeeping operations call for new and unfamiliar forms of information—detailed knowledge of the political, economic, and geographic topography of dozens of developing countries. Long-term socioeconomic assessments should help us predict famines, civil strife, the collapse of governments, and other events related to peacekeeping. Our difficulties in Somalia have again highlighted the need for better intelligence in such efforts.

Finally, the nature of large-scale warfare is changing dramatically. New technologies are transforming the way militaries fight, an effect seen dramatically in the Persian Gulf War. But the high-technology precision weapons used there represent just the first wave of new equipment that will produce what many are calling a "military-technical revolution."

The most telling features of this new era in warfare will be speed and precision. Modern technologies significantly increase the tempo of war: while before it might have taken hours, days, or even weeks to relay a message to deployed military forces, today battles are a real-time affair. The information loop of war, running from the detection of enemy forces to intelligence analysts, command headquarters, and eventually to friendly troops in the field, must now be compressed into a matter of minutes.

In order to remain relevant to this accelerated process of war, battlefield intelligence must be acquired, processed, analyzed, and disseminated with incredible speed. In fact, the distinction between intelligence and operations is becoming blurred. The revolution in warfare means that a number of military functions—intelligence, surveillance, targeting, and command and control—are collapsing into one another. This trend is graphically represented by such aircraft as the Airborne Warning and Control System and the Joint Surveillance and Targeting System, single platforms that perform many of these functions at once.

Operational intelligence must therefore become more readily available to combat forces and their commanders. Moreover, they should be fully integrated into the conduct of battle. At the same time, the providers of military intelligence must give more attention to the unique challenges posed by humanitarian, peacekeeping, and peace enforcement missions in the developing world.

In a larger sense, this same operational intelligence will be of great value in preventing other countries from achieving a decisive military advantage. By keeping track of the technologies, weapons, and tactics employed by potential adversaries, we can ensure that none of those capabilities will take us by surprise in a major war, that U.S. weapons will not suddenly be rendered obsolete by a stunning technological advance in another country. In this sense, operational intelligence will help us avoid a military-technical Pearl Harbor.

A NEW APPROACH TO INTELLIGENCE

The diffusion of intelligence requirements among a dizzying number of countries and issues highlights the value of a somewhat more centralized process of intelligence management. We need a stronger, unified hand at the helm of our analytical agencies, or we risk fracturing our efforts and duplicating our analysis at a time when our shrinking intelligence budgets make such inefficiency especially dangerous.

In many cases the forms of intelligence needed today cannot be gathered by high-tech satellites or aircraft. U.S. decision makers will more than ever need accurate estimates of the software rather than hardware of international politics—the beliefs, thought processes, and intentions of potential adversaries. Human intelligence, the much-praised but still neglected aspect of our intelligence apparatus, should receive more emphasis in the years ahead. This does not call for a profusion of new spies aimed at foreign governments, but for more analysts on the scene who understand the local dynamics.

Finally, any effort to reform the process of intelligence must keep in mind that the U.S. intelligence community is not a series of wire diagrams; it is a community of people. Their ability, dedication, and professionalism will determine the quality of the analysis that the community produces. The primary focus of any new plan for the intelligence community should be to improve even further the already admirable quality of its analysts, in part by making intelligence a more rewarding, stimulating, open, and uncontroversial career.

To do so, we must expand the exchange of information between analysts and colleagues outside the community; conduct more congressional briefings in open hearings (as was done with the CIA's July 1993 summary of conditions in Cuba); institutionally separate, to the degree possible, analysts from covert action; make individual analysts available to policy makers on a more regular basis; invite respected academics for sabbatical years or other short- to medium-term stints in the community; and encourage the wider use of open-source data and a reduction in the classification levels of intelligence community material. Each of these ideas carries risks, but they combat a greater danger—the gradual alienation of

the intelligence community from policy makers, the academic and business communities, and American society as a whole.

OUR FIRST LINE OF DEFENSE

The world is changing, and the way in which the United States targets and gathers its intelligence will change as well. The post–Cold War era calls for a leaner, more integrated, and above all more open U.S. intelligence community, with stronger lines of communication both to nongovernmental experts and to intelligence consumers. As suggested by the foregoing, this is an enormously difficult task. But the needed reforms have already begun, and with proper guidance, we can mold U.S. intelligence services into what they must be: our first line of defense against a disorderly world.

PREPARING FOR THE TWENTY-FIRST CENTURY

COMMISSION ON THE ROLES AND CAPABILITIES OF THE U.S. INTELLIGENCE COMMUNITY

The Commission on the Roles and Capabilities of the U.S. Intelligence Community was chartered by Congress in October 1994 to conduct a comprehensive review of American intelligence. The Cold War had ended, and it was prudent to reexamine a costly government activity closely tied to that era.

Legislative attempts in the early 1990s to restructure and reform intelligence had not been seen as producing significant change. Reform efforts within the executive branch had proceeded by fits and starts. Intelligence agencies touted new forays into areas such as intelligence on the environment, leading many observers to conclude they had lost focus and were searching for reasons to justify their existence.

In addition, new questions arose about the competence and accountability of intelligence agencies. The Aldrich Ames espionage case, in particular, raised concerns not only about the failure of the Central Intelligence Agency (CIA) to detect a rather clumsy spy in its midst but also about the degree to which the agency holds accountable those responsible.

By the fall of 1994 Congress decided the time had come for a "credible, independent, and objective review of the Intelligence Community" and established this commission to perform it. Nineteen separate areas were identified for assessment.

The commission began operations on March 1, 1995, and conducted a rigorous inquiry during the following twelve months. It received formal testimony from eighty-four witnesses, and its staff interviewed over two hundred other individuals. Members of the commission visited several foreign countries with which the United States has cooperative relationships in the intelligence area, and the commission reviewed a large amount of written opinion on intelligence issues.

OVERALL FINDINGS AND CONCLUSIONS

The commission concludes that the United States needs to maintain a strong intelligence capability. U.S. intelligence has made, and continues to make, vital contributions to the nation's security, informing its diplomacy and bolstering its defenses. While the focus provided by the superpower struggle of the Cold War has disappeared, there remain sound and important roles and missions for American intelligence.

At the same time, the performance of U.S. intelligence can be improved:

- Intelligence must be closer to those it serves. Intelligence agencies need better direction

This essay has been edited and is reprinted from Preparing for the 21st Century: An Appraisal of U.S. Intelligence, *Report of the Commission on the Roles and Capabilities of the United States Intelligence Community (Washington, D.C.: GPO, 1996), xv–xxv. Public Domain.*

from the policy level, regarding both the roles they perform and what they collect and analyze. Policy makers need to appreciate to a greater extent what intelligence can offer them and be more involved in how intelligence capabilities are used. Intelligence must also be integrated more closely with other functions of government, such as law enforcement, to achieve shared objectives.

- Intelligence agencies should function more closely as a "community." The present organizational arrangement does not provide sufficiently strong central direction. Authority is dispersed, and administrative barriers often prevent or impede cooperation between agencies.

- Intelligence can and should operate more efficiently. In some cases, organizational structures create inefficiencies. The process for allocating resources to intelligence is severely flawed. Greater use of modern management practices is needed. Some agencies find themselves with workforces that are not aligned with their current needs but lack the ability to correct the situation. Separate personnel and administrative systems among the agencies create additional inefficiencies. Meanwhile, the growing cost of these workforces precludes needed investments in new technologies and initiatives.

- The quality and utility of intelligence to the policy community should be improved. Intelligence producers need to build more direct relationships with their customers, take greater advantage of expertise and capabilities outside the government, and take additional measures to improve the quality and timeliness of their output. Some independent evaluation of this output needs to occur.

- Through expanded international cooperation, the United States should take advantage of its preeminence in the intelligence field to further its broader political and military interests, sharing the capabilities as well as the costs.

- The confidence of the public in the intelligence function must be restored. Ultimately, this will happen only as the intelligence community earns the trust and support of those it serves within the government, including the elected representatives of the people. Yet those responsible for directing and overseeing intelligence activities also can play a part by providing public recognition and support where appropriate.

While each of these problems is challenging, none is insuperable. This report reflects what, in the commission's view, needs to be done. The principal recommendations of the commission are summarized in the next section.

SUMMARY OF THE COMMISSION'S KEY RECOMMENDATIONS

THE NEED TO MAINTAIN AN INTELLIGENCE CAPABILITY

Without question, the United States needs information about the world outside its borders to protect its national interests and relative position in the world, whether as a Cold War superpower or a nation that remains heavily and inextricably engaged in world affairs. It needs information to avoid crises as well as respond to them, to calibrate its diplomacy, and to shape and deploy its defenses.

Much of that information is openly available, but much of it is not. Intelligence agencies attempt to fill the void. Their capabilities are costly. At times their activities are a source of embarrassment, even consternation. But they continue to provide information crucial to U.S. interests. Over the last five years, conflicts have been avoided, wars shortened, agreements reached, costs reduced, and lives saved as a result of information produced by U.S. intelligence agencies.

The commission concludes that the United States should continue to maintain a strong intelligence capability. U.S. intelligence has made, and continues to make, vital contributions to the nation's security. Its performance can be improved. It can be made more efficient. But it must be preserved.

THE ROLE OF INTELLIGENCE

The roles and missions of intelligence are not static. They are affected by changes in the world, in technology, and in the government's needs. Each president must decide where intelligence agencies should concentrate their efforts.

The commission perceives four functional roles for intelligence agencies—collection, analysis, covert action, and counterintelligence—as well as a number of missions in terms of providing substantive support to particular governmental functions.

There are complexities in each of the functional roles, but covert action (i.e., operations to influence conditions in other countries without the involvement of the United States being acknowledged or apparent) remains the most controversial. The commission concludes that a capability to conduct covert actions should be maintained to provide the president with an option short of military action when diplomacy alone cannot do the job. The capability must be utilized only where essential to accomplishing important and identifiable foreign policy objectives and only where a compelling reason exists why U.S. involvement cannot be disclosed.

Support to U.S. diplomacy, military operations, and defense planning should continue to constitute the principal missions of the intelligence community. Countering illicit activities abroad which threaten U.S. interests, including terrorism, narcotics trafficking, proliferation of weapons of mass destruction, and international organized crime are also increasingly important missions.

The increase in the availability of publicly available information may permit some diminution in the current level of effort to analyze the economies of other countries. The commission strongly supports the current policy prohibiting intelligence agencies from engaging in "industrial espionage," that is using clandestine means to obtain information from foreign commercial firms for the benefit of a U.S. competitor. It is appropriate, however, for intelligence agencies to report to cognizant officials at the Departments of State and Commerce evidence of unfair trade practices being undertaken by or with the knowledge of other governments to the disadvantage of U.S. firms.

Support to law enforcement and regulatory agencies is a legitimate mission, but requests for such support must be rigorously evaluated to ensure that intelligence agencies are able to make a useful contribution. The commission also sees the provision of support to U.S. agencies concerned with environmental and health problems outside the United States as a legitimate, albeit limited, mission.

THE NEED FOR POLICY GUIDANCE

By law, the principal source of external guidance for intelligence activities has been the National Security Council (NSC). In practice, however, the institutional functions of the NSC with respect to intelligence have varied from one administration to another. Moreover, the organizational structures created to perform these functions often have foundered due to lack of involvement by senior officials. This has resulted in inconsistent, infrequent guidance, and sometimes no guidance at all, leaving intelligence agencies to fend for themselves.

The institutional role played by the NSC with respect to intelligence activities should not change from administration to administration. This role should include providing overall guidance on what intelligence agencies are expected to do (and not do), establishing priorities for intelligence collection and analysis to meet the ongoing needs of the Government, and assessing periodically the performance of intelligence agencies in meeting these needs. Whatever NSC structure may be created to accomplish these ends, it should remain clear that the director of central intelligence reports directly to the president.

The commission recommends a two-tier structure to carry out the institutional role of the National Security Council. A Committee on Foreign Intelligence should be created, chaired by the assistant to the president for national security affairs, and including the director of central intelligence, the deputy secretary of defense, and the deputy secretary of state. This committee should meet at least semiannually and provide broad guidance on major issues. A subordinate Consumers Committee comprising representatives of the major consumers and producers of

intelligence, should meet more frequently to provide ongoing guidance for collection and analysis and periodically to assess the performance of intelligence agencies in meeting the needs of the government.

THE NEED FOR A COORDINATED RESPONSE TO GLOBAL CRIME

Global criminal activity carried out by foreign groups—terrorism, international drug trafficking, proliferation of weapons of mass destruction, and international organized crime—is likely to pose increasing dangers to the American people in the years ahead, as perpetrators grow more sophisticated and take advantage of new technologies.

Law enforcement agencies historically have taken the lead in responding to these threats, but where U.S. security is threatened, strategies which employ diplomatic, economic, military, or intelligence measures may be required instead of, or in collaboration with, a law enforcement response. In the commission's view, it is essential that there be overall direction and coordination of the U.S. response to global crime.

The commission recommends the establishment of a single element of the National Security Council —a Committee on Global Crime—chaired by the assistant to the president for national security affairs and including, at a minimum, the secretaries of state and defense, the attorney general, and the director of central intelligence, to develop and coordinate appropriate strategies to counter such threats to our national security.

For these strategies to be effective, the relationship between intelligence and law enforcement also must be substantially improved. In this regard, the commission recommends: (1) the president should designate the attorney general to serve as the spokesperson and coordinator of the law enforcement community for purposes of formulating the nation's law enforcement response to global crime; (2) the authority of intelligence agencies to collect information concerning foreign persons abroad for law enforcement purposes should be clarified by executive order; (3) the sharing of relevant information between the two communities should be expanded; and (4) the coordination of law enforcement and intelligence activities overseas should be improved.

THE ORGANIZATIONAL ARRANGEMENTS FOR THE INTELLIGENCE COMMUNITY

The position of director of central intelligence (DCI) was created to pull together and assess relevant information collected by the intelligence elements of the government. Over the past five decades, the number, size, and cost of those agencies grew. In 1971 President Richard Nixon gave the DCI explicit authority to establish requirements and priorities for intelligence-gathering, and to consolidate the budgets of all "national" intelligence activities into a single budget. Succeeding presidents issued orders reaffirming and, to a limited degree, expanding these authorities.

Nevertheless, over 85 percent of the intelligence budget is executed by agencies not under the DCI's control. He exercises no line authority over the personnel of agencies other than the CIA and has little recourse when these agencies choose to ignore his directives. He remains an advocate for "national" requirements, but his ability to influence other agencies is largely a function of his persuasiveness rather than his legal authorities. Partly because of their relatively weak position with respect to the intelligence community as a whole, most DCIs have devoted the bulk of their time to managing the CIA and serving as intelligence adviser to the president.

The commission considered many options for dealing with this problem, from abandoning the concept of centralized management altogether to giving the DCI line authority over "national" intelligence agencies within the Department of Defense (DOD). In the end, the commission concluded that a centralized framework should be retained and that it would be unwise and undesirable to alter the fundamental relationship between the DCI and the secretary of defense. The commission concluded the preferable approach is to strengthen the DCI's ability to provide centralized management of the intelligence community.

To give the DCI more time to manage, the commission recommends that the current position of deputy director of central intelligence should be replaced with two new deputies to the DCI: one for the intelligence community and one with day-to-day responsibility for managing the CIA. Both would be appointed by the president and confirmed by the Senate. The deputy for the CIA would be appointed for a fixed term. To give the DCI greater bureaucratic "weight" within the intelligence community, the DCI would concur in the appointment (or recommendation for appointment) of the heads of "national" intelligence elements within the Department of Defense and would be consulted with respect to the appointment of other senior officials within the intelligence community. The heads of two of the "national" intelligence elements—the director of the National Security Agency and the director of the Central Imagery Office (or its successor agency)— would be dual-hatted as assistant directors of central intelligence for signals intelligence and imagery, respectively. Their performance in those capacities would be evaluated by the DCI as part of their rating by the secretary of defense. In addition, the DCI would be given new tools to carry out his responsibilities with respect to the intelligence budget and new authority over the intelligence personnel systems.

THE CENTRAL INTELLIGENCE AGENCY

Although the CIA has had too many operational and management failures, those failures do not represent the norm. Indeed, the commission found that the CIA has had, and continues to have, important successes in what is a difficult and risky business. The commission concludes that the functions of the CIA remain valid and are not likely to be performed better elsewhere in the government. Substantial changes in the agency's management and method of operation are needed, however, to reduce the likelihood of additional internal breakdowns and instances of poor performance.

To provide greater continuity in the management of the CIA, the commission recommends that the deputy DCI responsible for the CIA be appointed to a fixed term with an overall length of six years, renewable by the president at two-year intervals. To improve the quality of management, the commission recommends a comprehensive approach to the selection, training, and career progression of CIA managers. Separate career tracks with appropriate opportunities for advancement ought to be provided for specialists who are not selected as managers. Clear guidelines should be issued regarding the types of information that should be brought to the attention of senior agency managers, including the DCI and deputy DCI.

THE NEED FOR A MORE EFFECTIVE
BUDGET STRUCTURE AND PROCESS

The DCI is responsible for approving the budget for "national intelligence," but 96 percent of the funding is contained in the budget of the Department of Defense. In addition, the DCI's budget is but one of three budgets or aggregations that make up the total funding for intelligence. The other two fund "defense-wide" and "tactical" intelligence activities of the Department of Defense.

Programs within the DCI's intelligence budget are not built around a consistent organizing principle. Activities of a similar nature are often funded in several "programs," making it difficult to assess trade-offs between programs or to know where best to take cuts, should cuts be necessary. Given that similar intelligence activities also may be funded outside the DCI's budget in either defense-wide or tactical intelligence aggregations, the potential for waste and duplication is exacerbated. The DCI also has had inadequate staff support, inadequate procedures, and inadequate tools to carry out effectively his budgetary responsibilities for "national" intelligence.

The commission recommends that the budget for national intelligence be substantially realigned. Programs grouping similar kinds of intelligence activities should be created under separate "discipline" managers reporting to the DCI. For example, all signals intelligence activities should be grouped under the "discipline management" of the director of the National Security Agency. These discipline managers also should coordinate the funding of activities within their respective disciplines in the defense-wide and tactical aggregations of the Defense Department, thus bringing greater consistency to all intelligence spending. The DCI should be provided a sufficient staff capability to enable him to assess trade-offs between programs or program elements and should establish a uniform, community-wide resource database to serve as the principal information tool for resource management across the intelligence community.

IMPROVING INTELLIGENCE ANALYSIS

Unless intelligence is relevant to users and reaches them in time to affect their decisions, the effort to collect and produce it has been wasted. Consumers in policy agencies in particular express dissatisfaction with the intelligence support they receive. While consumers often are uncooperative and unresponsive, producers must attempt to engage them.

The commission recommends that intelligence producers take a more systematic approach to building relationships with consumers in policy agencies. Key consumers should be identified and consulted individually with respect to the form of support they desire. Producers should offer to place analysts directly on the staffs of consumers at senior levels.

Relationships with consumers cannot be sustained, however, unless intelligence producers can over time demonstrate that they are bringing something of value to the table. While the commission found that intelligence analysis consistently adds value to that available from public sources, improving the quality of such analysis and ensuring it reaches users in a timely manner are continuing concerns.

The commission recommends that the skills and expertise of intelligence analysts be more consistently and extensively developed, and that greater use be made of substantive experts outside the intelligence community. A greater effort also should be made to harness the vast universe of information now available from open sources. The systems establishing electronic links between producers and consumers currently being implemented should be given a higher priority.

Estimative, or long-term, intelligence came in for particular criticism from consumers. The commission therefore recommends that the existing organization that prepares intelligence estimates, the National Intelligence Council, be restructured to become a more broadly based National Assessment Center. It would remain under the purview of the DCI but be located outside the CIA to take advantage of a broader range of information and expertise.

THE NEED TO "RIGHTSIZE" AND REBUILD THE COMMUNITY

Although there have been substantial personnel reductions in virtually every intelligence agency since the end of the Cold War, personnel costs continue to crowd out investments in new technologies and operational initiatives. In some agencies, this phenomenon is beginning to reach crisis proportions. Agencies find themselves with workforces that are not well aligned with their needs but lack the legal authority to streamline and reorient their workforces to current and future requirements.

The commission recommends the enactment of new legislation giving the most severely affected intelligence agencies a one-year window to "rightsize" their workforces to the needs of their organization. Such authority would be available only to the CIA and to intelligence agencies within the Department of Defense that determine that a reduction of 10 percent or more of their civilian workforce beyond the present congressionally mandated level of reduction is desirable. Agencies that avail themselves of this authority would identify positions no longer needed for the health and viability of their organization. The incumbents of such positions, if close to retirement, would be allowed to retire with accelerated eligibility. If not close to retirement, they would be provided with generous pay and benefits to leave the service of the agency concerned, or, with the concurrence of the agency affected, exchange positions with an employee not in a position identified for elimination who was close to retirement and would be allowed to leave under the accelerated retirement provisions. New employees would be hired to fill some, but not all, of the vacancies created, providing the skills necessary to satisfy the current and future needs of the agency involved.

Four separate civilian personnel systems exist within the intelligence community. These systems discourage rotation between intelligence agencies, which is key to functioning as a "community." In addition, many aspects of personnel and administration could be performed more efficiently if they were centralized.

The commission recommends the director of central intelligence consolidate such functions where possible or, if centralization is not feasible, issue uniform standards governing such functions. The commission also recommends the creation of a single senior executive service for the intelligence community under the overall management of the DCI.

MILITARY INTELLIGENCE

Responsibility for military intelligence is dispersed among the Office of the Secretary of Defense, the Joint Chiefs of Staff, the military departments, several defense agencies, and, to a lesser degree, the CIA. To provide coherence, a multitude of boards, committees, and working groups exist to develop policy and allocate resources. Although many witnesses suggested creating a single military official with overall responsibility for these activities, the commission does not endorse this suggestion.

The commission did find that progress had been made in reducing duplication in military intelligence analysis and production, but that the size and functions of the numerous organizations performing these functions continued to raise concern. The commission recommends that the secretary of defense undertake a comprehensive examination of the size and missions of these organizations.

The commission also found that the organizational arrangements for providing intelligence support to joint war fighting and for executing the functions of the Joint Chiefs of Staff as they pertain to intelligence should be improved. The commission recommends that the director for intelligence (J-2), who now is an officer assigned to the Defense Intelligence Agency, be constituted as part of the Joint Staff and be made responsible for these functions.

The commission also found that a problem continued to exist with respect to how information produced by national and tactical intelligence systems is communicated to commanders in the field. Such information has become increasingly important for the targeting of "smart" weapons and reconnaissance assets, but it is not always communicated in a timely way or in a form that can readily be used. Many organizations and coordinating entities within the DOD are working on aspects of this problem, but no one, short of the secretary of defense, appears to be in charge. The commission recommends that a single focal point be established on the staff of the secretary of defense to bring together all the relevant players and interests to solve these problems. It considers the assistant secretary of defense for Command, Control, Communications, and Intelligence to be the appropriate official for this purpose.

Finally, the commission believes the costs and difficulties involved in maintaining a separate infrastructure within the DOD for the conduct of clandestine human intelligence (HUMINT) operations are no longer justified. The commission recommends that the clandestine recruitment of human sources, now carried out by active duty military officers assigned to the Defense HUMINT Service, be transferred to the CIA, utilizing military personnel on detail from the DOD as necessary.

SPACE RECONNAISSANCE AND THE MANAGEMENT OF TECHNICAL COLLECTION

U.S. intelligence capabilities in space represent technological achievements of the highest order, and have, over time, served the nation's interests well. They are highly vulnerable to the failure of a single component system, however, and are very expensive to operate.

The commission recommends greater international cooperation in space reconnaissance through expanded government-to-government arrangements as a means of dealing with both the vulnerability and cost of U.S. space systems. In this regard, the commission proposes a two-tier approach as a model for such collaboration. The commission also recommends that the president reexamine certain restrictions on the licensing of commercial imaging systems for foreign sale in order to encourage greater investment by U.S. firms in such systems.

The commission endorses greater coordination between the space programs of the Defense Department and intelligence community in order to achieve economies of scale where possible but recommends the National Reconnaissance Office be preserved as a separate organization. The commission also endorses the creation of a National Imagery and Mapping Agency as recently proposed by the DCI and secretary of defense.

INTERNATIONAL COOPERATION

The commission found that the United States is deriving great benefit from its bilateral relationships in the intelligence area. Although other countries do not have technical capabilities to match those of the United States, they do provide expertise, skills, and access that U.S. intelligence does not have, and, for the most part, appear to be contributing within the limits of their respective national resources. Cooperation in intelligence matters also provides a tangible means of maintaining the overall political relationship with the countries concerned.

Increasingly, the United States acts through multinational organizations or as a part of multinational coalitions. Often it will be in the interest of the United States to share information derived from intelligence with such organizations or coalitions to achieve mutual objectives. While the intelligence community, when called upon, does attempt to satisfy these kinds of requirements, a more systematic, comprehensive approach is called for.

The commission recommends that the DCI and the secretaries of state and defense develop a strategy that will serve as the normal basis for sharing information derived from intelligence in a multinational environment.

THE COST OF INTELLIGENCE

The commission recommends a number of actions that it believes would, if implemented, reduce the cost of intelligence. In particular, the commission believes that until the intelligence community reforms its budget structure and process, it will remain poorly positioned to identify potential cost reductions.

At the same time, the intelligence community may have needs that are not funded in the projected program, especially in the area of research and development and investments in new technology. Given that downward pressure on spending will continue for the foreseeable future, these needs are not apt to be funded unless savings can be found to finance them within the existing budget. In the commission's view, it is therefore essential for the DCI and heads of agencies within the intelligence community to make a concerted effort to reduce the costs of their operations if they are to maintain their overall health and vitality.

ACCOUNTABILITY AND OVERSIGHT

Intelligence agencies, compared with other institutions of the federal government, pose unique difficulties when it comes to public accountability. They cannot disclose what they are doing to the public without disclosing what they are doing to their targets. Yet they are institutions within a democracy, responsible to the president, the Congress, and, ultimately, the people. Where accountability can be strengthened without damaging national security, the commission believes it should be.

The commission recommends that the president or his designee disclose the total amount of money appropriated for intelligence activities during the current fiscal year and the total amount being requested for the next fiscal year. The disclosure of additional detail should not be permitted.

Because intelligence activities cannot be openly discussed, special oversight arrangements have been created for intelligence agencies in both the legislative and executive branches. In Congress, principal day-to-day oversight is provided by special committees in the House of Representatives and the Senate, whose members serve on rotational assignments up to eight years in length. By and large, these committees appear to provide effective oversight. The commission believes, however, that their oversight would be strengthened if appointments to the committees were treated like appointments to other committees, with new members added as a result of normal attrition. The choice of new members, however, should continue to be made by the respective congressional leaders. If this is not feasible, the maximum period of service ought to be extended to at least ten years.

In the executive branch, the Intelligence Oversight Board, a standing committee of the President's Foreign Intelligence Advisory Board, has overall responsibility for oversight of intelligence agencies, and each agency either has an inspector general internal to its own organization or is part of an organization with an inspector general. Only the CIA has an independent statutory inspector general. The commission recommends a comprehensive review of these arrangements by the Intelligence Oversight Board to ensure effective performance of the oversight function.

CHAPTER 7

INTEREST GROUPS, THE MEDIA, AND PUBLIC OPINION

THE BUSINESS OF DEFENSE

GORDON ADAMS

The defense budget of the United States rose rapidly in the 1980s. Many justifications have been offered for its dramatic increase: inflation, the high price of increasingly sophisticated weapons, the rivalry between the military services, and the need for an arms buildup to protect U.S. interests in an unstable world.[1] Rarely mentioned, however, are the pressures that the defense contracting industry exert on the government, their chief "customer."

In approaching the government, contractors take advantage of both their opportunities as members of the "big business" community and their unique role and special access as manufacturers of weapons that guarantee "national security." The benefits to the industry of aggressive "government relations" practices are great. The cost to the country, however, in an inflated budget and a narrowing of the debate on strategic and foreign policy, is high.

BUSINESS AS USUAL

For over a century, private industry has asserted its power in American politics. Big business has both sought government favors and battled government efforts to control it.[2] Business leaders constantly warn that the government has become too large and exercises too much influence in the private sector. They castigate regulatory agencies as costly, restrictive, and inefficient. But alongside this apparent antagonism another, more cooperative set of relations has developed. During World War I business leaders were brought into the federal government as wartime production planners for virtually all sectors of U.S. industry. In the 1920s Secretary of Commerce Herbert Hoover organized permanent advisory commissions to the department composed of business representatives from different sectors of the economy. President Franklin Roosevelt attracted a number of businessmen into government positions first to combat the depression and later, in World War II, to plan wartime production. As the war ended, many government commissions and the new Council on Economic Advisers turned to business for staffing and ideas about postwar economic, foreign, and military policy.

Members of regulatory commissions are often drawn from the regulated industry; personnel move steadily between the agency, the industry being regulated, and its legal support community.[3] In certain areas, regulation—far from being the whipping boy of the business community—is welcomed. Much is gained by industry through regular federal involvement in price-setting and entry and exit from the markets.

Since 1946 America's corporations have expanded and developed practices and structures to influence congressional and executive policy makers. A growing number of major companies now have a corporate office responsible for "government relations." Most of the Fortune 500 companies have offices in Washington whose purpose is to gather information and exert political pressure. Government relations is the art of making connections: between the company's needs, its potential support at the grass roots (workers, communities, stockholders), its campaign spending, the key staff and members of Congress, and officials in agencies in the executive branch.

At a stunningly rapid pace, companies have taken advantage of the Federal Election Reform Act of 1971, as amended, to establish political action committees (PACs) to channel their campaign contributions. Increasingly, PACs are being used as the corporate forum for determining a company's government relations strategy.

A SPECIAL KIND OF BUSINESS

While the defense industry holds many characteristics in common with other members of the big business community, contractors play a unique role in American society. As manufacturers of strategic weapons, they are widely identified as guardians of national security. The federal government not only regulates their activities but serves as one of their best customers. The weapons they manufacture follow the specifications of their federal client; the procurement process is initiated and sustained by members of both the industry and the government. This close interdependence has made them pace-

This essay has been edited and is excerpted from Gordon Adams, The Politics of Defense Contracting: The Iron Triangle *(New Brunswick, NJ: Transaction Books, 1982), 19–29 and 43–54, by permission of Transaction Publishers. Copyright © 1982; all rights reserved.*

setters in developing government relations practices that safeguard their interests.

This intimacy developed early. Dependence on government procurement began during World War I; many firms disappeared between the wars when procurement declined. In response, defense industry leaders, the financial community, and government officials made vigorous efforts in the 1920s to establish national policies—air mail subsidies, federal regulation, and consistent defense procurement—that would help the industry survive. After World War II, industry pressure and government decisions led to federal support for a private defense capacity, in effect subsidizing industry to keep critical personnel in working teams and production facilities open. The decision to maintain a large, privately owned defense manufacturing capacity has led to a bewildering variety of federal procurement policies, many of which foster a high degree of intimacy between the Pentagon and its contractors and inhibit cost control.[4]

GOVERNMENT RELATIONS

Contractors' government relations, like those of other corporations, trade in two commodities: information and influence. A contractor seeks information from Congress and the executive in answer to many questions: what programs are forthcoming and where and how are they being defined; what are federal procurement plans and regulations going to look like, where do bureaucrats and members of Congress stand on particular systems, when will legislation be considered, and what form will it take? The company reworks this information, which flows in vast quantities, to focus on company needs and possibilities. In other words, it becomes intelligence.[5] The need for such intelligence is virtually endless, and contractors' government relations officers and Washington staff spend a substantial portion of their time talking on the phone, visiting Pentagon and congressional offices, reading documents, and deciphering information useful to the company. In addition, government relations specialists play a key role in providing information in the other direction—from the company to the government—on company plans and needs.

This flow of information facilitates the other principal task of government relations—the exerting of influence. Corporate officers for government relations advise their company on how to gain access and manipulate the government to serve its needs, often recommending changes in policy.[6] They manage the most important direction of communication: that toward the government, becoming expert at neutralizing opposition in Congress, selling a company plan in the executive branch, reversing unfavorable decisions and regulations, directing campaign contributions, focusing grass roots lobbying efforts, and even taking a hand in drafting proposed legislation.

Government relations efforts also aim at defending the industry and its views on policy from outsiders, critics, and alternative perspectives. The industry makes the most of its unique role: as a manufacturer of weapons it assumes a major role in defining national and global security. Industry spokesmen guard the terms of debate, challenging the legitimacy of alternative views and scoring participants who are not members of the fraternity.

THE IRON TRIANGLE

Over the years the defense industry has become a de facto participant in the policy-making process. As in other areas dominated by powerful corporate interests, a policy subgovernment or "iron triangle" has emerged.

Political scientists describe an "iron triangle" as a political relationship that brings together three key participants in a clearly delineated area of policy making: the federal bureaucracy, the key committees and members of Congress, and the private interest.[7] In defense, the participants are the Department of Defense (DOD), plus the National Aeronautic and Space Administration (NASA), and the nuclear weapons branch of the Department of Energy; the House and Senate Armed Services Committees and Defense Appropriations Subcommittee, as well as congressional members from defense-related districts and states; and the firms, labs, research institutes, trade associations, and trade unions in the industry itself.

The special interests and the federal bureaucracy interpenetrate. Policy makers and administrators move freely between the two arenas and policy issues are discussed and resolved among participants who share common values, interests, and perceptions. As Senator George Aiken has put it, "Agencies and their clientele tend to develop coincident values and perceptions to the point where neither needs to manipulate the other overtly. The confident relationships that develop uniquely favor the interest groups involved."[8] The distinction between public and private starts to disappear as a sector of industry begins to "appropriate" government authority.[9]

The creation of an iron triangle takes time and the active efforts of its participants. All three sides work to maintain it as economic circumstances change. There is continuous communication between the executive, Congress, and the industry, creating a community of interest in which it becomes difficult to answer the question, "Who controls whom?" Once molded, the triangle sets with the rigidity of iron. The three participants exert strenuous efforts to keep it isolated and protected from outside points of view. In time they become unwitting victims of their own isolation, convinced that they are acting not only in their own but in the public interest.

In the day-to-day performance of their tasks, administrators see very little of the more general public support which accompanied the establishment of the agency. The only people who are likely to come to the attention of administrators are those whose problems are uniquely a part of the administrative environment. . . . Under such circumstances it is not surprising that the administrator's perception of the public interest is in reality defined by the interests of the regulated parties.[10]

The development of the iron triangle has put an end to those brave days described by political theory when, in the "separation of powers," Congress legislated, the executive administered, and corporations did business with the government at arm's length. Instead, according to economist Murray Weidenbaum, "the close, continuing relationship between the Department of Defense and its major suppliers is resulting in convergence between the two, which is blurring and reducing much of the distinction between public and private activities in an important branch of the American economy."[11]

SELLING WEAPONS: A PARABLE

Description and analysis, the essential tools of the researcher, both reveal and distort reality. They stop the action and transpose many dimensions into a two-dimensional listing of facts and figures. Inevitably, they shift the emphasis from reality as process to reality as structure.

Yet in this discussion it is primarily process that interests us. Our focus centers on the practices that contractors have developed to influence government policy. Description and analysis alone cannot show how these blend together to affect a single DOD decision. This can only be done through narrative. To fill this gap we have invented a case study. It is hypothetical and fictional. No actual events, persons, or corporations are described.[12]

Jack Wilson, sitting at his desk in San Jose, was a company man. He had started his career with General Electronics International (GEI) in 1947, after wartime service in the air force. He had had only two brief stints elsewhere. Once, when GEI lost a major contract, he spent two years in Boston with United Electronics. Later, GEI seconded him for three years to the air force at Wright Patterson Air Force Base as a liaison officer on the company's supersonic-swing-wing (RPV) program. Promotions had come steadily—from engineer to production manager, to division chief for missile programs, and now, to corporate vice president for government relations. With steady raises, increasing corporate perks, and more power, Jack had developed a loyalty, a family feeling about GEI that would never die. He expected to retire, at least as a vice president or even—who knows. . . .

Samuel T. ("Chuck") Fuller had to go some day, leaving the president/chief operating officer job open. Chuck, too, had had a full career. In the 1930s, fresh out of Stanford Engineering, he had created a defense electronics firm, ERW, in the suburbs of San Jose—California's famous Silicon Valley. The sudden boom in Pentagon missile spending had made the firm's fortune and Chuck's career. Having engineered ERW's merger with Fargo Electronics, Chuck went to Washington as the second deputy to the Pentagon's director for defense research and engineering, one of the Pentagon's most powerful jobs. After four years with the administration, Chuck had returned to California and GEI, which had by then absorbed ERW/Fargo as part of a corporate diversification program. Chuck rose rapidly to the top and would retire in two years.

A key to promotion, Jack knew, was the procurement of a major Pentagon contract, which would establish him as the heir apparent for the top job.

Yet Jack knew that there was another strong candidate—and another route. Bruce Collins, the former astronaut and vice president for commercial markets, had tried to diversify GEI by developing commercial markets. His efforts had succeeded. If DOD contracts were slow in coming, GEI could build its future in commercial aviation.

For Jack, however, there was no choice. GEI's defense programs had been run separately from commercial business since the war. Company management had simply closed them off. Jack could not retool as a commercial man overnight.

Things were at a crucial point for GEI's defense work, moreover. Production on the giant Thunderbird ship defense missile for the navy was tailing off. Jack had design crews, researchers, engineers, looking for work. The end of the Thunderbird contract might force the company to lay them off. With any luck—for them—they would go to work for Thor Electron, or Rubicon, or another industry competitor, making the next contract even harder and more expensive for GEI to bid on. It could be worse, though. GEI did not have to worry about maintaining expensive overhead costs. The navy owned the building and machinery at Plant 5803 outside San Jose. GEI simply used it at minimal rent. If the Thunderbird contract ended, GEI could always give the plant back to the navy.

Still Jack needed a better option. With a new contract and a continued flow of defense funds into the company, he wanted to help create a humming production facility.

Jack knew he needed more information. What did the navy think it wanted? What could the company make? He reached for the phone and set up a meeting with George ("Smiley") Cooper, director of GEI's advanced research and development office, fondly called the Junk Works around GEI because it was located next to San Jose's city dump. He sat down with Cooper and went over the projections. They had to know what the navy had up its sleeve, what new missile systems it was thinking about. Cooper knew a lot on this score. For the past ten years, about $15 million a year had flowed into the Junk Works from the Pentagon's Independent Research and Development (IR&D) program. GEI scientists used the money to fund new weapons research ideas—ideas they could sell back to the Pentagon. As long as the ideas that came back were promising, the Pentagon kept a loose hand on the money reins.

For the past five years, Cooper had also been a member of the Navy Science Board's Advisory Committee on Ship Defense Systems. This committee brought together everybody—navy people, Green Aerospace, Rubicon, the McDavis Group, GEI. Most of the big contractors had a scientist or engineer member of the group, which was designed to pool ideas on ship defense systems. The navy used it as a sounding board, while the industry people used it to get to know each other and the navy and to push new ideas.

Several years ago, Cooper had done a concept paper at the request of the committee chairman. One of his old friends, Duffy McNee, who was now deputy assistant navy secretary for research and development, had taken a real interest in the proposed system: a new, all-weather missile with a 75- to 100-mile range, which could carry nuclear or conventional weapons. Just the thing the navy (and GEI) needed, thought Cooper. For three years he had been using IR&D to develop the concept, and it was near time to move toward real R&D contracts.

There was some risk in pushing this missile, Cooper told Jack. The navy had to be convinced. GEI's competitors, moreover, had seen Cooper's paper and could be working on their own designs. Rubicon Aerospace was said to be forging ahead. On the other hand, a success in pushing this system would make GEI's Missile Division golden for a decade to come. Cooper and Wilson agreed they needed more information on how to sell the navy and on the work of competitors. Cooper went off to call Deputy Assistant Secretary McNee.

Jack began sounding out some other key contacts. First, he called Buff Johnson, his deputy and government liaison officer in GEI's Washington office, which had been established ten years ago as a central location to gather information on Pentagon and NASA contracting and to guide GEI's out-of-town staff when they came to Capitol Hill for testimony and meetings with key members of Congress. Buff had many useful sources. Every couple of weeks, he would have lunch (Dutch treat, under the new entertainment guidelines from the Pentagon) with old friends in the Navy's Research Office. It had been seven years since he had retired from the staff there, moving immediately to GEI. But he had kept up his contacts.

He had also spent time on the Hill. While contracting for the navy, he had met many of the staff of the House and Senate Armed Services Committees who worked on naval R&D and procurement. He knew that they were important to getting future defense programs funded. His job now was to keep them informed on GEI programs and to keep a close ear to committee attitudes toward the defense budget. Though not officially registered as a lobbyist—the law was very loose—he did a fair amount of lobbyist's work.

Jack asked Buff for information about his Pentagon network. Had he talked recently with McNee or junior civilian and military people? Did he know where future ship missile defense systems were heading? Who was in charge of this work? Were there special advisory groups GEI ought to be in? Buff found the answers—the navy group working on ship defense was impressed with GEI's progress using IR&D money. But there were other competitors in the field, and he did not know how far along they were, or how interested the navy was in their work. Jack urged Buff to pin down more detailed information. He also asked him to do some sleuthing in the American Defense Preparedness Association (ADPA). GEI, along with other major defense firms, belonged to the ADPA, a trade group committed to serving "the defense needs of our nation." Jack asked Buff to attend the next meeting of ADPA's Missiles Committee to determine who among GEI's competitors had drawn a bead on the market.

Jack then focused in on the Navy Research and Development office. What kind of missile designs could they be sold? He made a call to Tony Lakeland at the Naval Weapons Center at China Lake. Lakeland had been with GEI's missile division for five years before moving to China Lake as an R&D program director. Jack suggested they meet for lunch when he came to GEI's China Lake office the following week. He knew that if GEI was to get in on the ground floor, he had to have some influence over the missile specifications the navy would draw up in preparing its request for bids for R&D contract work. The discussion with Tony gave him useful information and even more useful input into navy thinking.

After these preliminary calls Jack started to plan for a Washington trip. He put Buff to work on the schedule after clearing the trip and the program with an enthusiastic President Fuller. A courtesy visit to Deputy Assistant Secretary McNee was in order, which Cooper arranged. Buff set up detailed discussions with McNee's staff. In addition, there were meetings with the ADPA committee secretary and a friendly visit to the Aerospace Industries Association to discuss forthcoming changes in federal procurement policy.

Buff also arranged some meetings with Hill staffers, though it was early in the missile program to think about a congressional focus for GEI's effort. Jack did meet with Representative Claire Sampson from San Jose. GEI had made steady contributions to Sampson's last three campaigns through its Good Government Fund, a political action committee, and Buff had friendly access to Sampson's legislative assistant. As representative from GEI's district and a member of the Defense Appropriations Subcommittee that would consider the money requests for navy missile R&D, Sampson was doubly important to GEI. The Defense Subcommittee was famous on the Hill for going through Pentagon requests with a fine-toothed comb. In his visit, Jack explained that he was on a general information-gathering trip and described GEI's current R&D projects, including ship defense missiles. He pointed out to her how much GEI's 16,000 employees in San Jose supported her work and how important it was to the economy of the district that they be fully employed.

Jack took along a young employee of GEI's Washington office, Neil Jones, to meet with the R&D staff of the House and Senate Armed Services Committees. Jones was a presidential interchange executive with GEI. He knew missiles inside out and was very familiar with GEI's technical work. He was also intimately familiar with navy thinking, having been on the staff of the Navseasystcom tactical planning group for two years. He talked technical with the R&D staff and made strong arguments for the military need for GEI's missile.

During Jack's visit, the Washington office arranged a reception attended by several top brass and key civilian policy makers, as well as several members of Congress and staffers—a sort of informal, get-acquainted party. It was a quiet, cautious event. Jack could remember the old days before William Proxmire had uncovered abuses. GEI used to have a hunting lodge on Wye Island, off the Maryland coast, where they had full weekends with top Pentagon and Hill personnel—hunting, playing cards, drinking, and generally socializing. Press revelations and hearings on Thor Electron and Bow-Wing Electronics had changed all that. Now there was only the occasional cocktail party at a trade association meeting, free tickets to a Redskins' game, a lunch here and there, and—a rarity—a plane trip to the coast for a member of Congress or bureaucrat. The days of big entertainment and favors were gone, at least for now.

Buff called several weeks after Jack's return from Washington. One of McNee's key staffers was working up a draft request for proposals (RFP) for ship defense missiles, and GEI had to move fast. Jack called Smiley Cooper and urged him to arrange a meeting between the navy staffer and a Junk Works expert to go over GEI's ideas. A quick weekend conference in Washington was arranged, and GEI got its input into the RFP.

When the RFP came out, a month later, it took a middle line between GEI and Rubicon and implied that more than one contractor might be funded for designs. Both GEI and Rubicon bid and won contracts.

Jack's work, however, was just beginning; the production contract was no sure thing. Rubicon had a lot of missile experience and equally good contacts with the Pentagon and the Hill. As the design work proceeded, Jack picked up the pace, keeping up with advance information and bringing influence to bear in the Pentagon. The two design contracts were followed by two engineering development contracts and, in turn, two contracts for prototype development. The navy wanted to fly-off the two missiles against each other.

As the competition heated up and the program progressed, it became more visible, more expensive, and more controversial. The wider the circle of people involved, the more Jack had to do.

There were those both in the defense industry and in Congress who opposed a new missile. Thor Electron, which made the current ship defense missile, met regularly with Hill staffers to encourage Congress to accept a more modest program involving a redesign of the current weapon. Representative Jerry Friedman of Wisconsin worried about the cost of a new missile. Senator Scott Moran from Pennsylvania warned that the Pentagon budget was eating up social funding.

There was also opposition inside the Pentagon. A navy missile program was pushing the projected budget upward. Supporters of existing systems argued that the new expenditure was not needed and updates of current equipment were adequate. Outside the navy, the other services resisted the threat a growing Navy missile procurement program posed for growth in their own weapons buying.

Sometimes Jack felt like a duck stamping out a forest fire. Every time he thought he had one brush fire out, another jumped up a few feet, or a few offices away.

Jack mobilized everyone and everything to push through his program. He paid regular visits to Washington, visiting both the Hill and the Pentagon. He brought company specialists with him, who could make convincing technical cases for the GEI design. They met endlessly with navy people, some of whom had worked for GEI, discussing design changes, problems, cost, and the like. Jack had two goals: keep the missile in the DOD budget and encourage GEI's design into the winner's seat. He knew that for this to happen, he had to work both the Pentagon and Hill sides of the street.

Mobilizing the staff of GEI's Washington office, Jack and Buff outlined a campaign of visits to critical members of the House and Senate committees: the Armed Services and the Defense Appropriations Subcommittee, and their staffs. They sent their technical people to convince the R&D Subcommittee staff of the importance of the program. They reviewed campaign contributions from GEI's Good Government Fund, noting key members to whom contributions had been made. They looked at the pattern of GEI's subcontract awards. For some years the company had tried to be attentive to the economic and political impact of its subcontracts through which it farmed out over 40 percent of its prime contract dollars. The economic argument carried weight in Congress. Several million dollars in subcontracts in a district was hard to argue with. But, GEI could not make this argument directly. Its motives would be questioned.

Jack commissioned a study by a private economic consulting firm on the regional impact of the program. District by district, GEI could then forecast the results, tailoring individual presentations for specific members of Congress.

Special meetings were held with the two California senators and the San Mateo and San Jose representatives, Mattini and Sampson, respectively. The economic impact of the program would be largest in their districts. Past history had shown that Mattini, who generally took a critical stance on defense spending, had always been willing to go to bat for GEI when jobs in the district were at stake. The California delegation moved into action, calling on colleagues, sending staff around to encourage other staffers to support the program, and writing the Pentagon.

Representative Sampson was a major leader of this effort. Since she was a member of the House Defense Appropriations Subcommittee, her arguments commanded attention in the Pentagon. The Pentagon and the White House knew that her support was needed for other programs. Trade-off possibilities were endless. With an incumbent president up for reelection, Sampson's arguments about electoral support in her district found receptive listeners among the White House staff.

Turning to the Pentagon, Jack worked on other problems. GEI had to be sure its prototype came within close range of Rubicon in price, performance, and schedule. Buff's office and the California staff pursued contacts and discussions with the navy's technical and contracting people, acquiring up-to-date information on the missile test evaluation. Jack and Buff also marshaled every possible supporter to argue in the Office of the Secretary of Defense that the weapon was necessary. He made several calls to analysts of naval strategy in various universities, one of whom agreed to write an opinion piece on the missile in the *New York Times*, which the policy makers would read.

Jack aimed at other journals, making several phone calls a week to writers for *Aviation Week* and the *U.S. Naval Institute Proceedings*. He offered to provide information on recent developments in GEI's program and arrange visits to the plant for reporters. Several favorable write-ups resulted from these efforts, including a highly detailed, technical piece in *Aviation Week*. Jack mobilized the company's public relations people in San Jose who placed GEI's missile in the advertising copy of *Time* and *Business Week*.

Jack moved, too, to bring GEI's local dependents to put pressure on Congress and the executive branch. A company planning committee, Operation Common Good (OCG), had drawn up a plan aimed at mobilizing public opinion in San Jose. OCG prepared films and demonstrations for Fourth of July exhibits and American Legion meetings, provided speakers for meetings of men's and women's clubs to inform them about the nation's defense and the importance of a well-defended fleet. It sent press releases to local papers in all the key subcontracting locations and arranged for plant visits for important union and local government officials. It organized delegations of local citizens to visit Congress and the White House with statements of support. A nationwide campaign of ads urged readers to write GEI for an "Owner's Manual" for the missile, and Jack drafted a letter from President Chuck Fuller to employees, subcontractors, and stockholders, urging them to write Congress.

Decision time was near. Rubicon Aerospace and GEI kept pushing. White House and Hill pressures

won the day over the opposition of the secretary of defense: the missile was approved. Now came the question of funding. Jack and Rubicon's lobbyist turned to the Hill, with more visits to key staff, more reminders of campaign contributions and subcontracting benefits. The opponents of the missile lost in the Appropriations Committee, introduced a motion on the floor of the House amending the Defense Appropriations Act, but lost again, 207 to 142. The arena for the contestants now was moved to the Senate.

Senator Scott Moran from Pennsylvania led an effort in the Senate Appropriations Committee to delay a production decision on the missile until after the presidential campaign. The amendment barely squeaked through the committee, which meant a floor fight. Despite door-to-door lobbying and Pentagon phone calls, the amendment was passed.

The competing contractors united in their efforts to support the program. GEI and Rubicon pulled out all stops in the Conference Committee, calling members, orchestrating local employee, stockholder, subcontractor, and other grass roots pressures. Two GEI board members who formerly worked at high levels in the Pentagon, made personal calls to several key senators and representatives. One of them, the chairman of United Western Bank, also made some calls to former colleagues in the Treasury Department, pointing out the importance of funds to California's industrial sector. In response, congressional relations staff at Treasury made contact with key Appropriations Committee members. The battle in Conference was won; the amendment was removed; funding was approved.

Jack's attention turned back to the Pentagon and White House. He could not be sure that his missile would win. The two missiles were close in design and performance specifications. GEI had a slight lead in the fast schedule it could promise to the navy, but inside information from GEI's friends in Navy Research and Development suggested that Rubicon might come in with a slightly lower price. He would have to move carefully. In an election year, some pressure had to be directed toward the White House. All avenues would have to be carefully worked.

Jack called Dave Brahman, GEI board member, Harvard graduate, and partner in Shadly, Todd, Millbrook, and Coy, one of Washington's leading law firms. In the 1960s he had served as deputy secretary of the army and later put in two years as director of the Defense Intelligence Agency. His Washington network was wide, his reputation as an insider was unbeatable. Brahman gave Jack advice on how to approach the Republican National Committee and the White House in this election year and agreed to pay visits to some old friends on the White House staff to make the case for GEI's bid.

Meanwhile, in Washington Buff Johnson had come close to blowing the contract. In his anxiety to obtain information on the progress of the Navy evaluation, he had sent Gene McConnell, former navy engineer and GEI Washington technical specialist, to the navy program office. There, McConnell, who had a high security clearance, examined a memorandum going through the most recent technical discussions of the navy's missile needs. In it he found some valuable information for GEI's final bid. When Buff saw the notes Gene had taken, he could hardly wait to rush to the Telex and send word back to San Jose. A San Jose employee with lower security clearance, not realizing how sensitive the information was, called the Navy Research and Development office to double-check some points, inadvertently revealing the disclosure of classified information. The flap led to the suspension of two R&D office employees and the temporary withdrawal of Gene and Buff's security clearances. The bad publicity caused new headaches for Jack, as he fought off press inquiries and tried to dissipate the sense that GEI had special inside information.

From his friends at the Aerospace Industries Association, however, Jack had learned some good news. Rubicon was overloaded with missile work and planners in the Office of the Secretary of the Navy, worried about the state of the Navy Industrial Plant Reserve, wanted to keep GEI's technical work force and operating capacity in missiles alive. When a final contract recommendation reached the secretary of the navy's desk, this consideration could weigh in GEI's favor.

Turning back to national politics, Jack helped Dave Brahman set up meetings with finance people from the Republican National Committee to let them know about GEI's Good Government Committee contributions to the president's primary campaign. Brahman impressed on the national committee staff that an award in Santa Clara County would produce a good turnout for the president, while an award in Boston (site of Rubicon's plant) would not necessarily counter the natural tendency of that area's electorate to support the president's liberal challenger. Bob Sperling of GEI's Washington counsel, Worthington & Sperling, made several phone calls, reminding Republican Party officials of GEI's past services and support.

Once more Jack organized local groups who would send delegations to Washington. The San Jose delegation included the mayor, two council members, the head of the local Chamber of Commerce, and the local leader of the metalworkers' union, which organized part of GEI's plant. In Washington, they visited Representatives Sampson and Mattini, the chair of the House and Senate Armed Services Committees, and a staffer from the White House, impressing on each the economic and political benefit of a contract award to San Jose. A local San Francisco banker in the delegation paid a special visit to a friend at Treasury, carefully understating, while making clear, GEI's case.

Mattini approached the White House with a joint letter, made calls to friends in the Pentagon, urged other members of Congress to support the effort, and inserted pro-GEI material in the *Congressional Record,* which would be reprinted and distributed.

As the pressure built toward a decision and the contract award, Jack received a phone call from an insider in the Navy Research and Development office, who said Rubicon's missile looked like a winner because of its cost advantages. Jack relayed the bad news to Chuck Fuller, who looked over GEI's cost proposal and then asked Jack how the navy intended to write the contract—one contract for all of the missiles or one for a purchase in batches. Could GEI bid low for the first batch, take the loss, and make it up by getting a higher price for subsequent batches? Fuller knew this was a risky strategy—GEI could end up eating the loss as other contractors had in the past. Fuller's staff debated the issue and came up with a marginal price. Buff indicated that his navy sources felt a revised bid could save the day for GEI. The bid was lowered. A week later, to the popping of champagne corks in Washington and San Jose, GEI's Sting-Ray was announced the winner.

After a contract award, there are always a few protests. True to form, columnist Bill Sanderson suggested that political favoritism had won the day: President Hardy, wanting to curry the support of Californians for his campaign, had promised the congressional delegation the contract. Jack had already planned his strategy. He and Buff called the White House, prepared a statement that denied any such commitments and discussed a press release with the PR people at the Office of the Secretary of Defense pointing out the favorable evaluation of GEI's missile, its performance in the fly-off, and the price competitiveness with Rubicon. Gradually the public furor died down.

Once GEI had the production contract for the new Sting-Ray missile, Jack's operation became less central. In San Jose, GEI workers worked side by side with navy engineers and contract managers and an auditor from the Defense Contract Audit Agency (DCAA). This working relationship was made easy by the fact that over the years GEI had hired several former employees of the navy and DCAA. They knew the contract guidelines and procurement regulations, knew how to negotiate contract changes, understood the red tape and paperwork, and could help ease the relationship with the navy.

The calm did not last forever. Two years later, as part of a more general investigation into the relationship between contractors and the Pentagon, the Senate Banking Committee held hearings to examine efforts to stimulate grass roots support for their defense programs. The committee was concerned that the expenditures for such grass roots lobbying had been charged to contract costs. The Pentagon might be indirectly subsidizing lobbying aimed at Congress. A questionnaire to GEI, among others, asked about their grass roots lobbying. It was sent straight to Jack Wilson, who immediately got on the phone with the government relations officers of the other companies in the survey to see if they intended to respond. In the end, they all agreed that a failure to respond could lead to a subpoena of data and to negative PR for the companies. As a group, they prepared a general outline for each company to use in its response to the committee, providing a minimum of information, but trying to appear helpful.

Further work remained, though, since the committee was bound to proceed to hearings. The committee staff wrote President Fuller asking him to testify. Jack prepared the testimony. He knew that the facts were amply documented by the Defense Contract Audit Agency. He decided, therefore, to come clean and offer to negotiate a payback to the Pentagon. In addition, he drafted some possible questions and answers, prepared full data on GEI's many grass roots efforts for the Sting-Ray, and arranged Fuller's trip to Washington. He made sure that GEI's documentation went in at the last minute so as to limit the committee's time for careful perusal. Fuller's testimony went well, and Jack had to respond to only a few follow-up inquiries the president had thought it unwise to answer on the spot. By and large, Jack knew, the publicity from these kinds of hearings had a short shelf-life; in a few months it would be forgotten.

Jack's most important remaining job on the Sting-Ray program was to deal with the press about the increasing cost problem the company faced, as materials became more scarce and management cost control proved inadequate. By now, he knew, much of the public was numb to cost overrun problems. As long as the information could be kept fairly quiet, GEI's image was not likely to suffer.

The Sting-Ray was a success. Jack Wilson had played a key role in bringing a new major contract to GEI.

Two years later President Fuller retired. President Jack Wilson, tanned from the Caribbean holiday that his wife had insisted he take, sat down at his new desk. Zestfully, he leafed through the paper outlining his first item of business: plans for a successor missile to the Sting-Ray.

NOTES

1. There is a wide range of literature debating these various explanations for the growth and contents of the defense budget. Inflation and other elements of cost growth in weapons spending are discussed, for example, in A. Ernest Fitzgerald, *The High Priests of Waste* (New York: Norton, 1972); Jacques S. Gansler, *The Defense Industry* (Cambridge, Mass.: MIT Press, 1980); and Richard F. Kaufman, *The War Profiteers* (Garden City, N.Y.: Doubleday, Anchor Books, 1972). Cost increases of specific weapons systems are discussed in Gordon Adams, *The B-1 Bomber, An Analysis of Its Strategic Utility, Cost, Constituency and Economic Impact* (New York: Council on Economic Priorities, 1976); the space shuttle in *Aerospace Daily,* 11 February 1980, 217; and the F-18 fighter in "Options on F-18 Cancellation Weighed," *Aviation Week and Space Technology,* 20 June 1980. The weapons procurement process and the bureaucratic politics of the Pentagon are discussed in Morton J. Peck and Frederick M. Scherer, *The Weapons Acquisition Process: An Economic Analysis* (Cambridge, Mass.: Harvard Graduate School of Business Administration, Division of Research, 1962), 98–99; J. Ronald Fox, *Arming America: How the U.S. Buys Weapons* (Cambridge, Mass.: Harvard Graduate School of Business Administration, 1974), chap. 4; Harvey M. Sapolsky, *The Polaris System Development: Bureaucratic and Programmatic Success in Government* (Cambridge, Mass.: Harvard University Press, 1972), 77–78; Fitzgerald, *The High Priests of Waste,* 59–61; and Kaufman, *The War Profiteers,* xvi. Economic aspects of defense spending are covered by Paul Baran and Paul M. Sweezey in *Monopoly Capital* (New York: Monthly Review Press, 1968), chap. 7; United Nations Centre for Disarmament, *Economic and Social Consequences of the Arms Race and Military Expenditures,* Updated Report of the Secretary-General (New York: United Nations, 1978); and United Nations Centre for Disarmament, research reports commissioned by United Nations Group of Governmental Experts on the relations between disarmament and development, submitted to U.N. Secretariat, 1980; Seymour Melman, *The Permanent War Economy* (New York: Simon & Schuster, Touchstone Books, 1964); Lloyd Dumas, "Economic Conversion, Productive Efficiency and Social Welfare," *Journal of Sociology and Social Welfare* 4, nos. 3 and 4 (1977); David Gold and Gordon Adams, "The Military Budget, Politics and the American Economy," *URPE Newsletter* of the Union for Radical Political Economics 12, no. 4 (1980); and Michael Edelstein, *The Economic Impact of Military Spending* (New York: Council on Economic Priorities, 1977). International developments and U.S./Soviet military balance issues are discussed in Franklyn D. Holzman, "Are the Soviets Really Outspending the U.S. on Defense?" *International Security,* Spring 1980; Les Aspin, "Judge Not by Numbers Alone," *Bulletin of Atomic Scientists,* June 1980; U.S., C.I.A., *A Dollar Cost Comparison of Soviet and U.S. Defense Activities, 1968–78,* January 1979; and John Collins, *U.S.-Soviet Military Balance: Concepts and Capabilities, 1960–1980* (New York: McGraw-Hill, 1980). Weapons technologies are discussed in Richard Burt, *New Weapons Technologies, Debate and Directions,* International Institute for Strategic Studies, Adelphi Paper no. 126 (London: International Institute for Strategic Studies, 1976); and Daniel Goure and Gordon McCormick, "PGM: No Panacea," *Survival* (International Institute for Strategic Studies) 22, no. 1 (1980).

2. Arthur Bentley, *The Process of Government: A Study of Social Pressure,* 2d ed. (Evanston, Ill.: Principia Press, 1945); E. E. Schattschneider, *The Semi-Sovereign People,* 2d ed. (Hinsdale, Ill.: Dryden Press, 1975); David Truman, *The Governmental Process: Political Interests and Public Opinion* (New York: Knopf, 1975); and Edward Pendleton Herring, *Group Representation before Congress* (Baltimore, Md.: Johns Hopkins Press, 1929).

3. Marver Bernstein, *Regulating Business by Independent Commissions* (Princeton, N.J.: Princeton University Press, 1955); Grant McConnell, *Private Power and American Democracy* (New York: Knopf, 1967); and Common Cause, *Serving Two Masters, A Common Cause Study of Conflicts of Interest in the Executive Branch* (Washington, D.C.: Common Cause, 1976).

4. Senator William Proxmire, *Report from Wasteland* (New York: Praeger, 1970); Fox, *Arming America;* Kaufman, *The War Profiteers;* Fitzgerald, *High Priests of Waste;*

Peck and Scherer, *Weapons Acquisition Process;* Adam Yarmolinsky, *The Military Establishment* (New York: Harper & Row, 1971); and Dumas, "Economic Conversion, Productive Efficiency and Social Welfare."

5. Lewis Anthony Dexter, *How Organizations Are Represented in Washington* (Indianapolis: Bobbs-Merrill, 1969).

6. Phyllis McGrath, *Redefining Corporate-Federal Relationships* (Conference Board).

7. See Gordon Adams, "Disarming the Military Subgovernment," *Harvard Journal on Legislation* 14, no. 3 (1977); Lester V. Salamon and John J. Siegfried, "Economic Power and Political Influence: The Impact of Industry Structure on Public Policy," *American Political Science Review* 71, no. 3 (1977); Joel D. Auerbach and Burt Rockmen, "Bureaucrats and Clientele Groups: A View from Capitol Hill," *American Journal of Political Science* 22, no. 4 (1978); McConnell, *Private Power and American Democracy;* John Lieper Freeman, *The Political Process* (Garden City, N.Y.: Doubleday, 1955), 7 and 31; Charles Jones, *Introduction to the Study of Public Policy,* 2d ed. (North Scituate, Mass.: Duxbury Press, 1977), chap. 2; Stephen Bailey, *Congress in the Seventies,* 2d ed. (New York: St. Martin's Press, 1970), 61; and Douglas Cater, *Power in Washington* (New York: Random House, 1964).

8. Harmon Zeigler and Wayne G. Peak, *Interest Groups in American Society,* 2d ed. (Englewood Cliffs, N.J.: Prentice Hall, 1972), 172.

9. McConnell describes this as the "privatization of the state" in *Private Power and American Democracy,* 244; James O'Connor describes it as the "appropriation of a sector of state power by private interest" in *The Fiscal Crisis of the State* (New York: St. Martin's Press, 1973), 66. See also, Edward S. Flash, *Economic Advice and Presidential Leadership* (New York: Columbia University Press, 1965), 36–39; and Fred Block, *Origins of International Economic Disorder* (California: University of California Press, 1977), 102–8.

10. Michael T. Hayes, "The Semi-Sovereign Pressure Groups: A Critique of Current Theory and Alternative Typology," *Journal of Politics* 40 (1978): 134–61; Schattschneider, *Semi-Sovereign People;* and Zeigler and Peak, *Interest Groups in American Society,* 172. Auerbach and Rockmen note in their survey study, "Bureaucrats and Clientele Groups," that 84 percent of the members of Congress they polled felt that the influence of interests in the administrative process was at the expense of the public interest.

11. Weidenbaum, "Arms and the American Economy," 428.

12. We make no effort to describe, in depth, congressional or Defense Department processes, which also have an impact on such decisions. There are many case studies of weapons decisions, many of which focus on bureaucratic and legislative processes. See Michael H. Armacost, *The Politics of Weapon Innovation: the Thor-Jupiter Controversy* (New York: Columbia University Press, 1969); Robert J. Art, *The TFX Decision* (Boston: Little, Brown, 1968); Sapolsky, *The Polaris System Development.* Others provide helpful insights into the corporate side as well. See Adams, *The B-1 Bomber;* Fitzgerald, *The High Priests of Waste;* Michael Mann, "Rockwell's B-1 Promotion Blitz," *Business and Society Review,* Fall 1976; Proxmire, *Report from Wasteland;* Berkely Rice, *The C-5A Scandal* (Boston: Houghton Mifflin, 1971); Anthony Sampson, *The Arms Bazaar* (New York: Viking Press, 1977); U.S. Congress, Joint Committee on Defense Production, *DoD-Industry Relations: Conflicts of Interest and Standards of Conduct,* 94th Cong., 2d sess., February 1976; U.S. Cong., Joint Committee on Defense Production, Report by the Subcommittee on Investigations, *Conflict of Interest and the Condor Missile Program,* 94th Cong. 2d sess., September 1976.

SOLDIERS AND SCRIBBLERS: A COMMON MISSION

RICHARD C. HALLORAN

Ever since the invasion of Grenada in October 1983, military officers and members of the press have debated the role of the press in covering military affairs, including combat operations. At the war colleges in Washington, Carlisle Barracks, Newport, and Montgomery, as well as in other forums, that debate has roamed over the place of the press and television in American life, the pros and cons of military coverage, and how soldiers and scribblers should treat with one another. The objective has been to defuse the bitterness, rooted in Vietnam and manifest in the absence of firsthand coverage of Grenada, that has so divided two vital institutions.

Sad to report, there is not much evidence of progress. In session after session, the same questions and allegations come up from military officers, and many of the same answers are given by journalists. Granted, the audiences change from year to year, but few explanations from journalists seem to be getting through. Nor is there much evidence that

This essay has been edited and is reprinted from Parameters 17 (Spring 1987): 10–28, by permission of Parameters. *Copyright © 1987 by Richard Halloran.*

military concerns are getting through to editors who make day-to-day decisions.

After having taken part in about two dozen such sessions, I have come to at least one conclusion: military people really do not know much about the press and television. Random samples in seminars of fifteen people and audiences of three hundred officers, mostly field grade, show that only about half have ever talked seriously with a journalist, and less than a third more than once. Few military officers have done the factual research needed to determine whether their scant experience with the press is typical or atypical; few have done the content analyses to see whether their impressions can withstand scrutiny; few have examined the First Amendment, the development of the press and television, or the roles that gatherers of news have played in the military history of the United States.

Lieutenant Colonel Gerald W. Sharpe, a student at the Army War College in 1985–86, put together a useful—and revealing—study of the experience of his classmates with the press and their consequent attitudes. Colonel Sharpe reported that "more than half the respondents (53.5%) had never spent more than one day with the media." He found that 69 percent had spent no time with the media during their last assignments. In addition, he wrote, "more than one half of the officers indicated that they had less than one day of training in their careers about the media and more than 71 percent had three days or less."

Thus he concluded: "Many senior officers have had very little personal experience in a direct working relationship with the media and have had even less formal training about how the media works or its roles and missions in American society. In spite of this, they hold very strong negative views about the media."

In short, it would seem that the vast majority of military officers have vague impressions, emotional reactions, and gut feelings about the press and television but are, in fact, operating in ignorance. That is a harsh word, admittedly, but the facts would appear to justify it.

The reasons for the ignorance, which were beyond the scope of Colonel Sharpe's research, would seem to be three. First, American high schools and universities do little to teach young citizens about the function of the press and television. The schools teach political science, economics, and sociology but not much about the grease of communications that makes national institutions work. Second, the military educational system does little to teach officers about the various media. A "media day" at a war college and a half day in "charm school" for freshly minted generals and admirals are not enough.

And third, we in the press do a miserable job of explaining ourselves. As large segments of American society—military officers are far from alone in this— have recently questioned the ethics, motives, accuracy, fairness, and responsibility of the press and television, editors and reporters belatedly have come

to realize that their institutions are in deep trouble. Even so, we have been slow to respond and are still, in this correspondent's view, well behind the curve.

Here, then, is one reporter's summary of the questions asked, complaints made, and allegations charged by military officers since Grenada. These are my own replies based on three years of meetings with military people, seven years of covering the armed forces, and thirty years of experience in journalism. Let it be underscored that what follows represents the views of no one else even though it takes into account what other journalists have written or said. In addition, let it be understood that the battles of the press and the armed forces over Vietnam itself will not be fought again here. With the passage of time, that conflict between officers and journalists has become less germane to the issues of the day and is being shifted, rightly, to the province of historians.

THE MEDIA

Military officers and civilians alike talk about "the media" as if it were a single, monolithic, structured institution.

The institution is, in fact, quite the opposite. There is no such thing as "the media," no lockstep, all-encompassing institution, any more than there is "the military" or "the military mind." For one thing, "media" is plural, not singular. The media include an almost breathtaking diversity of channels of information. Among them are news agencies or wire services, radio, television, newspapers, weekly magazines, monthly magazines, quarterlies, books, and, in some definitions, motion pictures.

Within the realm of newspapers, there are major metropolitan papers like the *New York Times* and the *Los Angeles Times,* regional papers like the *Boston Globe* and the *Chicago Tribune,* a host of local dailies and weeklies, and not a few scandal sheets. Within newspapers are the news columns, features, analytical articles, editorials, and columnists. Radio and television include national networks and the local stations. National Public Radio and cable television add to the diversity. What is known as the trade press adds still another dimension. In the military field are, to mention but a few, *Defense Daily,* a newsletter; *Defense Week* and *Aviation Week; Armed Forces Journal* and similar monthlies; plus quarterlies like *Parameters,* the *Air University Review,* and, perhaps the latest on the scene, the *Naval Submarine Review.* In sum, "the media" is a myth.

THE POWER OF THE PRESS

Many Americans have asserted that the press and television have become too powerful. Perhaps the case most often cited is the resignation of President Richard Nixon under pressure.

Like "the media," the power of the press is a myth. The press has *influence,* not power, and the distinction is important. Military officers have power in that they have the legal and, if necessary, the physical force to have orders obeyed. The press has neither and cannot enforce anything.

On the other hand, the press and television exert enormous influence on the public agenda by what they select to publish or broadcast and what they choose to ignore. In some cases, a newspaper can set the public agenda for many months, as the *New York Times* did with the Pentagon Papers. Conversely, newspapers are often criticized by vested special interests for ignoring their particular causes, both right and left.

The determining factor in what is published and what is withheld is that elusive thing called news judgment. It is perhaps the most difficult element to define in all journalism. News judgment is a combination of deciding what the public needs to know, wants to know, and has a right to know. News judgment derives from an editor's or reporter's sense of history, experience, point of view, taste, and that intangible called instinct. It is, and journalists should acknowledge this freely, a subjective judgment on which two journalists will often disagree. Differing news judgments are the cause of differing front pages or differing ways in which an article is written. The saving grace is that, over time, extreme news judgments do not survive because competition provides a check and balance.

Regarding the press and President Nixon, history shows that the press, notably the *Washington Post*, influenced the public agenda by bringing the Watergate caper to public attention and by continuing to dig into the story. But there came a time in that episode when the press ran out of steam because it lacked the authority to issue subpoenas or to force testimony. The issue then passed to the Congress and the courts, following constitutional procedures, and it was those institutions, not the press, that forced Mr. Nixon to resign.

RIGHT TO KNOW

Many military officers hold that the concept of "the people's right to know" is not in the Constitution and has been made up for the convenience of the press.

Most journalists would argue that the people's right to know is implicit in the First Amendment and was among the basic reasons the Founding Fathers adopted the amendment. Just where the explicit phrase originated is not clear, but among the earliest references to it is one from an army officer, Brevet Major General Emory Upton, who wrote a book after the Civil War titled *The Military Policy of the United States*. In that work, General Upton sought to explain the lessons of the war and to seek improvement in the nation's military posture. In the introduction, he made a signal contribution to the understanding of the First Amendment:

The people who, under the war powers of the Constitution, surrender their liberties and give up their lives and property have a right to know why our wars are unnecessarily prolonged. They have a right to know whether disasters have been brought about through the neglect and ignorance of Congress, which is intrusted with the power to raise and support armies, or through military incompetency. Leaving their representatives free to pay their own salaries, the people have a right to know whether they have devoted their time to studying the art of government.

MOTIVES

In his research, Colonel Sharpe found that "written comments on the chief causes of the conflict between the Army and the media reveal a basic distrust of the media's motives and objectives." In discussions, many officers have asserted, "You do it for the money." Or, in a more general allegation, "Everything you do is just to sell newspapers."

The first charge, to be candid, is laughable and on a par with saying that an officer joined the army to get rich. A few television personalities, to be sure, drive to the bank each week in armored cars. Generally, salaries on major publications are behind those in the military service, given equivalent education, age, and time on the job. On smaller publications, salaries are far behind.

Young men and women become journalists for many reasons. Among them are a curiosity about the world, the chance to travel and to meet all sorts of people, and the opportunity for personal recognition. The newspaper byline is like the insignia of rank worn on an officer's shoulders. The unpredictable excitement and the driving pace appeal to many journalists, and the competition turns most on. For some, reporting and writing is a way of helping to set a national or state or local agenda and thus to influence the life of the republic, which is a form of public service.

On the second point, most publications exist on what is known as the three-legged stool of news, circulation, and advertising, a concept that appears to be little understood outside of journalism. The critical leg is content. To be successful, a publication must provide something people want to read or believe they need to read. Because different people want or must read different things, different publications cater to different audiences. Conversely, if a publication does not provide what people want or need, it will fail. The journalistic graveyard is full of monuments to publishers and editors who did not understand that point.

The provision of good or necessary or useful reading material is what builds a subscription list or newsstand sales, which add up to circulation. Because advertisers want to reach those same readers, they buy advertising space. In another little-understood point, it is the sale of advertising space, not the sale of newspapers, that provides far and away the largest part of a publication's income. That income, in turn, pays for salaries, travel, newsprint, and the other costs of publishing a paper.

The same cycle is true of television—content, viewers, advertising time—and of magazines. Only the wire services, which carry no advertising, earn their income from the sale of their product.

A legitimate question is whether a publication can be controlled by advertisers. In large publications, with many diverse advertisers, the answer is no. Local newspapers are more susceptible to pressure from a few dominant advertisers. But if the content of the paper is so good the community will not do without it, even smaller papers can withstand pressure from advertisers.

Critics assert that the press and television are merely commercial enterprises, implying that they should not have the place given them under the First Amendment. But that argument overlooks the reality that a news enterprise in America's capitalistic society must earn money to do its job. The alternative is government ownership. Down that road, as history as shown amply, lies the sort of totalitarian regime found in the Soviet Union.

ETHICS

At the Air War College, an officer rose in the auditorium to ask, "What a lot of us have on our minds is: Do you guys have any ethics?"

The answer is yes. Reflecting the independence of the press invested by the First Amendment, there is no sweeping code of ethics imposed on the press from the outside. Each publication or network fashions its own, some of which is written, other of which is understood. Professional groups, such as Sigma Delta Chi, have canons that have been published as voluntary guidelines.

At the *New York Times*, for instance, there is a thick file of policies, like case law, that has accumulated over the years. For example, top management recently circulated a memo updating the policy on conflicts of interest. No reporter may write about a company in which he or she has invested, or cover an institution with which he may be remotely connected. Business reporters may not trade or play the stock market. An education reporter may not run for the school board nor a political reporter for the city council. A sportswriter may not accept free tickets. Military correspondents should not own stock in a defense industry. No one may accept a gift or take a junket.

Beyond that are individual ethics learned from parents, teachers, churches, and role models. Like motives, they vary by person, with some journalists working with unquestioned integrity and others, unhappily for the craft, skating on thin ethical ice.

PROFESSIONALISM

The allegation holds that journalists, unlike doctors, lawyers, and military officers, are not professionals.

In a narrow sense, that is true. In keeping with the First Amendment, journalists are not licensed by government in the manner of the traditional profes-sions. The practice of journalism, moreover, is a highly skilled craft, perhaps even more art than science.

In the best journalists, professionalism is an attitude, a cast of mind, an instinct, and a demonstration of skill at reporting, writing, and explaining with integrity, accuracy, and fairness. The finest compliment one journalist can bestow on another is to say that he or she is a "pro." Conversely, to be labeled an amateur is to be scorned; unfortunately, journalism today has its share of amateurs.

ACCOUNTABILITY

A corollary to the questions of ethics and professionalism is the allegation that unlike military officers, the press is not accountable. Some assert that the press is irresponsible.

While members of the press and television are not accountable in the formal manner of military officers, they are definitely held accountable through a network of public opinion, constitutional and legal restraints, competitive pressures, and company policy. In many ways, the press is held as accountable as any institution in America, and perhaps more so, given its visibility. The people to whom a newspaper is most accountable are its readers. If they do not like what the paper reports, they stop reading it. If they do not like a TV news anchor, they switch him or her off. The comment is often made that nobody elected the press, which is true. But the press is voted on more than any other institution in America, and journalists more than any elected official. A daily newspaper or television network faces the voters every day and is given a thumbs up or thumbs down. If the thumbs continue to turn down, the journalist can be out of a job or the newspaper out of existence.

Second, the First Amendment, while broadly written, is not absolute and has been refined by the Supreme Court. Justice Oliver Wendell Holmes, an eloquent defender of the First Amendment, wrote perhaps the most famous and most useful test of freedom of speech and the press in the case entitled *Schenck* v. *The United States*. He said:

The character of every act depends upon the circumstances in which it is done. . . . [T]he most stringent protection of free speech would not protect a man in falsely shouting fire in a theatre and causing a panic. . . . [T]he question in every case is whether the words used are in such circumstances and of such a nature as to create a clear and present danger.

Libel laws, especially under recent court rulings, impose marked restraints on the press, particularly with regard to accuracy. Other checks come from competitors. A newspaper making a mistake can be almost certain that it will be corrected the next day in the opposing paper. Head-to-head newspaper competition, unfortunately, has declined in recent years because papers have failed or been merged with more successful publications. Even so, the various media compete with one another; the *New York Times* considers ABC News and *Time* magazine to be as much the competition as the *Washington Post* or *Newsday.*

Lastly, individual reporters are held accountable by their employers. Minor mistakes, if they are few, are tolerated in an imperfect world, but glaring or frequent mistakes are not. Janet Cooke, who wrote a fictitious story for the *Washington Post,* and Foster Winans, who fed inside information from the *Wall Street Journal* to a stock broker, no longer work in journalism.

INACCURACY

The allegation is that the press all too often just does not get things right.

This is probably the single most legitimate complaint among all of those heard. The press and television are rampant with errors of fact, many of them minor, such as getting an officer's rank wrong, or misquoting him slightly but enough to change the meaning of what he said, or leaving out an important qualifier that would have put the event or speech into perspective.

It is the accumulation of small error, moreover, that has so eroded the credibility of the press today. Worse, many editors and reporters are cavalier about it, passing off errors as inevitable given the amount of information that is gathered, collated, and printed against daily deadlines.

Mistakes are made for a multitude of reasons. Reporters may hear things wrong, or fail to check or follow up. An inexperienced reporter, like a second lieutenant or ensign, may not have understood the nuances of what he has heard or seen. Editors, whose view of the world often differs from that of their reporters, may insist that a story be written to conform with their views. Copy editors may make careless changes, cuts, or insertions that change facts and meaning, or allow the error of a reporter to slip by.

The culprits are mostly time and competition. There is a daily rush to judgment in which facts are assembled and decisions are made by reporters and editors with one eye on the clock. It is common for a reporter to learn something at 4 p.m., to have one hour to check it out and gather more facts, to begin writing at 5 p.m., and to finish a thousand-word article at 6 p.m. After that, a senior editor may have fifteen minutes to scrutinize the story for general content and a copy editor thirty minutes to get it ready for the printer. That is not much time.

Interestingly, and perhaps paradoxically, the public seems to forgive big errors more readily than small ones. The episodes involving Janet Cooke and Foster Winans are seen as aberrations; Cooke and Winans are seen as dishonest journalists who deliberately did something wrong but who do not represent the vast majority of journalists.

But readers and viewers, rightly, do not forgive mistakes of omission or commission, especially when the report is about something on which they are informed. Do we hear about it? You bet. There is always a reader out there who scrutinizes the paper with a dictionary in one hand and a microscope in the other, who takes considerable pleasure in catching the newspaper in the wrong and calls to say so. But, if truth be told, their admonitions are all too often received politely and then brushed aside with little lasting effect.

SLANTED NEWS

Many military officers charge that much in the press is not objective and thus is unfair.

What is said to be slanted news, however, often depends far more on the reader than the writer. It is a question, in the worn analogy, of seeing the bottle half empty or half full. Perhaps the objective way would be to describe the sixteen-ounce bottle as holding eight ounces of liquid and letting the reader decide for himself.

That is inadequate, however, when the writer seeks to explain what is going on. Increasingly, the role of journalism in America is not merely to describe what is in the bottle but to explain why and how it got that way and what it means to the community or the republic. What was once called "interpretive journalism" has gotten a bad name because of abuses. Today, many journalists seek to practice what might be called "explanatory journalism," which means assembling facts in a way that makes sense to a reader and then explaining them. Enter the element of judgment, which immediately puts the reporter on a slippery slope, with few ever being sure-footed enough to traverse it all of the time without taking a fall.

That reporters are not objective is partly true because no human being is fully objective. Each has a point of view that derives from his or her upbringing, education, and experience. That becomes a set of values that a journalist applies to his or her work. Some journalists covering military affairs, for instance, believe that military power is needed to protect the United States in a rough-and-tumble world. Others believe that military power is evil, and if the world were rid of it, prospects for the survival of the human race would be more promising. The point of view that a journalist brings to his or her work thus does much to determine what he or she chooses to cover and how. The journalist who thinks that military power is necessary will focus on one set of facts, while the journalist who dislikes military power will assemble a different set of facts. It should be said here that the "journalism of advocacy" found primarily in the "alternative press" is anathema to professional reporters.

Stripping a reporter of his or her point of view would be impossible, but good reporters acknowledge, to themselves and in the copy, that there are other points of view. It is there that balance, perspective, and fairness come into the writing. Achieving that balance may be the hardest thing in journalism, and journalists only deceive themselves and their readers if they think they do a good job of it every day.

BAD NEWS

A common cry: "You never print anything but bad news."

That is only partly true. Like slanted news, whether news is good or bad is determined far more by the reader or viewer than by the reporter. A headline reading "Nixon Resigns" may be bad news if the reader is a conservative Republican but good news if he is a liberal Democrat. Conversely, the headline "Reagan Wins Reelection by Landslide" is considered good by Republicans, not so good by Democrats.

Moreover, few people remember the good news. A suggestion for a war college research paper: establish criteria as to whether news is good, neutral, or bad. Take the main news section of any newspaper for a month and divide the articles into those categories. The majority will most likely be neutral. Then sample other officers to see which articles they remember.

The allegation is right, however, to the extent that things going wrong are newsworthy. Americans expect things to go right, and that is not necessarily news, because news is what makes today different from yesterday. Americans expect military officers to be competent, tanks to be bought at the lowest possible cost, and airplanes to fly right side up. Soldiers and sailors are the sons and daughters of the readers; they expect officers to care for the troops, and when that does not happen they want to know about it. When tanks cost too much or planes do not fly right, the readers want to know why the government has not spent their money well.

INVASION OF PRIVACY

Many Americans believe that journalists too often invade the privacy of prominent and private citizens alike.

There is some truth to this allegation, but less than meets the eye. Newspaper reporters and, more often perhaps, television cameramen set up what are known as "stakeouts" near the home of a person under investigation, or barge into living rooms at times of distress, or pursue people who wish not to be interviewed. Occasionally a reporter does not identify himself or herself when asking questions, which is particularly reprehensible when talking with people inexperienced in dealing with the press.

On the other hand, by far the majority of people who appear on camera or who are interviewed by a reporter do so willingly. No law forces people to talk when they do not want to, save under subpoena. Curiously, for some people who have just suffered a loss, such as the death of a member of the family at the hands of a terrorist, talking through the press to neighbors and compatriots has a cathartic effect. It helps people to get their grief out where it can be handled. It may also be a trait particular to Americans that we are ready to try to comfort neighbors, though they be strangers, in an hour of need, and we want to know who is hurting. Witness the outpouring of sympathy to the families of the marines killed in Beirut, or the hay sent by farmers in the Middle West to farmers in the South during the drought.

In addition, readers and viewers never know about the times a reporter asks to interview a person who has suffered a loss but backs off when that person says no. It happens, and often, but the only thing the reader may see is a line saying Mrs. Jones was not available.

HIDDEN SOURCES

The complaint is worded something like this: "When we read you in the paper, we don't know where you got your information or whom you've been talking to."

It is a fair comment and a valid criticism. Far too much in the press and on television today is hidden in what journalists call "blind sourcing." That is especially true in reports from Washington that cite "administration officials," "a policy-making official," "military officers," "congressional staff aides," "defense industry executives." For all the reader knows, those sources could have been office boys answering the telephones.

While the press is primarily to blame for blind sourcing, administration officials, military officers, and congressional staff aides who decline to speak for the record must assume some of the responsibility. More often than not, the reason for not going on the record has nothing to do with national security or government policy but has everything to do with protocol. The colonel does not want his name in the paper for fear the general will be upset; the general does not want to be quoted because the assistant secretary will be miffed; the assistant secretary thinks the secretary or even the White House should be the source.

Reporters, confronted with that, agree all too readily to take the information on "background," which is not background at all but not for attribution for reasons of protocol or politics. A careful reader will notice that the vast majority of nonattributed stories come from within the government, and mostly from within the administration. The press thus permits itself to be used by the administration to float trial balloons, to advocate or oppose policies without being held responsible for the comments, and to play all manner of diplomatic, political, and bureaucratic games.

Periodically, journalists in Washington try to tighten up the use of blind sourcing, but those efforts have failed so far because everyone fears losing a competitive advantage. One newspaper might say it will no longer accept blind sourcing; that will last until its competitor comes out with a hot story citing "administration sources."

ARROGANCE

Often the charge of arrogance seems to mean bad manners on the part of reporters, particularly reporters on television, who are more visible than those in print. But print reporters are also held culpable by officers who see them in action at press conferences, whether in Washington or elsewhere.

This, too, appears to be a legitimate complaint. Reporters have been caught up in, and probably have contributed to, the general decline of civility in American life. Many reporters, especially young reporters, seem to think that acting like tough guys out of the movie *Front Page* is necessary to do their jobs. In their defense, and it is admittedly a lame defense, reporters are no more rude than many lawyers, government officials, policemen, bicycle riders, secretaries, business executives, and diplomats.

Even so, the reporter who often asks the best and toughest questions in a Pentagon news conference, Charles Corddry of the *Baltimore Sun,* is a gentleman who rarely raises his voice and is consistently courteous. In his time, Mr. Corddry has skewered the most evasive senior political and military officials with penetrating questions that have left them mumbling like schoolboys. But it has been done in a civil manner.

LIBERALS

The allegation is that the media are controlled by liberals.

That must come as a shock to the *Wall Street Journal,* the *Los Angeles Times,* the *Chicago Tribune,* the *Washington Times,* the *Manchester Union Leader,* the *San Diego Union,* and several hundred other papers, not to say *U.S. News and World Report* and the *National Review.* Columnists such as William Safire of the *New York Times,* James J. Kilpatrick and George Will, whose work appears in the *Washington Post,* and William Buckley, whose views appear not only in *National Review* but in other outlets, must be amused.

There are several problems with the allegation that liberalism runs rampant in the press. First, few people agree on what a liberal is; definitions run from nineteenth-century liberalism to twentieth-century socialism. Second, even a 1981 study by two academicians, Robert Lichter and Stanley Rothman, did not make the case that what they called the "media elite" was heavily liberal. They found that barely half of the reporters considered themselves liberal, that the vast majority took conservative economic positions such as favoring private enterprise, and that many reporters were liberal primarily on social issues such as civil rights. A 1985 survey by William Schneider and I. A. Lewis in *Public Opinion,* published by the conservative American Enterprise Institute, addressed a more important question: "Do readers detect any bias when they read their daily newspapers?" The authors concluded: "Not really. . . . There is no evidence that people perceive the newspapers they read as strongly biased to the left." In a similar study in *Public Opinion,* Barbara G. Farah and Elda Vale asserted: "The professional standards of journalism dictate that no one gets a

break. Ask George McGovern, Edward M. Kennedy, or Geraldine Ferraro whether liberals are treated with special solicitude by the press."

Put another way, if the press is so pervasively liberal, how come Ronald Reagan won forty-nine of fifty states in the 1984 election?

OPERATIONAL SECURITY

Many officers assert that the presence of the press during a military operation jeopardizes security.

That is an allegation without basis in historical fact. An examination of the record in World Wars I and II, where there was censorship, and in Korea and Vietnam, where there were guidelines but no censorship, shows that rarely did the press endanger operational security. In Vietnam, Barry Zorthian, long the government's chief spokesman, has said he knows of only a half-dozen instances in which a correspondent broke the guidelines; three of those were inadvertent.

The record is not perfect. In a recent case, a wire service report disclosed a marine fire direction team's position in the mountains behind Beirut during the conflict in Lebanon. That did jeopardize the operation and perhaps the lives of those marines, and it should not have been printed. The dispatch could have been written in a way such that the facts were made known without giving information useful to an adversary.

Over the long run, however, the record shows that with a modicum of common sense, consultation, and planning, military forces can preserve operational security while correspondents go about their jobs. At the end of a long discussion of this issue at the Naval War College, a retired admiral asserted: "Operational security is not the issue. The issue is that when you write about us, you make us look bad."

The admiral had it exactly right—operational security is not the issue.

CLASSIFIED INFORMATION

Perhaps no single question is raised more, and with more heat, than the allegation: "You print classified information."

Right. The press has published classified information in the past and will in the future. For one thing, the classification system is almost a farce, is abused for political and bureaucratic reasons that have nothing to do with national security, and thus breeds contempt. For another, there are laws and court decisions that govern what may and may not be printed and the press is obliged to operate within those constraints, but they do not cover most classified information. Third, responsible publications are keenly aware that the release of sensitive information—which is not the same as classified information—could jeopardize lives, operations, intelligence sources, or technical capabilities.

Legally, it is important to understand that there is no law authorizing the classification of information, or forbidding the publication of classified information. The classification system is based in executive orders, the latest being Executive Order 12356, signed by President Ronald Reagan in April 1982. By definition, executive orders apply to members of the executive branch, and to no one outside it. A journalist or any other citizen, therefore, breaks no law by disclosing classified information.

Several narrowly written laws apply to journalists as well as to other citizens. One is found in sections 793 through 798 of Title 18 of the *U.S. Code,* forbidding the disclosure of intelligence gained by communications intercepts. Another is the law that forbids the public identification of intelligence agents. A third is in certain sections of the Atomic Energy Act pertaining to nuclear weapons.

What about the espionage laws? The Association of the Bar of the City of New York recently did a study of that statute, which forbids the unauthorized disclosure of information to a foreign nation with the intent to do harm to the United States. In its report, the association said: "We conclude that prosecution under the espionage laws is appropriate only in cases of transmission of properly classified information to a foreign power with the intent to injure the United States or to aid a foreign power."

Note several phrases: the association said "properly classified information," not just any classified information; "to a foreign power," not to American citizens, voters, and taxpayers; "with the intent to injure the United States," not to foster the public debate on serious issues confronting a democratic republic. The association went on to say: "Other uses of the statutes, such as prosecution of the media or those providing information for the sake of public debate, are inappropriate."

What about moral obligations? The journalist, indeed, must deal with serious moral obligations when he or she gains access to sensitive information that, if disclosed, would cause jeopardy to life, the security of troops, a piece of military technology, or a valuable intelligence source. The crux comes when the disclosure would cause direct, immediate, and irreparable damage. It would not make any difference whether the information was classified, but whether the disclosure would do genuine harm.

This view is rooted in the doctrine of "clear and present danger" enunciated by Justice Holmes and reinforced by other court rulings. In *Near* v. *Minnesota,* Justice Charles Evans Hughes said that in time of declared war, "no one would question but that a government might prevent . . . the publication of sailing dates of transports or the number and location of troops." In the case of the Pentagon Papers, one justice wrote that publication of national security information could be prohibited if the government could show that it would "inevitably, directly and immediately cause the occurrence of an event kindred to imperiling the safety of a transport at sea." Two other justices, in a concurring opinion, said the government must present proof that disclosure "will result in direct, immediate, and irreparable damage to our nation or its people."

There have been instances, not generally known because of their sensitive nature, in which journalists have withheld information that, if published, would have caused a clear and present danger. Several reporters in Washington, for instance, knew that American hostages had taken refuge in the Canadian Embassy in Teheran in 1979. To have printed that would surely have put those Americans in danger. The *New York Times* and other publications made a deliberate effort to determine which passengers aboard the hijacked TWA airliner in Beirut were military personnel so that their identity could be kept out of the paper. In another case, newspapers and networks for many months withheld information about the Central Intelligence Agency's attempt to raise a Russian submarine with the ship *Glomar Explorer.* Some of those decisions not to publish were made by editors who applied common sense and the standard of clear and present danger, while others were made after consulting with government authorities.

Editors have not always made the right decisions, but over the years many publications have been far more careful than anyone in the government has been willing to concede. Conversely, the government has failed to level with the press or has cried wolf so often that it has lost credibility. Both political parties have been guilty; it is not a partisan matter.

On classification itself, many journalists have little regard for the system because it is mindless. According to the 1985 report to the president from the Information Security Oversight Office, the latest report available, the Department of Defense alone made 22,322,895 original and derivative classification decisions that year. Of those, 446,458 were to classify something top secret.

Such numbers, on the face of it, are absurd. There are not nearly half a million things so secret that the disclosure of them would constitute a clear and present danger to the United States, nor would disclosure cause grievous damage to the national security. Justice Potter Stewart once wrote: "For when everything is classified, nothing is classified, and the system becomes one to be disregarded by the cynical or the careless, and to be manipulated by those intent on self-protection or self-promotion."

As an example of mindless classification, the following paragraph was taken from a navy budget document classified secret; the paragraph itself was also classified secret. It said, in full: "The Navy must continue to attract and retain sufficient numbers of high-quality, skilled and motivated people. Compensation and quality of life improvements must be competitive in the job market. Ways must be found to reduce requirements for administrative functions, reduce personnel turbulence and permanent change of stations moves." Had this paragraph been printed on every recruiting poster in the nation, it would not have harmed the national security.

Note, too, that complaints from government about classified information in the press usually describe the leak as "an unauthorized disclosure." In the eyes of many government officials and military officers, "authorized disclosure" is permissible if it serves their purposes. But that poses two different sets of ground rules, one for government, the other for journalists. Few journalists are willing to play in that rigged game; when the government cleans up the system and plays by the same rules it wishes to impose on journalists, then perhaps the system can be made to work.

LEAKS

An air force lieutenant colonel suggested that military people were baffled by leaks. "Just how does a leak work?" he asked.

The popular notion of a leak is a "Deep Throat" who signals a reporter with a flower pot and then meets him or her draped in a black cloak in an alley in the dark of night.

Not so. Most leaks occur in the light of day in the office of a senior political official or military officer, or someone on their staffs. The cliché holds that the ship of state is the only vessel that leaks from the top. It is a cliché, but it is also true. Relatively few leaks come from dissidents outside the government. Or, as a British official put it: "Briefing is what I do, and leaking is what you do."

A professor at Harvard, Martin Linsky, recently did a survey of nearly a thousand senior officials who held office from the Johnson through the Reagan administrations and he interviewed thirty-eight officials and journalists. From that, he concluded that 42 percent of the officials had at one time or another leaked information to a journalist. Professor Linsky also thought the percentage was really higher, saying: "Some who did would presumably not admit it and others would define their leaks narrowly enough so as to exclude their own practices."

The officials gave a variety of reasons for leaking: to counter a false report, to gain attention for a policy, to develop a good relationship with a reporter, to send a message to another branch of government, to undermine another official's position, to inform other officials and the public of a policy decision, to divert attention from another issue.

Stephen Hess, of the Brookings Institution, who has studied the operations and foibles of the press in Washington, identified six kinds of leaks in his book, *The Government/Press Connection:* the policy leak or pitch to gain or to erode support; the trial balloon, which discloses a proposal under consideration to see who supports and who opposes; the ego leak, in which the leaker shows off how important he is and how much he knows; the goodwill leak, in which the leaker hopes to accumulate credit with a reporter for use later; the animus or grudge leak that seeks to damage the reputation or programs of an opponent; and the whistle-blower leak, usually the last resort of a person who has been frustrated in getting changes inside the government.

One more should be added, the inadvertent leak, sometimes called a tip. It happens when a source drops a hint that flags a reporter that something newsworthy is going on. The reporter then uses that to lever out more information elsewhere. This happens more often than is realized, and the original leaker may never suspect whence the tip came.

Lastly, rarely do leaks appear in the paper as the leaker intended. Most good reporters, knowing that leaks are self-serving, seek more information from other sources before going into print. Moreover, reputable newspapers do not print pejoratives from an anonymous source. Either the source puts his name on it or it is not fit to print.

REPORTERS LACKING
MILITARY EXPERIENCE

Many officers complain that reporters, mostly young people, have not served in the armed forces and therefore are not competent to cover them.

The criticism does not hold. Capable reporters learn to cover politics without running for office, or business without having been entrepreneurs, or education without having taught school. Similarly, lawyers defend clients without having themselves stood trial and doctors treat patients for diseases they themselves have not suffered.

Having said that, a military reporter who has served in the armed forces can have an advantage over a competitor who has not. The reporter who has served may have a grasp of military culture and lingo that escapes his colleague and may have the credentials to establish rapport with military sources more easily. Remembering which end of the rifle the bullet comes out has rarely hurt a military correspondent.

On the other hand, the ranks of journalism today are full of reporters, editors, and producers who have been in military service—and hated every minute of it. They would not necessarily make better military correspondents than the reporter who has not served and would not be welcomed by military sources.

TAKING UP TIME

An army major in a military-media seminar leaned back from the table and said: "You're a pain in the ass. A media visit is more trouble than an inspection by a three-star general."

Maybe so. But that is a self-inflicted wound, as many reporters require only a few hours of time with informed officers and some time in the field with the troops. Television may need more, as producers can be demanding when it comes to pictures.

Comments like the major's, moreover, reflect a defensive attitude and a failure to understand that military officers are accountable to the voters and taxpayers through a variety of channels. The press is one of them—only one, to be sure, but still one of them.

Further, such comments indicate a failure to understand a principle of military life, especially in a democratic nation: the armed forces of the United States cannot long sustain a military operation without the consent and, indeed, the vigorous approval of the American people. Of all the lessons Americans should have learned from Vietnam, surely that must be high on the list.

It would be far better, for the nation and the armed forces, if officers looked more positively on the rare occasions they are called upon to deal with the press and saw them as opportunities to build support in the public. It should also be seen as a chance to show off the troops, who almost always like the attention they get.

In sum, talking with many journalists *is* worth an officer's time. It is also among his duties, and will become more so as he rises in rank.

THE PRESS IN WORLD WAR II

The allegation is that the press today is different from what it was in 1945.

Right. So are army officers, navy pilots, lawyers, doctors, and Indian chiefs, butchers, bakers, and candlestick makers. The whole world is different today, so the comparison is rather silly. Just as every other institution in America has changed, so have the media. Television, the speed of communications, the education of reporters, and the demands of readers are but a few of the differences.

Former Secretary of Defense James R. Schlesinger likes to assert that "the age of Ernie Pyle is dead." But that is another myth, for there never was an age of Ernie Pyle, the legendary correspondent of World War II who carved out a unique place covering the grunts. Ernie Pyle, who was killed in the Pacific just before the war ended, had the luxury of writing about the grunt's eye view of the war because hundreds of other reporters covered the daily news of the war.

Moreover, Ernie Pyle rarely covered what he called "the big picture" and thus was not confronted with the issues that military correspondents today must handle. He made his name writing about the relatively simple, focused existence of men in combat, not about the complexities of the military budget, or quality controls in defense plants, or whether women should be permitted in combat or the mysteries of fighting a nuclear war.

Reed Irvine, a critic of the press who runs an operation called Accuracy in Media, regularly lambastes journalists for not going to the field with the troops. The charge does not hold up—witness the number of reporters who were with troops in Vietnam, with about sixty getting killed and several winning combat decorations. Beyond that, Mr. Irvine and others who applauded the exclusion of reporters from Grenada cannot have it both ways. Journalists cannot be faulted for not being with the troops if the high command blocks them out.

LACK OF PATRIOTISM

Occasionally an officer or a civilian has charged that members of the press are unpatriotic because they uncover incompetence, fraud, lies, or other wrongdoing in government. Secretary of Defense Caspar W. Weinberger has come close to charging the press with treason and with giving aid and comfort to the enemy. Patrick Buchanan, the director of communications for President Reagan, questioned the loyalty of the press to the nation when details of the Iran-Contra affair were exposed.

Such accusations bear a tone of self-righteousness, as if to say that only the speaker is loyal to America and anyone who disagrees with him is unpatriotic. That attitude might be better suited to a Tory who believed in the divine right of kings than to an American with moral and intellectual roots in the Revolution's struggle for freedom from an oppressive government.

Accusing the press of disloyalty also betrays a lack of faith in the robust democracy that is America, the last best hope for human freedom on the face of the earth. Ours is an open society dedicated to the proposition that honest debate and dissent and a healthy distrust of the power of government are the order of the day. As an Irishman, John Curran, said in 1790, "The condition upon which God hath given liberty to man is eternal vigilance."

In a sense, soldiers and scribblers share a common mission. Under the Constitution, soldiers are charged with maintaining a vigil against external threats; journalists are charged with vigilance against internal enemies who would corrupt and destroy our way of life.

Contrast, for instance, the American handling of Watergate and the Soviet Union's handling of Chernobyl. It is a point overlooked that Watergate proved, perhaps more than anything else in the twentieth century, the strength of the American political system. America was able to withstand the shock and to have a peaceful transition of power that few other nations would have experienced. The Soviet Union, where the press is an arm of government, dealt with the accident at the nuclear power plant by trying to hide it from the Russian people and the world. In those cases, it would seem undeniable that the American press served American citizens far better than TASS, *Pravda,* and *Isvestia* served the Russians.

To close on a personal note, I do not question the patriotism of other Americans—and I do not permit anyone to question mine. If we cannot have that as a basis for treating with one another, then we as a nation will have lost something that makes America what it is.

PRESIDENTS, POLLS, AND THE USE OF FORCE

CATHERINE McARDLE KELLEHER

The crisis over Bosnia raises anew a debate that reaches back to the first days of the American republic: under what conditions will and should the United States be willing to use military force? It is a debate that most presidents have tried to avoid or to dominate quickly; President Bill Clinton is no exception. Yet for Bosnia or a new contingency, it is a debate that must now be joined as a superpower United States, clearly superior in military capability and far from its isolationist past, searches for new relations with former friends and foes, with competitors and clients, with the strong and the weak.

For much of the Cold War era, the arguments and the answers to these questions seemed reasonably straightforward: the United States had to be prepared to use force whenever and wherever an implacable ideological foe challenged its fundamental interests and those it shared with its free-world partners. In retrospect, Berlin, Korea, and Cuba appear predictable, if not necessarily inevitable, and in the tradition of World War II, "the good war." The worldwide threat of communism in all its forms meant the United States could no longer afford the luxury of slow, considered mobilization, of withdrawal to its hemisphere, or of shunning entangling military alliances.

But the decade of Vietnam and its aftermath, the debate over U.S. military intervention, and the legitimacy of both service and protest, divided the nation and ultimately marked a generation. Throughout the 1970s, most issues—military, political, and ethical—were left undiscussed or unresolved. The 1980s yielded few answers as arguments raged over whether to use American force in Nicaragua and Libya, and over the impact of military victories and defeats in Lebanon, Grenada, and Panama.

The debate over Bosnia goes to the heart of American assumptions about the utility of force and the factors that now must shape U.S. foreign and defense policy. What, in this post–Cold War era, are the appropriate yardsticks and instruments for U.S. national interest? How narrowly can or should we choose to interpret this concept? How are we now to balance our long-revered tradition as democracy's "city on the hill" and our proud claim as the first practical, nonideological polity in our approach to international issues? What of our legacy as the arsenal of democracy and the champion of human rights? What of our heritage as pragmatic problem solvers, faithful to case-by-case analysis and the trade-off of costs and benefits? Regarding Bosnia itself, how do we now choose between what some portray as our moral responsibility to intervene to prevent further atrocities and protect the innocent, and what others argue should be our principled avoidance of an involvement in an uncertain quagmire?

PUBLIC OPINION: TRENDS AND TENDENCIES

Understanding present trends concerning the use of force in Bosnia requires a step backward to more theoretical debates about the nature and disposition of American public opinion toward foreign policy more generally.

The dominant postwar interpretation was that Americans were largely uninformed and uninterested in international issues and affected more by mood and domestic conditions than by adherence to coherent worldviews.[1] Like most democratic populations, they were seen as slow to anger and generally noninterventionist, especially in the affairs of other democracies. But once mobilized by their political leadership, Americans were prone to rash or "moralistic" action, or the "spasm" use of military force. They wanted immediate action, the effective and immediate application of all-out military power "to get the job done," and the fastest possible return at the lowest costs of life to the "normal" status of domestic tranquility. Successful problem solving was the operational task; the preservation of democratic values in an uncertain world, the national preoccupation.

Analysis done during the 1980s and 1990s challenged this interpretation as outdated and far more reflective of the assumptions of the immediate postwar and even the prewar climate of opinion.[2] Whether once true or not, this traditional view is undermined by the nature of the post–Cold War international environment and the changing nature of domestic political patterns. Almost every general foreign policy survey shows the public is increasingly well informed about global issues, devotes attention to evolving international events, and has clear opinions on most major foreign and defense policy questions. Americans do take more account of moral issues in evaluating foreign policy choices than some other nationalities; they are more mobilizable for what William Schneider calls "valence" issues, or

This essay has been edited and is reprinted from Beyond the Beltway: Engaging the Public in U.S. Foreign Policy, *ed. Daniel Yankelovich and I.M. Destler (New York: W. W. Norton, 1994), 225–52, by permission of W.W. Norton & Company, Inc. Copyright © 1994 by The American Assembly.*

questions involving values, than for what seem matters of "position" or narrow policy advantage.[3] But they are overwhelmingly pragmatic in finally deciding on support for overseas initiatives, including the use of military force. Costs and risks count; case-by-case decisions outnumber the invocation of universal principles; short-term actions with a high probability of success are preferred to longer-term involvements with uncertain prospects for achievement. They are, in Bruce Jentleson's apt phrase, "the pretty prudent public."[4]

This reflects less the passing of the communist threat than a gradual evolution of post-Vietnam thinking about America's role. Jentleson argues, for example, that popular support for U.S. military ventures before the fall of the Berlin Wall reflects neither the block solidarity of the Cold War period nor the distraction and fragmentation of the "Vietnam trauma." Rather, Americans became more disposed to the use of military force for humanitarian ends or to counter blatantly aggressive behavior, while remaining resistant to military efforts at enforced nation building or intervention in civil wars.[5]

But the changes are clear even in public rhetoric or at the surface level of opinion. Unquestionably there is a special susceptibility in poll results to the manipulation of key words and symbols, but there is also increasing attention to practical utility—as is evident in recent surveys on attitudes about Bosnia. Americans are much more willing to offer their support for U.S. military involvement when it is mentioned in the context of an "allied" or "multilateral" or "U.N." mission. This signals a fundamentally different type of U.S. involvement, from unilateral action to collective effort, and it is not surprising that favorable responses increase by as much as 10 percent. Americans respond more subtly to words that play on sentiment such as "moral" or "humanitarian," and those that play on emotion by conjuring up graphic images of "ethnic cleansing" or "raping and murdering." Mention of words like "innocent" or "victim" may slightly increase support for American intervention, and phrases such as "send ground forces" or "risk casualties" have the opposite effect. The patterns indeed are quite stable—and far less variable than those reported in the past.

OVERVIEW: CURRENT OPINION ON THE
USE OF FORCE

In the abstract, Americans continue to view direct U.S. military involvement only as a last resort, reserved for the most desperate and extreme circumstances. The key descriptors are reluctance and caution. There is still a reservoir of support for the traditional U.S. commitment to the North Atlantic Treaty Organization (NATO) and to the use of military force to defend our allies in Western Europe. But there is an overwhelming reluctance, if not a fundamental aversion, to the use of force elsewhere. This dichotomy persists into the 1990s with two "hypothetical" exceptions. Americans report an increasing willingness to defend South Korea from an invasion by the North Koreans and Israel from an Arab attack.[6]

The Gulf War boosted public confidence in the military and fueled a greater tendency toward championing the cause of weaker nations confronted by aggression, and toward defending the human rights of the oppressed. But the apparent constraint of Saddam Hussein and the end of the Soviet Union have given new room for concerns about the severity of the budget deficit and heightened pressure to divert badly needed resources from defense to domestic programs. A majority of the American public objects to providing military aid overseas, and support for military assistance even to traditional allies has suffered since the Cold War ended. Despite the Gulf crisis, support has fallen for military and economic aid to Israel and Egypt, the two pillars of the Gulf strategy.[7]

Humanitarian assistance clearly outranks all other international initiatives in popular support—as it does in most European countries as well. The *Times Mirror* Center poll of October 11, 1990, for example, found that, while reluctant to send military aid, Americans are very willing to provide vital assistance to countries where basic vital necessities may not be available. Eighty percent of those surveyed responded that they would favor the United States offering "food and medical assistance" to those in need. By contrast, only 70 percent favored sending "economic and military aid to countries that are *important allies*" of the U.S.," and only 75 percent favored aid to encourage the purchase of U.S. products.

There is a good deal of evidence that while Americans reject an activist role for the U.S. military, they consistently support nonmilitary international involvement. A survey taken by the Chicago Council on Foreign Relations reveals an interesting trend in public support for an internationally engaged America. There was a steady decline in support for an active international role for the United States, from an all-time high in 1956 (71%) to an all-time low in 1982 (54%). From 1982 to 1986, however, there was a resurgence in support (to 64%) for an active United States. Ironically, in spite of the heightened attention given to domestic and economic issues, the 1990 survey indicates that the percentage of Americans favoring an active international role for the United States fell only slightly between 1986 and 1990 (see Table 1).

Americans also now see U.S. military prominence as only one aspect of our international interest and commitment. The 1991 *Times Mirror* Center poll, for example, found that 92 percent of those surveyed agreed it is best for the future of the United States to be active in world affairs. When asked directly about the statement, "The best way to ensure peace is through military strength," only 52 percent agreed, while 45 percent disagreed. For the most part, though, Americans still believe that a strong military is critical to the long-term security of the United

Table 1

Percentage of the American Public
"In Favor of Active Role"

Year	Percentage	Year	Percentage
1948	70	1978	59
1952	68	1982	54
1956	71	1986	64
1973	66	1990	62
1974	66		

Source: Chicago Council on Foreign Relations, 1990.

States. In a CBS News/New York Times poll of October 5–7, 1991, 67 percent of Americans agreed that it is "still important for (the) U.S. to be on guard with a strong military," while only 30 percent felt that it is "possible to reduce military strength."

Americans divide almost evenly on whether the United States is more influential today than it was in 1980; in the 1990 Chicago Council on Foreign Relations poll, 37 percent said the role of the United States is now more important, 35 percent said the role of the United States is now less important, and 24 percent said it is equally important. It is interesting to note that, traditionally, the views of the public with regard to the U.S. role in global affairs have fluctuated along with perceptions of the U.S. military vis-à-vis the Soviet Union. American opinion now is more closely correlated with public perceptions of the economic standing of the United States vis-à-vis Western Europe and Japan.[8] This plus the disparity between those who agree that an activist role for the United States is wise and those who agree that military power is the best way to fulfill our global mission illustrate that Americans are increasingly aware of the importance of economic and other nonmilitary power in safeguarding our national security.

Attitudes of the American public toward the use of force are strongly affected by whether the military action is unilateral, multilateral, or part of a U.N.-mandated effort. Throughout most of the Cold War, the American public supported the leadership role of the United States to balance the Soviet Union. Americans are now more likely to support U.S. military involvement as part of a coalition than when the United States is acting independently, and the public is even more supportive when the United States is acting as part of a U.N.-sanctioned effort. A Gallup poll taken December 3–4, 1992, found that 87 percent of Americans agreed that the "United States should commit its troops only as part of a United Nations operation," while 73 percent felt that the United States should commit "only with other allies." The percentage of the population willing to support U.S. military action "on its own in some cases" dropped to 62 percent.

A poll taken by Market Strategies and Greenberg-Lake between June 23 and July 1, 1991, found that 80 percent of Americans agreed with the statement: "When faced with future problems involving aggression, the United Nations should take the lead." In stark contrast to opinion at the height of the Cold War, only 17 percent responded that the "United States should lead." Asked what they would prefer if the United Nations refused to act, many (54%) felt the United States should then take the lead, but a clear 40 percent believed the United States should still wait for others to act or "stay out of it."

Clearly, most Americans now are more wary of unilateral military action. They seem reluctant but willing to join a multilateral effort to put an end to a genuinely ominous and threatening situation, and they are more willing to participate in an effort to fulfill a mission endorsed by the United Nations.

THE USE OF FORCE IN SPECIFIC COUNTRIES

During the Cold War, the continuing East–West struggle gave many countries some strategic significance that they otherwise would have lacked. Americans now consider a few select nations to be of special or vital interest, but most to be relatively insignificant in terms of U.S. security. Long-standing prejudices and preferences toward other countries and people, such as historical experience or cultural likeness, continue to affect public opinion regarding the use of force. Nonetheless, public attitudes toward many countries have changed dramatically since the end of the Cold War.

A Louis Harris and Associates poll taken in July of 1980 asked Americans which countries they felt "could be a threat to the security and well-being of the U.S." Eighty-four percent responded positively that the Soviet Union could pose a threat to the United States, while 56 percent cited Iran as a potential threat, and 41 percent named communist China. No other countries were mentioned by more than 17 percent of those surveyed as posing a potential threat to the United States. While the Soviet Union was seen as a serious threat to the United States and as its greatest rival during the Cold War, Americans now view Russia as being of critical importance to the United States. Whereas 84 percent of respondents in 1980 said the Soviet Union posed a threat to the United States, by 1990, 83 percent mentioned the Soviet Union as a nation of vital interest to the United States. In the Times Mirror polls of 1990 and 1992 as well, the perception of a Russian threat fell significantly from 32 percent in 1990 to 13 percent in 1992. Most striking was the increase in two years of the number of respondents who named Japan as representing the greatest threat to the United States—from 8 percent to 31 percent. The focus of public concern on an economic competitor rather than a traditional military rival suggests that the public has embraced the broader definition of U.S. security interests made a reality by the end of the Cold War.

The Chicago Council polls in 1986 and again in 1990 reflected other changes in how Americans view specific political-military relationships. Respondents

Table 2

Willingness of Americans to Use Force Overseas

Condition	Percentage
If Soviet troops invaded Western Europe	58
If Iraq invaded Saudi Arabia	52
If the government of Mexico were threatened by a revolution or civil war	48
If the Soviet Union tried to overthrow a democratic government in Eastern Europe	44
If North Korea invaded South Korea	44
If Arab forces invaded Israel	43
If Iraq refused to withdraw from Kuwait	42
If Japan were invaded by the Soviet Union	39
If the government of El Salvador were about to be defeated by leftist rebels	28
If the government of the Philippines were threatened by a revolution or civil war	22

Source: Chicago Council on Foreign Relations, 1990.

who saw Saudi Arabia as vital to the United States increased from 77 percent in 1986 to 83 percent in 1990. Those who said Japan was of vital interest to the United States increased from 77 percent in 1986 to 79 percent in 1990. Iran was mentioned by 51 percent in 1986 and 56 percent in 1990, while Poland was named as vital to the United States by 35 percent in 1986 and 43 percent in 1990. All other countries considered in the survey were thought to be less vital to the United States by 1990 than they had been in 1986. Most notably, the percentage of Americans viewing the countries of Western Europe (including Great Britain, Germany, and France) as vital to the United States fell significantly between 1986 and 1990.

Clearly, though, Americans retain a unique sense of commitment to our traditional allies in Western Europe. Although the immediate communist threat has receded, the special transatlantic relationship has endured and the economic and political ties have grown ever stronger over the years. The Chicago Council poll indicates that this majority willingness to use force extends to only four other American regional relationships: with Mexico, the Middle East, Korea, and Eastern Europe, and then only under direct threat (see Table 2).

THE USE OF FORCE IN BOSNIA

It is interesting to compare these general findings with the more specific opinion patterns in one particular time period with respect to the Bosnian crisis. Throughout the week of May 6, 1993, the day that the Bosnian Serbs rejected the Vance-Owen peace plan, a series of public opinion polls was conducted on the subject of U.S. military intervention in Bosnia. The results of three—a CBS News poll of May 4–5, a CNN/*USA Today* poll of May 6, and an ABC News poll of May 7—showed that Americans were paying closer attention to the crisis in the Balkans than they were earlier in the year, and that they were more supportive of President Clinton's efforts to bring a stop to the war. But although they were increasingly frustrated by the failure of the inter-

national community to take action, they were still unwilling to support any U.S. military action without European involvement.

Americans persisted in their belief that the United States is under no obligation to intervene. The CBS News poll of May 4–5, 1993, found that 52 percent of Americans did not believe that the United States has a responsibility there, while only 37 percent of Americans thought it does. The same poll found that a solid majority, 77 percent of Americans, felt that the war in Bosnia is the responsibility of the Europeans and that American involvement should follow only after a commitment by the Europeans. Many Americans indeed believe the United States has already done enough to stop the war in Sarajevo and Bosnia; Yankelovich surveys found 49 percent thought so in August 1992, while 59 percent took that position in January 1993.

The CNN/*USA Today* poll reported that in May 1993 a majority of Americans preferred that the United States not get involved in Bosnia at all. When asked about the possibility of the "United States conduct(ing) air strikes against Serbian military forces," 55 percent were opposed, while 36 percent favored such an action. But sentiment has been rising in support of sending U.S. forces as part of a multilateral operation. Indeed, the ABC poll found that a majority, 65 percent of Americans, favored air strikes against Bosnian Serb positions as long as these are carried out in conjunction with our European allies.

Throughout the fall and winter of 1992–93, a majority of Americans (58% according to ABC) still firmly opposed the use of U.S. ground forces under any circumstances. Americans were deeply divided on sending U.S. ground troops to the region even as part of a U.N. peacekeeping force because of the serious risks involved. The CBS poll found that 48 percent favored sending U.S. troops as part of a U.N. peacekeeping effort, but nearly as many (45%) opposed this action. Support went above the 50 percent level only when ground troops were not mentioned specifically and if an in-place peace agreement was posited.

There were many signals that the public was waiting for cues from the president as to the range of possible military options. Given President Clinton's reluctance to make a direct appeal to the American people in support of anything less than multilateral military action in Bosnia, there was mixed evidence relating to a "rallying 'round the president" effect. The May CBS poll found 35 percent approved of Clinton's efforts, 35 percent disapproved, and 30 percent offered no comment. Roughly equivalent CNN/USA Today results found 48 percent approved and 35 percent disapproved, while ABC reported 54 percent of Americans gave their approval and only 34 percent disapproved. These results seemed most directly influenced by the more general ratings of the president's performance in April and May 1993.

The CNN/USA Today poll asked Americans what they considered to be very good, good, or not good reasons for launching U.S. air strikes against Serbian forces. Sixty-three percent of Americans mentioned our "moral obligation" to stop ethnic cleansing; 57 percent cited stopping the spread of ethnic conflict in Europe. Only 49 percent claimed the U.S. "national security interests at stake in Bosnia" as a good or very good reason. Asked to give reasons why the United States should not launch air strikes, 73 percent mentioned avoiding American casualties, while 65 percent questioned their military efficacy. More tellingly, 71 percent sought to prevent the United States from getting drawn into the fighting, and 61 percent cited U.S. economic problems as a good or very good reason for the United States to stay out.

The shadow of Vietnam clearly hung over attitudes on Bosnia as some direct polling dramatically demonstrated. A Gallup poll of January 1993 found that 41 percent of Americans feared that U.S. intervention in Bosnia would end up like the war in Vietnam, while 47 percent saw an outcome more like that of the Gulf War. The CNN/USA Today poll of May 6, 1993, found similar responses to the same question: 43 percent feared an outcome more like Vietnam, and 49 percent speculated the war would be more like that in the Gulf. Public opinion remained polarized. Significantly, too, the CNN/USA Today poll found in early May that 84 percent of Americans would not approve of Clinton conducting air strikes without the approval of Congress.

COMPARISON WITH ATTITUDES ON THE GULF AND ON SOMALIA

Popular reluctance and misgivings over goals and instruments in Bosnia contrast sharply with the pattern of opinion with respect to the use of U.S. military force both in the Gulf and in Somalia. Although the story is far from over, the probable reasons for the differences seem clear and quite compelling.

Both the Gulf and Somalia enjoyed substantial popular support almost from the very first. Shortly after Iraq's brutal invasion of Kuwait, 70 percent of Americans polled by Hart and Teeter supported U.S.

military action. As the likelihood of war increased, there were some second thoughts—for example, by December a slip to only 63 percent. But as Desert Storm was launched and met with initial success, public support rose further. An ABC/Washington Post poll during military action garnered 85 percent approval, while a slightly later Gallup question elicited a remarkable 87 percent.[9]

The humanitarian use of military force in Somalia gained lower levels of support—only 66 percent approved of unilateral U.S. action in the weeks before the mission. Mention of humanitarian purposes or a possible multilateral framework—"a U.N. effort"—raised figures by another 10 percent. But it was the successful landing in Somalia and the demonstrated lack of risk that made the greatest difference. Subsequent polls showed 80 percent support and more.[10]

What Jentleson describes as the "halo effect" of success is clearly a very powerful factor in opinion trends.[11] Desert Storm's glow lasted almost two years. Five months after its end, 82 percent still declared it not to have been a mistake to send military force there. In the fall of 1991, 84 percent agreed that the U.S. military performance demonstrated that the United States could "still unite and accomplish things." A year after the invasion, 65 percent of Americans supported a potential second use of U.S. military force to compel Iraq's compliance with U.N. inspections of its military arsenal. In January 1993, 85 percent told ABC News/Washington Post interviewers that if Iraq continued to violate the no-fly zone, the United States should be prepared to attack Iraq again.

Unquestionably, public opinion rallied to the symbol of Saddam Hussein as an unscrupulous despot, bent on an anti-American course. The U.S. response to Iraq was also widely perceived as morally just; 56 percent of those interviewed in March 1991 cited moral reasons for the Gulf action, while only 34 percent cited economic factors.[12]

POLICY PARAMETERS: VIEWS ON THE MILITARY

It is important to put these attitudes on the use of force in specific cases into a more future-oriented policy context. A critical component is general public attitudes toward the military—as a profession and as an instrument of national action. Americans before World War II had generally held a low opinion of the military, particularly the professional cadre, and often were critical of them as outside the general democratic society. Patriotic feelings fastened rather on conscripts, raised only after a legitimate popular decision to use force and fashioned in the mold of the "citizen soldier."

The postwar period saw a radical change in this opinion profile, especially after the military buildup for Korea and the fixed military deployments in Europe and in Asia. Military forces—professional and conscript—became the embodiment of American values and American commitment against the communist threat. Approval ratings were high; and the military rose in status vis-à-vis civilian professions for perhaps the first time in peacetime history.

In the Vietnam decade, Americans were deeply divided on how they should now view the military; this division reflected their general views on the war itself. Some indeed held the military responsible for both the military defeat and the domestic unrest, and support for the Nixon decision to adopt an all-volunteer force reflected a substantial concern that fewer forces would be available for future interventions.

By the 1980s much of this criticism had waned, and public opinion toward the military was consistently favorable and generally in the 70–75 percent approval range. The end of the Cold War reduced this support in the 1990s by only a small fraction. Moreover, favorable opinion increased with evidence of military success; a poll taken during the Gulf War recorded support levels of 85 percent.[13] This paralleled the jump in support (again to 85%) recorded after the U.S. bombing of Libya in April 1986 in retaliation for terrorist activities.

Americans today are prepared to accept a reduction in troop levels, in response to the reduced overseas threat as well as to increasing economic constraints on spending. But public opinion is still divided over what that ideal level should be. In the past, opinion about the ideal level of U.S. forces was linked to popular perceptions of the balance between U.S. and Soviet military capability. But this is no longer seen as significant, and, as will be discussed below, the critical factor appears to be cost and the trade-off with domestic spending demands.

There are also post–Cold War changes not yet clearly crystallized in American opinion regarding the makeup of military forces and force structures. The causes seem to be perceptions that the evolving nature of the conflicts for which the U.S. military must be prepared and the increasingly technical and highly sophisticated weaponry and equipment employed in combat place new demands on soldiers and open new opportunities for men and women who do not meet the profile of traditional soldiers.

At this writing, the most contentious issue is President Clinton's argument that acknowledged homosexuals should be eligible to serve in the U.S. forces. The public has been quite vocal on this issue. Those who oppose lifting the ban believe that homosexuality is incompatible with the rigors and demands of life in the military. Some object to this legitimation of the gay lifestyle, fearing that it will be the first step down a slippery slope of specific rights demanded by gays. Those who favor allowing homosexuals in the military see the ban as blatant and unacceptable discrimination against individuals, based solely on sexual orientation. They embrace the parallel (readily rejected by the military establishment) between President Clinton's dilemma and President Harry Truman's 1948 executive order to racially integrate the U.S. military, pointing out that concerns about morale and discipline within the armed forces echo those objections voiced forty-five years earlier.

A *Newsweek* poll conducted on January 21 and 22, 1993, found that 72 percent of Americans surveyed believe gays can "serve effectively in the military if they keep their sexual orientation private." Only 22 percent of the people surveyed disagreed. When asked if Clinton should "delay his promise to lift restrictions on gays in the military if it will produce morale and readiness problems," 49 percent responded positively. Only 40 percent said that he should not delay his promise. Thus while most Americans are confident about the capabilities of gay soldiers, they are reluctant to force the military to accept homosexuals without proper consideration of the consequences of this decision.

In contrast, public attitudes on the inclusion of women in combat functions within the military have been generally positive throughout the late 1980s. The key issue seems to be the question of equity, and the majority support mirrors the support levels for the equal treatment of women in occupations throughout the society.

FRAMEWORK ISSUES: OPINION ON MILITARY SPENDING

Far more critical in framing the context of intervention is the question of support for military spending, for the continued acquisition of substantial military capability across the spectrum of military needs. It is an issue still in post–Cold War definition. The 1992 election campaign saw little mention of the level of defense spending, only somewhat ritualistic affirmations by both George Bush and Bill Clinton of the need for a strong defense. In the national campaigns, Democrats smarting from the impact of their proposed defense cuts on the 1988 Dukakis campaign and divided within their own ranks preferred to talk of gradual drawdowns; Republicans mentioned these issues only in general. Yet it is a Washington truism that continuing popular pressure means that defense spending must be reduced more drastically than any official proposal now contemplates. Cuts were an ever-present issue in a number of key congressional races.

Direct evidence on popular views is somewhat more complex. Public support for defense spending unquestionably increased in the late 1970s and early 1980s. The renewed hostility between the United States and the USSR fueled a willingness on the part of the American public to rebuild U.S. military power following a period of relative neglect in the early and mid-1970s. The shift in opinion toward increasing the defense budget was quite dramatic, reaching a level of 72 percent at the end of Ronald Reagan's first year.[14] Support then fell to 39 percent by December 1982 and declined gradually through the mid-1980s. Many Americans then preferred that the level of military spending be kept the same—a steady 43 percent. By 1987, indeed, a slight majority of Americans surveyed were willing to support substantial cuts in military spending to address the federal budget deficit problem.[15]

The end of the Cold War and the emergence of new pressures to lessen the budget deficit through reduced government spending convinced more Americans about defense cuts. A CBS News/*New York Times* poll of February 9–11, 1993, found, for example, that 50 percent of Americans agreed that the "share of tax dollars spent on military and defense programs is too much." By contrast, 6 percent of those surveyed felt that the share spent on military and defense is "too little," and 39 percent said that it is "about right."

This change in attitudes has come relatively quickly, revealing a marked shift from the traditional cautious and careful approach among Americans to defense questions. A Gallup poll, taken between March 30 and April 5, 1992, found that 39 percent of those surveyed "do not favor additional cuts in military spending." Seventeen percent responded that they "favor major cuts," 31 percent said they "favor moderate cuts," and 10 percent "favor minor cuts." Only three months later Gallup results showed 42 percent favored further deep cuts in the military budget beyond those then planned, with only 52 percent opposed to cuts, minor or major.

CONCLUSIONS

The sudden dismantling of an international system that had been in place for over forty years, rigidly defining the U.S. military posture and conduct, has left in its wake a nation not yet clear about what role the United States should assume in the post–Cold War world. The desire to curtail defense spending and to limit military involvement overseas clashes with the majority's commitment to global leadership and the fulfillment of international obligations. Americans in great numbers feel a moral compulsion to help countries in need and to defend the weak, but they are reluctant to be drawn into unpredictable and open-ended conflicts. They give new recognition to the economic dimensions of security, and they realize the importance of transnational relationships in an increasingly global economy. But they also struggle with how to balance international interests and responsibilities and domestic concerns.

In the abstract, Americans continue to regard the use of military force as a last resort in solving international crises. There is a consistently high level of confidence in the military, especially since the Gulf War of 1991. But much of the public is wary about U.S. involvement in unpredictable overseas ventures, especially without the support and contributions of allies and other countries. The general view is that in most cases, other options must be exhausted before direct military force is used. Even then, victory without exceedingly great sacrifice must be an attainable end. Moreover, Americans are increasingly aware of both the costs and risks involved in any overseas military option, and are increasingly unwilling to give blanket approval for military preparation against a range of unlikely threats.

In specific crises, Americans tend toward more pragmatic judgments about what is to be done, based on increasing attention and a growing fund of real-time information gained through television. They do review past history and are sensitive to earlier parallels, most particularly to continuities with the defining, if not yet resolved, Vietnam experience. They are also subject to halo effects—as approval for the rapid and successful use of force in the Gulf after the fact indicates—when they are convinced that a greater objective has been achieved.

On the whole, however, they look and weigh carefully probable outcomes, foreseeable risks, the projected length of involvement, options for multilateral action, and moral and humanitarian principles. The experience of the 1980s and the early 1990s suggests that within this generally conservative framework, most Americans render a relatively balanced and consistent set of judgments about the use of force in particular, and about the defense policy framework in general. The general expectation now—in contrast to the early Cold War period—is that there still is a need for a strong but reduced defense as insurance against uncertainty. But the use of military force is to be the exception in American foreign policy, it is rarely to be unilateral, and it is to involve limited goals and limited means.

The American people also are loyal and patriotic, and they will "rally 'round the flag" when convinced by an effective president that force is to be applied toward a worthy and achievable goal. The mobilization of opinion and support must be against a threat to values, or to the use of military force against an appropriate target of immediate significance. But among the electorate, perhaps even more than within the Congress, this is never an automatic reaction, and much depends on the specifics of the case. An interventionist president is held accountable for the course of the conflict—both directly and at the next election.

Barring a reversal of direction in Russia or an intensified Bosnia-like crisis, these trends will almost certainly continue and grow over the next decade. Memories of the military preparations and deployments judged normal in the Cold War era or even in Desert Storm will recede. Echoing earlier American patterns, the almost inevitable push will be for a smaller military at lower cost with fewer overseas deployments. Professionals will almost certainly press for the maintenance of American high-tech advantages, especially for intelligence and early warning of crisis or aggression. If economic conditions and presidential leadership are favorable, they may well win public acceptance.

Future questions about the conditions for the use of American force will very likely be two: what does the public know, and what does the president ask? If in harmony, these factors will allow for slow but sure decision; with even just a significant minority of the public and the Congress at odds with the president, there will be continuing debate and perhaps dead-lock. In the end, it may well turn on how quickly the shadow of Vietnam fades for succeeding genera-tions, and the kind of experience—multilateral or unilateral, interventionist or peacekeeping—that de-fines the post–Cold War era.

POLLS

A list of polls used follows:

ABC News: Somalia, 13 January 1993; Bosnia, 7 May 1993.

ABC News/*Washington Post:* 24 February 1991; 1–4 March 1991; 14–17 January 1993.

CBS News: The United States and Yugoslavia, 4–5 May 1993.

CBS/*New York Times:* 5–7 October 1991; 9–11 February 1993.

CNN/*USA Today:* Bosnia, 6 May 1993.

Chicago Council on Foreign Relations: "American Pub-lic Opinion and U.S. Foreign Policy 1991" (ed. John E. Reilly); "Use of U.S. Troops Overseas," 1990 (V-5); "Eco-nomic Aid, Military Aid and Arms Sales," 1990 (IV-7); "Preferred U.S. Role in World," 1990 (II-1); "Actual U.S. Role in World," 1990 (II-2); "Vital Interests," 1990, 1986 (III-2).

Communications Consortium: "Public Opinion Polls: Military Spending, An Update" (Dr. Ethel Klein), 12, 18, and 26 June 1987.

Gallup: 28 February–3 March 1991; 30 March–5 April 1992; 12–14 June 1992; 3–4 December 1992; 24 January 1993.

Newsweek: 21–22 January, 29–30 April 1993.

Hart and Teeter: 18–19 August, 8–11 December 1990.

Los Angeles Times: 12–14 August 1992.

Louis Harris and Associates: July 1980; 4–8 December 1992.

Market Strategies and Greenberg-Lake: 23 June–1 July 1991.

Times Mirror Center for the People & the Press: "The People, The Press & Politics 1990," A Times Mirror Politi-cal Typology, 11 October 1990; "The People, The Press & Politics on the Eve of '92: Fault Lines in the Electorate,"

4 December 1991; "The People, The Press & Politics Cam-paign '92: 1993—Priorities for the President, Survey XII—Part 2," 28 October 1992.

Yankelovich, for *Time*/CNN: August 1992; 13–14 Janu-ary 1993.

NOTES

1. See Gabriel A. Almond, *The American People and Foreign Policy* (New York: Praeger, 1960); and Russell F. Weigley, *The American Way of War: A History of United States Military Strategy and Policy* (Bloomington: Indiana University Press, 1973).

2. See Bruce W. Jentleson, *Foreign Military Interven-tion: The Dynamics of Protracted Conflict* (New York: Co-lumbia University Press, 1992); Page and Shapiro (1988); and Reilly (1991).

3. See Schneider (1992).

4. Jentleson, *Foreign Military Intervention,* 50.

5. Ibid., 53.

6. See Chicago Council on Foreign Relations, "Amer-ican Public Opinion and U.S. Foreign Policy 1991," ed. John Reilly, March 1991, 34.

7. Ibid., 29.

8. Ibid., 85.

9. On U.S. involvement in the Persian Gulf, see the Hart and Teeter poll of 18–19 August 1990; the ABC News/*Washington Post* poll of 24 February 1991; and the Gallup poll of 28 February–3 March 1991.

10. On Somalia, see the Gallup polls of 3–4 and 4–6 December 1992; and the Louis Harris poll of 4–8 De-cember 1992. Also see the ABC News/*Washington Post* poll of 11–14 December 1992; and the ABC News poll of 13 January 1993.

11. Jentleson, *Foreign Military Intervention,* 49.

12. On the Persian Gulf War, see the ABC/*Washington Post* poll of 1–4 March 1991.

13. Gergen (1990), 79.

14. Bartels (1991), 467.

15. See the CBS/*New York Times* poll of January 1987, which showed Americans more willing to cut money for defense (54%, yes; 40%, no) than to cut student loans or aid to farmers.

PART III

THE FORMULATION OF AMERICAN DEFENSE POLICY

INTRODUCTION

BRENDA J. VALLANCE

In this part of the book, we continue our examination of American defense policy by focusing on the interaction between the communications channels and conversion structures. The readings here outline several processes associated with defense policy. Chapters 8, 9, and 10 outline the details of each process in theory and in practice. Chapter 11 contains three classic discussions of what can go wrong in policy making. As the readings that follow illustrate, and the reader should come to recognize, the policy-making process is in fact highly dynamic and complicated, characteristics difficult to convey through a line drawing.

Chapters 8, 9, and 10 each open with an essay on a formal decision-making process commonly associated with defense policy as it is intended to work: namely, the interagency process, the defense acquisition process, and the defense budgeting process, respectively. Each of these discussions of ideal types is followed by a case study illustrating the process in actual practice and highlighting the political dynamics within it. As these cases show, when people

with differing interests, opinions, and needs come together to make policy, the means by which they do so become too complicated for a simple line drawing to portray. Add to this picture the inevitable "pulling and hauling" associated with bureaucratic politics, the reelection imperative that often drives members of Congress to place constituent interests before the broader concept of national interest, and the president's own program for national security that frequently conflicts with rival congressional plans, and the ideal types suddenly look sterile and distant from reality.

Chapter 8 discusses the National Security Council (NSC) and the interagency process that supports it, both of which involve high-level decision makers responsible for formulating policy and advising the president. Some participants in the interagency process may also participate in crisis policy making, although the exact makeup of the group is determined by the president, just as the president determines how he will use the interagency process. For example, President Harry Truman made limited use of the NSC, while his successor, Dwight Eisenhower, was

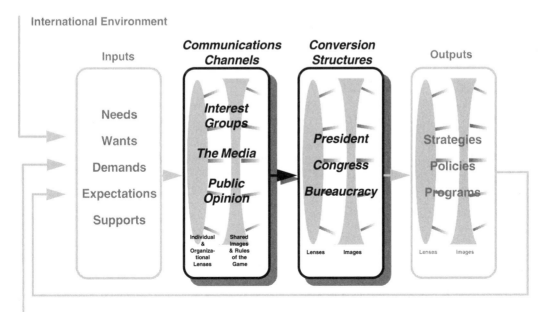

Defense Policy Process Model: Policy-Making Processes

much more active and formal in using the NSC as an advisory body. Both readings in this chapter are from the "Report of the President's Special Review Board," commonly referred to as the Tower Commission Report. This commission, composed of John Tower, Brent Scowcroft, and Edmund Muskie, was convened to examine the events surrounding the Iran-Contra affair during the Reagan administration. The first reading details the way the NSC and interagency process should work in order to provide the president sound advice and policy proposals. The second reading discusses what can go wrong when the interagency process is ignored or when proper responsibility and supervision are trivialized.

Chapter 9 examines the defense acquisition process. The first essay, detailing the numerous steps in this process, is written from an air force perspective, but the general concepts and steps it describes apply to all defense acquisition. Something that all readers are sure to note when reading Charles Nelson's "Keeping the Edge" is that the Department of Defense (DOD) excels at creating acronyms and an unusual lexicon! This also shows how specialized the actions associated with acquisition are. Again, the essay paints a relatively sterile picture of the acquisition process, with the steps neatly arranged as if immune to the pulling and hauling of politics. However, as Nick Kotz shows in "Wild Blue Yonder," his essay on air force bomber acquisition, nothing could be further from the truth. Kotz details what happens when the primary actors in the process—contractors, communities, members of Congress, and the DOD—have conflicting interests. From this, we see that defense acquisition is a highly competitive and complicated process compounded by an unpredictable threat and the challenge of fielding expensive technology designed to meet future needs.

In Chapter 10 we look at another complicated and lengthy process, the Department of Defense budgeting system. The planning, programming, and budgeting system (PPBS) consumes considerable time and effort in the DOD. The resulting budget affects a huge population, which includes military and civilian employees of the DOD, military communities, contractors, and subcontractors. It is not surprising, then, that this process is surrounded by a high level of interest and controversy. The first reading, "The ABCs of the PPBS," provides a general overview of the steps that must be mastered in order to understand and participate in this complicated process. The case used to examine the politics of the budget process is the defense Base Closure and Realignment Commission (BRAC), formed to facilitate the reduction in military facilities after the end of the Cold War. "The Politics of Base Closures," written during the base closing exercise of 1995, discusses the efforts of one community, Colorado Springs, Colorado, to save its army base, Fort Carson. While somewhat atypical of the budgeting process, the establishment of the BRAC demonstrates how contentious budgeting and especially budget cutting can be. This case also shows that the PPBS, driven by a

prioritization of military needs and requirements, is quite different from the actual process of funding and cutting defense requirements as they are driven by local interests, pork barrel politics, and DOD budget constraints.

The final chapter in this section, Chapter 11, discusses what can go wrong with decision making. In the first reading, "Crisis, Stress, and Decision Making," Ole Holsti deals specifically with the effects of crisis on the decision maker. Crisis, he points out, can distort one's perception of time and thus create a sense of pressure that can affect the rational search for alternative solutions. Under stress, actors tend to focus on the immediate, rather than seeing the long-term implications of their actions. In a crisis, the decision-making group tends to get smaller, while the amount of information the group must process may increase dramatically. If the group tries to negate information overload by constraining communication, they risk making decisions without the benefit of the vital information experts possess and without properly vetting alternatives. Establishing an effective decision-making process during a crisis is both critical and difficult.

In the second essay, "The Groupthink Syndrome," Irving Janis describes groupthink as "a mode of thinking that people engage in when they are deeply involved in a cohesive in-group, when the members' striving for unanimity override their motivation to realistically appraise alternative courses of action."[1] The primary characteristic of groupthink is a "strong concurrence-seeking tendency" among group members.[2] Groupthink alters the rational process of examining all alternatives and may occur in any type of decision making, whether during a crisis or in day-to-day operations. Groupthink also can exacerbate other decision-making problems and errors.

This section concludes with "Hypotheses on Misperception," in which Robert Jervis discusses how individuals process information on the basis of their existing images, theories, and perceptions. It is far easier for people to understand an action if they can relate it to their existing cognitive framework. It is also important to recognize that individuals process information and communications on the basis of these ideas. We have a tendency to assume that others understand our motivations and correctly interpret our intentions, although we are frequently guilty of sending confusing signals and misinterpreting the intentions of others. Misperception may occur in both peacetime and crisis decision making, although its effects are accentuated by the nature of a crisis.

After reading Chapter 11, students will find it useful to return to the cases in Chapters 8, 9, and 10 to see if they can identify any of the constraints to rational decision making there. As this section of the book demonstrates, defense policy is about the pulling and hauling of bureaucratic politics and the effects of images and perceptions on decision making. The neat blocks of our defense policy process model, in which communications channels and conversion structures are constrained and separated by thick black lines, can detract from understanding the controversy, inputs, and interests that are a part of the process. To many, bureaucratic politics connotes a slow, dinosaur-like process filled with red tape and uncaring bureaucrats. But when we consider that our system of government is designed to be slow and to allow for the voicing of numerous interests, bureaucratic politics gains new meaning. This section also demonstrates that in the difficult and often problem-ridden decision-making environment our leaders face, it is useful to have established processes for policy making. Although these processes are the ideal, the steps they outline are meant to preclude problems and facilitate rational decision making. The Tower Commission captured this well when it stated, "Process will not always produce brilliant ideas, but history suggests it can at least help prevent bad ideas from becoming Presidential policy."

NOTES

1. Irving L. Janis, *Groupthink: Psychological Studies of Policy Decisions and Fiascoes,* 2d ed. (Boston: Houghton Mifflin, 1982), 9.

2. Ibid., 10.

CHAPTER 8

THE INTERAGENCY PROCESS

ORGANIZING FOR NATIONAL SECURITY

JOHN G. TOWER, BRENT C. SCOWCROFT, AND EDMUND S. MUSKIE

Ours is a government of checks and balances, of shared power and responsibility. The Constitution places the president and the Congress in dynamic tension. They both cooperate and compete in the making of national policy.

National security is no exception. The Constitution gives both the president and the Congress an important role. The Congress is critical in formulating national policies and in marshaling the resources to carry them out. But those resources—the nation's military personnel, its diplomats, its intelligence capability—are lodged in the executive branch. As chief executive and commander in chief, and with broad authority in the area of foreign affairs, it is the president who is empowered to act for the nation and to protect its interests.

THE NATIONAL SECURITY COUNCIL

The present organization of the executive branch for national security matters was established by the National Security Act of 1947. That act created the National Security Council (NSC). As now constituted, its statutory members are the president, vice president, secretary of state, and secretary of defense. The president is the head of the National Security Council.

Presidents have from time to time invited the heads of other departments or agencies to attend National Security Council meetings or to participate as de facto members. These have included the director of central intelligence (the DCI) and the chairman of the Joint Chiefs of Staff (the CJCS). The president (or, in his absence, his designee) presides.

The National Security Council deals with the most vital issues in the nation's national security policy. It is this body that discusses recent developments in arms control and ballistic missile defense; that discussed whether or not to bomb the Cambodia mainland after the *Mayaguez* was captured; that debated the timetable for the U.S. withdrawal from Vietnam; and that considered the risky and daring attempt to rescue U.S. hostages in Iran in 1980. The National Security Council deals with issues that are difficult, complex, and often secret. Decisions are often required in hours rather than weeks. Advice must be given under great stress and with imperfect information.

The National Security Council is not a decision-making body. Although its other members hold official positions in the government, when meeting as the National Security Council they sit as advisers to the president. This is clear from the language of the 1947 act:

The function of the Council shall be to advise the President with respect to the integration of domestic, foreign, and military policies relating to the national security so as to enable the military services and the other departments and agencies of the Government to cooperate more effectively in matters involving the national security.

The National Security Council has from its inception been a highly personal instrument. Every president has turned for advice to those individuals and institutions whose judgment he has valued and trusted. For some presidents, such as President Dwight D. Eisenhower, the National Security Council served as a primary forum for obtaining advice on national security matters. Other presidents, such as President John F. Kennedy, relied on more informal groupings of advisers, often including some but not all of the council members.

One official summarized the way the system has been adjusted by different presidents:

The NSC is going to be pretty well what a President wants it to be and what he determines it should be. Kennedy—and these are some exaggerations and generalities of course—with an anti-organizational bias, disestablished all [the Eisenhower-created] committees and put a tight group in the White House totally attuned to his philosophic approach.... Johnson didn't change that very much, except certain difficulties began to develop in the informality which was [otherwise] characterized by speed, unity of purpose, precision.... So it had great efficiency and responsiveness. The difficulties began to develop in ... the informality of the thing.

The Nixon administration saw a return to the use of the National Security Council as a principal forum for national security advice. This pattern was continued by Presidents Gerald Ford and Jimmy Carter, and in large measure by President Ronald Reagan.

President's Special Review Board, Report of the President's Special Review Board *(Washington, D.C.: GPO, 1987), II-1 through II-5. Public Domain.*

Regardless of the frequency of its use, the NSC has remained a strictly advisory body. Each president has kept the burden of decision for himself, in accordance with his constitutional responsibilities.

THE ASSISTANT TO THE PRESIDENT FOR NATIONAL SECURITY AFFAIRS

Although closely associated with the National Security Council in the public mind, the assistant to the president for national security affairs is not one of its members. Indeed, no mention of this position is made in the National Security Act of 1947.

The position was created by President Eisenhower in 1953. Although its precise title has varied, the position has come to be known (somewhat misleadingly) as the national security adviser.

Under President Eisenhower, the holder of this position served as the principal executive officer of the council, setting the agenda, briefing the president on council matters, and supervising the staff. He was not a policy advocate.

It was not until President Kennedy, with McGeorge Bundy in the role, that the position took on its current form. Bundy emerged as an important personal adviser to the president on national security affairs. This introduced an element of direct competition into Bundy's relationship with the members of the National Security Council. Although President Lyndon Johnson changed the title of the position to simply "special assistant," in the hands of Walt Rostow it continued to play an important role.

President Richard Nixon relied heavily on his national security adviser, maintaining and even enhancing its prominence. In that position, Henry Kissinger became a key spokesman for the president's national security policies both to the U.S. press and to foreign governments. President Nixon used him to negotiate on behalf of the United States with Vietnam, China, the Soviet Union, and other countries. The roles of spokesman and negotiator had traditionally been the province of the secretary of state, not of the national security adviser. The emerging tension between the two positions was only resolved when Kissinger assumed them both.

Under President Ford, Lieutenant General Brent Scowcroft became national security adviser, with Henry Kissinger remaining as secretary of state. The national security adviser exercised major responsibility for coordinating for the president the advice of his NSC principals and overseeing the process of policy development and implementation within the executive branch.

President Carter returned in large part to the early Kissinger model, with a resulting increase in tensions with the secretary of state. President Carter wanted to take the lead in matters of foreign policy and used his national security adviser as a source of information, ideas, and new initiatives.

The role of the national security adviser, like the role of the NSC itself, has in large measure been a function of the operating style of the president. Nevertheless, the national security adviser has come to perform, to a greater or lesser extent, certain functions that appear essential to the effective discharge of the president's responsibilities in national security affairs.

- He is an "honest broker" for the NSC process. He ensures that issues are clearly presented to the president; that all reasonable options, together with an analysis of their disadvantages and risks, are brought to his attention; and that the views of the president's other principal advisers are accurately conveyed.

- He provides advice from the president's vantage point, unalloyed by institutional responsibilities and biases. Unlike the secretaries of state or defense, who have substantial organizations for which they are responsible, the president is the national security adviser's only constituency.

- He monitors the actions taken by the executive departments in implementing the president's national security policies. He asks the question whether these actions are consistent with presidential decisions and whether, over time, the underlying policies continue to serve U.S. interests.

- He has a special role in crisis management. This has resulted from the need for prompt and coordinated action under presidential control, often with secrecy being essential.

- He reaches out for new ideas and initiatives that will give substance to broad presidential objectives for national security.

- He keeps the president informed about international developments and developments in the Congress and the executive branch that affect the president's policies and priorities.

But the national security adviser remains the creature of the president. The position will be largely what he wants it to be. This presents any president with a series of dilemmas.

- The president must surround himself with people he trusts and to whom he can speak in confidence. To this end, the national security adviser, unlike the secretaries of state and defense, is not subject to confirmation by the Senate and does not testify before Congress. But the more the president relies on the national security adviser for advice, especially to the exclusion of his cabinet officials, the greater will be the unease with this arrangement.

- As the honest broker of the NSC process, the national security adviser must ensure that the different and often conflicting views of the NSC principals are presented fairly to the president. But as an independent adviser to the president, he must provide his own judgment. To the extent that the national security adviser becomes a strong advocate for a particular point of view, his role as honest broker may be compromised and the president's access to the unedited views of the NSC principals may be impaired.

- The secretaries of state and defense and the director of central intelligence head agencies of government that have specific statutory responsibilities and are subject to congressional oversight for the implementation of U.S. national security policy. To the extent that the national security adviser assumes operational responsibilities, whether by negotiating with foreign governments or becoming heavily involved in military or intelligence operations, the legitimacy of that role and his authority to perform it may be challenged.

- The more the national security adviser becomes an "operator" in implementing policy, the less will he be able objectively to review that implementation—and whether the underlying policy continues to serve the interests of the president and the nation.

- The secretary of state has traditionally been the president's spokesman on matters of national security and foreign affairs. To the extent that the national security adviser speaks publicly on these matters or meets with representatives of foreign governments, the result may be confusion as to what is the president's policy.

THE NSC STAFF

At the time it established the National Security Council, Congress authorized a staff headed by an executive secretary appointed by the president. Initially quite small, the NSC staff expanded substantially under President Eisenhower.

During the Eisenhower administration, the NSC staff assumed two important functions: coordinating the executive departments in the development of national policy (through the NSC Planning Board) and overseeing the implementation of that policy (through the Operations Coordination Board). A systematic effort was made to coordinate policy development and its implementation by the various agencies through an elaborate set of committees. The system worked fairly well in bringing together for the president the views of the other NSC principals. But it has been criticized as biased toward reaching consensus among these principals rather than developing options for presidential decision. By the end of his second term, President Eisenhower himself had reached the conclusion that a highly competent individual and a small staff could perform the needed functions in a better way. Such a change was made by President Kennedy.

Under President Kennedy, a number of the functions of the NSC staff were eliminated and its size was sharply reduced. The Planning and Operations Coordinating boards were abolished. Policy development and policy implementation were assigned to individual cabinet officers, responsible directly to the president. By late 1962 the staff was only twelve professionals, serving largely as an independent source of ideas and information to the president. The system was lean and responsive but frequently suffered from a lack of coordination. The Johnson administration followed much the same pattern.

The Nixon administration returned to a model more like Eisenhower's but with something of the informality of the Kennedy and Johnson staffs. The Eisenhower system had emphasized coordination; the Kennedy-Johnson system tilted to innovation and the generation of new ideas. The Nixon system emphasized both. The objective was not interdepartmental consensus but the generation of policy options for presidential decision, and then ensuring that those decisions were carried out. The staff grew to fifty professionals in 1970 and became a major factor in the national security decision-making process. This approach was largely continued under President Ford.

The NSC staff retained an important role under President Carter. While continuing to have responsibility for coordinating policy among the various executive agencies, President Carter particularly looked to the NSC staff as a personal source of independent advice. President Carter felt the need to have a group loyal only to him from which to launch his own initiatives and to move a vast and lethargic government. During his time in office, President Carter reduced the size of the professional staff to thirty-five, feeling that a smaller group could do the job and would have a closer relationship to him.

What emerges from this history is an NSC staff used by each president in a way that reflected his individual preferences and working style. Over time, it has developed an important role within the executive branch of coordinating policy review, preparing issues for presidential decision, and monitoring implementation. But it has remained the president's creature, molded as he sees fit, to serve as his personal staff for national security affairs. For this reason, it has generally operated out of the public view and has not been subject to direct oversight by the Congress.

THE INTERAGENCY COMMITTEE SYSTEM

The National Security Council has frequently been supported by committees made up of representatives of the relevant national security departments and agencies. These committees analyze issues prior to consideration by the council. There are generally several levels of committees. At the top level, officials from each agency (at the deputy secretary or undersecretary level) meet to provide a senior-level policy review. These senior-level committees are in turn supported by more junior interagency groups (usually at the assistant secretary level).

These in turn may oversee staff-level working groups that prepare detailed analysis of important issues.

Administrations have differed in the extent to which they have used these interagency committees. President Kennedy placed little stock in them. The Nixon and Carter administrations, by contrast, made much use of them.

THE REAGAN MODEL

President Reagan entered office with a strong commitment to cabinet government. His principal advisers on national security affairs were to be the secretaries of state and defense, and to a lesser extent the director of central intelligence. The position of the national security adviser was initially downgraded in both status and access to the president. Over the next six years, five different people held that position.

The administration's first national security adviser, Richard Allen, reported to the president through the senior White House staff. Consequently, the NSC staff assumed a reduced role. Allen believed that the secretary of state had primacy in the field of foreign policy. He viewed the job of the national security adviser as that of a policy coordinator.

President Reagan initially declared that the National Security Council would be the principal forum for consideration of national security issues. To support the work of the council, President Reagan established an interagency committee system headed by three senior interagency groups (or "SIGs"), one each for foreign policy, defense policy, and intelligence. They were chaired by the secretary of state, the secretary of defense, and the director of central intelligence, respectively.

Over time, the administration's original conception of the role of the national security adviser changed. William Clark, who succeeded Richard Allen in 1982, was a long-time associate of the president and dealt directly with him. Robert McFarlane, who replaced Clark in 1983, although personally less close to the president, continued to have direct access to him. The same was true for Vice Admiral John Poindexter, who was appointed to the position in December 1985.

President Reagan appointed several additional members to his National Security Council and allowed staff attendance at meetings. The resultant size of the meetings led the president to turn increasingly to a smaller group (called the National Security Planning Group, or NSPG). Attendance at its meetings was more restricted but included the statutory principals of the NSC. The NSPG was supported by the SIGs, and new SIGs were occasionally created to deal with particular issues. These were frequently chaired by the national security adviser. But generally the SIGs and many of their subsidiary groups (called interagency groups, or IGs) fell into disuse.

THE IRAN-CONTRA AFFAIR

JOHN G. TOWER, BRENT C. SCOWCROFT, AND EDMUND S. MUSKIE

The arms transfers to Iran and the activities of the National Security Council (NSC) in support of the Contras are case studies in the perils of policy pursued outside the constraints of orderly process. The Iran initiative ran directly counter to the administration's own policies on terrorism, the Iran–Iraq war, and military support to Iran. This inconsistency was never resolved, nor were the consequences of this inconsistency fully considered and provided for. The result taken as a whole was a U.S. policy that worked against itself.

WHAT WAS WRONG

The Tower Commission believes that failure to deal adequately with these contradictions resulted in large part from the flaws in the manner in which decisions were made. Established procedures for making national security decisions were ignored. Reviews of the initiative by all the NSC principals were too infrequent. The initiatives were not adequately vetted below the cabinet level. Intelligence resources were underutilized. Applicable legal constraints were not adequately addressed. The whole matter was handled too informally, without adequate written records of what had been considered, discussed, and decided.

This pattern persisted in the implementation of the Iran initiative. The NSC staff assumed direct operational control. The initiative fell within the traditional jurisdictions of the Departments of State and Defense, and the Central Intelligence Agency (CIA). Yet these agencies were largely ignored. Great reliance was placed on a network of private operators and inter-

---

President's Special Review Board, Report of the President's Special Review Board (*Washington, D.C.: GPO, 1987*), IV-1 through V-7. *Public Domain.*

mediaries. How the initiative was to be carried out never received adequate attention from the NSC principals or a tough working-level review. No periodic evaluation of the progress of the initiative was ever conducted. The result was an unprofessional and, in substantial part, unsatisfactory operation. In all of this process, Congress was never notified.

The record of the role of the NSC staff in support of the Contras is much less complete. Nonetheless, what is known suggests that many of the same problems plagued that effort as well.

The first section of this essay discusses the flaws in the process by which conflicting policies were considered, decisions were made, and the initiatives were implemented. The second section discusses the responsibility of the NSC principals and other key national security officials for the manner in which these initiatives were handled. The third section discusses the special problem posed by the role of the Israelis. And the fourth section outlines the board's conclusions about the management of the initial public presentation of the facts of the Iran initiative.

A FLAWED PROCESS

CONTRADICTORY POLICIES WERE PURSUED

The arms sales to Iran and the NSC support for the Contras demonstrate the risks involved when highly controversial initiatives are pursued covertly.

Arms Transfers to Iran

The initiative to Iran was a covert operation directly at odds with important and well-publicized policies of the executive branch. But the initiative itself embodied a fundamental contradiction. Two objectives were apparent from the outset: a strategic opening to Iran, and release of the U.S. citizens held hostage in Lebanon. The sale of arms to Iran appeared to provide a means to achieve both these objectives. It also played into the hands of those who had other interests—some of them personal financial gain—in engaging the United States in an arms deal with Iran.

In fact, the sale of arms was not equally appropriate for achieving both these objectives. Arms were what Iran wanted. If all the United States sought was to free the hostages, then an arms-for-hostages deal could achieve the immediate objectives of both sides. But if the U.S. objective was a broader strategic relationship, then the sale of arms should have been contingent upon first putting into place the elements of that relationship. An arms-for-hostages deal in this context could become counterproductive to achieving this broader strategic objective. In addition, release of the hostages would require exerting influence with Hizballah, which could involve the most radical elements of the Iranian regime. The kind of strategic opening sought by the United States, however, involved what were regarded as more moderate elements.

The U.S. officials involved in the initiative appeared to have held three distinct views. For some, the principal motivation seemed consistently a strategic opening to Iran. For others, the strategic opening became a rationale for using arms sales to obtain the release of the hostages. For still others, the initiative appeared clearly as an arms-for-hostages deal from first to last.

Whatever the intent, almost from the beginning the initiative became in fact a series of arms-for-hostages deals. The shipment of arms in November 1985 was directly tied to a hostage release. Indeed, the August-September transfer may have been nothing more than an arms-for-hostages trade. By July 14, 1985, a specific proposal for the sale of 100 TOW missiles to Iran in exchange for Iranian efforts to secure the release of all the hostages had been transmitted to the White House and discussed with the president. What actually occurred, at least so far as the September shipment was concerned, involved a direct link of arms and a hostage.

The initiative continued to be described in terms of its broader strategic relationship. But those elements never really materialized. While a high-level meeting among senior U.S. and Iranian officials continued to be a subject of discussion, it never occurred. Although Robert McFarlane went to Tehran in May of 1986, the promised high-level Iranians never appeared. In discussions among U.S. officials, the focus seemed to be on the prospects for obtaining release of the hostages, not on a strategic relationship. Even if one accepts the explanation that arms and hostages represented only "bona fides" of seriousness of purpose for each side, that had clearly been established, one way or another, by the September exchange.

It is true that, strictly speaking, arms were not exchanged for the hostages. The arms were sold for cash; and to Iran, rather than the terrorists holding the hostages. Iran clearly wanted to buy the arms, however, and time and time again U.S. willingness to sell was directly conditioned upon the release of hostages. Although Iran might claim that it did not itself hold the hostages, the whole arrangement was premised on Iran's ability to secure their release.

While the United States was seeking the release of the hostages in this way, it was vigorously pursuing policies that were dramatically opposed to such efforts. The Reagan administration in particular had come into office declaring a firm stand against terrorism, which it continued to maintain. In December of 1985 the administration completed a major study under the chairmanship of the vice president. It resulted in a vigorous reaffirmation of U.S. opposition to terrorism in all its forms and a vow of total war on terrorism whatever its source. The administration continued to pressure U.S. allies not to sell arms to Iran and not to make concessions to terrorists.

No serious effort was made to reconcile the inconsistency between these policies and the Iran initiative. No effort was made systematically to address the consequences of this inconsistency—the effect on U.S. policy when, as it inevitably would, the Iran initiative became known.

The board believes that a strategic opening to Iran may have been in the national interest but that the United States never should have been a party to the arms transfers. As arms-for-hostages trades, they could not help but create an incentive for further hostage taking. As a violation of the U.S. arms embargo, they could only remove inhibitions on other nations from selling arms to Iran. This threatened to upset the military balance between Iran and Iraq, with consequent jeopardy to the Gulf states and the interests of the West in that region. The arms-for-hostages trades rewarded a regime that clearly supported terrorism and hostage taking. They increased the risk that the United States would be perceived, especially in the Arab world, as a creature of Israel. They suggested to other U.S. allies and friends in the region that the United States had shifted its policy in favor of Iran. They raised questions as to whether U.S. policy statements could be relied upon.

As the arms-for-hostages proposal first came to the United States, it clearly was tempting. The sale of just 100 TOWs was to produce the release of all seven Americans held in Lebanon. Even had the offer been genuine, it would have been unsound. But it was not genuine. The 100 TOWs did not produce seven hostages. Very quickly the price went up, and the arrangements became protracted. A pattern of successive bargained exchanges of arms and hostages was quickly established. While release of all the hostages continued to be promised, in fact the hostages came out singly if at all. This sad history is powerful evidence of why the United States should never have become involved in the arms transfers.

NSC Staff Support for the Contras

The activities of the NSC staff in support of the Contras sought to achieve an important objective of the administration's foreign policy. The president had publicly and emphatically declared his support for the Nicaragua resistance. That brought his policy in direct conflict with that of the Congress, at least during the period that direct or indirect support of military operations in Nicaragua was barred.

Although the evidence before the board is limited, no serious effort appears to have been made to come to grips with the risks to the president of direct NSC support for the Contras in the face of these congressional restrictions. Even if it could be argued that these restrictions did not technically apply to the NSC staff, these activities presented great political risk to the president. The appearance of the president's personal staff doing what Congress had forbade other agencies to do, once disclosed, only touch off a firestorm in the Congress and threaten the administration's whole policy on the Contras.

THE DECISION-MAKING PROCESS WAS FLAWED

Because the arms sales to Iran and the NSC support for the Contras occurred in settings of such controversy, one would expect that the decisions to undertake these activities would have been made only after intense and thorough consideration. In fact, a far different picture emerges.

Arms Transfers to Iran

The Iran initiative was handled almost casually and through informal channels, always apparently with an expectation that the process would end with the next arms-for-hostages exchange. It was subjected neither to the general procedures for interagency consideration and review of policy issues nor the more restrictive procedures set out in a classified document, National Security Decision Directive (NSDD)-159, for handling covert operations. This had a number of consequences.

The Opportunity for a Full Hearing before the President was Inadequate. In the last half of 1985, the Israelis made three separate proposals to the United States with respect to the Iran initiative (two in July and one in August). In addition, Israel made three separate deliveries of arms to Iran, one each in August, September, and November. Yet prior to December 7, 1985, there was at most one meeting of the NSC principals, a meeting that several participants recall taking place on August 6. There is no dispute that full meetings of the principals did occur on December 7, 1985, and on January 7, 1986. But the proposal to shift to direct U.S. arms sales to Iran appears not to have been discussed until later. It was considered by the president at a meeting on January 17 that only the vice president, Donald Regan, Donald Fortier, and Vice Admiral John Poindexter attended. Thereafter, the only senior-level review the Iran initiative received was during one or another of the president's daily national security briefings. These were routinely attended only by the president, the vice president, Regan, and Vice Admiral Poindexter. There was no subsequent collective consideration of the Iran initiative by the NSC principals before it became public eleven months later.

This was not sufficient for a matter as important and consequential as the Iran initiative. Two or three cabinet-level reviews in a period of seventeen months was not enough. The meeting on December 7 came late in the day, after the pattern of arms-for-hostages exchanges had become well established. The January 7 meeting had the earmarks of a meeting held after a decision had already been made. Indeed, a draft Covert Action Finding authorizing the initiative had been signed by the president, though perhaps inadvertently, the previous day.

At each significant step in the Iran initiative, deliberations among the NSC principals in the presence of the president should have been virtually automatic. This was not and should not have been a formal requirement, something prescribed by statute. Rather, it should have been something the NSC principals desired as a means of ensuring an optimal environment for presidential judgment. The meetings should have been preceded by consideration by the NSC principals of staff papers prepared according to the procedures applicable to covert actions. These should have reviewed the history of the initiative, analyzed the issues then presented, developed a range of realistic options, presented the odds of success and the costs of failure, and addressed questions of implementation and execution. Had this been done, the objectives of the Iran initiative might have been clarified and alternatives to the sale of arms might have been identified.

The Initiative Was Never Subjected to a Rigorous Review below the Cabinet Level. Because of the obsession with secrecy, interagency consideration of the initiative was limited to the cabinet level. With the exception of the NSC staff and, after January 17, 1986, a handful of CIA officials, the rest of the executive departments and agencies were largely excluded.

As a consequence, the initiative was never vetted at the staff level. This deprived those responsible for the initiative of considerable expertise—on the situation in Iran, on the difficulties of dealing with terrorists, on the mechanics of conducting a diplomatic opening. It also kept the plan from receiving a tough, critical review.

Moreover, the initiative did not receive a policy review below the cabinet level. Careful consideration at the deputy and undersecretary level might have exposed the confusion in U.S. objectives and clarified the risks of using arms as an instrument of policy in this instance.

The vetting process would also have ensured better use of U.S. intelligence. As it was, the intelligence input into the decision process was clearly inadequate. First, no independent evaluation of the Israeli proposals offered in July and August appears to have been sought or offered by U.S. intelligence agencies. The Israelis represented that they had had contacts with elements in Iran for some time. The prospects for an opening to Iran depended heavily on these contacts, yet no systematic assessment appears to have been made by U.S. intelligence agencies of the reliability and motivations of these contacts, and the identity and objectives of the elements in Iran that the opening was supposed to reach. Neither was any systematic assessment made of the motivation of the Israelis.

Second, neither Manucher Ghorbanifar nor the second channel seem to have been subjected to a systematic intelligence vetting before they were engaged as intermediaries. Ghorbanifar had been known to the CIA for some time and the agency had substantial doubts as to his reliability and truthfulness. Yet the agency did not volunteer that information or inquire about the identity of the intermediary if his name was unknown. Conversely, no early request for a name check was made of the CIA, and it was not until January 11, 1986, that the agency gave Ghorbanifar a new polygraph, which he failed. Not-

withstanding this situation, with the signing of the January 17 finding, the United States took control of the initiative and became even more directly involved with Ghorbanifar. The issues raised by the polygraph results do not appear to have been systematically addressed. In similar fashion, no prior intelligence check appears to have been made on the second channel.

Third, although the president recalled being assured that the arms sales to Iran would not alter the military balance with Iraq, the board could find no evidence that the president was ever briefed on this subject. The question of the impact of any intelligence shared with the Iranians does not appear to have been brought to the president's attention.

A thorough vetting would have included consideration of the legal implications of the initiative. There appeared little effort to face squarely the legal restrictions and notification requirements applicable to the operation. At several points, other agencies raised questions about violations of law or regulations. These concerns were dismissed without, it appears, investigating them with the benefit of legal counsel.

Finally, insufficient attention was given to the implications of implementation. The implementation of the initiative raised a number of issues: should the NSC staff rather than the CIA have had operational control; what were the implications of Israeli involvement; how reliable were the Iranian and various other private intermediaries; what were the implications of the use of Richard Secord's private network of operatives; what were the implications for the military balance in the region; was operational security adequate? Nowhere do these issues appear to have been sufficiently addressed.

The concern for preserving the secrecy of the initiative provided an excuse for abandoning sound process. Yet the initiative was known to a variety of persons with diverse interests and ambitions—Israelis, Iranians, various arms dealers and business intermediaries, and Lieutenant Colonel Oliver North's network of private operatives. While concern for secrecy would have justified limiting the circle of persons knowledgeable about the initiative, in this case it was drawn too tightly. As a consequence, important advice and counsel were lost.

In January of 1985 the president had adopted procedures for striking the proper balance between secrecy and the need for consultation on sensitive programs. These covered the institution, implementation, and review of covert operations. In the case of the Iran initiative, these procedures were almost totally ignored.

The only staff work the president apparently reviewed in connection with the Iran initiative was prepared by NSC staff members, under the direction of the national security adviser. These were, of course, the principal proponents of the initiative. A portion of this staff work was reviewed by the board. It was frequently striking in its failure to present the record of past efforts—particularly past failures. Alternative ways of achieving U.S. objectives—other than yet another arms-for-hostages deal—were not discussed. Frequently it did not adequately present the risks involved in pursuing the initiative or the full force of the dissenting views of other NSC principals. On balance, it did not serve the president well.

The Process Was Too Informal. The whole decision process was too informal. Even when meetings among NSC principals did occur, often there was no prior notice of the agenda. No formal written minutes seem to have been kept. Decisions subsequently taken by the president were not formally recorded. An exception was the January 17 finding, but even this was apparently not circulated or shown to key U.S. officials.

The effect of this informality was that the initiative lacked a formal institutional record. This precluded the participants from undertaking the more informed analysis and reflection that is afforded by a written record, as opposed to mere recollection. It made it difficult to determine where the initiative stood, and to learn lessons from the record that could guide future action. This lack of an institutional record permitted specific proposals for arms-for-hostages exchanges to be presented in a vacuum, without reference to the results of past proposals. Had a searching and thorough review of the Iran initiative been undertaken at any stage in the process, it would have been extremely difficult to conduct. The board can attest firsthand to the problem of conducting a review in the absence of such records. Indeed, the exposition in the wake of public revelation suffered the most.

NSC Staff Support for the Contras

It is not clear how North first became involved in activities in direct support of the Contras during the period of the congressional ban. The board did not have before it much evidence on this point. In the evidence that the board did have, there is no suggestion at any point of any discussion of North's activities with the president in any forum. There also does not appear to have been any interagency review of North's activities at any level.

This latter point is not surprising given the congressional restrictions under which the other relevant agencies were operating. But the NSC staff apparently did not compensate for the lack of any interagency review with its own internal vetting of these activities. North apparently worked largely in isolation, keeping first McFarlane and then Poindexter informed.

The lack of adequate vetting is particularly evident on the question of the legality of North's activities. The board did not make a judgment on the legal issues raised by his activities in support of the Contras. Nevertheless, some things can be said.

If these activities were illegal, obviously they should not have been conducted. If there was any doubt on the matter, systematic legal advice should have been obtained. The political cost to the president of illegal action by the NSC staff was particularly high, both because the NSC staff is the personal staff of the president and because of the history of serious conflict with the Congress over the issue of Contra support. For these reasons, the president should have been kept apprised of any review of the legality of North's activities.

Legal advice was apparently obtained from the president's Intelligence Oversight Board. Without passing on the quality of that advice, it is an odd source. It would be one thing for the Intelligence Oversight Board to review the legal advice provided by some other agency. It is another for the Intelligence Oversight Board to be originating legal advice of its own. That is a function more appropriate for the NSC staff's own legal counsel.

IMPLEMENTATION WAS UNPROFESSIONAL

The manner in which the Iran initiative was implemented and North undertook to support the Contras are very similar. This is in large part because the same cast of characters was involved. In both cases the operations were unprofessional, although the board has much less evidence with respect to North's Contra activities.

Arms Transfers to Iran

With the signing of the January 17 finding, the Iran initiative became a U.S. operation run by the NSC staff. North made most of the significant operational decisions. He conducted the operation through Secord and his associates, a network of private individuals already involved in the Contra resupply operation. To this was added a handful of selected individuals from the CIA.

But the CIA support was limited. Two CIA officials, though often at meetings, had a relatively limited role. One served as the point man for North in providing logistics and financial arrangements. The other (Allen) served as a contact between North and the intelligence community. By contrast, George Cave actually played a significant and expanding role. However, Clair George, deputy director for operations at the CIA, told the board: "George was paid by me and on the paper was working for me. But I think in the heat of the battle, . . . George was working for Oliver North."

Because so few people from the departments and agencies were told of the initiative, North cut himself off from resources and expertise from within the government. He relied instead on a number of private intermediaries, businessmen and other financial brokers, private operators, and Iranians hostile to the United States. Some of these were individuals with questionable credentials and potentially large personal financial interests in the transactions. This made the transactions unnecessarily complicated and invited kickbacks and payoffs. This arrangement also dramatically increased the risks that the initiative would leak. Yet no provision was made for such an eventuality. Further, the use of Secord's private network in the Iran initiative linked those operators with the resupply of the Contras, threatening exposure of both operations if either became public. The result was a very unprofessional operation.

In November 1985, Secord undertook to arrange landing clearance for the Israeli flight bringing the HAWK missiles into a third-country staging area. The arrangements fell apart. A CIA field officer attributed this failure to the amateurish way in which Secord and his associates approached officials in the government from which landing clearance was needed. If Ghorbanifar is to be believed, the mission of McFarlane to Tehran was undertaken without any advance work, and with distinctly different expectations on the part of the two sides. This could have contributed to its failure.

But there were much more serious errors. Without adequate study and consideration, intelligence was passed to the Iranians of potentially major significance to the Iran-Iraq war. At the meeting with the second channel on October 5–7, 1986, North misrepresented his access to the president. He told Ghorbanifar stories of conversations with the president that were wholly fanciful. He suggested without authority a shift in U.S. policy adverse to Iraq in general and Saddam Hussein in particular. Finally, in the nine-point agenda discussed on October 26–28, he committed the United States, without authorization, to a position contrary to well-established U.S. policy on the prisoners held by Kuwait.

The conduct of the negotiators with Ghorbanifar and the second channel were handled in a way that revealed obvious inexperience. The discussions were too casual for dealings with intermediaries to a regime so hostile to U.S. interests. The U.S. hand was repeatedly tipped and unskillfully played. The arrangements failed to guarantee that the U.S. obtained its hostages in exchange for the arms. Repeatedly, North permitted arms to be delivered without the release of a single captive.

The implementation of the initiative was never subjected to a rigorous review. North appears to have kept Poindexter fully informed of his activities. In addition, Poindexter, North, and the CIA officials involved apparently apprised Director William Casey of many of the operational details. But North and his operation functioned largely outside the orbit of the U.S. government. Their activities were not subject to critical reviews of any kind.

After the initial hostage release in September 1985, it was over ten months before another hostage was released. This despite recurring promises of the release of all the hostages and four intervening arms shipments. Beginning with the November shipment, the United States increasingly took over the operation of the initiative. In January 1986 it decided to transfer arms directly to Iran.

Any of these developments could have served as a useful occasion for a systematic reconsideration of the initiative. Indeed, at least one of the schemes contained a provision for reconsideration if the initial assumptions proved to be invalid. They did, but the reconsideration never took place. It was the responsibility of the national security adviser and the responsible officers on the NSC staff to call for such a review. But they were too involved in the initiative both as advocates and as implementers. This made it less likely that they would initiate the kind of review and reconsideration that should have been undertaken.

NSC Staff Support for the Contras

As already noted, the NSC activities in support of the Contras and its role in the Iran initiative were of a piece. In the former, there was an added element of North's intervention in the customs investigation of the crash of the aircraft. Here, too, selected CIA officials reported directly to North. The limited evidence before the board suggested that the activities in support of the Contras involved unprofessionalism much like that in the Iran operation.

Congress Was Never Notified. Congress was not apprised either of the Iran initiative or of the NSC staff's activities in support of the Contras. In the case of Iran, because release of the hostages was expected within a short time after the delivery of equipment, and because public disclosure could have destroyed the operation and perhaps endangered the hostages, it could be argued that it was justifiable to defer notification of Congress prior to the first shipment of arms to Iran. The plan apparently was to inform Congress immediately after the hostages were safely in U.S. hands. But after the first delivery failed to release all the hostages, and as one hostage release plan was replaced by another, Congress certainly should have been informed. This could have been done during a period when no specific hostage release plan was in execution. Consultation with Congress could have been useful to the president, for it might have given him some sense of how the public would react to the initiative. It also might have influenced his decision to continue to pursue it.

Legal Issues. In addition to conflicting with several fundamental U.S. policies, selling arms to Iran raised far-reaching legal questions. How it dealt with these is important to an evaluation of the Iran initiative.

Arms Transfer to Iran

It was not part of the board's mandate to consider issues of law as they may pertain to individuals or detailed aspects of the Iran initiative. Instead, the board focused on the legal basis for the arms transfers to Iran and how issues of law were addressed in the NSC process.

The Arms Export Control Act, the principal U.S. statute governing arms sales abroad, makes it unlawful to export arms without a license. Exports of arms by U.S. government agencies, however, do not require a license if they are otherwise authorized by law. Criminal penalties—fines and imprisonment—are provided for willful violations.

The initial arms transfers in the Iran initiative involved the sale and shipment by Israel of U.S.-origin missiles. The usual way for such international retransfer of arms to be authorized under U.S. law is pursuant to the Arms Export Control Act. This act requires that the president consent to any transfers by another country of arms exported under the act and imposes three conditions before such presidential consent may be given:

(a) the United States would itself transfer the arms in question to the recipient country;

(b) a commitment in writing has been obtained from the recipient country against unauthorized retransfer of significant arms, such as missiles; and

(c) a prior written certification regarding retransfer is submitted to the Congress if the defense equipment, such as missiles, has an acquisition cost of 14 million dollars or more. (22 U.S.C. 2753 [a], [d])

In addition, the act generally imposes restrictions on which countries are eligible to receive U.S. arms and on the purposes for which arms may be sold.[1]

The other possible avenue whereby government arms transfers to Iran may be authorized by law would be in connection with intelligence operations conducted under the National Security Act. This act requires that the director of central intelligence and the heads of other intelligence agencies keep the two congressional intelligence committees "fully and currently informed" of all intelligence activities under their responsibility (50 U.S.C. 413). Where prior notice of significant intelligence activities is not given, the intelligence committees are to be informed "in a timely fashion." In addition, the so-called Hughes-Ryan Amendment to the Foreign Assistance Act requires that "significant anticipated intelligence activities" may not be conducted by the CIA unless and until the president finds that "each such operation is important to the national security of the United States" (22 U.S.C. 2422).

When the Israelis began transferring arms to Iran in August 1985, they were not acting on their own. U.S. officials had knowledge about the essential elements of the proposed shipments. The United States shared some common purpose in the transfers and received a benefit from them—the release of a hostage. Most importantly, McFarlane communicated prior U.S. approval to the Israelis for the shipments, including an undertaking for replenishment. But for this U.S. approval, the transactions may not have gone forward. In short, the United States was an essential participant in the arms transfers to Iran that occurred in 1985.

Whether this U.S. involvement in the arms transfers by the Israelis was lawful depends fundamentally upon whether the president approved the transactions before they occurred. In the absence of presidential approval, there does not appear to be any authority in this case for the United States to engage in the transfer of arms or consent to the transfer by another country. The arms transfers to Iran in 1985 and hence the Iran initiative itself would have proceeded contrary to U.S. law.

The attorney general reached a similar judgment with respect to the activities of the CIA in facilitating the November 1985 shipment by the Israelis of HAWK missiles. In a letter to the board, the attorney general concluded that with respect to the CIA assistance, "a finding under the Hughes-Ryan Amendment would be required."[2]

The board was unable to reach a conclusive judgment about whether the 1985 shipments of arms to Iran were approved in advance by the president. On balance the board believes that it is plausible to conclude that he did approve them in advance.

Yet even if the president in some sense consented to or approved the transactions, a serious question of law remains. It is not clear that the form of the approval was sufficient for purposes of either the Arms Export Control Act or the Hughes-Ryan Amendment. The consent did not meet the conditions of the Arms Export Control Act, especially in the absence of a prior written commitment from the Iranians regarding unauthorized retransfer.

Under the National Security Act, it is not clear that mere oral approval by the president would qualify as a presidential finding that the initiative was vital to the national security interests of the United States. The approval was never reduced to writing. It appears to have been conveyed to only one person. The president himself has no memory of it. And there is contradictory evidence from the president's advisers about how the president responded when he learned of the arms shipments which the approval was to support. In addition, the requirement for congressional notification was ignored. In these circumstances, even if the president approved of the transactions, it is difficult to conclude that his actions constituted adequate legal authority.

The legal requirements pertaining to the sale of arms to Iran are complex; the availability of legal authority, including that which may flow from the president's constitutional powers, is difficult to delineate. Definitive legal conclusions will also depend upon a variety of specific factual determinations that the board has not attempted to resolve—for example, the specific content of any consent provided by the president, the authority under which the missiles were originally transferred to Israel, the knowledge and intentions of individuals, and the like. Nevertheless, it was sufficient for the board's purposes to conclude that the legal underpinning of the Iran initiative during 1985 was at best highly questionable.

The presidential finding of January 17, 1986, formally approved the Iran initiative as a covert intelligence operation under the National Security Act. This ended the uncertainty about the legal status of the initiative and provided legal authority for the United States to transfer arms directly to Iran.

The National Security Act also requires notification of Congress of covert intelligence activities. If not done in advance, notification must be "in a timely fashion." The presidential finding of January 17 directed that congressional notification be withheld, and this decision appears to have never been reconsidered. While there was surely justification to suspend congressional notification in advance of a particular transaction relating to a hostage release, the law would seem to require disclosure where, as in the Iran case, a pattern of relative inactivity occurs over an extended period. To do otherwise prevents the Congress from fulfilling its proper oversight responsibilities.

Throughout the Iran initiative, significant questions of law do not appear to have been adequately addressed. In the face of a sweeping statutory prohibition and explicit requirements relating to presidential consent to arms transfers by third countries, there appears to have been at the outset in 1985 little attention, let alone systematic analysis, devoted to how presidential actions would comply with U.S. law. The board has found no evidence that an evaluation was ever done during the life of the operation to determine whether it continued to comply with the terms of the January 17 presidential finding. Similarly, when a new prohibition was added to the Arms Export Control Act in August of 1986 to prohibit exports to countries on the terrorism list (a list that contained Iran), no evaluation was made to determine whether this law affected authority to transfer arms to Iran in connection with intelligence operations under the National Security Act. This lack of legal vigilance markedly increased the chances that the initiative would proceed contrary to law.

NSC Staff Support for the Contras

The NSC staff activities in support of the Contras were marked by the same uncertainty as to legal authority and insensitivity to legal issues as were present in the Iran initiative. The ambiguity of the law governing activities in support of the Contras presented a greater challenge than even the considerable complexity of laws governing arms transfers. Intense congressional scrutiny with respect to the NSC staff activities relating to the Contras added to the potential costs of actions that pushed the limits of the law.

In this context, the NSC staff should have been particularly cautious, avoiding operational activity in this area and seeking legal counsel. The board saw no signs of such restraint.

FAILURE OF RESPONSIBILITY

The NSC system will not work unless the president makes it work. After all, this system was created to serve the president of the United States in ways of his choosing. By his actions, by his leadership, the president therefore determines the quality of its performance. By his own account, as evidenced in his diary notes, and as conveyed to the board by his principal advisers, President Reagan was deeply committed to securing the release of the hostages. It was this intense compassion for the hostages that appeared to motivate his steadfast support of the Iran initiative, even in the face of opposition from his secretaries of state and defense.

In his obvious commitment, the president appears to have proceeded with a concept of the initiative that was not accurately reflected in the reality of the operation. The president did not seem to be aware of the way in which the operation was implemented and the full consequences of U.S. participation.

The president's expressed concern for the safety of both the hostages and the Iranians who could have been at risk may have been conveyed in a manner so as to inhibit the full functioning of the system.

The president's management style was to put the principal responsibility for policy review and implementation on the shoulders of his advisers. Nevertheless, with such a complex, high-risk operation and so much at stake, the president should have ensured that the NSC system did not fail him. He did not force his policy to undergo the most critical review of which the NSC participants and the process were capable. At no time did he insist upon accountability and performance review. Had the president chosen to drive the NSC system, the outcome could well have been different. As it was, the most powerful features of the NSC system— providing comprehensive analysis, alternatives, and follow-up—were not utilized.

The board found a strong consensus among NSC participants that the president's priority in the Iran initiative was the release of U.S. hostages. But setting priorities is not enough when it comes to sensitive and risky initiatives that directly affect U.S. national security. He must ensure that the content and tactics of an initiative match his priorities and objectives. He must insist upon accountability. For it is the president who must take responsibility for the NSC system and deal with the consequences.

Beyond the president, the other NSC principals and the national security adviser must share in the responsibility for the NSC system.

President Reagan's personal management style placed an especially heavy responsibility on his key advisers. Knowing his style, they should have been particularly mindful of the need for special attention to the manner in which this arms sale initiative developed and proceeded. On this score, neither the national security adviser nor the other NSC principals deserve high marks.

It is their obligation as members and advisers to the council to ensure that the president is adequately served. The principal subordinates to the president must not be deterred from urging the president not to proceed on a highly questionable course of action even in the face of his strong conviction to the contrary.

In the case of the Iran initiative, the NSC process did not fail; it simply was largely ignored. The national security adviser and the NSC principals all had a duty to raise this issue and insist that orderly process be imposed. None of them did so.

All had the opportunity. While the national security adviser had the responsibility to see that an orderly process was observed, his failure to do so does not excuse the other NSC principals. It does not appear that any of the NSC principals called for more frequent consideration of the Iran initiative by the NSC principals in the presence of the president. None of the principals called for a serious vetting of the initiative by even a restricted group of disinterested individuals. The intelligence questions do not appear to have been raised, and legal considerations, while raised, were not pressed. No one seemed to have complained about the informality of the process. No one called for a thorough reexamination once the initiative did not meet expectations or the manner of execution changed. While one or another of the NSC principals suspected that something was amiss, none vigorously pursued the issue.

Donald Regan also shares in this responsibility. More than almost any chief of staff of recent memory, he asserted personal control over the White House staff and sought to extend this control to the national security adviser. He was personally active in national security affairs and attended almost all of the relevant meetings regarding the Iran initiative. He, as much as anyone, should have insisted that an orderly process be observed. In addition, he especially should have ensured that plans were made for handling any public disclosure of the initiative. He must bear primary responsibility for the chaos that descended upon the White House when such disclosure did occur.

Robert McFarlane appeared caught between a president who supported the initiative and the cabinet officers who strongly opposed it. While he made efforts to keep these cabinet officers informed, the board heard complaints from some that he was not always successful. John Poindexter on several occasions apparently sought to exclude NSC principals other than the president from knowledge of the initiative. Indeed, on one or more occasions Secretary George Shultz may have been actively misled by Poindexter.

Poindexter also failed grievously on the matter of Contra diversion. Evidence indicates that Poindexter knew that a diversion occurred, yet he did not take the steps that were required given the gravity of that prospect. He apparently failed to appreciate or ignored the serious legal and political risks presented. His clear obligation was either to investigate the matter or take it to the president—or both. He did neither. Director Casey shared a similar responsibility. Evidence suggests that he received information about the possible diversion of funds to the Contras almost a month before the story broke. He, too, did not move promptly to raise the matter with the president. Yet his responsibility to do so was clear.

The NSC principals other than the president may be somewhat excused by the insufficient attention on the part of the national security adviser to the need to keep all the principals fully informed. Given the importance of the issue and the sharp policy divergences involved, however, Secretary Shultz and Secretary Caspar Weinberger in particular distanced themselves from the march of events. Secretary Shultz specifically requested to be informed only as

necessary to perform his job. Secretary Weinberger had access through intelligence to details about the operation. Their obligation was to give the president their full support and continued advice with respect to the program or, if they could not in conscience do that, to so inform the president. Instead, they simply distanced themselves from the program. They protected the record as to their own positions on this issue. They were not energetic in attempting to protect the president from the consequences of his personal commitment to freeing the hostages. Director Casey appears to have been informed in considerable detail about the specifics of the Iranian operation. He appears to have acquiesced in and to have encouraged North's exercise of direct operational control over the operation. Because of the NSC staff's proximity to and close identification with the president, this increased the risks to the president if the initiative became public or the operation failed.

There is no evidence, however, that Director Casey explained this risk to the president or made clear to the president that North, rather than the CIA, was running the operation. The president does not recall ever being informed of this fact. Indeed, Director Casey should have gone further and pressed for operational responsibility to be transferred to the CIA.

Director Casey should have taken the lead in vetting the assumptions presented by the Israelis on which the program was based and in pressing for an early examination of the reliance upon Ghorbanifar and the second channel as intermediaries. He should also have assumed responsibility for checking out the other intermediaries involved in the operation. Finally, because congressional restrictions on covert actions are both largely directed at and familiar to the CIA, Director Casey should have taken the lead in keeping the question of congressional notification active.

Director Casey, and, to a lesser extent, Secretary Weinberger, should have taken it upon themselves to assess the effect of the transfer of arms and intelligence to Iran on the Iran-Iraq military balance, and to transmit that information to the president.

THE ROLE OF THE ISRAELIS

Conversations with emissaries from the government of Israel took place prior to the commencement of the initiative. It remains unclear whether the initial proposal to open the Ghorbanifar channel was an Israeli initiative, was brought on by the avarice of arms dealers, or came as a result of an American request for assistance. There is no doubt, however, that it was Israel that pressed Ghorbanifar on the United States. U.S. officials accepted Israeli assurances that they had had for some time an extensive dialogue that involved high-level Iranians, as well as their assurances of Ghorbanifar's bona fides. Thereafter, at critical points in the initiative, when doubts were expressed by critical U.S. participants, an Israeli emissary would arrive with encouragement, often a specific proposal, and pressure to stay with the Ghorbanifar channel.

From the record available to the board, it is not possible to determine the role of key U.S. participants in prompting these Israeli interventions. There were active and ongoing consultations between North and officials of the Israeli government, specifically David Kimche and Amiram Nir. In addition, Adolph Schwimmer, Yaacov Nimrodi, and Michael Ledeen, also in frequent contact with North, had close ties with the government of Israel. It may be that the Israeli interventions were actively solicited by particular U.S. officials. Without the benefit of the views of the Israeli officials involved, it is hard to know the facts.

It is clear, however, that Israel had its own interests, some in direct conflict with those of the United States, in having the United States pursue the initiative. For this reason, it had an incentive to keep the initiative alive. It sought to do this by interventions with the NSC staff, the national security adviser, and the president. Although it may have received suggestions from North, Ledeen, and others, it responded affirmatively to these suggestions by reason of its own interests.

Even if the government of Israel actively worked to begin the initiative and to keep it going, the U.S. government is responsible for its own decisions. Key participants in U.S. deliberations made the point that Israel's objectives and interests in this initiative were different from, and in some respects in conflict with, those of the United States. Although Israel dealt with those portions of the U.S. government that it deemed were sympathetic to the initiative, there is nothing improper per se about this fact. U.S. decision makers made their own decisions and must bear responsibility for the consequences.

AFTERMATH: THE EFFORTS TO TELL THE STORY

From the first hint in late October 1986 that the McFarlane trip would soon become public, information on the Iran initiative and Contra activity cascaded into the press. The veiled hints of secret activities, random and indiscriminate disclosures of information from a variety of sources, both knowledgeable and otherwise, and conflicting statements by high-level officials presented a confusing picture to the American public. The board recognized that conflicts among contemporaneous documents and statements raised concern about the management of the public presentation of facts on the Iran initiative. Though the board reviewed some evidence on events after the exposure, our ability to comment on these events remains limited.

The board found evidence that immediately following the public disclosure, the president wanted to avoid providing too much specificity or detail out of concern for the hostages still held in Lebanon and those Iranians who had supported the initiative. In doing so, he did not, we believe, intend to mislead the American public or cover up unlawful conduct. By at least November 20, the president took steps to ensure that all the facts would come out. From the president's request to Edwin Meese to look into the history of the initiative, to his appointment of this board, to his request for an independent counsel, to his willingness to discuss this matter fully and to review his personal notes with us, the board is convinced that the president did indeed want the full story to be told.

Those who prepared the president's supporting documentation did not appear, at least initially, to share in the president's ultimate wishes. McFarlane described for the board the process used by the NSC staff to create a chronology that obscured essential facts. McFarlane contributed to the creation of this chronology, which did not, he said, present "a full and completely accurate account" of the events and left ambiguous the president's role. This was, according to McFarlane, done to distance the president from the timing and nature of the president's authorization. He told the board that he wrote a memorandum on November 18 that tried to, in his own words, "gild the president's motives." This version was incorporated into the chronology. McFarlane told the board that he knew the account was "misleading, at least, and wrong, at worst." McFarlane told the board that he did provide the attorney general an accurate account of the president's role.

The board found considerable reason to question the actions of North in the aftermath of the disclosure. The board has no evidence to either confirm or refute that North destroyed documents on the initiative in an effort to conceal facts from threatened investigations. The board found indications that North was involved in an effort, over time, to conceal or withhold important information. The files of North contained much of the historical documentation that the board used to construct its narrative. Moreover, North was the primary U.S. government official involved in the details of the operation. The chronology he produced has many inaccuracies. These "histories" were to be the basis of the "full" story of the Iran initiative. These inaccuracies lend some evidence to the proposition that North, either on his own or at the behest of others, actively sought to conceal important information.

Out of concern for the protection of classified material, Director Casey and Vice Admiral Poindexter were to brief only the congressional intelligence committees on the "full" story; the DCI before the committees and Poindexter in private sessions with the chairmen and vice chairmen. The DCI and Poindexter undertook to do this on November 21, 1986. It appears from the copy of the DCI's testimony and notes of Poindexter's meetings, that they did not fully relate the nature of events as they had occurred. The result is an understandable perception that they were not forthcoming.

The board is also concerned about various notes that appear to be missing. Poindexter was the official note taker in some key meetings, yet no notes for the meetings can be found. The reason for the lack of such notes remains unknown to the board. If they were written, they may contain very important information. We have no way of knowing if they exist.

RECOMMENDATIONS

Not only . . . is the Federal power over external affairs in origin and essential character different from that over internal affairs, but participation in the exercise of the power is significantly limited. In this vast external realm, with its important, complicated, delicate and manifold problems, the President alone has the power to speak or listen as a representative of the nation.—*United States v. Curtiss-Wright Export Corp.*, 299 US 304, 319 (1936)

Whereas the ultimate power to formulate domestic policy resides in the Congress, the primary responsibility for the formulation and implementation of national security policy falls on the president.

It is the president who is the usual source of innovation and responsiveness in this field. The departments and agencies—the Defense Department, State Department, and CIA bureaucracies—tend to resist policy change. Each has its own perspective based on long experience. The challenge for the president is to bring his perspective to bear on these bureaucracies for they are his instruments for executing national security policy, and he must work through them. His task is to provide them leadership and direction.

The National Security Act of 1947 and the system that has grown up under it affords the president special tools for carrying out this important role. These tools are the National Security Council, the national security adviser, and the NSC staff. These are the means through which the creative impulses of the president are brought to bear on the permanent government. The National Security Act, and custom and practice, rightly give the president wide latitude in fashioning exactly how these means are used.

There is no magic formula that can be applied to the NSC structure and process to produce an optimal system. Because the system is the vehicle through which the president formulates and implements his national security policy, it must adapt to each individual president's style and management philosophy. This means that NSC structures and processes must be flexible, not rigid. Overprescription would either destroy the system or render it ineffective.

Nevertheless, this does not mean there can be no guidelines or recommendations that might improve the operation of the system, whatever the particular style of the incumbent president. We have reviewed the operation of the system over the past forty years, through good times and bad. We have listened carefully to the views of all the living former presidents as well as those of most of the participants in their own national security systems. With the strong caveat that flexibility and adaptability must be at the core, it is our judgment that the national security system seems to have worked best when it has in general operated along the lines set forth below.

ORGANIZING FOR NATIONAL SECURITY

Because of the wide latitude in the National Security Act, the president bears a special responsibility for the effective performance of the NSC system. A president must at the outset provide guidelines to the members of the National Security Council, his national security adviser, and the National Security Council staff. These guidelines, to be effective, must include how they will relate to one another, what procedures will be followed, what the president expects of them. If his advisers are not performing as he likes, only the president can intervene.

The National Security Council principals other than the president participate on the council in a unique capacity.[3] Although holding a seat by virtue of their official positions in the administration, when they sit as members of the council they sit not as cabinet secretaries or department heads but as advisers to the president. They are there not simply to advance or defend the particular positions of the departments or agencies they head but to give their best advice to the president. Their job—and their challenge—is to see the issue from this perspective, not from the narrower interests of their respective bureaucracies.

The National Security Council is only advisory. It is the president alone who decides. When the NSC principals receive those decisions, they do so as heads of the appropriate departments or agencies. They are then responsible to see that the president's decisions are carried out by those organizations accurately and effectively.

This is an important point. The policy innovation and creativity of the president encounters a natural resistance from the executing departments. While this resistance is a source of frustration to every president, it is inherent in the design of the government. It is up to the politically appointed agency heads to ensure that the president's goals, designs, and policies are brought to bear on this permanent structure. Circumventing the departments perhaps by using the national security adviser or the NSC staff to execute policy, robs the president of the experience and capacity resident in the departments. The president must act largely through them, but the agency heads must ensure that they execute the president's policies in an expeditious and effective manner. It is not just the obligation of the national security adviser to see that the national security process is used. All of the NSC principals—and particularly the president—have that obligation.

This tension between the president and the executive departments is worked out through the national security process described in the opening sections of this report. It is through this process that the nation obtains both the best of the creativity of the president and the learning and expertise of the national security departments and agencies.

This process is extremely important to the president. His decisions will benefit from the advice and perspective of all the concerned departments and agencies. History offers numerous examples of this truth. President John F. Kennedy, for example, did not have adequate consultation before entering upon the Bay of Pigs invasion, one of his greatest failures. He remedied this in time for the Cuban missile crisis, one of his greatest successes. Process will not always produce brilliant ideas, but history suggests it can at least help prevent bad ideas from becoming presidential policy.

THE NATIONAL SECURITY ADVISER

It is the national security adviser who is primarily responsible for managing this process on a daily basis. The job requires skill, sensitivity, and integrity. It is his responsibility to ensure that matters submitted for consideration by the council cover the full range of issues on which review is required, that those issues are fully analyzed, that a full range of options is considered, that the prospects and risks of each are examined, that all relevant intelligence and other information is available to the principals, that legal considerations are addressed, and that difficulties in implementation are confronted. Usually, this can best be accomplished through interagency participation in the analysis of the issue and a preparatory policy review at the deputy or under secretary level.

The national security adviser assumes these responsibilities not only with respect to the president but with respect to all the NSC principals. He must keep them informed of the president's thinking and decisions. They should have adequate notice and an agenda for all meetings. Decision papers should, if at all possible, be provided in advance.

The national security adviser must also ensure that adequate records are kept of NSC consultations and presidential decisions. This is essential to avoid confusion among presidential advisers and departmental staffs about what was actually decided and what is wanted. Those records are also essential for conducting a periodic review of a policy or initiative, and to learn from the past.

It is the responsibility of the national security adviser to monitor policy implementation and to ensure that policies are executed in conformity with the intent of the president's decision. Monitoring includes initiating periodic reassessments of a policy or operation, especially when changed circumstances suggest that the policy or operation no longer serves U.S. interests.

But the national security adviser does not simply manage the national security process. He is himself an important source of advice on national security matters to the president. He is not the president's only source of advice, but he is perhaps the one most able to see things from the president's perspective.

He is unburdened by departmental responsibilities. The president is his only master. His advice is confidential. He is not subject to Senate confirmation and traditionally does not formally appear before congressional committees.

To serve the president well, the national security adviser should present his own views, but he must at the same time represent the views of others fully and faithfully to the president. The system will not work well if the national security adviser does not have the trust of the NSC principals. He, therefore, must not use his proximity to the president to manipulate the process so as to produce his own position. He should not interpose himself between the president and the NSC principals. He should not seek to exclude the NSC principals from the decision process. Performing both these roles well is an essential, if not easy, task.

In order for the national security adviser to serve the president adequately, he must have direct access to the president. Unless he knows first hand the views of the president and is known to reflect them in his management of the NSC system, he will be ineffective. He should not report to the president through some other official. While the chief of staff or others can usefully interject domestic political considerations into national security deliberations, they should do so as additional advisers to the president.

Ideally, the national security adviser should not have a high public profile. He should not try to compete with the Secretary of State or the secretary of defense as the articulator of public policy. They, along with the president, should be the spokesmen for the policies of the administration. While a "passion for anonymity" is perhaps too strong a term, the national security adviser should generally operate offstage.

The NSC principals of course must have direct access to the president, with whatever frequency the president feels is appropriate. But these individual meetings should not be used by the principal to seek decisions or otherwise circumvent the system in the absence of the other principals. In the same way, the national security adviser should not use his scheduled intelligence or other daily briefings of the president as an opportunity to seek presidential decision on significant issues.

If the system is to operate well, the national security adviser must promote cooperation rather than competition among himself and the other NSC principals. But the president is ultimately responsible for the operation of this system. If rancorous infighting develops among his principal national security functionaries, only he can deal with them. Public dispute over external policy by senior officials undermines the process of decision making and narrows his options. It is the president's responsibility to ensure that it does not take place.

Finally, the national security adviser should focus on advice and management, not implementation and execution. Implementation is the responsibility and the strength of the departments and agencies. The national security adviser and the NSC staff generally do not have the depth of resources for the conduct of operations. In addition, when they take on implementation responsibilities, they risk compromising their objectivity. They can no longer act as impartial overseers of the implementation, ensuring that presidential guidance is followed, that policies are kept under review, and that the results are serving the president's policy and the national interest.

THE NSC STAFF

The NSC staff should be small, highly competent, and experienced in the making of public policy. Staff members should be drawn both from within and from outside government. Those from within government should come from the several departments and agencies concerned with national security matters. No particular department or agency should have a predominate role. A proper balance must be maintained between people from within and outside the government. Staff members should generally rotate with a stay of more than four years viewed as the exception.

A large number of staff action officers organized along essentially horizontal lines enhances the possibilities for poorly supervised and monitored activities by individual staff members. Such a system is made to order for energetic self-starters to take unauthorized initiatives. Clear vertical lines of control and authority, responsibility and accountability, are essential to good management.

One problem affecting the NSC staff is lack of institutional memory. This results from the understandable desire of a president to replace the staff in order to be sure it is responsive to him. Departments provide continuity that can help the council, but the council as an institution also needs some means to assure adequate records and memory. This was identified to the board as a problem by many witnesses.

We recognize the problem and have identified a range of possibilities that a president might consider on this subject. One would be to create a small permanent executive secretariat. Another would be to have one person, the executive secretary, as a permanent position. Finally, a pattern of limited tenure and overlapping rotation could be used. Any of these would help reduce the problem of loss of institutional memory; none would be practical unless each succeeding president subscribed to it.

The guidelines for the role of the national security adviser also apply generally to the NSC staff. They should protect the process and thereby the president. Departments and agencies should not be excluded from participation in that process. The staff should not be implementors or operators and staff should keep a low profile with the press.

PRINCIPAL RECOMMENDATION

The model we have outlined above for the National Security Council system constitutes our first and most important recommendation. It includes guidelines that address virtually all of the deficiencies in procedure and practice that the board encountered in the Iran-Contra affair as well as in other case studies of this and previous administrations.

We believe this model can enhance the performance of a president and his administration in the area of national security. It responds directly to President Reagan's mandate to describe the NSC system as it ought to be.

The board recommends that the proposed model be used by presidents in their management of the national security system.

SPECIFIC RECOMMENDATIONS

In addition to its principal recommendation regarding the organization and functioning of the NSC system and roles to be played by the participants, the board has a number of specific recommendations.

The National Security Act of 1947. The flaws of procedure and failures of responsibility revealed by our study do not suggest any inadequacies in the provisions of the National Security Act of 1947 that deal with the structure and operation of the NSC system. Forty years of experience under that act demonstrate to the board that it remains a fundamentally sound framework for national security decision making. It strikes a balance between formal structure and flexibility adequate to permit each president to tailor the system to fit his needs.

As a general matter, the NSC staff should not engage in the implementation of policy or the conduct of operations. This compromises their oversight role and usurps the responsibilities of the departments and agencies. But the inflexibility of a legislative restriction should be avoided. Terms such as "operation" and "implementation" are difficult to define, and a legislative proscription might preclude some future president from making a very constructive use of the NSC staff.

Predisposition on sizing of the staff should be toward fewer rather than more. But a legislative restriction cannot foresee the requirements of future presidents. Size is best left to the discretion of the president, with the admonition that the role of the NSC staff is to review, not to duplicate or replace, the work of the departments and agencies.

We recommend that no substantive change be made in the provisions of the National Security Act dealing with the structure and operation of the NSC system.

Senate Confirmation of the National Security Adviser. It has been suggested that the job of the national security adviser has become so important that its holder should be screened by the process of confirmation, and that once confirmed he should return frequently for questioning by the Congress. It is argued that this would improve the accountability of the national security adviser.

We hold a different view. The national security adviser does, and should continue, to serve only one master, and that is the president. Further, confirmation is inconsistent with the role the national security adviser should play. He should not decide, only advise. He should not engage in policy implementation or operations. He should serve the president, with no collateral and potentially diverting loyalties.

Confirmation would tend to institutionalize the natural tension that exists between the secretary of state and the national security adviser. Questions would increasingly arise about who really speaks for the president in national security matters. Foreign governments could be confused or would be encouraged to engage in "forum shopping."

Only one of the former government officials interviewed favored Senate confirmation of the national security adviser. While consultation with Congress received wide support, confirmation and formal questioning were opposed. Several suggested that if the national security adviser were to become a position subject to confirmation,it could induce the president to turn to other internal staff or to people outside government to play that role.

We urge the Congress not to require Senate confirmation of the national security adviser.

The Interagency Process. It is the national security adviser who has the greatest interest in making the national security process work, for it is this process by which the president obtains the information, background, and analysis he requires to make decisions and build support for his program. Most presidents have set up interagency committees at both a staff and policy level to surface issues, develop options, and clarify choices. There has typically been a struggle for the chairmanships of these groups between the national security adviser and the NSC staff on the one hand, and the cabinet secretaries and department officials on the other.

Our review of the operation of the present system and that of other administrations where committee chairmen came from the departments has led us to the conclusion that the system generally operates better when the committees are chaired by the individual with the greatest stake in making the NSC system work.

We recommend that the national security adviser chair the senior-level committees of the NSC system.

Covert Actions. Policy formulation and implementation are usually managed by a team of experts led by policy-making generalists. Covert action requirements are no different, but there is a need to limit, sometimes severely, the number of individuals involved. The lives of many people may be at stake, as was the case in the attempt to rescue the hostages in Tehran. Premature disclosure might kill the idea in embryo, as could have been the case in the opening of relations with China. In such cases, there is a tendency to limit those involved to a small number of top officials. This practice tends to limit severely the expertise brought to bear on the problem and should be used very sparingly indeed.

The obsession with secrecy and preoccupation with leaks threaten to paralyze the government in its handling of covert operations. Unfortunately, the concern is not misplaced. The selective leak has become a principal means of waging bureaucratic warfare. Opponents of an operation kill it with a leak; supporters seek to build support through the same means.

We have witnessed over the past years a significant deterioration in the integrity of process. Rather than a means to obtain results more satisfactory than the position of any of the individual departments, it has frequently become something to be manipulated to reach a specific outcome. The leak becomes a primary instrument in that process.

This practice is destructive of orderly governance. It can only be reversed if the most senior officials take the lead. If senior decision makers set a clear example and demand compliance, subordinates are more likely to conform.

Most recent administrations have had carefully drawn procedures for the consideration of covert activities. The Reagan administration established such procedures in January 1985, then promptly ignored them in its consideration of the Iran initiative.

We recommend that each administration formulate precise procedures for restricted consideration of covert action and that, once formulated, those procedures be strictly adhered to.

The Role of the CIA. Some aspects of the Iran arms sales raised broader questions in the minds of members of the board regarding the role of CIA. The first deals with intelligence.

The NSC staff was actively involved in the preparation of the May 20, 1985, update to the Spcial National Intelligence Estimate on Iran. It is a matter for concern if this involvement and the strong views of NSC staff members were allowed to influence the intelligence judgments contained in the update. It is also of concern that the update contained the hint that the United States should change its existing policy and encourage its allies to provide arms to Iran. It is critical that the line between intellgence and advocacy of a particular policy be preserved if intelligence is to retain its integrity and perform its proper function. In this instance, the CIA came close enough to the line to warrant concern.

We emphasize to both the intelligence community and policy makers the importance of maintaining the integrity and objectivity of the intelligence process.

Legal Counsel. From time to time issues with important legal ramifications will come before the National Security Council. The attorney general is currently a member of the council by invitation and should be in a position to provide legal advice to the council and the president. It is important that the attorney general and his or her department be available to interagency deliberations.

The Justice Department, however, should not replace the role of counsel in the other departments. As the principal counsel on foreign affairs, the legal adviser to the secretary of state should also be available to all the NSC participants.

Of all the NSC participants, it is the assistant for national security affairs who seems to have had the least access to expert counsel familiar with his activities.

The board recommends that the position of Legal Adviser to the NSC be enhanced in stature and in its role within the NSC staff.

Secrecy and Congress. There is a natural tension between the desire for secrecy and the need to consult Congress on covert operations. Presidents seem to become increasingly concerned about leaks of classified information as their administrations progress. They blame Congress disproportionately. Various cabinet officials from prior administrations indicated to the board that they believe Congress bears no more blame than the executive branch.

However, the number of members and staff involved in reviewing covert activities is large; it provides cause for concern and a convenient excuse for presidents to avoid congressional consultation.

We recommend that Congress consider replacing the existing intelligence committees of the respective Houses with a new joint committee with a restricted staff to oversee the intelligence community, patterned after the Joint Committee on Atomic Energy that existed until the mid-1970s.

Privatizing National Security Policy. Careful and limited use of people outside the U.S. government may be very helpful in some unique cases. But this practice raises substantial questions. It can create conflict-of-interest problems. Private or foreign sources may have different policy interests or personal motives and may exploit their association with a U.S. government effort. Such involvement gives private and foreign sources potentially powerful leverage in the form of demands for return favors or even blackmail.

The United States has enormous resources invested in agencies and departments in order to conduct the government's business. In all but a very few cases, these can perform the functions needed. If not, then inquiry is required to find out why.

We recommend against having implementation and policy oversight dominated by intermediaries. We do not recommend barring limited use of private individuals to assist in United States diplomatic initiatives or in covert activities. We caution against use of such people except in very limited ways and under close observation and supervision.

EPILOGUE

If but one of the major policy mistakes we examined had been avoided, the nation's history would bear one less scar, one less embarrassment, one less opportunity for opponents to reverse the principles this nation seeks to preserve and advance in the world. As a collection, these recommendations are offered to those who will find themselves in situations similar to the ones we reviewed: under stress, with high stakes, given little time, using incomplete information, and troubled by premature disclosure. In such a state, modest improvements may yield surprising gains. This is our hope.

NOTES

1. It may be possible to authorize transfers by another country under the Arms Export Control Act without obtaining the president's consent. As a practical matter, however, the legal requirements may not differ significantly. For example, section 614(2) permits the president to waive the requirements of the act. But this waiver authority may not be exercised unless it is determined that the international arms sales are "vital to the national security interests of the United States." Moreover, before granting a waiver, the president must consult with and provide written justification to the foreign affairs and appropriations committees of the Congress. See 22 U.S.C. 2374(3).

2. Apparently no determination was made at the time as to the legality of these activities even though serious concerns about legality were expressed by the deputy director of the CIA, a presidential finding was sought by CIA officials before any further CIA activities in support of the Iran initiative were undertaken, and the CIA counsel, Stanley Sporkin, advised that as a matter of prudence any new finding should seek to ratify the prior CIA activities.

3. The statutory members of the National Security Council are the president, vice president, secretary of state, and secretary of defense. By the phrase "National Security Council principals" or "NSC principals," the board generally means those four statutory members plus the director of central intelligence and the chairman of the Joint Chiefs of Staff.

CHAPTER 9

THE DEFENSE ACQUISITION PROCESS

KEEPING THE EDGE

CHARLES R. NELSON

It is not unusual to see people wince when the subject of acquisition is brought up for discussion. This is a typical reaction that is principally a result of lack of knowledge and even fear of having to delve into the subject. While I acknowledge the subject is technically complex, replete with acronyms, and seemingly always undergoing change, I do not subscribe to the belief the acquisition process is too hard to understand.

The question of importance always arises when the subject of acquisition is broached. Flyer, acquirer, loggie, contracting expert—everyone needs to understand how the services "keep the edge." If they do not think they do, then they should try fighting the next war with what the budgeter and the civilian economist buy. It may be at a lower cost and it may be delivered on time, but it also may not do the job it is needed to do.

This discussion introduces the acquisition process. It shows how the acquisition process is actually an extension of the national security policy process. After addressing this point, we will look at the acquisition structure; the in-depth acquisition process, differentiating between those parts of the process that are preparatory and those constituting the formal acquisition effort; and the relationship of the acquisition process to the biennial planning, programming, and budgeting system (PPBS).

ACQUISITION AND THE NATIONAL SECURITY PROCESS

The acquisition process is really an extension of the national security policy process. To facilitate discussion we draw on the model in Figure 1, adapted from one developed by Harold McCard, president of Textron Defense Systems. This model focuses only on the military instrument of power. It does not address plans or actions that use the economic and political instruments of power, which are, of course, possible alternatives for achieving national security objectives.

Walking our way through the model, we see that national security objectives, once translated into directives, require some sort of military response option. The formulation of these directives are affected by two conditions, the threat and the concept of operations.

National security objectives and their subsequent directives are derived from an assessment of the threat. The purpose of these directives is to ensure our national security will be maintained. An example of the influence of the threat on our national security objectives can be seen in the White House's *National Security Strategy of the United States*. The 1987 and 1988 publications identified Soviet expansion and military capability as the principal threat to our national security. However, the 1990 and 1991 publications make no mention of the Soviet Union being a direct threat.

Likewise, concepts of operations often determine the extent of our national security directives. For example, it would be meaningless to have as a directive to attack, take over, and govern some country. We do not have the capability, even if we had the desire, to accomplish such an unrealistic objective.

The threat and our concepts of operations also affect our strategies and missions. The recent Strategic Arms Reduction Treaty (START) and conventional forces reduction treaties reflect a perceived decrease in the threat.

With the reduction of strategic weapons and a likely increase in Third World conflicts, we will be planning for scenarios requiring rapid deployment, massive airlift, mobility, and high firepower systems instead of a European scenario between industrially advanced nations with high technology and heavy armor.

The same situation exists between strategies and missions, and our concepts of operations. One can readily see that strategies and missions (the plan for how we will meet our objectives) drive the kinds of operations for which we plan. However, the reverse is also a consideration. It serves no purpose to develop plans we cannot execute because of a lack of forces. Resource availability also sets limits on the planning of strategies and missions.

All of these are deciding factors, neither one singularly more important than any other, in the military response options available to our leaders. The analysts' assessment of the threat characteristics, our strategies and missions, and our concepts of opera-

This essay has been edited and is reprinted from Program Manager *(Jan-Feb 1992): 32–41, by permission of Defense Systems Management College Press.*

Figure 1
The National Security Model

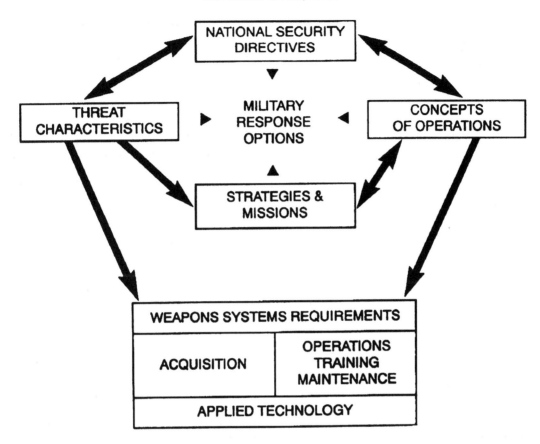

tions are reflected in the weapon systems we require. This should be intuitively obvious from McCard's model and the foregoing discussion. What is not readily obvious is the impact of a deficiency. What about the scenario where an assessment reveals a threat for which we have not prepared or an operational concept for which we do not have the necessary weapon capability?

When current capability is not enough to support response options for achieving our national security directives, we have the additional options of either changing our operations, training, and maintenance or acquiring a new weapon system. The former is usually the least costly and thus receives first consideration.

In the case of operations, if we have a bomber whose effective range has significantly decreased, we have the choice of stationing it closer to the intended target or modifying the aircraft with a newer and more efficient engine. In the case of training, suppose an adversary installs a new radar that will detect aircraft as low as 100 feet. One method of addressing this threat would be to train to fly missions at 50 to 75 feet. Another would be to employ some type of standoff penetrating missile. In the case of mainte-

nance, suppose we find the radios in our fighter-bombers achieve only half of the expected mean time between failure. One option could be to double the number of purchased contractor repairs or purchase an off-the-shelf, more technologically advanced radio.

If, after all of this, there is still a threat that cannot be met, acquiring a new, more technologically capable weapon system is likely to be the best way to keep the edge. This is, of course, a long-term solution requiring significant resources. As the model indicates, the application of new technology will probably undergird any alternative solutions that might be implemented.

Since Vietnam, we have been buying "smarter" and more technologically complex weapons. The cost of these weapons has been high, prompting critics to question their usefulness. Before Desert Storm, critics were asking if the benefits of the new weapon systems justified their enormous cost, especially since they had never been employed in combat. Desert Storm, however, changed this criticism. (It is not clear if it was a high-intensity, low-intensity conflict or a low-intensity conventional war. What is clear is that it was a "high-tech" conflict). Some of

Figure 2
The Acquisition Process

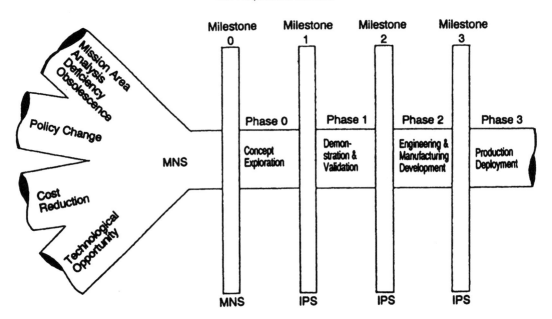

our newest and most sophisticated hardware was displayed, tested, and proven during Desert Storm. It also proved the wisdom of continually updating and modifying our mature weapon systems (B-52, F-111, AWACS, C-141, etc.). The lives saved and success of the operation reinforced the benefits of having high-technology weapons.

THE ACQUISITION STRUCTURE

Major acquisition programs are managed from a structure that is separate from the normal operational chains of command. Management of major weapon system acquisitions requires efficient decision making and effective implementation.

Program managers (PMs) are the individuals responsible for keeping acquisition costs within acceptable limits, meeting development and delivery schedules, and ensuring weapon systems perform as required. *They are not the advocates for the program—that is the responsibility of the operating command.* The PM reports directly to program executive officers (PEOs).

Program executive officers are key middle-level managers tasked with direct accountability for the execution and information validation of a limited group of mission-related major acquisition programs. The PEO positions were established as the command line between the service acquisition executive (SAE) and the PMs for major and selected acquisition programs. They devote full attention to this task and report only to the SAE.

The SAE is an assistant secretary with full-time responsibility for all service acquisition programs.

The SAE, although on the staff of the service secretary, is solely responsible to the defense acquisition executive for all service acquisition matters.

The undersecretary of defense for acquisition (USD[A]) has been designated the defense acquisition executive. According to the secretary of defense's *1991 Annual Report to the President and Congress,* the defense acquisition executive is ultimately responsible for acquisition within the Department of Defense (DOD), having *the authority for approving major defense programs at major milestones in the acquisition process, for directing the heads of the DOD components on all acquisition matters, and for directing the DOD comptroller to withhold funds if necessary to ensure program milestone criteria are met.*

THE ACQUISITION PROCESS

Now we shift to the process of acquisition (Figure 2). The acquisition process provides a logical means of progressively translating broadly stated mission needs into well-defined, system-specific requirements. *This is accomplished using an incremental commitment of resources, converting dollars into hardware.* As the alternative(s) progress through the process, resource consumption becomes greater and risks should become lower.

The process of acquisition can be divided into two distinct areas: *those that are considered preparatory and those that make up formal acquisition.* The preparatory part of acquisition consists of the requirements definition process and the concept exploration phase. The formal acquisition part of the process consists of the demonstration and validation phase, the engineering and manufacturing development phase, production and deployment phase, and the operation and support phase.

Although concept exploration is commonly considered part of the acquisition process, it is not part of the formal process. The formal acquisition process really begins with the Milestone I decision at the end of concept exploration. This is the first time alternative concepts are identified well enough to allow development and scrutiny.

PREPARATORY ACQUISITION ACTIVITIES

REQUIREMENTS DEFINITION

The requirements definition process precedes the Milestone O decision. It begins with an examination of the operational need, which leads to trade-offs in cost, schedule, and performance to determine the optimum system characteristics. Requirements are generated from four process activities: mission area analysis, changes in policy, cost reduction, and taking advantage of a technological opportunity. For example, mission area analysis might reveal a threat for which we have no capability to counter. Recall that projected improvements in Soviet radars, surface-to-air missiles, interceptors, and AWACS prompted the Air Force in the 1970s to purchase the B-1 as its survivable penetrating bomber.

Changes in policy can also result in a threat that is not countered. A good example is President Jimmy Carter's decision to cancel the B-1. The cancellation forced the air force to address the increased Soviet defensive threat through support for the alternative cruise missile program.

Cost reduction can also generate requirements. While this deficiency usually does not stand alone as a reason for undertaking an acquisition effort, there are very few requirements identified that do not emphasize cost reduction. An example is the development of the F-110 engine. While it promised increased performance and operational reliability over the F-100, it also promised greater operational cost efficiency.

The opportunity offered by a technological breakthrough can also lead to identification of a need. The development of stealth technology offered the possibility of decreasing pilot risk while increasing the potential for mission success. The success of the F-117 fighters during Desert Storm is ample testimony of the potential offered by taking advantage of new technology.

Any one, or all, of these *deficiencies can result in a major command preparing a mission need statement (MNS)*. This statement, when completed, is sent through the SAE to the Joint Requirements Oversight Council (JROC).

The JROC, chaired by the vice chairman of the Joint Chiefs of Staff, validates the threat assessment, examines the feasibility of the proposed approach to counter the threat, considers joint service require-

ments that might also be met, and assigns the proposed acquisition a priority. If the JROC concurs with the identified requirement, it requests that a Defense Acquisition Board be convened. This *Defense Acquisition Board constitutes the start of the Milestone O—Concept Studies Approval* decision process. (The USD(A) can approve the effort without convening a Defense Acquisition Board if he chooses to do so.) If after reviewing the requirement, the Defense Acquisition Board and the undersecretary of defense for acquisition concur with its validity, the USD(A) issues an acquisition decision memorandum (ADM). This ADM is sent to the service office responsible for acquisition to prepare a program management directive (PMD). This PMD conveys the USD(A)'s guidance along with alternatives to be considered, identification of participants, and special considerations such as joint or combined efforts. The PMD specifies what is to be done and who is to do it, not how it is to be done. Funding for this phase is provided by the submitting major command (MAJCOM) or a central studies fund controlled by the USD(A), or both, as directed in the ADM.

PHASE 0—CONCEPT EXPLORATION AND DEFINITION

The issuance of the Milestone O ADM and subsequent PMD initiates Phase 0—Concept Exploration (CE) and Definition. The emphasis during this phase is primarily on paper studies of alternatives. During this phase, the operating command initiating the mission need statement leads the study effort, establishes a concept action group to explore material alternatives, accomplishes a cost and operational effectiveness analysis (COEA), and prepares a brief operational requirements document (ORD).

The COEA provides an analytical basis to support milestone decision reviews. It allows comparison of each alternative solution on the basis of cost and operational effectiveness. The ORD is a formatted statement containing an assessment of operational effectiveness and suitability of each alternative while better defining operational requirements.

The implementing command will not activate a systems program office (SPO) until the development effort receives a Milestone I approval. However, in preparation for activation, the implementing command will establish a SPO cadre and nominate a program manager to the service acquisition executive for approval. For nominees in the rank of colonel, the SAE has approval authority. For general officers, the approval is coordinated with the chief of staff and service secretary. A deputy program manager for logistics (DPML) is also appointed and with the PM begins establishing what will become the systems program office and preparing the acquisition strategy, program management plans, and the acquisition program baseline (APB).

The acquisition strategy and the program management plans provide the information essential for milestone decisions. Acquisition strategy focuses on events, explicitly linking major contractual goals and milestone decisions with development and testing. Topics addressed in the acquisition strategy include competitive prototyping, competitive alternative development and production, live fire testing as appropriate, and estimated low-rate initial production quantities. Program plans provide for integrated, concurrent engineering of the system and its manufacturing, test, and support processes. The APB document identifies proposed cost, schedule, performance, and support parameters that establish the "contract" between the PM, the SAE, and the defense acquisition executive.

The DPML will be working with the operating command and the implementing command to prepare the integrated logistics support plan. This plan addresses the integrated logistics support elements for each alternative. These elements include maintenance planning; manpower and personnel; supply support; support equipment; technical data; training and training support; computer resources support; facilities; packaging, handling, storage, and transportation; and design interface.

With the operating command, the SPO cadre develops the system maturity matrix, the integrated program summary (IPS), and the test and evaluation master plan (TEMP) for the preferred solutions identified. The system threat-assessment report is prepared for the program by the service's intelligence command or agency.

The IPS document summarizes the results of the phase activities and communicates the preferred choice to the Defense Acquisition Board. *An IPS, prepared by the using command for Milestone I and by the systems program office at the end of the remaining phases, initiates the milestone review process. The TEMP helps to ensure testing of the proposed system is well thought out and planned.* It addresses test and evaluation for the entire program, including development test and evaluation (DT&E) and operational test and evaluation (OT&E). The TEMP begins identifying test approaches, facility requirements, and required resources.

The user prepares the concept exploration (CE) IPS when all of the alternatives have been evaluated, attaches supporting documentation prepared during the phase, and submits it to the JROC for Defense Acquisition Board review. This initiates the Milestone I—Concept Demonstration Approval decision process that signals Phase 0 is complete, and the program is ready to go to Phase I. At this decision point, the Defense Acquisition Board will review the threat assessment for validity and confirm that results warrant proceeding to the next phase. They will also approve the *concept baseline* that provides initial cost, schedule, and performance objectives for Phase I; verify completion of an environmental assessment with potential mitigating plans; confirm life cycle costs and annual funding requirements are affordable; and ensure adequate resources are programmed in the PPBS. This latter point is an important link between the acquisition process and the PPBS. The defense acquisition executive, throughout the entire acquisition process, will not permit a program to proceed into the next phase of acquisition unless sufficient funds have been identified and programmed for in the Future Years Defense Program (FYDP).

FORMAL ACQUISITION PROCESS

PHASE I—CONCEPT DEMONSTRATION AND VALIDATION

If the Defense Acquisition Board and defense acquisition executive agree with the assessment, and sufficient FYDP funding has been programmed, the defense acquisition executive issues a Milestone I ADM authorizing start of Phase I—Concept Demonstration and Validation (DEM/VAL). This ADM approves the acquisition strategy and concept baseline, establishes the requirements for the phase, and provides cost/affordability constraints.

Demonstration and validation further explores the most promising solutions identified in CE. For major acquisitions, usually two programs are considered in order to benefit from the advantages of competition. The competition and flyoff between the Lockheed, General Dynamics, and Boeing F-22 and the Northrop and McDonald Douglas F-23 provide an excellent example of using competition to obtain high-quality systems at the lowest price possible.

The objectives of this phase are to prove critical technologies and processes are understood; better define system characteristics and capabilities; establish a proposed development baseline containing better defined cost, schedule, and performance estimates; and identify the preferred system or best solution to the identified need.

Cost generally restricts the final choice to a single system, as in the case of the Advanced Tactical Fighter (ATF). Eleven F-22 aircraft will be purchased during engineering and manufacturing development (EMD) for flight and stress testing. At approximately $144 million a copy, the cost for carrying two contractors and purchasing twenty-two aircraft for testing would have added an additional $1.5 billion to the program costs. This illustrates it was simply cost prohibitive to take both aircraft into the next phase.

In addition to updating the documents initiated in the preceding phase, the SPO proves technical feasibility and reduces program risks; puts together a *development baseline* detailing proposed cost, schedule, and performance objectives; proposes low-rate initial production quantities; addresses live-fire testing requirements; and determines the applicability of using competitive alternative development and production. Competitive alternative development and production is the selection of a second contractor for full-scale development and production.

Prototyping and test and evaluation are used to demonstrate and validate the concept. The testing emphasis during this phase is almost completely on development test and evaluation. Operational test and evaluation efforts are usually limited to further definition of test approaches, schedules, facility requirements, and required resources.

The deputy program manager for logistics will be working with the implementing command and the operating command to better identify support requirements, updating life cycle cost estimates, and updating and refining the integrated logistics support plan.

When the above activities have been met and the PM believes the program is ready to go to the engineering and manufacturing phase, an IPS is prepared, which, in turn, triggers the *Milestone II— Development Approval decision review*. The Defense Acquisition Board thoroughly reviews program accomplishments at this time because from this point on significant resources will be committed. It reviews the threat assessment for validation by the Defense Intelligence Agency, the DT&E test results to confirm technologies and processes are attainable, the acceptability of the environmental assessment, the affordability of the life cycle and support costs, and the adequacy of programmed and budgeted resources (people and funding).

PHASE II—ENGINEERING AND MANUFACTURING DEVELOPMENT

The engineering and manufacturing development (EMD) phase begins with the issuance of the Milestone II ADM. The ADM will approve the proposed updated acquisition strategy, development baseline, low-rate initial production quantities, and specific cost, schedule, and performance criteria to be achieved.

The objectives of the EMD phase are to translate the design approach from DEM/VAL into a stable system design, validate the manufacturing and production processes, and demonstrate the system produced will meet contract specifications and satisfy minimum acceptable operational performance requirements. In this phase the weapon system design is scaled-up to full size. Full-scale development often presents difficult and technically complex challenges. The F-111 is a case in point. Although the engine-inlet design performed well in subscale testing, there were substantial airflow and cavitation problems when it was constructed on a full scale. The plane would not taxi without cavitating at least one of the engines in a turn. The problem was so difficult to correct that the air force finally had to accept the aircraft, even though it did not meet operational requirements and compromised employment scenarios.

During this phase the SPO will again have the threat revalidated by the Defense Intelligence Agency, test the design under as realistic operational conditions as possible, and refine the acquisition strategy and system cost estimates. It will also develop a *production baseline* that better portrays program cost, schedule, and performance objectives; develop a system configuration baseline; complete the environmen-

tal impact assessment; and confirm that life cycle and annual operational costs are affordable.

Major programs entering this phase, because of the magnitude of the resources expended, receive a tremendous amount of attention from Congress, the Office of Management and Budget, the Office of the Secretary of Defense, and the service chiefs. This interest makes support and advocacy by the operating command a necessity.

The operating command, because of the maturity of the system, is able to begin integrating the weapon into their strategy and tactics. There will also be an increase in logistics activities as the design of the support systems are finished and acquired, and training, reliability, maintainability, and manpower requirement estimates are refined.

Like DEM/VAL, testing constitutes a major part of the EMD phase effort. This testing, however, is not strictly DT&E, but a combination of DT&E and IOT&E (Figure 3). *The bulk of the testing effort is on IOT&E, because it must be completed and reported to the director of operational test and evaluation at OSD before a Defense Acquisition Board can be convened.* The articles used for this testing are produced by the manufacturer under the authorization for low-rate initial production obtained at Milestone II. The production of these articles at this time not only provide test articles but also prove the viability of the manufacturing process.

The EMD phase also marks a significant change in the life of the weapons program. Once the program has made it through Milestone II and into EMD, it takes on a life of its own. As design details are completed and the system readied for production, the program will begin to consume enormous resources. These resources translate into jobs not only for the prime contractor but also for a veritable army of subcontractors, vendors, and suppliers. The presence of these jobs in turn creates a certain level of political support in Congress. This is one reason a program that successfully enters EMD becomes extremely difficult to cancel.

When the program manager has demonstrated that all technical, operational, and funding thresholds have been met, an IPS will again be prepared and submitted to trigger a Defense Acquisition Board review. *The Milestone III Production Approval* decision review will evaluate the results of Phase III for acceptable completion and ratify the costs, schedule, and performance objectives provided in the proposed production baseline. Once this has been completed to the satisfaction of the Defense Acquisition Board and Defense Acquisition Executive, an ADM will be issued.

PHASE III—PRODUCTION AND DEPLOYMENT

The production and deployment phase begins with the issuance of the approving ADM and its subsequent PMD. *The objectives of this phase are weapon system quality and performance.* In the production phase, the system is produced in quantity using assembly line methods and fielded in large numbers. Trying to keep

Figure 3
Life Cycle of Major System Acquisitions

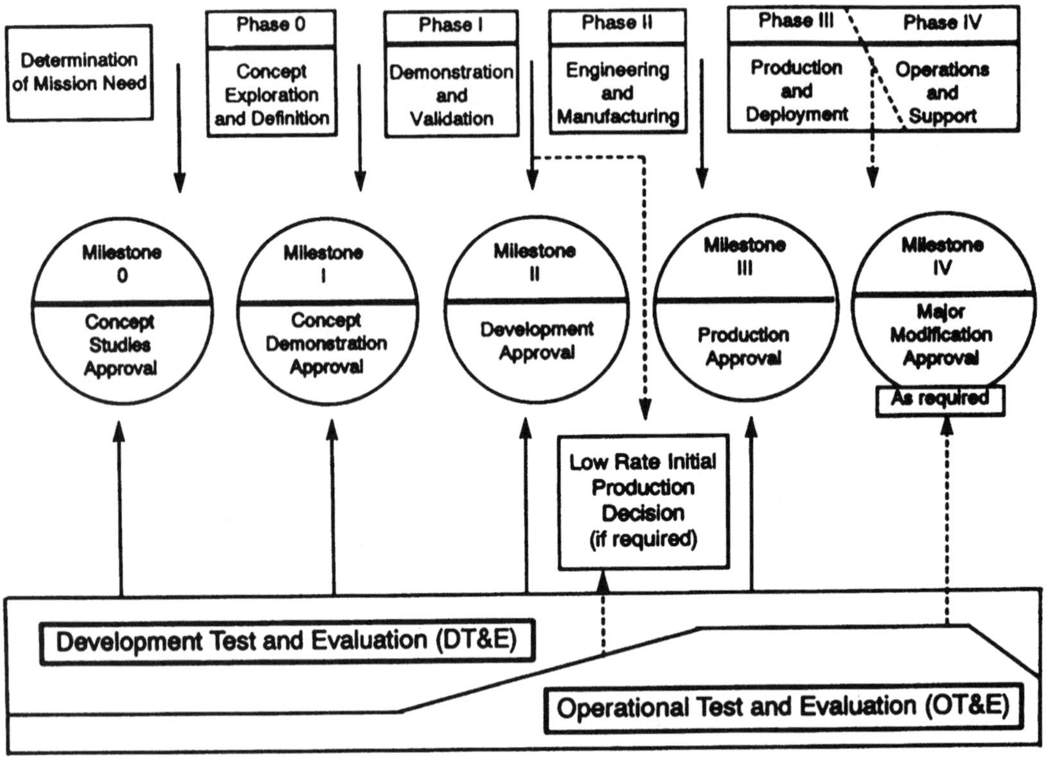

stable production rates in the face of annual budget perturbations becomes a major challenge.

Because production represents an even larger expense than EMD, there is great emphasis on acceptance testing of production line items and quality assurance methods to ensure production items meet article standards. *Follow-on IOT&E (FOT&E) will ensure that production articles meet effectiveness and suitability thresholds.* During this phase, user personnel will train extensively to learn how to operate and maintain the system. Throughout the phase, logistics support plans are implemented and tracked to ensure the system is properly supported.

Also during Phase III improvements not incorporated in the original design will be scheduled into future production lots to minimize delaying or adversely affecting the contractor. Problems or unplanned changes in this phase are extremely costly, because they often affect other areas of production and result in slips in the delivery schedule.

PHASE IV—OPERATIONS AND SUPPORT

The operations and support phase is really a continuation of Phase III, beginning after the system is fielded. Its objectives are to correct quality and safety problems, ensure the system continues to meet the threat, and identify shortcomings and deficiencies. Weapon systems are usually designed with a finite life. A deficiency results when a system will no longer sufficiently do the job because of an improved threat, a change in policy, prohibitive operational costs, technological obsolescence, or something as simple as aging. To address this deficiency, one can possibly make changes in operations, maintenance, or training.

If, however, these options are found to be insufficient, the systems PM along with the operating command will initiate an IPS and prepare proposed options, an acquisition strategy, and baseline. These actions initiate *the Major Modification Approval decision process; the newest milestone decision point.* For a system still in production, these options will then be submitted to the Defense Acquisition Board and defense acquisition executive for a decision on the acquisition phase in which the program will commence and approval of the proposed acquisition strategy and baseline. If the system is out of production, a mission need statement will be prepared that will then compete with other proposed programs in the requirements identification process. *The generation of the MNS, in essence, completes the tie between Phase IV and the requirements definition process for a new system start.*

THE BIENNIAL PLANNING, PROGRAMMING, AND BUDGETING SYSTEM

The PPBS is the process through which the DOD identifies what needs to be funded and for how much. Like DOD manpower, operations, and logistics activities, acquisition efforts are funded through this system. Acquisition efforts are directly linked to the PPBS in three specific ways; the program manager and the operating command, the Defense Planning and Resources Board, and the USD(A).

The PM is one direct link to the PPBS. He makes a program objective memorandum input *through the operating command for* inclusion into the budget. FYDP funding is obtained through this process.

Second, *the acquisition process is also tied to the PPBS through the DPRB.* The products of the PPBS provide the basis for making informed decisions on affordability and allocation of resources. The DPRB considers acquisition programs as well as other service funding programs. They must weigh all programs (acquisition, operations and maintenance, personnel, etc.) against each other and the total budget available. Programs, if found too expensive for the budget or too expensive for the benefit gained, can be unfunded in this process even if they have received milestone approval. Sometimes the only reason for canceling a program is the need to accommodate reductions in the budget. This difference in emphasis between the DPRB and the Defense Acquisition Board is the reason a weapon system program can be approved to enter the next phase one month and canceled the next.

Third, an acquisition program is *linked to the PPBS through USD(A) membership on the DPRB.* Many of the members of the DPRB are also members of the Defense Acquisition Board. The Defense Acquisition Board is chaired by the USD(A). The vice chairman of the Joint Chiefs of Staff serves as the vice chairman. The DPRB is chaired by the deputy secretary of defense and has the USD(A) as a key adviser on all resource decisions affecting acquisition program baselines.

Since the phases in the acquisition process can span several fiscal years, the progress of program implementation must be closely linked with the PPBS. While products of the PPBS provide the basis for making informed decisions on affordability and allocation of resources, there is no direct link between them and the Milestone decision-making activities. Milestone decision reviews occur when the program is ready for consideration regarding its move into the next phase, regardless of the PPBS activity going on at that time.

CONCLUSION

For over forty years we have been pursuing our national objectives through international relations backed by a superior military capability. Acquisition was the method that allowed the United States to "keep the edge" over the Soviet Union. The acquisition process is a vital alternative within the national security process. It is a methodical process, always trading off cost, schedule, and performance to field the best weapon system to meet the threat. Each phase of the process has as its goal the reduction of risks and the greater assurance of performance as specified. Effective acquisition is absolutely critical for keeping our military capability at peak readiness and effectiveness.

WILD BLUE YONDER

NICK KOTZ

On October 1, 1986, the U.S. Air Force proudly hailed a victory for which its generals had valiantly fought for thirty years: A new strategic bomber called the B-1 was taking its place in the American nuclear arsenal. Precisely on schedule, the first squadron of fifteen sleek planes stood poised for action at an air base in the mesquite-covered hills of north Texas. Over the next sixteen months, eighty-five more B-1s would roll off production lines in the desert near Palmdale, California. At a cost of more than $28 billion for the hundred-plane force, the B-1 was the most expensive airplane in aviation history.

The air force thought the bombers were worth every cent. General Lawrence Skantze, whose Air Force Systems Command had shepherded the plane through production, praised the B-1 down to its last rivet, calling it "the best, most capable manned penetrating bomber in the world." Carrying twenty nu-

This essay has been edited and is reprinted from The Washingtonian, *January 1988, 99–101, 155–60, and 162–64, by permission of Nick Kotz.*

clear missiles, each bomber could wreak two hundred times as much destruction as the bombs that leveled Hiroshima in World War II.

Taking air force spokesmen at their word, anchorman Dan Rather declared on the *CBS Evening News* that "a big new element of the U.S. nuclear weapons force went on line today." Pictures showed a breathtakingly beautiful airplane: The 127-foot span of its slim wings flowed into a long, narrow fuselage nearly half the length of a football field. A needle-sharp nose sloped downward from the cockpit like a beak. The B-1 bomber loomed in the sky like a graceful bird of prey.

Several months later a different story began to unfold. Prodded by congressional investigators, the air force admitted that despite the fanfare, not a single bomber had been battle-ready that October day. The B-1 was instead snarled in technical problems—problems the air force had known about for more than a year. The most serious malfunction would take at least four more years to correct—handicapping the B-1 during the critical period for which the air force had contended the plane was most needed.

Growing pains are inevitable in developing any complex weapons system. But the B-1 had more than its share, and if they were not remedied, the plane would be hamstrung in its principal mission—to penetrate the Soviet heartland and deliver a devastating nuclear blow. If some of its systems failed, how could the bombers overcome sophisticated Soviet defenses and reach their targets? The bird could fly, but could it reach its prey?

Revelation of flaws in the plane revived the partisans in a battle that stretched over the entire history of the air force's quest for a new bomber. After conducting its own investigation, the House Armed Services Committee reported in April 1987 that the B-1 bomber's chances of completing a wartime mission were only half as good as intended.

"Frankly, the Air Force screwed it up," said committee chairman Les Aspin, a Wisconsin Democrat and longtime B-1 critic. "They screwed it up and didn't tell us about it."

Some defense analysts labeled the bomber the Flying Edsel; others called it a "lead sled," because the 230-ton bomber was said to be hard to maneuver and unable to cruise fully loaded above a modest 20,000 feet. "An awful lot of that money [spent on the B-1] is down the tube," said Sam Nunn, Democratic senator of Georgia, who was chairman of the Senate Armed Services Committee.

Retired Air Force Colonel James Boyd, an innovator of fighter aircraft and critic of Pentagon procurement practices, sardonically told a fellow officer that the best use for the B-1 was "paint it yellow and use it as a line taxi" to carry equipment and crews from hangars to aircraft.

Stung by a barrage of what it considered politically motivated and grossly exaggerated criticism, the air force counterattacked. A stream of air force officers testified that the defects were being remedied rapidly, that even with its faults the B-1 could carry out its doomsday mission. Pilots who flew the plane, including Air Force Chief of Staff Larry Welch, issued testimonials to the B-1's remarkable performance and superiority to the aging B-52 it would replace.

Who was right—the air force or its critics? In one way, it did not much matter. It was too late to turn back.

The case of the B-1 raises fundamental questions: how did a thirty-year effort on a major weapons system manage to produce a $28 billion plane that did not seem to work very well, and why do such problems in military procurement recur so often?

Perhaps the most basic question is: how many weapons are needed to safeguard our nation? The dispute over how *many* weapons involves another: which are the right weapons? Besides the B-1, the air force is developing an even more expensive advanced-technology bomber, the Stealth, which is shrouded in greater official secrecy than any weapon since the atomic bomb. The bill for developing, producing, and operating the two bombers will come to well over $100 billion.

Advocates insist that both new bombers are needed to complement land-based and sea-based missiles as part of the strategic nuclear deterrent, and would also serve as vital weapons in fighting a war, whether nuclear or conventional. Yet a host of critics have questioned the need for both bombers—indeed for *any* new strategic penetrating bomber—in the age of intercontinental ballistic missiles. From Dwight Eisenhower, who had warned of the dangers of a "military-industrial complex" in his farewell address of January 1961, to Ronald Reagan, every American president has faced key decisions affecting the fate of B-1 and its experimental predecessor, the B-70.

Often clashing with these presidents, Congress has acted on the bomber during each of the past thirty years. Hanging in the balance have been huge economic benefits—for defense contractors, for labor unions, and for communities where the bombers would be built or based.

The tangled and controversial history of the bomber leads straight to the heart of defense politics.

THE BEST BASES POLITICS CAN BUY

On the Michigan shores of blustery Lake Huron, summers quickly fade and winter is a way of life. Sustaining the economy of the rural communities two hundred miles north of Detroit are two important industries: tourism and the U.S. Air Force. The tourists go home at Labor Day, but the air force will never leave.

At least that had always been the assumption of the hardy people of the towns of Tawas, Oscoda, Greenbush, and Harrisville. In winter, the giant Wurtsmith Air Force Base provides the payroll that keeps business humming in the banks, beauty parlors, auto lots, and Big Boy restaurants. The 5,200-

acre base houses the 379th Bombardment Wing, whose B-52H bombers stand poised to strike.

But on June 23, 1983, local business leaders received jolting news about their economic mainstay from an old friend, Air Force Lieutenant General Earl O'Loughlin. O'Loughlin, a decorated combat veteran, brought pride to his boyhood fishing companions in East Tawas. In his thirty-year career he rose from enlisted man to vice commander of the Air Force Logistics Command. He had come home to address a luncheon meeting of the chamber of commerce at the Waban Inn outside Oscoda.

O'Loughlin delivered an ominous message: Wurtsmith Air Force Base, with its 3,600 jobs and $78 million annual payroll, faced an uncertain future. As B-1 bombers came on line in the next few years, most B-52 squadrons would be retired. If Wurtsmith were to close down, the local economy would lose more than $100 million a year, including money spent by air force families, federal aid to schools with children of service personnel, and local construction contracts. "If you're not on the list to get the B-1," said O'Loughlin, "you're in trouble." The businessmen bombarded the general with questions. What should they do? What were their chances of getting one of the proposed B-1 squadrons for Wurtsmith?

In the year and a half after President Ronald Reagan decided to build the B-1, an alleged list had caused confusion and competition in Congress and in air force communities around the nation. The list would name the three or four bases chosen as homes for the 100 new bombers.

Competition for those bases had been intense—particularly among the communities near the thirteen bases already housing the Strategic Air Command's 349 B-52s. Even before the general's speech, rumors had been swirling in Michigan business circles that Wurtsmith had been removed from the number-two position on the B-1 base list.

Politics counted, O'Loughlin told his audience. "We have legislators in Michigan who have not defended the B-1 program—and those states with B-1 opponents will be the first to be cut!" Michigan's political problems, the general suggested, were its two U.S. senators, Democrats Carl Levin and Donald Riegle. Both men had opposed building the B-1, and Levin had been particularly outspoken, calling the plane "an unneeded waste of national resources."

General O'Loughlin urged the Chamber of Commerce to sponsor a letter-writing campaign to Levin and Riegle protesting their positions on the B-1, calling on them to support continuation of Wurtsmith and K. I. Sawyer, a base on Michigan's Upper Peninsula that the air force was considering closing. The letter-writing campaign had to be statewide to be effective, O'Loughlin said.

On that June day, the Michigan business leaders assumed they were just getting some helpful inside information from an old friend. They had no idea they were viewed as lobbying objectives in a well-orchestrated campaign the air force had been waging

across the country for at least ten years to build and sustain support for the B-1 bomber.

Lobbying pressure was applied at the grass roots as well as in Washington to win approval for the project from both the president and members of Congress. When an elected representative stood in the way of the B-1, the air force sometimes applied pressure through his or her constituents. Air force generals were booked to speak at gatherings of community leaders, such as the chambers of commerce, or at meetings sponsored by local Air Force Association chapters.

Earl O'Loughlin may have been visiting his old home on his own time and for purely personal reasons, but his message was vintage air force: support the air force's goals and it will support your community; oppose it and your economy might suffer.

Although production was under way on the B-1s in the summer of 1983, the air force was taking nothing for granted. The same week O'Loughlin spoke to the businessmen in Michigan, Levin was urging the Senate to cut $800 million from the B-1's 1984 funds; he pushed for building the Stealth bomber, designed to be almost invisible to radar, instead. But the air force wanted both planes.

In national politics, it is not unusual for the executive branch to menace the assets of a state or community if its elected representatives fail to cooperate. Nor is it unusual for members of Congress to support military projects in return for obtaining an installation for their region. But the political pushing and grabbing usually occurs behind the scenes, not in broad daylight. No one wanted it to appear that such issues of national defense as the location of strategic bases could be decided on narrow political grounds. But the Michigan fight took place in the open. O'Loughlin's blunt remarks, as reported in the weekly *Oscoda Press,* galvanized the assembled businessmen into action.

Before long, Bob Davis, the Republican representative of the region, prepared to go after Senators Levin and Riegle for endangering Wurtsmith by opposing the B-1. Word of the chamber meeting and Davis's impending political attack was relayed to Washington by staffer Chris Jewell in Levin's Alpena office, near Wurtsmith. Her message: "We've got trouble up here."

Levin's trouble included a tough reelection fight in 1984. His opponent, Jack Lousma, a former marine pilot and astronaut, ardently supported the B-1.

Levin tried to reassure his constituents that "the Pentagon makes its decisions based on national security, not on how an area's representative votes." The *Detroit News* replied in an editorial, "That's just plain naive. The air force generals who decide where new planes are to be based aren't likely to favor the home hearth of their most strident opponents."

Levin, a Harvard-educated former civil rights lawyer from Detroit, served as city council chairman before his election to the Senate in 1978. He was a member of the Senate Armed Services Committee, where the Pentagon viewed him as a typical antidefense liberal, sympathetic to nuclear freezes and arms-control agreements, and instinctively hostile to new strategic-weapons systems, whether the B-1 or the MX. The only time Defense Department officials felt they could count on Levin's active support was when major interests of his Michigan constituents were involved. Levin, for example, had been a vigorous advocate of the M-1 tank, which was being built by General Dynamics in the Detroit suburb of Warren.

Now, from his own base of power on the Armed Services Committee, Levin launched a counterattack. He persuaded the air force director of legislative liaison to write a letter flatly denying that General O'Loughlin had tied the fate of Wurtsmith to the Michigan senator's votes on the B-1. Not entirely satisfied with the tenor of the air force apology, Levin dictated the changes he wanted. He then convened a congressional hearing for the benefit of several hundred Michigan business and community leaders. A parade of Defense Department and air force officials, coached by Levin and his aides, reassured the home folks that Wurtsmith was being considered for a B-1 base and that neither Wurtsmith nor K. I. Sawyer would be closed.

In press conferences and committee hearings, Levin sent his own message back home: "I may have been against building the B-1s, but they are being built and Wurtsmith is the right place to base them."

In the end, Wurtsmith did not get its B-1 squadron, although the furor following General O'Loughlin's speech mobilized the Michigan congressional delegation to demand other benefits. Levin steered a resolution through Congress making it virtually impossible for the air force to close down K. I. Sawyer, and the air force added $100 million in new facilities there and at Wurtsmith.

Far to the south of Michigan, on June 29, 1985, the first B-1 arrived in a well-staged production at Dyess Air Force Base in Texas. Bands were playing, the sun was shining, and as a galaxy of Washington political and military stars applauded in the reviewing stand, the dark needle-nosed bomber suddenly appeared out of the northern sky. It roared over the welcoming crowd of 45,000, turned sharply over the mesquite-covered hills around the base, and made a perfect landing.

The pomp and ceremony at Dyess, outside Abilene, marked the delivery of that first bomber to its new home base. General John W. Vessey Jr., chairman of the Joint Chiefs of Staff, read a letter from President Reagan praising the patriotism of the local citizenry, who lined the sides of the 12,000-foot runway, cheering and drinking soft drinks from plastic cups emblazoned with a picture of the B-1.

One little-noticed incident marred the perfection of the day at Dyess. The plane that roared into Dyess was actually not the first production model of the bomber, as intended, but one of the research-and-demonstration planes. The first B-1 had sucked part of an air inlet into one of its jet engines on its flight from California to Texas and had to turn back.

More than anything else, the ceremony at Dyess was an air force "appreciation day" for former Republican Senator John Tower, the recently retired chairman of the Senate Armed Services Committee. Senator Tower had always fought for the B-1. When President Jimmy Carter canceled production of the B-1 in 1977, Tower helped keep the plane alive with continued development funds. In 1981, with the Reagan administration debating whether to bypass the B-1 in favor of the Stealth, the air force took no chances on keeping Tower's vital support: while the decision hung in the balance, an air force emissary told the committee chairman that Dyess, the base closest to his hometown of Wichita Falls, would be the first B-1 base. Tower was also promised that another Texas base would get the first B-52 squadron outfitted with cruise missiles. (Neither basing decision was made public: nearly two years later the air force would still insist to Senator Levin and his Michigan constituents that the B-1 bases had not yet been selected.)

Many in the air force and Congress believed that Dyess was chosen as the first B-1 base to please Tower. But a north-central Texas site for a B-1 base was considerably harder to justify on strategic grounds.

The air force's stated criteria for the B-1 bases were "pre-launch survivability, wartime considerations, facility availability, access to training routes, weather, community support, encroachment, and environment." In finally announcing the four bases selected—Ellsworth, in South Dakota; Grand Forks, in North Dakota; McConnell, at Wichita, Kansas; and Dyess—the air force stressed that all were aligned along the center of the American land mass. That way, each would have maximum warning—though only a few minutes at that—to escape a sneak Soviet submarine-missile attack from the Atlantic or Pacific.

Dyess was vulnerable on the most important criterion, "wartime considerations." Although all four bases are far from the oceans, air force officers noted privately that the Texas base would be vulnerable to short-range attack if Soviet submarines were to penetrate the Gulf of Mexico. The B-1's mission was to attack or threaten to attack the Soviet Union in a strategic crisis, and basing it in Texas would add several hours of flying time to the mission. Bombers taking off from Dyess would need an additional complex aerial refueling to carry out their mission, according to officers at Strategic Air Command (SAC) headquarters. From a wartime strategic viewpoint, other SAC bases—including Wurtsmith in Michigan—made a lot more sense.

One point in Dyess's favor as a training base for B-1 crews was its good weather. And Dyess met the criterion of "community support." But then, every other SAC base in the United States had good community support.

Politics also outweighed strategy in the selection of McConnell Air Force Base on the outskirts of Wichita, Kansas. Kansas senator Robert Dole began lobbying for McConnell in 1981 when he chaired the Senate Finance Committee, which controlled President Reagan's top legislative priority—tax reform.

McConnell had served as home base for personnel staffing a wing of aging Titan missiles. One of the Kansas Titans developed a leak in 1979, and one stationed in Arkansas exploded in 1980. The Kansas citizenry wanted the Titans removed immediately— but they also wanted to keep their base with 1,200 air force personnel, an economic resource worth about $100 million a year. The Wichita Chamber of Commerce pressed the Kansas congressional delegation to get one of the B-1 squadrons.

Despite Dole's entreaties, the air force equivocated. A number of air force officials bristled at the notion of "rewarding" Kansas, because the state's other senator, Republican Nancy Kassebaum, not only had opposed the B-1 but, as chairman of the Senate's Military Reform Caucus, was a constant thorn in the side of the Defense Department. The member of Congress from Wichita, Democrat Dan Glickman, also had opposed the B-1.

During the protracted tug-of-war over the B-1 bases, Dole played some slick politics of his own. He delighted in displaying his independence, taking swipes at the president on taxes and at the Defense Department on the B-1 and other issues. He prominently cosponsored legislation calling for a critical study of the B-1's high costs. Appearing on *Meet the Press,* he made page-one headlines by suggesting that perhaps the B-1 should be canceled to help combat the huge budget deficit.

The air force finally got the message, particularly when it became almost certain that Dole would become Senate Majority Leader in 1985 after Senator Howard Baker retired. McConnell got its squadron of B-1s. Announcing the prize, Dole stressed that the decision meant "that the employment and economic impact" of losing the Titan missiles would be neutralized and, "better yet, could be improved," with $115 million in new military construction coming to the base.

From both the strategic and economic points of view, McConnell had several serious drawbacks, according to some air force officers. The base shared its crowded runways with the Boeing Company plant—not the ideal setting for an instant launch of bombers in an emergency. The site, on the edge of a crowded city, created problems for base security, and did not satisfy the air force's own standards for "encroachment" or "environment" nearly as well as the more isolated SAC bases in rural Michigan, Montana, Wyoming, and the Dakotas. Finally, the Kansas base entailed extra costs of at least $40 million, because it had no facilities for storing nuclear weapons for bombers. The General Accounting Office cited the extra expense in recommending against McConnell as a B-1 base.

Nevertheless, Dole and McConnell got their B-1s.

Arkansas got its Little Rock Air Force Base in 1955 because of the combined power of that state's two senators, Democrats John McClellan and J. Wil-

liam Fulbright. Thirty years later, the base apparently became a political pawn in a still-unsettled battle between the air force and Arkansas senators who had opposed the B-1.

After a Titan missile exploded, Arkansas citizens wanted to get rid of the aging missiles based at Little Rock. But removing the Titans would mean losing base personnel, and the base also could lose its wing of 76 C-130 troop carriers. If it did not get the new C-17 carriers as a replacement, the base might be closed.

Base personnel and families comprised a population of almost 25,000. The annual base payroll of $250 million was the mainstay of the central Arkansas economy.

The well-organized Little Rock Community Base Council implored Arkansas Senators David Pryor and Dale Bumpers to help the base get a squadron of C-17s. The council, led by banker Pat Wilson, was one of the most effective grass roots base-support organizations in the country—it had raised the money to buy land for the base in the first place. Over the years, Wilson and his indefatigable band had befriended secretaries of the air force, congressional committee chairmen, and virtually every air force officer who had ever served at the base. Ever alert to shifting military currents, Wilson and his group began lobbying for the new C-17s when the plane was little more than a glint in the eyes of defense planners.

In Senator David Pryor, the council found a ready ally. Both Pryor and Bumpers, however, had antagonized the air force not only by opposing the B-1 but as advocates of arms control who also opposed other defense programs. In addition, Pryor raised hackles in the Pentagon as he became an effective leader of the congressional movement to reform Defense Department procurement practices.

On May 15, 1984, Pryor met in his office with Brigadier General James P. McCarthy, the air force's congressional director of legislative liaison, and Colonel Kenneth Anderson, the legislative liaison officer responsible for the Senate. For General McCarthy, who had flown 152 missions as a fighter pilot in Vietnam and commanded a strategic bomber wing, the meeting was just another encounter in a day's work. "Legislative liaison" was his job—seeking support for the air force from senators, and dealing with senators who wanted something from the air force.

Senator Pryor began by carefully spelling out why Little Rock should get the C-17s: not only was the base already a principal training facility for the airlift command, it enjoyed broad community support and was important to the local economy.

Finally he got to the point. "Well, general, how do our chances look on the C-17s?"

"You know, Senator," McCarthy said, "there are a lot of members of Congress interested in getting those planes."

"General, do you mean that politics are involved in these base decisions?" Pryor seemed shocked.

"Well, you know, Senator, your positions in many quarters are considered anti-military," replied McCarthy.

"General, why don't you give me some examples of what you are talking about?" said Pryor.

The general hesitated, then observed that Pryor had opposed construction of the B-1 bomber.

"We've been over that before," said Pryor. "You know that I've supported the Stealth bomber. What else?"

General McCarthy paused, then turned to Colonel Anderson, who was sitting next to him in a rocking chair. "Colonel, give me the senator's vote sheet," he ordered.

Anderson's face reddened as he reached into the inside pocket of his blue blazer and handed the general a thin folded document.

General McCarthy began ticking off issues on which the senator had differed with Defense Department policy.

"Let me see that thing," said Pryor.

What the general reluctantly handed him was a two-page computer printout titled "Senator Pryor: Floor Statements and News Items." It contained seventeen separate items. It noted that he had opposed the B-1 bomber, had "led the fight against nerve-gas production," had been "critical of defense contractors for hiring former Defense Department personnel," had criticized President Reagan for violating the War Powers Resolution, had voted against the MX missile, and had supported an amendment to increase competition in defense contracting. From a narrow Defense Department viewpoint, the only "pro-defense" items on Pryor's report card were his support for the Stealth bomber and three speeches in favor of the C-17.

"This sort of reminds me of an FBI dossier," said Pryor.

When the meeting ended, the base issue was still not settled. What Pryor had gained was an appreciation of how seriously the military plays politics. And three years later, in early 1988, Congress and the air force were still pushing and shoving to determine where the new air transports would be based.

General McCarthy had broken the rules of the game: exert pressure subtly, but never let a member of Congress know he or she is being "graded" by the Pentagon. For a general to tell a senator he had failed the test of Pentagon loyalty was a breach of etiquette.

But the Defense Department does keep careful track of its allies and opponents in Congress, and it examines their records as it bargains for support and reaches basing and production decisions. At times it has rated members of Congress on a point basis, much as labor unions or business groups rate congressmen on issues they deem important.

The rating system, lobbying of Congress by the military, and trading support for bases have gone on for years. The military, just like other executive departments of the government, routinely violates Title 18 of the U.S. Code, which forbids officials of the executive branch from lobbying members of Congress. According to law, military officers, just like officials of the Agriculture Department, should only supply information requested by Congress.

Dedicated air force officers would much rather locate B-1 bases where prudent national defense strategy, not politics, dictates. When they can speak anonymously, they rail against the unhealthy pressures of defense politics. They say that nothing undermines high standards of military leadership more than the pressures to make basing and procurement decisions on political grounds rather than on true military need. But they seldom speak out, even in the private councils of the air force. To question a decision can hurt one's career. It is easier to rationalize: there is not much difference in the military suitability of the different base sites. . . . One voice will not be heard. . . . These political cases are isolated.

THE DEMOCRATIC BOMBER AND THE REPUBLICAN BOMBER

In 1981 the Reagan administration brought to power a group of hard-line defense strategists who believed that in the face of a hostile and expansionist Soviet Union, the United States had to be prepared to fight and win a nuclear or conventional war.

President Reagan stressed that superiority over the Soviet Union, rather than sufficiency or parity of nuclear weapons, would be his policy. He said he sought to achieve for the nation "a margin of safety in nuclear weaponry." Defense Secretary Caspar Weinberger issued a secret directive calling for American nuclear forces that "must prevail and be able to force the Soviet Union to seek the earliest termination of hostilities on terms favorable to the United States."

When Air Force Deputy Chief of Staff Kelly Burke and a cadre of ranking generals marched into Caspar Weinberger's office in March 1981 to claim victory in the twenty-seven-year campaign for a new strategic bomber, they expected to be greeted by the most cooperative civilians ever to run the Pentagon.

The generals had good cause for optimism. Reagan had swept into office on a wave of promises that the nation's strategic defenses would be rebuilt. He had pledged to close the much-touted strategic window of vulnerability by building new weapons, including the B-1 bomber. Reagan's defense transition team had endorsed every proposal presented to it by the air force. In their first days in office, Reagan and Weinberger had agreed to a record $32 billion defense increase for 1981 and 1982—on top of the $20 billion increase already requested by Jimmy Carter before he left office.

General Burke had come to inform Weinberger and Frank C. Carlucci III, Weinberger's deputy secretary, how the air force planned to do its part in closing the window of vulnerability. The generals delivered an air force shopping list, confident that the only question to settle was the order in which they wanted their new weapons delivered. The first priority, Burke said, was to produce a hundred B-1B bombers.

The plane had reemerged in 1981 with another B to denote its important modifications—elimination of most of its supersonic capability; increase in its weight to include more fuel, weapons, and electronics; and new design features to make it less visible to Soviet radar as it swept into the Soviet Union armed with forty to sixty tons of nuclear missiles and bombs.

The B-1Bs would be backed up by a fleet of modernized B-52s standing off the edge of Soviet territory and firing cruise missiles. Production soon would follow on 132 advanced-technology bombers, the top-secret Stealths. When they were ready to take over the penetrator role in the 1990s, the B-1Bs would become cruise-missile carriers, freeing some B-52s for conventional warfare.

When Weinberger responded to General Burke, he was extremely skeptical about building two new bombers, especially the B-1B. Weinberger and Carlucci delivered a blast of probing, hostile questions that the generals had not anticipated: "Why can't we leapfrog the B-1B and just build the Stealth? How long will the B-1B be able to penetrate the Soviet Union? Why do you need both airplanes?"

As the air force leaders stumbled over their answers, Weinberger lost his patience and stormed out of the meeting. "They were totally unprepared," Carlucci recalled later. "They didn't have the facts or any good figures on what the planes would cost. They just assumed we would roll over and build it."

Weinberger was not pleased with the notion of spending more than $100 billion on two new bombers when many people thought bombers had only a marginal strategic utility anyway. He had become fascinated with the idea of skipping the B-1B, thereby saving billions, and opting for the newer technology of Stealth. In this, Weinberger was strongly influenced by conversations with his predecessor, Harold Brown, and with Stealth advocate William Perry, Brown's undersecretary for research and development, who stayed on for several months as a consultant to the Reagan administration. Other experts, including former Defense Secretary Melvin Laird, argued both to Weinberger and Reagan that the B-1B's time had passed. It represented the technology of the 1960s, they insisted—the country should invest in the plane of the future. In addition, Weinberger was captivated by the idea of a plane that was said to be virtually invisible to radar.

The air force had misjudged Caspar Weinberger—whose loyalties were to Ronald Reagan and his political needs, not to the air force. After Weinberger stalked out of the meeting with General Burke, Richard DeLauer, the newly appointed undersecretary of defense for research and development, took the stunned B-1B advocates to his office. DeLauer, a scientist who worked on the Atlas ICBM, was an executive of the defense conglomerate TRW before coming to the Pentagon.

"This is nonsense," he said. "You need to put together a program that makes sense." He told them

they had to cut the cost of their bomber program by retiring B-52s as new planes came on line. Most important, they needed to develop a much more convincing rationale for building the B-1B instead of bypassing it for a future Stealth bomber.

Like many new defense projects, the Stealth bomber had its origins not only in new technology but in defense politics. When President Carter turned down the B-1 in 1977, General Thomas Stafford, the air force deputy chief for research and development, decided to create a bomber that Jimmy Carter could like—one he could consider his own.

Until 1977, Stealth research had been aimed at developing a fighter plane. Special paints, rounded surfaces, and engines buried in the wings were some of the techniques Lockheed was experimenting with at its secret "Skunk Works" in California. Tiny Stealth fighter planes had been flown at the air force's secret installation at Nellis Air Force Base in the Nevada desert.

Tom Stafford decided the Stealth research should be directed at a penetrating strategic bomber that would be acceptable within the terms of the SALT II treaty Carter was then negotiating. Stafford put Northrop Aviation and other companies onto the project, which was financed with "black money" hidden within the budget. Only a few air force, Pentagon, and White House officials and heads of the defense committees in Congress knew about Stealth.

When he succeeded Stafford in late 1979, Kelly Burke continued the Stealth bomber research. Fighting desperately for years to get one new strategic bomber, the air force now found, much to its surprise, that it had created a brand new political dynamic: rival political constituencies for two different bombers. The B-1 was backed by Republicans, the House of Representatives, and Rockwell. The Stealth was supported by Democrats, the Senate, and Northrop. When Carter canceled the B-1, he made it a symbol for opponents who thought him weak on defense. The Stealth became a symbol for those politicians who had rejected the B-1.

The air force would have been grateful for *any* bomber after Carter's rejection of the B-1. Three years later, it suddenly saw the opportunity to get two new bombers. The B-1B was practically a bird in the hand, nearly ready for production, but Stealth held long-term promise as a penetrator far beyond the probable useful life span of the B-1B. Furthermore, the air force strategists realized that they now needed both planes for political reasons: to satisfy the rival constituencies.

To get both bombers, the generals would have to prove to Weinberger and the Stealth enthusiasts that the B-1B still was a strategic necessity and somehow also satisfy the new Stealth advocates. Some Stealth backers believed in the military merits of the nearly "invisible" plane; others were driven mainly by economic and corporate interests. For some Democrats, the Stealth provided a radarproof political shield for their opposition to the B-1B, deflecting criticism that they were soft on defense.

From a military standpoint, the air force calculated that the United States could use a force of about 350 to 400 strategic bombers. The number of planes actually requested—100 B-1Bs and 132 Stealths—was calculated almost entirely on economic and political factors. The air force decided that both Weinberger's and Congress's choke point for the B-1B was $20 billion, and Rockwell vice president Bastian "Buzz" Hello claimed he could produce 100 B-1Bs for that cost. The air force requested more Stealths than B-1Bs to satisfy the Senate—where a coalition of Stealth advocates and B-1B opponents might scuttle the B-1B.

Burke and his staff developed an analysis to show that the cost of building the B-1Bs and Stealths and operating them for twenty years would be only a little more than the cost of reconditioning and operating the aging B-52s—$93 billion for an all-B-52 fleet, $100 billion for all B-1Bs, and $114 billion for the combined B-1B and Stealth force. The analysis was debatable, but it made for a good selling point: "You can buy two new planes for little more than the cost of rehabilitating one old one."

The stage was set for a political and military debate and a bitter economic battle between two industrial combines. Lined up on one side was Rockwell International, with its twenty-seven-year effort to build a new air force bomber. On the other side were Northrop and its partners in Stealth: Boeing and LTV.

Leading the campaign for the Stealth in Congress was one of the last of the old-style aviation entrepreneurs, Northrop's sixty-year-old board chairman, Thomas V. Jones, a friend of Reagan who knew how to play high-stakes defense politics. Jones put together a potent industry team to lobby for and build the Stealth, as he joined forces with T. A. Wilson, chairman of Boeing, and Paul Thayer, chairman of the LTV Corporation. These executives waged an aggressive campaign to convince the powers in Washington to skip the B-1B and accelerate development of the Stealth. Leap-frogging the B-1B would mean billions in short-term revenue for Northrop, a windfall the company would happily share among its collaborators and subcontractors.

Buzz Hello of Rockwell set up a Washington command center to counter the Northrop challenge. One morning in May, he received an urgent call from a congressional ally on the House Defense Appropriations Subcommittee. "You wouldn't believe what's going on up here," his friend reported. "Northrop's Jones, Boeing's Wilson, and LTV's Thayer are telling the subcommittee that they can produce the first production squadron of Stealths in 1987—and furthermore, they'll do so at a fixed price."

Hello leaped into a taxicab and arrived at the entrance of the committee hearing room just as Thayer, Wilson, and Jones were departing. He tried to speak with Wilson and Thayer, but they ducked past him and out of the Rayburn House Office Building.

Hello had reason to feel betrayed. Boeing and LTV were both major partners with Rockwell in the B-1B program. Boeing would receive more than $2 billion for developing the B-1B bomber's offensive avionics and integrating all avionics (electronics) systems. LTV would be paid more than $1 billion for manufacturing part of the plane's fuselage. Furthermore, Hello believed the claims being made for the Stealth were preposterous. Jones was proposing a fixed price for a plane whose paper design had not yet been approved, and promising to deliver it in six years.

Boeing and LTV had valid economic reasons for pushing the Stealth, however, even if it meant sacrificing their B-1B contracts. For Boeing, which would help build the Stealth's revolutionary lightweight composite wing, the Stealth bomber would be a way for the company to acquire, at government expense, the technological expertise to pull ahead of the competition for the next generation of commercial jets. For LTV, and Boeing, income from Stealth contracts would far exceed any B-1B gains.

During the spring and summer of 1981, as partisans for each plane fought to win the votes of key members of the defense establishment in Congress, they also fought to convince Caspar Weinberger and Ronald Reagan. For the first seven months of 1981, Reagan remained silent and detached from the question of which bomber to choose: Cap Weinberger was making the defense decisions. Those who knew Reagan best said it would not be out of the question for him to reverse himself on the B-1B if Weinberger showed him that such an action made sense. And unlike Carter, Reagan knew how to reverse himself without causing an uproar.

In early May, Weinberger held private sessions with the rival aerospace groups. Tom Jones told Weinberger what he had told members of the congressional subcommittee: Northrop could meet the 1987 date for producing a squadron of fifteen Stealth planes, and would commit itself to a fixed price.

Weinberger subsequently met with Hello and his superiors, Rockwell board chairman, Robert Anderson, and president Donald Beall. Regarding the meeting as a "shoot-out" between the Stealth and B-1B, Anderson geared his presentation to showing the improbability of the Northrop promises. "Based on the experience we've had in eleven years of working on the B-1," he said, "I don't see how any new concept of an airplane could be ready in 1987. It would take at least until the mid-1990s."

Weinberger wanted to know exactly how much change would be required from the original B-1.

About 20 percent changed, Hello said.

"How much will it cost to build a hundred planes?" Weinberger asked.

Hello said it could be done for about $20 billion—an estimate considered far too low by some air force analysts.

"Will you guarantee that price and build the B-1B on a fixed-price contract?" Weinberger asked.

Anderson replied that he would not; there was still too much uncertainty in the plane.

"You've had a lot of experience already," said Weinberger. "You ought to be able to do it at a fixed price."

Anderson had told his own associates that he would not "bet the company" on one airplane. He knew that in any huge aerospace venture, costs could be difficult to control. In a $20 billion program, Anderson figured that a 10 percent cost overrun could cause losses for Rockwell of more than three times the value of the company's stock.

Weinberger then pressed the strong B-1B advocates in the Pentagon—DeLauer, Air Force Secretary Verne Orr, and the air force generals—for answers to the questions he considered crucial: How soon could the Stealth bomber become operational? How long could the B-1B be counted on to successfully penetrate Soviet defenses? How much would it cost to build the B-1B?

If the B-1B could serve only briefly as a viable penetrator, until Soviet radar was improved in the late 1980s, and if the Stealths could come on line in the late 1980s, or even the early 1990s, what was the point of spending $20 or $30 billion for a bomber that could at best meet a short-term need? The case for the B-1B was not helped by Rockwell's refusal to match Northrop's offer to build Stealth for a fixed price.

Furthermore, the air force itself harbored a strong opponent of the B-1B. In mid-May, just as the service leaders prepared to present their final, unanimous assessment to Weinberger, SAC commander Richard Ellis flew in from Omaha headquarters to register his dissenting opinion: the B-1B should be bypassed for Stealth, which, he said, had a far greater long-term potential to penetrate the Soviet Union. According to a SAC study, the B-1B could not penetrate what would be vastly improved Soviet defenses after 1988. Ellis, who helped invent the notion of the window of vulnerability, believed that a fleet of F-111 stretch bombers would suffice while the Stealth and MX missile were in development and production.

Ellis lost his case within the air force, so he took it to Congress. There, the rest of the air force leadership already was pushing the two-bomber program, even though neither Weinberger nor the president had approved it. Angered by the unruly generals, Weinberger ordered them back to the Pentagon. The decision would be difficult enough; Weinberger did not need the generals feuding in public and trying to preempt his decision.

Weinberger saw the issue as a classic case study for a business school. "It's got absolutely every element that leads to indecision," he said, "the kind of thing that normally you would put in the hold basket and look at again in five years." But if you were the secretary of defense, you could not.

The B-1B advocates thought the penetration issue was being given too much emphasis. The plane would be useful later as a cruise-missile carrier, they

contended, and would be able to serve for many years doing conventional bomber duty in its newly discovered capacity as a multipurpose long-range combat aircraft. They enlisted former Air Force Secretary Hans Mark and other aerospace experts to convince Weinberger that Northrop could not possibly meet its ambitious schedule, even if money were no object. They pointed out the aeronautical problems that would have to be overcome for an aircraft like Stealth, consisting mostly of wing. There was no such thing as a totally invisible aircraft, DeLauer argued. Rushing the Stealth could cause massive technological problems as well as huge cost overruns.

But the cost overruns on the B-1B were just as difficult a problem for the plane's supporters. For years its soaring costs had been a political sore point. Having been burned repeatedly, the analysts in the Air Force Systems Command now insisted that a hundred B-1Bs could not be built for less than $27 billion in 1981 dollars. When General Kelly Burke argued that this figure was too high, they refused to budge. Burke and Hello set up their own cost-study group, which came up with $20.5 billion.

Burke then took his figures to Air Force Chief of Staff Lew Allen. "It's a waste of time to propose the project at $27 billion," he told Allen. At that price neither Weinberger nor Congress would approve it. Allen called Rockwell's Anderson and told him there was a disagreement about the B-1B's cost, and that he should come to Washington.

At a Pentagon meeting, Anderson and Hello argued with the Systems Command officers, led by Lieutenant General Lawrence Skantze, that their $27 billion figure was too high. As Anderson recalled later, the meeting was "very vociferous. It was getting down to life or death for the B-1B, and we felt our numbers were right." Eventually, the Systems Command leaders backed down.

Nonetheless, Weinberger appeared ready to make his recommendation to the president that the B-1B be by-passed. In early June DeLauer made another appeal to his boss. "If we can get the B-1B for a fixed price, will you go for it?" he asked. Weinberger said that he might. He still had doubts about the need for the B-1B, but a price cap would ease his concern about the uncertainties in the total cost of two different bombers.

DeLauer immediately called Anderson in Paris, where he and everyone else in the aeronautical establishment were attending the Paris Air Show. "Bob, you've got to bite the bullet if you want the plane," DeLauer told him. "It's going to be fixed price or nothing."

Anderson reluctantly agreed to a fixed-price arrangement. The official price of the plane—$20.5 billion—now seemed to be settled. But the figure did not include a number of necessary items that would be billed later, at a cost of several billion dollars, and the "fixed-price" agreement had many loopholes and qualifications, including an indeterminate allowance for inflation. Before Anderson agreed "in principle to a fixed price" on June 9, General Skantze had reassured him in a June 3 letter that "we can do a fixed-price contract that can protect your interests." Even so, Anderson was taking a big gamble.

Anderson's capitulation kept the B-1B in contention, but the battle with the Stealth continued in both Washington and Paris. The air show was a perennial favorite of congressional junketeers, and Northrop's Jones was in Paris to collar every federal official who might have any influence on the decision. While Senator Barry Goldwater inspected Northrop's F-20 fighter, Jones lobbied Rhett Dawson, counsel to Goldwater's Senate Armed Services Committee and House legislative aide Tony Battista.

Tom Jones also worked the White House, including the president. In February, he was the only defense industry official at the president's birthday party. In May he hosted an intimate dinner honoring Reagan at the Georgetown Club.

Meanwhile, Rockwell's Bob Anderson called on presidential aides Edwin Meese, Richard Allen, and Michael Deaver to advocate the B-1B. Anderson stressed to Edwin Meese both the readiness of Rockwell to build the bomber and the economic benefits for California, home of both Meese and the president.

Congress did not wait for Weinberger and the president to make up their minds. In the House, Representatives Bill Chappell and Tony Battista moved the B-1B forward through the Armed Services and Appropriations committees.

Joseph Addabbo, a New York Democrat who chaired the House Defense Appropriations Subcommittee, was among the few influential House members still determined to stop the B-1B. Addabbo started an investigation into how the air force had slipped Stealth research money to Rockwell to help keep the B-1B alive during the Carter administration—but he stopped after Richard DeLauer reminded him that Stealth money had been used in an identical fashion to help the A-10 attack plane, manufactured on Long Island by Fairchild Industries—a major employer for workers who lived in Addabbo's district. Addabbo continued to oppose the B-1B, but he was defeated in his own committee. By June the House had authorized $2.4 billion to start production of the B-1B.

In the Senate, the B-1B faced tougher opposition—from partisans of Stealth, supporters of Northrop, Boeing, and Lockheed, and old B-1 foes.

On the other side, Ohio's John Glenn continued to lead the fight for the B-1B. At the request of General Burke, he held a special hearing to show that Northrop's promise to produce the Stealth by 1987 was totally unrealistic. Retired astronaut General Tom Stafford called on numerous senators to push the B-1.

Rockwell, the air force lobbyists, and the United Auto Workers (UAW) prepared masses of data showing that Ohio would benefit enormously from production of the B-1B. Contracts worth $7.5 billion would be spread among eight hundred companies in the state, including General Electric's engine plant outside Cincinnati and a principal Rockwell factory in Columbus. Their target was Glenn's fellow senator, liberal Democrat Howard Metzenbaum, who had previously opposed the B-1. Metzenbaum faced a tough reelection campaign in 1982, and the UAW let him know that its support hinged on his backing the B-1B. It was "a tough decision," but Metzenbaum switched to support of the B-1B.

In June, despite six months of intense pressure from the air force, Congress, and industry, Weinberger still hesitated. When it appeared that he might choose the Stealth, Rockwell's stock plunged from $43 to $36 in ten days.

Worried B-1B supporters stepped up their public advocacy for the bomber. If the Reagan administration did not build the B-1B, declared General Lew Allen Jr., the air force chief of staff, it would not be following through on its earlier defense pledge "to show resolve and determination quickly."

With Weinberger leaning toward the Stealth, the B-1B's hard-line supporters focused on President Reagan. One of them reminded the White House that the B-1B was "part of the Republican sacred litany, showing the determination of the Reagan administration to improve our defense posture." Representative Bill Dickinson, still the ranking Republican on the House Armed Services Committee, urged Reagan not to reject a "bird in the hand [the B-1B] for two birds in the bush." Representative Bill Chappell of Florida sought Reagan's commitment by suggesting that he could deliver the support of forty Southern Democrats for the president's tax and budget cuts.

Senator Tower was also pushing hard for the plane. That he had long been a supporter of the B-1 was well known. What was still secret was the fact that he had already received the air force's commitment to base a B-1 squadron at Dyess Air Force Base.

Most important, a group of Republican senators, led by Majority Leader Howard Baker of Tennessee, came to the White House to deliver a message: It would be politically disastrous for Reagan not to build the B-1B. Breaking his promise would be construed as an admission that Carter was right when he canceled the B-1. It was Carter, they reminded him, who advocated relying on cruise missiles and the Stealth. In the symbolism of Washington politics, Stealth was a Democratic bomber.

Baker had been approached earlier by General Burke and lobbied urgently by Rockwell officials to "get through to the president." He also had a strong parochial interest in the B-1B. The AVCO Corporation had a $1 billion contract to build the B-1B's wings, providing 2,600 jobs in Tennessee at its Nashville plant. For years, AVCO had counted on Baker to push its interest in the plane.

The White House heard increasingly from Reagan's hard-core conservative supporters, who complained that the administration had not taken a single action to close the window of vulnerability. The president had not made a decision on any of the key elements to modernize strategic defenses—the MX missile, a new Trident missile, and the B-1B.

With the administration apparently deadlocked on where to base the MX, other weapons would have to be used to satisfy nuclear hard-liners. The Trident II would not be ready for several years. The Stealth bomber was further in the future. Reagan and his political advisers began to realize that starting up production of the B-1B was the only dramatic action they could take.

In late July Reagan finally made his decision: America would build the B-1B. He told Weinberger, "People vote for you, and you make campaign pledges and you keep them." And the B-1B was the best available way to "do something in the here and now." Though Weinberger retained doubts, he was a good soldier. He accepted the decision.

On October 3, 1981, Reagan announced his strategic modernization program: the United States would build 100 B-1B bombers, to be followed by 132 Stealth bombers, what the air force had proposed from the beginning; 100 MX missiles would be located in hardened underground silos, at least until a better basing mode was found; the improved submarine-fired Trident II missile would be developed; the nuclear command and control system would be upgraded. The whole package was estimated to cost $180 billion.

As he announced his long-awaited strategic program to the news media, Reagan revealed an embarrassing lack of understanding of the military rationale underlying his decisions. Asked why the MX would be less vulnerable to Soviet attack in fixed rather than multiple silos, Reagan answered haltingly, "I don't know but what maybe you haven't gotten into the area that I'm going to turn over to the secretary of defense."

Questioned a few moments later about whether the revived B-1B could penetrate Soviet defenses, Reagan hastily fled the press briefing room, saying, "I think that my few minutes are up and I'm going to turn that question over to Cap."

Reagan may not have understood the strategic issues, nor how to explain them smoothly without a script, but he fully understood how to meet his own political needs. The B-1B met them. On the MX issue, he had deflected a barrage of criticism from opponents, including some of his own strongest political supporters in the West. With Rockwell ready to roll, he could demonstrate his resolve to take immediate action to produce new strategic weapons.

Reagan finally closed the window of vulnerability when he simply stopped talking about it, just as John F. Kennedy stopped talking about the missile gap after he took office. The president also settled the MX controversy by appointing a committee headed by Brent Scowcroft, which decided that submarine-based missiles and bombers were an adequate threat to keep the Soviets from exploiting any "window." So much for the window of vulnerability.

The president still had to justify to Congress his decision on the B-1B. When Weinberger appeared before the Senate Armed Services Committee on November 5, 1981, he still revealed a lack of confidence in the B-1B. He testified that the B-1B would not be able to penetrate the Soviet Union at all after 1990, and even by 1988 or 1989 could not penetrate "unless someone wants to direct suicide missions." He also said that Stealth would be ready by 1990. Robert Huffstutler, a CIA analyst, told the Senate Defense Appropriations Subcommittee that the old B-52s could do as well as B-1Bs in penetrating the Soviet Union until 1990.

The General Accounting Office and Congressional Budget Office both reported to Congress that the B-1B would cost far more than the air force estimate. The cost of the hundred-plane force would be $35 to $40 billion, counting inflation and the costs omitted by the air force, rather than the $20.5 billion in 1981 dollars that Rockwell and the air force had agreed on.

Taken at face value, all this information supported Weinberger's business-school case that skipping the B-1B might result in little strategic loss and would save billions of dollars. Influential senators, including some staunch Republicans, had reached this same conclusion.

To head off congressional opposition, the air force and the administration quickly reworked their testimony to justify the two-bomber program. Secretary Weinberger and William Casey, director of the CIA, issued a joint letter on November 11, 1981, refuting both Weinberger's and the CIA's earlier testimony. They now stated that the B-1B "would have the capacity to penetrate anticipated Soviet air defenses well into the 1990s."

The air force once again improvised a new mission for the plane. At the beginning of 1981, the air force plan called for B-1s to be converted to carry cruise missiles once the Stealths were ready. By the end of 1981, the air force was explaining how both planes would be used together as penetrators, creating a "synergistic effect," thereby compounding problems for Soviet defenders. Air force officers admitted privately that the new synergism had more to do with politics than with attacking the Soviet Union.

The late 1981 congressional debates over the bomber became irrelevant. A majority of members accepted the notion that Reagan had won a mandate for massive new defense spending.

The opposition fell apart. The grass roots coalition that effectively opposed the B-1 in 1976 and 1977 had fragmented. Some groups now fought the MX; others worked on a national nuclear-freeze movement. The bomber was yesterday's cause. Representative Downey of New York, a passionate B-1B opponent in 1976 and 1977, acknowledged its political inevitability in 1981. Shrugging off the B-1B as merely a waste of money and at least not a destabilizing weapon, he joined his liberal colleagues in focusing on the MX, a more dangerous weapon as well as a possibly more winnable political fight.

But the forces that sustained the B-1B remained intact. For Rockwell and the air force, the B-1B constituted a permanent interest. The bomber also represented a permanent interest to the states and communities that benefited from its production. Together they constituted the permanent B-1 lobby.

On November 18, 1981, the House of Representatives approved the two-bomber program by a vote of 335 to 61. On December 4 the Senate followed suit, defeating by 66 votes to 28 an effort to delete the B-1B's funds.

The final victory reflected the decisive power of the president of the United States to shape nuclear weapons policy. Presidents Eisenhower, Kennedy, Johnson, and Carter did not want to build a new strategic bomber, and under them none was built, although billions were spent in development. Because Richard Nixon and Ronald Reagan approved it, the bomber was started, under Nixon, and completed, under Reagan.

Over the course of almost thirty years, as individuals came and went and administrations changed, the air force and its allies kept the bomber alive. The federal funds that were the plane's lifeblood never stopped flowing. The ultimate strategy was patience, perseverance, and survival. Once the huge defense project developed momentum, it became as hard to stop as a driverless freight train rolling downhill, out of control.

BUT DOES IT FLY WELL ENOUGH?

With the parts from hundreds of subcontractors flowing into the huge desert plant at Palmdale, Rockwell finally began to build B-1 bombers, slowly at first, then with increasing speed and efficiency. The world's most expensive airplanes were assembled in a beige stucco plant taller than a seven-story building and larger than six football fields. By the fall of 1986, seven bombers at a time were rolling down the final assembly line, and four a month were being delivered to the air force.

For years, the air force and its allies in industry and labor had sought political support for the plane by stressing jobs and contracts, by trying to persuade members of Congress that its production would boost the economies of their states and congressional districts. During years of construction, from 1982 well into 1987, an average of about forty thousand workers kept busy on the B-1. Almost half of them were on the Rockwell payroll; the rest worked at several thousand companies in forty-eight states. In 1985, the peak production year, sixty thousand persons worked on the bomber.

The B-1 program indeed had economic impact, particularly in Southern California. In retrospect, it appears that B-1 supporters had exaggerated the economic benefits of the project, particularly in estimating the numbers of jobs created directly and indirectly, just as opponents had exaggerated the extent to which Rockwell cleverly placed subcon-

tracts for their political effect. But no one can doubt the impact on Rockwell International itself.

Rockwell delivered the bombers on schedule and at the agreed price of $20.5 billion—plus an additional $8 billion allowed for inflation from 1981 to 1988.

How much profit Rockwell made on the B-1 depended on the ability of the engineering team to improve its production performance with every airplane. The first bomber required 1.2 million manhours to construct; the fiftieth bomber, only 150,000. It took Rockwell ninety-two days to check out the thousands of complex parts in the first bomber, but only twenty days for the fiftieth. The improvements produced profits. In 1986, Rockwell International earned $516 million on total sales of $5.6 billion, with the B-1 bomber accounting for two-thirds of the income. Since Reagan revived the bomber in late 1981, Rockwell's stock had doubled in value. After all the crises and setbacks, the B-1 story seemed to be crowned with success.

Then, in early 1987, Congress discovered that the bomber was not all it was cracked up to be. The air force had in fact withheld $300 million in payments to the principal contractors because of shortcomings in the plane. It could not perform all the technological feats in its specifications, and therefore might not be able to carry out its mission of penetrating the Soviet Union.

It had problems of flight-control stability, which caused difficulty with aerial refueling—which in turn limited its range. The terrain-following radar navigation system malfunctioned, limiting the bomber's ability to attack at ground-hugging altitudes—so it would be vulnerable to Soviet radar. The mechanism for firing the bomber's twenty-four nuclear-armed short-range attack missiles did not work well. Added weight kept the B-1 from cruising at an altitude high enough for best fuel consumption.

Most troubling were problems with the bomber's defensive avionics system, a computerized method of detecting and deceiving enemy defenses.

The air force acknowledged to Congress that the defensive avionics did not work well enough to counter Soviet defenses already in place in 1987. It would take two to four years to fix the problem—which means that the system would not be operating properly during any of the window of vulnerability during which the air force had so strenuously argued that the plane was most needed. Even after they solved this problem, air force officers said, they still would have to spend several billion dollars to improve the system further—to match new Soviet defenses now in development.

A few critics within the air force had foreseen problems with the defensive avionics. They had argued unsuccessfully that the planned bomber mission had relied too heavily on complex and hard-to-perfect electronic countermeasures. The General Accounting Office (GAO) reported to Congress that some of the difficulties of the Eaton Corporation's Air Instruments Laboratory (AIL) of Long Island, which built and assembled the defensive avionics, stemmed from the fact that the company's principal experience had been in research and development, rather than in volume production of avionics equipment. Some air force officers privately questioned the choice of AIL, speculating that the company may have been chosen because of its politically strategic location in New York.

Whatever the B-1's flaws or its capabilities, its advocates won their long battle. The money was spent, the airplanes delivered to SAC bases, and military planners incorporated the B-1 into the nation's strategic nuclear war plans.

How much the B-1 is truly handicapped is a matter of conjecture. No one knows how it would perform in the chaos of a nuclear war. But if the Soviet Union believed that the B-1 could penetrate and cause horrible destruction, it presumably served its deterrent role—to help prevent a war from starting. Nonetheless, the flaws remain an important issue.

In December 1987, more than one year after the first fifteen-plane squadron was scheduled to join the nuclear force, only a single B-1 stood on lonely and symbolic alert. The other seventy-two bombers already delivered were undergoing testing, repairs, and revisions. GAO auditors criticized the air force for shortages of spare parts and lower-than-expected reliability. The cost of operating a B-1, $21,000 an hour, was much higher than planned for. The air force said the bombers could be readied for action in an emergency, but no one pretended that they were fully ready for combat.

On September 28, 1987, tragedy struck the program when one of the B-1s crashed while flying a low-level training mission over southeastern Colorado. One of the four demonstration-model B-1s had crashed in 1984, with the death of two crew members, in a loss that the air force attributed to pilot error. But the 1987 accident marked the first crash of the new production-model B-1s. Of the six crew members and instructors on board over Colorado, three died in the crash. The plane had plowed through a flight of migratory birds, a number of which were sucked into the jet engines. A crew member reported "multiple bird strikes," and radioed that the plane had "lost engines three and four with an engine on fire." His final transmission was "We're going down."

It is common for both commercial and military aircraft to hit birds; several thousand such incidents are reported each year. Most of the bird incidents occur at low altitudes—1,000 feet or less. And low altitudes are where the B-1 must function: Its strategy is based in large part on a low-level attack, on flying only 200 to 500 feet above the ground for more than 1,000 miles.

A spokesman for General Electric, manufacturer of the B-1 engines, said they had been built and tested to withstand strikes by one or two large birds. Experts said, however, that there is no way to prevent catastrophic damage if a plane rams through a flock of birds.

The 1987 crash provided new grist for B-1 critics. In a lead editorial headlined "The B-1 Fiasco," the *New York Daily News* wrote: "What good is a plane that may elude Russian missiles—but can't cope with one of the most common hazards of low-level flying?"

Days later, the B-1 fleet was temporarily grounded, to permit inspection of the emergency escape systems. Air force spokesmen said the inspection was an "outgrowth" of the crash. On December 4, the *New York Times* revealed that the Strategic Air Command had suspended low-level flights of the bomber. Air force spokesmen said the suspension applied only to peacetime training.

The air force, in its zeal to justify the continued role of the bomber in the missile age, had called for a plane with almost miraculous capabilities, one to meet every need, to answer every criticism. The B-1's original "gold-plated" requirements, including its Mach 2.6 supersonic speed, resulted in delays, cost overruns, and a series of changes in the bomber design. Even when performance requirements such as speed were gradually reduced, it was too late to change the basic design of the plane.

Some of the problems revealed in 1987 might have been averted if in 1981 the Reagan administration had followed a more cautious development procedure—"fly before you buy"—and built several B-1 test models before starting the hundred-plane production run. Instead, the bomber was developed and built on a rush schedule with considerable "concurrency"—that is, design changes were introduced as the bombers were being manufactured.

Congressional critics said the B-1 dramatized the problems inherent in trying to produce a new weapon before completing research, development, and testing to find and correct defects and inadequacies. But the air force, Rockwell, and their congressional allies had deliberately chosen this rush production schedule. At their instigation, legislation was passed in 1980 requiring initial deployment of a new bomber by 1987—largely to head off competition from the experimental Stealth, which could not be built that quickly. If the air force had been more cautious and delayed the deployment several years, Defense Secretary Weinberger and Congress would probably have by-passed the B-1 and waited for the Stealth.

Rigid efforts to control the B-1's costs also lessened its capability. Considering the project's long history of rising costs, Weinberger had good reason to prohibit any design or equipment changes that would further drive them up. An ironic result, however, was that the B-1 bombers were not equipped with an advanced new infrared navigation system that became available. Instead, it was installed on thirty-year-old B-52 bombers—making them in some ways more advanced than the B-1s.

The political and industrial competition between the B-1 and the Stealth was not halted by President Reagan's decision to build the B-1. With one contract finally in hand, Rockwell immediately began lobbying to build a second hundred B-1s. Northrop, which had the Stealth contract, fought to block any additional B-1s and to rush its bomber ahead faster.

In the midst of still another aerospace lobbying war, several key former government officials went through the defense community's revolving door to Rockwell. Michael Deaver, the White House aide considered closest to President Reagan, left government in 1985 to open his own Washington lobbying firm. Rockwell immediately hired him at $100,000 a year to persuade his former associates to buy the second hundred B-1s. (Deaver's efforts to lobby Reagan officials for the B-1 attracted the attention of the special prosecutor investigating whether he had violated federal conflict-of-interest laws.)

Rockwell also hired a new Washington consulting firm formed in 1982 by three retired air force generals—Kelly Burke, Tom Stafford, and Guy Hecker. Before retiring, all three had held high positions from which they helped to revive the B-1 after President Carter canceled it.

The revolving door has its legislative side, too. Robert Andrews, John Glenn's Senate aide, went onto Rockwell's payroll in 1982 to seek congressional approval for more B-1s. In the rival camp, Northrop hired Senate aide James Roche and retained as consultants recently retired Representative Jack Edwards, the ranking Republican on the House Defense Appropriations Committee, and Kenneth M. Duberstein, Reagan's former director for congressional relations who is now back at the White House.

Despite Rockwell's efforts, Defense Secretary Weinberger repeatedly rejected the proposal to build more B-1 bombers. Instead, he pushed ahead with the Stealth. The B-1 backers felt they were at a disadvantage, because the Stealth was being developed in almost total secrecy, with its hidden funds scattered throughout the defense budget. Rockwell wanted to show that building more B-1s would be a bargain, costing a fraction of the Stealth, but as Buzz Hello said, "I can't make a comparison with the [Stealth] because I'm not allowed to know anything about it."

The only aggressive attempts in Congress to puncture Stealth's veil of secrecy came from the B-1's principal advocates, particularly Ohio's Senator John Glenn, Representative Bob Dornan of California, and Representative Mike Synar of Oklahoma. They demanded that Congress be informed of the cost and development progress of the Stealth. The three represented places with the greatest economic stake in continued production of B-1 bombers.

A few members of Congress privy to information about the Stealth's progress estimated that the newest bomber might cost $450 to $600 million a plane, or $60 to $80 billion for a fleet of 132 bombers. By 1987, several billion dollars had reportedly already been spent on research and development—and the first test model was still not in the air. Senator Barry Goldwater, the air force's most faithful bomber advocate, told me that not only does the Stealth "face some very grave problems, both structural and aerodynamic, but the cost is climbing so high that I have begun to believe we may never be able to afford it for our fleet."

CHAPTER 10

THE DEFENSE BUDGETING PROCESS

THE ABCs OF THE PPBS

AIR COMMAND AND STAFF COLLEGE FACULTY

In a military world laced with jargon and acronyms, the acronym PPBS strikes fear into the hearts of many people. Actually, the planning, programming, and budgeting system is not quite the beast that these people would have us imagine. Although the magnitude of the system and the tremendous number of people involved produce some inherent complexities, the PPBS is merely a logical process of identifying needs, determining resource requirements, and allocating the resources.

Secretary of Defense Robert McNamara implemented the PPBS concept within the Department of Defense (DOD) in the early 1960s to provide a clearer relationship between defense plans and defense dollars. Before that time, defense planning was completely unrelated to fiscal reality. The PPBS addressed the problem by institutionalizing the planning and budgeting functions and by injecting the programming function to bridge the gap between them. The programming function defined plans in terms of forces and manpower. The budgeting function, in turn, translated the program package of forces and manpower into dollar requirements. Since its implementation in the sixties, this system has served numerous secretaries of defense. Periodic face-lifting has shifted the duties of certain participants, changed the titles and formats of documents, and rearranged timetables, but the basic PPBS structure and purpose have remained intact. There have been three recent changes. These include the biennial budget (a two-year budget instead of the traditional one-year budget), greater participation by unified and specified commanders in chief (CINCs) in the process, and a revision to the joint strategic planning system.

The end result of the PPBS cycle is a package of programs to be carried out over the six years as approved by the secretary of defense (SECDEF). This package of programs is called the Future Years Defense program (FYDP) and is often referred to as the "heart of PPBS." The FYDP, maintained as a computer database, is stratified in three ways: by military departments (army, navy, air force) and defense agencies, by major force programs, and by appropriations. The programs contained in the Future Years Defense program are defined in terms of

- *Manpower* for six years.

- *Dollars,* or program costs, for six years.

- *Forces* for nine years.

Since the first two years of the FYDP represent the upcoming budget years, each PPBS cycle also results in the biennial DOD budget request that goes to the president for inclusion in the budget he submits to Congress.

Although overall responsibility for the PPBS rests with the SECDEF, he relies heavily on the Defense Planning and Resources Board (DPRB) to assist him in managing the process. The DPRB (Figure 1) serves as a corporate review body for the SECDEF in each phase of the process. When Secretary Harold Brown established the board, he intended it to function in the programming and budgeting phases; however, Secretary Weinberger expanded its role to include oversight responsibility for the planning phase. Secretary Richard Cheney developed stronger links between national policies and the resources allocated to specific forces and programs. Besides the permanent members, other senior military and civilian officials may be called on to participate as the DPRB agenda dictates. They include the service chiefs, CINCs, and representatives from various parts of the Office of the Secretary of Defense (OSD). Representatives from the Office of Management and Budget (OMB) and the assistant to the president for national security affairs participate on a regular basis.

The following discussion describes the phases and documents involved in one biennial PPBS cycle. The discussion centers on the flow of events for each phase, the primary participants involved in the phase, and the contribution of each phase to the overall process. This interaction is depicted in Figure 2.

PLANNING PHASE

The objective of the planning phase is to identify threats to U.S. national security, develop the strategy necessary to meet national objectives, and determine the forces required to carry out the strategy. To

This essay has been edited and is reprinted from "The A-B-Cs of the PPBS," (Maxwell AFB, AL: Air University Press, n.d.), 23–21 through 23–28, by permission of Air Command and Staff College.

Figure 1
Membership of the Defense Planning and
Resources Board

> **Chairman: Deputy Secretary of
> Defense**
>
> **Chairman, Joint Chiefs of Staff
> Secretary of the Army
> Secretary of the Navy
> Secretary of the Air Force
> Under Secretary of Defense for Policy
> Under Secretary of Defense for
> Acquisition
> Assistant Secretary of Defense
> (Comptroller)
> Assistant Secretary of Defense
> (Program Analysis and Evaluation)**

achieve this objective, the services begin their "grass roots" planning about three years in advance of the budget execution year for a given PPBS cycle. The "formal" part of the planning phase begins over two years in advance of the first fiscal year being planned.

Everyone participates in the planning phase. The planning phase begins with several sources providing inputs in two major categories: policy, strategy, and force planning; and resource planning. The services, the Joint Chiefs of Staff (JCS) and Joint Staff, the CINCs of the unified and specified commands, and the OSD staff provide recommendations and advice, taking into account intelligence information and SECDEF guidance and policies. The CINCs then meet with the SECDEF and the DPRB in the summer to discuss their views and recommendations. The chairman of the JCS (CJCS) furnishes his input primarily through the national military strategy document (NMSD) discussed below. The services participate in the development, review, and coordination of the NMSD through their individual planning staffs. Various members of the OSD staff are responsible for providing guidance and forecasts to be considered in the planning phase. The DPRB oversees this phase and ensures the timely development of the key planning document—the defense planning guidance (DPG). Publication of this document in October completes the planning phase.

TWO KEY PLANNING DOCUMENTS

National Military Strategy Document. The NMSD contains the chairman's advice to the president, the National Security Council (NSC), and the SECDEF on the recommended national military strategy and fiscally constrained force structure needed to achieve

U.S. national security objectives. It includes an assessment of U.S. defense policy as stated in the last DPG and recommendations for change; recommended national military objectives; an intelligence appraisal; recommended fiscally constrained force levels; a presentation of military strategy force options; a CJCS net assessment of recommended strategy, forces, and military options; and a risk evaluation of those recommendations.

Planning Guidance. The DPG furnishes the SECDEF's planning guidance and fiscal constraints to the military departments for developing their programs. The OSD staff develops the document from inputs provided by the services, the CINCs, the JCS and Joint Staff, the DPG from the previous cycle, and the existing FYDP. Involvement of the DPRB throughout the planning phase ensures dialogue between the OSD staff, the CJCS, and the services before publishing the DPG. The final document consists of four elements: major planning issues and decisions, strategy and policy, the SECDEF's program planning objectives, and long-range road maps for defense programs. Issuance of the DPG to the services in October marks the end of the planning phase.

SUMMARY OF THE PLANNING PHASE

The PPBS planning phase establishes a framework within which the services build their programs and request their funds. Inputs from the services and several other sources are considered during the period of concentrated formal planning before the OSD publishes the DPG, the final product of the planning phase. The services then use the DPG to begin the programming phase.

PROGRAMMING PHASE

The purpose of the programming phase is to structure resources (forces and personnel) by mission to achieve the objectives established in the DPG. The process of determining forces and personnel for given programs involves the preparation of alternative mixes called "exercises." In the air force, these exercises are the responsibility of the headquarter U.S. Air Force resource allocation teams and the Air Force Council. The proper number of forces, munitions, training, and support must be determined to ensure proposed programs support and conform to SECDEF guidance. Successive iterations of the exercises continue until the service arrives at its final position as reflected in the program objective memorandum (POM), which is discussed below. The exercises are of special significance because it is at this point that trade-offs and competition for dollars begin among individual programs. An integral function of the exercises is to estimate the cost for each program since the top-line fiscal guidance received in the DPG cannot be exceeded.

The programming phase begins in October and ends the following August. The services have from October until April to prepare their POM and sub-

Figure 2

Biennial Planning, Programming, and Budgeting System

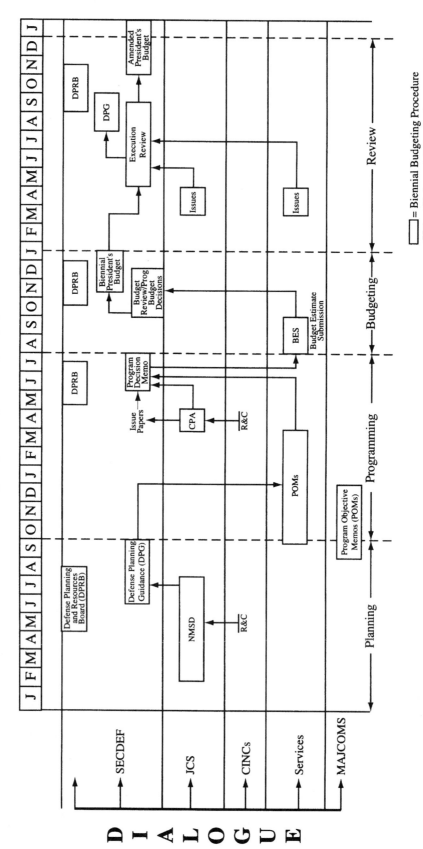

mit it to OSD. A copy of each service's POM also goes to the JCS and Joint Staff for their evaluation of the composite POM submission. The JCS and Joint Staff forward their evaluation to the SECDEF in the chairman's program assessment (CPA), which is discussed below. The remainder of the programming phase consists of evaluating the service POMs and considering alternative approaches proposed by the OSD staff. The alternatives to the service positions are grouped by topic and published in Issue Papers, also discussed below. Decisions that change the POMs are directed to the services by the SECDEF in the program decision memorandum (PDM). The programming phase ends in early August when the PDM goes out to the services.

FOUR KEY PROGRAMMING DOCUMENTS

Program Objective Memorandum. The POM represents the service's response to the DPG. Accordingly, the programs proposed by the service must be consistent with the objectives set forth in the DPG and still adhere to fiscal restraints. The POM expresses the service's total program requirements for the same period covered by the DPG. Since the POM represents an update to programs already approved and in the FYDP, it must include the rationale for the changes in the program. After submitting the POM, the FYDP computer database is updated. The POM also contains an assessment of the risk associated with current proposed forces and support programs. This risk represents the difference between planning ideals and limited resource realities. The services usually complete their POMs by the middle of May and submit them simultaneously to OSD and the JCS and Joint Staff.

Chairman's Program Assessment. The CPA provides the chairman's assessment of the composite POM to assist the SECDEF in making decisions on the defense program. In making this assessment, the chairman provides his views on the balance and capabilities of the aggregate force represented by all the POMs. The assessment is not intended to critique individual service POMs but rather to provide a "big picture" of military forces and capabilities as a whole.

Issue Papers. After receiving the services' POMs, officials in OSD, the JCS and Joint Staff, and the Office of Management and Budget (OMB) review them and propose issues or alternatives to approaches taken by the services in their POMs. Minor issues are settled "out of court" between the services and the OSD staff. Significant issues are written up and submitted to the executive secretary of the DPRB. Issues that merit the DPRB's attention are selected and published in Issue Papers.

Each Issue Paper discusses the feasibility of alternatives, identifies the cost and manpower effects, and sometimes recommends where any additional funding can be found by reducing other programs. Depending on the issue, it may be discussed within the DPRB, and a decision made by the chairman; or

the deputy secretary of defense (DEPSECDEF) will make a decision based solely on written responses from the service(s) and inputs from his staff.

Since services and the CINCs are represented on the DPRB, they are able to further argue their position on those issues about which they feel strongly. The DEPSECDEF, as chairman of the DPRB, then renders decisions on the issues. Those decisions are distributed to the military departments in the PDM. There is usually a PDM for each service and another that consolidates program decisions for all defense agencies. While these decisions can be appealed to the SECDEF, such appeals very rarely are successful.

Program Decision Memorandum. The PDM is the SECDEF's approval of service and defense agency programs (POMs) as modified by specific decisions. In essence, it consists of changes to the POM. Since the POM submission updates the FYDP computer database, changes to the POM (i.e., the PDM), also affect the FYDP database. The services rework their cost figures in the budgeting phase to reflect the PDM adjustments. Those adjustments are then used to update the FYDP database again. The POM and the PDM together serve as the basis for the final PPBS budgeting phase.

SUMMARY OF THE PROGRAMMING PHASE

As a recap, the programming phase begins in October when the services receive guidance from the SECDEF in the DPG. The services then build their POM, which goes to the SECDEF to explain how they plan to meet national security objectives. The CJCS provides his views on the service POMs through the CPA. The OSD staff, the JCS and Joint Staff, DPRB members, and OMB provide their views on the POMs through Issue Papers. The DPRB considers and resolves major issues. (The DPRB provides a very high level forum to air the issues and debate them, but it is not a voting body. The DEPSECDEF or SECDEF makes the final decision.) Final program decisions that change the POMs appear in the PDM. Issuance of the PDM signals the end of the programming phase and the beginning of the budgeting phase.

BUDGETING PHASE

The budgeting phase for DOD begins in August and continues until January. The purpose of the budgeting phase is to establish final program costs for preparation and submission of a detailed budget to the SECDEF. On the basis of the POM and the PDM, the services prepare and forward to the OSD their budget estimate submission (BES). The OSD staff analysts, as well as a representative of the OMB, evaluate the BES in an attempt to determine the adequacy of the estimates. Another objective of this evaluation, or budget review, is to identify less costly alternatives where possible. These changes are documented in program budget decisions (PBDs).

The DPRB irons out the final positions on disagreements that cannot be resolved between OSD
and the services. A major budget issue (MBI) is a
program or initiative priority or funding level in
which the service and OSD disagree and is of sufficient importance to warrant face-to-face discussions
at the highest levels (service chief and service secretary with the DEPSECDEF). The MBI process is
the budget final appeal arena for the services and
can result in OSD decisions being altered or (more
often) reaffirmed by the SECDEF or DEPSECDEF
personally. If the SECDEF or DEPSECDEF agrees
with the PBD by signing it, the service must accept
the program change.

The SECDEF then submits the final budget to
the OMB for its final review and inclusion in the
president's budget. In January, the president submits
his budget to Congress.

KEY BUDGETING DOCUMENTS

Budget Estimate Submission. The BES represents the service estimates of the cost of approved
programs. The cost estimates are presented in two
formats: by appropriation and by major force program. Although the services are not required to array
their programs according to priorities, they usually
identify "least dear" programs representing a small
percentage of their budgets. Decisions on the individual budget estimates are promulgated in PBDs
signed by the SECDEF or DEPSECDEF.

Program Budget Decisions. The purpose of the
PBD is to allow the OSD and OMB to document
their review of the services' budgets. As a result of
these reviews, a service's BES may be approved,
changed to incorporate fact-of-life and other last-
minute programmatic changes, or altered to reflect a
different program structure or cost. OSD forwards
draft PBDs to the services for review and comment.
The service may appeal the proposed OSD and
OMB changes through a formal appeal process that
is similar to the one used for the POM. Those PBDs
that are of very serious concern to the services can
be designated MBIs and appealed to the DPRB and
SECDEF. Usually those will amount to a few (five to
ten) of overriding concern to the service secretary.
After numerous exchanges of information, the
SECDEF signals the end of the reclama process by
approving and forwarding the budget to the OMB
for inclusion in the president's budget.

SUMMARY OF THE BUDGETING PHASE

Budgeting requires estimating and costing the
resources (forces, manpower, and dollars) needed to
execute the defense program approved by the
SECDEF. Since budgeting deals with future actions
and costs, it is subject to some uncertainty, and this
uncertainty leads to differences of opinion about
funding. The budget review offers a final opportunity to analyze budget requests before the loop is
closed. Then the SECDEF submits the defense
budget to the OMB, which puts it in the overall
president's budget.

EXECUTION REVIEW

The DOD portion of the president's budget covers two fiscal years. Therefore, DOD agencies theoretically can skip a year before they need to program
and budget for the next biennial cycle. During this
POM "off year," while Congress reviews the president's budget, OSD normally leads an execution review. The Office of the Undersecretary of Defense
for Policy has the lead to conduct this review. It is
similar to the DPRB review done in the programming phase, but the results are different. In the
programming phase, the OSD provides funding adjustments resulting in the PDM. The execution review is more policy oriented. During this time, the
OSD reviews current budget performance and
trends; discusses issues raised by the services, JCS
and Joint Staff, and CINCs; and directs studies and
policy decisions that affect development of the next
DPG and POM. The OSD publishes these decisions
in the program execution review decision memorandum (PERDM). This review process is not intended
to have a direct funding impact but can influence
future budgets through the DPG, various studies,
and the next POM.

The review process is still evolving, if for no other
reason than there has not been a real off year as envisioned in the legislation since the review was instituted.
Because of major perturbations in the budgeting process (a new administration or a new SECDEF with a
different view of defense priorities, or "real-world"
changes such as the recent events in Eastern Europe
and Operations Desert Shield and Desert Storm), the
DOD has consistently submitted an extensively
amended president's budget (in reality, a whole new
budget) for the second fiscal year of each biennial cycle.
The perturbations were so severe that no review was
conducted in fiscal 1991 or fiscal 1993.

THE BIG PICTURE

Now we have completed one biennial cycle in the
PPBS process. Each biennial budget is completed
every two years; however, budgets do not evolve in
isolation. Several cycles progress simultaneously, as
depicted in Figure 3. At any point in time, we are
dealing with up to four fiscal programs. For example,
in July 1991 we were executing (spending) fiscal
1991 funds and spending funds from prior years as
well, defending the fiscal 1992–93 budget through
the enactment process with Congress, supposedly
reviewing our execution of prior budgets, preparing
the fiscal 1993 amended president's budget (submitted in January 1992), and planning the fiscal 1994–
99 program. This overlap is significant because
unexpected events in one cycle can have an impact
on others. Sound complicated? It is not if one grasps

Figure 3
Cycle Overlap

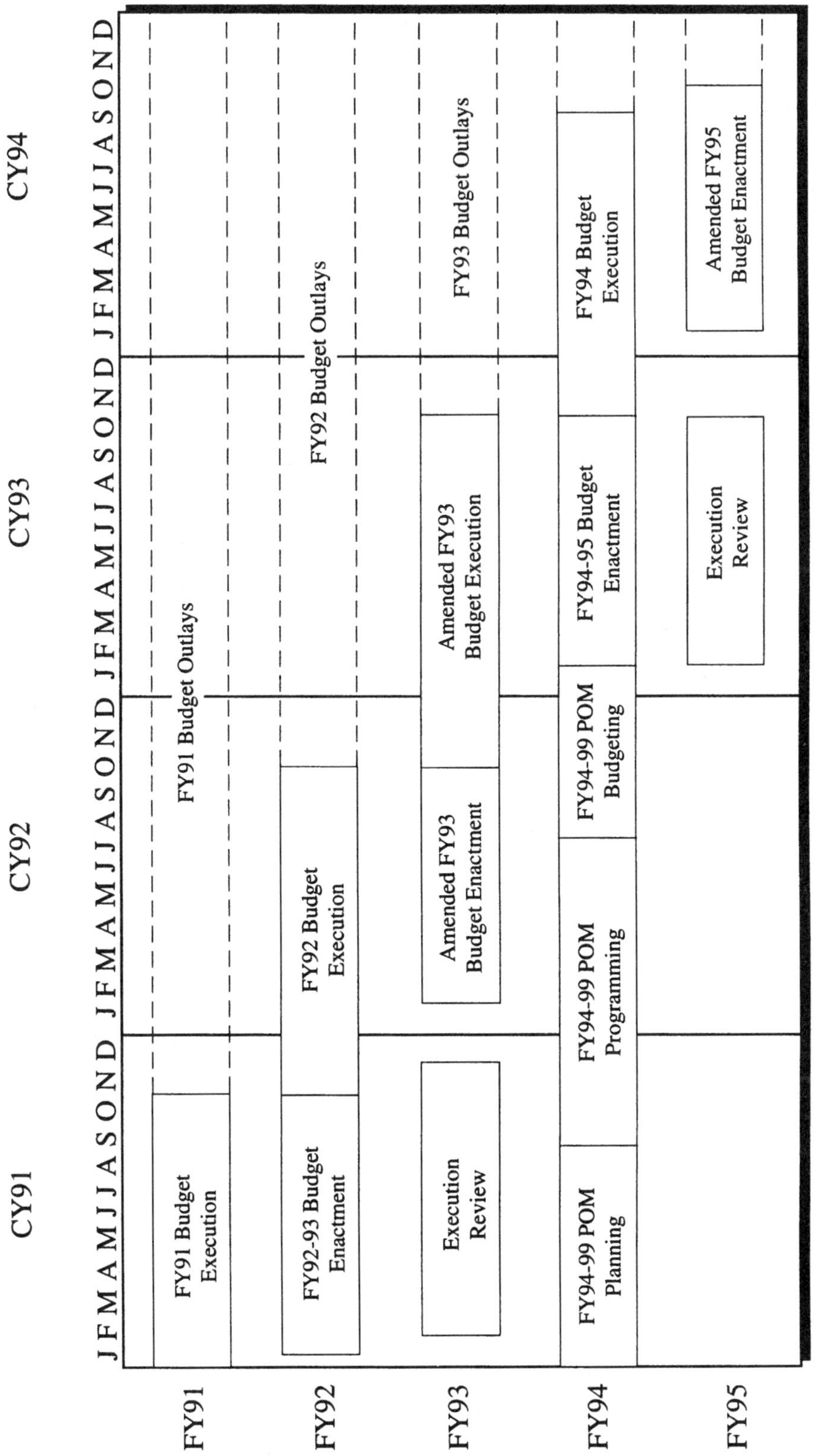

	CY91	CY92	CY93	CY94
	JFMAMJJASOND	JFMAMJJASOND	JFMAMJJASOND	JFMAMJJASOND

FY91 — FY91 Budget Execution — FY91 Budget Outlays

FY92 — FY92-93 Budget Enactment — FY92 Budget Execution — FY92 Budget Outlays

FY93 — Execution Review — Amended FY93 Budget Enactment — Amended FY93 Budget Execution — FY93 Budget Outlays

FY94 — FY94-99 POM Planning — FY94-99 POM Programming — FY94-99 POM Budgeting — FY94-95 Budget Enactment — FY94 Budget Execution

FY95 — Execution Review — Amended FY95 Budget Enactment

each step in the process and then steps back to look at the broad picture.

Figure 3 also shows how money from each year's budget is spent (outlayed) over many subsequent years. This outlay "bow wave" is a prime factor in the federal budget deficit reduction process. This is because the deficit is determined by the mismatch between government revenues and outlays—and the deficit reduction process attempts to reduce outlays by reducing the current year's appropriations and budget authority. Outlays from the past year's appropriations are not subject to control.

CONCLUSION

This essay has taken a broad-brush approach in looking at the planning, programming, and budgeting system. The PPBS is the overall structure through which the Defense Department allocates resources to meet mission needs. It is a far-reaching system that affects practically every member of the defense team in some way. This system ultimately determines the effectiveness of our military efforts to maintain a strong national defense posture in peace and war.

THE POLITICS OF BASE CLOSURES

GENEVIEVE ANTON AND JEFF THOMAS

Outside, it is cold. Inside the U.S. Capitol things are not, as debate rages over the need for new naval bases. Representatives from ship-building states smell jobs. But Representative Abe Clark of New Jersey complains that the "monstrous expense" flies in the face of defense cuts and tight finances. Lawmakers from port districts vote yes. Inland representatives vote no—and lose. It is February of '94—1794.

THE HISTORY

For more than two hundred years, Congress has created military bases. For more than two hundred years, military considerations have helped determine where to put them. And for more than two hundred years, the desire for the money that a base brings—and the politics that springs from it—have done just as much to secure a place in the U.S. military's vast empire. It is an American tradition.

A few men harnessed those forces fifty-three years ago to lure Fort Carson to Colorado Springs. Today a new generation hopes to harness them again—this time to save Fort Carson, Colorado's largest employer, from extinction.

As the Defense Base Closure and Realignment Commission geared up for a third round of cuts in 1995, the Colorado Springs area was in a cold sweat. The BRAC Commission, as it is known, had selected 250 domestic bases for closure since 1988, under orders from Congress. So far, Fort Carson had escaped the BRAC Commission's knife. But in 1995 the panel would grab a cleaver and lop off as many as

250 more bases in a single whack. Whether or not Fort Carson remained, 1995's hit list would reshape America's armed forces to a degree never seen in peacetime.

Military bases have long shaped America. Their names have become history: Bunker Hill, Fort Sumter, Pearl Harbor. Over two centuries, they and hundreds of other posts with less familiar names—Hope and Disappointment, Ranger and Tonto, Ord and Hitchepuckesassa—have made the United States the most heavily fortified nation on Earth.

Along the way, they have also pumped life into hundreds of cities, big and small. Sleepy hollows—such as Minot, North Dakota; Mountain Home, Idaho; Junction City, Kansas; and Colorado Springs —that might have dozed through the twentieth century instead have thrived on military jobs and payrolls. None wants to step off the gravy train. Certainly no member of Congress wants to anger voters by throwing thousands of rent-paying, grocery-buying neighbors out of work. Representative Ron Dellums (Democrat of California), an opponent of new weapons systems, had a fit when the naval bases in his Bay Area district were targeted for closure during the last round of cuts in 1993. Republican Representative Joel Hefley of Colorado Springs, a self-proclaimed porkbuster, pulled every string he could to save Fort Carson in 1995.

The fact is, however, that closing military bases is part of the tradition. The legendary Atlantic forts—Monroe, McHenry, Sumter—ultimately fell to obsolescence. Most frontier army encampments returned to the prairie. Bases were being closed

This essay has been edited and is reprinted from the six-part series, "The Fate of Fort Carson," in the Colorado Springs Gazette Telegraph: *2, 3, 9, and 23 October 1994, by permission of the* Gazette Telegraph.

until the eve of World War II, and once it ended, unfinished barracks were abandoned. Bases again closed by the hundreds after wars in Korea and Vietnam. Now, this part of the tradition is in full swing again, sparked by the need to cut the federal budget deficit and sustained by the end of the Cold War. As the military gets leaner, faster, and more nimble to land a quick punch to any spot on the globe, it wants to spend less on bases and more on training troops and operating planes, ships, and tanks.

Yet the stakes have never been higher for military towns. By the mid-1980s domestic bases employed more than 1.4 million troops and nearly 1 million civilians, pumping $60 billion a year into cities nationwide. And during an age when a college degree no longer guarantees a stable job, a military base is a prized neighborhood employer. Something worth fighting for.

STILL THE RULE: LOCATION, LOCATION

No one knows precisely where Jean Ribaut and his group of French explorers dropped anchor and waded ashore in May 1562. On an island bordering what they called the New World, they cut some trees and dug some earth to erect the first colonial fortification. They named it Charles Fort, after their king. But its walls could not protect the colonists from hunger, and it was soon abandoned. Today, on the same island, raw recruits from throughout the eastern United States get their first, gritty taste of military life at the Parris Island Marine Corps Recruit Depot in South Carolina.

As the number of U.S. military bases has grown and shrunk over the past two centuries, one fact has remained constant: a strategic location is the foremost consideration in the decision of where to put one. Some of those decisions, made long ago, are felt today.

The army cultivates officers at the spot where rebellious colonists erected a fort to deny the British control of the Hudson River Valley, a place called West Point. Norfolk, Virginia, gateway to vital Chesapeake Bay, has had a navy base as long as there has been a navy. The army's 1st Infantry Division lives and trains at Fort Riley, Kansas, built 141 years ago to help secure the frontier. Since the early days of aviation, the military has flown airplanes at San Diego's North Island, where the weather is almost always perfect for flying. Good ground, deep ports, clear skies. They are some of the reasons why bases are located where they are.

But there are other reasons why we have so many of them. There is fear: forts were built after the War of 1812, as Washington smoldered and Congress realized its pitiful coastal defenses needed more muscle. There is growth: from a porous line of army posts strung from Minnesota to Texas, new forts extended like fingers along the Oregon and Santa Fe trails in the 1840s and 1850s. There is trade: by the turn of the century, American interests stretched across the Pacific. Yankee traders sought elbow room among

the established European powers. Bases in Hawaii and places around the globe sprouted. And, of course, there is war: in 1917 the United States had 200,000 men in uniform. Eighteen months into World War I, it had 2.6 million. The war in Europe prompted the army to build thirty-two training camps almost overnight. Airplanes, an army experiment confined to six tiny fields before the war, buzzed over forty-four training fields by 1918. The navy opened twenty-five naval air stations. The United States proved it could fire up an awesome war machine.

But an important fact has been lost amid all the hand-wringing over the BRAC Commission's recent "unprecedented" cuts: The United States has, for most of its history, been a nation that would rather close bases than open them. Having won its independence, the new United States gave Henry Knox, the first secretary of war, only 718 soldiers to defend the vast nation. Having fought to a draw with Britain on home ground, the United States built sturdier coastal forts—but then cut the army in half as nationalistic fervor waned and the West beckoned. Having closed the frontier, the army closed its scattered posts and consolidated troops at remaining locations. And after World War I, the United States cut army manpower three times, to nearly prewar levels. Plans to resume a prewar expansion of the navy ran aground. By 1939 only a dozen army airfields remained.

The words of George Washington—to ensure peace, prepare for war—still had not sunk in completely. That changed with World War II. The attack on Pearl Harbor led the United States to decide, for the first time, that it needed a huge, permanent military—in wartime and even in peace. The army created nearly twice as many training camps as it did during World War I, including Camp Carson in Colorado Springs. The number of U.S. Army Air Force installations grew to nearly fifteen hundred, ranging from searchlight stations to air bases to rented hotels. Naval bases opened in Alaska, Washington, and California.

The United States came out of the war a superpower. Just a half-million strong before World War II, the U.S. armed forces kept about 1.5 million soldiers, sailors, and airmen after the war. They had to live and work somewhere. But in the nuclear age, it did not matter as much where. "You're vulnerable no matter where you are," said retired Admiral Eugene Carroll, former commander of U.S. forces in Europe and the Middle East. So by 1960 mammoth B-52 bombers were on constant alert in remote, inland places such as Grand Forks, North Dakota, and Gwynn, Michigan—not only distant targets, but well-placed for an over-the-pole trek into Soviet territory. At the height of the Cold War, the Strategic Air Command was the largest segment of the air force, operating forty-six domestic bases from Maine to Guam. By the time the BRAC Commission is done, only fourteen of those installations will remain. Overall, the air force is shedding 11 of the 24 wings it had in 1990. The army is going from 18 divisions to 10; the navy, from 546 combat ships to 346. Most of the remaining forces will be stationed in the United States, ready to move quickly to hot spots around the world.

Does that mean troops and planes and tanks will move toward the coasts? Or will they remain at large, inland bases, where there is plenty of room to practice? "It doesn't make much difference," said Allan Millett, a military historian at Ohio State University. "You still have to fly from here to there." That is a strategist talking. Bean counters think differently.

With the BRAC Commission ordered to get rid of some otherwise perfectly good bases in the name of budget cutting, it finds itself relying on old-fashioned qualities when separating the winners from the losers. After 432 years, we are back to what French explorer Jean Ribaut was looking for when he hit the South Carolina coast: good ground, deep ports, and clear skies.

MILITARY BASES, POLITICS TRAVEL HAND IN HAND

The location of military bases has always had as much to do with money as with strategy. The first colonial forts protected merchant ships. Later, they were never far from fur-trading posts. The young U.S. Navy charted the seas, chased pirates, escorted merchant ships, and with guns very visible, opened trade with Japan. Soldiers cleared the way for commerce. The army dispatched officers Meriwether Lewis and William Clark to chart the Northwest, and later, Lieutenant John Fremont to the Rocky Mountains. Soldiers dug canals, cleared roads, protected railroad crews, and built sawmills and blacksmith shops outside their encampments. Where there was money, politics was close behind.

After the navy's birth in 1794, Secretary of War Knox thought it "just and wise to proportion . . . benefits as nearly as may be to those places or states which pay the greatest amount to its support." Knox established navy yards in six cities that had supported the Naval Act to build the nation's first six warships. The yard at Philadelphia had long finished its work when Congress ordered new ships with "not less than 74 guns" each. It was a blank check, and the navy wrote Philadelphia a whopper. For fifteen years, Congress winked as the navy did nothing at the yard but build the world's most bloated gunship—one that barely sailed and was never used.

If pork barrel excesses continue to cause occasional embarrassment, they also reveal the huge appetite communities have for military installations. And the military has known it for a long time. When the army looked for a place to put its first major airplane base in 1915, it merely put the word out to local chambers of commerce and waited for the offers to roll in. Seizing the opportunity, several Hampton, Virginia, businessmen locked up thousands of acres and promised to provide a railroad and water. Hampton has prospered ever since. Today

Langley Air Force Base employs more than eleven thousand people and pumps an annual payroll of $358 million. Land for jobs. They have long been the terms of the deal, the essential transaction of a military base.

Colorado Springs, its tourist economy mired in the Great Depression, courted the army in 1941 for one purpose only: economic salvation. The city had land. The army had jobs. The negotiations began. The city bought the 5,533-acre Cheyenne Valley Ranch and offered it, along with gas, water, and electricity hookups, to the army. The Colorado congressional delegation and the assistant secretary of the interior—a Coloradan—twisted arms in Washington. Charles Tutt hosted army brass at his Broadmoor hotel. The golf was superb, the rare, pre-Prohibition liquor sublime. The army did not merely appreciate the gestures. The army expected them. As Fort Carson officials later wrote in a base history: "An Army post has to be wanted—wanted so much that the requesting community must provide countless reasons why it should be built at its doorstep rather than elsewhere. In addition, that community has to guarantee not only the soil on which future soldiers will live and train, but also a lifetime of water, utilities and a multitude of other necessities."

The army's final inspection of Colorado Springs was barely finished before the attack on Pearl Harbor sent the United States into World War II. Suddenly more desperate than selective, the army in one stroke approved new camps in Colorado Springs and twenty-two other cities. After the war, Camp Carson's population dropped sharply and bounced up and down with the army's constant reorganizations until 1970, when the 4th Infantry Division arrived. Uncertainty is the price of peace.

"During wartime, Congress merely asks the services how much they need, then turns them loose," says Paolo Coletta, a retired Naval Academy historian. "When the war's over and it's time to retrench, that's when the problems start." That is when it helps to have friends like Mendel Rivers. During Rivers's tenure from 1941 to 1970 representing Charleston, South Carolina, on the House Armed Services Committee, that city's naval yard became a major Atlantic Fleet base and acquired squadrons of destroyers and nuclear submarines. The base added submarine-training and maintenance centers, a hospital, supply and weapons depots, and a mine-warfare center. An army depot, air force base, marine air station, marine recruiting depot, Coast Guard station, and veterans hospital opened. Never was a campaign slogan truer than "Rivers Delivers." "You put anything else down there in your district, Mendel, it's gonna sink," a colleague once told him.

And that was before Rivers became committee chairman. After he did, Charleston's share of the annual navy construction budget more than doubled. In just two of Rivers six years as armed services chairman, the base received as much construction money as it had during the ten years before he took control of the committee. "What my people want is prosperity," Rivers said in 1969. "They want jobs. Money. And that's what I've brought them." Though perhaps more prolific than most, Rivers was just part of a long tradition of congressional interference when it comes to the placement of military bases.

Representative Felix Hebert of New Orleans persuaded President John Kennedy to twist the arm of Defense Secretary Robert McNamara to preserve the Eighth Naval District headquarters in his city. Senator Henry Jackson of Washington voted in 1972 to accelerate production of the new Trident submarine. In 1973 the navy announced that the Trident would be based at Bangor, Washington. The army tried repeatedly to close frontier relic Fort D. A. Russell in Cheyenne, Wyoming. But the chairman of the Senate Military Affairs Committee happened to be Francis E. Warren of Wyoming. Today his name adorns the base.

There is a reason why politicians for so long were so willing to throw their weight around: in the decades after World War II, their constituents had become deeply dependent on these bases. "The sheer growth of the military budget injected billions of dollars into local economies in a way that had never been done before," said economist Greg Bishak, executive director of the National Commission for Economic Conversion, which advocates putting military dollars toward other uses.

The Pentagon, aided by a Congress eager to earn points by spreading the wealth, ultimately opened installations in all fifty states—a monstrous federal jobs program that voters could support. At first, military towns considered the money a bonus. But it became a necessity when the postwar economic boom of the 1950s and 1960s faded. "There was more pressure at that point to not remove any of the existing economic foundations from communities," said Robert Pollin, an economist at the University of California at Riverside, where base closures have pushed unemployment to about 10 percent.

Not that the Pentagon did not try. The Kennedy administration closed bases, and Congress complained. The Johnson administration closed bases, and Congress demanded—but did not get—a say-so in choosing the doomed. The Carter administration tried to close bases, and Congress finally just shut down the process, requiring time-consuming studies that could be challenged in court. For the next decade, not a single military base closed.

It would take a congressional rookie from Texas, Dick Armey, and his clever invention of the BRAC Commission to finally break the deadlock in 1989. Now, the independent panel nominates bases for closure, and Congress and the president vote yes or no on the whole list. The system has defanged a Congress that historically had bared its teeth when bases were threatened. Still, the smell of money and politics remains in the air. Representative Dellums, who favored cutting funding for the B-2 bomber and the Strategic Defense Initiative, is claiming that the decision to close five naval installations in his district was "politically driven." Charleston is grumbling that

the Portsmouth Naval Shipyard between New Hampshire and Maine would have been chosen for closure if George Mitchell of Maine had not happened to be Senate majority leader. A newspaper in Florida, where voters supported George Bush in 1992, observes that the state is losing the Orlando Naval Training Center while Georgia and Louisiana, which voted for Bill Clinton, will gain military jobs under the 1993 round of base realignments.

With the BRAC Commission set to make more deep cuts in 1995, cities raised millions to pay lobbyists to keep their bases off the hit list. The Colorado Springs Chamber of Commerce "Keep Carson" campaign took donations. Idaho officials, trying to fortify Mountain Home Air Force Base against closure, offered to swap some land with the federal government to give the air force a bombing range it wants. Arizona promised to build the air force a $40 million runway if it spared Tucson's Davis-Monthan Air Force Base.

But today the charges of politics may just be sour grapes. The money may not sway any decisions. With the job of closing bases seemingly out of the hands of politicians, hundreds of communities across the country find themselves threatened. Threatened, too, is the tradition that, for more than two centuries, has protected so many.

THE FORMULA

It started out as an idea so ludicrous that nobody paid much attention to it. Today the consequences are so serious that everyone is obsessed with it. When Dick Armey told colleagues in 1987 he wanted to attack the federal budget deficit by forming an apolitical commission to close dozens of unneeded military bases, most said it could not be done.

To lawmakers, military bases were not just a collection of pork barrels—they were the whole, sloppy pig farm. They were expected to protect local bases and the jobs they provided—or risk the wrath of voters. Congress had thrown up so many roadblocks over the years, it was impossible to shut down any major base, much less dozens of them. A year later, however, Armey's crazy base closure idea had become law—one that continues to reshape not only the U.S. military, but hundreds of local economies. The nation targeted 250 bases for closure over the past six years, after a decade of not closing a single one. Meanwhile, the Defense Base Closure and Realignment Commission has gone from a few volunteers stuffed in a tiny office to a staff that swells up to a hundred people filling the fourteenth floor of a building near the Pentagon. "It is absolutely the most efficient piece of legislation that the United States Congress has ever passed," said base-closure consultant John Allen. "We'll never see anything like it again." Indeed, an array of political agendas needed to come together before politics could be taken out of the messy job of closing bases.

There was an aggressive new member of congress who saw closing bases as a way to make his mark on Capitol Hill. There was pressure on Congress to balance the budget. There was the Reagan administration's desire to shift military spending from bases to high-tech projects such as the Strategic Defense Initiative. And there was the Pentagon's long-simmering displeasure with lawmakers who twisted arms to keep hundreds of obsolete installations open. By the mid-1980s the military had some 3,800 facilities in the United States, including nearly 500 major installations that covered an area the size of Virginia. The cost to keep it all running: $20 billion a year—a fourth of which, the Pentagon said, contributed little or nothing to national defense. Then, suddenly, base closure became the story of the moment. The *New York Times,* which mentioned base closure just once in 1986, ran ten editorials pushing it in 1988.

It was as if people had just discovered that Fort Douglas, Utah, built to patrol stage coach routes, was now nothing more than a collection of historic buildings trapped in the middle of the University of Utah's campus. Or that no military ship had docked for decades at the Naval Station Puget Sound in Washington state. Or that the main attribute of Fort Sheridan outside Chicago was its sprawling golf course, a favorite among military retirees. Those bases were the first to go. But it would not stop there. Armey's Little Bill That Could had cracked open a door that the end of the Cold War would fling wide open.

The process has been tinkered with over the years, but the basic concept remains the same: the BRAC Commission submits a hit list of bases that the president and Congress can either accept or reject in total. "It gives lawmakers political cover and removes a burden from their shoulders," said Tom Houston, a former congressional aide who worked on the BRAC legislation. "They can stomp and scream and make all the speeches they want for the folks back home. But in the end, they can't get enough votes to reject the entire list. It was a thing of beauty, if you think about it."

In three rounds of closures—in 1988, 1991, and 1993—the BRAC Commission mothballed 15 percent of the nation's bases. The last scheduled round in 1995 is expected to close some 250 more bases—a final, monumental reshaping of the military for the twenty-first century. "Now we're essentially down to the big boys, the bases with deep histories and household names, the ones nobody ever thought would disappear," said Houston, now the BRAC Commission's staff director. Among the places that may be in the crosshairs next year is Fort Carson. And like other communities contemplating the loss of their biggest economic generator, Colorado Springs can no longer count on political clout to save its base. That is the way things work now—and the best evidence that the BRAC process has worked.

"There is only one yardstick to measure the success of BRAC," Houston said. "Are we closing bases?

Yes. Have we been fair and independent? I think so. Will we finish what we started? It looks like it."

PENTAGON, CAPITOL HILL
WRESTLE FOR CONTROL

In the days when the Pentagon called the shots, closing bases was easy. Defense Secretary Robert McNamara took on the biggest military housecleaning in history in the early 1960s, shuffling bases and closing more than sixty major installations—without consulting Congress. Near the end of the Vietnam War, hundreds more bases were closed. Congress howled. The Pentagon shrugged. Within a few years, though, lawmakers would wrest control of base closure from the generals in typical congressional fashion: by wrapping the whole process in a huge wad of red tape. After 1977 the Pentagon was required to, among other things, conduct lengthy and litigious environmental impact studies before closing a base. It worked. No base was closed for nearly a dozen years.

"It was unbelievable," said retired Lieutenant General Calvin Waller, who worked in the Pentagon office that handled base closures during the early 1980s. Once an officer told him the navy wanted to get rid of a five-man detachment in the Philadelphia Naval Shipyard. Waller told him to go ahead. When Waller's boss found out, he went ballistic. "Jesus Christ, you can't do that!" he told Waller. "We have to notify Congress! Philadelphia will be up in arms! Stop that guy right now!" For years, that was how things were done—or not done.

Then Dick Armey came along. The man who challenged one of the most sacred cows in Congress had almost no clout. But he did have an obsession: saving money. The forty-eight-year-old Republican economist from an affluent Dallas-area district won his first House seat in 1984 by pledging to cut waste. Once in Washington, Armey started searching for a cause, something that would save billions. Armey chose to attack unneeded military bases for a simple reason: "Base closure," he said, "was the one I could most easily get done."

To break a decade of gridlock, two things were needed: cut the red tape and shield lawmakers from the political pain that the economic pain of closing bases would bring. Armey's idea was the Defense Base Closure and Realignment Commission. It would do the work that Congress seemed incapable of doing. It would provide the president, and then Congress, with a list of bases to be closed. Lawmakers would vote on it—up or down. No picking, no choosing. No heavy thinking. No fear. No sweat.

Still, it was not an easy sell. "It was hand-to-hand combat," Armey said. "It was an intellectual battle. I had to convince them I had no ax to grind and no particular base in my gun sight." Armey got little support from the Pentagon or the White House, neither of which thought the bill had a chance. So, when a fellow Texan, Representative Jim Wright, helped Armey push his bill through, Armey was as surprised as anyone. "I didn't think you could win," Wright told Armey later. He was right—sort of. The bill failed the first time around, but by only seven votes. "It was a big surprise to me and everybody else," Armey said. "That vote sent up a signal it could be done."

MINOR PLAYER PLAYS MAJOR ROLE IN THE PROCESS

When Frank Carlucci became defense secretary in 1988, base closure topped his list of things to do. As deputy secretary in the early Reagan years, he had flirted with the idea, only to dismiss it as too difficult. "We were trying to grow and strengthen defense," Carlucci said. "It wasn't worth spending political capital on base closures when we needed Congress to give us the kind of buildup we wanted." But in 1988 the defense budget was in its third year of decline. And although Carlucci did not like the idea of Pentagon outsiders having the final say on which bases to close, he decided it was time to be pragmatic and support an independent base closure commission. "When I told Ronald Reagan I was going to do this, he kind of rolled his eyes," Carlucci said. "We all knew it would take an enormous amount of time and energy, and we still might lose." He persuaded the chairmen of the armed services committees to push a base closure proposal through Congress. It was Armey's proposal, yet it took him weeks to arrange a meeting with Carlucci, who says he brushed off the junior member of Congress as a "useful, though not pivotal" player.

For a second time, debate began over Armey's BRAC idea. And for a second time, key lawmakers tried to scuttle it. Something else was at work this time, however. Pressure was building on Congress to cut the federal deficit—the hot news item of the day. Closing bases promised huge savings, anywhere from $2 billion to $5 billion a year. (The estimate later proved to be grossly exaggerated.) "More and more lawmakers were being put on the defensive by voters or editorials in their hometown papers," said Houston, the former legislative aide. "They found themselves unable to justify voting against it." In fact, more than 90 percent of lawmakers voted for it. Yet few wanted any credit. Although Armey had enlisted 150 cosponsors, he was the only one who posed for a photograph when Reagan signed the bill.

COMMISSION'S FIRST HIT LIST SURPRISED FEW

When the BRAC Commission first went to work in 1988, everyone was skeptical whether it could scrub politics from a process so caked with the stuff. Even one of its chairmen, former Representative Jack Edwards refused to take the job unless key lawmakers pledged to support its recommendations. "Look," Edwards (Republican of Alabama) told colleagues. "I've got better things to do than waste my time on a nonpaying, time-consuming, friend-destroying kind of commission."

Because the BRAC Commission's work was so sensitive, security was tight. Its name was not listed at the building where it worked. Makeshift curtains covered the windows of its private conference room. The receptionist was an air force sergeant who let visitors in only after sweeping the tables clean of documents. "People complained about all the secrecy," said cochairman Abraham Ribicoff, a former Democratic senator from Connecticut. "But there was no monkey business going on. We called it the way we saw it."

BRAC commissioners waited until after the 1988 elections to visit some forty bases, trying to calm local fears by calling them "fact-finding" trips. The panel's spokesman—who spent twelve to fourteen hours a day answering panicked calls—typed a one-paragraph response for each commissioner saying a visit did not mean the base was at risk. But everyone knew the truth. A member of congress from Oklahoma toted bags stuffed with more than thirteen thousand letters to the BRAC Commission's office, begging that his local base be spared. A senator from Virginia swept through four bases in his state to check the commission's homework.

The week after Christmas, the BRAC Commission dropped its first bombshell: a recommendation that eighty-six installations be shut down. There were few surprises. Yet the list provoked banner headlines and protests. Some lawmakers criticized the commission, saying its research was shoddy and savings projections were inflated. However, outside of the two dozen congressional districts affected, there was not much howling—only relief. Many lawmakers who had dodged the BRAC Commission's bullet thought that base closure had come and now would go. They were wrong.

END OF COLD WAR GIVES RENEWED LIFE TO PANEL

True, the commission was never designed to survive. Its job was to save money, not reshape America's military. But then again, when the commission was created in 1988, the Berlin Wall was standing, Boris Yeltsin was a little-known politician, and the United States was pumping $300 billion a year into its arsenal. The end of the Cold War challenged the Department of Defense as much as the Soviet Union ever did. Generals suddenly found themselves poring over spreadsheets instead of maps. Within a few years, the military budget was being slashed 40 percent, the number of troops by a third. Around the Pentagon, tough choices became as common as short haircuts. "Everybody started to realize just how many bases we really had. It was shocking," said Keith Cunningham, director of Business Executives for National Security, a Washington, D.C.–based group that has lobbied for bases to be shut. "People in the Pentagon knew if they kept spending this kind of money on bases, there would be nothing left for weapons and training troops."

So the Pentagon and Congress agreed to resurrect the BRAC Commission, giving it five years to eliminate the waste that had built up in America's far-flung galaxy of fortresses. There were changes: today the commission is appointed by the president—not the Pentagon—and confirmed by the Senate. No more than one-third of its staff comes from the Defense Department.

In 1988 no one knew how the commission made its decisions. Today a base's military value must, by law, be given the greatest weight, and all BRAC Commission meetings and documents are public. "We bend over backwards to make sure everybody knows where we are and how to reach us," said Jim Courter, the panel's chairman. To some, however, the BRAC Commission's broad reach is still troubling. After shutting down 164 more bases in 1991 and 1993—and with the biggest, bloodiest round in 1995—a backlash emerged. Lawmakers said the 1995 round would be too painful; that the nation was still suffering from the last recession and could not handle it; that there was not yet proof that closing bases saves money. The Clinton administration and key lawmakers pushed to delay any more closings until after the 1996 election. They failed. In fact, the BRAC experiment has been so successful that it is now the vogue in Washington to call for similar commissions to handle other hard jobs—from cutting federal bureaucracies to choosing sites to dump hazardous waste. If Congress cannot run government, the argument goes, maybe a bunch of commissions can. It is an idea that disturbs some. "It circumvents the whole concept of American government," said one Washington lobbyist. "The president doesn't want to take responsibility, Congress doesn't want to take responsibility. I'm tired of nobody taking responsibility—it's antidemocratic."

THE POLITICS

When Congress set up an independent commission to take on the controversial job of closing military bases, lawmakers bragged that they had washed the stink of politics from the process. And that is true—sort of. Lawmakers on Capitol Hill no longer silently pull the strings that dictate which bases will be closed and which will remain open. Generals a few miles away in the sterile hallways of the Pentagon do. And try as they might to be objective, experts inside and outside the military say decisions by the top brass are colored by their likes and dislikes, their experience and emotions, their quirks and career worries. Congressional politics may be dead. But the fate of bases such as Fort Carson now rests in large part with the military, where politics still thrives.

"Base closure is not a scientific process," said retired Navy Admiral Eugene Carroll, director of the Center for Defense Information in Washington, D.C. "It is an art in which politics, money, service rivalry, and the subjective interests of the individuals making the decision are all factors." The Defense Base Closure and Realignment Commission checks Pentagon recommendations to make sure it sticks to the legal guidelines for judging bases. But in the past, it has changed only 15 percent of the Pentagon's choices. "The end result is still a list that looks very much like what the military wanted in the first place," said BRAC Commission staff director Tom Houston. The official line is that the military is not political. But every office has its politics, and the Pentagon is the biggest office building in the world. "There's no way you can wash politics out of the military services," said retired Army Lieutenant General Calvin Waller, who navigated the system over a thirty-two-year career that ended with his being second-in-command during the Persian Gulf War. "It's human nature for people with power to exert that power to get things done," said Waller, who headed up Colorado Springs's effort to save Fort Carson. "If anybody thinks that doesn't happen in the military—that politics plays no part in decision—they are pretty naive."

Pentagon officials have been accused by distraught lawmakers and community leaders of playing politics with base closure in 1988, 1991, and 1993. Protecting one base, undermining another. Tinkering with the data used to rate them. No one suggests that military politics drives the entire process, but it does play a quiet role—one that experts say may be more overt in 1995 when some 250 installations are expected to be closed. With most marginal bases already gone, the difference between winners and losers in 1995 will, in many cases, be thin. "If politics is going to rear its head, this will be the time," said a staffer for the House Armed Services Committee. "Whenever there are no clear choices, there is more political pressure. In some cases, the military simply has to pick one base over another that's just as good. It could justify almost any decision."

One indication of how susceptible the Pentagon may be to political pressure is the heavy lobbying of its officials. Civil leaders from communities where a base is threatened in 1995 have been courting Pentagon officials for more than a year. Consultants have been hired for their military—not congressional—contacts, and military retirees in towns, including Colorado Springs, have been asked to pick up the phone and call old friends. "I think most of the services would agree there is a tremendous amount of contact from communities right now, months before the list is actually finalized," said Barry Rhoads, a base closure consultant. Lobbyists hint that they can somehow influence the Pentagon's decision. But ask about specifics and they clam up. "I'd rather not talk about it," said Mark Greenbery, a consultant representing Colorado Springs. "We do as much as we can with the Pentagon in ways that benefit Fort Carson. I'm not willing to say more than that."

BRAC PROCESS SERVES TO KEEP MILITARY HONEST

From the outside, the military's deliberations seem as impenetrable as the Pentagon itself. For example, members of the army's base closure study group are hunkered down deep inside the building's bowels. There are no windows where they meet, a room behind an inconspicuous door sealed by a number-coded lock. Not even an army public affairs officer is allowed inside without clearance. The military, accustomed to working in secrecy under the cloak of national security, never before had to justify why it closed a base. The BRAC process requires that every scrap of paper, every number crunched, must eventually be made public. "It keeps the military honest," said Keith Cunningham. Yet the basic guidelines for base closure are intentionally vague; each service interprets them differently. In 1993 the BRAC Commission itself questioned the accuracy of the mathematical model used by the services to compare similar bases. "There were times when we thought that the services had arranged the data to support a foregone conclusion," said Peter Bowman, a retired navy captain who served on the BRAC Commission in 1991 and 1993. "I don't want to give specific examples, but we felt we were being misled a couple of times." "You can make statistics say anything you want," added a Pentagon official who spoke on condition of anonymity. "There are always shades of grey. Human judgment enters in at some point."

Consider the army's evaluation of bases in 1993. It listed Fort Stewart, Georgia, as having 144,500 acres of prime maneuver area. Nowhere was it mentioned that almost half the land was swamp. "You have to ask yourself 'What kind of moron submitted this information?'" said Waller, who was once chief of staff at Fort Stewart. "I defy anyone to go train on that kind of terrain. It's impossible." While it might have been an honest error, Waller is skeptical. "I just happen to be cynical enough to think someone was simply putting Fort Stewart in the best light they could. That's intellectually dishonest. But it happens all the time. It happens because communities aren't alone in having a stake in whether or not a base is closed."

From the secretary of defense—a presidential appointee—to officers in midcareer to base commanders who do not want to be at the helm of a sinking ship, national security is not always the only thing on the minds of military decision makers. For most, personal interests amount to nothing more than a soft spot for a certain base—a soft spot that is set aside to do a job impartially. But in the past, the actions of a few have raised questions.

In 1993 former Secretary of Defense Les Aspin took two California bases off the hit list drawn up by the services: McClellan Air Force Base in Sacramento and the Presidio in San Francisco. Aspin explained that northern California had been hit hard in previous rounds. "Frankly, this was piling on," he said. But, as one base closure expert put it, piling on is "difficult to define and harder to defend." After all, the economic impact of the 1993 round of base closures was far greater in small communities more dependent on military dollars. Critics claimed that President Bill Clinton, after a week of heavy lobby-

ing by California lawmakers, put pressure on his Pentagon chief to go easy on the state that sealed his 1992 election victory. Even sources on the BRAC Commission say Aspin's logic was vague and inconsistent. But the defense secretary got his way. And it sent a powerful message to the military services that the chain of command starts in the Oval Office.

Officers in uniform frown on such blatant favoritism by political appointees. But they, too, snap to attention when a powerful politician calls. As one retired four-star general put it: "As long as Senator Sam Nunn [the Democrat who chairs the Senate Armed Services Committee] is still in Washington, the Pentagon is going to think long and hard before it puts a major Georgia base on the closure list." And whether it is conscious or not, officers—or at least some retired ones—will say that the personal consequences of base closure are sometimes taken into account by decision makers.

When a base goes away, so do career opportunities. There are fewer posts to command, fewer slots for rising generals, fewer places to retire with commissaries and military hospitals nearby. "It could be as simple as a general who bought a nice piece of property near a base for investment purposes," said Carroll, the retired admiral. "Or maybe he wants to use his connections to get a job there after retirement." Generals who head military commands with several bases under their wing also may have personal motives to protect them from closure. General Ronald Yates, head of Air Force Materiel Command, has been accused of trying to transfer jobs from Peterson Air Force Base in Colorado Springs to one of his California depots—the same McClellan Air Force Base that barely escaped closure in 1993. Representative Joel Hefley (Republican of Colorado Springs) called it a "covert move" to bolster a vulnerable base. But a spokesman for Yates, who once described himself as a Tyrannosaurus Rex when it comes to protecting his depots, said the general's actions had nothing to do with base closure or the future of McClellan.

MILITARY JUDGMENT OUTWEIGHS EMOTIONS

Beefing up a base to save it may be unthinkable to military purists, but Air Force Secretary Sheila Widnall acknowledged the potential in a January letter to all her commanders. "We must avoid taking any actions which predetermine a closure or realignment selection decision for any installation," she wrote. The military forbids post commanders to take sides on base closure. They must remain silent despite any fondness for a base or community pressure. This tug of war between sentiment and duty was acknowledged by General Dennis Reimer. The former Fort Carson commander is now head of Forces Command, the post's higher headquarters. Reimer will make the initial recommendation to the army on which large "maneuver bases"—such as Fort Carson—should be closed. "Emotion does play a part. You become attached to a base," Reimer said during a visit to Fort Carson. "But I've got to try to strip out that emotion and make a decision based on sound military judgment." A tall order for any human being—even those with stars on their shoulders. Major General Randolph House has two of them on his. But he also finds himself in an awkward personal place as the 1995 round of base closures draws near. He once worked at Fort Carson, as an assistant division commander. Today he is commander of Fort Riley in Kansas. The two bases are seen as competitors. One of them, experts say, may be on the chopping block. "I'm not here to save Fort Riley," House said when asked where his loyalties lie, "any more than [Major General] Tom Schwartz is trying to save Fort Carson."

But House knows that he is only human, that politics itself is only human, and that because of that his superiors will not let him get anywhere near a decision that might affect the post he commands. "No one's going to ask me if I want to close Fort Riley," House said. "They know I'm going to say no."

THE MYTHS

On a sweltering summer afternoon in Washington D.C., a group of men and women who have gathered in a hotel conference room tug at their collars and dab their brows. But it is more than the hundred degree temperature outside making them sweat. Rather, these civic leaders from across the nation are each consumed with a single, anguished thought: that in 1995 the Defense Base Closure and Realignment Commission could shut their local military installation and gut their hometown economy. A thousand air conditioners could not cool the heat they feel. "I don't even want to think about it," says Michael Archer of the Spokane (Washington) Area Chamber of Commerce, where Fairchild Air Force Base is at risk. "But you can't just close your eyes and hope it doesn't happen." He is among seventy people who have paid $1,200 to attend this recent two-day conference on military base closure. Sponsored by a New York company, it is part of the cottage industry spawned by the anxiety of base closure. The bevy of consultants who are here, working the crowd to solicit new clients, is another part. They offer hard facts on how the complicated BRAC process works. Perhaps they will have a little inside information on what the competition is doing, something that might give one community an edge over its rivals.

But most important, these experts can help separate the myths from the realities when it comes to base closure. The myth that congressional clout can keep a base open—and the reality that it pays to begin lobbying Pentagon decision makers as early as possible. The myth that it is effective to argue that a base should not be closed because it will wreck a town's economy—and the reality that a base's importance to national defense is the only factor that will save it. The myth that a base is in the clear if it is left off the Pentagon's hit list—and the reality that a base is still at risk even if millions have been spent

recently to refurbish it. The year 1995 saw the fourth round of base closures since 1988, and according to some experts, most communities are getting better at distinguishing between what counts and what does not. "Sophomoric," is the way consultant Barry Rhoads describes community lobbying efforts of the past. "Most didn't lift a finger to defend themselves until the list came out."

In 1995, the stakes were higher than ever. The military has cut more than a third of its troops since the Cold War ended. In 1995 it was expected to shed itself of some 250 installations from coast to coast.

It is hot, and the temperature is only going to rise. "Is there anybody here from Fort Bragg, North Carolina?" Barry Steinberg, a base closure consultant, asks the community leaders who sweat before him at the Washington conference. No one answers. "Good," Steinberg says, "because you don't need to be here." He goes on: "I can quickly identify about a dozen bases—and Bragg is one of them—that are sacred bases. They aren't going away. Those are the only communities that don't have to worry about base closure. Everybody else may be making a fatal mistake if they're not prepared." This crowd does not need convincing. "It's expensive, but I felt we couldn't afford not to be here," says Jim Palmer of the Colorado Springs Chamber of Commerce, who is looking for tips on how to save Fort Carson. Tips on myths. Tips on realities. Those who do not know the difference between the two are shooting in the dark. And this is one target nobody wants to miss.

MYTH NO. 1: THE 1995 BASE CLOSURE PROCESS STARTS IN 1995

It does not. The process of deciding which bases to close has been under way for months. And smart community leaders know it. One day not long ago, the vice president of the Colorado Springs Chamber of Commerce got a call from a banker near Fort Knox, Kentucky. "He heard about what we've been doing to save Fort Carson and pleaded with me to send him some material," Jim Palmer said. The local "Keep Carson" campaign, conceived nearly two years ago, has raised $400,000 and logged thousands of hours trying to save the army post. But some communities waited until March 1 to see if their base was on the Pentagon's hit list to the BRAC Commission before getting to work. Big mistake, experts say. "Time is your enemy," says Paul Hirsch, a consultant and former BRAC Commission staffer. "If you wait until next spring, it's already too late." Now is the time to prepare a defense, because a community typically has only a few weeks to make its case after the Pentagon list becomes public.

Communities such as Colorado Springs are starting months, even years, in advance to map out strategies that would be the envy of military planners. They have raised money, hired lobbyists, and traveled to Washington to meet BRAC Commission staffers. Each military service is already at work comparing its bases, deciding which ones to recommend for closure. It is a secretive process that is difficult to influence. However, anyone can get a pretty good picture of where the military is headed by examining past decisions and be ready to deliver counterarguments when the BRAC Commission holds hearings next spring. The best way to do that is to find out what the military said about a base—and others like it—in past closure rounds.

"About 50 groups have come in this year alone asking us how the decisions are made and what they can do," says Tom Houston, the BRAC Commission's director. "Even in the off years it stays pretty busy." In the commission's cramped library in suburban Virginia, the hum of the copy machine never stops. People wait patiently in line, lugging stacks of heavy binders with marked pages, looking for clues to survive. Inside these four walls is every single document, transcript, or letter concerning the base closure process. Boxes full of comparisons and recommendations. Shelves stuffed with congressional letters and handwritten notes by BRAC Commission staff. One entire wall is obscured by documents from one service (the navy) from one year (1993). It is all public record, a peephole into the process. "The BRAC Commission is not your enemy," says Captain Peter Bowman, a retired navy officer who served on both the 1991 and 1993 panels. "It can be your best friend—if you know how to use it."

MYTH NO. 2: IF YOU'RE NOT ON THE HIT LIST, YOU'RE OUT OF THE WOODS

In 1993, on the day the Pentagon released its last list of recommended base closings, a sigh of relief arose from Plattsburgh, a community of 40,000 in upstate New York. The nearby air force base was not on it. In fact, the base was slated to double in size. "We were ecstatic," says Plattsburgh Mayor Clyde Rabideau. "Real estate boomed. Stores announced expansions. Everyone was walking on air, confident in our future." A few weeks later, it was as if all the air had been sucked out of Plattsburgh. The BRAC Commission voted to add the town's base to its list. "Just imagine our shock," Rabideau says. A shock, because many people do not realize there are *two* lists. One is put together by the Pentagon and released March 1. But that is only a recommendation for base closures that is reviewed by the BRAC Commission for mistakes or omissions. The commission can, and does, add similar bases to study for comparative purposes.

In 1991 the BRAC Commission looked at thirty-five additional bases not picked by the Pentagon but closed none of them. In 1993 it expanded the Pentagon's list by seventy-two—including Plattsburgh Air Force Base, which had fallen victim to a tactic popular among warring communities. Call it the "Don't take us, take them" defense. Plattsburgh became the target of two other air force bases on the chopping block: McGuire in New Jersey and Griffis, only 140 miles away from Plattsburgh in Rome, New York. "They were slinging mud like crazy, saying

terrible things about us," says Rick Dodge, who helped organize rallies in Plattsburgh. "Their mayor said something, our mayor said something. It got kind of personal." That was exactly what supporters of McGuire Air Force Base wanted: a civil war that would paralyze New York lawmakers by preventing them from taking sides. It worked. The commission closed both New York bases and kept McGuire. "We got screwed," Dodge says.

The same thing is expected to happen in 1995. If it does, Fort Carson may find itself in the same position Plattsburgh did. If another army base similar to Fort Carson—such as Fort Riley in Kansas—shows up on the Pentagon list, the BRAC Commission would probably add Colorado Springs's post and compare the two before deciding which to close. The BRAC Commission is urging communities to avoid smear campaigns this year. To discourage far-fetched arguments against other bases—there is a big hole in a competitor's runway, the land is a swamp, the port is filled with wreckage—Congress has ordered all testimony before the BRAC Commission to be under oath in 1995. Still, experts expect the rhetorical bombs to start flying soon after the Pentagon's list becomes public. "We can talk about doing this with dignity and decorum," says Steinberg, who has fought such battles for communities as a consultant. "But if you're talking about a community drying up without its base, the Marquess of Queensberry rules don't apply. It's going to be dirty, messy, and painful."

MYTH NO. 3: EMOTIONAL APPEALS SWAY THE COMMISSION

After the Pentagon hit list becomes public, the BRAC Commission begins visiting each major base recommended for closure and holds regional hearings where communities can tell their side of the story. Commissioners are often greeted by parades replete with fire trucks and pretty floats, signs professing undying support for the military, and auditoriums packed with patriots. Such passionate displays can tug at the hearts of commissioners, who, after all, are only human. But can it change their minds?

Jim Courter, BRAC Commission chairman in 1991 and 1993, remembers one man among ten thousand holding up a sign outside a threatened Georgia base: "You got the wrong base, baby. Uh-huh." That night he told U.S. Senator Sam Nunn (Democrat of Georgia) that sign took the prize. The next morning, a thousand people showed up at a hearing wearing T-shirts with the slogan. "It was impressive," Courter says.

Former commissioner Bob Stuart was deeply moved by what he saw in 1993 at K. I. Sawyer Air Force Base in Michigan, located in a struggling mining region that stood to lose $17 million if the base closed. "That one was particularly painful," Stuart says. "We arrived at night. Thousands of cars lined the road with lights blinking. I heard a chorus of 'Save our base.' They dumped 42,000 letters in our laps." The BRAC Commission closed the base anyway.

"I can't tell you we aren't moved by clever or poignant displays," says Houston. "It sticks in your mind. But the commissioners don't make up their minds in that moment. They do it much later, in the cold stillness of the hearing room. It is based on evidence, numbers, logic. Not emotion."

MYTH NO. 4: ALL CRITERIA ARE EQUAL

Most communities want to save their local base, not out of a sense of patriotism or national security. Rather, self-interest rules. Nobody wants to give up military payrolls. And the most common mistake community leaders make is thinking anybody cares. "You could not name a single community that wouldn't be economically hard hit by closure," says BRAC Commission director Houston. "So getting into a contest about who'll be worse off is simply a waste of time." Economic impact is among the eight criteria Congress ordered the military and the commission to consider before closing a base. But experts say it is one of the least important. The first four criteria, which deal with military value, are the ones that count. Unless there is a tie between two bases, those who have studied the BRAC Commission say, you can forget about the rest. Among them are return on investment, environmental impact, and community support.

"Military value is the heart and soul of the process," says Steinberg, the consultant. "The others are nice to talk about, easier to argue, but not what these base closure decisions are all about." Military value is determined by a complicated formula that weighs a base's strengths against its weaknesses. The army, for example, looks at such things as a base's location, its training land, proximity to docks or airports, and the opportunity to expand. Errors have been made. The Pentagon has in the past miscounted troops at bases and described acres of swamp as prime training land. In 1993 it rated Fort Carson as having the second-lowest quality of life among its eleven large maneuver bases—a conclusion that does not seem to fit with the fact that it is the most requested assignment among army officers. The burden of proof is on community leaders to convince the BRAC Commission there has been a mistake. "It's going to be an uphill fight because you need to convince us beyond any doubt the Pentagon made the wrong decision," Houston says. "But if you build an insurmountable case, and your base has extremely high military value, history has shown you can get off the list."

MYTH NO. 5: POLITICAL CLOUT CAN SAVE A BASE

Not so long ago, pork barrel politics had a lot to do with where the military set up shop. Military bases were the currency spread far and wide by the Pentagon to reward its friends in Congress. The common wisdom among voters is that a congres-sional powerhouse can save any base, as it has in the past. But most observers say the BRAC process has been surprisingly free—and often contemptuous—of congressional meddling. The BRAC Commission has shut down bases in half of the nation's fifty states, casting its net wide enough to snare even the most powerful of political kingfish. The list of losers is illustrative: Speaker of the House, Senate Majority Leader, ranking members of both armed services committees. Representative Ron Dellums of California, the Democratic chairman of the House Armed Services Committee, watched helplessly in 1993 as the naval installations in his district were sunk, taking ten thousand jobs down with them. California has lost more than one-fourth of its bases—nineteen in all. Yet Governor Pete Wilson is a close friend of past BRAC Commission chairman Courter.

"The most common misperception in the past has been that all you had to do was call up the governor or senator so-and-so and he'll take care of it," Courter says. "That's the way it used to be done. But it won't work anymore." Members of Congress may open a few doors and bend some ears, but they just cannot call the shots the way they used to. Congress is prevented from interfering because members cannot lobby to remove their hometown base from the BRAC Commission's hit list. They are only allowed to vote for or against the entire list. However, that does not stop lawmakers from bragging that they are doing everything possible to save their local base or taking unearned credit if it survives.

Whether it is Representative Joel Hefley (Republican of Colorado) calling a press conference outside Fort Carson's gate, or Representative Sonny Montgomery (Democrat of Mississippi) sitting in the front row at every public hearing of the 1993 BRAC Commission, it is mostly for show. The evidence is everywhere. Take, for example, Robert Dole of Kansas, the Senate's ranking Republican. Somebody with that kind of clout should be able to cut a deal to save a base in his state, right? "Let me tell you how significant Senator Dole thinks his clout with the commission will be in 1995," says Houston. Dole, he points out, is among a handful of senators who recently sponsored a bill that would have delayed the 1995 round of base closures. It went nowhere. "Does that," says Houston, "sound like someone with a great deal of confidence?"

MYTH NO. 6: THE MILITARY WON'T CLOSE A BASE IT'S PUMPING MONEY INTO

Some optimists in Colorado Springs draw comfort from the sound of hammers banging and bulldozers roaring over Fort Carson. Construction is under way on a $47 million complex for the 10th Special Forces Group, which began arriving at the post this summer. Combined with other new construction projects over the past six years—including an outdoor recreation center—the army will have invested $100 million in Fort Carson by next year. So a reasonable person might ask: the Pentagon would not flush all that down the toilet, would it? Sure it would.

Between 1988 and 1993 the military spent more than $1 billion on construction at bases that later were slated for closing. It has abandoned brand new commissaries, recently renovated barracks, and day-care centers. When it comes to waste, the navy wins hands down. Just look at the Staten Island Naval Station in New York. The brand new $300 million base was two-thirds finished in 1993 when the BRAC Commission ordered it closed. The army claims it is more careful, having poured only $71 million—10 percent of what the navy has spent—into bases that are being mothballed. "We try not to make stupid decisions for the taxpayer, or for us," says Colonel Bill Harvey, who is in charge of closing the army bases selected by the BRAC Commission.

The Pentagon says there is an intentional separation between those who decide which bases to close and those who order new construction, so as not to prejudice the BRAC process. But Harvey claims the army forwards its list of proposed construction contracts to the secretary of the army for review to make sure there is no reason to delay it. "So the army isn't going to start a big construction project at a place now that they're thinking about closing," he says.

That may bode well for Fort Carson, but it is no guarantee. "We try to do the best we can, but it's not a perfect system," Harvey says. "There are decisions out there waiting for us that we don't know about."

MYTH NO. 7: TRY HARD AND YOU'LL SUCCEED

If any community can brag it did everything right, it is Charleston, South Carolina. To preserve its naval installations in 1993, the city spent $1 million. It hired lawyers, public relations specialists, and a former navy captain-turned-lobbyist. In eighteen days, a group called In Defense of Charleston rounded up 140,000 signatures on petitions. The operation flooded the BRAC Commission with studies, and it choreographed a hard-hitting presentation that one commissioner called "the best I've ever seen." South Carolina's influential congressional delegation went to work, too. Senator Strom Thurmond used his seniority to take over as ranking Republican on the Senate Armed Services Committee. The state's other

senator, Democrat Ernest Hollings, a key member of the appropriations committee, reportedly took two BRAC commissioners out for tennis while they were in Charleston for a public hearing.

But all the intense lobbying did not help the city's bases. Each BRAC commissioner gave a long, heartfelt apology to the community. They acknowledged that Charleston had some fine naval facilities—then voted to close them, wiping away a third of the region's payroll. "It was simply redundant," commissioner Bob Stuart says. "We couldn't find another solution."

The Charleston effort was so impressive that Haidee Clark Stith of the South Carolina Department of Commerce was invited to share the lessons she learned at the recent base closure conference in Washington. Finally, one perspiring person in the crowd asked her the obvious question: if Charleston did such a good job at trying to dodge the heat of the BRAC process, why did it get burned? "You can do everything right and still end up with your base being closed," Stith says. "The reality is there are just too many bases, and even some good ones are going to go down."[1]

The BRAC Commission's director puts it more bluntly. "If we can close Charleston," Houston says, "there ain't nothing sacred anywhere." That may be hard to swallow for communities still dependent on the military of the past—the one with the fat checkbook that never ran dry. Nevertheless, if civic leaders went to the base closure conference looking for a magic bullet, they went home with a dose of realism: nobody can master this game. And amid all the myths of base closure, that is perhaps the most sobering reality.

NOTES

The history section was written by Jeff Thomas; the other sections were written by Genevieve Anton.

1. A total of 243 domestic military bases will eventually be closed as a result of the BRAC recommendations in 1991, 1993, and 1995. Through the end of 1995, the commission claims that its actions had already resulted in a savings of over $5 billion. The BRAC was disbanded following the 1995 round of closure recommendations. Fort Carson, Colorado, was not recommended for closure.

CHAPTER 11

FACTORS AFFECTING
DEFENSE POLICY MAKING

CRISIS, STRESS, AND DECISION MAKING

OLE R. HOLSTI

"What is relevant for policy" in times of crisis, according to Henry Kissinger, President Richard Nixon's principal foreign policy adviser, "depends not only on academic truths but also on what can be implemented under stress."[1] Observations by others who have experienced or studied international crises vary widely. Consider the following:

Hence, a decision-maker may, in a crisis, be able to invent or work out easily and quickly what seems in normal times to both the "academic" scholar and the layman to be hypothetical, unreal, complex or otherwise difficult.[2]

In every case, the decision [to go to war] is based upon a careful weighing of the chances and of anticipating consequences. . . . In no case is the decision precipitated by emotional tensions, sentimentality, crowd-behavior, or other irrational motivations.[3]

We have faith that man, who has been endowed with the wit to devise the means of his self-destruction, also has enough wit to keep those means under effective control.[4]

We create and enjoy crises. . . . Why? I don't know. I wish I knew. But all of us like them. I know I enjoy them. . . . There is a sense of elation that comes with crises.[5]

You see a poor, rather stupid fellow behind a desk and you wonder why he couldn't do better than that [in crisis situations]. Unfortunately, that picture comes up too often.[6]

I saw first-hand, during the long days and nights of the Cuban crisis, how brutally physical and mental fatigue can numb the good sense as well as the senses of normally articulate men.[7]

How *do* individuals and groups respond to the pressures and tensions of a crisis? Do we tend to approach such situations with high motivations, a keen sense of purpose, extraordinary energy, and enhanced creativity? Is necessity, as Herman Kahn suggests, the mother of invention? Or, is our capacity for coping with the problem impaired, perhaps even to the point suggested by Richard Neustadt's phrase, "the paranoid reaction characteristic of crisis behavior"?[8] When under intense pressure do we characteristically take the more cautious path, or are we more prone to taking high risks? Is our sense of what constitutes risk in any way altered?

CRISIS AND STRESS

The answers to these questions are always important for persons who find themselves faced with a crisis. They assume extraordinarily wide significance when the individuals are national leaders and the context is that of a contemporary international crisis: upon the ability of national leaders to cope with situations of intense stress may depend the lives of millions, if not the future of mankind. Despite the importance of these questions, many descriptive or prescriptive theories of international politics either ignore them or assume that the answers are self-evident. Consider, for instance, some of the basic premises of deterrence theories: that decisions by the nation to be deterred, as well as all others, will be based on dispassionate calculations of probable costs and gains, accurate evaluations of the situation, and careful assessments of relative capabilities: that the value hierarchies of national leaders are similar at least to the point that each places the avoidance of war at or near the top; and that all nations maintain tight centralized control over decisions that might involve or provoke the use of force.

Deterrence thus presupposes rational and predictable decision processes. No system of deterrence, however powerful the weapons, is likely to prove effective against a nation led by a trigger-happy paranoid, or by someone seeking personal or national self-destruction or martyrdom, or by decision makers willing to play a form of international Russian roulette, or by leaders whose information about and communication with an adversary are so incomplete that their decision-making processes are dominated by guesswork, or by those who regard the loss of most of their nation's population and resources as a reasonable cost for the achievement of foreign policy goals.

Clearly, the assumptions of deterrence are valid most of the time and under most circumstances, even in relations of considerable enmity such as "cold wars." Otherwise, we would be at war almost continuously. Most deterrence theories further assume, however, that threats and ultimata not only effectively influence an adversary's behavior but also enhance calculation, control, and caution while in-

---

This essay has been edited and is excerpted from Ole R. Holsti, Crisis, Escalation, War *(Montreal: McGill–Queen's University Press, 1972), 7–25, by permission of McGill–Queen's University Press.*

hibiting recklessness and risk taking. There may be a recognition that "the rationality upon which deterrence must be based is frangible,"[9] but there is also a tendency to assume that these rationalistic premises require little if any modification for crisis situations. Deterrence theorists, in short, tend to be sanguine about the ability of policy makers to be creative when the situation requires it—even when they are under stress.[10] To be sure, they often recognize some special features of crisis—for example, the difficulties of normal communication between adversaries.[11] But the lesson drawn from such examples is usually that lack of control over the situation may be used as a bargaining asset to force the adversary into a disadvantageous position, not only once, but in repeated encounters.

This is an oversimplified summary of the rich literature on deterrence. Nevertheless, there is a substantial element of truth in one critic's assertion that "the theory of deterrence . . . first proposes that we should frustrate our opponents by frightening them very badly and that we should then rely on their cool-headed rationality for our survival."[12]

The more general question is how crisis—defined here as *a situation of unanticipated threat to important values and restricted decision time*[13]—is likely to affect policy processes and outcomes. What are the probable effects of crisis upon abilities that are generally considered essential to effective decision making? These include the ability to

- Identify major alternative courses of action.

- Estimate the probable costs and gains of each alternative course.

- Resist premature cognitive closure.

- Distinguish between the possible and the probable.

- Assess the situation from the perspective of other parties.

- Discriminate between relevant and irrelevant information.

- Tolerate ambiguity.

- Resist premature action.

- Make adjustments to meet real changes in the situation (and, as a corollary, to distinguish real from apparent changes).

This list is by no means exhaustive.[14] Nor does it establish an unrealistic standard. It does, however, give us a checklist against which we can evaluate the probable consequences of stress on aspects of human performance relevant to foreign policy decisions.

The most important aspect of crises for our purposes is that these situations are characterized by high stress for the individuals and organizations involved. That a threat to important values is stress inducing requires little elaboration. The element of surprise is also a contributing factor; there is evidence that unanticipated and novel situations are generally viewed as more threatening.[15] Finally, crises are often marked by almost around-the-clock work schedules, owing to both the severity of the situation and the absence of extended decision time. During the Cuban missile confrontation, for instance, many American officials slept in their office for the duration of the crisis: "We had to go on a twenty-four hour basis here in the Department of State."[16] Premier Nikita Khrushchev also appears to have had little sleep during that week: "I must confess that I slept one night in my studio fully dressed on the sofa. I did not want to be in the position of one western diplomat who, during the Suez crisis, rushed to the telephone without his trousers."[17] Even during the much less intense Middle East situation created by the Six-Day War in 1967 the Soviet Politburo had at least one all-night meeting.[18] Lack of rest and excessively long working hours are likely to magnify the stresses inherent in the situation.

STRESS AND PERFORMANCE: THE EVIDENCE FROM PSYCHOLOGY

The central concern of this essay is to explore the possible consequences of crisis-induced stress on those aspects of individual and organizational performance that are most likely to affect the processes and outcomes of foreign-policy making. In this discussion stress is viewed as *the result of a situation that threatens important goals or values.* We shall measure stress by subjective responses to the situation rather than by attributes of the situation itself.

As a starting point we turn to the rich and voluminous body of theory and evidence from experimental psychology.[19] The advantages of precise measurement, easy replication, and tight control over the experimental variables have permitted psychologists to probe many aspects of human performance in various types of situations. Some emphasis is placed on the consequences of stress for the identification of alternatives and processes of choosing from among them, assessments of time factors, and patterns of communication. We also consider how time pressure, the number of perceived alternatives, and the volume of communications may affect the level of stress in a situation, and examine other relations between these variables—for example, between patterns of communications and identification of policy options. Theories and research on crises have generally demonstrated the importance of these variables.[20]

Some degree of stress is an integral and necessary precondition for individual or organizational problem solving; in its absence we lack any motivation to act. Low levels of pressure alert us to the presence of a situation requiring our attention, increase our vigilance and our preparedness to cope with it.[21] Increasing stress to moderate levels may heighten our propensity and ability to find a satisfactory solution to the problem. A study of research scientists has revealed, for example, that an environment of moderate stress, characterized by "uncertainty without anxiety," is the most conducive to creative work.[22] Indeed, for some elementary tasks a rather high degree of stress may increase performance, at least for limited periods of time. If the problem is qualitatively simple and performance is measured by quantitative criteria, stress can increase output. The threat of a severe flood may result in exceptional physical performance by emergency work crews who are filling and stacking sandbags, and a severe International crisis might give rise to improved output by foreign office clerical staffs.

Our present concern, however, is not with the effects of crisis on persons engaged in manual or clerical tasks, but with its consequences on the performance of top-ranking foreign policy officials. Foreign policy issues are nearly always marked by complexity, ambiguity, and the absence of stability; they usually demand responses which are judged by qualitative rather than quantitative criteria. It is precisely these qualitative aspects of performance that are most likely to suffer under high stress.[23]

Most research findings indicate a curvilinear relation between stress and the performance of individuals and groups. A moderate level of anxiety can be beneficial, but at higher levels it disrupts decision processes.[24] On the basis of a series of experiments, Herbert Birch determined that intermediate—rather than high or low motivation—was most conducive to the efficient solution of problems requiring both high and low insight. A related finding is that persons with moderate fear were better able to cope with the problems arising from major surgery than were those with high or low fear.[25] These results have been supported by other studies.[26] John Lanzetta, in an analysis of group behavior, found that "under increased stress there was a decrease in initiating behaviors, mainly in terms of 'diagnoses situation, makes interpretation' kinds of behavior; and an increase in more 'general discussions of the task' kind of behavior."[27] Following their analysis of the effects of stress on perception, Leo Postman and Jerome Bruner concluded: "Perceptual behavior is disrupted, becomes less well controlled than under normal conditions, and hence is less adaptive. The major dimensions of perceptual function are affected: selection of percepts from a complex field becomes less adequate and sense is less well differentiated from nonsense; there is maladaptive accentuation in the direction of aggression and escape; untested hypotheses are fixated recklessly."[28]

Other effects of stress that have been found in experimental research include increased random behavior; increased rate of error; regression to simpler and more primitive modes of response; problem-solving rigidity; diminished focus of attention, across both time and space; reduced ability to discriminate the dangerous from the trivial; diminished scope of complex perceptual activity; loss of abstract ability; disorientation of visual-motor coordination; and loss of complexity in the dimensions of political cognition.[29] A finding of special relevance for international crises is that tolerance for ambiguity is reduced when there is high stress. Under these conditions individuals made decisions before adequate information was available, with the result that they performed much less capably than those working under normal conditions. The combination of stress and uncertainty leads some persons to feel that "the worst would be better than this."[30]

To summarize, in situations of high stress "there is a narrowing of the cognitive organization at the moment; the individual loses broader perspective, he is no longer able to 'see' essential aspects of the situation and his behavior becomes, consequently, less adaptive."[31]

Some experimental studies have been criticized on both conceptual and methodological grounds, but the general conclusion that high stress inhibits rather than facilitates most aspects of human performance appears to be unassailable. Moreover, the capabilities that may be enhanced by moderate to high stress tend to have limited relevance in formulating foreign policy, whereas the skills that are inhibited under these conditions are usually crucial for such complex tasks.

A related aspect of international crises is the existence of time pressures that may become accentuated if either party believes that there are advantages to acting first. It should be pointed out that time pressure is not only a matter of clock time but also of the complexity and importance of the task to be accomplished. Given five minutes in which to choose between playing golf or mowing the lawn on Sunday, a person may feel no particular pressure, but a five-week deadline for deciding whether to change jobs may give rise to intense feelings of short decision time. Moreover, it is apparently the *perceptions* of time that are crucial: "The effects of a time limit appear to be due to perceived pressure rather than actual pressure brought on by an impossible time limit."[32]

Time perspectives are affected by high stress. For example, the ability to judge time is impaired in situations that increase anxiety.[33] Thus there appears to be a two-way relation between time and stress. On the one hand, the common use during crisis of such techniques as ultimata and threats with built-in deadlines is likely to increase the stress under which the recipient must operate. On the other hand, increasing levels of stress tend to heighten the salience of time and to distort judgments about it. It has been found in "real-life" crisis situations as well as experimentally that as danger increases there is a significant overestimation of how fast time is passing.[34] This suggests not only that short decision time distinguishes crises from other types of situations, but also that increasing stress will further heighten the salience of time.

Perceived time pressure may affect the search for alternatives in several ways. Foreign policy issues are rarely if ever analogous to the familiar multiple-choice question in which the universe of options is neatly outlined. The theoretically possible choices far exceed the number that can or will be considered. Especially in unanticipated situations such as crises, it is necessary to search out and perhaps create alternatives. A number of studies indicate that some time pressure can enhance creativity as well as the rate of performance, but most of the evidence suggests that beyond a moderate level it has adverse effects. Because complex tasks requiring feats of memory and inference suffer more from time pressure,[35] its effects on foreign policy decisions—which are usually marked by complexity—are likely to be particularly harmful. In such situations there is a tendency to fix upon a single approach, to continue using it whether or not it proves effective, and to hang on to familiar solutions, applying them even to problems that may be substantially different.[36]

Experimental research has shown that under severe time pressure normal subjects produce errors similar to those committed by schizophrenics. One study has revealed that, although a moderate increase in time pressure can increase the productivity of groups, an increase from low to high pressure has an adverse effect. N. H. Mackworth and J. F. Mackworth report that increasing the number of decisions required in a given period of time by a factor of five led to a fifteenfold rise in decision errors. There is, in addition, evidence that time pressure increases the propensity to rely upon stereotypes, disrupts both individual and group problem solving, narrows the focus of attention, and impedes the use of available information. Finally, short decision time tends to create early group agreement, thereby reducing incentives to search for and weigh other options.[37]

When decision time is short, the ability to estimate the range of possible consequences arising from a particular policy choice is likely to be impaired. There are several reasons why this should be so. Both experimental and field research indicate that severe stress is likely to give rise to a single-minded concern for the present and immediate future at the sacrifice of attention to longer-range considerations.[38] The uncertainties attending severe crisis make it exceptionally difficult to follow outcomes from a sequence of actions and responses very far into the future. Increasing stress also tends to narrow the focus of attention, thereby further limiting perceptions of time to the more immediate future. During the Korean war, for instance, it was observed that combat troops "cannot exercise complex functions involving the scanning of a large number of factors or long-term foresight because the stress is too massive and time too short for anything but the immediately relevant."[39] Moreover, if the present situation is perceived as extremely dangerous, the more distant future may appear to have little or no relevance unless a satisfactory solution can be found for the immediate problems. This may well be true, and placing a priority on the immediate often makes sense. After a drowning man has been pulled out of icy waters it would be foolish to take medical steps directed at warding off the longer-range dangers of pneumonia before giving artificial respiration to revive the victim.

There are also potential difficulties, however, in extreme concern for the immediate. Present actions alter future options, and decisions that provide immediate advantages may carry with them unduly heavy costs later. The price may be worth paying, but the balance sheet can scarcely be evaluated effectively if attention is fixed solely on the short-run benefits. There is also something seductively appealing about the belief that "if I can just solve the problem of the moment the future will take care of itself." This reasoning appears to have contributed to both Neville Chamberlain's actions during the Czech crisis of 1938 and to Lyndon Johnson's policies during the war in Vietnam.

Sustained time pressure may also give rise to significant changes in goals. The authors of a bargaining experiment concluded that "the meaning of time changed as time passed without the bargainers reaching an agreement. Initially the passage of time seemed to place the players under pressure to come to an agreement before their costs mounted sufficiently to destroy their profit. With the continued passage of time, however, their mounting losses strengthened their resolution not to yield to the other player. They comment: 'I've lost so much I'll be damned if I give in now. At least I'll have the satisfaction of doing better than she does.'"[40] This assertion and its underlying rationale are not unlike one of Kaiser Wilhelm's marginal notes, written when he finally recognized that his hopes of British neutrality in the rapidly approaching war were a delusion: "If we are to be bled to death, England shall at least lose India."[41]

The extent of the search for satisfactory solutions to a problem depends in part on the belief that the environment is benign and that such options in fact exist. But it is in the nature of crisis that most, if not all, policy alternatives are likely to be perceived as undesirable. The frying pan and the fire rather than Burian's ass (who starved to death when unable to choose between equally delectable bales of hay) is the appropriate metaphor for choices in an international crisis. As noted earlier, when stress increases, problem solving tends to become more rigid: the ability to improvise declines; previously established decision rules are adhered to more tenaciously, whether appropriate to the circumstances or not; and the ability to "resist the pull of closure" is reduced.[42] The evidence thus suggests the paradox that as the intensity of a crisis increases, creative policy making becomes both more important and less likely.

Identification of alternatives can also be related to the element of surprise in crises. Snyder has suggested that more options will be considered when the need for a decision is anticipated rather than suddenly imposed from without.[43] By the definition used here, crises are unanticipated, for at least one of the parties. Thus this attribute of the situation is itself likely to restrict inquiry and, as the crisis becomes more severe and stress increases, the search for options is likely to be further attenuated. In circumstances such as existed after the attack on Pearl Harbor we would not expect a lengthy review of potential responses by decision makers. Even during the Korean crisis of 1950, in which the situation was somewhat more ambiguous, only a single alternative course of action was considered: "The decision-making process in the Korean case was not characterized by the consideration of multiple alternatives at each stage. Rather a single proposed course of action emerged from the definition of the situation."[44]

The extreme situation occurs when only one course is perceived and the policy-making process is reduced to resigning oneself to the inevitable. If decision makers perceive that their options are reduced to only those with potentially high penalties—for example, "We have no alternative but to go to war"—considerable dissonance may be generated. The dissonance between what decision makers do (pursue policies that are known to carry a high risk of war) and what they know (that war can lead to disaster) can be reduced by absolving themselves from responsibility for the decision. This solution has been described by Leon Festinger: "It is possible, however, to reduce or even eliminate the dissonance by revoking the decision psychologically. This would consist of admitting to having made the wrong choice *or insisting that really no choice had been made for which the person had any responsibility.* Thus, a person who has just accepted a new job might immediately feel he had done the wrong thing and, if he had it to do over again, might do something different. Or he might persuade himself that *the choice had not been his; circumstances and his boss conspired to force the action on him.*"[45] This process may also be related to the widespread inability to perceive and appreciate the dilemmas and difficulties of others: "The grass is always greener on the other side of the fence." This has been noted with respect to the motives, general capabilities, and military strength ascribed to the adversary.[46]

One method of reducing dissonance is to believe that the only options that offer a way out of the dilemma rest with the opponent—only the other side can prevent the impending disaster. For example, during the frantic last-minute correspondence between the kaiser and the tsar, Wilhelm wrote: "The responsibility for the disaster which is now threatening the whole civilized world will not be laid at my door. In this moment it still lies in your [Nicholas] power to avert it."[47] Although it may at times be difficult to appreciate fully the dilemmas and difficulties of friends,[48] there is likely to be greater empathy with allies than with enemies. One way of coping with dissonance is to persuade oneself that the adversary is free from the very situational constraints that restrict the options available to self and allies.

What, finally, is the relation between crisis-induced stress, communication, and policy making? The adequacy of communication both in the physical sense of open channels of communication and in the sense of "pragmatics"—the correspondence between the sender's intent and the recipient's decod-ing—has been a major concern in studies of decision making. In this respect George Heise and George Miller have found that "the performance of a small group depends upon the channels of communication open to its members, the task which the group must handle, and the stress under which they work."[49]

Inadequate communication has received the greatest share of attention in crisis studies, with less concern for the effects of information overload.[50] Study of the latter appears to have been confined mostly to the laboratory rather than to historical situations. Yet information overload does appear to be an important consideration. The inception of a crisis usually gives rise to a sharply increased pace of individual and bureaucratic activities, virtually all of which are likely to increase the volume of diplomatic communication.

We noted earlier that high-stress situations tend to increase selective perception and to impair the ability to discriminate between sense and nonsense, the relevant and the irrelevant. Aside from the effects of stress, there are limits on our ability to process information. An experimental study of complex situations revealed that increased information loads resulted in fewer strategic integrated decisions and more unintegrated and simple retaliatory decisions.[51] As the volume of information directed at policy makers rises, the search for information within the communication system will tend to become less thorough, and selectivity in what is read, believed, and retained takes on increasing importance. Information that is unpleasant and that does not support preferences and expectations is most likely to fall by the wayside, unless it is of such an unambiguous nature that it cannot be disregarded. The experimental finding that selective filtering is often used at levels ranging from cells to human groups to cope with an unmanageable amount of information is apparently also valid for governmental organizations: "All Presidents, at least in modern times, have complained about their reading pile, and few have been able to cope with it. There is a temptation, consequently, to cut out all that is unpleasant."[52] Thus more communication may in fact result in less useful and valid information available to policy makers.

Although the volume of communication may rise during crises, the increase is likely to be uneven; there may be considerable disruption of communication with potential adversaries. In a simulation study, Richard Brody found that as perceived threat rose, the proportion of intra-alliance communication—as compared with interalliance messages—increased.[53] At the same time, both incoming and outgoing messages are likely to reflect increasingly simple and stereotyped assessments of the situation. If these expectations regarding changes, patterns, and content of communication in crisis are valid, the number of options that decision makers will consider is correspondingly restricted.

Certain other aspects of communications in a crisis may restrict the search for alternatives. There is a general tendency for a reduction in size of decision-making groups in such situations.[54] Technological and other factors have reduced decision time to a point where broad consultation with legislatures and other important groups may be virtually impossible. The limited membership of the "Excom," in which the decisions regarding missiles in Cuba were made, is a case in point. Decision groups in the crises concerning Korea (1950), Indochina (1954), Vietnam (1965), Cambodia (1970), and others were similarly restricted in size.[55]

There may be, moreover, a tendency to consult others less as the pressure of time increases, as well as to rely more heavily upon those who support the prevailing "wisdom." In his study of a governmental department, Dean Pruitt found a significant reduction in the number of people consulted by persons responsible for solving problems when time pressure increased.[56] One of the key decisions in the crisis leading up to World War I—the German decision to grant Vienna a blank check in support of the plan to punish Serbia—was made without any extended consultation.

On 5 July the Kaiser went for a stroll in the park at Potsdam with his chancellor, that bearded, sad-eyed giant Theobald von Bethmann-Hollweg, whom irreverent young officers called 'Lanky Theobald,' and Under-Secretary Zimmermann of the Foreign Office. By the time the walk was over, the Kaiser had made up his mind. Not another man had been consulted. The Foreign Minister was on his honeymoon and had not been recalled. The experienced, too subtle, too slippery ex-chancellor Bernhard von Bülow had not been called in. There in the park with Bethmann-Hollweg, whose judgment he despised, and Zimmermann, an official, the Kaiser reached his decision. He told the Austrian ambassador in Berlin that Germany would cover Austria should Russia intervene.[57]

Similarly, John Foster Dulles's decision to cancel a loan for the Aswan Dam, precipitating the 1956 Suez crisis, was made virtually on his own. He refused to consult with, much less accept the advice of, the American ambassador to Egypt, Henry Byroade, whose assessment of the situation—a correct one as it turned out—did not correspond to his own. During the months that followed Dulles's action, Anthony Eden believed that Nasser could not keep the Suez Canal open because European pilots would quit and there were no trained Egyptians to replace them. In contrast to the Norwegian government, which had learned from captains who had been through the canal that little training or skill was required to become a pilot, Eden made no effort to confirm or disconfirm his erroneous belief.[58]

Increasing stress may produce one potentially counteracting change in communication. In his studies of information overload, James Miller found that one of the widely used coping mechanisms is parallel channels of communication, particularly in higher-level systems such as groups or organizations, as opposed to cells, organs, or individuals.[59] Decision makers may seek to bypass both the effects of information input overload and of distortion of content in transmission by the use of improvised ad hoc channels of communication. These may take many forms, including direct communication between heads of governments and employment of special emissaries, or mediators.

It has been noted at various points that the rate of diplomatic and other activities tends to increase sharply during a crisis.[60] It remains to consider whether high stress increases risk taking, aggressiveness, and related aspects of foreign policy. Are we led to a position closely akin to the frustration-aggression hypotheses? The evidence is mixed. In some instances stress has resulted in higher risk taking; in other cases persons in such situations have become more cautious because they demanded greater certainty before committing themselves.[61] Assessments of what constitutes high and low risk may, however, change in circumstances of severe stress. During the tense days preceding the outbreak of World War I, many European statesmen came to believe that rapid mobilization of their armies was the "safe" choice, even though they may have recognized that doing so might be considered equivalent to an act of war. Or, to cite a more recent example, Dean Acheson, William Fulbright, and Richard Russell argued in October 1962 that President Kennedy's decision to blockade Cuba represented a far higher risk than their preferred strategy of bombing or invading to remove the Soviet missiles.

Thus high-stress situations may result in more aggressive policy choices, but the evidence presented here suggests a somewhat more complex process: crisis-induced stress gives rise to certain changes in perceptions of time, definition of alternatives, and patterns of communication. These, in turn, may reduce the effectiveness of both decision-making processes and the consequent policy choices, but not necessarily in the direction of higher risk taking.

It would be useful to specify the circumstances under which stress leads to aggression, appeasement, capitulation, attempts to withdraw from the situation, or other types of response. Unfortunately it is virtually impossible to do more than suggest some highly tentative hypotheses. For example, because stress often leads to a reduced ability to make fine distinctions, there may be a heightened tendency to see similarities between the present situation and previous events with which the decision makers have been associated. When faced with an intransigent Egypt in 1956, Anthony Eden drew an analogy between Nasser and Hitler. Harry Truman likewise saw a basic similarity between the Communist invasion of South Korea in 1950 and the expansion of other totalitarian systems during the 1930s. In these examples Eden and Truman drew upon the history of the 1930s—the period in which each reached national prominence—as a source of guidance, the latter far more successfully than the former.

A second very tentative hypothesis is that under conditions of high stress there will be a heightened tendency to maintain existing policies. This may appear to be a trite observation because there are always bureaucratic and other constraints that tend to act against sudden changes of policy. But because high-stress situations are often marked by reduced creativity and group pressures for conformity, we might suspect that only the presence of almost incontrovertible evidence of failure will give rise to substantial policy changes. It took the Nazi invasion of an already truncated Czechoslovakia in 1939 to cause Britain to abandon its conciliatory policy toward Hitler. Similarly, it was not until a conjunction of the Tet offensive, demands by General William Westmoreland for 206,000 additional troops in Vietnam, and evidence from the New Hampshire primary election of massive public dissatisfaction that a basic shift in American policy in Southeast Asia occurred. Note, however, that in the first example the change was from a policy of negotiation and conciliation toward a more aggressive stance, whereas the reverse was true of the second.

CONCLUSION

The evidence suggests that policy making under circumstances of crisis-induced stress is likely to differ in a number of respects from decision-making processes in other situations. More important, to the extent that such differences exist they are likely to inhibit rather than facilitate the effectiveness of those engaged in the complex tasks of making foreign policy choices.[62] Certainly this conclusion is consistent with the findings from experimental research.

While this literature is not lacking in empirical and quantitative findings, it is not wholly free from conceptual and operational problems. It cannot merely be assumed, for example, that results obtained with experimental subjects—usually students—are necessarily valid for persons of different age, culture, experience, and the like.[63] Nor is the usual technique of asking subjects to find the best answer to a problem or puzzle quite analogous to the task of the policy maker who may be confronted with a situation in which there is no single correct answer.

Perhaps an even more important question might be raised about the experimenter's ability to create a truly credible situation of high stress.[64] When human subjects are used the stress situation in the laboratory must of necessity be relatively benign and of short duration. It is usually induced by leading the subject to believe that he has failed at his assigned task. In contrast, a foreign policy official may perceive a crisis situation as a genuine threat to the continued existence of self, family, nation, or even mankind. Clearly, the ethical experimenter cannot create an identical situation in the laboratory.

In short, these experimental findings suggest some questions about the "conventional wisdom" underlying several aspects of strategy and diplomacy in crises. But the answers can only be found in the real world of international crises, not in the laboratory.

The crisis leading up to the outbreak of World War I in 1914 provides an almost ideal situation in which to assess the effects of stress on policy-making processes. As F. E. Horvath points out in discussing the limitations of experimental research, the knotty problem of defining stress operationally poses fewer difficulties when one studies a situation "which seems obviously stressful to most individuals."[65] Even a cursory reading of diaries, memoirs, and other eyewitness accounts of events during the culminating days of the crisis reveals the intense stress under which all European leaders were making foreign policy decisions. Admiral Alfred von Tirpitz wrote of his colleagues: "I have never seen a more tragic, more ravaged face than that of our Emperor during those days," and, "Since the Russian mobilization the Chancellor gave one the impression of a drowning man."[66] Walter Hines Page, the American ambassador in London, described even more vividly the effects of the crisis on Prince Lichnowsky: "I went to see the German Ambassador at 3 o'clock in the afternoon [August 5]. He came down in his pyjamas, a crazy man. I feared he might literally go mad. . . . the poor man had not slept for several nights."[67] Moreover, the rather widespread optimism about peace during the initial weeks after the assassination of the Austrian archduke, Franz Ferdinand, provides an opportunity to compare differences between circumstances of relatively high and low stress.

Nineteen fourteen is also an almost classic example of a diplomatic crisis that very rapidly escalated beyond the calculations and control of those responsible for making foreign policy decisions. This is not to say that in 1914 European nations were governed by monarchs, prime ministers, parliaments, and parties with a deep and unalterable devotion to peace. Nor is it to deny that competing imperial ambitions, trade rivalries, arms races, alliances, and rigid military plans may have been underlying sources of international instability; although these and many other attributes of the international system in 1914 were potent factors in shaping and constraining European diplomacy, the outbreak of war was the result of decisions that were made—or not made—by statesmen in Vienna, Belgrade, Berlin, St. Petersburg, Paris, and London. And the evidence indicates that general war in 1914 was not the goal of any European leaders, not even those who were willing to engage in diplomatic brinksmanship, or who sought the fruits of limited conflict, or who may have cherished long-range ambitions that could only be achieved by ultimate recourse to arms.[68] Finally, the documentation on the crisis probably surpasses in quality and quantity that of any comparable event in history. Thus the events of 1914 provide an exceptional opportunity for examining the effects of stress on selected aspects of policy making.

NOTES

1. Henry A. Kissinger, "Domestic Structure and Foreign Policy," in *International Politics and Foreign Policy,*

rev. ed., ed. James N. Rosenau (New York: Free Press, 1969), 265.

2. Herman Kahn, *On Escalation: Metaphors and Scenarios* (New York: Praeger, 1965), 38.

3. Theodore Abel, "The Element of Decision in the Pattern of War," *American Sociological Review* 6 (1941): 855.

4. John Foster Dulles, "The Problem of Disarmament," State Department Bulletin (Washington, D.C., 12 March 1956), 416.

5. Unidentified diplomat, quoted in Chris Argyris, *Some Causes of Organizational Ineffectiveness within the Department of State,* Department of State Publication 8180 (Washington, D.C.: Center for International Systems Research, 1967), 42.

6. Dwight D. Eisenhower, Address to *Washington Post* Book and Author Lunch, quoted in *Palo Alto Times,* 1 October 1965.

7. Theodore C. Sorensen, *Decision-Making in the White House* (New York: Columbia University Press, 1964), 76.

8. Richard E. Neustadt, *Alliance Politics* (New York: Columbia University Press, 1970), 116.

9. Bernard Brodie, quoted in Philip Green, *Deadly Logic: The Theory of Nuclear Deterrence* (New York: Schocken Books, 1966), 159.

10. See, for example, Thomas C. Schelling, *Arms and Influence* (New Haven: Yale University Press, 1966), 96; Kahn, *On Escalation,* 37–38; and Albert Wohlstetter and Roberta Wohlstetter, *Controlling the Risks in Cuba,* Adelphi Paper no. 17 (London: Institute of Strategic Studies, April 1965). This assumption has been valid in a number of important instances, including the Cuban missile crisis.

11. See especially Thomas C. Schelling, *The Strategy of Conflict* (Cambridge, Mass.: Harvard University Press, 1960).

12. Karl Deutsch, *The Nerves of Government* (New York: Free Press, 1963), 70.

13. This definition of crisis is taken from Charles F. Hermann, "Some Consequences of Crisis Which Limit the Viability of Organizations," *Administrative Science Quarterly* 8 (1963): 61–82. For extensive critical reviews of these, see Charles F. Hermann, *Crises in Foreign Policy* (Indianapolis: Bobs-Merrill, 1969); James A. Robinson, "Crisis: An Appraisal of Concepts and Theories," in *Contemporary Research in International Crisis,* ed. Charles F. Hermann (New York: Free Press, forthcoming); and Kent Miller and Ira Iscoe, "The Concept of Crisis: Current Status and Mental Health Implications," *Human Organization* 22 (1963): 195–201.

14. For a much more demanding list, see J. David Singer and Paul Ray, "Decision-Making in Conflict: From Inter-Personal to International Relations," *Bulletin of the Menninger Clinic* 30 (1966): 303. The literature on the limits of rationality in decision making is extensive. See, for example, Herbert A. Simon, *Administrative Behavior* (New York: Macmillan, 1957); James G. March and Herbert A. Simon, *Organizations* (New York: John Wiley and Sons, 1958); and Richard C. Snyder, H. W. Bruck, and Burton M. Sapin, *Foreign Policy Decision Making* (New York: Free Press, 1962).

15. Sheldon J. Korchin and Seymour Levine, "Anxiety and Verbal Learning," *Journal of Abnormal and Social Psychology* 54 (1957): 238.

16. Dean Rusk, "Interview of Secretary Rusk by David Schoenbrun of CBS News," in David Larson, *The "Cuban Crisis" of 1962* (Boston: Houghton Mifflin, 1963), 268.

17. Quoted in *New York Times,* 27 June 1967.

18. *San Francisco Chronicle,* 9 June 1967.

19. It should be noted that there is a lack of consensus on operational measures of stress among authors of the studies reviewed here. Some define it as the stimulus (e.g., a severe threat), whereas others view it as the perceptual and behavioral response to threat. We adopt the latter position, but the review here is not restricted to any single measure of stress. For further discussions, see Raymond B. Cattell and Ivan H. Scheier, "Stimuli Related to Stress, Neuroticism, Excitation, and Anxiety Response Patterns," *Journal of Abnormal and Social Psychology* 60 (1960): 195–204; Richard S. Lazarus, *Psychological Stress and the Coping Process* (New York: McGraw-Hill, 1966); and Margaret G. Hermann, "Testing a Model of Psychological Stress," *Journal of Personality* 34 (1966): 381–96.

20. See the studies cited in note 13, as well as Michael Haas, "Communication Factors in Decision Making," *Peace Research Society (International) Papers* 12 (1969): 65–86.

21. Some research findings indicate that just as "some degree of stress in infancy is necessary for the development of normal, adaptive, behavior, so the information we now have on the operation of the pituitary-adrenal system indicates that in many situations effective behavior in adult life may depend on exposure to some optimal level of stress." Seymour Levine, "Stress and Behavior," *Scientific American* 224 (January 1971): 26–31.

22. Cited in Kurt Back, "Decisions under Uncertainty: Rational, Irrational, and Non-rational," *American Behavioral Scientist* 4 (February 1961): 14–19. But in at least one study it was found that even mild stress interfered with problem solving. Wilbert S. Ray, "Mild Stress and Problem Solving," *American Journal of Psychology* 78 (1965): 227–34. Unless a specific study is cited, I have relied on two extensive reviews of the literature: Richard S. Lazarus, James Deese, and Sonia F. Osler, "The Effects of Psychological Stress upon Performance," *Psychological Bulletin* IL (1952): 293–317; and F. E. Horvath, "Psychological Stress: A Review of Definitions and Experimental Research," in L. von Bertalanffy and Anatol Rapoport, *General Systems Yearbook* (Ann Arbor: Society for General Systems Research, 1959).

23. Alfred Lowe, "Individual Differences in Reaction to Failure: Modes of Coping with Anxiety and Interference Proneness," *Journal of Abnormal and Social Psychology* 62 (1961): 303–8; Sara B. Kiesler, "Stress, Affiliation and Performance," *Journal of Experimental Research in Personality* 1 (1966): 227–35.

24. S. J. Korchin and others, "Visual Discrimination and the Decision Process in Anxiety," *AMA Archive of Neurology and Psychiatry* 78 (1957): 424–38; Robert E. Murphy, "Effects of Threat of Shock, Distraction, and Task Design on Performance," *Journal of Experimental Psychology* 58 (1959): 134–41; and Harold M. Schroder, Michael J. Driver, and Siegfried Streufert, *Human Information Processing* (New York: Holt, Rinehart and Winston, 1967), chap. 7.

25. Irving Janis, *Psychological Stress* (New York: John Wiley and Sons, 1958).

26. Herbert G. Birch, "Motivational Factors in Insightful Problem-Solving," *Journal of Comparative Psychology* 37 (1945): 295–317; and R. M. Yerkes, "Modes of Behavioral Adaptation in Chimpanzee to Multiple Choice Problems," *Comparative Psychological Monographs* 10 (1934): 1–108.

27. John T. Lanzetta, "Group Behavior under Stress," *Human Relations* 8 (1955): 47–48.

28. Leo Postman and Jerome S. Brunner, "Perception under Stress," *Psychological Review* 55 (1948): 322.

29. E. Paul Torrance, "The Behavior of Small Groups under Stress Conditions of 'Survival,'" *American Sociological Review* 19 (1954): 751–55; Sheldon J. Korchin, "Anxiety and Cognition," in *Cognition: Theory, Research, Promise,* ed. Constance Sheerer (New York: Harper and Row, 1964), 67; H. Kohn, cited in Enoch Callaway and Donald Dembo, "Narrowed Attention," *AMA Archive of Neurology and Psychiatry* 79 (1958): 85; L. T. Katchmas, S. Ross, and T. G. Andrews, "The Effects of Stress and Anxiety on Performance of a Complex Verbal-Coding Task," *Journal of Experimental Psychology* 85 (1958): 562; Ernst G. Beier, "The Effects of Induced Anxiety on Flexibility of Intellectual Functioning," *Psychological Monographs* 65 (1951): whole no. 326, 19; and Charles E. Osgood, G. J. Suci, and Percy H. Tannenbaum, *The Measurement of Meaning* (Urbana: University of Illinois Press, 1957).

30. C. D. Smock, "The Influence of Psychological Stress on the 'Intolerance of Ambiguity,'" *Journal of Abnormal and Social Psychology* 50 (1955): 177–82; and B. B. Hudson, quoted in Stephen B. Withey, "Reaction to Uncertain Threat," in *Man and Society in Disaster,* ed. George W. Baker and Dwight W. Chapman (New York: Basic Books, 1962), 118.

31. D. Krech and R. S. Crutchfield, quoted in Korchin, "Anxiety and Cognition," 63.

32. Roland L. Frye and Thomas M. Stritch, "Effects of Timed vs. Non-timed Discussion upon Measures of Influence and Change in Small Groups," *Journal of Social Psychology* 63 (1964): 139–43. For an intriguing discussion of "subjective time," see John Cohen, "Psychological Time," *Scientific American* (November 1964): 116–24.

33. Samuel I. Cohen and A. G. Mezey, "The Effects of Anxiety on Time Judgment and Time Experience in Normal Persons," *Journal of Neurology, Neurosurgery and Psychiatry* 24 (1961): 266–68.

34. Harry B. Williams and Jeannette F. Rayner, "Emergency Medical Services in Disaster," *Medical Annals of the District of Columbia* 25 (1956): 661; and Jonas Langer, Seymour Wapner, and Heinz Werner, "The Effects of Danger upon the Experience of Time," *American Journal of Psychology* 74 (1961): 94–97.

35. Jerome Bruner, Jacqueline J. Goodnow, and George A. Austin, *A Study of Thinking* (New York: John Wiley and Sons, 1956), 147.

36. Abraham S. Luchins, "Mechanization in Problem-Solving," *Psychological Monographs* 54 (1942): whole no. 248; and John Steinbruner, "The M.L.F.: A Case Study in Decision-Making" (Ph.D. diss., MIT, 1969).

37. George Usdansky and Loren J. Chapman, "Schizophrenic-like Response in Normal Subjects under time Pressure," *Journal of Abnormal and Social Psychology* 60 (1960): 143–46; Pauline N. Pepinsky and William B. Pavlik,

"The Effects of Task Complexity and Time Pressure upon Team Productivity," *Journal of Applied Psychology* 64 (1960): 34–38; N. H. Mackworth and J. F. Mackworth, "Visual Search for Successive Decisions," *British Journal of Psychology* 49 (1958): 210–21; Birch, "Motivational Factors"; Bruner, Goodnow, and Austin, *Study of Thinking;* Peter Dubno, "Decision Time Characteristics of Leaders and Group Problem Solving Behavior," *Journal of Social Psychology* 54 (1964): 259–82; Horvath, "Psychological Stress"; Donald R. Hoffeld and S. Carolyn Kent, "Decision Time and Information Use in Choice Situations," *Psychological Reports* 12 (1963): 68–70; and Frye and Stritch, "Effects of Timed vs. Non-timed Discussion."

38. Robert J. Alberts, "Anxiety and Time Perspectives," *Dissertation Abstracts* 26 (1966): 4848; James D. Thompson and Robert W. Hawkes, "Disaster, Community Organization, and Administrative Process," 283.

39. David Rioch, quoted in Korchin, "Anxiety and Cognition," 63.

40. Morton Deutsch and Robert M. Krauss, "The Effects of Threat upon Interpersonal Bargaining," *Journal of Abnormal and Social Psychology* 61 (1960): 189.

41. Max Montgelas and Walther Schücking, eds., *Outbreak of the War, German Documents Collected by Karl Kautsky* (New York: Oxford University Press, 1924), 401.

42. Korchin, "Anxiety and Cognition," 65–67; J. W. Moffitt and Ross Stagnher, "Perceptual Rigidity and Closure as a Function of Anxiety," *Journal of Abnormal and Social Psychology* 52 (1956): 355; S. Pally, "Cognitive Rigidity as a Function of Threat," *Journal of Personality* 23 (1955): 346–55; Sheldon J. Korchin and Harold Basowitz, "Perceptual Adequacy in Life Stress," *Journal of Psychology* 38 (1954): 501.

43. Richard C. Snyder, *Deterrence, Weapons and Decision-Making* (China Lake, Calif.: U.S. Naval Ordnance Test Station, 1961), 80.

44. Richard C. Snyder and Glenn D. Paige, "The United Nations Decision to Resist Aggression in Korea: The Application of an Analytical Scheme," *Administrative Science Quarterly* 3 (1958): 245; and Glenn D. Paige, *The Korean Decision* (New York: Free Press, 1968). See also March and Simon, *Organizations*. 154 ff.

45. Leon Festinger, *A Theory of Cognitive Dissonance* (Evanston: Row, Peterson, 1957), 43–44. Italics added.

46. See, for example, Kenneth Boulding, "National Images and International Systems," *Journal of Conflict Resolution* 3 (1961): 223–29; and Samuel F. Huntington, "Arms Races," in *Public Policy, 1958,* ed. Carl Friedrich and Seymour Harris (Cambridge, Mass.: Harvard University Press, 1958).

47. Montgelas and Schücking, *Outbreak of the World War,* 480.

48. Ole R. Holsti and Robert C. North, "The History of Human Conflict," in *The Nature of Human Conflict,* ed. Elton B. McNeil (Englewood Cliffs, N.J.: Prentice-Hall, 1965), 165–66.

49. George A. Heise and George A. Miller, "Problem Solving by Small Groups Using Various Communication Nets," *Journal of Abnormal and Social Psychology* 46 (1951): 335.

50. For exceptions, see Charles F. Hermann, "Some Consequences of Crisis Which Limit the Viability of Orga-

nizations," *Administrative Science Quarterly* 8 (1963): 61–82; James G. Miller, "Information Input Overload and Psychopathology," *American Journal of Psychiatry* 116 (1960): 694–704; and Harry B. Williams, "Some Functions of Communication in Crisis Behavior," *Human Organization* 16 (1957): 15–19.

51. Siegfried Streufert, Michael J. Driver, and Kenneth W. Haun, "Components of Response Rate in Complex Decision-Making," *Journal of Social Psychology* 3 (1967): 286–95. See also George A. Miller, "The Magical Number Seven Plus or Minus Two: Some Limits on Our Capacity for Processing Information," *Psychological Review* 63 (1956): 81–97.

52. Sorensen, *Decision-Making in the White House*, 38. See also, James G. Miller, "Information Input Overload and Psychopathology," *American Journal of Psychiatry* 116 (1960): 695–704. Theories of selective exposure to information are in dispute among psychologists, but they appear to fare better in field research than in the laboratory. See William J. McGuire, "Selective Exposure: A Summing Up," in *Theories of Cognitive Consistency*, ed. Robert P. Abelson (Chicago: Rand McNally, 1968), 797–800.

53. Richard A. Brody, "Some Systemic Effects of the Spread of Nuclear Weapons Technology: A Study through Simulation of a Multi-Nuclear Future," *Journal of Conflict Resolution* 7 (1963): 663–753.

54. This consequence of crisis may, however, actually improve some aspects of policy making: "The greater the emergency, the more likely is decision-making to be concentrated among high officials whose commitments are to the overall system. Thus it may be, paradoxically, that the model of means-ends rationality will be more closely approximated in an emergency when the time for careful deliberation is limited. Though fewer alternatives will be considered the values invoked during the decision period will tend to be fewer and more consistent, and decisions will less likely be the result of bargaining within a coalition." Sidney Verba, "Assumptions of Rationality and Non-rationality in Models of the International System," *World Politics* 14 (1961): 115. A more general argument along the same lines appears in Theodore J. Lowi, *The End of Liberalism: Ideology, Policy, and the Crisis of Public Authority* (New York: W. W. Norton, 1969), 158–60.

55. Snyder and Paige, "The United States Decision," 341–78; Glenn D. Paige, *The Korean Decision* (New York: Free Press, 1968); C. M. Roberts, "The Day We Didn't Go to War," *Reporter*, 14 September 1954; Hedrick Smith, "Cambodian Decision: Why President Acted," *New York Times*, 30 June 1970, 1, 14; Townsend Hoopes, *The Limits of Intervention* (New York: David McKay, 1969); and David R. Maxey, "How Nixon Decided to Invade Cambodia," *Look*, 11 August 1970.

56. Dean G. Pruitt, "Problem Solving in the Department of State" (Unpublished paper, Northwestern University, 1961), cited in Hermann, "Some Consequences of Crisis."

57. George M. Thomason, *The Twelve Days: July 24 to August 4, 1914* (New York: G. P. Putnam's Sons, 1964), 44–45.

58. This example was suggested by Robert Jervis.

59. James G. Miller, "Information Input Overload," *Self Organizing Systems—1962* (n.p.).

60. Paul Smoker, "Sino-Indian Relations: A Study of Trade, Communication and Defence," *Journal of Peace Research*, no. 2 (1964): 65–76.

61. Amia Lieblich, "Effects of Stress on Risk Taking," *Psychonomic Science* 10 (1968): 303–4; Korchin and Levine, "Anxiety and Verbal Learning," 238; Leonard Berkowitz, "Repeated Frustration and Expectations in Hostility Arousal," *Journal of Abnormal and Social Psychology* 60 (1960): 422–29; and Bruce Dohrenwend, "The Social Psychological Nature of Stress," *Journal of Abnormal and Social Psychology* 62 (1961): 294–302.

62. An alternative view is that "decision-makers do not perceive or behave differently in a crisis." That is, "they do not perceive hostility where none exists, and they express hostility directly in terms of their perception of hostility." Dina A. Zinnes, Joseph Zinnes, and R. D. McClure "Hostility in Diplomatic Communication: A Study of the 1914 Crisis," in *Contemporary Research in International Crisis*, ed. Charles F. Hermann (New York: Free Press, 1972). This does not demonstrate, however, that many other aspects of perception and behavior may not change in crisis situations. Moreover, their conclusion does not rule out the possibility that mutual perceptions of hostility may be sustained and magnified beyond their original causes.

63. Nor, of course, can it be assumed that they are *not* valid, or that the *converse* of the experimental findings are true.

64. For a further development of this point, see Horvath, "Psychological Stress"; and the pertinent observations about crisis "gaming" in Bernard Brodie, *Escalation and the Nuclear Option* (Princeton, N.J.: Princeton University Press, 1966), 37–39.

65. Horvath, "Psychological Stress," 208.

66. Alfred von Tirpitz, *My Memoirs* (London: Hurst and Blackett, 1919), 279, 280. For dramatic evidence of the consequences of protracted stress, see also the kaiser's marginal notes during the crisis.

67. Quoted in Luigi Albertini, *The Origins of the War of 1914*, vol. 3 (New York: Oxford University Press, 1953), 501.

68. Fritz Fischer has demonstrated that German war aims, as they developed during 1914–18, were imperialistic. No doubt the goals of other belligerents also expanded during the war, if only to justify the dreadful costs of the conflict. But I find quite unconvincing his severe indictment of German intentions during the *prewar* crisis. Fritz Fischer, *Germany's Aims in the First World War* (New York: W. W. Norton, 1967), chap. 2.

THE GROUPTHINK SYNDROME

IRVING L. JANIS

The first step in developing a theory about the causes and consequences of groupthink is to anchor the concept of groupthink in observables by describing the symptoms to which it refers.

SYMPTOMS OF GROUPTHINK

Eight main symptoms run through case studies of historic fiascoes and are seldom present in case studies of the nongroupthink decisions. Each symptom can be identified by a variety of indicators, derived from historical records, observers' accounts of conversations, and participants' memoirs. The eight symptoms of groupthink include group products and processes that reinforce each other. The symptoms can be divided into three main types, which are familiar features of many (although not all) cohesive groups observed in research on group dynamics.

TYPE I: OVERESTIMATIONS OF THE GROUP— ITS POWER AND MORALITY

1. An illusion of invulnerability, shared by most or all the members, which creates excessive optimism and encourages taking extreme risks.

2. An unquestioned belief in the group's inherent morality, inclining the members to ignore the ethical or moral consequences of their decisions.

TYPE II: CLOSED-MINDEDNESS

3. Collective efforts to rationalize in order to discount warnings or other information that might lead the members to reconsider their assumptions before they recommit themselves to their past policy decisions.

4. Stereotyped views of enemy leaders as too evil to warrant genuine attempts to negotiate, or as too weak and stupid to counter whatever risky attempts are made to defeat their purposes.

TYPE III: PRESSURES TOWARD UNIFORMITY

5. Self-censorship of deviations from the apparent group consensus, reflecting each member's inclination to minimize to himself the importance of his doubts and counterarguments.

6. A shared illusion of unanimity concerning judgments conforming to the majority view (partly resulting from self-censorship of deviations, augmented by the false assumption that silence means consent).

7. Direct pressure on any member who expresses strong arguments against any of the group's stereotypes, illusions, or commitments, making clear that this type of dissent is contrary to what is expected of all loyal members.

8. The emergence of self-appointed mindguards—members who protect the group from adverse information that might shatter their shared complacency about the effectiveness and morality of their decisions.

CONSEQUENCES

When a policy-making group displays most or all of the symptoms in each of the three categories, the members perform their collective tasks ineffectively and are likely to fail to attain their collective objectives as a result of concurrence seeking. In rare instances, concurrence seeking may have predominantly positive effects for their members and their enterprises. For example, it may make a crucial contribution to maintaining morale after a defeat and to muddling through a crisis when prospects for a successful outcome look bleak. But the positive effects are generally outweighed by the poor quality of the group's decision making. My assumption is that the more frequently a group displays the symptoms, the worse will be the quality of its decisions, on the average. Even when some symptoms are absent, the others may be so pronounced that we can expect all the unfortunate consequences of groupthink.

To be more specific, whenever a policy-making group displays most of the symptoms of groupthink, we can expect to find that the group also displays symptoms of defective decision making. Seven such symptoms are listed on the basis of prior research on decision making in government, industry, and other large organizations:

1. Incomplete survey of alternatives

This essay has been edited and is excerpted from Irving Janis, Groupthink: Psychological Studies of Policy Decisions and Fiascoes, *2d ed. (Boston: Houghton Mifflin Co., 1982), 174–97, by permission of Houghton Mifflin Company. Copyright © 1982.*

2. Incomplete survey of objectives

3. Failure to examine risks of preferred choice

4. Failure to reappraise initially rejected alternatives

5. Poor information search

6. Selective bias in processing information at hand

7. Failure to work out contingency plans.

A study by Philip Tetlock indicates that among the politically relevant consequences is the relatively poor quality of the thinking that goes into the public statements made by national leaders when they announce and try to explain policy decisions that are the products of groupthink. Tetlock did a comparative study of groupthink and nongroupthink decisions, using systematic content analysis techniques to assess the quality of thinking in public speeches made by the president of the United States or the secretary of state. For the sample of groupthink decisions, he found significantly lower scores on cognitive complexity than for the nongroupthink decisions, indicating more simplistic thinking about the issues.

ANTECEDENT CONDITIONS

In addition to stating the expected observable consequences, an adequate theory of groupthink must also specify the observable *causes*—that is, the antecedent conditions that produce, elicit, or facilitate the occurrence of the syndrome. A number of such antecedent conditions have been singled out by making inferences from case studies, which take account of findings from prior research on group dynamics. One major condition has to do with the degree of cohesiveness of the group. We would not expect to find the groupthink syndrome if the members dislike each other and do not value their membership in the group. Any such group that lacks cohesiveness is likely to display symptoms of defective decision making, especially if the members are engaging in internal warfare. But groupthink is not ever likely to be the cause of their poor decision making. Only when a group of policy makers is moderately or highly cohesive can we expect the groupthink syndrome to emerge as the members are working collectively on one or another of their important policy decisions. Even so, the symptoms of groupthink are unlikely to occur to such an extent that they interfere with effective decision making *unless certain additional antecedent conditions are also present.*

What are those additional conditions? Two of them pertain to administrative or structural features of the policy makers' organization. One condition involves *insulation of the policy-making group,* which provides no opportunity for the members to obtain expert information and critical evaluation from others within the organization. A second feature is *lack of a tradition of impartial leadership.* In the absence of appropriate leadership traditions, the leader of a policy-making group will find it all too easy to use his or her power and prestige to influence the members of the group to approve of the policy alternative he or she prefers instead of encouraging them to engage in open inquiry and critical evaluation. A third administrative or structural factor can also be inferred by comparing the conditions that prevailed during groupthink decisions with those during nongroupthink decisions: *the lack of norms requiring methodical procedures for dealing with the decision-making tasks.*

All three of the administrative or structural conditions can be regarded as factors that facilitate the occurrence of the groupthink syndrome; they involve lack of constraints on collective uncritical thinking. Insofar as they are long-standing features of the organization, each of the three conditions can be ascertained *before* the members of a policy-making group start their deliberations on whatever policy decision is under investigation. I mention this because it is pertinent to the question of whether the groupthink syndrome can be predicted in advance. My answer is that by ascertaining the presence of one or more of the three structural conditions as well as the level of group cohesiveness of the policy-making group (which can also be rated *before* the deliberations begin), such predictions can be made. If the predictions are confirmed in future studies on policy-making groups, we shall be able to conclude that the foregoing analysis of causal factors that lead to the groupthink syndrome is substantiated by empirical evidence.

HOW WIDESPREAD IS THE GROUPTHINK SYNDROME?

At present we do not know what percentage of all major fiascoes are attributable to groupthink. Some decisions of poor quality that turn out to be fiascoes might be ascribed primarily to mistakes made by just one man, the chief executive. Others arise because of a faulty policy formulated by a group of executives whose decision-making procedures were impaired by errors having little or nothing to do with groupthink. For example, a noncohesive committee may be made up of bickering factions so intent on fighting for political power within the government bureaucracy that the participants have little interest in examining the real issues posed by the foreign policy question they are debating; they may settle for a compromise that fails to take account of adverse effects on people outside their own political arena.

All that can be said from historical case studies is that the groupthink syndrome sometimes plays a major role in producing large-scale fiascoes. In order to estimate how large the percentage might be for various types of decision-making groups, we need investigations of a variety of policy decisions made by groups of executives who have grossly miscalculated the unfavorable consequences of their chosen courses of action. Such investigations should also provide comparative results that are valuable for helping to determine the conditions that promote groupthink.

GROUPTHINK VERSUS OTHER CAUSES OF MISCALCULATION

When carrying out an analysis of any defective policy decision, examine the available evidence carefully in order to answer a series of key questions before drawing any conclusion as to whether the groupthink syndrome provides at least part of the explanation for whatever errors were made. Obviously, one cannot assume that groupthink is the cause of practically all policy miscalculations and fiascoes. Anyone who relies on that naive assumption in preparing a case study would be carrying out a worthless exercise in unadulterated hindsight. A groupthink analysis of the Watergate cover-up or any other policy that has ended up as a fiasco could be discarded on the basis of the following devastating criticism: knowing in advance how bad the outcome was, the author simply assumed that it must be because the policy makers did a poor job; he also assumed that any poorly made decision (if more than one person was involved) must have been due to groupthink. So the author searched selectively for anecdotes that could be construed as illustrating the symptoms of groupthink. And behold!—he detected groupthink as the cause of the fiasco.

There is, however, a genuine problem of hindsight in analyzing case studies. Research by Baruch Fischhoff and others shows that "people consistently overestimate the predictability of past events once they know how they turned out." When one looks at fiascoes of the past, as Dostoyevsky pithily put it, "everything seems stupid when it fails." That is why I believe that one must examine all the available evidence bearing on each fiasco to see if it really was the product of stupidity, and if so, whether groupthink contributed to it.

In order to minimize psychological tendencies to indulge in hindsight and to find what one is looking for in case study material, I propose that the investigator should go through the somewhat tedious process of structuring the inquiry. It requires examining the facts carefully in order to answer the following series of four key questions before concluding that groupthink was a contributory cause of any fiasco:

1. Who made the policy decisions? Was it essentially the leader alone or did *group* members participate to a significant degree? If the members participated, were they in a *cohesive* group?

2. To what extent was the policy a result of *defective decision-making procedures* on the part of those who were responsible?

3. Can *symptoms of groupthink* be discerned in the group's deliberations? (Do the prime symptoms pervade the planning discussions?)

4. Were the *conditions* that foster the groupthink syndrome present?

There is also another question, which is intended to see if something new can be learned: if the answers to the four questions above are positive, can any leads be detected that suggest *new hypotheses* concerning the *conditions* that promote groupthink?

In examining case material for the purpose of answering the key questions, it is essential to seek evidence enabling one to make discriminations that separate facts from myths about how decisions are actually made. In America, according to traditional political doctrine, the president has sole responsibility for every decision authorized by the executive branch. This doctrine pertains to the accountability of the president, but it is often misunderstood as describing who actually made the decision. The doctrine places responsibility on President Dwight Eisenhower for the erroneous decision to send U-2 spy planes over the Soviet Union even though he was not even informed about them by the Pentagon until after he had publicly denied that the United States had launched any such flights. President Harry Truman, according to the doctrine, had sole responsibility for the Korean War decisions even though he was highly responsive to his advisers' recommendations and on at least one important decision was induced to change his mind completely. (It will be recalled that Truman had wanted to accept Chiang Kai-shek's offer to send Chinese Nationalist troops to Korea but was talked out of it by members of his inner circle.) John F. Kennedy reinforced the traditional doctrine by publicly assuming full responsibility for the Bay of Pigs fiasco. Nevertheless, his advisers knew that they shared the responsibility, and some of them acknowledged feeling personally humiliated. The known facts about how these decisions were arrived at certainly do not correspond to the myth stemming from the traditional doctrine of accountability.

The reverse situation must also be expected, perhaps even more often: the myth that is likely to be promoted by a leader and his followers is that an entire group participated in arriving at a decision, whereas, in fact, the choice was made only by the leader. The problem of discerning whether advisers participated as policy makers arises in connection with the major decisions made by any government, business firm, educational institution, or any other large organization, whenever a leader has nominal responsibility for the organization's policies. Only decisions in which the consensus of a stable in-group plays a crucial role in determining the chosen policy are relevant to investigations of the groupthink hypothesis.

The second and third key questions require most of the work that goes into the search for and appraisal of the available evidence used in case study reports. *Just because a policy turns out to have a bad outcome does not enable us to conclude that the group responsible for working out that policy did a poor job.* A disastrous outcome can be the result of unforeseeable sabotage, poor implementation by people outside the decision-making group, or unexpected accidents beyond the control of the policy makers, some of which have to be chalked up to just plain bad luck. There is also such a thing as good luck whereby poorly made decisions end up being undeservedly successful. Like many other social scientists, however, I assume that the more defects there are in making a decision (as specified by the seven criteria listed earlier), the greater the chances that unanticipated setbacks will occur and that the long-term outcome will fail to meet the decision maker's objectives.

Even when the members of a decision-making group select a defective course of action as a result of their own miscalculations, the main cause of their errors may prove to be misinformation from seemingly trustworthy experts, bolstered by seemingly sound supportive evidence from other sources of intelligence, which could lead even the most vigilant policy makers to draw the wrong conclusions. Unfavorable outcomes can result from such errors, even though the decision makers have made a fairly careful information search. In such instances, the miscalculations are not attributable to defective decision-making procedures and therefore are not candidates for an explanation in terms of groupthink. Nor are they candidates for explanation in terms of any other psychological causes involving emotional reactions, such as guilt, anger, or anxiety, which can reduce the cognitive efficiency of members of a decision-making group.

There are, in addition, as Leon Mann and I point out in our book *Decision Making,*

[various] flaws and limitations in human information processing, such as the propensity of decision makers to be distracted by irrelevant aspects of the alternatives, which leads to loose predictions about outcomes (Abelson, 1976); the tendency of decision makers to be swayed by the form in which information about risks is packaged and presented (Slovic and others, 1976); their reliance on faulty categories and stereotypes, which leads to erroneous decisions relating to social groups and ethnic minorities (Hamilton, 1976); and their illusion of control, which makes for overoptimistic estimates of outcomes that are a matter of chance or luck (Langer, 1975).

Tversky and Kahnemann (1974) describe various other illusions, some notorious and others not yet well known, that arise from intuitive assessments of probabilities that may incline all but the most statistically sophisticated of decision makers to make biased miscalculations in using evidence about the consequences of alternative courses of action.

All sorts of people, including experts trained in statistics, make mistakes in drawing inferences from the information available to them when they are making vital decisions—"overestimating the likelihood of events that can be easily and vividly imagined, giving too much weight to information about representatives, ignoring information about base rates, relying too much on evidence from small samples, and failing to discount evidence from biased samples." Even without all these sources of miscalculation, the mere fact that a huge overload of complicated information has to be processed in order to arrive at an optimal choice is sufficient to induce competent and highly efficient decision makers to resort to simple decision rules that fail to take account of the full complexity of the issues at hand. Then, too, there are ego-defensive tendencies and all sorts of self-serving biases that incline a person to lapse into wishful thinking rather than expending the effort to obtain the best available realistic information and to evaluate it critically.

Most of the sources of error I have just mentioned enter into a kind of "feedback loop" with groupthink. Informational overload, for example, contributes to groupthink tendencies, which in turn greatly aggravate the detrimental effects of the overload on the mental efficiency of decision makers. But the main point is that *blunders have all sorts of causes*—some, like informational overload, being magnified by groupthink; others, like sheer incompetence or ignorance, having nothing at all to do with groupthink. When one is analyzing any ill-conceived decision to find out whether the groupthink syndrome was a probable cause, it is essential to examine the evidence carefully to see if any alternative causal sequence, involving some other known sources of error, could account adequately for the decision makers' failure.

Now let us return for a moment to the unanswered question: How widespread is groupthink? Although nongroupthink sources of error may account for the majority of fiascoes that deserve to be fiascoes, I expect that investigations of a wide variety of group decisions on vital issues will probably show that clear-cut symptoms of groupthink are present in at least a substantial percentage of all miscalculated executive decisions—governmental and nongovernmental, American and foreign. Often, the groupthink syndrome is likely to be only a contributing cause that augments the influence of other sources of error, such as overestimating the probability of the threats that are most vividly presented and other such faulty inferences about possible outcomes. The groupthink syndrome, however, can sometimes turn out to be diagnosed as one of the *primary* causes. That diagnosis is made when there are numerous indications that groupthink played a crucial role, in the sense that if the group members had been less intent upon seeking for concurrence within the group they would have been able to correct their initial errors of judgment, curtail collective wishful thinking, and arrive at a much sounder decision.

HYPOTHESES ON MISPERCEPTION

ROBERT JERVIS

In determining how he will behave, an actor must try to predict how others will act and how their actions will affect his values. The actor must therefore develop an image of others and of their intentions. This image may, however, turn out to be an inaccurate one; the actor may, for a number of reasons, misperceive both others' actions and their intentions. In this essay I wish to discuss the types of misperceptions of other states' intentions that states tend to make. The concept of intention is complex, but here we can consider it to comprise the ways in which the state feels it will act in a wide range of future contingencies. These ways of acting usually are not specific and well-developed plans. For many reasons a national or individual actor may not know how he will act under given conditions, but this problem cannot be dealt with here.

PREVIOUS TREATMENTS OF PERCEPTION IN INTERNATIONAL RELATIONS

Although diplomatic historians have discussed misperception in their treatments of specific events, students of international relations have generally ignored this topic. However, two sets of scholars have applied content analysis to the documents that flowed within and between governments in the six weeks preceding World War I. But the data have been put into quantitative form in a way that does not produce accurate measures of perceptions and intentions and that makes it impossible to gather useful evidence on misperception.[1]

The second group of theorists who have explicitly dealt with general questions of misperception in international relations consists of those, like Charles Osgood, Amitai Etzioni, and, to a lesser extent, Kenneth Boulding and J. David Singer, who have analyzed the Cold War in terms of a spiral of misperception.[2] This approach grows partly out of the mathematical theories of L. F. Richardson[3] and partly out of findings of social and cognitive psychology, many of which are discussed in the following paragraphs.

These authors state their case in general, if not universal, terms but do not provide many historical cases that are satisfactorily explained by their theories. Furthermore, they do not deal with any of the numerous instances that contradict their notion of the self-defeating aspects of the use of power. They ignore the fact that states are not individuals and that the findings of psychology can be applied to organizations only with great care. Most important, their theoretical analysis is for the most part of reduced value because it seems largely to be a product of their assumption that the Soviet Union is a basically status quo power whose apparently aggressive behavior is a product of fear of the West. Yet they supply little or no evidence to support this view. Indeed, the explanation for the differences of opinion between the spiral theorists and the proponents of deterrence lies not in differing general views of international relations, differing values and morality,[4] or differing methods of analysis,[5] but in differing perceptions of Soviet intentions.

THEORIES—NECESSARY AND DANGEROUS

Despite the limitations of their approach, these writers have touched on a vital problem that has not been given systematic treatment by theorists of international relations. The evidence from both psychology and history overwhelmingly supports the view (which may be labeled Hypothesis I) that decision makers tend to fit incoming information into their existing theories and images. Indeed, their theories and images play a large part in determining what they notice. In other words, actors tend to perceive what they expect. Furthermore (Hypothesis Ia), a theory will have greater impact on an actor's interpretation of data (a) the greater the ambiguity of the data and (b) the higher the degree of confidence with which the actor holds the theory.[6]

For many purposes we can use the concept of differing levels of perceptual thresholds to deal with the fact that it takes more, and more unambiguous, information for an actor to recognize an unexpected phenomenon than an expected one. An experiment by Jerome Bruner and Leo Postman determined "that the recognition threshold for . . . incongruous playing cards (those with suits and color reversed) is significantly higher than the threshold for normal cards."[7] Not only are people able to identify normal (and therefore expected) cards more quickly and easily than incongruous (and therefore unexpected) ones, but also they may at first take incongruous cards for normal ones.

However, we should not assume, as the spiral theorists often do, that it is necessarily irrational for actors to adjust incoming information to fit more closely their existing beliefs and images. ("Irrational" here describes acting under pressures that the actor

This essay has been edited and is reprinted from World Politics 20 (1968): 238–54, *by permission of the Johns Hopkins University Press.*

would not admit as legitimate if he or she were conscious of them.) Robert Abelson and Milton Rosenberg label as "psycho-logic" the pressure to create a "balanced" cognitive structure—that is, one in which "all relations among 'good elements' [in one's attitude structure] are positive (or null), all relations among 'bad elements' are positive (or null), and all relations between good and bad elements are negative (or null)." They correctly show that the "reasoning [this involves] would mortify a logician."[8] But those who have tried to apply this and similar cognitive theories to international relations have usually overlooked the fact that in many cases there are important logical links between the elements and the processes they describe that cannot be called "psycho-logic." (I am here using the term "logical" not in the narrow sense of drawing only those conclusions that follow necessarily from the premises, but rather in the sense of conforming to generally agreed-upon rules for the treating of evidence.) For example, Charles Osgood claims that psycho-logic was displayed when the Soviets praised a man or a proposal, and people in the West reacted by distrusting the object of this praise.[9] But if a person believes that the Russians are aggressive, it is logical to be suspicious of their moves. When we say that a decision maker "dislikes" another state, this usually means that he believes that that other state has policies conflicting with those of his nation. Reasoning and experience indicate to the decision maker that the "disliked" state is apt to harm his state's interests. Thus in these cases there is no need to invoke "psycho-logic," and it cannot be claimed that the cases demonstrate the substitution of "emotional consistency for rational consistency."[10]

The question of the relations among particular beliefs and cognitions can often be seen as part of the general topic of the relation of incoming bits of information to the receivers' already established images. The need to fit data into a wider framework of beliefs, even if doing so does not seem to do justice to individual facts, is not, or at least is not only, a psychological drive that decreases the accuracy of our perceptions of the world but is "essential to the logic of inquiry."[11] Facts can be interpreted, and indeed identified, only with the aid of hypotheses and theories. Pure empiricism is impossible, and it would be unwise to revise theories in the light of every bit of information that does not easily conform to them.[12] No hypothesis can be expected to account for all the evidence, and if a prevailing view is supported by many theories and by a large pool of findings it should not be quickly altered. Too little rigidity can be as bad as too much.[13]

This is as true in the building of social and physical science as it is in policy making.[14] While it is terribly difficult to know when a finding throws serious doubt on accepted theories and should be followed up and when instead it was caused by experimental mistakes or minor errors in the theory, it is clear that scientists would make no progress if they followed Thomas Huxley's injunction to "sit down before fact as a mere child, be prepared to give up every preconceived notion, follow humbly wherever nature leads, or you will learn nothing."[15]

As Michael Polanyi explains, "It is true enough that the scientist must be prepared to submit at any moment to the adverse verdict of observational evidence. But not blindly. . . . There is always the possibility that, as in [the cases of the periodic system of elements and the quantum theory of light], a deviation may not affect the essential correctness of a proposition. . . . The process of explaining away deviations is in fact quite indispensable to the daily routine of research," even though this may lead to the missing of a great discovery.[16] For example, in 1795 the astronomer Joseph Lalande did not follow up observations that contradicted the prevailing hypotheses and could have led him to discover the planet Neptune.[17]

Yet we should not be too quick to condemn such behavior. As Thomas Kuhn has noted, "There is no such thing as research without counter-instances."[18] If a set of basic theories—what Kuhn calls a paradigm—has been able to account for a mass of data, it should not be lightly trifled with. As Kuhn puts it: "Lifelong resistance, particularly from those whose productive careers have committed them to an older tradition of normal science [i.e., science within the accepted paradigm], is not a violation of scientific standards but an index to the nature of scientific research itself. The source of resistance is the assurance that the older paradigm will ultimately solve all its problems, that nature can be shoved into the box the paradigm provides. Inevitably, at times of revolution, that assurance seems stubborn and pig-headed as indeed it sometimes becomes. But it is also something more. That same assurance is what makes normal science or puzzle-solving science possible."[19]

Thus it is important to see that the dilemma of how "open" to be to new information is one that inevitably plagues any attempt at understanding in any field. Instances in which evidence seems to be ignored or twisted to fit the existing theory can often be explained by this dilemma instead of by illogical or nonlogical psychological pressures toward consistency. This is especially true of decision makers' attempts to estimate the intentions of other states, since they must constantly take account of the danger that the other state is trying to deceive them.

The theoretical framework discussed thus far, together with an examination of many cases, suggests Hypothesis 2: scholars and decision makers are apt to err by being too wedded to the established view and too closed to new information, as opposed to being too willing to alter their theories.[20] Another way of making this point is to argue that actors tend to establish their theories and expectations prematurely. In politics, of course, this is often necessary because of the need for action. But experimental evidence indicates that the same tendency also occurs on the unconscious level. Bruner and Postman found that "perhaps the greatest single barrier to the recognition of incongruous stimuli is the tendency for perceptual hypotheses to fixate after receiving a minimum of confirmation. . . . Once there had occurred in these cases a partial confirmation of the hypothesis . . . it seemed that nothing could change the subject's report."[21]

However, when we apply these and other findings to politics and discuss kinds of misperception, we should not quickly apply the label of cognitive distortion. We should proceed cautiously for two related reasons. The first is that the evidence available to decision makers almost always permits several interpretations. It should be noted that there are cases of visual perception in which different stimuli can produce exactly the same pattern on an observer's retina. Thus, for an observer using one eye the same pattern would be produced by a sphere the size of a golf ball which was quite close to the observer, by a baseball-sized sphere that was further away, or by a basketball-sized sphere still further away. Without other clues, the observer cannot possibly determine which of these stimuli he is presented with, and we would not want to call his incorrect perceptions examples of distortion. Such cases, relatively rare in visual perception, are frequent in international relations. The evidence available to decision makers is almost always very ambiguous since accurate clues to others' intentions are surrounded by noise[22] and deception. In most cases, no matter how long, deeply, and "objectively" the evidence is analyzed, people can differ in their interpretations, and there are no general rules to indicate who is correct.

The second reason to avoid the label of cognitive distortion is that the distinction between perception and judgment, obscure enough in individual psychology, is almost absent in the making of inferences in international politics. Decision makers who reject information that contradicts their views—or who develop complex interpretations of it—often do so consciously and explicitly. Since the evidence available contains contradictory information, to make any inferences requires that much information be ignored or given interpretations that will seem tortuous to those who hold a different position.

Indeed, if we consider only the evidence available to a decision maker at the time of decision, the view later proved incorrect may be supported by as much evidence as the correct one—or even by more. Scholars have often been too unsympathetic with the people who were proved wrong. On closer examination, it is frequently difficult to point to differences between those who were right and those who were wrong with respect to their openness to new information and willingness to modify their views. Winston Churchill, for example, did not open-mindedly view each Nazi action to see if the explanations provided by the appeasers accounted for the data better than his own beliefs. Instead, like Neville Chamberlain, he fitted each bit of ambiguous information into his own hypotheses. That he was correct should not lead us to overlook the fact that his methods of analysis and use of theory to produce cognitive consistency did not basically differ from those of the appeasers.[23]

A consideration of the importance of expectations in influencing perception also indicates that the widespread belief in the prevalence of "wishful thinking" may be incorrect, or at least may be based on inadequate data. The psychological literature on the interaction between affect and perception is immense and cannot be treated here, but it should be noted that phenomena that at first were considered strong evidence for the impact of affect on perception often can be better treated as demonstrating the influence of expectations.[24] Thus, in international relations, cases like the United States' misestimation of the political climate in Cuba in April 1961, which may seem at first glance to have been instances of wishful thinking, may instead be more adequately explained by the theories held by the decision makers (e.g., communist governments are unpopular). Of course, desires may have an impact on perception by influencing expectations, but since so many other factors affect expectations, the net influence of desires may not be great.

There is evidence from both psychology[25] and international relations that when expectations and desires clash, expectations seem to be more important. The United States would like to believe that the USSR is ready to give up what the United States believe is its goal of world domination, but ambiguous evidence is seen to confirm the opposite conclusion, which conforms to the United States' expectations. Actors are apt to be especially sensitive to evidence of grave danger if they think they can take action to protect themselves against the menace once it has been detected.

SAFEGUARDS

Can anything then be said to scholars and decision makers other than "Avoid being either too open or too closed, but be especially aware of the latter danger"? Although decision makers will always be faced with ambiguous and confusing evidence and will be forced to make inferences about others that will often be inaccurate, a number of safeguards may be suggested that could enable them to minimize their errors. First, and most obvious, decision makers should be aware that they do not make "unbiased" interpretations of each new bit of incoming information, but rather are inevitably heavily influenced by the theories they expect to be verified. They should know that what may appear to them as a self-evident and unambiguous inference often seems so only because of their preexisting beliefs. To someone with a different theory the same data may appear to be unimportant or to support another explanation. Thus many events provide less independent support for the decision makers' images than they may at first realize. Knowledge of this should lead decision makers to examine more closely evidence that others believe contradicts their views.

Second, decision makers should see if their attitudes contain consistent or supporting beliefs that are not logically linked. These may be examples of true psycho-logic. While it is not logically surprising nor is it evidence of psychological pressures to find that people who believe that Russia is aggressive are very suspicious of any Soviet move, other kinds of consistency are more suspect. For example, in Finland in the winter of 1939, those who felt that grave consequences would follow Finnish agreement to give Russia a military base also believed that the Soviets would withdraw their demand if Finland stood firm. And those who felt that concessions would not lead to the loss of major values also believed that Russia would fight if need be.[26] In this country, those who favored a nuclear test ban tended to argue that fallout was very harmful, that only limited improvements in technology would flow from further testing, and that a test ban would increase the chances for peace and security. Those who opposed the test ban were apt to disagree on all three points. This does not mean, of course, that the people holding such sets of supporting views were necessarily wrong in any one element. The Finns who wanted to make concessions to the USSR were probably correct in both parts of their argument. But decision makers should be suspicious if they hold a position in which elements that are not logically connected support the same conclusion. This condition is psychologically comfortable and makes decisions easier to reach (since competing values do not have to be balanced off against each other). The chances are thus considerable that at least part of the reason why a person holds some of these views is related to psychology and not to the substance of the evidence.

Decision makers should also be aware that actors who suddenly find themselves having an important shared interest with other actors have a tendency to overestimate the degree of common interest involved. This tendency is especially strong for those actors (e.g., the United States, at least before 1950) whose beliefs about international relations and morality imply that they can cooperate only with "good" states and that with those states there will be no major conflicts. On the other hand, states that have either a tradition of limited cooperation with others (e.g., Britain) or a strongly held theory that differentiates occasional from permanent allies[27] (e.g., the Soviet Union) find it easier to resist this tendency and need not devote special efforts to combating its danger.

A third safeguard for decision makers would be to make their assumptions, beliefs, and the predictions that follow from them as explicit as possible. An actor should try to determine, before events occur, what evidence would count for and against his theories. By knowing what to expect he would know what to be surprised by, and surprise could indicate to that actor that his beliefs needed reevaluation.[28]

A fourth safeguard is more complex. The decision maker should try to prevent individuals and organizations from letting their main task, political future, and identity become tied to specific theories and images of other actors.[29] If this occurs, subgoals originally sought for their contribution to higher ends will take on value of their own, and information indicating possible alternative routes to the original goals will not be carefully considered. For example, the U.S. Forest Service was unable to carry out its original purpose as effectively when it began to see its distinctive competence not in promoting the best use of lands and forests but rather in preventing all types of forest fires.[30]

Organizations that claim to be unbiased may not realize the extent to which their definition of their role has become involved with certain beliefs about the world. Allen Dulles was a victim of this lack of understanding when he said, "I grant that we are all creatures of prejudice, including CIA officials, but by entrusting intelligence coordination to our central intelligence service, which is excluded from policy making and is married to no particular military hardware, we can avoid, to the greatest possible extent, the bending of facts obtained through intelligence to suit a particular occupational viewpoint."[31] This statement overlooks the fact that the CIA has developed a certain view of international relations that maximizes the importance of its information-gathering, espionage, and subversive activities. Since the CIA would lose its unique place in the government if it were decided that the "back alleys" of world politics were no longer vital to U.S. security, it is not surprising that the organization interprets information in a way that stresses the continued need for its techniques.

Fifth, decision makers should realize the validity and implications of Roberta Wohlstetter's argument that "a willingness to play with material from different angles and in the context of unpopular as well as popular hypotheses is an essential ingredient of a good detective, whether the end is the solution of a crime or an intelligence estimate."[32] However, it is often difficult, psychologically and politically, for any one person to do this. Since a decision maker usually cannot get "unbiased" treatments of data, he should instead seek to structure conflicting biases into the decision-making process. The decision maker, in other words, should have devil's advocates around. Just as Richard Neustad points out, the decision maker will want to create conflicts among his subordinates in order to make appropriate choices, so he will also want to ensure that incoming information is examined from many different perspectives with many different hypotheses in mind.[33] To some extent this kind of examination will be done automatically through the divergence of goals, training, experience, and information that exists in any large organization. But in many cases this divergence will not be sufficient. The views of those analyzing the data will still be too homogeneous and the decision maker will have to go out of his way not only to cultivate but to create differing viewpoints.

While all that would be needed would be to have some people examining the data trying to validate unpopular hypotheses, it would probably be more effective if they actually believed and had a stake in the views they were trying to support. If in 1941 someone had had the task of proving the view that Japan would attack Pearl Harbor, the government might have been less surprised by the attack. And only a person who was out to show that Russia would take objectively great risks would have been apt to note that several ships with especially large hatches going to Cuba were riding high in the water, indicating the presence of a bulky but light cargo that was not likely to be anything other than strategic missiles.

Of course all these safeguards involve costs. They would divert resources from other tasks and would increase internal dissension. Determining whether these costs would be worth the gains would depend on a detailed analysis of how the suggested safeguards might be implemented. Even if they were adopted by a government, of course, they would not eliminate the chance of misperception. However, the safeguards would make it more likely that national decision makers would make conscious choices about the way data were interpreted rather than merely assuming that they can be seen in only one way and can mean only one thing. Statesmen would thus be reminded of alternative images of others just as they are constantly reminded of alternative policies.

These safeguards are partly based on Hypothesis 3: actors can more easily assimilate into their established image of another actor information contradicting that image if the information is transmitted and considered bit by bit than if it comes all at once. In the former case, each piece of discrepant data can be coped with as it arrives and each of the conflicts with the prevailing view will be small enough to go unnoticed, to be dismissed as unimportant, or to necessitate at most a slight modification of the image (e.g., addition of exceptions to the rule). When the information arrives in a block, the contradiction between it and the prevailing view is apt to be much clearer and the probability of major cognitive reorganization will be higher.

SOURCES OF CONCEPTS

An actor's perceptual thresholds—and thus the images that ambiguous information is apt to produce—are influenced by what he has experienced and learned about.[34] If one actor is to perceive that another fits in a given category, he must first have, or develop, a concept for that category. We can usefully distinguish three levels at which a concept can be present or absent. First, the concept can be completely missing. The actor's cognitive structure may not include anything corresponding to the phenomenon he is encountering. This situation can occur not only in science fiction, but also in a world of rapid change or in the meeting of two dissimilar systems. Thus China's image of the Western world was extremely inaccurate in the mid–nineteenth century, its learning was very slow, and its responses were woefully inadequate. The West was spared a similar struggle only because it had the power to reshape the system it encountered. Once the actor clearly sees one instance of the new phenomenon, he is apt

to recognize it much more quickly in the future.[35] Second, the actor can know about a concept but not believe that it reflects an actual phenomenon. Thus Communist and Western decision makers are each aware of the other's explanation of how the Communist system functions, but do not think that the concept corresponds to reality. Communist elites, furthermore, deny that anything *could* correspond to the democracies' description of themselves. Third, the actor may hold a concept but not believe that another actor fills it at the present moment. Thus the British and French statesmen of the 1930s held a concept of states with unlimited ambitions. They realized that Napoleons were possible, but they did not think Hitler belonged in that category. Hypothesis 4 distinguishes these three cases: misperception is most difficult to correct in the case of a missing concept and least difficult to correct in the case of a recognized but presumably unfilled concept. All other things being equal (e.g., the degree to which the concept is central to the actor's cognitive structure), the first case requires more cognitive reorganization than does the second, and the second requires more reorganization than the third.

However, this hypothesis does not mean that learning will necessarily be slowest in the first case, for if the phenomena are totally new the actor may make such grossly inappropriate responses that he will quickly acquire information clearly indicating that he is faced with something he does not understand. And the sooner the actor realizes that things are not—or may not be—what they seem, the sooner he is apt to correct his image.[36]

Three main sources contribute to decision makers' concepts of international relations and of other states and influence the level of their perceptual thresholds for various phenomena. First, an actor's beliefs about his own domestic political system are apt to be important. In some cases, like that of the USSR, the decision-makers' concepts are tied to an ideology that explicitly provides a frame of reference for viewing foreign affairs. Even where this is not the case, experience with his own system will partly determine what the actor is familiar with and what he is apt to perceive in others. Louis Hartz claims, "It is the absence of the experience of social revolution which is at the heart of the whole American dilemma. . . . In a whole series of specific ways it enters into our difficulty of communication with the rest of the world. We find it difficult to understand Europe's 'social question'. . . . We are not familiar with the deeper social struggles of Asia and hence tend to interpret even reactionary regimes as 'democratic.'"[37] Similarly, George Kennan argues that in World War I the Allied powers, especially America, could not understand the bitterness and violence of others' internal conflicts: "The inability of the Allied statesmen to picture to themselves the passions of the Russian civil war [was partly caused by the fact that] we represent . . . a society in which the manifestations of evil have been carefully buried and sublimated in the social behavior of people, as in their very consciousness. For this reason, probably, despite our widely traveled and outwardly cosmopolitan lives, the mainsprings of political behavior in such a country as Russia tend to remain concealed from our visions."[38]

Second, concepts will be supplied by the actor's previous experiences. An experiment from another field illustrates this. DeWitt Dearborn and Herbert Simon presented business executives from various divisions (e.g., sales, accounting, production) with the same hypothetical data and asked them for an analysis and recommendations from the standpoint of what would be best for the company as a whole. The executives' views heavily reflected their departmental perspectives.[39] William W. Kaufmann shows how the perceptions of Ambassador Joseph Kennedy were affected by his past: "As befitted a former chairman of the Securities Exchange and Maritime Commissions, his primary interest lay in economic matters. . . . The revolutionary character of the Nazi regime was not a phenomenon that he could easily grasp. . . . It was far simpler, and more in accord with his own premises, to explain German aggressiveness in economic terms. The Third Reich was dissatisfied, authoritarian, and expansive largely because her economy was unsound."[40] Similarly it has been argued that Chamberlain was slow to recognize Hitler's intentions partly because of the limiting nature of his personal background and business experiences.[41]

The impact of training and experience seems to be demonstrated when the background of the appeasers is compared with that of their opponents. One difference stands out: "A substantially higher percentage of the anti-appeasers (irrespective of class origins) had the kind of knowledge which comes from close acquaintance, mainly professional, with foreign affairs."[42] Since members of the diplomatic corps are responsible for meeting threats to the nation's security before these grow to major proportions and since they have learned about cases in which aggressive states were not recognized as such until very late, they may be prone to interpret ambiguous data as showing that others are aggressive. It should be stressed that we cannot say that the professionals of the 1930s were more apt to make accurate judgments of other states. Rather, they may have been more sensitive to the chance that others were aggressive. They would then rarely take an aggressor for a status-quo power, but would more often make the opposite error.[43] Thus in the years before World War I the permanent officials in the British Foreign Office overestimated German aggressiveness.[44]

A parallel demonstration in psychology of the impact of training on perception is presented by an experiment in which ambiguous pictures were shown to both advanced and beginning police-administration students. The advanced group perceived more violence in the pictures than did the beginners. The probable explanation is that "the law enforcer may come to accept crime as a familiar personal experience, one which he himself is not surprised to encounter. The acceptance of crime as a

familiar experience in turn increases the ability or readiness to perceive violence where clues to it are potentially available."[45] This experiment lends weight to the view that the British diplomats' sensitivity to aggressive states was not totally a product of personnel selection procedures.

A third source of concepts, which frequently will be the most directly relevant to a decision maker's perception of international relations, is international history. As Henry Kissinger points out, one reason why statesmen were so slow to recognize the threat posed by Napoleon was that previous events had accustomed them only to actors who wanted to modify the existing system, not overthrow it.[46] The other side of the coin is even more striking: historical traumas can heavily influence future perceptions. They can either establish a state's image of the other state involved or can be used as analogies. An example of the former case is provided by the fact that for at least ten years after the Franco-Prussian War most of Europe's statesmen felt that Otto von Bismarck had aggressive plans when in fact his main goal was to protect the status quo. Of course the evidence was ambiguous. The post-1871 Bismarckian maneuvers, which were designed to keep peace, looked not unlike the pre-1871 maneuvers designed to set the stage for war. But that the post-1871 maneuvers were seen as indicating aggressive plans is largely attributable to the impact of Bismarck's earlier actions on the statesmen's image of him.

A state's previous unfortunate experience with a type of danger can sensitize it to other examples of that danger. While this sensitivity may lead the state to avoid the mistake it committed in the past, it may also lead it mistakenly to believe that the present situation is like the past one. George Santayana's maxim could be turned around: "Those who remember the past are condemned to make the opposite mistakes." As Paul Kecskemeti shows, both defenders and critics of the unconditional surrender plan of World War II thought in terms of the conditions of World War I.[47] Annette Baker Fox found that the Scandinavian countries' neutrality policies in World War II were strongly influenced by their experiences in the previous war, even though vital aspects of the two situations were different. Thus "Norway's success [during World War I] in remaining nonbelligerent though pro-Allied gave the Norwegians confidence that their country could again stay out of war."[48] And the lesson drawn from the unfortunate results of this policy was an important factor in Norway's decision to join NATO.

The application of the Munich analogy to various contemporary events has been much commented on, and I do not wish to argue the substantive points at stake. But it seems clear that the probabilities that any state is facing an aggressor who has to be met by force are not altered by the career of Hitler and the history of the 1930s. Similarly, the probability of an aggressor's announcing his plans is not increased (if anything, it is decreased) by the fact that Hitler wrote *Mein Kampf*. Yet decision makers are more sensitive to these possibilities and thus more apt to perceive ambiguous evidence as indicating they apply to a given case, than they would have been had there been no Nazi Germany.

Historical analogies often precede, rather than follow, a careful analysis of a situation (e.g., Harry Truman's initial reaction to the news of the invasion of South Korea was to think of the Japanese invasion of Manchuria). Noting this precedence, however, does not show us which of many analogies will come to a decision maker's mind. Truman could have thought of nineteenth-century European wars that were of no interest to the United States. Several factors having nothing to do with the event under consideration influence what analogies a decision maker is apt to make. One factor is the number of cases similar to the analogy with which the decision maker is familiar. Another is the importance of the past event to the political system of which the decision maker is a part. The more times such an event occurred and the greater its consequences were, the more a decision maker will be sensitive to the particular danger involved and the more he will be apt to see ambiguous stimuli as indicating another instance of this kind of event. A third factor is the degree of the decision maker's personal involvement in the past case—in time, energy, ego, and position. The last-mentioned variable will affect not only the event's impact on the decision maker's cognitive structure but also the way he perceives the event and the lesson he draws. Someone who was involved in getting troops into South Korea after the attack will remember the Korean War differently from someone who was involved in considering the possible use of nuclear weapons or in deciding what messages should be sent to the Chinese. Greater personal involvement will usually give the event greater impact, especially if the decision maker's own views were validated by the event. One need not accept a total application of learning theory to nations to believe that "nothing fails like success."[49] It also seems likely that if many critics argued at the time that the decision maker was wrong, he will be even more apt to see other situations in terms of the original event. For example, because Anthony Eden left the government on account of his views and was later shown to have been correct, he probably was more apt to see as Hitlers other leaders with whom he had conflicts (e.g., Nasser). A fourth factor is the degree to which the analogy is compatible with the rest of one's belief system. A fifth is the absence of alternative concepts and analogies. Individuals and states vary in the amount of direct or indirect political experience they have had that can provide different ways of interpreting data. Decision makers who are aware of multiple possibilities of states' intentions may be less likely to seize on an analogy prematurely. The perception of citizens of nations like the United States that have relatively little history of international politics may be more apt to be heavily influenced by the few major international events that have been important to their country.

The first three factors indicate that an event is more apt to shape present perceptions if it occurred recently, the statesman will then know about it at first hand even if he was not involved in the making of policy at the time. Thus if generals are prepared to fight the last war, diplomats may be prepared to avoid the last war. Part of the Anglo-French reaction to Hitler can be explained by the prevailing beliefs that the First World War was to a large extent caused by misunderstandings and could have been avoided by farsighted and nonbelligerent diplomacy. And part of the Western perception of Russia and China can be explained by the view that appeasement was an inappropriate response to Hitler.[50]

THE EVOKED SET

The way people perceive data is influenced not only by their cognitive structure and theories about other actors but also by what they are concerned with at the time they receive the information. Information is evaluated in light of the small part of the person's memory that is presently active—the "evoked set." My perceptions of the dark streets I pass walking home from the movies will be different if the film I saw had dealt with spies than if it had been a comedy. If I am working on aiding a country's education system and I hear someone talk about the need for economic development in that state, I am apt to think he is concerned with education, whereas if I had been working on, say, trying to achieve political stability in that country, I would have placed his remarks in that framework.[51]

Thus Hypothesis 5 states that when messages are sent from a different background of concerns and information than is possessed by the receiver, misunderstanding is likely. Person A and person B will read the same message quite differently if A has seen several related messages that B does not know about. This difference will be compounded if, as is frequently the case, A and B each assume that the other has the same background he does. This means that misperception can occur even when deception is neither intended nor expected. Thus Roberta Wohlstetter found not only that different parts of the U.S. government had different perceptions of data about Japan's intentions and messages partly because they saw the incoming information in very different contexts, but also that officers in the field misunderstood warnings from Washington: "Washington advised General [Walter] Short [in Pearl Harbor] on November 27 to expect 'hostile action' at any moment, by which it meant 'attack on American possessions from without,' but General Short understood this phrase to mean 'sabotage.'"[52] Washington did not realize the extent to which Pearl Harbor considered the danger of sabotage to be primary, and furthermore it incorrectly believed that General Short had received the intercepts of the secret Japanese diplomatic messages available in Washington which indicated that surprise attack was a distinct possibility. Another implication of this hypothesis is that if important information is known to only part of the government of state A and part of the government of state B, international messages may be misunderstood by those parts of the receiver's government that do not match, in the information they have, the part of the sender's government that dispatched the message.[53]

Two additional hypotheses can be drawn from the problems of those sending messages. Hypothesis 6 states that when people spend a great deal of time drawing up a plan or making a decision, they tend to think that the message about it they wish to convey will be clear to the receiver.[54] Since they are aware of what is to them the only important pattern in their actions, they often feel that the pattern will be equally obvious to others, and they overlook the degree to which the message is apparent to them only because they know what to look for. Those who have not participated in the endless meetings may not understand what information the sender is trying to convey. George Quester has shown how the German and, to a lesser extent, the British desire to maintain target limits on bombing in the first eighteen months of World War II was undermined partly by the fact that each side knew the limits it was seeking and its own reasons for any apparent "exceptions" (e.g., the German attack on Rotterdam) and incorrectly felt that these limits and reasons were equally clear to the other side.[55]

Hypothesis 7 holds that actors often do not realize that actions intended to project a given image may not have the desired effect because the actions themselves do not turn out as planned. Thus even without appreciable impact of different cognitive structures and backgrounds, an action may convey an unwanted message. For example, a country's representatives may not follow instructions and so may give others impressions contrary to those the home government wished to convey. The efforts of Washington and Berlin to settle their dispute over Samoa in the late 1880s were complicated by the provocative behavior of their agents on the spot. These agents not only increased the intensity of the local conflict, but led the decision makers to become more suspicious of the other state because they tended to assume that their agents were obeying instructions and that the actions of the other side represented official policy. In such cases both sides will believe that the other is reading hostility into a policy of theirs that is friendly. Similarly, Quester's study shows that the attempt to limit bombing referred to above failed partly because neither side was able to bomb as accurately as it thought it could and thus did not realize the physical effects of its actions.[56]

FURTHER HYPOTHESES FROM THE PERSPECTIVE OF THE PERCEIVER

From the perspective of the perceiver several other hypotheses seem to hold. Hypothesis 8 is that there is an overall tendency for decision makers to see other states as more hostile than they are.[57] There seem to be more cases of statesmen incorrectly believing others are planning major acts against their interest than of statesmen being lulled by a potential aggressor. There are many reasons for this that are too complex to be treated here (e.g., some parts of the bureaucracy feel it is their responsibility to be suspicious of all other states; decision makers often feel they are "playing it safe" to believe and act as though the other state were hostile in questionable cases; and often, when people do not feel they are a threat to others, they find it difficult to believe that others may see them as a threat). It should be noted, however, that decision makers whose perceptions are described by this hypothesis would not necessarily further their own values by trying to correct for this tendency. The values of possible outcomes as well as their probabilities must be considered, and it may be that the probability of an unnecessary arms-tension cycle arising out of misperceptions, multiplied by the costs of such a cycle, may seem less to decision makers than the probability of incorrectly believing another state is friendly, multiplied by the costs of this eventuality.

Hypothesis 9 states that actors tend to see the behavior of others as more centralized, disciplined, and coordinated than it is. This hypothesis holds true in related ways. Frequently, too many complex events are squeezed into a perceived pattern. Actors are hesitant to admit or even see that particular incidents cannot be explained by their theories.[58] Those events not caused by factors that are important parts of the perceiver's image are often seen as though they were. Further, actors see others as more internally united than they in fact are and generally overestimate the degree to which others are following a coherent policy. The degree to which the other side's policies are the product of internal bargaining,[59] internal misunderstandings, or subordinates' not following instructions is underestimated. This is the case partly because actors tend to be unfamiliar with the details of another state's policy-making processes. Seeing only the finished product, they find it simpler to try to construct a rational explanation for the policies, even though they know that such an analysis could not explain their own policies.[60]

Familiarity also accounts for Hypothesis 10: because a state gets most of its information about the other state's policies from the other's foreign office, it tends to take the foreign office's position for the stand of the other government as a whole. In many cases this perception will be an accurate one, but when the other government is divided or when the other foreign office is acting without specific authorization, misperception may result. For example, part of the reason why in 1918 Allied governments incorrectly thought "that the Japanese were preparing to take action [in Siberia], if need be, with agreement with the British and French alone, disregarding the absence of American consent,"[61] was that Allied ambassadors had talked mostly with Foreign Minister Motono, who was among the minority of the Japanese favoring this policy. Similarly, America's allies in the North Atlantic Treaty Organization may have gained an inaccurate picture of the degree to which the American government was committed to the multilateral force (MLF) because they had greatest contact with parts of the government that strongly favored the MLF. And states that tried to get information about Nazi foreign policy from German diplomats were often misled because these officials were generally ignorant of or out of sympathy with Hitler's plans. The Germans and the Japanese sometimes purposely misinformed their own ambassadors in order to deceive their enemies more effectively.

Hypothesis 11 states that actors tend to overestimate the degree to which others are acting in response to what they themselves do when the others behave in accordance with the actor's desires; but when the behavior of the other is undesired, it is usually seen as derived from internal forces. If the effect of another's action is to injure or threaten the first side, the first side is apt to believe that such was the other's *purpose*. An example of the first part of the hypothesis is provided by Kennan's account of the activities of official and unofficial American representatives who protested to the new Bolshevik government against several of its actions. When the Soviets changed their position, these representatives felt it was largely because of their influence.[62] This sort of interpretation can be explained not only by the fact that it is gratifying to the individual making it but also, taking the other side of the coin mentioned in Hypothesis 9, by the fact that the actor is most familiar with his own input into the other's decision and has less knowledge of other influences. The second part of Hypothesis 11 is illustrated by the tendency of actors to believe that the hostile behavior of others is to be explained by the other side's motives and not by its reaction to the first side. Thus Chamberlain did not see that Hitler's behavior was related in part to his belief that the British were weak. More common is the failure to see that the other side is reacting out of fear of the first side, which can lead to self-fulfilling prophecies and spirals of misperception and hostility.

This difficulty is often compounded by an implication of Hypothesis 12: when actors have intentions that they do not try to conceal from others, they tend to assume that others accurately perceive these intentions. Only rarely do they believe that others may be reacting to a much less favorable image of themselves than they think they are projecting.[63]

For state A to understand how state B perceives A's policy is often difficult because such understanding may involve a conflict with A's image of itself. Raymond Sontag argues that Anglo-German relations before World War I deteriorated partly because "the British did not like to think of themselves as selfish, or unwilling to tolerate 'legitimate' German expansion. The Germans did not like to think of themselves as aggressive, or unwilling to recognize 'legitimate' British vested interest."[64]

Hypothesis 13 suggests that if it is hard for an actor to believe that the other can see him as a menace, it is often even harder for him to see that issues important to him are not important to others.

While he may know that another actor is on an opposing team, it may be more difficult for him to realize that the other is playing an entirely different game. This is especially true when the game he is playing seems vital to him.[65]

The final hypothesis, Hypothesis 14, is as follows: actors tend to overlook the fact that evidence consistent with their theories may also be consistent with other views. When choosing between two theories we have to pay attention only to data that cannot be accounted for by one of the theories. But it is common to find people claiming as proof of their theories data that could also support alternative views. This phenomenon is related to the point made earlier that any single bit of information can be interpreted only within a framework of hypotheses and theories. And while it is true that "we may without a vicious circularity accept some datum as a fact because it conforms to the very law for which it counts as another confirming instance, and reject an allegation of fact because it is clearly excluded by law,"[66] we should be careful lest we forget that a piece of information seems in many cases to confirm a certain hypothesis only because we already believe that hypothesis to be correct and that the information can with as much validity support a different hypothesis. For example, one of the reasons why the German attack on Norway took both that country and England by surprise, even though they had detected German ships moving toward Norway, was that they expected not an attack but an attempt by the Germans to break through the British blockade and reach the Atlantic. The initial course of the ships was consistent with either plan, but the British and Norwegians took this course to mean that their predictions were being borne out.[67] This is not to imply that the interpretation made was foolish, but only that the decision makers should have been aware that the evidence was also consistent with an invasion and should have had a bit less confidence in their views.

The longer the ships would have to travel the same route whether they were going to one or another of two destinations, the more information would be needed to determine their plans. Taken as a metaphor, this incident applies generally to the treatment of evidence. Thus as long as Hitler made demands for control only of ethnically German areas, his actions could be explained either by the hypothesis that he had unlimited ambitions or by the hypothesis that he wanted to unite all the Germans. But actions against non-Germans (e.g., the takeover of Czechoslovakia in March 1938) could not be accounted for by the latter hypothesis. And it was this action that convinced the appeasers that Hitler had to be stopped. It is interesting to speculate on what the British reaction would have been had Hitler left Czechoslovakia alone for a while and instead made demands on Poland similar to those he eventually made in the summer of 1939. The two paths would then still not have diverged, and further misperception could have occurred.

NOTES

I am grateful to the Harvard Center for International Affairs for research support. An earlier version of this research note was presented at the International Studies Association panel of the New England Political Science Association in April 1967. I have benefited from comments by Robert Art, Alexander George, Paul Kecskemeti, Paul Leary, Thomas Schelling, James Schlesinger, Morton Schwartz, and Aaron Wildavsky.

1. See, for example, Ole Holsti, Robert North, and Richard Brody, "Perception and Action in the 1914 Crisis," in *Quantitative International Politics,* ed. J. David Singer (New York: Free Press, 1968). For a fuller discussion of the Stanford content analysis studies and the general problems of quantification, see my "The Costs of the Quantitative Study of International Relations," in *Contending Approaches to International Politics,* ed. Klaus Knorr and James N. Rosenau (Princeton, N.J.: Princeton University Press, 1969).

2. See, for example, Charles Osgood, *An Alternative to War or Surrender* (Urbana: University of Illinois Press, 1962); Amitai Etzioni, *The Hard Way to Peace* (New York: Collier, 1962); Kenneth Boulding, "National Images and International Systems," *Journal of Conflict Resolution* 3 (June 1959): 120–31; and J. David Singer, *Deterrence, Arms Control, and Disarmament* (Lanham, Md.: University Press of America, 1984).

3. L. F. Richardson, *Statistics of Deadly Quarrels* (Pittsburgh: Boxwood Press, 1960), and *Arms and Insecurity* (Pittsburgh: Boxwood Press, 1960). For nonmathematicians a fine summary of Richardson's work is Anatol Rapoport's "L. F. Richardson's Mathematical Theory of War," *Journal of Conflict Resolution* 1 (September 1957): 249–99.

4. See Philip Green, *Deadly Logic* (Columbus: Ohio State University Press, 1966); Green, "Method and Substance in the Arms Debate," *World Politics* 16 (July 1964): 642–67; and Robert A. Levine, "Fact and Morals in the Arms Debate," *World Politics* 14 (January 1962): 239–58.

5. See Anatol Rapoport, *Strategy and Conscience* (New York: Harper and Rowe, 1964).

6. Floyd Allport, *Theories of Perception and the Concept of Structure* (New York: Wiley, 1955), 382; Ole Holsti, "Cognitive Dynamics and Images of the Enemy," in David Finlay, Ole Holsti, and Richard Fagen, *Enemies in Politics* (Chicago: Rand McNally, 1967), 70.

7. Jerome Bruner and Leo Postman, "On the Perceptions of Incongruity: A Paradigm," in *Perception and Personality,* ed. Jerome Bruner and David Krech (Durham, N.C.: Duke University Press, 1949), 210.

8. Robert Ableson and Milton Rosenberg, "Symbolic Psycho-logic," *Behavioral Science* 3 (January 1958): 4–5.

9. Osgood, *An Alternative to War,* 27.

10. Ibid., 26.

11. I have borrowed this phrase from Abraham Kaplan, who uses it in a different but related context in *The Conduct of Inquiry* (San Francisco: Chandler, 1964), 86.

12. The spiral theorists are not the only ones to ignore the limits of empiricism. Roger Hilsman found that most consumers and producers of intelligence felt that intelligence should not deal with hypotheses but should only provide the policy makers with "all the facts" (*Strategic Intelligence and National Decisions* [Glencoe: Free Press, 1956], 46). The close interdependence between hypotheses and facts is overlooked partly because of the tendency to identify "hypotheses" with "policy preferences."

13. Karl Deutsch interestingly discusses a related question when he argues, "Autonomy . . . requires both intake from the present and recall from memory, and selfhood can be seen in just this continuous balancing of a limited present and a limited past. . . . No further self-determination is possible if either openness or memory is lost. . . . To the extent that [systems cease to be able to take in new information], they approach the behavior of a bullet or torpedo: their future action becomes almost completely determined by their past. On the other hand, a person without memory, an organization without values or policy . . . —all these no longer steer, but drift: their behavior depends little on their past and almost wholly on their present. Driftwood and the bullet are thus each the epitome of another kind of loss of self-control" (*Nationalism and Social Communication* [Cambridge, Mass.: MIT Press, 1954], 167–68). Also see Deutsch's *The Nerves of Government* (New York: Free Press, 1963), 98–109, 200–56. A physicist makes a similar argument: "It is clear that if one is too attached to one's preconceived model, one will miss all radical discoveries. It is amazing to what degree one may fail to register mentally an observation which does not fit the initial image. . . . On the other hand, if one is too open-minded and pursues every hitherto unknown phenomenon, one is almost certain to lose oneself in trivia" (Martin Deutsch, "Evidence and Inference in Nuclear Research," in *Evidence and Inference,* ed. Daniel Lerner [Glencoe: Free Press, 1958], 102).

14. Raymond Bauer, "Problems of Perception and the Relations between the U.S. and the Soviet Union," *Journal of Conflict Resolution* 5 (September 1961): 223–29.

15. Quoted in W. I. B. Beveridge, *The Art of Scientific Investigation,* 3d ed. (London, 1957), 50.

16. Michael Polyani, *Science, Faith, and Society* (Chicago: University of Chicago Press, 1964), 31. For a further discussion of this problem, see ibid., 16, 26–41, 90–94; Polanyi, *Personal Knowledge* (Chicago: University of Chicago Press, 1958), 8–15, 30, 143–68, 269–98, 310–11; Thomas Kuhn, *The Structure of Scientific Revolution* (Chicago: University of Chicago Press, 1964); Kuhn, "The Function of Dogma in Scientific Research," in *Scientific Change,* ed. A. C. Crombie (New York: Basic Books, 1963), 344–69; the comments on Kuhn's paper by Hall, Polanyi, and Toulmin, and Kuhn's reply in *Scientific Change,* 370–95. For a related discussion of these points from a different perspective, see Norman Storer, *The Social System of Science* (New York, 1960), 116–22.

17. "He found that the position of one star relative to others . . . had shifted. Lalande was a good astronomer and knew that such a shift was unreasonable. He crossed out his first observation, put a question mark next to the second observation, and let the matter go" (Jerome Bruner, Jacqueline Goodnow, and George Austin, *A Study of Thinking* [New York: Wiley, 1962], 105).

18. Kuhn, *The Structure of Scientific Revolution,* 79.

19. Ibid., 150–51.

20. Requirements of effective political leadership may

lead decision makers to voice fewer doubts than they have about existing policies and images, but this constraint can only partly explain this phenomenon. Similar calculations of political strategy may contribute to several of the hypotheses discussed below.

21. Bruner and Postman, "On the Perceptions of Incongruity," 221. Similarly, in experiments dealing with his subjects' perception of other people, Charles Dailey found that "premature judgment appears to make new data harder to assimilate than when the observer withholds judgment until all data are seen. It seems probable . . . that the observer mistakes his own inferences for facts" ("The Effects of Premature Conclusion upon the Acquisition of Understanding of a Person," *Journal of Psychology* 30 [January 1952]: 149–50). For other theory and evidence on this point, see Jerome Bruner, "On Perceptual Readiness," *Psychological Review* 64 (March 1957): 123–52; Gerald Davidson, "The Negative Effects of Early Exposure to Suboptimal Visual Stimuli," *Journal of Personality* 32 (June 1964): 278–95; Albert Myers, "An Experimental Analysis of a Tactical Blunder," *Journal of Abnormal and Social Psychology* 69 (November 1964): 493–98; and Dale Wyatt and Donald Campbell, "On the Liability of Stereotype or Hypothesis," *Journal of Abnormal and Social Psychology* 44 (October 1950): 496–500. It should be noted that this tendency makes "incremental" decision making more likely (David Braybrooke and Charles Lindblom, *A Strategy of Decision* [New York: Free Press, 1963]), but the results of this process may lead the actor further from his goals.

22. For a use of this concept in political communication, see Roberta Wohlstetter, *Pearl Harbor* (Stanford, Calif.: Stanford University Press, 1962).

23. Similarly, Robert Coulondre, the French ambassador to Berlin in 1939, was one of the few diplomats to appreciate the Nazi threat. Partly because of his earlier service in the USSR, "he was painfully sensitive to the threat of a Berlin-Moscow agreement. He noted with foreboding that Hitler had not attacked Russia in his *Reichstag* address of April 28. . . . So it went all spring and summer, the ambassador relaying each new evidence of the impending diplomatic revolution and adding to his admonitions his pleas for decisive "counteraction" (Franklin Ford and Carol Schorske, "The Voice in the Wilderness: Robert Coulondre," in *The Diplomats*, ed. Gordon Craig and Felix Gilbert, eds., vol. 3 [Princeton, N.J.: Princeton University Press, 1953], 573–74). His hypotheses were correct, but it is difficult to detect differences between the way he and those ambassadors who were incorrect, like Neville Henderson, selectively noted and interpreted information. However, to the extent that the fear of war influenced the appeasers' perceptions of Hitler's intentions, the appeasers' views did have an element of psycho-logic that was not present in their opponents' position.

24. See, for example, Donald Campbell, "Systematic Error on the Part of Human Links in Communications Systems," *Information and Control* 1 (1958): 346–50; and Leo Postman, "The Experimental Analysis of Motivational Factors in Perception," in *Current Theory and Research in Motivation*, Judson S. Brown (Lincoln: University of Nebraska, 1953), 59–108.

25. Dale Wyatt and Donald Campbell, "A Study of Interviewer Bias as Related to Interviewer's Expectations and Own Opinions," *International Journal of Opinion and Attitude Research* 4 (Spring 1950): 77–83.

26. Max Jacobson, *The Diplomacy of the Winter War* (Cambridge, Mass.: Harvard University Press, 1961), 136–39.

27. Raymond Aron, *Peace and War* (Garden City, N.Y.: Doubleday, 1966), 29.

28. Cf. Kuhn, *The Structure of Scientific Revolution*, 65. A fairly high degree of knowledge is needed before one can state precise expectations. One indication of the lack of international relations theory is that most of us are not sure what "naturally" flows from our theories and what constitutes either "puzzles" to be further explored with the paradigm or "anomalies" that cast doubt on the basic theories.

29. See Philip Selznick, *Leadership in Administration* (Evanston, Ill.: Row Peterson, 1957).

30. Ashley Schiff, *Fire and Water: Scientific Heresy in the Forest Service* (Cambridge, Mass.: Harvard University Press, 1962). Despite its title, this book is a fascinating and valuable study.

31. Allan Dulles, *The Craft of Intelligence* (New York: Harper and Row, 1963), 53.

32. Wohlstetter, *Pearl Harbor*, 302. See Beveridge, *The Art of Scientific Investigation*, 93, for a discussion of the idea that the scientist should keep in mind as many hypotheses as possible when conducting and analyzing experiments.

33. Richard Neustadt, *Presidential Power* (New York: Wiley, 1960).

34. Most psychologists argue that this influence also holds for perception of shapes. For data showing that people in different societies differ in respect to their predisposition to experience certain optical illusions and for a convincing argument that this difference can be explained by the societies' different physical environments, which have led their people to develop different patterns of drawing inferences from ambiguous visual cues, see Marshall Segall, Donald Campbell, and Melville Herskovits, *The Influence of Culture on Visual Perceptions* (Indianapolis: Bobbs-Merrill, 1966).

35. Thus when Bruner and Postman's subjects first were presented with incongruous playing cards (i.e., cards in which symbols and colors of the suits were not matching, producing red spades or black diamonds), long exposure times were necessary for correct identification. But once a subject correctly perceived the card and added this type of card to his repertoire of categories, he was able to identify other incongruous cards much more quickly. For an analogous example—in this case, changes in the analysis of serial reconnaissance photographs of an enemy's secret weapons-testing facilities produced by the belief that a previously unknown object may be present—see David Irving, *The Mare's Nest: The German Secret Weapons Campaign and Allied Counter-measures* (London: W. Kimber, 1964), 66–67, 274–75.

36. Bruner and Postman, "On the Perception of Incongruence" 220.

37. Louis Hartz, *The Liberal Tradition in America* (New York: Harcourt, Brace, 1955), 306.

38. George Kennan, *Russia and the West under Lenin and Stalin* (Boston: Little, Brown, 962), 142–43.

39. DeWitt Dearborn and Herbert Simon, "Selective Perception: A Note on the Departmental Identification of Executives," *Sociometry* 21 (June 1958): 140–44.

40. William W. Kaufman, "Two American Ambassadors: Bullitt and Kennedy," in *The Diplomats*, ed. Craig and Gilbert, 358–59.

41. Hugh Trevor-Roper puts this point well: "Brought up as a business man, successful in municipal politics, [Chamberlain's] outlook was entirely parochial. Educated Conservative aristocrats like Churchill, Eden, and Cranborne, whose families had long been used to political responsibility, had seen revolution and revolutionary leaders before, in their own history, and understood them correctly; but the Chamberlains, who had run from radical imperialism to timid conservatism in a generation of life in Birmingham, had no such understanding of history or the world: to them the scope of human politics was limited by their own parochial horizons, and Neville Chamberlain could not believe that Hitler was fundamentally different from himself. If Chamberlain wanted peace, so must Hitler" ("Munich—Its Lessons Ten Years Later," *Peace or Appeasement*, ed. Francis Loewenheim [Boston: Houghton Mifflin, 1965], 152–53). For a similar view see A. L. Rowse, *Appeasement* (New York, 1963), 117.

But Donald Lammers points out that the views of many prominent British public figures in the 1930s do not fit this generalization (*Explaining Munich* [Stanford: Hoover Institution, 1966], 13–140). Furthermore, arguments that stress the importance of the experiences and views of the actors' ancestors do not explain the links by which these influence the actors themselves. Presumably Churchill and Chamberlain read the same history books in school and had the same basic information about Britain's past role in the world. Thus what has to be demonstrated is that in their homes aristocrats like Churchill learned different things about politics and human nature than did middle-class people like Chamberlain and that these experiences had a significant impact. Alternatively, it could be argued that the patterns of child-rearing prevalent among the aristocracy influenced the children's personalities in a way that made them more likely to see others as aggressive.

42. Lammers, *Explaining Munich*, 15.

43. During a debate on appeasement in the House of Commons, Harold Nicolson declared, "I know that those of us who believe in the traditions of our policy, . . . who believe that one great function of this country is to maintain moral standards in Europe, to maintain a settled pattern of international relations, not to make friends with people who are demonstrably evil . . . —I know that those who hold such beliefs are accused of possessing the Foreign Office mind. I thank God that I possess the Foreign Office mind" (quoted in Martin Gilbert, *The Roots of Appeasement* [London: Weidenfeld and Nicolson, 1966], 187). But the qualities Nicolson mentions and applauds may be related to a more basic attribute of "the Foreign Office mind"—suspiciousness.

44. George Monger, *The End of Isolation* (London: T. Nelson, 1963). I am also indebted to Frederick Collignon for his unpublished manuscript and several conversations on this point.

45. Hans Toch and Richard Schulte, "Readiness to Perceive Violence as a Result of Police Training," *British Journal of Psychology* 52 (November 1961): 392 (original italics omitted). It should be stressed that one cannot say whether or not the advanced police students perceived the pictures "accurately." The point is that their training predisposed them to see violence in ambiguous situations. Whether on balance they would make fewer perceptual errors and better decisions is very hard to determine. For an experiment showing that training can lead people to "recognize" an expected stimulus even when that stimulus is in fact not shown, see Israel Goldiamond and William F. Hawkins, "Vexierversuch: The Log Relationship between Word-Frequency and Recognition Obtained in the Absence of Stimulus Words," *Journal of Experimental Psychology* 56 (December 1958): 457–63.

46. Henry Kissinger, *A World Restored* (New York: Grosset and Dunlop, 1964), 2–3.

47. Paul Kecskemeti, *Strategic Surrender* (Stanford, Calif.: Stanford University Press, 1964), 215–41.

48. Annette Baker Fox, *The Power of Small States* (Chicago: Chicago University Press, 1959), 81.

49. William Inge, *Outspoken Essays*, 1st ser. (London, 1923), 88.

50. Of course, analogies themselves are not "unmoved movers." The interpretation of past events is not automatic and is informed by general views of international relations and complex judgments. And just as beliefs about the past influence the present, views about the present influence interpretations of history. It is difficult to determine the degree to which the United States' interpretation of the reasons it went to war in 1917 influenced American foreign policy in the 1920s and 1930s and how much the isolationism of that period influenced the histories of the war.

51. For some psychological experiments on this subject, see Jerome Bruner and A. Leigh Minturn, "Perceptual Identification and Perceptual Organization," *Journal of General Psychology* 53 (July 1955): 22–28; Seymour Feshback and Robert Singer, "The Effects of Fear Arousal and Suppression of Fear upon Social Perception," *Journal of Abnormal and Social Psychology* 55 (November 1957): 283–88; and Elsa Sippoal, "A Group Study of Some Effects of Preparatory Sets," *Psychology Monographs* 46, no. 210 (1935): 27–28. For a general discussion of the importance of the perceiver's evoked set, see Postman, "Experimental Analysis," 87.

52. Wohlstetter, *Pearl Harbor*, 73–74.

53. For example, Roger Hilsman points out, "Those who knew of the peripheral reconnaissance flights that probed Soviet air defenses during the Eisenhower administration and the U-2 flights over the Soviet Union itself . . . were better able to understand some of the things the Soviets were saying and doing than people who did not know of these activities" (*To Move a Nation* [Garden City, N.Y.: Doubleday, 1967], 66). But it is also possible that those who knew about the U-2 flights at times misinterpreted Soviet messages by incorrectly believing that the sender was influenced by, or at least knew of, these flights.

54. I am grateful to Thomas Schelling for discussion on this point.

55. George Quester, *Deterrence before Hiroshima* (New York: Wiley, 1966), 105–22.

56. Ibid.

57. For a slightly different formulation of this view, see Holsti, "The Costs of the Quantitative Study of International Relations," 27.

58. The Soviets consciously held an extreme version of this view and seemed to believe that nothing is accidental.

See the discussion in Nathan Leites, *A Study of Bolshevism* (Glencoe: Free Press, 1953), 67–73.

59. A. W. Marshall criticizes Western explanations of Soviet military posture for failing to take this into account. See his "Problems of Estimating Military Power," a paper presented at the 1966 Annual Meeting of the American Political Science Association, 16.

60. It has also been noted that in labor–management disputes both sides may be apt to believe incorrectly that the other is controlled from above, either from the international union office or from the company's central headquarters (Robert Blake, Herbert Shepard, and Jane Mouton, *Managing Intergroup Conflict in Industry* [Houston, 1964], 182). It has been further noted that both Democratic and Republican members of the House tend to see the other party as the one that is more disciplined and united (Charles Clapp, *The Congressman* [Washington, D.C.: Brookings Institution, 1963], 17–19).

61. George Kennan, *Russia Leaves the War* (Princeton, N.J.: Princeton University Press, 1956), 484.

62. Ibid., 404, 408, 500.

63. Herbert Butterfield notes that these assumptions can contribute to the spiral of "Hobbesian fear. . . . You yourself may vividly feel the terrible fear that you have of the other party, but you cannot enter into the other man's counter-fear, or even understand why he should be particularly nervous. For you know that you yourself mean him no harm, and that you want nothing from him save guarantees for your own safety; and it is never possible for you to realize or remember properly that since he cannot see the inside of your mind, he can never have the same assurance of your intentions that you have" (*History and Human Relations* [New York: Macmillan, 1952], 20).

64. Raymond Sontag, *European Diplomatic History 1871–1932* (New York: Appleton-Century-Crofts, 1933), 124. It takes great mental effort to realize that actions that seem only the natural consequence of defending your vital interests can look to others as though you are refusing them any chance of increasing their influence. In rebutting the famous Crowe "balance of power" memorandum of 1907, which justified a policy of "containing" Germany on the grounds that it was a threat to British national security, Thomas Sanderson, a former permanent undersecretary in the Foreign Office, wrote, "It has sometimes seemed to me that to a foreigner reading our press the British Empire must appear in the light of some huge giant sprawling all over the globe, with gouty fingers and toes stretching in every direction, which cannot be approached without eliciting a scream" (quoted in Monger, *End of Isolation*, 315). But few other Englishmen could be convinced that others might see them this way.

65. George Kennan makes clear that in 1918 this kind of difficulty was partly responsible for the inability of either the Allies or the new Bolshevik government to understand the motivations of the other side: "There is . . . nothing in nature more egocentrical than the embattled democracy. . . . It . . . tends to attach to its own cause an absolute value which distorts its own vision of everything else. . . . It will readily be seen that people who have got themselves into this frame of mind have little understanding for the issues of any contest other than the one in which they are involved. The idea of people wasting time and substance on any other issue seems to them preposterous" (*Russia and the West*, 11–12).

66. Kaplan, *Conduct of Inquiry*, 89.

67. Johan Jorgen Holst, "Surprise, Signals and Reaction: The Attack on Norway," *Cooperation and Conflict*, no. 1 (1966): 34. The Germans made a similar mistake in November 1942 when they interpreted the presence of an Allied convoy in the Mediterranean as confirming their belief that Malta would be resupplied. They thus were taken by surprise when landings took place in North Africa (William Langer, *Our Vichy Gamble* [New York: Knopf, 1947], 365).

PART IV

AMERICAN DEFENSE POLICIES

INTRODUCTION

PETER L. HAYS

Part IV of this book examines specific outputs of the American defense policy process. Despite our best efforts to pare down the number of topics addressed, this is the longest part of the book. This alone indicates the volume, breadth, and complexity of many of the defense-related issues America faces today. We have divided these outputs into six broad conceptual headings and devoted a chapter to each: strategy, nuclear policy, conventional policy, special operations/low-intensity conflict (SOLIC) and operations other than war, arms control and proliferation, and civil–military relations. Factors that shape defense policy outputs such as emerging threats, regionally focused challenges, and the changing nature of warfare are reserved for Part V.

Chapter 12, "Strategy," provides the essential foundation for all subsequent discussions of American defense policy outputs. This chapter contains excerpts from the latest versions of the two most important official statements on U.S. national security: the Clinton administration's *National Security Strategy of Engagement and Enlargement* and the

Joint Chiefs of Staff's *National Military Strategy of the United States of America*. Both of these are recurring reports required by the Goldwater-Nichols Defense Reorganization Act of 1986.

The title of the Clinton administration's report reflects the two major themes of current U.S. national security strategy: U.S. interests will be best served if the United States remains *engaged* in a proactive, leadership role in world affairs while also seeking to *enlarge* the sphere of market democracies worldwide. Several aspects of Clinton's strategy are particularly noteworthy and controversial. First, this statement goes considerably beyond the Bush administration's national security strategy by defining national security quite broadly, including possible ecological threats. Second, by defining national security broadly and emphasizing the need for continuing U.S. engagement, Clinton's strategy raises the specter of an open-ended, interventionist American foreign policy. Finally, Clinton's strategy reinforces the priority placed by the Reagan and Bush administrations on attempting to enlarge the sphere of mar-

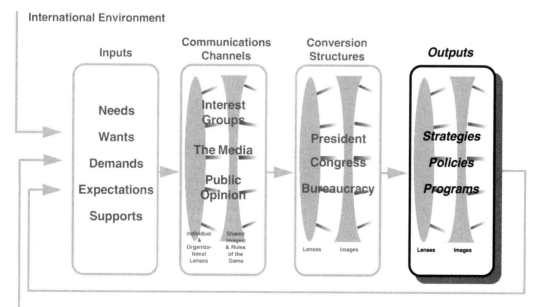

Defense Policy Process Model: Outputs

ket democracies worldwide but, like its predecessors, is less clear when explaining how or why the United States should attempt to achieve this objective.

Clinton's strong emphasis on enlarging the number of democratic states in the post–Cold War world may be the single most controversial element of his strategy. In practice, the specific criteria and modalities for intervention to promote democratic enlargement are extremely contentious. Moreover, the theory and empirical evidence supporting the pacific nature of democratic states in the international system remains inconclusive.[1] To date, it is not clear that we have seen much change in the actual amount of U.S. military and diplomatic emphasis on democratic enlargement as a result of Clinton's strategy.[2] From a broader perspective, the most interesting aspect of this strategy is its assumption that democratic states have a beneficial impact on the international system—a return to some of the earliest and most enduring themes in American political thought and American foreign policy.

The national military strategy released by Chairman of the Joint Chiefs of Staff General John Shalikashvili relates closely to the Clinton strategy document by outlining the tools available within the military dimension of the national security strategy. The military strategy identifies four principal security threats to the United States (regional instability, the proliferation of weapons of mass destruction, transnational dangers, and dangers to democracy and reform) and then highlights objectives and methods of countering these threats. It is also important to note that much of our latest national military strategy derives directly from the late Secretary of Defense Les Aspin's September 1993 *Bottom-Up Review* (BUR). For example, the strategy uses the two major regional conflict (MRC) standard first developed for the BUR as the basis for threat assessment, operations planning, and force sizing. The BUR, the national military strategy, and the national security strategy have all come in for their share of criticism for failing adequately to address issues such as military downsizing, the controversies surrounding roles and missions, and the appropriate U.S. nuclear posture for the post–Cold War era. Nonetheless, these documents represent an excellent point at which to begin defining and studying comprehensive and consistent approaches for U.S. national security in the changed international security environment.

U.S. nuclear policy is the focus of Chapter 13. The significant changes in and reduced emphasis on U.S. nuclear forces are among the most tangible military manifestations of the end of the Cold War. Former Secretary of Defense James Schlesinger's essay, "The Impact of Nuclear Weapons on History," helps remind us just how important nuclear weapons were in stabilizing and structuring the relationships among the United States, Western Europe, and the Soviet Union that led both to the Cold War and its eventual demise. Thus while nuclear weapons provided the essential subtext for understanding the Cold War, their role in today's international security

environment appears to be reduced but remains of critical importance. Three of the most important nuclear concerns today are the spread of fissile materials and the proliferation of nuclear weapons, paths toward stability and multilateral deterrence in a multipolar nuclear world, and the balance point and trade-offs between nuclear and high-technology conventional weapons systems. Roger Molander and Peter Wilson, in "On Dealing with the Prospect of Nuclear Chaos," present a clear and comprehensive analysis of the first two of these issues and their implications for American defense policy. The unlimited-duration extension of the Nuclear Nonproliferation Treaty (NPT) agreed to by most signatories at the April 1995 NPT Review Conference is a highly significant recent development in this area that may help to codify the two-tiered "have" and "have-not" system discussed as one of the alternative nuclear futures by Molander and Wilson.[3] The third major issue, the balance between nuclear and conventional deterrence, is the subject of "Extended Conventional Deterrence" by Charles Allan. The fundamental question addressed by Allan is how far the types of precision conventional weapons systems used by the United States during the Gulf War can go toward substituting for and perhaps even replacing nuclear weapons in deterring attacks on the United States and its vital interests. The role of nuclear weapons in international security and the very nature of deterrence following the revolution in military affairs[4] are certainly issues that deserve a great deal of attention as Americans formulate their defense policies for the post–Cold War world.

Chapter 14 shifts from nuclear issues to conventional U.S. military policy and the role that each of the services play in the national military strategy. This chapter contains the official U.S. Air Force and U.S. Navy white papers. These basic policy statements provide interesting insights into the institutional ethos of the air force and the navy and highlight their preferred roles and strategies for contributing to U.S. national security. The air force white paper, *Global Reach–Global Power*, asserts that the Gulf War demonstrated airpower's decisive impact on the revolution in military affairs. According to the air force, the dominance of airpower and the comprehensive organizational restructuring undertaken by that service in the early 1990s have combined to make air and space forces and the air force in particular "the pivotal contributors to our national military strategy—in deterrence, forward presence, and crisis response." An even more recent air force white paper, *Global Presence*, was released in February 1995. This document continues to build on the themes of *Global Reach–Global Power* by adding the concept of "virtual presence"— the "advantage obtained with space forces and information-based capabilities"—to the traditional concept of military presence.

Thus, as one would predict from Carl Builder's analysis of institutional personalities in Chapter 5, the newest and least established branch has taken the lead among the services in attempting to redefine itself in response to the end of the Cold War and the revolution in military affairs. Many of the air force's assertions in these areas have also served as lightning rods for critics who charge that the air force is moving too far, too fast, or that it is attempting to usurp the traditional roles and missions of the other services.[5]

Not surprisingly, *Forward . . . From the Sea* has a different approach to these issues, one that reflects the views of the navy and the Marine Corps. This latest naval policy statement builds on the themes first developed in the September 1992 *From the Sea* white paper. *Forward . . . From the Sea* examines the ability of naval forces to influence events in the littoral regions of the world and asserts that "the most important role of naval forces in situations short of war is to be *engaged* in forward areas, with the objectives of *preventing* conflicts and *controlling* crises."

Unfortunately, the army currently does not have a single version of its basic policy analogous to these air force and navy white papers. Still, the army traditionally has taken the development and use of its basic doctrine very seriously. The lack of an army white paper on its role in the post–Cold War U.S. national security strategy undoubtedly reflects the long-term perspective and confident character of the army's institutional culture as well as the difficult conceptual challenges associated with downsizing in the face of new types of security threats. Nonetheless, it must also be noted that the army has taken the lead in helping to define certain areas of today's national military strategy, such as operations other than war. Readers desiring more information on the army's current position should consult Field Manual 100-5, "Operations," the single document that probably comes closest to being the army's basic policy statement.

Chapter 14 also presents three discussions that critique several of the major points made in the air force and navy white papers. Eliot Cohen, in "The Mystique of U.S. Air Power," examines many of the general notions underlying the revolution in military affairs and questions whether airpower can provide a unique and virtually painless way to apply American power. Having directed the Gulf War Air Power Survey, Cohen is in an excellent position to assess the efficacy of airpower and the impact of the revolution in military affairs on the ability of the United States to use air forces for power projection. "The End of Naval Strategy" by Jan Breemer points out that the littoral focus in the navy's recent White Papers represents an enormous shift away from the blue-water focus of traditional sea-control strategy. Breemer raises many interesting issues about how naval forces should be used in the new international security environment and how the navy can adapt to these changes strategically and culturally. The final essay in this chapter, "Joint and Combined Operations in the Post–Cold War Era" by Representative Ike Skelton, provides a useful overview of the doctrinal and cultural changes in all the services following Goldwater-Nichols and the end of the Cold War.

Chapter 15 moves on to special operations/low-intensity conflict (SOLIC) and the emerging area of operations other than war (OOTW). General Carl Stiner, the former commander of U.S. Special Operations Command, provides a basic outline of the capabilities of special operations forces. He explains how these forces have adapted to the changing environment and how they have been used since the end of the Cold War. American defense policy planners must consider whether the U.S. SOLIC organizations and roles that have been shaped by factors such as Goldwater-Nichols remain appropriate today. Samuel Huntington examines these and other basic roles and missions issues in "New Contingencies, Old Roles." Huntington makes two broad points. First, he notes "that there are almost no conceivable roles in this new phase of our history that the Armed Forces have not performed in the past." However, he also argues forcefully that the U.S. military "should not be organized or prepared or trained to perform such [nonmilitary and nontraditional] roles." Senator Sam Nunn, former chairman of the Senate Armed Services Committee, mentions many of the same issues and safeguards as Huntington does but clearly has a different emphasis in "Domestic Missions for the Armed Forces." Senator Nunn's arguments for expanding the domestic role of the U.S. military should be kept in mind because these types of missions could have a large potential impact on civil–military relations. Many of these issues are revisited in Chapter 18 and figure prominently in the warning issued by Colonel Charles Dunlap in "The Origins of the American Military Coup of 2012."

The last two essays in this chapter turn to international roles and missions for U.S. forces as part of multilateral contingencies, especially under the auspices of United Nations peacekeeping operations. William Lewis, in "Peacekeeping: The Deepening Debate," questions the ability of the United Nations and its bureaucratic structures to provide useful peacekeeping capabilities in difficult real-world situations. Assistant Secretary of Defense Sarah Sewell, in "Peace Operations: A Department of Defense Perspective," provides an in-depth look at the specific mechanisms created by both the Department of Defense and the United Nations to deal with many of the criticisms leveled by Lewis and others. Given that peacekeeping has become an increasingly important part of U.N. operations and the U.S. preference for multilateral intervention emphasized in the Clinton administration's national security strategy, few aspects of American defense policy today are more relevant than the question of how the United States can better fit into multilateral peace operations.[6]

In Chapter 16 our attention turns to arms control and proliferation issues. This is yet another area in which the path of the United States is less certain owing to the changed international security environment and the revolution in military affairs. The essays by Gregory Rattray and Kerry Kartchner provide an overview of the objectives of arms control and analyze the adequacy of these objectives for the post–Cold War era. Their essays are supplemented by readings that briefly lay out the most important existing treaties and ongoing negotiations. This material will help students begin to understand how complex and multidimensional arms control has become. Heather Wilson's "Missed Opportunities: Washington Politics and Nuclear Proliferation" presents an insider's look at the actual state of U.S. policy implementation regarding critical nuclear proliferation issues. Wilson's exposé reminds us that the old adage "the devil is in the details" is never more true than when dealing with the specifics of complex and controversial challenges such as implementing the Nunn-Lugar Cooperative Threat Reduction program. The final essay in this chapter, Marc Dean Millot's "Facing the Emerging Reality of Regional Nuclear Adversaries," widens the discussion by examining both the political and the military ramifications of nuclear proliferation. Millot's analysis highlights several critical issues for current and future American defense policy: the many extreme difficulties in performing real-world counterproliferation missions, the growing nuclear aversion within the increasingly denuclearized U.S. military, and the resulting lack of strategies or military plans for dealing effectively with regional nuclear adversaries. Moreover, the emerging threat of new nuclear-armed adversaries clearly presents significant areas of conceptual overlap with several of the major issues raised earlier in Part IV, such as the balance between nuclear and conventional systems for deterrence and the differing views among the services concerning their preferred roles and contributions to the overall national security strategy.

Chapter 17 draws together many of the themes addressed above within the context of U.S. civil–military relations. Today there is a lively debate concerning the health of this relationship. Alarmists argue that factors such as the unintended consequences of Goldwater-Nichols, the end of the Cold War, and the revolution in military affairs have produced new and potentially severe strains in our current civil–military relations. Others assert that despite the changes and pressures, these relations are in good shape. In "The Political Dimension of Military Professionalism," John Garrison reviews the classic literature on this subject and compares the roots and basic tenets of the traditional and fusionist schools of thought as they relate to the proper role of the military within the American political system. As mentioned above, Colonel Dunlap's "Origins of the American Military Coup of 2012" creates a "darkly imagined excursion into the future" from many of the current themes and trends in civil–military relations. Dunlap's widely read and influential tale was the winner of the 1991–92 Chairman of the Joint Chiefs of Staff Strategic Essay Competition as the top paper from all the military's war colleges. The final essay, "Civil–Military Relations in the United States" by Douglas Johnson and Steven Metz, summarizes the current debate on the state of U.S. civil–

military relations with a comprehensive and insightful analysis of the roots and impact of the conflicting views on this subject. The health of U.S. civil–military relations is a crucial issue and an appropriate place to conclude our analysis of American defense policy outputs. The shape of this relationship will decisively influence the future of American defense policy and will help determine the kind of example the United States will set for other states struggling with this issue.

NOTES

1. The relationship between the domestic regime of a state and its international behavior has been a fundamental and controversial issue in political theory from at least Thucydides' *The Peloponnesian War* forward. Kenneth N. Waltz's analysis of his second image in *Man, the State and War* (New York: Columbia University Press, 1954) is particularly useful in tracing the development of these issues in political theory. Many aspects of this issue remain controversial among international relations scholars today. For example, there is little agreement on the theoretical rationale for why democratic states seem to fight each other (or other states) less frequently, there is no commonly accepted definition of democracy, and some even argue that the lower incidence of war between democratic states is not statistically significant. For recent analysis in these areas see "Give Democratic Peace a Chance?" *International Security* 19 (Fall 1994): 5–125.

2. For the argument that with the exception of Haiti there has been very little difference in the actual (but not rhetorical) promotion of democracy between the Bush and Clinton administrations, see Thomas Carothers, "Democracy Promotion under Clinton," *Washington Quarterly* 18 (Autumn 1995): 13–25. Carothers also argues that the American desire to replace our overarching containment strategy of the Cold War era with a similarly overarching strategy for the post–Cold War such as democracy promotion is itself an inappropriate vestige of the Cold War.

3. Recently, nuclear strategists from both the left and right sides of the political spectrum seem to be converging on the "virtual abolition" of nuclear weapons option discussed by Molander and Wilson as the best path forward for future nuclear arms control efforts by the United States. See Michael J. Mazarr, "Virtual Nuclear Arsenals," *Survival* 37 (Autumn 1995): 7–26.

4. The revolution in military affairs is addressed in detail in Chapter 19.

5. Many commentators were particularly critical of the air force's *Global Presence* White Paper and its emphasis on the controversial "virtual presence" concept. The critics also noted that *Global Presence* was released during the height of the roles and missions debate in the spring of 1995. See, for example, Glenn W. Goodman Jr., "The Power of Information: Air Force Clarifies Its Misunderstood Virtual Presence Concept," *Armed Forces Journal International* (July 1995): 24.

6. The United Nations' position on its role in worldwide peacekeeping operations in the optimistic afterglow of the Gulf War is spelled out in Secretary-General Boutros

Boutros-Ghali's *An Agenda for Peace: Preventative Diplomacy, Peacemaking, and Peace-Keeping* (New York: United Nations, 1992) and his "Empowering the United Nations," *Foreign Affairs* 72 (Winter 1992/93): 89–102. For an insightful critique of the U.N.'s peacekeeping prospects and the categories of peace operations developed by Boutros-Ghali see "Peacekeeping, Peace Imposition, and the United Nations" in Donald M. Snow's *National Security: Defense Policy for a New International Order,* 3d ed. (New York: St. Martin's Press, 1995), 253–83.

CHAPTER 12

STRATEGY

ADVANCING OUR INTERESTS THROUGH ENGAGEMENT AND ENLARGEMENT

WILLIAM J. CLINTON

The dawn of the post–Cold War era presents the United States with many distinct dangers, but also with a generally improved security environment and a range of opportunities to improve it further. The unitary threat that dominated our engagement during the Cold War has been replaced by a complex set of challenges. Our nation's strategy for defining and addressing those challenges has several core principles that guide our policy. First and foremost, we must exercise global leadership. We are not the world's police force, but as the world's premier economic and military power, and with the strength of our democratic values, the United States is indispensable to the forging of stable political relations and open trade.

Our leadership must stress preventive diplomacy—through such means as support for democracy, economic assistance, overseas military presence, military-to-military contacts, and involvement in multilateral negotiations in the Middle East and elsewhere—in order to help resolve problems, reduce tensions, and defuse conflicts before they become crises. These measures are a wise investment in our national security because they offer the prospect of resolving problems with the least human and material cost.

Our engagement must be selective, focusing on the challenges that are most relevant to our own interests and focusing our resources where we can make the most difference. We must also use the right tools—being willing to act unilaterally when our direct national interests are most at stake, in alliance and partnership when our interests are shared by others, and multilaterally when our interests are more general and the problems are best addressed by the international community. In all cases, the nature of our response must depend on what best serves our own long-term national interests. Those interests are ultimately defined by our security requirements. Such requirements start with our physical defense and economic well-being. They also include environmental security as well as the security of values achieved through expansion of the community of democratic nations.

Our national security strategy draws upon a range of political, military, and economic instruments and focuses on the primary objectives stressed throughout my administration:

- *Enhancing our security.* Taking account of the realities of the post–Cold War era and the new threats, a military capability appropriately sized and postured to meet the diverse needs of our strategy, including the ability, in concert with regional allies, to win two nearly simultaneous major regional conflicts. We will continue to pursue arms control agreements to reduce the danger of nuclear, chemical, biological, and conventional conflict and to promote stability.

- *Promoting prosperity at home.* A vigorous and integrated economic policy designed to stimulate global environmentally sound economic growth and free trade and to press for open and equal U.S. access to foreign markets.

- *Promoting democracy.* A framework of democratic enlargement that increases our security by protecting, consolidating, and enlarging the community of free-market democracies. Our efforts focus on strengthening democratic processes in key emerging democratic states including Russia, Ukraine, and other new states of the former Soviet Union.

These basic objectives of our national security strategy will guide the allocation of our scarce national security resources. Because deficit reduction is also central to the long-term health and competitiveness of the American economy, we have made it, along with efficient and environmentally sound use of our resources, a major priority. Under our economic plan, the deficit will be reduced over $700 billion by fiscal 1998. The present administration has also lowered the deficit as a percentage of the gross domestic product from 4.9 percent in fiscal 1992 to 2.4 percent in fiscal 1995—the lowest since 1979.

ENHANCING OUR SECURITY

The U.S. government is responsible for protecting the lives and personal safety of Americans, maintaining our political freedom and independence as a

William J. Clinton, A National Security Strategy of Engagement and Enlargement (*Washington, D.C.: GPO, February 1995*), 7–24. *Public Domain.*

nation, and promoting the well-being and prosperity of our nation. No matter how powerful we are as a nation, we cannot secure these basic goals unilaterally. Whether the problem is nuclear proliferation, regional instability, the reversal of reform in the former Soviet empire, or unfair trade practices, the threats and challenges we face demand cooperative, multinational solutions. Therefore the only responsible U.S. strategy is one that seeks to ensure U.S. influence over and participation in collective decision making in a wide and growing range of circumstances.

An important element of our security preparedness depends on durable relationships with allies and other friendly nations. Accordingly, a central thrust of our strategy of engagement is to sustain and adapt the security relationships we have with key nations around the world. These ties constitute an important part of an international framework that will be essential to ensuring cooperation across a broad range of issues. Within the realm of security issues, our cooperation with allies includes such activities as conducting combined training and exercises, coordinating military plans and preparations, sharing intelligence, jointly developing new systems, and controlling exports of sensitive technologies according to common standards.

The post–Cold War era presents a different set of threats to our security. In this new period, enhancing American security requires, first and foremost, developing and maintaining a strong defense capability of forces ready to fight. We are developing integrated approaches for dealing with threats arising from the development of nuclear and other weapons of mass destruction by other nations. Our security requires a vigorous arms control effort and a strong intelligence capability. We have implemented a strategy for multilateral peace operations. We have clarified rigorous guidelines for when and how to use military force in this era.

We also face security risks that are not solely military in nature. Transnational phenomena such as terrorism, narcotics trafficking, and refugee flows also have security implications both for present and long-term American policy. An emerging class of transnational environmental and natural resource issues is increasingly affecting international stability and consequently will present new challenges to U.S. strategy. The threat of intrusions to our military and commercial information systems poses a significant risk to national security and must be addressed.

MAINTAINING A STRONG DEFENSE CAPABILITY

U.S. military capabilities are critical to the success of our strategy. This nation has unparalleled military capabilities: the United States is the only nation capable of conducting large-scale and effective military operations far beyond its borders. This fact, coupled with our unique position as the security partner of choice in many regions, provides a foundation for regional stability through mutually benefi-

cial security partnerships. Our willingness and ability to play a leading role in defending common interests also help ensure that the United States will remain an influential voice in international affairs—political, military, and economic—that affect our well-being, so long as we retain the military wherewithal to underwrite our commitments credibly.

To protect and advance U.S. interests in the face of the dangers and opportunities outlined earlier, the United States must deploy robust and flexible military forces that can accomplish a variety of tasks:

- *Deterring and defeating aggression in major regional conflicts.* Our forces must be able to help offset the military power of regional states with interests opposed to those of the United States and its allies. To do this, we must be able to credibly deter and defeat aggression, by projecting and sustaining U.S. power in more than one region if necessary.

- *Providing a credible overseas presence.* U.S. forces must also be forward deployed or stationed in key overseas regions in peacetime to deter aggression and advance U.S. strategic interests. Such overseas presence demonstrates our commitment to allies and friends, underwrites regional stability, gains us familiarity with overseas operating environments, promotes combined training among the forces of friendly countries, and provides timely initial response capabilities.

- *Countering weapons of mass destruction.* We are devoting greater efforts to stemming the proliferation of weapons of mass destruction and their delivery means, but at the same time we must improve our capabilities to deter and prevent the use of such weapons and protect ourselves against their effects.

- *Contributing to multilateral peace operations.* When our interests call for it, the United States must also be prepared to participate in multilateral efforts to resolve regional conflicts and bolster new democratic governments. Thus our forces must be ready to participate in peacekeeping, peace enforcement, and other operations in support of these objectives.

- *Supporting Counterterrorism Efforts and Other National Security Objectives.* A number of other tasks remain that U.S. forces have typically carried out with both general-purpose and specialized units. These missions include counterterrorism and punitive attacks, noncombatant evacuation, counternarcotics operations, special forces assistance to nations, and humanitarian and disaster relief operations.

To meet all of these requirements successfully, our forces must be capable of responding quickly and operating effectively. That is, they must be ready to fight and win. This imperative demands highly qualified and motivated people; modern, well-maintained equipment; realistic training; strategic mobility; sufficient support and sustainment capabilities; and proper investment in science and technology.

Major Regional Contingencies

The focus of our planning for major theater conflict is on deterring and, if necessary, fighting and defeating aggression by potentially hostile regional powers, such as North Korea, Iran, or Iraq. Such states are capable of fielding sizable military forces that can cause serious imbalances in military power within regions important to the United States, with allied or friendly states often finding it difficult to match the power of a potentially aggressive neighbor. To deter aggression, prevent coercion of allied or friendly governments, and ultimately defeat aggression should it occur, we must prepare our forces to confront this scale of threat, preferably in concert with our allies and friends, but unilaterally if necessary. To do this, we must have forces that can deploy quickly and supplement U.S. forward-based and forward-deployed forces, along with regional allies, in halting an invasion and defeating the aggressor, just as we demonstrated by our rapid response in October 1994 when Iraq threatened aggression against Kuwait.

With programmed enhancements, the forces the administration is fielding will be sufficient to help defeat aggression in two nearly simultaneous major regional conflicts. As a nation with global interests, the United States must maintain forces with aggregate capabilities on this scale. Obviously, we seek to avoid a situation in which an aggressor in one region might be tempted to take advantage when U.S. forces are heavily committed elsewhere. More basically, maintaining a "two-war" force helps ensure that the United States will have sufficient military capabilities to deter or defeat aggression by a coalition of hostile powers or by a larger, more capable adversary than we foresee today.

We will never know with certainty how an enemy might fight or precisely what demands might be placed on our own forces in the future. The contributions of allies or coalition partners will vary from place to place and over time. Thus balanced U.S. forces are needed in order to provide a wide range of complementary capabilities and to cope with the unpredictable and unexpected.

Overseas Presence

The need to deploy U.S. military forces abroad in peacetime is also an important factor in determining our overall force structure. We will maintain a robust overseas presence in several forms, such as permanently stationed forces and pre-positioned equipment, deployments and combined exercises, port calls and other force visits, as well as military-to-military contacts. These activities provide several benefits. Specifically, they

- Give form and substance to our bilateral and multilateral security commitments.

- Demonstrate our determination to defend U.S. and allied interests in critical regions, deterring hostile nations from acting contrary to those interests.

- Provide forward elements for rapid response in crises as well as the bases, ports, and other infrastructure essential for the deployment of U.S.-based forces by air, sea, and land.

- Enhance the effectiveness of coalition operations, including peace operations, by improving our ability to operate with other nations.

- Allow the United States to use its position of trust to prevent the development of power vacuums and dangerous arms races, thereby underwriting regional stability by precluding threats to regional security.

- Facilitate regional integration, since nations that may not be willing to work together in our absence may be willing to coalesce around us in a crisis.

- Promote an international security environment of trust, cooperation, peace, and stability, which is fundamental to the vitality of developing democracies and free-market economies for America's own economic well-being and security.

Through training programs, combined exercises, military contacts, interoperability, and shared defense with potential coalition partners, as well as security assistance programs that include judicious foreign military sales, we can strengthen the local self-defense capabilities of our friends and allies. Through active participation in regional security dialogues, we can reduce regional tensions, increase transparency in armaments, and improve our bilateral and multilateral cooperation.

By improving the defense capabilities of our friends and demonstrating our commitment to defend common interests, these activities enhance deterrence, encourage responsibility sharing on the part of friends and allies, decrease the likelihood that U.S. forces will be necessary if conflict arises, and raise the odds that U.S. forces will find a relatively favorable situation should a U.S. response be required.

Counterterrorism, Fighting Drug Trafficking, and Other Missions

While the missions outlined above will remain the primary determinants of our general-purpose and nuclear force structure, U.S. military forces and assets will also be called upon to perform a wide range of other important missions. Some of these can be accomplished by conventional forces fielded primarily for theater operations. Often, however, these missions call for specialized units and capabilities.

Combating Terrorism. As long as terrorist groups continue to target American citizens and interests, the United States will need to have specialized units available to defeat such groups. From time to time, we might also find it necessary to strike terrorists at their bases abroad or to attack assets valued by the governments that support them.

Our policy in countering international terrorists is to make no concessions to terrorists, continue to pressure state sponsors of terrorism, fully exploit all available legal mechanisms to punish international terrorists, and help other governments improve their capabilities to combat terrorism.

Countering terrorism effectively requires close day-to-day coordination among executive branch agencies. The Departments of State, Justice, and Defense, the FBI, and CIA continue to cooperate closely in an ongoing effort against international terrorists. Positive results will come from integration of intelligence, diplomatic, and rule-of-law activities, and through close cooperation with other governments and international counterterrorist organizations.

Improving U.S. intelligence capacities is a significant part of the U.S. response. Terrorists, whether from well-organized groups or the kind of more loosely organized group responsible for the World Trade Center bombing, have the advantage of being able to take the initiative in the timing and choice of targets. Terrorism involving weapons of mass destruction represents a particularly dangerous potential threat that must be countered.

The United States has made concerted efforts to punish and deter terrorists. On June 26, 1993, following a determination that Iraq had plotted an assassination attempt against former President George Bush, the United States ordered a cruise missile attack against the headquarters of Iraq's intelligence service in order to send a firm response and deter further threats. Similarly, the United States obtained convictions against defendants in the bombing of the World Trade Center.

U.S. leadership and close coordination with other governments and international bodies will continue, as demonstrated by the U.N. Security Council sanctions against Libya for the Pan Am 103 and UTA 772 bombings, a new international convention dealing with detecting and controlling plastic explosives, and two important counterterrorism treaties—the Protocol for the Suppression of Unlawful Acts of Violence at Airports Serving International Aviation, and the Convention for the Suppression of Unlawful Attacks against the Safety of Maritime Navigation.

Fighting Drug Trafficking. The administration has undertaken a new approach to the global scourge of drug abuse and trafficking that will better integrate domestic and international activities to reduce both the demand and the supply of drugs. Ultimate success will depend on concerted efforts and partnerships by the public, all levels of government, and the American private sector with other governments, private groups, and international bodies.

The United States has shifted its strategy from an emphasis on transit interdiction to a more evenly balanced effort with source countries to build institutions, destroy trafficking organizations, and stop supplies. We will support and strengthen democratic institutions abroad, denying narcotics traffickers a fragile political infrastructure in which to operate. We will also cooperate with governments that demonstrate the political will to confront the narcotics threat.

Two new comprehensive strategies have been developed, one to deal with the problem of cocaine and another to address the growing threat from high-purity heroin entering this country. We will engage more aggressively with international organizations, financial institutions, and nongovernmental organizations in counternarcotics cooperation.

At home and in the international arena, prevention, treatment, and economic alternatives must work hand in hand with law enforcement and interdiction activities. Long-term efforts will be maintained to help nations develop healthy economies with fewer market incentives for producing narcotics. The United States has increased efforts abroad to foster public awareness and support for governmental cooperation on a broad range of activities to reduce the incidence of drug abuse. Public awareness of a demand problem in producing or trafficking countries can be converted into public support and increased governmental law enforcement to reduce trafficking and production. There has been a significant attitudinal change and awareness in Latin America and the Caribbean, particularly as producer and transit nations themselves become plagued with the ill effects of consumption.

Other Missions. The U.S. government is also responsible for protecting the lives and safety of Americans abroad. In order to carry out this responsibility, selected U.S. military forces are trained and equipped to evacuate Americans from such situations as the outbreak of civil or international conflict and natural or man-made disasters. For example, U.S. Marines evacuated Americans from Monrovia, Liberia, in August of 1990, and from Mogadishu, Somalia, in December of that year. In 1991 U.S. forces evacuated nearly 20,000 Americans from the Philippines over a three-week period following the eruption of Mount Pinatubo. Last year, U.S. Marines coupled with U.S. airlift, deployed to Burundi to help ensure the safe evacuation of U.S. citizens from ethnic fighting in Rwanda.

U.S. forces also provide invaluable training and advice to friendly governments threatened by subversion, lawlessness, or insurgency. At any given time, we have small teams of military experts deployed in roughly twenty-five countries helping host governments cope with such challenges.

U.S. military forces and assets are frequently called upon to provide assistance to victims of floods, storms, drought, and other humanitarian disasters. Both at home and abroad, U.S. forces provide emergency food, shelter, medical care, and security to those in need.

Finally, the United States will continue as a world leader in space through its technical expertise and innovation. Over the past thirty years, as more and more nations have ventured into space, the United States has steadfastly recognized space as an international region. Since all nations are immediately accessible from space, the maintenance of an international legal regime for space, similar to the concept of freedom of the high seas, is especially important. Numerous attempts have been made in the past to legally limit access to space by countries that are unable, either technologically or economically, to join space-faring nations. As the commercial importance of space is developed, the United States can expect further pressure from nonparticipants to redefine the status of space, similar to what has been attempted with exclusive economic zones constraining the high seas.

Retaining the current international character of space will remain critical to achieving U.S. national security goals. Our main objectives in this area include

- Continued freedom of access to and use of space.

- Maintaining the U.S. position as the major economic, political, military, and technological power in space.

- Deterring threats to U.S. interests in space and defeating aggressive or hostile acts against U.S. space assets if deterrence fails.

- Preventing the spread of weapons of mass destruction to space.

- Enhancing global partnerships with other spacefaring nations across the spectrum of economic, political, and security issues.

DECIDING WHEN AND HOW TO EMPLOY U.S. FORCES

Our strategy calls for the preparation and deployment of American military forces in the United States and abroad to support U.S. diplomacy in responding to key dangers—those posed by weapons of mass destruction, regional aggression, and threats to the stability of states.

Although there may be many demands for U.S. involvement, the need to husband scarce resources suggests that we must carefully select the means and level of our participation in particular military operations. And while it is unwise to specify in advance all the limitations we will place on our use of force, we must be as clear as possible about when and how we will use it.

There are three basic categories of national interests that can merit the use of our armed forces. The first involves America's vital interests, that is, interests of broad, overriding importance to the survival, security, and vitality of our national entity—the defense of U.S. territory, citizens, allies, and economic well-being. We will do whatever it takes to defend these interests, including—when necessary—the unilateral and decisive use of military power. This was demonstrated clearly in Desert Storm and more recently in Vigilant Warrior.

The second category includes cases in which important, but not vital, U.S. interests are threatened. That is, the interests at stake do not affect our national survival, but they do affect importantly our national well-being and the character of the world in which we live. In such cases, military forces should only be used if they advance U.S. interests, they are likely to be able to accomplish their objectives, the costs and risks of their employment are commensurate with the interests at stake, and other means have been tried and have failed to achieve our objectives. Such uses of force should also be limited, reflecting the relative saliency of the interests we have at stake. Haiti is the most recent example in this category.

The third category involves primarily humanitarian interests. Here, our decisions focus on the resources we can bring to bear by using unique capabilities of our military rather than on the combat power of military force. Generally, the military is not the best tool to address humanitarian concerns. But under certain conditions, the use of our armed forces may be appropriate: when a humanitarian catastrophe dwarfs the ability of civilian relief agencies to respond; when the need for relief is urgent and only the military has the ability to jump-start the longer-term response to the disaster; when the response requires resources unique to the military; and when the risk to American troops is minimal. Rwanda is a good case in point. U.S. military forces performed unique and essential roles, stabilized the situation, and then got out, turning the operation over to the international relief community.

The decision on *whether* and *when* to use force is therefore dictated first and foremost by our national interests. In those specific areas where our vital or survival interests are at stake, our use of force will be decisive and, if necessary, unilateral. In other situations posing a less immediate threat, our military engagement must be targeted selectively on those areas that most affect our national interests—for instance, areas where we have a sizable economic stake or commitments to allies, and areas where there is a potential to generate substantial refugee flows into our nation or our allies.

Second, in all cases the costs and risks of U.S. military involvement must be judged to be commensurate with the stakes involved. We will be more inclined to act where there is reason to believe that our action will bring lasting improvement. On the other hand, our involvement will be more circumscribed when other regional or multilateral actors are better positioned to act than we are. Even in these cases, however, the United States will be actively engaged at the diplomatic level. In every case, however, we will consider several critical questions before committing military force. Have we considered nonmilitary means that offer a reasonable chance of success? Is there a clearly defined, achievable mission? What is the environment of risk we are entering? What is needed to achieve our goals? What are the potential costs—both human and financial—of the engagement? Do we have reasonable assurance of support from the American people and their elected representatives? Do we have timelines and milestones that will reveal the extent of success or failure, and, in either case do we have an exit strategy?

The decision on *how* we use force has a similar set of derived guidelines.

First, when we send American troops abroad, we will send them with a clear mission and, for those operations that are likely to involve combat, the means to achieve their objectives decisively, having answered the questions: what types of U.S. military capabilities should be brought to bear, and is the use of military force carefully matched to our political objectives?

Second, as much as possible, we will seek the help of our allies and friends or of relevant international institutions. If our most important national interests are at stake, we are prepared to act alone. But especially on those matters touching directly the interests of our allies, there should be a proportionate commitment from them. Working together increases the effectiveness of each nation's actions, and sharing the responsibilities lessens everyone's load.

These, then, are the calculations of interest and cost that have influenced our past uses of military power and will guide us in the future. Every time this administration has used force, it has balanced interests against costs. And in each case, the use of our military has put power behind our diplomacy, allowing us to make progress we would not otherwise have achieved.

One final consideration regards the central role the American people rightfully play in how the United States wields its power abroad: the United States cannot long sustain a fight without the support of the public. This is true for humanitarian and other nontraditional interventions, as well as war. Modern media communications confront every American with images that both stir the impulse to intervene and raise the question of an operation's costs and risks. When it is judged in America's interest to intervene, we must use force with an unwavering commitment to our objective. While we must continue to reassess any operation's costs and benefits as it unfolds and the full range of our options, reflexive calls for early withdrawal of our forces as soon as casualties arise endangers our objectives as well as our troops. Doing so invites any rogue actor to attack our troops to try to force our departure from areas where our interests lie.

COMBATING THE SPREAD AND USE OF WEAPONS OF MASS DESTRUCTION AND MISSILES

Weapons of mass destruction—nuclear, biological, and chemical—along with their associated delivery systems, pose a major threat to our security and that of our allies and other friendly nations. Thus a key part of our strategy is to seek to stem the proliferation of such weapons and to develop an effective capability to deal with these threats. We also need to maintain robust strategic nuclear forces and seek to implement existing strategic arms agreements.

Nonproliferation and Counterproliferation

A critical priority for the United States is to stem the proliferation of nuclear weapons and other weapons of mass destruction and their missile delivery systems. Countries' weapons programs, and their levels of cooperation with our nonproliferation efforts, will be among our most important criteria in judging the nature of our bilateral relations.

Through programs such as the Nunn-Lugar Cooperative Threat Reduction effort and other denuclearization initiatives, important progress has been made to build a more secure international environment. One striking example was the successful transfer last fall of nearly six hundred kilograms of vulnerable nuclear material from Kazakhstan to safe storage in the United States. Kazakhstan was concerned about the security of the material and requested U.S. assistance in removing it to safe storage. The Departments of Defense and Energy undertook a joint mission to retrieve the uranium. Similarly, under an agreement we secured with Russia, it is converting tons of highly enriched uranium from dismantled weapons into commercial reactor fuel for purchase by the United States. The United States is also working with Russia to enhance control and accounting of nuclear material.

As a key part of our effort to control nuclear proliferation, we seek the indefinite and unconditional extension of the Nuclear Nonproliferation Treaty (NPT) and its universal application. Achieving a Comprehensive Test Ban Treaty as soon as possible, ending the unsafeguarded production of fissile materials for nuclear weapons purposes, and strengthening the Nuclear Suppliers Group and the International Atomic Energy Agency (IAEA) are important goals. They complement our comprehensive efforts to discourage the accumulation of fissile materials, to seek to strengthen controls and constraints on those materials, and over time to reduce worldwide stocks. As announced at last September's U.N. General Assembly, we will seek a global ban on the production of fissile material for nuclear weapons.

To combat missile proliferation, the United States seeks prudently to broaden membership of the Missile Technology Control Regime (MTCR). The administration supports the earliest possible ratification and entry in force of the Chemical Weapons Convention (CWC) as well as new measures to deter violations of and enhance compliance with the Biological Weapons Convention (BWC). We also support improved export controls for nonproliferation purposes both domestically and multilaterally.

The proliferation problem is global, but we must tailor our approaches to specific regional contexts.

We have concluded an agreed framework to bring North Korea into full compliance with its nonproliferation obligations, including the NPT and IAEA safeguards. We will continue efforts to prevent Iran from advancing its weapons of mass destruction objectives and to thwart Iraq from reconstituting its previous programs. The United States seeks to cap, reduce, and ultimately eliminate the nuclear and missile capabilities of India and Pakistan. In the Middle East and elsewhere, we encourage regional arms control agreements that address the legitimate security concerns of all parties. These tasks are being pursued with other states that share our concern for the enormous challenge of stemming the proliferation of such weapons.

The United States has signed bilateral agreements with Russia, Ukraine, and South Africa that commit these countries to adhere to the guidelines of the MTCR. We also secured China's commitment to observe the MTCR guidelines and its agreement not to transfer MTCR-controlled ground-to-ground missiles. Russia has agreed not to transfer space-launch vehicle technology with potential military applications to India. South Africa has agreed to observe the MTCR guidelines and to dismantle its Category I missile systems and has joined the NPT and accepted full-scope safeguards. Hungary, the Czech Republic, the Slovak Republic, and Poland have joined the Australia Group (which controls the transfer of items that could be used to make chemical or biological weapons). Hungary and Argentina have joined the MTCR, and Brazil has committed itself publicly to adhere to the MTCR guidelines. Argentina, Brazil, and Chile have brought the Treaty of Tlatelolco into force. We continue to push for the dismantlement of all intercontinental ballistic missiles located in Ukraine and Kazakhstan. With the United States and Russia, Ukraine is pressing forward on implementation of the Trilateral Statement, which provides for the transfer of all nuclear warheads from Ukraine to Russia for dismantlement in return for fair compensation.

Thus the United States seeks to prevent additional countries from acquiring chemical, biological, and nuclear weapons and the means to deliver them. However, should such efforts fail, U.S. forces must be prepared to deter, prevent, and defend against their use. As agreed at the January 1994 NATO Summit, we are working with our allies to develop a policy framework to consider how to reinforce ongoing prevention efforts and to reduce the proliferation threat and protect against it.

The United States will retain the capacity to retaliate against those who might contemplate the use of weapons of mass destruction, so that the costs of such use will be seen as outweighing the gains. To minimize the impact of North Atlantic Treaty Organization proliferation of weapons of mass destruction on our interests, however, we will need the capability not only to deter their use against either ourselves or our allies and friends but also, where necessary and feasible, to prevent it.

This will require improved defensive capabilities. To minimize the vulnerability of our forces abroad to weapons of mass destruction, we are placing a high priority on improving our ability to locate, identify, and disable arsenals of weapons of mass destruction, production and storage facilities for such weapons, and their delivery systems.

NUCLEAR FORCES

In September the administration approved the recommendations of the Pentagon's Nuclear Posture Review (NPR). A key conclusion of this review is that the United States will retain a triad of strategic nuclear forces sufficient to deter any future hostile foreign leadership with access to strategic nuclear forces from acting against our vital interests and to convince it that seeking a nuclear advantage would be futile. Therefore we will continue to maintain nuclear forces of sufficient size and capability to hold at risk a broad range of assets valued by such political and military leaders. The NPR's recommended strategic nuclear force posture was approved as the U.S. Strategic Arms Reduction Treaty (START) II force. The forces are 450–500 Minuteman intercontinental ballistic missiles (ICBMs), 14 Trident submarines all with D-5 missiles, and 20 B-2 and 66 B-52 strategic bombers. A nonnuclear role has been approved for the B-1s. This force posture allows us the flexibility to reconstitute or reduce further, as conditions warrant. The NPR also reaffirmed the current posture and deployment of nonstrategic nuclear forces; the United States will eliminate carrier and surface ship nuclear weapons capability.

ARMS CONTROL

Arms control is an integral part of our national security strategy. Arms control can help reduce incentives to initiate attack; enhance predictability regarding the size and structure of forces, thus reducing fear of aggressive intent; reduce the size of national defense industry establishments and thus permit the growth of more vital, nonmilitary industries; ensure confidence in compliance through effective monitoring and verification; and ultimately contribute to a more stable and calculable balance of power.

In the area of strategic arms control, prescribed reductions in strategic offensive arms and the steady shift toward less destabilizing systems remain indispensable. Ukraine's accession to the Nuclear Nonproliferation Treaty—joining Belarus's and Kazakhstan's decision to be nonnuclear nations—was followed immediately by the exchange of instruments of ratification and brought the Strategic Arms Reduction Treaty (START) into force at the December Conference on Security and Cooperation in Europe summit, paving the way for ratification of the START II Treaty. Under START II, the United States and Russia will each be left with between 3,000 and 3,500 deployed strategic nuclear warheads, which is a two-thirds reduction from the Cold War peak. Both nations agreed that once START II is ratified they will immediately begin to deactivate or otherwise remove from combat status those systems whose elimination will be required by that treaty, rather than waiting for the treaty to run its course through the year 2003. START II ratification will also open the door to the next round of strategic arms control, in which we will consider what further reductions in, or limitations on, remaining U.S. and Russian nuclear forces should be carried out. We will also explore strategic confidence-building measures and mutual understandings that reduce the risk of accidental war.

The full and faithful implementation of other existing arms control agreements, including the Anti-Ballistic Missile (ABM) Treaty, Strategic Arms Reduction Talks I, Biological Weapons Convention, Intermediate-range Nuclear Forces (INF) Treaty, Conventional Forces in Europe Treaty, several nuclear testing agreements, the 1994 Vienna Document on Confidence and Security-Building Measures, Open Skies, the Environmental Modification Convention, Incidents at Sea, and many others will remain an important element of national security policy. The ongoing negotiation initiated by the United States to clarify the ABM Treaty by establishing an agreed demarcation between strategic and theater ballistic missiles and to update the treaty to reflect the breakup of the Soviet Union reflects the administration's commitment to maintaining the integrity and effectiveness of crucial arms control agreements.

Future arms control efforts may become more regional and multilateral. Regional arrangements can add predictability and openness to security relations, advance the rule of international law and promote cooperation among participants. They help maintain deterrence and a stable military balance at regional levels. The United States is prepared to promote, help negotiate, monitor, and participate in regional arms control undertakings compatible with American national security interests. We will generally support such undertakings but will not seek to impose regional arms control accords against the wishes of affected states.

As arms control, whether regional or global, becomes increasingly multilateral, the Conference on Disarmament (CD) in Geneva will play an even more important role. The United States will support measures to increase the effectiveness and relevance of the CD. Arms control agreements can head off potential arms races in certain weapons categories or in some environments. We will continue to seek greater transparency, responsibility, and, where appropriate, restraint in the transfer of conventional weapons and global military spending. The U.N. register of conventional arms transfers is a start in promoting greater transparency of weapons transfers and buildups, but more needs to be done. The United States has proposed that the new regime to succeed the Coordinating Committee focus on conventional arms sales and dual-use technologies. Where appropriate, the United States will continue to pursue such efforts vigorously. Measures to reduce oversized defense industrial establishments, especially those parts involved with weapons of mass destruction, will also contribute to stability in the post–Cold War world. The administration also will pursue defense conversion agreements with the former Soviet Union states, and defense conversion is also on the agenda with China. The United States has also proposed a regime to reduce the number and availability of the world's long-lived antipersonnel mines whose indiscriminate and irresponsible use has reached crisis proportions. As another part of our effort to address this land mine problem, the administration has also submitted the Convention on Conventional Weapons to the Senate for advice and consent.

PEACE OPERATIONS

In addition to preparing for major regional contingencies, we must prepare our forces for peace operations to support democracy or conflict resolution. The United States, along with others in the international community, will seek to prevent and contain localized conflicts before they require a military response. U.S. support capabilities such as airlift, intelligence, and global communications have often contributed to the success of multilateral peace operations, and they will continue to do so. U.S. combat units are less likely to be used for most peace operations, but in some cases their use will be necessary or desirable and justified by U.S. national interests as guided by the Presidential Decision Directive (PDD) "U.S. Policy on Reforming Multilateral Peace Operations," and outlined below.

Multilateral peace operations are an important component of our strategy. From traditional peacekeeping to peace enforcement, multilateral peace operations are sometimes the best way to prevent, contain, or resolve conflicts that could otherwise be far more costly and deadly.

Peace operations often have served, and continue to serve, important U.S. national interests. In some cases, they have helped preserve peace between nations, as in Cyprus and the Golan Heights. In others, peacekeepers have provided breathing room for fledgling democracies, as in Cambodia, El Salvador, and Namibia.

At the same time, we must recognize that some types of peace operations make demands on the United Nations that exceed the organization's current capabilities. The United States is working with the U.N. headquarters and other member states to ensure that the United Nations embarks only on peace operations that make political and military sense and that the United Nations is able to manage effectively those peace operations it does undertake. We support the creation of a professional U.N. peace operations headquarters with a planning staff, access to timely intelligence, a logistics unit that can be rapidly deployed, and a modern operations center with global communications. The United States will reduce our peacekeeping payments to 25 percent while working to ensure that other nations pay their fair share. We are also working to ensure that peacekeeping operations by appropriate regional organizations such as NATO and the Organization for Security and Cooperation can be carried out effectively.

In order to maximize the benefits of U.N. peace operations, the United States must make highly disciplined choices about when and under what circumstances to support or participate in them. The need to exercise such discipline is at the heart of the administration's policy on reforming multilateral peace operations. Far from handing a blank check to the United Nations, the policy review on peace operations—the most thorough ever undertaken by an administration—requires the United States to undertake a rigorous analysis of requirements and capabilities before voting to support or participate in peace operations. The United States has not hesitated to use its position on the Security Council to ensure that the United Nations authorizes only those peace operations that meet these standards.

Most U.N. peacekeeping operations do not involve U.S. forces. On those occasions when we consider contributing U.S. forces to a U.N. peace operation, we will employ rigorous criteria, including the same principles that would guide any decision to employ U.S. forces. In addition, we will ensure that the risks to U.S. personnel and the command and control arrangements governing the participation of American and foreign forces are acceptable to the United States.

The question of command and control is particularly critical. There may be times when it is in our interest to place U.S. troops under the temporary operational control of a competent U.N. or allied commander. The United States has done so many times in the past—from the siege of Yorktown in the Revolutionary War to the battles of Desert Storm. However, under no circumstances will the president ever relinquish his command authority over U.S. forces.

Improving the ways the United States and the United Nations decide upon and conduct peace operations will not make the decision to engage any easier. The lesson we must take away from our first ventures in peace operations is not that we should forswear such operations but that we should employ this tool selectively and more effectively. In short, the United States views peace operations as a means to support our national security strategy, not as a strategy unto itself.

The administration is firmly committed to securing the active support of the Congress for U.S. participation in peace operations. It has set forth a detailed blueprint to guide consultations with Congress. With respect to particular operations, the administration will undertake consultations on questions such as the nature of expected U.S. military partici-

pation, the mission parameters of the operation, the expected duration, and budgetary implications. In addition to such operation-specific consultations, the administration has conducted regular monthly briefings for congressional staff and will deliver an Annual Comprehensive Report to Congress on Peace Operations. Congress is critical to the institutional development of a successful U.S. policy on peace operations, including the resolution of funding issues that have an impact on military readiness.

Two other points deserve emphasis. First, the primary mission of our armed forces is not peace operations; it is to deter and, if necessary, to fight and win conflicts in which our most important interests are threatened. Second, while the international community can create conditions for peace, the responsibility for peace ultimately rests with the people of the country in question.

STRONG INTELLIGENCE CAPABILITIES

U.S. intelligence capabilities are critical instruments of our national power and remain an integral part of our national security strategy. Only a strong intelligence effort can provide adequate warning of threats to U.S. national security and identify opportunities for advancing our interests. Policy analysts, decision makers, and military commanders at all levels will continue to rely on our intelligence community to collect information unavailable from other sources and to provide strategic and tactical analysis to help surmount potential challenges to our military, political, and economic interests.

Because national security has taken on a much broader definition in this post–Cold War era, intelligence must address a much wider range of threats and dangers. We will continue to monitor military and technical threats, to guide long-term force development and weapons acquisition, and to directly support military operations. Intelligence will also be critical for directing new efforts against regional conflicts, proliferation of weapons of mass destruction, counterintelligence, terrorism, and narcotics trafficking. In order to adequately forecast dangers to democracy and to U.S. economic well-being, the intelligence community must track political, economic, social, and military developments in those parts of the world where U.S. interests are most heavily engaged and where overt collection of information from open sources is inadequate. Finally, to enhance the study and support of worldwide environmental, humanitarian, and disaster relief activities, technical intelligence assets (principally imagery) must be directed to a greater degree toward the collection of data on these subjects.

The collection and analysis of intelligence related to economic development will play an increasingly important role in helping policy makers understand economic trends. That collection and analysis can help level the economic playing field by identifying threats to U.S. companies from foreign intelligence services and unfair trading practices.

This strategy requires that we take steps to reinforce current intelligence capabilities and overt foreign service reporting within the limits of our resources, and similar steps to enhance coordination of clandestine and overt collection. Some key goals are

- Provide timely warning of strategic threats, whether from the remaining arsenal of weapons in the former Soviet Union or from other nations with weapons of mass destruction.

- Ensure timely intelligence support to military operations.

- Provide early warning of potential crises and facilitate preventive diplomacy.

- Develop new strategies for collection, production, and dissemination (including closer relationships between intelligence producers and consumers) to make intelligence products more responsive to current consumer needs.

- Improve worldwide technical capabilities to detect, identify, and determine the efforts of foreign nations to develop weapons of mass destruction.

- Enhance counterintelligence capabilities.

- Provide focused support for law enforcement agencies in areas like counternarcotics, counterterrorism, and illegal technology trade.

- Streamline intelligence operations and organizations to gain efficiency and integration.

- Revise long-standing security restrictions where possible to make intelligence data more useful to intelligence consumers.

- Develop security countermeasures based on sound threat analysis and risk management practices.

To advance these goals the administration significantly restructured counterintelligence policy development and interagency coordination. The PDD on U.S. counterintelligence effectiveness took immediate steps to improve our ability to counter both traditional and new threats to our nation's security in the post–Cold War era. Further, the administration directed a comprehensive restructuring of the process by which our security policies, practices, and procedures are developed and implemented. The PDD on security policy coordination ensures the development of security policies and practices that realistically meet the threats we face as they continue to evolve, at a price we can afford, while guaranteeing the fair and equitable treatment of all Americans upon whom we rely to guard our nation's security. Consistent with the provisions of the fiscal 1995 Intelligence Authorization Act, the Chairman of the Foreign Intelligence Advisory Board was directed to conduct a comprehensive review of the roles and missions of the intelligence community and fundamentally evaluate and define the need for intelligence in the post–Cold War environment.

[Editor's note: The executive summary of this review is in Chapter 6.]

THE ENVIRONMENT AND SUSTAINABLE DEVELOPMENT

The more clearly we understand the complex interrelationships between the different parts of our world's environment, the better we can understand the regional and even global effects of local changes to the environment. Increasing competition for the dwindling reserves of uncontaminated air, arable land, fisheries and other food sources, and water, once considered "free" goods, is already a very real risk to regional stability around the world. The range of environmental risks serious enough to jeopardize international stability extends to massive population flight from man-made or natural catastrophes, such as Chernobyl or the East African drought, and to large-scale ecosystem damage caused by industrial pollution, deforestation, loss of biodiversity, ozone depletion, desertification, ocean pollution, and ultimately climate change. Strategies dealing with environmental issues of this magnitude will require partnerships between governments and nongovernmental organizations, cooperation between nations and regions, and a commitment to a strategically focused, long-term policy for emerging environmental risks.

The decisions we make today regarding military force structures typically influence our ability to respond to threats twenty to thirty years in the future. Similarly, our current decisions regarding the environment and natural resources will affect the magnitude of their security risks over at least a comparable period of time, if not longer. The measure of our difficulties in the future will be settled by the steps we take in the present.

As a priority initiative, the United States successfully led efforts at the September Cairo Conference to develop a consensus Program of Action to address the continuous climb in global population, including increased availability of family planning and reproductive health services, sustainable economic development, the empowerment of women to include enhanced educational opportunities, and a reduction in infant and child mortality. Rapid population growth in the developing world and unsustainable consumption patterns in industrialized nations are the root of both present and potentially even greater forms of environmental degradation and resource depletion. A conservative estimate of the globe's population projects 8.5 billion people on the planet by the year 2025. Even when making the most generous allowances for advances in science and technology, one cannot help but conclude that population growth and environmental pressures will feed into immense social unrest and make the world substantially more vulnerable to serious international frictions.

PROMOTING PROSPERITY AT HOME

A central goal of our national security strategy is to promote America's prosperity through efforts both at home and abroad. Our economic and security interests are increasingly inseparable. Our prosperity at home depends on engaging actively abroad. The strength of our diplomacy, our ability to maintain an unrivaled military, the attractiveness of our values abroad—all these depend in part on the strength of our economy.

ENHANCING AMERICAN COMPETITIVENESS

Our primary economic goal is to strengthen the American economy. The first step toward that goal was reducing the federal deficit and the burden it imposes on the economy and future generations. The economic program passed in 1993 has restored investor confidence in the United States and strengthened our position in international economic negotiations. Fiscal 1995 will be the first time that the deficit has been reduced three years in a row since the Truman administration. We are building on this deficit reduction effort with other steps to improve American competitiveness: investing in science and technology; assisting defense conversion; improving information networks and other vital infrastructure; and improving education and training programs for America's workforce. We are structuring our defense research and development effort to place greater emphasis on dual-use technologies that can enhance competitiveness and meet pressing military needs. We are also reforming the defense acquisition system so that we can develop and procure weapons and material more efficiently.

PARTNERSHIP WITH BUSINESS AND LABOR

Our economic strategy views the private sector as the engine of economic growth. It sees the government's role as a partner to the private sector—acting as an advocate of U.S. business interests; leveling the playing field in international markets; helping to boost American exports; and finding ways to remove domestic and foreign barriers to the creativity, initiative, and productivity of American business.

To this end, on September 29, 1993, the administration published its report creating America's first national export strategy and making sixty-five specific recommendations for reforming the way government works with the private sector to expand exports. Among the recommendations were significant improvements in advocacy, export financing, market information systems, and product standards education. The results of these reforms could enable U.S. exports to reach the trillion dollar mark by the turn of the century, which would help create at least six million new American jobs.

Another critical element in boosting U.S. exports is reforming the outdated export licensing system.

That reform began with significant liberalization of export licensing controls for computers, supercomputers and telecommunications equipment. The administration is also seeking comprehensive reform of the Export Administration Act, which governs the process of export licensing. The goal of this reform is to strengthen our ability to prevent proliferation and protect other national interests, while removing unnecessarily burdensome licensing requirements left over from the Cold War.

ENHANCING ACCESS TO FOREIGN MARKETS

The success of American business is more than ever dependent upon success in international markets. The ability to compete internationally also ensures that our companies will continue to innovate and increase productivity, which will in turn lead to improvements in our own living standards. But to compete abroad, our firms need access to foreign markets, just as foreign industries have access to our open market. We vigorously pursue measures to increase access for our companies—through bilateral, regional, and multilateral arrangements.

The North American Free Trade Agreement

On December 3, 1993, the United States signed the North American Free Trade Act (NAFTA), which creates a free-trade zone among the United States, Canada, and Mexico. NAFTA has already created more than 100,000 American jobs. NAFTA has increased Mexico's capacity to cooperate with our nation on a wide range of issues that cross our two-thousand-mile border—including the environment, narcotics trafficking, and illegal immigration.

Asia Pacific Economic Cooperation

Our economic relations depend vitally on our ties with the Asia Pacific region, which is the world's fastest-growing economic region. In November 1993 the United States convened the first-ever summit of the leaders of the economies that constitute the Asia-Pacific Economic Cooperation (APEC) forum. U.S. initiatives in the APEC forum will open new opportunities for economic cooperation and permit U.S. companies to become involved in substantial infrastructure planning and construction throughout the region. The trade and investment framework agreed to in 1993 provided the basis for enhancing the "open regionalism" that defines APEC. At the second leaders' meeting in November 1994, the leaders of APEC further drove the process by accepting the goal of free and open trade and investment throughout the region by early in the twenty-first century and agreeing to lay out a blueprint for achieving that goal by the Osaka APEC leaders meeting.

Uruguay Round of GATT

The successful conclusion in December 1993 of the Uruguay Round of the negotiations under the General Agreement on Tariffs and Trade (GATT) significantly strengthened the world trading system. The Uruguay Round accord is the largest, most comprehensive trade agreement in history. It will create hundreds of thousands of new U.S. jobs and expand opportunities for U.S. businesses. For the first time, international trade rules will apply to services, intellectual property, and investments, and effective rules will apply to agriculture. The Uruguay Round also continued the cuts in tariff rates throughout the world that began just after the Second World War. Working with Congress, the administration secured U.S. approval of this pathbreaking agreement and the resulting World Trade Organization, which provides a forum to resolve disputes openly. The administration remains committed to ensuring that the commitments in the Uruguay Round agreement are fulfilled.

U.S.–Japan Framework Agreement

While Japan is America's second-largest export market, foreign access to the Japanese market remains limited in important sectors, including automobiles and automobile parts. Japan's persistent current account surpluses are a major imbalance in the global economy. The U.S.-Japan Framework for Economic Partnership was established in July 1993 to redress the imbalances in our economic relationship. In October 1994 the United States and Japan reached framework agreements regarding government procurement of medical technologies and telecommunications (including Nippon Telephone and Telegraph [NPP] procurement). In December we concluded a further agreement on flat glass. We have also reached framework agreements on financial services and intellectual property rights. The administration is committed to ensuring that competitive American goods and services have fair access to the Japanese market. We will continue to work to ensure that Japan takes measures to open its markets and stimulate its economy, both to benefit its own people and to fulfill its international responsibilities.

Summit of the Americas

America's economy benefits enormously from the opportunity offered by the commitment of the democratic nations of the Western Hemisphere to negotiate a free-trade agreement for the region by 2005. The Western Hemisphere is our largest export market, constituting over 35 percent of all U.S. sales abroad. The action plan will accelerate progress toward free, integrated markets, which will create new high-wage jobs and sustain economic growth for America. The invitation to Chile to begin negotiations to join NAFTA is the first step toward the summit of the Americas goal of reaching a hemispheric free-trade zone.

Expanding the Realm of Free Trade

The conclusion of NAFTA, the Uruguay Round, the Bogor Declaration of the 1994 APEC leaders meeting, and the Summit of the Americas' action plan represents unprecedented progress toward more open markets both at the regional and global levels. The administration intends to continue its efforts in further enhancing U.S. access to foreign markets. The World Trade Organization will provide a new institutional lever for securing such access. Emerging markets, particularly along the Pacific Rim, present vast opportunities for American enterprise, and APEC now provides a suitable vehicle for the exploration of such opportunities. Similarly, the United States convened the Summit of the Americas to seize the opportunities created by the movement toward open markets throughout the hemisphere. All such steps in the direction of expanded trading relationships will be undertaken in a way consistent with protection of the international environment and with the goal of sustainable development here and abroad.

STRENGTHENING MACROECONOMIC COORDINATION

As national economies become more integrated internationally, the United States cannot thrive in isolation from developments abroad. International economic expansion is benefiting from Group of Seven (G-7) macroeconomic policy coordination. To improve global macroeconomic performance, we will continue to work through the G-7 process to promote growth-oriented policies to complement our own efforts.

PROVIDING FOR ENERGY SECURITY

The United States depends on oil for more than 40 percent of its primary energy needs. Roughly 45 percent of our oil needs are met with imports, and a large share of these imports come from the Persian Gulf area. The experiences of the two oil shocks and the Gulf War show that an interruption of oil supplies can have a significant impact on the economies of the United States and its allies. Appropriate economic responses can substantially mitigate the balance of payments and inflationary impacts of an oil shock; appropriate foreign policy responses to events such as Iraq's invasion of Kuwait can limit the magnitude of the crisis.

Over the longer term, the United States' dependence on access to foreign oil sources will be increasingly important as our resources are depleted. The U.S. economy has grown roughly 75 percent since the first oil shock; yet during that time our oil consumption has remained virtually stable and oil production has declined. High oil prices did not generate enough new oil exploration and discovery to sustain production levels from our depleted resource base. These facts show the need for continued and extended reliance on energy efficiency and conservation and development of alternative energy sources. Conservation measures notwithstanding, the United States has a vital interest in unrestricted access to this critical resource.

PROMOTING SUSTAINABLE
DEVELOPMENT ABROAD

Broadly based economic development not only improves the prospects for democratic development in developing countries, but also expands the demands for U.S. exports. Economic growth abroad can alleviate pressure on the global environment, reduce the attraction of illegal narcotics trade, and improve the health and economic productivity of global populations.

The environmental aspects of ill-designed economic growth are clear. Environmental damage will ultimately block economic growth. Rapid urbanization is outstripping the ability of nations to provide jobs, education, and other services to new citizens. The continuing poverty of a quarter of the world's people leads to hunger, malnutrition, economic migration, and political unrest. Widespread illiteracy and lack of technical skills hinder employment opportunities and drive entire populations to support themselves on increasingly fragile and damaged resource bases. New diseases such as AIDS and epidemics, often spread through environmental degradation, threaten to overwhelm the health facilities of developing countries, disrupt societies, and stop economic growth. These realities must be addressed by sustainable development programs that offer viable alternatives. U.S. leadership is of the essence. If such alternatives are not developed, the consequences for the planet's future will be grave indeed.

Domestically, the United States must work hard to halt local and cross-border environmental degradation. In addition, the United States should foster environmental technology targeting pollution prevention, control, and cleanup. Companies that invest in energy efficiency, clean manufacturing, and environmental services today will create the high-quality, high-wage jobs of tomorrow. By providing access to these types of technologies, our exports can also provide the means for other nations to achieve environmentally sustainable economic growth. At the same time, we are taking ambitious steps at home to better manage our natural resources and reduce energy and other consumption, decrease waste generation, and increase our recycling efforts.

Internationally, the administration's foreign assistance program focuses on four key elements of sustainable development: broad based economic growth, the environment, population and health, and democracy. We will continue to advocate environmentally sound private investment and responsible approaches by international lenders. At our urging, the multilateral development banks are now placing increased emphasis on sustainable development in their funding decisions, to include a commitment to perform environmental assessments on projects for both internal and public scrutiny. In particular, the Global Environmental Facility, established last year, will provide a source of financial assistance to the developing world for climate change, biodiversity, and oceans initiatives.

The United States is taking specific steps now in all of these areas:

- In June 1993 the United States signed the Convention on Biological Diversity, which aims to protect and utilize the world's genetic inheritance. The Interior Department has been directed to create a national biological survey to help protect species and to help the agricultural and biotechnical industries identify new sources of food, fiber, and medications.

- New policies are being implemented to ensure the sustainable management of U.S. forests by the year 2000, as pledged internationally. In addition, U.S. bilateral forest assistance programs are being expanded, and the United States is promoting sustainable management of tropical forests.

- In the wake of the 1992 United Nations Conference on Environment and Development, the United States has sought to reduce land-based sources of marine pollution, maintain populations of marine species at healthy and productive levels, and protect endangered marine mammals.

- The United States has focused technical assistance and encouraged nongovernmental environmental groups to provide expertise to the republics of the former Soviet Union and Central and Eastern European nations that have suffered the most acute environmental crises. The Agency for International Development, the Environmental Protection Agency, and other U.S. agencies are engaged in technical cooperation with many countries around the world to advance these goals.

- The administration is leading a renewed global effort to address population problems and promote international consensus for stabilizing world population growth. Our comprehensive approach will stress family planning and reproductive health care, maternal and child health, education, and improving the status of women. The International Conference on Population Development, held in September in Cairo, endorsed these approaches as important strategies in achieving our global population goals.

PROMOTING DEMOCRACY

All of America's strategic interests—from promoting prosperity at home to checking global threats abroad before they threaten our territory—are served by enlarging the community of democratic and free-market nations. Thus working with new democratic states to help preserve them as democracies committed to free markets and respect for human rights is a key part of our national security strategy.

One of the most gratifying and encouraging developments of the past fifteen years is the explosion in the number of states moving away from repressive governance and toward democracy. Since the success of many of those experiments is by no means assured, our strategy of enlargement must focus on the consolidation of those regimes and the broadening of their commitment to democracy. At the same time, we seek to increase respect for fundamental human rights in all states and encourage an evolution to democracy where that is possible.

The enlargement of the community of market democracies respecting human rights and the environment is manifest in a number of ways:

- Over the past ten years, more than thirty nations in Central and Eastern Europe, the former Soviet Union, Latin America, Africa, and East Asia have adopted the structures of a constitutional democracy and held free elections.

- The nations of the Western Hemisphere have proclaimed their commitment to democratic regimes and to the collective responsibility of the nations of the Organization of American States to respond to threats to democracy.

- In the Western Hemisphere, only Cuba is not a democratic state.

- Nations as diverse as South Africa, Cambodia, and El Salvador have resolved bitter internal disputes with agreement on the creation of constitutional democracies.

The first element of our democracy strategy is to work with the other democracies of the world and to improve our cooperation with them on security and economic issues. We also seek their support in enlarging the realm of democratic nations.

The core of our strategy is to help democracy and markets expand and survive in other places where we have the strongest security concerns and where we can make the greatest difference. This is not a democratic crusade; it is a pragmatic commitment to see freedom take hold where that will help us most. Thus we must target our effort to assist states that affect our strategic interests, such as those with large economies, critical locations, nuclear weapons, or the potential to generate refugee flows into our own nation or into key friends and allies. We must focus our efforts where we have the most leverage. And our efforts must be demand driven—they must focus on nations whose people are pushing for reform or have already secured it.

Russia is a key state in this regard. If we can support and help consolidate democratic and market reforms in Russia (and the other newly independent states), we can help turn a former threat into a region of valued diplomatic and economic partners. Our intensified interaction with Ukraine has helped move that country on to the path of economic reform, which is critical to its long-term stability. In addition, our efforts in Russia, Ukraine, and the other states support and facilitate our efforts to achieve continued reductions in nuclear arms and compliance with international nonproliferation accords.

The new democracies in Central and Eastern Europe are another clear example, given their proximity to the great democratic powers of Western Europe, their importance to our security, and their potential markets.

Since our ties across the Pacific are no less important than those across the Atlantic, pursuing enlargement in the Asian Pacific is a third example. We will work to support the emerging democracies of the region and to encourage other states along the same path.

Continuing the great strides toward democracy and markets in our hemisphere is also a key concern and was behind the decision to host the Summit of the Americas in December 1994. As we continue such efforts, we should be on the lookout for states whose entry into the camp of market democracies may influence the future direction of an entire region; South Africa now holds that potential with regard to sub-Saharan Africa.

How should the United States help consolidate and enlarge democracy and markets in these states? The answers are as varied as the nations involved, but there are common elements. We must continue to help lead the effort to mobilize international resources, as we have with Russia, Ukraine, and the other new independent states. We must be willing to take immediate public positions to help staunch democratic reversals, as we have in Haiti and Guatemala. We must give democratic nations the fullest benefits of integration into foreign markets, which is part of why NAFTA and the GATT ranked so high on our agenda. And we must help these nations strengthen the pillars of civil society, improve their market institutions, and fight corruption and political discontent through practices of good governance.

At the same time as we work to ensure the success of emerging democracies, we must also redouble our efforts to guarantee basic human rights on a global basis. At the 1993 United Nations Conference on Human Rights, the United States forcefully and successfully argued for a reaffirmation of the universality of such rights and improved international mechanisms for their promotion. In the wake of this gathering, the United Nations has named a high commissioner for human rights, and the rights of women have been afforded a new international precedence. The United States has taken the lead in helping the United Nations set up international tribunals to enforce accountability for the war crimes in the former Yugoslavia and in Rwanda.

The United States also continues to work for the protection of human rights on a bilateral basis. To demonstrate our own willingness to adhere to international human rights standards, the United States ratified the international convention prohibiting discrimination on the basis of race, and the administration is seeking Senate consent to ratification for the convention prohibiting discrimination against women. The United States will play a major role in promoting women's rights internationally at the U.N. Women's Conference in September.

In all these efforts, a policy of engagement and enlargement should take on a second meaning: we should pursue our goals through an enlarged circle not only of government officials but also of private and nongovernmental groups. Private firms are natural allies in our efforts to strengthen market economies. Similarly, our goal of strengthening democracy and civil society has a natural ally in labor unions, human rights groups, environmental advocates, chambers of commerce, and election monitors. Just as we rely on force multipliers in defense, we should welcome these "diplomacy multipliers," such as the National Endowment for Democracy.

Supporting the global movement toward democracy requires a pragmatic and long-term effort focused on both values and institutions. The United States must build on the opportunities achieved through the successful conclusion of the Cold War. Our long-term goal is a world in which each of the major powers is democratic, with many other nations joining the community of market democracies as well.

Our efforts to promote democracy and human rights are complemented by our humanitarian assistance programs, which are designed to alleviate human suffering and to pave the way for progress toward establishing democratic regimes with a commitment to respect for human rights and appropriate

strategies for economic development. We are also exploring ideas such as the suggestion of Argentina's President Carlos Saúl Menem for the creation of an international civilian rapid-response capability for humanitarian crises, including a school and training for humanitarian operations.

Through humanitarian assistance and policy initiatives aimed at the sources of disruption, we seek to mitigate the contemporary migration and refugee crises, foster long-term global cooperation and strengthen involved international institutions. The United States will provide appropriate financial support and will work with other nations and international bodies, such as the International Red Cross and the U.N. High Commissioner for Refugees, in seeking voluntary repatriation of refugees—taking into full consideration human rights concerns as well as the economic conditions that may have driven them out in the first place. Helping refugees return to their homes in Mozambique, Afghanistan, Eritrea, Somalia, and Guatemala, for example, is a high priority.

Relief efforts will continue for people displaced by the conflict in Bosnia and other republics of the former Yugoslavia. We will act in concert with other nations and the United Nations against the illegal smuggling of Chinese into this country. Working with the tools of diplomatic, economic, and military power, our humanitarian and refugee policies can bear results, as was evident in Haiti. We provided temporary safe haven at Guantanamo Naval Base for those Haitians who feared for their safety and left by sea until we helped restore democracy.

THE NATIONAL MILITARY STRATEGY OF THE UNITED STATES OF AMERICA

JOHN M. SHALIKASHVILI

INTRODUCTION

With the end of the Cold War, international relations have entered a new era. New democracies are evolving within the former Soviet Union and Europe; old rivalries are being transformed. For the United States this unsettled period provides both opportunities and risks as we seek to promote our values and protect our interests worldwide.

In *A National Security Strategy of Engagement and Enlargement,* the president described our security objectives and provided the armed forces the guidance to shape our military strategy. Drawing also from the guidance developed in the *Bottom-Up Review,* this military strategy outlines how best to use U.S.

military capabilities to help achieve national goals. This military strategy of flexible and selective engagement prescribes a selective employment of military capabilities in peace and the use of decisive military force in war to achieve our national military objectives in this new international environment.

National military strategy addresses the main dangers that threaten U.S. security interests, identifies the national military objectives, determines the military tasks we must accomplish to achieve these objectives, and examines the capabilities and forces required.

This is a strategy that applies day-to-day to guide our activities in the near term, even when we are at peace. But let there be no doubt about one fundamental fact: military forces exist—are organized, trained, and

John M. Shalikashvili, National Military Strategy of the United States of America *(Washington, D.C.: GPO, 1995), 1–20. Public Domain.*

Figure 1
Military Capabilities

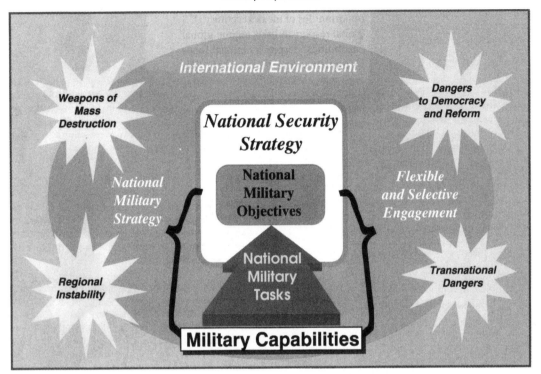

equipped—first and foremost to fight and win America's wars. Within this overriding requirement, this strategy also embodies a number of associated priorities.

INTERNATIONAL ENVIRONMENT

We have recently passed from a longstanding bipolar order to a still unsettled multipolar world. This was a welcome development, bringing promising opportunities to advance our interests and values but also ushering in new and diverse challenges.

Today the United States faces no immediate threat to its national survival. However, global interdependence and transparency, coupled with our worldwide security interests, make it difficult to ignore troubling developments almost anywhere on earth. In fact, in the five years since the fall of the Berlin Wall we have deployed our forces to assist in security or humanitarian crises about forty times—a far greater pace than in the preceding twenty years. This level of activity, a measure reflective of these unsettled times, suggests a continuing need for flexible and robust military capabilities.

It is also true that the intentions of other nations can change, sometimes very rapidly, and thus our national military strategy must account for the military capabilities of other nations as well as their current intentions.

In surveying the international environment, the national security strategy as articulated by the president recognizes four principal dangers that our military, in combination with other elements of national power, must address: regional instability, the proliferation of weapons of mass destruction, transnational dangers, and the dangers to democracy and reform in the former Soviet Union, Eastern Europe, and elsewhere (see Figure 1).

REGIONAL INSTABILITY

Regional instabilities are, and will remain, a recurring challenge, from nations that explode into internal conflict, as happened in Yugoslavia, Somalia, and Rwanda, to attacks against neighboring states, as we saw when Iraq invaded Kuwait. Many antagonisms that were buried by the frozen relationships of the Cold War have now surfaced, adding to those that carried over from that era.

The revival of age-old religious, ethnic, and territorial quarrels, in many cases compounded by the more contemporary tensions stemming from the disintegration of the Soviet Union, may present an even wider threat: the risk that they may engulf neighboring states. Among the former Soviet republics, in the Balkans, in the Maghreb, and throughout Africa, dangerous instabilities litter the landscape. Additional challenges are posed by Iraq, Iran, and North Korea, each of which is an imminent threat to the security of its neighbors and region.

WEAPONS OF MASS DESTRUCTION

The threat of nuclear attack against the American homeland today has diminished, but there are still thousands of nuclear warheads and strategic delivery systems in the world. Despite the internal political and economic changes under way in the states of the former Soviet Union, we must remain mindful of these capabilities. For as long as these weapons exist, they will remain a threat to our security.

Especially troubling is the prospect that some of these weapons or their component materials might be stolen or otherwise acquired by third parties. Thus the security and accountability of all nuclear warheads, weapon systems, and materials remain a grave concern.

Indeed, the proliferation of weapons of mass destruction—nuclear, chemical, and biological—is one of the most troubling dangers we face. The ongoing efforts to obtain such weapons by a number of countries present great and growing risks for the United States and its allies. The continuing diffusion of missile delivery technology is increasing the risks we face. Even the prospect of a hostile regional power or terrorist group gaining access to nuclear, chemical, or biological weapons contributes to regional insecurities and increases the difficulty of settling disputes peacefully.

TRANSNATIONAL DANGERS

Increasing global interdependence has made every nation more vulnerable to growing transnational threats. Spreading diseases, fleeing refugees, international crime syndicates, and drug lords are several of the more serious transnational threats that bleed across our own and other nations' borders. What gives these threats unique character is that combating them lies beyond the reach of any single government. But the damage they might inflict on our health, children, prosperity, and societies could be significant.

DANGERS TO DEMOCRACY AND REFORM

The community of democratic nations and free-market economies is growing throughout the world—a trend consistent with important U.S. interests. The United States is committed to supporting nations transitioning into this community and therefore will assist in efforts to defend against threats to democratic and economic reform in the former Soviet Union, Eastern Europe, and elsewhere. However, the transition process in these emerging democracies remains susceptible to setbacks and reversals. The failure of democratic reform in the newly independent states, particularly in Russia itself, would not necessarily return us to the bipolar standoff that characterized the Cold War, but it would in all likelihood adversely affect the United States and its interests.

NATIONAL MILITARY OBJECTIVES

Since the birth of the nation our military strategy has been anchored to the same core purpose: to protect our nation and its interests, while maintaining fundamental American values intact. Throughout the latter half of the century this has required a strategy of global engagement. This engagement is no less required today, even though our national military strategy has continued to evolve.

In addressing the four dangers discussed earlier, U.S. military strategy must be intrinsically constructive, proactive, and preventive, helping to reduce the sources of conflict and at the same time blocking the effective use of force by potential adversaries. In military terms, we have translated these purposes as two complementary objectives: promoting stability and thwarting aggression (see Figure 2).

PROMOTE STABILITY

We must not expect an easy transition to the stable, multipolar world we seek. The last transition of such magnitude, at the end of World War II, took years and saw numerous conflicts; and the form of that stability posed a threat to our nation for nearly forty years.

A primary thrust of our strategy must be to promote a long-term stability that is advantageous to the United States. There is ample historical precedent in this century that regional instability in military, economic, and political terms can escalate into global conflict. Our strategy further promotes stability in order to establish the conditions under which democracy can take hold and expand around the world. We intend to use the daily, peacetime activities of the armed forces to pursue this effort. U.S. forces stationed overseas, as well as those temporarily deployed, participate with allies at all levels in cooperative and defensive security arrangements that help preclude conflict and foster the peaceful enlargement of the community of free-market nations.

In carefully selected cases, where our interests so dictate, we must be prepared in peacetime to use our vast capabilities to transport, communicate, support, assist, and manage to address our regional security needs and counter emerging instabilities. When more significant interests are at stake and our capabilities would make a difference, we must also be prepared to deploy forces, usually in conjunction with allies and friends, but alone if we must.

THWART AGGRESSION

The most serious measure of engagement is our commitment to protect U.S. extended interests and our allies. We will be prepared to respond promptly in the Persian Gulf area, in Northeast Asia, and other regions where U.S. interests or allies are threatened. Through this preparation we seek to prevent conflict and reassure allies and friends of our commitment and capabilities.

Should war nevertheless occur, our forces, in concert with those of our allies and friends, must be capable of defeating any potential adversary and es-

Figure 2
Achieving National Military Objectives

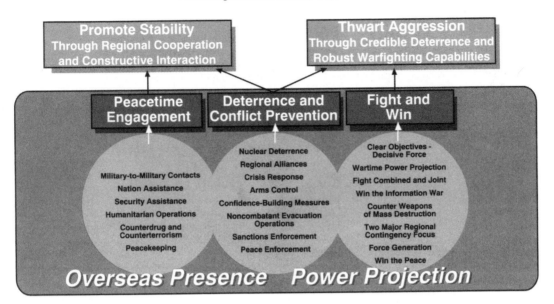

tablishing the decisive conditions which lead to long-term solutions.

Because the United States has important national interests throughout the world, we must avoid any situation in which a hostile power in one region might be tempted to take advantage when U.S. forces are heavily committed elsewhere. Consequently, we must have forces of sufficient size and capabilities, in concert with regional allies, to defeat potential enemies in major conflicts that may occur nearly simultaneously in two different regions. Maintaining this capability also provides a hedge against the emergence of a hostile coalition or a more powerful or resurgent adversary.

STRATEGY

The end of the Cold War has further tightened the close, complementary relationship that must exist between military activities and other elements of U.S. national power. The president's national security strategy describes this relationship and prescribes a set of integrated regional approaches to meet U.S. interests in different parts of the globe. The strategic military objectives described above will thus be achieved in concert with other elements of power and by military activities that may vary from region to region, depending on U.S. interests and particular conditions.

This strategy of flexible and selective engagement comprises three sets of tasks: remaining constructively engaged in peacetime, acting to deter aggression and prevent conflict, and fighting and winning our nation's wars when called upon. To facilitate performing these tasks, we continue to refine the two fundamental and complementary strategic concepts

of overseas presence and power projection. Our strategy for accomplishing our national military objectives is best understood by examining these two strategic concepts and the three components of the strategy: peacetime engagement, deterrence and conflict prevention, and war fighting.

STRATEGIC CONCEPTS

Overseas Presence

Overseas presence forces, including some tailored for specific missions, perform a variety of activities that promote stability and prevent conflict. In addition, through overseas presence we maintain mobile, combat-ready forces capable of responding to a wide range of threats throughout the world. U.S. forces overseas provide visible proof of our commitment to defend American interests with our allies and friends worldwide. Overseas presence is not a crutch for friends who refuse to bear their share of the burden; rather, it is an essential mechanism to support our fundamental interests in forward regions where the support of these interests can best be developed.

Overseas presence takes the form of permanently stationed forces and forces temporarily deployed, some on a regular, rotational basis. In addition, we maintain an overseas presence through a broad program of routine air, ground, and naval deployments, as well as various contingency operations.

In accordance with our security needs, the bulk of our overseas presence forces are deployed in Western Europe, Japan, and South Korea, with smaller capabilities elsewhere in the Pacific, the Middle East and Southwest Asia, and Latin America.

Approximately 100,000 U.S. military members serve in Europe in ground forces consisting of substantial elements of two army divisions along with a corps headquarters, associated corps troops, and other supporting elements; in air forces consisting of about two and one-third fighter wings; and in a Mediterranean naval ashore presence sufficient to support a carrier battle group and an amphibious ready group.

In Northeast Asia we also retain close to 100,000 troops. In South Korea they serve in one army division and one wing of combat aircraft. In Japan we maintain a marine expeditionary force, an army special forces battalion, one and one-half wings of combat aircraft, and forward deploy an aircraft carrier, amphibious assault ship, and their support ships.

In the Middle East we maintain only a small presence. The bulk of our overseas presence commitment in this area, as well as in Southwest Asia, is reflected in the significant periodic deployments of forces, to include participation in contingency operations. Our forces deploy to Africa to participate in humanitarian or peace operations as national interests dictate. In Latin America small numbers of our armed forces help to promote democratic growth in many countries and work to halt the import of drugs into our country.

Our overseas presence helps to keep important infrastructure available and ready. Permanently stationed forces maintain support and basing that are vital for receiving reinforcement and for throughput and onward movement in time of crisis and conflict.

Although the size of our forces permanently stationed overseas and the size of some deployments have decreased in recent years, and in Europe dramatically, their importance has not diminished. They signal our commitment to the region in which they are deployed and are a visible reminder to those who would threaten our interests.

Power Projection

With fewer U.S. forces permanently stationed overseas, we must increase our capability to project forces abroad. Credible power projection capability complements our overseas presence in acting as a deterrent to potential adversaries. Effective power projection capabilities also provide greater flexibility in employing military force. Coupled with overseas forces, the ability to project tailored forces through rapid, strategic mobility gives national leaders additional time for consultation and increased options in response to potential crises and conflicts.

Our ability to rapidly project power worldwide depends on four strategic mobility enhancements: increased airlift capability, additional pre-positioning of heavy equipment afloat and ashore, increased surge capacity of our sealift, and improved readiness and responsiveness of the ready reserve force.

Power projection is essential for performing the required tasks of all components of the strategy. However, it is most critical in the deterrence and conflict prevention and war-fighting portions of our military strategy.

Components of the Strategy

Peacetime Engagement

Overseas presence and power projection provide the basis for executing the tasks required by our strategy. The first group of these tasks, peacetime engagement, describes a broad range of noncombat activities undertaken by our armed forces that demonstrate commitment, improve collective military capabilities, promote democratic ideals, relieve suffering, and in many other ways enhance regional stability. On any given day, tens of thousands of the men and women of our armed forces are engaged worldwide across the range of peacetime engagement activities.

Military-to-Military Contacts. Military-to-military contact programs are one of the most effective instruments in our efforts to create a more stable security order. Today there are opportunities to forge new and more cooperative security relationships both with former adversaries and with formerly nonaligned nations. Moreover, there has been a vast increase in our participation in multinational operations whose members include many nontraditional allies, as we saw in the Gulf War and in recent humanitarian and peace operations such as in Haiti. The success of these operations hinges on mutual trust, effective communications and interoperability, and doctrinal familiarity, precisely the results we seek from ongoing military-to-military contacts.

These programs are also a platform for imparting influence and democratic values to militaries in reforming or newly democratic nations. The militaries of Central and Eastern Europe are a particular priority. U.S. military-to-military joint contact teams are at work in twelve of these countries today, and we are expanding this program to other regions this year.

Combined training exercises provide particularly useful military-to-military contacts. Their benefits are many: combined training, joint readiness and interoperability, and military professionalism. Our sponsorship of such exercises also helps to shape our basing, prepositioning, logistics support, and security agreements.

We also maintain an active exchange program between military units and regularly assign individual personnel to work for limited periods with other armed forces. Exchanges of personnel, both as students and teachers, at military academies and professional military schools foster understanding between our respective military establishments.

Nation Assistance. Our forces participate selectively in a variety of activities to assist friendly nations as they combat lawlessness, subversion, and insurgency. These efforts are carefully orchestrated to reinforce the host nation's developmental programs. Specific activities that involve our armed forces include bilateral and multilateral exercises, civil–military operations, intelligence and communications sharing, and logistics support.

Security Assistance. Security assistance involves the selective use of cooperative programs with allied and friendly armed forces that furnish these countries with the means to defend themselves from aggression and to fight alongside U.S. forces in a coalition effort. Providing vital training and U.S.-manufactured weapons systems increases the access and influence of the U.S. military and improves the interoperability of potential coalition members. In addition, these contacts help to build and solidify relationships with emerging democracies and security partners. Security assistance also deters aggression in unstable regions and provides a cost-effective alternative to maintaining larger U.S. forces in the region.

A very important avenue for interaction between U.S. military personnel and their foreign counterparts is the International Military Education and Training program. Last year students from more than a hundred foreign countries studied at U.S. military schools, learning not only technical skills but also gaining a broader appreciation for American values and perspectives.

Our regional commanders in chief are unanimous in stating that security assistance programs, along with military-to-military contacts, produce gains that far exceed their costs, and we seek to reenergize and expand these important programs.

Humanitarian Operations. Our armed forces stand ready to participate in humanitarian and disaster relief operations at home and abroad. The U.S. military can offer unique capabilities in terms of logistics (transport, supply, and distribution), communications, and security. Often, our greatest contribution to these operations resides in our ability to rapidly respond when more traditional relief agencies are overwhelmed. After these organizations are "up and running," military forces can be withdrawn. A prime example of this concept is the recent U.S. assistance operation in Rwanda.

Counterdrug and Counterterrorism. The armed forces, working in close cooperation with law enforcement agencies, will use all means authorized by the president and the Congress to halt the flow of illegal drugs into this country. We will also act both unilaterally and in concert with security partners to fight international terrorism.

Peacekeeping. We remain prepared to support traditional peacekeeping operations on a case-by-case basis. When warranted by circumstances and national interests, this support may include participation of U.S. combat units. When appropriate, we prefer to share the burden of peacekeeping with allies and friends.

When the United States does participate, we will follow the guidelines of Presidential Decision Directive 25, to include seeking a clear delineation of the objectives of each operation, ensuring an unbroken chain of command to the president, and ensuring rules of engagement to protect our forces and permit the proper execution of assigned tasks. The capabilities we provide will be carefully tailored, usually to reinforce and supplement the resources of our international partners. We recognize that peace operations are often different from traditional military operations in the tasks and capabilities they require of our armed forces. We are continuing to develop appropriate doctrine and training for these operations.

Reserve component elements will take on increased responsibility for participating in and supporting peacekeeping missions.

Deterrence and Conflict Prevention

Deterrence and conflict prevention, the second component of the strategy, is a combination of efforts to deter threats to our security and interests as well as a series of other actions we can take to restore stability, security, and adherence to international law. Our military strategy envisions vigorous efforts in each of the following tasks in order to secure our interests and reduce the potential for conflict.

Nuclear Deterrence. The highest priority of our military strategy is to deter a nuclear attack against our nation and allies. Our survival and the freedom of action that we need to protect extended national interests depend upon strategic and nonstrategic nuclear forces and their associated command, control, and communications.

We have recently concluded a comprehensive nuclear posture review that looked into the next century and validated those systems we will need for the foreseeable future. Though we are continuing to pursue reductions under the Strategic Arms Reduction Treaty (START) I and II, we still need to maintain a survivable triad of strategic delivery systems. This serves both to deter still very powerful strategic arsenals and to convince possible adversaries that any attempt to seek a nuclear advantage would be futile. We still need to maintain a mix of forward-deployed and deployable nonstrategic nuclear weapons, both to provide deterrent coverage for our allies, and because extended deterrence in many cases is a decisive factor in our nonproliferation efforts.

Regional Alliances. Our regional strategies, and the global strategy of which they are a part, are built on the foundation of strong and effective alliances. Our goal of a stable, multipolar world hinges on both the ability to preserve and adapt our existing alliances to challenges we confront today and anticipate tomorrow and on the capacity to develop new relationships as necessary.

American forces in Europe continue to demonstrate a strong commitment to this area of significant national interests. In addition, we provide the North Atlantic Treaty Organization (NATO) with key leadership, critical intelligence and communications support, and much of the nuclear force that guarantees European security. Our capability to conduct military operations is sustained through frequent exercises and interoperability training that ensures the effectiveness of coalitions both in and beyond the treaty area.

The end of the Cold War has seen NATO's military focus evolve from deterring aggression by the Soviet-led Warsaw Pact to dealing with today's diverse security challenges. The alliance has embraced a new strategic concept that recognizes the changes in the geostrategic environment and is adjusting its missions, command arrangements, and forces accordingly. Implementing the Combined Joint Task Force concept will facilitate NATO's participation in nontraditional, out-of-area operations such as peace operations, sanctions enforcement, and humanitarian assistance. It will also enable NATO to provide timely operational support to other bodies such as the United Nations and the Western European Union.

Today many of our former adversaries have expressed a desire to join NATO—an indicator of NATO's success in adapting to meet new security challenges. More than twenty nations, including Russia and other former Soviet republics, have already joined NATO's Partnership for Peace program. These countries seek to align their defense programs and policies more closely with NATO's—and to forge stronger ties to the West. The United States fully supports and participates in the Partnership for Peace initiative, which fosters regional stability and is essential to the eventual enlargement of the NATO alliance.

Five of the seven U.S. mutual defense treaties are with partners in the Asia Pacific region, helping to underpin the relative stability of an area that is home to the world's fastest-growing economies. We will remain engaged with the Association of Southeast Asian Nations, the sponsor of the largest security forum (involving eighteen countries) in that region.

In Northeast Asia our bilateral security relationship with Japan remains fundamental to U.S. security. Our forces in Japan are a visible demonstration of our commitment to the peace and stability of the entire region and are available for short-notice deployment throughout the theater. Frequent combined U.S. and Japanese military exercises continue to enhance professional interaction between our militaries.

The defense of the Republic of Korea will remain a key element of U.S. strategy in this region. Our forward-stationed forces there represent an unambiguous demonstration of that commitment. We will continue to conduct a vigorous exercise program with Korean forces to ensure that we are ready and able to work together and to reinforce the theater, if necessary.

In Southwest Asia, we must remain alert to the dangers posed by a still aggressive Iraq and a revolutionary Iran that continues to fan the flames of social, political, and economic dissent among neighboring states. U.S. commitment to peace and security in the critical Persian Gulf region is demonstrated through bilateral defense cooperation agreements, security assistance, pre-positioning, forward presence, and combined exercises. These activities

in a region vital to U.S. and global security and prosperity assist our friends in improving their self-defense while deterring aggression.

We will continue to support the deepening of democracy throughout the Western Hemisphere. We are strengthening our relationships with Latin America and Mexico and are working with the Organization of American States to promote stability and mutual security.

Crisis Response. Should our resolve to protect vital national interests be challenged, we must be able to respond rapidly through a wide spectrum of deterrent options and preventive measures. We intend to respond initially to crises using our forces stationed and deployed overseas but will be prepared to deploy all necessary forces to threatened areas as we demonstrated in October 1994 when Saddam Hussein once again moved forces south and threatened Kuwait. Critical to such reinforcement requirements are sea- and land-based pre-positioned equipment sets, enhanced airlift and sealift capabilities, and air refueling forces. Rapid power projection, from the United States to overseas areas and between regions, remains key to crisis response.

Arms Control. Arms control efforts contribute significantly to our security by limiting and reducing the number and types of weapons that can threaten us and by reducing regional arms buildups that can raise tensions and risks. Among the fundamental arms control agreements are the Antiballistic Missile Treaty, START I and II, the Treaty on Intermediate-Range Nuclear Forces, and the Nuclear Nonproliferation Treaty. The Treaty on Conventional Armed Forces in Europe is a landmark agreement that has significantly reduced conventional forces for the first time in our generation and has greatly enhanced security in this area vital to U.S. interests.

Recognizing the contributions that arms control agreements can make to national security, we seek to broaden the range of arms control efforts to address chemical and biological weapons. When implemented, the Chemical Weapons Convention will mandate the destruction of all chemical weapons and their production facilities.

Confidence-Building Measures. Our military forces will continue to be directly involved in confidence-building efforts to foster openness and transparency in military affairs. Implementation of Vienna Document 1994 is a concrete example of such efforts that include information exchanges, exercise limits and observations, and demonstrations of military capability. Agreements governing Dangerous Military Activities and regional initiatives, such as the Open Skies regime that permits aerial overflight of participating nations' territories, directly support our goal of preventing conflict.

Noncombatant Evacuation Operations. The U.S. government is responsible for protecting the lives and safety of its citizens abroad. Often, that task falls to our armed forces. When conditions of violence or disorder in foreign countries threaten American lives, U.S. forces, in support of the Department of

State, will use all appropriate means to extract American citizens promptly and safely.

Sanctions Enforcement. Military forces are increasingly used to enforce economic sanctions resulting from national policy decisions and U.N. Security Council resolutions. U.S. forces will participate in operations to search, divert, delay, or disrupt transport vessels and to assist in the compliance of guidelines set by either U.S. or U.N. authorities. Effective enforcement requires efficient coordination of military operations at sea, on land, and in the air and space.

Peace Enforcement.   On occasion, U.S. forces may be directed to participate in peace enforcement operations or other operations in the gray zone between peace and war. These operations are characterized by the use of force or the threat of the use of force, and are interwoven with diplomatic and economic efforts, often involving both governmental and nongovernmental organizations. Such actions may be undertaken to maintain or restore international peace and security, or to respond to acts of aggression.

We continue to incorporate the lessons learned from our recent experiences in Iraq, Somalia, and the former Yugoslavia. For example, when significant U.S. forces are directed to participate in a major peace enforcement operation likely to involve combat, our guidelines will continue to be to:

- Commit sufficient forces to achieve clearly defined objectives.

- Plan to achieve those objectives decisively.

- Reassess and adjust, as necessary, the size, composition, and disposition of our forces to achieve our objectives.

Application of these guidelines is clearly exemplified by our Operation Uphold Democracy in Haiti commencing in September 1994.

During peace enforcement operations, command and control arrangements are critical. Ordinarily in such instances, a U.S. command will be established or the mission will be conducted through a competent, established regional organization such as NATO or an ad hoc coalition. The greater the U.S. military contribution and the greater the likelihood of combat, the more inclined we will be to lead the operation. The president, however, will never relinquish command authority over U.S. forces.

Fight and Win

The ability of U.S. armed forces to fight and win, the third component of our strategy, serves as the ultimate guarantor of our vital interests. This ability is crucial to deter aggression and prevent conflict, and if challenged, it ensures that we will in fact prevail. Being ready to fight and win remains our foremost responsibility and the prime consideration governing all our military activities. It is for this reason, fundamentally, that our nation has raised and sustained its armed forces.

In war, our use of military force will follow the principles outlined below.

Clear Objectives: Decisive Force. In any application of force, military objectives will be clearly defined to support our national political aims in the conflict. We intend to commit sufficient force to achieve these objectives in a prompt and decisive manner.

Wartime Power Projection. If we have forces deployed to the threatened area when crisis turns to conflict, these forces will assist our regional allies in creating a viable defense to halt the invasion rapidly and will form the basis for the subsequent buildup of combat power needed to defeat the aggressor decisively. But we anticipate that, for the most part, we will project air, land, and sea forces from the United States and, in some cases, from overseas areas, to augment forward-deployed forces or to establish U.S. presence in the theater of operations. This power projection could ultimately entail the transport of large numbers of personnel and their equipment. Such an effort requires detailed plans to provide the necessary intelligence, logistics, and communications support, as well as capabilities to protect our forces during deployment.

We continue to build on the lessons learned in Operation Desert Storm to strengthen our power projection capabilities. During the September 1994 deployment of forces to Haiti, roll-on/roll-off shipping was proved exceptionally ready and significantly more reliable as a result of post–Gulf War improvements. Early access to combat, combat support, and combat service support capabilities in the reserve component is also vital to meet our power projection requirements for any major regional contingency. We have demonstrated in recent operations in both Haiti and Kuwait that we have the ability to gain this prompt access to the reserves, clearly indicating improved wartime capabilities.

Fight Combined and Fight Joint. While we maintain the unilateral capability to wage decisive campaigns to protect U.S. and multinational security interests, our armed forces will most often fight in concert with regional allies and friends, as coalitions can decisively increase combat power and lead to a more rapid and favorable outcome to the conflict. Combined operations capitalize on our peacetime training, help generate and sustain international support, and enable our forces to provide the high-leverage capabilities required to achieve decisive outcomes against any adversary.

Modern warfare requires U.S. forces to fight as a joint team whether operating unilaterally or as part of an international coalition. Accordingly, each of the services provides trained and ready forces to support the combatant commanders' war-fighting plans and operations. Success in joint and combined military operations requires bringing to bear, at the right times and places, the unique and complementary capabilities of each of the services.

Each service has both a role and primary and collateral functions to execute, for which it must

Figure 3
Interactive Information Sharing Is Key to Modern Battlefield Success

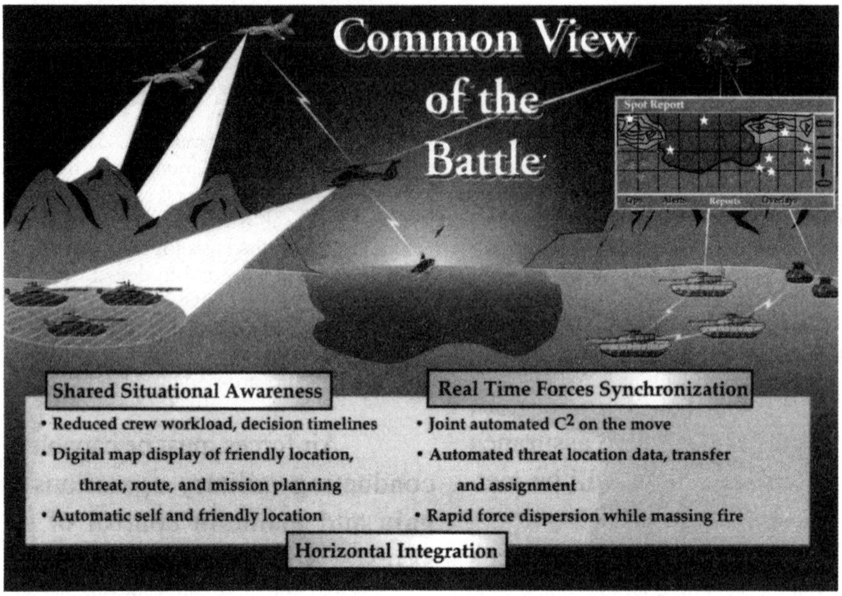

train, organize, and equip its forces. Land forces are mainly involved with prompt and sustained combat operations on land; naval and marine forces with operations at or from the sea; air forces with military operations in the air. Each of our services leverages the benefits of unhindered access to space (see Figure 3).

Land forces must be capable of deploying rapidly and, if necessary, executing forcible entry to seize the initiative and close with and destroy enemy forces through synchronized maneuver and precision fires throughout the breadth and depth of the battle area. They must be capable of achieving operational and tactical freedom of maneuver and be sufficiently agile to achieve their objectives before opponents can effect countermeasures. Land forces must possess the capabilities necessary to dominate the land battle. In addition, they must provide the combat support and combat service support necessary to sustain the land battle as well as provide critical elements of support to joint forces deployed in theater. Ultimately, land forces can occupy territory, control populations, and provide on-the-scene assurance that political objectives will be met.

Naval and marine forces must be capable of conducting naval and amphibious war-fighting operations. Forward-deployed naval expeditionary forces can respond immediately to a crisis, execute forcible entry or reinforce other forward-deployed elements, and through prompt action help halt an enemy offensive and enable the flow of follow-on ground and land-based air contingents. These forces assist in providing protective cover from air, land, sea, or missile intrusion. By ensuring freedom of the seas

and controlling strategic choke points, naval and marine forces provide strategic freedom of maneuver and thus enhance deployment and sustainment of joint forces in theater.

Air forces must be capable of conducting military operations to gain and maintain control of the skies, holding vital enemy capabilities at risk throughout the theater, and helping to destroy the enemy's ability to wage war. Air superiority is essential so we can quickly move forces into theater and attack the enemy at will. Air control provides the joint force numerous operational and tactical advantages while facilitating land and naval maneuver. Air forces provide sustained, precise firepower, reconnaissance and surveillance, critical refueling, and global lift to rapidly deploy and sustain joint forces in theater.

Space forces play an increasingly important role in prosecuting modern warfare. They provide global and battlefield surveillance, ballistic missile warning, precise navigation, secure communications, weather, and intelligence information. Space assets facilitate effective command and control and enhance the joint utilization of our land, sea, and air forces.

Special operations forces from all three military departments provide combatant commanders and deployed forces with unique capabilities to conduct direct action, special reconnaissance, unconventional warfare, counterterrorism, psychological operations, and civil affairs activities. Properly employed, special operations forces provide commanders capabilities that extend their vision of the battlefield, increase their flexibility, and enhance their initiative. These forces will be fully integrated into military operations by the combatant commanders.

Win the Information War. The remarkable leverage attainable from modern reconnaissance, intelligence collection and analysis, and high-speed data processing and transmission warrants special emphasis. The services and combatant commands require such fused information systems. These systems enhance our ability to dominate warfare. We must ensure that this leverage works for us and against our adversaries. New doctrine is being developed and training and control programs are under way to ensure that advantages, built on the early success of Operation Desert Storm, are being exploited.

Countering Weapons of Mass Destruction. Potential adversaries should recognize our capability to dominate any escalation of conflict should weapons of mass destruction be employed against us. In addition, we will maintain and strengthen our defensive capabilities against such weapons. We continue efforts to prevent the use of mass destruction weapons and make preparations to operate effectively in environments marked by biological, chemical, or radioactive contamination.

Two Major Regional Contingency Focus. When entering any regional conflict, we will fully apply all the principles addressed above to ensure decisive victory. At the same time, however, we will remain aware that risks and dangers exist in other regions. While projecting forces to one contingency, we will be enhancing the readiness of other assets to handle a challenge elsewhere. Some high-leverage capabilities could be used in one major regional contingency and then reallocated and redeployed to another, as conditions permit. Other capabilities essential to fighting and winning the first conflict will remain in the theater where they are committed.

Force Generation. We will quickly generate combat power in wartime. Active forces engaged overseas in lower-priority missions may be recalled, reorganized, retrained, and redeployed. Normally our armed forces will withdraw from operations other than war when the security situation is stabilized and other organizations are prepared to assume responsibility for relief or security. In times of crisis, we will need to accelerate this process. As our first forces react to a major regional crisis, we will begin actions to ensure forces are ready to meet a second contingency should it arise. Activities not involving critical U.S. interests will be turned over to the United Nations or other responsible regional security organizations while we attend to higher-priority taskings.

Substantial reserve forces will be committed to combat and combat support missions early in any major regional contingency. To backfill active forces elsewhere and to prepare for unforeseen contingencies, some reserve component forces can expect to be mobilized immediately and to remain on active duty throughout the conflict, even though they are not directly involved in operations.

Win the Peace. In the wake of any major theater conflict, our forces will likely encounter numerous demands to attend to the needs of the indigenous population. This may well include activities such as providing humanitarian relief and nation assistance that are included in the peacetime engagement component of our military strategy. Planning for postconflict operations will begin prior to and continue throughout any conflict. Close coordination and cooperation between military and other governmental and nongovernmental agencies will be particularly critical during the transition period following war as some functions are transferred to nonmilitary organizations and while our forces are being redeployed and reconstituted.

MILITARY CAPABILITIES

POSTURE AND SIZE

The U.S. armed forces are now in their eighth year of drawdown and will continue to be reduced and reshaped in accordance with the *Bottom-Up Review.* By 1999 the total active end strength will be 1,445,000 people, down from 2,130,000 in 1989. Over the next few years, active army divisions will continue to decline from 18 to 10, active air force fighter wings from 24 to 13, and navy battle force ships from 567 to 346. Active Marine Corps structure will remain at three marine expeditionary forces, but end strength will continue to decline from 197,000 personnel to 174,000. Selected reserve personnel will decline from 1,170,000 in 1989 to 893,900 in 1999, with a proportionate decline in force structure. The Coast Guard will reduce its active end strength from 44,000 to 36,300.

Nevertheless, the United States will retain formidable forces. While smaller, we must become pound-for-pound more capable through enhancements and selected modernizations. Our ability to execute this strategy of flexible and selective engagement will be put at risk without these required force upgrades.

The dynamic and unpredictable post–Cold War environment demands that we maintain military capabilities flexible and responsive enough to cope with unforeseen threats. Thus, U.S. forces will be sized and structured to achieve decisive victory in two nearly simultaneous major regional conflicts and to conduct combat operations characterized by rapid response and a high probability of success.

Our military forces are being sized and structured using scenario-based planning and assessments initiated during the *Bottom-Up Review.* Although no one can predict with certainty where the next conflict will occur, the use of plausible, illustrative scenarios against postulated threat forces enables comparisons and analyses to determine the relative values of different forces and capabilities across a range of circumstances. While the two nearly simultaneous major regional contingency requirement most challenges the force structure, other needs—such as forces to provide adequate overseas presence, space capabilities to support a wide range of activities in peace and war, and secure nuclear forces for deterrence—have also been taken into account.

Combat support capabilities, including transportation, logistics, intelligence, communications, and medical, remain vital to our success and will be strengthened.

FORCE-BUILDING FOUNDATIONS

The combat forces and supporting capabilities must be built on five fundamental foundations.

Quality People

The experience of Operation Desert Storm confirmed that there is no substitute for high-quality men and women in our armed forces. In a smaller force with diverse requirements, quality people provide the fundamental edge over any adversary.

The requirement for quality people is not an abstraction. It reflects the fundamental reality of military operations: despite intense planning and high technology, military operations are nevertheless marked by ambiguity, uncertainty, and chance and are driven by emotion; they normally continue twenty-four hours a day, in any conceivable terrain or climate, and in conditions of extreme stress. Under these circumstances, leadership, courage, initiative, flexibility, and skill will remain essential to victory. No foreseeable change in technology will diminish the importance of high-quality men and women in our military.

We are working hard to maintain excellence among our recruits. But we must also develop and retain these quality young people in the armed forces. Developing this talent requires enlightened leadership as well as realistic and challenging training. Retaining good people requires paying attention to the quality of life for our service men and women and their families. This involves not only providing adequate military compensation and family programs but ensuring that our operating tempo and planned deployments are kept within reasonable bounds.

Readiness

Experience shows that crises can emerge quickly and unpredictably. Our forces currently maintain a range of readiness postures to meet possible contingencies, from American aircraft aloft on combat air patrol over the Adriatic Sea and elsewhere to large reserve component forces in the United States.

Our forces must be sufficiently ready—manned, equipped, trained, and sustainable—to meet the deployment requirements our strategy demands and to provide a hedge against uncertainty. They must be ready to fight today. We are working to strengthen readiness through better understanding and prediction of requirements as we restructure the force.

War-fighting plans require us to strengthen joint readiness and to exercise routinely with our allies and friends. Traditional measures of readiness were defined in service-specific terms. Today we are strengthening joint and allied doctrine and educa-tion, developing joint readiness measures, and improving joint and coalition training and exercises.

Enhancements

Enhancement of our strategic mobility capability, including airlift, sealift, and pre-positioning, is already under way. We have taken delivery of the first eighteen of the initial procurement of forty C-17 advanced transport aircraft. One army heavy brigade equipment set is pre-positioned aboard ships now on station to cover contingencies from Northeast Asia to the Persian Gulf. Our plans call for three additional brigade sets to be pre-positioned ashore, two in Southwest Asia and one in South Korea. We are procuring more sealift, including medium-speed roll-on/roll-off ships. In combination, these assets will greatly improve the power projection capability of our forces.

Battlefield surveillance will continue to be upgraded with the integration of systems such as the joint Surveillance and Target Attack Radar System, the upgraded Airborne Warning and Control System, the RC-135 Rivet Joint intelligence platform, and unmanned aerial vehicles.

Enhancements to provide a robust, globally capable and interoperable communications architecture are also required. These include the jam-resistant MILSTAR satellite communications system and the Global Command and Control System. In addition, the appropriate mix of U.S. military and commercial space systems will be integrated to reduce costs and optimize support for the war fighter. We must retain a decisive advantage in these areas.

Planned firepower enhancements include the Joint Standoff Weapon, Joint Direct Attack Munitions, sensor-fuzed weapons, ATACMS, and other strike enhancements for early arriving bombers and fighter-bombers.

Modernization

We intend to remain the best-equipped force in the world. Modernization programs preserve the essential combat edge that U.S. forces now possess. Through a program of recapitalization, we are consciously retiring certain weapons systems and platforms in order to afford more capable and modern equipment. Modernization programs provide the technological foundation for future capabilities and readiness.

Defense investments during the Cold War have provided us the necessary foundation in terms of platforms, systems, and research and development. We now seek the greatest value added under a more constrained budget. Major modernization programs involving significant investment are being undertaken only where there is clearly a substantial payoff. Continued modernization of existing platforms will take advantage of rapid technological change, particularly in the areas of reconnaissance and information warfare. Operational prototyping will be used to rapidly field small numbers of high-leverage systems.

Balance

Despite their smaller size, our armed forces must retain an appropriate mix of forces and capabilities to provide versatility and a hedge against the unknown. Force structure must support land, sea, air, and space requirements, combat forces must be balanced with capable supporting forces, active duty forces must be balanced with appropriate reserve capabilities, and force structure must be balanced with infrastructure.

As roles, missions, and functions are reexamined in an effort to attain greater efficiency, we must ensure that the balance among critical combat, combat support, and other supporting capabilities is retained.

CONCLUSION

Today's national military strategy builds on its predecessors and continues the evolution from the strategies developed during the Cold War. Despite the breakup of the Soviet Union and the subsequent drawdown of U.S. forces, this is a strategy of continued global engagement. Flexibly and selectively applied, U.S. military power will remain a fundamental factor in ensuring national security.

In keeping with the broad outlines of military strategy developed over nearly half a century, we see the United States with worldwide responsibilities that re-quire flexible military capabilities. As before, we will stand together with our allies and friends to ensure stability in a troubled world. Deterrence and conflict prevention are central elements of our strategy. A balanced force structure (including air, land, naval, and space elements), a strategic nuclear force, and correctly sized overseas presence are essential to maintaining the required deterrent and war-fighting capabilities.

The days of the familiar bipolar competition with the former Soviet Union are now in the past. Security issues are more complex and increasingly regional in nature. Our actions must be appropriate to meet specific needs across a broad range of potential challenges. This requires a high tempo of military activity, including military operations, with a significant risk of hostile action. The forces to meet our security needs will be largely based in the United States. Even though smaller than before, they will need to remain highly capable. Quality people, readiness, enhancements, selected modernization, and balance will provide the critical edge.

This military strategy is one of flexible and selective engagement, designed to protect U.S. interests throughout the world and to help meet the security needs of our partners in key regions. This strategy requires a ready American military force capable of responding quickly and decisively to protect our nation's security.

CHAPTER 13

NUCLEAR POLICY

THE IMPACT OF NUCLEAR WEAPONS ON HISTORY

JAMES SCHLESINGER

I have entitled this essay "The Impact of Nuclear Weapons on History," consciously, if somewhat immodestly, emulating Alfred Thayer Mahan's monumental *The Influence of Sea Power on History*. To be sure, seapower affected the survival or fall of empires for more than two and one-half millennia, while nuclear weapons have been with us but a scant half century. Yet in that brief period of five decades, nuclear weapons have had as dramatic an impact on the course of history as anything in the annals of seapower. Nuclear weapons shaped the outcome of the international confrontation known as the Cold War. For the Western world, the principal domain of freedom and personal liberty, and especially for Western Europe, the role of nuclear weapons has been crucial.

It seems appropriate to reflect upon this dramatic impact, however brief, on the occasion of the fiftieth anniversary of what undoubtedly was the first overt incident in international nuclear competition, the sabotage action by the Norwegian underground directed against the heavy-water plant of Norsk Hydro at Rjukan. We must ignore the conversations among scientists and between scientists and statesmen. The sabotage in Telemark was the first *public act* of the nuclear age, designed to preclude Germany from being the first to develop nuclear explosives. Although later evidence revealed that the German government was far less focused on atomic weapons than was once feared, had Hitler's Germany "won the race," today few would question how great had been the impact of nuclear weapons on history.

Nonetheless, with the end of the Cold War (and because nuclear weapons were never employed in it), the question may be posed: would history have been substantially different if nuclear weapons had not existed? Did the existence of nuclear weapons—and all of the strategic reasoning and strategic games that they provoked—really affect anything? Any attempt to rerun history conceptually is a risky business—as uncertain, for example, as was the future of nuclear explosives or nuclear energy at the time of the sabotage effort at Rjukan in 1943. The brief answer to the question, would history have been different? is, not necessarily. If, in the absence of nuclear weapons, the United States had been as willing and as able to be both engaged and committed to preserving international stability; if Western Europe had quickly regained its confidence after World War II and been prepared stalwartly to resist pressures from the East; and if the Soviet Union had been highly circumspect and refrained from applying pressures to targets of opportunity such as West Berlin, then indeed history might not have been affected by the existence of nuclear capabilities. To pose so stark a set of requirements, however, reveals how very low is the probability that history was not decisively affected (and, indeed, favorably affected) by the existence of nuclear weapons. The likelihood that in the absence of nuclear weapons America would have been so deeply engaged internationally, that Europe would have been self-confident and stalwart, and that the Soviet Union would have exhibited continuous restraint is so low that it points to a clear and definitive answer. The unavoidable conclusion is that the existence of nuclear weapons not only affected history in general, but most decisively the history of Western Europe.

Those who would argue the contrary can do so only now that the existential pressures of the Cold War have been removed. The belief that nuclear weapons were not a principal determinant of the flow of history rests in my judgment on the premise—the dubious premise—that the Soviet Union was a relatively benign and contented power. These days it is becoming increasingly difficult to recall how formidable a military threat and (in the early years) a political threat the Soviet Union once was. It becomes necessary to recall how fearful Western Europe was in 1947 and 1948, the alarm that led European leaders to foster the North Atlantic Treaty in 1949, the panic that ensued after the invasion of South Korea in 1950, the various and regular crises over Berlin, the pressure on Norway and Turkey, the fears generated by the growing Soviet nuclear capabilities, reinforced by the Soviet Union's growing conventional strength, the renewed alarms over the invasions of Hungary and Czechoslovakia, the attempted flanking movements in the Middle East, the renewed pressures during the last years under Leonid Brezhnev, and so on, and so on. It is, I believe, quite implausible to argue that, in the absence of nuclear weapons, the Western nations would

This essay has been edited and is reprinted from The Washington Quarterly 16 (Fall 1993): 5–12, *by permission of MIT Press.*

have, with equal fortitude, resisted these and other pressures. One must also recall to what extent the hinge of Western defense (and of Soviet pressures) was a defeated and divided Germany, whose self-confidence was only slowly, gradually, and partly restored. To resist Soviet pressures Germany required the continued and unequivocal backing of its Western allies, particularly the United States.

If these events are forgotten or dimly remembered, it becomes somewhat easier to believe that in the absence of nuclear weapons, history would have been unaffected. Already I have delineated the three principal variables and the three principal players. Let me address them in greater detail:

- Would the United States have been equally committed to preserving the international fabric and international stability?

- Would Europe have been equally stalwart in resisting Soviet pressures?

- Would the Soviet Union have been equally restrained and equally circumspect in using and threatening the use of its massive conventional forces?

THE ROLE OF THE UNITED STATES

I start with the United States, whose course of future action was unpredictable, to say the least, in 1945. The United States had had a long history of intervening abroad and then returning to North America. After World War I it had explicitly embraced a policy of isolationism, which was later enshrined in the Neutrality Acts of the 1930s. The decision of the new president, Harry Truman, to terminate Lend-Lease the day after the war ended was hardly auspicious regarding an American embrace of its new international responsibilities. In the first year or so after the close of the war, the United States almost totally demobilized its forces. Indeed, at the time of the Berlin crisis and of the invasion of South Korea, it was somewhat surprised—and pleasantly surprised—to discover how effective its nuclear monopoly appeared to be as a deterrent of substantial aggressive moves by the Soviet Union.

One must go somewhat further back in history, into the wartime period itself, to recognize the full role that nuclear weapons played in the postwar period. Had nuclear weapons not existed, or had President Truman been unwilling to demonstrate their use at Hiroshima and Nagasaki, the Japanese war would have continued, perhaps for a long time, and Japanese resistance would have been bitter. The struggle for the Japanese Home Islands would probably have been long and certainly bloody—for which Iwo Jima and Okinawa were but harbingers. America would have been far more bloodied; its combat losses would have been substantial.

Mr. Truman's decision to use the atomic bomb terminated the war—without the necessity of an invasion of the Japanese Home Islands. The U.S.

losses were sharply reduced. The United States did not leave the war exhausted. Indeed, it ended the war remarkably undamaged, especially compared to the other belligerents. For our purposes here, it needs to be underscored that without the use of the bomb and without the quick termination of the war, America's ability and willingness to play so substantial and generous a postwar role would likely have been significantly reduced.

If once again we examine the developments that occurred after the close of the war, it seems unquestionable that both America's ability and its willingness to assume the international role that it did reflected the existence of and prior use of nuclear weapons. Without Mr. Truman's decision to employ the bomb, the United States would have been far later in concentrating on the revitalization of Europe and far less able to do so—if it had ever gotten around to it at all. The prolongation of the Pacific war would have riveted the American public's attention on the Far East—it would inevitably have resulted in a reversal of Franklin Roosevelt's courageous and controversial decision in 1941 to treat Europe as the primary theater and the focus of America's initial war effort. Had the United States continued to be absorbed in the Far East, it would have left the Soviet Union in a position to continue to apply pressure to the weakened nations of Western Europe, while the United States remained absorbed elsewhere.

Of perhaps even greater importance, America's willingness and ability to play so large an international role, particularly on the Eurasian continent, reflected the confidence that came from its exclusive possession of nuclear weapons. The pell-mell demobilization of U.S. forces that took place in the year or so after the close of the war would likely have taken place even if the United States had not possessed the atomic bomb, because it was driven largely by domestic attitudes and pressures. After the demobilization, and with only token forces left in Europe and the Far East, the United States would have been far less willing to challenge the Soviet Union on political or strategic issues had it not possessed a counterweight to the massive Soviet military establishment in the form of the bomb. I personally doubt that the United States would, in the absence of nuclear weapons, have been ready to play the role that it did in the postwar period.

Moreover, the American ability to lead a rather fractious Europe also depended on nuclear weapons. Implicitly in the late 1940s and explicitly in the 1950s Europe's defense depended upon the American nuclear umbrella. The nations of Europe were ready, if not always eager, to follow America's lead, because the United States was essential to their security. As we shall see, over time nuclear weapons became the glue of the North Atlantic Treaty Organization (NATO). Both symbolically and militarily they became essential to NATO's cohesion. Not only were nuclear weapons a prerequisite to America's willingness to play so large an international role, but they were also essential to the European nations' playing their necessary part and remaining stalwart.

WESTERN EUROPE AND
SOVIET PRESSURE

I turn now to my second variable: Western Europe's ability to stand up to Soviet pressure. In the aftermath of the war Europe's own self-confidence was understandably modest. In simple fact, the European nations remained pretty wobbly for a long time after 1945 and were never in a position—without the support of the American superpower—either collectively or, even more so, individually to withstand the pressures from the East. Europe's self-confidence took a long time to be restored, and Germany's self-confidence, shattered by defeat in the war, was not wholly restored until the Soviet empire began to disintegrate at the close of the 1980s. No doubt, the talk about "Finlandization" became both excessive and tasteless, yet even with firm American support, whether one or more of the European nations might succumb to Soviet intimidation remained an unresolved question. In the absence of the nuclear umbrella, which undergirded the American guarantee of protection for Western Europe, there is little question in my mind that a number of the European states would have been far more susceptible to Soviet pressures. Overall the cohesion of the alliance, perhaps regrettably, continued to depend upon nuclear weapons.

AMBITIONS OF THE SOVIET UNION

I turn now to my third variable: how ambitious was the Soviet Union? To what extent did its policy of restraint represent genuine moderation and to what extent did it reflect the clear military counterweight represented by NATO? I do not believe, as some have argued, that Soviet recalcitrance and intransigence were driven primarily by fear. Such crucial elements as Leninist ideology, Russian nationalism, and Moscow-as-the-Third-Rome also drove Soviet policy, along with Stalin's own special paranoia. In this connection the eminent Finnish statesman, Max Jakobson, cites some observations made by Stalin in a conversation with Tito in April 1945, in which Stalin rather revealingly stated:

This war is not as in the past. . . . Whoever occupies a territory also imposes on it its social system. Everyone imposes his own system as far as his army can reach. . . . Where the Russian flag has once been hoisted it must not be lowered.[1]

Clearly Stalin's objective was to extend Soviet control as far as possible. Whether his successors shared his ambitions to the same degree is debatable. The Brezhnev Doctrine, enunciated in 1968, may be interpreted as a defensive statement: we will hold on to what we have. Nevertheless, that pronouncement coincided with the repeatedly expressed conviction that "the correlation of forces" was steadily moving in favor of the Soviet Union and against the West. Thus I find it hard to accept a judgment, which is based upon a conviction of an underlying moderation in Soviet

policy, that the outcome in Europe was not affected by the existence of the nuclear deterrent.

THE WEST AND NUCLEAR WEAPONS

Although the ramifications of nuclear weapons were worldwide, nowhere did they have an impact as great as in Europe. For example, the security of Japan was not significantly affected by the existence of nuclear weapons—even though it affected Japan's political psychology and was a troubling element in that country's relations with the United States. By contrast, the United States became exposed to political developments overseas and to foreign military forces in a way that it had not been throughout most of its history. As the Soviet Union developed its nuclear counterdeterrent during the 1960s and 1970s, the United States became vulnerable to direct attack, as it never had been before. To be sure, the notion of a nuclear Pearl Harbor, an unprovoked, surprise attack on the United States, was always rather far-fetched, given America's own deterrent posture. Nonetheless, the United States had become vulnerable—as a result of a hypothetical escalation from a European war—because it had pledged to respond to any attack on NATO Europe. Thus the task for U.S. and NATO strategy was to close off any possibility that might lead to war by miscalculation.

Yet the strategy of the West adjusted only belatedly and perhaps insufficiently to the evolution of military capabilities. In the late 1940s the West, unwittingly and rather by chance, became dependent upon the U.S. nuclear monopoly for its protection. In the late 1950s, even as the Soviet Union took its first steps toward developing a counterdeterrent, the West came to depend upon nuclear deterrents to an even greater extent. The European allies signally failed to develop the conventional forces to defend Europe that they had pledged at Lisbon in 1952. The Americans, after the Korean War, reduced their own conventional forces—and embraced a doctrine of "massive retaliation."

In brief, the West became "hooked" on reliance on nuclear weapons—even after the Soviet development of the counterdeterrent made a nuclear response increasingly risky. And, for a variety of reasons, Europe was far more hooked than was the United States. In part, this reflected differing assessments of the threat. The Europeans (most of the time) thought the Soviet Union to be risk-averse and disinclined to initiate risky military action. They were less inclined than the Americans to expend the resources to close off hypothetical military vulnerabilities. Thus they perennially resisted American entreaties to build a conventional deterrent sufficient to stop a Warsaw Pact onslaught.

Although motivations differed, most of the European states preferred continued reliance on the threat of nuclear retaliation. Under Charles de Gaulle and his successors, France's independent nuclear capability became synonymous with French grandeur and France's "place in the sun"—irrespective of the complications that assumption introduced into alliance strategy. Germany, as a presumed target of a Warsaw Pact thrust, was most important of all. From the days of Konrad Adenauer on, Germany tended to believe that only the clear threat of an immediate nuclear response could provide security for Germany. A nuclear strategy was believed to be synonymous with German security, and a conventional strategy meant a destructive conventional war devastating to Germany. Although dependent upon American protection, Germany gave ground only grudgingly on the issues of nuclear strategy and conventional forces. The British, too, persuaded that the Soviets would not move, long embraced the threat of early nuclear response as providing defense on the cheap. Most of the smaller allies, whatever their inhibitions, did not want to make additional sacrifices and thus were also hooked on dependency on nuclear weapons.

In the late 1980s, in large measure because Mikhail Gorbachev, conditions began to change rapidly. The dependence of Western security on nuclear weapons first eased and then fell away almost entirely. In 1989 the Soviet Union's grip on its empire in Eastern Europe began to relax, and in 1990 the satellite nations were, at long last, freed. The Warsaw Pact dissolved. In 1990 and 1991 the Soviet Union dissolved into its constituent states. Russia itself was weakened. For all intents and purposes the prospect, and the occasional reality, of the nuclear confrontations of the Cold War were now over. Whatever role nuclear weapons had played in the preservation of the states of Western Europe was now almost entirely completed.

LOOKING TO THE FUTURE

What of the future? As the Cold War has ended, so have the disciplines that were a part of that long international confrontation. The world is a more chaotic place, most notably in those regions formerly part of the Soviet empire. One consequence is that the inhibitions imposed on the acquisition of nuclear capabilities by countries other than the five permanent members of the Security Council have now been eased. A spread of weapons, particularly into the Third World, would add to the probabilities of, and would unquestionably lower the inhibitions on, the actual employment of nuclear weapons. Thus in the wake of the Cold War, preventing nuclear proliferation becomes one of the most significant challenges to international security. Yet without that fundamental challenge to the United States represented by the Soviet ideological thrust and military threat, it is questionable whether the credibility that the United States achieved in Europe can be transferred to this new mission. It will take different and, in some respects, greater efforts on our part to provide comfort to nonweapon states. Thus to prevent a spread of nuclear capabilities will require firm purpose and decisive action. One wonders whether the international community is prepared for such action.

My purpose here is to examine the role of nuclear weapons during the Cold War. I wish only, without indulging in any false nostalgia, to point out that however grave the risks, the disciplines of the Cold War had their uses. During the Cold War nuclear capabilities, awesome as they were, were to a large extent offsetting and served to sustain a strategic stalemate. No one can run history over again. Historical what-might-have-beens are always intriguing, rarely persuasive. If nuclear weapons had not existed, and consequently had not played their role during the Cold War, what would have been the result? We do know that Warsaw Pact military capabilities represented a substantial threat for almost four decades, that Western Europe was politically and militarily vulnerable and economically weak for a substantial period after World War II, and that the Western allies were unwilling to provide conventional forces to match those of the East. We also know that nuclear weapons were central to the strategy of the Western alliance, that they served as the glue that bound that alliance together, and that they were critical to and fortified the role of the United States as military protector and leader of the Western nations. To contemplate a world without nuclear weapons was frightening for the governments of Europe. That was dramatically demonstrated as late as the Reykjavik Summit in 1986, when President Ronald Reagan toyed with the idea that both sides might rid themselves of nuclear weapons. The alarm that overtook Europe at the bare hint of such an outcome underscores a fundamental truth: that during the Cold War nuclear weapons may well have been the salvation of a free Europe.

SUMMING UP

In the long sweep of history, it is arguable that mankind would have been better off had nuclear explosives never been developed. But that is *only* in the long sweep of history. It is far, far harder to argue that the West generally, and Western Europe in particular, would have been better off without nuclear weapons. Without the nuclear deterrent, the kind of semidarkness that held the nations of Eastern Europe in its grip for more than four decades might also have afflicted much of Western Europe. Despite the worries of the past and the prospect of concern about nuclear weapons in the future, in this century their benefits have exceeded their costs.

I started this discussion with a reference to Admiral Mahan's classic work on the role of seapower. Let me close by citing Mahan's eloquent tribute to that line of British ships that forever barred Napoleon from achieving his ambitions. His words are equally fitting in this modern context for those indispensable yet vulnerable elements of our strategic forces that held Soviet ambitions in check. It is one that I used many years ago in paying tribute in Omaha, Nebraska—home of the Strategic Air Command—to those who for so long had sustained the deterrent that protected the West from another despotic regime:

Those far distant, storm-beaten ships, upon which the Grand Army never looked, stood between it and the dominion of the world.[2]

NOTES

This paper was delivered at the Conference on Nuclear Technology and Politics commemorating the fiftieth anniversary of the sabotage action against the Norsk Hydro heavy-water plant, Rjukan, Norway, 17 June 1993.

1. Max Jakobson, *Finland: Myth and Reality* (Helsinki: Otava, 1988), 46. In that last sentence, Stalin was deliberately quoting Czar Nicholas I.

2. Alfred Thayer Mahan, *The Influence of Sea Power upon the French Revolution and Empire, 1793–1812*, vol. 2 (Boston: Little, Brown, 1892).

ON DEALING WITH THE PROSPECT OF NUCLEAR CHAOS

ROGER C. MOLANDER AND PETER A. WILSON

The following essay represents an attempt to stand back and take stock of the possible role of nuclear weapons in the international security environments that may unfold in the course of the next generation—say, the next twenty to twenty-five years.[1]

Although considerable rhetorical emphasis has of late been given to concern about the threat of nuclear weapons proliferation—and the Clinton administration has taken action in the case of North Korea and Ukraine in an effort to roll back two troubling new nuclear arsenals—it is not clear that President Bill Clinton and his senior advisers or the national security leadership in Congress have a strategic vision as to the ultimate objective of efforts in this critical post–Cold War strategy and policy arena. Yet the United States faces a major, urgent challenge. It must foster and sustain a process leading to a new post–Cold War strategy and associated policies regarding nuclear weapons. This requires moving the post–Cold War global nuclear security environment toward greater international integration by both declaratory policy and perceptible measures and by an accompanying deemphasis of nuclear weapons as a flagship element of national security. The initiatives called for to achieve such ends will almost certainly demand considerable political, economic, and military investment, if not sacrifice, in the face of powerful secular trends that appear to be moving the planet more toward conditions of chaos, especially in the political arena.

OVERVIEW

The first fifty years of the nuclear age were dominated by the Cold War. Its end, wrought by the spectacular and by any historical measure dramatically fast collapse of the Soviet Union, created a *profound* discontinuity in the international security environment. The unexpectedly abrupt disappearance of the bipolar international security framework that had guided national security thinking in so many countries for so long caught nations and alliances by surprise—and wholly unprepared to consider the menu of security options that events now thrust before them. Nations once secure in the framework and discipline of a bipolar Cold War standoff were abruptly forced, guided by the instinct of survival, not just to look at new alliances, but also to reassess self-reliance for security—and therefore to consider or reconsider obtaining some measure of nuclear weapons capability.

In its triggering events, the end of the Cold War also unleashed centrifugal forces that not only immediately increased the number of states possessing nuclear weapons but also set in motion a virtually certain dispersion of nuclear weapons–related know-how and personnel. That dispersion—the telltale signs of which are starting to appear—will surge into a world that already had the character (thanks to the global spread of commercial nuclear power) of a nuclear supersaturated system—a virtual nuclear weapons cloud chamber where the entry of a small team (and plausibly even an individual) from the former Soviet nuclear weapons or ballistic missile development/production complex could dramatically alter a nation's nuclear weapons capability and thus its strategic position regionally or globally.[2]

Further complicating the challenge posed by this image of the future is what might be called the legacy of Rio—the inescapable global turning away from fossil fuels that is dictated by deteriorating global atmospheric conditions, punctuated politically by the United Nations Conference on Environment and Development held in Rio de Janeiro in 1992. This "why take the chance?" imperative to

This essay has been edited and is reprinted from The Washington Quarterly 17 (Fall 1994): 19–39, *by permission of MIT Press.*

reduce dependence on fossil fuels occurs, unfortunately, in a context in which nuclear power is still the only universally available alternative with the potential to meet projected energy and energy security demands in many important parts of the developed and developing world.[3]

It seems clear that within the next two or three decades, maybe four at the very outside, we will move rapidly as a civilization through what might be called the middle years of the learning curve of the nuclear age. This will bring us to a state in which virtually any industrialized nation will have the scientific infrastructure and other wherewithal necessary to produce indigenously both nuclear weapons and associated modern delivery vehicles (probably, if deemed necessary, covertly by current inspection standards), and at an economically affordable cost.[4]

How many nations will maintain nuclear arsenals "at-the-ready"—available for use in minutes or a day or two at most—when the planet reaches that state? How many will openly maintain virtual nuclear arsenals—arsenals that by plan (pre-positioning of materials, training of personnel, etc.) can be reliably built or assembled inside a nation's particular notional strategic warning time (that time, presumably a matter of weeks or months, for the appearance of dire political-military threats)? Which of these will be overt, and which covert? What military role or function will nations proclaim to themselves and others for their at-the-ready or consciously planned virtual nuclear arsenals? What uncertainty will there be—and what might be "acceptable" to national security planners or treaty monitors—about the degree to which a nation is nuclear armed?

In thinking through these questions, we begin with a certain premise: for the future of conflict between human beings, the most important issue is *choosing* an asymptotic long-term goal (or plausibly achievable end state) for the nuclear weapons component of the nuclear age.[5] This choice must be squarely faced now.

By its nature the above premise demands that careful attention be given to the articulation and consideration of alternative nuclear asymptotes or end states *and* the ability of the United States to effect one or another of these possible futures. The body of this essay is directed to the framing of this alternative end-states problem analytically and politically.

Four illustrative asymptotes are presented for consideration (and by implication for interpolation and extrapolation):

- *"High-entropy" deterrence:* a highly proliferated world with few rules of the nuclear road, save possibly an enduring (if successful) cultural taboo on nuclear use that relies, among other things, on an expanding web of bipolar or multipolar international deterrence relationships to keep the nuclear peace.

- An *ever*-slowly-expanding *nuclear club:* acceptance of an inexorable slow growth in the number of nuclear-armed states, with new members of the club grudgingly (or sometimes willingly) integrated into the existing nuclear order and carefully educated to a set of nuclear norms of behavior and associated concepts of deterrence and balance.

- *A two-tiered* static *"have-a-lot/have-none" international system:* a handful of "haves" maintain substantial (but limited by treaty) at-the-ready nuclear arsenals and commit themselves individually or collectively (most likely through the U.N. Security Council) as explicitly as necessary to maintaining the security of the "have-nots."

- *The "virtual abolition" of nuclear arsenals:* virtual elimination of existing at-the-ready nuclear arsenals (a handful of states maintain tens to hundreds of nuclear weapons at-the-ready) underwritten by an unprecedented comprehensive and highly intrusive international inspection and collective enforcement regime.

In essence, the four asymptotic states, with their emphasis on the nuclear dimension of the international environment, are consistent with the broader view that each end state represents different levels of planetary political and economic integration or disintegration. Table 1 displays a summary description of these four states. An elaboration of their major features follows.

ALTERNATIVE FUTURES

HIGH-ENTROPY DETERRENCE

The high-entropy deterrence state could well be the product of a post–Cold War era during which the United States turns progressively inward and away from forceful involvement in an increasingly turbulent world that is slowly accelerating away from the order of the Cold War and into a period of increased international, political, economic, and military fragmentation. In such a world, many states could conclude that the possession of a nuclear arsenal is a reasonable answer to the real or imagined threat of regional or global predators. Although bilateral or multilateral nuclear arms-control agreements might seek to stabilize the size and character of at least at-the-ready nuclear arsenals, nations possessing such nuclear arsenals or substantial virtual nuclear arsenal capability would presumably go to great lengths to make such arsenals survivable against preemptive attack. In the worst case there might even be a number of small arsenals controlled by nonstate entities, such as international criminal organizations and political or religious groups, that would take advantage of the increasingly challenging nuclear weapons control problem—or that might in a crisis (like the loss of central control in some nuclear-armed state) appear out of nowhere. Defining international stability would be problematic.

Table 1

Alternative Nuclear End States

Plausible nuclear asymptotes (end states)	At-the-ready arsenals		Virtual arsenals	Other key characteristics
High-entropy deterrence				
Highly nuclear proliferated world	U.S./Russia	5,000+	Not relevant to major nuclear powers; state of many virtual arsenals unknown	Weak international security system
Many at-the-ready and virtual nuclear arsenals	China/Ukraine	1,000+		Mixed national counterproliferation responses (defenses, counterforce, power projection adaptation, or neo-isolationism)
Few "rules of the nuclear road"	UK/France	100s		
Bilateral and multilateral deterrence relationships	Israel/India /Pakistan	100+		
	Ten+ nations	10s		
An ever-slowly expanding nuclear club				
Inexorable growth in number of nuclear-armed states	U.S./Russia	3,000	Not of concern to major nuclear powers; relevant to minor powers and others (e.g., Japan, Germany, Ukraine)	No major change in current international security system
New nuclear "club" members integrated and educated on "norms of behavior"	China	1,000		Little improvement in IAEA
	UK/France	500+		Some counterproliferation responses constrained by arms control
	Israel	200		
	India/Pakistan	100+		
Little improvement in NPT inspection regime	Others	10s–100s		
A two-tiered static have-a-lot/have-none international system				
"Idealized NPT"	U.S./Russia	2,000	300–1,000 in months	Strengthened international security system with new security guarantees
"Haves" (presumably UNSC permanent five) maintain substantial but treaty-limited arsenals	China	600	100–300 in months	
	UK/France	400	100–300 in months	Improved NPT regime (inspection and enforcement)
	Others	0	10s in weeks to months	Counterproliferation deemphasized
Virtual abolition of nuclear arsenals				
Deemphasis of military nuclear roles/missions	U.S./Russia	300	200–400 in months	Robust international security system (great powers agree on "nuclear order")
A few states maintain up to hundreds of at-the-ready nuclear weapons (e.g., a global total of 1,000) to deter breakout	China	200	50–100 in months	Comprehensive/ intrusive/relentless inspection and enforcement regime
	UK/France	100	50–100 in months	
	Others	0	10s in months	Robust counter-proliferation investment

The world of many nuclear-armed entities might emerge slowly over a transition period during which there is no use of nuclear weapons—in which case there could be growing confidence in the lasting viability, and the breadth of application, of nuclear weapons–based deterrence.[6]

Some variant of this end state might emerge from a dramatic demonstration of the military and political utility of nuclear weapons, for example, a war that leaves a clear victor *thanks to* the use of nuclear weapons and no meaningful punitive response from the international community. In this situation nuclear weapons would be given a powerful legitimacy, especially if the use had not been catastrophic. Such an outcome would shatter any nuclear use taboo and could trigger a period of hyperproliferation as many states moved deliberately designed or inherent virtual arsenals much closer to operational status.

AN EVER-*SLOWLY*-EXPANDING NUCLEAR CLUB

By definition the asymptote of an ever-*slowly*-expanding nuclear club is a slow growth curve along which the major powers of the international community *slowly* accept new nuclear-armed states. In essence, this end state is a description of the history of nuclear weapons proliferation during the first fifty years of the nuclear age and the current, late-twentieth-century circumstance. The fundamental assumption of this possible end state is that the process of nuclear proliferation can remain a slow-motion affair, with new entrants achieving acceptance in the nuclear club only after a protracted period.

In all cases, the security concerns of the new entrants to this choice of regime would take on broader legitimacy as the major powers (and, more important, the declared nuclear weapon states) tolerated and even helped rationalize the gradual appearance of a new nuclear-armed state or states.

To facilitate this process of gradual expansion, a variety of regional arms-control arrangements might well be negotiated by the new entrants to achieve new regional nuclear deterrence balances. The success of this strategy would be highly contingent upon the new entrants' accepting an internationally defined set of rules of the nuclear road and possibly some rationalized deterrence relationship(s). An underlying rationale for considering this kind of asymptote is the perspective that the United States may well be in the position of trying to make a virtue of necessity—that the process of the proliferation of nuclear-armed states is inevitable, and especially so in an environment or under conditions where the United Nations or a nuclear-armed power like the United States is not prepared to provide insecure states with credible extended deterrence guarantees. As with any two-tiered system, the international political legitimacy of this approach, in which "some will sit in judgment on others' needs," is somewhat shaky and viable only insofar as tested by time and experience.

The obvious first step under this asymptote would be to accept Pakistan, India, and Israel as official members of the nuclear club, legitimizing the Israeli and Pakistani arguments that a state without powerful and reliable allies should be able to compensate for its conventional military inferiority vis-à-vis some threat by deploying a nuclear arsenal. India would presumably find the rationale for its arsenal in classic bilateral nuclear deterrence concepts vis-à-vis Pakistan or China.[7]

Overt acceptance of Israel as a nuclear-armed state would undoubtedly further stimulate nuclear weapons programs among the Arab states and Iran so that a predictable sequel would be the eventual demand to grant legitimacy to, say, nuclear arsenals in Iraq and Iran. Crafting a three-party strategic nuclear balance among these three "greater Middle East" regional adversaries (which would rationalize the size of their at-the-ready arsenals) exemplifies the challenges that could be faced in the relative near term if the rate of expansion of the nuclear club remains slow.

A TWO-TIERED *STATIC* HAVE-A-LOT/HAVE-NONE SYSTEM

A two-tiered, *static*, have-a-lot/have-none (hereinafter "have" and "have-not") international system is still the implicit goal (and at times somewhat shakily proclaimed status quo) of the current international nonproliferation regime. One fundamental problem of this two-tiered system as currently constituted is the fading legitimacy of its basis: the five major powers on the winning side in World War II and the five permanent members of the U.N. Security Council are the five declared nuclear-armed states—the haves that this choice of preferred end state would presumably try to perpetuate.

One key to the viability of this kind of two-tiered system is thus the viability of the current composition of the Security Council. The difficulty of changing this arrangement, for instance, by adding Japan, Germany, and possibly India and Brazil as permanent members, will only be made more complex by the nuclear issue.[8]

In terms of the problems posed by India, Israel, and Pakistan, the existence of nuclear weapons in these nations is no longer questioned in public or private debate and discussion. Thus as a variant of the basic approach of this alternative asymptote it might be possible to grandfather these three nations into the Nuclear Nonproliferation Treaty (NPT) in a second tier of haves that agree, maybe in an NPT II, to accept severe limits on the size of their at-the-ready arsenals, greater transparency in their nuclear programs so as to limit their potential to mobilize a virtual nuclear arsenal, and a commitment to become a have-not in some long term. Whether the global community would insist on more explicit and restrictive limits on the size of the arsenals of the permanent five, or on greater transparency in their nuclear weapons programs, would remain to be seen.

Whether it would prove enforceable is another open question. It is important to acknowledge that the ongoing effort to eliminate Iraq's weapons of mass destruction capability is probably unique and may not amount to a real precedent. A posture among the permanent five that will permit their taking action in future regional crises of this character or on challenges of suspect violators cannot necessarily be guaranteed.

THE VIRTUAL ABOLITION OF NUCLEAR ARSENALS

The virtual abolition option reflects a view that in the post–Cold War world the United States and other nuclear-armed nations could, and maybe in their own long-term interests should, abandon their current degree of dependence on nuclear weapons. In the U.S. military, for example, there appears to be a rising belief that a United States properly armed with conventional weapons may not need to rely on thousands of at-the-ready nuclear weapons to satisfy its future defense and deterrence needs (*assuming* continued improvement, however slow, in the U.S.–Russian political-military relationship); indeed, there appears to be a preference for this state of affairs. At the same time, looking to the future threat environment, there is a rapidly growing appreciation that a small nuclear arsenal in the hands of a regional predator (such as Iraq in 1991) would present any U.S. or U.S.-led military force with a daunting set of basic military problems. From this conjunction of factors there emerges an interest in exploring what it would take to deemphasize in a profound fashion the role of at-the-ready nuclear arsenals in international security.[9]

In such a context of nuclear deemphasis, one clear question is how far existing at-the-ready arsenals would need to be reduced to market the concept versus how far such arsenals can or should be reduced against an array of stability concerns. One possible approach along such lines would be to eliminate all nuclear weapons save for a handful of very small nuclear arsenals (e.g., a total of no more than a thousand weapons worldwide) in the hands of a carefully chosen set of nations, for example, the permanent members of the U.N. Security Council. Such an approach would require a body such as the Security Council to assume far-reaching, unprecedented, and highly intrusive responsibilities associated with early warning and the attendant enforcement measures as part of a new grand bargain on the nuclear weapons dimension of international security. Such roles might be extrapolated from the measures taken in Desert Shield/Desert Storm and the U.N. Special Commission created by Security Council resolution 687 in Iraq.

The constellation of very small (and highly survivable) nuclear arsenals would be designed to be the lid on the jar—a deterrent and hedge against any nuclear arsenal breakout. Accompanying this at-the-ready force would be careful, conscious thought and sustained attention to virtual nuclear arsenals. Two questions should stand out:

- What level of nuclear monitoring and thus intrusiveness and persuasiveness is necessary to ensure adequate early warning (e.g., months) of breakout efforts in any nation (including in those nations that possess small at-the-ready arsenals)?

- What virtual nuclear capability would be necessary to enable the United States, other nations with small at-the-ready arsenals, and possibly other selected nations (e.g., other U.N. Security Council members), faced with the necessity of responding to particularly heinous nuclear breakout scenarios, to be able to rebuild or build large nuclear arsenals (into the thousands if necessary) with full production beginning in a relatively short time (e.g., a matter of months)?

In providing very early warning of illegal nuclear weapons programs, the highly intrusive inspections would be designed to give the international community time for diplomatic action and to build consensus for emergency sanctions, and if necessary urgent (conventional) military actions, against newly discovered outlaw programs.

It is implicit in the level of nuclear order that would exist in this end state that substantial cooperation between the major powers—however armed— would be an imperative. The sturdy child of this common interest should be a sustaining major power interest in (and responsibility for) a broader range of global order and especially the *containment* of regional or even national crises in terms of the character, degree, geographical extent, and geographical impact of their violence. A nuclear civil war would likely be tragic for more than just the nation in turmoil.

The feasibility of this potential end state rests on the notion that potential proliferators can be convinced that at-the-ready nuclear weapons are in fact unnecessary to ensure their national security—that under a virtual abolition regime, threats to national security, whether conventional or nuclear, would diminish sufficiently to render conventional defense and multifaceted security guarantees viable means of maintaining security and independence.

THE PRESENT NUCLEAR VANTAGE POINT

In order to evaluate these alternatives, and to underscore the importance now of seeking to choose among them, a long-term perspective is necessary, one that starts at the very beginning of the nuclear age in order to reveal the potential role of nuclear weapons in the context of current challenges and opportunities. This will also help to define a strategy for getting from here to there.

Nuclear Weapons Production

In the immediate aftermath of the bombing of Hiroshima and Nagasaki, as the world confronted the implications of the development and use of atomic bombs to end World War II, it was poignantly clear to the Manhattan Project scientists that they stood on the cusp of an inescapable global nuclear weapons learning curve. Although there was considerable uncertainty as to when that curve would steepen and the number of nations with the indigenous wherewithal to build nuclear weapons rapidly would increase, there was little doubt in their minds that humanity would in time, be it over decades or generations, reach such a point. They clearly recognized that the biggest atomic secret of all—that weapons that harnessed the energy of the atomic nucleus could actually be built—was out of the box with Alamagordo and demonstrated for all to see at Hiroshima. They understandably wondered where it would end.

On the heels of the question of the rate of growth in indigenous capability came the companion question of just how many countries would exploit their newfound nuclear capability and build and maintain nuclear weapons for at-the-ready nuclear arsenals (see Figure 1). A derivative concern was the question of how many nations might not appear nuclear armed but might consciously and covertly lay plans

Figure 1

Detailed Global Nuclear-Weapons-Capability Learning Curve

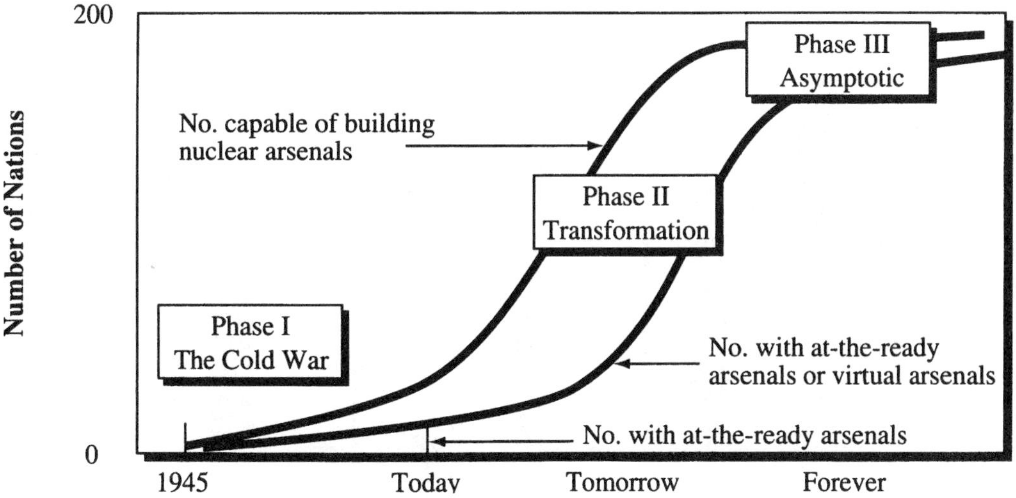

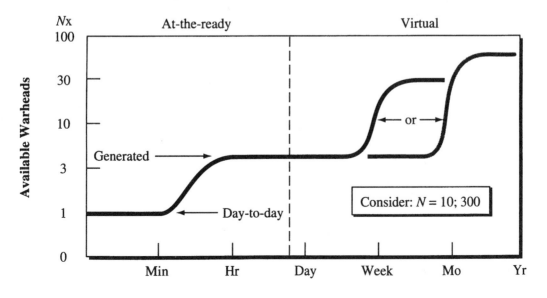

to take a virtual nuclear arsenal to an at-the-ready state inside some notional strategic warning time.

As the United States considers where such learning curves stand today, it must recognize that the point may soon be reached at which a nation's virtual nuclear arsenal capability will be almost as important a metric as that nuclear arsenal it maintains at-the-ready. Figure 2 portrays the virtual arsenal concept as a function of the time required to bring nuclear forces to a ready-to-shoot status.

Figure 3 bears further testimony to this potential by highlighting the prospect that Japan's growing plutonium stockpile (and associated handling facilities), married to its substantial and growing satellite launch capability, could form the basis for an impressive virtual nuclear arsenal within the next twenty to thirty years (assuming that the Japanese would be prepared to accept the reduced yields of weapons made of reactor-grade plutonium).

The success of the Manhattan Project and of nuclear weapons in quickly ending the war with Japan drove home for everyone both the feasibility of developing nuclear weapons and their value. The United States immediately went to extraordinary ends—manifest in the 1947 Atomic Energy Act—to deny the acquisition of nuclear weapons know-how and capability by other nations for as long as possible. The Soviet nuclear test in 1949, however, and

Figure 2

Sizing and Timelines for a Virtual Nuclear Arsenal

Figure 3

A Notional Comparison of U.S. and Japanese At-the-Ready and Virtual Nuclear Arsenals

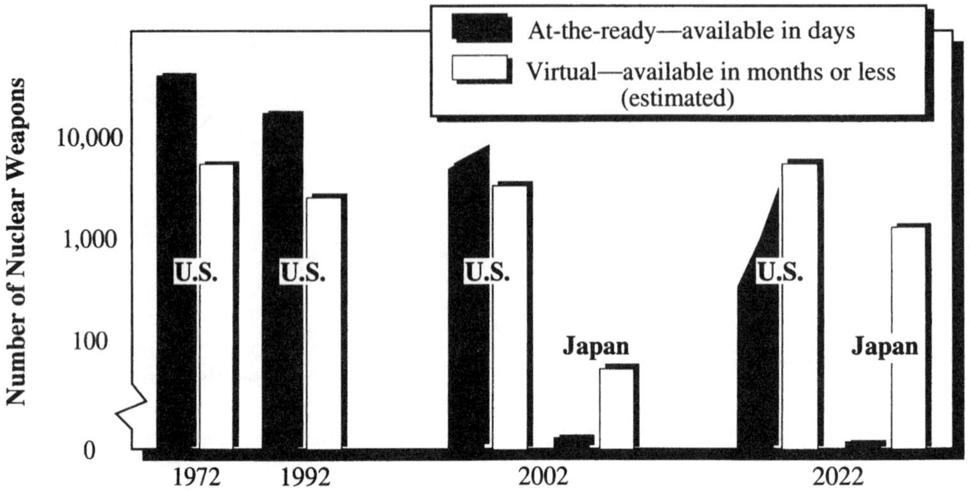

the British test in 1952 made it clear that there was going to be no U.S. monopoly on nuclear weapons, and U.S. efforts shifted to establishing and maintaining global superiority in this military realm.

In this same time frame the idea emerged in the United States that nations that might otherwise get on a nuclear weapons path could be enticed onto a more appealing commercial nuclear power path through the utopian reward of energy too cheap to meter. With the clarity of hindsight, pursuit of this idea—manifest in the mid-1950s in the U.S. Atoms for Peace plan—looks like one of the worst decisions of the nuclear age. Although the plan did draw many nations into the world of commercial nuclear power, the promised yellow brick road to cheap power (and peace) faded with the recognition of the complexity and cost of producing safe nuclear power plants and the challenge of disposing of nuclear waste—leaving in its wake a host of countries with a maturing nuclear infrastructure and unfortunately much of the basic nuclear know-how required to launch a serious nuclear weapons program. France unambiguously proved the dual-use value of this technology by exploding a nuclear weapon in 1960.

During this period, U.S. policy makers and military strategists were becoming increasingly concerned that the long-feared steepening of the at-the-ready or virtual nuclear arsenal curves of Figure 1 was about to take place. It did not. President John F. Kennedy was not alone in his oft-cited estimate or admonition that there could be as many as twenty nuclear-armed states in twenty years, but the nations that might have launched nuclear weapons programs in this time frame were instead bought off or politically fenced off from such development by the U.S. deployment of theater nuclear weapons and the extended deterrence promise of shelter under the U.S. nuclear umbrella—or by the imposed nuclear umbrella of the Soviet-controlled Warsaw Pact. Nations

that might otherwise have built nuclear weapons were persuaded not only to keep their nuclear efforts directed to nuclear power, but also to join in a global effort—eventually labeled the nuclear nonproliferation regime—to erect a comprehensive set of limitations (treaties, inspections, export constraints, etc.) that would deny or restrain access to key nuclear weapons–related technologies and materials.

The nuclear nonproliferation regime, anchored by the NPT completed in 1968, at least for a time did its job. Although China's explosion of a nuclear weapon in 1964 was not good news, it was no real surprise that the Chinese had made this political commitment and were able to mount the scientific and industrial effort to achieve nuclear club status. The fact that Israel in this same time frame was also achieving nuclear weapons capability—and that Sweden was planning a virtual nuclear arsenal—would have been more troubling and a clearer intimation of things to come if the Israeli and Swedish secrets had been less well kept.

India's explosion of a nuclear device in 1974, clearly with the aid of technology and materials procured under the guise of a peaceful nuclear power program, was a profoundly troubling development. It demonstrated that a nation with a sound scientific infrastructure and a nuclear power program, even if economically strapped, could covertly develop nuclear weapons. (Almost twenty years later Iraq, only in the middle tier of nations in terms of gross national product and also burdened by the cost of a long and difficult war with Iran, proved that point even more starkly with a highly advanced nuclear weapons program—and that achieved covertly in spite of being an NPT signatory.)

In this same period two other Asian states—South Korea and Taiwan—also pursued serious nuclear weapons programs, but in the mid-1970s they were leaned on heavily by the United States and the programs were halted, or at least went underground. The prospect that in spite of the NPT and safeguards imposed by the International Atomic Energy Agency (IAEA) nations other than Iraq might have advanced covert nuclear weapons programs is one of the intangible but worrisome problems of the steep part of the growth curve in the global spread of the ability to build nuclear weapons. This capacity for clandestine development by a medium-size power was also revealed by South Africa during 1993 with its confession that it had developed six nuclear weapons in a home-grown program in the face of severe international economic sanctions.

Contrary to this growth trend are the three nonproliferation success stories—Brazil, Argentina, and most recently South Africa. To all appearances, all three have now abandoned active nuclear weapons programs and appear ready to accept inspection programs that would provide substantial warning if they were to restart them. All three countries now presumably view their regional security circumstances as much improved compared with the period in which they launched their programs.

The shock of the extraordinarily advanced character of the covert Iraqi program has shattered confidence in the ability of the IAEA and other nuclear-intelligence collection capabilities to know just what is going on globally in this realm. This no-confidence condition can be rectified among political (and military) leaders only through repeated future detection successes—a daunting challenge.

In confronting the reality of the inexorable spread of nuclear weapons know-how, it is also critically important to recognize that the actual production of nuclear weapons is becoming monotonically easier. Largely as a consequence of improvements in technologies relating to commercial nuclear power, with every year it can be assumed that the size of the key facilities is getting smaller, as is the required number of scientists and technicians, the education level of this technical cohort, the amount of electrical power consumed, the release of telltale radionuclides, and the time for each key step in the nuclear weapons development process. (A two-story centrifuge facility covering a single city block can annually produce enough highly enriched weapons-grade uranium for roughly ten nuclear weapons—well within the size of facilities that could be hidden in existing mountain caves or readily constructed deep underground chambers.) The South African nuclear weapons program carried on under international embargo stands out as the current most efficient effort in this nuclear olympiad; running about ten years and involving roughly four hundred key scientists and technicians, it cost an estimated $900 million in total expenditures (a minor fraction of South Africa's annual defense expenditures).[10]

LONG-RANGE BOMBARDMENT

Long-range delivery systems have spread simultaneously with the diffusion of nuclear weapons pro-

duction capability. Another technology of fifty years ago, the ground mobile tactical ballistic missile, has now matured as the long-range bombardment means of choice for many regional powers. Although the U.S.-led coalition gained air supremacy during the 1991 Persian Gulf War, the allied forces were unable to neutralize Iraq's ground mobile tactical ballistic missile, the Scud, a variant of the German V-2. Scuds and their launchers were very hard to find even with the exploitation of advanced surveillance means, several thousand tactical air sorties, and special forces in suspected launch sites. Public reports indicate that the United States had no confirmed kills of a Scud missile and launcher during the counterforce campaign in spite of aircraft sorties numbering in the thousands. Although the strategic psychological performance of the Patriot surface-to-air missile was impressive, after-action reports suggest that the number of Scud warhead kills it achieved was abysmally low compared with what would be required for a serious strategic defense.[11]

Moreover, future proliferators should be able to take advantage of extant cruise missile technology to produce (possibly in very large numbers) a potent alternative to the long-range ballistic missile.

Through deployment of a large ground mobile missile force in concealed or heavily fortified sites (e.g., hardened, deep underground tunnels with multiple blind portals), a medium-size regional power will be able to field a long-range strike force that would be difficult if not impossible to kill or neutralize by regional adversaries or possibly even by a major effort by a global power like the United States backed by coalition partners.[12]

The military performance of both ballistic and cruise missiles will also improve substantially with the full global exploitation of the Global Positioning Satellite navigation aid. This constellation of navigation satellites, along with its competitors, such as the Russian Federation's GLONASS, will provide missile accuracies measured in the tens of meters as against the near-kilometer miss distance of the Scud.

Aside from the major powers that have the capacity to build intercontinental-range (greater than 5,500 kilometer) ballistic missiles—for example, the Russian Federation, the United States, and China—there are a wide range of states that can produce theater-range (500 to 2,000 kilometer) missiles. Notable entrants into the long-range missile club include North Korea, India, Pakistan, Iran, Israel, and Egypt. The ongoing effort to restrict the flow of missile development and production-related technology through the Missile Technology Control Regime (MTCR) has made little difference here.[13]

A BOTTOM LINE

It can be seen from the above assessment that a rapid maturing of inherent or readily obtainable national strategic nuclear capability is now taking place within a highly dynamic international security environment. This situation enables nations—or possible peoples—that for hundreds if not thousands of years have sought a means of guaranteeing their security to see within their grasp a powerful means by which possibly to achieve strategic security—the chance of a millennium. An unusual historical moment such as this, a testimony to the common Chinese character for chaos and opportunity, could easily, for good luck or bad, be a quick path to the world of Frank Herbert's *Dune* where the tribes explored the galaxy with the "family atomics," in whatever real or virtual state, stored safely away.

NUCLEAR WEAPON USE

In this post–Cold War context of rapidly evolving weapons capabilities and international politics, it is important to examine the potential role of nuclear weapons in conflict—and especially how they might be used by new nuclear powers. The following sections assess the character and implications of an evolving spectrum of potential scenarios regarding post–Cold War nuclear weapons use.

The Prospect of Nuclear Conflict: Generic Next-Use Cases

With the end of the Cold War, there is now the real prospect that local or regional conflicts (some unleashed in part by the end of the bipolar standoff) will be the most likely route to nuclear war. Three generic circumstances would appear to capture the spectrum of such scenarios for the next use of nuclear weapons and supersede in all likelihood the classic superpower nuclear exchange scenarios of the Cold War:[14]

- The loss of central control, in which a national command authority fragments during the breakup of a heretofore unitary state, raising the prospect of a nuclear civil war.

- The emergence of a nuclear-armed regional predator, in which a major power (or a major power-led alliance) intervenes to thwart some nation's expansionist or hegemonistic efforts.

- A regional war between two newly nuclear-armed states, the so-called Nth on Nth nuclear war problem.

Each of these cases represents a class of events characteristic of the post–Cold War security environment. Note that this dynamic and uncertain international security context will most likely prevail through the first decade of the twenty-first century if not well beyond. Conventional wisdom suggests that future nuclear weapon use by a new regional nuclear state is unlikely unless that state is directed by a madman.[15] Contrary to this expectation, a wide range of use scenarios are plausible and may range from brandishing a nuclear arsenal, to a variety of crisis maneuvers, to outright use of one or more nuclear weapons to bring about a powerful regional strategic effect.

Over the course of the past three years the RAND Corporation has been exploring the policy implications of future nuclear crises in a post–Cold War context through a series of policy exercises. Several major insights have been gained from these exercises.

- Even a very small number of nuclear weapons in the hands of an adversary will affect the behavior of the United States and its coalition partners in future regional crises. Their impact is expected to be so strong as to call into question major conclusions in the Department of Defense's 1993 *Bottom-Up Review,* which assumes that the U.S. military should prepare to fight two *nonnuclear* major regional contingencies and dictates major changes in the operational concept, organization, and equipment of future U.S. expeditionary forces.[16]

- A regional predator will find a small nuclear arsenal a powerful tool for collapsing regional military coalitions that the United States might craft to oppose such a future opponent.

- Design and deployment of military forces capable of destroying a small nuclear arsenal or even simply neutralizing that arsenal for a time represent a prodigious military-intelligence operational challenge. This problem is even further complicated by severe budgetary restraints.

- There are no apparent technological or operational silver bullets by which to defeat the "tyranny of small numbers" manifest in small regional strategic nuclear arsenals. A robust counterproliferation capability will require a large-scale investment in a new generation of sensors, active defenses, strike systems, and special operations capabilities.

- The conduct of a future counterproliferation campaign to neutralize a small nuclear force is likely to call for an all-service capability organized by a unified command that can conduct this high-performance mission with little operational warning and at a transoceanic distance.[17]

Non- and Counterproliferation

It seems clear at this writing that the Clinton administration's nonproliferation/counterproliferation strategy remains a work in progress, hampered to some degree by the lack of consensus (and a perpetuated and increasingly sterile debate) on the distinctions between nonproliferation and counterproliferation.[18] At the presidential level, the administration has so far emphasized somewhat traditional nonproliferation initiatives and in three main areas: (1) pressing for the indefinite and unchanged renewal of the NPT treaty document during the 1995 Review and Extension Conference; (2) negotiating a global comprehensive nuclear test ban; and (3) ending the global production of weapons-grade fissile material.

The counterproliferation concept has to date been manifest formally only in a speech made by then Secretary of Defense Les Aspin on December 7, 1993, in which he announced and described a Defense Counterproliferation Initiative (DCI).[19] Although he embraced traditional nonproliferation efforts and the ongoing antitactical ballistic missile program within counterproliferation, the major new elements in Aspin's speech were the call for improved counterforce capability against weapons of mass destruction and a charge to the military services and the regional commanders in chief to describe how they would propose to fight wars against adversaries who had weapons of mass destruction. At the same time traditional nonproliferation advocates within the Department of State and the Arms Control and Disarmament Agency question whether the concept of counterproliferation is appropriate and constructive in the face of current nonproliferation concerns.[20]

What seems needed at this stage is a vigorous and more disciplined White House–led, administration-wide effort to develop a new U.S. national security strategy that integrates and conforms with the long-term objectives of (1) an evolving U.S. regional security strategy as articulated originally in the Bush administration and further embraced and emphasized in the 1993 *Bottom-Up Review;* (2) the more traditional U.S. strategic nuclear posture with respect to the Russians and China; and (3) the U.S. nonproliferation/counterproliferation strategy. If the United States does not decide where it is going, all roads lead there.

ALTERNATIVE PATHWAYS TO AN UNCERTAIN EARLY TWENTY-FIRST CENTURY

We turn now to the strategic road map from here to there. "Here" is the intellectual crashing together of the three strategy components cited above. "There" is, for example, one or another of the four exemplary asymptotic states.

FROM HERE TO HIGH ENTROPY

There would appear to be two separable and still credible paths to a state of nuclear high entropy that are worthy of consideration. One is very rapid, the other is in slow motion. In both cases the pathway into a nuclear well-armed future for the planet would be cleared by a conscious national and international decision to step aside and *not* invest the energy and political leverage necessary to rein in the prevailing trends in the nuclear realm. Such a posture might credibly be adopted by default by an inward-turning United States.

The domino that is likely to decide the path that a world of relatively unfettered access to nuclear weapons will take—rapid or slow—is the ongoing struggle in Eurasia between the twin forces of integration and fragmentation. In this regard the appearance of an extreme nationalist and expansionist regime in Russia would be a disaster for the prospect of containing nuclear weapons proliferation.[21]

If the outcome on that supercontinent is a return to fragmentation and extreme nationalism, it is logical that many nations will be very quick to (re)consider nuclear weapons. It is not far from the view that "the best defense is self-defense" to that of "the best (and cheapest) means of self-defense is nuclear weapons"—on the grounds (probably correct) that nobody is likely to attack a nation that has a nuclear arsenal that is survivable and reliably deliverable—the iron logic of Charles de Gaulle.

Then we face a new dilemma. Once a nation has stepped over the line from nuclear weapons potential to nuclear weapons at-the-ready (or is about to do so), is it in the broader global interest to make that new nuclear-armed state a more competent club member—as experienced drivers would, for example, a novice at the Indianapolis 500? Should that nation get the latest safety equipment—safing, fusing, and firing mechanisms? Should it be educated in how best to hide its arsenal and be given the (almost?) latest in tactical warning systems as a means of helping ensure the survivability of its nuclear deterrent in the name of regional crisis stability?

If nuclear proliferation unfolds in this way, then the United States might be much more inclined to ensure that those nations that choose to become nuclear armed are safely so, a policy that itself might further accelerate an already rapid process. In any event, the world that would result would either be highly turbulent—one worthy of the label "nuclear anarchy" or "nuclear Hobbesian world"—or very quiescent, with the widespread deployment of nuclear weapons creating an interstitial nuclear force field that keeps adversary nations apart.

Even if the forces for global integration gain dominance in Eurasia, a world with a more laissez-faire attitude toward nuclear arsenals would still move unambiguously toward a state of high entropy, but presumably at a more deliberate pace, stimulated not by a continental trend but by region-specific security problems. For example, failure to resolve the security problems of the Middle East and Persian Gulf in the relatively near future is likely to see Iran convert its growing nuclear potential as a minimum to the brink of an at-the-ready nuclear arsenal and similar steps by Iraq once it is freed from the U.N. inspection and monitoring regime. Similarly, in South Asia, an unfettered India and Pakistan are likely to move over time to unambiguous deployment of small arsenals and a sustained debate over an appropriate nuclear asymptote for South Asia. In East Asia, failure to achieve peaceful Korean reunification in the near term is likely to lead to an unambiguously nuclear-armed North Korea, with South

Korea hard on its heels. We can only speculate whether in this situation (or one in which a reunited Korea drags its feet in dismantling North Korea's nuclear weapons production capability) Japan would feel compelled to take its virtual nuclear weapons capability a few steps closer to an at-the-ready state. Of course, such a step may not be disclosed, much less rationalized.

The above assessment shows by credible examples already well known that the number of nuclear-armed nations could be at least eleven in ten to fifteen years, with more almost certain to follow—each generating policy questions such as those cited above.

HERE IS THERE: AN EVER-*SLOWLY*-EXPANDING NUCLEAR CLUB

If the United States and other key major powers were instead to adopt a more activist role in international affairs, a strong coalition could emerge that would seek to rein in—but not necessarily halt—the proliferation of at-the-ready nuclear arsenals. Such a coalition could conceivably include the United States, the major powers of Europe, Russia, India, Japan, and China.

As noted, the world is currently proceeding along the path of slow motion nuclear proliferation. With some additional effort it might be kept there.

A key early issue along this path—and the testing ground for getting down to cases on the policy questions regarding nuclear force safety and survivability cited above—would be how the undeclared nuclear-armed states, Israel, Pakistan, and India, are brought into this "slow-growing" nuclear club. This step of formally acknowledging these nations' existing (or imminent) status as nuclear weapon states might even be taken in the context of the 1995 NPT Review and Extension Conference.

FROM HERE TO A TIGHT "FIVE-HAVES," TWO-TIERED SYSTEM

To effect a future nuclear proliferation regime based on the logic of maintaining a small but finite number of nuclear-armed special nations—presumably (at least for now) the U.N. Security Council permanent five—would require convincing Israel, Pakistan, and India to give up their nuclear arsenals. This would no doubt require both new and credible security commitments to and guarantees for all three parties *and* substantial progress on diminishing the sources of the conflicts that stimulated these arsenals in the first place. In theory, this commitment could be made through the vehicle of a modified and reinforced U.N. Security Council framework supplemented by regional collective security guarantees.

If no such international commitment at present proves satisfactory, these states could in principle be grandfathered into the NPT on a one-time-only basis as temporary overt nuclear weapon states. Such temporary membership might be conditioned, for exam-

ple, on agreement to limits or a freeze on arsenal size and nuclear infrastructure inspection procedures akin to the full-scope safeguards of the IAEA.

The maintenance of any such basically two-tiered system would require that all of the significant actors accept the international political status quo. Not surprisingly, a major war in which nuclear weapons came into play, either through brandishing or outright use, could rapidly collapse such a two-tiered system.

FROM HERE TO VIRTUAL ABOLITION

Of those end states presented, the one that requires the greatest engagement and input of energy on the part of the major nations of the world is virtual abolition. This follows from two imperatives: (1) five major (and several other) nations must go through the wrenching experience of rethinking their own security situation without at-the-ready nuclear arsenals as a flagship element; and (2) unprecedented and far-reaching inspection and enforcement and other security guarantee elements in a new multifaceted security system based on the U.N. Security Council must be formulated and marketed.

A strategy of virtual abolition is grounded in the concept that the threat to global peace posed by nuclear weapons proliferation is so great that the major powers will take heroic steps to make nuclear weapons illegitimate—to keep them off the list of weapons with which nations fight. These steps would include adding fundamental new elements to the existing international security system, including a highly intrusive global inspection regime and new and unambiguous security commitments to some nations as they need it. For the international community to head down this path, especially during this critical and difficult early phase of the post–Cold War era, the United States in particular would have to become very active in promoting such a security structure to the major economic and military powers, in particular in Eurasia, possibly as a trial balloon as early as the run-up to the 1995 NPT Review and Extension Conference.

In further testing of the viability of such a concept, the United States and other like-minded nuclear-armed nations, by their own weapons procurement and posturing actions, might demonstrate their willingness to move away from large at-the-ready nuclear arsenals as a flagship element of a security posture and to expend the resources to develop the conventional forces wherewithal—whatever that might be—to play a lead role in extending deterrence to insecure nations and in the enforcement of a virtual abolition regime.[22]

FROM HERE TO THE 1995 NPT REVIEW AND EXTENSION CONFERENCE

In all four of the above road maps, the 1995 NPT Review and Extension Conference looms large as a forum that could reveal the direction that many leading nations, and most notably the United States, will take on the nuclear proliferation problem.

If the 1995 conference is a repeat of 1990, 1985, and previous conferences—with the United States and other key nations basically paying homage to an unchanged NPT and engineering a political escape to a relatively short-term treaty extension—then one can infer that an implicit decision tantamount to global acquiescence to the force of nuclear entropy has essentially been made.

If the run-up to the conference is characterized by a strong effort to bring Israel, India, and Pakistan into the NPT as nuclear weapon states—or by no serious effort whatever to lobby these countries on NPT membership—then one can infer that the implicit choice is an ever-expanding nuclear club, with the first expansion beyond the core permanent five possibly tolerable as a separate category.

If the run-up to the conference is characterized by (1) a strong international effort to persuade India and Pakistan to rein in their nuclear arsenal building programs before it is too late to turn back and to join the NPT as nonnuclear weapon states in return for some new international security guarantees or change of international status (e.g., for India with respect to its concerns over China, the "payment" may be permanent membership in the U.N. Security Council); (2) a strong effort to forge a regional settlement in the Middle East within which Israel makes a commitment eventually to forgo at-the-ready nuclear weapons (although it may retain a significant, acknowledged, and well-planned virtual nuclear arsenal); and (3) attention to an improved IAEA inspection regime—then one can infer an effort at rollback and eventually holding the line on the permanent five (for now) as the only nations with at-the-ready nuclear weapons.

Finally, if the run-up to the conference is marked by seriously debated proposals among the permanent five for radical reductions in nuclear arsenals and the extending of new or reinforced security guarantees by that body—and the opening of their nations to the kind of intrusive inspection that would characterize a virtual nuclear arsenal regime—and if the 1995 conference sees the tabling of a new permanent five "interim" nuclear forces reduction package (say to 1,500 to 2,000 warheads apiece for the United States and Russia and 300 to 400 for the other three nations), then serious steps toward setting an asymptotic goal akin to virtual abolition will probably have been taken.

THE CHALLENGE

The successful constraint of the inherent entropy in the spread of nuclear weapons know-how and wherewithal will require a major sustained effort by the international community and especially leadership by key nations like the United States, Russia, China, France, and the United Kingdom, whose political leverage is essential if a far more effective regime of nuclear containment is to emerge. With-

out such a major input of energy now, the natural end state of the nuclear age asymptote is almost assuredly high entropy. Such a wide diffusion of nuclear weapons in the hands of many states and probably some nonstate actors in a dynamic political soup would place before the international community the perpetual and ever more complex task of constructing multiple stable nuclear deterrence relationships and the strongest possible global cultural taboo on the use of nuclear weapons. Containing this tendency will require nothing less than an urgent commitment to the development of a broad international consensus on some asymptotic goal that reflects a concept of containment of such entropic forces and of an appropriate associated strategy.

With the end of the fifty-year "national emergency" (December 1941–December 1991) the U.S. public and the political elites clearly would like to focus the nation's energies on long-neglected domestic concerns. This poses a special challenge for those concerned about the international security dynamic, because the burden of proof will be on those who argue for investing always precious presidential time and energy in an effort to build a strong and aggressive U.S. leadership posture in these crucial international matters, and in devising the necessary policies. Containing nuclear entropy in the long term will require nothing less.

[Editor's note: During the April-May 1995 NPT Review and Extension Conference, the treaty was extended for an indefinite period by consensus of the parties. In addition, the conference called for a strengthening of the treaty review process with review conferences every five years, agreed on a set of principles and objectives for nuclear nonproliferation and disarmament, set the goal of achieving a comprehensive nuclear test ban by 1996, and called for the states in the Middle East to agree to the creation of a weapons of mass destruction–free zone. This outcome contains many elements discussed by Molander and Wilson but does not correspond directly to any of the four paths through the review conference envisioned in this essay.]

NOTES

The views expressed in this article are those of the authors and not necessarily those of RAND or any of its sponsoring organizations.

1. This essay summarizes a longer monograph, Roger C. Molander and Peter A. Wilson, *The Nuclear Asymptote: On Containing Nuclear Proliferation*, MR-214-CC (Santa Monica, Calif.: RAND, 1993). Its substance flows from three years of policy exercises and analyses conducted at RAND for various elements of the U.S. national security community during which Marc Dean Millot played a major role.

2. For a description of the likely diffusion of nuclear and missile expertise from the former Soviet Union see Kathleen C. Bailey, *Strengthening Nuclear Non-Proliferation* (Boulder, Colo.: Westview Press, 1993), 37–47.

3. The very success of the new economic "elephants"—the People's Republic of China, India, and Brazil—will place heavy demands on the regional and global ecosystem as their consumption of fossil fuels for energy production and transportation rises. All three are short of domestic petroleum supplies and will rely heavily on the construction of a civilian nuclear power infrastructure. For an overview of China's explosive and therefore geostrategically significant economic growth see William H. Overholt, *The Rise of China: How Economic Reform Is Creating a New Superpower* (New York: W. W. Norton, 1994).

4. For a description of the South African nuclear weapons program, see Peter D. Zimmerman, "Proliferation: Bronze Medal Technology Is Enough," *Orbis* 38 (Winter 1994): 75–78.

5. The term *asymptote* is used in this essay in its mathematical sense of a limit—in this case, a steady state or a goal—that a curve or function approaches ever closer, but never quite reaches.

6. The contrarian view that nuclear proliferation is stabilizing was articulated by Pierre Gallois and André Beaufre, both leading French strategic theoreticians favoring Charles de Gaulle's decision to build an independent nuclear deterrent. More recent advocates of this thesis include Kenneth N. Waltz, *The Spread of Nuclear Weapons: More May Be Better,* Adelphi Paper 171 (London: International Institute for Strategic Studies, 1981); K. Subrahmanyan, ed., *Nuclear Myths and Realities* (New Delhi: ABC Publishing, 1981); and Martin van Creveld, *Nuclear Proliferation and the Future of Conflict* (New York: Free Press, 1993). Van Creveld's view is more subtle in that he believes that for state-to-state relations nuclear weapons have stabilized regional conflicts, while there remains the grave risk that nuclear weapons will fall into the hands of nonstate organizations that arise out of the disintegration of the nation-states.

7. For a sophisticated articulation of the case for an overt Indian minimum deterrent capable of reaching China's heartland see K. Sundarji, *Blind Men of Hindoostan* (New Delhi: USS Publishers' Distributors, 1993). Sundarji, a former Indian chief of staff, makes the case for an overt Indian nuclear weapons program and an appropriate political military planning mechanism, which does not exist at this time.

8. During the first few months of the Clinton administration, there was talk about adding Japan and Germany as new permanent members to the Security Council as part of a reform effort to revitalize the United Nations. Enthusiasm for such major changes has faded in the face of objections from France and the United Kingdom as well as other large states such as India.

9. One of the major findings of the RAND "The Day After" exercise series was the strong view held by many U.S. military participants that nuclear weapons no longer provide the United States with a net national security benefit. It was in this context that the early concept of virtual abolition was articulated. See Marc Dean Millot, Roger Molander, and Peter A. Wilson, *"The Day After . . ." Study: Nuclear Proliferation in the Post–Cold War World,* vol. 1, *Summary Report* (MR-266-AF); vol. 2, *Main Report* (MR-253-AF); vol. 3, *Exercise Materials* (MR-254-AF) (Santa Monica, Calif.: RAND, 1993).

10. Zimmerman, "Proliferation," 77–78.

11. During the 1960s it became an article of faith within the U.S. strategic analytical community that small nuclear forces were dangerous and destabilizing owing to their vulnerability to preemption. This was one of the central tenets of the nonproliferation argument that new nuclear-armed states could deploy only small and vulnerable forces. The Scud campaign and the U.S. failure to identify the full range of installations associated with Iraq's nuclear weapons program suggest that a medium-size power may have a wide range of options to deploy a small and survivable nuclear arsenal that cannot be easily neutralized by a counterforce attack. One can only note the current debate within the U.S. national security community about the feasibility of "taking out" the North Korean nuclear weapons program and associated missile infrastructure.

12. For an analysis of the anti-Scud campaign see Thomas A. Keaney and Eliot A. Cohen, *Gulf War Air Power Survey* (Washington, D.C.: GPO, 1993), 83–90. This study and others concluded that the allied air forces gained no confirmed kills of a Scud and its associated launcher after 1,000 attack sorties. Other reports suggest that some Scud missiles and their launchers were destroyed by special operations forces in the Western Iraqi desert. See Christopher Bellamy, *Expert Witness: A Defence Correspondent's Gulf War 1990–91* (New York: Brassey's, 1993), 107–8. The mobile missile challenge has a precedent; the lack of success of allied World War II air forces in destroying mobile German V-2 launchers. See David Irving, *The Mare's Nest: The German Secret Weapons Campaign and Allied Counter-measures* (Boston: Little, Brown, 1964), 304–13.

13. For an excellent survey of the status of the MTCR and the diffusion of ballistic missile development and production capability see William C. Potter and Harlan W. Jencks, eds., *The International Missile Bazaar: The New Suppliers' Network* (Boulder, Colo.: Westview Press, 1994). Noteworthy is the description of long-standing cooperative relations between North Korea and Egypt and Iran.

14. For a summary and analysis of the findings derived from the policy exercises conducted during 1991 and 1992 see Millot, Molander, and Wilson, *"The Day After . . ." Study,* vols. 1 and 2. All of these exercises involved scenarios that led to the detonation of one or more nuclear weapons during a regional strategic crisis. During 1993 and 1994, the coauthors conducted a second generation of exercises that explored a broader range of scenarios including direct nuclear threats to the United States.

15. As an example of the conventional wisdom that only a madman would use nuclear weapons see Bailey, *Strengthening Nuclear Non-Proliferation,* 101.

16. Les Aspin, *The Bottom-Up Review: Forces for a New Era* (Washington, D.C.: Department of Defense, 1993).

17. For a further elaboration of these points see Millot, Molander, and Wilson, *"The Day After . . ." Study,* vol. 1.

18. For a detailed discussion of the first-year evolution of the Clinton administration's non- and counter-proliferation policy see Marc Dean Millot, "Facing the Emerging Reality of Regional Nuclear Adversaries," *Washington Quarterly* (Summer 1994). For a detailed critique of the strategic and budgetary planning assumptions of *The Bottom-Up Review* see Andrew F. Krepinevich, *The Bottom-Up Review: An Assessment* (Washington, D.C.: Defense Budget Project, 1994).

19. For an outline of the DCI see "Remarks by Defense Secretary Les Aspin to the National Academy of Sciences Committee on International Security and Arms Control," *Federal News Service*, 7 December 1993, LEXIS.

20. For a critique of giving too much emphasis to counterproliferation at the expense of a vigorous enforcement of the NPT regime see Rupert Pengelley, "Betting Each Way on Proliferation," *International Defense Review* 2(1994):1.S.

21. Hopes to gain a consensus among the permanent five on far-reaching nuclear disarmament and arms-control initiatives will be shattered if the Russian Federation is headed by a regime that frightens many of its Eurasian neighbors, who in turn call for collective defense guarantees from the United States or the North Atlantic Treaty Organization. If these are not forthcoming, several might execute a nuclear weapons option, and others such as China might carry out a major expansion of their nuclear arsenals.

22. Even if Russia does not go sour, it will be a major diplomatic challenge for the United States to convince the Russian Federation, China, the United Kingdom, and France to consider a radical downgrading of their nuclear arsenals as part of a very ambitious post-1995 non- and counterproliferation regime of virtual abolition. The Russian Federation, for example, has announced a new military doctrine that renounces the Soviet no-first-use declaratory policy and highlights the need for nuclear forces. See Brigitte Sauerwein, "Russia Adopts New Military Doctrine," *International Defense Review* 12(1993): 931. Furthermore, the French government is in the process of deciding whether to *expand* the deterrent role of its nuclear forces as a counterproliferation option. See Pierre Sparaco, "French Defense White Paper Paves Way for Six-Year Plan," *Aviation Week & Space Technology*, 7 March 1994, 39.

EXTENDED CONVENTIONAL DETERRENCE

CHARLES T. ALLAN

General Colin Powell, former chairman of the Joint Chiefs of Staff, observed in 1992 that "deterrence remains the primary and central motivating purpose underlying [U.S.] national military strategy" (1992, 6). The end of the Cold War, however, and the overwhelming U.S.-led victory in the Persian Gulf War have sparked a new discourse on the meaning, tools, and targets of U.S. deterrence strategy.

In 1993, then Secretary of Defense Les Aspin succinctly defined the changed national security environment in his *Bottom-Up Review* (1993a, 7):

During the Cold War, our military planning was dominated by the need to confront numerically superior Soviet forces in Europe, the Far East, and Southwest Asia. Now, our focus is on the need to project power into regions important to our interest and to defeat potentially hostile regional powers such as North Korea and Iraq.

This statement has three major implications for deterrence strategy. First, the demise of the Soviet threat has significantly decreased the risk of war in Europe or direct attack on the United States. Thus the central role of *nuclear* deterrence has declined. Second, deterrence strategy can no longer focus on a single adversary but must be tailored to a number of regional powers. And third, as during the Cold War, the U.S. deterrent shield will be *extended* to interests far from the United States but very close to its potential adversaries (Arquilla and Davis 1992).

The overwhelming victory of the U.S.-led coalition forces over Iraq has also had major implications for deterrence. In analyzing the impact of Desert Storm, William Perry (1991, 66) has observed:

This new conventional military capability adds a powerful dimension to the ability of the United States to deter war. While it is certainly not as powerful as nuclear weapons, it is a more credible deterrent, particularly in regional conflicts vital to U.S. interests. . . . It should also strengthen the already high level of deterrence of a major war in Europe and Korea. The United States can now be confident that the defeat of a conventional armored assault in those regions could be achieved by conventional military forces, which could enable the United States to limit the role of its nuclear forces to the deterrence of nuclear attack.

In light of the increased lethality of conventional weapons and President George Bush's 1991 decision to eliminate ground- and sea-based tactical nuclear weapons, this analysis indicates that *conventional* weapons may form the basis of U.S. extended deterrence.

The purpose of this research survey is to determine the outline of U.S. post–Cold War thinking on deterrence, while focusing on extended conventional deterrence. The survey does not attempt to parse the lengthy and complex Cold War deterrence debate, which focused almost entirely on the North Atlantic Treaty Organization (NATO), the Soviet Union, and

This essay has been edited and is reprinted from The Washington Quarterly 17 *(Fall 1994): 203–33, by permission of MIT Press.*

nuclear issues. To thoroughly address the issue of extended conventional deterrence, the survey falls into three sections.

Deterrence. The first section addresses the meaning of deterrence in the post–Cold War era. It reviews recommendations to expand the meaning of deterrence to incorporate nonmilitary instruments of power and examines the debate over the types of military threats best suited to a post–Cold War deterrence strategy. Here, the debate focuses on whether deterrence is purely punitive (i.e., incorporates only threats of countervalue punishment) or contains elements of both punishment and denial (i.e., defense). Finally, it asserts that a third form—dynamic deterrence—is emerging in the post–Cold War, post–Desert Storm world.

Conventional Deterrence. The second section addresses current thinking on conventional deterrence. It delineates the rationale for conventional deterrence and its strengths and weaknesses. In addition, this section reviews the debate over the roles of conventional and nuclear weapons in extended deterrence.

Extended Conventional Deterrence. This section outlines the implications of the regional emphasis of U.S. national security policy on deterrence. It addresses the following issues:

- The necessity for clear commitments

- The inadequacy of the classic "rational actor" model as a foundation for deterrence strategy

- The role of coalitions in U.S. deterrence strategy

- The role of reputation in supporting long-term U.S. deterrence stability

- Potential counterstrategies to U.S. deterrence.

The survey concludes with a discussion of how the deterrence debate may affect U.S. national security policy and force structure and makes recommendations for future research.

WHAT DOES DETERRENCE MEAN?

After forty years at the center of the national security debate, deterrence is no longer frozen in its Cold War constructs. Traditionally analysts have focused on deterrence as the use of threats of military retaliation to "prevent an adversary from using military force to achieve foreign policy objectives" (Huth 1988a, 15). The definition of deterrence is expanding to include more than military threats. In fact, the types of military threats that constitute deterrence are themselves the subject of debate. Ongoing deterrence studies focus on an expanded meaning of deterrence and its integration into overall national security strategy.

Expansionists believe the definition of deterrence should be modified to include all instruments of national security, not merely the threat of military force (Blackwell, Mazarr, and Snider 1993; Buchanan 1993). The new definitions are not limited to

forms of coercion but incorporate positive inducements as part of deterrence strategy (J. Mueller 1992; K. Mueller 1991). This expansion of deterrence to include positive inducements would subsume a body of scholarship, represented primarily by the work of Janice Gross Stein (1991) and Richard Lebow (1985), that they refer to as "reassurance theory."

Paul Huth and Bruce Russett (1990) maintain that a key area for future deterrence study is how military threats, nonmilitary sanctions, and positive inducements may be integrated to prevent aggression. Robert Jervis (1994) supports this line of inquiry, noting that the concepts of deterrence, reassurance, and positive inducements are essentially complementary. John Arquilla and Paul Davis (1992) and George Quester (1993) believe that the integration of military threats and other foreign policy instruments has synergistic effects that have not been adequately researched. Other writers feel that foreign policy initiatives, economic measures, and nonlethal forms of coercion will be essential deterrent tools in the post–Cold War era (Buchanan 1993; Engstrom 1993; Starr 1993). The deterrent value of both nonlethal weapons and the growing field of information warfare are the subjects of intense study and war-gaming. Although the purpose of this discussion is to illuminate current thinking on deterrence, it should not be construed as asserting that the relations between the United States and developing powers will be ones of confrontation and deterrence. On the contrary, most evidence indicates that cooperative engagement will be the primary mode of relations between the United States and the developing world. States will still compete militarily, however. The type of military forces and the modes of their application required to underpin national security remain the focus of the public debate on deterrence (Nitze 1994).

Punishment. The type of military threats that constitute deterrence will have a significant impact on military force posture and structure decisions (Cimbala 1991; Palmer 1992; Jervis 1994). The two prevailing schools of thought on these threats differ over whether deterrence should include only threats of punishment, commonly referred to as countervalue targeting, or both punishment and a defensive strategy known as denial. During the Cold War, deterrence was perceived as a primarily punitive strategy (Blackwell, Mazarr, and Snider 1993).

The Cold War punitive definition of deterrence emphasized the devastating effects on the targeted society and regime. According to Stephen Cimbala (1991, xii), "A deterrent threat is a threat to inflict unacceptable *punishment* to the society or government of the opponent, regardless of whether or not his forces prevail in battle." Large-scale societal punishment, for many Cold War strategists, was the sine qua non of a credible deterrent (Cimbala 1991; Friedberg 1991). This form of punishment rejects defensive forces and instead requires forces that are simultaneously irresistible in their application and instantaneously devastating in their effects. The Cold War notion of punishment derived its strength from societal vulnerability to the incredible power of nuclear weapons (Cimbala 1991) and a lack of ballistic missile defenses (Davis 1993b). As Richard Harknett (1991) asserts, an aggressor faced with such a deterrent threat would theoretically have no way to contest the costs associated with challenging it. Because the outcome of war would not be determined on the battlefield, and the costs would be clearly perceived by the adversary as devastating to him and his society, resorting to force would be irrational. As long as the credibility of use remains perceptibly higher than zero, a devastating punitive deterrent should hold.

In fact, as David Abshire (1993) notes, the forceful component of the North Atlantic Treaty Organization's (NATO's) deterrence of the Soviet Union was effective for precisely this reason. If societal destruction is the primary basis for a strategy of deterrence through punishment, then paradoxically it holds that the most destructive weapons will ensure the strongest and most enduring deterrent (Betts 1988; Cimbala 1991; Harknett 1991; Jervis 1992). Beyond deterrence based on societal devastation are strategies that incorporate threats of less devastating punishment.

Denial. Although massive retaliatory punishment was the underlying theme of Cold War strategy, deterrence can also obtain through denial—the recognized ability to defeat the enemy's forces on the battlefield, thus denying him his military objectives and deterring aggression (Gray 1992; Quester 1992a; Jervis 1994).

Denial in its purest form, however, implies that the adversary is not punished for attempted aggression, only that his attempt to achieve his aims through force is denied. Thus classical denial focuses on territorial defense (Jervis 1994). A deterrent based solely on denial eschews offensive capabilities in favor of concepts such as "nonoffensive defense" (Boeker 1990; Nokkala 1991). A primarily defensive strategy would provide the type of deterrence described by John Mearsheimer (1983) and supported by Huth's analysis (1988a). Mearsheimer postulates that conventional deterrence is most likely to hold if it denies the aggressor a successful blitzkrieg option, thereby forcing a protracted conflict.

A New Approach. These forms of punishment and denial have constituted, and to some are still adequate as, the basis for developing deterrence strategy (Gray 1992). An emerging school of thought, however, advocates fundamental changes.

To the post–Cold War advocates of conventional deterrence, the concepts of punishment and denial alone are insufficient to support deterrence in the new era. Two factors appear to mandate changes. First, in contrast to the Cold War NATO scenario, enduring, significant U.S. ground forces will not be present at the beginning of future regional crises nor will these forces stay in a region once a crisis has ended (Arquilla and Davis 1992; Haffa 1992; Hooker and Waddell 1992). Second, precision guided munitions have demonstrated the capability to be discriminate in attacking a wide variety of targets. Consequently, a new, third deterrence modality is required. This new modality—here called *dynamic deterrence*—has three characteristics: (1) punishment need not be and no longer should be societal but tailored to the values of the targeted regime; (2) denial should not be a purely defensive concept but primarily offensive; and (3) the credible use of force should be viewed as essential to deterrence, not merely as a sign of its failure. For Robert Haffa (1992, 19) this new modality means that

a strategy of effective conventional deterrence must be . . . asymmetrical in threat and application, intense and overwhelming in its threat, offensive with a capability for punishment as well as denial, and extended globally through new technologies and weapons systems.

Paul Nitze (1994) and a Washington Strategy Seminar (WSS) study group (1993) have articulated almost identical views of conventional deterrence. The latest thinking postulates that punishment may be made more discriminating through targeting those things that a regime values most or possibly the leadership itself (Haffa 1992; Quester 1992a; WSS 1993). Even advocates of societal punishment cite precision strikes against a regime's leadership as an example of precision punishment (Harknett 1992). If punishment can be made more precise, then the moral and political dilemmas associated with the loss of innocent life can be avoided, thus making punishment more usable for U.S. deterrence strategy (Cropsey 1994).

Although punishment is to be more precise, denial will be more offensive in nature. Dynamic deterrence must include significant offensive counterforce capabilities because the long-term presence of large U.S. forces in a region will be problematic for both regional (Hess 1993; WSS 1993) and U.S. domestic (Sloan 1992) reasons. Conventional Cold War deterrence concepts implied primarily the capability to deny an enemy a swift victory and were essentially defensive in nature (Mearsheimer 1983). To the current advocates of extended conventional deterrence, mere denial of a blitzkrieg is inadequate and antiquated (Haffa 1992). Because future deployments of powerful U.S. forces will be temporary (Hooker and Waddell 1992), as they were during the Persian Gulf War, U.S. decision makers will face the policy dilemma that forces either must be used to effectively eliminate the military threat that triggered their deployment or face pressures to leave with the threat still intact (Garfinkle 1991; George 1991; Record 1993). Defensive denial would require the long-term deployment of substantial U.S. forces. Dynamic deterrence would therefore reject exclusively "nonoffensive defense." Of course, the advocates of dynamic deterrence are not proposing that the United States became an aggressive power. Just as NATO sought the capabilities to use offensive operations to strike deep against advancing Soviet forces in response to an initial act of aggression, so the advocates of dynamic deterrence would be prepared to strike deep in response to aggression. For the advocates of dynamic deterrence, however, U.S. forces must be projected from long range and force would be applied strategically to create the environment for long-term regional stability.

During the Cold War, war between the superpowers was an unacceptable outcome to deterrence. The advocates of dynamic deterrence believe the use of force may be necessary to demonstrate that the United States has the will, operational skill, and technical prowess required to defeat even the most powerful threats rapidly and at minimal cost (Haffa 1992). The consequence of overwhelming U.S.-led victories would be an extended period of deterrence stability while potential adversaries search for real or perceived weaknesses in U.S. strategy, operational art, or technology (Guertner 1993). Robert Art (1992–93) concurs that the periodic use of force may be essential for a broader, general deterrence to remain credible.

CONVENTIONAL DETERRENCE

The advocates of *conventional* deterrence (conventionalists) propose that now is the time for deterrence to break its nuclear chains. Nitze (1994, C-1) has stated that

the United States should consider . . . converting its principal strategic deterrent from nuclear weapons to a more credible deterrence based at least in part upon "smart" conventional weapons. It is a shift that could be justified as a coldly rational approach to a new security strategy and equally so as a morally correct foreign policy choice.

In their extensive study of potential U.S. responses to nuclear proliferation and attack, three RAND analysts (Millot, Molander, and Wilson 1993) note that participants in their "Day After . . ." series of war games have provided supporting rationale to Nitze's arguments. Many participants, drawn from government, industry, and academe, offered two reasons for increased dependence on a conventionally based deterrent: as a result of Desert Storm U.S. conventional dominance would deter regional adversaries by nonnuclear means; and it is "counterproductive . . . to base extended deterrence on nuclear guarantees, even in the face of possible nuclear provocation by an opposing regional power" (pp. x–xi). Other participants believed that "conventional weapons are or will soon enough be, nearly perfect substitutes for nuclear weapons in terms of military effectiveness, deterrent value, and reassurance" (p. 19). Thus two arguments support the shift to a conventionally based deterrent: (1) conventional weapons have attained counterforce and countervalue capabilities previously achievable only with nuclear forces, and (2) nuclear threats are not credible in regional contingencies.

Improved Conventional Capabilities. Overwhelming conventional superiority is the key to increased reliance on conventionally based deterrence. The dynamic modality of conventional deterrence embodies the perceived characteristics of U.S. conventional dominance. Dynamic deterrence had its genesis in the drive to use technology to overcome the conventional imbalance in Europe and to delay resorting to nuclear weapons to counter Soviet aggression, thus making the active defense of Europe a more credible deterrent. This early effort to shift deterrence to a greater reliance on conventional weapons was the basis for *discriminate* deterrence as proposed in 1988 by the Commission on Integrated Long-term Strategy headed by Fred Iklé and Albert Wohlstetter (Kaufman, Clark, and Sheehan 1991). The commission emphasized two concepts: stealth and precision guidance would allow conventional munitions to replace nuclear weapons for many missions, and new technologies and operational concepts would allow NATO strategy to be more offensive in nature.

The overwhelming success of Desert Storm and the post–Cold War regional context of U.S. foreign policy provided the break between discriminate deterrence and dynamic deterrence. The advocates of discriminate deterrence could not foresee an era when the United States would have both conventional superiority over its primary adversaries and the ability to conduct a comprehensive counterforce and countervalue strategic conventional attack throughout the opponent's territory. The Soviet Union was too powerful and too vast to allow such possibilities. Perry (1991) emphasized the counterforce aspects of the new technologies in his assessment of the Gulf War. For him, Desert Storm provided a clear vindication of the advocates of discriminate deterrence by emphasizing how the new technologies had proven their ability to defeat armored forces. In this sense, Perry's thinking is transitional. The advocates of true dynamic deterrence would emphasize not only the destruction of battlefield targets but also the capability of conventional forces to strike strategically throughout the depth of an aggressor state (Haffa 1992; Drew 1993; Nitze 1994).

The proponents of dynamic deterrence believe that conventional weapons have not only become more effective in their counterforce roles but also incorporate significant countervalue capabilities. Conventionalists assert that current U.S. conventional capabilities are so overwhelming that they should intimidate any prospective regional adversary for the foreseeable future (Gray 1992; Guertner 1993). Haffa (1992, 11) notes:

For example, the development and deployment of survivable conventional delivery platforms and very precise munitions recently displayed in the Gulf War—the F-117s, with a probability of target destruction of .8, approximated the requirements of the strategic nuclear-SIOP—suggest that conventional force has immediately become more punishing, more usable, and, therefore more credible.

Haffa and James Patton, writing together in 1991 and separately in 1992 and 1993, respectively, believe that the combination of stealthy platforms (e.g.,

F-117s, B-2s, and attack submarines) and precision munitions make conventional deterrence essentially uncontestable (no third-world country will be able to challenge the survivability of these platforms) and devastating (hundreds of targets will be destroyed in a single day). Applying a similar rationale, Seth Cropsey (1994) proposes a deterrence strategy based on thousands of conventional cruise missiles. For the advocates of dynamic deterrence, conventional weapons can realistically replace nuclear weapons as the basis for deterrence because they have a devastating counterforce (denial) capability; precise munitions and stealthy platforms give conventional weapons a powerful countervalue (punishment) capability; and the low collateral damage associated with conventional munitions means the United States can and will use them effectively—making deterrence more credible (WSS 1993).

The advocates of conventional deterrence acknowledge, however, that conventional weapons will require improvements in two areas to convince U.S. adversaries and reassure U.S. allies that conventional deterrence can hold. First, as Haffa (1993) notes, weapons of mass destruction (WMDs) pose a serious challenge to the applicability of conventional deterrence. In the counterproliferation arena, former Secretary of Defense Les Aspin (1993b) outlined three major requirements: improved capability to locate, identify, and attack mobile missile launchers; theater ballistic missile defense; and improved hard target kill capability. Second, as noted in a RAND study of future force requirements, forces armed with current munitions may have been unable to establish an assured defense of key facilities in Saudi Arabia if Saddam Hussein's armored forces had continued south instead of stopping in Kuwait (Bowie and others 1993). Both of these deficiencies have been highlighted in Korea, where the exposed position of Seoul makes a conventional defense extremely problematic, and where North Korea's deeply buried nuclear facilities are inaccessible to U.S. conventional weapons (McPeak 1993). The RAND study (Bowie and others 1993) proposes possible solutions to the problem of defeating rapid armored advances while U.S. Air Force (Engstrom 1993) and U.S. Navy (Buchanan 1993) studies offer approaches to developing forces to support deterrence and counterproliferation. Even if the United States obtains the technological solutions to these problems, new, untried capabilities may have little deterrent impact (Lewis 1989). Despite the requisite U.S. capabilities to deter, an adversary may still choose war.

Critics point out that a conventionally based deterrent is prone to failure. They cite evidence that conventional deterrence has failed even when a defender has clear preponderance of forces (Lebow 1989; Stern and others 1989; Wolf 1991). There are two salient explanations for these failures. First, it may be difficult to apprise a potential adversary of the elements of conventional war fighting that would allow the United States to win decisively in a regional conflict, such as long-range aviation, strategic lift capability, and battlefield reconnaissance. Indeed, it is the capabilities that most contribute to U.S. conventional dominance that may be hardest to communicate (Harknett 1991; Arquilla and Davis 1992; Hooker and Waddell 1992). The skills required to employ and integrate new technologies as well as the technologies themselves are essential to U.S. dominance in conventional warfare (Perry 1991; Cohen 1994). Successful conventional war-fighting is a contest of skill and professionalism and requires an understanding of the operational art (Harknett 1992). An adversary may be unable to know, much less appreciate, these subtle but very real components of successfully waging conventional war (Cimbala 1991).

Second, conventional weapons may not be sufficiently destructive to deter the most risk prone and desperate of adversaries. Certain leaders will be unmoved by the magnitude of destruction that the United States is able to inflict through conventional means (Pape 1992). The destructive power of conventional weapons is after all finite and therefore contestable, and some aggressors may be inclined to believe that they will succeed despite evidence to the contrary (Cimbala 1991; Harknett 1991). Many critics of conventional deterrence believe that it will be unable to prevent a desperate adversary from using WMDs to avoid a decisive conventional defeat. Critics of conventionally based deterrence maintain that the inability to communicate both the quality of one's forces and the devastating power of new weapons is one of its key failings.

Conventionalists agree that adversaries will test conventional deterrence. Indeed, they argue the effective use of force is an essential element of conventional deterrence (Guertner 1992; Nitze 1994).

Deterrence failures [wars or crises] provide the opportunity to demonstrate the price of aggression, rejuvenate the credibility of deterrence (collective or unilateral), and establish a new period of stability (Guertner 1992, 3).

Conflicts demonstrate new technologies and the skills to use them. Thus both critics and advocates of dynamic deterrence agree that potential aggressors are very likely to assess improperly or totally ignore the value of technological and operational improvements without demonstrations of U.S. capabilities.

For the proponents of extended conventional deterrence, the character of war termination is a critical component of deterrence strategy. For some, U.S. responses to aggression must be disproportionate in order to convey the seriousness of challenging U.S. interests and preventing the United States from becoming involved in a protracted conflict (Buchanan 1993). Less than decisive outcomes may be interpreted either as a lack of capability or, possibly more seriously, a lack of U.S. will (Garrity 1993a).

The destruction of combat forces as well as the countervalue (punishment) targets of the regime should demonstrate the depth and breadth of U.S.

conventional dominance. In the age of instant communications, all potential aggressors would observe the results (Haffa 1992). A new general deterrence environment would be established for the affected region and potentially globally. For the dynamic deterrence advocates, the more disproportionate the U.S. victory in breadth, depth, cost, and political implications, the broader and more persistent the new postwar deterrent will be. Because conventional force does not carry the global, national, or personal taboos that nuclear weapons do, its use is far more likely and credible than the use of nuclear weapons in any crisis (Dunn 1994; Nitze 1994).

Credibility. The greater apparent willingness of U.S. leaders to use conventional weapons is the second underpinning of the conventional deterrence argument. Operationally, the United States retains a dramatic lead over any potential regional nuclear challenger. Other than the states of the former Soviet Union, none of the potential regional adversaries of the United States possesses a force capable of countering U.S. nuclear forces. In fact, except for vulnerability to unconventional entry—cargo ship, small civil aircraft, or advanced emplacement (Carnesale 1993; Levine 1993)—the United States is currently immune from nuclear attack by renegade states. Thus the United States no longer faces the problem of self-deterrence resulting from the lack of credibility of trading "Boston for Bonn."

Yet concern over the adequacy of the "coupling" of U.S. strategic nuclear weapons to NATO has periodically undermined U.S. efforts to reassure its European allies about the reliability of its nuclear umbrella. Throughout the history of Cold War deterrence, the United States sought to give its conventional and nuclear defense of Europe a greater war-fighting character. Until the end of the Cold War, however, the Europeans opposed most efforts to alter the fundamentally punitive and retaliatory characteristics of deterrence (Bitzinger 1989). Some believe, despite the profound asymmetry between U.S. nuclear forces and those of possible adversaries, a nuclear deterrent may not be credible in regional conflicts (Spector 1992; Flournoy 1993; Nitze 1994). This may be true even if the adversary uses nuclear weapons first (Guertner 1993; Odom 1993; Cropsey 1994). For the *antinuclear* conventionalists, nuclear threats are not credible in regional contexts in general because U.S. interests there will not be sufficiently vital, and it is in the U.S. interest to maintain a taboo against nuclear use, even when confronted by a nuclear attack against its forces or allies (Mazarr 1993; Cropsey 1994; Dunn 1994).

Despite efforts to give U.S. and NATO nuclear deterrence a war-fighting character, that form of deterrence succeeded in Europe precisely because of the devastating effects of failure (Quester 1992b). But for those who would delegitimize U.S. nuclear use (Kaysen, McNamara, and Rathjens 1991; Cropsey 1994; Dunn 1994; Nitze 1994), nuclear weapons are nearly unusable as a policy tool because their employment would cause morally and politically un-

acceptable noncombatant casualties and environmental destruction. For example, although the Center for Strategic and International Studies (CSIS) Nuclear Strategy Study Group would retain the *threat* to use nuclear weapons in retaliation for nuclear attacks against U.S. forces and territory, it further states "in the actual event there may be good reasons for the U.S. leaders not to follow through on their threats" (Mazarr 1993, 52). Significantly, the group's report would provide no U.S. nuclear guarantees to support U.S. regional allies under the threat of WMD blackmail or to retaliate for WMD attack against those allies (p. 54). Consequently, conventional weapons should form the basis for future U.S. extended deterrence strategy (Cropsey 1994).

The credibility of U.S. nuclear use may be further degraded by both the asymmetries of stake in regional conflicts and the loss of the automaticity considered characteristic of the Cold War environment. Lewis Dunn (1994) contends that the less vital interests involved in regional conflicts, the more relaxed time constraints placed on presidential decision making, and the intense U.S. aversion to innocent casualties combine to drastically reduce the credibility of a U.S. nuclear deterrent, even to an opponent's first use of WMDs.

Dunn makes a further argument against the continued credibility of U.S. extended nuclear deterrence. He contends that the withdrawal of theater nuclear weapons has eliminated the main symbol of U.S. nuclear commitment. Over time, he feels the ability to employ theater nuclear weapons will atrophy, seriously undercutting "the perceived willingness of the United States to use nuclear weapons again" (Dunn 1994, 13). Because Dunn believes that conventional weapons can replace nuclear weapons with little loss of capability and their use has far more credibility, he does not recommend rectifying this situation. The final argument against extended nuclear deterrence postulates that even if nuclear threats could be made credible, maintenance of a taboo against nuclear proliferation and use would be in the interest of the United States (Mazarr 1993; Nitze 1994).

If, as some analysts insist, U.S. conventional dominance is almost unassailable, then preventing the spread of WMDs and maintaining a taboo against their use is clearly in the U.S. interest. Unfortunately, half of this problem may already be beyond solution. North Korea may already possess a nuclear weapon and chemical and biological threats are spreading (Roberts 1993). Thus the threat is present today (Aspin 1993b). With nonproliferation only slowing the expansion of nuclear possession, only the taboo against nuclear use remains salient, and then only if new nuclear powers accept it.

Aside from the substitution of extended conventional deterrence for extended nuclear deterrence and equipping forces for combat in a nuclear major regional contingency, the advocates of tightly constrained nuclear deterrence propose strong collective security measures by the international community as the best source of enforcement for a global ban on the use of nuclear weapons (Fetter 1991; Swiecicki 1992; Levine 1993; Mazarr 1993; Dunn 1994). The CSIS Nuclear Strategy Study Group concluded that

a robust global agreement that provided for crippling political, economic, and military sanctions, in the event of nuclear use could in effect take the place of a credible nuclear retaliation in deterring nuclear war. (Mazarr 1993, 54)

The general components of this international regime are

- An unequivocal U.S. renunciation of first use

- Universally enforced economic sanctions against the offending state

- A strong presumption of action by the United Nations to include the ultimate military sanction of destroying the offending regime with conventional forces

- Overall reduction in internationally perceived utility of force through expanded use of international forums for settling disputes.

Some supporters of reduced nuclear dependency add a fifth option for enforcing the nuclear taboo—preemption.

Normally, the definition of deterrence would not include the concept of preemption or preventive war. Gary Guertner (1993) includes preemption of a rogue state's WMD capabilities in his definition of conventional deterrence. For McGeorge Bundy (1991), one of the most important results of the Gulf War was the elimination of Iraq's WMD capabilities, which could not have occurred without the conflict. In addition, with the increased efficacy of conventional weapons in a counterproliferation role, Colin Gray (1992) postulates that if the United States does not wish to rely on nuclear deterrence and conventional means for preemption are available, then there will be an increased temptation to preempt. Preemption is emerging as an essential element of current deterrence thinking (Buchanan 1993; Davis 1993a; Engstrom 1993; Levine 1993; Strain 1993). Without preemption of rogue WMD capabilities, the United States and its coalition partners might not have confidence that conventional deterrence would hold. Michele Flournoy (1993) and Philip Zelikow (1993) both recommend that preemption be considered against nuclear-armed adversaries or those striving for a nuclear capability. Zelikow believes an internationally supported declaratory policy of preemption might slow rogue state WMD proliferation. The inclusion of preemption, while somewhat inconsistent with the older modalities of deterrence, is essentially compatible with the concept of dynamic deterrence.

Thus the arguments for conventionally based extended deterrence are mutually supporting. If conventional weapons can attain the strategic capabilities once held exclusively by nuclear weapons and the use of nuclear weapons is politically and

morally unacceptable, then the United States can and should shift the basis of its deterrence strategy from nuclear to conventional weapons. For the conventionalists, such as Guertner (1993, 149), "Direct retaliation is one of the few credible missions for strategic nuclear forces in the post–cold war world. Extending deterrence should be a function of conventional forces."

It's Too Early. Despite significant support for a growing reliance on conventional deterrence even in the face of nuclear threats, extended nuclear deterrence still has advocates. According to Keith Payne (1992, 270):

Past U.S. policy has not been guided by the notion that nuclear weapons serve only to deter the use of other nuclear weapons, and it should not be so restricted in the future. Because deterring conflict is far superior to the actual use of force in most instances, we should continue to pursue nuclear policies that attempt to cast as long a deterrence shadow as is likely to be credible, including the deterrence of conventional, chemical, biological, or nuclear provocations.

The CILS report on discriminate deterrence, despite advocating increased reliance on conventional capabilities, saw a continuing role for nuclear weapons in deterring the massing of forces necessary for launching a "no warning" conventional offensive (Kaufman, Clark, and Sheehan 1991, 112), as many believe is possible in Korea. Support for continued reliance on nuclear deterrence is based on essentially three arguments.

- The vast destructiveness of nuclear weapons and the inability to defend against them makes it easy to communicate their effect to even the most desperate opponents.

- The retrenchment of U.S. forces makes nuclear weapons essential to maintaining an extended deterrence and discouraging WMD proliferation.

- Nuclear weapons are essential for reassuring regional allies faced by significant conventional or WMD threats.

The first of these arguments focuses on the punishment modality of deterrence. Its central theme is that the costs of challenging a nuclear deterrent are both uncontrollable and irrevocable for the aggressor. Robert Pape (1992, 429) supports this position:

In practice the vast gap in destructive power between nuclear and conventional weapons means that coercion in these two circumstances operates differently. Nuclear weapons can nearly always inflict more damage than any victim can withstand. Assuming the assailant's threat is credible, the resistance of even the most determined opponents can be overwhelmed. Conventional munitions can only inflict limited damage compared to the pain thresholds of modern nation states, so [conventional] punishment strategies are rarely effective.

For the supporters of continued reliance on some form of nuclear deterrence (nuclearists), this means nuclear deterrence may hold even in cases where the aggressor is irrational in Western political terms (Harknett 1991; Payne 1992). Conversely,

Because the destructive potential of conventional weapons can be degraded significantly to the point that the challenger can perceive—correctly or incorrectly—that it is contestable, the costs associated with a conventional deterrent threat can be perceived as manageable [by the aggressor]. (Harknett 1991, 255)

Hence, nuclear weapons should disabuse a future adversary of an overly optimistic assessment of the outcome of conventional aggression or WMD use (Payne 1992). But deterring conventional aggression or WMD-based coercion may not be the most important use of U.S. nuclear weapons.

One of the key functions advocated for nuclear weapons in the post–Cold War conflicts may be to provide intrawar dissuasion of the use of WMDs. A potential adversary faced with decisive conventional defeat or intolerable conventional punishment may choose to use WMDs in the absence of a credible U.S. nuclear deterrent (Arquilla and Davis 1992; Payne 1992). For nuclearists, there is the chance that a WMD-armed adversary will choose even a decisive conventional defeat rather than face the societal and personal devastation resulting from a U.S. nuclear attack.

To many analysts, the post–Cold War retrenchment of U.S. forces makes nuclear weapons essential to maintaining extended deterrence and discouraging WMD proliferation among potential adversaries and friends. George Quester and Victor Utgoff (1993, 133) argue that (1) the extreme concern over the proliferation of nuclear weapons demonstrated by the world community is itself a strong incentive for regional aggressors to proliferate; and (2) instead of letting the U.S. theater nuclear arsenal atrophy, the United States should maintain the quality of its theater nuclear forces to allow the United States to reverse the advantages of any aggressor's initial WMD use with finely tuned escalation designed to cause "minimum damage to innocent civilians." For Quester and Utgoff, maintaining a qualitatively superior U.S. theater nuclear capability in conjunction with highly capable conventional forces would reduce the significance of the rudimentary nuclear stockpiles acquired by rogue states and make proliferation unattractive. Others (Dowler and Howard 1991; Strain 1993) advocate that although theater nuclear capabilities are required, they must be significantly improved to give them political and moral credibility for use. These improvements would include very low-yield warheads, nuclear earth-penetrating weapons (Dowler and Howard 1991), and the revival of neutron weapons (Strain 1993). Thomas Dowler and Joseph Howard (1991) and Frederick Strain (1993) assert that such improvements are essential to provide a credible nuclear deterrent to conventional regional aggression or WMD use.

The advocates of the continuing utility of nuclear weapons not only disagree with the *antinuclear* conventionalists over the types of nuclear weapons required for deterrence but also over the criteria for their use. The CSIS Nuclear Strategy Study Group report (Mazarr 1993) and Robert Levine (1993) advocate an unconditional no-first-use policy for the United States. Conversely, the nuclearists establish a variety of criteria for first use: deterrence of conventional attack on the United States and its allies (Dowler and Howard 1991; Payne 1992; Strain 1993); prevention of the destruction of a major U.S. military unit (Dowler and Howard 1991; Watman 1994); and retaliation for the use of biological weapons (Quester and Utgoff 1994; Watman 1994). Dowler and Howard (1991) are particularly concerned that the first U.S. forces to arrive in a theater during a crisis will be too light to stand up to the heavily armored units of local powers and must have some nuclear backup to prevent their conventional defeat. Quester and Utgoff (1993) assert that "no-first-use" would assure proliferators of the advantage of the first nuclear strike. They further state that, in conjunction with consultation with the UN Security Council,

for the time being at least, the United States may also need to retain an option for exceptional first use of nuclear weapons in situations where allies and friends worry that they could be overwhelmed by hostile conventional forces (Quester and Utgoff 1994, 112).

Payne (1992) and Quester and Utgoff (1993, 1994) are especially concerned that U.S. nuclear capabilities should reassure U.S. regional allies against coercion and keep them from seeking their own nuclear capabilities.

Ultimately, the U.S. nuclear umbrella has been an essential tool for preventing U.S. allies from seeking their own nuclear capabilities (Quester and Utgoff 1993, 1994). As Kathleen Bailey (1991) notes, in the absence of a nuclear umbrella the threat of conventional forces will become dominant, and U.S. allies may consider acquiring nuclear weapons as a deterrent against conventional attack. If, as is almost universally accepted, nuclear weapons can only be used to deter threats against vital U.S. interests, "the issues are, first, how to make an interest appear vital and, second, how to convince others that one's nuclear forces are adequate to the task" (Art 1992–93). Although Art believes that strategic nuclear forces can serve to extend deterrence to U.S. allies, for Quester and Utgoff (1993, 1994) the forward deployability of U.S. theater nuclear forces and their credibility for tactical application may provide the perception to allies and adversaries alike that defense of an interest is vital and under the protection of the U.S. extended nuclear deterrence.

Although there is a wide divergence in views over the dominance of conventional or nuclear weapons in deterrence, there is some convergence. Guertner (1993, 147) states:

There is, however, a potential paradox of success [for extended conventional deterrence] if aggressive Third World leaders believe that only weapons of mass destruction can offset U.S. advantages in conventional military power. Under such circumstances, theater nuclear weapons can have important signaling functions that communicate new risks and introduce greater costs for nuclear aggression that inflicts high casualties on U.S. forces or on allied countervalue targets.

Although they support continued reliance on extended nuclear deterrence, Quester and Utgoff (1993, 139) believe that

if the United States deploys a menu of conventional options comparable to that shown in Desert Storm, it enhances the impression that it can hold its own nuclear forces in reserve to retaliate for any use of nuclear forces by its adversaries, and that it can in the meantime punish and/or defeat such countries on the nonnuclear battlefield.

These views differ primarily over the character of nuclear forces. Guertner advocates a nuclear force adequate only for signaling, while Quester and Utgoff (1993) advocate nuclear forces whose deterrence value is enhanced by their quality, flexibility, and availability.

Implications. Whether conventional weapons or nuclear weapons will dominate U.S. extended deterrence strategy in the post–Cold War era has significant implications for defense force structure. Given the capabilities of currently available conventional weapons, the United States would have difficulty providing an assured extended defense of regional allies against large-scale, rapid conventional invasions. Neither can the United States conventionally counter WMD-equipped ballistic missile attack with confidence. This situation poses three policy choices for U.S. decision makers:

- Pursue the requirements of a purely conventional extended deterrence strategy while maintaining a near-term nuclear component for theater deterrence.

- Take advantage of improved conventional and nuclear technologies to simultaneously reduce dependence on nuclear weapons and increase the credibility of their use.

- Improve the capability of conventional forces to defeat conventional invasion while ensuring the credibility of the existing nuclear forces to deter use of WMDs by adversaries.

This choice will determine the cost of U.S. force structure and its flexibility in meeting global U.S. commitments.

EXTENDED CONVENTIONAL DETERRENCE: REGIONAL IMPLICATIONS

With the end of the Cold War, a world of relative order enforced by the bipolar superpower relationship has given way to one of global disorder in which regional powers pursue their own security arrangements. If deterrence is to play a role in this new world disorder, then it must apply in these regional contexts. No longer will forty years of competition provide a modus vivendi between the United States and its potential adversaries (Gray 1992; Pfaltzgraff 1993). Determining the efficacy of extended *conventional* deterrence in the regional context will require the examination of five questions:

1. Where must the United States apply deterrence strategy?

2. How will the adversary react to U.S. deterrent threats?

3. How will coalitions affect U.S. deterrence efforts?

4. What will be the role of U.S. reputation in developing a "dynamic," "general" deterrence environment?

5. What strategies will adversaries use to circumvent U.S. conventional deterrence?

In a post–Cold War regional context, determining who should be deterred will be far more difficult than before.

DETERRENCE STRATEGY: WHERE TO APPLY IT

In contrast to circumstances during the Cold War, a U.S. decision to intervene in a particular regional conflict will depend on the assessment of U.S. interests in that conflict and not on any impact the U.S. intervention might have on a global competitor (Jervis 1994). In fact, because of the breakdown of the superpower relationship and its concomitant restraints on client state objectives, challenges to U.S. interests may become more frequent (Haass 1991; Nitze 1994). The outline of the debate over the locations of U.S. interests has been effectively delineated in a *Washington Quarterly* research survey by Don Snider and Gregory Grant (1992). As Art (1992–93, 7) states, "Clarity about a nation's foreign policy goals is the fundamental prerequisite to the development of sound strategy." The outcome of this debate is crucial for the success of a U.S. strategy of extended conventional deterrence.

Regional powers will generally view their interests in a local conflict as more vital than those of the United States and therefore will tend to place less credence in U.S. deterrent threats (Gray 1992; Palmer 1992; Flournoy 1993; Mahnken 1993; Jervis 1994). The perception of weak U.S. commitment will be magnified where the United States has failed to explicitly identify or clearly communicate its interests. The muddled signals sent to Saddam Hussein prior to the Gulf War are a well-documented example of this failure (Gray 1992; Stein 1992; Blackwell, Mazarr, and Snider 1993). Deterrence threats are most effective when made before the attacker fixes his decision to move (Davis and Arquilla 1991; Jervis

1994). The lateness of U.S. decision making is a primary cause of confused signals of commitment.

Arquilla and Davis (1992) have noted that late expressions of commitment are endemic in U.S. efforts to deter and are a primary cause of deterrence failure. These late communications result from a failure of the U.S. foreign policy establishment to identify the commitment to itself. Only after a crisis has started does the United States assess its interests and decide to attempt deterrence. The lateness of these commitments attenuates their importance to an aggressor who has already decided to attack.

How Will the Adversary React?

More powerful states have failed to deter weaker states, even when their commitment was clearly expressed and the power imbalance between the deterrer and the attacker was obvious (Wolf 1991). Although U.S. will, commitment, and credibility may be readily apparent to all observers, ultimately the target of deterrence is a free actor who must decide to be deterred (Gray 1991; Cimbala 1992). Richard Hooker and Ricky Waddell (1992, 81) feel that "The psychology of deterrence is . . . its most elemental feature."

In deterrence theory, as opposed to deterrence practice, the opponent is assumed to be a "rational actor." Rational actors use an essentially economic "cost-benefit" analysis to determine whether or not to challenge a deterrent threat (Achen and Snidal 1989). Most post–Cold War analysts of deterrence would argue that the archetypical rational actor model is unsatisfactory for developing deterrence strategy and must be tailored to a wide variety of behavioral characteristics (Payne 1992; Davis 1993b; Grier 1993; Dunn 1994). Deterrence analysts have proposed a variety of more complex models to replace the rational actor (Lebow and Stein 1989; Arquilla and Davis 1992; Metz 1993, 1994). Kenneth Watman (1994) has proposed that the ability to deter an actor should be evaluated on a continuum from "hardest-to-deter" to "easiest-to-deter." Steven Metz expands on the same paradigm, adding that an actor's susceptibility to deterrence will be determined by placement on eight continuums, each based on a given factor. Synthesizing Metz's analysis with those of other deterrence analysts, this survey addresses four such factors:

- Quantity and quality of information available
- Cultural influences
- Assessment of the status quo
- Psychological states.

One or more of these factors is likely to impede U.S. efforts to deter aggressors. At the high end of these continuums actors will be easy to deter. The low ends demonstrate a concept that permeates post–Cold War deterrence literature, the "undeterrables."

Information. As we have seen, imperfect information about a defender's commitment may be present for both the defender and the attacker. Prior to the crisis, the "intended deterrees [themselves] will not know how much of a politically and technically credible threat it would take to deter them" (Gray 1991, 14). In addition, as Arquilla and Davis point out (Davis and Arquilla 1991; Arquilla and Davis 1992), adversaries have historically discounted key elements of U.S. power such as strategic mobility, precision weapons, maritime power, and airpower owing to a lack of familiarity with these systems. Without understanding these elements of U.S. military strength, the regional aggressor will view the absence of U.S. heavy ground forces as evidence of a lack of both capability and commitment. Moreover, Adam Garfinkle (1992) asserts that Third World leaders are frequently misled into overly optimistic views of their own forces' capabilities. Without clear recognition of U.S. power, deterrence cannot hold.

Cultural Influences. Even in the presence of clear signals of commitment and unmistakable credibility, cultural differences between the United States and its potential opponents could sabotage a deterrence strategy (Jablonsky 1991). Thomas Mahnken (1991, 198) places the impact of these cultural differences in the starkest light: "It is naive to expect cultures that place supreme value upon martyrdom, or regimes that slaughter their own citizens to embrace Western precepts of deterrence and stability." More subtly, cultural differences may make the format of a threat crucial. Garfinkle (1992) provides an example from the Arab world, where loud, public deterrent threats are generally discounted as bluffs and a sign of weakness. Moreover, disrespect backs the attacker into a corner where his honor must be defended without regard to the apparent outcome. Understanding an adversary's thinking and reactions to threats may be as important as the will and credibility to back up those threats.

Assessment of the Status Quo. Yet an appropriately couched, credible threat may still not deter. An adversary's assessment of the status quo will determine how well an immediate deterrent threat will succeed. If in the estimate of attackers, the long-term status quo presents an intolerable condition, they may choose to go to war regardless of the current balance of power. The impetus to go to war may come from internal distress (Blackwell, Mazarr, and Snider 1993), or it may be the result of an assessment that the correlation of forces is shifting even more dramatically toward the defender and, therefore, opportunities for success will only decline (Lebow 1989; Arquilla and Davis 1992). Clearly, these circumstances are not the result of the opponent's irrationality, but of different perspectives on costs, benefits, and time.

Psychological States. Rejection of the rational actor model as a prescriptive tool does *not* imply that Third World leaders are "crazy." As David Jablonsky (1991, 3) correctly states, the "pure rationality model . . . is impossible to achieve since it presupposes omniscience and a capability for comprehensive analysis that time, cost and other factors do not permit. Arquilla and Davis (1992) refer to this condition as "limited" rationality.

Although none of the obstacles to rational decisions in a deterrence crisis listed above are truly irrational, "crazy" thinking can be present in crises. This apparently mad thinking is caused by three factors: cognitive dissonance; ideological, nationalistic, or religious values; and true psychopathology. Cognitive dissonance in a crisis results when decision makers are faced with unacceptable alternatives and filter out unpleasant information in order to increase the value of a chosen course of action (Lebow and Stein 1989; Jablonsky 1991; Wolf 1991). The dedication of adversaries to religious, nationalistic, or ideological forces may make them immune to threats that would be credible in U.S. eyes. Finally, Barry Wolf (1991) asserts that actual psychopathology among national leaders may be present at a relatively high rate. Such leaders may be willing to accept massive military or societal devastation to maintain themselves and their self-image (Record 1993). These leaders tend to be more common in the undemocratic or revolutionary states that will challenge the United States in regional contingencies (Jablonsky 1991).

The demise of the rational actor model has given rise to a replacement, the *strategic personality* (Engstrom 1993; Flournoy 1993). The strategic personality, which is a composite of the actor's position on the deterrability continuums, has significant implications for deterrence. The composition of a regional power's strategic personality will help to

- Establish the correct mix of reassurance and threat required to deter.

- Assess the probability of successful deterrence.

- Determine the utility to deterrence of instruments that affect the opponent's situational perception.

If the strategic personality is to serve a prescriptive function, then the U.S. intelligence community must accept the task of determining its components on a case-by-case basis. Ultimately, strategic personality should reveal a regime's or nation's perceptions and values, allowing them to be manipulated or targeted. Utgoff (1993) asserts that developing research centers that focus on the strategic personality of regional powers may have extremely high leverage for U.S. deterrence strategy. If punishment is to be part of a U.S. strategy to deter, then the regime, its symbols, and possibly the leadership itself may be the only appropriate targets (WSS 1993; Cohen 1994). Understanding the regime's strategic personality will assist in precise target selection.

If a credible threat is not feasible, then exploitation of an adversary's strategic personality may offer an alternative. Some analysts (Cimbala 1993), U.S. Navy studies (Buchanan 1993), and U.S. Air Force studies (Engstrom 1993) propose that emerging information-based capabilities designed to modify an opponent's strategic personality may have the highest future deterrence leverage. Finally, if there is a reasonable probability, as Wolf (1991) and Payne (1992) indicate, that a future adversary might prove "undeterrable" even in the face of nuclear deterrence, active defenses and preemptive capabilities will be essential elements of U.S. force structure.

MULTILATERAL VERSUS UNILATERAL DETERRENCE

As Jervis (1994, chap. 9) notes, "the question of whether policy is to be pursued multilaterally or unilaterally may be only slightly less important than the question of what interests are worthy of defense." Advocates of a multilateral approach offer two reasons for depending more on international efforts and less on U.S. unilateral capabilities:

- U.S. power must be bound by international controls to assure other nations about its use and to prevent its abuse.

- The United States requires coalition bases and capabilities to conduct decisive, low-cost operations in a regional conflict.

For those who oppose reliance on coalitions:

- Collective security is a chimera: states will always act in their perceived best interests.

- Reliance on allies will be too constraining to U.S. policy in political, strategic, and tactical terms.

- The regional coalitions will be prone to fracture in the face of severe coercive threats.

The debate over the role of coalitions in deterrence is not one of absolutes, but of degrees.

Multilateralists. The advocates of multilateralism emphasize the value of coalitions as demonstrated in Desert Storm. They view Desert Storm as an extremely successful application of both the collective security powers of the United Nations and the power of the ad hoc Desert Storm coalition. It was also a harbinger of the future. "The United Nations, not the United States, will threaten a response to a North Korean attack south or an Iranian attack on Saudi Arabia" (Blackwell, Mazarr, and Snider 1993, 175). They see the U.N. role as vital in providing political legitimacy to U.S. actions in the Persian Gulf, creating an environment conducive to both international and domestic support for U.S. intervention. The leaders of regional powers viewed "the ability to act as an integrator of nations and policies" as a key element of U.S. power (Garrity 1993b, 154).

Others would add that the predilection to act unilaterally is too destabilizing and might result in coalitions rising against the United States (Jervis 1994; Art 1992–93). Gary Guertner (1993, 145) states:

Even though collective action and shared capabilities may limit U.S. freedom of action, these limits are reassuring to others and may contribute more to stability than attempts by the world's only superpower to unilaterally impose deterrence—nuclear or conventional.

Quester and Utgoff (1993, 138) adopt a similar position, pointing out that the international community's fears of U.S. nuclear or conventional dominance "can be assuaged if the United States continues to develop confidence in its willingness to exercise power only on behalf of, and with, the world community." Although support from the world community may be politically useful, coalitions may be militarily indispensable.

In addition to political legitimacy, coalition partners provide two essential requirements for deterrence credibility: in-place forces with capabilities that complement those of the United States, and basing access (Guertner 1993). As noted in Huth (1988a), the local balance of forces has historically been a key to deterrence success in a crisis. In immediate deterrence crises, in-country coalition forces can complement U.S. capabilities (Odom 1993) and when combined with enhanced perceptions of U.S. long-range power may tip the balance in favor of deterrence. The Saudis, recognizing this fact, are currently modernizing and expanding their ground forces (Atkenson 1992; Simon 1992). Long-term force structure agreements with key coalition partners could enhance the complementarity of U.S. and coalition forces.

Without access to en route and in-theater logistical and basing support, the United States could not have brought overwhelming power to bear in the Persian Gulf (Stein 1992; Blackwell, Mazarr, and Snider 1993). As Garrity (1993b, 157) notes,

In many cases, intervention in some regional conflicts will be so demanding that [the United States and its traditional allies] will require the support of many other states, which support is often most readily called upon through an international mechanism. This support—including bases, overflight rights, and logistical support—may be necessary to apply *decisive* force (i.e., at a level that ensures a quick conflict with low casualties and low collateral damage).

Although the Cold War has ended, the geostrategic quandary for the United States has not. U.S. interests in Eurasia are thousands of miles from the United States but within easy striking distance of regional powers. Michael Desch (1992) and William Odom (1993) assert, therefore, that overseas bases are vital for U.S. power projection capabilities.

Limits of Multilateralism. The opponents of extensive U.S. reliance on coalitions argue that the advocates of tying U.S. power to collective security are making a virtue out of necessity. First, they would argue that only the United States had the power to forge the Desert Storm coalition and that apart from U.S. capabilities only the availability of the Saudi bases was essential to U.S. success (Gray 1992; Garrity 1993a; Mahnken 1993). More gener-

ally, Josef Joffe (1992) and Gray (1992) argue that collective security has never really protected anyone and is doomed to failure because states will always act in their own self-interest. This has been true even in NATO, the most enduring of modern coalitions. The strength of the NATO alliance rested on the cohesion derived from confrontation with a central adversary, but NATO cohesion has sometimes failed when the alliance pursued problems of a peripheral or ambiguous nature (Kaufman, Clark, and Sheehan 1991; Garrity 1993a; Mahnken 1993). Policy differences with coalition partners may prove so constraining that the United States may be unable to deter aggression effectively or protect its vital interests.

The policies of its partners in a coalition may prove constraining to the United States in three ways: (1) their internal domestic policies may prevent deployment of U.S. forces prior to an immediate crisis; (2) coalition partners may honestly disagree with the U.S. assessment of the threat and the actions necessary to diffuse it; and (3) fear of the threat itself, particularly WMDs, may prevent the coalition partner from giving the United States access and cause threatened states to succumb to coercion. U.S. friends in Southwest Asia are particularly vulnerable to internal pressures to limit any permanent U.S. presence (Simon 1992; Hess 1993; WSS 1993). U.S. forward-presence forces in the region could act as a lightning rod for social unrest. They could, for instance, undermine the legitimacy of the Saudi royal family (Hess 1993). Thus U.S. forces must remain over the horizon (Garrity 1993b). A major goal of U.S. deterrence strategy must be to communicate the capability of its long-range forces to defeat aggression and cast the shadow of what Haffa (1992) calls their "virtual presence" as a replacement for forward-deployed forces.

Regardless of internal constraints, coalition partners may agree with U.S. objectives but disagree with U.S. tactics, making deterrence impossible. Prior to the Iraqi invasion of Kuwait, "The most persistent disbelievers in the possibility of an Iraqi invasion were other Arab leaders who continually cautioned President George Bush and others not to take any action that might provoke Saddam" (McCausland 1993, 7). A disagreement over tactics could also arise over counterproliferation efforts aimed at North Korea. Flournoy (1993) avers that efforts to gain collective approval could compromise preemption. There is little the United States can do except wait if its coalition partners prefer to take a passive or conciliatory position (Blackwell, Mazarr, and Snider 1993). Coalition partners may also restrain U.S. efforts to produce decisive victory by refusing to allow the destruction of the offending regime (Hess 1993). Thus even if the possibility of attack is clear, the attacker's intentions are unmistakable, and decisive victory is possible, U.S. coalition partners may still balk at accepting U.S. forces or supporting en route U.S. deployment efforts and may limit the extent of the victory.

The contents of the threat itself may imply that a U.S. presence will provoke an attack. If waging war in alliance with the United States is too costly for the coalition partner compared to accepting the attacker's demands, then the partner may acquiesce even if the U.S. commitment is highly credible (Wu 1989). Most analysts, including some supporters of collective security, agree that the possession of WMDs by a regional aggressor will make forming coalitions extremely difficult if not impossible (Swiecicki 1992; Flournoy 1993; Garrity 1993a; Mahnken 1993; Zelikow 1993). Conversely, a powerful conventional threat, such as that posed by North Korea against the South, may provide a deterrent shield against preemption of the North's nuclear program (Spector 1992; Zelikow 1993). Consequently, despite credible U.S. commitment and capabilities, dependence on reluctant allies may allow a vital U.S. interest to be successfully challenged.

Although coalitions may offer the United States political advantages and in-place forces to provide assistance in immediate deterrence, reluctant coalition partners are likely to be an ingredient of regional conflict. This implies that the United States should retain a significant capability for unilateral intervention.

THE ROLE OF U.S. REPUTATION

Analysts of reputation since the Cold War have addressed three factors: the end of bipolar competition, the role of reputation in and out of crises, and the impact of war termination on reputation. Of these factors, the first has had the greatest impact on the current understanding of reputation.

For the United States, the strategic motivation for supporting or creating commitments in order to develop an image of U.S. credibility has disappeared with the end of the Cold War. Gains and losses in the developing world were important during the Cold War because of their impact on the perception of U.S. reputation by the central adversary and its allies (Desch 1992). The United States fought to defend areas of less than vital interest attempting to ensure its reputation in more vital regions (Gray 1991; Jervis 1994). U.S. decision makers viewed contests in peripheral areas as only parts of a larger conflict; a U.S. willingness to fight in these places, therefore, both supported containment and the reputation required for deterrence. But as Jervis (1989, 192) observes, "It appears [other states] do not perceive commitments as so tightly linked and that the outcomes of confrontations are determined to a greater extent by each side's intrinsic interest in the issue at stake." Consequently, U.S. decision makers will not improve their reputation for acting decisively in regions of vital interest by creating and supporting commitments in peripheral areas.

If extended conventional deterrence is to protect vital interests, it must both effectively prevent and defuse crises. The most effective deterrence strategy will prevent threats from arising—an approach frequently called general deterrence (Wu 1989). For many analysts, the crushing defeat of Iraq by the U.S.-led coalition has created the reputation for U.S. will and capability that provides the basis for a long-term general deterrence environment (Perry 1991; Gray 1992; Guertner 1993). Yet failures to support commitments or effectively apply force may rapidly undermine this general reputation (Haffa 1993). Saddam Hussein has been broadly quoted as citing the failures of U.S. policy in Vietnam and the U.S. withdrawal from Beirut in the aftermath of the 1983 bombing of the marine barracks as his rationale for discounting the U.S. commitment to liberate Kuwait (Stein 1992).

Because of its intense media coverage and lopsided outcome, the Gulf War may have had greater impact than past conflicts in establishing a general U.S. reputation for the capacity and will to protect its interests (Haffa 1992). For reputation to be useful in an immediate extended deterrence crisis, it must be based on previous confrontations between the defender and the attacker (Huth 1988b; Wu 1989). But in an immediate crisis, a general reputation for will and capability to retaliate is apparently of questionable utility (Huth 1988a). Once an opponent has threatened to use force, the defender's general reputation has already been factored into the decision.

Finally, reputation depends upon the effective and decisive use of force. For deterrence to be effective, U.S. forces must be able to win decisively with low cost (Jervis 1994). Declines in U.S. defense spending will be closely followed by possible opponents and any perceived inability of the United States to conduct a Desert Storm–style operation will undermine deterrence (Garrity 1993a). In addition, U.S. decision makers must have a reputation for being willing to not merely reverse an adversary's aggression but to severely punish it as well (Haffa 1992; Buchanan 1993). Because of the propensity of conventional deterrence to fail, the character of the war that followed the last "deterrence failure" will affect how long deterrence credibility lasts after that war. To many analysts, the decision not to destroy the Republican Guards at the end of the Gulf War, whether emanating from humanitarian or strategic impulses, will affect the way potential aggressors will view the U.S. willingness to destroy regimes (Blackwell, Mazarr, and Snider 1993). To produce long periods of stability, conventionalists contend, dynamic deterrence must create a reputation for credibility, effectiveness, and decisiveness.

COUNTERSTRATEGIES

Although a powerful reputation may help sustain a strong general deterrence regime, a U.S. deterrence strategy must ultimately be effective against specific opponents. The targets of U.S. efforts to deter will seek strategies to counter the overwhelming U.S. military dominance displayed in the Persian Gulf. Eliot Cohen (1993, 40) criticizes Secretary Aspin's "bottom-up review" for focusing on enemies who had learned nothing at all from Saddam's debacle. Nothing about playing on American sensitivity to casualties, nothing about using weapons of mass destruction to scare off America's allies, nothing about engaging in ambiguous aggression rather than Saddam's incompetent brutality.

The same general criticism applies to current thinking on extended deterrence. Advocates and critics of conventional deterrence have acknowledged that the victory in Desert Storm does not indicate any significant capability to combat guerrilla warfare, terrorism, or ambiguous challenges to U.S. interests.

Two studies have focused on regional counters to U.S. conventional dominance. Garrity (1993a) has integrated the thinking of numerous regional area experts to determine how U.S. enemies and friends are reassessing their national security strategies in light of the Gulf war. Mahnken (1993) has analyzed the strategies that a regional adversary might employ to deter U.S. intervention in a regional conflict. These studies and others suggest five broad categories of counterstrategies to U.S. conventional deterrence. An adversary could seek to (1) control the threshold of conflict, (2) control the spectrum of conflict, (3) exclude the United States from the region, (4) raise the costs of intervention, or (5) ensure the survival of its regime. Intelligent adversaries will not use these strategies in isolation but will seek an optimum mix to achieve their objectives. Because the bulk of U.S. power will be outside the area when a crisis starts, local powers will focus on strategies to keep the United States out of the region.

Control the Threshold. As most observers acknowledge, it is much easier for U.S. political leadership to develop the domestic political support to combat blatant adventurism than to deter ambiguous aggression (Blackwell, Mazarr, and Snider 1993). Future adversaries may seek to avoid the appearance of threatening U.S. interests in a region by employing limited aims strategies (Stern and others 1989; Paul 1991), by incremental achievement of aims, and by obscuring the causes of conflict (Mahnken 1993). In a limited aims strategy, an adversary will use conventional means to take as much as possible of its objective without provoking U.S. intervention. An incremental approach is an expanded form of the limited aims strategy. Because the adversaries do not have a priori knowledge of the threshold for U.S. intervention, they will use limited probes to find it. Successes will be followed by periods of evaluation. U.S. threats will be honored with tactical retreats followed by attempts to find the limits of U.S. patience (Garrity 1993a). The probes would be calibrated never to exceed a newly established U.S. tolerance of the status quo.

Finally, by obscuring the source of the threat either through support of internal dissent or insurgency in the target state or assertions of self-defense, the aggressor may make the conflict sufficiently ambiguous to avoid triggering U.S. intervention. But because regional aggressors are unsure of the thresholds that may also trigger U.S. intervention, they will seek methods of negating U.S. conventional dominance.

Control the Spectrum of Conflict. Rogue states have two avenues by which to negate U.S. conventional dominance: control of the spectrum of conflict, and direct counters to U.S. capabilities. To control the spectrum of conflict the adversary will either concentrate on guerrilla warfare or threaten the use of WMDs. In Desert Storm the United States demonstrated the ability to roll an armored force back over territory it had taken. Even the most ardent supporters of the deterrent role of conventional weapons note that the forces and tactics that prevailed in Desert Storm are not readily adaptable to guerrilla warfare (Perry 1991). Metz (1993) believes that the utility of deterrence declines rapidly at levels of conflict below conventional warfare. Adversaries may also choose to leap over the conventional level of conflict by threatening to use WMDs (Cimbala 1993).

If faced with fighting the conventional forces of the United States, its rivals will also attempt to counter U.S. conventional dominance directly through technological and asymmetric means. Technological challenges will range from sea mines to disrupt U.S. logistics to improved air defenses and command and control. Advanced conventional weapons with improved accuracy may present new challenges to fixed U.S. bases and eventually to surface maritime power (Patton 1993). According to the CILS report, if the United States is to retain the technological edge needed to deter or defeat regional powers, it must assess future adversaries' acquisition of advanced conventional capabilities (Kaufman, Clark, and Sheehan 1991). How readily regional powers will be able to absorb these advanced technologies remains the source of continued debate (Garfinkle 1992; Roberts 1993).

Adversaries will also seek passive and low-technology solutions to U.S. conventional supremacy. In the passive mode, the adversary will use mobility, hardening, foul weather, and dispersal to counter U.S. air supremacy and precision guided munitions. Finally, special operations forces may be the tool of choice to attack air bases and logistics facilities (Garrity 1993a).

Strategies of Exclusion. If an adversary believes that it will be unable to control the conflict spectrum it may be able to deny the United States access to the region. Regional powers have noted U.S. dependence on en route logistics support, transit rights, and in-theater bases to support Desert Storm. To keep U.S. power out of a region, two strategies could prove effective: capturing or destroying vital logistics nodes, or fracturing the coalition (Mahnken 1993; Dunn 1994). A fait accompli strategy could deny U.S. access to key facilities in the region (Stern and others 1989; Paul 1991). This could be a high-risk strategy for the aggressor because it would threaten vital U.S. interests. If the United States chose to reverse the fait accompli through a long conventional war, then its war aims may not be limited. The regime itself would be threatened with destruction. To destroy ports of entry or render them useless through use of nuclear weapons or other WMDs would also be high risk because the United States maintains such overwhelming nuclear asymmetry with its potential regional opponents. *Threats* of terrorism or WMDs against coalition partners may be successful, however, in denying U.S. access to in-theater bases or en route facilities without activating a U.S. response. Finally, potential adversaries may attempt to extend their reach through coalitions with other rogue states (WSS 1993).

Raising the Costs. Even without the capability to deny the United States access to a region of vital interest, a local power may nonetheless prevent U.S. intervention by raising its perceived costs. If the United States perceives the costs in blood, national cohesion, and treasure as too high when compared with the value of the interests involved in a conflict, then an aggressor may deter U.S. intervention. Perceived costs can be raised by the continued U.S. distaste for protracted, guerrilla warfare (Blackwell, Mazarr, and Snider 1993; Pfaltzgraff 1993) and military casualties (Mahnken 1993; Safire 1993) and a generally greater willingness on the part of potential adversaries to accept high casualties (Mahnken 1993). Part of this strategy may be threats of direct WMD attack against the United States either through ballistic missiles in the future (Mahnken 1991; WSS 1993) or terrorism (Dunn 1994). The specter of WMD use will also raise the perceived level of cost to U.S. forces. The U.S. aversion to casualties applies not only to its own and allied forces and civilians but also to the civilian society of the adversary (Glosson 1993; Cohen 1994). The decision to disperse military equipment to civilian neighborhoods or the actual use of civilians as human shields may further contribute to dissuading U.S. intervention (Garrity 1993b).

Finally, a belligerent may attempt to dissuade intervention by threatening critical economic disruptions or environmental destruction. Although there may have been tactical considerations to the Iraqi release of oil into the Persian Gulf (preventing an amphibious landing) and the igniting of the Kuwaiti oil wells (obscuring and hindering the allied land forces), these actions have been recognized as the first case of environmental "terrorism." In the future, a potential aggressor may threaten to cause environmental destruction as part of a strategy to dissuade U.S. intervention in a regional conflict.

Economic cartels and coalitions have generally proved ineffective at stopping intervention. In the future, belligerents may threaten or attempt new and different means of economic disruption. Robert Steele (1993) has done an extensive study of U.S. vulnerabilities to warfare in the information age. He points out that a belligerent may threaten to disrupt national or international trade, financial transactions, and communications through attacks on vital communications links and computer systems. Such attacks could take the form of overt destruction of critical rail links, air traffic control systems, communications links, electrical grids, and computer systems or could be more subtly affected by electronic infiltration and disruption (Steele 1993; Toffler and Toffler 1993).

Strategies of Regime Survival. Third-world leaders consider the survival of their regime to be paramount (Garrity 1993a; Mahnken 1993; Dunn 1994). Regional aggressors will seek to prevent the United States from expanding its war aims to destruction of the regime and may view threats of WMD use as the ultimate guarantee of its survival (Arquilla and Davis 1992; Payne 1992; Cimbala 1993). With nuclear weapons ensuring the regime's survival, a rogue state may discount the risks of war and resort to force.

The recognition by regional powers of the strength of U.S. conventional capabilities is the central theme of the studies of counterstrategies to U.S. conventional dominance. This perception will effectively support deterrence of conventional conflict as long as the United States maintains the will to use the force, extreme technological asymmetry, and the quantitative sufficiency demonstrated in Desert Storm. Other powers will continue to seek strategies that allow them to regain strategic independence by avoiding direct confrontations with the United States and will challenge U.S. deterrence through asymmetric means.

CONCLUSIONS AND IMPLICATIONS

The end of the Cold War and the U.S.-led victory in the Persian Gulf have established a new security environment. Four characteristics of this new era will affect U.S. deterrence strategy. First, U.S. security policy will have a regional focus. Second, although the United States will be militarily dominant it will significantly reduce its in-place forces overseas. Third, and arguably, U.S. nuclear weapons will have little or no role in regional conflicts. Finally, just as in the Cold War, likely U.S. adversaries will enjoy the advantage of proximity to the theaters of potential conflict, while the United States must project power thousands of miles to protect its interests.

This new security environment has profound implications for the future of U.S. deterrence theory, strategy, and practice. This survey has approached the problem by addressing the meaning of deterrence, assessing the deterrent roles of conventional and nuclear weapons, and reviewing the ramifications of a regionally oriented security policy for U.S. deterrence strategy. Four issues have emerged from this analysis that will dominate the deterrence debate and establish the basis for further research:

- If deterrence is to be based on conventional weapons, what form of deterrence will overcome the twin U.S. dilemmas of distance from its vital security interests and retraction of U.S. forces from overseas? How will deterrence and the use of force interact? Is preemption of adversary WMD capabilities essential to the success of extended conventional deterrence?

- What will be the role of nuclear weapons in an era of U.S. conventional dominance, and how will that role be affected by the proliferation of weapons of mass destruction? If U.S. allies require a nuclear umbrella, are strategic nuclear forces adequate for the task or must the United States retain robust theater nuclear capabilities? Finally, will U.S. pledges of "no-first-use" or "negative security guarantees" promote or undermine nonproliferation?

- To what extent should or must U.S. deterrence strategy depend on multilateral or collective security? Can U.S. military supremacy be brought to bear without coalition support? Will the ability of the United States to act decisively unilaterally drive states to oppose it in order to retain some level of strategic independence? Can U.S. coalition partners withstand WMD coercion without U.S. nuclear guarantees?

- How will potential adversaries react to U.S. deterrence strategies? How will they attempt to circumvent the conventional dominance displayed in Desert Storm? How will a conventionally based deterrence strategy overcome strategies of exclusion, U.S. aversion to casualties, or ambiguous aggression?

This survey has shed light on contemporary thinking on these questions and identified areas of divergence and convergence. The question of the role of nuclear weapons in extended deterrence and the level of multilateralism required in U.S. strategy have stirred up the greatest controversies in the policy analysis community. Conversely, there is more general agreement on the criteria for U.S. forces necessary to underwrite U.S. deterrence strategy.

Any U.S. deterrence strategy must rely on credible forces. Areas of convergence in the deterrence discourse imply several requirements for their structure. Credible U.S. forces must

- Promptly project sufficient firepower to reassure threatened allies against rapid conventional defeat.

- Deter and defend against WMD attack in order to ensure coalition cohesion and protect forward-deployed U.S. forces.

- Have the capability to fight a WMD-equipped adversary either through long-range attack or damage-limiting procedures.

- Be discriminate in order to avoid civilian casualties while punishing a rogue regime and destroying its fielded forces and its war-making potential. and

- Minimize dependence on overseas basing to circumvent strategies of exclusion.

The capabilities of the forces that meet these requirements must be clearly communicated to potential adversaries.

Neither current U.S. conventional nor nuclear capabilities satisfy all of these criteria. Although the military can design the necessary forces, the broader security policy community must establish the general signaling, dialogue, and posture required to make these forces an effective deterrent. The outcome of the deterrence debate will determine the configuration of U.S. force structure, the doctrine for its application, and the policies for its use.

Deterrence is no longer frozen in its cold war construct. Yet two factors may constrict its formerly preeminent role in U.S. strategy: the changing form of warfare itself, and increased cooperative international engagement. If for no other reason than the potential spread of weapons of mass destruction, however, it is not clear that deterrence is out of the nuclear fire. Ultimately, deterrence cannot be a stand-alone strategy in the post–Cold War era and must be flexibly applied to meet the demands of the new security environment.

The views expressed here are those of the author and do not reflect the official policy or position of the U.S. Air Force, the U.S. Department of Defense, or the U.S. government. The author wishes to thank Mike Cantagallo for his assistance with this essay.

REFERENCES

Abshire, David. 1993. Interview by author. Washington, D.C., 29 December.

Achen, Christopher H., and Duncan Snidal. 1989. "Rational Deterrence Theory and Comparative Case Studies." *World Politics* 41 (January): 143–69.

Arquilla, John, and Paul K. Davis. 1992. *Extended Deterrence, Compellence and the "Old World Order."* Santa Monica, Calif.: RAND.

Art, Robert J. 1992–93. "A U.S. Military Strategy for the 1990s: Reassurance without Dominance." *Survival* 34 (Winter): 3–23.

Aspin, Les. 1993a. *The Bottom-Up Review: Forces for a New Era.* Washington, D.C.: Department of Defense.

———. 1993b. "The Defense Department's New Nuclear Counterproliferation Initiative." Address to the National Academy of Sciences, Washington, D.C., 7 December.

Atkenson, Edward B. 1992. *A Military Assessment of the Middle East, 1991–1996.* Carlisle Barracks, Pa.: Strategic Studies Institute, U.S. Army War College.

Bailey, Kathleen C. 1991. *Doomsday Weapons in the Hands of Many: The Arms Control Challenge of the '90s.* Urbana: University of Illinois Press.

Betts, Richard K. 1988. "Nuclear Peace and Conventional War." *Journal of Strategic Studies* 11 (March): 79–95.

Bitzinger, Richard A. 1989. *Reconstructing NATO Strategy for the 1990s: A Conference Report,* Santa Monica, Calif.: RAND.

Blackwell, James A., Michael J. Mazarr, and Don M. Snider. 1993. *Desert Storm: The Gulf War and What We Learned.* Boulder, Colo.: Westview Press.

Boeker, Egbert. 1990. "A Non-Provocative Conventional Posture in Europe with No First Use of Nuclear Weapons." In *Life beyond the Bomb: Global Stability without Nuclear Deterrence,* edited by Elmer Schmalling. New York: St. Martin's Press.

Bowie, Christopher, and others. 1993. *The New Calculus: Analyzing Airpower's Changing Role in Joint Theater Campaigns.* Santa Monica, Calif.: RAND.

Buchanan, Richard A. 1993. Presentation to CSIS Extended Conventional Deterrence Working Group, Washington, D.C., 6 December.

Bundy, McGeorge. 1991. "Nuclear Weapons and the Gulf." *Foreign Affairs* 70 (Fall): 83–110.

Carnesale, Albert. 1993. *"Defenses against New Nuclear Threats."* In *New Nuclear Nations: Consequences for U.S. Policy,* edited by Robert D. Blackwill and Albert Carnesale. New York: Council on Foreign Relations.

Cimbala, Stephen J. 1991. *Strategy after Deterrence.* New York: Praeger.

———. 1992. *Force and Diplomacy in the Future.* New York: Praeger.

———. 1993. "Nuclear Weapons in the New World Order." *Journal of Strategic Studies* 16 (June): 173–79.

Cohen, Eliot A. 1993. "Beyond Bottom Up." *National Review* 45 (15 November): 40–43.

———. 1994. "The Mystique of U.S. Air Power." *Foreign Affairs* 73 (January–February): 109–24.

Cropsey, Seth. 1994. "The Only Credible Deterrent." *Foreign Affairs* 73 (March–April): 14–20.

Davis, Jacquelyn. 1993a. *Deterrence Planning for Regional Conflict and Crisis Management: Setting Priorities for the 1990s.* Director's Workshop Report, Washington, D.C.: Institute for Foreign Policy Analysis.

———. 1993b. "Deterrence in the Twenty-first Century: Roles and Missions for Naval Forces." In *Naval Forward Presence and the National Military Strategy,* edited by Robert L. Pfaltzgraff and Richard H. Schultz Jr. Annapolis, Md.: Naval Institute Press.

Davis, Paul K., and John Arquilla. 1991. *Deterring or Coercing Opponents in Crisis: Lessons from the War with Saddam Hussein.* Santa Monica, Calif.: RAND.

Desch, Michael C. 1992. "Conventional Deterrence and U.S. Post–Cold War Military Base Requirements in the Third World." Paper presented to the conference "Conventional Deterrence in the Post–Cold War Era," U.S. Naval Postgraduate School, Monterey, Calif., 13–14 August.

Dowler, Thomas W., and Joseph S. Howard III. 1991. "Countering the Threat of the Well Armed Tyrant: A Modest Proposal for Small Nuclear Weapons." *Strategic Review* 19 (Fall): 34–40.

Drew, Dennis M. 1993. *Airpower in the New World Order.* Carlisle Barracks, Pa.: Strategic Studies Institute, U.S. Army War College.

Dunn, Lewis A. 1994. "Rethinking the Nuclear Equation: The United States and the New Nuclear Powers." *Washington Quarterly* 17 (Winter): 5–25.

Engstrom, Peter. 1993. Presentation to the CSIS Extended Conventional Deterrence Working Group, Washington, D.C., 6 December.

Fetter, Steve. 1991. "Ballistic Missiles and Weapons of Mass Destruction: What Is the Threat? What Should Be Done?" *International Security* 16 (Summer): 5–42.

Flournoy, Michele A. 1993. "Implications for U.S. Military Strategy." In *New Nuclear Nations: Consequences for U.S. Policy,* edited by Robert D. Blackwill and Albert Carnesale. New York: Council on Foreign Relations.

Friedberg, Aaron L. 1991. "Is the United States Capable of Acting Strategically?" *Washington Quarterly* 14 (Winter): 5–23.

Garfinkle, Adam. 1991. "The Gulf War: Was It Worth It?" *World & I* 6 (October): 70–79.

———. 1992. "Arab Political Culture and Deterrence." Paper presented to the conference "Conventional Deterrence in the Post–Cold War Era," U.S. Naval Postgraduate School, Monterey, Calif., 13–14 August.

Garrity, Patrick J. 1993a. *Does the Gulf War (Still) Matter? Foreign Perspectives on the War and the Future of International Security.* Los Alamos, N.M.: Center for National Security Studies.

———. 1993b. "Implications of the Persian Gulf War for Regional Powers." *Washington Quarterly* 16 (Summer): 153–70.

George, Alexander L. 1991. *Forceful Persuasion: Coercive Diplomacy as an Alternative to War.* Washington, D.C.: U.S. Institute of Peace.

Glosson, Buster C. 1993. "Impact of Precision Weapons on Air Combat Operations." *Airpower Journal* 7 (Summer): 4–10.

Gray, Colin S. 1991. "Deterrence Resurrected: Revisiting Some Fundamentals." *Parameters* 21 (Summer): 13–21.

———. 1992. "Deterrence in the New Strategic Environment." *Comparative Strategy* 11 (July–September): 247–67.

Grier, Peter. 1993. "In Nukes Strategy Review, U.S. Eyes 'Undeterrables.'" *Christian Science Monitor,* 9 November, 1, 4.

Guertner, Gary L. 1992. "Introduction." In *Conventional Forces and the Future of Deterrence,* edited by Guertner, Robert P. Haffa Jr. and George H. Quester. Carlisle Barracks, Pa.: Strategic Studies Institute, U.S. Army War College.

———. 1993. "Deterrence and Conventional Military Forces." *Washington Quarterly* 16 (Winter): 141–51.

Haass, Richard N. 1991. "Regional Order in the 1990s: The Challenge of the Middle East." *Washington Quarterly* 14 (Winter): 181–88.

Haffa, Robert P. Jr. 1992. "The Future of Conventional Deterrence: Strategies and Forces to Underwrite a New World Order." In *Conventional Forces and the Future of Deterrence,* edited by Gary L. Guertner, Robert P. Haffa Jr., and George H. Quester. Carlisle Barracks, Pa.: Strategic Studies Institute, U.S. Army War College.

———. 1993. Letter to author. 21 November.

Haffa, Robert P. Jr., and James H. Patton. 1991. "Analogues of Stealth: Submarines and Aircraft." *Comparative Strategy* 10 (July–September): 257–71.

Harknett, Richard J. 1991. "Conventional Deterrence and Strategic Change." Ph.D. diss., Johns Hopkins University, Baltimore, Md.

———. 1992. "Integrating Tomahawk into a Conventional Deterrence Strategy: Inherent Flaws, Blunt Solutions." Paper presented to the conference "Conventional Deterrence in the post–Cold War Era," U.S. Naval Postgraduate School, Monterey, Calif., 13–14 August.

Hess, Andrew C. 1993. "Cultural and Political Limits on Forward Presence in Southwest Asia." In *Naval Forward Presence and the National Military Strategy*, edited by Robert L. Pfaltzgraff and Richard H. Schultz Jr. Annapolis, Md.: Naval Institute Press.

Hooker, Richard D. Jr., and Ricky L. Waddell. 1992. "The Future of Conventional Deterrence." *Naval War College Review* 45 (Summer): 78–87.

Huth, Paul K. 1988a. *Extended Deterrence and the Prevention of War*. New Haven, Conn.: Yale University Press.

———. 1988b. "Extended Deterrence and the Outbreak of War." *American Political Science Review* 82 (June): 423–43.

Huth, Paul K., and Bruce Russett. 1990. "Testing Deterrence Theory: Rigor Makes a Difference." *World Politics* 42 (July): 466–501.

Jablonsky, David. 1991. *Strategic Rationality Is Not Enough: Hitler and the Concept of Crazy States*. Carlisle Barracks, Pa.: Strategic Studies Institute, U.S. Army War College.

Jervis, Robert. 1989. "Rational Deterrence: Theory and Evidence." *World Politics* 41 (January): 183–207.

———. 1992. "The Utility of Nuclear Deterrence." In *International Politics: Enduring Concepts and Contemporary Issues*, edited by Jervis and Robert J. Art. New York: Harper-Collins.

———. 1994. "What Do We Want to Deter, and How Do We Deter It?" In *Turning Point: The Gulf War and Future U.S. Military Strategy*, edited by L. Benjamin Ederington and Michael J. Mazarr. Boulder, Colo.: Westview Press.

Joffe, Josef. 1992. "Collective Security and the Future of Europe: Failed Dreams and Dead Ends." *Survival* 34 (Spring): 36–49.

Kaufman, Daniel J., David S. Clark, and Kevin P. Sheehan, eds. 1991. *U.S. National Security Strategy for the 1990s*. Baltimore, Md.: Johns Hopkins University Press.

Kaysen, Carl, Robert S. McNamara, and George Rathjens. 1991. "Nuclear Weapons after the Cold War." *Foreign Affairs* 70 (Fall): 95–110.

Lebow, Richard Ned. 1985. "The Deterrence Deadlock: Is There a Way Out?" In *Psychology and Deterrence*, edited by Robert Jervis, Richard Ned Lebow, and Janice Gross Stein. Baltimore, Md.: Johns Hopkins University Press.

———. 1989. "Deterrence: A Political and Psychological Critique." In Stern and others *Perspectives on Deterrence*.

Lebow, Richard Ned, and Janice Gross Stein. 1989. "Rational Deterrence Theory: I Think, Therefore I Deter." *World Politics* 41 (January): 208–23.

Levine, Robert A. 1993. *Uniform Deterrence of Nuclear First Use*. Santa Monica, Calif.: RAND.

Lewis, Kevin N. 1989. *Getting More Deterrence out of Deliberate Capability Revelation*. Santa Monica, Calif.: RAND.

McCausland, Jeffrey. 1993. "The Gulf Conflict: A Military Analysis." *Adelphi Papers* 282 (November) (London: Brassey's for the IISS).

McPeak, Merrill A. 1993. Quoted in Barton Gellman, "Trepidation at Root of U.S. Korea Policy, Conventional War Seen Catastrophic for South." *Washington Post*, 12 December, A-1, A-49.

Mahnken, Thomas G. 1991. "The Arrow and the Shield: U.S. Responses to Ballistic Missile Proliferation." *Washington Quarterly* 14 (Winter): 189–203.

———. 1993. "America's Next War." *Washington Quarterly* 16 (Summer): 171–84.

Mazarr, Michael J. 1993. *Toward a Nuclear Peace: The Future of Nuclear Weapons in U.S. Foreign and Defense Policy*. Report of the CSIS Nuclear Strategy Study Group. Washington, D.C.: CSIS.

Mearsheimer, John. 1983. *Conventional Deterrence*. Ithaca, N.Y.: Cornell University Press.

Metz, Steven. 1993. Letter to author, 14 December.

———. 1994. Letter to author, 14 January.

Millot, Marc Dean, Roger Molander, and Peter A. Wilson. 1993. *"The Day After . . ." Study: Nuclear Proliferation in the Post–Cold War World*, vol. 1, *Summary Report*, MR-266-AF. Santa Monica, Calif.: RAND.

Mueller, John. 1992. "The Obsolescence of War in the Modern Industrialized World." In *International Politics: Enduring Concepts and Contemporary Issues*, edited by Robert Jervis and Robert J. Art. New York: Harper-Collins.

Mueller, Karl P. 1991. "Strategy, Asymmetric Deterrence and Accommodation: Middle Powers and Security in Modern Europe." Ph.D. diss., Princeton University, Princeton, N.J.

Nitze, Paul H. 1994. "Is It Time to Junk Our Nukes?" *Washington Post*, 16 January, C1–C2.

Nokkala, Arto. 1991. "Non-offensive Defense: A Criteria Model of Military Credibility." Helsinki: War College.

Odom, William E. 1993. *America's Military Revolution: Strategy and Structure after the Cold War*. Washington, D.C.: American University Press.

Palmer, Glenn. 1992. "Conventional Deterrence and Alliances: Three Models of U.S.-Allied Relations." Presentation at the conference "Conventional Deterrence in the Post-Cold War Era," U.S. Naval Postgraduate School, Monterey, Calif., 13–14 August.

Pape, Robert A. Jr. 1992. "Coercion and Military Strategy: Why Denial Works and Punishment Doesn't." *Journal of Strategic Studies* 15 (December): 123–75.

Patton, James H. 1993. "The Impact of Weapons Proliferation on Naval Forces." In *Naval Forward Presence and the National Military Strategy*, edited by Robert L. Pfaltzgraff and Richard H. Schultz Jr. Annapolis, Md.: Naval Institute Press.

Paul, T. V. 1991. "Asymmetric Conflicts: A Study of War Initiation by Lesser Powers." Ph.D. diss., University of California at Los Angeles, Los Angeles, Calif.

Payne, Keith B. 1992. "Deterrence and U.S. Strategic Force Requirements after the Cold War." *Comparative Strategy* 11 (July–September): 269–82.

Perry, William J. 1991. "Desert Storm and Deterrence." *Foreign Affairs* 70 (Fall): 66–82.

Pfaltzgraff, Robert L. 1993. "Change and Continuity in the 1990s." In *Naval Forward Presence and the National Military Strategy*, edited by Pfaltzgraff and Richard H. Schultz Jr. Annapolis, Md.: Naval Institute Press.

Powell, Colin L. 1992. *The National Military Strategy—1992*. Washington, D.C.: GPO.

Quester, George H. 1992a. "Conventional Deterrence: The Past Is Prologue." In *Conventional Forces and the Future of Deterrence*, edited by Gary L. Guertner, Robert

P. Haffa Jr., and George H. Quester. Carlisle Barracks, Pa.: Strategic Studies Institute, U.S. Army War College.

———. 1992b. "The Future of Nuclear Deterrence." *Survival* 34 (Spring): 74–88.

———. 1993. Interview by author. College Park, Md., 9 December.

Quester, George H., and Victor A. Utgoff. 1993. "U.S. Arms Reductions and Nuclear Nonproliferation: The Counterproductive Possibilities." *Washington Quarterly* 16 (Winter): 129–40.

———. 1994. "No-First-Use and Nonproliferation." *Washington Quarterly* 17 (Spring): 103–14.

Record, Jeffrey. 1993. "Defeating Desert Storm (and Why Saddam Didn't)." *Comparative Strategy* 12 (April–June): 125–40.

Roberts, Brad. 1993. "From Nonproliferation to Antiproliferation." *International Security* 18 (Summer): 139–73.

Safire, William. 1993. "The Fault Dear Brutus, Is Not. . . ." *New York Times,* 18 October, 17.

Simon, Steven. 1992. "U.S. Strategy in the Persian Gulf." *Survival* 34 (Autumn): 81–97.

Sloan, Stanley R. 1992. *The U.S. Role in the Post–Cold War World: Issues for a New Great Debate.* Washington, D.C.: Congressional Research Service.

Snider, Don M., and Gregory Grant. 1992. "The Future of Conventional Warfare and U.S. Military Strategy." *Washington Quarterly* 13 (Winter): 203–26.

Spector, Leonard. 1992. *Deterring Regional Threats from Nuclear Proliferation.* Carlisle Barracks, Pa.: Strategic Studies Institute, U.S. Army War College.

Starr, Barbara. 1993. "The Jane's Interview: Rear Admiral Thomas Ryan." *Jane's Defence Weekly* 19 (29 May): 32.

Steele, Robert D. 1993. "War and Peace in the Age of Information." Presentation to the U.S. Naval Postgraduate School, Monterey, Calif., 17 August.

Stein, Janice Gross. 1991. "Reassurance in International Conflict Management." *Political Science Quarterly* 106 (Fall): 431–51.

———. 1992. "Deterrence and Compellence in the Gulf, 1990–91: A Failed or Impossible Task?" *International Security* 17 (Fall): 147–79.

Stern, Paul C., Robert Axelrod, Robert Jervis, and Roy Radner, eds. 1989. *Perspectives on Deterrence.* New York: Oxford University Press.

Strain, Frederick R. 1993. "Nuclear Proliferation and Deterrence: A Policy Conundrum." *Parameters* 23 (Autumn): 85–95.

Swiecicki, Juliet A. 1992. "Severing the Ties That Bind: Moving beyond Deterrence." *Comparative Strategy* 11 (July–September): 283–306.

Toffler, Alvin, and Heidi Toffler. 1993. *War and Anti-War: Survival at the Dawn of the 21st Century.* Boston: Little, Brown.

Utgoff, Victor A. 1993. Interview by author. Alexandria, Va., 22 November.

WSS (Washington Strategy Seminar). 1993. *Persian Gulf Working Group Report.* Washington, D.C.: Washington Strategy Seminar.

Watman, Kenneth. 1994. Presentation to the CSIS Extended Conventional Deterrence Working Group, Washington, D.C., 27 January.

Wolf, Barry. 1991. *When the Weak Attack the Strong: Failures of Deterrence.* Santa Monica, Calif.: RAND.

Wu, Samuel S. 1989. *Extended Deterrence and the Onset of War.* Rochester, N.Y.: University of Rochester.

Zelikow, Philip. 1993. "Offensive Military Options." In *New Nuclear Nations: Consequences for U.S. Policy,* edited by Robert D. Blackwill and Albert Carnesale. New York: Council on Foreign Relations.

CHAPTER 14

CONVENTIONAL POLICY

GLOBAL REACH–GLOBAL POWER

DONALD B. RICE

In the public eye, the U.S. Air Force is most often identified with specific systems—fighters, bombers, missiles, satellites—and events such as the successful air campaign in Desert Storm. Yet the heart of what the air force contributes to national security is not captured by a narrow focus on specific programs and operations. *Aerospace power*—a maturing, precise and flexible instrument of national power—is what the air force contributes. Within the air force it is called simply *global reach–global power.*

The June 1990 white paper titled *Global Reach–Global Power* was the first official statement of the air force's role in national security since 1947. It laid out a vision of aerospace power and a strategic planning framework for the air force, building on the unique characteristics of aerospace forces—speed, range, flexibility, precision, and lethality.

More than any other single event, the decisive role of airpower in the Gulf War validated these concepts and pointed toward an even more capable force, uniquely well placed to draw on advances in technology and doctrine. Today air forces combined with space forces are the pivotal contributors to our national military strategy—in deterrence, forward presence, and crisis response. Beyond this, aerospace power gives America unique strengths for building influence and extending a helping hand around the globe.

The air force is in the process of reshaping to meet the requirements of an era where smaller, more capable forces must meet unpredictable threats. *Global Reach–Global Power* has been the blueprint of this reshaping and has become a part of our day-to-day operations, our resource allocation decisions, and our vision of future air- and spacepower. This companion white paper on the evolution of global reach–global power expands and elaborates upon its underlying tenets and points toward aerospace power's maturing role for a future filled with new challenges and opportunities.

NEW ENVIRONMENT, NEW NATIONAL STRATEGY

In the fifty years from Pearl Harbor to the collapse of the Soviet Union, Americans acted on the belief that the United States was safest in a world in which ideas, goods, and people could move freely—and that such a world was not possible without substantial, persistent American engagement in it. Generations of citizens did their part to meet the special responsibilities of this nation to nurture such a world.

The events of 1991—from the Persian Gulf War to the end of the Cold War—reaffirmed, yet redefined, the context in which America's global leadership is conducted. In 1991 the great global threat to our security passed. But dangers of a different sort remain, and conflict persists in many regions. More nations possess sophisticated weapons and technologies, and in other nations the roots of democratic government are still taking hold. For the 1990s and beyond—as for much of this century—there will be no substitute for American leadership.

To support this leadership, American military forces must find the right balance of complementary roles, functions, and force structure for a new security environment. Many features of this environment are already taking shape, and the Department of Defense (DOD) is responding. A regional focus is replacing decades of preoccupation with the Cold War standoff. The new security environment will not be defined by planning for a major war in Europe or a spiralling arms race. Although emerging threats will not be easy to foresee or fully evaluate in the same way as the NATO–Warsaw Pact confrontation, the likelihood that U.S. military forces will be called upon to defend U.S. interests in a lethal environment is high. The new definition of global engagement focuses on countering these regional hot spots and on preserving collective security in a fragmenting world.

The demands of the new environment play to the inherent strengths of air- and spacepower. In an age of uncertainty, with the location and direction of future challenges almost impossible to predict, spacecraft allow us to monitor activities around the world and to know the battlefield even before our forces arrive. With smaller forces overall and fewer deployed overseas, airpower's ability to respond around the globe—within hours, with precision and with effect—is an invaluable capability that is America's alone.

Donald B. Rice, Global Reach—Global Power: The Evolving Air Force Contribution to National Security (*Washington, D.C.: The Department of the Air Force, December 1992*), *1–15. Public Domain.*

Aerospace power has become central to the way that our nation uses the military instrument. Our global power assures our friends that they are not alone. With our global reach, potential adversaries understand that distance does not mean disinterest. In all of its forms *Global Reach–Global Power* is a formula for American engagement. The principles outlined below enable the air force to keep the watchful eye, offer the helping hand, or deliver the clenched fist that the situation may demand and that the nation has come to expect.

GLOBAL REACH–GLOBAL POWER: FIVE PRINCIPLES

A clear view of aerospace power's inherent strengths guided us through rapid changes in response to the end of the Cold War and the beginning of the defense drawdown. At the same time, the concepts of global reach and power point forward, toward future programs and planning to further develop these strengths. Since 1990, global reach–global power has become the overarching structure under which we program and evaluate air force funding and operations. Spanning the spectrum from versatile combat forces to building U.S. influence through operations short of war, the maturation of air- and spacepower is evident in each of the five pillars of global reach–global power:

- Sustain deterrence: nuclear forces.

- Provide versatile combat capability: theater operations and power projection.

- Supply rapid global mobility: airlift and tankers.

- Control the high ground: space and C3I systems.

- Build U.S. Influence: strengthen security partners and relationships.

Sustaining global reach and power in the long term depends on pursuing the innovative technologies and concepts of operations that offer the highest payoff in capability. Air and space forces possess an almost unparalleled potential to capitalize on advanced technologies—more so than most other forms of military power that are more constrained by limits of geography and physics. Technology and other factors are driving a change in the relative value of forces, opening up more roles for air- and spacepower. Correspondingly, air and space forces are becoming instruments of choice for rapid, tailored responses in a range of contingencies.

Airpower—which includes spacepower—is a seamless whole that delivers a remarkable set of tools. Many of these tools—such as precision and stealth—were for the first time used *together* on a large scale in the Gulf. Other tools—such as real-time processing and dissemination of information to combat forces—are being improved at a rapid pace. Some, particularly in the area of space, will reach their full potential after the turn of the century.

Qualitative improvements in each area add up to a major evolution in aerospace power *as a whole.* Instead of just reacting to events, aerospace power in the evolving post–Cold War world is a flexible tool that can help shape events.

To stay abreast of this evolution in the basic attributes of airpower, we have implemented several major changes in our organization. One of the most dramatic examples is the shift away from a primary emphasis on strategic nuclear roles for long-range bombers. B-1 crews that once spent most of their training time in the nuclear role now fly more than two-thirds of their training sorties practicing a variety of demanding conventional missions. This is part of a broader process of eliminating outdated distinctions between "strategic" and "tactical" systems—for airframes and for major commands. Separating strategic systems from tactical systems no longer serves as a sound basis for organizing, training, and equipping air and space forces.

Finally, we have defined a concise mission that gives focus to our capabilities and efforts. The mission of the air force is *to defend the United States through control and exploitation of air and space.* The five pillars of global reach and global power implement this demanding charge.

SUSTAIN DETERRENCE

Nuclear deterrence is a bedrock requirement of national security. Even at reduced force levels, the triad of bombers, land-based missiles, and sea-based missiles remains the most stable and adaptable form of sustained deterrence. At the same time, changing nuclear requirements have freed some forces for primary conventional roles.

Two presidential nuclear arms reduction initiatives, the ratification of Strategic Arms Reduction Treaty (START), and the 1992 Washington Summit Agreement, reshaped nuclear forces and redefined the role of nuclear strategy for the Air Force. The newly inaugurated United States Strategic Command in Nebraska took over responsibility for joint air force and navy nuclear planning. Both services cooperating closely in one command creates the right setting for integrated force structure and strategy decisions.

With the many positive changes since the end of the Cold War, the nuclear deterrent is still a fundamental aspect of our national security and a key underpinning of our new strategic partnership with Russia and the other nuclear states of the former Soviet Union. Flexibility in deterrence will be more important than ever as the world navigates through a decade in which many predict the emergence of weapons of mass destruction in more countries around the world. Of the many uncertain threats the future may hold, nuclear proliferation is one of the most disturbing. Nuclear deterrent forces must be so constituted as to give any potential nuclear adversary second thoughts.

PROVIDE VERSATILE COMBAT FORCE

Modern aircraft and precision weapons have transformed the battlefield and the relative value of weapon systems. While complementary forces of all the services will be essential, the air force offers, in most cases, the quickest, longest-range, leading-edge force available to the president in a fast-breaking crisis. Conventional airpower provides exceptional flexibility across the spectrum of conflict. The air force can deter, provide a presence, or put ordnance on a target set anywhere in the world in a matter of hours.

Providing forces tailored for the theater air campaign is the foremost challenge for air force power projection forces. Air superiority is the foundation. When it comes to air superiority, the air force is not interested in an even match. We want to win the air battle over enemy territory, and we want no enemy air attacks on our forces. Our ability to move forces into theater, to refuel, to reach out, depends on guaranteed control of the air. Modern fighter forces move forward fast, bringing persistent firepower to seize and hold control of the air or strike ground force targets with lethal effect. F-15s from Virginia were the first forces to touch down in Saudi Arabia in August 1990 in response to the invasion of Kuwait. Flexibility and lethality enable air forces to hedge or eliminate risk in the period before other forces can reach the fight. The F-22 will ensure America sustains these capabilities into the twenty-first century.

A truly versatile power projection force for theater operations cannot focus on old stereotypes of how air- and spacepower are applied. Aircraft are platforms designed to achieve effects—it is how they are used that determines whether the effect will be strategic or tactical. Desert Storm planners took advantage of this fact. "Strategic" B-52s attacked armor concentrations and conducted obstacle breaching. "Tactical" F-15s and F-16s struck nuclear and chemical facilities, and F-117s hit key targets in downtown Baghdad. Labels can be counterproductive in an era of regional conflicts—and in light of the flexibility of modern airpower. Increased speed, flexibility, and lethality reinforce the concept that it is the effects—not the systems—that matter.

Power projection forces focus on increasing their ability to provide initial response and sustained firepower for an air campaign in any theater. Long-range bomber forces have unmatched potential to provide both. B-52s launched from Louisiana delivered conventional air-launched cruise missiles on targets in Iraq on the first night of the war. With fewer bombers dedicated to the nuclear role, enhanced conventional capabilities will yield long-range platforms capable of striking critical targets in the first days of any campaign—and of sustaining operations over the long term.

Advanced conventional capabilities and smart employment tactics are the keys to operational success for all power projection forces. A rising curve of technological sophistication in areas from precision munitions to information processing is already increasing the effectiveness of platforms in a range of missions. Enhanced survivability is another boost. With stealth, F-117, B-2, and F-22 crews can identify with Winston Churchill's sentiments: "There is nothing more exhilarating than to be shot at without result," while most of the time denying the enemy any opportunity to shoot at all. Survivable platforms with precision weapons command decisive force and can wield it to great effect in a highly compressed period of time.

Intelligence is another crucial variable for combat forces. As important as collection is, dissemination of intelligence to the right people at the right time is the ultimate measure of success. Robust information architectures and a partnership between operators and suppliers enable power projection forces to better achieve the flexible, effective operations that air and space forces are capable of providing.

Mature use of airpower in the future will rely not just on advanced technology and concepts, but on ever-increasing complementarity between land and sea-based airpower, and between land, sea, air, and space forces. . . . Tight budgets put a premium on choosing the right upgrades and new systems. The air force and the navy have both an opportunity and a responsibility to hone their cooperation for future air operations. As our national strategy depends more and more on control from the air, leading-edge land and sea-based air forces will rely on compatible communications and planning systems. Precise direct-attack and standoff munitions from the same family will increase effectiveness and operational flexibility for all air forces. At the operational level, navy expertise in operating "from the sea" and against the littoral complements air force advantages in deep strike missions, large-scale air operations, and massive firepower. True jointness is using the right tools at the right time.

Both land and sea-based air forces are stepping up to a widening role in forward presence operations. Forces deployed permanently or temporarily overseas provide a flexible tool, ready to watch and monitor, or to form the tip of the spear for response to a crisis. Even with reduced force structure and overseas bases, long-term presence in Europe and the Asia Pacific region is central to our defense strategy. Global reach and power also means maintaining the ability to deploy forward from the United States. The composite wings in Idaho and North Carolina are structured to deploy within hours. Forces based in and operating from the continental United States also have a widening role in projecting power and presence forward as needed. B-2s on the ramp in Missouri can deliver precise firepower anywhere in the world, within hours.

SUPPLY RAPID GLOBAL MOBILITY

Mobility is the sinew of global reach—and a capability that will serve our strategic interests well into the future, especially with a reduced overseas presence. Our national security strategy calls on us "to be able to deploy substantial forces and sustain them in parts of the world where prepositioning equipment may not always be feasible, where adequate bases may not be available, and where there is a less-developed industrial base and infrastructure to support our forces once they have arrived." Mobility forces preserve a tremendous asset: the ability to operate from the continental United States and to move rapidly to any spot on the globe, whether building an air bridge for ground forces or speeding support for air forces already on the scene.

Rapid deployment is a combat force multiplier. Fighter forces paired with precision weapons are a formidable combination that our mobility fleet can deploy worldwide and sustain at high in-theater sortie rates. Just two C-5 sorties per day could deliver all the precision guided munitions (PGMs) used by the F-117s in the Gulf. About four days worth of the airlift at the peak of Operation Desert Shield could supply *all* the PGMs used by *all* aircraft during the war. New systems such as the F-22 will be able to operate with even less support, packaging ready airlift with advanced firepower into a truly leaner, meaner force. In other cases, supplying global mobility *is* the air campaign. The Berlin airlift in the winter of 1948–49 accomplished vital strategic objectives. Rapid delivery of supplies during the 1973 Yom Kippur War kept Israeli forces in the fight.

Tankers are the lifeblood of global reach and global power. Air refueling assumes increasing importance as a force multiplier in a period of smaller forces and declining forward basing. Tankers build air bridges to sustain high rates of airlift to any point on the planet, sometimes flying more sorties than the airlifters. Strike packages rely on tankers to extend range and payload and guarantee air forces the global reach to deploy rapidly and to employ effectively. Land-based tanker forces are indispensable to support a range of theater air operations. In Southwest Asia, joint U.S. and coalition forces depended on U.S. Air Force tankers for operations beyond the littoral. Because of these requirements, tankers and airlifters have received a proportionally smaller cut than other elements of our force structure.

Control the High Ground

Control of the air has become a prerequisite for the American way of war. Similarly, at the dawn of the new century, space forces' superiority of speed and position over surface and air forces points to control of space as a prerequisite for victory. Control of the high ground is the means to provide information on the disposition of enemy forces, bomb damage, the time and location of ballistic missile launches, precise navigation, secure communications, and more. The air force's space sentinels and our U-2s, RC-135s, JSTARS, and AWACS aircraft provide the United States with the real-time information necessary to anticipate and monitor a crisis and act, when necessary, with a decisive information advantage over our adversaries. AWACS deployments provide another form of presence, by improving situation awareness in cases where a large presence is inappropriate or not possible. JSTARs will serve as the eyes and ears of the joint force commander. These forces complement and support land, sea, and air forces—giving the United States the edge in combat and helping to achieve our national security goals throughout the spectrum of conflict.

During the Persian Gulf War, America's de facto control of space allowed us to keep continuous watch on the enemy—providing commanders with situational awareness that allowed them to cut through the fog of war. Extending this kind of control into the future means both ensuring access to space—one of the fundamental national interests of the United States—and ensuring our exploitation of space in situations even when an adversary challenges us there. Space superiority is joining air superiority as a sine qua non of global reach and power.

Protecting our forces, deployed or at home, from ballistic missile attack is another essential. As weapons of mass destruction proliferate, the air force must extend its ability to protect our theater forces, our allies, and our homeland by holding ballistic missiles at risk—all the way from prelaunch through space to reentry. With one-quarter of the budget spent on space, the air force is uniquely well-positioned to provide all aspects of spacepower. Over 90 percent of the trained forces, most of the infrastructure, and about 80 percent of funding for the DOD's space-related assets come from the air force. The air force conducts 90 percent of all DOD operational launches and currently has command and control of ninety-nine active satellites.

While the basic concepts are understood and being applied, there is still tremendous potential for growth in our thinking, hardware, control, and exploitation of space. Space is breaking the confines of its research and development heritage and becoming more integrated with terrestrial forces. As space becomes more and more integrated with our day-to-day operations, we will create the new concepts, doctrine, and strategies that will be required to support the joint forces commander.

Space forces are today where airpower was before World War II. The mission of space forces, long considered support for combat or mobility "customers," is now an integral part of combat operations. Tomorrow, control of the high ground will draw space forces more fully into the versatile combat force, decreasing the time required to respond to aggression and allowing air forces to strike anywhere on the surface of the Earth with overwhelming but discriminate power.

Build U.S. Influence

Effective military instruments need not always be used for war. Part of global reach and power is employing air and space forces to accomplish national security objectives by building influence abroad. Air force professionals make an impact when they share their knowledge of defense organization and civilian control with counterparts in newly democratic states. Other tools—from training to airlift to air occupation—offer great flexibility that no other nation can match.

Part of global power is the means to extend a helping hand, and to use airpower for diplomatic and humanitarian purposes, or in support of international objectives. In one particular week during the autumn of 1992, air force planes were supporting fire-fighting operations in California and Idaho; humanitarian relief efforts in Somalia, Turkey, and Yugoslavia; and peacekeeping forces in Angola. Airlifting relief supplies to Russia in the winter of 1992 put global reach to work to build strategic partnership. Operation Provide Comfort offers another example: the same forces that participated in the Gulf War shifted to providing relief supplies to Kurdish refugees in northern Iraq. As always, air force planes are on hand in the United States—disaster relief to Florida's victims of Hurricane Andrew was just one example of their application.

Air- and spacepower are also reaching into new arenas. Peacekeeping represents one area where global reach—backed up by access to global power—is making a growing contribution. Operation Olive Branch dedicated U-2s to collect information to implement U.N. Security Council Resolution 687's provisions for destroying nuclear capabilities and missile weaponry in Iraq. Without stationing masses of troops on the ground, the threat of airpower enables us to back up the small teams conducting inspections and control the behavior of Iraqi forces. In Southern Watch, air force and navy aircraft are enforcing a no-fly zone over Southern Iraq. Peacekeeping operations demand tailored responses—to monitor, inspect, and enforce diplomatic solutions. Airlift, surveillance, and ready, tailored combat power to deter or defend are among the contributions air and space forces can bring to international peacekeeping efforts.

Global access and influence ultimately depend on the bonds of alliance and international cooperation. Extensive programs with partners like Great Britain and Japan provide a conduit for air force professionals to share expertise and are a bulwark of global security. Security assistance, exercises with security partners, military-to-military contacts, and foreign military sales are all part of the air force's global commitments. German F-4s and Tornados operate side by side with an American squadron at Holloman Air Force Base in New Mexico. Emphasizing regional defense strategies underscores the need for continued commitment to building influence with friends and allies through the flexible tools of airpower.

U.S. security relationships during the Cold War extended to a relatively fixed set of formal allies and friends. In 1992 fighter and bomber exchanges with the Russians broke the last of that mold. Today, there is hardly a nation anywhere that does not want to deepen its military contacts with the United States.

This offers us an unprecedented opportunity to enhance our own security as well as to encourage the cause of democracy globally. We stand preeminent today as a military power, yet the military flourishes within an open society, responding to a democratic government. Attributes that we take for granted are a reservoir of practical experience to offer emerging democracies in Central Europe, the Soviet successor states, and elsewhere. Carefully tailored programs of military contacts are one way to advise new democracies on processes for a modern military—from pay, promotion, and recruitment to military justice, public affairs, and legislative liaison—as they build structures that will defend, not imperil, their newly won freedoms.

GLOBAL REACH–GLOBAL POWER IN ACTION

DESERT STORM

Global reach–global power was validated under fire in the Gulf War. In thirty-nine days, airpower grounded the Iraqi Air Force and systematically stripped the Iraqi Army of its combat power—making possible the fastest land offensive of the twentieth century. Airpower technology caught up with airpower theory in Southwest Asia. Air and space forces achieved a degree of effectiveness that earlier airpower pioneers foresaw but that the technology of their day could not yet deliver. The air campaign paralyzed Iraq's capability to wage war, achieving effects that simply were not within the scope of earlier campaigns. In several categories, from air defense to oil production, the 1991 air campaign produced effects on a greater scale than did the Combined Bomber Offensive in two and a half years of costly strikes on Nazi Germany. "The decisive factor in the war with Iraq was the air campaign," said House Armed Services Committee Chairman Les Aspin.

Several new factors made the air campaign decisive. In the Gulf, the role of the joint forces air component commander (JFACC), the single commander for air assets, confirmed the revolution in employment and effectiveness of airpower—and the success of unified command. The JFACC and his staff had options available to them that went so far as to bear only a distant conceptual relation to the conduct of the air war in Europe or the Pacific fifty years earlier.

With stealth, the JFACC used his forces to strike the enemy across the length and breadth of his territory, on the first night, with no losses among the F-117s. With the air supremacy that stealth helped achieve, the coalition struck the enemy by day with near impunity. Forces loitered over the target, using precision weapons to destroy aimpoint after aimpoint in the same target complex. The same strike aircraft "plinked" armored vehicles, killed enemy aircraft in their hardened shelters, and destroyed bunkers that served as the nerve centers of the Iraqi war machine. The commander's freedom to moderate losses and accomplish objectives was an advantage the JFACC could exercise consistently for the first time. Strikes unfolded in real time as the JFACC watched on a display data linked to him in his headquarters by AWACS and other sensors. Precision weapons and high assurance of mission success confidently linked strategic objectives with aimpoints—making strategic bombing more discriminate, reducing losses, and achieving measurable results with fewer missions.

Allied aircrews shut down Iraq's oil production, electricity, transportation, communications, and ability to produce weapons of mass destruction with a mere 1 percent of the bombs dropped in eleven years in Vietnam. Iraq's leaders could not effectively reinforce or maneuver their military forces. Discriminate and simultaneous attacks inflicted paralysis—not devastation.

The success of the air campaign revolutionized the conduct of war. General Colin Powell spoke to the role of airpower: "I will say this—and I've said it before and I'll say it again: airpower was decisive in that war." Modern airpower demonstrated that it can undercut the enemy's basic ability to wage war and deny opposing ground forces the ability to execute their scheme of maneuver, while also inflicting heavy damage on those forces to cripple their operational effectiveness. With precise and rapid application of airpower to paralyze and wear down enemy forces early on, ground forces have relatively less to do and can move quickly to consolidate gains when ground operations begin. In the future the role of air and space forces will be part of a new form of combat where, in the words of Vice Chairman of the Joint Chiefs of Staff David Jeremiah, "it will no longer be necessary to close with the enemy in order to destroy him."

The experience of Southwest Asia challenges the air force to concentrate precision and refine simultaneity to expand the contribution of airpower to the joint conduct of war. Five and ten years from now, the force will be smaller than it was in 1991, but more lethal, and hence more capable. Signs of the response to that challenge are visible in the major procurement programs, the new air force doctrine manual, the command organization, and the commitment to quality in personnel and training.

The winning edge in the Gulf War came from strategy, technology, and most of all, our people. Competence and years of realistic training made the difference in the success of air- and spacepower. The quality of our highly trained people is essential to carrying out the missions of global reach–global power.

SHAPING THE FUTURE

Visions succeed through implementation as well as articulation. The experience of Desert Storm was the final impetus that led us to reexamine and change some old practices to better structure the air force for a new era. As General Merrill A. McPeak explained: "The real test of an institution is how it handles success. Everyone recognizes the need for change after failure. What should make us proud is that . . . we are way ahead in crafting an Air Force that fits the needs of the next century."

The air force reshaped to apply global reach and power in circumstances where theater warfare—not a global Soviet threat—is the emphasis. Strategic Air Command, Tactical Air Command, and Military Airlift Command divided airmen into separate communities, so in 1992 the three merged into the new Air Combat Command and Air Mobility Command. Air Force Materiel Command melded Systems and Logistics commands into a single organization for cradle-to-grave weapon system management. In Air Force Intelligence Command, one commander now has responsibility for functions once scattered across the air force. The scope of these changes was enormous. In terms of resources and personnel, the restructuring of major air force commands dwarfed any of the mergers, acquisitions, divestitures, and consolidations that took place in the private sector over the preceding decade. More important, reshaping positioned the air force to decentralize and to take down the walls that divided airmen and the functions of airpower into limiting categories.

Air Combat Command (ACC) blends the firepower of the air force into one command. As a result the air force is better prepared to respond to new challenges in any theater. Composite wings are one feature that carries this philosophy to the level of day-to-day operations. Different aircraft can combine in one wing to train together in peacetime, preparing to fight the way they would in war. Under this structure, the commands no longer support the outdated distinctions that matched tactical aircraft to armies and long-range aircraft to a primarily strategic nuclear mission. ACC's crews train for a variety of conventional roles—both fighters and bombers aiming to be as proficient at hitting tanks as they are at hitting enemy war-making capacity. Factors like range and payload type outweigh command culture when a theater commander needs responsive, effective firepower.

Air Mobility Command lines up most of our mobility and refueling assets on the same team, thereby enabling the American response to reach its destination anywhere on the globe. Integrating airlift and tankers enhances mobility, reach, and combat power across the breadth of America's armed forces. The uniquely American capabilities to airlift anything, anywhere and to extend the range of our firepower are the foundation of global reach and power.

The merger of Systems Command and Logistics Command into the new Air Force Materiel Command (AFMC) reflects these organizational changes and infuses modern management principles into every aspect of the business of the air force. AFMC's job is to turn global power and reach concepts into capabilities—to design, develop, and support the world's best air and space weapon systems. AFMC has laid its cornerstone in the Integrated Weapon System Management concept, giving us cradle-to-grave management of our systems.

Finally, we are responding to a new security environment and building on the excellent performance of U.S. Air Force Guard and Reserve forces in the Gulf by giving them new missions and expanding their roles in traditional tasks. Although active manpower has been reduced by more than a quarter since the mid-1980s, guard and reserve personnel strengths will maintain their current levels. In our fighter force, air reserve component units will grow from one-third to over 42 percent of the total force by 1995. If one includes the air defense interceptors of our National Guard, fully 48 percent of air force fighter cockpits will be filled by reservists and guardsmen. Similarly, nearly half of all our strategic and tactical airlift aircraft are in the guard and reserve, as are 56 percent of all our airlift flight crews. The restructuring of our bomber forces will also allow us to transfer some B-52s and B-1s to guard and reserve units where citizen-airmen can contribute to the bomber's expanding conventional role.

CONCLUSION

In its most simplified terms, the goal of our national military strategies during the Cold War was *to contain*. A new era demands that we sharpen our ability *to shape* the international environment. Shaping our alliances, ensuring a favorable security climate, and crafting the most effective response to crises are the core objectives our military strategies must support.

Two challenges confront the U.S. Air Force as we strive to enhance our contribution to national security. The first is to maintain the forces we will need to deal with residual or emerging threats around the globe. The second is to create, steadily and affordably, the backbone of our forces for after the year 2000. Both challenges demand that our nation maintain a superior core of military capabilities that guarantee the flexibility and effectiveness of our military response to a wide variety of situations.

Core capabilities for the nation range across service lines. They include the ability to maintain global situational awareness and to inflict strategic and operational paralysis on adversaries by striking key nodes in their war-making potential. At the same time, we must hold emerging strategic capabilities in potentially hostile states at risk, while being prepared to defend against limited missile attack. Another core capability is maintaining sufficient, quality forces that can be deployed worldwide to deter or defend. Assured access to air and space is as important to the nation's economic well-being as to its security. Access to any region requires air, maritime, and space supremacy. As a new range of challenges arise, we will be called upon to assist international efforts for relief, peacekeeping, and drug interdiction and a range of other missions short of war. To ensure success for the long haul, we will also need to sustain a research and industrial base sufficient to keep our technological edge.

One of the most important aspects of the global reach–global power planning framework is that it shows us how to prudently trade some force structure to maintain a high level of readiness and investment in critical modernization programs. Ongoing review of the roles and functions of the services is indispensable, and will create a climate in which each can perform at its best and bring the optimum contribution to the joint conduct of warfare. The U.S. Air Force of the 1990s is smaller in numbers, yet more capable of sustaining core capabilities and countering a wide variety of challenges to our nation's security and our interests abroad. Air and space forces must be prepared to shoulder increased responsibility for bringing decisive capabilities to bear in a range of combat operations and in military operations short of war.

America is an aerospace nation. Our aerospace forces and technology are a national treasure and a competitive edge, militarily and commercially. Now, more than ever, we have the opportunity to mature the abilities of air force air and space forces and make them even more useful tools for meeting our national security objectives—through global reach–global power.

GLOBAL PRESENCE

SHEILA E. WIDNALL AND RONALD R. FOGLEMAN

As America approaches the next century, it faces both an uncertain world and a promising future. Our challenge as an air force and as a nation is to sustain that promise and secure the future.

In the years to come, America's military will continue to play a pivotal role. That role will be a stabilizing one, founded on the shared principles and traditions of all the services. Increased cooperation is the cornerstone for success.

The primary responsibility of America's military is to deter potential adversaries or fight and win wars decisively. To improve the way we do business, we must reconsider this core responsibility in terms of how America's military forces actually project power.

At the foundation of this approach is *power projection*. Power projection is a means to influence actors or affect situations or events in America's national interest. It has two components: *war fighting* and *presence*. War fighting is the direct use of military force to compel an adversary. Presence is the posturing of military capability, including nonbelligerent applications and the leveraging of information to deter or compel an actor or affect a situation. A sound national military strategy depends on coherent war-fighting and presence strategies.

Changes in the international security environment, advances in technology, and reductions in America's military force structure require a fresh consideration of America's presence strategy. This discussion provides a reconceptualization of presence. It expands traditional notions of presence to correspond with the emerging international security picture and to match current and future applications.

GLOBAL PRESENCE: A NEW APPROACH

America's approach to evolving national security concerns has changed over the years to meet the needs of a shifting geopolitical environment. During the Cold War, America's vital national interests seemed to be more easily defined. Our nation faced a monolithic threat to its national security, and our political and military leaders were able to contain and counter that threat with effective strategies for ensuring America's security. *Forward defense* was a key component of our containment strategy and amounted to what today is called presence.

The thrust of forward defense was to deter potential aggressors, and if that failed, to engage those aggressors' forces close to their borders, halting and repelling the aggression. As such, presence equated

to and was ensured by bipolar alliances, heavy overseas troop commitments, frequent political and military-to-military interaction with America's allies, and the continual courting of "on-the-fence" nations. In short, part of America's Cold War strategy was "being there." It was a strategy most Americans understood.

As the 1980s ended and the Cold War subsided, the basis for the traditional definition of presence began to dissolve. America moved from the Cold War's bipolar arrangement toward what was perceived to be a new, less threatening political environment. As forward defense lost its rationale, *forward presence* and *overseas presence* emerged. The goal of each was to assure America's allies of our nation's continued commitment to their security while responding to the reality of the decreasing threat to America's national existence.

Today the global international system has become a more diverse panorama of political, military, and economic concerns confronting the United States. Consequently, it is more difficult to achieve consensus on what Americans consider "vital" national interests. Despite this, America's military forces are involved in more operations of greater duration than at any time in the past twenty years; and, these operations have been conducted with 25 percent of the total force and 40 percent fewer forward deployed forces than the services possessed in 1989.

In the face of increasing demands on U.S. military forces, smaller force structures, and shrinking defense budgets, we can no longer afford to physically deploy forces in every region of concern. Concurrent with changes in the international security environment are significant advances in technology, most notably information technologies. The ability to create, disseminate, access, and manipulate information for one's own ends and to control information available to competitors or adversaries produces a potential for decisive advantage. Much as the introduction of the airplane moved us into the three-dimensional battlefield, information technologies lead us to consider the potential of operations in a four-dimensional, virtual battlespace. This battlespace is not defined in terms of traditional, centralized, geopolitical boundaries, but in terms of a decentralized, global web of networks. As a result, we must examine new methods of characterizing the threat—including the use of technology-based analysis—and determine appropriate responses.

Sheila E. Widnall and Ronald R. Fogleman, Global Presence, 1995 (*Washington, D.C.: The Department of the Air Force, 1995), 3–16. Public Domain.*

To use an analogy, during the Cold War, America was like a cop permanently guarding the door of every bank around the globe. Changes in the security environment coupled with technological improvements and force reductions altered America's need to continue in this role. Hence America replaced "the cop on the beat" with "video monitoring and alarm systems" linked to joint military capabilities that can be brought to bear wherever and whenever necessary. This monitoring and alarm network consists of space-based and air-breathing platform sensors and other information-gathering systems. In most instances, information, combined with forces that can rapidly respond with the right mix of capabilities, can achieve U.S. goals. On occasion, information alone may be enough to attain U.S. objectives. Of course, in some regions of the world a physical presence is imperative; however, there may be circumstances when such a presence is counterproductive. In instances where a physical presence is not preferred, information capabilities provide America the option to visit the "bank" as often as it wishes to check the integrity of the system.

In an environment influenced by so many variables, how should America best pursue the continuing need for presence? One way is through *global presence*.

Global presence expands the definition of presence to include the advantages of physical and virtual means. Global presence considers the full range of potential activities from the physical interaction of military forces to the virtual interaction achieved with America's information-based capabilities.

FUNDAMENTALS OF GLOBAL PRESENCE

Three tenets are key to moving beyond traditional conceptions of presence:

- All military forces can exert presence.

- Forces have unique attributes that affect the scope and quality of the presence they exert and complement each other when appropriately applied.

- Technological advances are enhancing the contributions of military forces to presence missions.

ALL MILITARY FORCES CAN
EXERT PRESENCE

The suitability of forces to exert presence is conditional. The task is to match the right combination of capabilities to achieve the desired objective. For forces to exert presence, the actors we wish to influence must understand that we

- Have national interests involved.

- Have the political will to support or defend those interests.

- Can monitor and assess their actions accordingly.

- Have sufficient force to achieve our objectives.

Without fulfilling these four conditions, military forces are not likely to influence an actor.

U.S. efforts to persuade Israel not to respond to Iraqi Scud attacks during the Persian Gulf War can help illustrate these conditions. America's objective was to preserve the political and military coalition opposing Iraq. To accomplish this objective, the United States had to satisfy the four conditions mentioned above.

First, to ensure Israel understood and appreciated American interests, which included Israeli security, the U.S. deputy secretary of state and undersecretary of defense for policy delivered personal assurances from the president of the United States to the Israeli prime minister. Thereafter, the Department of Defense established a secure communication link with the Israeli Ministry of Defense to enable immediate and frequent contact between U.S. and Israeli officials.

Second, to ensure Israel understood America intended to support those interests, the president ordered the immediate transfer of two Patriot air defense missile batteries to Israel and the training of Israeli crews for their operation.

Third, to assure Israel that America could monitor and assess activities throughout the region, the United States provided near-real-time warning of Iraqi Scud missile attacks on Israel. Near-real-time warning offered the Israeli populace as much as five minutes to take shelter before missile impact.

Fourth, to assure the Israeli leadership that America had sufficient force to achieve its objectives, the president offered four additional Patriot batteries to be operated by U.S. troops. Likewise, U.S. Central Command devoted a substantial amount of its air, space, and special operations assets to combat the Scud threat.

In this instance, America succeeded by ensuring U.S. objectives were clearly understood, by demonstrating U.S. commitment to Israel's security, and by coordinating a common response to the crisis. Space-based assets aided this response and were part of the process that included all four conditions for exerting presence. These four conditions are enduring requirements, guiding America's political and military leaders when considering presence operations. Because every operation is fundamentally different, political and military leaders should choose forces with the attributes each case warrants.

MILITARY FORCES EMPHASIZE
DIFFERENT ATTRIBUTES

America's military forces emphasize different attributes depending on the medium in which they operate. These attributes magnify a theater commander's ability to exert presence in accordance with the *principles of war*. They also enable theater commanders to develop alternative joint force packages. These attributes include:

- Responsiveness: the ability to arrive quickly where needed.

- Persistence: the ability to maintain or adjust operational tempos over an extended period of time.

- Flexibility (versatility): the ability to configure forces for a particular set of conditions.

- Survivability: the ability to limit risks when employing forces.

- Economy: the ability to efficiently allocate resources required to deploy and employ capabilities.

Employing the proper alternative joint force package depends on numerous factors, beginning with an assessment of national security objectives. An example of this can be drawn from the situation in Kuwait in 1994.

The possibility of a resurgent Iraqi threat posed a serious danger to the region's stability and America's interests in the Persian Gulf. This required more than just a physical presence; it required a global presence, combined with diplomatic initiatives, to contain Iraqi adventurism. When Iraq mobilized a significant ground force near Kuwait's border, the United States quickly responded with Operation Vigilant Warrior. On short notice, air and ground forces deployed from the United States to Saudi Arabia and Kuwait to deter incursions into these territories. Likewise, naval forces moved from the Mediterranean Sea and Indian Ocean into the Persian Gulf. Space forces and other information-based capabilities enabled air, ground, and naval force operations and provided American, coalition, and other world leaders a window through which they could monitor, assess, and, with a variety of means, attempt to manipulate behaviors. Concurrently, global media coverage of America's military mobilization and deployment presented Saddam Hussein and the world with an unmistakable statement of U.S. intentions and resolve. In this case, U.S. efforts capitalized on the complementary attributes of air, ground, sea, and space forces to successfully secure U.S. objectives. In the future, when demonstrating similar resolve, our nation's leaders will benefit from forces increasingly influenced by technological innovations.

TECHNOLOGICAL INNOVATIONS ENHANCE U.S. ABILITY TO EXERT PRESENCE

Technological advances enhance the role of all military forces in exerting presence. Improvements in three specific areas enable forces to exert influence with less political and military risk:

- *Situational awareness:* Advances in information-based technologies allow military forces

to monitor and assess most global conditions rapidly and efficiently.

- *Strategic Agility:* Improvements in transport technologies enable rapid responses with a variety of military forces to distant locations.

- *Lethality:* Enhancements in weapon system technologies make it possible to achieve desired effects more quickly and at less cost.

Situational awareness results from advances in information-based technologies that allow military forces to monitor and assess global conditions rapidly and efficiently. This is more than hitching a ride on the information highway. Political and military leaders have come to depend upon advances in space-based and air-breathing platform sensors and other information-based systems deployed around the globe. These forces are an increasingly vital component of national policy implementation. For example, these capabilities were critically important during 1994, when determining and executing appropriate responses to events in Korea, Iraq, Bosnia, Somalia, Rwanda, and Haiti.

Situational awareness gives America the ability to anticipate crises and prepare appropriate responses to them. Improvements in space-based and air-breathing platform sensors and information-based systems in the coming years will steadily increase the situational awareness of military leaders and military forces at all echelons. Today, situational awareness improves our ability to generate military options before crises erupt. Once the use of military capabilities is necessary, the full range of recent technological advances comes into play.

Improvements in transport technologies enable the United States to respond rapidly to national security concerns anywhere in the world with a variety of military capabilities. This is strategic agility. With strategic agility, U.S. military forces can operate unconstrained by geographic barriers and can reach 100 percent of the world's population. We gain strategic agility with such national assets as our air mobility fleet, that is, our airlift and air refueling forces. When these assets are combined with Army Civil Affairs units, for instance, air mobility becomes a means for demonstrating U.S. benevolence. When combined with the 82d Airborne, air mobility becomes a means for demonstrating U.S. resolve.

Strategic agility also gives us the ability to anchor forces in one location and rapidly swing them, if needed, to other locations. This enables military forces far removed from any target to deliver aid or combat capabilities within minutes or hours of a national decision to act.

Enhancements in weapon systems and related technologies make it possible to achieve desired effects more quickly and at less cost. For example, *Gulf War Air Power Survey* analysis revealed precision munitions were twelve times more effective than nonprecision munitions.[1] As a result, air forces minimized their exposure to enemy defenses and experienced significantly fewer aircraft losses. At the same time, the use of precision weapons significantly decreased collateral damage. When combined with the advantages of stealth technologies, precision munitions become even more potent. Consequently, increased lethality enables America to maintain a credible deterrent threat with a reduced force structure.

The synergistic benefits achieved when combining situational awareness and strategic agility with lethality allow America to consider a wide range of military responses to worldwide circumstances. These capabilities, inherent in our war-fighting forces (forces that possess the attributes of responsiveness, persistence, flexibility, survivability, and economy) form the cornerstone of global presence.

PRESENCE IS A TEAM EFFORT

America's military services have always fought as a team. Goldwater-Nichols legislation codified jointness, and recent historical trends have reinforced this concept. Today few would dispute the efficacy of joint war fighting, which Desert Storm clearly validated.

Like war fighting, presence is a team effort. Just as theater commanders define their war fighting requirements, they have the responsibility to determine presence requirements as well. As such, they must retain access to the military means that enable them to obtain the balance of forces and capabilities needed to exert presence. Global presence facilitates that process. Global presence acknowledges that all military capabilities contribute to presence with physical and virtual means.

SUMMARY

Whether forces operate globally or from forward areas, they operate as a team. Together, they offer America's leadership a mechanism for modulating responses to global, regional, or local situations to achieve national objectives while controlling risk. Global presence acknowledges this interdependency. It reconceptualizes presence to correspond with the emerging international security picture and expands presence to match current and future applications.

Today America's military forces are more mobile, more lethal, and more omnipresent than ever before. These features enhance traditional conceptions of military presence by allowing theater commanders to employ the advantages of all military options, forces, and capabilities.

As we peer into the future, we should view global presence as one route the services can take to achieve our country's ever evolving national security objectives. We in the military possess the means, physical and virtual, to provide America continuous awareness of world events and a force capable of projecting military power worldwide, in minutes or hours, with little or no warning. In so doing, we meet our responsibility to our civilian leadership and the American people to deter potential adversaries or fight and win wars decisively.

NOTE

1. *Gulf War Air Power Survey*, vol. 2 (Washington, D.C.: GPO, 1993), 352–53.

THE MYSTIQUE OF U.S. AIRPOWER

ELIOT A. COHEN

Airpower is an unusually seductive form of military strength, in part because, like modern courtship, it appears to offer gratification without commitment. Francis Bacon wrote of command of the sea that he who has it "is at great liberty, and may take as much and as little of the Warre as he will." A similar belief accounts for airpower's attractiveness to those who favor modest uses of force overseas. Statesmen may think that they can use air attacks to engage in hostilities by increments, something ground combat does not permit. Furthermore, it

appears that the imminent arrival of so-called nonlethal or disabling technologies may offer an even more appealing prospect: war without casualties.

This rise in airpower's stock comes from its success in the Persian Gulf War. In the view of some, that conflict represented the opening shot of a fundamental transformation in the nature of warfare, a "military-technical revolution" as the Russians have termed it for more than a decade. Thus the Russian military sadly read the outcome of a war that vindicated their predictions even as it sealed their pro-

This essay has been edited and is reprinted from Foreign Affairs 73 *(January/February 1994): 109–24, by permission of* Foreign Affairs. *Copyright 1994 by the Council on Foreign Relations, Inc.*

found sense of inferiority vis-à-vis the United States. Secretary of Defense Richard Cheney agreed: "This war demonstrated dramatically the new possibilities of what has been called the 'military-technological revolution in warfare.'" Others, outside the Bush administration, expressed this view no less enthusiastically. William Perry, now secretary of defense, wrote in *Foreign Affairs* that "a new class of military systems . . . gave American forces a revolutionary advance in military capability."[1]

WAS THE GULF WAR A REVOLUTION?

The lopsided struggle with Iraq has already affected the way Americans understand modern war, inducing the ornithological miracle of doves becoming hawks. More than one distinguished commentator who had reservations about aerial bombardment in the Persian Gulf expressed a newfound belief in its utility as a tool of American foreign policy in the Balkans. Thus Anthony Lewis of the *New York Times* wrote during the Persian Gulf War in disgust at the ruin wrought by aerial bombardment, "We should never again tolerate anyone who talks about 'surgical strikes.'" Since then he has developed a keener appreciation of airpower, asserting that "a few air strikes in Dubrovnik" would have stopped the Yugoslav horrors in 1991. There is a "straightforward way to apply force" in Bosnia that involves "minimum risk" and provides a course that is not merely right but "clear and doable"—precision air attacks.[2]

Many of these individuals came away from the Persian Gulf War with a far healthier respect for airpower, believing it had made all the difference. Indeed it had.[3] Some 52,000 air-to-surface sorties delivered approximately 210,000 unguided bombs, 9,300 guided bombs, 5,400 guided air-to-surface missiles, and 2,000 antiradar missiles; American forces also hurled more than 300 cruise missiles at the enemy. To what effect? Of its 700 aircraft, the Iraqi air force lost 33 in the air; approximately 140 perished in hardened aircraft shelters, and more than 120 were flown to Iran. The Iraqi air defense system succumbed within days—really, hours—to an extremely sophisticated attack, and it managed to shoot down only a tiny fraction of the attacking aircraft. The Iraqi electrical grid, oil refineries and most of the telephone and communications system stopped functioning. The Iraqi ground forces in the Kuwait theater attracted the most attention from coalition air forces. Before the ground war began on February 24, the Republican Guard located in the northern part of the theater had lost nearly a quarter of its armor to air attacks, and frontline units had suffered even heavier losses. Moreover, airpower had completely disrupted Iraqi logistics and immobilized the Iraqi army. Aircraft operating around the clock crushed the one attempt by the Iraqis to launch a large-scale operation—the two-division thrust southward that barely got over the Saudi border at the town of Khafji. Although ground action necessarily consummated the final victory for coalition forces, airpower had made the final assault as effortless as a wartime operation can be.

The Persian Gulf War has an importance that goes beyond its immediate (and considerable) effects on politics there. If the claims of airpower advocates are correct, the United States has acquired a military edge over conventional opponents comparable to that exercised in 1898 by the soldiers of Lord Kitchener against the sword-wielding dervishes of the Sudan. The way would lie open to a reorientation of the defense budget toward an air-dominated force structure.[4] Indeed, if airpower performed as spectacularly as first appeared in the Persian Gulf, the way to an American-policed world order might look remarkably smooth. Was, then, the Persian Gulf War a major departure in the history of warfare, and does it point the way to unshakable American military preeminence?

TOOLS OF WAR

The war saw the first extensive use of some new technologies. The F-117 stealth fighter penetrated the Iraqi radar system safely and secretly. The Joint Surveillance Target Attack Radar System, still undergoing testing, detected Iraqi trucks and tanks along highways in Kuwait, and an array of satellites provided unparalleled support to military commanders for intelligence gathering, mapmaking, communication, navigation, meteorology, and missile-launch detection. Still, the bulk of the work came from much older systems and mundane technologies such as air refueling (which was required for three-fifths of all combat missions). Most of the weapons used in the Persian Gulf dated back two decades or more. The airframes of air force B-52 and navy A-6 bombers had seen at least twenty years of active service, although they employed newer electronics. Guided bombs first appeared in the Vietnam War, when American aircraft dropped 4,000 or so on the Vietnamese communists. Even modern, first-line aircraft such as the F-16 have been in use for almost a decade. The "military-technical revolution" sparkled in the new systems, but it drew as much on considerably more mature technologies.

The most profound change in military technology, however, was the vast increase in usable and communicable information. This war saw, for example, the first combat use of the Global Positioning System (GPS), which allows units to locate their position in three dimensions by a mere press of a button. (The Gulf War was the last war in which only one side will have this knowledge. The technology for tapping into the GPS is widespread, easy to use and relatively low cost. And even if American operators were to attempt limiting access by degrading the GPS satellite signals, a clever enemy could largely circumvent such spoofing.) Space-based information-gathering systems also churn out vast quantities of information, and even a Third World country, for example, can tap into international weather satellites or buy militarily useful commercial imagery from the

French satellite imaging system, commonly known as SPOT.

Conventional warfare depends increasingly on the skillful manipulation of electronically transmitted information. The advantage goes overwhelmingly to combatants who can bring together information from many sources, updating old databases (e.g., removing from the target list a radar station already destroyed) and acting on perishable information. Countries such as the United States or, to a lesser extent, Israel have enormous and growing advantages in these areas. In the future, the struggle for information may take the place that the contest for geographic position took in the past. But the information explosion does not mean, as a casual observer might think, that war will become more transparent to those who conduct it. Clausewitz's "fog of war" may now descend on the battlefield not so much from a paucity of good information as from a plethora of half-knowledge. A fog it remains, however, and it lay heavily over the Persian Gulf War.

Any editor knows that the advent of the personal computer and facsimile machine has prompted authors to fiddle with articles constantly and to submit them at the very last moment. Similarly, the flood of combat information prompts commanders to change targets or tactics at the last moment. In the Gulf War commanders changed one-fifth of all missions during the few hours between the time staffs printed the centralized air tasking order (ATO) and the time aircraft took off. They made many more changes before the ATO was officially issued and still more after aircraft had left their bases. Sometimes these decisions made sense; other times they did not. In all cases they created great uncertainty among the pilots flying the missions.

Despite the wisdom of proverbs, pictures sometimes lie, or at least deceive. Coalition air planners in Riyadh tried to do their own bomb damage assessment by looking at videotape footage of laser-guided bomb strikes. Lacking time (and, in some cases, experience in photo interpretation), they sometimes misinterpreted what they saw—mistaking an exploding fuel truck or decoy for a mobile missile launcher, for example, or thinking that a bomb bursting on a concrete roof meant that the contents of the building had been destroyed. The short decision times created by modern weapons can also force quick decisions on the basis of electronically gathered information whose ambiguity may not be readily apparent. The shooting down of an Iranian airliner in 1988 by an American naval cruiser is a case in point. Time pressure created by an abundance of data breeds longer-term problems as well. The constant pressure of the data stream, together with the growth of nighttime operations, means that leaders try to keep on top of events at the cost of sleep and acuity.

Combat information increasingly takes the form of abstract representations of reality compiled from multiple sources. It becomes harder to discriminate between different types of information when a distant, anonymous expert or even a machine has done the sifting. Since the Vietnam War, American generals have decried civilian micromanagement of military operations, an indictment only partly warranted but accepted uncritically by politicians as well as soldiers. Today, however, the danger of *military* micromanagement looms much larger. A general in Washington, an admiral in a command ship, or a theater commander in rear headquarters may have access to almost the same information as a forward commander, and in some cases more. Those distant commanders will often succumb to the temptation to manipulate individual units in combat accordingly.

Dependence on vast quantities of electronic information, of course, poses certain risks. During the war, pilots complained of having to fly missions without the kind of target graphics they had used in training. In the future, soldiers may become overly dependent on detailed, well-presented, and accurate information that simply may not exist in wartime. And as the verisimilitude of computer simulators and war games increases, future warriors may paradoxically find themselves all the more at a loss when the real world differs sharply from a familiar cyberworld.

Furthermore, the more sophisticated and expensive the information-gathering system, the greater the premium opponents will put on disabling it with anything from electronic attack to homing missiles. The payoff for shooting down a state-of-the-art radar surveillance aircraft, for example, will surely attract intense efforts to do so. The Persian Gulf War also demonstrated a trend toward what one might call the *speciation*—that is, the evolution of distinct families—of munitions. The new munitions can, in theory and often in practice, achieve effects unimaginable with the conventional, high-explosive bomb. Antiradiation missiles, for example, not only destroyed Iraqi radars, but intimidated air defense crews from turning them on in the first place. Specially tipped laser-guided bombs punctured hardened aircraft shelters immune to regular high explosives.

But as air-delivered munitions have become increasingly specialized in their effects, they have become susceptible to unintentional misuse. Air campaign planners expected extremely high kill rates against Iraqi armor, for example, on the basis of the use of a scatterable mine, CBU-89. But the projected lethality of CBU-89 relied on calculations made for a war in Europe, fought against Soviet tank armies on the move. Against static, dug-in Iraqi tanks, CBU-89 had much less to offer. The speciation of munitions brings unusual capabilities, but it also poses the risk of creating forces so specialized that they lack flexibility, and weapons so expensive that commanders will have only slender inventories to use when a war starts. Moreover, "dumb" (or at least relatively unintelligent) weapons will keep a place. Massive raids by B-52s raining down conventional bombs helped crush the morale of Iraqi soldiers and smash the large military-industrial facilities that figured so prominently in Saddam Hussein's aspirations for power.

WAR AND ORGANIZATION

The successes of the air campaign in the gulf rested almost as much on organizational innovations as on technology. To speak of a revolution in warfare as a purely technological affair is to miss half the significance of the war. In the Gulf War, for example, Lieutenant General Charles Horner, the commander of CENTAF (the air force component of U.S. Central Command), also controlled in some measure the airplanes of all the services, as well as helicopters flying above 500 feet and navy Tomahawk cruise missiles. In this respect he embodied a doctrine dear to airmen for half a century: "Control of available airpower must be centralized and command must be exercised through the air force commander if this inherent flexibility and ability to deliver a decisive blow are to be fully exploited."[5] "Centralized planning, decentralized execution" remains a catchphrase of air force doctrine, much as "don't divide the fleet" preoccupied American naval strategists in earlier times.

In practice, though, Horner's authority had its limits. The navy controlled maritime air operations, the marines determined the assignments of their short take-off and landing aircraft plus at least half of their fighter-bombers, while the allies exercised discretion regarding which targets they would attack. Special operations forces—which in effect constitute a fifth armed service—continued to struggle for control of their own air operations.

Horner, directing 1,800 combat aircraft, had a staggering fleet at his command. Nonetheless, even his gently wielded centralized control elicited suspicion and hostility from officers in other services who feared an air force attempt to dominate all aerial warfare. Grudgingly conceding the necessity of a single command center, they argued that in theory it could dilute the synergy of, for example, marine air and ground forces, and that in practice it proved cumbersome and slow.

The centralized control of airpower made for a much more coherent campaign than would otherwise have occurred. But, as officers from the other three services bitterly observed, the centralized control rested overwhelmingly in the hands of air force officers. Although the core planning staff, the so-called Black Hole, included representatives from the navy, army, and Marine Corps, as well as the British and Saudi air forces, its membership came predominantly from the air force. In theory a joint targeting board should have selected targets; in practice it did very little. Furthermore, much of the inspiration for the Black Hole's targeting decisions came from an air force staff in the Pentagon, an organization known as Checkmate led by Colonel John Warden, a fervent believer in airpower.

Thus an air force staff (nominally under Joint Staff auspices) dominated the flow of targeting information and proposals to the theater. This certainly violated the intent if not the letter of a command system that in theory excluded the service staffs from operational activity. But in fact this arrangement proved fortuitous because the air staff could tap a far wider range of expertise than could General Norman Schwarzkopf's understaffed and overworked air force staff in Riyadh, which had to cope first with the task of deploying a vast force to the Persian Gulf and then with the myriad chores of daily flight activity and defensive planning. Furthermore, air force dominance in both Washington and Riyadh meant that the plan was conceptually consistent. Normal procedures, which give each service an equal voice in the name of cooperative participation, would not have done nearly so well.

The procedurally orthodox abhor the notion of Washington service staffs feeding operational suggestions to a theater staff. Such a practice subverts the idea—enshrined in the Goldwater-Nichols Act of 1986—of theater commanders as semiautonomous warlords who take only the broadest strategic direction from Washington. But American defense planners should look at what happened and ask whether these improvisations do not point the way to greater effectiveness. After several decades of insisting that the word "service" means "parochial," military reformers might ponder the individual merits of the services, each of which can pool a great deal of operational expertise along with a common worldview and an esprit de corps difficult to find among a mélange of officers.

The abundance of reliable and secure voice, data, and facsimile communications to (and within) the theater transformed command and control. Communications technology subverted hierarchies and rendered abundant exchanges between the theater and the United States both inevitable and desirable. During the Persian Gulf War, staffs in Colorado relayed warnings of Scud launches to Riyadh and Tel Aviv, and the now-defunct Tactical Air Command near Norfolk, Virginia, managed CENTAF logistical accounts. Watching CNN and using other sources of instantaneous news, the chairman of the Joint Chiefs of Staff (and, to only a slightly smaller degree, his civilian superiors) monitored the day-to-day activities of U.S. Central Command's (CENTCOM's) forces. The new technologies threaten age-old principles such as unity of command and delegation of authority. Those pieces of military folk wisdom have so much authority that they will persist in peacetime even if they must disappear in war. A new concept of high command, one that acknowledges that technology inevitably diffuses authority, will have to take root.

Information gathering and processing technology can help but not solve the problem of bomb damage assessment. In many cases, commanders sent out sorties uncertain about the degree of damage a target had already received. Part of the problem stemmed from excessive reliance on intelligence derived from satellites rather than locally controlled reconnaissance aircraft. The theater intelligence staff was small in number and had little experience in tasking the array of satellites at its disposal. There remained, moreover, the sheer difficulty of knowing what damage has been done. From an overhead photograph, for example, it may prove difficult to figure out whether a small black hole on top of a hardened aircraft shelter indicates a hit by a dud bomb, an explosion in the thick, rubble-filled space between the shelter's inner and outer walls, an explosion within the shelter, or an artful paint job by Iraqi camouflage experts. And unless reconnaissance units can keep targets under near-constant surveillance from many angles and with different kinds of sensors, intelligence analysts may not know which projectile did what kind of damage. Finally, functional damage may differ sharply from physical damage. Air force planners desired the first, hoping, for example, that a few hits on a command post would discourage the Iraqis from using it, even if according to normal measures of damage (which depend mainly on engineering criteria) the facility had not received a mortal blow. Not surprisingly, they became increasingly frustrated with intelligence reports that paid more attention to physical than functional damage.

The problem of bomb-damage assessment means that the fog of war will persist, although intelligence services will work to develop ever more sophisticated means of interpreting imagery and cross-checking damage through different sources of information. These individual uncertainties can add up to much higher aggregate levels of confusion. Hard as it may be to figure out what a particular *target* consists of and how to strike it, figuring out a *target system*—for example, how destruction of one microwave relay affects an entire telephone network—is even more difficult. It is depressing to recall that the United States began the war with two known Iraqi nuclear facilities on its target list, that it added six during the conflict, and that another dozen were uncovered by U.N. inspectors only after the war. Furthermore, it appeared that the Iraqis had vitiated the effects of bombing by stripping these buildings of equipment and materials used in the nuclear program. This, too, was not known until after the war.

Although some aircraft, such as the F-117, had excellent videotape recorders, most could not take pictures of where their bombs or missiles had landed. Nor did the coalition have nearly enough unmanned aircraft or manned reconnaissance aircraft to do a proper job, given the magnitude of the effort. These shortfalls revealed an institutional failure before the war to accept the notion that knowing what a bomb has done is almost as important as delivering it. In future conflicts, where commanders might have less time or much smaller forces, an inability to track damage to an enemy could prove crippling. Even in retrospect it has proven extremely difficult to decipher the air war's effects. There was no comprehensive survey of the battlefield conducted in the wake of advancing coalition forces, in part because of deficient prewar planning and in part because of CENTCOM's antipathy to visiting study teams. The American armed forces could have done a far more thorough job of recording and analyzing battles as they unfolded, and certainly after they were over.

THE WAR AND AMERICAN INFLUENCE

Reliance on airpower has set the American way of war apart from all others for well over half a century. Other countries might field doughty infantry, canny submariners, or scientific artillerists comparable in skill and numbers to America's. Only the United States, however, has engaged in a single-minded and successful quest for air superiority in every conflict it has fought since World War I. Air warfare remains distinctively American—high-tech, cheap in lives, and (at least in theory) quick. To America's enemies—past, current, and potential—it is the distinctively American form of military intimidation.

Air warfare plays to the machine-mindedness of American civilization. Aircraft can direct massive and accurate destructive force at key points without having to maneuver cumbersome organizations on land or sea. Airpower can indeed overawe opponents, who know quite well that they cannot hope to match or directly counter American strength. On the other hand, these enemies will find indirect responses. The Saddam Husseins of the world have surely learned that they need not take American children hostage to deter bombardment; they can take their own citizens' young with no less effect. When F-117s struck the so-called al-Firdos bunker—a perfectly appropriate military target—on February 13, they apparently killed the wives and children of Iraqi leaders using the facility as a shelter. For the next four days all air operations against Baghdad ceased, and when they resumed, politically motivated controls reduced the number of targets to the barest handful. Mobility, when abetted by camouflage and tight communications security, can also shield a potential opponent from harm. Publicly available evidence does not suggest that air attacks destroyed any Scud missile launchers, for example.

The soldier or marine will surely say to the airpower enthusiast that nothing can substitute for the man with the bayonet. True, but some politically desired effects (elimination of electrical power in Baghdad, for example) required no use of ground forces. And in some cases the United States has proved unwilling to use ground forces to achieve its objective (for example, the overthrow of Saddam). Airpower may not decide all conflicts or achieve all of a country's political objectives, but neither can land power.

All forms of military power seem likely to benefit from the imminent arrival of "nonlethal" or "disabling" technologies, which offer the prospect of war without casualties. But here, perhaps, lies the most dangerous legacy of the Persian Gulf War: the fantasy of near-bloodless uses of force. Set aside, for the moment, the question of so-called nonlethal weapons. No military technology (indeed, no technology at all) works all the time. Inevitably, even the best-aimed laser-guided bomb will lose its fix on a target because of a passing cloud or a steering mechanism failure and hurtle into an orphanage or hospital. As one wise engineer puts it, "The truly fail-proof design is chimerical."[6]

In many cases, so-called nonlethal weapons will prove just the reverse. The occupants of a helicopter crashing to earth after its flight controls have fallen prey to a high-power microwave weapon would take little solace from the knowledge that a nonlethal weapon had sealed their doom. Some of these weapons (blinding lasers for example) may not kill but have exceedingly nasty consequences for their victims. And in the end a disabling weapon works only if it leaves an opponent vulnerable to full-scale, deadly force.

WAR IS CRUELTY

The simple and brutal fact remains that force works by destroying and killing. In the Gulf War the commanding generals ostentatiously, indeed obsessively, abjured Vietnam-style body counts, but that did not diminish the importance of terrifying enemy soldiers through the fear of violent death from tons of ordnance raining down on them. And fear of violent death only comes from the imminent possibility of the real thing. True, in the Gulf War relatively small numbers of Iraqis (perhaps 2,300 civilians and up to 10,000 soldiers) died before the ground war, although others suffered indirectly from the combined effects of air attack and the coalition embargo. That so few died reflects, among other things, the potential of the new technologies and the scrupulous regard for civilian life shown by coalition planners. But the essential ingredient of fear remained constant.

Sometimes fear does not suffice. The objectives of conflicts such as the war with Iraq will frequently mandate killing. The destruction of some 50 percent of the Republican Guard's armor (in roughly equal proportions by air and ground action) made little difference outside the Kuwait theater. The Republican Guard remained at war's end an organized force and, after drawing on ample stocks of weapons in Iraq proper, put down the Kurdish and Shi'ite uprisings. To stop that and to undermine Saddam's regime (which the Bush administration certainly wished to do) would have required killing or wounding the men who constituted the bulwark of the regime. This uncomfortable fact, long known to the Israelis, who have had few scruples about killing German rocket scientists in the past or rogue super-gun designers in more recent years, sits poorly with Americans. When General Michael Dugan, chief of staff of the U.S. Air Force, hinted to journalists in September 1990 that the most effective use of airpower might consist of attacks on Saddam Hussein, his intimate associates, and key members of the Iraqi general staff and Ba'ath Party, he only pointed to the truth, impolitic as his outraged superiors found it.

It appears likely that civilian populations or large portions of them will continue to be the objects of terror. General William Tecumseh Sherman described the grim purpose of his 1864 march through Georgia and South Carolina thus: "My aim then was, to whip the rebels, to humble their pride, to follow them to their inmost recesses, and make them fear and dread us. 'Fear of the Lord is the beginning of wisdom.'" Sherman's troops did not massacre the inhabitants of the South: they merely ruined their private and public possessions, attacking (as a contemporary strategic analyst might antiseptically observe) the region's "economic infrastructure." In many cases today, war means bringing power, particularly airpower, to bear against civil society. Those who hope for too much from airpower desire to return to a mode of warfare reminiscent of the mid–eighteenth century in western Europe—war waged by mercenary armies isolated from society; war with (by modern standards, at any rate) remarkable efforts to insulate civilians from its effects. Sherman, reflecting the character of armed struggle in his century as well as ours, believed that in modern conditions civil society must inevitably become a target.

As leaders attempt to use their civilians as hostages against American airpower this will become ever more true, whether we like it or not. Moreover, throughout the nineteenth and twentieth centuries military power has become increasingly intertwined with civil society. The electric generators that keep a defense ministry's computers running and its radars sweeping the skies also provide energy for hospitals and water purification plants. The bridges indispensable to the movement of military forces support the traffic in food, medicine, and all other elements of modern life for large civilian populations. Sherman faced a similar situation when he besieged Atlanta. "You cannot qualify war in harsher terms than I will," he told the hapless leading citizens of that city. "War is cruelty, and you cannot refine it."

THE USE OF AIRPOWER

American airpower dominated the Persian Gulf War as no other conflict since World War II. Special circumstances helped account for this achievement, but in the end airmen were probably correct in their belief that this war marked a departure. No other nation on Earth has comparable power, nor will any country accumulate anything like it, or even the means to neutralize it, for at least a decade and probably much longer. American airpower has a mystique that it is in the American interest to retain. When presidents use it, they should either hurl it with devastating lethality against a few targets (say, a full-scale meeting of an enemy war cabinet or senior-level military staff) or extensively enough to cause sharp and lasting pain to a military and a society. But both uses of force pose problems. The first type represents, in effect, the use of airpower for assassination, a procedure not without precedent (American pilots stalked and slew Japan's Admiral Isoroku

Yamomoto in 1943.) But it sets troubling precedents and invites primitive but nonetheless effective forms of revenge. The second involves the use of airpower in ways bound to offend many, no matter what pains commanders take to avoid the direct loss of human life. To strike hard, if indirectly, at societies by smashing communication or power networks will invite the kind of wrenching television attention that modern journalists excel at providing.

Still, to use airpower in penny packets is to disregard the importance of a menacing and even mysterious military reputation. "The reputation of power is power," Hobbes wrote, and that applies to military power as well as to other kinds. The sprinkling of air strikes over an enemy will harden him without hurting him and deprive the United States of an intangible strategic asset. American leaders at the end of this century indeed have been vouchsafed with a military instrument of a potency rarely known in the history of war. But glib talk of revolutionary change obscures the organizational impediments to truly radical change in the conduct of war and, worse, its inherent messiness and brutality. In the end, students of airpower will serve the country well by putting the Persian Gulf War in a larger context, one in which the gloomy wisdom of Sherman tempers the brisk enthusiasm of those who see airpower as a shining sword, effortlessly wielded, that can create and preserve a just and peaceful world order.

NOTES

This essay represents the author's opinion solely, and not the views of the U.S. Air Force or any other government agency.

1. Department of Defense, *The Conduct of the Persian Gulf War* (Washington: GPO, 1992), 164; William Perry, "Desert Storm and Deterrence," *Foreign Affairs* (Fall 1991): 66.

2. See his columns in the *New York Times*, 8 February 1991; 14 June, 3 August, and 7 December 1992; and 12 April 1993.

3. See Thomas A. Keaney and Eliot A. Cohen, *Gulf War Air Power Summary Report* (Washington, D.C.: GPO, 1993).

4. Such a possibility seems implicit in Christopher Bowie and others, *The New Calculus: Analyzing Air Power's Changing Role in Joint Theater Campaigns* (Santa Monica, Calif.: RAND), 1993.

5. War Department, *Command and Employment of Air Power Field Manual 100-20* (Washington, D.C.: GPO, 1943), 3–4.

6. Henry Petroski, *To Engineer Is Human: The Role of Failure in Successful Design* (New York: Vintage, 1992), 217.

FORWARD . . . FROM THE SEA

JOHN H. DALTON, JEREMY M. BOORDA, AND CARL E. MUNDY JR.

With the publication of *. . . From the Sea* in September 1992, the U.S. Navy and Marine Corps announced a landmark shift in operational focus and a reordering of coordinated priorities of the naval service. This fundamental shift was a direct result of the changing strategic landscape—away from having to deal with a global maritime threat and toward projecting power and influence across the seas in response to regional challenges.

In the two years since *. . . From the Sea* became our strategic concept, the administration has provided expanded guidance on the role of the military in national defense. A major review of strategy and force requirements resulted in a shift in the Department of Defense's focus to new dangers—chief among which is aggression by regional powers—and the necessity for our military forces to be able to rapidly project decisive military power to protect vital U.S. interests and defend friends and allies. In defining our national strategy for responding to these new dangers, the review emphasized the importance of maintaining forward-deployed naval forces and recognized the impact of peacetime operational tempo on the size of navy and Marine Corps force structure. In addition to recognizing the unique contributions of the navy and Marine Corps in the areas of power projection and forward presence, it restated the need for the navy to support the national strategic objectives through our enduring contributions in strategic deterrence, sea control and maritime supremacy, and strategic sealift.

Forward . . . From the Sea addresses these naval contributions to our national security. Most fundamentally, our naval forces are designed to fight and win wars. Our most recent experiences, however, underscore the premise that the most important role of naval forces in situations short of war is to be

John H. Dalton, Jeremy M. Boorda, and Carl E. Mundy Jr., Forward . . . From the Sea *(Washington, D.C.: Department of the Navy, 1995), 1–10. Public Domain.*

engaged in forward areas, with the objectives of *preventing* conflicts and *controlling* crises.

Naval forces thus are the foundation of peacetime forward presence operations and overseas response to crisis. They contribute heavily during the transitions from crisis to conflict and to ensuring compliance with terms of peace. At the same time, the unique capabilities inherent in naval expeditionary forces have never been in higher demand from U.S. theater commanders—the regional commanders in chief—as evidenced by operations in Somalia, Haiti, Cuba, and Bosnia, as well as our continuing contribution to the enforcement of United Nations sanctions against Iraq.

THE STRATEGIC IMPERATIVE

The vital economic, political, and military interests of the United States are truly global in nature and scope. In many respects these interests are located across broad oceans, and to a great extent they intersect those of current and emergent regional powers. It is in the world's littorals where the naval service, operating from sea bases in international waters, can influence events ashore in support of our interests.

Because we are a maritime nation, our security strategy is necessarily a transoceanic one. Our vital interests—those interests for which the United States is willing to fight—are at the end point of "highways of the seas" or lines of strategic approach that stretch from the United States to the farthest point on the globe. Not surprisingly, these strategic lines and their end points coincide with the places to which we routinely deploy naval expeditionary forces: the Atlantic, Mediterranean, Pacific, Indian Ocean, Red Sea, Persian Gulf, and Caribbean Sea. Reductions in fiscal resources, however, dictate that we must refocus our more limited naval assets on the highest priorities and the most immediate challenges, even within these areas of historic and vital interest to the United States.

Naval forces are particularly well-suited to the entire range of military operations in support of our national strategy. They continue the historic role of naval forces engaged in preventive diplomacy and otherwise supporting our policies overseas. Moreover, forward-deployed naval forces—manned, equipped, and trained for combat—play a significant role in demonstrating both the intention and the capability to join our North Atlantic Treaty Organization (NATO) and other allies, as well as other friendly powers, in defending shared interests. Finally, if deterrence fails during a crisis and conflict erupts, naval forces provide the means for immediate sea-based reaction. This could include forcible entry and providing the protective cover essential to enabling the flow of follow-on forces that will be deployed, supported, and sustained from the continental United States. In short, forward-deployed naval forces will provide the critical operational linkages between peacetime operations and the initial requirements of a developing crisis or major regional contingency.

PEACETIME FORWARD PRESENCE OPERATIONS

Naval forces are an indispensable and exceptional instrument of American foreign policy. From conducting routine port visits to nations and regions that are of special interest, to sustaining larger demonstrations of support to long-standing regional security interests, such as with UNITAS exercises in South America, U.S. naval forces underscore U.S. diplomatic initiatives overseas. Indeed, the critical importance of a credible overseas presence is emphasized in the president's 1994 National Security Strategy: "presence demonstrates our commitment to allies and friends, underwrites regional stability, gains U.S. familiarity with overseas operating environments, promotes combined training among the forces of friendly countries, and provides timely initial response capabilities."

In peacetime U.S. naval forces build "interoperability"—the ability to operate in concert with friendly and allied forces—so that in the future we can easily participate fully as part of a formal multinational response or as part of "ad hoc" coalitions forged to react to short-notice crisis situations. Participation in both NATO Standing Naval Forces and in a variety of exercises with the navies, air forces, and land forces of coalition partners around the Pacific rim, Norwegian Sea, Arabian Gulf, and Mediterranean basin provide solid foundations for sustaining interoperability with our friends and allies.

In addition, the outreach to the former Warsaw Pact countries in the NATO Partnership for Peace program will further build solidarity and interoperability. We have already made solid progress in expanding and intensifying our cooperation with the navies in Eastern Europe with exercises such as BALTOPS 94 and BREEZE 94, which included units from Bulgaria, Estonia, Latvia, Lithuania, Poland, Romania, Russia, and Ukraine. U.S. forward-deployed naval forces have also contributed to humanitarian assistance and disaster-relief efforts—from the Philippines to Bangladesh to Rwanda—with similar, very positive, results.

Although naval presence includes a wide range of forward-deployed navy and Marine Corps units afloat *and* ashore in friendly nations, our basic presence "building blocks" remain aircraft carrier battle groups—with versatile, multipurpose, naval tactical aviation wings—and amphibious ready groups—with special operations-capable marine expeditionary units. These highly flexible naval formations are valued by the theater commanders precisely because they provide the necessary capabilities forward. They are ready and positioned to respond to the wide range of contingencies and are available to participate in allied exercises, which are the bedrock of interoperability.

We have also turned our attention to examining the naval capabilities that could contribute to extending conventional deterrence. In this regard, forward-deployed surface warships—cruisers and destroyers—with theater ballistic missile defense capabilities will play an increasingly important role in discouraging the proliferation of ballistic missiles by extending credible defenses to friendly and allied countries. By maintaining the means to enhance their security and safety, we may reduce the likelihood that some of these nations will develop their own offensive capabilities. Our efforts will thereby slow weapons proliferation and enhance regional stability.

In addition, even as we have shifted our emphasis to forward presence and power projection from sea to land, the navy continues to provide a robust strategic nuclear deterrent by maintaining strategic ballistic missile submarines at sea. As long as it is U.S. policy to ensure an adequate and ready strategic nuclear deterrent, our highly survivable strategic ballistic missile submarines will remain critical to national security.

CRISIS RESPONSE

U.S. naval forces are designed to fight and win wars, as are all elements of our military arsenal. To successfully deter aggressors, we must be capable of responding quickly and successfully in support of U.S. theater commanders. Forces deployed for routine exercises and activities undergirding forward presence are also the forces most likely to be called upon to respond rapidly to an emerging crisis. The potential for escalation dictates that presence forces must be shaped for missions they may encounter. This provides theater commanders with credible crisis-response capabilities in the event normal conditions or outcomes do not turn out as we expect.

Building on normally deployed forces, we can mass, if the situation requires, multiple aircraft carrier battle groups into carrier battle forces, amphibious ready groups with embarked marine expeditionary units, and as needed project our naval expeditionary forces ashore using the afloat maritime pre-positioning force. Such a massing of naval units can be complemented by the deployment of army and air force units to provide a joint force capable of the full range of combat operations that may be required.

A U.S. warship is sovereign U.S. territory, whether in a port of a friendly country or transiting international straits and the high seas. U.S. naval forces, operating from highly mobile "sea bases" in forward areas, are therefore free of the political encumbrances that may inhibit and otherwise limit the scope of land-based operations in forward theaters. The latter consideration is a unique characteristic and advantage of forward-deployed naval forces. In many critical situations, U.S. naval forces alone provide theater commanders with a variety of flexible options—including precise measures to control escalation—to respond quickly and appropriately to

fast-breaking developments at the operational and tactical levels.

Whether surging from adjacent theaters or from continental U.S. deployment bases, naval forces are uniquely positioned, configured, and trained to provide a variety of responses in the event of an unexpected international crisis. Their operational flexibility and responsiveness are a matter of record.

REGIONAL CONFLICT

Naval forces make a critical contribution in a major regional contingency during the transition from crisis to conflict. Forward naval forces deployed for presence and reinforced in response to an emerging crisis can serve as the transition force as land-based forces are brought forward into theater.

Using a building-block approach, U.S. naval forces can be "tailored" with specific capabilities. The resulting naval expeditionary force—conceptually built around fleet operational forces and a forward-deployed marine expeditionary force—can provide a highly flexible force for a wide range of missions, including long-range strike operations and early forcible entry to facilitate or enable the arrival of follow-on forces.

Focusing on the littoral area, navy and Marine Corps forces can seize and defend advanced bases—ports and airfields—to enable the flow of land-based air and ground forces, while providing the necessary command and control for joint and allied forces. The power-projection capabilities of specifically tailored naval expeditionary forces can contribute to blunting an initial attack and, ultimately, ensuring victory. The keys to our enabling mission are effective means *in place* to dominate and exploit littoral battlespace during the earliest phases of hostilities.

Moreover, the unique capabilities inherent in naval tactical aviation operating from our sea bases or expeditionary airfields, as well as the capability to contribute to sustained land combat operations, provide theater commanders with flexibility in the conduct of littoral operations. Throughout the twentieth century, marine air-ground task forces, placed ashore initially as enabling forces, have fought and contributed decisively in every major ground conflict. Similarly, naval tactical aviation has made pivotal contributions when the nation's airpower was needed in combat.

In the event of a future regional conflict, U.S. naval forces will assume critical roles in the protection of vital sealift along the strategic lines of approach to the theater of conflict, including the air and sea ports of debarkation. Our success in a major regional contingency will depend upon the delivery of heavy equipment and the resupply of major ground and air elements engaged forward. Sealift is the key to force sustainment for joint operations, and we are committed to a strong national capability.

JOINT AND COMBINED OPERATIONS

No single military service embodies all of the capabilities needed to respond to every situation and threat. Our national strategy calls for the individual services to operate jointly to ensure both that we can operate successfully in all warfare areas and that we can apply our military power across the spectrum of foreseeable situations—in peace, crisis, regional conflict, and the subsequent restoration of peace.

The enhanced combat power produced by the integration of all supporting arms, which we seek to attain through joint operations, is inherent in naval expeditionary forces. For example, the aircraft carrier battle group integrates and focuses diverse technologies and combat capabilities to ensure the dominance of the air, surface, and subsurface battle space necessary for the prosecution of subsequent campaigns. Further, marine expeditionary forces, employing marine air-ground task force (MAGTF) combined-arms doctrine, are the most versatile expeditionary forces in existence. Established by law to be "forces of combined arms, together with supporting air components," MAGTFs are expeditionary, rapidly expandable air-ground formations, capable of operating from sea bases, ashore, or both, simultaneously. They are the model for the joint air-ground task forces evolving as conflicts grow smaller and the forces available grow fewer.

Naval expeditionary forces have long operated as integral elements of joint forces acting with other joint or allied sea, land, air, and space forces. Just as the complementary capabilities of navy and Marine Corps forces add to our overall strength, combining the capabilities and resources of other services and those of our allies will yield decisive military power.

MAINTAINING OUR NEW DIRECTION

The new direction for the naval service remains focused on our ability to project power from the sea in the critical littoral regions of the world. We remain committed to structuring our naval expeditionary forces so that they are inherently shaped for joint operations, with the emphasis on operations forward from the sea, tailored for national needs. Recent Department of the Navy budget decisions, which

resulted in a real increase in spending on littoral warfare and the means for power projection, are illustrative of the shift in priorities we have undertaken since the publication of . . . *From the Sea*. As we continue to improve our readiness to project power in the littorals, we need to proceed cautiously so as not to jeopardize our readiness for the full spectrum of missions and functions for which we are responsible.

In the two years since . . . *From the Sea* was published, we have expanded on and capitalized upon its traditional expeditionary focus. "Expeditionary" implies a mind-set, a culture, and a commitment to forces that are designed to be deployed forward and to respond swiftly. Our new direction provides the nation naval expeditionary forces shaped for joint operations, tailored for national needs, operating *forward . . . from the sea.*

CONCLUSION

. . . *From the Sea* was the initial step in demonstrating how the navy and Marine Corps responded to the challenges of a new security environment. Our strategy and policies continue to evolve as we learn from our recent experiences and prepare for the new challenges and opportunities of this highly dynamic world. Naval forces have five fundamental and enduring roles in support of the national security strategy: projection of power from sea to land, sea control and maritime supremacy, strategic deterrence, strategic sealift, and forward naval presence. We will continue to carry out these roles to protect vital U.S. global interests, citizens, allies, and friends, wherever they may be at risk.

The Cold War may be over, but the need for American leadership and commensurate military capability endures. Many of our most vital interests remain overseas where the U.S. Navy and the Marine Corps are prepared for new challenges—*forward* deployed, *ready* for combat, and *engaged* to preserve the peace.

THE END OF NAVAL STRATEGY

JAN S. BREEMER

Two kinds of revolutionary change have historically altered the way navies think about their functions. The first, change "from the bottom up," is triggered by technological innovation, for example, the airplane or the submarine. The response to tech-

nological change is at first confined to minor doctrinal adjustments in an effort to preserve the familiar doctrinal framework. As evidence accumulates that the new weapons do not abide by the old rules and that trying to make them fit is, in fact, counter-

This essay has been edited and is reprinted from Strategic Review 22 (Spring 1994): 40–53, *by permission of the United States Strategic Institute.*

productive, strategic concepts and doctrine eventually undergo revolutionary change.

The second and less common revolutionary change follows a reverse course. The catalyst for this "top-down" revolution often is a systemic shift in the international security environment. Such a shift may be the result of the rise or fall of an opponent capable of challenging the continued relevance of the existing naval strategic planning framework. If the gap between the new environment and the older naval strategic culture proves too wide to bridge by means of adjustments in force levels and force composition alone, the strategic culture must be changed in order to accommodate the environment.

The U.S. Navy last experienced a top-down revolution one century ago when it discarded coastal defense and commerce raiding in favor of Mahan's vision of naval power as the struggle for command of the sea by battlefleets.[1] That vision, central to the navy's professional culture since the birth of the "new navy," is challenged today by the end of the Cold War and the demise of the Soviet naval menace. The navy's recent white paper, *From the Sea,* is the service's response to this challenge; it gives notice that the service is about to go through the most fundamental top-down revolution since the birth of the new navy one hundred years ago. As the navy prepares to shift its strategic and doctrinal essence away from planning for war at sea toward support for battle on land, it must come to grips with the revolutionary implications of this change for its traditional self-image as the sole, autonomous provider of oceanic security.

As part of this shift, the naval profession will need to radically reinterpret its role in national security. This essay proposes that as part of this reidentification the navy adopt a narrow interpretation of its responsibilities for warfare on the littoral landmass and that it restructure its forces accordingly.

NAVAL POWER FROM THE SEA: ONCE AGAIN

In 1954 Samuel Huntington laid out the U.S. Navy's new "transoceanic" strategy for fighting the Cold War.[2] This "New Naval Doctrine," he wrote, recognized the "obvious fact that international power is now distributed not among a number of basically naval powers but rather between one nation and its allies which dominate the land masses of the globe and another nation and its allies which monopolize the world's oceans."[3] According to the author, the hostility between Western maritime power and Soviet continental predominance spelled the end of the Mahanian concept of seapower as the struggle between great fleets for command of the oceans. Instead, now that American naval power faced a continental rival without a fleet to speak of, it would fight its future battles away from the sea and on and over the opponent's "littoral" land zone.[4]

Huntington also wrote that this transition had not come easily but only after an acute identity crisis that went to the "depths of the Navy's being."[5] That crisis centered on the question of what the world's most powerful fleet, armed with the Mahanian philosophy of the "decisive battle," was to do when it had no seagoing rival on the horizon, and when a strategic air force armed with nuclear bombs seemed to have "absolutely" replaced it as the nation's first line of defense. Huntington concluded that the navy's determination to solve the crisis by looking beyond Mahan and switching its doctrinal focus away from blue water and toward the Eurasian landmass, proved its "flexibility and vigor" in adapting to new circumstances.

Forty years later, the navy's ability to adapt to revolutionary change is again being tested.[6] This revolution will compel the navy to revise completely the way it has traditionally identified itself as a provider of national defense and international security. At the center of this revolution will be the question of how an organization whose professional norms, values, and operating routines have customarily been identified with the Mahanian view of naval power can accommodate itself to a post–Cold War security environment in which the struggle for "command of the sea" will no longer be its *essential* charge.[7]

NAVIES AND "BOTTOM-UP" CHANGE

Over the past 150 years or so, the face of naval power has been repeatedly and radically transformed by dramatic material changes.[8] Between 1860 and 1890, steam propulsion, iron and steel construction, and scientific gunnery turned fleets from collections of wooden sailing vessels with firepower not much different from Elizabethan days into "fighting machines" with unheard of destructive power.[9] Even before the naval profession had fully grasped the strategic and doctrinal implications of the new machine-age fleets, the submarine and the airplane unleashed a second material revolution. Next came the most controversial revolution of all, the impact of nuclear weapons on the character of naval power.[10]

Although very different in kind, these revolutions had one thing in common: they were *technological* transformations that, for a time at least, did not seem to threaten the blue-water culture that dominated the naval profession. Autopropulsion, submarines, aircraft, and, albeit with greater difficulty, even the atomic bomb, could be "piggy-backed" to the customary vision of naval warfare as merely new and better ways for doing the old task of securing command of the sea.[11]

Attempts to graft large-scale technological change onto "old thinking" can only be a temporary expedient; new weapons demand their own operational culture and, along the way, ultimately revolutionize the very thinking about naval power. And it is in the "explosion of ideas," of course, not in the refinement of techniques or tactics, that the true revolutionary significance of a new weapon must be found.[12] When the dust has settled, the outcome may be a new doctrine, the emergence of new war-making "principles," or even, in the case of the atomic bomb, the rejection of the Clausewitzian concept of war as the pursuit of politics by other means.[13] Cultural change that has its roots in technological innovation takes place *from the bottom up*.[14]

REVOLUTIONARY TECHNOLOGICAL CHANGE

Since the mid–nineteenth century, revolutionary changes from the bottom up have thoroughly transformed our concept of naval power, of how it works, and how it relates to other forms of military force. Thus, the machine-age fleets that were created in the Victorian era and whose controllability Mahan thought portended a much closer match between the (offensive) principles and the practice of war at sea, actually produced the opposite effect. The prospect of a truly annihilating sea battle made possible by modern gunnery also brought the sobering thought that a victory might well be of Pyrrhic proportions. The upshot for the naval strategy of World War I was that rather than seeking to defeat the enemy in compliance with the "sounder military understanding of a navy," [15] both the British and the Germans turned their "decisive battle" forces into fleets-in-being that waited for the other side to make a mistake that would place its forces at a disadvantage.[16]

The submarine and the airplane revolutionized thinking about seapower even more profoundly; both inventions vastly complicated the command-of-the-sea concept. In the case of the submarine, World War I ended the notion that command of the sea could be gained through victory in one or more decisive battles between surface fleets. The submarine also undermined the view of naval warfare as one or a series of battles between massed fleets. This image was necessarily part and parcel of a war-fighting practice that insisted on the importance of concentration of forces. The submarine denied this principle; it fought alone and had to be defeated alone. This fact, plus the relative ease with which a submarine adversary could replace its losses, meant that the struggle for sea control would henceforth be a *campaign of exhaustion*.

The airplane further diluted the ship's monopoly on command of the sea; indeed, World War II demonstrated that just as the success of armies on land had come to depend on air superiority, so fleets could no longer aspire to command the sea without commanding the air. Even more important in the long run, aircraft (and later missiles) obliterated the dividing line that had always separated land warfare from sea warfare, and armies from navies. A few years before the Great War, Winston Churchill, then first lord of the admiralty, had sought to assure the Germans that, no matter how powerful the Royal Navy, it could not endanger a single continental hamlet.[17] He was correct then—or at least almost so. He could have added that the obverse was true as well: as long as armies were confined to terra firma not even the Kaiser's divisions could threaten the island kingdom's safety or its fleet. The airplane terminated this historical truism in World War II as naval aviation repeatedly struck inland, and land-based aviation became the fleet's most dangerous enemy. A corollary implication was that technology had conspired to create the *integrated* theater of war. In the past, the geography of warfare was necessarily divided between land and sea theaters; the only place the two intermingled was on the beach (hence the centuries-long controversy between armies and navies over who should be responsible for its defense), which usually occurred only momentarily during an amphibious landing. Airpower *routinized* this crossover between the land and the sea.

Perhaps the most revolutionary consequence of the airplane for seapower was that by the time of World War II, it had broken the latter's historical monopoly on sea control. Land-based airpower proved not only its "negative" ability to deny the opponent the use of the seas but also the "positive" wherewithal to secure and keep the sea.[18] To be sure, there was another side to this coin as well. By embracing the airplane as its own, naval forces possessed, for the first time in history, the means to strike against land forces.[19] Yet this development also contributed to the dilution of the old naval strategic concept that held that fleets existed solely to fight other fleets. In any case, the ability to strike inland gave navies merely a *competitive* capability; it was not clear that this compensated for the loss of the erstwhile *unique* ability to secure the seas.

Little remains to be said about the impact of nuclear weapons on naval strategic thought. It did not require the limited war theorists of the late 1950s to persuade naval officers that atomic warfare would not be business as usual. If the naval planners of World War I were deterred from all-out battle by the *cost* of victory, their nuclear successors were stymied by its apparent *impossibility*.

"FROM THE TOP DOWN"

While navies, along with other military forces, may stand on the brink of a new revolution from the bottom up, a more fundamental challenge for naval power is the impending top-down revolution of naval roles and missions as articulated in *From the Sea*. This revolution is more fundamental because it *overturns the very foundation of our modern concept of naval power and strategy*, that is to say, its *essential* preoccupation with command of the sea. Unlike the technology-induced changes of the past, this top-down revolution is dictated by the necessity for naval power to adapt to systemic changes in the international security environment. It calls for "a fundamental shift away from open-ocean war fighting *on* the sea toward joint operations conducted *from* the sea."[20]

Top-down revolutions that start with wholesale changes in military roles, doctrines, and strategic concepts are rare.[21] The dynamics of the navy's conversion to a blue-water fleet one century ago were varied, but one notable feature was the expectation that the United States, along with the rest of the globe, was about to enter into a new "world order" of heightened competition very likely to embroil America in foreign conflicts.[22] The other top-down revolution has already been mentioned: the post–World War II period during which there was no prospective oceanic opponent. The fleet appeared ready to step back from its Mahanian lineage and become "a navy oriented away from the oceans and towards the land masses on their far side."[23] But the doctrinal revolution that Huntington wrote about in 1954 never quite came to fruition. True, for a while nuclear "power projection" took pride of place alongside sea control during the era of "massive retaliation." However, two events ensured that sea control would remain "*the* fundamental function of the U.S. Navy," and that therefore naval power projection, though always available to a land campaign on a "collateral" basis, would continue to serve the ends of sea control first.[24]

The first event was the emergence of the Soviet submarine fleet. Contrary to Huntington's assertion, the size of this force and apparent intent to duplicate the onslaught of the U-boats of World War II, made antisubmarine warfare (ASW) a primary *sea control* mission.[25] Next came the emergence in the 1960s of a "real" Soviet fleet, complete with cruisers and aircraft carriers. For many Western observers this development signaled that traditional naval strategy had lost none of its relevance after all. Former U.S. Navy Secretary John Lehman thought so. Mahan's views, he wrote in 1981, "are being followed by the Soviet Union today," resulting in a blue-water navy "patently Mahanian in design."[26]

There is irony in the fact that the progeny of Lehman's reborn naval strategy, the U.S. Navy's "Maritime Strategy," was rendered null and void by events in Eastern Europe and the Soviet Union at the very moment the strategy's goal of a "600-ship navy" was about to be reached. Made public by the navy and Marine Corps in 1986, the Maritime Strategy will probably be remembered as the high-water mark of "blue-water" naval thinking in the postwar era.[27] When the Maritime Strategy's successor, *From the Sea*, was unveiled six years later, the 600-ship fleet target had already been reduced to 451, and further reductions by 1999 are forthcoming as part of the Clinton administration's *Bottom-Up Review.*[28] This kind of force cutting alone is more than sufficient grounds for a dramatic revision of the way the navy has done business for the past forty-five years. The real catalyst for change, however, rests with the revolutionary shift in the navy's strategic culture embedded in *From the Sea.*

FROM THE SEA

The document's message is short and straightforward. It argues that given the demise of the Soviet threat and therefore that of the specter of a far-ranging campaign for control of the transatlantic sea lines of communications, classic "sea control" need no longer be the navy's first priority. In the words of then Acting Navy Secretary Sean O'Keefe, sea control has become "in some ways—a given" that the United States has "covered at this point."[29] It followed, reported the commander in chief of the newly established U.S. Atlantic Command, that the navy was now "permitted . . . to have a wider field of view and operational thought."[30] The focal point of this "wider field of view," says *From the Sea,* will be the so-called littoral, or near-land areas of the world oceans. Specifically, the document announces that the navy will be reshaped into an instrument of crisis management and an "enabling" force on behalf of other military forces operating on the landward side of the littoral.

Using navies for purposes other than outright war at sea is not a novel development. On the contrary, sea battles and oceanic campaigns have historically been the exception, so that other than preparing for the next "big" war, fleets have always spent most of their useful service life on "littoral" duties—showing the flag, suppressing piracy, intervening in local crises, and so on. This was precisely the role of the Royal Navy for nearly one century after the defeat of Napoleon, and again after the two world wars.[31] The same has been true for the U.S. Navy since World War II.[32] Although its strategic concept, training, and tactical routines, and weapons procurement were guided throughout by the scenario of a war at sea with the Soviet Union, its practical business has been to project its "moral effect" and shape events in the Third World.[33] The navy has been more than happy to highlight its value as a naval-diplomatic and "crisis-response" tool, but few of its officers took seriously the occasional suggestion that "presence" be elevated to an official function alongside sea control and that this be reflected in the makeup of the fleet.[34]

Given that intervention in local crises and conflicts has been the bread and butter of the navies of the major powers all along, it may be concluded that there is nothing unique or revolutionary about *From the Sea.* Nothing can be further from the truth. The document is without precedent in that *it explicitly defines littoral operations to contain crises or support land forces in "small" wars as the primary task for navies in the foreseeable future.* Never before has a major navy relegated sea control and the preparation for the next "big" war at sea to a secondary consideration. Even at the height of *Pax Britannica,* when successive generations of Royal Navy officers had never seen a sea fight, spending their careers instead "policing" the empire (oftentimes fighting native uprisings on *land*), the latter was never thought to be more than a passing collateral duty. Throughout this period, ships were built and crews trained for "fleet action."[35] The same has been true for the principal blue-water fleets after both world wars.

The reasons for this consistent mismatch between fleet theory and fleet practice were sound enough. During the era of *Pax Britannica,* Great Britain's Victorian navy had to keep a wary eye on France, its traditional rival across the channel, and, to a lesser extent, the navies of Russia and the United States. After World War I, it took the Washington Naval Treaty of 1922 to break up the triangle of mutual suspicion over fleet-building policies that had developed among the United States, Great Britain, and Japan.[36] And after World War II an increasingly powerful Soviet navy cast its shadow over the U.S. Navy's policing activities. It must be recalled that the crises and conflicts of the past forty years usually had Cold War overtones, so that offsetting demonstrations of U.S. and Soviet naval power always carried the risk of escalation to full-scale war.[37]

Circumstances are entirely different today: for the first time in centuries, the world's largest fleet is without an actual or foreseeable competitor on the high sea. It can therefore focus its energies on "operations other than war at sea" without having to look over its shoulder for the next blue-water challenge.[38] True, there still exists a very large Russian navy that, outwardly at least, still has all the material qualifications to endanger the seas. Nevertheless, despite the cautionary note that "intentions can change overnight," even the navy's intelligence director acknowledged in 1992 that the main preoccupation of the former Soviet fleet was to "survive." With the exception of the ballistic missile submarines, its mission is no longer offensive and will not become so for at least twenty years.[39] To paraphrase Admiral Miller, an ocean without challengers has forced the U.S. Navy to confront a "big change in operational culture."[40]

THE END OF NAVAL STRATEGY

From the Sea writes the epitaph to the command of the sea "system" that has dominated naval thought since the late sixteenth century when, thanks to the growth of seaborne commerce and the development of warships capable of keeping the sea, "true naval war" replaced "cross-ravaging" as the main purpose of military power at sea.[41] For the next three hundred years the fleets of the principal maritime powers fought by the unwritten rule that "nothing can be done of consequence in naval war till one side secures the control of the water area."[42] The rule was codified at the turn of this century in the great navalist writings of Corbett, Colomb, and Mahan.[43] Their body of writings also spelled out how navies went about securing command of the sea, that is, *naval strategy.*[44]

Naval strategy is concerned, by definition, with the maneuvering of naval forces in order to win (or deny) command of the sea.[45] There have been very few sea wars in which the opposing strategies were purely naval and therefore command of the sea the sole issue.[46] In most conflicts with a large seagoing dimension, naval strategy and the struggle for command have been subordinated to a larger *maritime* strategy.[47] The distinction between "naval" and "maritime" strategy and the role of navies in both is often overlooked, but it is an important one. Corbett explained the relationship between the three in 1911: maritime strategy, he wrote, pertained to the "principles which govern a war in which the sea is a substantial factor." This relationship is particularly important today. Calling it the "problem of coordination," Corbett stressed that the foremost principle of *maritime strategy* was "to determine the mutual relations of your army and navy in a plan of war."[48] In today's jargon this is called "jointness."

Corbett went on to explain that naval strategy was a subset of maritime strategy: it was concerned with how the fleet could best carry out the seagoing portion of the overarching maritime strategy. Naval tasks might include protection against invasion, blockading the enemy's ports, or projecting the army against enemy territory.[49] But no matter how varied the tasks, success or failure rested on a common prerequisite that was at the core of what Corbett called the "theory of naval war," namely, to secure and exercise command of the sea.[50] There was nothing mysterious about this; command of the sea meant nothing more than control of the sea lines of communications, whether for military or commercial purposes.[51]

The implications were far-reaching, however. For one, wrote Corbett, the principles of naval strategy "should be found giving shape not only to strategy and tactics, but also to material, whatever methods and means of naval warfare may be in use at any given time."[52] In other words, if command of the sea is the fleet's foremost, indeed sole, naval (as opposed to maritime) strategic purpose, it follows that the capabilities required to command the sea will determine fleet size and structure, strategic orientation and tactical routines, and even ship and weapon characteristics. For another, since naval strategy was solely concerned with the contest for control of the maritime communications, it followed that once the latter was resolved, *"pure naval strategy comes to an end"*[53] (emphasis added). It was not that the successful fleet went out of business, but rather that winning (and keeping) command of the sea meant that the victorious fleet had fulfilled its naval purpose, had ceased to fight pure naval war, and could now turn all its attention to what Mahan called the "ulterior objects" of the nation's broader maritime (or continental) strategy. This is precisely where the U.S. Navy finds itself today and why *From the Sea* lays such great stress on the need for the navy to satisfy the requirements of *national,* as opposed to naval, strategy.

FROM SEA CONTROL TO LAND CONTROL

The history of sea warfare is full of instances in which fleets were used to fight a maritime strategy sans naval strategy. To reiterate: naval strategy is possible only if there is an opponent who is able and willing to contest the command of the sea; if there is not, the fleet is directly subordinate to the necessities of war on land. The Crimean War is an auspicious example. Shortly after war broke out in 1854, the Russians chose not to use their considerable fleet to oppose a threatened Anglo-French invasion at sea, but to turn their ships instead into floating coastal defense batteries. The Crimean peninsula was the center of hostilities, but the same policy was carried out in the Baltic and even in far-away Petropavlovsk on the Pacific coast.[54] The result was allied command of the sea by default, which meant that the question before the naval commanders was not how to defeat the Russian fleet, but how to best influence events on land from the sea.

The use of a fleet to support land operations was known at the time of the Crimean war as a "conjunct" operation. One century later the term "combined operation" had come into vogue. Today's military planners speak of "joint" warfare. Jointness became the legislated modus operandi for the American military with the passage of the Goldwater-Nichols Department of Defense Act of 1986.[55] The reasons for its passage were perceived inefficiencies in the existing, service-focused command structure. The end of classic naval strategy reinforces the strategic logic of jointness. *From the Sea* acknowledges that the new strategic order—and therefore the service's institutional health—dictates that the navy become a full-time player in land warfare. This is vastly different from naval power's conjunct or combined role in the past. Rather than a collateral and temporary association, a diversion, if you will, from the fleet's primary purpose *on* the sea. Jointness signifies a reverse order of priorities; it connotes *fusion* of effort in place of ad hoc arrangements, and, most important, it subordinates all seagoing naval operations directly to events on land.

The navy's new "battlespace" concept highlights the new primacy of land warfare in fleet operations. Battlespace is defined as the sea, air, and land areas that the navy must dominate in order to conduct operations ashore; it encompasses the "area from the open ocean to the shore which must be controlled to support operations ashore," as well as the "area inland from shore that can be supported and defended directly from the sea."[56] What is important here is the pivotal role of operations on *land:* battlespace dominance matters for the ability of naval power to control military events *ashore.* Superficially, this may not sound terribly revolutionary; but it represents a 180-degree reversal from the classic relationship between sea control and naval power projection. In the past, the navy valued the ability to project power ashore primarily for its contribution to sea control—not to control operations on land. Admiral Holloway could therefore report, in 1977, that the "capability to project power was developed in naval forces largely as an adjunct to strategic sea control."[57] The battlespace concept overturns this hierarchy—battlespace dominance and power projection are now subordinate to naval (and joint!) *land control!*

HOW MUCH LAND CONTROL?

During the "golden age" of navalism, when Mahan, Corbett, and others wrote their great works, naval thinkers carried on an endless debate over the exact meaning of "command of the sea." The question was whether a fleet should be strong enough to win "absolute" command, or whether it merely needed to be capable of establishing control at times and places as dictated by the nation's "ulterior objects" at the time. The answer was important, for on it depended how large (and expensive) a fleet should be built. The navy's new strategic concept of land control poses a somewhat similar question—namely, *how much* land control should be the aim of warfare from the sea? Should it be sufficient to underwrite the navy and Marine Corps' traditional, over-the-beach "enabling" role in order to "lay the doormat" for follow-on heavy air force and army units; or should it include the wherewithal to conduct operations throughout the land theater of action, especially "deep strikes" by carrier aviation?[58] The signals so far are mixed.

Part of the problem has to do with the ambiguous definition of the word "littoral."[59] Many authorities, notably the former chairman of the Joint Chiefs of Staff, have identified it with "coastal."[60] When still in office, Acting Navy Secretary O'Keefe seemed to agree, when he commented in an interview that *From the Sea* "focuses on the kinds of scenarios that call for shorter-range strike capabilities . . . pointed more toward close-air support missions."[61] The document itself, on the other hand, does not quite say that. The initial publication gave no details on how far inland the navy's battlespace might reach, other than to say that it "expands and contracts and has limits."[62] A later (undated) version of the document is more explicit, however. It includes a map of the world that shows the "littoral region" as lying anywhere within the 650 nautical miles of naval strike capabilities. The only areas of the world thus excluded are the very central portions of Canada, South America, Africa, and Siberia. Some question whether the navy should stake out such a comprehensive land control claim.

THE MEANING OF "LITTORAL"

There are at least three reasons for the navy's land-control claim. First, it can be argued that a theater-wide strike capability is necessary to defeat enemy airplanes or missiles that threaten the "doormat" from rear areas hundreds of miles away. Next, the navy may be "hedging" against an uncertain operational and organizational future. There is the long-standing argument that land bases for Air Force "strategic" bombers may not always be available.[63] *From the Sea* might also represent a transitional strategy, a stepping stone as it were, in a continuing debate over the future of separate military services. By claiming a broad land control role the navy may be positioning itself for its share of a future unified service. In addition, it makes perfect sense for a military organization, especially a navy that has long been accustomed to operating self-sufficiently in all forms of warfare, to cast its mission "net" as widely as possible. Service mission responsibilities translate into budgets and joint command opportunities, and military organizations measure their "health" by both.

Equally weighty arguments can be advanced *against* "deep" littoral control. A navy deep strike capability may not conflict with the *letter* of jointness, but it certainly tests its *spirit*.[64] It may also be wiser for the navy to borrow from the economic theory of comparative advantage and focus its efforts on what it has always done best, that is, amphibious forcible entry, instead of spreading its resources between "tactical" and "strategic" tasks and competing with the air force's strategic forte.[65] In fact, mission and burden allocation based on the idea of comparative advantage may hold the solution to a balanced yet joint-spirited navy land control capability.

The theory of comparative advantage (sometimes called the "factor endowment" model for the particular natural and other "endowments" that give a nation a competitive edge in the production and export of certain goods) does not propose that nations will specialize in the production of endowed goods to the exclusion of all other, nonendowed, products. By the same token, even if it is agreed that naval airpower can be used most cost-effectively for amphibious forcible entry (e.g., close air support, battlefield air interdiction, and general over-the-beach air superiority), it would still be worthwhile for it to keep *some* capacity for control of the "deep" littoral landmass. Why not make the Tomahawk cruise missile the navy's deep strike "silver bullet?"[66] This would provide an on-call ability to strike against those enemy rear area targets that pose an immediate danger to the success of an expeditionary lodgment.

Conversely, deep targets whose control might be critical to the overall war effort but that do not threaten the amphibious doormat, would be left for follow-on land-based aircraft to deal with.[67] The reasoning behind this distribution of effort is clear: if sea-launched Tomahawks are not enough to contain the opponent's "strategic" threat, chances are that the contingency at hand is probably too large for assault from the sea alone.

In any event, an important task for today's naval planners is to consider the likelihood of "from-the-sea-only" contingencies that will require more than a few Tomahawk salvos. If the chances are high, it should next be asked whether those contingencies will be important enough to warrant the opportunity costs of a continued heavy investment in deep strike carrier aviation.

CONCLUSION: A DIALECTIC OF SEAPOWER?

When Huntington wrote about the navy's new transoceanic doctrine, he commented how its adoption had come only after a crisis that went to "the depths of the Navy's being."[68] The navy's uncertainty of purpose in the immediate post–World War II years pales in comparison with today's identity crisis. The crisis then was that the only potential opponent appeared immune to the pressure of seapower; today's problem is the absence altogether of an identifiable enemy.[69] Even this is only a part of the radically different security environment with which blue-water naval power must come to grips. Equally unfamiliar phenomena include the prominence of "ethno-strife" as a source of armed conflict and intervention, the new legitimizing role of the United Nations in crisis and conflict management, and the heightened importance of multinational peacekeeping and peace enforcement operations. Collectively, these trends will no doubt create a very different "system" of sea warfare.[70]

There remains one concluding observation, or rather, question: how final is the end of naval strategy? What are the chances that naval power's landward orientation is a passing episode, and that its epicenter will be found at sea again? The answer seems to hinge on three factors. The first has to do with the historic interconnection between land- and seapower on the one hand, and between the offense and defense on the other. History reveals that landpowers threatened from the sea have always resorted to the sea themselves and aimed to ward off attack *on* the sea. The reason is simple: it is less destructive to the nation, and therefore cheaper in the long run, to defend oneself through offensive action away from home than by defending the beaches. That is why Sparta built a fleet to defeat the Athenians, why Rome took its military prowess onto the sea to fight Carthage, and why, two thousand years later, the Soviet Union pushed its strategic defenses onto the oceans. Taken in isolation, this trend suggests that a successful American strategy of intervention "from the sea" may eventually spur nations thus threatened to create their own seagoing countervailing capabilities, and contest *on* the sea the American ability to freely use the seas.

Whether or not this will happen depends on the second factor, the outcome of what Peter Schwartz has called a "critical uncertainty" about the existing international system.[71] Namely, few nations other than a united Europe, Japan, and China perhaps will have the financial and technical ability to counter American naval might at oceanic distances from their shores. The critical uncertainty concerns America's future relationship with Europe and Japan. If the global security environment continues to be defined by U.S. unipolarity and a (U.S.-led) "security community" among the major industrialized powers, the rise of competitors with enough resources to force U.S. naval power away from the littoral and defend itself on blue waters is unlikely.[72] This could happen, however, if, as has been claimed by some authors, U.S. unipolarity is bound to give way to balance of power competition, including possibly war, between the United States, Europe, and Japan.[73]

Transatlantic or transpacific great power rivalry need not necessarily lead to a return of blue-water strategy, at least not in its classic form. The third factor and second critical uncertainty is the evolution of technology, especially the range and endurance of aircraft and unmanned flying systems. While it is unlikely that aircraft will ever become more cost-effective than ships for the transportation of very large quantities of men and materiel, it is at least conceivable that improved design and more powerful engines will permit aircraft to reach out and compete for sea control across increasingly wider expanses of water. In that case, a future great power struggle for control of the "deep blue" may come in the form of power projection from opposing littorals.[74]

What is the likelihood of this scenario? Slim for the foreseeable future. This and the coming generation of naval officers will have to think about the uses and usefulness of naval force in an entirely different way than their predecessors did. This shift of vision will be more difficult and more controversial than the navy's last top-down revolution. The fleet's cultural transformation one century ago from "an alphabet of floating washtubs" to the "New American Navy" was easy, because centuries of fleet-against-fleet fighting had long produced a familiar bundle of ideas about the proper role of blue-water fleets.[75] Mahan and his navalist *confreres* merely codified this experience. By contrast, the naval officer who must now be indoctrinated to fight for land control has very few historical lessons, let alone "principles," to consult. True, there is a long tradition of amphibious operations, but these were never central to the blue-water culture or naval strategy per se.

It may be that the closest analogy to the navy's doctrinal vacuum today is to be found in the period when fighting ships first turned from cross-ravaging to naval strategy on the sea. By the end of the sixteenth century, naval warfare had "settled into form," on the idea that the best way to impose one's will on a seagoing opponents was to defeat their warfleets.[76] But it took most of the next century for this basic proposition to mature and become the centerpiece of a unique professional culture with a strategic code and tactical rules peculiar to war on the sea. Thus, the first naval "fighting instructions" were issued in the 1650s while decades later it was still common for fleets to be commanded by generals.[77] The navy finds itself in somewhat similar circumstances: it has acknowledged the new shape of naval warfare, but it is still far from completing the necessary cultural transformation. This, more than anything else, is the challenge of the end of naval strategy.

NOTES

1. The terms "command of the sea" and "sea control" are used interchangeably throughout this discussion, the sole difference between the two being that the second is of more recent origin. The author fully recognizes that command of the sea (or sea control) is not a "generic" condition,

that instead its geographic and temporal scope can vary greatly, depending on the particular military-strategic situation and the ultimate purpose of such command. It is also recognized that, strictly speaking, command is not peculiar to "blue-water" operations, and that it may be just as necessary for "brown-water" missions. This said, though, it is clear that in the case of the U.S. Navy at least, its post–World War II concept of sea control has been defined by the specter of an oceanic struggle with the Soviet Union. See *U.S. Navy Analysis of Congressional Budget Office Budget Issue Paper "General Purpose Forces: Navy,"* Report prepared for the Committee on Armed Services, House of Representatives, 95th Cong., 1st sess., 1977, 6.

2. Samuel P. Huntington, "National Policy and the Transoceanic Navy," U.S. Naval Institute *Proceedings* (Washington, D.C.: GPO, May 1954), 483–93.

3. Ibid., 488–89.

4. Ibid., 490.

5. Ibid., 484.

6. Department of the Navy, *From the Sea: Preparing the Naval Service for the 21st Century* (henceforth cited as *From the Sea*) (Washington, D.C.: GPO, September 1992). The document has been published in several editions, as well as in the November 1992 issue of the U.S. Naval Institute *Proceedings* (Washington, D.C.: GPO), 93–96. All subsequent references pertain to the September 1992 edition unless noted otherwise.

7. The term "essential charge" is adapted from Morton Halperin's "organizational essence," which he described as "the view held by the dominant group in the organization of what the missions and capabilities should be." The U.S. Navy's organizational essence, according to Halperin, is to maintain combat ships whose primary mission is to control the seas against enemies. Morton H. Halperin, *Bureaucratic Politics and Foreign Policy* (Washington, D.C.: Brookings Institution, 1964), 28.

8. The best overall account of naval technological change during the hundred years leading up to World War II is Bernard Brodie's *Sea Power in the Machine Age* (Princeton, N.J.: Princeton University Press, 1941).

9. *The Navy as a Fighting Machine* was the title of Rear-Admiral Bradley A. Fiske's book, published in 1916 (New York: Charles Scribner's Sons). Fiske, one of the "fathers" of modern gunnery in the U.S. Navy, wrote of the unprecedented firepower of the early–twentieth century battleship, how it could "whip an army of a million men just as quickly as it could get hold of its component parts . . . , knock down all the buildings in New York afterward, smash all the cars, break down all the bridges and sink all the shipping" (p. 60).

10. Averting, not winning war, being the main purpose of the American military was Bernard Brodie's classic 1946 statement on the essence of nuclear deterrence.

11. Bernard Brodie is one of those who have observed that military organizations tend to have much less difficulty with accepting new weaponry than their adaptation, and will therefore often, to use Barry Posen's phrase, "graft new pieces of technology on to old doctrines." See Bernard Brodie, "Technological Change, Strategic Doctrine, and Political Outcomes," in *Historical Dimensions of National Security Problems*, ed. Klaus Knorr (Lawrence: University Press of Kansas, 1976), 299. Cited in Barry R. Posen, *The*

Sources of Military Doctrine: France, Britain, and Germany between the World Wars (Ithaca, N.Y.: Cornell University Press, 1984), 55.

12. Admiral of the Fleet Sir John Fisher's famous remark on the relevance of history was that, "in regard to the Navy . . . history is a record of exploded ideas." Cited in Paul M. Kennedy, "The Relevance of the Pre-War British and American Maritime Strategies to the First World War and Its Aftermath, 1898–1920," in *Maritime Strategy and the Balance of Power: Britain and America in the Twentieth Century,* ed. John B. Hattendorf and Robert S. Jordan (New York: St. Martin's Press, 1989), 183.

13. Soviet military theoreticians, more so than their Western colleagues, stressed the materialist sources of change in the "principles" of war. For example, they concluded in the early 1950s that nuclear weapons had given rise to the principle of "surprise" as a new decisive factor in war.

14. Morris Janowitz, in *The Professional Soldier* (New York: Free Press, 1960), did not use the same term, but it was implied in his observation that there is a "cultural lag" between technological innovation and its adoption by the military.

15. According to Mahan, writing in 1911, "Happily, the last twenty years has seen the conception of a navy 'for defense only' yield to sounder military understanding of the purposes of a navy; and that understanding, of the navy's proper office in offensive action, results as certainly in battleships as the defensive idea does in small vessels." Captain A. T. Mahan, *Naval Strategy: Compared and Contrasted with the Principles and Practices of Military Operations on Land* (Boston: Little, Brown, 1911), 151–52.

16. The charge that overcautiousness and fear of excessive losses led pre–World War I Admiralty planners to forsake naval strategy's offensive principles and to rely instead on the deterrent effect of the Grand Fleet's superior numbers, was at the heart of the so-called Jutland Scandal. For the view of one critic, see Arthur Hungerford Pollen, *The Navy in Battle* (London: Chatto & Windus, 1918), esp. 55.

17. Winston S. Churchill, *The World Crisis, 1911–1918,* vol. 1 (London: Odhams Press, 1938), 76.

18. The best illustration, drawn from World War II, of how land-based airpower could dominate the struggle for command of the sea, was the ebb and flow of the Allied and Axis fortunes in the Mediterranean theater. Both sides sought to supply by sea their respective expeditionary forces in Africa; for both, success and failure depended almost entirely on the control of the North African airfields. See, for example, Captain S. W. Roskill, *The War at Sea 1939–1945,* vol. 2: *The Period of Balance* (London: Her Majesty's Stationery Office, 1956), 46.

19. In congressional testimony in 1945, Navy Secretary James Forrestal told how, in a "struggle . . . unique in the history of war," U.S. naval aviation was fighting the Japanese land-based air force for air superiority over the Japanese islands. Cited in Vincent Davis, *Postwar Defense Policy and the U.S. Navy, 1943–1946* (Chapel Hill: University of North Carolina Press, 1966), 148.

20. *From the Sea,* 1.

21. Organizational theory offers an explanation why top-down revolutions are a sporadic occurrence, namely, the tendency of organizations to be excessively rigid, incapable of purposeful adaptation, and constrained by inertia. For this view, see Michael T. Hannan and John H. Freeman, "The Population Ecology of Organizations," *American Journal of Sociology,* no. 82 (1977): 929–64; and Herbert Kaufman, *The Limits of Organizational Change* (University of Alabama Press, 1971). The author is indebted to Emily O. Goldman for directing him to this observation in her "Thinking about Strategy Absent the Enemy," draft paper presented at the 1993 International Studies Association Annual Meeting, Acapulco, Mexico, 23–28 March 1993.

22. A report by the U.S. Navy's Policy Board in 1890 painted a remarkable degree of maritime security. The country had "no colonies, nor any apparent desire to acquire them;" its overseas commerce was largely carried in foreign vessels; exports competed with those of other nations in but a few overseas markets; and it was considered highly improbable that even the world's strongest naval power, Great Britain, could "detach all [its] effective navy from [its] own coast for distant operations" while it had to safeguard its own commerce. Nevertheless, the board urged the immediate construction of 200 warships of all types because of "indications" that the country was entering an era of "commercial competition" in which it was "certain to reach out and obstruct the interests of foreign nations." In any case, the report continued, the opening of an Isthmian canal was bound to become a "fruitful source of danger." Cited in Harold and Margaret Sprout, *The Rise of American Naval Power 1776–1918* (Princeton, N.J.: Princeton University Press, 1944), 209–10.

23. Huntington, "National Policy," 488.

24. *U.S. Navy Analysis of Congressional Budget Office Budget Issue Paper, "General Purpose Forces: Navy,"* 8, 12, 13–14.

25. Huntington thought that because it was a defensive operation, antisubmarine warfare "can never become the primary mission of the Navy." It is also surprising that, writing in 1954 (when the scenario of a Soviet submarine assault against the Atlantic sea lines of communications had already gained wide credence), Huntington thought that the navy only needed to be concerned with what he called submarine "raiding operations" against its combatants. Huntington, "National Policy." 491–92.

26. John F. Lehman Jr., "Rebirth of a U.S. Naval Strategy," *Strategic Review* (Summer 1981): 11.

27. The public version of the Maritime Strategy was published as a special supplement to the January 1986 U.S. Naval Institute *Proceedings.*

28. Secretary of Defense Les Aspin, *Report on the Bottom-Up Review* (Washington, D.C.: October 1993), 28.

29. "Be Careful What You Ask for . . . ," interview with Acting Secretary of the Navy Sean O'Keefe. U.S. Naval Institute *Proceedings* (January 1993): 73.

30. Interview with Admiral Paul David Miller, Commander in Chief U.S. Atlantic Command and Supreme Allied Commander Atlantic, *Jane's Defence Weekly,* 13 March 1993, 32.

31. For accounts of the British navy's "policing" activities in the nineteenth century, see C. J. Bartlett, *Great Britain and Sea Power 1815–1853* (Oxford: Clarendon Press, 1963); and by the same author, "The Mid-Victorian

Reappraisal of Naval Policy" in *Studies in International History,* ed. K. Bourne and D. C. Watt (Hamden: Archon Books, 1967), 189–208. A good account of the Royal Navy's naval diplomatic and crisis management activities during the interworld war years, especially in the Mediterranean, is Kenneth Edwards, *The Grey Diplomatists* (London: Rich & Gowan, 1938). For an account of the Royal Navy's "return to normalcy" in the first decade after World War II see Eric Grove's *Vanguard to Trident: British Naval Policy since World War II* (Annapolis, Md.: Naval Institute Press, 1987).

32. The standard—though now outdated—account of the U.S. Navy's post–World War II crisis management activities is Barry M. Blechman and Stephen S. Kaplan, *Force without War: U.S. Armed Forces as a Political Instrument* (Washington, D.C.: Brookings Institution, 1978).

33. In a classic statement on naval suasion, Lord Palmerston, then Great Britain's foreign minister, wrote Prime Minister Melbourne in 1835 that he wanted to keep a fleet in the Mediterranean in spite of a threatening buildup of Russian naval power in the Baltic because, "We want to act by the moral effect produced by the presence of our fleet, and the uncertainty in the minds of others, what the fleet may do; and thus to prevent the necessity of its having to act by force of arms." Cited in Bartlett, *Great Britain and Sea Power 1815–1853,* 107.

34. For example, a report by the Congressional Budget Office in 1978 recommended that the navy build small V/STOL carriers for presence purposes "in less threatening Third World environment" so that the large-deck carriers could be held back for war with the Soviet Union. *U.S. Naval Forces: The Peacetime Presence Mission* (Washington, D.C.: GPO, December 1978). Writing a few years earlier, Admiral Stansfield Turner, too, wondered whether "the presence mission [is] becoming sufficiently important to warrant building or designing forces for that purpose." "Missions of the U.S. Navy," *Naval War College Review* (September–October 1974): 16.

35. Writing at the end of the nineteenth century, one British naval author said of this period in his service's history that, compared with Trafalgar and "though notable enough," it "need not detain us." Commander Charles N. Robinson, *The British Fleet: The Growth, Achievements and Duties of the Navy of the Empire* (London: George Bell and Sons, 1895), 47.

36. For accounts of the post–World War I naval rivalry between the United States, Great Britain, and Japan see, for example, Hector C. Bywater, *Navies and Nations: A Review of Naval Developments since the Great War* (Boston: Houghton Mifflin, 1927); Frederick Moore, *America's Naval Challenge* (New York: Macmillan, 1929); and Harold and Margaret Sprout, *Toward a New Order of Sea Power: American Naval Policy and the World Scene, 1918–1922* (Princeton, N.J.: Princeton University Press, 1946).

37. The Jordanian crisis in September 1970 triggered a standoff between the U.S. Sixth Fleet and the Soviet Mediterranean *eskadra* that prompted the chairman of the Joint Chiefs of Staff to predict that if shooting started it would quickly spread to both the Atlantic and Pacific. Three years later, the commander of the Sixth Fleet, Vice Admiral Daniel Murphy, wrote that his fleet's confrontation with the Soviets at the height of the Arab-Israeli October War had

set "the stage for the hitherto unlikely 'war at sea' scenario." Reported in Elmo R. Zumwalt Jr., *On Watch* (New York: Quadrangle, 1976), 297, 447.

38. The words "operations other than war at sea" are a liberal paraphrase of the U.S. Army's term "operations other than war." The army defines the latter as including acts of violence and hostilities other than conventional combat ("war") between nation-states or coalitions of nation-states. *Preliminary Draft Field Manual FM100-5: Operations* (Washington, D.C.: GPO, 21 August 1992), 5-1 through 5-6. Cited in General Gordon R. Sullivan and Lieutenant Colonel James M. Dubik, *Land Warfare in the 21st Century* (Carlisle, Pa.: U.S. Army War College, Strategic Studies Institute, February 1993), 9.

39. Statement of Rear Admiral Edward D. Shaefer Jr., Director of Naval Intelligence, before the Seapower, Strategic, and Critical Materials Subcommittee on Intelligence Issues (Washington, D.C., 5 February 1992) 2, 8. Shaefer testified in 1992 that it might be another twenty years before a new Eurasian power might rise and challenge U.S. interests. He based his estimate on what he saw as a twenty-year cycle in the fall and rise of Germany and the United States as great military powers in this century. If, on the other hand, the cyclical fortunes of Russian and Soviet naval power over the past three hundred years is used as a clue, it may be fifty years before the world will see another Eurasian fleet to be reckoned with. For the history of the ups and downs of Russian naval aspirations, see Admiral of the Fleet of the Soviet Union S. G. Gorshkov, *The Sea Power of the State* (Annapolis, Md.: Naval Institute Press, 1976), 66–92; Fred T. Jane, *The Imperial Russian Navy,* 2d ed. (London: Conway Maritime Press, 1983), 44–306; and Mairin Mitchell, *The Maritime History of Russia 1848–1948* (London: Sigwick and Jackson, 1948), 310–39.

40. Interview with Admiral Paul David Miller.

41. See Vice Admiral P. H. Colomb, *Naval War Warfare: Its Ruling Principles and Practice Theoretically Treated,* 2d ed. (London: W. H. Allen, 1895), 1–24. The author defined cross-ravaging as a "system of retaliatory expeditions attacking territory, destroying towns, burning property, and laying waste with fire and sword."

42. Ibid., 21.

43. For the best single-volume study of the influence of Corbett, the Colomb brothers, Mahan, and others on turn-of-the-century naval thought, see Donald M. Schurman, *The Education of a Navy: The Development of British Naval Strategic Thought, 1867–1914* (London: Cassell, 1965).

44. The only competitive "system" of naval warfare was the French *jeune école* theory of guerre de course of the late nineteenth century. It, too, promoted the "blue-water" use of naval power, but wanted to substitute raider warfare against enemy commerce for fleet-against-fleet battle.

45. Of course, this can only be the strategy of the stronger power; the "correct" strategy for the weaker fleet is to *deny* its opponent the use of the sea.

46. The most prominent, arguably sole, instances of pure opposing naval strategies are the Anglo-Dutch wars of 1652–54 and 1665–67. The third war between the two (1672), included a French land invasion of the United Republic, forcing the Dutch to divide their resources. Strictly speaking, therefore, this was a *maritime* conflict.

47. Naval strategy can also be a subset of a continental strategy, the difference being that naval power makes a relatively smaller contribution to the continental belligerent's overall strategic purposes.

48. Sir Julian S. Corbett, *Some Principles of Maritime Strategy* (1911; reprint, Annapolis: Naval Institute Press, 1972), 13, 14.

49. British foreign minister Sir Edward Grey is credited with referring to the British army as "a projectile to be fired by the Navy." Cited in Samual R. Williamson Jr., *The Politics of Grand Strategy: Britain and France Prepare for War, 1904–1914* (London: Ashfield Press, 1990), 107.

50. In fairness to Corbett, it must be added that unlike many of his contemporary navalists, he warned against deifying the importance for command of the sea as an absolute necessity. He wrote: "That this feature of naval warfare should be consecrated in a maxim is well, but when it is caricatured into a doctrine, as it sometimes is, that you cannot move a battalion oversea till you have entirely overthrown your enemy's fleet, it deserves gibbeting." Corbett, *Some Principles*, 101.

51. Ibid., 90.

52. Ibid., 110.

53. Ibid., 87.

54. For an account of the little-known Pacific dimension of the Crimean war, see Barry M. Gough, *The Royal Navy and the Northwest Coast of North America, 1810–1914* (Vancouver: University of British Columbia Press, 1971), 108–30.

55. *Goldwater-Nichols Department of Defense Reorganization Act of 1986*, Public Law 99-433, 1 October 1986.

56. *From the Sea*, 3, 5.

57. *U.S. Navy Analysis of Congressional Budget Office Budget Issue Paper. "General Purpose Forces: Navy,"* 4. Holloway drew a distinction between "strategic" and "tactical" sea control. The first, he said, involved sea control operations at some distance from the seagoing units to be protected, for example, carrier air strikes or amphibious raids against enemy naval bases. He described "tactical" sea control as local self-defensive operations. Admiral Holloway deliberately stressed the primary sea control purpose of the navy's aircraft carrier power projection capabilities in order to dispel the impression left by his predecessor, Admiral Elmo Zumwalt, that sea control and power projection forces entailed distinct capabilities and functions. The author is indebted to Captain Peter Swartz, U.S. Navy (ret.), for leading him to this observation. For Zumwalt's claim that the navy's "sea control forces" had been underfunded to benefit its power projection fleet, see his *On Watch*, 63.

58. Charles E. Myers Jr. proposed that the sea services "should concentrate on being prepared to lay a doormat across any littoral and be ready to guarantee that it can be maintained." Myers thought that an area 20 miles inland or 400 square miles altogether should reasonably be the aim of the navy's littoral land control aspiration. See his "Littoral Warfare: Back to the Future," U.S. Naval Institute *Proceedings* (Washington, D.C.: GPO, November 1990): 54.

59. The word "littoral" comes from oceanography and technically includes only that part of the coast that falls dry between high and low tides.

60. See, for example, *Report on the Roles, Missions, and Functions of the Armed Forces of the United States*, III-17.

61. "Be Careful What You Ask For . . . ," 74. O'Keefe added that the "long-range strike mission is one we still must be prepared for," but that the navy could now rely more on the air force and cruise missiles.

62. *From the Sea*, 5.

63. This is a realistic concern. It should be noted, however, that there are some observers of the post–Cold War international scene who maintain that as future contingencies will increasingly come in the form of U.N.-sponsored collective security actions, it will become relatively easier to find countries willing to host coalition land-based aircraft. The *Economist* thus wrote that "the old cold-war excuse for dithering—'We can't let you in because the other superpower wouldn't like it'—no longer applies." "Defence in the 21st Century," *Economist*, 5 September 1992, 15.

64. Jointness recognizes the advantages of different services owning complementary capabilities, but a key aim is to overcome redundancy and duplication of effort between the services.

65. For a discussion of "comparative advantage," applied to service roles and missions, see Mackubin T. Owens, "After the Gulf War: The Marine Corps and the New National Military Strategy," in *Fundamentals of Force Planning*, vol. 2: *Defense Planning Cases*, ed. Force Planning Faculty (Newport: Naval War College Press, 1991), 352–55. A legitimate analysis of the comparative advantage of sea- vs. land-based airpower in "tactical" and "strategic" roles would have to consider the relative cost of each in both roles.

66. For a similar recommendation, see Charles E. Myers Jr., "Time to Fold 'Em," U.S. Naval Institute *Proceedings* (Washington, D.C.: GPO, July 1991): 37–41.

67. The distinction that is made here is analogous to the one between the commander's "area of influence" and "area of interest." The first is the geographical area in which a commander is directly capable of influencing operations through maneuver of fire support systems normally under his control. The second encompasses the commander's area of concern in general, including the area adjacent to his area of influence, which might be controlled by enemy forces that could jeopardize his mission. See JCS Pub. 1-02. Cited in Department of the Navy, Headquarters, U.S. Marine Corps, FMFM 1: *Warfighting* (Washington, D.C.: GPO, 6 March 1989), 87.

68. Huntington, "National Policy," 484.

69. General Powell put it succinctly: "The real threat we now face is the threat of the unknown, the uncertain." *National Military Strategy of the United States* (Washington, D.C., January 1992), 4.

70. For example, if multinational crisis operations, whether sponsored by the United Nations or not, are going to be the wave of the future, U.S. national and navy planners will need to become much more accustomed to the "culture" of coalition decision making.

71. Peter Schwartz, *The Art of the Long View* (New York: Doubleday, 1991), 105–23.

72. Barry Bazun, referencing Karl Deutsch and S. A. Burrell, has argued that the dominant feature of the post–Cold War security environment is a tacit "capitalist security

community" among Europe, North America, Japan, and Australia. He defines such a community as a group of states that do not expect, or prepare for, the use of military force in their relations with each other. "New Patterns of Global Security in the Twenty-First Century," *International Affairs* (London), July 1991, 16–18.

73. For an argument why U.S. unipolarity cannot last, see Christopher Layne, "The Unipolar Illusion: Why New Great Powers Will Rise," *International Security,* Spring 1993, 5–51.

74. A 1982 report by the Naval Studies Board of the National Research Council forecast the technological feasibility of very high endurance aircraft with the ability to fly at 70,000 feet for two or three days. Naval Studies Board, *The Implications of Advancing Technology for Naval Avia-*tion (Washington, D.C.: National Academy Press, 1982), 29.

75. U.S. Representative John D. Long of Massachusetts has been credited with labeling the post–Civil War U.S. Navy "an alphabet of floating washtubs." Cited in Peter D. Karsten, *The Naval Aristocracy: United States Naval Officers from the 1840's to the 1920's—Mahan's Messmates* (Ph.D. diss., University of Wisconsin, 1968), 340. *The New America Navy* is the title of a two-volume book written by John D. Long, who was secretary of the navy from 1897 to 1902 (New York: Outlook, 1903).

76. Colomb, *Naval War Warfare,* 25.

77. See Julian S. Corbett, *Fighting Instructions 1530–1816* (1905). Reprinted by Burt Franklin, New York, 1967.

JOINT AND COMBINED OPERATIONS IN THE POST–COLD WAR ERA

IKE SKELTON

Three years ago, prior to the disintegration of the Soviet Union, former Secretary of Defense Richard B. Cheney, General Colin L. Powell, former chairman, Joint Chiefs of Staff (JCS), and their respective staffs crafted a new "National Military Strategy."[1] The new strategy envisioned the end of the Cold War. It differed from the earlier Cold War strategy in many ways. First, it saw the primary threat as regional rather than global. Possible confrontations with Iraq, Iran, and North Korea occupied the attention of planners rather than a possible world war with the Soviet Union. Second, the new strategy also emphasized conventional forces rather than nuclear weapons. For example, the air force reconfigured much of its bomber force for conventional use in regional crises. Third, forward presence replaced forward deployment as one of the key policies by which to secure American interests around the globe. Overseas basing would be significantly reduced, and intermittent presence would be increased. The American military would become a primarily continental United States (CONUS)–based force, especially the army and air force.

The base force, as articulated by Department of Defense (DOD) officials, accompanied the new military strategy and called for reducing the size of all four military services.[2] It envisioned roughly a 25 percent reduction in the size of American military forces and the size of the defense budget by the middle of this decade.

THE NEW WORLD DISORDER

In the midst of these plans, in fact on the same day that former President George Bush was giving a major speech on the new National Military Strategy in Aspen, Colorado, on August 2, 1990, Iraqi armed forces invaded and occupied Kuwait.

The ensuing Persian Gulf War was a stunning victory. Sailors in the Gulf, soldiers and marines ashore, and airmen in the skies defeated a brutal foe. All of the world witnessed the great skill, determination, and professionalism of the American military. Among other things, the war showed that our investment in quality people, tough training, and first-rate weapon systems, both combat and support systems, in the 1980s was money well spent. Those who fought in the Gulf helped write another magnificent chapter in American military history.

Despite the end of the Cold War, the Kuwait invasion and the subsequent war revealed that the world was still a dangerous and uncertain place. The kaleidoscope of the future is still unpredictable.

The end of the Cold War has been accompanied by a resurgence of nationalism—in some places militant nationalism. This resurgence poses a major challenge to the established political and economic order. The disintegration of states—Yugoslavia, the Soviet Union, and Ethiopia—will generate conflict about the distribution of assets.

This essay has been edited and is reprinted from Military Review 73 *(September 1993): 2–12, by permission of the Honorable Ike Skelton.*

This is the fourth great wave of state creation since the end of the Napoleonic Wars in 1815. The first was in Latin America after the withdrawal of Spanish power; the second occurred in Europe and the Middle East after the collapse of the Austro-Hungarian, Turkish, and Russian empires. The third took place after World War II, when Britain, France, and the Netherlands relinquished control of their respective empires, some more willingly than others. The end of communist rule in what was the Soviet Union marks the fourth great period of state creation. In short, the world will not be a particularly stable place.

The fault lines of international security are shifting in many directions: Eastern Europe has now become Central Europe; Southwest Asia has given way to Central Asia. The continued utility of military force for good or evil has not been eliminated, nor have the principles of deterrence (conventional, as well as nuclear) lost strategic relevance. But the non-military aspects of security—social, economic, and political—will now assume greater importance in the strategist's appreciation of the forces at play.

THE SERVICES REORGANIZE

In the midst of these momentous political developments, the three service departments began their respective efforts to reorganize for the future.

AIR FORCE

The air force issued its white paper, *Global Reach–Global Power*, in June 1990.[4] This visionary document outlined a strategic planning framework for the air force in the post–Cold War era. Such venerable institutions as the Strategic Air Command, the Tactical Air Command, and the Military Airlift Command passed into history. The Air Combat Command incorporated all the winged firepower of the service—fighter, bomber, reconnaissance, command and control (C^2), tactical airlift, and rescue aircraft. Air mobility command acquired most of the mobility and refueling assets—strategic transport aircraft, tankers, and medical evacuation aircraft. Other changes included the streamlining and elimination of organizations. The air force will reduce the number of major commands from thirteen in June 1991 to eight by October 1993.

More than a fundamental management reorganization of the air force, *Global Reach–Global Power* symbolized a new way of thinking for airmen. Artificial distinctions between tactical and strategic were done away with and airpower is now considered a unified whole. At the same time, the air force discovered some old truths that have been important to the army as an institution for many years—the importance of professional military education (PME) and, closely tied in with education, the importance of doctrine.

NAVY

The navy, the service that traditionally has been most resistant to change, has also responded to the end of the Cold War and its experience in the Persian Gulf War with its own white paper, . . . *From the Sea.*[5] Issued in September 1992, after about a year's study, the new strategy incorporated two assumptions. First, the authors of the new strategy believed that the United States and its allies would have uncontested control of the seas. Second, they thought that most future military operations would be "joint," involving more than one service.

The document symbolized a new way of thinking for the navy in a number of respects. The focus for future operations has shifted from the open sea to the coastlines of the world. In close cooperation with the Marine Corps, the emphasis on littoral warfare "is a new doctrine that marries Navy and Marine forces and priorities. . . . The Navy and Marine Corps will now respond to crises and can provide the initial, 'enabling' capability for joint operations."[6]

Similar to the air force approach, the navy's change in strategy was accompanied by a change in structure. The staff of the chief of naval operations (CNO) was rearranged on a functional basis to mirror the organization of the Joint Chiefs of Staff (JCS). The CNO's new N1 through N8 organizations conform to the JCS's J1 through J8. Power has shifted from the three separate baronies—air, surface, and submarine warfare—to the new N8, the deputy CNO for resources, warfare requirements, and assessments. Rather than dividing budgetary resources into roughly equal shares as in the past, the new arrangement allows one individual to control the money flow. As a result, the navy has already made plans to try to protect amphibious and carrier assets by reducing the attack submarine fleet by half and retiring all thirty-five Oliver Perry–class frigates. Similar to the army and air force, the navy has finally come to understand the importance of doctrine. It will establish a naval doctrine command to help smooth the integration of navy and Marine Corps forces in a joint power–projection role, building doctrine for expeditionary warfare.

ARMY

In many ways, the army instituted a number of far-reaching changes twenty years ago, in the waning years of the Vietnam War. The outcome of that bitter conflict was reflected in three crucial decisions that affected the army more than any other service—the end of the draft and beginning of the all-volunteer force (AVF), the creation of the total force concept and the establishment of the U.S. Army Training and Doctrine Command (TRADOC), Fort Monroe, Virginia.

Although many military leaders expressed great misgivings about the AVF, by the early 1980s the services had finally learned how to make it work. Recruiting high school graduates and paying them well helped create the army of excellence that proved itself in Panama and Iraq. The importance of the total force concept was also vindicated in the Persian Gulf War. Since much of the active army's combat support and combat service support was found in the reserve components (RCs), the requirement to activate those forces helped bring along the support of the American public. It worked just as Army Chief of Staff Creighton Abrams had designed it back in the early 1970s. And the third decision, the creation of TRADOC, revealed the U.S. Army in the deserts of the Middle East fighting with the synthesis of excellent people, first-rate equipment, and top-notch military thinking for the employment of forces.

While less prone to issuing white papers showing the great changes it is undertaking, the army is indeed undergoing fundamental changes as it shapes itself as a strategic force for the twenty-first century. The army is coming home. It will be primarily a CONUS-based force rather than the forward-deployed force it was during the Cold War. In addition to substantial force reductions that have produced the inactivation of four divisions and one corps along with the consolidation of fifty-one war reserve stocks to five, the army has recently issued the latest version of U.S. Army Field Manual (FM) 100-5, *Operations*, its bible. Understanding the new world in which it finds itself, the army has seen fit to include a chapter titled "Operations Other than War." One need only read today's newspapers to see army forces involved in such operations in Zagreb, Macedonia, Somalia, northern Iraq, and Latin America to see the need to address such contingencies.

Although there is no army version of *Global Reach–Global Power* or . . . *From the Sea* that the army can point to as a blueprint for the future, FM 100-5 is a major step in the right direction. However, more needs to be done to explain the army's future.

While each of the services is reorganizing for the post–Cold War era, each understands that most military operations in the future will be joint, multiservice efforts. This viewpoint has been underscored by the November 1991 publication of Joint Pub 1, *Joint Warfare of the US Armed Forces*. Joint Pub 1 and the related effort to develop joint doctrine will help the services work more closely together in a period of declining budgets and force structure. There will be room for leading thinkers from each of the four services to offer their creative talents for melding the disparate ways the services think about the employment of their respective forces. The recent publication of *Joint Force Quarterly*, under the auspices of the Institute for National Strategic Studies at the National Defense University, is still another indication that jointness has finally come of age.

While the services have been busy adjusting to the changing political circumstances of the world since the fall of the Berlin Wall in 1989, the chairman of the JCS has also been busy reviewing defense policies. Earlier this year, as a result of the Goldwater-

Nichols Department of Defense Reorganization Act of 1986, the chairman of the JCS issued the latest report titled "Roles, Functions and Missions of the Armed Forces of the United States." Two considerations predominated in the effort to put together the report: improving the way the armed forces fight, and saving money in the process.[7] The report noted the dramatic changes that have taken place already: the creation of the U.S. strategic command, the elimination of nuclear weapons in the army and Marine Corps, and the end of the requirement to maintain chemical weapons because of the signing by the United States of the chemical weapons convention in Paris in January 1993. The report also highlighted the savings that can take place by further consolidation among the four services in the matter of depot maintenance and flight training.

Other changes on the horizon include the creation of a unified command for all units of the four armed services based in the United States, and the possible consolidation of space and strategic commands. Yet two of the key issues that were raised by then chairman of the Senate Armed Services Committee, Sam Nunn, in a significant speech on July 2, 1992, were not addressed in the report of the chairman: the trade-offs between land-based versus sea-based power projection (air force bombers versus navy carriers) and the ambitious tactical aviation modernization programs of the air force and navy (four separate aircraft when there may be funds for only two at most).[8]

Testifying before the House Armed Services Committee in March 1993, General Powell described the roles and missions report as "simply a snapshot of a continuous process of self-evaluation that occurs every day. The Joint Staff will continue to examine other areas for possible consolidation or elimination."[9] The Joint Staff will not be the only group involved in this effort. The Congress, think tanks, and other defense specialists will also be studying the matter of roles and missions. The end of the Cold War and the dramatic reduction in the size of U.S. military forces have ensured that this issue will be around for the next few years. In much the same way that the issue of defense reorganization took time to gather steam in the 1980s—from 1982, when former Chairman of the Joint Chiefs of Staff David Jones called for dramatic change, until late 1986, when the Goldwater-Nichols Act became law—it will take a few years to deal with the issue of roles and missions.

ARRIVAL OF A NEW ADMINISTRATION

The arrival of any new administration in Washington signals change. This is especially so with the election of President Bill Clinton, who promised change during the campaign. He is the first individual elected to the presidency born after World War II and the first president to begin his term of office after the end of the Cold War.

His choice of Les Aspin, the former chairman of the House Armed Services Committee, as secretary of defense meant that one of Washington's leading defense thinkers would now be in the position to institute many of the changes he had promoted in his former position in Congress.

The new secretary signaled his effort to institute change almost immediately upon assuming office. He did so by redesigning the Office of the Secretary of Defense (OSD) and choosing a high-powered team of seasoned defense intellectuals to assist him. OSD has always been considered the weakest of the bureaucratic players at DOD, taking third place to the uniformed service staffs and the newly strengthened joint staff. A second, and maybe more important effort was the "bottom-up review" to chart the course for national defense for the future. The secretary has given a series of speeches explaining the overall effort of reducing defense spending and force structure, yet maintaining an adequate defense capability to secure American global interests.

One of the early trial balloons that got shot down quickly was the proposed strategy to fight two regional wars on a sequential basis. Known as "Win-Hold-Win," the strategy called for fighting a first regional conflict while essentially using airpower to hold off a second adversary. Once the first regional conflict was won, those forces would then be redeployed to help win the second regional conflict.

Criticized, justly in my opinion, by some as "Win-Hope-Win" or "Win-Hold-Lose," the strategy seemed reminiscent of the mistake made by President Harry S Truman's administration. In a major policy statement at the National Press Club in early 1950, Secretary of State Dean Acheson left South Korea outside the American defense perimeter in the Pacific.[10] The House of Representatives compounded the mistake by rejecting (193 to 192) a defense assistance program that would have provided five hundred army officers to supervise the equipping of South Korean troops.[11]

Joseph Stalin, dictating North Korean war plans, interpreted the American statement as a green light to begin preparations to invade South Korea. Obviously, the Truman administration had not intended, by way of Acheson's speech, to encourage North Korea to attack the south in its effort to reunify the peninsula. Yet that was the unintended consequence of the speech.

Similarly, Aspin would not want to encourage a second regional adversary to attempt to take advantage of a situation in which American forces were engaged in a regional conflict elsewhere. Why telegraph one's weaknesses?

Upon reflection, the secretary came to the same conclusion. "After much discussion and analysis, we've come to the conclusion that our forces must be able to fight and win two major regional conflicts. . . . First, . . . we don't want a potential aggressor in a second region to believe that we're vulnerable. . . . Second, we want to be prepared in case an adversary emerges with larger or more capable forces than today's regional powers."[12]

Equally important, the secretary has talked about the importance of maintaining a strong peacetime presence of U.S. military forces around the world. He recognized the fact that such presence contributes to regional stability, sending the signal that the United States is committed to protecting American and allied interests. And yet the dilemma we face is doing all this with a military force structure that is shrinking. The secretary admitted that "creative thinking" will be needed. Some of the ideas being considered are rotating air force squadrons to forward bases for limited periods; having navy ships, air force long-range bombers, and Airborne Warning and Control System aircraft operate together as part of the same joint task force; and conducting more but smaller military exercises with allies.

If nothing else, the OSD is wrestling with some very tough issues. The new leadership at the DOD realizes that as the American military reduces in size it must maintain its readiness and remain a quality force, ready to fight. It has identified the three major challenges to readiness:

- Maintaining good people in the military.
- Keeping up training and maintenance.
- Ensuring the proper esprit de corps.

Truth be told, the American military establishment is under great stress. The reductions experienced by each of the services caused turbulence and uncertainty. In addition, the debate over removing the ban on homosexuals serving in the armed forces has caused great anxiety among those in uniform. And the recommendation in the proposed fiscal 1994 defense budget not to include a cost-of-living allowance increase was penny wise and pound foolish and sent the wrong signal to those in uniform. At the end of the day, I believe that the Congress will take action on homosexuals and pay, which will find favor among the vast majority of service members.

PROPOSALS TO MAINTAIN AND STRENGTHEN THE MILITARY

Peering into the future is not easy, but some outlines on the horizon are visible. First, we know that defense spending will continue to decline over the next few years. Second, the world remains a dangerous place despite the disappearance of the Soviet Union, so the need for capable American military forces remains. Third, joint operations among the services and combined operations with friends and allies will more and more characterize future American military efforts as we seek to maintain American military power despite force reductions.

Among the various proposals to maintain military capability I would include the following. First, the army needs to continue improving the relationship between its active and reserve components. Much that is positive has happened, including the army's *Bold Shift* initiative and the Title XI Army National Guard Combat Reform Initiative in the fiscal 1993

Defense Authorization Act. More needs to be done, especially in the area of reserve PME. If more responsibilities are to be placed on RC forces, they must be provided greater opportunities to become more proficient through PME.

An even greater opportunity awaits the army if it views the RC combat units as a genuine asset to be developed rather than as simply another requirement it must address. Such units could be fashioned as building blocks to allow the army to expand the number of divisions in case a hostile world-class military power arises over the next generation—a Fascist Russia or an expansionist China. Many army personnel who are leaving the service may be just the kind of people that the army could place in such RC units in order to have an officer and noncommissioned officer corps made up of experienced personnel. The army would do itself a great service to look at another ground-oriented fighting force, the Marine Corps, to copy some of the elements that have made the active-reserve relationship among marines a very healthy and effective one.

These are very difficult problems to address because of the RC time constraints. Yet creative thinking combined with a positive attitude among senior uniformed army leaders are the ingredients necessary if progress is to be made on these two important issues.

Second, ongoing efforts to make the army and air force more mobile and rapidly deployable, similar to the sea services, need to be maintained at the current tempo and maybe even accelerated. The Mobility Requirements Study validated the C-17 program, reaffirmed enhancement of the ready reserve force of transport ships, and called for twenty additional large roll-on, roll-off ships. This would allow the deployment of one light and two heavy army divisions worldwide within thirty days. The formation of air force composite wings at Mountain Home Air Force Base (AFB), Idaho, and Pope AFB, North Carolina, is the air force's solution to finding new ways to prepare its forces for rapid deployment. Such forces train together at home in the way they would fight when deployed overseas. The former, designated an air intervention wing, includes bombers, fighters, tankers, and C^2 aircraft. The latter is considered a battlefield support wing and includes fighters, close air support aircraft, and tactical transports. It works closely with the army's 82d Airborne Division at Fort Bragg, North Carolina.

Third, PME needs to be stressed even more during a time of diminishing resources, especially joint PME. There is a need for both field experience and education among military officers. Sir William Francis Butler, noted British soldier and nineteenth-century author, said it well: "The nation that will insist upon drawing a broad line of demarcation between the fighting man and the thinking man is liable to find its fighting done by fools and its thinking done by cowards."[13] PME is central to the effort of maintaining a first-rate officer corps.

Lord Ernest Rutherford, British nuclear physicist and Nobel Peace Prize winner was once quoted as saying, "We are short of money, so we must think." That is not a bad description of where the armed forces stand today. Education stimulates thinking. The challenge in these next few months and years will be not to cut education to such an extent that we actually find ourselves guilty of eating our own seed corn. Education, it must be remembered, is the foundation upon which the future is built. As Sir Francis Bacon noted, "Knowledge is power," and a strong military must have wise leaders who have not suffered because of excessive cuts in education.

Finally, I caution this generation of military officers not to be complacent about the next war. Success sometimes is seductive. The great victory won in the Persian Gulf region two years ago cannot be allowed to contribute to complacency in the years to come.

As a nation, we emerged victorious from World War II in no small measure because of the moral and intellectual strengths at the highest levels of the American officer corps. Unfortunately, after World War II, we became complacent. Strategic thinking atrophied after 1945. In the nuclear age, many believed that the ideas and thoughts associated with classical military history and strategy had been rendered obsolete.

Maurice Comte de Saxe, the famous French military analyst, noted: "Few men occupy themselves in the higher problems of war. They pass their lives drilling troops and believe this is the only branch of the military art. When they arrive at the command of armies they are totally ignorant, and in default of knowing what should be done . . . they do what they know."[14]

Doing what one knows, rather than what should be done, is a problem that many military commanders have faced throughout history. It is a problem not unfamiliar to the American military in the recent past. I would contend that in Vietnam the American military did what it knew—fighting the conventional war that it had fought in World War II and Korea—rather than knowing what to do, fighting the revolutionary war in which it became engaged. It took ten years to put together a strategy to win the war. By that time it was too late. The patience of the American public had come to an end.

The bitter experience of Vietnam, which resulted from a loss of strategic vision, sent American military men back to the study of war and military history. Students at the five command and staff colleges and the five war colleges are the beneficiaries of this renewed interest in the study of war. For some, there has been much to catch up on. For all, however, this educational opportunity has meant extensive reading, serious research, written analysis, seminar discussions, and old-fashioned thinking.

The U.S. military must not lose the ability to fight the big war. In light of the victory in the Persian Gulf War, I am reasonably confident that it will maintain this ability. At the same time, the U.S. military must devote more attention to the difficult problems posed by small wars—or to use the more current phrase, low-intensity conflict and operations other than war. Over our short history, we have had difficulty dealing with unconventional warfare—in the late 1800s fighting the Indians, early this century pacifying the Philippines, and most recently in Vietnam. Operations other than war will pose similar difficulties.

As I look close to our shores, at Peru, Colombia, Haiti, and the drug war, these are the kinds of conflicts that will require more of our attention in the years to come. Such conflicts have a military dimension, but they are overwhelmingly political by nature. We have not understood this great truth on previous occasions when we have involved ourselves in such struggles. These will be the conflicts that will engage more of our attention and efforts in the coming years.

We should have learned from history that wars—even major ones—can come about when least expected. The peace and tranquility of a European summer in 1914 was suddenly shattered by an assassin's bullet. The world was ill prepared for the tragic events that followed. We must maintain a ready, modern, and sufficiently powerful military that can meet any unexpected contingency.

We need to remind ourselves that despite all the problems we have America is the richest and most productive nation in the world today. No other nation comes close in terms of economic output and none seems likely to overtake us for at least a generation, if then. We have both the ability and resources to continue leading the free world. All we need is the will. Those who would pose a false choice between meeting our responsibilities abroad and meeting the needs of our people at home do our nation a disservice. For the truth is, we either meet both responsibilities or we shall meet neither.

In the post–Cold War era, leadership will not be easy. But the United States will have a leading role to play far into the twenty-first century. Now is the time to realize that taking the initiative is preferable to inaction, that leadership is preferable to self-doubt,

that securing the gains democracy has made in the past decade is within our reach. We can do all this if we look upon the design of the future not as a threat but as a challenge.

NOTES

1. John M. Collins, "The DOD Base Force, and U.S. Unified Command Plan: An Assessment," *National Military Strategy*, Congressional Research Service Report (Washington, D.C.: Library of Congress, 11 June 1992).

2. General Colin L. Powell, *The Base Force: A Total Force Presentation to the House Appropriations Committee,* Subcommittee on Defense, 25 September 1991.

3. John M. Collins, *U.S. Military Force Reductions: Capabilities versus Requirements,* Congressional Research Service Report (Washington, D.C.: Library of Congress, 8 January 1992).

4. *The Air Force and U.S. National Security Policy: Global Reach—Global Power,* a White Paper, June 17, 1990.

5. . . . *From the Sea: Preparing the Naval Service for the 21st Century,* September 1992, 12.

6. Ibid., 2.

7. Chairman, Joint Chiefs of Staff, *Report on the Roles, Missions and Functions of the Armed Forces of the United States* (Washington, D.C.: GPO, February 1993).

8. Sam Nunn, *Congressional Record* (2 July 1992), S9559–64.

9. Statement from Powell, Chairman of the Joint Chiefs of Staff, before the Committee of Armed Services, U.S. House of Representatives, 30 March 1993, 10.

10. William Manchester, *The Glory and the Dream* (New York: Bantam, 1990), 518–19.

11. Ibid., 519.

12. Remarks from Les Aspin, U.S. Air Force Senior Statesman Symposium, 24 June 1993, 1.

13. U.S. Congress, House Armed Services Committee, *Panel on Military Education Report,* Report to the Committee on Armed Services, House of Representatives, 101st Cong., 1st sess., 21 April 1989, 18.

14. Ibid.

CHAPTER 15

SOLIC AND OPERATIONS
OTHER THAN WAR

U.S. SPECIAL OPERATIONS FORCES: A STRATEGIC PERSPECTIVE

CARL W. STINER

We could easily end up with more than we need for contingencies that are no longer likely, and less than we must have to meet emerging challenges.—President George Bush, August 2, 1990

The post–Cold War international environment presents the United States with security challenges that are unprecedented in ambiguity, diversity, risk, and—opportunity. For the first time since the 1930s, no single power confronts the United States as a clear and present military danger. However, the failure of communism and the end of the Cold War do not eliminate threats to U.S. interests, negate U.S. responsibilities to friends and allies, nor void the necessity for potent U.S. military forces.

In recent years, we have witnessed momentous events—dramatic progress in strategic arms control negotiations, the end of the Cold War, a stunning military victory in the Middle East by a coalition led by the United States, the withdrawal of Soviet forces from Eastern Europe, the collapse of the Warsaw Pact, and the demise of the Soviet Union as we have known it for the past forty years. But in the midst of all this change, there remain certain constants that force us to temper hope with realism.

Improved relations with the countries of Eastern Europe and the republics of the former Soviet Union, and the accompanying reduced risk of global nuclear warfare, should not obscure the realities of a world that will continue to grow more uncertain. The only thing definite is that the United States no longer faces a large monolithic national force intent on defeating it. International turmoil and aggression, however, remain with us.

Drives for regional hegemony, resurgent nationalism, ethnic and religious rivalries, rising debt, drug trafficking, and terrorism will challenge the international order as it has seldom been challenged before. Widely available and sophisticated conventional, nuclear, biological, and chemical armaments, coupled with new means to deliver them, will render the international arena even more volatile. Within developing nations, dramatic increases in population and growing dissatisfaction with the perpetual gap between rich and poor will continue to be causes of unrest; the problems associated with rising political and economic expectations will be even more pro-

nounced. Social upheaval could lead to the establishment of repressive regimes that may threaten the security interests the United States is trying to nurture and preserve.

As a result of these conditions, the number of prominent players in international politics will increase significantly. New combinations of power will develop while traditional international relationships will be called into question. In a world marked by competing political, social, and economic systems, there will always be those who consider their interests at odds with those of the United States.

These realities present diverse security challenges to the United States. They range from immediate to long-term challenges, from overt aggression to the latent fomenting of political instability, from the resurgence of powerful repressive governments to the continuance of a variety of renegade regimes and unstable rulers, from terrorism to narcotrafficking. Capabilities for countering one threat may be ineffective or unusable against another.

A primary objective of the United States in today's international system is to champion "a stable and secure world, where political and economic freedom, human rights, and democratic institutions flourish."[1] In this regard, the ability of the United States to provide leadership and exert military and economic influence globally is unmatched. International security cannot rest on the good intentions of individual countries and leaders; Iraq's bold invasion of Kuwait demonstrates the perils of such security approaches. The challenges to global stability are such that they are unlikely to be managed without active engagement by the United States. The distinctive role of the United States is rooted not only in its power, but also in its values. The United States cannot solve all the world's security problems. However, it must remain the country to which others turn in distress.

U.S. DEFENSE POSTURE AND SPECIAL OPERATIONS FORCES

The armed forces of the United States, in concert with other elements of U.S. strategy, are an effective means for contributing to a stable world based on the rule of law, self-determination, political and eco-

This essay has been edited and is reprinted from Parameters 22 (Summer 1992): 2–13, *by permission of* Parameters.

nomic pluralism, and regional cooperation. In this evolving international era, our military forces continue to support U.S. and allied security interests with versatile and ready land, maritime, and air forces. The U.S. military responds to threats to U.S. interests with forward-based forces under unified commands, reinforced as needed with rapid-deploying forces from the continental United States. In addition, our military forces are employed in peacetime military activities requested by, and in support of, Third World governments aimed at fostering political legitimacy, democratic values, and civic infrastructures.

The special operations forces (SOF) of the United States, comprising special operations, psychological operations, and civil affairs forces from the army, navy, and air force, are essential to a balanced national defense posture in this complex international environment. Special operations forces are uniquely capable of operating in all political-military environments—from peacetime training, internal defense, and nation assistance all the way up to full-blown conventional warfare. As such, our nation's special operations forces can be used as an instrument of U.S. national policy in its efforts to promote international stability, foster economic and political pluralism, and alleviate conditions that create human misery and fuel insurgencies in various countries around the world. Language skills and regional and cultural familiarity enable special operations forces to make unique contributions toward protecting and promoting U.S. interests across the entire operational continuum. Special operations forces offer the National Command Authorities and defense policy makers a low-cost capability for expressing U.S. interest and resolve in every region of the world.

Today, in addition to the special operations forces that remain employed in the Persian Gulf region in support of Operation Provide Comfort and who are caring for displaced Haitian refugees and supporting Operation Guantanamo at Guantanamo Bay, Cuba, there are special operations forces employed in thirty-six countries in every region of the world. These soldiers, sailors, and airmen are professional instruments of U.S. policy. They are forward-employed and performing their missions every day of the year, from the grass roots level—where the problems are—up to the ambassadorial level, giving advice and assistance and coordinating requirements in behalf of American interests. Many of these employments provide a significant and needed presence in areas where no other U.S. military forces are stationed or regularly deployed.

Long before the end of the Cold War, growing nontraditional threats to U.S. interests prompted the revitalization of special operations assets as an essential component of our nation's defense capabilities. The United States Special Operations Command has been given broad responsibility to maintain special operations forces to support theater unified commands and, if directed by the National Command Authorities, to exercise command of selected special

operations.[2] U.S. special operations forces provide the National Command Authorities and the theater unified commanders with the flexibility required to execute options ranging from specialized peacetime capabilities to equally specialized wartime support, while at the same time aggressively preparing for a demanding and challenging future.

SPECIAL OPERATIONS FORCES—VERSATILE AND READY

Former Chairman of the Joint Chiefs of Staff Admiral William J. Crowe Jr. in 1987 set forth the prescription for bringing special operations forces securely into the military establishment:

First, break down the wall that has more or less come between special operations and the other parts of the military. . . . Second, educate the rest of the military—spread a recognition and understanding of what SOF does . . . and how important that it is done. . . . Last, integrate SOF efforts into the full spectrum of our military capabilities.[3]

Those tasks have now been accomplished. Since December 1989 the United States has fought two major combat operations—Just Cause in Panama and Desert Shield/Desert Storm in the Gulf. Operating in conjunction with conventional forces in both cases, special operations forces contributed directly to the achievement of decisive victories. When employed properly and synchronized with other battlefield assets, special operations forces provide to commanders capabilities that extend their vision of the battlefield, increase their flexibility, and enhance their initiative.

While Operations Just Cause and Desert Shield/Desert Storm were under way, other special operations forces continued to serve worldwide in peacetime military activities involving foreign internal defense, security assistance, civic action, counterdrug and counterterrorism, and humanitarian relief operations. Using specific skills requested by and tailored to support host nations and theater commanders in chief (CINCs), these special operations forces were employed to improve a host nation's capability to provide services and carry out other governmental functions. In the process, these special operations forces enhanced host-nation and international support for U.S. regional objectives.

Simultaneous employment of special operations forces in these peacetime military assistance activities, in contingency operations like Just Cause, and in full-scale war like Desert Storm demonstrates the versatility and readiness that are the hallmarks of special operations forces.

VERSATILITY

Versatility will be an essential characteristic of all U.S. armed forces in the coming decades, not just special operations forces. Our nation's leaner military forces will be challenged by a growing number and variety of potential threats and opportunities.

Each service offers unique capabilities to the National Command Authorities and the unified commanders that, when properly focused and integrated, advance U.S. security interests.

Special operations forces offer their own brand of versatility particularly applicable in an uncertain international environment. The capability either to forward-employ special operations forces or to base them in the United States for rapid overseas movement provides significant flexibility to U.S. defense planners.

In most developing countries, there are discrete economic, social, and security problems affecting both the quality of life and a regime's ability to carry out the basic obligations of governance. Helping a country meet the fundamental needs of its populace is the crux of any nation-assistance effort. Special operations forces are particularly adept at nation-assistance tasks that require cultural familiarity, linguistic skills, and long-term commitment. Characterized by small, flexible units with a wide variety of specialized skills and regional expertise, special operations forces provide numerous forms of training and assistance to host countries. U.S. participation in nation-assistance initiatives often works best when it remains inconspicuous; the relatively low profile of special operations forces is especially appropriate when U.S. presence is a sensitive issue with the host country. The use of special operations forces in focused nation-assistance programs, coordinated with country teams and in support of theater unified commanders, can advance the interests of the United States while assisting developing countries.

Special operations forces have been a critical ingredient in theater CINC efforts to implement country-specific programs that apply military resources to ameliorate conditions leading to subversion, lawlessness, insurgencies, and even regional conflict. For example, in Dominica, navy SOF provided medical and dental care to over three hundred patients, repaired local medical facilities, presented classes to Dominican health care providers, and gave basic health self-help instruction to the local populace. In Nepal, a small thirteen-person army SOF team trained Nepalese nurses and medics in field medical and trauma tasks. Seminars were conducted on advanced trauma techniques for Nepalese doctors and nurse specialists. In both of these cases, host governments and U.S. ambassadors were enthusiastic about the expanded role of the U.S. military working with host-country military and government officials as a means for providing essential services to the local populace and educating the military on the contributions it can make to society during peacetime.

In Bangladesh, army and air force SOF continue to train the Bangladesh armed forces in disaster relief operations. The training, according to the U.S. ambassador, "has helped advance the interests of world peace . . . cement(ed) a solid relationship between the United States and the Peoples Republic of Bangladesh . . . enhanced Bangladeshi self-sufficiency for disaster relief operations . . . and raised the level of technical expertise in the Bangladesh military."[4] Thousands of Bangladesh's isolated villages are now within an hour of assistance in case of another natural disaster.

In several African and Central and South American countries, special operations forces are working with the host-nation military, government officials, and, where appropriate, police in civic action programs and internal defense. For example, in Zimbabwe, Namibia, Niger, and the Ivory Coast in Africa and in Colombia, Peru, Bolivia, and Ecuador in South America, special operations forces are training host-nation military and government officials in counterpoaching skills, basic soldier training, small-unit tactics and techniques, communications systems and procedures, basic medical skills, and programs for food and water distribution.

Special operations forces continue to be active in the ongoing war against narcotics trafficking. As a supporting command in the Department of Defense counterdrug effort, U.S. Special Operations Command provides personnel and resources when requested. Typical counterdrug support includes communications support, training with host-nation forces on riverine and small-boat operations and military skills, and peacetime psychological operations training directed at gaining support for U.S. counterdrug efforts, defeating narcotrafficking, and educating the local populace.

In addition, special operations forces can be employed to counter terrorism, subversion, or insurgencies, consistent with the requirements of U.S. national security policy and objectives. Special operations forces are also capable of conducting complex crisis-response contingency operations on short notice with great precision—from personnel recovery missions to larger operations.

READINESS

The international security environment exposes vital resources to threats that could jeopardize the U.S. economy, the well-being of our friends and allies, and our overall national security position. Contingency operations in the future will most likely require some form of special operations early in execution, including special reconnaissance or direct-action missions, psychological operations, and either clandestine or forcible entry.

Special operations forces engaged in peacetime assistance programs in foreign countries may, with little warning, be required to transit to mid- or high-intensity combat in support of rapidly deploying conventional forces. In such cases, immediate demands for special operations skills and regional expertise will not allow time for retraining. Accordingly, maintenance of high combat-readiness standards while special operations forces are participating in peacetime military assistance activities is imperative. Other special operations forces, normally based in the United States, are available to reinforce theater unified commanders on a timely basis, or to execute missions under control of the National Command Authorities. All special operations forces are organized and trained to operate in a mutual support posture vis-à-vis conventional forces.

Special operations forces also provide technologically advanced command and control capabilities to unified commanders. These communications and data processing capabilities operate at every level of joint and allied command. They are ready and rapidly deployable and can be tailored to specific requirements.

Sustainment of forward-employed special operations forces in conflict and peacetime military assistance activities contributes to a high state of national readiness. As the forward presence of conventional forces is reduced, special operations leaders will continue to work closely with the services to meet the essential sustainment requirements for forward-employed special operations forces.

SOF SUPPORT OF CONVENTIONAL FORCES

Special operations forces perform their missions at the strategic, operational, and tactical levels to influence operations throughout the theater. SOF can no longer be placed in their own box or operational area on the battlefield, separate and distinct from other forces. Rather, special operations forces must be integrated into the campaign at every stage of planning and execution.

In Panama, special operations forces proved critical in providing the precombat intelligence necessary for commanders to successfully neutralize twenty-seven essential targets during the crucial opening phase of Operation Just Cause. In addition, army and air force SOF worked together to secure critical bridges, communication sites, and terrain to deny access by the Panama Defense Forces (PDF). An excellent example of this was the Rangers' airborne assault on Torrijos-Tocumen Airport during the early minutes of hostilities. By securing this airfield, the Rangers provided initial on-the-ground intelligence and prevented the PDF from interfering with future operations. Fire support for this mission consisted of an air force special operations. AC-130 Spectre gunship and army special operations AH-6 attack helicopters. Navy special operations forces played an equally critical role. Navy Sea-Air-Land teams (SEALs) and special boat units secured critical waterways and shore target areas to preclude PDF use.

These joint SOF operations were essential to prevent the PDF from sending reinforcing troops and material to critical areas in the theater of operations, as well as to isolate the PDF leadership. Integrated with conventional forces in support roles, special operations forces prevented the PDF from mounting effective resistance and contributed to the overall success of the combat operations.

In Operations Desert Shield and Desert Storm, the United States Central Command effectively employed SOF in support of its campaign plan. Army special operations forces and Navy SEALs were among the first contingents employed in the theater of operations, providing coalition forces training in individual and small-unit skills. This training program focused on nuclear, biological, and chemical techniques, integrating joint and combined arms into tactical plans, land navigation, beach surveillance and reconnaissance, and close air support. In addition, special operations forces were the primary trainers for the reconstitution of the Kuwaiti armed forces.

With every coalition Middle Eastern battalion that went into battle in Desert Storm, there were special forces units with them. These were the same special forces units that had lived and trained with the coalition units since the beginning of Desert Shield in early August. Their role proved critical for the successful command and control of the coalition forces.

Just prior to the beginning of the ground war, special operations forces were inserted deep into Iraqi territory on special reconnaissance missions. The intelligence provided by these special operations teams supplemented the battlefield data previously received by the operational and tactical commanders—and proved essential to the success of the ground tactical plan. Navy SEALs actively supported deception operations and maritime embargo operations, conducted area reconnaissance missions, and supported countermine warfare operations. Special operations direct-action missions were also implemented to support the Desert Storm campaign plan.

Although not normally considered a special operations mission, army, navy, and air force SOF were tasked by General Norman Schwarzkopf to conduct all combat search and rescue missions for downed pilots in the Kuwaiti theater of operations. Of the four pilots rescued, special operations forces rescued three, the fourth being rescued by Kuwaiti resistance forces. Throughout Operations Just Cause, Desert Shield, and Desert Storm, the operational leadership understood the capabilities and limitations of special operations forces during the changing phases; the end result was optimum employment.

SPECIAL OPERATIONS FORCES— THE FUNDAMENTAL PRINCIPLES

The distinctive characteristics of special operations forces rest on five fundamental principles that prepare the force for any mission:

- High-quality personnel
- Specialized training
- Advanced technology
- Forward-looking doctrine
- Versatile force structure.

HIGH-QUALITY PERSONNEL

The most important of these fundamentals is the selection and retention of mature, high-quality soldiers, sailors, and airmen. High-quality people enable special operations forces to meet challenges across a broad spectrum of mission requirements. The long-term readiness of special operations forces requires the development of personnel programs, with the military services and U.S. Special Operations Command working closely together, that promote the growth of a vigorous force.

Volunteers for most special operations units must first demonstrate their maturity, intelligence, combat skills, and physical toughness in their parent services, and then successfully complete a rigorous selection process. Such a selection process produces special operators ready to work under the most demanding conditions, often in circumstances where the reputation of the United States hangs in the balance. Experiences in recent years confirm that it is the caliber of the special operations personnel that proves decisive in mission accomplishment.

SPECIALIZED TRAINING

The second fundamental principle of special operations forces is the necessity for rigorous training to exacting standards in a variety of specialized skills. Only first-class training guarantees readiness for war. Training must include not only autonomous special operations exercises, but routine joint training with conventional land, maritime, and air forces. Special operations forces train for missions in contingency operations and war that, in accordance with joint and service doctrine, *only they conduct*. Therefore, special operations training in peacetime must prepare them realistically for the challenges they will face in war.

Examples abound. A special operations soldier recently provided linguistic and information support for the U.S. ambassador to the People's Republic of Mongolia during a humanitarian/medical assistance operation. In Cameroon, a small team of regionally focused special operations civil affairs forces inoculated over 58,000 people against the deadly meningitis bacteria and treated an additional 1,700 people for a wide range of ailments. For many of these Cameroonian people, it was the first time in their lives they had seen a doctor. These same skills serve well in conflict, especially in combined operations with allies and international partners.

Leader training, especially midcareer professional development, is of particular importance. In addition to the outstanding leadership training provided by the services, special operations leaders must refine their tactical and technical skills, sharpen their focus on the integration of special operations forces in joint operations, and increase their understanding of the unique requirements inherent in peacetime military assistance activities. Integrating special operations capabilities into computer-driven command post exercises and battle simulations will also enhance the cooperation and mutual understanding of conventional and special operations leaders.

ADVANCED TECHNOLOGY

The exploitation of emerging technology is vital to special operations forces because it can be decisive in offsetting enemy superiority in numbers, firepower, and mobility. High-technology research and development (R&D) is a key component in special operations modernization planning. Special operations and service R&D programs are closely coordinated to preclude wasteful duplications and to take advantage of shared capabilities. Special emphasis is given to developing improved mobility programs, flexible command and control systems, enhanced night-vision capabilities, and integrated communications systems for special operations and conventional forces at every level of command. These programs increase the ability of special operations forces to respond rapidly and to conduct deep penetrations in denied areas.

Technological exploitation is enhanced by the relatively smaller size of the special operations community, which permits quicker decisions and implementation. To develop and field the right systems on time, special operations R&D programs must be aggressively managed. A primary challenge in this area is to discriminate among emerging technologies and to select those that, through further development, provide the greatest benefit for the resources expended.

FORWARD-LOOKING DOCTRINE

Doctrine for special operations forces must be sufficiently flexible to permit operations in a joint or combined environment, or as an autonomous joint force. Special operations doctrine must also focus on the coordinated integration of special operations capabilities with conventional forces to achieve maximum combat power and effectiveness. To successfully meet these requirements, it must address the broad range of special operations capabilities, from mid-high intensity conflict such as Desert Storm to humanitarian and security assistance programs symbolized by Operation Provide Comfort in northern Iraq. In these operations, special operations forces were required to transition overnight from a combat role to a provider of humanitarian and security assistance.

While special operations doctrine proved effective during operations in Panama, the Gulf, and northern Iraq, continuous updating is needed to provide a framework for future special operations force structure and modernization decisions.

VERSATILE FORCE STRUCTURE

An effective force structure must posture special operations forces to operate in the face of an uncertain threat environment, that is, to meet the entire range of potential requirements of the theater unified commands. Reserve component special operations forces play an important role in enhancing the versatility of the total special operations force. In addition to combat capabilities, reserve component special operations forces possess individual and unit civil affairs and humanitarian assistance skills uniquely suited to peacetime military assistance activities supporting friendly governments. Force planning must continue to ensure that reserve component capabilities appropriately meet anticipated strategic requirements and modernization plans.

Adjustments may be needed in the active/reserve special operations force mix to reflect the changing requirements demanded by a different kind of strategic environment than that which served as a basis for force structure decisions during the Cold War. U.S. Special Operations Command must have the active component capabilities to meet requirements for short- or no-notice contingency and humanitarian assistance operations in more than one theater of operation at a time. The simultaneous and widely separated employment of large contingents of special operations forces in the year 1991 alone demonstrates the need for this capability.

An area meriting particular concern is the requirement for in-theater logistical support. In the past, special operations forces have depended on the services' in-place logistical support structures to provide for the bulk of SOF sustainment. However, as service infrastructures are drawn down, it can be expected that forward-deployed logistical assets will be reduced. This will require SOF to deploy its own tailored support and sustainment organization with forward-employed special operations forces.

Maintaining an effective mix of active ground, maritime, and air forces, with a corresponding reserve structure to provide for sustainment and depth, is a cornerstone of U.S. national security strategy and a tenet for special operations planners.

CONCLUSION

Today the United States is in a position to influence positively the overseas security environment by fostering economic progress and political stability. In pursuit of such goals, special operations forces are an ideal instrument. The versatility and readiness of U.S. special operations forces provide the National Command Authorities and defense policy makers with a wide range of feasible alternatives, including simultaneous operations on several fronts.

The United States must continue to field a robust special operations force capable of deterring and countering an unprecedented range of hostile threats to U.S. interests. At the same time, the United States must field special operations forces for involvement in peacetime military assistance activities to promote the multiple objectives of U.S. foreign and national security policies.

NOTES

1. George Bush, *National Security Strategy of the United States, 1991–1992* (Washington: Brassey's, 1991), 15.

2. Activated on 1 April 1987, USSOCOM was formed as a result of the Cohen-Nunn Amendment to the 1986 Defense Reorganization Act. Some of the tasks assigned to USSOCOM include: (a) responsible for all joint SOF doctrine, tactics, techniques, and procedures; (b) train assigned forces and ensure interoperability of forces and equipment; (c) monitor preparedness of SOF worldwide; (d) develop and acquire unique SOF equipment, materiel, supplies, and services (RD&A authority); (e) responsible for SOF Program (MFP 11) and budget.

3. William J. Crowe Jr., USSOCOM Headquarters Activation Ceremony, 1 June 1987, MacDill Air Force Base, Florida.

4. William B. Milam, Ambassador to Bangladesh, letter to Commander, 3d Battalion, 1st Special Forces Group, 29 January 1991.

NEW CONTINGENCIES, OLD ROLES

SAMUEL P. HUNTINGTON

Few issues are more important than the roles and missions of the armed forces in the post–Cold War era. We are in the midst of major changes in the structure of the international system and of serious challenges to national security. This is not, however, the first time the nation has faced such challenges. At the birth of the Republic we had to establish the military and naval forces to deal with threats from Europe. With the end of the Napoleonic era our national defense changed dramatically, as did the

This essay has been edited and is reprinted from Joint Forces Quarterly 2 (Autumn 1993): 38–43, *by permission of* Joint Forces Quarterly.

armed forces. This situation remained fixed in its essentials until the close of the nineteenth century when America emerged as a world power. At that time the nation consigned the Indian-fighting army and the commerce-protecting navy to history and in their stead created an army designed for big wars and a navy for big battles. That system served us well throughout two world wars. But by the late 1940s with the advent of the Cold War we needed a new defense establishment. Now *that* conflict is over, and once again the nation must debate the nature of our national interests and the roles of the armed forces, just as earlier generations did in 1784, 1815, 1898, and 1946. In effect, we have to move on to a fifth phase of American defense policy.

NONTRADITIONAL AND NONMILITARY

The term "nontraditional roles" obviously implies a distinction between traditional and nontraditional military roles. The traditional roles of the armed forces will presumably continue, but in this fifth phase of American military history the services will perform new nontraditional roles. Some new roles have evolved, others have been promoted by the Congress, in particular by Senator Sam Nunn, the former chairman of the Senate Armed Services Committee. It was largely due to his leadership that the Defense Authorization Act of 1993 encouraged the armed forces to conduct an antidrug campaign targeted at inner-city youths, to provide role models for youth and health care to underserved communities, and to address domestic ills by improving the environment and economic and social conditions. In a speech in the Senate, Senator Nunn stated:

While the Soviet threat is gone, at home we are still battling drugs, poverty, urban decay, lack of self-esteem, unemployment, and racism. The military certainly cannot solve these problems. . . . But I am convinced that there is a proper and important role the armed forces can play in addressing these pressing issues. I believe we can reinvigorate the military's spectrum of capabilities to address such needs as deteriorating infrastructure, the lack of role models for tens of thousands if not millions of young people, limited training and education opportunities for the disadvantaged, and serious health and nutrition problems facing many of our citizens, particularly our children.[1]

These clearly seem to be nontraditional roles. But are they really? The fact is that there are almost no conceivable roles in this new phase of our history that the armed forces have not performed in the past. The distinction to be made is not between traditional and nontraditional roles but between military and nonmilitary roles or, more precisely, between combat missions and noncombat missions. The purpose of the armed forces is combat: to deter and defeat enemies of the United States. That is their principal role or raison d'être, the justification for expending the resources needed to establish and maintain them. Forces created to perform that role,

however, can be—and have been throughout our history—employed in noncombat, nonmilitary uses.

For over three decades the United States Military Academy at West Point trained all of the nation's engineers, civilian as well as military. Throughout the nineteenth century the army engaged in the economic and political development of the country. It explored and surveyed the West, chose sites for forts and planned settlements, built roadways, and developed waterways. And for years the army performed roles that now are performed by agencies like the National Weather Service and the Geological Survey. In the latter part of the last century, the Army Signal Corps pioneered the development of the telegraph and telephone. The navy was equally active in exploration and scientific research. Naval ships explored the Amazon, surveyed the coastlines of North and South America, laid cables on the ocean floor, and gathered scientific data from around the world. They also policed the slave trade. Naval officers negotiated dozens of treaties and oversaw lighthouses, life-saving services, coastal surveys, and steamboat inspection. The army ran civil governments in the South during Reconstruction and at the same time governed Alaska for ten years. It was, of course, frequently called upon to intervene in labor strikes and domestic unrest. The Army Corps of Engineers constructed public buildings and canals and other civil works including the Panama Canal. Soldiers helped to combat malaria in Panama and cholera, hunger, and illiteracy in Cuba, Haiti, and Nicaragua. They also established schools, built works projects, promoted public health, organized elections, and encouraged democracy in those countries. In the 1930s the army took on the immense task of recruiting, organizing, and administering the Civilian Conservation Corps.

After recent hurricanes in Florida and Hawaii many people hailed the superb contributions of the armed forces to disaster relief as evidence of a *new* role. Nothing could have been more incorrect. The services have regularly provided such relief in the past. As an official army history puts it, in the decades of the 1920s and 1930s, "the most conspicuous employment of the Army within the United States . . . was in a variety of tasks that only the Army had the resources and organization to tackle quickly. In floods and blizzards and hurricanes it was the Army that was first on the spot with cots, blankets, and food."[2] This has been true throughout our history. It is hard to think of a nonmilitary role without precedent for such roles are as American as apple pie.

FUTURE ROLES AND MISSIONS

Throughout our history, however, nonmilitary roles have never been used to justify maintaining the armed forces. The overall size, composition, and organization as well as recruitment, equipping, and training of the services have been based on our national interests and the missions—the combat missions—to be performed. In this fifth phase of

American defense policy the roles of the Armed Forces remain as important as ever. There are three roles that present themselves today.

MAINTAINING SUPERIORITY

For the first time in sixty years, no major power, no rival, poses a national security challenge to the United States. We need defense policy and the capability not to contain or deter an existing threat as was the case during the Cold War, but rather to prevent the emergence of a new threat. To accomplish this goal, we must maintain a substantial, invulnerable nuclear retaliatory capability and deploy forces in both Europe and Asia to reassure allies and to preclude German or Japanese rearmament. We must also maintain both technological and maritime superiority, and provide a base for the rapid and effective development of a new enhanced defense capability if a major threat should begin to emerge.

REGIONAL SECURITY

Significant threats exist to our national interests in Southwest and East Asia, and we must have the capability to deal with them as we did in the Gulf War. To deter or defeat regional aggression the United States needs light and heavy land forces, tactical aviation, naval and marine forces designed to fight from the sea against enemies on land, and the sealift and airlift to deploy forces rapidly to the scene of combat. Ideally the United States should be able to fight the equivalent of the Gulf War. The late Secretary of Defense Les Aspin's "Option C" purportedly would provide this capability. Whether in five years the armed forces will be able to mount an operation like Desert Storm against an enemy similar to Iraq remains to be seen.

Our decisive victory in the Persian Gulf, however, makes it unlikely that we will be able to repeat that victory. Major regional aggressors in the future are likely to possess and use nuclear weapons. This reality was reflected in the reply of the Indian defense minister who, when asked what lesson he drew from the Gulf War, said: "Don't fight the United States unless you have nuclear weapons."[3] Likely aggressors—North Korea, Iran, Iraq—are intent on acquiring nuclear weapons. But until they get them the probability of stability in their respective regions is reasonably high. Once they do acquire these weapons, however, the likelihood they will use them is also high. In all probability the first sure knowledge the world will have that such powers possess a usable nuclear weapon will be the explosion of a weapon on the territory of one of their neighbors. Such an act is likely to be accompanied by a massive conventional offensive to quickly occupy Seoul, Saudi oil fields, or whatever other target the aggressor has in mind. That is the most serious type of regional threat that we may confront, and perhaps the most probable.

Coping with that kind of aggression will place new demands—nontraditional demands—on the armed forces. They will have to fight an enemy who has a small number of nuclear weapons and little or no inhibition to use them. To deter this first use by a rogue state, the United States will have to threaten massive retaliation, possibly nuclear. The principal role of Strategic Command in the coming years will be to maintain nuclear peace in the Third World.

FOREIGN INTERNAL DEFENSE

The armed forces may have to intervene quickly and effectively in countries important to our national security interests in order to restore a government to power that has been overthrown, remove a hostile regime, protect American lives and property abroad, rescue hostages, eliminate terrorists, destroy drug traffickers, or engage in other actions that normally fall under the rubric of low-intensity conflict. Whether or not a state is aggressive or pacific, reasonably decent or totally threatening, depends overwhelmingly on the nature of its government. President Clinton has appropriately said that the promotion of democracy should be a central, perhaps even the central, theme of U.S. foreign policy. In those areas critical to our national security, the United States has to be prepared to defend governments that are friendly and democratic and to overthrow those that are unfriendly and undemocratic.

This requirement also emphasizes a new role for the armed forces: targeting dictatorships and their leaders. In the Gulf War, the U.S.-led coalition degraded by more than 50 percent the capability of the Iraqi military, and also brought Iraqi society to a virtual standstill. But that tremendous use of force failed to eliminate the true villains of peace, Iraq's government. The elimination of Saddam Hussein was an established U.S. objective, although not one endorsed by the United Nations, and it was not achieved. Indeed, during the last decade, we have attempted to eliminate three hostile dictators: Muammar Qaddafi, Manuel Noriega, and Saddam Hussein. We only succeeded in the case of Noriega, and that took time and caused us some embarrassment because it involved a tiny country about which American intelligence must have been the best in the world. Targeting and incapacitating dictatorial governments will be an important role for the armed forces in the coming years, and it is one with respect to which our capabilities are now sadly deficient.

FUTURE CHALLENGES

Besides the military roles that the armed forces can expect to perform in the post–Cold War world, what are the appropriate nonmilitary—or civilian—roles that loom on the horizon? As indicated previously, these roles have been historically numerous and diverse, and no reason exists to suggest that they will not be continued. Future missions could involve the following:

- Domestic activities as highlighted by Senator Nunn and in the Defense Authorization Act.

- Humanitarian assistance at home and abroad when welcomed by local governments.

- Peacekeeping at the invitation of the parties involved in the conflicts.

There is another type of mission—one about which questions have arisen—illustrated by the crisis in Somalia. Should the armed forces provide humanitarian assistance in those situations where such efforts are likely to be opposed by one or more of the conflicting parties? Clearly some form of international authorization, presumably approval by the United Nations, is a prerequisite for action by the United States. This occurred with the precedent-breaking U.N. Security Council Resolution 688 that authorized intervention by U.S., British, and French forces in order to protect the Kurds in northern Iraq. The United Nations has also given approval to deploy outside military forces in Bosnia as well as in Somalia to provide humanitarian assistance to the innocent victims of civil war and anarchy.

DEFINING THE LIMITS

The goal of our involvement in such situations is presumably to ensure that relief supplies reach the intended beneficiaries. This means that the armed forces should be able to act militarily to prevent or eliminate hostile action against efforts to deliver relief supplies. While that is certainly an appropriate response, there is a need to define the limits of U.S. involvement in such missions, and this gives rise to two problems.

First, so long as the conditions in the country concerned remain violent, external military force will be required to ensure that food and medical supplies reach their intended recipients. If the United Nations is unable to provide those forces, this could mean an extended if not indefinite American commitment. This is not a Gulf War–type situation where it was possible to drive the invading Iraqi forces out of Kuwait and then pack up and go home. In the case of Bosnia it could mean waiting for the South Slavs or other conflicting parties to resolve their differences by political or military means before extricating ourselves. And that could take a very, very long time.

Second, there is the problem of becoming an active participant in the conflict in the country concerned. One or more parties in that conflict may perceive any outside involvement as a hostile act. Thus by deploying American troops, from the viewpoint of the local combatants, we become the enemy. Inevitably while we are there for humanitarian purposes our presence has political and military consequences. The United States has a clear humanitarian interest in preventing genocide and starvation, and Americans will support intervention to deal with such tragedies within limits. When Somali clans or Slavic factions fight each other, we may attempt to mitigate the horrendous consequences that flow from the violence. Under such circumstances the nation may even accept some American casualties. But the United States has no interest in which clan dominates Somalia, or where boundary lines are drawn in the Balkans. Americans will not support intervention that appears to be directed toward political goals. It is morally unjustifiable and politically indefensible that members of the armed forces should be killed to prevent Somalis from killing one another.

The armed forces can and should, if it is appropriate, be put to a variety of civilian uses, including domestic social and economic renewal, humanitarian and disaster relief both at home and abroad, and peacekeeping operations. The military should only be given military missions that involve possible combat, however, when they advance national security interests and are directed against a foreign enemy of the United States.

The possible nonmilitary roles of the armed forces have recently received a good amount of attention. Arguments have been made that the military should be organized and trained in order to perform such roles. A proposal has been made, for instance, that a unified command should be established for humanitarian assistance operations. In a somewhat similar fashion, a commission of former government officials has proposed creating a military command headed by a three- or four-star officer to provide support for U.N. peacekeeping operations and to develop doctrine, carry out planning, and train U.S. forces for such operations. The United States, another group argued, "should retain and promote officers whose expertise includes peacekeeping, humanitarian administration, and civilian support operations."[4]

Such proposals are basically misconceived. The mission of the armed forces is combat, to deter and defeat enemies of the United States. The military must be recruited, organized, trained, and equipped for that purpose alone. Its capabilities can, and should, be used for humanitarian and other civilian activities, but the military should not be organized or prepared or trained to perform such roles. A military force is fundamentally antihumanitarian: its purpose is to kill people in the most efficient way possible. That is why nations have traditionally maintained armies and navies. Should the military perform other roles? Absolutely, and as previously stated they have done so throughout our history. Should these roles define the armed forces? Absolutely not. All such roles should be spillover uses of the armed forces that can be performed because the services possess the organization, training, and equipment that are only maintained to defend the nation.

NOTES

1. Public Law 102-484, 28 October, 1992, secs. 376, 1045, and 1081; Sam Nunn, *Congressional Record* 138, no. 91 (1992): S 8602.

2. Maurice Matloff, editor, *American Military History* (Washington, D.C.: GPO, 1969), 413.

3. Quoted in Les Aspin, "From Deterrence to Denuking: Dealing with Proliferation in the 1990s," Memorandum, 18 February, 1992, 6.

4. Carnegie Endowment for International Peace and Institute for International Economics, Memorandum to the President-Elect, Subject: "Harnessing Process to Purpose" (Washington: Carnegie Endowment for International Peace, 1992), 17; Thomas G. Weiss and Kurt M. Campbell, "Military Humanitarianism," *Survival* 33 (September–October 1991): 457.

DOMESTIC MISSIONS FOR THE ARMED FORCES

SAM NUNN

The end of the cold war has created a number of opportunities, as well as challenges, for our nation. The collapse of the Warsaw Pact and the Soviet Union give us a chance to make significant reductions in the size of our military forces and our defense budget. Recent nuclear weapons agreements have diffused a portion of the world's arsenal of weapons of mass destruction. But tremors of instability and outright regional conflict are continuing to shake many parts of the globe. These volatile situations, coupled with the changing nature of the world's balance of power, mean that we must still maintain a strong, and perhaps, even more flexible military force.

FORGING CIVIL–MILITARY COOPERATION FOR COMMUNITY REGENERATION

Over the next few years, the nation will continue the debate over what size the base force should be, what roles and missions it should undertake, and how it should be structured. There is considerable uncertainty at this time on just what kind of a military capability we will need in the future and what size force will be adequate.

We are leaving a security era that demanded large numbers of U.S. combat forces stationed overseas or operating in forward locations at high states of combat readiness in order to confront a large and quantitatively superior opponent. That era has ended. We are entering a security era that permits a shift in our overall strategy more toward smaller force levels, with fewer overseas deployments and lower operating tempos. The exact size and organization of this future base force is still taking shape. It will be a smaller force than we have today. We all know that. It will have to be just as professional—and even more flexible. The force will still need a basic amount of combat and operations training to sustain

maximum proficiency as well as readiness. But there will be a much greater opportunity than in the past to use military assets and training to assist civilian efforts in critical domestic needs.

The Los Angeles riots of May 1992, with their terrible cost in life and property, should remind us all that our society faces numerous domestic challenges that in many respects are as daunting as any potential foreign threat to our national security. While the Soviet threat is gone, we are still battling at home drugs, poverty, urban decay, lack of self-esteem, unemployment, and racism. The military certainly cannot solve all of these problems, and I do not propose any magic solution to the numerous problems we have at home. But I am totally convinced that there is a proper and important role the armed forces can play in addressing many of these pressing issues. I believe we can reinvigorate the military's spectrum of capabilities to address such needs as deteriorating infrastructure, the lack of role models for tens of thousands, indeed hundreds of thousands if not millions, of young people, limited training and education opportunities for the disadvantaged, and serious health and nutrition problems facing many of our citizens, particularly our children.

THE ARMY'S DOMESTIC ACTION PROGRAM

There is a solid precedent for civil–military cooperation in addressing domestic problems. Army Regulation 28-19, developed under the leadership of Secretary Howard "Bo" Callaway in the Ford administration and issued in 1975, authorized a Domestic Action program. The purpose of the program was to authorize "use of Department of the Army human and physical resources to assist and support the continued improvement and development of society." Under this program, local military commanders

This essay has been edited and is reprinted from Domestic Missions for the Armed Forces *(Carlisle Barracks, PA: U.S. Army War College, February 1993), 1–13, by permission of the Army War College.*

helped communities with activities such as fixing up recreation facilities and conducting summer programs for disadvantaged young people. The program was decentralized, however, and, of course, in many respects needed to be decentralized. But it had very little management emphasis from the army's leadership. In the 1980s, as the army increased its focus on military training, interest in the Domestic Action program faded, and the regulation was rescinded in 1988.

ASSIST IN MEETING DOMESTIC NEEDS WITH INNOVATIVE MILITARY TRAINING

As we restructure our armed forces over the next decade, the attention of civilian and military leadership at the Department of Defense (DOD) must remain focused on training the armed forces for their primary mission, which is the military mission. But that goal, in my view, is compatible with enhancing the military's ability to assist in meeting domestic needs. Creative commanders have always devised numerous innovative activities for their units—beyond routine training—to build morale and also to build unit cohesion. Community service projects present an excellent opportunity for them to do so while providing important services to our society. The military involvement in counternarcotics activities is a good example of a mission that enhances military skills, helps address an important domestic problem, and improves the morale of the people involved.

During markup of the National Defense Authorization Act for fiscal 1993, I offered a proposal to authorize the armed forces to engage in appropriate community service programs. The basic concept is outlined below.

PRINCIPLES AND OBJECTIVES OF A CIVIL–MILITARY COOPERATIVE ACTION PROGRAM

I want to stress at the outset that any such programs must be governed by three essential principles:

1. Any such project must be undertaken in a manner that is consistent with the military mission of the unit in question.

2. The project must fill a need that is not otherwise being met and must not compete with the private sector or with services provided by other government agencies.

3. The program cannot become a basis for justifying additional overall military expenditures or for retaining excess military personnel. Projects should be undertaken only with personnel, resources, and facilities that exist for legitimate military purposes.

Building on the army's experience with its Domestic Action program, I would envision a new Civil–Military Cooperative Action program with the following objectives:

- Enhancing individual and unit training and morale through meaningful community involvement.

- Encouraging cooperation between civilian and military sectors of our society.

- Advancing equal opportunity in the nation and helping to alleviate racial tension and conflict and strife and misunderstandings in our nation.

- Enriching the civilian economy by transfer of technological advances and manpower skills.

- Improving the ecological environment and economic and social conditions of the areas that are within the reach of our existing military base structure.

- Increasing the opportunities for disadvantaged citizens, particularly children, to receive employment, training, education, and recreation.

The program would be organized under the supervision of the assistant secretary of defense for force management and personnel. I believe that we should give the military departments and the Department of Defense broad discretion to manage the program in a manner consistent with their military missions, who would in turn grant flexibility to local commanders in the implementation of the program. Every base will be different–different missions, different talents, different capabilities, different geographic areas. There will not be one model for the country.

To ensure that projects meet important community needs and do not compete with the private sector and other government organizations, local installations would establish advisory councils on civil–military cooperation. In these groups, officials from the military installations; representatives of appropriate local, state, and federal agencies; leaders of civic and social service organizations; and business and labor representatives from the private sector would meet to provide advice to local commanders in planning and executing civilian military projects.

If we commit ourselves to it, this plan, as I view it, can make a major contribution to community restoration and regeneration efforts across the country. Over the years American taxpayers have invested in and have built a great stockpile of innovative ideas, knowledge, trained and talented people, and equipment in the military. These resources, if properly matched to local needs and coordinated with civilian efforts, can make a useful contribution to addressing the problems we face in blighted urban areas, in neglected rural regions, in schools, and elsewhere.

OPPORTUNITIES FOR MILITARY ASSISTANCE

Depending on the capabilities and availability of specific units, and the needs of local communities, the armed forces can assist civilian authorities in addressing a significant number of domestic problems.

ROLE MODELS

I would put at the top of the list role models. One of the key strengths of the armed forces is developing role models. Hard-working, disciplined men and women who command respect and honor in their very presence can serve as a very powerful force among our young people—especially where family structures are weakened by poverty, drugs, and crime. We should enhance opportunities for good role models to interact with our young people.

Take, for example, the case of Sergeant First Class Lenard Robinson, stationed at Fort Bragg, North Carolina, who actively corresponded with learning-handicapped children at a school in California while he was overseas during Operation Desert Storm. Typically, learning-handicapped children have great difficulty expressing themselves in writing. Sergeant Robinson's vivid descriptions of his experiences overseas, combined with photos and videos that he sent, have inspired many children to read his letters. And many of the children, who never wrote more than a few words before they heard of Sergeant Robinson, now write long letters to him. We have thousands of Sergeant Robinsons in our military services today.

The YESS program in Michigan is a collaborative effort between the private sector, nonprofit organizations, and the Michigan National Guard to provide disadvantaged young people with role models and specific educational skills. Young people live on a military base for five days, receive science and math tutoring, and are exposed to military hardware and operations. This provides an exciting, stimulating environment not only to enhance their educational skills, but also to provide them with role models that encourage these young people to set goals for their own lives. It enables them to look at others who have come from similar circumstances and say, "If they did it, I can do it also."

The nation is familiar with our senior military leaders, many of whom are black who served our nation so well during Operation Desert Storm, such as General Colin Powell and Lieutenant General Calvin Waller. Over 400,000 members of the armed forces today who serve our nation well and ably who are black, and over 90,000 who are Hispanic, whose service, in Operation Desert Storm and elsewhere, represent a model for every citizen in our country. These include marines such as Captain Ed Ray, a light infantry company commander whose testimony before our committee about combat in Operation Desert Storm demonstrated the professionalism and competence of our junior officers. Or Specialist Jonathan Alston of the Second Armored Division whose heroism in Desert Storm earned him the Silver Star and who is featured in the television docudrama "The Heroes of Desert Storm." These individuals can serve, not just those who have been in Desert Storm but thousands of others who have achieved great professionalism. They can serve as a role model in community service programs throughout our country.

But there must be a structured program to enable community organizations to benefit from the capabilities and qualities of military role models. Military leadership, at both the officer and enlisted level, is an example of unique national resources. Why not use this resource as an example to tens of thousands of inner-city and rural youth who, for example, may never have had a father in their own home?

REHABILITATION AND RENEWAL OF COMMUNITY FACILITIES

All across this country, schools, public housing, and recreational facilities, as well as roads and bridges, need repair in areas where government funds and private sector involvement are simply not available. Active duty and reserve units, particularly those with engineering capabilities, could participate in restoring part of our infrastructure in this country. Military construction units may need to be beefed up and perhaps redistributed to ensure that capabilities exist in all geographic areas to meet this important need.

Bill Guilfoil of the Atlanta Project at the Carter Center in Georgia reported to me that at least 1,500 public housing units are boarded up and unoccupied in Atlanta because of their state of disrepair. Meanwhile, the city's homeless population numbers at least 12,000. I think this story would be repeated in city after city after city across our land.

There are dozens of combat engineer units, located in Georgia, that really need to do construction and maintenance training in order to keep up their proficiency because that is what they do. That is what they have to do in any kind of conflict. I think it makes sense to put those domestic needs and our military engineering resources together. Army combat engineering units could be effectively used to repair dilapidated public housing, repair aging schools, and refurbish old recreational facilities. They could also provide temporary facilities to meet pressing public needs. The Women's Infants and Children program center that served the south central Los Angeles area was destroyed in the riots, leaving the area without the capability to ensure that children and pregnant mothers receive vital nutrition. The military has the capability to provide temporary buildings on a very short notice. Why not use this capability to deal with such an emergency?

Last year, in Operation Provide Comfort in Iraq, military maintenance and construction units built housing, laid cement roads, put in plumbing systems—and the list goes on and on—for the desperate Kurds. We have desperate people in America. Why not put those resources to work at home? In many areas, these units are located right next door to blighted areas.

NATIONAL GUARD BUREAU FOR A NATIONAL GUARD YOUTH CORPS

The military should examine ways to refocus local reserve component training on local community support initiatives whenever feasible and operationally justified. I will be proposing a pilot program to be implemented by the National Guard Bureau for a National Guard Youth Corps.

In the Department of Defense Appropriations Act for fiscal 1992, Congress appropriated funds for the National Guard Bureau to develop a program designed to demonstrate how disadvantaged youth can be aided through a program, based on a military model, of education, personal and skills development, and work in service to their communities. The National Guard Bureau has since completed its work on designing a pilot program. I think it is very promising. As it is currently envisioned, the chief of the National Guard Bureau would be authorized to enter into agreements with the governors of ten states to operate a military-based training program to improve basic skills and employability of high school dropouts.

The program would require a relatively modest investment of the talent that is already available in National Guard units. I also have been informed that General Colin Powell is interested in expanding the Junior ROTC training program, an effort, which I applaud, that could benefit from the types of assistance that I have outlined in these remarks. An expansion of the Junior ROTC program, particularly in our inner cities, could be very beneficial.

If these plans are implemented, they could do much to help the young people of our country. Why not put our military resources to work on this type endeavor?

SUMMER PROGRAMS

Our young people need other kinds of help. I believe we should investigate ways to refocus DOD summer hire programs to recruit disadvantaged students where feasible. In areas where the DOD operates schools, teachers and perhaps facilities could be involved in summer school outreach to disadvantaged children. Why not put these resources to work in areas of greatest need?

JOB TRAINING AND EDUCATION

There is a dire need for job training and education—especially in the inner cities—to enable men and women to meet the needs of the evolving workplace. While our educational system and private industry must bear the primary responsibility for training and education, there may be opportunities in specific locations for civil–military cooperation in the use of military training facilities to assist in meeting these needs. Why not look at our military resources as a resource for this kind of training and education?

MEDICAL TRANSPORT

Our ability to transport people to medical facilities in an emergency can never be fast enough, particularly for trauma victims. Every day, military medevac units must log certain hours of flight training. That is what they train for all year long, to be ready in a contingency. That is what they are in business to do, to help evacuate people in a conflict situation. I submit that they should be allowed to do so while helping our own citizens at the same time. Currently, 97 percent of the aeromedical evacuation units are in the Air National Guard and Air Force Reserve. These units provide long-distance medical evacuation. In addition, one reserve and seventeen active helicopter units in the army and one air force reserve helicopter unit provide short-distance emergency medical evacuation under the Military Assistance to Safety and Traffic program already available in a number of states. In Georgia, for example, the 498th medical company at Fort Benning has provided critical emergency medical support to assist communities throughout southwest Georgia, particularly in rural areas. I believe that these units can be more centrally integrated and managed as they train to provide even more assistance to our communities.

Communities that do not have access to current military or civilian medical transportation services need these resources. Why not look at the inventory of our military resources, determine which areas can be matched up, determine where the private sector is not able to provide this kind of service, and use the military in meeting these critical needs?

PUBLIC HEALTH OUTREACH

In a similar vein, there are many citizens in both urban and rural areas who lack the very basics of health and medical services. There may be opportunities in specific locations to use DOD medical capabilities to assist civilian authorities in providing public health outreach to these urban areas. The Centers for Disease Control in Atlanta estimates that fewer than half of all American children are fully immunized against diseases such as polio, diphtheria, tetanus, measles, and rubella. Infant vaccination and basic medical treatment are services that the military provides routinely in humanitarian missions abroad. Why not use these resources at home?

NUTRITION

There may be areas in which the military could even play a useful role by assisting civilian authorities in addressing the serious problem of hunger in America. The Food Research and Action Center has estimated that five million children under the age of twelve—one in eight in America—suffer from hunger.

An old military saying is that "the army travels on its stomach." The military has extensive food storage, preparation, and distribution systems. Military units responsible for these systems, including those in the National Guard and Reserves, could play an important role in the distribution of surplus food. They could help provide transportation, storage, and preparation assistance to federal, state, and local agencies while they are preparing for their basic mission.

Where civilian agencies need this assistance, and military units are capable of providing it, why not put these resources to work?

AN OPPORTUNITY FOR POSITIVE CHANGE

The time to turn these ideas into action, I think, is now—during this window of change and flexibility. As we reconfigure our military forces for our future defense requirements, I believe that we can reduce some of the combat missions that have been assigned to the National Guard and Reserves. At the same time, because warning times will be much longer, we should realign more of the military's support missions to the National Guard and Reserves. These support units must be distributed in a regionally balanced way to provide a more effective capability for each state, with the added benefit of facilitating the opportunities for civil–military cooperation. Pentagon officials should put greater emphasis on coordinating military training with the potential benefits that such training can have in improving our communities. They need authority to do so and they need an expression from the congressional branch of government to do so.

I am confident that this Civil–Military Cooperative Action program can be structured in a manner consistent with our military needs, without competing with the private sector or other government agencies. It is imperative that we not undercut private enterprise. But we can all look at the cities of our country today, we can look at the problems in Los Angeles and the problems in Atlanta and the problems in Chicago and the problems in New York and Boston, and on and on, and we can easily say, without any fear of being repudiated, that the private

sector cannot handle the job that needs to be done. All we have to do is look at the federal budget deficit and know that there is not going to be an instant solution with huge—billions and billions of dollars—of new expenditures.

There are many opportunities for the military to get involved. I do not pretend the military can solve all these problems. They would have to be carefully tailored to each individual base, each individual unit's capability, and we would have to keep our focus on the military mission, first and foremost, but there are many opportunities for military assistance to community needs that cannot be met with current private sector or civilian public resources.

I watched the faces of the people who fought in Desert Storm. I watched the faces of those who provided relief to people who were dying on the desert and who they had been fighting with a few minutes before, and I watched the young people, and the satisfaction they had in helping people who were dying in need. I also talked to many people who came back from helping the Kurds. I talked to people who had come back from helping in Bangladesh. Nothing gives military people more pride than carrying out a mission of humanity, a mission of peace, a mission of mercy. This is something they enjoy doing. It gives them tremendous satisfaction and it is something they do well.

By using the capabilities we have in the military, we can assist civilian authorities in addressing the critical fundamentals upon which a healthy society, a healthy economy, and a healthy military are built. I believe this is a sensible investment we can make in our future, and a vital one. I believe that working together we can develop a vibrant Civil–Military Cooperative Action program to begin working on some of these problems that afflict our nation.

PEACEKEEPING: THE DEEPENING DEBATE

WILLIAM H. LEWIS

Commentators, scholars, and policy practitioners have devoted increasing attention to the question of providing the United Nations with enhanced capabilities in the fields of peacemaking, peace enforcement, and peacekeeping.[1] This attention, which appears to be replacing arms control and strategic studies in intensity of interest, may prove no more than a passing fad. But it is my view that, with the collapse of the Soviet empire and evaporation of the notion of a "new world order," the potentialities and

limitations of the United Nations system in coping with an increasingly volatile international security environment will prove of more enduring concern to the American foreign policy community.

The purposes of the United Nations, as stated in its charter, are "to maintain international peace and security, and to that end to take effective collective measures for the prevention and removal of threats to the peace, and for the suppression of acts of aggression or other breaches of the peace."[2] To these

This essay has been edited and is reprinted from Strategic Review 21 (Summer 1993): 26–32, *by permission of the United States Strategic Institute.*

ends, U.N.-sponsored military forces fought two major wars (Korea and Kuwait) over the past forty-five years, launched more than a dozen peacekeeping operations, and mediated a comparable number of international disputes. In the United States, however, official views about the United Nations have generally oscillated between the "euphoric and the cynical"—for some, it is the ultimate mechanism for the resolution of international conflict, for others, a "dangerous place" in which U.S. freedom of action can only be constrained by the machinations of "foreigners" whose goals and objectives clash with those of the United States.

Somalia could well prove the test case for U.S. collaboration and U.N. competence. The latter stumbled badly in 1991–92 when, in the wake of the overthrow of a petty tyrant, Siad Barre, civil war spread and the last strands of organized government vanished. The world body could mount neither an effective peacemaking operation nor a coherent humanitarian relief effort. As Somalia descended into chaos with thousands of defenseless Somalis dying of starvation, President George Bush ordered 25,000 American troops into the area to ensure safe delivery of food and medical assistance. By the end of 1992, local U.S. commanders and U.N. Secretary-General Boutros Boutros-Ghali were in open disagreement concerning the goals and missions of the U.S. forces, their length of stay, and the mandate of the United Nations in replacing U.S. forces.[3] Finally, agreement was reached early in 1993 that a U.N. coalition force, under a Turkish general, would replace U.S. troops deployed there on or about May 1, 1993, with a mandate to enforce the peace and to help establish the foundations of a national political system. The U.S. government, for its part, agreed to retain four to five thousand American military personnel in Somalia under U.N. command.

Several policy issues have arisen as a by-product of this arrangement. Most immediate and pressing for the Clinton administration is the "precedent" of placing U.S. forces under foreign command. Some observers and commentators have objected, contending that "never before has there been foreign command of U.S. military units."[4] Second, they hold that such action represents a derogation of U.S. national sovereignty, a challenge to the Constitution—and the War Powers Act—and an erosion of the responsibilities of the president as commander in chief.[5] In addition, critics perceive proposals to justify U.S. involvement in peacekeeping operations under the terms of Article 43 of the United Nations Charter as being at odds with Article 51, which affirms each member state's right to individual or collective self-defense. The U.N. commander's takeover of responsibility for security and nation building in Somalia, with U.S. forces in a subordinate position, is viewed by these critics as merely the opening chapter in a post–Cold War age of U.N. ascendancy.

A REJUVENATED UNITED NATIONS?

Opponents of American acquiescence to a "unique chain of command" under U.N. leadership and direction point to Boutros-Ghali as the *deus ex machina*, most particularly, his reliance on Article 43 of the charter. As one critic wrote:

On Article 43 rest the extravagant aspirations of Boutros-Ghali and the equally extravagant hopes of those Americans who think the United Nations could relieve the United States of the burdens of being the only superpower.[6]

The critics, perhaps inadvertently, have struck on a central question confronting both the U.S. government and other U.N. member states. Put simply, whether the U.N. system for peacekeeping (in the generic sense) should rely on ad hoc coalitions led by the United States (or some other "leader" nation) or on an institutionalized arrangement fashioned under the direction of the secretary-general and the Security Council.

Secretary-General Boutros-Ghali, in a June 1992 report to the Security Council, followed by an article in *Foreign Affairs,* has called for U.S. endorsement of his efforts to strengthen U.N. capabilities to "maintain peace and stability."[7] The secretary-general identifies U.N. objectives in broad social terms—to maintain the peace by "securing justice and human rights" through "social progress and better standards of living." In his view, security and socioeconomic issues form part of a seamless web. With this as a conceptual framework for action, he holds that the organization's energies should be directed toward (1) *preventive diplomacy*—to mediate disputes or, if required, prevent their escalation; (2) *peacemaking*—to initiate military and diplomatic actions aimed at resolving contentious issues peacefully (through measures envisaged in Chapter VI of the charter); and (3) *peacekeeping*—to preserve the peace by dispatching U.N. forces, "with the consent of the parties concerned," to assist in implementing agreements concluded by the peacemakers. The secretary-general also suggests a fourth field, *peace building*—to "identify and support structures which will tend to strengthen and solidify peace in order to avoid a relapse into conflict."

Each of the fields has distinctive imperatives. For example, preventive diplomacy requires measures to create a climate of confidence among potential adversaries; it also requires establishment of an early warning system to alert the United Nations and regional organizations to impending crises; finally, it might necessitate deployment of military units to crisis areas for deterrent purposes. Boutros-Ghali notes that just as diplomacy can be expected to cover all four fields of activity, "so there may not be a clear dividing line between peacemaking and peacekeeping."

ENHANCING THE U.N.'S CONFLICT RESOLUTION ROLE

The secretary-general's goals are clearly delineated. He wishes to have the United Nations assume an internationally accepted, enhanced conflict resolution role. To achieve this, three criteria must be met—greater control over planning and execution of military operations by the United Nations, creation of standby and standing forces that would be placed at the disposal of the Security Council and the secretary-general, and sufficient funding and logistics to underwrite demands placed on the United Nations to stabilize and control conflict situations as they arise. As for U.S. "input," Boutros-Ghali is guarded; he clearly wishes to avoid a repetition of the Gulf War experience, during which the Security Council "chose to authorize member states to take measures on its behalf."

In addressing future crisis situations, the secretary-general proposes to bring into being the special arrangements "foreseen" in Articles 42 and 43 of the charter:

- Member states should provide assurance that they will undertake to make armed forces, assistance, and facilities available to the Security Council "not only on an *ad hoc* basis but on a permanent basis."

- To ensure the availability of these forces, the Security Council is urged to initiate negotiations with the member states.

- The Military Staff Committee should be encouraged to play an active role involving support for military planning and diplomatic negotiations.

As envisaged by the secretary-general, the mission of on-call forces under Article 43 would be to respond to aggression, "imminent or actual." Their assigned responsibility—designated peace enforcement—would exceed the traditional missions of United Nations peacekeeping forces. Because of the financial burdens associated with the formation and maintenance of these and other military formations, Boutros-Ghali strongly supports proposals by some member states for "peacekeeping contributions to be financed from defense, rather than foreign affairs, budgets."

The secretary-general's recommendations have been greeted with enthusiasm by a wide range of American private organizations. Several have called for the formation of a small standby force of several battalions under permanent U.N. command, others propose the creation of a rapid deployment force of even larger size, while some would merely seek to have member states earmark national contingents for deployment at Security Council behest when circumstances warrant.[8] In almost all instances, they propose to revive the nearly defunct Military Staff Committee and urge that it provide separate direction for these earmarked forces, oversee their training, and secure needed logistical and financial support preparatory to their mobilization.

INSTITUTIONAL REFORMS

If the United Nations is to establish effective arrangements for an enhanced post–Cold War collective security role, proponents contend that several institutional reforms and collaborative arrangements will have to be solidified. The secretary-general will have to be assured that consensus on the part of the Security Council's five permanent members can be sustained over the coming years to ensure parsimonious use of veto power. Second, Article 43 will have to be brought to life if ad hoc military arrangements are to be eschewed, which clearly means the earmarking of standby forces by member states. The article is quite explicit in this regard:

All U.N. members undertake to make available to the Security Council, on its call and in accordance with a special agreement or agreements, armed forces, assistance and facilities, including rights of passage, necessary for the purpose of maintaining international peace and security. . . . Such agreement or agreements shall govern the number and types of forces, their degree of readiness and general location, and the nature of the facilities and assistance to be provided.[9]

Boutros-Ghali and his predecessor, Perez de Cuellar, frequently have called on member states to meet their obligations under the terms of Article 43; however, they have received little more than token or verbal support. Nations that have traditionally earmarked forces for peacekeeping as opposed to aggressive enforcement missions—notably the Canadians, the Irish, and the Nordics—have expressed official reservations concerning involvement in a U.N. collective security system entailing casualty-heavy military actions upon demand of the Security Council.

Traditional peacekeeping contributors also have greeted with undisguised skepticism proposals that forty or fifty member states from "different parts of the world" designate units of brigade strength (2,000 to 3,000 men) that would be at the disposal of the Security Council as a prototype Rapid Deployment Force (UNRDF). Numbering in the aggregate somewhat less than 100,000, the RDF would have several missions, purposes, and roles. It would

- Be dispatched to member state border areas to deter acts of aggression by neighbors.

- Defend against any such acts should they arise.

- Forcefully terminate "repression against civilian populations" when such acts constitute a threat to international peace and security.

- Provide humanitarian assistance when natural disasters occur.

- "Combat acts of terrorism and international drug trafficking."[10]

These proposals, not surprisingly, have generated a firestorm of criticism reminiscent of the disillusionment that attended efforts by the permanent five to negotiate agreement on implementation of Article 43 over a four-year period shortly after the conclusion of World War II. Their negotiations yielded total policy disagreement and paralysis.

Among the permanent five members, basic divergences emerged from 1946 to 1949 over what guidelines to establish regarding the scope, reach, and automaticity of Article 43 with respect to the provision of on-call forces. Since the major powers were expected to make the bulk of such forces available, their failure to reach agreement sealed the fate of Article 43. Because war-making decisions were viewed as sovereign prerogatives to be jealously guarded, virtually all the permanent five negotiators entertained objections on the matter of automaticity. On the other hand, they recognized that automaticity did not entirely undermine sovereign rights, given the veto power of the permanent five. Of more than passing interest, the United States then argued that veto rights should not obtain when the aggressor member state was one of the permanent five—a position strenuously contested by the Soviet Union. With respect to command arrangements for on-call forces, Moscow contended that Article 43 did not necessarily mean "at the direction" of the secretary-general or the Headquarters Secretariat. All of the permanent five agreed that Article 43 was silent on command arrangements, but in consequence thereof, this too ultimately became a divisive issue.

THE MILITARY STAFF COMMITTEE

The U.N. Charter does, in theory, provide a mechanism for sorting out issues relating to command of forces. Article 46 dictates: "Plans for the application of armed force shall be made by the Security Council" with the assistance of a "Military Staff Committee." The functions of the committee are delineated in Article 47:

There shall be established a Military Staff Committee to advise and assist the Security Council on all questions relating to the Security Council's military requirements. . . the employment and command of forces placed at its disposal, the regulation of armaments, and possible disarmament.[11]

The committee is also charged with responsibility "for the strategic direction of any armed forces" under the oversight of the Security Council. As to its composition, the committee is to consist of the chiefs of staff of the permanent members of the Security Council, with provision to be made for participation of others when "the efficient discharge of the Committee's responsibilities" so demands.

It is not surprising that the disagreements inevitably crystallized among the permanent five as an accompaniment to the emergence of the Cold War. Key among them were (1) the location and length of stay on foreign territory of on-call forces; (2) the right of passage of these forces through member state territory; (3) the nature and size of military facilities to be made available to permanent five on-call forces; (4) the material assistance to be provided, including financial contributions; and (5) the size and composition of these forces (an equal or comparable issue). In 1947 the following estimates were provided by the Military Staff Committee to the Security Council:[12]

	France	United Kingdom –China	United States
Airforce	1,275	1,200	3,800
Gound forces (divisions)	16	8–12	20
Naval forces			
Battleships	3	2	3
Carriers	6	6	6
Cruisers	9	6	15
Destroyers	18–24	24	84
Submarines	12	12	90

The Soviet Union refused to provide an estimate of required forces despite repeated requests by the other committee members and the secretary-general. As a result, American suspicion of Soviet intentions grew—since the United States itself was engaged in substantial demobilization of its World War II armed forces. This fed growing concern in Washington over Moscow's purposes in retaining prepossessing Red Army formations. For his part, Stalin professed to believe that the American design was to "encircle the Soviet Union under the guise of foreign bases and U.N. forces." With the eruption of war on the Korean peninsula and the organization of collective security systems outside the U.N. framework, the Military Staff Committee, ineluctably, became moribund.

THE ISSUES REVIVED

The demise of the former Soviet Union has led to a shift in the analytical lenses of American foreign policy specialists. There is renewed interest in the crisis prevention roles the United Nations might play in an increasingly conflict-ridden world. As previously mentioned, the linkage of a revived Military Staff Committee to standby forces has become a matter of intense interest. For the Clinton administration, peacekeeping is becoming a focal point for policy discussion, with a wide array of questions under discussion: Should the United States become involved in intrastate conflicts under U.N. auspices? What range of military support should we be prepared to provide? Under what circumstances and whose command? Should there be a central executive agent in the Department of Defense responsible for coordination of U.S. peacekeeping?

The strategic choices confronting the United States in the years immediately ahead involve

- Whether to allocate substantial military and financial resources to collective security operations over which the United States has limited influence or control.

- Whether to confine U.S. military support to logistics, lift, and communications.

- Whether the United States should extend support for a revived (and expanded) Military Staff Committee with terms of reference that dictate the nature and scope of "strategic guidance" to be provided to U.N. forces.

In a speech presented to the U.N. General Assembly in September 1992, President Bush was careful to avoid wholehearted U.S. support for Boutros-Ghali's proposals to enhance U.N. military capabilities. The president acknowledged the need for member states to train soldiers for peacekeeping duties, but he was emphatic in insisting that governments must retain final decision on the use of their troops. On the other hand, the president pledged to place U.S. military "lift, logistics, communications, and intelligence capabilities" at the service of U.N. peacekeepers.

Mr. Bush finessed a fundamental question. If troops theoretically at the disposal of the Security Council are not also placed under its direction, why bother creating an Article 43 relationship and seek to revive the Military Staff Committee? Chapter VII of the U.N. Charter contains sufficient basis for the council to request ad hoc military assistance from members in the event of a clear-cut act of aggression. A partial (positive) answer reposes in the deterrent nature of effective Article 43 arrangements, which, if supported by the major powers, would strengthen respect for Security Council resolutions (so long as the offender is not a permanent five member). A contrary view is that the secretary-general should not press others on the troop contribution issue but rely instead on promises of availability and deal with member state contributions on a case-by-case basis —that is, as the need arises.

Resolution of this issue would have a significant bearing on prospects for revival of the Military Staff Committee. In this context, there is a fundamental need to assess future requirements for coalition forces. Manifold analytical issues demand to be addressed, including how to overcome the reluctance of member states to place troops under the command and authority of others in hostile environments where there is high expectation of casualties. Failure to establish effective command arrangements, on the other hand, could have disastrous consequences for future U.N. operations. A technologically sophisticated but weakly unified joint U.N. force could confront significant disadvantages against a low-tech but well-directed adversary, as in present-day Bosnia.

At another level of analysis, interoperability of forces and equipment must be ensured to remove handicaps to military operations that inevitably arise when incompatibility of doctrine and equipment is present. Achieving even a modest level of interoperability requires a prolonged effort to harmonize, through military-to-military agreements, and by joint training exercises, commonly accepted war-fighting doctrine and rules of engagement, intelligence sharing, and integrated system building.

Achieving harmonization outside the framework of the North Atlantic Treaty Organization would necessitate a degree of military openness and willingness to share burdens and resources hitherto unknown in the post–Cold War world. Future enforcement missions directed or delegated by the United Nations must meet the test of feasibility, including unity of command, rapid deployment, and integrated operational doctrine. Under all foreseeable circumstances, effective Military Staff Committee strategic oversight is problematic at best, particularly in rapidly evolving situations. Under combat conditions, local commanders cannot await tactical guidance. Even under optimum battlefield circumstances, the Military Staff Committee would be in a position to serve as little more than a conduit for progress reports to the Security Council and the secretary-general. On the other hand, without altering chain of command relationships, a consultative committee link might serve as a useful vehicle for receiving and digesting the views of member states concerning war aims of mission coalition forces and general rules of engagement that should guide them.

On balance, it is my view that recourse to Article 43 and a revived Military Staff Committee does not necessarily serve as a starting gate for the derogation of sovereignty or limitation of sovereign choice. The United States enjoys a veto power that vouchsafes protection of its interests in this area. Second, Article 43 language, "on its call"—with reference to the Security Council—should not be construed as "at its direction." The inescapable conclusion is that U.S. policy should be cautious but flexible, as the secretary-general seeks to develop appropriate diplomatic and military strategies to deal with today's tumultuous international arena.

NOTES

1. Considerable semantic confusion exists with regard to these terms. For the purposes of this discussion, I define "peacekeeping" as the use of military forces to monitor cease-fires or truces under strictly enforced (limited) rules of engagement by U.N. contingents; "peacemaking" as the introduction of contingents, without invitation if required, to create conditions conducive to peace; "peace enforcement" connotes the use of force to terminate aggression by a member state. Peacemaking is most applicable in intrastate conflicts, whereas enforcement tends to apply to interstate conflicts.

2. U.N. Charter, chap. 1, art. 1.

3. Andrew Katell (Associated Press), "U.N. Would Oversee Somalia Force: Decisions Not in U.S. Hands," *Washington Times,* 3 December 1992, 1.

4. George F. Will, "Sovereignty and Sophistry," *Washington Post,* 11 April 1993, 24.

5. Ibid.

6. Ibid.

7. Boutros Boutros-Ghali, "Empowering the United Nations," *Foreign Affairs* (Fall 1992): 89–102.

8. See Indar Rikhye, *Strengthening U.N. Peacekeeping* (Washington, D.C.: United States Institute of Peace,

May 1992); William H. Lewis, ed., *The Security Roles of the United Nations* (Washington, D.C.: National Defense University, October 1991); *Partners for Peace—Strengthening Collective Security for the Twenty-First Century* (New York: United Nations Association of the USA Global Policy Project, October 1992).

9. U.N. Charter, art. 43.

10. Richard N. Gardner, "Collective Security and the 'New World Order': What Role for the United Nations?"

in *Two Views on the Issue of Collective Security* (Washington, D.C.: United States Institute of Peace, June 1992), 9–12.

11. U.N. Charter, art. 47.

12. See Jane Boulden, "The U.N. Charter, Article 43 and the Military Staff Committee," *Guide to Canadian Policy on Arms Control, Disarmament, Defence and Conflict Resolution* (Ottawa: Canadian Institute for International Peace and Security, April 1991).

PEACE OPERATIONS: A DEPARTMENT OF DEFENSE PERSPECTIVE

SARAH B. SEWALL

Today, over eight hundred U.S. troops are participating in United Nations peace operations, helping prevent the Balkan conflict from engulfing Macedonia and supporting U.N. efforts in Bosnia and Croatia, the Middle East, Kuwait, Western Sahara, and Georgia. Several thousand Americans also joined the U.N. mission in Haiti to see the country through inauguration of a new president in early 1996. American participation in these operations reflects the fact that peace operations, employed selectively, can promote our national security objectives. This is the basic premise of Bill Clinton's Presidential Decision Directive (PDD) establishing U.S. policy toward peace operations.[1] The policy emphasizes the critical need to make peace operations more effective and sets out a variety of initiatives toward that end.

The PDD has engendered heated criticism from two very different perspectives. One side has characterized the policy as an ineffective and misguided approach that will harm U.S. national security interests, possibly leading to the "subordination of American military forces and U.S. foreign policy prerogatives to the UN."[2] Another collection of voices accuses the United States of failing to help the United Nations effectively meet post–Cold War security challenges. Charging that the policy renounces participation in U.N. security operations, they conclude that the United States has "washed its hands of responsibility and abandoned the mantle of leadership."[3]

Unfortunately, both sides misconstrue the administration's stated policy and ignore the reality of American actions in support of current peace operations. More fundamentally, both miss the point.

The United States is now the single greatest power in a world that has been transformed by the end of the Cold War; we want to help shape a stable world order in which democracy and economic growth can flourish. The political and military constraints once imposed by the existence of the Soviet empire and superpower competition have evaporated. This has contributed to the reemergence of internal ethnic, religious, and nationalist conflicts that characterize today's world. In addition, other states have experienced the absolute failure of a functioning government and have devolved into lawless anarchy. The end of the Cold War has not ushered in a period of peace, or even a different form of stability; some regions are experiencing a significant increase in violence, with its attendant economic, political, and human costs.

Few internal conflicts in distant lands will directly affect vital U.S. interests. But they do affect our national security in a broader sense. We have an interest in upholding international norms of behavior, such as respect for human rights, which promote justice and stability. More important, internal conflicts can affect our security interests. Fighting, weapons trade, and terrorized populations often cross national borders. The expansion of internal conflicts into neighboring states can erode stability in regions that are important to us for strategic, political, or economic reasons. Moreover, the cumulative impact of such conflicts is significant, undermining our objectives of expanding economic growth and the ranks of democratic nations. Continuing ethnic, nationalist, and religious conflicts risks can gradually erode the sinews of international community.

This essay has been edited and is reprinted from SAIS Review 15 *(Winter-Spring 1995): 113–33, by permission of* SAIS Review. *Copyright © 1995 by the Johns Hopkins Foreign Policy Institute, Paul H. Nitze School of Advanced International Studies.*

The United States, as it focuses attention upon challenges within our nation and reduces its armed forces, has neither the desire nor the ability to act as the world's police force. Yet there are many challenges to international peace and security that we believe should be prevented, contained or resolved. The United Nations—by building coalitions of the willing—offers an alternative, collective response to these challenges. The United States directly or indirectly benefits from U.N. efforts to achieve peace in El Salvador, usher in a new state in Namibia, relieve suffering and contain fighting in the former Republic of Yugoslavia, monitor Commonwealth of Independent States peacekeeping operations in Georgia, promote stability in Lebanon, or observe cease-fires along the India-Pakistan border and in Cyprus.

Many observers focus on the costs of U.N. peace operations. Yet the cost to the United States is a very small percentage of our expenditures on defense or foreign assistance.[4] As former Secretary of State James Baker said, "United Nations peacekeeping operations are a pretty good buy, and we ought to recognize that . . . we have spent trillions of dollars to win the Cold War, and should be willing to spend millions of dollars to secure the peace."[5] Peace operations are a means of burden sharing, since the United States provides roughly 1 percent of U.N.-helmeted forces worldwide and pays less than one-third of the cost of operations.[6] We want to avoid always being called upon to lead and organize international coalitions to address all emerging conflicts. Thus it is fundamentally in U.S. interests to support these operations and build the capabilities of international institutions and other countries to conduct peace operations effectively. Failure to do so could mean either increasing costs and risks to Americans, or countenancing the spread of violence to the detriment of U.S. interests.

For these reasons, the Clinton administration has developed a comprehensive policy to make peace operations more selective and effective tools of U.S. national security. First, the policy establishes "factors for consideration" when the U.S. government is deciding to support or participate in peace operations in order to ensure disciplined and coherent policy decisions. It also enunciates U.S. practice regarding command and control in multilateral operations, as applied since the American Revolution and reaffirmed by the chairman of the Joint Chiefs of Staff. It proposes that the Department of Defense (DOD) play a larger role in guiding—and paying U.N. assessments for—certain U.N. peace operations. It also seeks to improve cooperation with the Congress in formulating peace operations policy. Finally, the policy recommends extensive improvements to U.N. peacekeeping capabilities and outlines initiatives to reduce the cost of these operations to the United Nations and the United States.

From the Department of Defense's perspective, the policy is both positive and necessary because it directly addresses the key issues of concern to the U.S. military. It stresses the need to seek clearly defined mandates; to secure adequate resources; to integrate political, military, and economic/humanitarian efforts; and to reassess missions and objectives in light of developments on the ground. The policy's emphasis on strengthening international peace operations capabilities also reflects the armed forces' desire to ensure that the United States can participate in effective operations, and that other nations can conduct operations successfully without the need for U.S. participation.

The PDD on peace operations complements existing strategic guidance embodied in the National Security Strategy, the National Military Strategy and the bottom-up review of military forces and systems. As the 1994 National Security Strategy states: "The dissolution of the Soviet Union has radically transformed the security environment and our allies . . . [y]et there remain a complex array of old and new security challenges America must meet as we approach a new century."[7] The primary purpose of the U.S. armed forces is to fight and win wars, and the main regional danger is large-scale aggression by major regional powers. The centerpiece of our military preparedness therefore is maintaining forces ready to deploy, fight, and "achieve decisive victory in two nearly simultaneous major regional conflicts."[8]

Yet it is evident that smaller, often internal, conflicts based on ethnic or regional animosities will pose other dangers.[9] What is more significant, perhaps, these conflicts remain far more likely than a major regional contingency, just as conventional war remained more probable than nuclear conflict during the Cold War. Therefore we will ensure that our forces are capable of conducting smaller-scale interventions, as well as humanitarian and peace operations. Multilateral peace operations can help prevent, contain, or resolve conflicts before they spread and potentially require more costly action. But the U.S. military cannot police the globe. We will preserve the ability to act unilaterally, and we will act multilaterally when it serves our interests. Promoting collective mechanisms for enhancing international security when our vital interests are not directly threatened is a key means of enhancing our ability to protect vital U.S. interests. Peace operations are an important and cost-effective means of confronting challenges that we do not wish to address unilaterally. This is why military officers refer to peace operations as constituting an "economy of force."

Support for peace operations, while not a strategy unto itself, is an important component of our national security strategy. This is demonstrated by greater U.S. participation in peace operations and in support of U.N. Security Council resolutions.[10] Yet we cannot underestimate the challenges we face as a department, a government, and one member of an international system in helping peace operations fulfill their potential. As the U.N.'s Shashi Tharoor has stated, we need to change the focus from "doing the right thing to doing the thing right."[11]

This work is important to the DOD because the United States will continue acting multilaterally in many contexts. The DOD therefore has a direct interest and a role to play in helping establish more capable institutions and procedures within which to participate and in improving the capabilities of other nations with whom we will cooperate. The DOD also understands that U.S. armed forces can better develop their own capabilities to conduct effectively the full range of peace operations.

IMPROVING CAPABILITIES OF U.S. ARMED FORCES

Responding to . . . [crises] means forces that can act unilaterally, but more likely in the future can act as part of a great international coalition such as the United Nations. It means a force that can participate more fully in peacekeeping and humanitarian operations.—General Colin Powell, former Chairman of the Joint Chiefs of Staff, 1994

The use of overwhelming and decisive force, the central tenet of our war-fighting doctrine, has little relevance to peace operations. The enemy is no longer easily identified approaching in a tank or armored personnel carrier. Even the military tasks common to the work of both war and peace—such as patrolling or escorting convoys—may have a fundamentally different purpose and be conducted in a vastly changed environment. We are still developing our understanding of the unique challenges associated with preparing armed forces to participate effectively in peace operations.

Institutions, like people, are often slow to change. The DOD is no exception—and it faces new challenges in the face of shrinking manpower and budgets. In this light, the pace of the DOD's response to the demands of peace operations is impressive. These efforts began under the former chairman of the Joint Chiefs of Staff, General Powell. The current chairman, General Shalikashvili, is accelerating and expanding what is becoming a comprehensive process of change.

DOCTRINE

Organizational change in the U.S. military is usually reflected first in doctrine. As Army Chief of Staff General Gordon Sullivan states, "To change doctrine is to . . . change the Army culture."[12] The Joint Staff and the services have reassessed military doctrine covering the full spectrum of operations.[13] Published in 1993, current doctrine for the first time includes an entire chapter on military operations other than war (OOTW)—including peace operations. Expanding on this chapter, Joint Pub 3-07, *Joint Doctrine for Military Operations Other than War,* is expected to be published in the Spring of 1995. More specific peacekeeping guidance, *Joint Tactics, Techniques, and Procedures for Peacekeeping* (Joint Pub 3-07.3), was published in April 1994 and currently is being revised to include the full range of peace operations.

The army has revised its capstone doctrine, Field Manual 100-5 and has just published the follow-on FM 100-23, *Peace Operations.* Recognizing that success in peace operations is measured in terms of political settlement, not victory on the battlefield, the army's new doctrine emphasizes that peace operations are "designed principally to create or sustain the conditions in which political and military activities may proceed."[14] Further, the doctrine warns commanders that the use of excessive force may result in a tactical success but ultimately result in long-term strategic failure because such actions could serve to "heighten tensions, polarize opinion, foreclose negotiating opportunities, prejudice the perceived impartiality of the peace operation contingent, and escalate the overall level of violence."[15] The Marine Corps is currently evaluating this document to determine its potential relevance for Marine Corps doctrine. In addition, the U.S. Army Infantry School has drafted a white paper addressing brigade and battalion conduct of peace enforcement operations. The Army Center for Lessons Learned published a handbook for soldiers participating in peace operations and produced one designed specifically for forces deploying to Haiti.[16] These efforts clearly signify what General Sullivan would call a change in culture.[17]

TRAINING

While peace operations doctrine has been emerging, the services have focused their training more directly on peace operations. The first assessment of U.S. military training for peace operations, released in September 1994 by the DOD inspector general, concluded that well-trained, disciplined combat soldiers and current combat planning, training, staffing, and decision-making processes are necessary preparation for peacekeeping operations.[18] But the report also noted the growing understanding within the U.S. military that "peace operations confront our Armed Forces with a requirement for different knowledge, skills, attitude, and environmental considerations than warfighting . . . [and] confirm the need for special peace operations training to successfully conduct peace operations missions."[19] Lessons learned from Somalia, discussions with other militaries, and information gained from joint exercises and peace operations training have given the U.S. military a more detailed understanding of how to tailor training to the requirements of peace operations.

The combatant commands and the services have initiated a variety of activities, most of which have been mission-specific training tailored to actual or anticipated deployments to peace operations. The unified commands have developed exercise programs that focus on staff planning, command and control, simulated deployments, and training with other government agencies, non-governmental agencies, private voluntary organizations, and militaries from other countries.[20]

The army has led the way in developing unit training designed specifically for peace operations.

This is most clearly exemplified by the innovations taking place at the army's combat training centers. In recent years, the army has developed peace operations scenarios in its combat training centers that employ the full range of state-of-the-art training technologies to train armored and light infantry units as well as division and corps staffs.[21]

In November 1993, for example, a brigade from the 82nd Airborne Division, augmented by a company of German airborne soldiers, participated in a training exercise at Fort Polk that replicated a peace enforcement operation on the mythical island of Cortina. This training was conducted with army units, special operations forces, representatives from various U.S. government agencies, and representatives from the International Red Cross, Save the Children, the United Nations Department of Humanitarian Affairs, a Disaster Assistance Relief Team, and the media—all playing their respective roles.[22] Such training includes maintaining buffer zones, dealing with armed civilians and civilian militia, working with irregular forces manning checkpoints, operating within restrictive rules of engagement, and responding to sniper fire along supply routes.[23] Unfortunately, such intensive peace operations training is still available only for a relatively small number of units. Nonetheless, it is recognized as an unparalleled experience. Nations such as the Netherlands and Germany have arranged special peace operations rotations for their forces at the U.S. Combat Maneuver Training Center in Hohenfels, Germany.

When possible, unit training is being provided to U.S. forces in preparation for deployment to a particular peace operation. Emerging army doctrine holds that deploying units should be provided four to six weeks of additional specialized training.[24] In preparation for deployment to Haiti during Operation Uphold Democracy, soldiers in the 10th Mountain Division (Light) were given extensive training on crowd control, establishing check points, conducting security patrols in a city, interaction and coordination with representatives of non-governmental organizations, separating belligerents, and operating with restrictive rules of engagement.[25]

The Marine Corps, while emphasizing combat preparation, is also making adjustments to training, adding emphasis on organizational integration, staff interfaces, military operations in cities and towns, and cultural awareness.[26]

EDUCATION

The professional military education system is incorporating instruction about peace operations into the curricula for our military leaders. Army education efforts begin in its precommissioning program; as officers advance, they are exposed to more specific instruction about peace operations. Both the Command and General Staff College and the Army War College have reorganized their core curricula to expand the treatment of the operational and strategic characteristics of peace operations. Peace operations elective courses increasingly appear in the army curricula.

The Marine Corps is building training for peace operations into its officer education base. The U.S. Marine Corps' school for lieutenants has developed an urban patrolling course incorporating lessons learned from U.S. operations in Somalia and British activities in the Balkans. Exercises focused on interaction between "civilians" and marines compel officers to make rapid decisions about whether to use deadly force. The Marine Corps Command and Staff College has modified its curricula to include a specific course on peace operations.

Although the air force and the navy report that they have not made any formal changes in how they conduct unit training for peace operations, they have included OOTW in the core curricula of their service schools.[27]

EQUIPMENT

The DOD is in the process of identifying equipment requirements that are unique to peace operations, recognizing that some of the technology applied to major regional contingencies may also be applicable to peace operations. The services already have begun modifying existing equipment to meet the demands of peace operations. The army has installed armored "belly plates" on armored personnel carriers to counter the threat posed by antiarmor mines and has affixed special gunshields to protect M-113 gunners when operating in an urban environment. Reactive armor has been installed on Bradley Fighting Vehicles to counter the threat from rocket-propelled grenades, providing protection to peacekeepers without requiring the use of firepower. The air force has modified its parachutes, delivery systems, and procedures to ensure more accurate delivery of humanitarian relief supplies to besieged enclaves in Bosnia-Hercegovina. Some equipment requirements already have been identified: U.S. Special Operations Command is developing a Kevlar blanket for the floors of humvees to increase mine protection, as well as new weapons based on nonlethal technologies.

FORCE COMPOSITION AND READINESS

As the DOD evaluates the demands that peace operations place on U.S. forces, we are determining whether adaptations of U.S. force structure will be required in the years ahead. The administration already has rejected the proposal to dedicate specific U.S. forces to a standing U.N. force.[28] This idea draws support from many quarters, including former President Ronald Reagan, but the administration opposes committing forces to a U.N. army.[29]

We do support the U.N.'s "standby arrangements initiative" to establish a database of national forces and capabilities that might be available for use in a Chapter VI peacekeeping operation. This effort is intended to help the United Nations avoid having to ask every nation for every capability, starting from scratch each time and thereby delaying deployments.

The United Nations is now seeking to develop a database of forces or capabilities nations might provide to U.N. peacekeeping efforts. In September the U.S. informed the United Nations that our most effective contributions usually are highly technical and resource intensive capabilities. While prepared to consider the full range of support, we believe it most appropriate for the United States to consider providing strategic lift, logistics, communications, civil affairs, psychological operations, engineering, information, contracting, contract management services, and personnel for U.N. headquarters staff functions. Of course, the provision of any such support remains contingent upon a U.S. government decision. We believe this standby arrangements initiative—unlike a standing U.N. army—is a useful way to help the United Nations improve its capabilities.

In examining the current U.S. force structure's adaptability for peace operations, an obvious limitation emerges. Capabilities that are central to peace operations—including combat service support, transportation, civil affairs, and psychological operations forces—are available predominantly in the reserve components. Some critical systems—such as specialized aircraft—also are limited in the active force. Although relatively small numbers of military personnel are involved in peace operations at any one time, the strain on limited capabilities can be felt in the active component. It also is clear that the mix of combat support forces, tailored to the requirements of confrontation with the former Soviet Union, may require adjustments to meet current operational challenges. As the demands of peace operations are better understood, modest changes in the composition of both active and reserve components may better prepare us for the requirements of peace operations and other likely contingencies.

The Department of Defense currently is focusing on innovative and responsible use of the national guard and reserve components. Because it is difficult to gain access to these capabilities, the administration has sought more flexible and responsive authority to employ both individual volunteers and unit deployments as required.[30] While active forces will continue to bear the primary responsibility for initial responses to peace operations, we believe that reserve forces can play a critical role by providing individual volunteers for select low-density specialties, and a rotational base for some active forces deployed for extended periods.[31]

This concept is now ready to be tested by the army. For over a decade the United States has deployed an infantry battalion task force as part of the Multinational Force and Observers (MFO) mission that monitors the border between Egypt and Israel in the Sinai. Through the Pilot MFO Initiative, the army has formed a composite task force consisting predominantly of Army National Guard and U.S. Army Reserves.[32] Only 20 percent of the force is from the active component. Two months of unit training will prepare the task force for its peacekeeping mission. This trial concept is one example of the military's efforts to respond flexibly to operational requirements in the face of a downsized active force.

Greater use of the reserve and guard components is one means of responding to the demands for participation in peace operations. In addition, we must address the way we finance participation in these operations. We will need innovation here, too, because current budget practices make it difficult to protect readiness accounts from the impact of increased operations.

Preserving readiness is a top priority of this administration. But readiness for what? Our core requirement is to sustain the capability to fight and win the nation's wars, but readiness for an MRC is not our only concern. The military must be prepared to participate in a wide range of operations, including the most likely contingencies. And while units participating in peace operations may not have the opportunity to retain proficiency in all critical war-fighting skills, other capabilities (e.g., combat support, combat service support) may become more "ready" through real-life exercise. Nonetheless, the way we finance participation in peace operations can negatively affect our forces' training and maintenance activities, particularly toward the end of the fiscal year.

Peace operations, like wars, are unanticipated. The DOD does not budget in advance for the incremental costs of conducting these operations. While the United Nations reimburses the United States for its costs of participation in a U.N. peace operation, there is often a significant time lag.[33] Operations that are not conducted as blue-helmeted operations under the United Nations, such as the activities of the multinational force in Haiti, are generally paid for by those nations that participate. In either case, the services finance their participation in peace operations through their operations and maintenance accounts—the funds that are budgeted for daily operations, training, and other ongoing requirements. They draw down these funds, awaiting reimbursement from the United Nations, congressional approval of DOD-recommended reprogramming, or supplemental appropriations from Congress.

In its fiscal 1994 defense budget proposal, the Clinton administration sought to establish a separate fund to reimburse the services for their incremental costs of participating in peace operations, but Congress rejected this proposal. Ensuring more timely supplemental funding is another potential solution. Clearly this issue deserves further attention; we must find a more effective means of ensuring prompt financing for military operations. The wrong answer would be to halt involvement in operations that advance American interests. The right answer is to find a way to reduce the short-term financial impact of these activities so that the services will not have to sacrifice necessary training and maintenance. Our concerns about preserving readiness require that we continue working with the Congress to find a solution to this problem.

IMPROVING INTERNATIONAL
CAPABILITIES

I think the United Nations has in the past and can in the future perform an extraordinarily important role . . . [but it] is often ill equipped to deal with the more challenging operations and that therefore we ought to consider what it is that we can do to strengthen their ability to deal with it, other than just pure peacekeeping operations.—General John Shalikashvili, Chairman of the Joint Chiefs of Staff, 1993

The challenge that the U.S. armed forces face in responding to peace operations certainly is dwarfed by that facing the United Nations. The United Nations was simply unprepared to assume such a significant operational role in addressing conflicts around the globe. U.N. peace operations nearly doubled from ten in 1990 to seventeen in 1994. The cost of U.N. operations exploded from less than $500 million in 1990 to nearly $4 billion in 1994. The value of procurements to support these operations increased 1,400 percent between 1988 and 1993. U.N. forces increased sevenfold to roughly seventy thousand in the same period.[34] Moreover, these operations expanded significantly in their size, complexity, and difficulty—from the straightforward monitoring of an existing peace agreement into such objectives as the creation of a secure and stable environment for the delivery of humanitarian relief, or the organizing and monitoring of elections and transition to statehood. In the past few years, the organization has initiated more operations than it had conducted throughout its entire prior history.

The administration believes that the United Nations cannot conduct a large-scale peace enforcement operation that is likely to involve combat; capable regional organizations such as NATO or ad hoc coalitions should assume this responsibility. But the international community, including the United States, likely will continue asking the United Nations to undertake large operations in unstable conditions against unpredictable threats, potentially requiring the use of force. We stand to benefit from efforts to ensure that the United Nations has the expertise and tools to accomplish what the U.N. Security Council directs.

While much attention has focused—appropriately—on the U.N.'s significant limitations in planning, organizing, deploying, and conducting military operations, not enough notice has been taken of the changes under way in the U.N.'s Department of Peacekeeping Operations (DPKO). Under the dynamic leadership of Undersecretary-General for Peacekeeping Kofi Annan, the DPKO has begun adapting to its new role. A simple example is most symbolic. For the first time, the United Nations has a twenty-four hour monitoring cell, known as the Situation Center, which connects field commanders and New York at all times and provides a regular flow of information in both directions. Reorganization within the DPKO has rationalized functions and ac-

commodated new requirements in the field. Logistical and financing support for peace operations has been streamlined by moving the Field Operations Division out of the independent Department of Administration and Management into the DPKO.

The DPKO has grown from 60 personnel in September of 1993 to 350 in June of 1994. While impressive, this growth does not adumbrate the creation of a global military command. In some respects, the United Nations still makes do with far fewer resources than we would consider necessary to carry out its responsibilities.[35] Bureaucratic "stovepiping" and burdensome internal procedures governing everything from budgets to contracting continue to hobble the organization's efficacy. But the United Nations has begun to develop the manpower, expertise, and processes vital for conducting the work with which it is charged. The direction of change reflects recommendations of the administration's policy on peace operations, and the PDD formalizes our commitment to helping the United Nations in what will be a significant, continuing effort.

OPERATIONAL SUPPORT

Although the contribution of American troops to U.N. operations is most visible, the DOD also has been providing other operational support to the United Nations. Whether flying a contingent of foreign peacekeeping troops to Rwanda or leasing counterbattery radar equipment to U.N. forces in Bosnia, the United States is a flexible and reliable provider of key goods and services to U.N. peace operations. While we first satisfy our own national requirements, we have the ability to help meet U.N. operational requirements. In 1993 the United States contracted to lease or sell more than $120 million of equipment, services, and expertise to the United Nations. The United States provided more than half of all such national support to U.N. peace operations. These goods and services reflect the special capabilities of American forces—our ability to airlift items to nearly any spot on the globe, the reserves of equipment from which we can draw, and our specially trained personnel. We do not see this trend diminishing; in the first half of 1994, the DOD provided nearly $70 million of such goods and services.[36]

In urgent cases, our support extends beyond meeting U.N. requests for assistance. In the case of the UNAMIR operation in Rwanda, the DOD—in addition to providing transportation and equipment—worked behind the scenes to help speed deployments of other national contingents, identify specific equipment requirements, and otherwise buttress the U.N.'s efforts to deploy and equip the peacekeeping force.

Like the United Nations, the DOD has had to make major internal adjustments to meet the rapid increase in demands for peace operations support. The DOD lacked dedicated organizations and efficient procedures for approving, executing, and managing financial data regarding the provision of support. One of our challenges in the last year has been formalizing and streamlining internal systems to enable a rapid response to these new requirements. This process will continue because the department is committed to using its special capabilities to support U.N. operations.

PERSONNEL AND EXPERTISE

For many years, the DOD has detailed military officers to the United Nations in a variety of capacities. Eleven U.S. officers currently serve in the DPKO on a permanent basis, working on military planning, procurement, logistics, budget reform, and finance.[37] This level of support is likely to increase slightly and become a routine American contribution to enhancing U.N. effectiveness. In addition, the DOD has provided special teams of technical experts on a temporary basis to assist the United Nations in developing key capabilities through tools such as logistics templates and computerized budgeting systems.

The immediate benefits of these low-cost investments are readily apparent. Instead of creating each budget estimate from scratch—a process that took six or more weeks—the United Nations now uses a basic computer program. Entering key assumptions, DPKO staff can generate within minutes a rough planning figure that comes within 10 percent of the more detailed budget estimates. The U.N.'s draft logistics plan for the U.N. operation in Haiti was ready months in advance of most prior planning efforts. The United Nations also has expanded its use of standing sea and airlift contracts, providing faster and more reliable transportation for U.N. forces and equipment.

The DPKO already has asked the DOD to build on this promising beginning. Future efforts may include development of more sophisticated budget tools and assistance in designing logistics support kits that can be rapidly deployed to the field to start up a new operation.

The DOD also conducted an analysis of the DPKO's command, control, and communications requirements to determine how the U.N.'s information and communications systems could be improved. The United States has since provided the United Nations with a detailed blueprint for purchasing a commercially available system to vastly improve its information and communications capabilities. If the United Nations chooses, it can streamline and improve its command and control capabilities and implement a series of cost-savings measures, ranging from creating a database of available forces to speeding its procurement process.

U.N. TRAINING

One of the key challenges facing the United Nations is ensuring that the national forces participating in peace operations have the requisite military capabilities and share a common approach to their mission. Nations participating in peace operations arrive with very different skills and attitudes. They have been exposed to differing training and doctrine; they may have had little experience in either peace operations or multinational operations. This can create significant problems on the ground.

The United Nations is addressing this issue by helping coordinate national peacekeeping training, and the DOD has been assisting in these efforts.[38] The DPKO's Training Unit is developing guidelines, instructions, and performance goals for units and individuals that will participate in U.N. peacekeeping operations. The DOD recently detailed an army major to serve as the manual and instruction officer within the Training Unit. The United Nations has also made available to member states recently developed videotapes and accompanying training manuals.[39] The United Nations plans to conduct multinational command and staff exercises to prepare key individuals for the demands of a multinational operation and to create mobile training teams to assist national or regional training programs.[40]

Expanding the pool of capable troop-contributing nations will enhance the international community's ability to conduct peace operations and will reduce demands for U.S. forces for such operations. It is important that member states work with the United Nations, within regional organizations, and in their bilateral programs to strengthen the capabilities of military forces that are likely to participate in peace operations.

The Clinton administration recognizes the importance of adapting our foreign and military aid programs, which were created during the Cold War, to accomplish a broad range of new goals. We have the opportunity to use our bilateral programs—Military-to-Military Contact program, International Military and Education Training, and joint exercises—to increase the number of foreign forces that are well prepared for peace operations. Because peacekeeping has become a new focus of the regional organizations in which we participate, enhancing peacekeeping capabilities is likely to become a larger element of our bilateral programs as well as our multilateral initiatives.

Regional organizations already have begun to focus on peace operations. NATO expanded its mission to include peace operations in 1992 and has set in motion a series of related initiatives to improve its members' and partners' ability to conduct peace operations. Internally, NATO's Military Committee has endorsed a planning document for NATO support to peacekeeping activities, which offers definitions, guidelines, and steps for future actions regarding preparing for and participating in peace operations. Development of formal peace operations doctrine remains a major political challenge, but it would be a logical and useful development. The North Atlantic Cooperation Council, at NATO direction, is developing recommendations for peace operations exercises, command and control procedures, communications, and planning. Training activities among members are being coordinated, and the Supreme Headquarters Allied Powers Europe has developed peacekeeping courses. Greater harmonization with the work of other international organizations would maximize the impact of NATO's actions.

An obvious benefit of the administration's Partnership for Peace (PFP) initiative is that it employs NATO resources to help prepare Central and East European countries for peacekeeping. NATO is cooperating with PFP members to develop multinational planning, training, and exercises for peacekeeping, search and rescue, and humanitarian operations. The United States has been pushing to make exercises a reality since the fall of 1993, when we hosted a seminar on exercise planning for NATO and the partner states. Most of NATO's planning for peacekeeping activities now takes place under the auspices of PFP. In September six NATO and six PFP states took part in "Cooperative Bridge '94" near Posznan, Poland, NATO's first training exercise on non-NATO territory with non-NATO forces. Several such exercises have occurred and more are planned. In fact, of the $100 million President Clinton has proposed for the Partnership for Peace in fiscal 1996, nearly half would be used to support participation in future joint peacekeeping exercises. In a related initiative, the administration also plans to support (through assistance such as communications and transportation equipment, uniforms, and language training) Latvia, Lithuania, and Estonia in their efforts to form a joint 750-person Baltic Battalion for peacekeeping purposes.

Finally, we expect our bilateral peacekeeping exercises with other nations to expand. The United States has extended its military cooperation with Russia to include peacekeeping exercises. Last September, the two nations took part in "Peacekeeper '94," which focused on supervision of a U.N. mediated truce. In preparation for that exercise, U.S. and Russian staff developed a combined tactics, techniques, and procedures manual for the operation, which we believe could be adapted by other nations for bilateral peacekeeping exercises. Planning already has begun for a U.S.–Ukraine combined peacekeeping training exercise next year in Ukraine. Many of our allies share our interest in promoting regional and bilateral efforts to enhance international peace operations capabilities. We will expand our own activities and encourage those of others because this work is an important strand in the web of activities needed to strengthen collective security mechanisms.

As we look toward building these improved multilateral capabilities, we must incorporate the lessons of the past. There is no doubt that peace operations, and in particular the more ambitious undertakings of recent years, are fraught with difficulties. There is no formulaic concept of operations for missions with such a potentially broad range of functions, each conducted in a unique historical, political, military, geographic, and cultural context, each carried out with a different constellation of political/military leadership, national forces, and national capabilities.

The United States and the international community continue to learn by doing in what remains significantly uncharted territory. The United States is keenly aware of the problems that the international community has faced and the mistakes we have made. The lessons we have learned are reflected in the administration's new peacekeeping policy and in our national efforts to prepare our forces to participate in such operations. This learning process will continue; no undertaking of this magnitude could be smooth and certain. But the United States has committed itself to a comprehensive effort to reform the conduct of peace operations.

The U.N.'s authorization of a multinational force to restore democratic processes in Haiti, and its commitment ultimately to assume responsibility for that operation, are just the most recent demonstration of how United Nations actions can advance U.S. foreign policy goals. A survey of ongoing peace operations only underscores the utility of multilateral actions to prevent, contain, or resolve conflicts, thereby reducing the demand for direct U.S. involvement and minimizing the destabilizing impact of these conflicts.

The price the United States pays to support these operations is very small compared with the benefits that we accrue, or compared with the costs and risks entailed in addressing these problems unilaterally. The U.N. Security Council's greater willingness to support peace operations should be considered one of the many benefits of the end of the Cold War. The Clinton administration wants to exploit this opportunity to ensure that the United Nations achieves its fullest potential as a means of enhancing U.S. and international security. The PDD on reforming multilateral peace operations formalizes this U.S. commitment and provides a comprehensive framework for achieving it.

In several respects, the Department of Defense benefits most directly from the president's new peace operations policy. Military forces may have the most to gain by ensuring that missions are clearly conceived, that operations are well organized, that the chain of command is sound, and that other military partners are competent. Self-interest, not foggy idealism, makes the DOD an advocate of selective and effective peace operations. Our efforts to contribute to the success of peace operations, by improving our own preparedness and by improving the capabilities of other nations and institutions, reflect this reality.

NOTES

1. "Peace operations" is a term used to describe actions taken by the United Nations under the authority of Chapter VI or Chapter VII of the United Nations Charter, by regional arrangements pursuant to Chapter VII of the U.N. Charter or by ad hoc coalitions pursuant to a U.N. Security Council resolution or consistent with Chapter VI

of the U.N. Charter. The umbrella term encompasses both peacekeeping operations, pursuant to Chapter VI of the U.N. Charter, which involve the deployment of forces with the consent of the parties to the dispute to assist in preserving or maintaining the peace (generally noncombat operations to monitor or facilitate implementation of an existing truce agreement), and peace enforcement operations pursuant to Chapter VII of the U.N. Charter, which do not require consent of the parties to the conflict and include the threat or use of force to preserve, maintain, or restore international peace and security.

2. Report of the Senate Armed Forces Committee on the Senate Defense Authorization Bill, 103d Cong., 2d sess., June 1994, 311.

3. Thomas Weiss, "Triage at the UN," *Washington Quarterly 17* (Autumn 1994): 153.

4. In 1993 U.S. assessments for U.N. peacekeeping operations were $832 million, compared with the fiscal 1993 annual defense budget of $276.1 billion (0.3 percent) and a gross domestic product of $6,340.3 billion (0.01 percent).

5. Secretary of State James Baker, testimony before the House Appropriations Committee, 3 March 1992.

6. Even at the height of U.S. involvement in Somalia, U.S. forces constituted only about 5 percent of U.N. peacekeepers. Similarly, the anticipated U.S. participation in UNMIH would again raise the U.S. contribution to roughly 5 percent of blue-helmeted forces worldwide.

7. *National Security Strategy of Engagement and Enlargement,* (Washington, D.C.: The White House, July 1994), 1.

8. Les Aspin, *Report on the Bottom-Up Review* (Washington, D.C.: U.S. Department of Defense, October, 1993), 7–8.

9. Ibid., 2.

10. In addition to directly participating in U.N. peace operations as noted above, thousands of U.S. forces operate in support of U.N. Security Council Resolutions. In Turkey and northern Iraq, about 1,500 U.S. troops participate in humanitarian Operation Provide Comfort. In the Persian Gulf, some 11,000 U.S. military personnel help impose a no-fly zone over Iraq (Operation Southern Watch) and enforce the Iraq embargo through the multilateral maritime intercept force. In the former Yugoslavia, about 2,000 air force and navy personnel join our NATO allies in Operation Deny Flight enforcing the no-fly zone over Bosnia, providing close air support to U.N. peacekeepers, and enforcing the NATO-instituted exclusion zones. Roughly 8,000 other U.S. personnel in the Adriatic help enforce sanctions against Serbia. In addition, since 1982 the United States has provided 800 soldiers to the multinational force and observers in the Sinai to monitor implementation of the Camp David accords. This is a multinational mission conducted independently of the United Nations.

11. Presentation at "A Practitioners' Conference Coordinating U.N. Peace Support Operations," London, 2 June 1994.

12. General Gordon R. Sullivan, *America's Army: Into the Twenty-First Century,* Institute for Foreign Policy Analysis, National Security Paper no. 14 (Hollis, N.H.: Puritan Press, 1993), 23–24.

13. Once approved, joint doctrine guides the employment of forces from two or more services toward a common objective and, as such, provides guidance to all services and combatant commands.

14. Department of The Army, *Peace Operations,* Field Manual (FM) 100-23 (December 1994), iii–iv.

15. Ibid., 4–3. Despite the clarity of this directive, a *New York Times* editorial incorrectly charged that the army's doctrine "reflects its traditional dislike of occupation and its strong preference for overwhelming force used decisively."

16. *Handbook for the Soldier in Operations other than War (OOTW),* Center for Army Lessons Learned no. 94-4 (Fort Leavenworth, Kans.: U.S. Army Combined Arms Center, July 1994); *Haiti,* Center for Army Lessons Learned no. 94-3 (Fort Leavenworth, Kans.: U.S. Army Combined Arms Center, July 1994). These handbooks were provided to soldiers in both the 82nd Airborne Division and the 10th Mountain Division (Light).

17. These major steps rebut charges that the military is unwilling to prepare for such operations. See, for example, John G. Ruggie, "The UN: Stuck in a Fog between Peacekeeping and Enforcement," in *Peacekeeping the Way Ahead,* Institute for National Strategic Studies (Washington, D.C.: National Defense University, November, 1993).

18. *Specialized Military Training for Peace Operations: Program Evaluation* (Washington, D.C.: Department of Defense, Inspector General, September 1994).

19. Ibid., 50.

20. Exercises such as Tradewinds '94, conducted by USACOM, Elder Brave conducted by USPACOM, and Atlantic Resolve conducted by USEUCOM provide our headquarters and staffs the opportunity to participate in a combined peace operation exercise with military units from other nations.

21. Sullivan, *America's Army,* 20–21. The two centers that conduct peace operations training are the Joint Readiness Training Center (JRTC) at Fort Polk, Louisiana, and the Combat Maneuver Training Center (CMTC) at Hohenfels, Germany. The Battle Command Training program (BCTP) is conducted at Fort Leavenworth, Kansas.

22. General Gordon R. Sullivan and Andrew B. Twomey, "The Challenges of Peace," *Parameters* 24, no. 3 (1994): 11–12.

23. Department of Defense, *Catalog of Peace Operations Training* (Washington, D.C.: GPO), 8–9.

24. Department of the Army, *Peace Operations* (Draft), Appendix C (Training), C-1.

25. Units assigned to the 10th Mountain Division began to conduct individual, leader, and unit training specifically oriented toward their missions in Haiti nearly five weeks prior to deployment.

26. Department of Defense, *Specialized Military Training for Peace Operations,* ii.

27. Ibid.

28. Boutros Boutros-Ghali, *An Agenda for Peace Preventive Diplomacy, Peacemaking, and Peace-keeping,* Report of the Secretary-General (New York: United Nations, 31 January 1992, 17 June 1992), para. 43.

29. Ronald Reagan, "Democracy's Next Battle," Address to the Oxford Union Society, 4 December 1992.

30. To facilitate greater utilization of the reserve component (RC), the administration requested authority for the secretary of defense to activate up to 25,000 members

of the RC for a period of 180 days (plus an extension of another 180 days). While Congress has yet to approve this request, it has allowed the president to call up RC personnel for a period of 270 days instead of 90 days (with a 90-day extension option). For a more detailed discussion see "Accessibility of Reserve Component Forces, *Defense Issues* 9, no. 45 (1994).

31. Reserve call-ups may still be necessary for larger operations or if active units already are heavily engaged. The former case was demonstrated in the call-up of reserves for the multinational force in Haiti, where over 900 members of the RC were activated to serve in military police, transportation, psychological operations, civil affairs, and port security and harbor defense units. In addition to this call-up, another 800 personnel volunteered in specialties such as air traffic control, communications, and airfield refueling.

32. There are some similarities between peace operations and the activities of the National Guard in providing disaster relief and securing urban areas in the United States.

33. The U.N.'s delay in reimbursement is partly due to the fact that nations like the United States are so late in paying their share of U.N. peacekeeping assessments. The Department of State pays the U.S. share of U.N. peacekeeping assessments. In fiscal 1995, the administration proposed that the DOD pay U.N. assessments for operations involving U.S. forces or potentially involving combat, but Congress did not support this approach.

34. It is worth noting U.N. records that state U.S. firms obtained fully 28 percent—or some $132 million—of commercial contracts let by U.N. headquarters in New York.

35. For example, while NATO headquarters employs more than one thousand officers to handle procurement valued at almost $400 million annually, U.N. headquarters has only a staff of thirty to manage procurement that totals $470. These comparative data were drawn from a pamphlet provided by the United Nations Association of the United States announcing a new publication entitled *How to Do Business with the United Nations: A Complete Guide to UN Procurement* (New York: UNA/USA, forthcoming).

36. This represents a significant increase in the level of U.S. support. In 1992 less than $4 million worth of reimbursed support was provided.

37. The United States provides roughly 15 percent of foreign national military detailees to the United Nations.

38. Barry M. Blechman and Matthew Vaccaro, *Training for Peacekeeping: The United Nations' Role* (Washington, D.C.: Henry L. Stimson Center Report no. 12, July 1994).

39. This series was produced by the United Nations Institute for Training and Research (UNITAR) in April 1993 and has already been distributed to member states. Copies of this material have been reviewed by those who are currently writing U.S. doctrine, and their assessment is that it is fully compatible with the emerging U.S. and NATO doctrine. In addition to videotapes and manuals, the United Nations will soon offer correspondence courses to member states.

40. For an excellent review of the status of U.N. training for peace operations, see Blechman and Vaccaro, *Training for Peacekeeping*.

CHAPTER 16

ARMS CONTROL AND PROLIFERATION

INTRODUCTION TO ARMS CONTROL

GREGORY J. RATTRAY

Given the changing international system and uncertainty about how states will achieve security in this environment, a brief examination of arms control is both timely and necessary. To that end, this essay defines arms control and distinguishes it from disarmament. It also discusses the history of arms control and its prospects in the post–Cold War era.

THE SECURITY DILEMMA AND ARMS RACES

In a system of sovereign states with the capability to build and maintain sizable armed forces, a situation known as a security dilemma exists. States cannot ensure that rival states will not attempt to achieve undue influence through the pursuit and maintenance of military superiority. Trust often does not exist. States, therefore, interpret incoming information on the military capabilities of rival states in the worst light. Evidence of a new military program or spending by one state "requires" other states to respond in a similar fashion to avoid the other side achieving superiority whether through larger forces or technological breakthroughs. An upward spiral, or arms race, can ensue, even at the cost of a state neglecting its domestic needs; for example, many experts view huge defense expenditures as a primary contributing cause of the collapse of the Soviet Union. In addition, an arms race increases political tension between states, raising the probability and severity of crises and possibly causing war. Arms control tries to address the negative effects of the security dilemma.[1]

Early arms control theorists defined arms control in the broadest sense to refer to all forms of military cooperation between potential enemies in the interest of reducing the likelihood of war, the political and economic costs of preparing for war,[2] and the scope and violence of war if it were to occur. Yet, until recently, our political leaders and media seem to have had a more limited definition. They generally confined arms control to a limited set of activities dealing with specific steps to control a class or related classes of weapons systems, codified in formal agreements or treaties.

The impetus for controlling arms is not limited solely to constraining arms competitions or prolifer-ation. Another common motive is to disarm perceived aggressors—as was done with Germany after World War I, Germany and Japan after World War II, and Iraq after the Gulf War. Quite possibly, states and international organizations may attempt to accomplish such punitive arms control in the post–Cold War era. However, this type of action falls outside the focus of the definition that we outline for this essay and therefore is not a major topic of discussion.

For the purposes of this essay arms control is defined as *a process involving specific, declared steps by a state to enhance security through cooperation with other states*. These steps can be unilateral, bilateral, or multilateral. Cooperation can be implicit as well as explicit. In considering what steps states might be taken to achieve security objectives, it is important to keep this broad definition in mind and not think of arms control as dealing only with numbers and types of weapons.

ARMS CONTROL VERSUS DISARMAMENT

There is a difference between conceiving of arms control as a means to achieving a larger goal and seeing arms control as an end unto itself. As defined earlier, the arms control process is intended to serve as a means of enhancing a state's national security. Arms control is one of a number of approaches a nation has available for achieving this goal. Arms control could even lead states to agree to increases in certain categories of armaments if such increases would contribute to crisis stability and thereby reduce the chance of war. This concept of arms control should be distinguished from that of general and complete disarmament. Proponents of disarmament as an end in itself see the goal of arms control as more simply reducing the size of military forces, budgets, explosive power, and other aggregate measures.

One way of illustrating the difference between complete disarmament and arms control is to examine the prospects for eliminating all nuclear weapons. To proponents of general disarmament, the prospect of a world free of nuclear weapons seems very desirable. The world's political leaders apparently support such a goal. Former Soviet president Mikhail Gorbachev pledged to work toward the

This essay has been edited and is reprinted from Arms Control: Toward the 21st Century, *edited by Jeffrey A. Larsen and Gregory J. Rattray. Copyright © 1996 by Lynne Rienner Publishers, Inc. Reprinted by permission of the publisher.*

elimination of all nuclear weapons by the year 2000. The goals of the U.S. Arms Control and Disarmament Agency (ACDA) include achieving general and complete disarmament. Substantial progress toward reducing the number of nuclear weapons has been made recently (although most of the actual reductions will not be complete until after the turn of the century).

Yet many worry about the consequences of ever achieving a nuclear-free world. Nagging questions exist. If all nations pledged to give up their weapons, would the United States take them at their word or would it require some means of ensuring their commitment had been carried out? Could the United States verify such a pledge? Does the technology currently exist to accomplish such verification? Even if the international community could verify at some point in the future that no nuclear weapons existed, would humankind be forever free from nuclear destruction? Could the world ever eradicate the technical knowledge required to construct such weapons? In a conflict involving national survival, might nations again attempt to build and use such weapons? Would not great incentives exist to use newly constructed nuclear weapons to maintain a nuclear monopoly if rival states were also trying to build these weapons? Could the world ensure that nonstate actors never developed and used such weapons? The goal of complete disarmament, nuclear and otherwise, may appear desirable at first glance. However, the apparent barriers to achieving such a goal and its possible consequences force one to examine less radical, though still important, steps to improving national security through arms control.

Of course, advocacy of disarmament as part of a state's arms control policy can also be part of a "means to an end" approach. For example, the United States and other countries have negotiated global conventions that endeavor to rid the world of chemical and biological weapons. The United States unilaterally decided that neither chemical nor biological weapons would enhance its security, even if they were possessed by other states. Efforts to rid the world of such weapons generally are perceived to enhance the security of all states. Similarly, in recent years, the United States and the Soviet Union (now Russia) have managed to agree to eliminate certain classes of strategic arms. The important distinction centers on what arms control is intended to achieve—lower numbers of weapons or improved security for the parties involved.

HISTORICAL BACKGROUND

Humankind's efforts to control the consequences of the possession and use of weapons followed quickly upon the heels of weapons development. History records negotiations between the Greek city-states of Sparta and Athens concerning limitations to fortifications in the fifth century B.C.[3] During the Middle Ages, the Catholic church issued canons proscribing violence against clerics and women, banned jousting tournaments (which tended to turn into battles), and attempted to ban weapons such as the crossbow.[4] In 1817 the United States and Great Britain signed the Rush-Bagot Agreement calling for the virtual removal of armed warships from the Great Lakes. The potential for devastation inherent in the armed might of newly industrialized countries prompted the 1899 and 1907 Hague Conventions to outlaw weapons such as dumdum bullets and asphyxiating gases, in the hope of mitigating the impact of future wars.

World War I fully exposed the horrors and totality of modern interstate conflict and the limits to controlling arms through agreements. President Woodrow Wilson called it "the war to end all wars." Attempts to prevent the recurrent use of poison gas prompted the 1925 Geneva Protocol to again prohibit the use of chemical and biological weapons. The 1928 Kellogg-Briand Pact, signed by sixty-three countries, went even further by attempting to completely abolish aggressive war as a legitimate right of states. In more focused negotiations, such as the Washington Naval Conference of 1922 and the London Naval Conferences of 1930 and 1935, treaties were made in an effort to balance the naval strength of the major powers. These agreements constrained the size of the fleets of the United States, the United Kingdom, Japan, France, and Italy.

The limitations of such efforts were again made clear by the outbreak and massive scope of World War II. As this conflict concluded with the dropping of the first atomic weapons on Hiroshima and Nagasaki, humankind faced an even more insistent challenge to control the possibilities for violence and destruction unleashed in the pursuit of weapons and national security.

ARMS CONTROL DURING THE COLD WAR

These efforts to limit the pursuit and acquisition of weapons became known as arms control. Despite the failure of early efforts to control the nuclear genie, arms control during the Cold War eventually assumed a high priority on the national security agenda as a way of managing the superpower nuclear rivalry. The new importance of arms control was a reaction to the bipolar structure of the international system and the new and, many argued, revolutionary nature of nuclear weapons. In general, these negotiations were limited in scope and focused on increased strategic nuclear stability between the superpowers. The Strategic Arms Limitation Talks (SALT) and the Strategic Arms Reduction Talks (START) held center stage during this period. Other important multilateral negotiations and agreements occurred that limited nuclear testing and deployment, particularly the Nonproliferation Treaty (NPT). Efforts were conducted in other areas, such as the Biological and Toxin Weapons Convention (BWC) and the Mutual and Balanced Force Reduction (MBFR) talks covering conventional weapons in Europe.

As the United States and the Soviet Union faced one another as military, political, and ideological rivals, the conduct of bilateral negotiations became very formal. Agreements took years to reach. Every possible implication for the strategic balance was scrutinized, while increasingly complex provisions for verification became part of the process to guard against cheating. Even when a treaty was concluded, the benefits and pitfalls of arms control were hotly debated among the national security elites. SALT II was never ratified by the U.S. Senate, even after its signing in 1979 following seven years of painfully slow negotiations. The pros and cons of the Antiballistic Missile (ABM) Treaty became a perennial issue after President Ronald Reagan renewed the U.S. quest for strategic defenses. Soviet (and later, Russian) nationalists argued that too many concessions had been made to the United States during the START process and the agreements undermined their own security.

<h3 style="text-align:center">ARMS CONTROL AND THE
CLOSE OF THE COLD WAR</h3>

The dissolution of the Soviet Union and of the Warsaw Pact has transformed the content and perceived importance of arms control in just a few short years. As the Iron Curtain fell and the former republics of the Soviet Union declared independence, the ideological and military threats to the United States from the East dissipated. The imperative to manage the strategic nuclear balance between the superpowers faded. The place of arms control on the national security agenda began to drop. By the early 1990s, commentators began to question whether the lengthy, formalistic negotiations and highly structured forums established for arms control during the Cold War were causing nations to wait for a treaty before undertaking actions already planned and thereby slowing the pace of defense reductions. The utility of past arms control agreements has been debated in light of the changed strategic situation in Europe.[5] Others have questioned whether arms control remains a useful tool for national security at all.[6]

Meanwhile, the Gulf War brought a new set of issues into the limelight. Iraqi pursuit of a range of advanced arms—including nuclear weaponry, ballistic missiles, and super-long-range artillery—affected the conduct of the war, as well as leaving most of the industrialized members of the United Nations coalition chastised for helping to build the Iraqi war machine, however unwittingly. Iraq's progress toward a nuclear weapons capability while remaining a member of the nuclear NPT regime and subject to International Atomic Energy Agency (IAEA) inspections frightened many observers. At the same time, the dissolution of the Soviet military machine has created opportunities for weapons, military technologies, and know-how to flow to other states and even nonstate actors: Su-27 fighters and surface-to-air missiles have been sold to China,[7] Russia transferred cryogenic engine technology to the Indian space program,[8] smugglers have been caught in Germany with small quantities of (presumably) Russian pluto-

nium.[9] Proliferation has risen quickly to the top of the security agenda of the United States and other Western nations.

The Gulf War led the way in pointing to other new security concerns. The breakdown of the bipolar international system coincided with a rise in regional instability. Conflict has begun to break out around the globe. Domestic conflicts are spilling over the borders of crumbling, multiethnic states. Vicious, even genocidal, fighting in Africa, in Yugoslavia, and within the confines of the former Soviet Union make some observers long for the relative calm of the latter stages of the Cold War. Tensions are high in other areas, such as the Korean peninsula. Humanitarian and moral imperatives have led to U.N. and U.S. intervention in many of these situations.

Yet the early 1990s also saw the refocusing of public attention within the United States on problems at home. Revitalizing the economy and improving U.S. economic competitiveness became central focuses of the 1992 presidential race. Other countries in the developed and developing worlds confront similar challenges. Japan has faced political scandals and numerous changes in government. Germany has the daunting task of integrating a formerly Communist-ruled region suffering from decay of work incentives, an outdated industrial base, and massive environmental problems. Defense needs compete with other crucial priorities in an era of shrinking federal budgets and economic competition from abroad.[10] Environmental issues have also pushed their way onto the security agenda. The defense establishment increasingly must concern itself with the need to limit and clean up the impact of its activities. Others see transnational problems such as pollution and global warming as new sources of potential conflict.[11] The post–Cold War nature of national security and the role of military forces have yet to be clearly defined.

<h3 style="text-align:center">ARMS CONTROL IN THE
POST–COLD WAR ERA</h3>

As the Cold War ended, the conception and execution of what was referred to as arms control began to change, first with an increase in the number and types of bilateral arrangements between the superpowers, starting with the Intermediate-Range Nuclear Forces (INF) Treaty signed in December 1987. After the precedent set by the INF Treaty, negotiations on nuclear arms control began to pick up pace, resulting in the START I agreement in July 1991. This treaty was expanded to include Ukraine, Belarus, and Kazakhstan through the Lisbon Protocol signed in May 1992. START II mandated even deeper cuts in strategic forces and was agreed to in January 1993. In addition, numerous unilateral declarations and reductions have been made by both sides regarding their nuclear forces. Increasingly, the United States and Russia have moved away from a competitive approach to security based on deterrence to a cooperative approach based on re-assurance.[12]

As rapprochement between the superpowers deepened, the forums and scope for other negotiations began to broaden. Under the auspices of the Conference on Security and Cooperation in Europe (CSCE), multilateral agreements were reached in Europe, beginning with confidence- and security-building measures (CSBMs). CSBMs were first included in the Helsinki Final Act in 1975. Interest in these measures picked up momentum during the 1980s, leading to the 1986 Stockholm and 1992 Vienna Documents, which laid out extensive sets of CSBMs. Negotiations on conventional forces culminated in the Conventional Forces in Europe (CFE) Treaty in December 1990 and the CFE 1A Agreement in July 1992; these two agreements dramatically limited the size and structure of conventional forces.

Regions beyond Europe also began to turn to arms control as a means to build security. The Middle East peace talks under the direction of the United States and Russia after the Gulf War had a very significant security component. In May 1991, the Bush administration proposed the Middle East Arms Control Initiative, calling on the five permanent members of the U.N. Security Council to "establish guidelines for restraints on destabilizing transfers of conventional arms" to the region.[13]

Numerous regional nuclear confidence-building agreements have been pursued, with varying degrees of success. Despite ongoing tensions, India and Pakistan have managed to reach a series of agreements since 1985, including pacts not to attack each other's nuclear facilities and notification of military exercises. In Latin America, Brazil and Argentina signed an agreement with the IAEA renouncing the pursuit of nuclear weapons and allowing for the inspection of facilities. This agreement renewed progress toward full compliance with the Latin American nuclear-free zone established by the Treaty of Tlatelolco in 1967. In 1992, the two Koreas signed a Joint Declaration on the Denuclearization of the Korean Peninsula, although further progress toward cooperation proved difficult.

Significant progress was made on global regimes as well. The U.N. Conference on Disarmament negotiated a Chemical Weapons Convention (CWC), which was opened for signature on 1 January 1993. In December 1991, a U.N. General Assembly resolution also established a Register on Arms Transfers providing for the voluntary provision of information on arms exports and imports. Over eighty states provided reports during the first year of operation, and the register may become an increasingly important tool in tracking conventional arms around the world. After the September 1991 Third Review Conference of the 1972 Biological and Toxin Weapons Convention (BWC), the secretary-general established a group of government experts to analyze the possibility of strengthening the convention through the creation of verification procedures.

NEW APPROACHES TO ARMS CONTROL

Other aspects of arms control are changing to accommodate the new arms control agenda. The very formal, structured approach to reaching agreement has been broadened to include more informal modes of cooperation. In particular, the use of unilateral and reciprocal declarations such as those made by the superpowers regarding tactical nuclear weapons and the cancellation of new strategic systems between September 1991 and January 1992 resulted in dramatic steps outside formally established negotiating procedures.[14] Numerous similar types of commitments—such as unilateral declarations by states such as Israel, South Africa, Russia, and China to abide by the provisions of the Missile Technology Control Regime (MTCR)—may presage a major change in how states approach arms control.

Security negotiations between states have also developed an increasingly operational focus; they no longer simply pursue agreements to limit types and numbers of weapons. The growing interest in transparency is highlighted by the increasingly strict verification provisions written into treaties pioneered by the on-site inspection portions of the INF Treaty, as well as new agreements to share data—such as in the CFE Treaty and through the U.N. Register of Conventional Arms. As mentioned earlier, since 1975 the CSCE accords have included ever-broadening CSBMs to include advance notification, limits on size and number, and observation of military exercises. The Open Skies Treaty allows at least twenty-five countries to conduct, and be obligated to receive, observation flights by unarmed aircraft carrying optical and video cameras as well as infrared sensors and side-looking radar.[15] Efforts to deal with growing concerns about the leakage of nuclear materials to potential proliferants are likely to be dealt with through CSBMs rather than formal treaties.

New international organizations have evolved to implement agreements. U.N. Security Council Resolution 687 created a U.N. Special Commission in 1991 to monitor and eliminate Iraq's ballistic missile and weapons of mass destruction capability. CWC provisions include the creation of the Organization for the Prohibition of Chemical Weapons (OPCW) based in The Hague to monitor and enforce the treaty. Other international institutions with an arms control role, particularly the IAEA, have received renewed attention as proliferation concerns became prominent in light of new information on Iraq's activities prior to the Gulf War. Similarly, the MTCR has assumed an increasingly important role in efforts to limit technological diffusion in the missile area.

Certainly, as of 1996 the news is not all good. Proliferation concerns remain prominent in dealing with almost all the former Soviet republics. Ukraine demonstrated great intransigence in ratifying START and accepting the NPT regime. Russia complains of difficulty implementing chemical weapons agreements because of a lack of resources. The Middle East Arms Control Initiative died after China pulled out to protest U.S. F-16 sales to Taiwan.[16] The United States has accused both Russia and China of violating their pledges to adhere to MTCR restrictions. The future of the CWC in the Middle East is very uncertain because some Arab states intend to withhold ratification based on Israel's suspected possession of nuclear weapons. North Korea has stalled IAEA inspections numerous times, has threatened withdrawal from the NPT, and has raised tensions on the peninsula. The U.S. Senate keeps a close eye on these situations in deciding whether to ratify agreements. This causes delays in the entry into force and implementation of agreements. Arms control has resolved some, but certainly not all, of the diverse security challenges that face today's states.

However, no one can deny that a great deal of progress has been made through activities usually labeled "arms control." Arms control has a place in dealing with the new concerns of advanced weapons proliferation, regional instability, and economic and environmental security. The new and old arms control approaches will coexist while important dimensions of the exercise are redefined. The future of arms control as a means of achieving security needs rigorous examination.

NOTES

1. Two classics dealing with arms races are Samuel P. Huntington, "Arms Races Prerequisites and Results," *Public Policy: Yearbook of the Graduate School of Public Administration* (Cambridge, Mass.: Harvard University Press, 1958); and Colin Gray, "The Arms Race Phenomenon," *World Politics* (October 1971).

2. Thomas C. Schelling and Morton H. Halperin, *Strategy and Arms Control* (Washington, D.C.: Pergamon Brassey's, 1985), 3.

3. Christopher J. Lamb, *How to Think about Arms Control, Disarmament and Defense* (Englewood Cliffs, N.J.: Prentice Hall, 1988), 11.

4. Richard D. Burns, ed., *The Encyclopedia of Arms Control and Disarmament* (New York: Charles Scribner's Sons, 1993), 568.

5. See Richard K. Betts, "Systems for Peace or Causes of War? Collective Security, Arms Control and the New Europe," *International Security* (Summer 1992): 5–43; and the ensuing debate between Betts and Michael J. Mazarr in "Correspondence: A Farewell to Arms Control?" *International Security* (Winter 1992–93): 188–200.

6. See Colin S. Gray, *House of Cards: Why Arms Control Must Fail* (Ithaca, N.Y.: Cornell University Press, 1992), and *Weapons Don't Make War: Policy, Strategy and Military Technology* (Lawrence: University of Kansas Press, 1993).

7. Steven Erlanger, "Russia Sells War Machine to Pay the Cost of Peace," *New York Times*, 3 February 1993, p. 1; and "Su-27 Fighter Aircraft Sold to China," FBIS-SOV-92-242, 16 December 1992, p. 16.

8. *Arms Control Reporter* (Cambridge, Mass.: Institute for Defense and Disarmament Studies), p. 706.A.3.

9. Numerous press reports have detailed four incidents that occurred between May and August 1994. For example, see "Officials Say Contraband Not a Threat," *Washington Post*, 28 August 1994, pp. A1, A20; and "Nuclear Smugglers Spark Worries over Russian Safeguards," *Arms Control Today*, September 1994, 25.

10. See Peter G. Peterson, "The Primacy of the Domestic Agenda," in *Rethinking America's Security: Beyond the Cold War to New World Order* (New York: W. W. Norton, 1992), 57–93. More specifically, two major works address the impact of disproportionately high defense expenditures: Paul Kennedy, *The Rise and Fall of Great Powers: Economic Change and Military Conflict 1500–2000* (New York: Random House, 1987); and David Calleo, *Beyond American Hegemony* (New York: Basic Books, 1987).

11. For a discussion of this evolving area of national security studies see W. Harriet Critchley and Terry Teriff's chapter "Environment and Security" in *Security Studies for the 1990s* (Washington, D.C.: Brassey's, 1993), 327–45.

12. Various experts have commented on this evolution. In particular, see Ivo Daalder, "The Future of Arms Control," *Survival* (Spring 1992).

13. Malcom Chambers, Owen Greene, Edward J. Laurance, and Herbert Wulf, eds., *Developing the U.N. Register of Conventional Arms* (United Kingdom: University of Branford Press, 1994), 3.

14. The possibilities for implicit agreement and unilateral initiatives were discussed in the seminal work of Schelling and Halperin, *Strategy and Arms Control*, originally published in 1961. Schelling reinforces this point with an article entitled "What Went Wrong with Arms Control" in *Foreign Affairs* (Winter 1985–86), 219–33.

15. Science Applications International Corporation, "Open Skies," *Profile Summaries of Arms Control Treaties* (McLean, Va.: Science Applications International Corporation, 1994), 1.

16. Chambers and others, Developing the UN Register, 3.

THE OBJECTIVES OF ARMS CONTROL

KERRY M. KARTCHNER

Because arms control is an instrument of national security strategy, its objectives are integrally linked to those of a nation's overall defense priorities. For planning purposes, defense priorities are developed and applied on at least two levels: the grand strategy level, representing general security aspirations, and the operational level, where the broadly stated objectives of grand strategy are translated into more specific goals to guide actual military operations. The same is true for arms control, where objectives have been articulated at the grand strategy and operational levels as well.[1]

The basic grand strategic objectives of arms control as an instrument of national security remain virtually unchanged, at least in general terms. U.S. national security interests at the highest level of abstraction are essentially the same as during the Cold War: to protect and preserve the fundamental freedoms and institutions of the United States by deterring or preventing attack on U.S. national interests at home and abroad. New threats, nonetheless, have necessitated reordering the priorities among traditional U.S. national security objectives. Deterring nuclear attack is now less urgent than preventing or countering proliferation of weapons of mass destruction, for example.

However, the conceptual problems now facing defense planners and arms control policy makers at the operational level are fundamentally different from those that confronted the founders of traditional arms control theory in the late 1950s and early 1960s. During that time, the strategic planners' task was to manage an escalating nuclear arms competition between two superpowers locked in an ideological and geopolitical rivalry on a global scale. The stakes were unambiguous and absolute because the survival of the United States itself was at risk and the adversary was clearly identifiable. Every military and diplomatic maneuver of that era was animated and overshadowed by the prospect of a shockingly swift surprise nuclear attack with the potential for unthinkably devastating consequences. The paramount task of political and military policy makers was, therefore, to reduce, deter, or eliminate the prospect of mutual and instantaneous annihilation by surprise nuclear attack. Classical (or, traditional) arms control theory was developed in direct response to the "surprise attack imperative"—the urgent need to find and institutionalize whatever means possible to mitigate the threat of a surprise nuclear attack.[2]

The surprise attack imperative has receded into history and has lost the urgency it once commanded.

The superpower rivalry has all but disappeared with the disintegration of the former Soviet empire, and mutual nuclear deterrence no longer seems so urgent or relevant. Indeed, new and emerging sources of danger do not appear susceptible to traditional deterrence. There is no global arms race to speak of, only a myriad of regional arms competitions. The near-term survival of the United States itself is not at risk. The stakes in terms of U.S. national interests are now fraught with ambiguity and uncertainty. Most important, the threat of a surprise nuclear attack, which was the touchstone of traditional arms control theory, can no longer be considered even a viable planning scenario.[3]

These considerations raise some obvious questions. If arms control was initially the product of the surprise attack imperative, and that imperative is now obsolete, are the original objectives of arms control still relevant? Are the assumptions and conceptual framework developed by the founders of traditional arms control now inapplicable? If not, must these assumptions and objectives be reprioritized and adapted to meet the immediate and pressing security dilemmas facing today's defense and foreign policy decision makers?

This essay reviews the basic objectives of arms control as originally espoused in traditional arms control theory and explains how the theory was developed to support overall U.S. national security goals during the Cold War. It also proposes a reprioritization of objectives at the grand strategy level, as well as new objectives at the operational level, in light of U.S. defense and security priorities on the eve of the twenty-first century.[4]

ARMS CONTROL AND NATIONAL SECURITY

The founding premise of traditional arms control theory—that arms control can be an important adjunct to national security strategy—has not always been obvious nor consistently observed in practice because arms control is inherently a counterintuitive approach to enhancing security. Consider the following: arms control makes national security dependent to some degree on the cooperation of prospective adversaries. It often involves setting lower levels of arms than would otherwise appear prudent based on a strict threat assessment. It mandates establishing a more or less interactive relationship with putative opponents and, in the case of mutual intrusive verification and data exchanges, exposing sensitive national security information and facilities to scrutiny

This essay has been edited and is reprinted from Arms Control: Toward the 21st Century, *edited by Jeffrey A. Larsen and Gregory J. Rattray. Copyright © 1996 by Lynne Rienner Publishers, Inc. Reprinted by permission of the publisher.*

by foreign powers. It requires seeking and institutionalizing areas of common ground where the potential for conflicts of interest seemingly far outweigh objectives in common. Arms control is fundamentally a high-stakes gamble, mortgaging national survival against little more than the collateral of trust and anticipated reciprocal restraint, often in a geopolitical context fraught with political hostility and tension. It is, in fact, a voluntary (and not always reversible) delimitation of national sovereignty. Viewed from this perspective, arms control is not obviously better than its alternative—unilaterally providing for one's own security.

What compels the United States and other nations, then, to structure so much of their national security posture on an approach that seemingly contradicts a country's natural instincts toward self-sufficiency and self-preservation? The answer to this apparent paradox is that the theory of arms control as developed in the late 1950s and early 1960s—if conceptually valid and faithfully implemented—allows us to anticipate that an otherwise equivalent degree of security may be established by negotiation at weapons levels lower than would be the case if these levels were determined unilaterally.

THE DEVELOPMENT OF ARMS CONTROL THEORY

The phrase *traditional arms control theory* refers to the assumptions and premises of those strategic analysts who first developed the objectives and possibilities of arms control as an adjunct to national security during 1958–62.[5] Traditional arms control theory was the product of a unique confluence of factors, and it reflected the assumptions, analyses, and policy priorities of defense analysts and policy makers of the late 1950s and early 1960s. Of course, seeking negotiated solutions to national security dilemmas was not new, but the rethinking of arms control in this period was part of a general reevaluation of U.S. defense and foreign policy that was precipitated, first of all, by considerable dissatisfaction with the postwar diplomatic and arms control stalemate. The United States had sought to establish through diplomatic means a variety of disarmament arrangements since 1945 (e.g., the Baruch Plan, the Open Skies Treaty), but long negotiations and multiple proposals had yielded no tangible results, primarily because of Soviet objections to those verification regimes deemed essential by the Western allies. In the mid-1950s, policy makers began to rethink an approach that had emphasized general and complete disarmament and to consider instead limited, partial measures that would gradually enhance confidence in cooperative security arrangements. Thus, more modest goals, under the rubric of "arms control," came to replace the propaganda-laden disarmament efforts of the late 1940s and early 1950s.

In addition, each major war seems to precipitate the rise, ten to fifteen years later, of a new generation of military leaders and strategic theorists who are free of traditional biases and who promulgate a revisionist outlook on strategy, tactics, and technology. In this case, the development of traditional arms control theory benefited from the emergence of leaders who were predisposed to favor arms control as a cooperative approach to enhancing security, who were under political pressure to seek diplomatic solutions and reduce defense budgets, and who recognized the public's growing fear of nuclear weapons.

Finally, by far the most important factors leading to the development of traditional arms control theory were the Soviet launching of Sputnik in 1957 and the reverberations this event had for U.S. thinking about defense and security in the nuclear age. This stunning technological achievement on the part of the Soviet Union stripped the U.S. psyche of its traditional sense of insular security and profoundly affected everything from U.S. educational priorities to U.S. defense and foreign policy. More specifically, it caused considerable anxiety regarding the long-term viability of nuclear deterrence and sensitized U.S. defense intellectuals to the danger of technological threats to strategic stability. Beginning with this event, U.S. political and military leaders collectively turned their attention to thwarting the new danger of a surprise nuclear attack. In fact, the very first modern arms control effort, incorporating the basic assumptions of emerging arms control theory, was the 1958 Surprise Attack Conference, held in the immediate aftermath of Sputnik.[6]

BASIC TENETS OF TRADITIONAL ARMS CONTROL THEORY

The period that began with the Surprise Attack Conference and ended with the publication in 1962 of the proceedings of the 1960 Woods Hole Summer Study produced the basic canons of modern arms control theory.[7] From the literature of this golden era of arms control thinking emerged a virtual consensus on several key assumptions, which may be considered the basic tenets of traditional arms control theory.

First, arms control was conceived as an instrument whose purpose was to enhance national security. As Hedley Bull, one of the founders of traditional arms control theory, succinctly explained: "Arms control or disarmament was not an end in itself but a means to an end and that end was first and foremost the enhancement of security, especially security against nuclear war."[8] And as Thomas Schelling and Morton Halperin state near the end of their book: "The aims of arms control and the aims of a national military strategy should be substantially the same."[9] This principle established as the dominant goal of arms control the enhancement of national security, not the reduction of arms per se. In fact, it was understood that not all reductions were necessarily useful. There was an explicit recognition that arms control could be harmful if not properly guided by overall national security strategy: "It is not to be assumed that the level of forces and weapons most favorable to international security is the lowest one."[10] This meant that arms control policies should be developed with national security strategy clearly in mind.

Second, the superpowers shared a common interest in avoiding nuclear war; this common interest could and should be the basis for effective arms control agreements. According to Bull, "The fact that the United States and the Soviet Union were locked in a political and ideological conflict, one moreover that sometimes took a military form, did not mean that they could not recognize common interests in avoiding a ruinous nuclear war, or cooperate to advance these common interests."[11] This assumption was one of the most important (and controversial) conceptual departures from past thinking promulgated by the new arms control theory. Previously, it was assumed that relaxation of political tensions had to precede achieving substantive arms control agreements. The founders of traditional arms control theory, on the other hand, believed that the threat of global nuclear annihilation was so paramount that it transcended political and ideological differences. If true, this meant that it was not necessary to fully resolve political conflicts before proceeding to negotiate arms control agreements—solutions to both could be advanced simultaneously. Nevertheless, original arms control theorists also recognized that where too much political tension existed, arms control would be impossible, and where there was little tension between countries, arms control would be superfluous: "Only the existence of international tension . . . makes arms control relevant. It is relevant when tension is at a certain point, above which it is impossible and beneath which it is unnecessary. . . . When the relations between nations are marked by sympathy and amity, arms control appears to be irrelevant."[12] Moreover, certain political conditions were essential. According to Bull, "Unless the powers concerned want a system of arms control; unless there is a measure of political détente among them sufficient to allow of such a system; unless they are prepared to accept the military situation among them which the arms control system legitimizes and preserves, and can agree and remain agreed about what this situation will be, there can be little place for arms control."[13]

Third, arms control and military strategy should be used together to promote national security. The unity of strategy and arms control was a central tenet of traditional arms control theory. Such unity was essential if arms control theorists and defense policy strategists were to avoid working at cross-purposes. For example, if the implementation of U.S. defense strategy required deploying certain types of weapons that were restricted by arms control agreements, this could defeat the overall purpose of U.S. national security posture and erode the legitimacy of both the arms control process and U.S. defense policy. The founders of traditional arms control theory asserted that arms control negotiators and defense policy makers should strive toward the same goals and operate on the basis of the same general assumptions regarding which weapons were desirable and which were destabilizing.

Finally, arms control regimes need not be limited to formal agreements but could also include informal, unilateral, and verbal agreements. To cite Bull again: "If arms control was cooperation in military policy between antagonistic states to advance interests that they perceived to be common ones, then this included not only the attempt to negotiate formal agreements to limit the character, deployment, or use of their arms, but also informal agreements to restrain arms competition and indeed to restrain military conflicts themselves, and also unilateral actions that advanced perceived common interests and were not merely directed toward the advantage of one side."[14]

THE ORIGINAL OBJECTIVES OF TRADITIONAL ARMS CONTROL THEORY

For arms control to be an effective instrument of national security, its objectives must be determined by, and be in close harmony with, the broader objectives of overall national security strategy.[15] At the most basic level of abstraction, three grand conceptual dilemmas dominated strategic thinking and the formulation of U.S. national security objectives during the Cold War: (1) What deters? (2) How much is enough? (3) What if deterrence fails? These dilemmas involve (1) determining how best to deter whom from doing what, (2) assessing and establishing the adequacy of weapons and resources committed to deterrence, and (3) grappling with the unthinkable consequences should deterrence fail and a (nuclear) war actually occur.[16]

The founders of traditional arms control theory realized that if arms control were to be an adjunct of national security it should address these same grand conceptual dilemmas, and they believed that negotiated solutions could effectively contribute to resolving them. Traditional arms control theory was based on the premise that the superpowers inherently shared an area of common ground (i.e., avoiding nuclear war) and that this "element of mutual interest" could serve as the basis for limited, cooperative arrangements involving reciprocal restraint in the acquisition of weapons of mass destruction. In defining the scope and application of arms control, theorists set forth three general objectives for arms control that directly corresponded with the three grand conceptual dilemmas of the Cold War:

We believe that arms control is a promising, but still only dimly perceived, enlargement of the scope of our military strategy. It rests essentially on the recognition that our military relation with potential enemies is not one of pure conflict and opposition, but involves strong elements of mutual interest in *the avoidance of a war that neither side wants, in minimizing the costs and risks of the arms compe-*

tition, and in curtailing the scope and violence of war in the event it occurs.[17] (emphasis added)

Clearly, establishing the requirements of deterrence must precede and form the basis for the creation of policies for reducing the risk of nuclear war, the goal of reducing defense spending must be informed by some notion of what constitutes sufficient levels of weapons, and any scheme for limiting damage should war occur must presuppose at least some thought as to the nature of warfare and the way forces are to be employed in combat. Thus, the primary objectives of traditional arms control theory—reducing the risk of war, reducing the costs of preparing for war, and reducing the damage should war occur—are necessarily determined by the three major dilemmas of military policy.

THE FIRST OBJECTIVE: REDUCING THE RISK OF WAR

In practice, U.S. defense strategy sought to reduce the risk of nuclear war through some form of deterrence. It followed logically that arms control should therefore promote deterrence as the principal means of reducing the risk of war. The task for arms control negotiators became, then, to establish means and methods for enhancing and institutionalizing mutual nuclear deterrence and to restrict to the extent possible any threat to the preservation or stability of that deterrence.

Defining the essence of deterrence for purposes of arms control was relatively straightforward. Given the state of technology at the time and the lack of suitable means for limiting damage from, or defending against, nuclear attack, this necessarily meant codifying a condition of mutual assured destruction. However, restricting to the extent possible threats to the preservation (or stability) of deterrence was more complicated. One possible threat to strategic stability involved uncontrolled arms races, which could result in the development of unilateral military advantages for one side or the other. Arms control was seen as a prime means for setting limits on and restraining strategic arms race behavior. Thus, arms race stability became a component objective of traditional arms control theory at the operational level.

Moreover, for early arms control theorists, restraining certain types of technology was practically synonymous with reducing the risk of war and enhancing deterrence: "A main determinant of the likelihood of war is the nature of present military technology and present military expectations."[18] Again, the underlying premise was that war is most likely to begin with a surprise nuclear attack made possible by modern developments in ballistic missile, guidance and control, and nuclear weapons technology. Therefore, those weapon systems employing technologies that in theory most contributed to the ability to execute a surprise nuclear attack against the nuclear retaliatory forces of the other side, or that undermined the ability of either side to

hold deterrent targets at risk, became principal candidates for arms limitation agreements.

THE SECOND OBJECTIVE: REDUCING THE COSTS OF PREPARING FOR WAR

The assumptions underlying the second objective proceeded logically from the basic theory of arms control. This objective presumed that arms control "releases economic resources: that armaments, or armaments races, are economically ruinous or profligate, and that disarmament or arms control would make possible the diversion of resources now squandered in armaments into other and worthier channels."[19] If arms control succeeded in providing the same degree of security at lower levels of weapons than would otherwise be the case, it could lead to the necessity of fielding fewer weapons and thus lower overall defense spending. Further, if certain types of technology were mutually outlawed, there would be fewer costs associated with defense research and development, weapons production, force deployment, operations, and maintenance. The savings thus realized would be diverted to domestic economic priorities and would promote overall prosperity.

THE THIRD OBJECTIVE: REDUCING THE DAMAGE SHOULD WAR OCCUR

The theoretical postulations behind the third objective likewise seem self-evident, but they present something of a conundrum. If fewer weapons were fielded as a result of arms limitation agreements, should war nevertheless occur, overall damage would be less than it would otherwise have been. But fielding fewer weapons is not the only way to reduce damage in the event of war. Damage could be limited by also developing certain types of strategies and technologies, such as ballistic missile defense, which is designed to limit damage from ballistic missile attack. Therefore, arms control agreements that permitted, even encouraged, ballistic missile defenses would seem compatible with the goal of reducing damage should war occur.

However, there was an inherent contradiction between this arms control objective and the operationalization of the first objective. The first objective was translated in practice into promoting mutual assured destruction (or, in other words, mutual societal vulnerability), which derives its deterrent value from the threat of inflicting massive damage. By definition, this contradicts the goal of limiting damage. Furthermore, the option of reducing or limiting damage through active defenses was discarded by arms control and defense policy makers alike because of the presumed technological infeasibility and strategic provocativeness of missile defenses. Consequently, the objective of reducing damage should deterrence fail and war occur fell by the wayside of arms control practice. Reducing damage should war occur nevertheless remained an important goal of arms control negotiations.

PRIORITIZING ARMS CONTROL'S OBJECTIVES

In practice, the first of the three main objectives proposed by traditional arms control theory came to eclipse and overshadow the other two. Achieving the first objective would indirectly satisfy or render mute the other two. Stabilizing mutual nuclear deterrence at lower levels of forces than would otherwise be the case would necessarily result in reduced defense costs, with fewer weapons to field and maintain. And, it was implied, avoiding a nuclear war altogether would obviate the necessity of limiting damage should a war occur (but still begs the question of what to do if, for whatever reason, deterrence fails). Again, the Cold War focus on strategic arms control generally left untouched the issue of reducing damage during conventional conflicts. Thus, reducing the risk of war, or the risk of war through surprise nuclear attack, became the paramount objective of traditional arms control thinking.

RETHINKING THE OBJECTIVES OF TRADITIONAL ARMS CONTROL THEORY

The objectives established by traditional arms control theory transcend any given historical era. These objectives apply equally to weapons of mass destruction and conventional weapons systems and scenarios. They must, however, be adapted at the operational level to the prevailing circumstances if arms control is to remain a viable instrument of national security strategy.

As noted earlier, the three principal objectives of arms control as they were interpreted operationally were closely linked to the three main conceptual dilemmas of strategic thinking in the nuclear age: What deters? How much is enough? What if deterrence fails? However, the answers to these three questions have changed dramatically since the end of the Cold War. Therefore, to evaluate the current relevance of the basic objectives we must fundamentally reexamine the traditional answers to these dilemmas.

WHAT DETERS? OR, REDUCING THE RISK OF WAR

The implementation of traditional arms control theory came to embrace an assured destruction approach to deterrence and strategic stability that relied exclusively on the offensive threat of punitive retaliation. Traditional arms control theorists assumed defense was neither a technologically feasible nor strategically viable option. Both of these assumptions are now subject to reconsideration for several reasons.

First, the technologies may now exist to create militarily effective ballistic missile defenses at sustainable cost.[20] However, suggesting that technology is no longer the obstacle it once was is not to say that it is strategically or politically prudent to proceed with deploying ballistic missile defenses at the pres-

ent time. Myriad difficult and complicated issues need further clarification before making such a decision, including the likely impact of such deployments on current and prospective nuclear arms reduction agreements. Nevertheless, great strides in interceptor and target acquisition technology have convinced political leaders to pursue full-scale development of theater ballistic missile defenses while deferring the question of strategic missile defenses to a later date.

Second, given the deteriorated and exhausted state of the Russian economy, the real progress to date in U.S.–Russian relations, and the domestic preoccupations of the Russian leadership, it is difficult to take seriously the danger of a renewed strategic nuclear arms race between East and West. In other words, the action-reaction dynamic is no longer operative, and consequently deployment of a U.S. ballistic missile defense system is unlikely to trigger a massive Russian offensive force buildup.[21] Thus, the two major objections to reducing the risk of war through damage limitation strategies and capabilities—technological infeasibility and strategic instability—are less supportable than they might have been during an earlier era.

Most important, the assured destruction approach may not be effective in deterring the principal regional threat scenarios faced by the United States and its allies in the post–Cold War era. In the future, the United States is increasingly likely to face regional crisis situations where local animosities are intense, risk-taking propensities are high, the willingness to absorb casualties is great, a rogue power faces imminent defeat or other powerful incentives to resort to using nuclear or other weapons of mass destruction, and the stakes involved are infinitely greater for the regional players than for the United States, whose interests will be relatively limited. In such circumstances, how viable is U.S. possession of nuclear weapons as a deterrent without overt threats to use them? Furthermore, the United States is unlikely to make such threats for fear of legitimizing the pursuit of weapons of mass destruction on the part of regional hegemonies, undermining international normative constraints against all types of proliferation, and squandering the moral high ground in world politics. Bear in mind that U.S. nuclear weapons, with an overwhelming capability to completely obliterate Iraq many times over, did not deter Saddam Hussein from invading Kuwait. Nuclear use in this situation was simply not a credible threat.

Finally, since surprise attack is no longer the dominant threat scenario, the United States no longer needs an emphasis on punitive retaliation as a deterrent. The danger of surprise nuclear attack was deemed amenable only to the threat of punitive retaliatory strikes that would inflict unacceptable damage. With this requirement now greatly diminished, the United States can consider shifting the emphasis of its security policy to developing those capabilities necessary to deter attacks and to reducing the risk of war by limiting, rather than inflicting, wholesale damage.

How Much Is Enough? Or, Reducing the Cost of Preparing for War

The second major objective of traditional arms control theory has been to reduce the burden of maintaining a large defense establishment. This objective is traditionally interpreted at the operational level in economic terms, but it is inseparable from considerations of force sizing, or strategic adequacy, since maintaining the size, composition, and posture of deployed forces largely contributes to the cost of our defense establishment.

It is generally accepted that arms control as practiced during the Cold War never fulfilled the aspiration of reducing defense budgets. However, this objective of arms control remains quintessentially relevant in the aftermath of the Cold War and is perhaps even more achievable than ever before.

The collapse of the Soviet threat is dramatically altering our calculations of defense sufficiency, with profound implications for arms control. These calculations have recently been addressed in Department of Defense reports in both the "Nuclear Posture Review" of strategic force requirements and the "Bottom-Up Review" of conventional force requirements. In all likelihood, these assessments are only the beginning of an ongoing process that will result in even further downsizing and restructuring of U.S. forces. The matter of military sufficiency will, therefore, be of continuing relevance for the foreseeable future.

The "Bottom-Up Review" outlined the U.S. need for the capability to fight two near-simultaneous major regional contingencies anywhere in the world. The planning baseline for these contingencies was a Gulf War scenario. Along with maintaining preparedness for these contingencies, U.S. forces have become heavily involved in supporting peacekeeping, peacemaking, and humanitarian operations with varying degrees of success. Finally, major technological changes—such as the evolution of stealth techniques, the development of precision-guided weapons, and the growing importance of information on the battlefield—are prompting serious consideration of how we will conduct warfare in the future. These considerations must be reflected in assessing strategic sufficiency for arms control purposes.

Whatever the final outcome of deliberations over nuclear or conventional sufficiency in terms of long-range policies, clearly the United States in the near future will dramatically reduce its overall level of strategic weapons and its degree of reliance on nuclear deterrence as an instrument of national security. Arms control can codify and multilateralize such considerations to help deter any reversal in the process of global denuclearization and demilitarization now under way.

What If Deterrence Fails? Or, Reducing Damage Should War Occur

As noted earlier, the objective of actively limiting damage (a form of war fighting) was categorically rejected by the arms control community during the Cold War, in part because of a belief that the notion of deterrence failing was unthinkable, because of technical obstacles facing ballistic missile defense, and a fear of aggravating the nuclear arms race. Any contribution of past arms control efforts to the objective of reducing damage should war occur, then, was necessarily an indirect by-product of actually reducing weapons.

In the aftermath of the Cold War, limiting damage should be the paramount objective (at least at the strategic level) of both arms control efforts and military strategy. The prospect of regional powers, who are undeterred by threats of punitive retaliation, acquiring their own weapons of mass destruction or advanced conventional weapons argues for developing the means to limit the damage that could be inflicted by such rogue states. Since it cannot always be anticipated where or when such threats will emerge, nor can it always be known what threats such regional powers will find credible or persuasive, the United States can never be totally confident of successfully deterring every eventual threat to its territory or that of its allies. The United States must recognize that deterrence could fail—and should deterrence fail, it must be prepared to limit damage to itself and its allies and interests abroad.

CONCLUSION

As noted at the outset, the problems and dilemmas confronting defense planners and arms control policy makers today are in many ways different from those that faced the original founders of traditional arms control theory in the late 1950s and early 1960s. These theorists were principally concerned with the danger of a civilization-threatening surprise nuclear attack; they developed arms control as one mechanism for suppressing and confining that danger, which has receded with the passing of the Cold War. Nevertheless, the general objectives of traditional arms control theory at the grand strategy level remain applicable to the full range of contemporary arms control efforts, including arms control aimed at regional stabilization and the regulation of conventional, chemical, and biological weapons. After all, we still want to reduce the likelihood of war; only the probable location, nature, and participants in future wars have changed, meaning that how we deter or prevent these future wars must change as well. Minimizing the burden of security and defense will always be a high priority in democratic societies that consider warfare to be a deviation from normal international relations. And reducing the damage and violence should war occur also continues to be a desirable objective. Ultimately, the success or failure of arms control must be evaluated in terms of its contribution to these three objectives.

Reducing the risk of war remains an important objective of U.S. national security strategy, but the sources and causes of war are now so diffuse and complex that no single strategy can address all of them. Moreover, deterrence is no longer a viable threat-reduction strategy, at least in many of the regional situations of greatest concern, since many of the new and emerging sources of danger cannot be deterred by traditional assured-destruction-type blandishments (i.e., punitive threats of massive attacks against populations). Because the United States is faced with the prospects of not always being able to prevent regional conflicts from erupting and not always being able to deter emerging threats to the U.S. homeland from proliferating weapons of mass destruction and long-range delivery systems, future U.S. defense strategy must emphasize the ability to limit damage to U.S. territory, to protect U.S. forces deployed abroad, and to safeguard the vital interests of U.S. allies. If arms control is to effectively fulfill its preordained mission of enhancing national security and to remain a viable instrument of broader national defense strategy, it must be adapted to promote the objective of limiting damage during conflicts. This mandate raises one of the traditional arms control objectives, previously forsaken by arms control policy makers of the Cold War era, to a new position of preeminence as a hedge against deterrence failure in an unstable and unpredictable world.

Concluding that there is a need to limit damage means that ways must be found to surmount the traditional incompatibilities between the requirements of verifiable arms control (i.e., open and observable forces) and the requirements of an operational damage limitation strategy (which necessarily requires protected and survivable forces). As a preliminary answer, arms control may contribute to the new requirement for limiting damage to U.S. interests and assets in the following ways: by avoiding unnecessary restrictions aimed at U.S. defensive capabilities; by encouraging the deployment of residual nuclear or conventional forces (i.e., those that remain after implementing arms reduction agreements) in survivable basing modes; by facilitating the conversion of defense industries in the newly independent states of Eastern Europe and the former Soviet Union; and by fostering cooperative regimes aimed at controlling the spread of weapons of mass destruction and other destabilizing technologies.

To remain a vital and sustainable component of U.S. national security, arms control must expand its charter into the arenas of democratization, demilitarization, defense conversion, regional stabilization, and countering proliferation. In short, arms control must be, in form and substance, responsive to U.S. national security priorities on the eve of the twenty-first century.

NOTES

1. Military writings often refer to a third level of abstraction, the tactical level. In arms control terms, tactical objectives would be those applied in the context of specific negotiations or treaties. They are not discussed here.

2. Note the emphasis given to arms control as a response to the danger of surprise attack in Thomas C. Schelling and Morton H. Halperin, *Strategy and Arms Control* (New York: Twentieth Century Fund, 1961), 10–14. See also the chapter on surprise nuclear attack in Hedley Bull, *The Control of the Arms Race* (New York: Praeger Press, 1961), 158–74. These two books are part of the original canon of classical arms control theory.

3. Although Russia retains (and will retain for the foreseeable future) a nuclear arsenal sufficiently large to physically threaten the utter destruction of the United States, many strategic planners are convinced that a Russian surprise attack against the United States is an extremely remote possibility at this time, given improving U.S.–Russian relations, the internal preoccupations of Russian policy makers, and the scarcity of resources in a devastated and exhausted economy.

4. For a thorough and insightful survey of the history of nuclear arms control during the Cold War period that also traces the myriad revisions and adaptations in the theory of arms control as applied in practice, see the chapter titled "Strategic Arms Control" by Joseph DeSutter in *American Defense Policy*, 6th ed., ed. Shuyler Foerster and Edward Wright (Baltimore, Md.: Johns Hopkins University Press, 1990), 349–81.

5. One of the key founders of traditional arms control theory uses the term "classical" when referring to the assumptions and premises: see Hedley Bull, "The Classical Approach to Arms Control Twenty Years After," in *Soviet Power and Western Negotiating Policies,* vol. 2, ed. Uwe Nerlich (Cambridge: Ballinger, 1983), 21–30.

6. A thorough history of the Surprise Attack Conference and its relationship to contemporary arms control endeavors can be found in Johan J. Holst, "Strategic Arms Control and Stability: A Retrospective Look," in *Why ABM? Policy Issues in the Missile Defense Controversy*, ed. Johan J. Holst and William Scheider Jr. (New York: Pergamon Press, 1969), 245–84.

7. The three basic canons of traditional arms control theory were published in 1961: Schelling and Halperin, *Strategy and Arms Control;* Bull, *The Control of the Arms Race;* and Donald G. Brennan, ed., *Arms Control, Disarmament, and National Security* (New York: George Braziller, 1961); earlier published as a special issue of *Daedalus: Proceedings of the American Academy of Arts and Sciences* (Fall 1960).

8. Bull, "The Traditional Approach to Arms Control Twenty Years After," 21.

9. Schelling and Halperin, 142.

10. Bull, *The Control of the Arms Race,* 37.

11. Bull, "The Traditional Approach to Arms Control Twenty Years After," 22.

12. Bull, *The Control of the Arms Race,* 75.

13. Ibid., 10.

14. Bull, "The Traditional Approach to Arms Control Twenty Years After," 24.

15. In the introduction to their seminal book, Schelling and Halperin state: "There is hardly an objective of arms control to be described in this study that is not equally a continuing urgent objective of national military strategy— of our unilateral military plans and policies" (p. 3).

16. Throughout much of the Cold War, these three dilemmas were elaborated mostly in nuclear terms (e.g.,

What deters nuclear war? How many nuclear weapons are enough? What if nuclear deterrence fails?), but they are equally applicable to the full range of defense scenarios, including policies and threats involving conventional, chemical, biological, and other types of weapons.

17. Schelling and Halperin, 1.

18. Ibid., 3.

19. Bull, *The Control of the Arms Race,* 3.

20. Few would dispute the fact that the advances over the past few years in ballistic missile defense technologies have been remarkable. For example, coatings have been developed that make mirrors for space-based lasers so reflective that they need no cooling, thus reducing their weight. See William J. Broad, "From Fantasy to Fact: Space-Based Laser Nearly Ready to Fly," *New York Times,*

6 December 1994, B5. Of all the prospective ballistic missile defense options, space-based lasers are the most technologically demanding. For a broader treatment of the development and maturation of ballistic missile defense technologies, including computers, optical sensors, interceptors, kinetic kill vehicles, and directed energy weapons, see Donald R. Baucom, *The Origins of SDI, 1944–1983* (Lawrence: University of Kansas Press, 1992), esp. 97–106.

21. Nevertheless, the Russians are not eager for the United States to proceed in this direction without mutual consultations, so deploying such a system could exacerbate or undermine recent progress in the U.S.–Russian relationship and jeopardize implementation of START and ratification of START II. A decision to initiate such a deployment would have to involve a careful weighing of these considerations.

EXISTING ARMS CONTROL TREATIES

JEFFREY A. LARSEN AND GREGORY J. RATTRAY

TREATY BANNING NUCLEAR WEAPON TESTS IN THE ATMOSPHERE, IN OUTER SPACE AND UNDER WATER, ALSO CALLED PARTIAL TEST BAN TREATY (PTBT) AND LIMITED TEST BAN TREATY (LTBT)

BRIEF DESCRIPTION

The signatories agreed not to carry out any nuclear weapon test explosion in the atmosphere, in outer space, under water, or in any other environment that would cause radioactive debris to spread outside the territorial limits of the state that conducted the test.

KEY DATES/SIGNATORIES

Signed:	5 August 1963
Ratified:	7 October 1963
Entry into force:	10 October 1963
Duration:	Unlimited
Original Parties:	United States, United Kingdom, Soviet Union

125 Follow-on Parties

TREATY ON THE PRINCIPLES GOVERNING THE ACTIVITIES OF STATES IN THE EXPLORATION AND USE OF OUTER SPACE, INCLUDING THE MOON AND OTHER CELESTIAL BODIES, ALSO CALLED OUTER SPACE TREATY

BRIEF DESCRIPTION

This treaty, negotiated primarily between the United States and the Soviet Union, serves to limit the militarization of outer space and celestial bodies. The treaty prohibits any state from placing weapons of mass destruction in outer space or deploying them on celestial bodies. In addition, all celestial bodies are to be used solely for peaceful purposes and may not be used for military bases, fortifications, or weapons testing of any kind.

KEY DATES/SIGNATORIES

Signed:	27 January 1967
Ratified:	25 April 1967
Entry into force:	10 October 1967
Duration:	Unlimited

115 Parties

This essay has been edited and is reprinted from Arms Control: Toward the 21st Century, *edited by Jeffrey A. Larsen and Gregory J. Rattray. Copyright © 1996 by Lynne Rienner Publishers, Inc. Reprinted by permission of the publisher.*

TREATY ON THE NONPROLIFERATION OF NUCLEAR WEAPONS, ALSO CALLED NONPROLIFERATION TREATY (NPT)

BRIEF DESCRIPTION

The nuclear Nonproliferation Treaty (NPT) obligates nuclear weapon states party to the treaty (originally the United States, the Soviet Union, and the United Kingdom) to three main principles: not to transfer nuclear weapons or control over such weapons to any recipient, directly or indirectly; not to assist, encourage, or induce any nonnuclear weapon state to manufacture or otherwise acquire such weapons or seek control over them; and to actively work toward complete nuclear disarmament. In addition, the nuclear weapons states are required to assist the nonnuclear weapon states in the use of nuclear energy for peaceful purposes, including the benefits of peaceful nuclear explosions.

Nonnuclear weapon states also agree to several provisions. They may not receive the transfer of nuclear weapons or control over them. They are also prohibited from manufacturing, seeking help in manufacturing, or otherwise obtaining nuclear weapons.

All states must accept the safeguards negotiated with the International Atomic Energy Agency (IAEA) to prevent the diversion of nuclear energy from peaceful purposes to nuclear weapons. The IAEA is tasked as the treaty's implementation and compliance body; it meets in Vienna.

At the 1995 Review and Extension Conference in New York, the treaty parties adopted three decisions and one resolution. The treaty review process was strengthened, and review conferences will continue to take place every five years. A set of principles and objectives for nuclear nonproliferation and disarmament was agreed to, including the goal of achieving a comprehensive nuclear test ban by 1996. The treaty was extended for an indefinite period by consensus of the parties. Finally, the conference called upon the states in the Middle East to agree to the creation of a zone free of weapons of mass destruction.

KEY DATES/SIGNATORIES

Signed: 1 July 1968
Ratified: 24 November 1969
Entry into force: 5 March 1970
Duration: Extended indefinitely
                    11 May 1995

NUCLEAR STATE PARTIES

United States, Soviet Union (Russian Federation assumes successor status), United Kingdom, France (March 1992), China (September 1992)

NONNUCLEAR STATE PARTIES

Afghanistan[a]   Algeria   Antigua and
Albania[b]   Barbuda

Argentina
Armenia
Australia[a]
Austria[a]
Azerbaijan
Bahamas
Bahrain
Bangladesh[a]
Barbados
Belarus[c]
Belgium[a]
Belize
Benin
Bhutan[a]
Bolivia
Bosnia and
  Herzegovina
Botswana
Brunei[a]
Bulgaria[a]
Burkina Faso
Burma
  (Myanmar)
Burundi
Cambodia
Cameroon
Canada[a]
Cape Verde
Central
  African
  Republic
Chad
Chile
Colombia[b]
Comoros
Congo
Costa Rica[a]
Côte d'Ivoire[a]
Croatia
Cyprus[a]
Czech
  Republic[a]
Denmark[a]
Dominica
Dominican
  Republic[a]
Ecuador[a]
Egypt[a]
El Salvador[a]
Equatorial
  Guinea
Eritrea
Estonia[a]
Ethiopia[a]
Fiji[a]
Finland[a]
Gabon
Gambia[a]
Georgia
Germany
Ghana[a]
Greece[a]

Grenada
Guatemala[a]
Guinea
Guinea-Bissau
Guyana
Haiti
Holy See[a]
Honduras[a]
Hungary[a]
Iceland[a]
Indonesia[a]
Iran[a]
Iraq[a]
Ireland[a]
Italy[a]
Jamaica[a]
Japan[a]
Jordan[a]
Kazakhstan[c]
Kenya
Kiribati[a]
People's
  Democratic
  Republic of
  Korea
Republic of
  Korea[a]
Kuwait
Kyrgyzstan
Laos
Latvia
Lebanon[a]
Lesotho[a]
Liberia
Libya
Liechtenstein[a]
Lithuania
Luxembourg[a]
Macedonia
Madagascar[a]
Malawi
Malaysia[a]
Maldives[a]
Mali
Malta[a]
Marshall
  Islands
Mauritania
Mauritius[a]
Mexico[a]
Micronesia
Moldova
Monaco
Mongolia[a]
Morocco[a]
Mozambique
Namibia
Nauru[a]
Nepal[a]
Netherlands[a]
New Zealand[a]
Nicaragua[a]

Niger
Nigeria[a]
Norway[a]
Palau
Panama
Papua New
  Guinea[a]
Paraguay[a]
Peru[a]
Philippines[a]
Poland[a]
Portugal[a]
Qatar
Romania[a]
Rwanda
St. Kitts and
  Nevis
St. Lucia[a]
St. Vincent
  and the
  Grenadines
San Marino
São Tomé and
  Principe
Saudi Arabia
Senegal[a]
Seychelles
Sierra Leone
Singapore[a]
Slovakia
Slovenia
Solomon
  Islands
Somalia
South Africa[a]
Spain[a]
Sri Lanka[a]
Sudan[a]
Suriname[a]
Swaziland[a]
Sweden[a]
Switzerland[a]
Syria
Taiwan
Tajikistan
Tanzania
Thailand[a]
Togo
Tonga
Trinidad and
  Tobago
Tunisia[a]
Turkey[a]
Turkmenistan
Tuvalu[a]
Uganda
Ukraine[c]
United Arab
  Emirates
Uruguay[a]
Uzbekistan
Vanuatu

Venezuela[a]	Western	Zaire[a]
Vietnam[a]	Samoa[a]	Zambia
	Yemen	Zimbabwe

a. NPT safeguards agreements that have entered into force as of 1992.

b. Non-NPT full safeguards agreement.

c. Agreed to sign as a nonnuclear state under the START I Lisbon Protocol.

BIOLOGICAL AND TOXIN WEAPONS CONVENTION (BWC)

BRIEF DESCRIPTION

Building on the Geneva Protocol of 1925, which bans the use of biological weapons in war, the Biological and Toxin Weapons Convention (BWC) bans the development, production, stockpiling, and acquisition of biological weapons and the delivery systems of such agents.

An ad hoc group met in several sessions between March 1992 and September 1993 to identify, examine, and evaluate potential methods of verification. Twenty-one potential verification measures, including on-site inspections, were identified and evaluated. An effective verification regime would have to rely on several different measures. The need to protect sensitive commercial property and intellectual information was also identified.

Although the United States declared that it had destroyed all of its biological weapons by December 26, 1975, it has become increasingly clear that the Soviet biological weapons program violated the BWC. In September 1992, trilateral negotiations between the United States, the United Kingdom, and the Russian Federation began in an effort to resolve compliance concerns and improve verification methods.

KEY DATES/SIGNATORIES

Signed:	10 April 1972
Ratified:	26 March 1975
Entry into force:	26 March 1975
Duration:	Unlimited
139 Parties	

TREATY BETWEEN THE UNITED STATES OF AMERICA AND THE UNION OF SOVIET SOCIALIST REPUBLICS ON THE LIMITATION OF ANTIBALLISTIC MISSILE SYSTEMS, ALSO CALLED ANTIBALLISTIC MISSILE (ABM) TREATY

BRIEF DESCRIPTION

The basic premise of the ABM Treaty is stated in its preamble: "Effective measures to limit antiballistic-missile systems would be a substantial factor in curbing the race in strategic offensive arms and would lead to a decrease in the risk of outbreak of war involving nuclear weapons." The purpose of the treaty is stated in Article I, which prohibits the deployment of an ABM system for "the defense of the territory" or the provision of "a base for such a defense." The former prohibition includes a nationwide defense, whether on land or sea or in air or space; the latter encompasses items such as powerful, large phased-array radars (LPARs), which are the long-lead-time items of a deployed land-based ABM system.

An ABM system is defined for treaty purposes as a system "to counter strategic ballistic missiles or their elements in flight trajectory." An ABM system is described as "currently consisting" of three components: ABM launchers, ABM interceptor missiles, and ABM radars. The word *strategic* was included to preserve the option to deploy antitactical ballistic missiles (ATBMs).

ABM components are defined as either "constructed and deployed for an ABM role" or of "a type tested in an ABM mode." These definitions are linked with treaty prohibitions against the testing in an ABM mode of non-ABM systems such as surface-to-air missile systems (SAMs).

The treaty limited each side to two ABM deployment sites (later reduced to one site by the 1974 protocol). The authorized deployment area, with a radius of 150 kilometers, must be centered either on the national capital area or on an intercontinental ballistic missile (ICBM) field; each side has the right to switch the site one time. All deployed ABM components must be located within the designated deployment area, and they must be fixed and land-based. The United States chose to locate its site at the Grand Forks, North Dakota, ICBM fields, while the Soviet Union selected Moscow.

Provisions for ABM test ranges prohibit, among other things, ABM deployments in various locations around the country under the guise of test facilities. The numerical limitation of fifteen launchers at an ABM test range reinforces this purpose. The United States has two ABM test ranges from which fixed land-based ABM components may be tested: White Sands, New Mexico, and Kwajalein Island in the Pacific.

The treaty prohibits space-based, air-based, sea-based, and mobile land-based ABM systems and components. The ban covers development and testing as well as deployment. No restraints are placed on research that precedes field testing.

The treaty imposes a ceiling of 100 ABM launchers and 100 ABM missiles at launch sites in the ABM deployment area. It prohibits certain capabilities of fixed land-based components, such as automatic, semiautomatic, or rapid-reload ABM launchers and launchers that could launch more than one ABM interceptor missile at a time. Agreed Statement E extends these prohibitions to ABM interceptors with more than one independently guided warhead. There are no limits on the range or velocity of the ABM interceptors.

During the ABM Treaty negotiations, the U.S. government was concerned about the Soviet Union's potential for upgrading its extensive SAM systems to give them ABM capabilities. Article VI(a) prohibits non-ABM systems, such as SAMs, from having "capabilities to counter strategic ballistic missiles" or from being "tested in an ABM mode."

The treaty limits the location of ABM radars to authorized ABM deployment areas or ABM test ranges. Early warning radars constructed after the treaty entered into force must be located on the periphery of the country and oriented outward. The periphery requirement assumed that a radar so located was vulnerable to military attack and therefore not strategically effective. The outward orientation was intended to prohibit the over-the-shoulder coverage necessary for an effective ABM radar providing coverage of incoming ballistic missiles within territorial boundaries. The explicit exceptions to these rules are radars for space tracking or for national technical means (NTM), which are not limited in terms of power, location, orientation, or other factors.

Space-based sensors and LPARs raise many similar treaty compliance issues, since both can perform many different functions. The U.S. negotiators understood that some space-based sensors were akin to early warning or NTM radars, and their deployment in space was fully consistent with the purpose and letter of the treaty. On the other hand, although not then available, space-based sensors capable of substituting for ABM radars are banned.

Provisions of the treaty are to be verified solely by NTM; each party agrees not to interfere with the other's NTM and not to use deliberate concealment measures that would impede verification by NTM.

The Standing Consultative Commission addresses compliance issues and ongoing problems and challenges. It meets in Geneva, Switzerland.

KEY DATES/SIGNATORIES

Signed: 26 May 1972
Ratification advised
  by U.S. Senate: 3 August 1972
Entry into force: 3 October 1972
Duration: Unlimited, with five-year reviews
Parties: United States, Soviet Union

A resolution was signed in Bishkek, Kyrgyzstan, on 9 October 1992 that obligated the members of the Commonwealth of Independent States (CIS) to abide by the treaty. This agreement did not include Azerbaijan, which refused to sign, nor the Baltic states nor Georgia, which were not CIS members. However, the Russian Federation signed a bilateral agreement in March 1994 with Latvia, allowing the

Russians to retain control of the radars there for four years, after which they will be dismantled.

INTERIM AGREEMENT BETWEEN THE UNITED STATES OF AMERICAN AND THE UNION OF SOVIET SOCIALIST REPUBLICS ON CERTAIN MEASURES WITH RESPECT TO THE LIMITATION OF STRATEGIC OFFENSIVE ARMS, ALSO CALLED STRATEGIC ARMS LIMITATION TREATY I (SALT I)

BRIEF DESCRIPTION

The interim agreement, like the ABM Treaty, was the result of the first series of Strategic Arms Limitation Talks, which lasted from November 1969 to May 1972. The agreement freezes the number of strategic ballistic missile launchers and prohibits the conversion of older launchers to accommodate modern heavy ICBMs. An increase in SLBMs was allowed provided an equal number of land-based launchers was destroyed. The United States was authorized up to 710 SLBMs, while the Soviet Union was allowed 950. Mobile ICBMs were not covered by the agreement.

The agreement was perceived as a holding action, and its duration was limited to five years in the hope that a more comprehensive agreement would be reached. The U.S. Congress passed a joint resolution supporting the agreement, instead of the Senate passing ratification.

KEY DATES/SIGNATORIES

Signed: 26 May 1972
Joint resolution
  passed: 30 September 1972
Entry into force: 3 October 1972
Duration: Five years
Parties: United States, Soviet Union

TREATY BETWEEN THE UNITED STATES OF AMERICA AND THE UNION OF SOVIET SOCIALIST REPUBLICS ON THE LIMITATION OF UNDERGROUND NUCLEAR WEAPONS TESTS, ALSO CALLED THRESHOLD TEST BAN TREATY (TTBT)

BRIEF DESCRIPTION

This treaty prohibits signatories from the underground testing of nuclear weapons with a yield greater than 150 kilotons at declared testing sites. Because of U.S. concerns about possible Soviet violations of the treaty, negotiations were undertaken from 1987 to 1990 to strengthen the methods of verification and to address the possibility of accidentally exceeding the 150-kiloton limit. The resulting protocol requires notification of explosions and provides various options for measuring the yield of the explosions, including on-site inspection for tests with a planned yield greater than 35 kilotons.

The United States has only one declared testing site, located in Nevada. The former Soviet Union maintained two testing sites, one within the Russian Federation and the other in Kazakhstan.

KEY DATES/SIGNATORIES

Signed:	3 July 1974 (treaty)
	1 June 1990 (protocol)
Duration:	Five years, with five-year extensions
Ratified:	11 December 1990
Entry into force:	11 December 1990
Parties:	United States, Soviet Union (Russian Federation assumes successor state status)

TREATY BETWEEN THE UNITED STATES OF AMERICA AND THE UNION OF SOVIET SOCIALIST REPUBLICS ON UNDERGROUND NUCLEAR EXPLOSIONS FOR PEACEFUL PURPOSES, ALSO CALLED PEACEFUL NUCLEAR EXPLOSIONS TREATY (PNET)

BRIEF DESCRIPTION

The Peaceful Nuclear Explosions Treaty (PNET) between the United States and the former Soviet Union was signed in 1976. As with the TTBT, its protocol on the verification of compliance was not completed until 1990. The treaty allows peaceful nuclear explosions outside declared testing sites but prohibits any individual explosion exceeding a yield of 150 kilotons. Group explosions are limited to a yield of 1.5 megatons, provided that each individual explosion's yield can be verified and does not exceed 150 kilotons. The protocol for PNET requires notification of explosions and allows for on-site inspections and other methods of measuring the yield of the detonation.

KEY DATES/SIGNATORIES

Signed:	28 May 1976 (treaty)
	1 June 1990 (protocol)
Ratified:	11 December 1990
Entry into Force:	11 December 1990
Duration:	Five years, with five-year extensions

Parties:	United States, Soviet Union (Russian Federation assumes successor state status)

TREATY BETWEEN THE UNITED STATES OF AMERICA AND THE UNION OF SOVIET SOCIALIST REPUBLICS ON THE LIMITATION OF STRATEGIC OFFENSIVE ARMS, ALSO CALLED STRATEGIC ARMS LIMITATION TREATY II (SALT II)

BRIEF DESCRIPTION

The SALT II talks lasted from November 1972 until June 18, 1979, when the treaty was signed in Vienna. The treaty places limits on ballistic missiles and their launchers but does not require the reduction of such items. Each country was limited to 2,250 launchers, with a sublimit of 1,320 launchers for multiple independently targetable reentry vehicle (MIRVed) missiles. MIRVed ballistic missiles were limited to 1,200, of which only 820 could be ICBMs. In addition, new ICBMs and air-to-surface ballistic missiles (ASBMs) were limited to 10 warheads, while sea-launched ballistic missiles (SLBMs) were allowed to carry up to 14 warheads. The treaty prohibited spaced–based nuclear weapons, fractional orbital missiles, and rapid reload missile launchers.

A protocol to the treaty was signed at the same time and was to remain in effect until 31 December 1981. The protocol prohibited the deployment of ground-launched cruise missiles (GLCMs) and sea-launched cruise missiles (SLCMs) with a range of over 600 kilometers, as well as ASBMs and mobile ICBMs. Additionally, MIRVed GLCMs and SLCMs with a range of over 600 kilometers could not be tested.

President Jimmy Carter submitted the treaty to the Senate immediately following the signing, but because of congressional concerns and the Soviet invasion of Afghanistan he was forced to remove it from consideration. Since the treaty was never ratified, it became a politically, not legally, binding agreement. On 27 May 1986, Ronald Reagan, after citing Soviet violations, declared that the United States would no longer abide by the limits of the SALT agreements.

KEY DATES/SIGNATORIES

Signed:	18 June 1979
Submitted to Senate:	22 June 1979
Withdrawn from Senate:	3 January 1980
United States exceeds limits:	28 November 1986
Parties:	United States, Soviet Union

TREATY BETWEEN THE UNITED STATES OF AMERICA AND THE UNION OF SOVIET SOCIALIST REPUBLICS ON THE ELIMINATION OF THEIR INTERMEDIATE-RANGE AND SHORTER-RANGE MISSILES, ALSO CALLED INTERMEDIATE-RANGE NUCLEAR FORCES (INF) TREATY

BRIEF DESCRIPTION

This treaty provided for the complete elimination of all U.S. and Soviet intermediate-range (1,000–5,500 kilometers) and shorter-range (500–1,000 kilometers) ground-launched ballistic and cruise missiles. Although the final elimination of missiles was completed by June 1, 1991, the on-site inspection regime will continue until the year 2001 to ensure compliance with the treaty. This includes continuous monitoring of the missile final assembly facilities at Magna, Utah, and Votkinsk, Soviet Union (now in the Russian Federation). Additionally, on-site inspections of former missile operating bases and missile support facilities are allowed at a rate of fifteen per year until 1996 and ten per year until 2001. Some of these facilities are now located in successor states other than the Russian Federation (Belarus, Ukraine, Kazakhstan, Uzbekistan, Turkmenistan, Lithuania, Latvia, and Estonia) and states of the former Warsaw Pact. The Special Verification Commission is tasked with overseeing verification and compliance; it is based in Geneva, Switzerland.

KEY DATES/SIGNATORIES

Signed: 8 December 1987
Ratified: 27 May 1988
Entry into force: 1 June 1988
Duration: Unlimited (thirteen years for
             the inspection regime)
Parties: United States, Soviet Union
             (Russian Federation assumed
             successor state status); Belarus,
             Kazakhstan, and Ukraine have
             also accepted inspections

TREATY ON CONVENTIONAL ARMED FORCES IN EUROPE (CFE)

BRIEF DESCRIPTION

The CFE Treaty was originally signed by the twenty-two members of North Atlantic Treaty Organization (NATO) and the former Warsaw Pact on 19 November 1990. However, due to the breakup of the Soviet Union and other changes in Europe, thirty states are now parties to the treaty. The area of application (AOA) for the CFE Treaty is commonly referred to as the Atlantic to the Urals, or ATTU. For countries that do not fall within this area, such as the

United States and Canada, or those that have territory extending outside of the AOA, such as Russia, Turkey, and Kazakhstan, the limits apply only to forces stationed in the ATTU zone. However, an agreed statement requires Russia to destroy 14,500 pieces of equipment that were moved east of the Urals during the negotiations. The treaty only limits the amount of equipment in the AOA; troop limits were addressed in follow-on negotiations, which resulted in the CFE 1A document.

The treaty divides Europe into two groups: NATO and the members of the former Warsaw Treaty Organization (WTO), imposing conventional arms limitations equally to both. Each of the groups' total holdings are limited in five major categories: tanks, artillery pieces, armored combat vehicles (ACVs), combat aircraft, and attack helicopters. Three of these categories were further defined as follows:

- Artillery: guns/howitzers, mortars, and multiple-launch rocket systems

- ACVs: armored personnel carriers, armored infantry fighting vehicles, and heavy armament combat vehicles

- Helicopters: specialized attack and multipurpose attack.

Sublimits were also placed on the most threatening ACVs, including armored infantry fighting vehicles and heavy armament combat vehicles. An additional group of equipment is not limited by the treaty yet is still subject to the treaty. The equipment in this category includes trainer aircraft, combat support and transport helicopters, river bridging vehicles, and armored vehicle look-alikes, all of which are subject to operational constraints and information exchanges.

Four nested zones were also created, each one encompassing the preceding zone plus adjacent territory or districts, resulting in a Russian matryoshka doll effect. Specific limits are placed on the ground equipment allowed in each zone, the smallest of which is the central zone (see Table 1). These limits allow for free movement away from, but not toward, the center of Europe, thus decreasing the threat of a surprise attack. Aircraft and helicopters, while limited in the AOA, are not affected by the zoning limits. Additionally, there were limits put on the number of forces that could be stationed in the so-called flank zone. This zone includes Armenia, Georgia, Azerbaijan, and Moldova, as well as the southeastern third of Ukraine and the Leningrad and northern Caucasus military districts in the Russian Federation. This was done to prevent the Soviet Union from repositioning its forces previously located in Central Europe to the borders of Turkey and Norway, forcing them instead to be moved deep within Russia. In the northern sector of this zone, a portion of the Soviet Union's forces had to be allocated to designated permanent storage sites (DPSSs).

Table 1

CFE Equipment Limits by Zone

Treaty-limited equipment	Overall	One country	Central zone	Expanded central zone	Extended zones	Flank zones
Tanks[a]	20,000	13,300	7,500	10,300	11,800	4,700
Artillery pieces[a]	20,000	13,700	5,000	9,100	11,000	6,000
Armored combat vehicles[a]	30,000	20,000	11,250	19,260	21,400	5,900
Combat aircraft[b]	6,800	5,150				
Attack helicopters[c]	2,000	1,500				

Source: CFE Treaty.

a. As a result of an agreement anounced on 14 June 1991, equipment assigned to naval infantry or costal defense forces is counted against the total authorized.

b. No state is permitted to maintain more than 400 permanently land-based naval aircraft; no group total is to exceed 430 aircraft.

c. No state is permitted to maintain any permanently land-based naval helicopters.

Although each group was left to decide the equipment levels allotted to each country, limits on the amount a single country could possess are stated in the treaty (see Table 1). These single party limits, roughly one-third of the total allowed for the AOA, stress the importance of no one nation being able to dominate the continent. Additionally, restrictions were placed on the amount of equipment that one state could station on the territory of another. Before signing the treaty at the November 1990 summit meeting in Paris, both groups met separately to develop individual country limits. While the results of NATO's meeting in Brussels remain relatively unchanged (see Table 2), political events have signifi-

cantly altered the agreement reached by the countries of the former Warsaw Pact in Budapest (see Table 3). In May 1992 the eight members of the Commonwealth of Independent States (CIS) that had territory within the AOA met in Tashkent to decide how to divide the former Soviet Union's allotment of equipment. Russia and Ukraine also agreed to sublimits within the flank zone, including percentages for active and permanently stored ground equipment. The Russian Federation is now permited to place 600 tanks, 400 artillery pieces, and 800 ACVs in DPSSs along the northern portion of the flank zone. Kazakhstan pledged not to station any of its forces west of the Ural River, thus in the

Table 2

CFE Equipment Limits by State (NATO)

States	Tanks	Artillery	Armored combat vehicles	Attack helicopters	Combat aircraft
Belgium	334	320	1,099	46	232
Canada	77	38	277	13	90
Denmark	353	553	316	12	106
France	1,306	1,292	3,820	352	800
Germany	4,166	2,705	3,446	306	900
Greece	1,735	1,878	2,534	18	650
Italy	1,348	1,955	3,339	142	650
Netherlands	743	607	1,080	69	230
Norway	170	527	225	0	100
Portugal	300	450	430	26	160
Spain	794	1,310	1,588	71	310
Turkey	2,795	3,523	3,120	43	750
United Kingdom	1,015	636	3,176	384	900
United States	4,006	2,492	5,372	518	784
Total	19,142	18,286	29,822	2,000	6,662
Treaty limits	20,000	20,000	30,000	2,000	6,800

Source: CFE Treaty.

Table 3

CFE Equipment Limits by State (Former WTO)

States	Tanks	Artillery	Armored combat vehicles	Attack helicopters	Combat aircraft
Armenia[a]	220	285	220	50	100
Azerbaijan[a]	220	285	220	50	100
Belarus[a]	1,800	1,615	2,600	80	260
Bulgaria	1,475	1,750	2,000	67	235
Czech Republic[b]	957	767	1,367	50	230
Georgia[a]	220	285	220	50	100
Hungary	835	840	1,700	108	180
Kazakhstan[a]	0	0	0	0	0
Moldova[a]	210	250	210	50	50
Poland	1,730	1,610	2,150	130	460
Romania	1,375	1,475	2,100	120	430
Russian Federation[a]	6,400	6,415	11,480	890	3,450
Slovakia[b]	478	383	683	25	115
Ukraine[a]	4,080	4,040	5,050	330	1,090
Total	20,000	20,000	30,000	2,000	6,800
Treaty limits	20,000	20,000	30,000	2,000	6,800

Source: CFE Treaty.
a. As a result of the Tashkent agreement, 15 May 1992.
b. As a result of the Prague agreement, 5 February 1993.

AOA. Russia assumed responsibility for the former Soviet Union's forces outside the CIS, such as in Poland, Germany, and the Baltics. In a separate agreement, signed on February 5, 1993 in Prague, the Czechs and Slovaks agreed to a 2:1 split of the equipment allocated to the former Czechoslovakia.

Implementation of the treaty is divided into four phases: baseline validation, 0–120 days after entry into force (concluded November 1992); reduction, three years after baseline validation phase; residual-level validation, 120 days after reduction phase; and residual, which is indefinite because it covers the remaining life of the treaty. Within the reduction phase, a schedule for reduction was established to ensure that each country would reach its reduction limits 40 months after entry into force. The timetable has three parts, each with a corresponding percentage of the parties' reduction requirement that must be completed: 25 percent after 16 months (November 1993), 60 percent after 28 months (November 1994), and 100 percent by 40 months (November 17, 1995). All the equipment must be destroyed except for a very limited number that can be decommissioned, converted to trainers or target drones, or converted to nonmilitary uses.

The treaty allows for several methods of ensuring compliance, including national/multinational technical means, information exchanges, and on-site inspections, all of which are supervised by the Joint Consultative Group, based in Vienna. There are several types of inspections described in the treaty: announced inspections of declared sites, challenge inspections within a specified area (a country may refuse, but then a reasonable assurance of compliance is required), and inspections to verify the destruction or reclassification of equipment. The number of allowed inspections is based on percentages and varies depending on the type of inspection and the current phase of implementation.

The treaty makes an important distinction between objects of verification (OOVs) and declared sites. OOVs are units holding conventional armaments subject to the treaty, while declared sites are where the units are located, usually a military base or facility. Announced inspections require only that the site be announced, thus the team could wait until arrival to decide which one of the several units that might be located at the base would be inspected.

KEY DATES/SIGNATORIES

Signed: 19 November 1990
Ratified: 15 November 1991
Entry into force: 9 November 1992
(17 July 1992 is the date used to determine the timing of all treaty rights and obligations)

Duration: Unlimited; review after forty-six months and five-year intervals thereafter

Parties:

Armenia[a]	Bulgaria	Denmark
Azerbaijan[a]	Canada	France
Belarus[a]	Czech	Georgia[a]
Belgium	Republic	Germany

Hellenic	Netherlands	Spain
Republic	Norway	Turkey
Hungary	Poland	Ukraine[a]
Iceland	Portugal	United
Italy	Romania	Kingdom
Kazakhstan[a]	Russia[a]	United States
Luxembourg	Slovak	
Moldova[a]	Republic	

a. Part of the former Soviet Union that is located in AOA.

TREATY BETWEEN THE UNITED STATES AND THE UNION OF SOVIET SOCIALIST REPUBLICS ON THE REDUCTION AND LIMITATION OF STRATEGIC OFFENSIVE ARMS, ALSO CALLED STRATEGIC ARMS REDUCTION TREATY I (START I)

BRIEF DESCRIPTION

The START I Treaty, which was signed on July 31, 1991, will reduce U.S. and former Soviet Union strategic offensive arms (SOAs) (ICBMs, SLBMs, and heavy bombers) to 1,600 and attributed warheads (an agreed-upon number of warheads that are associated with each weapon system) to 6,000. There are additional sublimits for attributed warheads: 4,900 warheads on deployed ballistic missiles and 1,100 warheads on deployed mobile ICBMs. The former Soviet Union is also limited to 154 deployed heavy ICBMs (down from 308 before the treaty), each carrying 10 warheads. In addition, an aggregate limit of 3,600 metric tons was placed on ballistic missile throw weight. The treaty also provides for the right to reduce (download) the number of warheads attributed to three existing types of ICBMs and SLBMs. No single type may have more than 500 downloaded warheads, with a sublimit of four warheads downloaded per missile. Overall, no more than 1,250 warheads may be downloaded at any one time.

Warheads carried by heavy bombers, including those in long-range, nuclear air-launched cruise missiles (LRNAs), will be counted at a discount rate.

Especially significant is the discounted rate for penetrating bombers, which count as only one warhead regardless of how many missiles they are capable of carrying. Politically binding side agreements will also limit the number of deployed nuclear SLCMs and the number of Soviet Backfire bombers.

An extensive series of on-site inspections and an exchange of locational and technical data for all systems, with regular updates, will complement each party's NTM to monitor compliance with the treaty. An additional important verification measure is the agreement to exchange telemetric information from all test flights of ICBMs and SLBMs, including the equipment necessary to interpret the data. The Joint Compliance and Inspection Commission (JCIC) is tasked with monitoring compliance with the treaty and has been meeting in Geneva, Switzerland, since 1991.

Although the Russian Federation assumed successor status to the treaty after the breakup of the Soviet Union, a significant number of SOAs were also located in Belarus, Kazakhstan, and Ukraine (see Table 4).

On May 23, 1992, a protocol was signed in Lisbon that makes START I a five-nation, multiparty treaty instead of a bilateral treaty. The protocol and appended presidential letters would also obligate three of those parties (Belarus, Kazakhstan, and Ukraine) to become nonnuclear state parties to the Nonproliferation Treaty. This provision was also mandated by the U.S. Senate's START I ratification bill. The Ukraine parliament (Rada), while conditionally ratifying the START I Treaty, proved hesitant in declaring Ukraine a nonnuclear state under the NPT. On January 14, 1994, in Moscow, the presidents of Ukraine, the Russian Federation, and the United States signed the Trilateral Agreement, which promised Ukraine financial and security assistance as a means of persuading the Rada to unconditionally ratify START I and the NPT. Finally, on February 3, 1994, the Rada unconditionally ratified START I, and on December 5, 1994, Ukraine deposited its instruments of ratification for the NPT, allowing START I to enter into force. Table 5 presents the ratification dates.

Table 4

Systems Deployed Outside the Russian Federation at Signature

State	ICBMs/warheads	Heavy bombers/warheads	Total: SOAs/warheads
Belarus	81/81		81/81
Kazakhstan	104/1,040	40/320 (370)[a]	144/1,360 (1,410)[a]
Ukraine	176/1,240	42/336 (596)[a]	218/1,576 (1,836)[a]

Source: START I.

a. Number in parentheses is based on maximum number for which the bomber is actually equipped. The preceding value is START I discount attribution number.

Table 5

START I and NPT Ratification Dates

Treaty	United States	Russian Federation	Kazakhstan	Belarus	Ukraine
START I	1 Oct 1992	4 Nov 1992	2 Jul 1992	4 Feb 1993	3 Feb 1994
NPT	5 Mar 1970	5 Mar 1970 (Soviet Union)	14 Feb 1994	23 Jul 1993	16 Nov 1994

Source: Arms Control Reporter (Cambridge, Mass.: Institute for Defense and Disarmament Studies, 1995).

KEY DATES/SIGNATORIES

Signed:	31 July 1991
Ratified:	See Table 5
Protocol to obligate Soviet Union Successor States:	23 May 1992
Entry into force:	5 December 1994
Duration:	Fifteen years with option to extend at five-year intervals
Parties:	United States, Soviet Union (but now the following successor states: Belarus, Kazakhstan, Russian Federation, Ukraine)

TREATY ON OPEN SKIES

BRIEF DESCRIPTION

The Open Skies Treaty was signed in Helsinki on March 24, 1992, by members of NATO and the former Warsaw Pact. Each participating state will have the right to conduct, and the obligation to receive, overhead flights by unarmed fixed-wing observation aircraft. Each aircraft will be authorized to carry the following equipment: panoramic, still-frame, and video cameras; infrared scanning devices; and side-looking synthetic aperture radars. The inspecting party will provide the aircraft used in the overflight; however, the host nation may impose the "taxi option," which requires the host aircraft to be used in the overflight. Prior to their use, all aircraft and sensor suites must undergo certification inspections.

The number of flights each country can conduct and must receive is limited on the basis of negotiated annual quotas. The U.S. quota is forty-two overflights per year; however, during the first three years only thirty-one are permitted annually. Any states may acquire the data from any overflight.

KEY DATES/SIGNATORIES

Signed:	24 March 1992
Ratified:	3 November 1993
Provisional period of application:	Initially 24 March 1992–

March 1993 (extended to February 1995)

Estimated entry into force:	Sixty days after deposit of twenty instruments of ratification (expected in 1996)
Duration:	Unlimited, with initial review after three years after entry into force and at five-year intervals thereafter
Parties:	

Belarus	Hungary	Russian Federation
Belgium	Iceland	Slovak Republic
Bulgaria	Italy	
Canada	Kyrgyzstan	
Czech Republic	Luxembourg	Spain
Denmark	Netherlands	Turkey
France	Norway	Ukraine
Georgia	Poland	United Kingdom
Germany	Portugal	
Greece	Romania	United States

THE CONCLUDING ACT OF THE NEGOTIATION ON PERSONNEL STRENGTH OF CONVENTIONAL ARMED FORCES IN EUROPE, ALSO CALLED CONVENTIONAL ARMED FORCES IN EUROPE 1A (CFE 1A) TREATY

BRIEF DESCRIPTION

The CFE 1A Agreement is a politically, not legally, binding document and therefore is not subject to ratification. The goal of the agreement is to limit and/or reduce personnel levels in the AOA of the CFE Treaty. Each state sets its own limits. These are open to discussion but not subject to negotiation (see Table 6).

The personnel counted against the limits fall into several categories: (1) land or air forces (including ground-based air defense) and the command and staff for these units; (2) other forces that hold equipment limited under the CFE Treaty, including land-based naval aircraft and naval infantry forces, as well as coastal defense units; and (3) reserve personnel called up for full-time service for more than ninety

Table 6

CFE 1A Troop Limits

North Atlantic Treaty Group			Budapest/Tashkent Group		
State	Ceilings	Holdings	State	Ceilings	Holdings
Belgium	70,000	68,688	Armenia	Not reported	32,682
Canada	10,660	1,408	Azerbaijan	Not reported	56,000
Denmark	39,000	29,893	Belarus	100,000	92,664
France	325,000	332,591	Bulgaria	104,000	98,930
Germany	345,000	314,688	Czech Republic	93,333	92,893
Greece	158,621	163,705	Georgia	40,000	Not reported
Italy	315,000	290,224	Hungary	100,000	75,294
Netherlands	80,000	66,540	Kazakhstan	0	0
Norway	32,000	26,100	Moldova	20,000	11,123
Portugal	75,000	42,534	Poland	234,000	269,670
Spain	300,000	168,346	Romania	230,000	230,000
Turkey	530,000	575,963	Russian Federation	1,450,000	1,110,578
United Kingdom	260,000	192,547	Slovakia	46,667	54,223
United States	250,000	137,271	Ukraine	450,000	495,156

Source: CFE 1A Treaty.

days. Exempted are sea-based naval personnel, internal security units, and forces serving under U.N. command.

Additional stabilizing measures are also listed in the agreement. A forty-two-day advance notification is required to increase the personnel strength of any ground force unit by more than 1,000, to increase any air force unit by more than 500, or to call up more than 35,000 reservists (except call-ups made in response to emergency situations such as natural disasters). Additionally, any personnel reassigned to a unit not subject to limitation will still be counted for one to two years.

The national ceilings declared by each state must be reached within forty months after entry into force. Personnel information is provided during pre-inspection briefings for CFE declared site inspections or in response to inspectors' requests during a CFE challenge inspection.

KEY DATES/SIGNATORIES

Signed:　　　　　17 July 1992
Ratified:　　　　　Not required
Entry into force:　17 July 1992
Duration:　　　　Unlimited; initial review after
　　　　　　　　　six months, then at five-year
　　　　　　　　　intervals

Parties:

Armenia[a]	Czech	Hellenic
Azerbaijan[a]	Republic	Republic
Belarus[a]	Denmark	Hungary
Belgium	France	Iceland
Bulgaria	Georgia[a]	Italy
Canada	Germany	Kazakhstan[a]

Luxembourg	Romania	Ukraine[a]
Moldova[a]	Russian	United
Netherlands	Federation[a]	Kingdom
Norway	Slovakia	United States
Poland	Spain	
Portugal	Turkey	

a. Part of the former Soviet Union that is located in AOA.

TREATY BETWEEN THE UNITED STATES
OF AMERICA AND THE RUSSIAN
FEDERATION ON FURTHER REDUCTION
AND LIMITATION OF STRATEGIC
OFFENSIVE ARMS, ALSO CALLED
STRATEGIC ARMS REDUCTION TREATY II
(START II)

BRIEF DESCRIPTION

In 1991 and 1992, Presidents George Bush and Mikhail Gorbachev made a series of presidential initiatives reducing nuclear stockpiles and lowering the alert status of several weapon systems. These set the foundation for the signing of a Joint Understanding at the June 1992 summit between President Bush and Russian Federation president Boris Yeltsin in Washington. The Joint Understanding called for the elimination of all MIRVed ICBMs and deep cuts in SLBMs, forming the basis of the START II Treaty. This treaty was signed at the January 1993 Moscow summit by Presidents Bush and Yeltsin. It relies heavily on START I for definitions, procedures, and verification and, as such, cannot legally enter into force before START I.

Table 7

START I and II Limits and Completion Dates

	START I	START II Phase 1	START II Phase 2
Reduction completion date	Seven years after entry into force	2000	2003
Total attributed warheads	6,000	3,800–4,250	3,000–3,500
Ballistic missile warheads	4,900	3,800–4,250	3,000–3,500
MIRVed ICBMs	Not addressed	1,200	0
Heavy ICBMs	1,540	650	0
Mobile ICBMs	1,100	1,100	1,100
SLBMs	Not addressed	2,160	1,700–1,750

Source: START II Treaty.

The eliminations are to take place in a two-phase process (see Table 7). By the year 2000, each side must reduce its deployed strategic forces to 3,800–4,250 attributed warheads, within which the following sublimits apply: 1,200 warheads for MIRVed ICBMs, 650 warheads for heavy ICBMs, and 2,160 warheads for SLBMs. Phase II limits must be reached by the year 2003 (or by the year 2000 if the United States can contribute to the financing of the destruction or elimination of strategic offensive arms in Russia). At that time, each party must have reduced its deployed strategic forces to 3,000–3,500 attributed warheads, within which the following sublimits apply: zero warheads for MIRVed ICBMs, 1,700–1,750 total warheads for SLBMs, and elimination of all heavy ICBMs.

To reach the lower warhead ceilings, the downloading procedures identified in START I have been modified. The Russian Federation is allowed to download 105 SS-19 ICBMs by five warheads, leaving only one warhead per missile (all other downloading is still limited to four warheads per missile). Additionally, the overall ceilings on the aggregate numbers of downloaded warheads were removed. As a result, any missile that was previously equipped with six warheads or more, except the SS-19s, must be destroyed, while those equipped with five or fewer may be retained, provided they are downloaded to only one warhead.

Since the treaty eliminates the entire class of heavy ICBMs (SS-18), special provisions were made regarding the reuse of that hardware. All the missiles and their launch canisters may be converted to space launch vehicles, while up to ninety of the silos may be converted to launch single-warhead ICBMs. Any nonconverted equipment must be destroyed.

The treaty also has several provisions regarding bombers. The B-2 must now be exhibited and will be inspectable, whereas under START I, the B-2 was subject to neither condition unless it was tested/equipped with long-range nuclear ALCMs (LRNA). A one-time reorientation of up to one hundred nuclear heavy bombers to a conventional role is allowed without adhering to the START I conversion procedures as long as they were never accountable as LRNA heavy bombers. The United States chose this option for its B-1 fleet. Additionally, conventional and nuclear bombers must be based separately and crews must be separately trained, and bombers must have differences observable by NTM and visible during inspection. The treaty also removes the "discount" provisions from START I bomber warhead counting rules but allows an increased number of bombers to be retained. START II also specifically provides the right to change the number of nuclear warheads the treaty attributes to a bomber, if there is a visible change in the plane's configuration. Approximately 1,300 warheads may be attributed to bombers in each country, depending on the number of ICBMs and SLBMs retained by each party.

Although this treaty builds on START I, some additional verification measures are included. START II significantly increases the number of on-site inspections, mostly relating to the retention of converted Russian heavy ICBM (SS-18) silos and the conversion of heavy bombers. The compliance regime is governed by the Bilateral Implementation Commission, which meets in Geneva, Switzerland.

KEY DATES/SIGNATORIES

Signed: 3 January 1993
Ratified: Not yet ratified
Estimated entry
  into force: 1996
Duration: As long as START remains in force
Parties: United States, Russian Federation

CHEMICAL WEAPONS CONVENTION (CWC)

BRIEF DESCRIPTION

The Chemical Weapons Convention (CWC) is a multilateral agreement to ban the production, possession, transfer, and use of chemical weapons by all parties to the convention. It was negotiated by the 39 nations (with 36 additional nations in observer status) of the Conference on Disarmament (see separate entry). Initial treaty signature was in Paris on 13

January 1993, when 130 nations signed the convention. While the number of signatories continues to grow, very few countries have ratified the treaty. Both the United States and the Russian Federation, whose bilateral agreements provided the impetus for the talks, have yet to ratify the treaty.

The convention bans the development, production, stockpiling, transfer, acquisition, and both retaliatory and first use of chemical weapons. It also prohibits a state from aiding any other state, regardless of whether they are a party to the convention, in the pursuit of treaty-banned activities, which effectively institutes a nonproliferation regime. Additionally, parties are required to declare all chemical weapons and facilities no later than thirty days after entry into force and to destroy all chemical weapons within ten years of entry into force. The convention will also require declarations on the production of other types of precursor and dual-purpose chemicals.

The verification regime will include routine, intrusive on-site inspections of declared government chemical weapons facilities, as well as civilian facilities that use certain chemicals that could be used or converted to make weapons. In addition, challenge inspections may be conducted at any facility where a party suspects illegal activities. These inspections will be on short notice. Inspectors will be allowed to visit the site and investigate whether banned activities are taking place. The CWC will be implemented by the Organization for the Prohibition of Chemical Weapons (OPCW), in The Hague, Netherlands.

KEY DATES/SIGNATORIES

Signed:	13 January 1993
Ratified:	Not yet ratified
Entry into force:	180 days after 65th ratification
Duration:	Unlimited
159 Parties	

ONGOING ARMS CONTROL NEGOTIATIONS

JEFFREY A. LARSEN AND GREGORY J. RATTRAY

FISSILE MATERIAL CUTOFF TALKS

The idea of a fissile material production cutoff gained prominence from 1956 through 1969, when it became the basis for U.S. arms control negotiations. Limited success was realized in 1964 when the United States, the United Kingdom, and the Soviet Union announced reductions in the production of weapons-grade fissionable materials. The success of superpower arms control initiatives, a U.S. halt in production of fissile material, and President Bill Clinton's speech to the United Nations in September 1993 provided the impetus for a cutoff convention.

The Conference on Disarmament (CD) began preliminary discussions on a fissile material cutoff convention during its 1994 session. Ambassador Gerald Shannon, Canada's representative to the CD, was appointed special coordinator for the talks. In tandem with these negotiations, technical discussions were held in Vienna, with IAEA assistance, to address technical and verification issues. The format and scope of the talks have yet to be determined. While the nuclear weapon states want to address only future production of fissile material, many nonnuclear weapon states, including the Group of twenty-one "nonaligned" nations, wish to include limits on existing stocks of weapons-grade nuclear material.

CONFERENCE ON DISARMAMENT (CD)

The Conference on Disarmament (CD), which before 1983 was called the Committee on Disarmament, is the independent negotiating body of the U.N. for arms control treaties. It is one of three international disarmament forums (with the U.N. Disarmament Commission and the U.N. General Assembly First Committee) but the only body that negotiates treaties. The conference consists of thirty-two members, including all five nuclear weapon states. Additionally, numerous nations are allowed to participate as nonmembers. Although they maintain an open agenda, participants normally discuss weapons of mass destruction, conventional weapons, reduction of military budgets and armed forces, and confidence-building measures. Most of the work on these topics is accomplished in ad hoc committees. The CD is located in Geneva, Switzerland.

COMPREHENSIVE TEST BAN TALKS

The concept of a comprehensive test ban can be found in the Preamble to the Limited Test Ban Treaty, signed in 1963. Later negotiations resulted in more restrictions on testing, such as those in the TTBT and PNET. Trilateral negotiations among the

This essay has been edited and is reprinted from Arms Control: Toward the 21st Century, *edited by Jeffrey A. Larsen and Gregory J. Rattray. Copyright © 1996 by Lynne Rienner Publishers, Inc. Reprinted by permission of the publisher.*

United States, the United Kingdom, and the Soviet Union from October 1977 to November 1980 on a comprehensive ban ended without result. A reopening of the talks was then delayed until the verification issues of existing treaties could be resolved. Currently, four of the five nuclear powers (excluding China) have enacted unilateral testing moratoriums. The Chinese continued to conduct nuclear tests into 1995. In addition, in mid-1995 France resumed testing in the South Pacific. The U.S. moratorium was initiated by Congress on September 4, 1992, and was extended until September 1995 by President Clinton.

After initial consultation between the five nuclear powers, the First Committee of the U.N. General Assembly on 19 November 1993 approved a resolution by consensus that advocated a global treaty to ban all nuclear weapons tests. As urged by the U.N. resolution, the Conference on Disarmament created the Nuclear Test Ban Ad Hoc Committee, which held several negotiating rounds during 1994. The result was the creation of a "rolling text," which contained agreed treaty text as well as bracketed disputed text, which will be the basis for a final treaty. The verification regime may include a global network of seismic stations and radionuclide sensors and the right to conduct on-site inspections. The verification oversight agency has not been selected.

The 1995 NPT review conference called on all nuclear weapon states to sign a Comprehensive Test Ban Treaty (CTBT) no later than 1996, which all five nuclear weapon states agreed to do.

NUCLEAR-FREE ZONES

There have been several efforts by both international and regional organizations to ban or limit the use of nuclear material in specific regions of the world. Three separate treaties, which have been signed by almost all the nations of the world, prohibit nuclear materials from being stored or tested in outer space, on the seabed floor, and in Antarctica. Additionally, efforts are currently under way to establish nuclear-free zones in the Middle East, South Asia, Northeast Asia, and Africa. Two regional nuclear-free zones, in Latin America and the South Pacific, have already been established through treaties.

SOUTH PACIFIC NUCLEAR-FREE ZONE

The South Pacific Nuclear-Free Zone, created in 1986, is a multilateral treaty that bans the stationing, manufacturing, testing, and dumping of nuclear weapons or nuclear waste within the zone. The issue of ship and aircraft traffic is left up to individual countries. There are eleven parties to the treaty, including Australia and New Zealand. There are three protocols to the treaty that are open for signature to the nuclear weapon states. The first bans the manufacturing, testing, and storing of nuclear weapons in areas for which the state is responsible. The second bans the use or threatened use of nuclear weapons against parties to the treaty. The third bans nuclear testing in the region. China and the Russian Federation have signed the second and third protocols, while the United States, the United Kingdom, and France have refused to sign any of the protocols.

LATIN AMERICAN NUCLEAR-FREE ZONE

The Latin American Nuclear-Free Zone was formalized in the Treaty of Tlatelolco, signed on February 14, 1967. The treaty bans the storage and testing of nuclear weapons within the signatory countries but allows for the peaceful use of nuclear material. The treaty has two protocols: one that obligates states with colonies to adhere to the treaty and another that calls for nuclear weapon states to recognize the zone. All Latin American states except Cuba have ratified the treaty.

CONFIDENCE- AND SECURITY-BUILDING MEASURES (CSBMs)

As opposed to structural arms control measures designed to limit, reduce, or eliminate numbers of weapons systems, CSBMs are intended to foster transparency and trust through purposely designed cooperative measures. CSBMs are intended to help clarify states' military intentions, reduce uncertainties about potentially threatening military activities, and constrain opportunities for surprise attack or coercion. Specific examples of CSBMs in the European context are discussed below.

The Conference on Security and Cooperation in Europe (CSCE)—as of December 1994 the Organization on Security and Cooperation in Europe (OSCE)—established a series of agreements and procedures designed to increase the security of members through increased military transparency and cooperation. The Helsinki Final Act, signed in 1975, was the first of these measures. It was signed by the United States, Canada, and all European nations except Albania. In addition to recognizing existing borders and the need for economic cooperation, the act required advance notification of military maneuvers involving more than 25,000 troops. This agreement set the foundations for the complicated and increasingly intrusive measures that followed.

The CSCE later formed a subcommittee named the Conference on Disarmament in Europe (CDE), which met from 1984 to 1986. One of the results of this conference was the Stockholm Document, which entered into force in January 1987 and expanded the requirements for notification and provided for observation of military activities. Members of the CSCE met from March 1989 to November 1990 to strengthen the existing CSBMs in line with the Stockholm agreement. The result was the Vienna Document 1990, which entered into force on January 1, 1991. The Vienna Document 1992, negotiated between November 26, 1990, and March 4, 1992, supplemented these measures and entered into force on May 1, 1992.

The following is a summary of existing measures within the OSCE's confidence-building regime, as established by the Vienna Documents:

- Forty-two-day advance notification of ground exercises involving more than 9,000 troops or 250 tanks, or more than 3,000 airborne or amphibious assault troops.

- Observation rights to all countries for ground maneuvers involving more than 13,000 troops or 300 tanks or more than 3,500 airborne or amphibious assault troops.

- Limits the number of exercises a country can conduct with more than 40,000 troops or 900 tanks to one per two years.

- Limits the number of exercises a country can conduct with 13,000–40,000 troops or 300–900 tanks to six per year, of which only three can involve more than 25,000 troops or 400 tanks.

- Each party may be inspected by any other party but is only obligated to accept three short warning inspections and 15 information verification inspections each year.

- Exchanges of military information by December 15 that will be accurate for the following year, including the location, manpower levels, major weapon systems employed, and commanding organizations for any unit at or above regiment/brigade level.

- Invitations to air bases and demonstrations of new weapons and equipment.

At the July 1992 Helsinki summit meeting of the CSCE, a decision was made to form the Forum for Security Cooperation. This organization, which meets weekly in Vienna, is tasked with carrying out follow-on negotiations to CFE/CFE 1A and the Vienna CSBMs. In addition, this body oversees implementation, implementation assessment, discussion, and clarification of existing CSBMs.

MISSILE TECHNOLOGY CONTROL REGIME (MTCR)

In April 1987 the United States, Canada, France, West Germany, Italy, Japan, and the United Kingdom created the Missile Technology Control Regime (MTCR) to restrict the proliferation of missiles and missile technology. The MTCR is the only multilateral missile nonproliferation regime. It is a voluntary arrangement, not an international agreement or a treaty, among countries that have an interest in stopping the proliferation of missile technology. The regime develops export guidelines that are applied to a list of controlled items and implemented according to each nation's procedures. In January 1993 the MTCR guidelines were expanded to restrict the spread of missiles and unmanned air vehicles, with a range of at least 300 kilometers, capable of deliver-

ing a 500-kilogram payload or a weapon of mass destruction. The guidelines are sensitive to the fact that ballistic missile and space launch vehicle technology are virtually identical. They are designed not to impede a nation's space program as long as it does not contribute to the delivery of weapons of mass destruction. Membership in the MTCR is open to any country that commits to the principles of nonproliferation and has a record of effective export controls. The MTCR currently has twenty-five members.

BILATERAL CHEMICAL WEAPON AGREEMENTS

The United States and the Soviet Union entered into two bilateral agreements regarding chemical weapons to facilitate the Chemical Weapons Convention. The memorandum of understanding, signed at Jackson, Wyoming, in 1989, called for two phases of data exchanges and visits/inspections of facilities. Phase I was completed in December 1989, when the United States and the Soviet Union declared that they had 29,000 and 40,000 agent metric tons, respectively. Phase II called for more detailed exchange of information and more thorough inspections. The second agreement is the Bilateral Destruction Agreement (BDA), signed in June 1990. The BDA bans chemical weapons production, provides a schedule for the destruction of all chemical weapons, and allows for on-site inspections.

In a series of summit meetings between President Boris Yeltsin and Presidents George Bush and Bill Clinton, several advances were made. Yeltsin committed Russia to abide by the existing agreements and signed implementing documents, including a time line, for Phase II of the Wyoming memorandum. Additionally, the BDA schedule was altered to delay reduction to 5,000 agent tons until December 2004. Financial assistance to help Russia meet these deadlines was provided by the United States under the Nunn-Lugar Act. An additional agreement signed at Tashkent by some CIS states (Azerbaijan, Armenia, Kazakhstan, Kyrgyzstan, Moldova, Russian Federation, Tajikistan, Turkmenistan, and Uzbekistan), commits these parties to similar goals regarding chemical weapons and the CWC.

While the Russian implementation of the Wyoming memorandum has been problematic, the United States attributes this to substantive differences within the Russian government on how to handle the chemical weapons data declaration; the United States continually presses the Russian Federation for complete compliance. The United States is technically ready to destroy chemical weapons and is required to do so under a congressional mandate; however, it faces opposition from environmental groups.

PRESIDENTIAL INITIATIVES

Between September 1991 and January 1992 a series of presidential initiatives were announced by the presidents of the United States and Russia that significantly affected the nuclear force structure. Some of the measures were simply accelerations of those mandated by START I, while others were incorporated into START II. However, additional binding actions are not addressed in either treaty.

SEPTEMBER/OCTOBER 1991

On 27 September 1991, President Bush announced the following U.S. actions:

- All U.S. strategic bombers and 450 Minuteman II ICBMs removed from day-to-day alert.

- All tactical nuclear weapons on surface ships, attack submarines, and land-based naval aircraft removed for destruction or central storage.

- Nuclear short–range attack missile (SRAM II), Peacekeeper Rail Garrison ICBM, and mobile portion of small ICBM (SICBM) canceled.

- Elimination of all MIRVed U.S. and Soviet ICBMs proposed.

- Discussions on nonnuclear ABM systems requested.

On October 5, 1991, President Mikhail Gorbachev declared the following similar reductions:

- Heavy bombers and 503 ICBMs remained off alert.

- All tactical nuclear weapons on surface ships, attack submarines, and land-based naval aircraft removed for destruction or central storage.

- Bomber nuclear arms and rail-mobile ICBMs placed in storage.

- Short Range Attack Missile (SRAM), small mobile ICBM, and rail-mobile ICBM modernization and expansion programs canceled.

- Seven Strategic Nuclear Submarines (SSBNs) decommissioned

- Nuclear arsenal reduced to 5,000 warheads (below START I limit of 6,000 warheads).

- Reduction of strategic offensive arms by approximately one-half suggested.

- Discussions requested on nonnuclear (ABM) systems.

- One-year moratorium on nuclear testing.

JANUARY 28–29, 1992

In his State of the Union Address to the U.S. Congress on January 28, 1992, President Bush announced further reductions in the U.S. strategic forces to include the following:

- B-2 bomber production limited to 20.

- Advanced cruise missile production limited to 640.

- Small ICBM and production of Peacekeeper missiles and W-88 warhead for Trident missiles canceled.

In addition, he stated that if Russia were to eliminate all MIRVed ICBMs, the United States would take the following actions to cut strategic nuclear warheads to approximately 4,700:

- Peacekeeper missiles eliminated.

- Minuteman III missiles reduced to one warhead per missile.

- Trident submarine warheads reduced one-third.

- Large number of strategic bombers converted to primarily conventional use.

Russian Federation president Yeltsin (who stated that his remarks had been prepared in consultation with other leaders of the CIS) responded in a televised speech in Moscow on January 29, 1992. He stated Russia's intention to abide by all arms control agreements signed by the Soviet Union, as well as his support for the NPT, MTCR, CTBT, and the fissionable material cutoff talks. He then made public the following reductions in CIS strategic offensive forces:

- Approximately 600 ICBMs and SLBMs off alert.

- Advanced bombers, long-range air launched cruise missiles, and nuclear SLCM production and development halted.

- Strategic bomber exercises with more than thirty heavy bombers eliminated.

- 130 ICBM silos and six SSBNs eliminated/prepared for elimination.

- SSBN combat patrols cut in half.

- Strategic nuclear weapons in Ukraine to be dismantled earlier than planned.

- Extension of nuclear testing moratorium.

- Weapons-grade plutonium production reduced by 1993, halted by 2000.

Last, he proposed the following U.S.-Russian reciprocal actions:

- Eliminate all SSBN patrols.

- Reduce strategic nuclear warheads to 2,000–2,500.

- Retarget strategic offensive forces away from one another.

- Reach START limits three years early.

- Long-range nuclear SLCMs and new long-range nuclear air launched cruise missiles eliminated.

COOPERATIVE THREAT REDUCTION (CTR) PROGRAM

In the fall of 1991, conditions in the disintegrating Soviet Union created a global threat to nuclear safety and stability. The U.S. Congress, having recognized a window of opportunity to materially reduce the threat from nuclear weapons in the former Soviet Union and the proliferation potential they represented, enacted the Soviet Nuclear Threat Reduction Act—also called the Nunn-Lugar legislation. Subsequently, the program has expanded to include all weapons of mass destruction (WMD), assistance for defense conversion, and facilitation of military-to-military contacts.

The CTR program currently provides assistance to reduce or eliminate the threat posed by the thousands of existing WMD and associated infrastructure remaining in the former Soviet Union. Primary program objectives are to accelerate WMD dismantlement and destruction while ensuring a strong chain of custody for fissile material transport and storage. These objectives also foster compliance with the START agreement, the Lisbon Protocol, the NPT, the CWC, and the January 1994 Trilateral Statement. As of December 1994, the United States had authorized over $1.2 billion for the program, and agreements were in effect in Russia, Ukraine, Belarus, and Kazakhstan.

TRILATERAL BIOLOGICAL WEAPON TALKS

The trilateral working group was initiated because of U.S. concerns that the Russian offensive biological weapons program inherited from the Soviet Union was in violation of the BWC. The first meeting was in September 1992, when delegations of the United States, the United Kingdom, and the Russian Federation met in Moscow to review steps taken to resolve compliance concerns regarding the former Soviet Union. The result was the Trilateral Statement, in which Russia listed the steps taken to resolve BWC compliance concerns. The statement further called for Russia to allow unrestricted access visits to nonmilitary sites, which were to be followed by reciprocal Russian visits to the United States and the United Kingdom.

In April 1994 Russia submitted its annual BWC data declaration to the United Nations pursuant to voluntary confidence-building measures adopted at past BWC review conferences. However, the declaration provided no more information than the 1992 declaration on past Russian offensive biological weapons activities. In mid-1994 the trilateral working group met in Vienna to assess the status of the Trilateral Statement implementation process. The countries' commitment to the process was underscored by a statement at the September 1994 Washington summit by Presidents Yeltsin and Clinton on the importance of continued implementation of the Trilateral Statement.

MISSED OPPORTUNITIES: WASHINGTON POLITICS AND NUCLEAR PROLIFERATION

HEATHER WILSON

In his first press conference after winning the election, Bill Clinton listed his top five foreign policy priorities. Third on his list, after cutting the defense budget and reducing nuclear arsenals, was "working hard to stop the proliferation of weapons of mass destruction." That President Clinton gave this task such salience reflected the increasing seriousness of the proliferation threat.

In recent months, the proliferation problem has become specific and acute. In early November, as North Korea made menacing noises about the possibility of U.N. sanctions, and increased its troops along the Demilitarized Zone, President Clinton acknowledged that North Korea's likely development

of nuclear weapons is a "grave issue" for the United States. At the same time, he admitted that there is "a lot of disagreement about what we should do" to stop them.

The determination of one of the world's least rational regimes to build nuclear weapons highlights the importance of developing an effective policy to control proliferation and to respond to proliferants when our efforts at control fail.

This same lesson should have been learned from the Gulf War. Through the mechanism of U.N. inspections, we discovered after the war that our intelligence about the Iraqi nuclear weapons program had woefully underestimated the progress the Iraqis

This essay has been edited and is reprinted from The National Interest *34 (Winter 1993/94): 26–36, by permission of* The National Interest.

had made. While the intelligence community spent months on lessons learned, the most important lesson did not require much analysis: countries like Iraq can build nuclear weapons and we cannot be confident we know about it. The cold reality of fighting a war against a regional power that was on the verge of having weapons of mass destruction revealed our vulnerabilities, even if we were fortunate enough to have escaped paying a huge price.

In the months following the Gulf War, the collapse of the Soviet Union reduced the danger of a global thermonuclear war almost to zero. But in an ironic twist of fate, its collapse also ushered in an era of disorder in which the proliferation of weapons of mass destruction and the expertise to build them has accelerated.

In response to this growing threat, the United States should by now have adopted a comprehensive nonproliferation program. Such a program would have focused, to begin with, on developing new defensive technologies and enhancing and integrating intelligence capabilities. This should have been coupled with an effective emergency assistance program to accelerate safe and secure dismantlement of the former Soviet arsenal and to ensure that former Soviet bomb builders do not ply their trade in hostile countries. An active regional strategy should have been combined with a strengthening of export controls to deter potential proliferants. Finally, single Washington agencies should have been empowered to coordinate and implement the different elements of the nonproliferation program, with specific policy guidance from the White House. None of this has happened.

THE GRAVITY OF THE THREAT

For a long time, the nuclear club was one of the world's most exclusive: the United States, the Soviet Union, China, France, and Britain were the only acknowledged members. Even before proliferation became a significant concern in the late 1980s, there was a handful of states that probably qualified for membership in this exclusive group, most notably India, Israel, South Africa, and Pakistan. But the neighborhood around the club is changing and more states are aspiring to membership. The spread of computers and advanced technology and the growth of scientifically trained elites is making it possible for less wealthy states to begin to develop and maintain a nuclear capability.[1]

While states engaged in nuclear weapons research may choose to terminate their programs before they actually develop weapons, Taiwan, Iran, Algeria, and Libya are conducting such research. Argentina and Brazil went beyond research and began to develop nuclear material production facilities before their widely praised decisions to refrain from further development. Iraq actually had succeeded in producing nuclear weapons material, and North Korea not only has produced it, but is probably developing nuclear weapons in which to use it. Most of the countries that are developing nuclear weapons are also developing or already have ballistic missiles. Even when sounding rockets and space launch programs are excluded, most Middle Eastern countries, North and South Korea, India and Pakistan, South Africa, Brazil and Argentina, Libya and Tunisia have or are developing ballistic missiles of varying ranges and payloads.

Germany, Japan, and Canada could almost certainly develop nuclear weapons in a fairly short period of time but have chosen not to do so. Japan's recent flirtation with the idea of developing its own nuclear deterrent in response to the North Korean threat illustrates how proliferation can fuel regional arms races.

The collapse of the Soviet Union and the aftershocks that continue to rock the successor republics have increased the risk of proliferation. In a process that might be described as proliferation by disintegration, the Soviet Union went from a single unified military command structure with control over an arsenal of some twenty-eight thousand warheads, to a loosely affiliated commonwealth that included four nuclear-armed republics.[2]

It is difficult to describe the magnitude of the proliferation threat caused by the collapse of the Soviet Union. Potential proliferation threats used to be discussed in terms of grams of special nuclear material that might be in the wrong hands.

It takes only about 15 kilograms of highly enriched uranium or 6 kilograms of plutonium to make a nuclear weapon. Just as a result of the arms control agreements already signed, by the end of the decade between 300,000 and 500,000 kilograms of uranium and 60,000 kilograms of plutonium will have been released from the arsenal of the former Soviet Union.

Building a nuclear weapon is relatively easy compared with the difficulty of refining uranium and plutonium to the concentrations required to make a nuclear explosion. The breakdown of central control in the Soviet Union and the surfeit of weapons-grade nuclear material raise the prospect that countries determined to develop nuclear weapons will not have to make their own nuclear material; they will just buy it.

There have been too many reports of attempts to sell or buy nuclear material from the former Soviet Republics to be complacent about the security of the former Soviet stockpile. Just based on its value for use as nuclear fuel, the uranium and plutonium in warheads from the former Soviet stockpile destined to be dismantled is worth an estimated $7 billion. In a country where inflation was 1000 percent in 1993, where the currency is worthless, scientists are going unpaid by the institutes that employ them, and selling state property for private gain is common, the temptation to sell "just a little bit" of this valuable material is very great indeed.[3]

Even if our diplomatic efforts to limit proliferation are reasonably successful, we must anticipate that over the next ten years more states will join the nuclear club. Some of them will have interests very different from our own.

PLANE TICKETS TO MOSCOW

In the closing months of 1991, the Bush administration and several members of Congress recognized that the failed August coup and the triumph of the reformers in Russia offered an opportunity to influence the future composition and posture of the nuclear forces in the former Soviet Union. Senators Sam Nunn and Richard Lugar sponsored the Soviet Nuclear Threat Reduction Act of 1991. Signed by the president in December of 1991, the act allowed $400 million of reprogrammed Defense Department funds to be used to ensure the safety and security of weapons of the former Soviet Union, to accelerate dismantlement of those weapons, and to prevent proliferation. In the fiscal 1993 and 1994 budgets $800 million more was added for a total of $1.2 billion available to make secure and dismantle former Soviet weapons.

Designed as an emergency effort to deal with a critical problem, the Nunn-Lugar program has failed in practice. Two years after its establishment, about $100 million has been spent on a laundry list of peripheral activities. Legalistic arrangements for implementation remain uncompleted and unratified, and missiles remain targeted against the United States. With further aftershocks rocking the collapsed Soviet empire, our failure to act decisively may become one of the greatest lost opportunities of this decade.

In a classic example of Washington bureaucratic politics, no senior official in the Bush administration actively supported Nunn-Lugar, but every agency wanted to be in charge of it. While the bill specified that the Department of Defense (DOD) was to be the executive agent for the program, in a move that spelled disaster for rapid action, the DOD ceded control to an interagency arms control policy working group with participants from the State Department, the Department of Energy, the National Security Council Staff, the Joint Chiefs of Staff, the Arms Control and Disarmament Agency, and the intelligence community. Within the State Department, at least three offices vied for leadership responsibility for the program.

While this interagency group had effectively managed complex arms-control negotiations like the Strategic Arms Reduction Treaty (START) and the Conventional Forces in Europe (CFE), it was entirely incapable of the rapid decision making needed for a program like Nunn-Lugar. At a time when the Russian government was reeling with rapid changes and internecine suspicions, and the governments of other republics were just forming, the U.S. team chose to use formal bilateral arms control as the diplomatic paradigm for running the Nunn-Lugar program. Delegations of dozens, representing all agencies, trooped to Moscow in November and December 1991 and January 1992, forcing the Russians to sit across the table similarly represented but reluctant to talk because of the distrust and disagreement among players on their own side.

A less charitable view of this arrangement can also be offered. By bogging the program down in bureaucracy in Washington and putting the Russians in a forum where it was virtually impossible for them to articulate their needs, senior administration officials could ensure the program's failure. While plausible, this explanation ignores the fact that these same senior officials were under increasing political pressure from the Congress to show some progress.

By late January 1992 Secretary of State James Baker had made it clear that he wanted to reach initial agreement on areas of cooperation when he went to Moscow in February. Now feeling the heat, the bureaucracy developed a laundry list compiled largely of notions picked up from cocktail party conversation with members of the Russian delegation. The intent was not to promote U.S. security interests, but to make some progress that was politically sustainable with the Congress.

Baker and his delegation of dozens went to Moscow in February 1992. Sitting across the table from a phalanx of men who distrusted each other, Baker recited a list of possibilities to prompt a discussion. There was none. The Russians did not know what they needed, and each item on the list appealed to the parochial interest of one or another Russian ministry. Boris Yeltsin said all of the ideas sounded good to him, and Baker was able to announce a shopping list of initial areas of assistance: fissile material containers, armored blankets, conversion of Russian rail cars, accident response equipment, nuclear materials storage, and reprocessing of uranium and plutonium.

Throughout this process, there was never an attempt to evaluate the weaknesses in the Russian system in order to identify where U.S. assistance might make the most difference. Likewise, the United States never evaluated its own security interests so as to target programs in a way that would maximize benefits to the United States.

Divisions and competing agendas on the Russian side provided opportunities that the United States could have seized if it had evaluated its own interests and had been prepared to act more flexibly to pursue them. In a tradition that will be familiar to Americans who have dealt with corrupt city machine politics, the minister for atomic energy, Victor Mikhailov, wanted the $400 million turned over to him to build a storage facility, with a percentage certain to go into unrelated projects and the pockets of functionaries. Academician Velikov, adviser to Yeltsin and vice president of the Russian Academy of Sciences, wanted to use the money to keep his scientists employed at his institutes. General Zelentsov of the Ministry of Defense was less self-serving than the rest but initially insisted that storage for warheads must be hardened against nuclear attack—presumably from the United States. The Russians were divided and did not know what they needed. The February agreement in principle on areas of assistance was a classic case of providing the solution without knowing the problem or knowing our own interests. Once the shopping list was publicly announced by Secretary Baker, the bureaucracy was committed to pursuing and defending this agenda, even if the programs made no sense.

The next mistake the United States made was to negotiate detailed formal agreements on each area of assistance. Instead of signing a general agreement and moving forward with practical assistance, Baker turned his agreement in principle over to technical working groups to work out details. What began as emergency assistance became full employment for arms controllers. As one member of the U.S. delegation commented some months later, "What we'll get for the $400 million is a lot of plane tickets to Moscow." These technical teams spent months negotiating details in formal government-to-government agreements, some of which are still unfinished or unratified. With a plausible story to report to Congress and a course of cooperation charted, much of the political pressure abated and senior officials paid little attention to the implementation of the Nunn-Lugar program.

NUCLEAR SCIENTISTS

While the control of nuclear warheads was the initial focus of attention when the Soviet Union collapsed, the future of Russian nuclear weapons scientists quickly became an area of concern. Repressive Soviet policies that kept bomb designers in their closed cities in Cheliabinsk and Arzamas dissolved with the union. In testimony before Congress in early 1992, the Central Intelligence Agency estimated that there were some one million people employed in the Russian nuclear weapons complex, some one to two thousand of whom had the ability to make a nuclear device.

In January of 1992, while the U.S. government was reviewing visa requirements and exploring possible cooperation between U.S. and Russian national laboratories, a consortium of three American Fortune 200 companies proposed to the U.S. government that they absorb large numbers of these scientists and retain them to do commercial work while remaining in Russia. At that time, a top Russian scientist could be retained for about $1,000 a year. These companies, which already had operations in Russia and could use their infrastructure to provide basic supplies and foodstuffs to employed scientists, believed that access to food, the opportunity to get commercial experience, and a chance to stay in their own country would be very attractive to many nuclear weapons scientists even if they were paid considerably less than they might get if they emigrated to a country trying to develop nuclear weapons. With the consortium's combined revenues of $15 billion per year and 100,000 employees, gainfully employing 1,000 to 2,000 scientists at these rates would not have been difficult.

Senior officials in the Bush administration were not interested in this kind of private sector initiative. Instead, in February 1992, they announced their intent to establish a $25 million science center jointly with the European Community and Japan that would accept grant applications from former weapons scientists. The bureaucratic application and sponsorship procedures established by the United States, the European Community, and Japan have not yet delayed any applications because the sponsors chose to negotiate a formal government-to-government agreement to establish the center, and it has not been approved yet. Almost two years after the problem was identified, *not one dollar* of Nunn-Lugar funds has been used to redirect Russian nuclear weapons scientists to nonweapons work.

Senator Hank Brown (Republican of Colorado) was eager to ensure that Russian nuclear weapons builders would have the opportunity to come to the United States if they were determined to emigrate. He sponsored the Soviet Scientist Immigration Act, which became law in October of 1992. The law allows 750 unused immigration slots to be used by scientists formerly employed in the Soviet nuclear weapons program. Unfortunately, the Immigration and Naturalization Service cannot decide how to write the regulations. Over a year after the passage of the law not one former Soviet bomb builder had been allowed to come to the United States under this special rule. One assumes countries like Iraq do not have these kinds of problems.

THE UKRAINIAN BLUNDER

In December 1991 Secretary Baker visited the capitals of all four of the former Soviet republics that had nuclear weapons. He succeeded in getting the three non-Russian republics to agree to give up their strategic nuclear weapons and return the warheads to Russia for dismantlement. This agreement was formalized in May 1992 at a meeting in Lisbon, where the three non-Russian republics agreed to implement START I and accede to the 1968 Nonproliferation Treaty (NPT) as nonnuclear weapons states.

After we got a commitment from the Ukrainians to become nonnuclear, we ignored them. Large delegations continued to go to Moscow to discuss financing the Russian arms reduction program, and in Washington aid to Russia was a major issue. All the while, the Russians made clear that they intended to keep their nuclear weapons. But there was no assistance for—or even a foreign policy toward—Ukraine.

In April 1992 Ukraine formally requested assistance from the United States for destroying intercontinental ballistic missiles (ICBMs). While continuing to threaten to block any assistance unless Ukraine ratified START and acceded to the NPT, in the summer the United States began discussions with Ukraine on providing assistance.

As right-wing resistance to giving nuclear warheads to Russia without recognition of Ukrainian borders grew in the Rada, the United States reached agreement with Russia to buy highly enriched uranium from dismantled warheads. Because some of the uranium would come from warheads now in Ukraine, the Ukrainians argued that they deserved some compensation. In addition, they were balking at implementing some of the expensive technical requirements of START I unless they received some assistance. While continuing to dangle carrots for the Russians, the United States used a stick on the Ukrainians, threatening no assistance unless Ukraine went nonnuclear. The contrast with our policy toward the Russians only served to inflame the political problem in Kiev. In November 1992, when Prime Minister Leonid Kuchma formally announced that Ukraine was unwilling to give strategic nuclear weapons on its soil to the Russians, the United States finally offered $175 million in dismantlement assistance to Ukraine if and only if Ukraine ratified START and acceded to the Nonproliferation Treaty.

From the administration's perspective, linking financial assistance to START ratification and NPT accession was leverage to get Ukraine to go nonnuclear. In reality, this linkage made little sense. The assistance the United States would provide, if used properly, would bring Ukraine into de facto compliance with the terms of the START treaty even if the Rada did not ratify it. Rather than work the practical problem, de-mate the warheads, and destroy the ICBMs and their silos, the United States held out for Ukrainian ratification of a document negotiated before Ukraine existed as an independent state.

The Clinton administration continued the policy of linking aid to START ratification and NPT accession. In the spring of 1993, Clinton refused to meet with Prime Minister Kuchma, fueling the perception in Kiev that the United States was so fixated on the need to give political and economic support to Russia that it was turning a blind eye to Russia's relations with its neighbors.

In April 1993, while talks on Ukrainian compliance with START and the NPT were clearly stalled, a U.S. company that had been working quietly with Ukraine to develop a program for the safe destruction of ICBMs received a letter from Ukrainian Minister of Engineering V. Antonov, who has responsibility for implementing the missile destruction program. Antonov said that Ukraine was now prepared to proceed with a joint venture to remove nuclear warheads from SS-19s so that liquid fuel could be removed and the missiles destroyed. The company informed the U.S. government. While key U.S. officials thought the Antonov letter was a positive indication that the Ukrainians were now prepared to move forward, the company was told that formal agreements between the United States and the Ukrainian governments were not finalized. Without an agreement to provide assistance as well as ratification of START I and NPT accession, the United States would not contract to provide assistance. The U.S. company informed the Ukrainian government that it was unable to proceed and another opportunity was lost.

In June of 1993 the Clinton administration did initiate a more reasonable approach to Ukraine. Secretary of Defense Lee Aspin proposed to accelerate dismantlement by de-mating warheads, destroying the ICBMs, and putting the warheads under international control in Ukraine, pending transportation to Russia. The uranium in the warheads would be purchased by the United States or returned to Ukraine as reactor fuel. While initially promising, the United States took the position that the details of this arrangement must be worked out by Ukraine and Russia, and that the United States would remain on the sidelines. Without U.S. follow-through, this initiative quickly lost momentum.

In July, Ukraine confirmed that it had asked the Russians to return to Ukraine to de-mate the warheads from a field of ten ICBMs for safety reasons. Published reports in September 1993 illustrate the need for a more active U.S. policy. Apparently, the de-mated warheads were stored in a poorly designed storage shelter or a shelter not designed for the number of warheads deposited there. The bunker began to overheat. At a recent conference in Kiev, Ukrainian government officials suggested that the Russians had overdramatized the problem to illustrate the need to return the warheads to Russia promptly, but they never denied that there had been a problem and that the warheads had been improperly stored.

The Kravchuk-Yeltsin agreement in early September 1993 to relinquish the Black Sea fleet and return all nuclear weapons to Russia was a surprise. The agreement requires ratification and Kiev is unlikely to take any further action until the outcome of the current political crisis in Russia becomes clear.

A SLOW START

In the year since President Clinton made his pronouncement that preventing the proliferation of weapons of mass destruction was one of his top three foreign policy priorities, the rhetoric about the importance of nonproliferation has continued unabated. But the administration has by and large failed to develop coherent policies to meet this new challenge.

To be fair, Clinton did not inherit a well-oiled policy machine as far as nonproliferation is concerned. During the campaign, the Clinton team correctly identified nonproliferation as a foreign policy area in which changes were needed, changes for which the new president could take credit. But aside from creating some new offices and position titles and turning up the volume about the importance of the problem, very little of substance has been done.

In the summer of 1993 an administration task force attempted to develop a new policy for nonproliferation. Unfortunately, to do the job they relied on the same interagency mechanisms and many of the same people who had been running nonproliferation policy previously. Announced by President Clinton in his speech to the U.N. General Assembly on September 27, 1993, this new policy contains some new initiatives, but has several serious flaws. Far from providing a new framework, the policy rehashes current programs with a few new twists and steps gingerly around the bureaucratic knots that have hindered decisive action for the past two years. More important, the general preference for multilateralism that characterizes much of the Clinton foreign policy threatens to sidetrack the development of adequate defenses against proliferants in the event that diplomacy fails—and in the area of proliferation, it is very likely that our diplomacy will fail. Finally, responding to pressure from industry and the Commerce Department, the Clinton administration will relax controls on exporting missile technology. The parameters of these new export control rules are still being developed, but the direction is troublesome. America, in a state of denial and bureaucratic stasis for nearly two years, can no longer afford idle rhetoric about proliferation.

Clinton's new policy emphasizes multilateral strategies including harmonization of export controls and coordination of sanctions. While an activist diplomacy to strengthen nonproliferation norms is not, on its own, objectionable, there are elements of the administration that consider multilateral diplomacy to be inconsistent with developing the military capability to defend against proliferants when diplomacy fails.

The last White House policy document from the Bush administration on nonproliferation, NSD-70, broke new ground by directing the Defense Department to develop capabilities to defend against proliferants, including capabilities for preemptive military action. Reportedly, in last summer's review, there were strong disagreements between State and Defense about whether we should develop this counterproliferation capability. As far as the policy is concerned, it appears that State won. Improving our defenses and developing military options has received almost no support from the White House.

To their credit, Defense Department officials are continuing to pursue counterproliferation programs. They are proceeding from the reasonable assumption that if we are involved in a conflict with a regional power in the future, it is likely that it will be armed with nuclear weapons. Defense is identifying gaps in our current program so that they may be filled. The question is whether DOD officials can sustain a program to fill those gaps without the policy support of the White House, and with open opposition from State.

For all the rhetoric about making nonproliferation a higher priority, the new policy loosens constraints on exports of missile technology in deference to U.S. industry that wants to enter the international commercial space market. Even with all its caveats about selling only to countries that support nonproliferation norms, it will be more difficult for the United States to convince other countries not to export missile technology to their friends if we export to ours. Moreover, today's friends can become tomorrow's enemies. Would the United States have sold missile technology to the Shah of Iran before his

fall? If so, we would certainly regret that decision today.

Bureaucratic politics continues to bedevil U.S. nonproliferation strategy. Because everyone wants to be in charge of a presidential priority, turf fights emerged anew as the Clinton team took office. There are now at least three directorates on the National Security Council Staff with overlapping responsibilities for nonproliferation. The intelligence community's nonproliferation center claims to be the focal point for intelligence policy but does not coordinate closely with the DOD and the Department of Energy, which spend millions each year on research, analysis, and collection on nonproliferation. In an effort to put one person in charge, Strobe Talbott at the State Department was named the focal point for all matters relating to the former Soviet Union, but he is not actively involved in nonproliferation matters, leaving this to Ambassador Jim Goodby. At the same time, Undersecretary of State Lynn Davis has responsibility for political-military affairs, which include nonproliferation and arms control. Predictably, there have been serious turf fights between State and Defense where Assistant Secretary of Defense Ash Carter has attempted to take a leadership role in ways that the State Department thinks is within its purview.

The summer policy review failed to cut through this bureaucratic Gordian knot. It is not unusual for the White House to direct certain departments to take responsibility for particular programs or initiatives. Clinton's nonproliferation policy, however, is silent on agency responsibility. According to one insider, "That was just in the too-hard pile." As a result, we can expect policy by committee and consensus to continue to be the painfully slow mechanism for action.

Finally, Clinton's nonproliferation policy says virtually nothing about the arsenal of the former Soviet Union. While this may initially appear to be a curious omission, the sad truth is that it is probably a reflection of arbitrary bureaucratic lines of demarcation. It may be difficult to believe, but the people who work on nonproliferation are not the same people who work on the Nunn-Lugar program. Rather than develop a comprehensive policy, the Clinton administration accepted the turf as it found it and circumscribed its policy accordingly.

TOWARD A PROACTIVE POLICY

In February 1992, in testimony before Congress, Undersecretary of State for International Security Affairs Reginald Bartholomew said, "In sum, I think the prospects are good for beginning some tangible assistance efforts [for the Former Soviet Union] in the next several weeks." Almost two years later, virtually nothing has been done. We have delivered five hundred armored blankets, some emergency response equipment, and a few prototype nuclear material containers to the Russians. We have also experimented with safety modifications to a Russian rail car and done some work on designs for a storage facility. It is difficult to see how any of these activities have accelerated dismantlement, helped prevent proliferation, or even contributed measurably to the safety and security of the Russian stockpile.

With another political crisis rocking Russia, the opportunity to facilitate the dismantlement of the former Soviet stockpile and prevent proliferation from that program may have already passed. Nevertheless, the United States still needs a comprehensive nonproliferation policy and the will to implement it.

We must anticipate that the enemies we are likely to face in any regional conflict in the future will be armed with weapons of mass destruction. The acquisition of these weapons will be driven by regional factors largely beyond U.S. influence. It is also probable that the United States will be unable to deter the use of these weapons simply by possessing a nuclear deterrent of its own. It is therefore essential that the United States develop the capability to defend itself against proliferants. At a minimum, we must develop more accurate real-time intelligence capabilities to locate precisely nuclear warheads and delivery vehicles, and integrate that information with weapons systems capable of destroying them. In a war against a nuclear-armed enemy, "Scud busting" cannot be left to luck. We must also develop the capability to intercept ballistic missiles in the ascent phase. Intercepting warheads in the last moments before impact, a sight made familiar as Patriot missiles fired at incoming Scuds in the Gulf War, is not good enough if a nuclear weapon is on board. Finally, we must develop and deploy more sophisticated chemical and biological detection systems, and we must develop and acquire vaccines and continue our chemical warfare defense program.

The development of a military capability to defend ourselves against proliferants raises controversial questions about how and when that capability should be used. There are circumstances in which the United States should be prepared to use military force preemptively to destroy the weapons of mass destruction of another state. Likewise, we should have the capability to act covertly to disable or destroy those weapons. It is not necessary to spell out in advance the precise circumstances in which the United States would act preemptively. But proliferants must never be allowed to assume that the United States will wait to be attacked with nuclear weapons before we will act. More important, we should not fail to develop these military capabilities because we are afraid of the controversy that might ensue.

The Clinton administration's preoccupation with multilateralism to the exclusion of the unilateral pursuit of U.S. interests is a problem much broader than our nonproliferation program. Proliferation *is* a multinational problem that requires coordination and cooperation among like-minded states. However, as with other areas of our foreign policy, the United States should be prepared to act alone if it is in our national interest to do so.

The United States must abandon its bureaucratic approach to providing assistance to the former Soviet Union for the safeguarding and dismantlement of nuclear weapons. The Washington interagency community should agree on a general policy approved by the president; and one agency, probably the Department of Defense, should be empowered to carry it out. We should have abandoned the notion of negotiating formal government-to-government agreements requiring ratification long ago. Instead, the United States should facilitate practical assistance, using the resources of private corporations wherever reasonable, and focus its efforts on areas where U.S. assistance can make the most difference fastest. In particular, this would include efforts to improve accountability and safe storage of nuclear materials and environmentally safe destruction of ICBMs and their fuel.

The inability of the Immigration and Naturalization Service to write regulations is a scandalous excuse for failing to allow former Soviet bomb designers to come to the United States. The United States must coordinate its intelligence and immigration activities to ensure that bomb builders who are leaving the former Soviet Union can come to America. More directly, some Nunn-Lugar funds should be used to redirect the efforts of former Soviet bomb builders, not through a bureaucratic multinational science center, but through private industry, universities, and National Science Foundation grants.

The United States should seek to strengthen the Missile Technology Control Regime, rather than weaken it by trying to distinguish between acceptable commercial space launch sales and unacceptable missile activities. These limitations will continue to be unpopular with the U.S. space and missile industry, but to do otherwise sends the wrong message to other suppliers of missile technology.

Finally, the United States should pursue an active regional strategy to combat proliferation with a three-part approach that would seek to lessen the motivation to develop weapons of mass destruction, cause political and economic pain to those regimes that do choose to develop them, and, where possible, extend the U.S. counterproliferation defensive umbrella to the threatened neighbors of proliferants. For example, the United States should ensure that any ascent-phase ballistic missile interception capability is made available for the defense of Japan and South Korea, either based on land or at sea.

The principles on which the Clinton nonproliferation policy is based are misguided and follow on the heels of a Bush administration policy that was outdated. Countering proliferation is not about "building a new consensus" that nonproliferation is important. Rather, having accepted its importance, we must decide to use U.S. resources and influence to prevent proliferation where possible, to assist countries in a rapid and flexible way when opportunities arise to dismantle weapons, and to defend against proliferants when our diplomatic efforts fail.

NOTES

1. See Tom Clancy and Russell Seitz, "Five Minutes Past Midnight and Welcome to the Age of Proliferation," *National Interest* (Winter 1991/92).

2. Belarus, armed with 81 single warhead SS-25 ICBMs at the time of the collapse, has ratified START I and acceded to the Nonproliferation Treaty in February 1993 as a nonnuclear weapons state. Kazakhstan has 1,410 warheads on 104 SS-18 missiles and 40 Bear-H bombers. While Kazakhstan has ratified START I, it has not ratified the NPT as it committed itself to do in the Lisbon Protocols of May 1992. Ukraine was left with 46 SS-24 and 130 SS-19 ICBMs, in addition to 30 Bear-H and Blackjack bombers, and has some 1,656 strategic nuclear warheads. While Ukraine initially agreed to relinquish its nuclear weapons and comply with START I and the NPT, it has been equiv-

ocating on that commitment for eighteen months, in part because of inept American diplomacy.

3. While the proliferation of nuclear weapons is the subject of this discussion, chemical and biological agents are also a threat. The proliferation of chemical and biological weapons is harder to characterize because these weapons are so much easier to produce. A country sophisticated enough to produce fertilizer can produce chemical weapons. Likewise, biological toxins are relatively easy to produce, if more difficult to use discriminately on the battlefield. In the wake of the collapse of the Soviet Union, Russia acknowledged that the Soviet Union had continued its offensive biological warfare research well into the Gorbachev era. Like their counterparts at nuclear weapons research facilities, these experts may be tempted to take lucrative positions in countries that would like to benefit from the post-Soviet military yard sale.

FACING THE EMERGING REALITY OF REGIONAL NUCLEAR ADVERSARIES

MARC DEAN MILLOT

Drawing in part on the Clinton administration's experience during 1993 and early 1994 with North Korea's nuclear program, this essay reviews nuclear proliferation from a strategic perspective. It turns first to the prospects for a nonproliferation policy aimed at preventing potential nuclear powers from acquiring a nuclear arsenal, either by denying them access to the relevant capabilities or by destroying their weapons programs. All evidence suggests that neither approach is likely to succeed. Nuclear weapons capabilities are proliferating, and the United States will have to deal with some of the new nuclear powers as nuclear adversaries. Moreover, by placing overwhelming emphasis on the ideal of prevention, U.S. policy tends to deny the emerging reality of proliferation and obstruct thinking about its consequences, particularly the military threat to U.S. allies.

The next topic of concern is the current state of U.S. planning for conflict with regional nuclear adversaries. Many military officers believe that nuclear weapons are obsolete in the post–Cold War period and thus the United States is unprepared to fight a Major Regional Conflict (MRC) under the shadow of nuclear attack. This situation could create problems for the United States: there is a danger that its security guarantees to its allies will deteriorate and the possibility that they too will "go nuclear."

One approach to countering this proliferation was proposed by the late Secretary of Defense Les Aspin in a speech given shortly before his resignation and, unfortunately, overshadowed by it.[1] This approach recognizes that the United States and its allies are confronted by regional nuclear adversaries and places emphasis on improving the United States' ability to cope with the threat by military means. Several actions must be taken to realize Aspin's vision and to arrive at a more comprehensive and balanced national policy toward the emerging reality of nuclear proliferation.

THE PROLIFERATION OF NUCLEAR WEAPONS CAPABILITIES IS HERE AND NOW

The first serious obstacle to thinking about how to deal with the consequences of proliferation is the policy of nonproliferation as currently formulated. Its principal means are

- The Nuclear Nonproliferation Treaty (NPT), with its exchange of promises by the acknowledged nuclear powers to work toward nuclear disarmament and offer technical assistance in peaceful nuclear technology in return for a pledge by nonnuclear weapon states to forswear

This essay has been edited and is reprinted from The Washington Quarterly 17 *(Summer 1994): 41–71, by permission of MIT Press.*

nuclear weapons and submit their peaceful nuclear programs to certain safeguards designed to monitor adherence to that covenant.

- A system of unilateral and multilateral controls by Western nations on the export of nuclear weapons–related technologies.

In essence, the strategy underlying this traditional conception of nonproliferation has been to prevent nuclear proliferation by denying potential proliferators unobstructed access to the relevant technologies and materials.

Few would argue against the proposition that a world free of nuclear weapons capabilities would be to the United States' advantage. But the strong demand for nuclear weapons and the explosive spread of nuclear weapons capabilities suggest that the proposition should not constitute the guiding principle of U.S. policy toward proliferation.

The Demand for Nuclear Arsenals Remains Strong

The demand side of nonproliferation has always been strong. In terms of state behavior, there is nothing aberrant about nuclear weapons proliferation. The motivations are as diverse as those of humanity itself: fear; the drive for power, influence, and prestige; and the desire to ensure security and control one's destiny. Some combination of these impelled the acknowledged nuclear powers—the United States, the Soviet Union, Great Britain, France, and the People's Republic of China—to acquire their arsenals.

These motivations have also driven other states down the same path. In a few of these cases, the policy of denial seems to have worked. Argentina, Brazil, and South Korea have renounced their nuclear weapons programs. In some cases, prevention has not been achieved. Israel, India, and Pakistan remain essentially unacknowledged nuclear powers. In other cases, nonproliferation has been advanced, but for reasons unrelated to either the NPT or export controls. Iraq was denied the nuclear option by a war with the United States. South Africa developed nuclear weapons without U.S. knowledge, but as it moved to settle its domestic problems, it gave up its nuclear weapons.

In still other cases, the prospect of nonproliferation remains quite unclear. Some days U.S. leaders have reason to hope that the Ukrainians will deny themselves the nuclear option; some days they have reason to be less hopeful.[2] In several cases, states continue to harbor the desire to acquire nuclear weapons. According to Lynn Davis, undersecretary of state for international security affairs. Iran is one such state.[3] Libya and Algeria are also widely believed to want the bomb.

In at least one case, the prospect of nonproliferation is quite dim. In 1992 the Bush administration's director of central intelligence, Robert Gates, said that North Korea was between "a few months and a couple of years" of possessing a nuclear weapon.[4] In 1993 Director R. James Woolsey stated "there is a real possibility that North Korea has manufactured enough fissile material for at least one nuclear weapon."[5] The Central Intelligence Agency (CIA) reportedly now claims that the North "probably has developed one or two bombs."[6] Aspin estimated "maybe a bomb and a half at the outside."[7] At his confirmation hearings, Secretary of Defense William J. Perry conceded that North Korea could have as many as two weapons.[8] Meanwhile U.S. intelligence analysts argue over how many months will pass before the North could place nuclear warheads on the Nodong missile, a rocket capable of striking Japan.[9]

North Korea's program demonstrates how a dirt-poor pariah, isolated from the world by sanctions and multilateral technology controls, and sometimes operating under an International Atomic Energy Agency (IAEA) inspections regime pursuant to the NPT, can nevertheless prove quite capable of acquiring or developing nuclear weapons. It constitutes a threshold test for the policy of prevention. If North Korea can get the bomb, how can the United States be expected to deny other potential adversaries?

The Supply of Nuclear Weapons Materials, Technology, and Expertise Is Exploding

Looking to the "supply side," the prevention of nuclear proliferation by means of denial is becoming increasingly infeasible.

The Inexorable Advance of Technological Sophistication. Less than two weeks before he resigned, in a now largely forgotten speech given before the National Academy of Sciences, Secretary Aspin explained that the industrial and technological basis of a nuclear weapons arsenal has come well within the reach of the states mentioned above.

Many potential aggressors no longer have to import the sophisticated technology they need. They are growing it at home. The growth of indigenous technology can completely change the nonproliferation equation. Potential proliferators are sometimes said to be, quote "several decades behind the West," end quote. That's not much comfort nowadays. A would-be nuclear nation is . . . four decades behind the West. Then in 1993 it is at the same technology level as the United States was in 1953. By 1953, the United States had fission [sic] weapons. We were building intercontinental-range bombers, and we were developing intercontinental missiles. Realize too that most of the thermonuclear weapons in the United States' arsenal were designed in the 1960s using computers which were then known as "supercomputers." However, these same computers are no more powerful than today's laptop personal computers that you can pick up at the store or order through the catalog.[10]

The Trade among China and the Pariah States. The supply of nuclear weapons materials, technology, and expertise has expanded well beyond the reach of the United States and other Western countries that share its views on nuclear proliferation. Senator John Glenn (Democrat of Ohio), who has spent a good part of his career working for nonproliferation, told the Senate Armed Services Committee:

We've seen the North Koreans and the Chinese, the People's Republic of China, out willing to sell whatever to anybody in these areas of mass destruction. We know the connection with Pakistan through the years and what's developed there. We now see varying sales going on not only to Pakistan but Iran, Algeria, Libya and Syria.[11]

Reports in 1993 suggest that North Korea and Iran may be jointly developing the Nodong medium-range ballistic missile.[12] The United States has had its occasional successes in restraining Chinese sales, but it is proving unable to halt the expanding nuclear weapons cooperation among the pariahs.

The Many Sources of Former Soviet Nuclear Weapons-Related Capabilities. The breakup of the Soviet Union created an enormous potential source of nuclear weapons–related technology, materials, expertise, and even of weapons. We have no conception of its actual extent. In 1992 Secretary of Defense Richard B. Cheney told the House Foreign Affairs Committee:

There's such a demand for that kind of capability out around the world, they'll pay any price in Libya or Tehran or elsewhere, I have to assume that some of that capability in the form of technical experts with significant knowhow will in fact find its way into capitals where we'd rather it not be. We . . . shouldn't be foolish enough to think it's not going to happen.[13]

And in late 1993 Aspin said:

People working on the nuclear weapons in the Soviet Union are now available for hire in other parts of the world. . . . It is possible that nuclear weapons or the materials that go into making nuclear weapons could find their way into some kind of a nuclear black market.[14]

The Unavoidable Leakage of "Dual-Use" Technology from the West. The promotion of highly advanced, military-related—that is, "dual-use"—technology is an important element of the Clinton administration's economic strategy.[15] The strategy explicitly integrates the military industrial capabilities of the Departments of Energy (DOE) and Defense (DOD) in domestic economic renewal:

For example, the Oak Ridge National Laboratory's once highly secretive Y-12 plant made components for nuclear warheads. . . . Now outside researchers have access to one Y-12 plant's engineering center, prototyping facility, and ultraprecision manufacturing equipment that were formerly reserved for military work.[16]

The entire Y-12 complex is to become a Center for Defense and Manufacturing Technology.

President Bill Clinton's second secretary of defense doubts that the export of such dual-use technologies should be controlled. In 1992 Perry succinctly stated his position during his confirmation hearings to be deputy secretary.

We have to draw a clean distinction between defense-unique systems, and between dual-use technology. [In] the former we can and should control the sale whenever we think that's going to damage our proliferation goals. But in the latter, the dual-use technology, I think it's a hopeless task, and it only interferes with a company's ability to succeed internationally if we try to impose all sorts of controls in that area.[17]

If the Y-12 complex exemplifies dual-use, rather than "defense-unique," technology, the barrier between potential proliferators and nuclear weapons–related capabilities is low indeed. During 1993, the administration decided to relax controls on a broad range of telecommunications technology and computer exports; to allow sales of supercomputers, satellite technology, and nuclear power plant parts to China, despite that country's nuclear weapons-related exports; and to reconsider exports related to space-launch vehicles and remote sensing satellites.[18] As President Clinton explained to a group of business executives, the administration is unwilling to pursue nonproliferation to the point where we "cut off our nose to spite our face."[19]

DENIAL IS NOT WORKING, AND CANNOT WORK

In a very basic sense, reliance on the policy of nonproliferation based on the denial of nuclear weapons-related capabilities cannot provide adequate national security to the United States. The policy may have succeeded in the past, it may prevent some U.S. friends and allies from going nuclear today, but it is failing to prevent the spread of nuclear weapons capabilities to hostile states in the very regions in which U.S. military forces are most likely to become engaged in war.

Aspin provided a straightforward explanation of the consequence of this failure.

The new nuclear danger we face is perhaps as little as a handful of nuclear weapons in the hands of rogue states. . . . [O]ur commanders in the field have to assume that U.S. forces are threatened. . . . So the threat is real, and the threat is upon us today, not in the future; it's here and now.[20]

COPING WITH THE GAP BETWEEN THE REALITY OF PROLIFERATION AND THE IDEAL OF NONPROLIFERATION

THE MORAL TONE OF U.S. NONPROLIFERATION POLICY

At a June 1991 Heritage Foundation seminar, Daniel Poneman, the National Security Council staff member in charge of nonproliferation in both the Bush and Clinton administrations, characterized U.S. nonproliferation policy as a declaration of "global norms that essentially it is a bad thing to obtain these sorts of weapons."[21] This tone was echoed by President Clinton in remarks at the Los Alamos National Laboratory, the birthplace of the atomic bomb, less than four months after taking the oath of office.

There are still too many nations who seem determined to define the quality of their lives based on whether they develop a nuclear weapon . . . that can have no other purpose but to destroy other human beings. It is a mistake and we should try to contain it and to stop it.[22]

There is a strong moralistic quality to U.S. nonproliferation policy that inhibits realistic appraisal of the state or prospects of nuclear proliferation. The sentiment expressed by Poneman and the president is reminiscent of arguments that abstinence should be the basis of domestic policies toward AIDS, teen pregnancy, and drug use. Those who accept this approach tend to argue against efforts to mitigate the effects of these ills by promoting, for example, safe sex, the abortion option, or the use of clean needles. Ameliorating the consequence of evil is taken to suggest that society will "allow" the ills to continue. By signaling that it will allow the evil, it is argued, society ultimately encourages it.

Efforts to deal with the problem of proliferation by focusing on the immorality of nuclear weapons have had a similar effect on U.S. national security policy. The policy of prevention by denial finds it practically impossible to openly recognize the reality of nuclear possession. Thus India, Israel, and Pakistan are officially unacknowledged nuclear powers. In the face of ongoing proliferation, a nonproliferation policy starting with the proposition that it is morally unacceptable for countries other than the acknowledged nuclear powers of the NPT to obtain nuclear status is driven either to deny that such a process is occurring, or to consider extreme means to halt its progress. Both tendencies can be seen in the Clinton administration's approach to nuclear proliferation in North Korea.

COPING WITH THE GAP: FOCUSING ON THE PAST SUCCESS OF NONPROLIFERATION

Confronted with the growing evidence of strong demands for nuclear arsenals and expanding sources of supply, advocates of prevention struggle to resolve the gap between the actuality of proliferation and the supposed norm of nonproliferation. Perhaps the foremost technique has been to discuss nonproliferation as history, and in the abstract, global terms of "international security," rather than in the context of foreseeable and concrete military threats to U.S. national security. Thus, nonproliferation has been touted as a great success for the world, and so for the United States, because Argentina, Brazil, and South Africa have apparently denied themselves their nuclear weapons programs. At the same time, the widely acknowledged nuclear weapons programs of those nations the United States is most likely to engage in war—Iraq, Iran, and North Korea—are characterized as a few problem cases.[23]

A similar approach is taken by U.S. government officials when they refer to the failure of early predictions that many more states would become nuclear powers than have actually done so as evidence of the nonproliferation regimes' success. Poneman took this tack in his remarks to the Heritage Foundation when he stated:

I will not belabor the famous predictions from back in the '60s . . . 25 powers by year X. Needless to say, we are not anywhere near that stage, and I think, it is due to the fact that we have addressed what I would call the demand side of the equation in nuclear weapons through such norms as the Nonproliferation Treaty.[24]

The historical approach would have the United States judge the efficacy of nonproliferation policy by looking to what it has done for the nation in the past, rather than its relevance to the present.

COPING WITH THE GAP: CONSIDERING FORCIBLE NONPROLIFERATION

As North Korea threatened to completely shatter the illusion of a no-nuclear norm in late fall 1993, the Clinton administration attempted to close the gap between ideals and reality by demanding the troublemaker's compliance with the NPT and threatening to enforce it. The failure of a policy of prevention by denial momentarily yielded to a policy of denial by force.

In a November 7, 1993, interview from the Oval Office televised on *Meet the Press,* the president insisted that

North Korea cannot be allowed to develop a nuclear bomb. We have to be very firm about it. I spend a lot of time on this issue. . . . We have got to stop the proliferation of nuclear weapons, and in particular North Korea needs to stay in the control regime.[25]

On November 17, Secretary of State Warren Christopher warned North Korea that the United States had "options other than negotiation" if it did not submit to inspections of its suspected nuclear weapons facilities.[26] Given U.S. actions in the war over Kuwait, such "options" were widely understood to include war.

In early December, Clinton told reporters

I hope we are not headed toward a full blown crisis. I hope that we can avoid one, but I am not positive that we can. . . . I am confident that if, God forbid, any kind of a conflict should come we could do what we need to do.[27]

On December 11, while appearing on *Meet the Press,* Secretary Aspin agreed with *Washington Post* correspondent Bob Woodward that President Clinton had given the North an "ultimatum."

Woodward: Just so we make this clear. The president issued an ultimatum, didn't he? He said, like George Bush in the Iraqi invasion of Kuwait, this will not stand. We will not let them get the bomb.

Aspin: We will not let the North Koreans become a nuclear power, yes.

Woodward: Period.

Aspin: I believe that's correct.

. . . .

Aspin: . . . We have a policy that has been consistent from the very beginning, and that is, as I just outlined to Bob Woodward here, is the policy that says, look, nuclear weapons in the hands of North Korea is not acceptable.[28]

Taken as a whole, the remarks strongly suggest that the administration was willing to consider the pursuit of nonproliferation on the Korean peninsula by means of war.[29]

THE OPTION OF FORCIBLE NONPROLIFERATION IS GENERALLY UNREALISTIC

Translated into the narrowest possible military objective, President Clinton's demand that "North Korea cannot be allowed to develop a nuclear bomb" requires the destruction of North Korea's weapons-grade material and its means of producing such material. At a minimum, this calls for destruction of the reactor at Yongbyon, assuming that it is the sole facility for the production of weapons-grade material and that it is also the only location where any materials already produced are stored. It is certainly possible to destroy the reactor site and, if it constituted the entire nuclear weapons production complex, to at least delay North Korea's nuclear program.

So narrowly defined, this is an operation the U.S. military can accomplish unilaterally, quickly, and stealthily, with sea-launched cruise missiles and long-range bombers. The promise of no U.S. casualties would be very credible. But there would be Korean and, in the long run, Japanese casualties. An attack on the reactor could spew radioactive material across parts of North Korea. It could send a radioactive cloud over Japan. It could result in a nuclear disaster analogous to Chernobyl.

The attack could also start a second Korean War. Even without nuclear weapons, North Korea might well take Seoul, destroy substantial portions of South Korea, and kill many American soldiers. Of course, the strike on the North Korean facility could be preceded by a substantial buildup of U.S. forces in the region, as Operation Desert Shield preceded Operation Desert Storm in the war with Iraq. A buildup of U.S. forces, however, might also lead the North to invade South Korea, rather than wait for the United States to attack at full strength.

Moreover, such a buildup would give the North warning to disperse its nuclear materials and to dismantle and disperse equipment, if it has not done so already. The United States could respond by expanding the target set to include the places North Korea might hide its nuclear program and suspected missile production facilities, storage sites, and dispersed field locations. Given the uncertainties surrounding the assumption of a single North Korean nuclear weapons production facility and materials storage site, considerations of military prudence are likely to lead operational planning in that direction in any event. But many of these facilities are likely to be deeply buried. One Defense Intelligence Agency estimate reportedly claimed the North's underground facilities are "virtually invulnerable to allied air attack."[30]

At the end of this analysis of move and countermove, which could go many steps beyond the points made here, a president considering military options against even a small nuclear program is likely to find that although virtually every uncertainty or problem can be answered to some extent with an additional increment of U.S. military power, forcible nonproliferation will quickly take on the character of a substantial military operation, involving enormous costs and risks.

In the case of North Korea, the operation will not be "surgical"; it may precipitate a preemptive attack on South Korea and eventually require the United States to invade and occupy the North. It will not be quick; finding and destroying the North Korean nuclear weapons infrastructure will take time. It will not be stealthy or unilateral; it will certainly require the active cooperation of South Korea and Japan, and the acquiescence of China and Russia. There is a substantial risk of significant U.S. casualties. Unless he is prepared to follow up even the limited attack with an invasion leading to removal of the regime and occupation of the country, President Clinton will also have to accept the risk of an eventual nuclear revenge against the United States, perhaps delivered by unconventional means. And there is one uncertainty for which no amount of U.S. military power can compensate; the possibility that North Korea has developed one or more nuclear weapons and put them on its missiles.

These costs and risks must be weighed against the consequences of a successful military operation. They might be acceptable if the result is that potential proliferators see the futility of pursuing the nuclear weapons option and give up their programs. But no one can say with any certainty that by attacking North Korea in the name of nonproliferation, the United States will actually reverse the international trend toward further proliferation. Israel's highly successful raid on the nuclear facility at Osirak did not convince Iraq to abandon its nuclear weapons program. On the contrary, the Iraqis subsequently enlarged their program and dispersed and hid their nuclear facilities. Even a highly successful U.S. attack is as likely to cause other would-be proliferators to redouble their efforts as it is to convince them to abandon their programs. A less successful attack could remove from the calculations of these onlookers a nagging fear that might otherwise tend to discourage pursuit of the nuclear option.

It is unlikely that the president will choose to risk war when he has no reason to believe that, absent his threat to destroy North Korea's nuclear program, North Korea is likely to start a war on its own. The cause of nonproliferation is simply not worth that risk. But having threatened at least implicitly to consider such an attack on North Korea, if the president fails to make good on that threat, other potential proliferators will tend to be emboldened to follow in North Korea's footsteps.

COPING WITH THE GAP: SIDESTEPPING THE QUESTION OF A PROLIFERATOR'S NUCLEAR STATUS

The most frightening way to close the gap between the reality of proliferation and the ideal of preventing proliferation would be to create circumstances that foster an impression that a proliferator is complying with the no-nuclear norm and to avoid actions that tend to contradict that impression. Unfortunately, elements of this approach can be found in the Clinton administration's dealings with North Korea.

To understand the problem it is important to recall how the North Korean crisis began. In March 1993, just a few months after coming to office, the new administration became so concerned about North Korea's nuclear weapons program that it insisted that routine inspections of the North's nuclear facilities by the IAEA were completely inadequate to monitor compliance with the NPT.[31] The United States convinced the IAEA to demand intrusive inspections, particularly of nuclear disposal sites, that would enable nuclear engineers to better determine whether the North had processed weapons-grade materials in violation of the treaty. The North refused, withdrew from even the limited inspections, and the crisis ensued.

In the following months the administration declared it would not allow North Korea to become a nuclear power; that it was "not acceptable" to the United States for the North to acquire nuclear weapons. The clear implication of U.S. policy pronouncements was that the North was not adhering to the no-nuclear norm and that special inspections were necessary to prove it to the world. When the North remained intransigent, the administration implied it might well be prepared to resolve the impasse by force.

The administration then reviewed the military options and apparently found them wanting.[32] Instead, the administration considered canceling Team Spirit, an annual joint U.S.–South Korean military exercise of plans to reinforce and protect the South in times of crisis, and offering economic incentives to North Korea, if it would return to the inspections regime considered unacceptable just a few months earlier.[33] By January 1994 the administration had abandoned plans to increase pressure on North Korea by various economic sanctions, perhaps including a blockade, because it seemed highly likely to move the United States closer to the unthinkable war option. Instead, it came to a settlement with North Korea. The North agreed to at least a one-time inspection of its declared sites, with the details to be worked out with the IAEA.[34]

According to Under Secretary Davis, the United States reportedly agreed to cancel Team Spirit and is "prepared to help bring North Korea into the family of nations, but only if they meet our conditions" in their negotiations with the IAEA.[35] Davis reportedly also claimed that the agreement would permit international inspectors to "tell the rest of the world that there are no dangerous activities occurring in North Korea with respect to nuclear weapons."[36] At present, something like a return to the previously unacceptable inspections regime seems a tolerable outcome to the Clinton administration.[37] There has been no suggestion from the administration that it is prepared to resume its position that routine inspections are unacceptable and return to the crisis atmosphere of 1993.

By arriving at a compromise with the North, the administration avoided the stark choice between starting down the road to war and stepping away from its commitment to nonproliferation. More important for the purpose of this discussion, the evidence necessary to prove that more likely than not the North has nuclear weapons, or at least the material to make them, will remain out of reach. As described in a January 1994 *Washington Post* editorial, the administration's policy "pushes into a foggy future the previous and prime American thrust to ensure that North Korea builds no bombs at all."[38] Thus, the compromise with North Korea enables the administration to continue to treat proliferation as a possibility rather than something to be faced today.

Allowing the nuclear status of states like North Korea to remain ambiguous amounts to pretending that they are not nuclear powers. Psychologists call the phenomenon "avoidance." A policy of avoidance enables potential proliferators to continue to proceed with their nuclear weapons programs in the dark. It also discourages the United States from taking actions urgently needed to deal with the military consequences of regional nuclear adversaries.

THE U.S. MILITARY IS UNPREPARED FOR OPERATIONS AGAINST A REGIONAL NUCLEAR ADVERSARY

A second obstacle to clear thinking about the consequences of nuclear proliferation for U.S. national security lies in the U.S. military. The DOD's civilian leadership, Democrat and Republican, has recognized the threat a regional nuclear adversary could pose to future U.S. military operations. Secretary Cheney spelled it out in testimony before the House Foreign Affairs Committee in March 1992.

There are a growing number of nations in the world that have balistic missile capability, it's going to expand significantly between now and the end of the century and increasingly there will be nations that will have nuclear warheads to put on those missiles. Our biggest loss in the Gulf, 28 people in one event, was when a Scud, a very crude 1950s technology missile, hit one of our barracks in the rear area in Dhahran. Now that was a small scale but it represents the kind of problem that we have got to deal with long term. The next time we deploy forces like we did against Saddam Hussein, we have got to anticipate it will be in an environment in which our adversaries will be able to launch more sophisticated missiles, better guidance systems, bigger payloads and maybe weapons of mass destruction deployed on that.[39]

Les Aspin also recognized the danger posed by regional nuclear adversaries. In February 1992, while chairman of the House Armed Services Committee, he stated: "The proliferation of nuclear weapons is now the chief threat we face in the post-Soviet era." Reflecting on the aftermath of the war with Iraq, Aspin pointed out that

proliferation . . . has continued for the last 20 years, largely obscured by the shadow of superpower competition. The extent of Saddam Hussein's nuclear ambitions, and near success in achieving them, should be a wake up call not just about Iraq, but about other countries as well.[40]

In his speech of December 7, 1993, Secretary Aspin outlined the message in that "wake up call" and put it in historical perspective.

During the Cold War, our principal adversary had conventional forces in Europe that were numerically superior to the West. For us during those years nuclear weapons were the great equalizer. . . . Now today . . . nuclear weapons can still be the equalizer against conventional forces . . . but today, the United States . . . is the biggest kid on the block when it comes to conventional military forces, and it is our potential adversaries who may attain nuclear weapons. So nuclear weapons may still be the great equalizer; the problem is the United States may now be the equalizee.[41]

Aspin's bottom line was that "the policy of prevention through denial won't be enough to cope with the potential of tomorrow's proliferators."[42] Nevertheless, and despite the fact that the countries violating the supposed global norm of nonproliferation are the very nations the U.S. military is most likely to fight, the uniformed military has not joined the DOD's civilian leadership in challenging the preeminence of "prevention through denial." Nor has it challenged the viability of prevention by forcible denuclearization. The reason is a post–Cold War trend in U.S. military thinking that has devalued nuclear weapons as an element of U.S. military strategy in particular, and of military strategy in general. As a result, the United States is not preparing seriously for conflicts with regional nuclear adversaries.

THE U.S. MILITARY IS GETTING OUT OF THE NUCLEAR BUSINESS

From fall 1991 to summer 1993, Roger Molander, Peter Wilson, and I conducted a RAND study examining the emerging debate within the U.S. government over the consequences of nuclear proliferation for U.S. national security policy.[43] The focus of "The Day After . . ." study was a series of case-study defense planning exercises on regional nuclear warfare assuming U.S. force postures similar to those later proposed in the Pentagon's *Bottom-Up Review* (discussed below). Roughly two hundred forty people from throughout the U.S. government participated, including nearly fifty active duty officers drawn primarily from various defense planning staffs in the Pentagon.

Two of the scenarios dealt with U.S. military interventions against regional adversaries armed with small arsenals of nuclear-tipped mobile missiles, specifically Iran and North Korea. Observing the exercises, I was impressed by the widespread confidence of military participants in the efficacy of the advanced conventional weaponry employed with such success in the war with Iraq against the forces of a regional nuclear adversary.[44] This impression was not contradicted when the Iranian exercise was rerun with hundreds of officers attending the National War College.

Apparently Operation Desert Storm has left many in the U.S. military convinced that nuclear weapons are largely unnecessary in the post–Cold War world. Conventional weapons are considered able to destroy virtually every military target that used to be assigned to nuclear weapons, from buried command centers to hardened aircraft shelters, and even large concentrations of armor. Military planners point out that the precision of modern conventional weapons allows the user to reduce civilian casualties to incredibly low levels, particularly compared to nuclear weapons. This capacity for discrimination gives commanders far greater operational flexibility than nuclear weapons could ever offer. The ability to reduce the collateral damage of attacks to adjacent populations also promises to minimize the "interference" of American civilian officials during the course of a war. Apart from recognition of a need to retain some number of warheads on U.S. land- and submarine-based ballistic missiles to balance those of whoever remains in charge of the former Soviet Union's intercontinental nuclear arsenal, there is a widespread belief in the military that U.S. armed forces can do without a nuclear capability.

These attitudes are consistent with changes to the nation's nuclear force posture made over the last several years. Aside from strategic forces, nuclear weapons are on their way out of the U.S. arsenal. And with the Clinton administration's agreement not to automatically target the former Soviet Union, even strategic nuclear weapons lack an immediate and compelling military rationale. Nuclear weapons have been withdrawn from U.S. ground forces. It is no exaggeration to say that the U.S. Army is out of the nuclear business. It is only a slight exaggeration to say that the U.S. Navy and Marines are out. Nuclear weapons have been withdrawn from U.S. surface ships and attack submarines. It would take weeks to rearm those vessels and the navy appears eager to rid itself of the cost of maintaining that option. The Strategic Command retains control of U.S. intercontinental nuclear forces, but the U.S. European Command is the only combatant command with nuclear forces at the ready, roughly 1,000 air-delivered weapons dedicated to the North Atlantic Treaty Organization (NATO). Because NATO has no adversary, the weapons have no mission, and the

U.S. Air Force is seriously contemplating the option of returning them to the continental United States.

At a breakfast meeting of defense journalists on September 23, 1993, on the eve of his retirement as chairman of the Joint Chiefs of Staff (JCS), General Colin L. Powell looked back on the role of the military in the dismantlement of the U.S. nuclear arsenal with great pride.

I'm enormously pleased to sort of put it in the column for the four years I've been chairman that we have put in place arms control agreements and we have done unilateral things within the armed forces reflecting the post–Cold War environment that has resulted in us reducing in due course our nuclear weapons level by about 70 percent. I mean, it was the United States armed forces without a whole lot of prompting from anybody that decided let's get rid of artillery-fired projectiles in the Army. It was within the leadership of the armed forces that we bit the bullet on taking tactical nuclear weapons off our ships at sea. . . . [Y]ou know, the Navy, the Marine Corps, and the Army now totally rely on the Air Force for any potential future nuclear weapons they need in the battlefield. . . . So I'm very pleased that the JCS has stayed ahead of the curve with respect to nuclear weapons. In fact, they've been in the forefront of getting rid of capability that is no longer needed in the post–Cold War environment and that was costing us money to keep.[45]

With the ongoing disassembly of the theater nuclear stockpile, and the de facto closure of much of the nuclear weapons production complex, the United States will find it difficult to get back into the nuclear weapons business quickly in a time of crisis. As a consequence, the guarantee of security the United States extends to its regional allies is based increasingly on conventional military power. My experience with "The Day After . . ." study implies that this prospect worries few in the U.S. military. In place of nuclear deterrence they suggest that the United States offer its allies a promise to repeat Operation Desert Storm if they are attacked.

THE U.S. MILITARY IS NOT PLANNING TO FIGHT NUCLEAR MRCS

Accompanying the U.S. military's belief that its own military strategy no longer requires nuclear forces is a more general sense that nuclear weaponry is essentially obsolete and unusable. In December 1992 General Powell reflected this attitude in remarks following a speech at American University: "I also think nuclear weapons have much less political utility than anyone thinks they do, particularly those who are trying to develop them."[46] This position was not new to the chairman. In January 1992 he was also quoted disparaging the value of nuclear weaponry.

I think there is far less utility to these weapons than some Third World countries think there is. What they hope to do militarily with weapons of mass destruction I can increasingly do with conventional weapons, and far more effectively.[47]

These remarks also reflect a widespread attitude among military planners we encountered in "The Day After . . ." study that because nuclear weapons have less value to the United States than they did during the Cold War, they ought to be of less value to potential proliferators as well. Many in the military reject Secretary Aspin's notion that if nuclear weapons fall into the hands of its regional adversaries the United States may become the "equalizee." Instead, they see nuclear weapons as weapons of the Cold War and, because the Cold War is over, the rationale for nuclear weapons has ended.

The results of this attitude can be found in the DOD's *Bottom-Up Review* (BUR), a study initiated almost at the outset of the Clinton administration and released in October 1993.[48] The review was intended to provide coherence to the administration's military strategy and guidance for downsizing the U.S. force structure under a reduced defense budget. The Joint Staff, under General Powell, played a substantial role in the effort, and the report was unveiled to the press at a joint conference by Aspin and Powell.

The most disturbing aspect of the BUR report is the disconnect between its review of the threat posed by the proliferation of nuclear weaponry, on the one hand, and its discussion of force-sizing scenarios and their implications for the U.S. force structure on the other. The threat and policy-oriented sections are consistent with Secretary Aspin's perspective, but the force-sizing scenarios and force structure implications are more in line with the views of General Powell.

The Report Reflects a Clear Conception of the Regional Nuclear Threat.   The briefest review of Operations Desert Storm and Desert Shield suggests that future power projection operations based on that experience will be seriously vulnerable to even a small nuclear arsenal. The coalition flew thousands of sorties against a handful of Iraqi mobile Scud missile launchers without a single confirmed kill.[49] The Patriot antiballistic missile system destroyed far too few Scud warheads.[50] As President Clinton said in his speech before the United Nations General Assembly in September 1993, Iraqi missile attacks "would have been far graver in their consequences if they had carried nuclear weapons."[51]

The BUR reports review of the proliferation threat discussed some of the larger consequences of a potential conflict with a regional nuclear adversary. Specifically, "a hostile nuclear-armed state could threaten . . . its neighbors, perhaps dissuading friendly states from seeking our help to resist aggression[;] concentrations of U.S. forces deployed in the region[;] regional airfields and ports critical to U.S. reinforcement operations[; and] American cities—either with covertly delivered weapons or, eventually, ballistic or cruise missiles" (p. 5). Thus "weapons in the hands of a hostile power not only threaten U.S. lives but also challenge our ability to use force to protect our interests" (p. 5).

In keeping with this assessment, the BUR establishes a requirement to "ensure that U.S. armed forces can successfully carry out operations in a [regional] conflict involving the use of nuclear . . . weapons" (p. 73). The report describes the demanding requirements of military operations designed to ensure a successful intervention against a regional nuclear adversary. It highlights some of the force structure implications of these requirements, including improvements to intelligence in support of battlefield operations against nuclear adversaries; the ability to seize, disable, and destroy nuclear arsenals; and the development of nuclear and conventional forces to assure a credible threat of retaliation to nuclear attack (pp. 6, 73).

The report also implies the possibility of war with a nuclear-armed Iran or North Korea. Indeed, it explicitly states that "chief among the new dangers is . . . aggression by regional powers" (p. iii) described elsewhere in the report as "set on regional domination through military aggression while simultaneously pursuing nuclear, biological, and chemical weapons capabilities" (p. 1). The BUR concludes that "countering proliferation is central to addressing . . . regional dangers in the Post–Cold War world. Strengthening the U.S. military's capabilities for meeting the threat of . . . proliferation . . . is one of the Department's most important responsibilities in the new security environment" (p. 74).

The Threat Is Not Reflected in the Analysis of Force Posture. When he presented the BUR to the public, Secretary Aspin noted that the most important factor in sizing and shaping the future U.S. military posture is the prospect of simultaneously fighting two MRCs against such states as Iran and North Korea. The report's initial discussion of MRCs is consistent with the more general policy sections noted above. It describes a "potential regional aggressor" armed with "100–1,000 Scud-class ballistic missiles, some possibly [armed] with nuclear . . . warheads" (p. 13). It notes the need to protect friendly forces from missile attacks and to "destroy high-value targets, such as weapons of mass destruction" (p. 16).

But beyond this verbal nod in the direction of a power projection operation fought under a nuclear shadow, the quantitative analysis of MRCs assumes the adversary does not employ nuclear weapons. The MRC operation is portrayed as a repeat of Desert Shield and Desert Storm. As a result, aside from a decision to retain the theater missile defense component of the otherwise defunct Strategic Defense Initiative, the report makes no mention, and there is no evidence of, any serious effort to focus resources on the capabilities required to fight nuclear MRCs.

The unmistakable implication of the BUR's analysis of MRCs is that a version of the force structure employed in the war against Iraq is sufficient for operations against regional nuclear adversaries. This conclusion is completely at odds with the rest of the report. It is also at odds with Secretary Aspin's December 7 remarks that U.S. military commanders must assume they are threatened by nuclear weapons, that the threat is "upon us today," that "it's here

and now." The disconnect between the discussion of the consequences of nuclear proliferation and the analysis of essentially nonnuclear MRCs suggests that while some in the DOD have recognized the nature of the threat posed by regional nuclear adversaries, the department as a whole has been unable to respond decisively.

An Adequate Response May Be Perceived as Too Expensive. One reason for this failure may be the cost of a military capability to fight a credible nuclear MRC. In military campaigns against regional adversaries, U.S. defense planners contemplating the next Desert Storm face what Roger Molander and Peter Wilson call "a tyranny of small numbers."

For example, as noted in the BUR, a handful of nuclear weapons can destroy the few ports and airfields U.S. contingency plans now rely upon to reinforce a threatened ally. During Secretary Perry's confirmation hearing, Senator William S. Cohen (Republican of Maine) suggested that even with the nuclear weapons it might already have, North Korea could seriously undermine U.S. plans to defend South Korea.

[Given] the limited number of ports and airfields that the United States would be required to [use to] reinforce [South Korea], I would respectfully suggest that even one or two nuclear weapons would constitute a militarily-significant arsenal in the region.

Secretary Perry agreed. "We are very concerned about the possibility that North Korea has even one nuclear weapon. We're not sanguine about that at all."[52]

Ensuring the survival of U.S. forces arriving in theater and the success of power projection operations requires a combination of highly effective defensive and offensive capabilities. Given its experience against Iraqi mobile Scuds, the U.S. military understands that guaranteeing the destruction of a small arsenal of nuclear-tipped, mobile, medium-range missiles like the Nodong is likely to be a very expensive undertaking. Yet even under BUR assumptions, the DOD is reportedly underfunded by $40 to $50 billion over the next five years.[53] A U.S. military establishment attempting to adjust to a massive downsizing may be psychologically unable to contemplate the additional cuts to the traditional force structure that will undoubtedly be necessary to rapidly develop and field entirely new capabilities to conduct nuclear MRCs. Declaratory policies denying the reality of proliferation or relying on forcible denuclearization may be more palatable.

REGIONAL NUCLEAR PROLIFERATION PLACES U.S. ALLIANCE STRUCTURE IN JEOPARDY

The result of the Clinton administration's failure to accept the emergence of nuclear arsenals in the states most likely to threaten U.S. vital interests and recognize that the U.S. military is not prepared to deal with a regional nuclear adversary could be disastrous.

The most dangerous consequence is that the most important regional allies of the United States may be taking the first tentative steps toward reconsidering their decisions to forswear nuclear arsenals and rely on U.S. security guarantees. Japan, South Korea, Germany—indeed almost any of the nations considered U.S. allies—have the capacity to acquire a nuclear arsenal in a matter of months. Given their industrial capabilities, technological expertise, financial strength, organizational capacity, and military sophistication, U.S. policy makers would do well to think of these allies as "virtual" nuclear powers. The only thing standing in the way of their acquiring an actual nuclear arsenal is their decision not to do so.

Again the North Korean crisis provides us with a view of the future. Close observers of Japan sense the first signs of what might become a serious debate over the nuclear option. Beginning with outgoing Foreign Minister Kabun Muto in July 1993, senior officials in Japan have openly, albeit somewhat indirectly, raised the possibility that North Korea's nuclear weapons capability may require Japan to follow suit. "If it comes down to a crunch, possessing the will that we can do it is important," Muto said.[54] On January 30, the London *Sunday Times* reported that the British Defence Ministry had informed the prime minister that "Japan has acquired all the parts necessary for a nuclear weapon and may even have built a bomb which requires only enriched plutonium for completion."[55] Japan has enormous stockpiles of plutonium for its nuclear power program.[56] On February 4, 1994, Japan launched its H-2 rocket, a missile capable of carrying large satellites into orbit and a potential nuclear weapons delivery vehicle.[57] This is the stuff of virtual nuclear power. Only a political decision is needed to make it real.

Allied nuclear weapons options have acquired a certain degree of legitimacy as a response to the emerging reality of regional nuclear adversaries.[58] Secretary Perry admitted as much at his confirmation hearing. "[If] North Korea becomes a nuclear power—not as defined by us but as defined by the Japanese and the South Koreans and the Taiwanese—there is every possibility that they will then want to become nuclear powers as well." U.S. policy makers are beginning to realize that decisions to formalize, preserve, or move ahead with the nuclear weapons option could soon enter the mainstream of policy debate in allied capitals.

THE CREDIBILITY OF EXTENDED DETERRENCE IS IN DECLINE

A critical factor in allied decisions about nuclear weapons options is the credibility of U.S. security guarantees. No country is predisposed to place its survival in the hands of another. During the Cold War the United States convinced its allies to place much of their hope for security in its hands, convincing them that their local problem was also part of the U.S. global strategic problem. U.S. treaty commitments were of course couched in phrases that left

Congress with its constitutional right to declare war. But the United States built an integrated structure of coalition defense, placing hundreds of thousands of U.S. soldiers along its allies' borders with the Soviet bloc, basing thousands of nuclear weapons that could reach Soviet territory on allied soil, sharing responsibility for the release and delivery of those weapons with its allies' political authorities, and interlocking U.S. plans for intercontinental nuclear warfare with the theater nuclear plans. In so doing, the United States created a situation in which for all practical purposes, regardless of how a war against U.S. allies might start, it was automatically committed to their defense. Through these efforts it created a unique situation, in which in any debate over national security in any allied capital the burden of proof was placed on those who argued against relying on U.S. security guarantees.

With the end of the Cold War that situation has changed. U.S. leaders do not view today's threats as being on the order of that posed by the Soviet Union. Regional security problems are now treated by the United States more as local problems of secondary concern, particularly when compared to domestic issues such as the economy, health care, and the federal budget deficit. Against the backdrop of a much reduced U.S. military presence overseas, Americans must take care not to exacerbate fears among the allies that the United States is becoming disconnected from their own perceptions of their security requirements.

With this admonition in mind, the apparent desire of many in the U.S. military to replace extended nuclear deterrence with a promise to repeat Desert Storm is likely to be taken as a sign of a declining U.S. commitment to their security. However effective Desert Storm was as a military campaign from the U.S. perspective, Kuwait was first entirely overrun and pillaged by Iraqi forces.[59] The fact that the United States is offering this conventional deterrent as the answer to wars that its allies must assume will be conducted against adversaries armed with at least small nuclear arsenals is even less reassuring. And when U.S. officials suggest that they might give up the military exercises that give operational plausibility to U.S. promises to reinforce those allies, as the Clinton administration did when it suggested that Team Spirit could be canceled, U.S. credibility is eroded still further.[60]

On the other hand, and as the earlier reactions of South Korean and Japanese officials to Secretary Aspin's November 1993 trip to the Far East show, hints by U.S. officials of policies that might well lead to strikes on the nuclear facilities of the neighbors of U.S. allies raise the possibility that the United States might start a regional nuclear war.[61] This fear can only be reinforced when U.S. defense analysts voice their own concerns about the vulnerability of allied conventional forces to a short-warning attack by the North, and about the prospect of losing Seoul. Suggestions that U.S. leaders lack prudence and good judgment undermine allied confidence in U.S. leadership.

On reflection, allies of the United States may find the intensity of the administration's reaction to North Korea's nuclear program even more unsettling. There is no question that the United States has the military power to defeat North Korea in a nuclear war, perhaps even while refraining from nuclear use. But as Senator Cohen suggested, U.S. political leaders consider even two North Korean weapons to be "militarily significant." Even two nuclear weapons could not save North Korea from utter defeat, but their use would be a political disaster of enormous proportions for the United States and its president. The prospect of that disaster may be a source of deep fear on the part of U.S. leaders. Recognition that this fear can be manipulated—as perhaps it has been by North Korea—could become a powerful factor motivating nuclear proliferation. And if U.S. allies come to believe that a fear of nuclear conflict may cause the United States to hesitate at some moment when they must depend absolutely on its support to assure their own survival, the credibility of U.S. security guarantees will suffer tremendously.

If the allies of the United States come to believe that it no longer shares their view of regional security, is no longer automatically committed to their defense, can no longer be counted as prudent, and may suffer from a paralytic fear of nuclear conflict, the burden of proof in any debate over national security in any allied capital will shift to those who argue for continuing to rely on U.S. security guarantees. Decisions to pursue national nuclear weapons programs may not be far behind.

THE DISINTEGRATION OF U.S. ALLIANCES WILL EXACERBATE REGIONAL MILITARY INSTABILITY

The lack of credible security assurances will push allies of the United States toward nuclear arsenals of their own to restore the military equilibrium upset by their local nuclear adversaries or by more general regional nuclear instabilities. These allies may well see a realization of their virtual nuclear arsenal as the only alternative to losing all influence over their own national security. This development, however, would lead down a worrisome path, with dangerous implications for regional stability and ultimately for the security of the United States itself.

One lesson U.S. defense decision makers should take from the growing understanding of U.S.–Soviet crises is that nuclear stability is not automatic. By the end of the Cold War nuclear stability was practically an institution; in the beginning it was barely a concept. As historians report their findings on such events as the Cuban missile crisis, it is becoming apparent that the superpowers learned to create stability on the basis of trial and error.[62] Reading the results of this research it is difficult to not conclude that, particularly in the early days of U.S.–Soviet competition, luck played an uncomfortably significant role in avoidance of nuclear war.

It is possible that the new nuclear powers will learn from the history of U.S.–Soviet nuclear crises, just as they have learned to take advantage of U.S. technological innovations in the development of their own nuclear weapons programs. Perhaps the relatively rapid development of a stable regional nuclear balance is feasible. On the other hand, U.S. leaders should be concerned that nations with widely varying values, thought processes, and cultures may go through the learning experience without their own good fortune. It is hard to know where any nuclear war might end, or what lessons onlookers will take away from it.

It is doubtful that anyone is eager to run a real world experiment on the universality of the superpowers' nuclear logic. Indeed the vision of experimental failure on a massive scale has probably influenced U.S. decision makers to give prevention its privileged role in the national response to the proliferation threat. But now that regional adversaries of the United States are going nuclear, the experiment will begin if U.S. allies follow suit. As perhaps several of these experiments play themselves out, the odds increase that one will lead to nuclear war.

When U.S. leaders come to recognize that these experiments are out of their hands, they will face the question of what to do with the remaining forward presence of their forces on allied territories. If they stay, the United States runs the risk of being sucked into nuclear wars that are not of its making against its will. If they leave, the United States will lose any hope of regional influence, but may at the same time precipitate a crisis that may itself increase the risk of nuclear conflict. Neither choice is appealing; both hold grave risks for U.S. national security. Preventing the need of future leaders to confront that choice should be the goal of U.S. policy.

U.S. NATIONAL SECURITY POLICY MUST COUNTER THE CONSEQUENCES OF PROLIFERATION

National security decision makers must recognize that the United States and its allies will face several regional nuclear adversaries in the next decade. They must focus on the need to reassure regional allies that the best counter to this threat lies in defense arrangements with the United States, rather than in pursuing their own nuclear options. To succeed, U.S. leaders must back up their security assurances by giving regional nuclear conflict the highest priority in defense planning. Countering the consequences of proliferation should replace nonproliferation, and particularly the ideal of prevention, as the focus of U.S. policy to deal with the new nuclear threat.

A NEW NATIONAL POLICY SHOULD MOVE PREVENTION FROM CENTER STAGE

The first step toward a counterproliferation policy is to recognize that, however successful it may have been in the past, the policy of prevention is now failing to protect U.S. national security. Regional nuclear adversaries are emerging. Appeals to idealism, moral suasion, trade controls, and preventive strikes cannot continue to be the centerpiece of a strategy to deal with ongoing proliferation. A presidential decision directive should be promulgated, describing the reality of proliferation and placing the development of military means and alliance plans to conduct nuclear MRCs at the center of a national counterproliferation program.

The directive must also address the NPT, and particularly the 1995 Review Conference. That treaty has some value as the embodiment of an ideal, but maintaining it inviolate should not be the U.S. goal if the price is denying the reality of ongoing proliferation. At a minimum the United States should not seek an indefinite extension of the treaty, which remains the administration's position.[63] Such an objective is simply too much at odds with the reality of ongoing proliferation and reflects a blindness to that reality that can only undermine U.S. credibility.

A policy is needed that allows U.S. decision makers—and forces the U.S. bureaucracy—to recognize the emergence of regional nuclear powers. The United States must relate to the new nuclear powers as nuclear powers, not pariahs. Perhaps they will have to be admitted to the NPT as nuclear weapon states. This would at least allow U.S. policy makers to begin to develop the kind of dialogue they engaged in with the Soviets. This dialogue would tend to enhance a U.S. ability to predict the behavior of these new powers. It might also speed up their acculturation to the responsibility of nuclear power, a responsibility that even radical states like the Soviet Union eventually came to accept. It would also form the basis for formal negotiations to promote nuclear stability that might lead, for example, to meaningful arms-control treaties. Without recognition of the nuclear status of these new nuclear powers, no such negotiations are possible.

As for export controls, the president's directive must openly recognize the rising tide of global technological sophistication and the extent to which advanced and dual-use technologies are vital to the export strategy to fuel the economic growth of the United States itself and provide Americans with quality, high-wage employment. In these circumstances, the best U.S. leaders can hope for is that national and multilateral export controls will slow the spread of some uniquely nuclear weapons-related technologies and at least provide a mechanism for warning intelligence and defense analysts of the acquisition strategies of potential proliferators.[64]

Of far greater importance to U.S. policy than NPT renewal or export controls is the expression of an unambiguous intention to help U.S. allies defend themselves against regional nuclear predators. Indeed, the directive should make clear a policy determination by the president that a serious effort by the United States and its allies to reduce the military value of small nuclear arsenals is the best means of deterring regional nuclear adversaries from employing their arsenals for political benefit and of dissuading potential proliferators from pursuing the nuclear option. Admittedly, this is a far less ambitious policy than prevention by denial or force. It recognizes that some countries will acquire nuclear arsenals, despite U.S. best efforts. But given the ongoing proliferation of nuclear weapons capabilities, the limited goal is realistic; prevention is not.

THE DEFENSE COMPONENT OF COUNTERPROLIFERATION REQUIRES PLANNING FOR NUCLEAR MRCs

The second and most important step is to convince the allies of the United States that its leaders understand the strategic threat regional nuclear adversaries present to their survival and consider it to be an equivalent threat to U.S. security. The United States must renew the faith of its allies in its promises to assure their security.

The *Bottom-Up Review* constituted the first of three opportunities Secretary Aspin created for the DOD to address the consequences of proliferation for the U.S. military establishment and move forward with programmatic responses. The second was the Counterproliferation Initiative (CPI), an effort initiated in spring 1993 to identify programs that might address the proliferation threat. Some of the CPI's early findings must have been folded into the BUR effort before the report was released in October, but the initiative's results were not announced until Secretary Aspin's December 7 speech.

In his speech, Aspin listed five elements of the DOD's counterproliferation policy: the adoption of counterproliferation as a new DOD "mission," plans to "fight wars differently," plans to change "what we buy to meet the threat," changes in "how we collect intelligence and what intelligence we collect," and "do[ing] all of these things with our allies."[65] Less than two weeks after launching this initiative, Aspin was forced from office. Given the strong tendency in the Clinton administration to downplay the emerging reality of regional nuclear adversaries and the military's preference to downplay the threat of regional nuclear conflicts, the CPI's future is questionable. In the wake of Aspin's resignation, the burden of turning words into action falls on his successor, William J. Perry.

Planning for Nuclear MRCs

Convincing regional allies of the credibility of U.S. security guarantees necessitates a major revision of U.S. operational planning. The United States must be prepared to conduct MRCs under the nuclear gun. The DOD must reanimate policy and operations analysis of the consequences of proliferation for U.S. defense planning. Aspin noted that the department was "preparing guidance for dealing with this new threat—fighting a Desert Storm kind of war with the opponent actually having a handful of nuclear weapons." He also stated that the JCS and regional commanders in chief were "developing a military planning process for dealing with adversaries who have weapons of mass destruction."[66]

The most important near-term response to the regional threat of a small nuclear arsenal is in the area of operational planning. Even as part of a high-priority effort, U.S. military capabilities tailored to the threat may take years to develop and deploy; the threat is here and now. At a minimum, the U.S. military must be able to deny a potential regional nuclear adversary the military advantages that Iraq would have had if its Scuds had been tipped with nuclear warheads.

In future power projection operations, the United States cannot rely on a few local ports and airfields to receive reinforcements as it did in Desert Shield, or as it would today to reinforce South Korea. Nor can it rely on a small number of airfields relatively close to enemy lines to conduct a massive air offensive as it did in Desert Storm, or as it would today to defend South Korea. The survival of any such facility cannot be guaranteed and its loss could be an enormous blow to any U.S. military effort planned along the lines of Desert Shield and Desert Storm. In power projection operations fought under the nuclear shadow, U.S. military planners must seek to limit the importance of any one potential target to the success of the mission and to increase the number of nuclear warheads the adversary must use to destroy that facility.

The objective of these changes to operational planning should be to limit the damage a regional nuclear predator can do to U.S. and allied military capabilities in the theater with its small arsenal, and to deny the adversary the advantages that might accrue to him from first-use early in the conflict. In general terms, the near-term operational response to the new nuclear threat requires

- The dispersal of allied facilities, logistics support, and forces in the theater, in order to reduce the military effect of a successful nuclear attack on any one target.

- An increase in the number of nuclear-hardened facilities such as aircraft shelters, in order to increase the number of warheads required for a successful nuclear strike.

- At least a limited ability to preferentially defend military targets, in order to increase the uncertainties facing an enemy attack planner.

A regional nuclear adversary facing this problem would be unable to do what Iraq might have done if it had possessed a handful of nuclear weapons. Operational planners must ensure that two nuclear weapons in the hands of North Korea are not "militarily significant," as Secretary Perry and Senator Cohen believe they are today.

Acquiring New Means to Defeat a Regional Nuclear Adversary. Aspin also stated that "acquisition . . . has to be readjusted in the light of the new emphasis."[67] In keeping with this admonition, Secretary Perry should reopen the BUR by initiating a thorough study of nuclear MRCs. The results of the revised BUR should inform decisions on changes to force structure and the reallocation of defense resources to accelerated development of military forces specifically designed for regional nuclear contingencies.

In particular, the DOD must begin to redirect substantial defense resources to the research, development, and acquisition of weapon systems that will give U.S. leaders a high-confidence, conventional, damage-limiting capability against regional adversaries. This capability should consist of intelligence collection and analysis systems directed particularly at the location of mobile missiles and concealed facilities, highly responsive and accurate offensive weapon systems to destroy enemy nuclear forces and deeply buried facilities, missile defense systems that in combination permit only a small percentage of warheads to leak through, and the command and control arrangements necessary to coordinate the employment of these systems in time-sensitive operations.

The capability must be of high confidence and damage-limiting because the consequences of nuclear attack are so devastating. Perfection is not possible and probably not necessary to deter regional adversaries from aggression, but the U.S. Air Force must do far better in attacking mobile missile launchers than it did against the Scud carriers during the war with Iraq, and the follow-ons to the U.S. Army's Patriot missile defense must be far more capable of intercepting incoming warheads. The capability must be conventional, because U.S. leaders may be forced to use it in the early hours of a regional war. They should not be self-deterred from using the capability because they or their allies are unwilling to conduct nuclear operations.

Elements of this capability exist in various stages of development in each of the armed services. What is missing from these programs is overall coherence and a sense of urgency. As the *Economist* noted in late 1993, in the area of acquisition, the CPI "is still, as yet, a collection of hitherto disparate ideas rather than big-budget innovations."[68]

A Meaningful Line Item for Counterproliferation. Adequate funding of counterproliferation is a critical issue facing Secretary Perry. The DOD requested only $40 million specifically for counterproliferation in 1994: $9.5 million to support the Defense Technology Security Assistance Agency, $25 million to support improved export control activities in the former Soviet bloc, and $9 million for studies[69]—in short, nothing for the research, development, and acquisition of counterproliferation capabilities described in Secretary Aspin's speech. Indeed, that particular budget request predates Aspin's remarks by months and is largely derivative of the prevention approach to nonproliferation the former secretary decried.

Aspin thought of the $40 million as the first step in developing a serious line item for counterproliferation. "It's just the beginning," he told House

Armed Services Committee chairman Ronald V. Dellums (Democrat of California).[70] Secretary Perry should work to create a meaningful counterproliferation line item for future defense budgets.

A Counterproliferation Organization. The conventional damage-limiting capability must be thought of as a comprehensive system of systems. It needs unified command and control to operate in war. It needs its own concept of operations. It also needs a substantial budget, which, in the current fiscal environment, will have to come from elsewhere in the DOD. This will probably result in further cuts to the traditional force structure of air wings, carrier battle groups, and divisions and will probably be resisted by the military.[71]

To achieve programmatic and budgetary coherence, the secretary of defense must create an organizational structure dedicated to that objective. Currently, responsibility for pulling together the programmatic information on counterproliferation lies with the assistant to the secretary of defense for atomic energy, the official responsible for the reliability of the U.S. nuclear stockpile and the secretary's principal adviser on matters related to nuclear weapons. That arrangement may be appropriate for information gathering, but the assistant's charter is too narrow to cover development of the conventional damage-limiting capability.

A better option would be to reorient the staff and resources once devoted to the Strategic Defense Initiative and now to the reduced Ballistic Missile Defense Organization (BMDO) to this new mission, under the leadership of someone with the confidence of the secretary, Congress, and the uniformed military. An even more radical option, suggested by Roger Molander, would be to merge the activities and resources of the BMDO and the Defense Nuclear Agency to create a Defense Strategic Weapons Agency. This new agency would combine the DOD's sources of technological and organizational expertise most relevant to development of counterproliferation capabilities.

Reinterpreting the ABM Treaty. Secretary Aspin noted that development of the defensive portion of the damage-limiting capability requires a reinterpretation of the Antiballistic Missile (ABM) Treaty.[72] That artifact of the Cold War prohibited the development of systems capable of intercepting strategic missile payloads under the guise of "theater" missile defense programs in order to close off a "back door" route to nationwide strategic missile defenses, thus maintaining the condition of mutual assured destruction between the superpowers and containing their arms race. To limit the damage from such medium-range ballistic missiles as North Korea's Nodong, ballistic missile defense systems must be developed to specifications that give them capabilities against some classes of former Soviet submarine-launched ballistic missiles. The Clinton administration is contemplating changes in its interpretation of the treaty's requirements that would allow one such system—the Theater High-Altitude

Area Defense—to be developed and deployed beginning in 1996.[73] The political conditions that underlay the ABM treaty no longer exist, and Secretary Perry should push the administration to change its interpretation of the treaty, preferably with the approval of the nuclear successor states of the former Soviet Union, but without their leave if necessary.

Reevaluating the Role of U.S. Nuclear Forces. The third opportunity Secretary Aspin created for the DOD to address the consequences of proliferation for the U.S. military establishment and move forward with programmatic responses is the Nuclear Policy Review, a reexamination of the U.S. nuclear posture initiated in fall 1993. Unfortunately, it appears that this effort will examine nuclear proliferation only to the extent that it has implications for U.S. nuclear forces.[74] Work on the CPI should be coordinated with the Nuclear Policy Review to ensure that the United States has the combination of nuclear and conventional weapons programs necessary to counter the regional nuclear threat. The critical problems cutting across the two efforts are the extent to which conventional defense can serve as a military and political substitute for nuclear deterrence in the perception of U.S. adversaries and allies and, to the extent it cannot, a definition of the nuclear forces required to meet U.S. extended deterrence commitments. As discussed below, this analysis should be a joint venture with U.S. allies.

THE DIPLOMACY OF COUNTERPROLIFERATION IS COLLECTIVE DEFENSE

Developing U.S. military capabilities that improve prospects of U.S. victory in nuclear MRCs is only part of the answer to nuclear proliferation. Reorienting the alliances of the United States to address the consequences of proliferation should be seen as a crucial task of U.S. diplomacy in the coming years. To reassure its allies of its commitment to their security, the United States must reconsider—from a political perspective—the matter of forward presence and the extent to which conventional deterrence can substitute for nuclear deterrence.

The allies must be intimately involved in this review, for only they can judge what kind of local U.S. military presence will meet their needs and whether they prefer the threat of nuclear retaliation to aggression to the promise of Desert Storm. Certainly the United States cannot allow its allies to blackmail it into protecting them by even an implicit threat to go nuclear, nor can it afford to bear the brunt of the financial burden as it did throughout the Cold War. But it must recognize that its allies will respond to the nuclear threat posed by regional adversaries or unstable neighbors. If the United States does not accept their problem as its own, the allies will be forced to go it alone.

Sharing the Risk of Regional Nuclear Conflict. For the United States to accept the allies' problem as its own demands more than declaring a state of "deterrence" that is somehow inherent in the mere existence of the U.S. strategic nuclear arsenal. The fact that the United States is capable of utterly destroying any of its regional nuclear adversaries is well known to Iraq, Iran, and North Korea. It did not deter them from pursuing their nuclear arsenals. The United States must take active measures to dispel any perception they may have that by threatening a regional nuclear war they can separate the United States from its allies.

Thus, a successful counterproliferation policy requires more than a theoretical ability to dominate the escalation ladder. It requires that the United States share the risk of war with its allies in such a way that both they and U.S. regional adversaries are convinced that the United States is unequivocally committed to allied defense. Conceptualizing this structure and seeing that it is implemented is a task that combines diplomacy and defense analysis. As noted above, the United States was highly successful in building a physical and organizational structure of collective defense during the Cold War that deterred its adversaries and reassured its allies. Finding a way of recreating the character of that commitment to allies and giving it physical qualities should be the central focus of U.S. alliance institutions in the post–Cold War era.

Joint Development of Counterproliferation Capabilities. Part of the answer probably lies in collective development and deployment of the high-confidence, conventional, damage-limiting capability, building on the theater ballistic missile defense systems Secretary Aspin proposed to NATO, South Korea, and Japan in November 1993, and again at NATO in December.[75] Commenting on the possibility of joint development in his December 7 speech, Aspin recognized that U.S. "allies and security partners around the world have as much to be concerned about in these areas as we do."[76] Aspin also emphasized the economies of an alliance initiative during his visit to NATO.

The advantage of cooperation, of course, is that it reduces the cost to any one member but is able to spread the benefits. . . . We could cooperate, for example on research and development in methods to counter weapons of mass destruction, we could cooperate on intelligence efforts, we could cooperate on missile defense.[77]

Secretary Perry should continue the push for joint activities, because it makes U.S. expressions of allied solidarity concrete.

Theater Nuclear Forces. Part of the answer also may lie in maintaining some U.S. theater nuclear capability that can be deployed to allied territory in time of crisis and over which U.S. and allied political authorities would share control.[78] Such a deployment could send a strong message to a potential military foe that the United States and its ally are unified in their resolve to resist nuclear intimidation. It would also give a regional nuclear adversary pause if it knew that its local opponent also had access to nuclear weapons. And the option raises the specter of a proportionate retaliation in kind. Perhaps allied

planning for the deployment of theater nuclear warheads to bolster deterrence against nuclear predator states ought to begin. Whatever its form, effective reassurance requires the United States to shoulder real risks on behalf of its allies.

SUMMARY AND CONCLUSION

The threat posed by North Korea's ballistic missile and nuclear weapons programs offers U.S. policy makers insights into an emerging reality. Efforts to deny even minor, isolated countries nuclear weapons capabilities are becoming problematic as the world catches up to the level of technological sophistication achieved by the United States in the 1950s and 1960s, the sources of nuclear weapons-related supplies expand, and modern dual-use technologies become a ubiquitous feature of the global economy. Similarly, there is little reason to believe in the efficacy of forcible nonproliferation. For military and political reasons, the prospects of destroying even a small nuclear weapons program before it yields a nuclear arsenal are not good. As a result, small survivable arsenals of nuclear weapons in the hands of regional adversaries are likely to become an important obstacle to U.S. military operations in the post–Cold War world.

There is little evidence that the United States takes this new threat seriously. The Clinton administration has largely denied the emerging reality of regional nuclear adversaries with high-minded statements about an international "norm" of nonproliferation, stern warnings to those who violate the norm, tough talk about military strikes on nascent nuclear arsenals, and redefinitions of nonproliferation that accommodate the actuality of ongoing proliferation.

The U.S. military has largely cooperated in this refusal to accept the possibility of regional nuclear war because of an assessment that nuclear weapons are an obsolete vestige of the Cold War. The only serious statement that the U.S. military establishment might actually have to be prepared to fight regional nuclear adversaries has been former Secretary of Defense Les Aspin's December 7 speech to the National Academy of Sciences. Little has been said on the matter before or since those remarks.

The outcome of this refusal to face the emerging reality of regional nuclear adversaries is that the United States is not preparing seriously for the possibility of having to fight in a regional nuclear war. If it continues down this path, it will be unable to cope with the potential threat of nuclear aggression against its allies. If it cannot ensure the security of its allies against this threat, the result is likely to be further proliferation among these allies, highly unstable regional military situations, a severe reduction of the United States' international influence, and a growing probability of regional nuclear wars involving U.S. forces.

Proliferation by regional allies of the United States is not inevitable. If it first recognizes that the threat of regional nuclear war threatens its own survival in ways no less meaningful than the threat presented to its allies by the Soviets and then convinces its allies that it understands this fact, the United States can dissuade them from deciding to follow their regional adversaries down the nuclear path. If the United States takes these steps, it has some hope of steering its way safely through the uncertain times ahead.

U.S. policy should embrace Aspin's analysis of the proliferation problem. It should proceed from the assumption that the United States will face several regional nuclear adversaries in the next decade, emphasize the need to reassure regional allies that the best counter to this threat lies in collective defense arrangements with the United States, and give regional nuclear conflict high priority in U.S. military planning. This approach would reduce the prospect of proliferation by regional allies of the United States, improve regional military stability, maintain U.S. influence, and reduce the chances of U.S. military forces being dragged into a regional nuclear conflict. Turning Aspin's words into action requires a serious effort on the part of Secretary Perry, and even his efforts will be effective only if President Clinton changes national policy.

NOTES

I would like to thank Marten Van Heuven, Jonathan Pollack, Chris Bowie, Paul Davis, and Brad Roberts for their comments on earlier drafts of this essay. I would also like to thank Roger Molander and Peter Wilson for the many hours of spirited debate that drove me to write it. The views expressed here are mine and are not intended to reflect those of The RAND Corporation or any of its sponsors.

NOTES

1. "Remarks of Defense Secretary Les Aspin to the National Academy of Sciences Committee on International Security and Arms Control," Federal News Service. 7 December 1993, available in LEXIS. Nexis Library, Current News File. The speech was entitled "The Defense Department's New Nuclear Counterproliferation Initiative: Dealing with the Spread of Weapons of Mass Destruction in the Post–Cold War, Post-Soviet Era."

2. John Dunn, "The Ukrainian Nuclear Weapons Debate," Jane's Intelligence Review (August 1993): 339–42.

3. "United States Will Not Have Veto Power in New Export Control Regime, Official Says," International Trade Reporter, Current Reports, 17 November 1993, 1923; Jack Kelley, "Nuclear Program in the Works," USA Today, 4 January 1994, 6.

4. Mark Matthews and Charles Corddry, "U.S. Warns North Korea over Nukes," Baltimore Sun, 18 November, 1993, 1 (quoting Gates).

5. Jon Swain and James Adams, "Kim Goes to Brink on Frontier of Hate," Sunday Times (London), 21 March 1993 (quoting Woolsey).

6. Stephen Engelberg with Michael Gordon, "Intelligence Study Says North Korea Has Nuclear Bomb," New York Times, 26 December 1993, 1.

7. "Newsmaker," MacNeill Lehrer News Hour, Educational Broadcasting and GWETA, 7 December 1993, Tuesday Transcript no. 4814, available in LEXIS, Nexis Library, Current News File.

8. "Hearing of the Senate Armed Services Committee: Confirmation of William Perry to be Secretary of Defense," Federal News Service, 2 February, 1994, available in LEXIS, Nexis Library, Current News File.

9. See Paul Beaver, "Nodong-1 Details Fuel New Fears in Asia," Jane's Defence Weekly, 15 January, 1994, 4; John Fialka, "Check of North Korea Nuclear Sites Won't Provide Comfort Clinton Wants," Wall Street Journal, 31 January 1994, 14.

10. "Remarks by Defense Secretary Les Aspin."

11. "Hearing of the Senate Armed Services Committee: The START Treaty and the US–Russia Joint Understanding on Further Reductions in Strategic Offensive Arms," Federal News Service, 28 July 1992, available in LEXIS, Nexis Library, Current News File.

12. Kevin Rafferty, "Iran and North Korea 'to Test Missile,'" Guardian (Manchester), 26 October 1993, 20.

13. "Hearing of the House Foreign Affairs Committee, Foreign Military Aid," Federal News Service, 4 March 1992, available in LEXIS, Nexis Library, Current News File.

14. "Remarks by Defense Secretary Les Aspin."

15. Technology for Economic Growth: President's Progress Report (Washington, D.C.: The White House, November 1993).

16. Ibid., 34–35.

17. "Mixed Signals on Proliferation," Middle East Defense News, 22 March 1993 (quoting Perry).

18. Henry Sokolski, "Unseen Dangers in China," Armed Forces Journal International, February 1994, 25; Andrew Lawler, "Lawmakers Rap Clinton's Policy on Missile Sales," Defense News, 10 October 1993, 3; "U.S. Will Continue to Ease Export Controls on China Despite Nuclear Test, Official Says," International Trade Reporter, Current Reports, 13 October 1993, 1709; John Mintz, "The Satellite Makers' China Card: Martin Marietta Warns U.S. Sales Ban Will Cause Massive Layoffs," Washington Post, 20 October 1993, C-11; Elaine Sciolino. "U.S. Will Court China in a Sale of Big Computer," New York Times, 19 November 1993, 1.

19. "Remarks by President Bill Clinton and Vice President Al Gore to a Group of Business CEO's." Federal News Service, 29 September 1993, available in LEXIS, Nexis Library, Current News File.

20. "Remarks by Defense Secretary Les Aspin."

21. "Heritage Foundation Asian Studies Center Panel Discussion: Missile and Nuclear Weapons Proliferation in East Asia," Federal News Service, 24 June 1991, available in LEXIS, Nexis Library, Current News Library.

22. Ronald A. Taylor, "Clinton: U.S. Will Block Nukes Abroad," Washington Times, 18 May 1993, 3 (quoting Clinton).

23. This approach is most openly taken by those with a long-standing interest in the cause of nonproliferation. A typical example is "NPT 1995: Time to Shift Gears," an article in the November 1993 issue of Arms Control Today by Lewis Dunn, a former assistant director of the Arms Control and Disarmament Agency, and U.S. ambassador to

the 1985 NPT Review Conference. Assessing the effectiveness of the NPT, Dunn wrote: "The overall record is very good and getting better, but not untarnished" (p. 15). China's unwillingness to adopt tight export controls, and the position of North Korea, Ukraine, India, and Pakistan are referred to as "wild cards," as exceptions to the rule, and certainly not indications of any trend (p. 17).

24. "Heritage Foundation . . . Missile and Nuclear Weapons Proliferation in East Asia."

25. Martin Walker and Kevin Rafferty, "U.S. Warns Off North Korea," *Guardian*, 8 November 1993 (quoting Clinton).

26. Matthews and Corddry, "U.S. Warns North Korea over Nukes."

27. Quoted in Carl P. Leubsdorf, "Clinton Somber about Impasse on N. Korea Nuclear Program," *Dallas Morning News*, 9 December 1993, 1-A.

28. "Broadcast Interview with Defense Department Personnel," Federal News Service, 11 December 1993, available in LEXIS, Nexis Library, Current News File.

29. The concept of forcible denuclearization may go well beyond rhetoric. Major General Robert Linhard, director of plans and policy at the Strategic Command, is an important player in the development of military responses to proliferation. In an unclassified briefing given at a conference on emerging nuclear actors against the backdrop of the escalating crisis with North Korea, and drawing on administration statements as potential guidance, he identified "rollback of proliferation where it has occurred" as one of the DOD's "counterproliferation objectives." Linhard noted the department's "unique responsibility to develop plans/options involving direct military action, especially preemptive military action." These military options would support political objectives including to "punish illegal proliferation and eliminate acquired capabilities" and "preemptively destroy capabilities." Among the administration pronouncements Lindhard drew on was a statement made by Secretary of State Warren Christopher in January 1993. In it, the secretary outlined a general approach to nonproliferation in which "we must work assiduously with other nations to discourage proliferation through improved intelligence export controls incentives, sanctions, and even force when necessary." Robert Linhard, "Counterproliferation Strategies," in *Counterproliferation: Deterring Emerging Nuclear Actors*, Proceedings of the Strategic Options Assessments Conference (Offutt AFB, Nebraska, 7–8 July 1993), Appendix A (briefing charts).

30. Barton Gellman, "Trepidation at Root of U.S. Korea Policy; Conventional War Seen Catastrophic for South," *Washington Post*, 12 December 1993, A-1 (quoting the Defense Intelligence Agency monograph, "North Korea: The Foundations for Military Strength").

31. Swain and Adams, "Kim Goes to Brink on Frontier of Hate."

32. Secretary of State Christopher suggested as much on ABC television on 21 November when he cautioned that Israel's raid on Osirak might be "too easy an analogy" to possible strikes on Youngbyon. David Sanger, "U.S. Revising North Korea Strategy," *New York Times*, 22 November 1993, 5. General Merrill McPeak, chief of staff of the air force, told reporters that "a preemptive attack would not be totally successful, because American intelligence could not

locate North Korea's hidden caches of plutonium and because attacks on North Korea's . . . nuclear reactor core with conventional bombs could cause radioactive pollution." Quoted in Michael Gordon, "Pentagon Begins Effort to Combat More Lethal Arms in Third World," *New York Times,* 8 December 1993, 15. But McPeak was even more concerned about the conventional defense of South Korea. "The worst nightmare," he said, "is that Seoul would come under attack almost immediately. . . . I just can't answer whether we could stop them before they got to Seoul or not." Quoted in Gellman, "Trepidation at Root of U.S. Korea Policy."

33. Thomas L. Friedman, "U.S. and Seoul Differ on Offer to North," *New York Times*, 2 November 1993, A-16.

34. Steven Greenhouse, "U.S. Backs Off on Atomic Sites in North Korea," *New York Times*, 5 January 1994, A-1.

35. Lynn Davis, "Korea: No Capitulation," *Washington Post*, 26 January 1994, A-21.

36. John J. Fialka, "Check of North Korean Nuclear Sites Won't Provide Comfort Clinton Wants," *Wall Street Journal*, 31 January 1994, 14 (quoting Davis).

37. On February 15, after some stalling, the North once again agreed to IAEA inspection of its seven declared sites, but not of the suspect sites so important to determining whether the North has been developing nuclear weapons. Carol J. Williams and Jim Mann, "N. Korea Agrees to Inspection of 7 Nuclear Sites," *Los Angeles Times*, 26 February 1994, 1.

38. "No North Korean Bomb?" *Washington Post*, 6 January 1994, A-16.

39. "Hearing of the House Foreign Affairs Committee, Foreign Military Aid," Federal News Service, 4 March 1992, available in LEXIS, Nexis Library, Current News File.

40. Les Aspin, "From Deterrence to Denuking: Dealing with Proliferation in the 1990s" (monograph), 18 February 1992, 5.

41. "Remarks by Defense Secretary Les Aspin."

42. Ibid.

43. The results of this research are documented in Marc Dean Millot, Roger Molander, and Peter A. Wilson, *"The Day After . . ." Study: Nuclear Proliferation in the Post–Cold War World*, vol. 1, *Summary Report* (MR-266-AF); vol. 2, *Main Report* (MR-253-AF); vol. 3, *Exercise Materials* (MR-254-AF) (Santa Monica, Calif.: RAND, 1993).

44. Ibid., vol. 2, 39–110, esp. 69–70, 109; and vol. 3. At least one former senior civilian official also appears to accept this line of argument. See Paul H. Nitze, "Is It Time to Junk Our Nukes?" *Washington Post*, 16 January 1994, C-1.

45. "Defense Writers Group Breakfast Meeting," Federal News Service, 23 September 1993, available in LEXIS, Nexis Library, Current News File.

46. "Joint Chiefs of Staff Chairman Gen. Colin Powell Address Sponsored by American University's Kennedy Political Union," Reuters Transcript Record, 1 December 1992, available in LEXIS, Nexis Library, Current News File.

47. Stephen Budiansky and Bruce Auster, "Tackling the New Nuclear Arithmetic," *U.S. News and World Report*, 20 January 1992, 38.

48. Les Aspin, *Report on the Bottom-Up Review* (Washington, D.C.: Department of Defense, October 1993) (hereinafter referred to as BUR).

49. On some of the problems of "Scud-hunting" see Rick Atkinson, *Crusade: The Untold Story of the Persian Gulf War* (Boston, Mass.: Houghton Mifflin, 1993), 145–48.

50. On the debate over Patriot operations see "Playing Patriot Games," *U.S. News and World Report,* 22 November 1993, 16.

51. "President Bill Clinton Addresses the General Assembly of the United Nations, the United Nations, New York," Federal News Service, 27 September 1993, available in LEXIS, Nexis Library, Current News File.

52. "Hearing of the Senate Armed Services Committee; Confirmation of William Perry to be Secretary of Defense."

53. "Clinton to Complete '95 Budget Meetings with Cabinet, Agency Heads by This Week." Daily Report for Executives (Washington, D.C.: Bureau of National Affairs, 13 December 1993), A-237.

54. Selig S. Harrison, "A Yen for the Bomb?" *Washington Post,* 31 October 1993, C-2.

55. Nick Rufford, "Japan to 'Go Nuclear' in Asian Arms Race," *Sunday Times* (London), 30 January 1994, 1.

56. See generally, Harrison, "A Yen for the Bomb?"

57. Andrew Pollack, "Japan Launches Rocket, Cutting Reliance on U.S.," *New York Times,* 4 February 1994, A-17.

58. See Ken Adelman, "The Nuclear Domino Threat," *Washington Times,* 20 October 1993, 21.

59. The comment concerning the outcome of another Korean conflict attributed to General Gary Luck, a veteran of the war with Iraq and commander of U.S. forces in Korea, that "I can win a war, I just can't do it right away" is unlikely to make South Koreans feel more secure. Gellman, "Trepidation at Root of U.S. Korean Policy."

60. Friedman, "U.S. and Seoul Differ on Offer to North."

61. The headline of the newspaper article on the trip read, "Seoul's Big Fear: Pushing North Koreans Too Far," as a North Korean buildup along the demilitarized zone reportedly placed 70 percent of its forces within range of the South. David Sanger, *New York Times,* 7 November 1993, 16. See also R. Jeffrey Smith, "North Korea Bolsters Border Force," *Washington Post,* 6 November 1993, 19.

62. See James G. Blight and David A. Welch, *On the Brink: Americans and Soviets Reexamine the Cuban Missile Crisis* (New York: Hill and Wang, 1989). One interesting means of accessing this record is the *Cold War International History Project Bulletin* (Woodrow Wilson International Center for Scholars, Washington, D.C.). For example, the fall 1993 issue contains a fascinating debate over the extent of the local Soviet military commander's authority to initiate the use of nuclear weapons in Cuba during the missile crisis.

63. "State Department Regular Briefing," Federal News Service, 8 December 1993, available in LEXIS, Nexis Library, Current News File.

64. Indeed, this appears to be the likely outcome of the multilateral talks to replace the West's export control Coordinating Committee (COCOM) with a regime (including the former Soviet Republics) to control the spread of technologies associated with weapons of mass destruction. "Eagleburger Says Allied Pressure Will Force End to COCOM Relatively Soon," *International Trade Reporter, Current Reports,* 29 September 1993, 1609. In her November 1993 testimony to Congress, Undersecretary Davis noted that the United States had been unable to retain the right of COCOM members to veto proposed exports. "United States Will Not Have Veto Power," 1923. Members of the new system will be able to approve exports after notifying the other members. Consequently, export controls are likely to be a marginal component of counterproliferation.

65. "Remarks by Defense Secretary Les Aspin."

66. Ibid.

67. Ibid.

68. "Cold War II," *Economist,* 11–17 December 1993, 29.

69. Statement of Walter B. Slocombe, principal deputy undersecretary of defense (policy), before the Senate Armed Services Committee hearing on Arms Control Treaty Verification, Nunn-Lugar Programs, and Counterproliferation, 23 June 1993 (mimeograph), 26.

70. "Hearing of the House Armed Services Committee, Fiscal Year 1994 Defense Authorization Bill," Federal News Service, 30 March 1993, available in LEXIS, Nexis Library, Current News File.

71. For one example of the continuing competition between the services over a more integrated defense against ballistic missiles see "Army Stands by Status Quo for Its Role in Air Defense," *Defense Daily,* 5 November 1993, 195.

72. "Remarks by Defense Secretary Les Aspin."

73. Jeffrey Smith, "Officials Say U.S. Wants to Change ABM Treaty to Buttress Missile Defense," *Washington Post,* 4 December 1994, A-22.

74. "Press Briefing with Secretary of Defense Les Aspin; Ash Carter, Assistant Secretary of Defense for Counter-Proliferation; Lieutenant General Barry McCaffery Regarding Defense Nuclear Posture Review, The Pentagon," Federal News Service, 29 October 1993, available in LEXIS, Nexis Library, Current News File.

75. See generally, "Aspin Pitches TMD to Japanese, S. Koreans," *BMD Monitor,* 5 November 1993, 297.

76. "Remarks by Defense Secretary Les Aspin."

77. Charles Aldinger, "Aspin Urges Allies to Develop New Nuclear Defenses," Reuters, 9 December 1993, available in LEXIS, Nexis Library, Current News File.

78. In remarks before the Indianapolis Press Club on 6 December, which were subsequently broadcast on C-SPAN, Senator Richard G. Lugar (Republican of Indiana) proposed a return of U.S. nuclear artillery shells to South Korea. On 1 February 1994, the Senate passed a nonbinding amendment to State Department legislation, urging the United States to "enhance the defense capability of United States forces by preparing to reintroduce tactical nuclear weapons in South Korea," if the North refused to submit to inspections. "Senate Calls For Isolation Of North Korea," Reuters, 1 February 1994, available in LEXIS, Nexis Library, Current News File.

CHAPTER 17

CIVIL–MILITARY RELATIONS

THE POLITICAL DIMENSION OF MILITARY PROFESSIONALISM

JOHN H. GARRISON

Since the mid-1960s the military profession in America has been faced with a crisis of identity and purpose. At first dimly perceived, but coming into sharper focus since 1968, this crisis centers upon two grossly general questions about the nature of the profession: "What are we to be?" and "What are we to do?" The first of these two questions concerns itself with the substance of military professionalism—the attributes, characteristics, and attitudes of the professional soldier. What are they? What should they be? The second question—"What are we to do?"—concerns itself with the functions of the military profession—the missions assigned, the tasks performed, the actions undertaken. What are they and what should they be?

The very crisis nature of the issue indicates that there is less than unanimous agreement, both within and outside of the military, about the answers to these crucial questions. This has led to much soul-searching and a large amount of self-criticism within the profession itself. In rather general terms, opinion within the military seems to have crystallized around two basically different positions. One is a traditionalist view that sees the profession as having quite narrow, well-defined boundaries that restrict it to purely military qualities, attitudes, and functions. The second is a more contemporary or modernist view that defines the profession in terms of much wider, less well-defined boundaries encompassing a variety of different attributes, concerns, and activities beyond the purely military. These schools of thought are known by many names: Traditionalist/Modernist, Separatist/Fusionist, Professional Soldier/Soldier-Statesman, and the like. No matter how they are labeled, these two positions are quite contradictory in their views on many issues and aspects of military professionalism. And none is more contradictory than their interpretation of the proper political dimension of the profession.

TRADITIONAL VIEW

The traditional view of the American military profession is perhaps most clearly stated in Samuel Huntington's classic work *The Soldier and the State.* Written in 1956, this book was the first modern scholarly examination of the profession of arms in America, and as such it became something of a benchmark against which more recent studies have been compared.

One of Huntington's central theses is that the true American professional military ethic is a peculiar product of the years of extreme military isolation and rejection from American society between the Civil War and World War I:

> The very isolation and rejection which reduced the size of the services and hampered technological advance made these same years the most fertile, creative, and formative in the history of the American armed forces. . . . Withdrawing into its own hard shell, the officer corps was able and permitted to develop a distinctive military character. The American military profession, its institutions and its ideals, is fundamentally a product of these years.[1]

A basic tenet of the traditional professional military ethic that emerged from this period is the belief that the professional soldier is, and should be, apolitical—above politics. Politics and officership do not mix; there exists between military affairs and politics a sharp, clear line that must be observed and maintained! (It might be added that the traditionalist belief in a sharp, distinct division between war and diplomacy is a logical corollary to this apolitical view.)

This attitude had as its founder and strongest proponent General William T. Sherman, commanding general of the army from 1869 to 1883. Sherman was adamant in stressing the complete separation of the military from politics; he is quoted by Huntington as stating that the principle should be to "keep the Army and Navy as free from politics as possible," and that "no Army officer should form or express an opinion" on party politics. A contemporary of Sherman's, Rear Admiral Stephen B. Luce, fostered the same apolitical tradition in the navy during the immediate post–Civil War years.[2]

In summarizing the traditional view of the relationship between the military profession and politics, it is useful to once again examine *The Soldier and the State.* Describing various attributes of the professional military ethic, Huntington states:

This essay has been edited and is reprinted from American Defense Policy, 6th ed., *Schuyler Foerster and Edward N. Wright, eds. (Baltimore: Johns Hopkins University Press, 1990), 606–13, by permission of Johns Hopkins University Press.*

Politics deal with the goals of state policy. Competence in this field consists in having a broad awareness of the elements and interests entering into a decision and in possessing the legitimate authority to make such a decision. Politics is beyond the scope of military competence, and the participation of military officers in politics undermines their professionalism, curtailing their professional competence, dividing the profession against itself, and substituting extraneous values for professional values. The military officer must remain neutral politically.[3]

TOWARD POLITICAL INVOLVEMENT

This belief that professional officers should be apolitical or above politics was almost universally accepted within the profession from Sherman's day up until World War II. However, the situation began to change under the pressures of waging a truly global conflict. The leading wartime military commanders—George C. Marshall, William Leahy, Henry Arnold, Ernest King, David D. Eisenhower, Douglas MacArthur—were drawn into extensive political involvement, including the making of the highest national policies relative to war production, surrender terms, zones of occupation, and the governing of occupied territories.

This trend continued into the post–World War II period as America was confronted with a drastically changed international environment, with a revolutionary and frightening threat posed by nuclear weapons and long-range delivery vehicles, and ultimately with the Cold War. American foreign policy became very concerned with national security considerations, and as Professor Sam Sarkesian of Loyola University (and a retired army officer) states, "The preoccupation with national security and a proper defense posture stimulated the growth of a vast defense establishment and concomitant political power and involvement in the political process."[4] In the years after the end of World War II, military men bore much of the responsibility for the reconstruction of Germany and Japan; administered many U.S. economic and social programs overseas, moved into key positions in Washington's extensive foreign policy establishment, began representing the United States and dealing with foreign powers as members of military assistance missions, defended administration defense budget requests before Congress, and generally began actively to seek public support for a strong defense establishment.

Most of these activities continued, and expanded, from the late 1940s on into the 1970s. And as this political involvement by military men persisted, a different view of the relationship between the military profession and politics gradually emerged to challenge the traditional apolitical standard. Huntington identified this new attitude as early as 1956, calling it "political-military fusion," the idea that military considerations could no longer be realistically separated from political considerations.[5] However, it has only been in the last ten years or so that this view has come to compete seriously and openly (within the military) with the long-standing apolitical image.

This more recent and drastically different approach has been given many labels—"political soldiers," "soldier-statesmen," and "military policy advisers," to name just a few. They all stem, however, from Huntington's concept of "fusionism." This theme has appeared with increasing regularity in recent works, authored by civilians and military men alike, discussing civil–military relations and contemporary military professionalism. It has become quite common to see assertions that "military and nonmilitary factors in national security policy are so closely interrelated that they may be thought of as inseparable," "the traditional distinction between civil and military affairs has become quite tenuous," and "there are no purely political or military solutions to our national problems."[6] One of the clearest statements of this "fusionist" view of the relationship between the military profession and politics has been offered by Sarkesian:

The nature of professionalism in the U.S. military is undergoing significant change under the impact of changing domestic and international forces. . . . To the [traditional] professional concept of manager-technician, and the diminished heroic leader role, must now be added the political dimension, since the pressures of the new forces require political skills and responses. . . .

The military in the United States, although steeped in professionalism, has a political dimension which needs to be recognized if the military is to serve national security goals and if effective civilian control is to be maintained.[7]

The key to understanding this approach, however, lies not only in recognizing that the political dimension exists but also in accepting this dimension as a proper one for the military profession. Advocates of the "political soldier" school enthusiastically welcome this interpretation as both necessary and fitting. Professor Sarkesian's assessment is indicative of this attitude: "Professionalism must now incorporate considerations of political skills as part of the individual role, and political effectiveness as part of institutional patterns. In other words, a new military ethos is developing which is a manifestation of an emergent military whose institutional role and professional status are tempered by political consciousness."[8] Rather naturally, this also leads to a belief by such advocates that professional officers must attain greater political sophistication and training in order that they may better understand and participate in the political as well as the military aspects of national defense. Colonel Don Bletz, U.S. Army, represents a sizable number of middle-grade officers from all services who adhere to this view. Writing in *Military Review* in 1971, Colonel Bletz summarized this thinking quite clearly:

Military professionals must fully accept the fact that military force can only be a means to an end and that end is, in the final analysis, the eventual resolution of some political problem. . . .

It is not suggested that the military officer develop the same type of expertise as his civilian colleague [in the Foreign Service]. . . . However, [military professionals] must be fully capable of participating in the formulation and implementation of viable politico-military policies by appropriate weighting of the dynamic politico-military equation.[9]

Although many military professionals have accepted the idea of "political-military fusion," it must be said that there is less than complete agreement among all interested parties, military and civilian, as to the desirability of this political dimension of the profession. There is a great deal of controversy and disagreement between followers of the traditional, apolitical approach and supporters of the "political soldier" school. Most who think it is undesirable for the professional officer to become practiced and involved in politics do so for one (or both) of two reasons: there is concern that such activity will dilute the unique *military* expertise and qualities of the professional, thereby degrading the essential *military* capabilities of the profession, and second, there is fear that such activity will threaten civilian control of the military by making it possible for military men to have excessive influence or control over defense and foreign policy.

Many supporters of the traditional view, desirous of an apolitical military, proceed from the belief that there are certain qualities, skills, and attitudes that are essentially military and are, in fact, necessary for the effective accomplishment of the purely military tasks required of the armed forces. These qualities, skills, and attitudes are not only essential, they are quite difficult and demanding, focusing as they do upon armed combat. Maintaining these attributes and capabilities in a high state of readiness is a constant and time-consuming job. From this point, the argument leads to the conclusion that the time and effort spent by professional officers preparing for, or actively involved in, other lessor nonessential functions (such as political activity) reduce the readiness and effectiveness of the profession in its primary mission area—combat.

The second line of reasoning, the fear of the usurpation of civilian control, is somewhat less rigorous, and more emotional, in its development. It really stems from the long-standing fear of excessive and unchecked military power in American society, dating from colonial times. The principle of firm and constant civilian control of the military, generally understood to mean ultimate and complete subordination of the armed forces to elected and appointed federal government officials, has been upheld as the necessary safeguard against such an eventuality. Critics of the "political soldier" school of thought believe that this essential civilian control can be (will be? is being?) circumvented or subverted by the greater involvement of the military in political activities. According to this argument, such involvement can lead (will lead? is leading?) to the military, rather than their civilian masters, determining how, where, when, and with what resources the armed forces of the United States will be used—to the potential (possible? actual?) detriment or danger of the rest of society.

THE MEANING OF "POLITICS"

Any useful assessment of these two approaches—traditional and fusionist—to the military profession and its relationship with politics must really include some discussion of the meaning of that term "politics" as it applies to military professionalism. In general, as understood and used by the traditional school, "politics" refers to partisanship. As has already been mentioned, being apolitical means, in General Sherman's words, that "no Army officer should form or express an opinion" on party politics. Or, as Professor Huntington put it, the professional officer must maintain strict political neutrality, refusing to become embroiled in partisan questions of who will be elected or what party's proposals will be supported.[10] In his landmark book *The Professional Soldier*, Morris Janowitz concisely supports this interpretation, explaining that "under democratic theory, the 'above politics' formula requires that, in domestic politics, generals, and admirals do not attach themselves to political parties or overtly display partisanship." He goes on to say, "In practice, with only isolated exceptions, regulations and traditions have worked to enforce an essential absence of political partisanship."[11]

This assessment of the effectiveness of the "above politics" formula is widely held to be true. The military profession and its professionals in America have remained remarkably free from partisan party politics. Since World War II, the relatively few instances where individual professional officers, almost invariably retired, have sought political office (the most prominent examples being MacArthur, Eisenhower, Edwin Walker, Curtis LeMay, and Elmo Zumwalt) have been exceptions rather than the rule. And in no instance, whether involving a military man or a civilian, has the military profession as an organization involved itself in a partisan contest for political office.

However, partisanship is not the only meaning of the term "politics" applicable to the military. The noted political scientist, David Easton, provided a definition of politics more than twenty years ago that has come to be one of the most widely accepted in the field of social science. Easton said that politics is "the authoritative allocation of values,"[12] where values are simply anything valued by society, such as resources (money, raw materials, manpower, etc.), power, or prestige. The process of determining how such things of value will be allocated among competing segments of society, and doing so in a way that is accepted as legitimate (though not necessarily desirable) by society as a whole, is the process of politics. Every day, decisions are made by government officials concerning policy choices, budget expenditures, and program implementation that are all, in fact, authoritative value allocations. Put very simply, then, politics is nothing more than the process of determining who in society gets what!

If the term "politics" is understood in this light, it is quite obvious that the military is involved. The military profession, as an organization, is most certainly involved in the process of determining how the federal government and American society will allocate values. Military professionals are participants in this process as advisers to political decision makers, as advocates of particular policy alternatives, as implementers of final political decisions, and even as decision makers themselves. Every time a military leader determines, from the military point of view, that a particular weapon system (or force level, or foreign commitment, etc.) is advisable or required for the nation's security, he is helping to determine how the nation's financial, material, and manpower resources will be allocated. It is not really important that this military leader is not often the final decision maker on the issue. Even as adviser, or as nothing more than implementer of the decision, he influences the outcome—and that is politics!

INEVITABILITY OF POLITICAL INVOLVEMENT

According to these two, distinct meanings of the term "politics," it is clear that the military profession has not been and is not now involved in politics of the partisan party politics variety. It is also quite clear that the military profession is deeply involved in politics in terms of decision making or value allocation politics.

This type of involvement was probably inevitable! At least, it was probably inevitable given the combination of two circumstances—the constitutional provisions for civilian control of the military that were established more than 185 years ago, and the massive growth in the size, responsibilities, and functions of the federal government since the 1940s, particularly in the field of international relations. These two factors have combined to establish patterns of political interaction and pressures for involvement that in all likelihood made military participation in the political decision-making process inevitable.

As has already been mentioned, the concept of civilian control of the military is deeply rooted in American tradition, stemming from colonial experience and solidified into basic principles of law incorporated into the Constitution. This concept was really the product of a vital concern that our Founding Fathers had with efforts to "overcome and contain the exercise of arbitrary military power. England's experience pointed out the dangers of embodying the powers both to declare and to wage war in one office" (i.e., the King).[13] From the very founding of our Republic, Americans have been particularly worried about the "exercise of arbitrary military power." It was, after all, the arbitrary use of British military power in the North American colonies that was considered by many to be a factor contributing to the Revolution.

If this were the only military concern of the Founding Fathers, a simple answer was available—do away with the military entirely! However, there was another concern on their minds; they clearly recognized the need to have a strong, capable military arm to protect the new nation against the British, the French, and the Indians. In the words of Professor Elmer Mahoney of the U.S. Naval Academy, this led the Founding Fathers to a "dichotomy of the country's need for military strength coupled with fear that the power given and the institutions created [by this military strength] could be inherently destructive if arbitrarily used."[14]

The solution to this dichotomy involved the incorporation of two basic principles into the Constitution. The first was the concept of civilian control; to guard against the basic distrust of the military, reliance was put in the principle of strictly subordinating the military arm of the government to the civilian. Beyond this, there was still the danger of vesting the powers of both declaring and waging war in the same office, making it possible for one civilian in government to arbitrarily use the military arm. To prevent this, reliance was placed on the second basic principle, a principle used by the framers throughout the Constitution to guard against the excessive concentration of power in any one official or element of the government. This was the basic principle of separation of powers and checks and balances. Specifically, civilian control of the military was divided between the federal government and the states, on the one hand, and between branches within the federal government on the other. The U.S. Congress was given the power to declare war, and to raise and support military forces (Article I, Section 8). The president was given the power actually to conduct military operations (i.e., wage war) as commander in chief (Article II, Section 2). Control over the state militias was divided between the state governors and the federal government (Article I, Sections 8 and 10; Article II, Section 2). The result of all of this was the establishment of a system of divided civilian control of the military.

This arrangement has had some interesting implications for the resulting operation and effectiveness of civilian control, and, collaterally, for the involvement of the military in politics. To begin with, this system of divided civilian control has not, according to some students of civil–military relations, resulted in effective military subordination to the civilian voice in government. Samuel Huntington believes:

The very aspects of the Constitution which are frequently cited as establishing civilian control are those which make it difficult to achieve. Civilian control would be maximized if the military were limited in scope and relegated to a subordinate position in a pyramid of authority culminating in a single civilian head. The military clauses of the Constitution, however, provide for almost exactly the opposite. They divide civilian responsibility for military affairs and foster the direct access of the military authorities to the highest levels of government.[15]

The reason for this lies in an understanding of the intentions of the Founding Fathers in establishing divided civilian control. Huntington believes that "the Framers' concept of civilian control was to control the uses to which *civilians* might put military force rather than to control the military themselves. *They were more afraid of military power in the hands of political officials* than of political power in the hands of military officers" (emphasis added).[16]

Whether or not Huntington is correct in assuming that the *primary* concern was to limit *civilian* use of military force, it is fairly evident that it was a *concern* of the framers. And as long as it was a concern, a problem existed. "The simplest way of minimizing military power" would be the "maximizing of the power of civilian groups in relation to the military." However, "the maximizing of civilian power always means the maximizing of the power of some particular civilian group."[17] Consequently, control was divided among multiple civilian groups so that no one group or individual would have absolute authority over the military.

The result of this arrangement has been a struggle among the various groups sharing divided control, primarily the president and Congress, for dominance. This struggle is not related solely to the issue of control of the armed forces; rather, it is part of a more general power struggle between the executive and congressional branches resulting from the broad principle of separation of powers and checks and balances. What makes the civilian control issue such an important one is the fact that federal government activities in the field of international relations have become so extensive since the 1940s, and that the military has played such a major role in those activities. This, of course, has had great influence on the size of the military establishment and its impact on the nation's economy and society. The struggle itself is such that, in Huntington's view, "The Chief Executive identifies civilian control with presidential control" while "Congress . . . identifies civilian control with congressional control." However, "both Congress and the president are fundamentally concerned with the distribution of power between executive and legislative rather than between civilian and military."[18]

Huntington's belief in the inherent failings of divided civilian control is not universally accepted. Others, such as Professor Mahoney, claim that military subordination to civilian control is ineffective not because the designed system is faulty, but rather because the appropriate civilian officials fail to exercise the constitutional powers given them! "There is not that much wrong with the present system that faithful adherence to the letter and spirit of civil supremacy will not correct. The power to control is there, but the civilians have failed to use it, and the electorate has not held them accountable for their omission."[19] And, there are still others who contend that civilian control is not ineffective; that it is functioning as it should.

Whatever the point of view, the congressional-executive power struggle aspect of divided civilian control is a fact, and it is this very struggle for power between civilian branches of the government that has made military involvement in politics inevitable. In the years since World War II, the executive branch has gained the upper hand in this tug of war with Congress, and every effort is made by the president and Defense Department officials to maintain the power over the military that has been acquired, as well as to acquire still more. Congress, on the other hand, has resisted this accretion of power by the executive, and, more recently, has made vigorous attempts to restrict the exercise of some of that power (witness the 1973 War Powers Resolution) and to reassert greater congressional control over the military.

As both parties to this struggle have maneuvered for an advantage, the military itself has been drawn into the controversy. Each side seeks to enlist the support and assistance of military leaders, the services, and even the entire profession. Executive branch leaders call upon the Joint Chiefs of Staff and senior commanders to support administration proposals for reorganizing the Defense Department, while congressional committees call upon the service chiefs and their deputies to oppose Defense Department efforts to increase centralized control over the services by the Office of the Secretary of Defense. As a result, the military is compelled to become involved in what is essentially a political power struggle—a power struggle that takes the form of disputes over policy decisions. In Huntington's words, "The separation of powers" between Congress and the president "is a perpetual invitation, if not an irresistible force, drawing military leaders into political conflicts."[20]

NECESSITY OF POLITICAL INVOLVEMENT

Beyond the probable inevitability of political involvement by the military, a strong case can be made for its necessity. Many articles have been written by proponents of the "political-military fusion" school in which multiple and detailed arguments are offered in support of the necessity of this involvement.[21] Rather than catalog the various points made in those papers, it might be useful to focus attention on two fairly broad reasons that demonstrate why involvement by military professionals in decision making or value allocation politics is necessary.

The first reason has to do with decision making itself—the process by which alternatives are examined and assessed, and one or more are chosen as policy to be pursued. To begin with, in the area of national security virtually all policy alternatives available to political decision makers today relate in some way to the use, the threatened use, or the condition of military forces. During the decision-making process, each of the various competing policy alternatives must be analyzed and appraised to determine suitability (will the alternative accomplish the desired objectives?), feasibility (is the alternative compatible with available resources?), and acceptability (what are the relative costs of the alternative, and are they acceptable?).

This process of analysis and appraisal must, if it is to be meaningful and helpful to the decision maker, be accomplished by experts having the knowledge and experience to make realistic judgments of relative merit from among the alternatives being considered. Since virtually all such alternatives in the national security policy field involve some aspect of military force, it follows that experts in the development and application of such force—military professionals—*must* be involved in the decision-making process. If they are not included, serious overcommitments of available resources or serious policy shortcomings are possible. Therefore, military professionals must be involved in political decision-making since, in the words of Lieutenant Colonel William Simons, "military officials are uniquely qualified to describe the resources and costs demanded by available strategic alternatives."[22]

The second reason is closely related to the first. The availability of resources (money, matériel, manpower) has a major, even determining impact on the national security policies that are selected and implemented by the government. Policy alternatives for which there are inadequate resources available are not really feasible and should not be selected. In effect, they are not even available as options.

In recent years, two trends have developed that greatly affect the resources that are available to the defense establishment. To begin with, many vital resources have become quite scarce (and costly); the oil embargo and subsequent energy crisis are a prime example. In addition, the competition for these scarce resources has increased dramatically—among nations, among segments of American society, and among the agencies of government. Greater competition for scarcer resources means that it will be harder and harder for the defense establishment to obtain the resources necessary to provide viable policy alternatives and to ensure the ability to accomplish assigned missions.

All this means that expert advice must be made available to those officials in both the executive and legislative branches responsible for determining the allocation of resources, and that this advice must be effectively supported and defended. Once again, since military professionals are the only real source of a particular type of expert advice needed—that concerning the development and application of military force—it stands to reason that military professionals must be involved in the political process of resource allocation. In the words of Professor Sarkesian:

The military will find itself in a position in which it will have to defend its policies and programs to a suspicious Congress. . . .

Politically astute and technically knowledgeable officers will be a *sine qua non* for the effective representation of the military in external political activities. . . . By necessity, the military will have to engage in the "kinds" of politics, and on a scale and intensity, characteristic of politically active interest groups.[23]

Therefore, the question of the necessity of professional military involvement in the political decision making process should be answered with a firm "yes." The two reasons that have just been discussed amply demonstrate the need for military participation in the analysis and appraisal of security policy alternatives, and in the resource allocation process. If professional officers do not, or cannot, participate in such political decision-making processes, the national security policy that *is* formulated and implemented runs the risk of being less appropriate and less effective than it should, or could be.

DEVELOPING POLITICO-MILITARY EXPERTISE TO ENSURE "PROPER AND EFFECTIVE" POLITICAL INVOLVEMENT

This, then, brings us back to the two questions asked at the beginning of this discussion concerning the nature of the military profession: "What are we to be?" and "What are we to do?" A partial answer to the second question must be that one function of the military profession is participation in the political decision-making process as it relates to national security policy. This is, in all likelihood, an inevitable function, but it is also a necessary and proper function.

What, then, of the first question: "What are we to be?" In answering this question, full recognition must be made of the profession's involvement in the political process. Part of what officers must be as military professionals must necessarily relate to that political involvement. The military must accept, both individually as professionals and institutionally as a profession, the new political dimension of military professionalism. Professional officers must become aware of the proper political role that the military should play—a very definite and limited role, but a legitimate one nonetheless. But much more than this, professional officers must also become knowledgeable in the purposes and procedures of the political process in which they participate. They must know how and why the process operates if they are truly to understand it; and they must understand it if their involvement in the political process is to be effective. The objective of this process is the security of the nation, and it is vital that the military be effective in performing its role toward achieving that objective.

NOTES

This essay represents the views of the author and does not necessarily reflect the official opinion of the Armed Forces Staff College.

1. Samuel P. Huntington, *The Soldier and the State* (New York: Vintage Books, 1964), 229.

2. Ibid., 230–32.

3. Ibid., 71.

4. Sam C. Sarkesian, "Political Soldiers: Perspectives on Professionalism in the U.S. Military," *Midwest Journal of Political Science* 16, no. 2 (1972): 240.

5. Huntington, *Soldier and State,* 350–51.

6. Sources of quotations are, in order: Rocco M. Paone, "Civil–Military Relations and the Formulation of U.S. Foreign Policy," in *Civil–Military Relations,* ed. Charles L. Cochran (New York: Free Press, 1974), 83; Lieutenant Colonel Jack L. Miles, "The Fusion of Military and Political Considerations," *Marine Corps Gazette* 52, no. 8 (1968): 28; Colonel Donald F. Bletz, "Military Professionalism," *Military Review* 51, no. 5 (1971): 12.

7. Sarkesian, "Political Soldiers," 239.

8. Ibid., 258.

9. Bletz, "Military Professionalism," 16–17.

10. Huntington, *Soldier and State,* 71, 231–32.

11. Morris Janowitz, *The Professional Soldier* (New York: Free Press, 1971), 233.

12. David Easton, *The Political System* (New York: Knopf, 1953), 134.

13. Elmer J. Mahoney, "The Constitutional Frame-work of Civil–Military Relations," in *Civil–Military Relations,* ed. Cochran, 34.

14. Ibid., 35.

15. Huntington, *Soldier and State,* 163.

16. Ibid., 168.

17. Ibid., 80.

18. Ibid., 81.

19. Mahoney, "Constitutional Framework," 38.

20. Huntington, *Soldier and State,* 177.

21. Among some of the better ones are: Lieutenant Colonel William E. Simons, "Military Professionals as Policy Advisers," *Air University Review* 20, no. 3 (1969); Charles Wolf Jr., "Is United States Foreign Policy Being Militarized?" *Orbis* 14, no. 4 (1971). See also Sarkesian, "Political Soldiers"; Bletz, "Military Professionalism"; and Miles, "Fusion of Military and Political Consideration."

22. Simons, "Military Professionals," 5.

23. Sarkesian, "Political Soldiers," 255.

THE ORIGINS OF THE AMERICAN MILITARY COUP OF 2012

CHARLES J. DUNLAP JR.

The letter that follows takes us on a darkly imagined excursion into the future. A military coup has taken place in the United States—the year is 2012—and General Thomas E. T. Brutus, commander in chief of the Unified Armed Forces of the United States, now occupies the White House as permanent military plenipotentiary. His position has been ratified by a national referendum, though scattered disorders still prevail and arrests for acts of sedition are under way. A senior retired officer of the Unified Armed Forces, known here simply as Prisoner 222305759, is one of those arrested, having been convicted by court-martial for opposing the coup. Prior to his execution, he is able to smuggle out of prison a letter to an old War College classmate discussing the "Origins of the American Military Coup of 2012." In it, he argues that the coup was the outgrowth of trends visible as far back as 1992. These trends were the massive diversion of military forces to civilian uses, the monolithic unification of the armed forces, and the insularity of the military community. His letter survives and is here presented verbatim.

It goes without saying (I hope) that the coup scenario above is purely a literary device intended to dramatize my concern over certain contemporary developments affecting the armed forces, and is emphatically *not* a prediction.—The Author

Dear Old Friend,

It's hard to believe that twenty years have passed since we graduated from the War College! Remember the great discussions, the trips, the parties, the people? Those were the days!!! I'm not having quite as much fun anymore. You've heard about the Sedition Trials? Yeah, I was one of those arrested—convicted of "disloyal statements," and "using contemptuous language toward officials." Disloyal? No. Contemptuous? You bet! With General Brutus in charge it's not hard to be contemptuous.

I've got to hand it to Brutus, he's ingenious. After the president died he somehow "persuaded" the vice president not to take the oath of office. Did we then have a president or not? A real "Constitutional Conundrum" the papers called it.[1] Brutus created just enough ambiguity to convince everyone that as the senior military officer, he could—and should—declare himself commander in chief of the Unified Armed Forces. Remember what he said? "Had to fill the power vacuum." And Brutus showed he really knew how to use power: he declared martial law, "postponed" the elections, got the vice president to "retire," and even moved into the White House! "More efficient to work from there," he said. Remember that?

This essay has been edited and is reprinted from Parameters 23 (Winter 1992/93): 2–20, *by permission of* Parameters.

When Congress convened that last time and managed to pass the Referendum Act, I really got my hopes up. But when the Referendum approved Brutus's takeover, I knew we were in serious trouble. I caused a ruckus, you know, trying to organize a protest. Then the Security Forces picked me up. My quickie "trial" was a joke. The sentence? Well, let's just say you won't have to save any beer for me at next year's reunion. Since it doesn't look like I'll be seeing you again, I thought I'd write everything down and try to get it to you.

I am calling my paper the "Origins of the American Military Coup of 2012." I think it's important to get the truth recorded before they rewrite history. If we're ever going to get our freedom back, we've got to understand how we got into this mess. People need to understand that the armed forces exist to support and defend government, not to *be* the government. Faced with intractable national problems on one hand, and an energetic and capable military on the other, it can be all too seductive to start viewing the military as a cost-effective solution. We made a terrible mistake when we allowed the armed forces to be diverted from their original purpose.

I found a box of my notes and clippings from our War College days—told my keepers I needed them to write the confession they want. It's amazing; looking through these old papers makes me realize that even back in 1992 we should have seen this coming. The seeds of this outrage were all there; we just didn't realize how they would grow. But isn't that always the way with things like this? Somebody once said that "the true watersheds in human affairs are seldom spotted amid the tumult of headlines broadcast on the hour."[2] And we had a lot of headlines back in the '90s to distract us: The economy was in the dumps, crime was rising, schools were deteriorating, drug use was rampant, the environment was in trouble, and political scandals were occurring almost daily. Still, there was some good news: the end of the Cold War as well as America's recent victory over Iraq.

All of this and more contributed to the situation in which we find ourselves today: a military that controls government and one that, ironically, can't fight. It wasn't any single cause that led us to this point. Instead, it was a combination of several developments, the beginnings of which were evident in 1992. Here's what I think happened:

Americans became exasperated with democracy. We were disillusioned with the apparent inability of elected government to solve the nation's dilemmas. We were looking for someone or something that could produce workable answers. The one institution of government in which the people retained faith was the military. Buoyed by the military's obvious competence in the First Gulf War, the public increasingly turned to it for solutions to the country's problems. Americans called for an acceleration of trends begun in the 1980s: tasking the military with a variety of new, nontraditional missions, and vastly escalating its commitment to formerly ancillary duties.

Though not obvious at the time, the cumulative effect of these new responsibilities was to incorporate the military into the political process to an unprecedented degree. These additional assignments also had the perverse effect of diverting focus and resources from the military's central mission of combat training and warfighting. Finally, organizational, political, and societal changes served to alter the American military's culture. Today's military is not the one we knew when we graduated from the War College.

Let me explain how I came to these conclusions. In 1992 not very many people would've thought a military coup d'etat could ever happen here. Sure, there were eccentric conspiracy theorists who saw the Pentagon's hand in the assassination of President Kennedy,[3] President Nixon's downfall,[4] and similar events. But even the most avid believers had to admit that no outright military takeover had ever occurred before now. Heeding Washington's admonitions in his farewell address about the dangers of overgrown military establishments,[5] Americans generally viewed their armed forces with a judicious mixture of respect and wariness.[6] For over two centuries that vigilance was rewarded, and most Americans came to consider the very notion of a military coup preposterous. Historian Andrew Janos captured the conventional view of the latter half of the twentieth century in this clipping I saved:

A coup d'etat in the United States would be too fantastic to contemplate, not only because few would actually entertain the idea, but also because the bulk of the people are strongly attached to the prevailing political system and would rise in defense of a political leader even though they might not like him. The environment most hospitable to coups d'etat is one in which political apathy prevails as the dominant style.[7]

However, when Janos wrote that back in 1964, 61.9 percent of the electorate voted. Since then voter participation has steadily declined. By 1988 only 50.1 percent of the eligible voters cast a ballot.[8] Simple extrapolation of those numbers to last spring's Referendum would have predicted almost exactly the turnout. It was precisely *reversed* from that of 1964: 61.9 percent of the electorate did *not* vote.

America's societal malaise was readily apparent in 1992. Seventy-eight percent of Americans believed the country was on the "wrong track." One researcher declared that social indicators were at their lowest level in twenty years and insisted "something [was] coming loose in the social infrastructure." The nation was frustrated and angry about its problems.[9]

America wanted solutions and democratically elected government wasn't providing them.[10] The country suffered from a "deep pessimism about politicians and government after years of broken promises."[11] David Finkle observed in the *Washington Post Magazine* that for most Americans "the perception of government is that it has evolved from something that provides democracy's framework into something that provides obstacles, from something to celebrate into something to ignore." Likewise, politicians and their proposals seemed stale and repetitive. Millions of voters gave up hope of finding answers.[12] The "environment of apathy" Janos characterized as a precursor to a coup had arrived.

Unlike the rest of government, the military enjoyed a remarkably steady climb in popularity throughout the 1980s and early 1990s.[13] And indeed it had earned the admiration of the public. Debilitated by the Vietnam War, the U.S. military set about reinventing itself. As early as 1988 *U.S. News & World Report* heralded the result: "In contrast to the dispirited, drug-ravaged, do-your-own-thing armed services of the '70s and early '80s, the U.S. military has been transformed into a fighting force of gung-ho attitude, spit-shined discipline, and ten-hut morale."[14] After the U.S. military dealt Iraq a crushing defeat in the First Gulf War, the ignominy of Vietnam evaporated.

When we graduated from the War College in 1992, the armed forces were the smartest, best-educated, and best-disciplined force in history.[15] While polls showed that the public invariably gave Congress low marks, a February 1991 survey disclosed that "public confidence in the military soar[ed] to 85 percent, far surpassing every other institution in our society." The armed forces had become America's most—and perhaps only—trusted arm of government.[16]

Assumptions about the role of the military in society also began to change. Twenty years before we graduated, the Supreme Court confidently declared in *Laird* v. *Tatum* that Americans had a "traditional and strong resistance to any military intrusion into civilian affairs."[17] But Americans were now rethinking the desirability and necessity of that resistance. They compared the military's principled competence with the chicanery and ineptitude of many elected officials, and found the latter wanting.[18]

Commentator James Fallows expressed the new thinking in an August 1991 article in *Atlantic* magazine. Musing on the contributions of the military to American society, Fallows wrote: "I am beginning to think that the only way the national government can do anything worthwhile is to invent a security threat and turn the job over to the military." He elaborated on his reasoning:

According to our economic and political theories, most agencies of the government have no special standing to speak about the general national welfare. Each represents a certain constituency; the interest groups fight it out. The military, strangely, is the one government institution that has been assigned legitimacy to act on its notion of the collective good. "National defense" can make us do things—train engineers, build highways—that long-term good of the nation or common sense cannot.[19]

About a decade before Fallows's article appeared, Congress initiated the use of "national defense" as a rationale to boost military participation in an activity historically the exclusive domain of civilian government: law enforcement. Congress concluded that the "rising tide of drugs being smuggled into the United States . . . present[ed] a grave threat to all Americans." Finding the performance of civilian law enforcement agencies in counteracting that threat unsatisfactory, Congress passed the Military Cooperation with Civilian Law Enforcement Agencies Act of 1981.[20] In doing so Congress specifically intended to force reluctant military commanders to actively collaborate in police work.[21]

This was a historic change of policy. Since the passage of the Posse Comitatus Act in 1878, the military had distanced itself from law enforcement activities.[22] While the 1981 law did retain certain limits on the legal authority of military personnel, its net effect was to dramatically expand military participation in anti-drug efforts.[23] By 1991 the Department of Defense was spending $1.2 billion on counternarcotics crusades. Air force surveillance aircraft were sent to track airborne smugglers; navy ships patrolled the Caribbean looking for drug-laden vessels; and National Guardsmen were searching for marijuana caches near the borders.[24] By 1992 "combating" drug trafficking was formally declared a "high national security mission."[25]

It wasn't too long before twenty-first-century legislators were calling for more military involvement in police work.[26] Crime seemed out of control. Most disturbing, the incidence of violent crime continued to climb.[27] Americans were horrified and desperate: a third even believed vigilantism could be justified.[28] Rising lawlessness was seen as but another example of the civilian political leadership's inability to fulfill government's most basic duty to ensure public safety.[29] People once again wanted the military to help.

Hints of an expanded police function were starting to surface while we were still at the War College. For example, District of Columbia National Guardsmen established a regular military presence in high-crime areas.[30] Eventually, people became acclimated to seeing uniformed military personnel patrolling their neighborhood.[31] Now troops are an adjunct to almost all police forces in the country. In many of the areas where much of our burgeoning population of elderly Americans live—Brutus calls them "National Security Zones"—the military is often the only law enforcement agency. Consequently, the military was ideally positioned in thousands of communities to support the coup.

Concern about crime was a major reason why General Brutus's actions were approved in the Referendum. Although voter participation by the general public was low, older Americans voted at a much higher rate.[32] Furthermore, with the aging of the baby boom generation, the block of American voters over forty-five grew to almost 53 percent of the voters by 2010.[33] This wealthy,[34] older electorate welcomed an organization that could ensure their physical security.[35] When it counted, they backed Brutus in the Referendum—probably the last votes they'll ever cast.

The military's constituency was larger than just the aged. Poor Americans of all ages became dependent upon the military not only for protection against crime, but also for medical care. Again we saw the roots of this back in 1992. First it was the barely defeated proposal to use veterans' hospitals to provide care for the nonveteran poor.[36] Next were calls to deploy military medical assets to relieve hard-pressed urban hospitals.[37] As the number of uninsured and underinsured grew, the pressure to provide care became inexorable. Now military hospitals serve millions of new nonmilitary patients. Similarly, a proposal to use so-called underutilized military bases as drug rehabilitation centers was implemented on a massive scale.[38]

Even the youngest citizens were coopted. During the 1990s the public became aware that military officers had the math and science backgrounds desperately needed to revitalize U.S. education.[39] In fact, programs involving military personnel were already under way while we were at the War College.[40] We now have an entire generation of young people who have grown up comfortable with the sight of military personnel patrolling their streets and teaching in their classrooms.

As you know, it wasn't just crises in public safety, medical care, and education that the military was tasked to mend. The military was also called upon to manage the cleanup of the nation's environmental hazards. By 1992 the armed services were deeply involved in this arena, and that involvement mushroomed. Once the military demonstrated its expertise, it wasn't long before environmental problems were declared "national security threats" and full responsibility devolved to the armed forces.[41]

Other problems were transformed into "national security" issues. As more commercial airlines went bankrupt and unprofitable air routes dropped, the military was called upon to provide "essential" air transport to the affected regions. In the name of national defense, the military next found itself in the sealift business. Ships purchased by the military for contingencies were leased, complete with military crews, at low rates to U.S. exporters to help solve the trade deficit.[42] The nation's crumbling infrastructure was also declared a "national security threat." As was proposed back in 1991, troops rehabilitated public housing, rebuilt bridges and roads, and constructed new government buildings. By late 1992, voices in both Congress and the military had reached a crescendo calling for military involvement across a broad spectrum of heretofore purely civilian activities.[43] Soon, it became common in practically every community to see crews of soldiers working on local projects.[44] Military attire drew no stares.

The revised charter for the armed forces was not confined to domestic enterprises. Overseas humanitarian and nation-building assignments proliferated.[45] Though these projects have always been performed by the military on an ad hoc basis, in 1986 Congress formalized that process. It declared overseas humanitarian and civic assistance activities to be "valid military missions" and specifically authorized them by law.[46] Fueled by favorable press for operations in Iraq, Bangladesh, and the Philippines during the early 1990s, humanitarian missions were touted as the military's "model for the future."[47] That prediction came true. When several African governments collapsed under AIDS epidemics and famines around the turn of the century, U.S. troops—first introduced to the continent in the 1990s—were called upon to restore basic services. They never left.[48] Now the U.S. military constitutes the de facto government in many of those areas. Once again, the first whisperings of such duties could be heard in 1992.[49]

By the year 2000 the armed forces had penetrated many vital aspects of American society. More and more military officers sought the kind of autonomy in these civilian affairs that they would expect from their military superiors in the execution of traditional combat operations. Thus began the inevitable politicization of the military. With so much responsibility for virtually everything government was expected to do, the military increasingly demanded a larger role in policy making. But in a democracy policy making is a task best left to those accountable to the electorate. Nonetheless, well-intentioned military officers, accustomed to the ordered, hierarchial structure of military society, became impatient with the delays and inefficiencies inherent in the democratic process. Consequently, they increasingly sought to avoid it. They convinced themselves that they could more productively serve the nation in carrying out their new assignments if they accrued to themselves unfettered power to implement their programs. They forgot Lord Acton's warning that "all power corrupts, and absolute power corrupts absolutely."[50]

Congress became their unwitting ally. Because of the popularity of the few military programs—and the growing dependence upon them—Congress passed the Military Plenipotentiary Act of 2005. This legislation was the legacy of the Goldwater-Nichols Defense Reorganization Act of 1986. Among many revisions, Goldwater-Nichols strengthened the office of the chairman of the Joint Chiefs of Staff and mandated numerous changes intended to increase "jointness" in the armed services.[51] Supporters in the Military Plenipotentiary Act argued that unity of command was critical to the successful management of the numerous activities now considered "military" operations. Moreover, many members of Congress mistakenly believed that Goldwater-Nichols was one of the main reasons for the military's success in the First Gulf War.[52] They viewed the Military Plenipotentiary Act as an enhancement of the strengths of Goldwater-Nichols.

In passing this legislation Congress added greater authority to the military's top leadership position. Lulled by favorable experiences with chairmen like General Colin Powell,[53] Congress saw little danger in converting the office of the chairman of the Joint Chiefs of Staff into the even more powerful Military Plenipotentiary. No longer merely an adviser, the

Military Plenipotentiary became a true commander of all U.S. services, purportedly because that status could better ameliorate the effects of perceived interservice squabbling. Despite warnings found in the legislative history of Goldwater-Nichols and elsewhere, enormous power was concentrated in the hands of a single, unelected official.[54] Unfortunately, Congress presumed that principled people would always occupy the office.[55] No one expected a General Brutus would arise.

The Military Plenipotentiary was not Congress's only structural change in military governance. By 2007 the services were combined to form the Unified Armed Forces. Recall that when we graduated from the War College greater unification was being seriously suggested as an economy measure.[56] Eventually that consideration, and the conviction that "jointness" was an unqualified military virtue,[57] led to unification. But unification ended the creative tension between the services.[58] Besides rejecting the operational logic of separate services,[59] no one seemed to recognize the checks-and-balances function that service separatism provided a democracy obliged to maintain a large, professional military establishment. The Founding Fathers knew the importance of checks and balances in controlling the agencies of government: "Ambition must be made to counteract ambition. . . . Experience has taught mankind the necessity of auxiliary controls . . . [including] supplying opposite and rival interests."[60]

Ambition is a natural trait of military organizations and their leaders.[61] Whatever might have been the inefficiencies of separate military services, their very existence served to counteract the untoward desires of any single service. The roles and missions debates and other arguments, once seen as petty military infighting, also provided an invaluable forum for competitive analysis of military doctrine. In addition, they served to ensure that unscrupulous designs by a segment of the military establishment were ruthlessly exposed. Once the services were unified, the impetus to do so vanished, and the authority of the military in relation to the other institutions of government rose.[62] Distended by its pervasive new duties, monolithic militarism came to dominate the Darwinian political environment of twenty-first-century America.

Why did the uniformed leadership of our day acquiesce to this transformation of the military? Much of the answer can be traced to the budget showdowns of the early 1990s. The collapse of the Soviet Union left the U.S. military without an easily articulated rationale for large defense budgets. Billions in cuts were sought. Journalist Bruce Auster put it bluntly: "Winning a share of the budget wars . . . require[s] that the military find new missions for a post—Cold War world that is devoid of clear military threats."[63] Capitulating, military leaders embraced formerly disdained assignments. As one commentator cynically observed, "The services are eager to talk up nontraditional, budget-justifying roles."[64] The Vietnam-era aphorism, "It's a lousy war, but it's the only one we've got," was resuscitated.

Still, that doesn't completely explain why in 2012 the military leadership would succumb to a coup. To answer that question fully requires examination of what was happening to the officer corps as the military drew down in the 1980s and 1990s. Ever since large peacetime military establishments became permanent features after World War II, the great leveler of the officer corps was the constant influx of officers from the Reserve Officers Training Corps program. The product of diverse colleges and universities throughout the United States, these officers were a vital source of liberalism in the military services.[65]

By the late 1980s and early 1990s, however, that was changing. Force reductions decreased the number of ROTC graduates the services accepted.[66] Although General Powell called ROTC "vital to democracy," 62 ROTC programs were closed in 1991 and another 350 were considered for closure.[67] The numbers of officers produced by the service academies also fell, but at a significantly slower pace. Consequently, the *proportion* of academy graduates in the officer corps climbed.[68] Academy graduates, along with graduates of such military schools as the Citadel, Virginia Military Institute, and Norwich University tended to feel a greater homogeneity of outlook than, say, the pool of ROTC graduates at large, with the result that as the proportion of such graduates grew, diversity of outlook overall diminished to some degree.

Moreover, the ROTC officers that did remain increasingly came from a narrower range of schools. Focusing on the military's policy to exclude homosexuals from service, advocates of "political correctness" succeeded in driving the ROTC from the campuses of some of our best universities.[69] In many instances they also prevailed in barring military recruiters from campus.[70] Little thought was given the long-term consequences of limiting the pool from which our military leadership was drawn. The result was a much more uniformly oriented military elite whose outlook was progressively conservative.

Furthermore, well-meaning attempts at improving service life led to the unintended insularity of military society, representing a return to the cloistered life of the pre–World War II armed forces. Military bases, complete with schools, churches, stores, child care centers, and recreational areas, became never-to-be-left islands of tranquility removed from the chaotic, crime-ridden environment outside the gates.[71] As one reporter put it in 1991: "Increasingly isolated from mainstream America, today's troops tend to view the civilian world with suspicion and sometimes hostility."[72] Thus a physically isolated and intellectually alienated officer corps was paired with an enlisted force likewise distanced from the society it was supposed to serve. In short, the military evolved into a force susceptible to manipulation by an authoritarian leader from its own select ranks.

What made this all the more disheartening was the wretched performance of our forces in the Second Gulf War.[73] Consumed with ancillary and nontraditional missions, the military neglected its fundamental raison d'etre. As the Supreme Court succinctly put it more than a half century ago, the "primary business of armies and navies [is] to fight or be ready to fight wars should the occasion arise."[74] When Iranian armies started pouring into the lower Gulf states in 2010, the U.S. armed forces were ready to do anything but fight.

Preoccupation with humanitarian duties, narcotics interdiction, and all the rest of the peripheral missions left the military unfit to engage an authentic military opponent. Performing the new missions sapped resources from what most experts agree was one of the vital ingredients to victory in the First Gulf War: training. Training is, quite literally, a zero-sum game. Each moment spent performing a non-traditional mission is one unavailable for orthodox military exercises. We should have recognized the grave risk. In 1991 the *Washington Post* reported that in "interview after interview across the services, senior leaders and noncommissioned officers stressed that they cannot be ready to fight without frequent rehearsals of perishable skills."[75]

The military's antidrug activities were a big part of the problem. Oh sure, I remember the facile claims of exponents of the military's counternarcotics involvement as to what "valuable" training it provided.[76] Did anyone really think that crew members of an AWACS—an aircraft designed to track high-performance military aircraft in combat—significantly improved their skills by hours of tracking slow-moving light planes? Did they seriously imagine that troops enhanced combat skills by looking for marijuana under car seats? Did they truly believe that crews of the navy's sophisticated antiair and antisubmarine ships received meaningful training by following lumbering trawlers around the Caribbean?[77] Tragically, they did.

The problem was exacerbated when political pressures exempted the guard and the reserves from the harshest effects of the budgetary cutbacks of the early 1990s.[78] The First Gulf War demonstrated that modern weapons and tactics were simply too complex for part-time soldiers to master during their allotted drill periods, however well motivated.[79] Still, creative guard and reserve defenders contrived numerous civic-action and humanitarian assignments and sold them as "training." Left unexplained was how such training was supposed to fit with military strategies that contemplated short, violent, come-as-you-are expeditionary wars.[80] Nice-to-have guard and reserve support-oriented programs prevailed at the expense of critical active-duty *combat* capabilities.[81]

Perhaps even more damaging than the diversion of resources was the assault on the very ethos of military service. Rather than bearing in mind the Supreme Court's admonition to focus on war fighting, the military was told to alter its purpose. Former Secretary of State James Baker typified the trendy new tone in remarks about the military's airlift of food and medicine to the former Soviet republics in early 1992. He said the airlift would "vividly show the peoples of the former Soviet Union that those who once prepared for war with them now have the courage and the conviction to use their militaries to say, 'We will wage a new peace.'"[82]

In truth militaries ought to "prepare for war" and leave the "peace waging" to those agencies of government whose mission is just that. Nevertheless, such pronouncements—seconded by military leaders[83]—became the fashionable philosophy. The result? People in the military no longer considered themselves warriors. Instead, they perceived themselves as policemen, relief workers, educators, builders, health care providers, politicians—everything but warfighters. When these philanthropists met the Iranian 10th Armored Corps near Daharan during the Second Gulf War, they were brutally slaughtered by a military that had not forgotten what militaries were supposed to do or what war is really all about.

The devastation of the military's martial spirit was exemplified by its involvement in police activities. Inexplicably, we ignored the deleterious effect on combat motivation suffered by the Israeli Defense Forces as a result of their efforts to police the West Bank and Gaza.[84] Few seemed to appreciate the fundamental difference between the police profession and the profession of arms. As Richard J. Barnet observed in the *New Yorker,* "The line between police action and a military operation is real. Police derive their power from their acceptance as 'officers of the law'; legitimate authority, not firepower, is the essential element."[85]

Police organizations are understandably oriented toward the studied restraint necessary for the end sought: a judicial conviction. As one Drug Enforcement Administration agent noted: "The military can kill people better than we can [but] when we go to a jungle lab, we're not there to move onto the target by fire and maneuver to destroy the enemy. We're there to arrest suspects and seize evidence."[86] If military forces are inculcated with the same spirit of restraint, combat performance is threatened.[87] Moreover, law enforcement is also not just a form of low-intensity conflict. In low-intensity conflict, the military aim is to win the will of the people, a virtually impossible task with criminals "motivated by money, not ideology."[88]

Humanitarian missions likewise undermined the military's sense of itself. As one navy officer gushed during the 1991 Bangladesh relief operation, "It's great to be here doing the opposite of a soldier."[89] While no true soldier relishes war, the fact remains that the essence of the military is war fighting and preparation for the same. What journalist Barton Gellman has said of the army can be extrapolated to the military as a whole: it is an "organization whose fighting spirit depends . . . heavily on tradition."[90] If that tradition becomes imbued with a preference for "doing the opposite of a soldier," fighting spirit is bound to suffer. When we first heard editorial calls to "pacify the military" by involving it in civic projects,[91] we should have given them the forceful rebuke they deserved.

Military analyst Harry Summers warned back in 1991 that when militaries lose sight of their purpose, catastrophe results. Citing a study of pre–World War II Canadian military policy as it related to the subsequent battlefield disasters, he observed that

instead of using the peacetime interregnum to hone their military skills, senior Canadian military officers sought out civilian missions to justify their existence. When war came they were woefully unprepared. Instead of protecting their soldiers' lives they led them to their deaths. In today's post–Cold War peacetime environment, this trap again looms large. . . . Some today within the US military are also searching for relevance, with draft doctrinal manuals giving touchy-feely prewar and postwar civil operations equal weight with warfighting. This is an insidious mistake.[92]

We must remember that America's position at the end of the Cold War had no historical precedent. For the first time the nation—in peacetime—found itself with a still-sizable, professional military establishment that was not preoccupied with an overarching external threat.[93] Yet the uncertainties in the aftermath of the Cold War limited the extent to which those forces could be safely downsized. When the military was then obliged to engage in a bewildering array of nontraditional duties to further justify its existence, it is little wonder that its traditional apolitical professionalism eventually eroded.

Clearly, the curious tapestry of military authoritarianism and combat ineffectiveness that we see today was not yet woven in 1992. But the threads were there. Knowing what I know now, here's the advice I would have given the War College Class of 1992 had I been their graduation speaker:

- *Demand that the armed forces focus exclusively on indisputably military duties.* We must not diffuse our energies away from our fundamental responsibility for war fighting. To send ill-trained troops into combat makes us accomplices to murder.

- *Acknowledge that national security does have economic, social, educational, and environmental dimensions but insist that this doesn't necessarily mean the problems in those areas are the responsibility of the military to correct.* Stylishly designating efforts to solve national ills as "wars" doesn't convert them into something appropriate for the employment of military forces.

- *Readily cede budgetary resources to those agencies whose business it is to address the nonmilitary issues the armed forces are presently asked to fix.* We are not the Drug Enforcement Agency, Environmental Protection Agency, Peace Corps, Department of Education, or Red Cross—nor should we be. It has never been easy to give up resources, but in the long term we—and the nation—will be better served by a smaller but appropriately focused military.

- *Divest the defense budget of perception-skewing expenses.* Narcotics interdiction, environmental cleanup, humanitarian relief, and other costs tangential to actual combat capability should be assigned to the budgets of DEA, EPA, State, and so forth. As long as these expensive programs are hidden in the defense budget, the taxpayer understandably—but mistakenly—will continue to believe he's buying military readiness.

- *Continue to press for the elimination of superfluous, resource-draining guard and reserve units.* Increase the training tempo, responsibilities, and compensation of those that remain.

- *Educate the public to the sophisticated training requirements occasioned by the complexities of modern warfare.* It's imperative we rid the public of the misperception that soldiers in peacetime are essentially unemployed and therefore free to assume new missions.[94]

- *Resist unification of the services not only on operational grounds, but also because unification would be inimical to the checks and balances that underpin democratic government.* Slow the pace of fiscally driven consolidation so that the impact on less quantifiable aspects of military effectiveness can be scrutinized.

- *Ensure that officer accessions from the service academies correspond with overall force reductions (but maintain separate service academies) and keep ROTC on a wide diversity of campuses.* If necessary, resort to litigation to maintain ROTC campus diversity.

- *Orient recruiting resources and campaigns toward ensuring that all echelons of society are represented in the military, without compromising standards.*[95] Accept that this kind of recruiting may increase costs. It's worth it.

- *Work to moderate the base-as-an-island syndrome by providing improved incentives for military members and families to assimilate into civilian communities.* Within the information programs for our force of all-volunteer professionals (increasingly U.S.-based), strengthen the emphasis upon such themes as the inviolability of the Constitution, ascendancy of our civilian leadership over the military, and citizens' responsibilities.

Finally, I would tell our classmates that democracy is a fragile institution that must be continuously nurtured and scrupulously protected. I would also tell them that they must speak out when they see the institution threatened; indeed, it is their duty to do so. Richard Gabriel aptly observed in this book *To Serve with Honor* that

when one discusses dissent, loyalty, and the limits of military obligations, the central problem is that the military represents a threat to civil order not because it will usurp authority, but because it does not speak out on critical policy decisions. The soldier fails to live up to his oath to serve the country if he does not speak out when he sees his civilian or military superiors executing policies he feels to be wrong.[96]

Gabriel was wrong when he dismissed the military's potential to threaten civil order, but he was right when he described our responsibilities. The catastrophe that occurred on our watch took place because we failed to speak out against policies we knew were wrong. It's too late for me to do any more. But it's not for you.

Best regards,

Prisoner 222305759

NOTES

1. The Twenty-fifth Amendments to the Constitution provides that in the case of "death . . . the Vice President shall become the President." But Section 1 of Article II requires the taking of the oath before "enter[ing] the Execution of his office."

2. Daniel J. Boorstin, "History's Hidden Turning Points," *U.S. News & World Report,* 22 April 1991, 52.

3. Oliver Stone's movie, *JFK,* is one example. See Joel Achenbach, "JFK Conspiracy: Myth vs. Facts," *Washington Post,* 28 February 1992, C5.

4. See Len Colodny and Robert Gettlin, *Silent Coup* (New York: St. Martin's, 1991).

5. George Washington in his "Farewell Address" dated 19 September 1796 counseled: "Overgrown military establishments . . . under any form of government are inauspicious to liberty and . . . are to be regarded as particularly hostile to republican liberty." As quoted in *The Annals of America* (Chicago: Encyclopedia Britannica, 1976), 609.

6. Author Geoffrey Perret expressed the traditional view as follows: "The antimilitaristic side of the American character is forever on guard. Americans are so suspicious of military ambition that even when the armed forces win wars they are criticized as robustly as if they had lost them." *A Country Made by Wars* (New York: Vintage, 1989), 560.

7. Andrew C. Janos, "The Seizure of Power: A Study of Force and Popular Consent," Research Monograph no. 16 (Princeton, N.J., Center for International Studies, Princeton University, 1964), 39.

8. Mark S. Hoffman, ed., The World Almanac & Book of Facts 1991 (New York: Pharo Books, 1990), 426; Royce Crocker, *Voter Registration and Turnout 1948–1988,* Congressional Research Service Report no. 89-179 (Washington, D.C.: Library of Congress, 1989), 11.

9. E. J. Dionne Jr., "Altered States: The Union & the Campaign," *Washington Post,* 26 January 1992, C1. Fordham University researcher Marc Miringoff reports that the Index of Social Indicators fell to its lowest point in twenty years. He describes the index, which is an amalgamation of social and economic data from government sources, as "sort of a Dow Jones of the national soul." See Paul Taylor, "'Dow Jones of the National Soul' Sours," *Washington Post,* 16 January 1992, A25. The nation's frustration was the cause, according to columnist George F. Will, of a rising level of collective "national stress." George F. Will, "Stressed Out in America," *Washington Post,* 16 January 1992, A27. See also Charles Krauthammer, "America's Case of the Sulks," *Washington Post,* 19 January 1992, C7.

10. A 1989 Harris poll revealed that 53 percent of Americans believed that Congress was not effectively fulfilling its responsibilities. See Robert R. Ivany, "Soldiers and Legislators: Common Mission," *Parameters* 21 (Spring 1991): 47.

11. Mortimer B. Zuckerman, "Behind Our Loss of Faith," *U.S. News & World Report,* 16 March 1992, 76. Many believed that democracy's promise did not include them. Ninety-one percent of Americans reported that the "group with too little influence in government is people like themselves." See "Harper's Index," *Harper's Magazine,* January 1991, 17.

12. David Finkle, "The Greatest Democracy on Earth," *Washington Post Magazine,* 16 February 1992, 16. Forty-three percent of those who failed to vote did not see any important differences between the two major parties. See "Harper's Index," *Harper's Magazine,* March 1992, 13. One in eight Americans was so pessimistic as to conclude that the country's domestic problems were "beyond solving." "Harper's Index," *Harper's Magazine,* October 1991, 15.

13. A ten-year rise in public confidence was reported by Tom Morganthau and others in "The Military's New Image," *Newsweek,* 11 March 1991, 50.

14. Michael Satchell and others, "The Military's New Stars," *U.S. News & World Report,* 18 April 1988, 33.

15. A survey of 163 new army brigadier generals revealed that their IQ was in the 92d percentile of the population. See Bruce W. Nelan, "Revolution in Defense," *Time,* 18 March 1991, 25. In many instances the curriculum vitae of military personnel was more impressive than that of their civilian counterparts. For example, over 88 percent of brigadier generals had an advanced degree compared with 19 percent of top civilian business leaders. See David Gergen, "America's New Heroes," *U.S. News & World Report,* 11 February 1991, 76. Similarly, 97 percent of enlisted personnel were high school graduates, the highest percentage ever. See Grant Willis, "DoD: Recruits in '91 Best Educated, Most Qualified," *Air Force Times,* 27 January 1992, 14. The services "had become practically a drug-free workplace." See David Gergen, "Bringing Home the Storm," *Washington Post,* 28 April 1991, C2. Military sociologist Charles Moskos explained that the reason for the great decline in disciplinary problems is "simply better recruits." Peter Slavin, "Telling It Like It Is," *Air Force Times,* 14 March 1988, 60.

16. Ivany, "Soldiers and Legislators," 47; Gergen, "America's New Heroes," 76; Grant Willis, "A New Generation of Warriors," *Navy Times,* 16 March 1991, 12.

17. 408 U.S. 1, 17 (1972).

18. At least one observer sensed the peril that arises when power and respect converge in the military: "Our warriors are kinder and gentler, and have not shown the slightest inclination to lust for political power. But that potential always lurks where power and respect converge, and the degree of military influence in society is something

to watch carefully in the years ahead." Martin Anderson, "The Benefits of the Warrior Class," *Baltimore Sun*, 14 April 1991, 3F.

19. James Fallows, "Military Efficiency," *Atlantic*, August 1991, 18.

20. Civilian law enforcement agencies were intercepting only 15 percent of the drugs entering the country. See *U.S. Code Congressional & Administrative News* (St. Paul: West, 1981), 1785; Public Law 97-86 (1981) codified in 10 U.S.C. 371 et seq.

21. *Newsweek* reports: "The Pentagon resisted the [counternarcotics] mission for decades, saying that the military should fight threats to national security, and the police should fight crime." Charles Lane, "The Newest War," *Newsweek*, 6 January 1992, 18. See also *U.S. Code Congressional & Administrative News*, 1785.

22. The original purpose of the Posse Comitatus Act (10 U.S.C. 1385) was to restrain Federal troops who had become deeply involved in law enforcement in the post–Civil War South—even in areas where civil government had been reestablished. See *U.S. v. Hartley*, 486 F. Supp. 1348, 1356 fn. 11 (M.D. Fla. 1980). The statute imposes criminal penalties for the improper uses of the military in domestic law enforcement matters. See *U.S. Code Congressional & Administrative News*, 1786.

23. Additional amendments were added in 1988. See Public Law 100-456 (1988).

24. Although antidrug spending decreased in fiscal 1993, the rate of decline was slower than that of the DOD budget as a whole. William Matthews, "Counternarcotics Request Increased," *Air Force Times*, 24 February 1992, 2. See also Lane, "Newest War," 18.

25. "Combatting Drugs," *National Military Strategy of the United States* (Washington, D.C.: GPO, 1992), 15.

26. Some were suggesting the need for greater military authority in 1992. See Dale E. Brown, "Drugs on the Border: The Role of the Military," *Parameters* 21 (Winter 1991–92): 58–59.

27. The rise in the rate of violent crime continued a trend begun in the 1980s when such offenses soared by 23 percent. See "Crime and Punishment," in *The Universal Almanac 1992*, ed. John W. Wright (Kansas City: Andrews and McMeel, 1991), 255.

28. "Harper's Index," *Harper's Magazine*, July 1991, 15.

29. George Will observed that "urban governments are failing to perform their primary function of protecting people from violence on streets and even in homes and schools." "Stressed Out in America," A27.

30. Using guardsmen in a law enforcement capacity during riots and other emergencies was not unusual, but a regular presence in a civilian community in that role was unusual in those days. Guard members usually performed law enforcement activities in their status as state employees. This is distinct from their federalized status when they are incorporated into the U.S. military. See *U.S. Code Congressional & Administrative News*, 2583; and K. R. Clark, "Spotlighting the Drug Zone," *Pentagram*, 30 January 1992, 20–21.

31. Indeed, one of the specific purposes of the D.C. program was to "work with police to increase the uniformed presence in the neighborhood at night to cut down

on illegal activity." See Clark, "Spotlighting the Drug Zone," 21.

32. For example, persons over the age of sixty-five vote at a rate 50 percent higher than that of the eighteen to thirty-four age group. See Will, "Stressed Out in America," A27.

33. The number of baby boomers in the population is expected to peak in 2020. See Marvin J. Cetron and Owen Davies, "Trends Shaping the World," *Futurist*, September–October 1991, 12. Persons over sixty-five were estimated to constitute 18 percent of the electorate by 2010. This group, together with the boomers over forty-five years, would constitute 53 percent of the electorate by 2010. These percentages were computed from statistics found in "The U.S. Population by Age," *Universal Almanac 1992* ed. John W. Wright, (Kansas City: Andrews and McMeel, 1991), 207.

34. Deidre Fanning, "Waiting for the Wealth," *Worth*, February/March 1992, 87, 89.

35. A 1990 poll of Americans aged fifty years and older showed that nearly 23 percent believed that use of the military was the best way to combat the growing problems of drug abuse and crime. See Mark S. Hoffman, ed., *The World Almanac Book of Facts 1991* (New York: Pharo Books, 1990), 33.

36. "Plan to Open Veterans Hospitals to Poor Is Dropped," *New York Times*, 23 February 1992, 17.

37. Scott Shuger, "Pacify the Military," *New York Times*, 14 March 1992, 25.

38. Andy Tobias, "Let's Get Moving!" *Time*, 3 February 1992, 41.

39. *U.S. News & World Report* noted that "a third of the officers leaving the Army are qualified to teach high school math, and 10 to 20 percent can teach physics." David Gergen, "Heroes for Hire," *U.S. News & World Report*, 27 January 1992, 71.

40. For example, a District of Columbia National Guard unit entered into a "Partnership in Education" agreement with a local school district. Under the memorandum the guard agreed to "institute a cooperative learning center providing tutoring in science, English, mathematics, and other basic subjects." See "Guard Enters Partnership with School," *Pentagram*, 13 February 1992, 3. For another example, see "Arlington Schools Join Forces with Defense Department Agency," *Washington Post*, 12 December 1991, Va1.

41. The DOD budget for environmental cleanup for fiscal 1993 was $3.7 billion. Anne Garfinkle, "Going Home Is Hard To Do," *Wall Street Journal*, 27 January 1992, 12. See also Peter Grier, "US Defense Department Declares War on Colossal Pollution Problem," *Christian Science Monitor*, 2 March 1992, 9. The army, at least, saw this activity as a "vital mission" as early as 1991. The *National Journal* reported: "Outside the Storm, a pamphlet heralding the Army's post–Persian Gulf war 'vital missions and important work' touches on the war on drugs and 'protecting the planet Earth' even reprinting a syrupy ode to environmentalism from the 1989 Sierra Club Wilderness Calendar." David C. Morrison, "Operation Kinder and Gentler," *National Journal*, 25 May 1991, 1260.

42. In February 1992 Trans World Airlines became the eighth major airline to go bankrupt since 1989. Martha M.

Hamilton, "Trans World Airlines Files for Bankruptcy," *Washington Post,* 1 February 1992, C2. By 1992 U.S.-flagged commercial shipping had virtually disappeared. See James Bovard, "The Antiquated 1920 Jones Act Slowly Sinks U.S. Shipping," *Insight,* 6 January 1992, 21. In the wake of Desert Storm, $3.1 billion was spent to build and convert ships for the military's cargo fleet. Michael Blood, "An Idea to Use Shipyard as a U.S. Sealift Base," *Philadelphia Inquirer,* 6 February 1992, B-1. The precedent for "leasing" military resources can be traced to 1992. Just such an arrangement occurred in Germany following reunification: "A shortage of German [air] controllers and their unfamiliarity with newly reunified Berlin's busy skies prompted Germany to hire a squadron from the US Air Force at a cost of $35 million for four years. . . . It is the only US military unit that guides civilian air traffic on foreign soil." Soraya S. Nelson, "AF Controllers in Berlin Keep Eye on Civilian Sky," *Air Force Times,* 10 February 1992, 22.

43. See, for example, Helen Dewar, "Nunn Urges Military Shift: Forces Would Aid Domestic Programs," *Washington Post,* 24 June 1992, A17; Rick Maze, "Nunn Urges Military to Take Domestic Missions, *Army Times,* 21 September 1992, 16; Mary Jordan, "Bush Orders U.S. Military to Aid Florida," *Washington Post,* 28 August 1992, A1; George C. Wilson, "Disaster Plan: Give Military the Relief Role," *Army Times,* 21 September 1992, 33; and Rick Maze, "Pentagon May Get Disaster-relief Role Back," *Army Times,* 21 September 1992, 26. See also note 64.

44. See Shuger, 25. Similarly, noting the growing obsolescence of the guard's combat role, a National Guard officer proposed an alternative: "The National Guard can provide a much greater service to the nation by seeking more combat support and combat service support missions and the structure to support them. Such units can participate in nation building or assistance missions throughout the world, to include the United States. . . . Much of our national infrastructure, streets, bridges, health care, water and sewer lines, to name just a few, particularly in the inner cities of the United States, are in disrepair. Many of the necessary repairs could be accomplished by National Guard units on a year-round training basis." Colonel Philip Drew, "Taking the National Guard Out of Combat," *National Guard,* April 1991, 38. Also jumping on the bandwagon are National Guard officers Colonel Philip A. Brehm and Major Wilbur E. Gray in "Alternative Missions for the Army," SSI Study "Pacify the Military," (Strategic Studies Institute, USAWC, 17 July 1992).

45. Eric Schmitt, "U.S. Forces Find Work as Angels Of Mercy," *New York Times,* 12 January 1992, E3.

46. See the legislative history of Public Law 99-661, *U.S. Code Congressional & Administrative News,* 6482. Public Law 99-661 codified in 10 U.S.C. 401 et seq.

47. Ken Adelman, "Military Helping Hands," *Washington Times,* 8 July 1991, D3; Bruce B. Auster with Robin Knight, "The Pentagon Scramble to Stay Relevant," *U.S. News & World Report,* 30 December 1991/6 January 1992, 52.

48. It was predicted that the AIDS epidemic would hit Africa especially hard with infection rates in some cities as high as 40 percent by the year 2000. See Marvin J. Cetron and Owen Davies, "Trends Shaping the World," *Futurist,* September–October 1991, 12. Some experts have predicted that African famine might present a requirement for a military humanitarian mission (Weiss and Campbell, 451–52). See also Richard H. P. Sia, "U.S. Increasing Its Special Forces Activity in Africa," *Baltimore Sun,* 15 March 1992, 1. Long-term military commitments to humanitarian operations have been recommended by some experts (Weiss and Campbell, 457).

49. U.S. troops assigned to African countries in the early 1990s were tasked to "help improve local health-care and economic conditions." See Sia, "U.S. Increasing Its Special Forces," p. 1. Similarly, the notion of using the expertise of U.S. military personnel to perform governmental functions in foreign countries was also suggested in the 1990s. For example, when the food distribution system in the former Soviet Union broke down during the winter of 1991–92, there were calls for Lieutenant General Gus Pagonis, the logistical wizard of the First Gulf War, to be dispatched to take charge of the system. See "A Man Who Knows How," editorial, *Los Angeles Times,* 5 February 1992, 10.

50. As quoted in Robert Debs Heinl Jr., ed., *Dictionary of Military and Naval Quotations* (Annapolis, Md.: U.S. Naval Institute, 1966), 245.

51. Public Law 99-433 (1986). Under the Goldwater-Nichols Defense Reorganization Act, the chairman of the JCS was given much broader powers. Not only is he now the primary military adviser to the president, he is also responsible for furnishing strategic direction to the armed forces, strategic and contingency planning, establishing budget priorities, and developing joint doctrine for all four services. Edward Luttwak and Stuart L. Koehl, eds., *The Dictionary of Modern War* (New York: Harper Collins, 1991), 320. The law also mandated that joint duty be a requirement for promotion to flag rank. See Vincent Davis, "Defense Reorganization and National Security," *The Annals of the American Academy of Political Science,* September 1991, 163–65. This facilitated development of senior military cliques that transcended service lines.

52. Many praised Goldwater-Nichols as the source of success in the Gulf War. See, for example, "Persian Gulf War's Unsung Hero," editorial, *Charleston (South Carolina) News & Courier,* 4 April 1991, 6. See also Sam Nunn, "Military Reform Paved Way for Gulf Triumph," *Atlanta Constitution,* 31 March 1991, G5. But the Gulf War was not a true test of either Goldwater-Nichols or joint warfare. About all that conflict demonstrated was that poorly trained and miserably led conscript armies left unprotected from air attack cannot hold terrain in the face of a modern ground assault.

53. One study concluded that because of Powell's background he was "especially well qualified" for the politically sensitive role as chief of the JCS. See Preston Niblock, ed., *Managing Military Operations in Crises* (Santa Monica, Calif.: RAND, 1991), 51.

54. Representative Denton stated as to Goldwater-Nichols: "This legislation proposes to reverse 200 years of American history by, for the first time, designating by statute . . . a single uniformed officer as the 'Principal Military Advisor' to the President. That change in the role of the Chairman of the Joint Chiefs of Staff is profound in its implications. Similar proposals have been specifically and overwhelmingly rejected in the past—in 1947, 1949,

1958—on the grounds that, in a democracy, no single military officer, no matter what his personal qualifications, should have such power." *U.S. Code Congressional & Administrative News,* 2248. See also Robert Previdi, *Civilian Control versus Military Rule* (New York: Hippocrene Books, 1988).

55. In *The Federalist No. 51* the Founding Fathers warned against the folly of constructing a governmental system based on assumptions about the good character of individuals who might occupy an office.

56. William Matthews, "Nunn: Merge the Services?" *Air Force Times,* 9 March 1992, 6.

57. This belief was enshrined in Joint Pub 1, *Joint Warfare of the United States* (Washington: Office of the JCS, 11 November 1991). It states (p. iii) that "joint warfare is essential to victory." While joint warfare might usually be essential to victory, it cannot be said that it is essential in every instance. For example, rebels—composed entirely of irregular infantry—defeated massive Soviet combined-arms forces in Afghanistan. Equipped only with light arms, Stinger missiles, and light antiaircraft guns, they triumphed without benefit of any air or naval forces, and indeed without unity among themselves. Furthermore, even in the case of Western nations, there are likely to be plenty of hostilities involving single-service air or naval campaigns.

58. Former Secretary of the Navy John Lehman described the value of this creative tension in discussing his criticism of the "unified" Chairman of the Joint Chiefs of Staff occasioned by Goldwater-Nichols. According to Lehman: "Franklin Roosevelt . . . wanted to hear Admiral King argue with Marshall in front of him. He wanted to hear MacArthur argue against Nimitz, and the Air Corps against the Army, and the Navy against all in his presence, so that he would have the option to make the decisions of major strategy in war. He knew that any political leader, no matter how strong, if given only one military position, finds it nearly impossible to go against it. Unfortunately . . . now the president does not get to hear arguments from differing points of view." "U.S. Defense Policy Options: The 1990s and Beyond," *Annals of the American Academy of Political and Social Science* (September 1991), 199–200.

59. See, for example, Arthur C. Forster Jr., "The Essential Need for An Independent Air Force," *Air Force Times,* 7 May 1990, 25.

60. Alexander Hamilton, James Madison, and John Jay, *The Federalist,* as reprinted in the *Great Books of the Western World,* ed. Robert M. Hutchins (Chicago: Encyclopedia Britannica, 1952), vol. 63, 163.

61. Shakespeare called ambition "the soldier's virtue." *Antony and Cleopatra,* Act III, Scene 1, as reprinted in the *Great Books of the Western World,* ed. Hutchins, vol. 27, 327.

62. Samuel P. Huntington, *The Soldier and the State* (Cambridge, Mass.: Harvard University Press, 1959), 87, said: "If the officer corps is originally divided into land, sea, and air elements, and then is unified under the leadership of a single, overall staff and military commander in chief, this change will tend to increase its authority with regard to other institutions of government. It will speak with one voice instead of three. Other groups will not be able to play off one of the officer corps against another."

63. Bruce B. Auster with Robin Knight, "The Pentagon Scramble to Stay Relevant," *U.S. News & World Report,*

December 1991/6 January 1992, 52. Despite the Gulf War, defense outlays were scheduled by 1997 to shrink to their lowest percentage of the federal budget since the end of World War II. Sara Collins, "Cutting Up the Military," *U.S. News & World Report,* 10 February 1992, 29. See also John Lancaster, "Aspin Seeks to Double Bush's Defense Cuts," *Washington Post,* 27 February 1992, A16; and Helen Dewar, "Bush, Mitchell Take Aim at Slashing the Defense Budget," *Washington Post,* 17 January 1992, B1.

64. Morrison, "Operation Kinder and Gentler," 1260. Most revealing, on 1–2 December 1992 the National Defense University at Fort McNair in Washington, D.C., hosted a symposium titled "Non-Traditional Roles for the U.S. Military in the Post–Cold War Era," featuring presentations on disaster relief, refugee evacuation, humanitarian medical care, engineering assistance to infrastructure and environment, counternarcotics, riot control, emergency preparedness, civil unrest, national assistance, and so on.

65. Military analyst Harry Summers insists that ROTC is a key reason military coups have not occurred in the United States as they have in other countries. He notes: "ROTC was designed to produce a well-rounded officer corps inculcated in the principles of freedom, democracy, and American values through close contact with civilian students on an open college campus, and through a liberal education taught by a primarily civilian academic faculty. And that's just what has happened." "Stalking the Wrong Quarry," *Washington Times,* 7 December 1989, F-3.

66. The army plans to cut ROTC officer acquisitions from 7,778 in 1990 to 5,200 in 1995. See Peter Copeland, "ROTC More Selective in Post–Cold War Era," *Washington Times,* 27 May 1991, 3.

67. David Wood, "A Breed Apart, Volunteer Army Grows Distant from Society," *Newark (New Jersey) Star Ledger,* April 1991, 1.

68. The armed services will shrink at least 25 percent by 1995. Richard Cheney, "U.S. Defense Strategy for an Era of Uncertainty," *International Defense Review,* 1992, 7. But service academy graduates are expected to decline by only 10 percent during the same period. Eric Schmitt, "Service Academies Grapple with Cold War Thaw," *New York Times,* 3 March 1992, 12. Just after the Vietnam War, West Point was supplying about 8 percent of new army officers, compared to the current 24 percent, a new study by the congressional General Accounting Office (GAO) suggests. To roll back the officer stream from West Point, the GAO says, enrollment might have to be limited to 2,500 cadets, a 40 percent drop from today. Larry Pardon, "Changing Cadence at West Point," *Los Angeles Times,* 25 March 1992, 1.

69. See, for example, Tom Philip, "CSUS May End ROTC over Anti-Gay Policy," *Sacramento Bee,* 15 February 1992, 1.

70. As of November 1991, eighty-nine law schools prohibit or restrict on-campus military recruiting. See "Sexual Preference Issue," *HQ USAF/JAX Professional Development Update,* November 1991, 9. Such bans are not legal in most cases. The 10 U.S.C. 2358; and *U.S. v. City of Philadelphia,* 798 F.2d 81 (3d Cir. 1986). Furthermore, by condoning the exclusion of military recruiters from campuses—billed as "marketplaces of ideas"—these universities legitimized censorship of "politically incorrect" views.

71. An article by journalist David Wood grasped this trend. He quoted an army officer as stating, "We are isolated—we don't have a lot of exposure to the outside world." Wood goes on to observe: "The nation's 2 million active soldiers are a self-contained society, one with its own solemn rituals, its own language, its own system of justice, and even its own system of keeping time. . . . Only a decade ago, life within the confines of a military base might have seemed a spartan existence. But improving the garrison life has been a high priority. As a result, many bases have come to resemble an ideal of small-town America. . . . There is virtually no crime or poverty. Drug addicts and homeless are mere rumors from the outside." "Duty, Honor, Isolation: Military More and More a Force unto Itself," *Newark (New Jersey) Star Ledger,* 21 April 1991, 1. See also Laura Elliot, "Behind the Lines," *Washingtonian,* April 1991, 160.

72. Wood, Duty Honor Institution, 1.

73. Studies indicate that defeat in war may actually increase the likelihood of a military coup. Ekkart Zimmermann, "Toward a Causal Model of Military Coups d'Etat," *Armed Forces and Society* 5 (Spring 1979): 399.

74. *United States ex rel. Toth* v. *Quarles,* 350 U.S. 11, 17, 76 S. Ct. 1 (1955). Of course, Carl von Clausewitz had put it even better: "The end for which a soldier is recruited, clothed, armed, and trained, the whole object of his sleeping, eating, drinking, and marching, is simply that he should fight at the right place and the right time." *On War,* Michael Howard and Peter Paret, eds. (Princeton: Princeton University Press, 1976), 95.

75. Barton Gellman, "Strategy for the '90s: Reduce Size and Preserve Strength," *Washington Post,* 9 December 1991, A10.

76. See, for example, Brown, "Drugs on the Border: The Role of the Military," 50.

77. According to one report, the effort was futile and wasteful: "We're getting so little of the drug traffic for such a great expenditure of effort," lamented one navy officer: "We're pouring money into the ocean, at a time when resources are scarce." William Matthews, "Drug War Funds Would Shrink under Budget Proposal," *Air Force Times,* 17 February 1992, 33.

78. John Lancaster reported that proposals to cut guard and reserve funding "inflame passions on Capitol Hill," causing Congress to resist cutting the part-time forces. "Pentagon Cuts Hill-Favored Targets," *Washington Post,* 24 January 1992, A6. Art Pine reported that the guard and reserves "exercise stunning political power and influence, both among state and local governments and in the power centers of Washington." Pine quoted Brookings Institution expert Martin Binkin as saying that the guard/reserve lobby "makes the gun lobby led by the National Rifle Association look like amateurs." Art Pine, "In Defense of 2nd Line Defenders," *Los Angeles Times,* 13 March 1992, 1.

79. Former director of operations for the Joint Staff, Lieutenant General Thomas Kelly, believed there was simply not enough training time to keep guard units ready for the kind of highly complex warfare the army now conducts. He said, "There is nothing on earth harder to teach than the maneuver function in combat." As quoted by Grant Willis, "A New Generation of Warriors," *Navy Times,* 16 March 1991, 12. The motivation of some guardsmen toward fulfilling their military responsibilities was called into question when up to 80 percent of the guardsmen in California units called up for Desert Storm reported for duty unable to meet physical fitness standards. Steve Gibson, "Guards Flunked Fitness," *Sacramento Bee,* 18 June 1991, B1.

80. "Decisive Force," *National Military Strategy of the United States* (Washington, D.C.: GPO, 1992), 10; "Contingency Forces," *National Military Strategy of the United States* (Washington, D.C.: GPO, 1992), 23. Secretary of Defense Richard Cheney and Chairman of the Joint Chiefs of Staff Colin Powell testified before the Senate Armed Services Committee on 31 January 1992 that the military of the future "would be smaller and more mobile and flexible. . . . Its likely target would be regional conflicts, in which American firepower might still be needed on short notice." As reported by Eric Schmitt, "Pentagon Says More Budget Cuts Would Hurt Combat Effectiveness," *New York Times,* 1 February 1992, 9.

81. Military analyst and decorated combat veteran David Hackworth sized up the guard and reserves as follows: "Except for the air and Marine combat components, these forces aren't worth the billions paid each year to them. The combat service and support units are great, but there are too many of them." "A Pentagon Dreamland," *Washington Post,* 23 February 1992, C3.

82. Operation Provide Hope was a two-week humanitarian aid effort involving sixty-four U.S. Air Force sorties carrying approximately 4.5 million pounds of food and medicine. Michael Smith, "First of up to 64 Relief Flights Arrives in Kiev," *Air Force Times,* 24 February 1992, 8. For Baker quotation, see David Hoffman, "Pentagon to Airlift Aid to Republics," *Washington Post,* 24 January 1992, A1.

83. The vice chairman of the Joint Chiefs of Staff also saw the military's future role in noncombat terms. Stating that there was "no plausible scenario" in which the United States would be involved in a military conflict in Europe or with elements of the former Soviet Union, he maintained that the likeliest use of military forces would be to address instability that could arise from migrations by poor peoples of the world to wealthier regions. He envisioned the military's role: "You would like to deal with this on a political and social level. The military's role should be subtle, similar to the role it plays now in Latin America— digging wells, building roads, and teaching the militaries of host nations how to operate under a democratic system. . . . When prevention fails, the military can be called to the more active role of running relief operations like the current one at Guantanamo Bay, Cuba, for fleeing Haitians. Operation Provide Comfort, the giant US military rescue mission to save Kurdish refugees who fled from the Iraqi army to the snow-covered mountains of southeastern Turkey last spring, may have been a precursor of what we can look forward to in the next decade if not the next century." As quoted by William Matthews, "Military Muscle to Shift to Humanitarian Help," *Air Force Times,* 6 January 1992, 14.

84. Leon Hader, "Reforming Israel—Before It's Too Late," *Foreign Policy,* No. 81 (Winter 1990/91): 111.

85. Richard J. Barnet, "Reflections—The Uses Of Force," *New Yorker,* 29 April 1991, 82.

86. Charles Lane, "The Newest War," 18.

87. *Newsweek* reported the following incident: when a Marine reconnaissance patrol skirmished with smugglers near the Arizona-Mexico border last December—firing over their heads to disperse them—one colonel near retirement age shook his head. He argued that combat-trained marines shouldn't be diminishing hard-learned skills by squeezing off warning shots. "That teaches some very bad habits," he said. Bill Torque and Douglas Waller, "Warriors without War," 19 March 1990, 18.

88. Charles Lane, "The Newest War," 18.

89. As quoted by Morrison, "Operation Kinder and Gentler." This relief operation involved 8,000 sailors and marines tasked to help millions of Bangladesh survivors of a 30 April 1991 cyclone. See Morrison, 1260.

90. Barton Gellman, "Strategy for the '90s: Reduce Size and Preserve Strength," *Washington Post,* 9 December 1991, A10.

91. Shuger, "Pacify the Military," 25.

92. Harry Summers, "When Armies Lose Sight of Purpose," *Washington Times,* 26 December 1991, D3.

93. See "Warnings Echo from Jefferson to Eisenhower to Desert Storm," *USA Today,* 1 March 1991, 10A.

94. A caller to a radio talk show typified this view. She stated that while she appreciated the need for a military in case "something like Iraq came up again," she believed that the military ought to be put to work rebuilding the infrastructure and cleaning up the cities instead of "sitting around the barracks." "The Joel Spevak Show," Station WRC, Washington, D.C., 11 March 1992.

95. One example of the dangers of lowering standards to achieve social goals is Project 100,000. Conceived as a Great Society program, youths with test scores considered unacceptably low were nevertheless allowed to enter the armed forces during the 1966–72 period. The idea was to give the disadvantaged poor the chance to obtain education and discipline in a military environment, but the results were a fiasco. See Marilyn B. Young, *The Vietnam Wars, 1945–1990* (New York: Harper Collins, 1991), 320.

96. Richard A. Gabriel, *To Serve with Honor* (Westport, Conn.: Greenwood, 1982), 178.

CIVIL–MILITARY RELATIONS IN THE UNITED STATES

DOUGLAS V. JOHNSON AND STEVEN METZ

For Americans, few national security issues are more enmeshed in tradition and emotion than civil–military relations. An important problem for the Founding Fathers, the relationship between the citizenry and the forces that protect it continues to touch intensely sensitive beliefs about the proper distribution of political power in a free society. Cries have sporadically emerged that the equilibrium between the military and its civilian overseers is skewed in the military's favor. Such a "crisis school" is again coalescing, led by writers such as Richard Kohn (1994).

It is easy to understand why a "crisis school" should emerge. Civil-military relations, like most aspects of U.S. national security, are changing, and change always demands adjustment. This is nothing new: the relationship of civilian leaders and the uniformed military has often been adjusted to reflect alterations in the global strategic environment, the nature of warfare, domestic politics, sociocultural trends, and the capabilities and institutional values of the military and the civilian institutions that control it (Finer 1975). If there is anything unusual about the current readjustment, it is the activism of the military. More than at any time in the past, the U.S. military is helping define its relationship to civil authorities and to the American public. To assess whether there is, in fact, a crisis in U.S. civil–military relations, it is necessary to know both what is written *about* the military and what is written, thought, and discussed *by* it.

THE TRADITION

The framers of the Constitution never anticipated the controversy that eventually surrounded military involvement in making national policy and strategy (Huntington 1957, 164–65). As in Europe, the American political and military elites were coterminous during the early years of the Republic. The Founding Fathers certainly intended civilian control of the military (Kohn 1991), but in a time when the bulk of the American military was composed of militia citizen-soldiers, it made no sense to think that a George Washington or an Andrew Jackson brought a fundamentally different approach to policy and strategy because they had held military command. By the mid–nineteenth century, this had begun to change. The importation of military ideas from Europe, the creation of the military academies at West Point and Annapolis, and the formation of permanent (if small) armed forces to patrol the frontier and to suppress

This essay has been edited and is reprinted from The Washington Quarterly *18 (Winter 1995): 197–213, by permission of* MIT Press.

piracy and smuggling gave birth to a discrete group of military professionals. But before the Civil War, the notion of a uniquely military perspective on policy and strategy had not fully formed. Even George McClellan's run for the presidency in 1864 was traumatic not because he was a military officer but because he was a popular figure who seemed less dedicated than Lincoln to outright military victory and the abolition of slavery. In fact, the presence of many generals on both sides whose credentials for command were elected office rather than military training showed that the separation of political and military leadership was not yet firm in the minds of Americans.

After the Civil War, the notion arose that political participation and military professionalism were incompatible. This attitude was less imposed by distrustful civilians than generated *within* the military. Most officers felt that professionalism required aloofness from politics to a degree bordering on disdain. In fact, Samuel Huntington (1957, 258) notes that not one in five hundred professional military officers had ever cast a ballot. At a higher level, military involvement in policy and strategy making was not an issue, mostly because the military did not seek an active role. "By the eve of the Second World War," Russell Weigley (1993, 41) writes, "the respect of the American military for civil supremacy was perhaps at its highest, reaching a degree of self-denial that even ardent champions of the principle might in retrospect regard as excessive." Because military power was a relatively unimportant element of prewar American statecraft—or at least less important than it would later become—this was readily accepted.

Civil–military relations during World War II, "though judged defective, were relatively harmonious and reasonably effective" (Hendrickson 1988, 27). Analysts differ as to the basis of this harmony. Weigley (1993, 43) attributes it to "remarkably silent military acquiescence." Army planners, he notes, considered the Philippines indefensible but did not question the Roosevelt administration's pledge of protection. They also opposed the diversion of supplies to China and Operation Torch (the invasion of North Africa) but buckled before the dictates of President Franklin D. Roosevelt's diplomacy. Huntington (1957, 315–20), by contrast, considers the weakness of civilian officials other than Roosevelt the basis of wartime comity between the military and civilians. Civilians, including those in the State Department, simply ceased to consider grand strategy, thus augmenting the role of the military.

By the end of the war, the military had fully abandoned its self-imposed isolation from questions of policy or higher strategy. In reaction, the notion that military influence on policy and strategy was inherently bad or dangerous was revived. Part of its basis was the theme that led the Founding Fathers to enshrine the notion of civilian control of the military—the belief that military influence over national policy was a threat to democratic values. Post–World War II writers such as Harold Lasswell warned that the United States might be transformed into a "garrison state" with an erosion of democracy and civil rights (Huntington 1957, 346–54). This line of thinking still persists. For instance, David R. Segal (1994, 375) sees

a continuing pragmatic attempt to balance fundamental democratic values and ideals against elements of their defense that have at times intruded upon the rule of law, individual freedoms, and popular participation in policy debate and decision-making by an informed citizenry.

Even Huntington (1957)—the dean of scholars of American civil–military relations—stressed the enduring importance of managing the tension between the dominant liberalism of the American political culture and the conservatism of the military.

But the idea that military influence in policy making might challenge democratic values was never the most important argument of those who sought to constrain the military during the Cold War. More important was the perception by some civilians that the military was unable to fully grasp the role of military force in the modern security environment. The military, according to this notion, was still imbued with the traditional American tendency to see a rigid separation between war and peace, could not accept the notion of limited war, and was unable to apply force subtly in support of statecraft. The military was seen as a guard dog so thoroughly trained to attack that it became unsuitable as a pet or companion. In the Cold War security environment, major conventional war—which the U.S. military understood—seemed a less pressing threat than new forms of conflict. The appearance of nuclear weapons, for instance, meant that the use of conventional military force often ran the risk of escalation to annihilation (Flint 1991, 261; Feaver 1992, 87–106). At the other end of the conflict spectrum, Marxist "people's war" posed equal conundrums.

Both nuclear strategy and Marxist people's war thus obviated the old balance of responsibility that had left the military in charge of war and civilians in charge of nonwar policy and strategy. U.S. national security strategy was forced to become holistic, making a clear delineation of functions and responsibilities difficult. The Cold War was a total struggle requiring—in André Beaufre's (1974, ix) term—a "total strategy" integrating military, political, economic, moral, and ideological elements. Weigley (1993, 56) notes:

The era of the Cold War brought an unprecedented frequency of decisions to be made at [the] political-diplomatic-strategic intersection. Of necessity, this Cold War circumstance also produced an unprecedented mingling of civilian and military leaders in the course of the policy-making process.

To many civilian policy makers it appeared that the military insisted on seeing all uses of military force through the lens of full-scale conventional war. General Douglas MacArthur, for example, seemed oblivious to the risk of escalation to the nuclear level, thus precipitating one of the most serious civil–military crises in U.S. history (James 1988; Flint 1991; Rovere and Schlesinger 1992). In Vietnam, the army continued to treat Marxist people's war like a conventional struggle (Krepinevich 1986). Even today Harry Summers's work *On Strategy* (1982), which argues that Vietnam was essentially a conventional war, retains a tremendous following within the U.S. military.

The perception on the part of civilians that the military was unable or unwilling to grasp the nature and role of military force in modern statecraft—whether or not it was accurate—might have inspired a return to the pre–World War II quarantine of the military from policy making. Other factors supported such an effort. The rise of a community of civilian strategists in universities and think tanks, for instance, broke the military's monopoly on strategic wisdom (Gray 1982). It also provided a perspective at odds with mainstream military thinking. According to Weigley (1973, 406), "American scholars and intellectuals tended to be more deeply imbued with suspicion of the military than the general run of civilians, and in the past there had been especially little scholarly investigation of military problems."

But several factors counterbalanced the pressure to quarantine the military from policy making during the early Cold War years. The most important of these was the Soviet military threat. The Soviet Army (and People's Liberation Army) did more to increase the political influence of the U.S. military than any other single organization. This was particularly true after the informal acceptance of a version of containment with heavy emphasis on military strength. Second was the popularity and prestige of the military, especially its senior leaders (Huntington 1957, 354). Third was the dramatic increase in defense spending that made the military a much more important element of the U.S. economy. Eventually a tenuous equilibrium was reached between the desire to limit military influence and the need for it. This was codified in the seminal National Security Act of 1947 and other pieces of legislation.

By the early 1960s, several trends had combined to complicate civil–military relations if not to spark a full-blown crisis. First, the maturity of U.S. strategic nuclear forces, strategy, and employment doctrine appeared to further decrease the chances of a large-scale conventional war—the military forte. Second was a widespread perception of financial profligacy on the part of the military. Fear of excessive military spending was central to President Dwight D. Eisenhower's national security strategy; his solution was "massive retaliation" (Metz 1991, 53–54). Although the army opposed this, the air force and navy generally supported it, thus dividing the services and weakening their opposition. President John F. Kennedy picked up on the same theme but had a different approach: managerial efficiency as engineered by Secretary of Defense Robert S. McNamara. In contrast to massive retaliation, this threatened all the

services equally, thus forcing them to form a united front in opposition (although with uneven success). McNamara eroded the military's quantitative brainpower advantage by dramatically enlarging his own staff and brought to the Pentagon a new way of thinking about military affairs—operations research —that the uniformed services initially did not understand. The dynamic and confident secretary of defense "ignored or dismissed military advice, disparaged military experience and expertise, and circumvented or sacked generals and admirals who opposed him" (Kohn 1994, 6).

The trend unsettling civil–military relations in the early 1960s was the rapid spread of Marxist people's war throughout the Third World. Frustrated by the military's apparent unwillingness to grapple with this, Kennedy instigated a number of reforms such as the expansion of Army Special Forces and the formation of the Special Warfare School (Simpson 1983, 65–68). But, Krepinevich (1986) argues, such efforts were marginalized by the conventional thinking of military leaders. Even General Maxwell Taylor (1972, 200) admits, "It took some time for most American officials in Washington, myself included, to sense the full significance of the threat of Wars of National Liberation as President Kennedy viewed it." Coming on the heels of the McNamara reforms, Vietnam thus represented the nadir of comity between senior military leaders and civilian policy makers. The civilians believed they needed to control the military tightly in order to mold military operations to political objectives; the military leaders believed that civilians prevented the winning of the war and squandered both resources and lives (Kohn 1994, 6).

In other countries, such a precipitous decline in the power and autonomy of the military might have sparked a coup: the U.S. military embarked on reform. Luckily for the military, eight years of GOP control of the White House gave it breathing space because Republicans traditionally accord the military freer rein than Democrats (Hendrickson 1988, 34; Kohn 1994, 6). This effort took several forms. The services forged a common front, because interservice differences had often been used by civilians to play one service off against another and thus to control them all. The military built and sustained alliances with supporters in the executive and in Congress (Kohn 1994, 6). At the same time, the military cultivated political and strategic expertise within its ranks so as to leave no doubt about its competence in modern politico-military strategy. Sam Sarkesian and John Williams (1994, 219; also Graves, 1990), for instance, note the importance of full-time, civilian graduate education—which became a de facto requirement for higher rank in the air force and army—in giving officers intellectual flexibility. Similarly, the curricula at the four war colleges and, to a lesser extent, at the command and staff colleges, paid greater attention to world politics, strategy, and national security policy making. Initiatives like the army's Foreign Area Officer Program, which gave selected officers regional expertise through a combination of graduate education and assignments in their areas, contributed to the process. And in the 1970s the strategic-level service journals—*Naval War College Review, Parameters,* and *Air University Review*—began to devote greater space to foreign policy and national strategy. According to Admiral William J. Crowe Jr. (1993, 23)—a Princeton Ph.D.—by the 1980s few officers "made it into the higher ranks without a firm grasp of international relations, congressional politics, and public affairs."

Some writers find the inspiration for this reform movement inside the military and attribute it to the normal (albeit dangerous in the case of the military) bureaucratic desire to gain greater institutional prerogative and influence. Mark Perry (1989, xvii), for instance, sees the Joint Chiefs of Staff (JCS) waging a "forty-year battle to gain a larger role in making decisions on American foreign policy." Weigley (1993, 57) places greater stress on Vietnam; after the war, he wrote

the Joint Chiefs campaigned consistently both to secure statutory authority for a military voice in deliberating on national policy and strategy, and through public pronouncements to influence policy-making in ways that will guard them against a repetition of waging war under the constraints against the application of overwhelming power that prevailed in Korea and Vietnam.

There were, then, two struggles under way: a broad one to determine the proper role of military power in U.S. strategy, and a more specific one to determine the particular way in which military power would be used.

In addition to the intramilitary drive for greater political acumen and, by default, a greater role in determining national policy and strategy, an active military reform movement in Congress and the defense intellectual community also pushed for change. This group argued that not only had the military failed to develop a coherent notion of modern strategy, but it also needed to be forced to alter its organization, doctrine, force structure, manpower policy, and methods of weapons acquisition (Hendrickson, 1988; Art, Davis, and Huntington, 1985). Writers such as Edward N. Luttwak (1985) advocated not just change, but "drastic, fundamental reform." But unlike defense intellectuals who could cajole but not coerce, the reformers in Congress such as Senators Gary Hart (Democrat of Colorado) and Sam Nunn (Democrat of Georgia) had the power to directly change the structure and attitudes of the military. Their apogee—and the most influential single determinant of American civil–military relations since the National Security Act of 1947—was the 1986 Department of Defense Reorganization Act (Public Law 99-433), sponsored by Senators Barry Goldwater (Republican of Arizona) and Congressman Bill Nichols (Democrat of Alabama).

Goldwater-Nichols assumed that the weakness of military advice to national policy makers did not reflect shortcomings in the actual thinking of senior officers, but in the structure for the articulation of this advice. Despite opposition from Secretary of Defense Caspar W. Weinberger and many within the military (Crowe 1993, 146–161), the act greatly strengthened the chairman of the JCS and named him the principal military adviser to the president, the National Security Council, and the secretary of defense. According to Perry (1989, 340),

By making the chairman an official member of the NSC, Congress endorsed long-held JCS beliefs that civilian decisions on military questions had often led to disaster. The JCS chairman had the right to give advice not only when asked, but also when not asked. The nation's military leaders were no longer disqualified from being included in foreign policy discussions simply because they wore uniforms.

Critics of the strengthening of the chairman quickly made themselves heard. An unintended side effect of Goldwater-Nichols, they argued, was to dramatically increase the power of the uniformed military and thus challenge the degree of civilian control imposed by McNamara. According to former Secretary of the Navy John Lehman,

Civilian control, as the term is generally understood and certainly as it was intended by the Founding Fathers, has been eliminated by years of well-meaning reform legislation, culminating in the Goldwater-Nichols Act, drafted almost entirely by military staff officers from the Joint Chiefs of Staff and the committee staffs. . . . In their understandable quest for efficiency, the military reformers have consolidated the power previously separated between the military departments, disenfranchised the civilian officials of each service, and created autocracy in the Joint Staff and arbitrary power in the person of the Chairman. (Powell and others 1994, 23, 24)

The contemporary "crisis school" of civil–military relations thus grew from the military's internal reforms and from Goldwater-Nichols.

THE DEBATE

Appearing soon after implementation of Goldwater-Nichols, Robert Previdi's *Civilian Control versus Military Rule* (1988, 9) called the new law "the most important piece of military legislation passed by the Congress in the last forty years . . . [and] the most dangerous." An alarmist work intended for the public rather than scholars of civil–military relations, Previdi's book claimed that Goldwater-Nichols "represents the first potential challenge to civilian control of the military in the history of the United States" (p. 10). His basis was a contention that "a civilian is best qualified to understand political policy" (PMO). In a 1994 *Commentary* article, Edward Luttwak (1994, 29)—a persistent connoisseur of controversy—amplified the alarmist critique, and his impressive credentials as a strategic thinker gave his argument greater weight than Previdi's. Luttwak considered "the collapse of civilian control over the military policies and military strategy of the United States . . . the biggest Washington scandal by far." "The Great Pentagon Reform," he continued, "has since shown us that the only thing worse than interservice rivalry is interservice harmony" (p. 30). We are, he argued, in "the reign of the Joint Staff" and, in the Persian Gulf War, saw a military ducking civilian control by skillful manipulation of the media and by only briefing civilian decision makers on war plans after they were worked out in too much detail to change.

The assumption of the JCS chairmanship by Colin Powell in 1989 added fuel to charges that the civil—military balance was skewed in favor of the military. Crowe—the first post–Goldwater-Nichols chairman—concluded that the chairman was obligated to give overall rather than simply military advice to the president (Woodward 1991, 39). He preferred, however, to act behind the scenes (Kohn 1994, 8–9). Powell, with his vast experience in international affairs as the president's national security adviser, was a different breed (Means 1992; Roth 1993). He saw himself, Bob Woodward (1991, 154) wrote, as "the action officer connecting the military forces to the political system and the political system back to the forces." Often accused of being a "political general," Powell responded, "there isn't a general in Washington who isn't political, not if he's going to be successful, because that's the nature of our system" (p. 155).

With the combination of the legal power flowing from Goldwater-Nichols and his own tremendous political skill, Powell became the most influential JCS chairman in U.S. history. He was, according to Kohn (1994, 9), "the most powerful military leader since George C. Marshall, the most popular since Dwight D. Eisenhower, and the most political since Douglas MacArthur." During the Bush administration, the president's personal interest in national security and the firm control of the military by Secretary of Defense Richard B. Cheney contained any worries that Powell was too political, too influential. When Bill Clinton assumed office with "less experience, interest, understanding, and credibility in military affairs" than any president since the 1920s (Kohn 1994, 4), there were warnings that Powell's influence was too great. In a melodramatic screed, Colman McCarthy (1993) called Powell "just one more warlord" who "knows the art of self-lionization" and "is a cunning myth builder." Somewhat more seriously, Kohn (1994, 9), in a widely discussed essay in *The National Interest*, wrote, "it was under Colin Powell's tenure that civilian control eroded most since the rise of the military establishment in the 1940s and 1950s."

The basis of this fear is not entirely clear. Kohn seems more concerned by the very fact that a uniformed officer developed a national security strategy that he then pushed in influential venues like *Foreign Affairs* (Powell 1992/93) than in the actual content of his positions. Powell's "defiance of a young, incoming president with extraordinarily weak au-

thority in military affairs," Kohn feels, set the stage for "resistance all down the line." "No commander-in-chief," he wrote, was "ever so disliked or so reviled or spoken of with such contempt and dislike by the professional military, as Bill Clinton" (1994, 13–14). To the extent that there were discernible differences in Powell's approach to policy and strategy and that of his civilian superiors, they concerned the appropriate use of military force. But in contrast to the liberal warnings of the early Cold War that military officers would overmilitarize U.S. foreign policy, Powell subscribed to the restrictive set of conditions for the use of military force first presented in Weinberger's November 1984 speech to the National Press Club (Weinberger 1990, 433–45) and well analyzed by Sabrosky and Sloane (1988). As part of the U.S. military's post-Vietnam rebuilding of internal morale and public support, it sought to avoid the use of force where there were no clear and attainable objectives. Driven by this credo, Powell opposed the use of force in Bosnia, thus appearing at odds with the Clinton administration. On this issue as well as on force cuts and the issue of gays in the military, Powell held such strong beliefs that some administration officials thought "the general was guilty of something close to insubordination" (Lacayo 1993, 32).

Kohn's *National Interest* article prompted a number of retorts. Colin Powell himself wrote, "Of all the problems facing the nation, a crisis in civil–military relations is not one of them and things are not out of control. . . . Presidents Bush and Clinton, and Secretaries Cheney and Aspin, exercised solid, unmistakable control over the Armed Forces and especially me" (Powell and others 1994, 23). William Odom and Samuel Huntington also deny that the United States is experiencing a crisis in civil–military relations (Powell and others 1994). As evidence of the constrained role of even the post–Goldwater-Nichols chairman, Crowe pointed to "the ease with which the Iran-Contra conspirators circumvented the JCS" (Crowe 1993, 300). And, as Perry (1989, 341) noted, Goldwater-Nichols ensures that the nation's top military officers will be *heard* by civilian policy makers, but not that they be *heeded*. That depends on the quality and needs of the individuals involved. Writers of the "crisis school" like Previdi, Luttwak, and, especially, Kohn, have not demonstrated that there is a military approach to national policy and strategy that is incongruent with nonmilitary approaches, or that military involvement in policy making changes the outcome in some undesirable way. The basis of their argument thus seems based primarily on nostalgia and fear of change.

But even if we are not in the midst of a crisis, an ongoing adjustment in U.S. civil–military relations is clearly taking place. The primary issues seem to be, first, whether the solutions are structural or attitudinal and, second, whether the key to reestablishing equilibrium is military self-restraint or increased civilian competence. The heart of support for structural adjustments is, of course, the Congress because legislation can change structure directly but only alter attitudes indirectly as when, for example, Congress changed military attitudes toward joint duty by making it a prerequisite for flag rank. Lehman takes the structuralist approach when he advocates making the military service secretaries "operating executives" through whom the secretary of defense exercises civilian control, including control of promotions and assignments (Powell and others 1994, 25). Political scientist David Hendrickson (1988, 28) follows the alternate tack when he argues, "An appropriate pattern of civil–military relations . . . depends not so much on the formal institutional arrangements among civilian and military leaders as on the attitude each adopts toward the other."

On the second question, Kenneth Kemp and Charles Hudlin (1992) approach civil–military relations as an ethical issue and focus on respect for civilian control as a moral obligation of soldiers rather than on institutional or legal frameworks. Huntington also stresses self-restraint within the military. "The military must," he writes, "abandon participation in public debate about foreign and military policy, stop building alliances amongst the public and in Congress for defense spending and resist the temptation to maneuver in the bureaucracy to achieve its own ends, however commendable" (Powell and others 1994, 30). But Huntington also expresses a more prevalent opinion: that increased military activity in policy making is largely due to inadequacies on the part of civilian strategists and those charged with overseeing the military. Huntington first noted the problem of weak civilian leadership in national security strategy in his classic *The Soldier and the State* (1957, 263). More recently, he has written:

Military establishments want political leaders to set forth reasonably clear goals and policies. If political leaders fail to do this, chiefs of staff have to make their own assumptions and develop their plans and programs accordingly. . . . It is to the great credit of the American military that it did not attempt to perpetuate Cold War strategies and instead took the initiative in attempting to redefine its missions and restructure its forces. It was the top political leadership which failed to adapt rapidly to the changed conditions. (Powell and others 1994, 28)

Even Richard Kohn (1994, 10), while sounding the claxon of crisis, admits that Colin Powell took the lead in crafting a new national military strategy largely because the National Security Council, Department of State, and Office of the Secretary of Defense were "so devoid of a vision of the future international system." The failure of the Clinton administration to release a national security strategy document until July 1994 (Clinton 1994) or to produce a new national military strategy document to replace the 1992 version (Powell 1992) perpetuated the impression that the military must take the lead in the massive post–Cold War transformation of U.S. national security policy.

Some observers attribute the decline of civilian effectiveness to recent reform legislation. According to James Kitfield (1994, 72),

Tight ethics restrictions have discouraged good candidates for top civilian posts at the Pentagon from serving. And as an unintended result, the pendulum of power over defense affairs has swung from the civilian to the military side of the government's national security apparatus.

This is an important point. Even more than a vacuum, the military abhors disorder defined as inadequate or inconsistent attention to important problems and the absence of logical, sequential planning procedures. In making national policy and strategy, military officers are often frustrated by the failure of civilians to adopt similarly rigorous methods for defining objectives and allocating resources. Social scientists have long noted the linkage of frustration and aggression. For the U.S. military, frustration, in combination with a naturally aggressive institutional culture, spawned organizational aggression. The dominant pattern of civil–military relations is for the military to accept or attempt to seize functions that it perceives civilian leaders or agencies as not performing or not performing adequately. It is not that the military has some deep-set desire to increase its power, but rather that it feels compelled to do so. For supporters of the position that civilian inadequacies rather than military power lust is the root of the problem, the onus is on civilian leaders and agencies to either show why these functions do not need to be performed or to perform them adequately.

THE MILITARY VOICE

The military's influence on civil–military relations is indirect and attitudinal. Officers can lobby for or against legislation that will affect the military's internal organization. They can also form alliances with like-minded officials and members of Congress. But probably the most important way the military affects civil–military relations is through cultivation of attitudes among its ranks. Often this is codified in doctrine. Military doctrine is the official, usually consensual, statement of what a service is and does. It is a basic guide book. Most services incorporate some notion of civil–military relations in basic doctrine. For example, the U.S. Navy's newly released, first comprehensive doctrinal statement, Naval Doctrine Publication 1, *Naval Warfare,* emphasizes the civil–military relationship: "Doctrine guides our actions . . . and provides a basis for mutual understanding within and among the services and the national policymakers" (Department of the Navy 1994). No other doctrinal statement is quite as explicit as this in addressing the necessity of informing "national policymakers."

Inside the front cover of the U.S. Army's lead doctrinal statement, Field Manual 100-1, *The Army,* is a historical vignette describing how George Washington rebuked officers who suggested that he seize authoritarian power. Their primary concern was the government's failure to pay them; Washington's was the principles for which the Revolution had been fought. The selection of this particular event to open the army's foundation doctrine illustrates its attitude toward civilian control of the military. Continuing this theme, the foreword states, "We are an Army that is rooted in the traditions of our democracy" (Department of the Army 1994, ii). The preface then begins, "FM 100-1, The Army, expresses the Army's fundamental purpose, roles, responsibilities, and functions, as established by the Constitution, Congress and the Department of Defense" (p. v). Chapter 2, "The American Army," discusses in detail "The Constitutional and Legal Basis" of the army and then continues its focus on the use of military force as an instrument of national power in support of national purpose. This idea has been present in every edition of this field manual. The theme of military subordination to civilian control reappears in Chapter 5 with a discussion of the manner in which army forces may be employed by the National Command Authorities in support of national security goals. Army subordination to civil authority is described in the subsection "Command and Control of the Armed Forces," which emphasizes the change growing from Goldwater-Nichols. A new subsection entitled "Employment Considerations" was added to the 1994 edition. This is intended to integrate the precepts of just war, national security policy, and the professional responsibilities of senior military leaders while at the same time making it clear that the key decisions are the responsibility of the civilians.

Although neither air force nor Marine Corps doctrine manuals stress civilian control of the military in this fashion, they all clearly note the subordination of military activity to national strategic goals (see, for example, Department of the Air Force [1992] and Department of the Navy [1989], 19–20).

If the services were in revolt, as the "crisis school" suggests, it would be reasonable to see some indication in the pages of the extensive military press, but there is no such evidence. More common are criticisms of the military, and enjoinders to serving officers about the importance of civilian control. For example, the most provocative article to appear recently in *Parameters*, the organ of the U.S. Army War College, has been "The Origins of the American Military Coup of 2012" by Charles J. Dunlap Jr. (1992–93). This is a fictional account of a future military coup told from the perspective of a prisoner of the government. It can thus be considered a contribution to the "crisis school" of civil–military relations from a serving officer, but it dramatically expands the horizons of the critique. The upcoming crisis, as the author sees it, will derive from changes made in the core missions of the U.S. military during the 1990s. He writes,

When the military was then obliged to engage in a bewildering array of nontraditional duties to further justify its existence, it is little wonder that its traditional apolitical professionalism eventually eroded. (p. 14)

Dunlap is certainly correct in the advice he believes a hypothetical graduation speaker for an Army War College class of 1992 ought to have given:

- Demand that the armed forces focus exclusively on indisputably military duties.

- Acknowledge that national security does have economic, social, educational, and environmental dimensions but insist that this doesn't necessarily mean the problems in those areas are the responsibility of the military.

- Readily cede budgetary resources to those agencies whose business it is to address the nonmilitary issues the armed forces are presently asked to fix.

- Divest the defense budget of perception-skewing expenses.

- Continue to press for the elimination of superfluous, resource-draining Guard and Reserve units.

- Educate the public to the sophisticated training requirements of modern warfare.

- Resist unification of the services both on operational grounds and because unification would be inimical to the checks and balances that underpin democratic government.

- Assure that officer accessions from the service academies correspond with overall force reductions (but maintain separate service academies) and keep ROTC on a wide diversity of campuses.

- Ensure that all echelons of society are represented in the military without compromising standards.

- Encourage military members and families to assimilate into civilian communities. (p. 14)

Dunlap errs, however, in his description of things he calls nontraditional. As the past commandant of the U.S. Army War College, Major General William Stofft, made clear in remarks to the officers drafting Field Manual 100-1, *The Army*, most of what is described today as nontraditional activity has been what the army has done for most of its existence. The Cold War was but 44 years of history; the U.S. Army is 218 years old. What is truly disturbing about Dunlap's article is the author's failure to grasp the complexity of the U.S. government. It is a fact of history and the will of the Congress that the army not be restricted to purely war-fighting duties. Were such a thing to take place, the pressure from the people would be overwhelming to disband the organization or reduce it to minimal proportions during time of peace. Dunlap's opposition to service unification moves in exactly the opposite direction to Goldwater-Nichols. Insofar as Goldwater-Nichols accomplished a great deal of what the army has sought since the National Security Act of 1947, and the army sought these changes in the interest of greater rationality in the national security process, it would appear that Dunlap is out of step. Even as the services again argue over roles and missions, there seems little likelihood that any of them will be disbanded.

All in all, there is little in the pages of any of the service journals to indicate unrest above what is normal for a bureaucratic institution struggling for its existence or seeking resources it feels necessary to accomplish its tasks and missions. If one seeks controversy, look in the *Parameters* "Comments and Reply" section, particularly of the winter 1992–93 issue. The closing comment is from a retired officer who asks that the contributors attempt a higher level of civility in their discourse rather than the savagery recently demonstrated. Moving on to the book review section one encounters some rather sharp opinions also. But all of this is well within the legitimate sphere of interest of a professional body, arguing the merits and warts of positions that have an impact upon the performance of its duties.

FUTURE DEBATES

U.S. civil–military relations evolve through a distinct pattern. First changes in the domestic and international political environment make existing attitudes and structures obsolete. Then there is usually dramatic change, either through galvanizing events such as Truman's firing of MacArthur and Cheney's public rebuttal of Air Force Chief of Staff Larry Welch or through key legislation such as the National Security Act of 1947 or the Goldwater-Nichols Department of Defense Reorganization Act. This is shaped by individuals—a Powell, a McNamara—who are the product of those organizations but somehow become more. Throughout the process, there is an attempt to sustain equilibrium and balance between the military and its civilian overseers. This is natural; balance is the absolute essence of the U.S. political system. U.S. civil–military relations, though, are built on an ingrained asymmetry between the military, organized as a coherent, corporate body, and its civilian overseers, who are not. A well-structured career pattern makes it easier for the military to deliberately improve its political skill and strategic acumen. Officers can be required to study world politics and strategy before attaining senior positions. Civilians are largely self-taught, their knowledge often less systematic than that of their military counterparts. But the array of tools held by civilians more than counterbalances the military's more coherent method for cultivating individual skill. Civilians control the military's budget, can fire individual military leaders, and must approve senior-level promotions and assignments. The equilibrium between the military and civilians thus reflects an asymmetry of resources where military acumen is matched by the civilians' wide array of tools.

The lifeblood of this equilibrium is constant adjustment shaped by open, informed debate from all segments of the national security community. During times of strategic change, the need for such debate increases. This is certainly true today—it is time

to "let a hundred schools of thought contend." But there has been no benchmark, full-scale scholarly examination of U.S. civil–military relations since Hendrickson (1988). This means that the impact of the end of the Cold War has not been evaluated. Peter Feaver (1992) has provided the most profound recent assessment, but his analytical framework may not apply outside the realm of nuclear strategy. In general, then, the post–Cold War literature on U.S. civil–military relations is thin, particularly in terms of future-oriented thinking and the questioning of basic assumptions. Although not all changes in the global security environment affect U.S. civil–military relations, there is a particular need for study of six important trends.

Changes in the Nature of Armed Conflict. During the Cold War, civil–military relations reflected a set of assumptions about the distinction between military and nonmilitary thinking, attitudes, and behavior. Analysts believed that it was possible to have either a militarized foreign policy or a nonmilitarized one, and that there was a "military mind" distinct from a nonmilitary mind (Bletz 1972, 186–203). In the future, these assumptions may not hold as the nature of armed conflict changes. Some writers predict a melding of law enforcement and traditional military functions in response to "gray area" threats, the privatization of security, and new forms of high-technology terrorism (Van Creveld 1991, 192–227; Metz 1994, 71–73). Protection of cyberspace, the ecology, and public health are becoming important national security issues. We may also be at the beginning of a high-technology "revolution in military affairs" that will change the nature of essential military skills, further eroding the distinction between things military and nonmilitary (Metz and Kievit 1994, 20–21). Civil–military relations were simplified in the nineteenth century by the quarantine of the military, both intellectually and geographically, and by the rigid distinction between war and peace. The Cold War demanded a holistic strategy, but the future is likely to require an even more inclusive notion, possibly leading to a fundamental transformation of U.S. civil–military relations.

Changes in U.S. National Security Strategy. The broad role of military power in U.S. national security strategy helps shape civil–military relations. Today, two strategic changes in particular could dramatically alter those relations. First, it is possible that the United States will move toward disengagement from many parts of the world leaving responsibility for security to regional powers or international organizations. This could greatly lessen the need for U.S. military force, especially power projection capabilities, and erode the rationale for a major role for the armed forces in formulating national policy. Second, the ongoing tendency to use U.S. military force in operations other than war, whether peace operations, disaster relief, or counter-narcotrafficking, could have long-term effects on civil–military relations. U.S. military involvement in ambiguous, protracted operations like Somalia could erode some of the support and popularity that the armed services earned in the Gulf War, thus altering the political balance of power between the military and its civilian overseers. Recognizing this, the military might oppose their use in operations other than war, thus sparking a true crisis with civilian policy makers. Analysts must assess the potential for this and, more important, suggest ways to prevent it.

Changes in U.S. Political Leadership. The changing composition of Congress and of executive branch civilians may affect relations with the military. As fewer and fewer U.S. political leaders have experienced military service, they may understand the military less. By the same token, tendencies among the U.S. political leadership toward greater gender and ethnic diversity can do the same. These issues are amenable to empirical testing to see if, for instance, time as an enlisted soldier, seaman, marine, or airman truly affects the attitudes that a representative, senator, or executive branch official holds toward the military.

Sociocultural and Normative Changes. Huntington (1957) argued that the U.S. military is essentially and necessarily a conservative organization nested in a liberal society. It is not clear whether U.S. society is becoming more liberal, but if it is, problems will emerge in civil–military relations. The Cold War constrained liberal tendencies in U.S. society by forcing an outward orientation, encouraging acceptance of, if not acquiescence to, the military, and amplifying the need for national consensus. The tendency to "rally round the flag" papered over deep schisms. The end of the Cold War, in conjunction with the ongoing sociocultural diversification of the United States, may further isolate the military from mainstream U.S. culture and affect civil–military relations.

Economic Changes. In the past, declining defense budgets often set the military services against one another as they competed for resources. This eased civilian control of the military, but complicated the process of offering coherent military advice to policy makers. It is possible that "jointness"—cooperation among the armed services—has now become so fully ingrained that they will continue to cooperate even as budgets decline. The intensity of service debate during the ongoing "roles and missions" study, however, suggests that under the veneer of interservice comity lurks the potential for conflict. If this explodes into the open, civil–military relations will be affected, but how is not clear. Similarly, changes in the defense industrial and technological base may also change civil–military relations. During the Cold War, defense spending touched most parts of the United States—a fact not lost on Congress. Today, the old military-industrial complex is greatly weakened if not altogether dead. This may lessen the military's influence in Congress.

Changes in the Military. Sometimes changes within the military not designed to affect civil-military relations end up doing so. Two examples are clear today. First, the ongoing closure of military bases was intended to make the services more effective and efficient. An unintended side effect has been the end of military presence in many parts of the United States. Rather than a truly national distribution, the military seems to be moving toward location solely on the southern and western littoral of the nation. This simplifies power projection, but also means that an increasing number of Americans in the Northeast and Midwest—as well as their representatives in Congress—have little or no firsthand experience with the military. The impact of this on attitudes and perceptions needs to be explored. Second, in response to declining resources, the armed services, particularly the army, are beginning to reconsider or adjust the relationship between active and reserve components. Some military leaders and defense analysts feel that during a time of frugality for the armed services, a large reserve component is a luxury. Dollar for dollar, the argument goes, more is gained from money spent on active forces, especially as warfare becomes increasingly complex and crisis reaction more central to U.S. national security strategy. But the reserve components have long been one of the primary connections between the military and U.S. society. Thus decisions to diminish reserve forces—even if made solely on the grounds of military effectiveness—may have unintended side effects for civil–military relations. Other things designed to increase military effectiveness and efficiency—training techniques, methods of leader development, doctrine—can also shape civil–military relations, but the precise way this happens has not been fully analyzed.

Finally, analysts of civil–military relations also need to turn the equation around. Most often, civil–military relations are treated as the *dependent* variable, shaped by other forces and trends. But the state and form of civil–military relations is also an *independent* variable helping define the limits of the possible in U.S. national security strategy. In any case, one thing is clear: the current adjustment of U.S. civil–military relations, whether it constitutes a crisis or not, is inconsequential compared to the much more fundamental changes to come. By speculating on these now, defense analysts can ease the transformation and speed the adjustment of the vital equilibrium between the military and civilian leaders.

The views expressed in this essay are those of the authors and do not necessarily reflect the official policy or position of the Department of the Army, the Department of Defense, or the U.S. government.

REFERENCES

Art, Robert J., Vincent Davis, and Samuel P. Huntington, eds. 1985. *Reorganizing America's Defense: Leadership in War and Peace.* Washington, D.C.: Pergamon-Brassey's.

Beaufre, André. 1974. *Strategy for Tomorrow.* New York: Crane, Russak.

Bletz, Donald F. 1972. *The Role of the Military Professional in U.S. Foreign Policy.* New York: Praeger.

Clinton, William J. 1994. *A National Security Strategy of Engagement and Enlargement.* Washington, D.C.: The White House.

Crowe, William J. Jr. 1993. *The Line of Fire: From Washington to the Gulf, the Politics and Battles of the New Military.* New York: Simon and Schuster.

Department of the Air Force. 1992. *Basic Aerospace Doctrine of the United States Air Force.* Air Force Manual 1-1, vol. 2. Washington, D.C.: Department of the Air Force.

Department of the Army. 1994. *The Army.* Field Manual 100-1. Washington, D.C.: Department of the Army.

Department of the Navy. 1989. *Warfighting.* Fleet Marine Force Manual 1. Washington, D.C.: Department of the Navy.

———. 1994. *Naval Warfare.* Naval Doctrine Publication 1. Washington, D.C.: Department of the Navy.

Dunlap, Charles J. Jr. 1992–93. "The Origins of the American Military Coup of 2012." *Parameters* 22 (Winter): 2–20.

Feaver, Peter Douglas. 1992. *Guarding the Guardians: Civilian Control of Nuclear Weapons in the United States.* Ithaca, N.Y.: Cornell University Press.

Finer, S. E. 1975. *The Man on Horseback: Military Intervention into Politics.* Harmondsworth: Penguin.

Flint, Roy K. 1991. "The Truman–MacArthur Conflict: Dilemmas of Civil–Military Relations in the Nuclear Age." In *The United States Military under the Constitution of the United States, 1789–1989,* edited by Richard H. Kohn. New York: New York University Press.

Graves, Howard D. 1990. "Education of U.S. Army Officers." In *The U.S. Army in a New Security Era,* edited by Sam C. Sarkesian and John Allen Williams. Boulder, Colo.: Lynne Rienner.

Gray, Colin S. 1982. *Strategic Studies: A Critical Assessment.* Westport, Conn.: Greenwood.

Hendrickson, David C. 1988. *Reforming Defense: The State of American Civil–Military Relations.* Baltimore, Md.: Johns Hopkins University Press.

Huntington, Samuel P. 1957. *The Soldier and the State: The Theory and Politics of Civil–Military Relations.* Cambridge, Mass.: Belknap.

James, D. Clayton. 1988. "Command Crisis: MacArthur and the Korean War." In *The Harmon Memorial Lectures in Military History, 1959–1987,* edited by Harry R. Borowski. Washington, D.C.: Office of Air Force History.

Kemp, Kenneth W., and Charles Hudlin. 1992. "Civil Supremacy over the Military: Its Nature and Limits." *Armed Forces and Society* 19 (Fall): 7–26.

Kitfield, James. 1994. "Pentagon Power Shift." *Government Executive* (April):72.

Kohn, Richard H. 1991. "The Constitution and National Security: The Intent of the Framers." In *The United States Military under the Constitution of the United States, 1789–1989,* edited by Richard H. Kohn. New York: New York University Press.

———. 1994. "Out of Control: The Crisis in Civil-Military Relations." *National Interest,* no. 35 (Spring): 3–17.

Krepinevich, Andrew F. Jr. 1986. *The Army and Vietnam.* Baltimore, Md.: Johns Hopkins University Press.

Lacayo, Richard. 1993. "The Rebellious Soldier." *Time,* 15 February, 32.

Luttwak, Edward N. 1985. *The Pentagon and the Art of War: The Question of Military Reform.* New York: Touchstone.

———. 1994. "Washington's Biggest Scandal." *Commentary* (May): 29–33.

McCarthy, Colman. 1993. "Colin Powell Just One More Warlord." *National Catholic Reporter,* 15 October, 23.

Means, Howard. 1992. *Colin Powell: Soldier/Statesman, Statesman/Soldier.* New York: Donald I. Fine.

Metz, Steven. 1991. "Eisenhower and the Planning of American Grand Strategy." *Journal of Strategic Studies* 14 (March): 49–71.

———. 1994. "Insurgency after the Cold War." *Small Wars and Insurgencies* 5 (Spring): 63–82.

Metz, Steven, and James Kievit. 1994. *The Revolution in Military Affairs and Conflict Short of War.* Carlisle Barracks, Pa.: U.S. Army War College Strategic Studies Institute.

Perry, Mark. 1989. *Four Stars: The Joint Chiefs of Staff in the Post-War Era.* Boston, Mass.: Houghton Mifflin.

Powell, Colin L. 1992. *National Military Strategy of the United States.* Washington, D.C.: Joint Staff.

———. 1992/93. "U.S. Forces: Challenges Ahead." *Foreign Affairs* 20 (Winter): 32–45.

Powell, Colin, John Lehman, William Odom, Samuel Huntington, and Richard H. Kohn. 1994. "Exchange on Civil–Military Relations." *National Interest,* no. 36 (Summer): 23–31.

Previdi, Robert. 1988. *Civilian Control versus Military Rule.* New York: Hippocrene.

Roth, David. 1993. *Sacred Honor: A Biography of Colin Powell.* Grand Rapids, Mich.: Zondervan.

Rovere, Richard H., and Arthur Schlesinger Jr. 1992. *General MacArthur and President Truman: The Struggle for Control of American Foreign Policy.* New Brunswick, N.J.: Transaction.

Sabrosky, Alan Ned, and Robert L. Sloane, eds. 1988. *The Recourse to War: An Appraisal of the "Weinberger Doctrine."* Carlisle Barracks, Pa.: U.S. Army War College Strategic Studies Institute.

Sarkesian, Sam C., and John Allen Williams. 1994. "Civil–Military Relations in the New Era." In *U.S. Domestic and National Security Agendas: Into the Twenty-First Century,* edited by Sam C. Sarkesian and John Mead Flanagin. Westport, Conn.: Greenwood.

Segal, David R. 1994. "National Security and Democracy in the United States." *Armed Forces and Society* 20 (Spring): 375–93.

Simpson, Charles M. III. 1983. *Inside the Green Berets: The First Thirty Years.* Novato, Calif.: Presidio.

Summers, Harry G. Jr. 1982. *On Strategy: A Critical Analysis of the Vietnam War.* Novato, Calif.: Presidio.

Taylor, Maxwell D. 1972. *Swords and Plowshares.* New York: W. W. Norton.

Van Creveld, Martin. 1991. *The Transformation of War.* New York: Free Press.

Weigley, Russell F. 1973. *The American Way of War: A History of United States Military Strategy and Policy.* Bloomington: Indiana University Press.

———. 1993. "The American Military and the Principle of Civilian Control from McClellan to Powell." *Journal of Military History,* Special Issue, 57 (October): 27–58.

Weinberger, Caspar W. 1990. *Fighting for Peace: Seven Critical Years at the Pentagon.* New York: Warner Books.

Woodward, Bob. 1991. *The Commanders.* New York: Simon and Schuster.

PART V

THE FUTURE OF AMERICAN DEFENSE POLICY

INTRODUCTION

BRENDA J. VALLANCE

We conclude our examination of American defense policy by looking at the primary challenges the United States faces today and into the future: changes to the international system and technological innovations that influence the international and domestic environments. As illustrated in our model, these challenges act both as inputs to and outputs of the defense policy process.

As inputs into the political system model, the international and domestic environments determine the threats we face and our ability to deal with those threats. At the same time, when we formulate our national security and military strategies, we establish policies and programs to implement these strategies. In many cases, the policies and programs call for the development of new technologies, and these innovations feed back into the environment, altering previous technological limitations. Our strategy decisions also may alter the international environment by changing the distribution of power in a region, solving a regional dispute, or failing to resolve a conflict successfully, perhaps allowing it to escalate and in-

volve an increasing number of states. In all of these cases, today's decisions, whether successful or not, alter the international environment and serve as new inputs to the defense policy process model and the formulation of future strategies, policies, and programs.

Chapter 18 in this section addresses the challenges we face in today's international environment. The first essay, "Integrated Regional Approaches," presents the last section of the Clinton administration's national security strategy, which is based on the concepts of engagement and enlargement discussed in Part IV. This excerpt deals with the regional contingencies that have become the focus of defense policy since the end of the Cold War. In the absence of a single dominant threat (the Soviet Union during the Cold War), analysts now envision the primary threat "as aggression by potentially hostile regional powers . . . capable of fielding sizable military forces that can cause serious imbalances in military power within regions important to the United States."[1] In its attempts to achieve engage-

Defense Policy Process Model: Future Environment, Inputs, and Feedback

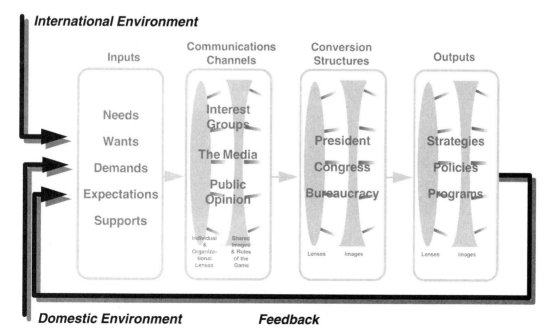

ment and enlargement, the United States is pursuing several security goals: ensuring military security for itself and its allies, increasing the number and strength of democracies, and opening markets in each of the world's regions. This essay briefly outlines the challenges each region presents with regard to these goals.

The subsequent essays in this chapter provide more detail about these challenges and the regional complexities American defense policy must address. In contrast to the regional contingencies discussed in the Clinton administration's national security strategy, these essays paint a very complicated picture of the United States' regional challenges. They focus on four regions of the world: Asia and the Pacific, Europe, Russia and its neighbors, and the Middle East. The Western Hemisphere and Sub-Saharan Africa are excluded because diplomatic and economic measures, not armed force, are the predominant national security tools used to deal with these regions. In addition, although Africa presents a variety of significant challenges for U.S. foreign policy, it is likely to remain at the periphery of American defense policy.

The descriptions of the regional challenges reveal just how difficult a task the United States is facing. It must try to ensure military security, democracy, and open markets in an uncertain world confronted with such varied issues as ethnic conflict, market integration in Europe, and the Islamic revival in Southwest Asia. It also must formulate a defense policy that can deal with the proliferation of weapons of mass destruction, help keep the peace in an area of ethnic conflict, and help resolve regional conflict in a distant location. In an era of defense budget cuts, base closings, and troop drawdowns, what is the appropriate security strategy to deal with these multiple and complex problems?

To complicate matters further, analysts have different views of how best to approach the international environment. As an example, some European specialists believe that the North Atlantic Treaty Organization (NATO) is still a legitimate and viable security alliance that will continue to play the primary role in European defense policy. Others counter that NATO is an anachronism of the Cold War, no longer viable in the current European environment. To take another example, some say the best strategy to deal with Islam is to suppress all Islamic movements, whether mainstream or militant. Others distinguish between the two and suggest that mainstream movements should be allowed to participate in the political process. Which view is correct? Which should the United States adopt? The neat lines representing the international environment's input to the defense policy process model give no hint of how difficult it is to interpret correctly complex political issues.

It is equally difficult to make sure the nation's defense strategies, policies, and programs keep pace with the rapidly changing world. International events occur at a fast pace, and assessments of regional issues become quickly dated. The essays in this section were written in late 1994, but some of the information they present has already been overtaken by time and events.

In Chapter 19, we examine technology and its role in defense policy, another important aspect of the international and domestic environments. As technological developments spread throughout the world, they affect the threats we face and the way we fight. In today's world, computers and communications systems are integral to our armed forces and those of other nations. Global positioning systems, precision-guided munitions, and stealth technologies were an important part of the Persian Gulf War, and more advanced systems are already planned for the military of the future. These types of systems are particularly important in the post–Cold War era. During the Cold War, we believed the threat we faced required a massive response. Nuclear weapons and large conventional forces made up of heavy armor were meant to present such a destructive blow that the enemy would be deterred from acting. But in the post–Cold War era the threat has changed. Forces designed to inflict massive destruction with large numbers of casualties are not appropriate for fighting the types of regional conflicts we now see as the threat. Instead, if the use of military force is necessary, our goal now is to end the conflict as quickly as possible by striking precise targets and keeping casualties to a minimum, both among civilians in the region and among our own forces.

The combination of technological advances and new military requirements leads some analysts to conclude that we are at the dawn of (some would argue we are already in the midst of) tremendous change in the military. This military technical revolution (MTR), or what more recently has been labeled the revolution in military affairs (RMA), may be the answer to the converging realities of regional conflict and military downsizing. Currently, the RMA is a popular theme in defense-oriented journals, with entire volumes dedicated to discussing the issue. The first essay in this chapter, "The Military Technical Revolution" by Michael Mazarr (with Jeffrey Shaffer and Benjamin Ederington), examines how the RMA can increase the combat effectiveness of our forces and meet the challenge of a global threat in our budget-constrained environment. Making the RMA work, however, requires not only smart and exotic weapons and advanced technology platforms, but also the doctrine and organizational concepts that will maximize their effectiveness. In short, the RMA requires a new way of thinking about military strategy.

The second essay in this section discusses "cyberwar," or what many refer to as information warfare, another important aspect of the RMA. In "Cyberwar Is Coming!" John Arquilla and David Ronfeldt argue that because of technological innovations in communications and intelligence, "the side that knows more, that can disperse the fog of war yet shroud an adversary in it, will enjoy decisive advantages." The ability to field large maneuver armies will no longer determine the military outcome, and the destruction of societies will no longer be the key to warfare. Rather, success in warfare will go to the side that possesses knowledge and is able to deny knowledge to its opponent. Arquilla and Ronfeldt also note that organizational changes will be needed to incorporate this concept into our war-fighting arsenal.

The final essay in this chapter discusses many of the challenges we face in incorporating RMA concepts into our war-fighting doctrine and forces. In "The Coming Military Revolution," James Fitz-Simonds suggests that despite its interest in the RMA, the military has not explored many of the problems such technology may create. For instance, while the RMA may result in increased knowledge about the enemy, will our forces be able to utilize this information quickly, or will they be overwhelmed and lose the advantage of speed and knowledge? Can we afford both the cost and the organizational change necessary to accommodate the concepts associated with the RMA? The author also discusses the strategic challenges presented by the RMA. Although purposely designed as a nonnuclear strategy, the RMA, he notes, may cause nations to develop nuclear weapons to challenge our advanced conventional capabilities. He also questions whether during war political decisions can be made as rapidly as

large volumes of information are received and processed.

In Chapter 20, "The Future of American Defense Policy," the editors briefly review the material presented in the preceding chapters by returning to the defense policy process model and offer some final thoughts. What these chapters have shown is that although the Cold War has ended, the defense policy process will not change dramatically. Bureaucratic politics and its associated "pulling and hauling" will remain an important element in defense policy, as will the primary actors already a part of the process. This does not mean, however, that the defense policy of today will not change. Changes in the international and domestic environments present challenges to which American defense policy must respond. Resource limitations, new threats, changing roles and missions, and technological innovation must all be considered in the debate. Under these circumstances, American defense policy will undoubtedly continue to be challenging, complex, and difficult to predict.

NOTE

1. William J. Clinton, *A National Security Strategy of Engagement and Enlargement* (Washington, D.C.: GPO, July 1994), 7.

CHAPTER 18

EMERGING THREATS AND REGIONAL CHALLENGES

INTEGRATED REGIONAL APPROACHES

WILLIAM J. CLINTON

The United States is a genuinely global power. Our policy toward each of the world's regions reflects our overall strategy tailored to their unique challenges and opportunities. This essay highlights the application of our strategy to each of the world's regions; our broad objectives and thrust, rather than an exhaustive list of all our policies and interests. It illustrates how we integrate our commitment to the promotion of democracy and the enhancement of American prosperity with our security requirements to produce a mutually reinforcing policy.

EUROPE AND EURASIA

Our strategy of enlargement and engagement is central to U.S. policy toward post–Cold War Europe. European stability is vital to our own security, a lesson we have learned twice at great cost this century. Vibrant European economies mean more jobs for Americans at home and investment opportunities abroad. With the collapse of the Soviet empire and the emergence of new democracies in its wake, the United States has an unparalleled opportunity to contribute toward a free and undivided Europe. Our goal is an integrated democratic Europe cooperating with the United States to keep the peace and promote prosperity.

The first and most important element of our strategy in Europe must be security through military strength and cooperation. The Cold War is over, but war itself is not over.

As we know, war continues in the former Yugoslavia. While that war does not pose a direct threat to our security or warrant unilateral U.S. involvement, U.S. policy is focused on five goals: achieving a political settlement in Bosnia that preserves the country's territorial integrity and provides a viable future for all its peoples, preventing the spread of the fighting into a broader Balkan war that could threaten both allies and the stability of new democratic states in Central and Eastern Europe, stemming the destabilizing flow of refugees from the conflict, halting the slaughter of innocents, and helping to support the North Atlantic Treaty Organization's (NATO's) central role in post–Cold War Europe while maintaining our role in shaping Europe's security architecture.

Our leadership paved the way to NATO's February 1994 ultimatum that ended the heavy Serb bombardment of Sarajevo, Bosnia's capital. Our diplomatic leadership brought an end to the fighting between the Muslims and Croats in Bosnia and helped establish a bicommunal Bosnian-Croat Federation. Since April 1994 we have been working with the warring parties through the contact group (United States, Russia, United Kingdom, France, and Germany) to help the parties reach a negotiated settlement. Our goal is to bring an end to the war in Bosnia consistent with the contact group plan, which would preserve Bosnia as a single state within its existing borders while providing for an equitable division of territory between the Muslim-Croat Federation and the Bosnian-Serb entity. While we have not yet succeeded in achieving a political settlement, diplomatic efforts in the final months of 1994 helped produce a cease-fire and a cessation of hostilities agreement that took effect on January 1, 1995. On this basis, efforts are now under way with our contact group partners to renew negotiations on a political settlement based on the contact group plan.

Should these new diplomatic efforts falter, we remain prepared to move forward with our proposal at the United Nations to lift the arms embargo on Bosnia-Herzegovina, multilaterally. We remain strongly opposed to a unilateral lifting of the arms embargo as a step that would have grave consequences for NATO and U.S. interests. Should large-scale fighting resume and U.N. troops need to be withdrawn, we have agreed, in principle, to provide U.S. support, including the use of ground forces, to a NATO-led operation to help ensure a safe withdrawal. We also remain prepared to help implement a final peace settlement in Bosnia.

As we work to resolve that tragedy and ease the suffering of its victims we also need to transform European and transatlantic institutions so they can better address such conflicts and advance Europe's integration. Many institutions will play a role, including the European Union, the Western European Union, the Council of Europe, the Organization for Security and Cooperation in Europe, and the United Nations. But NATO, history's greatest political-military alliance, must be central to that process.

William J. Clinton, A National Security Strategy of Engagement and Enlargement *(Washington, D.C.: GPO, February 1995), 25–32. Public Domain.*

The NATO alliance will remain the anchor of American engagement in Europe and the linchpin of transatlantic security. That is why we must keep it strong, vital, and relevant. For the United States and its allies, NATO has always been far more than a transitory response to a temporary threat. It has been a guarantor of European democracy and a force for European stability. That is why its mission endures even though the Cold War has receded into the past. And that is why its benefits are so clear to Europe's new democracies.

Only NATO has the military forces, the integrated command structure, the broad legitimacy, and the habits of cooperation that are essential to draw in new participants and respond to new challenges. One of the deepest transformations within the transatlantic community over the past half century occurred because the armed forces of our respective nations trained, studied, and marched through their careers together. It is not only the compatibility of our weapons, but the camaraderie of our warriors that provide the sinews behind our mutual security guarantees and our best hope for peace.

Since the end of the Cold War, the United States has significantly reduced the level of U.S. military forces stationed in Europe. We have determined that a force of roughly 100,000 U.S. military personnel assigned to U.S. European command will preserve U.S. influence and leadership in NATO and provide a deterrent posture that is visible to all Europeans. While we continue to examine the proper mix of forces, this level of permanent presence, augmented by forward-deployed naval forces and reinforcements available from the United States, is sufficient to respond to plausible crises and contributes to stability in the region. Such a force level also provides a sound basis for U.S. participation in multinational training and preserves the capability to deter or respond to larger threats in Europe and to support limited NATO operations "out of area."

With the end of the Cold War, NATO's mission is evolving; today NATO plays a crucial role helping to manage ethnic and national conflict in Europe. With U.S. leadership, NATO has provided the muscle behind efforts to bring about a peaceful settlement in the former Yugoslavia. NATO airpower enforces the UN-mandated no-fly zone and provides support to UN peacekeepers. NATO stands ready to help support the peace once the parties reach an agreement.

With the adoption of the U.S. initiative, Partnership for Peace (PFP), at the January 1994 summit, NATO is playing an increasingly important role in our strategy of European integration, extending the scope of our security cooperation to the new democracies of Europe. Twenty-five nations, including Russia, have already joined the partnership, which will pave the way for a growing program of military cooperation and political consultation. Partner countries are sending representatives to NATO headquarters near Brussels and to a military coordination cell at Mons—the site of Supreme Headquarters Allied Powers Europe. Joint exercises have taken place in Poland and the Netherlands. In keeping with our strategy of enlargement, PFP is open to all former members of the Warsaw Pact as well as other European states. Each partner will set the scope and pace of its cooperation with NATO.

The North Atlantic Treaty has always looked to the addition of members who shared the alliance's purposes and its values, its commitment to respect borders and international law, and who could add to its strength; indeed, NATO has expanded three times since its creation. In January 1994, I made it plain that the question is no longer whether NATO will take on new members, but when and how we will do so. Last December we and our allies began a steady, deliberate, and transparent process that will lead to NATO expansion.

During 1995, we came to agreement with our allies on the process and principles, and we will share our conclusions with the members of the Partnership for Peace. Once this effort is complete, NATO can turn to the question of candidates and timing. Each nation will be considered individually. No nonmember of NATO will have a veto.

Expanding the alliance will promote our interests by reducing the risk of instability or conflict in Europe's eastern half—the region where two world wars and the Cold War began. It will help ensure that no part of Europe will revert to a zone of great power competition or a sphere of influence. It will build confidence and give new democracies a powerful incentive to consolidate their reforms. And each potential member will be judged according to the strength of its democratic institutions and its capacity to contribute to the goals of the alliance.

NATO expansion will not be aimed at replacing one division of Europe with a new one, but at enhancing the security of all European states, members and nonmembers alike. In this regard, we have a major stake in ensuring that Russia is engaged as a vital participant in European security affairs. We are committed to a growing, healthy NATO–Russia relationship and want to see Russia closely involved in the Partnership for Peace. Recognizing that no single institution can meet every challenge to peace and stability in Europe, we have begun a process that will strengthen the Organization for Security and Cooperation in Europe and enhance its conflict prevention and peacekeeping capabilities.

The second element of the new strategy for Europe is economic. The United States seeks to build on vibrant and open market economies, the engines that have given us the greatest prosperity in human history over the last several decades in Europe and in the United States. To this end, we strongly support the process of European integration embodied in the European Union and seek to deepen our partnership with the European Union in support of our economic goals, but also commit ourselves to the encouragement of bilateral trade and investment in countries not part of the European Union.

The nations of the European Union face particularly significant economic challenges with nearly twenty million people unemployed and, in Germany's case, the extraordinarily high costs of unification. Among the Atlantic nations, economic stagnation has clearly eroded public support in finances for outward-looking foreign policies and for greater integration. We are working closely with our West European partners to expand employment and promote long-term growth, building on the results of the Detroit Jobs Conference and the Naples G-7 Summit. A White House-sponsored Trade and Investment Conference for Central and Eastern Europe took place in Cleveland in January 1994.

In Northern Ireland, the administration is implementing a package of initiatives to promote the peace process. The secretary of commerce led a trade and investment mission to Belfast in December 1994, and in April will host a White House conference in Philadelphia on trade and investment in Northern Ireland.

As we work to strengthen our own economies, we must know that we serve our own prosperity and our security by helping the new market reforms in the new democracies in Europe's East that will help to deflate the region's demagogues. It will help ease ethnic tensions. It will help new democracies take root.

In Russia, Ukraine, and the other new independent states of the former Soviet Union, the economic transformation undertaken will go down as one of the great historical events of this century. The Russian government has made remarkable progress toward privatizing the economy (over 50 percent of the Russian gross domestic product is now generated by the private sector) and reducing inflation, and Ukraine has taken bold steps of its own to institute much-needed economic reforms. But much remains to be done to build on the reform momentum to assure durable economic recovery and social protection. We have given strong and consistent support to this unprecedented reform effort and have mobilized the international community to provide structural economic assistance, for example, securing agreement by the G-7 to make available four billion dollars in grants and loans as Ukraine implemented economic reform.

The short-term difficulties of taking Central and Eastern Europe into Western economic institutions will be more than rewarded if they succeed and if they are customers for America's and Western Europe's goods and services tomorrow. That is why this administration has been committed to increasing support substantially for market reforms in the new states of the former Soviet Union, and why we have continued our support for economic transition in Central and Eastern Europe, while also paying attention to measures that can overcome the social dislocations which have resulted largely from the collapse of the Soviet-dominated regional trading system.

Ultimately, the success of market reforms to the East will depend more on trade than aid. No one nation has enough resources to markedly change the future of those countries as they move to free market systems. One of our priorities, therefore, is to reduce trade barriers with the former communist states.

The third and final imperative of this new strategy is to support the growth of democracy and individual freedoms that has begun in Russia, the nations of the former Soviet Union, and Europe's former communist states. The success of these democratic reforms makes us all more secure; they are the best answer to the aggressive nationalism and ethnic hatreds unleashed by the end of the Cold War. Nowhere is democracy's success more important to us all than in these countries.

This will be the work of generations. There will be wrong turns and even reversals, as there have been in all countries throughout history. But as long as these states continue their progress toward democracy, respect the rights of their own and other people, and understand the rights of their minorities and their neighbors, we will support their progress with a steady patience.

EAST ASIA AND THE PACIFIC

East Asia is a region of growing importance for U.S. security and prosperity; nowhere are the strands of our three-pronged strategy more intertwined, nor is the need for continued U.S. engagement more evident. Now more than ever, security, open markets, and democracy go hand in hand in our approach to this dynamic region. Last year, we laid out an integrated strategy—a new Pacific community—that links security requirements with economic realities and our concern for democracy and human rights.

In thinking about Asia, we must remember that security is the first pillar of our new Pacific community. The United States is a Pacific nation. We have fought three wars there in this century. To deter regional aggression and secure our own interests, we will maintain an active presence and we will continue to lead. Our deep bilateral ties with allies such as Japan, South Korea, Australia, Thailand, and the Philippines and a continued American military presence will serve as the foundation for America's security role in the region. Currently, our forces number nearly 100,000 personnel in East Asia. In addition to performing the general forward deployment functions outlined above, they contribute to regional stability by deterring aggression and adventurism.

As a key element of our strategic commitment to the region, we are pursuing stronger efforts to combat the proliferation of weapons of mass destruction on the Korean Peninsula and in South Asia. In October 1994 we reached an important agreed framework with North Korea—stopping, and eventually eliminating, its nuclear weapons program—and an agreement with China, limiting its sales of ballistic missiles.

Another example of our security commitment to the Asia Pacific region in this decade is our effort to develop multiple new arrangements to meet multiple threats and opportunities. We have supported new regional exchanges—such as the Association of Southeast Asian Nations Regional Forum—on the full range of common security challenges. These arrangements can enhance regional security and understanding through dialogue and transparency. These regional exchanges are grounded on the strong network of bilateral relationships that exist today.

The continuing tensions on the Korean Peninsula remain the principal threat to the peace and stability of the Asian region. We have worked assiduously with our South Korean and Japanese allies, with the People's Republic of China and with Russia, and with various U.N. organizations to resolve the problem of North Korea's nuclear program. We have also engaged in extensive negotiations with the Pyongyang government, and have worked out an agreed framework for replacing—over a ten-year period—North Korea's dangerous, plutonium-producing reactors with safer light water reactors. That effort will be accompanied by a willingness to improve bilateral political and economic ties with the North, commensurate with their continued cooperation to resolve the nuclear issue and to make progress on other issues of concern. Our long-run objective continues to be a nonnuclear, peacefully reunified Korean Peninsula. Our strong and active commitment to our South Korean allies and to the region is the foundation of this effort.

We are developing a broader engagement with the People's Republic of China that will encompass both our economic and strategic interests. That policy is best reflected in our decision to delink China's most-favored-nation status from its record on human rights. We will also facilitate China's entry into international trade organizations, such as the General Agreement on Tariffs and Trade, if it undertakes the necessary obligations. Given its growing economic potential and already sizable military force, it is essential that China not become a security threat to the region. To that end, we are strongly promoting China's participation in regional security mechanisms to reassure its neighbors and assuage its own security concerns. We have also broadened our bilateral security dialogue with the Chinese and we are seeking to gain further cooperation from China in controlling the proliferation of weapons of mass destruction. We are also in the early stages of a dialogue with China on environmental and health challenges.

The second pillar of our engagement in Asia is our commitment to continuing and enhancing the economic prosperity that has characterized the region. Opportunities for economic progress continue to abound in Asia and underlie our strong commitment to multilateral economic cooperation, principally through Asia Pacific Economic Cooperation (APEC). Today, the eighteen member states of APEC—comprising about one-third of the world's population—produce $14 trillion and export $1.7 trillion of goods annually, about one-half of the world's totals. U.S. exports to APEC economies reached $300 billion last year, supporting nearly 2.6 million American jobs. U.S. investments in the region totaled over $140 million—about one-third of total U.S. direct foreign investment. A prosperous and open Asia Pacific is key to the economic health of the United States. The first meeting of APEC leaders is vivid testimony to the possibilities of stimulating regional economic cooperation as we saw in their recent statement at the second leaders' meeting, which accepted the goal of free trade within the region by early in the twenty-first century.

We are also working with our major bilateral trade partners to improve trade relations. The United States and Japan successfully completed a preliminary accord in September to bring about the implementation of the 1993 Framework Agreement, designed to open Japan's markets more to competitive U.S. goods and reduce the U.S. trade deficit. Since we delinked China's most-favored-nation trade status from specific human rights considerations in May, U.S.–China trade has grown significantly. We continue to work closely with Beijing to resolve remaining bilateral and multilateral trade problems, such as intellectual property rights and market access. Unless the issue of intellectual property rights is resolved, economic sanctions will be imposed.

The third pillar of our policy in building a new Pacific community is to support democratic reform in the region. The new democratic states of Asia will have our strong support as they move forward to consolidate and expand democratic reforms.

Some have argued that democracy is somehow unsuited for Asia or at least for some Asian nations—that human rights are relative and that they simply mask Western cultural imperialism. These arguments are wrong. It is not Western imperialism, but the aspirations of Asian peoples themselves that explain the growing number of democracies and the growing strength of democracy movements everywhere in Asia. We support those aspirations and those movements.

Each nation must find its own form of democracy, and we respect the variety of democratic institutions that have grown in Asia. But there is no cultural justification for torture or tyranny. Nor do we accept repression cloaked in moral relativism. Democracy and human rights are universal yearnings and universal norms, just as powerful in Asia as elsewhere. We will continue to press for respect for human rights in countries as diverse as China and Burma.

THE WESTERN HEMISPHERE

The Western hemisphere, too, is a fertile field for a strategy of engagement and enlargement. Sustained improvements in the security situation there, including the resolution of border tensions, control of insurgencies, and containment of pressures for arms proliferation, will be an essential underpinning of political and economic progress in the hemisphere.

The unprecedented triumph of democracy and market economies throughout the region offers an unparalleled opportunity to secure the benefits of peace and stability, and to promote economic growth and trade. At the Summit of the Americas, the thirty-four democratic nations of the hemisphere committed themselves for the first time to the goal of free trade in the region. They also agreed to a detailed plan of cooperative action in such diverse fields as health, education, environmental protection, and the strengthening of democratic institutions. To ensure that proposals in this plan are implemented, they called for a series of follow-on ministerial meetings over the next year and requested the active participation of the Organization of American States and the Inter-American Development Bank. The Summit ushered in a new era of hemispheric cooperation that would not have been possible without U.S. leadership and commitment.

The North America Free Trade Agreement (NAFTA), ratified in December 1994, has strengthened economic ties, with substantial increases in U.S. exports to both Mexico and Canada, creating new jobs and new opportunities for American workers and business. The United States, Mexico, and Canada have begun discussions to add Chile to NAFTA.

We remain committed to extending democracy to all of the region's people still blocked from controlling their own destinies. Our overarching objective is to preserve and defend civilian elected governments and strengthen democratic practices respectful of human rights. Working with the international community, we succeeded in reversing the coup in Haiti and restoring the democratically-elected president and government. Our challenge now is to help the Haitian people consolidate their hard-won democracy and rebuild their country. With the restoration of democracy in Haiti, Cuba is the only country in the hemisphere still ruled by a dictator. The Cuban Democracy Act remains the framework for our policy toward Cuba; our goal is the peaceful establishment of democratic governance for the people of Cuba.

We are working with our neighbors through various hemispheric organizations, including the OAS, to invigorate regional cooperation. Both bilaterally and regionally, we seek to eliminate the scourge of drug trafficking, which poses a serious threat to democracy and security. We also seek to strengthen norms for defense establishments that are supportive of democracy, respect for human rights, and civilian control in defense matters. Finally, protecting the region's precious environmental resources is an important priority.

THE MIDDLE EAST AND SOUTHWEST AND SOUTH ASIA

The United States has enduring interests in the Middle East, especially pursuing a comprehensive breakthrough to Middle East peace, ensuring the security of Israel and our Arab friends, and maintaining the free flow of oil at reasonable prices. Our strategy is harnessed to the unique characteristics of the region and our vital interests there, as we work to extend the range of peace and stability.

We have made solid progress in the past two years. We have helped bring about many historic firsts—the handshake of peace between Prime Minister Yitzhak Rabin and Chairman Yasser Arafat on the White House lawn has been followed by the Jordan-Israel peace treaty, progress on eliminating the Arab boycott of Israel, and the establishment of ties between Israel and an increasing number of its Arab neighbors. But our efforts have not stopped there; on other bilateral tracks and through regional dialogue we are working to foster a durable peace and a comprehensive settlement, while our support for economic development can bring hope to all the peoples of the region.

In Southwest Asia, the United States remains focused on deterring threats to regional stability, particularly from Iraq and Iran as long as those states pose a threat to U.S. interests, to other states in the region, and to their own citizens. We have in place a dual containment strategy aimed at these two states, and will maintain our long-standing presence which has been centered on naval vessels in and near the Persian Gulf and prepositioned combat equipment. Since Operation Desert Storm, temporary deployments of land-based aviation forces, ground forces, and amphibious units have supplemented our posture in the Gulf region. Operation Vigilant Warrior demonstrated our ability to rapidly reinforce the region in time of crisis.

We have made clear to Iraq it must comply with all the relevant Security Council resolutions, and we remain committed to supporting oppressed minorities in Iraq through Operations Provide Comfort and Southern Watch. Our policy is directed not against the people of Iraq, but against the aggressive behavior of the government. The October 1994 deployment, Vigilant Warrior, demonstrated again the need and our ability to respond quickly to threats to our allies.

Our policy toward Iran is aimed at changing the behavior of the Iranian government in several key areas, including Iran's efforts to obtain weapons of mass destruction and missiles, its support for terrorism and groups that oppose the peace process, its attempts to undermine friendly governments in the region, and its dismal human rights record. We remain willing to enter into an authoritative dialogue with Iran to discuss the differences between us.

A key objective of our policy in the Gulf is to reduce the chances that another aggressor will emerge who would threaten the independence of existing states. Therefore we will continue to encourage members of the Gulf Cooperation Council (GCC) to work closely on collective defense and security arrangements, help individual GCC states meet their appropriate defense requirements, and maintain our bilateral defense agreements.

South Asia has experienced an important expansion of democracy and economic reform, and our strategy is designed to help the peoples of that region enjoy the fruits of democracy and greater stability through efforts aimed at resolving long-standing conflict and implementing confidence building measures. The United States has engaged India and Pakistan in seeking agreement on steps to cap, reduce, and ultimately eliminate their weapons of mass destruction and ballistic missile capabilities. Regional stability and improved bilateral ties are also important for America's economic interest in a region that contains a quarter of the world's population and one of its most important emerging markets.

In both the Middle East and South Asia, the pressure of expanding populations on natural resources is enormous. Growing desertification in the Middle East has strained relations over arable land. Pollution of the coastal areas in the Eastern Mediterranean, the Red Sea, and the Gulf of Aqaba has degraded fish catches and hindered development. Water shortages stemming from overuse, contaminated water aquifers, and riparian disputes threaten regional relations. In South Asia, high population densities and rampant pollution have exacted a tremendous toll on forests, biodiversity, and the local environment.

AFRICA

Africa poses one of our greatest challenges and opportunities to enlarge the community of market democracies. Throughout Africa, U.S. policy supports democracy, sustainable economic development, and resolution of conflicts through negotiation, diplomacy, and peacekeeping. New policies will strengthen civil societies and mechanisms for conflict resolution, particularly where ethnic, religious, and political tensions are acute. In particular, we will seek to identify and address the root causes of conflicts and disasters before they erupt.

The nexus of economic, political, social, ethnic, and environmental challenges facing Africa can lead to a sense of "Afro-pessimism." However, if we can simultaneously address these challenges, we create a synergy that can stimulate development, resurrect societies, and build hope. We encourage democratic reform in nations like Nigeria and Zaire to allow the people of these countries to enjoy responsive government. In Mozambique and Angola, we have played a leading role in bringing an end to two decades of civil war and promoting national reconciliation. For the first time, there is the prospect that all of southern Africa could enjoy the fruits of peace and prosperity. Throughout the continent—in Rwanda, Burundi, Liberia, Sudan, and elsewhere—we work with the United Nations and regional organizations to encourage peaceful resolution of internal disputes.

Last year South Africa held its first nonracial elections and created a Government of National Unity. We remain committed to addressing the socioeconomic legacies of apartheid to ensure that democracy fully takes root in South Africa. During the state visit of Nelson Mandela, we announced formation of a bilateral commission to foster new cooperation between our nations. We must support the revolution of democracy sweeping the continent—on center stage in South Africa, and in quieter but no less dramatic ways in countries like Malawi, Benin, Niger, and Mali. We need to encourage the creation of cultures of tolerance, flowering of civil society, and the protection of human rights and human dignity.

Our humanitarian interventions, along with the international community, will address the grave circumstances in several nations on the continent. The U.S. Agency for International Development's new "Greater Horn of Africa" initiative got ahead of the curve on a potential famine that threatened twenty-five million people, and moved beyond relief to support reconstruction and sustainable development. In Somalia, our forces broke through the chaos that prevented the introduction of relief supplies. U.S. forces prevented the death of hundreds of thousands of Somalis and then turned over the mission to U.N. peacekeepers from over a score of nations. In Rwanda, Sudan, Angola, and Liberia, we have taken an active role in providing humanitarian relief to those displaced by violence.

Such efforts by the United States and the international community must be limited in duration and designed to give the peoples of a nation the opportunity to put their own house in order. In the final analysis, the responsibility for the fate of a nation rests with its own people.

We are also working with regional organizations, nongovernmental organizations, and governments throughout Africa to address the urgent issues of population growth, spreading disease (including AIDS), environmental decline, enhancing the role of women in development, eliminating support for terrorism, demobilization of bloated militaries, relieving burdensome debt, and expanding trade and investment ties to the countries of Africa.

Central to all these efforts will be strengthening the American constituency for Africa, drawing on the knowledge, experience, and commitment of millions of Americans to enhance our nation's support for positive change in Africa. For example, the White House Conference on Africa, the first such gathering of regional experts ever sponsored by the White House, drew together more than two hundred Americans from the administration, Congress, business, labor, academia, religious groups, relief and development agencies, human rights groups, and others to discuss Africa's future and the role that the United States can play in it. The president, vice president, secretary of state, and national security adviser all participated in the conference, which produced a wealth of new ideas and new commitment to Africa.

ASIA PACIFIC

RONALD N. MONTAPERTO

The Asia Pacific region presents a paradox. Despite the threat of conflict on the Korean Peninsula, opposing claims in the South China Sea, and the low boil in Cambodia, the region is more stable and more peaceful than at any time in this century. On the other hand, there is a pervasive sense of uncertainty about the future.

A number of factors contribute to the sense of regional unease. Owing to the collapse of the Cold War framework, regional powers now compete more directly than in the past. (Russia is years away from exerting an influence even approximating that of the former Soviet Union.) Record-setting achievements in national economic development have brought with them a new desire on the part of regional powers to gain the strategic depth required to safeguard their growing prosperity.

More specifically, Beijing's obdurate pressing of its territorial claims in the South China Sea provokes a measure of anxiety, particularly in light of China's growing air and naval power. There is also fear that a halt in China's economic growth or a hitch in the transfer of power after the death of Deng Xiaoping could threaten China's political stability, and with it, the stability of the whole region. The region also faces the prospect of a nuclear-armed North Korea, whose unpredictable leadership sees itself as besieged on all sides.

But the most troubling uncertainty of all concerns the presence and role of the United States. Despite high-level assurances and continued forward deployments, there exists a broad perception in Asia that U.S. power is declining, at least in relative terms, and that the U.S. military presence in Asia is bound to decline as well. This raises doubts about the future of the U.S. role as the region's strategic anchor and balancer. More important, it raises questions about a new regional balance of power.

DEFINING TRENDS

The national security policies of the major regional powers increasingly reflect efforts to come to terms with these and other uncertainties. During the next few years, as these policies continue to evolve in response to regional and global developments, a new regional security order will emerge. The new system will be shaped by five major trends that define the Asia Pacific region today.

THE STRATEGIC IMPORTANCE OF THE REGION WILL CONTINUE TO INCREASE IN LINE WITH THE INCREASE IN ITS ECONOMIC IMPORTANCE

Since the mid-1970s, many Asian nations have taken advantage of a stable regional political order to implement market- and trade-oriented economic policies that have produced the most rapid rates of economic growth in history. A number are now poised to join the community of prosperous market democracies.

By the next century, the global center of economic gravity may well have shifted to this region. In 1992, regional gross national product accounted for 25 percent of the gross world product (calculated on a purchasing power parity basis or at official exchange rates). Japan and China represented the world's second- and third-largest economies, respectively. Barring some political calamity, the region will produce approximately one-third of the gross world product in 2001 (on a purchasing power parity basis). The region is also a major source of the investment capital required to spark and sustain the global economy. Current official reserves in the region now exceed $250 billion, equal to those in all of Europe; more than three-quarters of those reserves are held by China, Hong Kong, and Taiwan.

The ultimate effect of the Asian economic miracle on intra-regional relations is not clear. On the one hand, economic success creates forces for divisiveness. The need for raw materials and access to markets breeds competition, which is intensifying as the interests of individual nations expand. Often, as in the case of China and Japan, competition is complicated by historical animosities and conflicting territorial claims. Also, such powers as North Korea, Burma, Laos, Vietnam, and Cambodia, which do not yet share in the general prosperity, remain sources of tension.

On the other hand, the positive response of Japan, South Korea, and the Association of Southeast Asian Nations (ASEAN) to Beijing's efforts to reconstruct and expand relations illustrates that Asia's economic coming of age is also producing an impulse toward stability and integration. This principle is increasingly evident in efforts to develop regional frameworks for economic and security cooperation, ranging from the Asia Pacific Economic Cooperation (APEC) accord to the ASEAN Regional Forum (ARF), to South Korean proposals for a conference on security and cooperation in Northeast Asia.

This essay has been edited and is reprinted from Strategic Assessment 1995: U.S. Security Challenges in Transition, *ed. Patrick Clawson (Washington, D.C.: Institute for National Strategic Studies, 1995), 17–30, by permission of National Defense University Press.*

REGIONAL POWERS WILL CONTINUE TO FOCUS ON DOMESTIC AGENDAS

Domestic economic, political, and social problems have become the primary concerns of regional leaders. In Japan, a succession of weak governments has had little success in developing policies to deal effectively with a stubborn recession, while in China the leadership continues to grapple with the political consequences of market economics. Beijing is also concerned about growing disparities in income levels among the nation's different regions, which may eventually threaten the unity of the People's Republic. Both China and Japan are experiencing a slow transition to a new, younger generation of political leaders. China already faces significant social unrest, which may well increase as the succession unfolds. In both cases, completing the transition will require a number of years.

On the Korean Peninsula, the real test of Seoul's still-new democratic political institutions will not be passed until the succession to Kim Young Sam is completed by constitutional means. In the North, a new leadership is emerging. The outcome is uncertain, and much depends upon the final issue. Political implosion in the North would be destabilizing at the very least and could result in a conflict that would destroy many of the recent political and economic achievements of the region.

This concern with domestic matters means that for the next few years at least, Asian political leaders will, more than ever, tend to view foreign and national security policy needs through the prism of pressing domestic political requirements. Domestic political preoccupations and internal political weakness have been known to result in destabilizing behavior in other times and places. Considering the stakes, however, it is more likely that the regional leaders most affected by these conditions will seek to avoid potentially destabilizing confrontations.

REGIONAL LEADERS WILL INTENSIFY EFFORTS TO DEVELOP A MORE PERMANENT STRUCTURE OF SECURITY RELATIONS

Doubts about the future U.S. role and presence, the absence of any external military threat to replace the former Soviet Union, and the persistence of potential flashpoints all contribute to a desire to achieve a new structure of regional security relations. At present, however, the characteristics of the evolving regional order are unclear. Whether there will be one system, or one for Northeast Asia and one for Southeast Asia (and, if the latter, the nature of the relationship between the two) is a major uncertainty.

The end of Chinese stonewalling on regional security dialogue, the Clinton administration's call for a new Pacific community, and the achievements of APEC and ARF all suggest that, in principle, multilateralism is a preferred approach to dealing with regional security problems. This, in turn, raises questions about the future of the present approach, which relies upon a network of bilateral security ties between the United States and Japan, South Korea, Australia, the Philippines, and Thailand, as well as agreements providing the United States with access to support facilities in Malaysia and Singapore.

REGIONAL POWERS WILL TRY TO SIDESTEP CONFRONTATIONAL ISSUES

Because of domestic economic and political priorities, no nation—with the possible exception of North Korea—has an interest in disrupting the overall stability that prevails in the region. For example, despite strains in U.S. relations with China (over human rights and trade issues) and Japan (over market access), all three countries continue to cooperate in order to avoid any serious disruption of their bilateral ties.

The possibility of conflict in Taiwan, the South China Sea, and especially the Korean Peninsula will, of course, continue to affect the security planning of every regional power. Given China's strong interest in maintaining stability, however, Beijing is likely to remain conciliatory. Conflict would be likely to occur only if Taiwan were to declare its independence, or if one or more parties to the territorial dispute in the South China Sea were to directly challenge China's sovereignty claim.

Nor is a conventional conflict between India and Pakistan likely to create instability beyond South Asia. Even though China would face pressure to assist Pakistan in such a conflict, Beijing would almost certainly prefer to avoid direct involvement and work with other major external powers to promote a diplomatic settlement. If, however, such a conflict were to escalate to the nuclear level, the impact on the region would be much more difficult to manage.

The Korean Peninsula will be the major source of concern, particularly if the isolation and inaccessibility of the North Korean regime persists. A top priority of all of the regional powers will be to avoid the outbreak of conflict, and the powers most directly concerned will wish to avoid taking any actions that might provoke the North Korean leadership. At the same time, secondary attention will be directed toward achieving a smooth and gradual process of reunification, even if this means tolerating some ambiguity about North Korean nuclear capabilities and intentions.

REGIONAL POWERS WILL CONTINUE TO ADJUST THEIR MILITARY STRATEGIES AND IMPROVE THEIR MILITARY CAPABILITIES

The emphasis on domestic priorities and a regionwide desire to maintain stability will not prevent regional security planners from reexamining and redefining their military strategies and improving their force structures. This is illustrated by China's relatively new focus on limited regional conflict and its ongoing program of military modernization, Japan's recently completed reevaluation of its National Defense Program Outline, South Korea's defense modernization plan, and the continuing efforts of the ASEAN nations to modernize their military equipment and capabilities.

Between 1985 and 1992 increasing prosperity made it possible for regional powers to increase their spending on defense. Nations with the highest rates of economic growth also showed the largest increases in spending for defense. Overall, Asian defense spending grew at about 22 percent. This exceeds the rates for the Middle East and the rest of the less developed world, and almost matches European levels for the same period—although since 1992 European defense spending has declined, while Asia's has not. As might be expected, Northeast Asian defense spending is the highest, owing to the size of the economies of China, Japan, and South Korea, and to the scale of the strategic challenges they face. During the next few years, Chinese and South Korean expenditures will probably continue to show the largest increases, while the rates of increase for Japan and North Korea can be expected to hold steady or decline slightly. Expenditures by Southeast Asian nations also may be beginning to level off.

Acquisition patterns reflect a desire to modernize forces in order to deter or prosecute any limited regional conflicts that might arise. Regional powers are seeking the kinds of high technology systems and capabilities that proved effective during the Gulf War. Areas for improvement include air and naval capabilities; command, control, and communications systems; tactical intelligence systems; electronic warfare capabilities; and rapid deployment forces.

China is actively engaged in improving the quality of its nuclear forces. Evidence available at this time suggests that Beijing is committed to modernizing its small strategic force, rather than mounting an effort to substantially increase the size of that force. Because Beijing still has some distance to travel on this path, it is likely that China's testing program will continue. North Korea's nuclear intentions continue to be a subject of serious regional and global concern.

There is much discussion about whether these developments constitute an arms race or not. Citing the generally good political relations among Asian nations, most observers believe that regional security planners are not basing their force structure improvements on the need to deal with a particular "threat," and there is no indication of an action-reaction dynamic at work. Excepting the Korean Peninsula, it is therefore probably misleading to think in terms of a regional arms race.

In virtually every case, doubts about the future U.S. role and military presence in the region are a major factor stimulating change. With the obvious exception of North Korea, most nations view the prospect of a diminishing U.S. military presence with varying degrees of dismay. Considering Bei-

jing's worries about future relations with its historic competitor Japan, even China probably would prefer that such a decline occur only after the Chinese have achieved considerable improvement in their own military capabilities. Regional powers that have hitherto relied to some extent upon U.S. security guarantees are beginning to develop "hedging strategies" to prepare for possible future contingencies, designing and deploying more self-sufficient forces capable of operating with less direct U.S. support.

U.S. SECURITY INTERESTS

With the exception of the Korean flashpoint, none of the trends that define the region at present is necessarily threatening to U.S. interests. They do, however, indicate that a new security order is emerging to replace the Cold War system—an order that reflects the rising economic power and political aspirations of the major regional powers. South Korea and the ASEAN countries—and perhaps China as well—are examples of former Third World nations that are well on the way to joining the market democracies. Meanwhile, Japan, which has long been numbered among the ranks of market democracies but has refrained from exercising leadership, is making an effort to come to terms with the responsibilities of its position.

The challenge for the United States is to maintain a stabilizing presence in the region during this time of transition, and thereby to secure its interests for the future. Because of its past actions, its high standing within the region, and its national power, the U.S. remains well-positioned to meet this challenge.

DETERRING CONFLICT BY MAINTAINING AN EFFECTIVE SECURITY PRESENCE

An effective U.S. security presence remains key to maintaining the peace in Asia. A credible U.S. commitment to the security of both Korea and Japan helps to deter conflict on the Korean Peninsula. A perceived diminution of the U.S. military commitment to Japan, including the nuclear umbrella, would encourage a more independent Japanese military, which would cause alarm throughout the region, given vivid memories of Japan's brutal aggression earlier in this century. The U.S. military presence has helped to make the ASEAN region peaceful, and regional actors expect that the United States will remain engaged for the foreseeable future.

EXPANDING U.S. ACCESS TO ASIA PACIFIC ECONOMIES AND SUPPORTING THEIR GROWTH

The United States has a vital national interest in maintaining access to the region's vibrant economic systems. The Asia Pacific region is emerging as the center of global economic activity, and the economic welfare of the United States is deeply intertwined with the economic future of this region. Continuing strong economic growth in this region serves U.S. interests by providing expanding markets for U.S.

exports, new investment opportunities and sources of capital, and a stimulus to the development of new technologies and marketing strategies. More important, such access is also a positive indicator of a long-term U.S. commitment to expanding its regional presence.

PREVENTING THE DOMINATION OF THE REGION BY ANY HOSTILE POWER

The rise of a hostile hegemon in Asia would threaten vital U.S. interests. If China, India, Japan, or Russia were to make such an effort, the effect would, at a minimum, be destabilizing. It would also threaten conflict, potentially degrade the material quality of U.S. life, and undermine the ability of the United States to maintain its position globally.

Although there is no possibility that any hostile power will achieve hegemony in the region in the next few years, the situation in the future might be different. Whether the United States is challenged by a hostile or potentially hostile power at some point in the future depends, in part, upon U.S. actions in the next four to five years.

PREVENTING THE PROLIFERATION OF WEAPONS OF MASS DESTRUCTION AND THE SYSTEMS FOR DELIVERING THEM

At present, the major challenge to U.S. interests and regional stability resides in the Korean Peninsula, where North Korea now faces the need either to fish or cut bait with respect to its nuclear program. A North Korean nuclear capability would raise the stakes of war on the peninsula, and increase the pressure on Japan and South Korea to mount nuclear weapons programs of their own. Either of these events would threaten the global interests of the United States and would probably destroy the Nonproliferation Treaty.

PROMOTING THE GROWTH OF DEMOCRATIC POLITICAL SYSTEMS

It is in the long-term U.S. interest to promote the development of governments that share its democratic values and market-oriented approach to economics. The nations of the region are only beginning to come to terms with the issues that divided them in the past, and a shared democratic orientation and commitment to market economies would promote their willingness to take measures to offset years of mistrust. Also, such a commitment can help to establish a basis for restructuring civilian/military relations, which, despite progress, continues to be a problem in many Asian states.

KEY U.S. SECURITY POLICY ISSUES

THE KOREAN PENINSULA

The Korean issue is perhaps the most challenging and important of all of the issues facing the United States in the region. U.S. interactions with Pyongyang have a direct impact on the vital interests of Japan, China, and South Korea. Therefore Washington will be challenged to consider the positions of these powers very carefully.

Leadership Succession

The death of Kim Il Sung, and the uncertainties surrounding the succession of Kim Chong Il, affect every aspect of the Peninsula's security; the fate of North Korea's nuclear program, the dynamic of North/South relations, and the future U.S. role in Korea will all be influenced by events now unfolding in Pyongyang. The policies of the United States and the other concerned powers—mainly China, Japan, and of course South Korea—are of crucial importance in shaping future events in ways that may channel North Korean behavior in more positive directions.

Like so much about the North, the final outcome of the succession remains full of uncertainty. Some analysts hold that planning and preparation for the succession, which began as early as the mid-1970s, was essentially complete by the time of Kim Il Sung's death. Indeed, the absence of early signs of real opposition suggests that the younger Kim may be well on the way to consolidating his position as leader. But questions about the longevity of his tenure and the direction of his policies remain.

Some observers believe that, because Kim Chong Il is dependent upon the extremely conservative elites of the Korean People's Army and Korean Worker Party, there will be no major policy changes in the short term. Others note that the younger Kim is well connected with the technocratic circle in the North that has long argued for greater flexibility in economic and foreign policies, and that is now poised to regain the ascendancy it enjoyed at the end of the last decade. In this view, the regime change holds some promise for the future.

Clarity is probably years away. In the meanwhile, the United States and its allies will have to make decisions on the basis of uncertain information.

The Nuclear Issue

Efforts to come to terms with the nuclear problem, which have the highest priority for all interested parties, have two components: to secure a freeze on all North Korean nuclear activity, and to evaluate—and, if necessary, roll back—any progress the North may have made toward developing nuclear weapons. If, as appears likely, the purpose of the nuclear program is to secure the existence of the North Korean regime in some form, Pyongyang can be expected to make every effort to sustain the ambiguity that surrounds its nuclear accomplishments. Further, there is some tension between efforts to learn about and roll back the program, on the one hand, and the process of maintaining a freeze, on the other. The effort to accomplish the former could well impact negatively on the latter, as North Korea makes cooperation on a freeze contingent upon a reduction in demands for clarification of past activities.

The August 1994 Geneva agreement provides some ground for optimism. In effect, the North agreed to freeze its nuclear program and observe its commitments to the Nonproliferation Treaty and the International Atomic Energy Agency (NPT/IAEA). Pyongyang also promised it would not reprocess the eight thousand fuel rods now in storage or refuel its reactors. In return, the United States offered to facilitate North Korean acquisition of light water reactors and eventually to consider steps toward some form of diplomatic recognition of the North. Pyongyang now has positive inducements to move ahead in expanding relations with Washington and Seoul, and with the region in general. The agreement does much to defuse concerns in Beijing, Tokyo, and even Southeast Asia about the potentially divisive course of events before the meeting in Geneva.

Prior to Geneva, the United States tended to part ways with China, Japan, and South Korea on the question of priorities in dealing with the nuclear issue. Washington's stance, in which deterrence was central, reflected a deep concern about the international proliferation dimensions of the problem, particularly the potential impact on the future of the Nonproliferation Treaty regime. Japan, China, and South Korea also appreciated the proliferation threat, but, as the powers that stand to lose the most in the event of conflict, were more concerned than Washington to avoid antagonizing the regime in Pyongyang. The Geneva agreement has relieved some of the immediate pressures engendered by these differences. However, the differences remain, and in the future, Tokyo, Beijing, and Seoul will probably continue to be more willing than Washington to tolerate the ambiguity surrounding nuclear activities in the North.

Even though some aspects of the problem may be easier to manage after the Geneva agreement, others remain undiminished. For example, while verification of the North's agreements on reprocessing are verifiable, assessing compliance with NPT/IAEA standards ultimately requires investigation of two waste facilities, which North Korea adamantly rejects. Solving this problem through negotiation will be difficult. Another source of difficulty, which directly affects U.S.–South Korean relations, is that Seoul does not want U.S. negotiations with Pyongyang to impinge upon its own prerogatives in dealing with the North. One way in which it manifests this concern is by raising the issue of "challenge inspections" (demanding, in effect, that Pyongyang open virtually all of its military bases to ad hoc inspection) in the process of North–South dialogue. Finally, Pyongyang retains a card it has played with success in the past: the ability to use the ambiguity surrounding its past nuclear accomplishments to influence the pace and content of the negotiation process.

Pyongyang's high stake in its nuclear program, when coupled with the uncertainties surrounding the leadership succession, make for a tense situation. Internal political instability in the North still carries with it the possibility of an attack upon the South, and prudence dictates that every effort be made to foreclose the North's military option for achieving its goals. This, in turn, argues for adopting an array of diplomatic and military measures designed to enhance deterrence without undercutting the negotiations.

South Korean Confidence

In the longer run, the major uncertainties on the Korean Peninsula concern the questions of North–South dialogue and reunification. There is a firm regional consensus in favor of preserving stability. Part and parcel of that conviction is the judgment that an incremental approach to reunification is best. All concerned parties agree their interests would be best served by gradual, peaceful progress toward reunification—the so-called soft landing.

Since the election of President Kim Young Sam in December 1992, South Korean politics has evolved in ways that have surprised many observers. By implementing a series of adroit domestic measures and holding the line on foreign policy, President Kim has managed to project an air of competence. Most notable in this regard have been the twin successes of convincing the public that he is willing to deal with corruption and winning acceptance by the military. Combined with the general perception that South Korea's economic future is bright, this has created considerable confidence about the effectiveness of South Korean political and economic institutions. There is also a general feeling that if a smooth constitutional transfer of power follows President Kim, South Korean politics will have turned an important corner.

Further, the Republic of Korea Army has begun to address historical problems related to intelligence, command and control, air defense, and air and naval capabilities. Scheduled improvements and air and naval procurement programs will eventually help to remove remaining weaknesses, and very probably give the South an overall military advantage. In the short term, however, U.S. assistance will continue to be necessary. It is increasingly likely that the outcome of a North Korean attack would be the destruction of the Pyongyang regime. However, such a victory would be achieved only at the cost of the temporary loss of Seoul and widespread destruction throughout the peninsula.

The South Korean approach to reunification remains optimistic. The predominant view is that the goal of a united Korea is best achieved by using South Korea's increasing diplomatic, economic, and military strength to enhance deterrence and by patiently encouraging the political and economic evolution of the Pyongyang regime. Seoul's belief that time is on its side influences its stance in the dialogue with the North, because it feels less pressure to make concessions than in the past. This view, along with Seoul's concern that it not be marginalized, contains the potential for some friction with the United States. The challenge will be for Washington to find the proper overlay between its dialogue with Pyongyang and the process of North–South dialogue.

PREPARING FOR AN UNSTABLE OR ASSERTIVE CHINA

The Stability Question

The course of economic and political evolution in China is of concern to U.S. policy simply because China's size, resource base, and growing national strength mean that its influence extends into every corner of the region. Some observers, citing a marked rise in strikes, peasant protests against government inefficiency and corruption, and urban discontent over inflation and corruption, judge that Beijing will not be able to both sustain economic development and maintain a stable unitary state, and thus China is a potential source of considerable regional instability.

Others hold that despite obvious problems that are characteristic of all developing societies, China's leaders will in the long run successfully use sustained economic growth to offset dissenting voices, buttress their position, and eventually forge a new, effective relationship between the center and the provinces. Indeed, since his "Southern Journey" at the beginning of 1992, Deng and the proponents of market-oriented reform have staked much on the gamble that continued economic growth will guarantee both stability and the continued leadership of the Chinese Communist Party.

A third view, related to the second, emphasizes the possibility that pressures engendered by China's experience with market economics will ultimately result in greater pluralism, which will in turn be manifested in more democratic political institutions. Most proponents of this view hold that a more democratic China will emerge as a force for regional stability.

Early in 1995, Beijing acknowledged the intensity of the problems it faces by announcing a shift in national priorities from pursuing economic growth to maintaining social stability, which had previously been merely a corollary of economic development. Under the new formulation, however, stability takes precedence, even if it means that some growth must be sacrificed in the short run. The threat to stability in China has two basic sources: uncertainties surrounding the leadership succession and fissiparous pressures engendered by uneven economic development in various areas.

A successful transfer of leadership requires the emergence of an individual who, like Deng Xiaoping, can forge an authoritative consensus among divergent interests. The impending succession will also involve the empowerment of a younger generation of leaders who owe their positions more to mastery of technical skills than to associations developed in the revolutionary environment of the past. Most important of all, a successful succession will require the restoration of a measure of legitimacy to the rule of the Chinese Communist Party.

At this time, it is not clear whether Jiang Zemin will be able to consolidate his position after Deng passes from the scene. Although he now holds all of the most important official leadership positions, a significant number of party and government officials regard him as more of a passive respondent to emerging events than a strong leader who actively defines the policy environment.

It is more likely that Deng's passing will usher in a period of collective leadership that will persist for a number of years, and during which individuals will jockey for position until one is able to gain power. Most observers consider it unlikely that this process will produce changes in the basic direction of domestic or foreign policies. More than 80 percent of prices in China are now set primarily by market mechanisms, and it would be nearly impossible to reverse course without major, regime-threatening dislocations. Similarly, domestic imperatives will encourage China to pursue moderate foreign policies designed to avoid confrontations that might upset regional stability. Moves toward a more aggressive or confrontational foreign policy would endanger economic progress, again with dire consequences for the Beijing regime. However, U.S. policy makers must be prepared to face the possibility that the imperatives of succession politics may motivate China's leaders to harden positions on sensitive U.S.–China issues such as Taiwan, trade, and human rights.

China's Growing Assertiveness

The main long-term Chinese foreign policy objective will be to secure what Beijing sees as China's rightful position as a leading force in regional and global affairs. To that end, Beijing faces a challenge with two dimensions, one immediate and tactical, and one strategic and future oriented.

In an immediate and tactical sense, Beijing will focus on the national interests that are most pressing and keep potential challenges to those interests under control. Specifically, the Chinese leadership seeks to use diplomatic means and the specter of improving Peoples Liberation Army military capabilities to put teeth into Chinese claims in the South China Sea. Beijing also seeks to deploy military forces that are capable of reinforcing Chinese demands on Taiwan, even though the Chinese remain fairly sanguine about future developments in both of these areas.

The second, more strategic dimension is the challenge to create an economy that is capable of supporting the wide range of economic, political, and military options that will guarantee that China has a major voice in creating the new regional structure of security relations. Although China's recent economic growth has been spectacular, the economy may be reaching the point at which deficiencies in its legal, energy, transportation, and communications infrastructures will begin to inhibit future growth. In the late 1980s similar deficiencies in the rural infrastructure brought a virtual halt to increases in agricultural productivity, raising problems that have yet to be overcome.

Beijing's firm declaratory positions on Taiwan, Hong Kong, and the South China Sea and its military modernization program (with its emphasis on force projection) provide concrete manifestations of Beijing's commitment to have a strong voice in the region. In light of this, U.S. relations with Beijing assume critical importance. If U.S.–China relations remain stable, they will provide a force for stability in the region. If the relationship were to deteriorate, on the other hand, then other powers would face pressure to choose sides, thus making it difficult to avoid tensions. Washington's 1994 decisions to restore military-to-military ties with China and to separate economic and trade issues from human rights concerns may have set the stage for a recovery from the deterioration of Sino-American relations that occurred after Beijing's violent suppression of the student democracy demonstrations of 1989.

However, there are politically powerful constituencies within China, most notably within the military, who feel that China may be paying too high a price for Washington's favor. According to this view, the United States is anxious to prevent the rise of a powerful China as a new peer competitor in the region. This judgment that Washington has tacitly adopted the view of China as an enemy clouds Beijing's evaluation of other aspects of U.S. China policy.

Taiwan is potentially the most disruptive issue in bilateral relations. China's senior leadership already judges that continuing U.S. political, military, and economic support fosters the increasingly independence-minded political culture that characterizes the island today. Anti-U.S. factions among the Chinese leadership portray Washington's Taiwan policy as the means by which the United States perpetuates the division of China, prevents the integration of the two economies, and retards China's economic development. They hold similar views with respect to U.S. human rights policies, Washington's position on China's entry into the General Agreement on Tariffs and Trade (GATT)/World Trade Organization, Beijing's military technology transfer and arms control policies, and the U.S. position on the Spratly Islands/South China Sea question. In each of these cases, concerns about a putative U.S. effort to constrain China has had a crucially important influence on Beijing's assessment of the situation.

Thus far, economic and political considerations have prevented Beijing from taking the openly confrontational stance advocated by the proponents of this view. Moreover, it is most unlikely that this will change dramatically in the next few years, since China has so much to lose. However, anti-U.S. forces are already a potent factor in policy deliberations and may enjoy increased influence in the future. Much, therefore, will depend upon the evolution of U.S. policies in particular areas of friction. As the dominant regional power, the United States faces the challenge of accommodating to China's rise in ways that do not threaten its own economic position or its relations with its friends and allies.

DEALING WITH A CHANGING JAPAN

Political Weakness and the Domestic Focus

During the next few years, Japanese leaders, like their counterparts elsewhere in the region, will focus primarily on domestic issues and problems. Overcoming Japan's stubborn economic recession is the most immediate problem facing the fragile coalition of Socialist Prime Minister Tomiichi Murayama. Neither former Prime Minister Miyazawa's 13 trillion yen package, passed in the spring of 1993, nor the 6 trillion yen plan proposed by former Prime Minister Hosokawa in September of that year produced any significant economic upturn.

In the opinion of many observers, the fact that Japan's economic performance remains sluggish despite such initiatives signals that nothing short of basic reform—involving market opening and a dramatic loosening of regulatory strictures—will be sufficient to achieve results. This view is reinforced further by continuing pressure from the United States, Europe, and China to be more forthcoming in market access, technology sharing, and investment practices. And yet, despite the outcome of the Framework Talks with the United States, Tokyo apparently remains unwilling, and probably unable, to implement such a program.

This is a result of a second problem now confronting the Japanese political system: the political vacuum created by the end of the thirty-eight-year reign of the Liberal Democratic Party (LDP) in early 1993. Unless the Japanese are able to forge a new consensus of political forces to replace the defunct LDP-based system, it is highly unlikely that any government will be able to undertake thoroughgoing economic reform measures. Even with the benefit of a new electoral reform law that reduces the number of candidates that any party might field, that process will require a number of years, as conservatives, socialists, and middle-of-the-road forces all compete for advantage. Political weakness is likely to remain a feature of the Japanese political landscape for the next two or three years at least. In the meantime, Tokyo will find it difficult to respond to the pressure for change emanating both from within and without. Washington should expect Japanese movement on issues of concern to the U.S. to proceed in a frustrating series of starts, stops, and reversals.

Foreign Policy Aspirations

In foreign policy, Japan is seeking to acquire a role in international affairs that is commensurate with its economic strength and influence. Tokyo's campaign to gain a permanent seat on the U.N. Security Council, its willingness to participate in U.N. peacekeeping operations, and the opening of its rice market to better prepare for participating in GATT and the World Treaty Organization all illustrate this aspiration, as well as a willingness to begin changing established customs in order to achieve it.

Another possible indicator of things to come is the effort begun during the Hosokawa administration to expand and solidify political and economic ties with Asia. Japan now surpasses the United States in trade and investment in China. Also, Tokyo was quick to distance itself from the U.S. position on Chinese human rights policies. In a similar way, Hosokawa's apology to South Korea for the injustices of Japanese colonial rule have paved the way for an improved relationship between the two powers. Such actions, along with Prime Minister Murayama's September travels in Southeast Asia, represent an attempt by Tokyo to create options as it confronts regional uncertainties.

Japan's foreign policy aspirations provide the United States with opportunities, such as obtaining a more active Japanese role in peacekeeping and disaster relief operations. At the same time, a more internationally assertive Japan could feed worries in the region that Tokyo seeks to fill the power vacuum created by U.S. withdrawal.

Shifting Security Priorities

Tokyo is also facing a number of major decisions about its defense and national security policies. Although Japanese defense planners have been slow to acknowledge it publicly, the collapse of the Soviet Union removed the need to include a specific military threat in Tokyo's unspoken defense calculus. Although relations with Russia continue to be a source of tension, there is little expectation that these will be expressed in military terms. Concerns about a possible Chinese military threat remain similarly unconvincing with the Japanese public. In fact, depending on events in North Korea, Japan may face no military threat at all in the next few years. In these circumstances, the need to structure the self-defense forces for the "defense of Japan" rings increasingly hollow.

No serious consideration is given to ending Japan's Mutual Security Treaty with the United States. However, within Japanese defense circles, there is a lively discussion about defining a new rationale for the alliance, one that will replace the imperatives of Cold War containment strategy with a formulation more in tune with present and future realities.

Such thinking is based upon two considerations, one positive and one more negative. On the positive side, there is a feeling that Japan must be more responsible for safeguarding its own prosperity and interests. On the negative side, there is a sense that the United States will have neither the capability nor the political will to come to Japan's aid in any but the most extreme circumstances. For example, while it is accepted that the United States would do its part to defend Japan from any actual attack, and that the U.S. nuclear umbrella remains effective, there is considerably less confidence that Washington would provide military support to Japan if Tokyo had to deal with a crisis in the South China Sea or the Senkaku Islands. In other words, the alliance may not be useful to Tokyo's efforts to deal with the military contingencies Japan is most likely to face.

Irrespective of the path traveled, whether positive or negative, the end point is the same. Increasing numbers of Japanese officials believe that while Tokyo should continue to cooperate with Washington and other regional powers to maintain the peace and stability of the region, Japan should develop a force that is able operate more independently of the United States, in order to deal with the military contingencies Tokyo is most likely to face.

Much of this thinking is reflected in the report of the Prime Minister's Advisory Group on Defense Issues, published in August 1994. Convened by former Prime Minister Hosokawa and accepted, albeit with reservations, by Prime Minister Murayama, the blue ribbon panel affirms the centrality of the alliance to Japan's defense posture, but also calls for upgrading consultation mechanisms, improving joint training and logistics mechanisms, and enhancing cooperation in command, control, and communications. More significantly, the report calls for Japan to play an active role in shaping the new regional security order by participating in cooperative security efforts, and for allowing regular self-defense force units to participate in U.N. peacekeeping operations. Finally, the report in effect advocates reducing force size in order to permit qualitative improvements in weapons systems, including theater missile defense.

It is extremely unlikely that the present socialist-led coalition has the strength or the inclination to effect a wholesale change in Japan's defense posture. However, defense policy eventually could be the issue that separates the socialists from their LDP partners in the coalition. Moreover, as new coalitions evolve, this new view of defense issues is likely to persist, and there is reason to believe that it will be reflected in acquisition and research and development policies. If events in fact do develop in this direction, the United States will face the necessity of making some hard decisions of its own about the way the alliance operates, and especially about channels of communication between the alliance partners and new roles, missions, and capabilities for the self-defense force. Dealing with the North Korean nuclear issue will test this capability. Also, it will be necessary to consider very carefully the reactions of other regional powers who, mindful as they are of the past, will be concerned about any changes in Japan's defense posture.

DEFINING THE PLACE OF MULTILATERALISM IN THE REGIONAL SECURITY ORDER

Washington's bilateral security alliances and access agreements form the backbone of the U.S. presence in East Asia. Whether this system will continue to offer the best guarantee of regional security, or whether the security environment would be improved if a larger degree of multilateralism were to evolve, is a major question now confronting the United States. However, extreme caution is required in approaching this issue, as U.S. efforts to assess the advantages of multilateralism could raise additional questions in the region about the durability of U.S. security commitments and thus encourage speculation about a diminishing U.S. role and presence.

The Trend Toward Multilateralism

Since 1980, eight multilateral organizations, associations, or agreements have developed or been concluded. Although levels of institutionalization vary and are in some cases quite rudimentary, all of these new institutions appear to have achieved permanent status. Multilateralism has become a fact of regional political life, especially on economic issues, and to a lesser degree in security matters. The interest in multilateralism provides the United States with an opportunity to become an integral part of an emerging Asia Pacific community.

Among the factors accounting for the rise of multilateralism, two stand out as being most important. Both have direct implications for U.S. policy.

The first is the broad perception that the U.S. military presence is likely to be reduced significantly before the end of the decade. Regional analysts assess that the force of approximately 100,000 U.S. troops in East Asia envisioned by the *Bottom-up Review* will not become a reality. It is also generally perceived that even if U.S. forces were to remain present in some numbers, the domestic focus of the Clinton administration, the U.S. Congress, and the U.S. public will reduce Washington's willingness to become involved in disputes in Asia, with the possible exception of Korea. In this context, multilateralism becomes, in the view of some regional powers, a means of placing limits on the influence of any potential hegemon such as China or Japan by enmeshing them within a larger consensual framework. The challenge for Washington is to convince the region's leaders that the U.S. commitment to the security of East Asia is not in doubt.

Second, the momentum generated by success in the economic sphere will continue to spur the growth of organizations devoted to expanding and managing trade, and success in economic coordination may encourage efforts to adopt multilateral approaches to security issues as well. As economic and national security concerns continue to converge, multilateralism in economic affairs will naturally tend to move into the security sector. Issues such as overlapping Exclusive Economic Zones, technology transfer regimes, arms sales, access to trade routes, and environmental security all have both an economic and a security dimension requiring multilateral consultations. Officials in Singapore, Malaysia, and Thailand were frankly surprised at the alacrity

with which participants joined discussions at the recent ASEAN Regional Forum. As a result, the organizing committee is reportedly considering a more specific agenda for the next session, which may well convene with an expanded ASEAN membership including Vietnam and Laos. If this occurs, the momentum of the impulse toward multilateral security cooperation will continue its increase.

The Limits of Multilateralism

At present, the effort to promote multilateralism is centered where it began, in Southeast Asia and ASEAN. At its core, it retains the original focus on consultative mechanisms and economic concerns. Indeed, there is surprising unanimity about the potentialities and limits of this approach. For example, most nations, including the United States, agree that multilateral activity should continue to emphasize economic issues. They also feel that, where security issues are concerned, multilateralism is most appropriately viewed as a means of enhancing comprehensive security by consultation and cooperation. Although some players, such as Australia and Canada, argue for more rapid progress toward institutionalization of security cooperation and have offered plans for building such institutional frameworks, this call is regarded with considerable skepticism elsewhere in the region as being premature. Nor does any participant see multilateral approaches to security as an immediate replacement for the present system, which centers on the United States and its network of bilateral security alliances. Even China, which may embrace a different view in the future, recognizes that for the present the U.S. forward military presence provides an essential component of regional stability. Virtually all regional analysts agree that multilateral approaches to managing security concerns must be based upon a reliable U.S. military presence manifested in strong bilateral security relations.

One explanation for this "least common denominator" approach is that it is difficult for nations to agree on any specific agenda for consideration by multilateral fora. For example, with respect to the two major regional flashpoints—the Korean Peninsula and the South China Sea—neither China nor North Korea is willing to accept multilateral management. On the contrary, China defines its claims in the Spratly Islands as a sovereignty issue, while North Korea, for reasons of its own, remains committed to dealing directly with the United States. Because of such limitations, bilateral relations between the region's nations and the United States are likely to remain the most important factor in the Asia Pacific security scene for the rest of this decade.

EUROPE

JAMES W. MORRISON, JEFFREY SIMON, AND CHARLES L. BARRY

With the end of the abnormal stability that the Cold War imposed on Europe, the diverse nature of the continent has once again come to the fore. Europe has some of the world's most modern societies, well-established democracies, advanced economies, and cooperative international systems. At the same time, it is home to many relatively poor states, states in which democracy and market economies are struggling to gain a foothold, and regions with ethnic tension and conflict.

This essay deals with Western, Central, and Eastern Europe, as well as the North Atlantic Alliance, to which the United States and Canada belong. It also covers the Baltic States and Turkey. Russia, Ukraine, and other former Soviet Eurasian states are addressed in the next essay. Dividing the Eurasian area in this way may tend to restrict discussion of broad issues such as those dealt with by the fifty-three states in the Conference on Security and Cooperation in Europe (CSCE), but it breaks up what would otherwise be an inordinately long analysis.

Significant changes are under way in Europe and the North Atlantic Treaty Organization (NATO); some changes predate the end of the Cold War but many flow from its termination. The perceived threat of a massive Soviet military attack has been replaced by new challenges from turmoil in the East and the South. Allies are discussing a new transatlantic relationship reflecting a reduced U.S. military presence in Europe and an enhanced European pillar. Western Europe is increasingly integrating, and Central and East European states are pressing for integration with the West.

Differences in security perspectives have emerged. Northern and Central European states tend to focus primarily on the threat of instability in the East, while Mediterranean states worry more about developments to the south. States in Central and Eastern Europe seek security assurances from the West, primarily out of concern about actual and potential developments in Russia and other states of the former Soviet Union. Conflict in the Balkans raises the specter of European national conflicts so familiar in the past.

There is a range of perceptions of the situation in Europe. Some optimistically see Europe as the wealthiest, most progressive, cooperative, and secure region in the world. They see no real threat to Europe and believe that NATO no longer has a mission and will or should fade away.

Other analysts are relatively pessimistic. They point to the difficulties in achieving European unity. They emphasize continuing economic problems in Western Europe, such as low economic growth and high unemployment, which adversely affect relations among European Union (EU) states, limit assistance to the East, and increase pressure for reductions in defense budgets and forces. They perceive a lack of leadership within Europe itself and fear the United States is no longer as interested or willing to lead the alliance. They point to a number of problems within individual countries and in their bilateral and multilateral relations, often focusing on the roles of Germany and France. They see the continuing conflict in the former Yugoslavia as calling into question the credibility of the European Union and NATO and fear ethnic conflict may spread.

This analysis acknowledges the difficulties faced in Europe but is relatively bullish on the ability of institutions such as NATO, the European Union, the Western European Union (WEU), and the CSCE to address the problems successfully. This web of security-related institutions with overlapping memberships is increasingly reaching out to states in the East as well as to European states formerly viewed as "neutral."

DEFINING TRENDS

NATO IS ADJUSTING BETTER THAN EXPECTED

Some observers maintain that NATO is eroding or that it is an anachronism that should go the way of the Warsaw Pact. Most observers, however, believe that the alliance has been adapting itself—some would say admirably—for a new era, steadily transforming its political focus, security agenda, and military structures. In NATO's forty-five year history, there have been a dozen summits involving heads of state and government; half of these have occurred in the last seven years, launching major initiatives that demonstrate NATO's desire to stay relevant in a rapidly evolving security environment.

NATO has developed a substantial outreach program through the North Atlantic Cooperation Council (NACC) and the Partnership for Peace (PFP) program, in which NATO's sixteen members have engaged in cooperation with more than twenty states in Central and Eastern Europe, Western Europe, and the Commonwealth of Independent States.

This essay has been edited and is reprinted from Strategic Assessment 1995: U.S. Security Challenges in Transition, *ed. Patrick Clawson (Washington, D.C.: Institute for National Strategic Studies, 1995), 31–50, by permission of National Defense University Press.*

While some people have advocated immediate NATO membership for the Czech Republic, Hungary, Poland, and Slovakia, it became apparent at the NATO summit in January 1994 that the NATO allies were not ready immediately to accept new members into NATO, that further work was needed to develop the NATO relationship with Russia, and that the ground had not been laid for NATO expansion with the U.S. Senate and European parliaments. An evolutionary, step-by-step process leading to the point where NATO expansion seems only natural may stand the best chance of success.

The expectations raised in 1991 by the rhetoric of the Rome NATO summit declaration and the new alliance strategic concept, calling for NATO to promote stability throughout the transatlantic region, have yet to be fulfilled. NATO, however, now supports the initiative to establish a European Security and Defense Identity (ESDI), which is to strengthen the alliance's European pillar while reinforcing the trans-Atlantic link and enable European allies to take greater responsibility for their common security and defense. NATO has also launched an initiative to develop a concept for Combined Joint Task Forces (CJTF). More will be said later about each of these. The alliance has also moved from a near-dogmatic belief that it must never tread outside of NATO territory to the conviction that to remain relevant it must be prepared to operate out-of-area. The experience in the former Yugoslavia, however, may dampen allies' enthusiasm for out-of-area operations.

The alliance's 1991 new strategic concept and related declarations lay down a whole new set of missions. NATO's military was told to expand its horizons to include roles in peacetime and in crisis management, as well as to retain the ability to go to war. In 1992 NATO declared itself prepared to support peacekeeping under the auspices of the CSCE and the United Nations. By 1994 NATO was heavily involved in peace operations in the former Yugoslavia and had drafted a new doctrine for peace operations that is to provide the foundation for future training, exercises, and planning.

NATO's intervention in the former Yugoslavia has been criticized by some as too little and too late, and serious policy differences have emerged among allies. Nonetheless, NATO has had limited success and, more important, has gained valuable operational experience in crisis response. NATO has been on extended duty in the Adriatic blockade Operation Sharp Guard and in Operation Deny Flight over Bosnia. The alliance's military operations in the former Yugoslavia mark the first time NATO has engaged in combat operations since its founding in 1949. NATO forces were largely responsible for the lifting of the siege of Sarajevo in February 1994. [Editor's note: With the signing of the Dayton accords in November 1995, NATO has deployed an implementation force (IFOR) of 60,000 troops to monitor the cease-fire and separation of forces in Bosnia.]

As NATO's military missions have changed, forces and command structure have been reduced, reflecting the decreased threat of general war. NATO itself has few assigned forces, and the militaries of nearly all its member states are shrinking. This indicates a strategy of anticipating and managing crises and a growing reliance on reserve forces. NATO's integrated military structure has reduced both the number and size of its commands, consolidating areas of responsibility and streamlining command links.

The focus on political tasks and, for the military, the shift to peace operations and crisis intervention and smaller, more flexible forces are intended to improve NATO's capability for effective crisis management and prevention of war. There is, nevertheless, growing concern that the continued reductions in defense budgets of the allies may forestall the technological modernization necessary to give these smaller forces the needed flexibility and mobility. Such a development would have serious repercussions for the path NATO is committed to following.

Finally, NATO is making a concerted drive to address emerging tensions and crises before they erupt into military conflict. Evidence of this broader political and economic focus can be found in the NACC work plans. The NACC has set out an ambitious agenda for activities related to defense conversion, privatization, environmental reclamation, economics, and other issues. NACC meetings have issued position statements on conflicts and situations far removed from NATO itself, such as the armed confrontation along the Tajik-Afghan border and the nuclear crisis in North Korea. The respective roles of NACC and PFP are still evolving.

DEFENSE BUDGETS ARE DECLINING IN MOST NATO COUNTRIES

In real terms, defense budgets in the United States and most other NATO member states peaked in the latter half of the 1980s and have been in steady decline since. The U.S. defense budget began its decline early (in 1986) and since 1990 has fallen faster (13 percent versus 10 percent) than the aggregate budgets of other NATO countries. Defense budgets of NATO member states have followed measured, deliberate reductions, and many expect reductions to continue for several more years, with some exceptions. While the aggregate of the allies' real spending on defense is in decline, some countries—Turkey, Norway, and Luxembourg—for differing reasons have actually increased their defense budgets in recent years, and some states may strive to maintain current real levels of defense spending.

The reasons for declining budgets are not surprising: the lack of a threat of attack by hostile forces, competing domestic demands long subordinated to Cold War defense priorities, the economic recession, and a perceived urgency to invest in restructuring and "reinvention" of governments and industries in preparation for greater economic competition in the future. Of these reasons, the first—the absence of a visible threat—is the basic rationale that allows consideration of all the rest.

At the same time, reductions are unlikely to gain greater momentum owing to concerns over defense industry job losses, the time necessary to effect defense conversion to commercial enterprise, the recent ebbing of recessions (especially in the United States), and the growing realization that there are greater and more costly demands for military power in the post–Cold War era than initially perceived. For the United States, the many post–Cold War contingencies, both outside and inside the NATO region, and the costs of all-volunteer forces have imposed great strains on U.S. military manpower and equipment.

The trend in declining budgets in NATO is most evident in the area of active force reductions. Overall, the forces of NATO nations have declined by 15 percent since 1990, although in some force indicators (e.g., maneuver brigades, fighter aircraft, and combatant ships) those states with the most modern forces have taken reductions of up to 30 percent (Germany) and 40 percent (United Kingdom and United States).

A less visible yet telling effect of reduced budgets and smaller forces is the reduction in opportunities for NATO forces to train together. Exercises now are fewer and smaller and often rely on simulation technology.

The arsenal of NATO integrated forces and infrastructure, which has been ready for Europe's defense and often tapped for contingencies from the Middle East to Africa to the Falkland Islands, is dwindling significantly, and NATO's superior multinational experience from decades of collective training is waning even more quickly.

WESTERN EUROPE IS DEEPENING AND BROADENING ITS INTEGRATION

The transformation of the European Community into the European Union is the most recent achievement of a long, often tedious, and yet persistent integrative process that has been under way since shortly after World War II. Before 1991, integration in Europe was confined to trade and related economic policies. With the creation of a single market—which was officially inaugurated on January 1, 1993, although not all aspects have yet been fully implemented—economic integration reached a new plateau and now appears to be all but irreversible, though the tendency to suffer occasional setbacks can be expected to continue.

In the early 1990s the integrative process spread to the social, political, security, and defense arenas. With the signing of the Treaty on European Union—the Maastricht Treaty—in December 1991, integration was broadened to include both cooperation on justice and home affairs and development of a common foreign and security policy, with provision for an eventual defense component. A common defense policy is now envisaged. How deep such integration

will go and how quickly it will progress are matters for speculation. While few expect Europe to stop at the single-market stage, progress is likely to be cautious and evolutionary, with periods of apparent backsliding, as EU members struggle to compromise on the way forward. The unexpected delays in ratifying the Maastricht Treaty in 1992–93 and the weeks of public debate over a new successor EU Commission president in spring 1994 are examples of the difficulties faced in integration. The most important challenges for the European Union in the next several years will be addressed at the Intergovernmental Conference set for 1996.

As the European Union pursues deeper internal integration, it is also broadening its geographic reach. The twelve members in 1994 became fifteen in 1995, with the addition of Austria, Finland, and Sweden. Six countries from Central and Eastern Europe have signed association agreements and could start entering the Union by the beginning of the next century. How effectively the European Union could coordinate its activities with in excess of twenty members is a major question, but the Union does seem committed to further expansion.

The accession to the European Union of Austria, Finland, and Sweden will increase its economic power. On the other hand, it will also take some adjusting to accommodate the three new "neutral" states; with current member Ireland, more than a quarter of EU membership will comprise states formerly described as "neutral." The European Union will also share a new long border with Russia in Scandinavia. If East European states are eventually admitted, this will have even greater implications in the context of addressing issues beyond those traditionally discussed by NATO allies.

Parallel to integration in the European Union, the Western European Union, since 1987, has gradually expanded its activities, both operationally (participating in the Persian Gulf War and operations in the former Yugoslavia) and politically (moving its headquarters to Brussels and absorbing the functions of the defense-oriented Eurogroup and the armaments cooperation-oriented Independent European Program Group). The WEU has also expanded its membership from the seven states that founded it in 1954 to nine members (with a tenth—Greece—awaiting membership ratification), two observers, three associate members, and nine associate partners. At half the WEU's meetings, when all are invited to attend, there are twenty-four states represented.

The Western European Union is now the most visible embodiment of the ESDI and the strengthening of the European pillar within the alliance. Most observers expect ever-closer WEU ties with both the European Union and NATO.

The trend in U.S.–European Union relations is toward increased ties and greater collaboration on global issues. Potentially, the European Union has the collective strength to be Washington's most significant partner, and the United States and European Union already work together on many security issues. In 1990, the United States and the European Union agreed to establish high-level bilateral contacts, and there are indications that both sides would like to see cooperation grow after the 1996 EU Intergovernmental Conference.

CENTRAL AND EAST EUROPEANS ARE STRUGGLING FOR INTERNAL REFORM WHILE SEEKING INTEGRATION WITH THE WEST

Events in Central and Eastern Europe have been in fast-forward over the past five years. Having experienced three distinct periods since the revolutions of 1989–90, the region is now poised for another shift.

Initial Euphoria. In 1989–90, Central and Eastern Europeans experienced euphoria, stemming from their successful revolutions and optimism about establishing democracies and market economies and joining NATO and the European Community. This period saw German unification and NATO's extension of a "hand of friendship" to the East.

Return to More Cautious Optimism. In 1991 came the disintegration of the Warsaw Pact, withdrawal of Soviet forces from Hungary and Czechoslovakia, the failed coup in the Soviet Union, and a NATO Summit that resulted in the new NATO strategic concept, the creation of the NACC to engage the East, and the initiation of military ties with the East. Central and Eastern Europe's initial euphoria turned to more cautious optimism.

Increasing Skepticism. By 1992 and 1993, the Soviet Union had disintegrated, and Boris Yeltsin initially acquiesced in, but subsequently opposed, the bids of several nations in Central and Eastern Europe to join NATO. NATO and EU hesitancy to embrace Central and Eastern Europe contributed to pessimism about the prospects for the extension of Western security institutions and economic support to the East, while Russia's domestic turmoil and entanglements in the "near abroad" led to increased skepticism about Russia's democratic development. Greater realism about the time frame for a successful economic transformation began to set in. Voters in Lithuania and Poland in 1993—and in Hungary, Slovakia, and Bulgaria in 1994—expressed their frustration at the ballot box, returning ex-communists to power.

Testing NATO. The fourth period, beginning in 1994, has seen Central and East Europeans reluctantly resigned to a slower process of integration than they wish but willing to participate in cooperative arrangements, testing Western intentions. NATO's Summit in Brussels in January 1994 adopted the PFP program, suggesting possible eventual membership in NATO through PFP participation and the possible inclusion of forces of PFP partners in the newly conceived Combined Joint Task Forces, presumably for out-of-area contingencies. Central and East Europeans, increasingly skeptical about Western intentions, are pressing NATO to clarify whether participation in the alliance's new PFP program is truly considered a step toward NATO membership.

If NATO (and the European Union) appear to defer indefinitely membership for new entrants from the East, Central and East Europeans could become disillusioned and seek some alternative security arrangements, although working out such arrangements would not be easy. Poland, for example, has been establishing ties with Germany and France, which could provide the basis for a trilateral security group. Poland has also been developing ties with Ukraine; if Ukraine remains independent, a Polish-Ukrainian relationship could provide security assurances in the future vis-à-vis larger neighbors. Finally, a strong pan-Slavic pull within the Polish military could provide the basis for some accommodation with Russia, depending on what happens there.

ETHNIC TENSIONS ARE WIDESPREAD BUT LARGELY UNDER CONTROL EXCEPT IN THE FORMER YUGOSLAVIA

Europe has a mixture of ethnic situations, including states that are nearly ethnically homogenous and states with a high degree of ethnic heterogeneity. Many European states also have increasing numbers of immigrants, some coming from former colonies but many increasingly coming from Southern and Eastern Europe seeking jobs and relief from ethnically based conflict.

Ethnic tensions are, in general, being managed peacefully in Western Europe. The German government has been able to reduce domestic violence against immigrants and foreigners. In Northern Ireland, the cease-fires by the Irish Republican Army and armed Protestant militants are promising, although it remains to be seen whether this signals the beginning of the end of twenty-five years of sectarian violence there.

The CSCE has been helpful in developing conflict-prevention mechanisms focused on diplomatic measures to keep potential conflicts from erupting into violence. The fruits of these efforts can be seen in the Baltics, in the mitigation of problems between Slovakia and Hungary, and in Macedonia. The French initiative on stability talks also seeks to use diplomacy to prevent conflicts between states.

In Central and Eastern Europe, three types of ethnic minorities can be distinguished:

- National minorities in border regions where boundary lines separate elements of a group from the main body of their ethnic nation (such as Hungarians in Vojvodina, Transylvania, and Slovakia).

- National minorities separated by great distances from their home country (such as German minorities in Romania).

- Exceedingly mixed ethnic populations in certain regions (such as the former Yugoslavia).

These three types of situations give rise to different problems and conflict resolution approaches. The problem of frontier minorities can be addressed by special agreements between neighboring states or negotiated revisions to existing frontiers, although the latter are politically difficult. Tensions arising from the presence of isolated minorities can be reduced by providing adequate legal protection for minority rights. In mixed regions, guarantees of minority rights from the government in control of the region are also crucial, as is promoting peaceful coexistence among the groups that consider the region their home.

Although several areas of ethnic tension remain in Central and Eastern Europe, violence has generally been avoided, with the glaring exception of the former Yugoslavia. In most areas, the interests of ethnic minorities have been accommodated by peaceful means.

Poland exemplifies a twentieth-century Central European trend toward ethnic homogenization within national borders. When Poland achieved independence in 1918, Poles made up only 60 percent of the population. By 1990, as a result of border adjustments and mass migrations, they make up nearly 98 percent. A good-neighbor treaty with Germany has addressed the concerns of the 1.3 percent German minority.

The January 1993 division of Czechoslovakia into a generally ethnically homogenous Czech Republic and a somewhat less homogenous Slovakia took place on peaceful, if perhaps not entirely amicable, terms. However, ethnic tensions could evolve concerning the Hungarian and Czech minorities in Slovakia.

Hungary is also nearly ethnically homogenous. Tensions arise, however, over the status of Hungarian minorities in neighboring states—notably in Romania (2.3 million Hungarians), Slovakia (600,000 ethnic Hungarians), and the former Yugoslavia (400,000 ethnic Hungarians, primarily in the Vojvodina autonomous republic of Serbia). Hungary and Romania have not yet signed a good-neighbor treaty, and Hungarian relations with Slovakia and Serbia have not always been cordial.

Romania is nearly 90 percent ethnic Romanian but also has a relatively large ethnic Hungarian population (8.9 percent). Issues involving Hungarians in the Transylvania area have been the most contentious.

Bulgaria has potential ethnic problems with the 8.5 percent of its population who are ethnic Turks, as well as with several smaller minorities. Official discrimination against Turks was terminated under a new Bulgarian government, and this has contributed to warming of Turkish-Bulgarian relations. However, Bulgaria risks being drawn into conflict in the former Yugoslavia over ethnic issues, particularly if hostilities extend to Macedonia.

Sizable ethnic Albanian populations exist in states neighboring Albania, including Serbia and Montenegro (where 14 percent of the population is ethnic Albanian, concentrated in the Kosovo region), and Macedonia (which is 21 percent ethnic Albanian).

Finally, the treatment of large ethnic Russian minorities in the three Baltic states was a major issue in negotiations on Russian troop withdrawals from that region, especially in Latvia and Estonia.

EUROPE'S SOUTHERN REGION FACES INCREASING INSTABILITY

Instability in and near Europe's southern region is an increasing security concern. Of immediate and primary concern is the conflict in Bosnia and the danger that it will expand. Beyond this, instability in North Africa and terrorism from the Middle East pose a number of risks to Europe. Tensions between Greece and Turkey have also increased significantly.

Former Yugoslavia

The bloody four-year conflict and ethnic hatred among and within the successor states to Tito's Yugoslavia present a major challenge to post–Cold War Europe. Not since World War II has Europe experienced the types of horrors seen in the former Yugoslavia—ethnic cleansing, indiscriminate shelling of civilian centers, concentration camps, organized rape as an instrument of intimidation, and mass movements of refugees. Beyond what has already been experienced, there is the potential that the conflict could expand across borders.

The institutions created by the international community during the Cold War to manage crises failed to end the violence in the former Yugoslavia in a timely fashion, although they helped to moderate it. The inability of the European Union and its Atlantic and Eurasian partners to stop the violence casts a shadow over the concept of a new European security order.

North Africa and the Near East

The risk of civil war in Algeria, instability elsewhere in North Africa, and the security risks posed by the irresponsible Libyan regime have serious implications for security in Southern Europe. To the east, the Middle East peace process has lessened the threat of full-scale war in the Levant but has increased the threat of terrorist reactions by opponents of the peace process. The situation in Iraq remains a major concern to neighboring Turkey and others.

This instability poses risks in the Mediterranean basin and to Southern Europe itself. The safety of Americans, Europeans, and others in the North African states is an increasing concern, as is the waxing potential for terrorism emanating from this part of the world. Many countries in Southern Europe rely on natural gas and oil from North Africa and would be seriously affected by any disruption. Major conflict or civil war in North Africa could also result in a massive flow of refugees to Southern Europe; there are already hundreds of thousands of North African immigrants in Southern Europe, and some estimate that a major conflict in North Africa could lead to 500,000 to 1,000,000 refugees.

Greece and Turkey

Tensions between Greece and Turkey have increased lately; if not moderated, these could pose significant problems for cooperation in NATO. Activity by each nation's air and naval elements in the Aegean are cause for concern, and the situation in

Cyprus continues to be a source of tension. The conflict in the former Yugoslavia, with the potential for Turkish support for Muslim elements in Bosnia (in tension with Greek ties to Serbia), has made it increasingly difficult to moderate the tensions between Greece and Turkey. Efforts by NATO allies and others to persuade Greece to drop its blockade of the former Yugoslav Republic of Macedonia have been unsuccessful to date.

Turkey also faces instability in neighboring Iraq under Saddam Hussein, as well as from terrorists among its own sizable Kurdish minority.

U.S. SECURITY INTERESTS

Europe is of vital importance to the United States and has been a central focus of American defense efforts. Because of the strategic importance of Europe and its resources and the close ties between America and Europe, the United States three times in this century—in World War I, World War II, and the Cold War—has sent American military forces to Europe to help prevent aggressive powers from dominating Europe by force.

Europe includes many of the most politically, economically, and militarily advanced countries in the world, countries fully engaged and influential at the highest levels in international politics, trade and commerce, assistance programs, and defense and security collaboration. European states outnumber any other region of the world in the U.N. Security Council and the two institutions of the most advanced economic states—the G-7 economic summit structure and the Organization for Economic Cooperation and Development.

The United States has strong political, economic, social, and cultural ties to Europe. In many areas of economic activity, Europe is of greater importance to the United States than any other region of the world; trade is a notable exception, as U.S. trade with Asia now exceeds U.S. trade with Europe.

The majority of Americans claim European ancestry or ethnic origin. In the 1990 U.S. Census when 249 million people were counted, 164 million indicated specific foreign ancestries or ethnic origins; 143 million of these—87 percent of those indicating specific foreign ancestries and 57 percent of the total population—indicated European ancestries. Moreover, historical and political-philosophical ties between the United States and Europe are obvious, deep, and too numerous to mention.

Many European states have modern, deployable militaries capable of contributing to collective security in NATO and outside the NATO area. In the Persian Gulf War, for example, European NATO allies and friends in Europe contributed significantly to coalition efforts. Many countries in Europe provided rights for coalition partners to overfly their territory en route to and from Southwest Asia.

At least six key U.S. security interests can be identified for the Europe and NATO area.

ENSURING A FREE, SECURE, PEACEFUL, AND COOPERATIVE EUROPE

The United States has a vital interest in a free, secure, peaceful, and cooperative Europe and North Atlantic area. Ancillary to this is a Europe that is democratic and prosperous, open to U.S.-European trade and investment opportunities, and supportive of political, economic, and military cooperation with the United States in Europe and other important parts of the world. The United States wants a Europe that abides by international law and humanitarian principles endorsed by the United Nations and the Conference on Security and Cooperation in Europe. The United States seeks an expanded zone of peace and security throughout Europe. The president has cited as goals "a free and undivided Europe" and "an integrated democratic Europe cooperating with the United States to keep the peace and promote prosperity."

Trends in transatlantic cooperation, integration in Western Europe, and outreach to the East are favorable to these interests, while the continuation and possible expansion of conflict in the Balkans and growing instability to the east and south are not.

MAINTAINING MUTUAL SECURITY COMMITMENTS AND A STRONG, ADAPTIVE NATO

Commitments to the security of Europe and the North Atlantic area are enshrined in the North Atlantic Treaty, in which the United States and its NATO allies have agreed that an attack against one would be considered an attack against all, and that each ally would take whatever action it deemed necessary, including the use of force, to restore and maintain security. The United States has a strong interest in maintaining support among signatory countries for the security commitments reflected in the NATO treaty, as well as in other security instruments.

The continued U.S. military presence in Europe reflects Washington's commitment. At the end of fiscal 1993, of 308,000 U.S. military personnel deployed in foreign areas, nearly half—149,000—were stationed in Germany or elsewhere in Europe. President Bill Clinton has made a commitment to maintain approximately 100,000 U.S. military personnel in Europe for as long as the European allies want them there. (There are in addition some 17,000 personnel afloat in the Europe area.)

Critical to these wider interests is maintaining the viability and vitality of NATO as an institution that is able, as necessary, to deter and defend against any attacks on its members. NATO has been a key element in maintaining general peace in Europe for the last forty-five years, an unprecedented phenomenon in modern times. A strong NATO can also play a critical role in promoting peace and security beyond NATO's borders. Invaluable for this are NATO's integrated command structure, its forces that cooperate in areas of intelligence and warning, command

and control, doctrine, equipment and joint training, and the base structure in Europe and the Atlantic.

The general trend in maintaining the alliance's viability and vitality is favorable to U.S. interests, although differences among allies on issues such as policy regarding the former Yugoslavia can sometimes challenge alliance cohesion. Programs to reach out to the East, promote European integration and ESDI, develop new security concepts such as CJTF, engage carefully and effectively within policy limitations in the Balkans, and pursue arms control and counterproliferation initiatives can help to maintain a strong NATO, if managed properly. An unfavorable trend is the increased tension between Greece and Turkey, which diminishes the cohesion and strength of the alliance in its strategically important southeast corner. Alliance interests would be served by efforts to ameliorate relations between these two allies and promote their sense of security.

ENCOURAGING EUROPEAN INTEGRATION, CONSISTENT WITH OPEN RELATIONS WITH THE UNITED STATES AND A STRONG NATO

The United States has long supported European economic and political integration. With the January 1994 NATO Summit, the United States convinced the European allies that it fully and firmly supported both an ESDI that could be "separable but not separate" from NATO and the role of the WEU as embodying the European pillar of NATO. Concerned that if not managed correctly European integration could freeze out the United States and Canada and undercut NATO, the United States encourages European integration through a transparent process that permits continued close relations and collaboration between Europe and the United States and Canada. The United States supports establishment of an ESDI that is consistent with maintaining a strong NATO.

Close cooperation on security issues between NATO and the WEU, including transparency of planning and activity and reciprocal access to information on such issues as development of concepts for CJTF, will be critical.

MAINTAINING ACCESS TO MILITARY FACILITIES IN EUROPE AND THE NORTH ATLANTIC

About 70 percent of all the military sites used by U.S. forces in foreign territories are located in Europe and the North Atlantic. These facilities have played important roles supporting U.S. forces in Europe and operations outside Europe. For example, in the Persian Gulf War, sixteen states in Europe provided en route staging support at ninety airfields as the buildup accelerated. More than 95 percent of flights to Southwest Asia were staged through Europe, consisting of about 2,200 tactical and 15,402 strategic airlift stories. In addition, tanker aircraft operated from ten air bases in seven European countries. Coalition forces operating from Turkey used

NATO-developed bases there; bases in the United Kingdom and elsewhere supported B-52 bomber operations. More recently, bases and facilities in Europe have played indispensable roles in U.S. humanitarian and other peace operations in areas of the former Yugoslavia, the Middle East, Africa, and even the former Soviet Union. As the United States reduces its forces in Europe, it has been reducing the number of facilities used there.

PROMOTING SUCCESSFUL REFORM AND INCREASED SECURITY FOR CENTRAL AND EASTERN EUROPE

It is in the U.S. interest to promote within Central and Eastern Europe democracy, market-based economies, and effective, defensively oriented militaries responsible to duly elected civilian governments. Democracies and defensively oriented militaries tend not to fight each other, and market economies offer the best chance for prosperous and peaceful societies.

It is also in the U.S. interest to encourage countries of Central and Eastern Europe to pursue, as a way of improving security, increased bilateral and multilateral ties—a web of contacts extending to the United States, other NATO members, and regional neighbors and institutions. On balance, the trends are favorable, with the exception of developments in former Yugoslavia.

HELPING TO PREVENT, CONTAIN, AND RESOLVE ETHNIC CONFLICTS

The United States has an interest in helping to prevent, contain, and resolve conflicts in Europe, with particular emphasis now on ethnic quarrels, which are most prevalent. Interests can best be served by early diplomatic efforts to defuse tensions before they erupt into violence; once lives are lost, it is far more difficult and costly to contain or stop a conflict. Trends are generally favorable in both Western and Eastern Europe, with the notable exception of Bosnia.

KEY U.S. SECURITY POLICY ISSUES

DEVELOPING NATO'S PARTNERSHIP FOR PEACE PROGRAM

NATO began its outreach program to the East in July 1990 with a declaration issued at the NATO Summit in London, followed by the establishment of the NACC at the November 1991 Summit in Rome. While the NACC had laudable goals of establishing security contacts and providing technical assistance to Eastern states, its limitations immediately became apparent. The immense diversity among NACC partners (say, between Poland and Uzbekistan) led to calls for a more differentiated approach and to increasing demands for membership in NATO by the westernmost NACC members. At the same time, disagreements among the allies over how far NACC should go in satisfying operational requirements of the partner states (as opposed to serving mainly as a consultative body) further limited the scope of NACC activities.

In January 1994 NATO Summit leaders in Brussels adopted the PFP program, the goals of which are to (1) enhance operational cooperation between NATO and the partner states, (2) develop defense transparency among partner states, (3) advance the development of democratic means of control over the military in the newly emerging democracies, and (4) provide a vehicle to help the partners realize that (unlike NACC, where NATO foots the bill) participation in NATO activities has obligations as well as benefits.

Since January 1994 more than twenty states have become PFP partners, including the Central and East European states, Sweden, Finland, Slovenia, Russia, Ukraine, and several other former Soviet Eurasian states. Offices have been constructed at both NATO headquarters in Brussels and at the Supreme Headquarters Allied Powers Europe in Mons, Belgium, to accommodate representatives of these states. Exercises involving forces of NATO members and new PFP partners have been planned, and some have already been conducted. Implementation of PFP, if not handled carefully, could, to one degree or another, have some unwanted, unintended consequences.

Subregional Cooperation

Rather than encouraging forms of subregional cooperation and stability—such as that established by the Czech Republic, Hungary, Poland, and Slovakia (the so-called Visegrad states)—the PFP program could have an unintended, unfortunate effect of transforming the region's potential security partners into competitors, diverting attention from cooperation with neighbors toward a race to see which nations are most willing and able to meet the West's standards and expectations.

NATO could minimize the potential negative consequences of its bilateral ("16 to 1") agreements with each PFP partner by encouraging partners to cooperate directly with their neighbors, ensuring that each agreement remains transparent to neighbors, and supporting Visegrad, Balkan, and Baltic common security activities.

Democratic Reformers

By deferring the NATO membership question in developing the PFP, NATO leaders appear partly to have responded to a perceived need to placate Russia and support Yeltsin and reformers in that country. NATO must work now to ensure that the PFP also supports democratic reformers in Central and Eastern Europe and does not have the unintended effect of undermining their political bases of support, thereby undermining the credibility of the United States and NATO in Central and Eastern Europe.

Russians and Central and East Europeans have traditionally seen security as a zero-sum game where one side wins and the other loses. To the extent that Central and East Europeans perceive the PFP as the West succumbing to Russian pressure in terms of the PFP being used as a stalling device against NATO membership, the West will lose credibility and influence.

If the PFP does not soon generate highly visible programs that bolster support for the region's reform-oriented leaders, then the prestige, influence, and support that NATO enjoys at present may be lost on future Central and East European leaders and publics. For such projects to be successful and visible, financial resources will be necessary. President Clinton recognized this when he announced on a trip to Poland in July 1994 that he would request $100 million for fiscal 1996 to support PFP programs, of which $25 million would go to Poland and $10 million to the Baltic states. The challenge for the United States is to energize other NATO allies and partners to commit resources to PFP programs, and to work with those allies to initiate cooperative programs with PFP partners, as Great Britain and Denmark have done with the Baltic states.

Civil-Military Relations

Military rather than political forms of cooperation have been emphasized in the PFP. As a result, the PFP could have a number of unwanted and unintended consequences. First, states with stronger military traditions and institutions could have an advantage. Second, pushing the military to the forefront in the East–West partnership could work against efforts in Central and East European states to establish control over their militaries. Emphasizing the political dimension of the PFP and working to ensure a civilian Ministry of Defense component would moderate this potential negative effect.

Security Perceptions—Ideals and Reality

By intentionally leaving vague any detailed criteria and time frame for NATO admission in order not to exclude anyone, the PFP suggests an undifferentiated Europe, which does not have much credibility in Central and Eastern Europe. Many Central and East Europeans believe that democratic reform has already failed in most of the former Soviet Union, and that some form of authoritarian rule there is likely for the foreseeable future. They also fear that Russia is moving toward an imperial foreign policy that threatens their security and their democratic governments.

The PFP, if provided adequate resources and implemented properly, may reinvigorate NATO and herald a new European security architecture. If it is not provided adequate resources and is implemented carelessly, however, the PFP could undermine European security and widen the gulf that separates East from West.

MANAGING THE NATO EXPANSION ISSUE

Though NATO has resisted the Central and East European nations' desire for immediate membership in the alliance, the PFP proposal has expressed NATO's long-term commitment to expand. Active participation in the PFP is seen as a necessary—although not sufficient—condition for eventual NATO membership. NATO has left vague the time frame for possible expansion and has not provided any detailed criteria for determining qualification for membership beyond the NATO Treaty's Article 10 reference to a state being in a position to further the principles of the treaty and contribute to security in the North Atlantic area.

As the alliance moves forward with its study on implications of NATO expansion and what it takes for a state to join NATO, and as it eventually makes decisions on NATO expansion, it will face several key questions, such as why NATO expansion is necessary when few perceive any immediate military threat to the East, whether NATO expansion will be counterproductive in terms of drawing new dividing lines in Europe and isolating states left out, whether expansion will cause adverse reactions against NATO and against reformers in those states not included, and what demands expanding NATO defense commitments will place on Western forces and defense budgets, which are now being reduced.

NATO will want to proceed carefully, balancing the desires of Central and East European states to be fully reintegrated into Europe and the desire of NATO allies to project security eastward, with concerns about the seriousness of extending new security guarantees. NATO will also have to balance the view that NATO expansion can help keep NATO vibrant and alive, with the view that NATO expansion will be a divisive issue in an alliance of sixteen members already seriously troubled over Bosnia and in need of clarifying a new transatlantic (West–West) relationship. NATO will need also to balance its intent to control its own destiny and not be subject to a veto by outside states such as Russia, with its concern not to undercut reformers and promising developments in countries that are not invited immediately or even eventually to join NATO. Russian President Boris Yeltsin has warned of a "cold peace," and much will depend here on the nature and strength of relationships that NATO and others in the West establish with Russia and other Eastern states.

To balance these interests, NATO is taking careful and measured steps to strengthen the PFP. NATO is also moving to identify the internal steps required in NATO to eventually expand membership and to assess the implications of expanded membership. NATO will also help prospective members understand what NATO membership entails. Consultations will be required to determine how to frame the expansion debate in NATO publics and parliaments, how eventually to decide which interested states should be admitted to NATO and when, and how to advance NATO relationships not only with those states that may initially join NATO but also with other PFP partners not expected to join NATO at the outset or even eventually.

DEVELOPING COMBINED JOINT TASK FORCES

The CJTF initiative, approved at the January 1994 NATO summit, is intended to provide NATO a powerful, new organizational concept for responding to crises by rapid deployment of forces. This initiative is designed to (1) satisfy the requirements of the NATO strategic concept for more flexible and mobile forces, (2) provide a vehicle for NATO participation in crisis management and peace support operations, (3) facilitate operations with non-NATO nations such as the PFP partners, and (4) permit the use of NATO infrastructure and forces to support the evolution of ESDI.

While no official definition of a CJTF has been adopted, NATO Summit language suggests that the term refers to a multinational, multiservice task force consisting of NATO—and possibly non-NATO—forces capable of rapid deployment to conduct crisis management and peace operations of limited duration under the control of either the NATO military structure or the WEU. There is a presumption in NATO that CJTF operations would be beyond NATO's borders. NATO CJTFs are expected to be a hybrid capability that combines the best attributes of coalition and alliance forces: rapid flexible crisis response and a trained, ready, multinational, multiservice force backed by an in-place infrastructure.

The WEU is also working on the CJTF concept and appears to envisage CJTFs that are smaller than what NATO has in mind but employed for similar missions. The WEU may want to address early on the possibility of working with NATO and seeking the use of NATO assets, such as the SHAPE Technical Center, for its own CJTF planning. NATO insistence on fully developing the CJTF concept would help guard against NATO's slipping into the role of "Europe's military hardware store." Fully developing the concept would require resolving the thorny issue of command and political control over operations involving NATO forces in operations beyond the direct defense of NATO territory addressed in Article 5 of the NATO Treaty or under WEU. Systematic cooperation between NATO and the WEU in assembling and deploying CJTFs will be crucial to preserving the transatlantic nature of the alliance.

While the geographical areas in which NATO would deploy a CJTF is first of all a political question, military capabilities and limitations will also shape the decision. In contemplating the regions where NATO CJTFs might be deployed, it can be assumed that any mission will aim to protect alliance interests. Likely interests include preservation of peace in the lands and waters immediately adjacent to NATO territory. Similar security interests might extend to distant areas where conflict could threaten European security and stability.

CJTF logistical support will be a major challenge for an alliance that has known only interior lines of communication, fixed bases, and a wealth of host nation support. NATO will have to adjust to rapid deployments, long and potentially unsecured lines of supply and communication, and minimal base facilities.

Another major challenge will be the creation of requisite communications and information systems. A deployed CJTF headquarters must have not only the traditional rearward, lateral, and forward military linkages, but also links with local governments, nongovernment organizations, and international agencies. For the time being, CJTFs will be heavily dependent on U.S. national assets for strategic and operational support in communications and intelligence.

Many questions surrounding the implementation of the CJTF concept are virgin territory for NATO military planners, among them the division of labor among major NATO commands, major subordinate commands, and a CJTF during operations; the degree of interoperability of on-hand communication; the availability of intelligence; training and exercise requirements and their costs; and the need for a detailed assessment of movement requirements of a CJTF. NATO military staffs have begun to tackle these issues.

A special aspect of adapting a rapid development capability to a consensus-based alliance is the case in which a nation assigns personnel to a CJTF headquarters in peacetime but withholds consent to deploy them to a certain out-of-area crisis. This and other issues will take time to resolve; one such concern is the dearth of English-speaking commanders and staff officers in East European militaries.

MODIFYING NATO STRUCTURES AND ACTIVITIES

Although from 1991 to 1994 NATO made a number of bold decisions at its summit meetings, many of those decisions have yet to be implemented, and more changes will be required as the security situation evolves.

One area for possible further change is the NATO integrated military structure. Although NATO staffs have already been streamlined, many have called for another review to ensure that the command structure is fully oriented toward the new missions. A number of questions arise. Are all the current headquarters still necessary? Have they been reduced in active strength to the minimum necessary? Are they mobile, flexible, and kept up to date by essential investment in modern command and control and information equipment?

A second issue is preparing for the new missions of the alliance, such as peace operations and humanitarian relief. Forces such as the ACE Rapid Reaction Corps, the Standing Naval Forces, and the ACE Mobile Forces need to be trained and equipped to perform new tasks. Deploying and sustaining forces in out-of-area operations require significant planning and training.

Another area where further modification of NATO may be on the agenda is balancing burdens and responsibilities between the European and North American pillars of the alliance. This requires the development of effective political and military ties with the WEU and the emergence of an ESDI that works in tandem with the United States and Canada. The task of crafting an ESDI that is a partner and not a competitor to NATO has fallen on the WEU. Transparency will be essential to building a trusting and productive relationship. It will not be enough for WEU and NATO representatives to hold occasional meetings; systematic coordination and information sharing is needed. The United States and Canada will be the only NATO allies not routinely seated at the WEU table to deliberate security issues. The WEU must take care that its positions are not presented in NATO fora as *faits accompli*. In turn, Washington must demonstrate trust in its European allies in order to allow the ESDI to develop.

Finally, NATO's increasing political role suggests a new approach that seeks to identify and resolve tensions that may affect the alliance before they become crises, as well as to employ the alliance's formidable infrastructure and resources to respond to unexpected contingencies. For example, NATO's Senior Civil Emergency Planning Committee, Civil Emergency Planning Directorate, and Committee on Challenges of Modern Society might be chartered to plan for responses to natural and man-made disasters. While initial planning could concentrate on the NATO and NACC regions, the alliance could eventually tackle similar issues in regions beyond Europe. The associated requirement to move from reactive to proactive planning would not be easy for a consensus-based organization like NATO.

RESOLVING OR CONTAINING CONFLICT IN THE BALKANS

Precipitated by a lethal mixture of economic backwardness, historical animosity, exploitative leaders, and the suppression of human and minority rights, the conflict in the former Yugoslavia has become a case study of the local consequences of the breakdown of the Cold War international system and the pains associated with the emergence of another.

- It has highlighted the complexity of ethnonational conflicts and the interconnections among the political, economic, social, cultural, and security problems associated with the end of communism.

- It raises serious questions about the international ramifications of intrastate conflicts.

- It presents challenges to a number of wellestablished principles of international order, such as nonintervention in the internal affairs of sovereign states, the right of national self-determination, and the inviolability of borders.

- It underscores the limitations of existing European institutions to deal with the international fallout of such conflicts and the need to develop institutions for effective and timely conflict prevention and management.

- It poses fundamental questions about the viability of a Euro-Atlantic community based upon a system of nation-states and dedicated to democratic values and open societies.

The efforts of European institutions failed to avert conflict in former Yugoslavia. Indeed, early European diplomatic recognition of secessionist states may have exacerbated the situation. The efforts of other countries and international organizations similarly failed.

Involvement of the United States and Others

The United States and other powers have been caught in a dilemma. They feel a moral obligation to assist victims and to help resolve the conflict. Yet they are well aware of the long history of bloody ethnic conflict in the Balkans and are leery of sending their military forces to the area, especially when warring factions doggedly continue to fight and do not appear interested in a peace arrangement.

The United States and other states are thus cautious about their involvement. They have pursued four courses of action: humanitarian relief, containment of the conflict, diplomatic initiatives to resolve the conflict, and making plans to help maintain the peace with military forces once a peace agreement is reached. All of these measures aim to moderate the damage caused by the conflict while limiting exposure of U.S. or other foreign military forces to hostilities.

The United States, under Operation Provide Promise, and some allies have flown humanitarian assistance to people in Bosnia. The United States, NATO allies, and members of the WEU under Operation Sharp Guard have been willing to commit maritime forces in the Adriatic to maintain U.N. sanctions, and these and other states have taken other measures to restrict trade with certain of the parties. In late November 1994, in response to congressional interest in lifting the embargo on arms for the Bosnian government forces and Croatia, the United States ceased enforcing the arms embargo with regard to Bosnian government forces. Under Operation Deny Flight, the United States and NATO allies have also been willing to commit airpower to deny military flights to warring parties, to protect U.N. Protection Forces (UNPROFOR) on the ground in Bosnia, and to enforce U.N. exclusion zones. Coordination with the United Nations of the employment of these forces has had some difficulties. The naval forces are now operating under the NATO integrated military command structure, as are allied forces involved in the airpower operations, demonstrating the value and capability of the NATO command structure.

Some states committed ground force units to UNPROFOR in Bosnia, which were used to help ensure humanitarian relief is delivered and to keep certain equipment from being used by warring parties. The United States was leery of deploying American ground forces into the former Yugoslavia. Under Operation Able Sentry, U.S. and Nordic ground forces have been deployed in Macedonia to help deter the spread of conflict.

Following earlier unsuccessful international efforts to negotiate a settlement in the former Yugoslavia, an international contact group, consisting of representatives from France, Germany, Russia, the United Kingdom, and the United States, launched a diplomatic initiative to reach a peace settlement in Bosnia. This initiative proposed that the Muslim-Croat Federation in Bosnia be given control of 51 percent of Bosnia's territory and the Bosnian Serbs—who now control about 70 percent of Bosnia—be given 49 percent.

[Editor's note: As noted earlier in the essay, the Dayton accords, signed in 1995, are an attempt to resolve the conflict and separate the warring sides through the deployment of the implementation force (IFOR).]

Kosovo and Macedonia

Developments in the Kosovo autonomous province of Serbia and in the former Yugoslav Republic of Macedonia could trigger an escalation of conflict in the Balkans and even beyond. In Kosovo, Serbian repression continues, and an increasing number of people appear to believe that moderation in resisting Serbia is achieving few if any results. Conflict in Kosovo could lead to a scenario that involves massive refugee flows and a spillover of conflict to many states in the region, with implications far beyond. In Macedonia, the economic situation is disastrous, given the disruption of trade with embargoed Serbia and the Greek economic blockade of Macedonia. Some 25 percent of wage-earners in Skopje have not been paid for months, and labor troubles could lead to ethnic strife.

The West has taken some steps such as the deployment of troops into northern Macedonia under Operation Able Sentry. Efforts by the United States and the European community to provide greater assistance and to help develop an east-west infrastructure for Macedonia, so it is not so dependent on north-south commerce and ties, would help alleviate the pressure on Macedonia; encouraging Greece to end its blockade would be even more immediately significant.

The Future in Former Yugoslavia

With the signing of the Dayton accords and the deployment of 20,000 U.S. personnel as part of the 60,000-person NATO-led peacekeeping force, the question now is whether peace can be sustained and the lives of peacekeepers protected. The failure of the Euro-Atlantic community to enforce a settlement earlier in Yugoslavia's ethnonational conflicts and to help establish an arrangement through which the successor states may live in security cast a shadow on the notion of building a collective security system to manage change and crises in Europe and beyond.

Implications for U.S. Relations with Allies and Friends

Past differences between the United States and its allies, especially the United Kingdom and France, on such issues as deploying ground forces in Bosnia and lifting or enforcing the arms embargo on the Bosnian government and Croatia have led to much speculation about the implications for U.S.–allied relations and even the future of NATO. These differences may add to other incentives European allies have to pursue close defense cooperation in Europe; the United Kingdom and France, for example, reportedly are creating a joint air command for peacekeeping missions. The United States appears to recognize the priority a strong NATO has in U.S. national security interests and the need to relate policy on the former Yugoslavia to this higher interest in maintaining a cohesive alliance.

RUSSIA AND NEIGHBORS

JAMES H. BRUSSTAR

The disintegration of the USSR left in its wake fifteen successor states, each struggling to cope with the demands of statehood and the need to define a role in the international system. After three years of independence, it is by no means certain how many of these entities will be viable states within their present borders. Nor is it clear whether the two largest, Russia and Ukraine, will seek integration with the Western security system. Major factors underlying these uncertainties include

- Growing doubts in the region about the wisdom of the December 1991 decision to dismantle the USSR.

- The failure of many new leaders in the region to gain legitimacy in the eyes of their citizens.

- Uncertainty within many of the new states regarding their potential to achieve economic independence and political sovereignty (a trend bolstered by a growing backlash against economic hardships and rampant corruption).

- Conflicts in the Caucasus and Central Asia.

- A general awakening to the fact that the major Western countries may not be able to reduce the dislocations associated with the transition from a Soviet-style command economy to a market system.

These developments have forced many of the Soviet successor states to reevaluate their future in the international system. This in turn challenges the West to reassess its own policies regarding these states.

DEFINING TRENDS

RUSSIA IS INTERVENING IN THE SECURITY MATTERS OF OTHER FORMER SOVIET STATES

In 1992 Russia was reluctant to interfere in the security problems of other members of the Commonwealth of the Independent States (CIS). Former Russian Foreign Minister Andrey Kozyrev initially established a policy of noninterference, in an apparent effort to curry favor with the West—on which, Kozyrev believed, Russia was critically dependent for economic assistance. Kozyrev believed that the foremost threat to Russia's security was economic and political isolation, and that Russia could overcome this threat only through economic and diplomatic integration into the Western dominated international system.

This policy, however, was soon challenged by those who believed that Russia had to rely upon itself for its security and place in the international community. This group argued that Russian security policies should focus on protecting Russia's vital interests—especially in the area they called the "near abroad" (that is, the former Soviet Union)—rather than on integrating into an international system controlled by the West.

The debate between Kozyrev and the advocates of a foreign policy based on defending Russia's own vital interests continued for almost two years. It ended abruptly early in the morning of October 4, 1993, when President Boris Yeltsin rushed to the Ministry of Defense to implore the military to put down the rebellion in the streets of Moscow. In

---

This essay has been edited and is reprinted from Strategic Assessment 1995: U.S. Security Challenges in Transition, *ed. Patrick Clawson (Washington, D.C.: Institute for National Strategic Studies, 1995), 51–66, by permission of National Defense University Press.*

exchange for the military's support, Yeltsin evidently made several concessions—including acceptance of a security policy based on Russia's vital interests.

Despite the Ministry of Foreign Affairs' position prior to October 1993, however, many of Russia's policies regarding the CIS during that period were apparently made by individual ministries based on bureaucratic interests and proclivities, not official state policy. At the same time, moreover, Russia displayed a tendency to provide military support throughout the region in a manner that weakened the authority of the other Soviet successor states.

It is important to note, however, that Russia's determination to be involved in security matters throughout the "near abroad" has not been entirely unwelcome. Many Soviet successor states in the Caucasus and Central Asia are having major problems in establishing their sovereignty and look to Moscow for support. This is reflected in the fact that Russia has sought and achieved troop-stationing agreements with most of the states in the near abroad, and in the increased interest within the CIS in new forms of political, economic, and security cooperation.

Moldova

Immediately after the dissolution of the Soviet Union in December 1991, former Soviet armed forces stationed in the Trans-Dniester Region of Moldova began to actively support Dniester activists seeking independence from Moldova. In May 1992 Russia asserted its control over these units, and in June Major General Aleksandr Lebed was placed in charge of the Russian forces of the 14th Army stationed in the Trans-Dniester region. On July 29 Russian peacekeeping forces were deployed to the Trans-Dniester region in accord with a Moldovan-Russian agreement. Russian forces remain in the region, and negotiations between Russia and Moldova indicate that they will remain there for several more years.

Georgia

In June 1992 President Yeltsin and Georgian leader Eduard Shevardnadze signed an agreement on settling conflicts in the region. A month later, they agreed to send Russian, Georgian, and Ossetian peacekeeping forces into South Ossetia, where they remain today.

In August 1992 Russia also sent forces into Abkhazia, a former autonomous republic under Moscow's control that has resisted integration into an independent Georgian state, in order to evacuate Russian tourists caught between Georgian and Abkhazian warring factions. After the evacuation, Russian forces remained in Georgia, ostensibly to keep the peace, after Georgia and Russia signed an agreement on September 3, 1992, calling for the complete neutrality of Russian forces and pledging Moscow's respect for Georgia's borders. Nevertheless, the Russian military reportedly provided support to Abkhazian forces throughout late 1992 and

1993. Moreover, Russia actively sought to broker a negotiated settlement to the Georgian-Abkhazian conflict during the winter of 1992–93, and even refused to finalize a friendship treaty with Georgia in the spring of 1993 until progress was made in settling the Abkhazia conflict.

Russian involvement in the conflict took a turn in October 1993, when Georgia sought Russia's help in overcoming internal armed opposition to the Georgian government. This led to a treaty between the two countries regarding Russian basing rights in Georgia, which in turn paved the way for Russia to perform peacekeeping functions along the Georgian-Abkhazian border. Russia's role as peacekeeping "facilitator" was recognized by the U.N. Security Council on July 21, 1994, in UNSC Resolution 937.

Tajikistan

Russia also became involved in Tajikistan's conflicts after anti-Islamic, old-guard political forces achieved victory in the Tajik civil war in December 1992. On January 22, 1993, Russia, Kazakhstan, Kyrgyzstan, and Uzbekistan agreed at the Minsk CIS Summit to send primarily Russian troops to the CIS border between Tajikistan and Afghanistan, in order to defend against Tajik opposition attacks from Afghan territory. In a separate operation, the CIS authorized Russian forces to perform peacekeeping functions within Tajikistan.

Armenia and Azerbaijan

Russian military activities in Armenia and Azerbaijan have been limited. In accordance with CIS agreements, Russia turned over Soviet military equipment to both countries, and has not become actively involved in their dispute over the Nagorno-Karabakh region. In late January 1994, Russia offered to provide peacekeeping forces to patrol a security zone between the two countries. This offer was not accepted, however, and while Russia continues to express concern over the conflict, it has limited its involvement.

DOMESTIC PRESSURES AND MUTUAL APPREHENSIONS IMPAIR RUSSIA–UKRAINE RELATIONS

On December 1, 1991, 76 percent of Ukrainian voters supported Ukrainian independence from the Soviet Union, as urged by the newly elected Ukrainian president, Leonid Kravchuk. The primary objective at the time was to wrest control of Ukraine's political and economic destiny from the Soviet central government. Russian and Belorussian political leaders shared this desire to do away with the Soviet central government mechanism. As a result, agreements were signed that abolished the Soviet Union and established the much more amorphous CIS in its place.

Russian political leaders who pushed for the formation of the CIS had intended for the commonwealth to succeed the Soviet Union as a confederation of states. It was not their intention that the successor states should go their own ways on security matters. Rather, Russia advocated a CIS military structure that would subordinate a major portion of the old Soviet military—including all of the strategic nuclear and naval forces—to a CIS military command responsible to the collective heads of state of the commonwealth. In January 1992 Russia even went so far as to proclaim that it would not establish its own army, but would rely on forces controlled by the CIS to defend Russian territory. Political leaders in Moscow believed that Russia's political and economic weight would give it the strongest voice in CIS security decisions. Moreover, they feared that the creation of a separate Russian military would upset and alienate the other Soviet successor states.

Moscow was not ready for the Soviet Union to break up so quickly and completely; Russia had merely wanted to replace the mechanism by which the republics were joined together with something less objectionable. Ukraine's declaration in January 1992 that all military forces stationed on Ukrainian territory belonged to Kiev—and its subsequent efforts to convert these forces into an Ukrainian army and navy—came as a surprise to many in Moscow, and presented a major challenge to Moscow's plans for the CIS. In May 1992 Moscow countered by creating its own army, which included many Russian forces stationed in other CIS states. Moscow also challenged Ukraine's claim to nuclear forces and the Black Sea Fleet stationed in the Crimea.

Good Russian–Ukrainian relations require mutual trust on security matters, which has been in short supply. Ukraine's unilateral demands for independence in security matters have hurt communications and understanding. This distrust has nearly turned into open rancor during the negotiations over ownership of the Black Sea Fleet. In particular, the disruptive behavior of the fleet's Russian commanders—such as Admiral Kasatonov, who openly resisted the efforts of Moscow and Kiev to divide the fleet in a mutually acceptable way—has prevented negotiations from taking place in a calm and conciliatory environment. Agreements regarding the fleet reached in August 1992, April 1993, and June 1993 were quickly repudiated by at least one of the parties to the dispute.

In short, relations between Russia and Ukraine have been strained since soon after the CIS agreement was signed in December 1991. Many Russian leaders have not reconciled themselves to the breakup of the Soviet Union. They believe that their own security will be placed in jeopardy if Ukraine moves out of Moscow's sphere of influence on security matters.

Furthermore, domestic problems have distracted them from the task of building good relations with Ukraine. Throughout 1992 and 1993, Yeltsin clashed repeatedly with the more conservative Russian legislature over policy issues and the division of political power between the branches of government.

This confrontation, which was punctuated by threats to close down the legislature and counterthreats of impeachment, practically paralyzed the Russian government. Moreover, the struggle for power spread to the provinces, where many locally elected officials were recycled Communist Party leaders who resisted the reform efforts pushed by the president.

Ukrainian leaders, on the other hand, have been hesitant to compromise with Russia, fearing this might open them to the charge of diminishing Ukrainian independence. They tend to blame Russian interference for domestic problems that have not been resolved. And they are paralyzed by major differences within the country regarding how closely Ukraine should be connected to Russia.

The Rukh political party, based in western Ukraine, spearheaded the drive for independence and had a major influence on Ukrainian politics immediately after the break with Soviet Moscow. However, a large number of Ukrainians, particularly in the central and eastern parts of the country, soon began to question the wisdom of policies designed to sever Ukraine from Russia. In November 1992, USIA polls showed 52 percent of all Ukrainians agreeing with the statement that it was "a great misfortune" that the Soviet Union no longer existed.

Russian concerns about possible Ukrainian entry into Western economic and security circles have led it to take steps that undermine Ukrainian independence, such as maintaining economic and political pressure on Kiev as Ukraine struggles with its domestic problems. A prominent example of this economic pressure has been Russia's frequent interruption of oil and gas deliveries to Ukraine, which has resulted in major production problems within Ukrainian industry. Moreover, some political groups within each country have sought to gain political advantages for their cause by pitting the grievances of ethnic Russians in the Ukraine against the resentment many ethnic Ukrainians harbor against Russia.

Further, controversial boundary decisions made during Soviet times—when borders were often drawn without regard to historical and geographic logic—have been revisited, fueling mutual distrust. Of particular note in this regard is the issue of Crimea's political status. Historically a part of Russia, Crimea was arbitrarily removed from Russia's jurisdiction by Nikita Khrushchev in 1954 and made part of Ukraine. The population, however, remains largely Russian and the region has strong ties with Russia. The peninsula is also the historic home of the Black Sea Fleet, and as such has major naval bases and support facilities that are of value to both countries.

Crimean political activists who favor increased autonomy and even independence gained a major victory in the local Crimean presidential elections of January 30, 1994, when Yuriy Meshkov—an outspoken advocate of Crimea's return to Russian control—won with 73 percent of the vote. Those favoring increased autonomy also easily won the parliamentary election conducted on March 20. Crimea's new parliament voted on May 20, 1994, to restore the controversial Crimean constitution of 1992, which had been put aside because Kiev objected to the degree of autonomy it claimed for Crimea. Crimean regional leaders tend to look to Moscow, not Kiev, as their protector.

The split between the western part of the country and the central and eastern parts has plagued Ukrainian politics since independence, causing policy gridlock and hamstringing Kravchuk's administration. The western part of the country has been primarily concerned with establishing Ukrainian independence from Moscow and moving the country into Western Europe's sphere of influence to the greatest extent possible. In contrast, the eastern part of Ukraine, in which most of Ukraine's ethnic Russians live, has been more willing to cling to Russia for economic as well as cultural reasons. The economic base of the eastern part of Ukraine was strongly connected to Russia—and heavily subsidized by Moscow—in the Soviet Union. Thus, managers in this part of the country have been unprepared and unwilling to reorient their largely obsolete industries in the direction sought by the Ukrainian nationalists of the west.

Resistance in the eastern part of Ukraine to the economic reforms and nationalism favored in the west led to the openly stated suspicion that Moscow was using ethnic Russians in the east to sabotage Ukrainian independence. Political infighting between the nationalists of western Ukraine and the pro-Russian and reform-resistant population of central and eastern Ukraine have stymied policy making in Kiev, leading to economic stagnation, domestic strife, and the diplomatic suspension of Ukraine between Eastern and Western Europe—without a clear foothold in either.

On July 10, 1994, Leonid Kuchma won Ukraine's presidential runoff election, gaining 9.8 million votes to Leonid Kravchuk's 8.9 million. Kuchma, who stood for closer relations with Russia, won in all regions of eastern, east central, and southern Ukraine, while Kravchuk, who ran as a nationalist, won in all western and west central regions. While this outcome may help to defuse tensions with Moscow on some issues, it may also lead to increased internal tension if Ukrainian nationalists push to the fore the issue of asserting their country's independence vis-à-vis Russia. External tensions with Russia may also increase if the nationalists turn their spotlight on Russian interference in Ukrainian domestic affairs.

LEADERS SUPPORTING A STRONG RUSSIA ARE GAINING POWER IN RUSSIA

The results of the December 1993 Duma elections were a severe political blow to President Yeltsin, decreasing his ability to exercise the powers he gained under the new constitution and forcing him to make major concessions to more conservative forces. Russia's more open actions in the near abroad and increased role in the former Yugoslavia are a direct result of these concessions.

Since 1992 conservative and even moderate Russian politicians had loudly complained that the Russian Foreign Ministry was allowing the U.N. secretary-general and NATO to exclude Russia from playing a role in resolving the civil war in Bosnia. On February 15, 1994, Yeltsin announced that Russia would no longer tolerate exclusion, and unilaterally injected Russia into the negotiating process by sending a special envoy, Vitaliy Churkin, to Serbia. Churkin's immediate success in getting the Bosnian Serbs to withdraw heavy weapons from Sarajevo not only obviated the need for NATO air strikes against Serbian positions, but inaugurated a new era of Russian involvement in the Bosnian peace process. Russia's subsequent participation in the contact group addressing the Bosnia problem and in providing forces for peacekeeping in Bosnia reflects an apparent intention to act in concert with the other major powers, rather than as an independent force.

During the last three years, Russian military leaders—particularly Major General Lebed—have also spoken out on regional politics, expressing political views at odds with those of the Russian leadership, even when ordered not to by the Russian president and minister of defense several times since July 1992.

FORCE REDEPLOYMENTS, REORGANIZATIONS, AND REDUCTIONS ARE AFFECTING THE READINESS OF RUSSIAN FORCES

Starting with Soviet President Mikhail Gorbachev's December 1988 announcement at the United Nations of unilateral force reductions in Eastern Europe, the Soviet—and now Russian—military has experienced a series of major redeployments, reorganizations, and reductions. The completed force withdrawals from Germany and the Baltic states at the end of August 1994 did not end the process. Russia is still involved with internal redeployments and troop reductions.

The reductions in nuclear arms called for by the Strategic Arms Reduction Talks (START) Treaty are being implemented on schedule, considerably reducing the number of deployed strategic nuclear missiles under Moscow's command. The reduction has also been accompanied by retargeting agreements with the United States that eliminate peacetime targeting of U.S. sites and reduce the combat alert status of some units. Russia and China have also agreed not to target each other in peacetime.

General-purpose forces, whose training has been severely reduced, have experienced considerable degradation in their combat readiness. Those units that have maintained a high degree of readiness have been used to conduct domestic and international peacekeeping missions.

Moscow also lost control of some of the Soviet Union's best military equipment when Ukraine and Belarus declared their ownership of all general-purpose forces stationed on their territory. For the most part, these forces had been formed from equipment evacuated from Eastern Europe in accordance with the 1988 Soviet unilateral reduction announcement and the 1990 Conventional Forces in Europe (CFE) Treaty. Additional, newer items of equipment were removed and stored east of the Ural mountains in order to meet the CFE limits, considerably diminishing the military forces west of the Urals under the control of Russia in comparison with its Soviet predecessor of a few years before.

The current Russian active duty military force, while capable of protecting Russia's borders from any short-term threat, no longer has the ability to project force into the heart of Europe. Russia's navy has also lost much of its power projection and sustainability capabilities.

Russia is, however, fully capable of rebuilding a force that could threaten its neighbors. With four or five years of determined mobilization, Russia could reassemble a force capable of threatening other countries located near its borders. Remobilization, however, does not appear to be high on the agenda of any of Russia's present political leaders. Reductions in Russia's active duty military force do not threaten Russia's stated defensive goals, even though the Russian general staff undoubtedly feels a need to improve combat training. Moreover, shifts in Moscow's military intentions would undoubtedly be preceded by perceptible changes in political leadership.

U.S. SECURITY INTERESTS

In the former Soviet Union, numerous political and ethnic entities have declared their independence and have started the process of nation building. Some of these states appear to be successful, while others do not. Boundaries and political affiliations have been settled in some regions, but not everywhere. Instability plagues the region, and will likely continue to do so for several years.

The process of political and economic reform in many of the new states has been characterized by indecisiveness, acrimony, and open conflict. Democracy and market economies were originally the goals of all states in the region, but little or no progress has been made toward these goals in many of these nations. In some cases, the banner of democracy has simply been hoisted over traditional forms of government by the few for the few. The principles of the market economy are not universally accepted or completely understood in most of the new states. Moreover, the drive for political and economic independence from the former Soviet central authorities has started to give way in some areas to serious thoughts of political and economic reassociation.

PREVENTING A MILITARY THREAT

While the development of democracy and market economies is the long-term solution to the region's instability, the United States has an interest in preventing the reemergence in the region of a military threat to U.S. interests. The risk of a new Soviet-type military-ideological threat, fortunately, appears to be small, since Russia—which would have to be the nucleus of such a threat—is making progress with political and economic reforms, thus reducing the possibility that it will reemerge as an adversary.

ENCOURAGING THE GROWTH OF DEMOCRACY

In the long term, the success of democratic reforms—particularly in Russia and Ukraine—will enhance U.S. security. In turn, the establishment of democratic values will profoundly reduce the chances of conflict. Democratic reforms are the best long-term answer to the aggressive nationalism and ethnic hatreds unleashed at the end of the Cold War.

PROMOTING ECONOMIC REFORMS

Promoting economic reforms in the former Soviet Union will significantly increase the chances that democracy will take root in the region. In addition, economic reforms in the region, undergirded by political reforms, will open foreign markets for the United States, as secure, democratic, market-oriented nations are more likely to support and engage in free trade.

PROMOTING REGIONAL STABILITY

Ethnic and border disputes present a real threat to the stability of the former Soviet Union. Many of the Soviet successor states—including Ukraine—are having problems establishing their sovereignty, are embroiled in violent conflict, or are ignoring democratic reforms. It is in the U.S. interest that ethnic feuds and the uneven development of reforms throughout the region not be allowed to threaten positive developments within the former Soviet Union or other parts of Central and Eastern Europe.

KEY U.S. SECURITY POLICY ISSUES

FUTURE SECURITY COOPERATION WITH THE WEST

Late 1993 proved to be a watershed year in shaping the U.S. attitude toward Russian participation in post–Cold War international security problems. Russia's decision that securing its own vital interests had to take precedence over cooperation with the West, and the specter of ultranationalists rising to power in Moscow, made it clear that the West was incorrect in its assessment that Russia was too preoccupied by domestic problems to be interested in international affairs.

While always acknowledging that Russia was a major power, the United States and the rest of the West often tended to address international security problems without fully taking stock—or advantage—of Moscow's interest in such matters. The situation began to change in early 1994, when Russia inserted itself into the situation in Bosnia.

Consequently, Washington has started to consult more with Moscow on a variety of problems. In the spring of 1994 the United States welcomed Russia as a fifth member of the Quadripartite Contact Group addressing the Bosnia problem. Similarly, it consulted with Russia on the North Korea nuclear problem and worked in the U.N. Security Council to acknowledge Russia's peacekeeping role in Georgia after Russia showed a readiness to conform to international norms.

The U.S. approach toward security cooperation with Russia is best represented by the Partnership for Peace program, which envisions broader European cooperation on security matters, while at the same time hedging against the appearance of a new threat to European security. The United States encourages Russia's contribution to international security but at the same time recognizes that Russia is not yet ensconced in the democratic and market traditions, and a Russia turned hostile or unstable would present a major challenge for European security. Nevertheless, security cooperation between Russia and the West will continue to expand as political and economic reforms take root in Russia and other areas of the former Soviet empire. At least six factors will affect future cooperation between the states of the former Soviet Union and the West on security matters:

Security cooperation within the CIS. There is a growing acceptance in most of the non-Russian states that their security depends on cooperation— even alliance—with Moscow. This has led to a number of bilateral military cooperation treaties between Russia and the other successor states. Russian security cooperation with its neighbors, as a rule, will come with a stipulation that those receiving Moscow's assistance or guarantees will not allow other major military powers to station troops on their territory without approval from Moscow. Consequently, non-Russian states of the region—with the possible exception of Ukraine—will tend to shy away from forms of cooperation with the West that might meet with Russian disapproval.

Ukraine's position. Ukraine has cooperated with the United States and with Russia on some nuclear issues, especially the U.S.-Russian-Ukrainian trilateral agreement facilitating Ukraine's denuclearization and ratification of the Nuclear Nonproliferation Treaty. On the other hand, Ukraine could seek a security position that is independent of Russia, in which case Kiev will want to cooperate as much as possible with the West on security matters. A Ukraine that is fully independent of Moscow on security matters and cooperative with the West will likely increase strains and decrease cooperation between Russia and the West in the near term.

Russia's vital interests. Cooperation with the West will also hinge on Russia's assessment of its vital interests. Moscow's new policy of defending its vital interests regardless of the West's attitude on a given problem may well lead to situations in which cooperation between Russia and the West is not possible— even to situations where confrontation is possible.

The West's intentions in the near abroad. Another key factor is Moscow's perception of the intentions of other major powers towards the area of the near abroad and Russia itself. Like the West, Russia comes out of the Cold War with lingering doubts about the trustworthiness of its former opponent. This inclination to distrust the West was heightened in 1993 when NATO first seemed ready to expand to the borders of the former Soviet Union, and the Western powers talked of mediating conflicts within the Caucasus and Central Asia. President Yeltsin's strong objection to additional NATO eastward expansion plans reflects Russia's continued extreme sensitivity to proposals or policies that appear to be aimed at isolating Russia or decreasing Russia's influence in the regions along its borders.

Russia will continue to promote European security agreements that boost Russia's role while devaluing the role of NATO. Russia's decision to join the Partnership for Peace program should be viewed as a tactical step in Moscow's long-term plans for reorganizing and expanding Europe's security structures.

The West's willingness to treat Russia as a partner. Russia's leeriness of Western intentions will be also affected by the West's willingness to include Russia as an equal partner in resolving international problems of interest to Moscow. If Moscow's participation is sought early in future planning processes, the West can expect Russia to cooperate as long as the West is not pushing a position at odds with Russia's vital interests. However, if the West is seen to be excluding Russia from the planning process—as Russia believed was the case in Bosnia in 1993—then Moscow may obstruct Western activity, using its veto authority in the U.N. Security Council if necessary.

The power of ultranationalists. The ascent to power of ultranationalists in Russia would for all practical purposes end any possibility of cooperation between the West and Russia. Ukraine, on the other hand, would be even more eager to cooperate with the West under such circumstances, assuming it still believed that its security depended on its ability to remain free of Moscow's domination.

THE POSSIBLE RISE OF
ULTRANATIONALISM IN RUSSIA

The results of the December 1993 parliamentary election in Russia raised the specter of ultranationalists gaining political control in Moscow, followed by Russian soldiers marching south and west to reestablish the old Czarist and Soviet empires. The statements of Vladimir Zhirinovsky were well known in the West before the elections but were of little concern because he had no power base in government. But the recent vote—and the efforts by several states in Central Europe to use the ultranationalists' election success to add urgency to their pleas to gain entry into NATO—changed the West's perception of the ultranationalist threat, making it a major topic of discussion.

The possibility of an ultranationalist government in Russia does exist—and has for two to three years. The appeal of the ultranationalists can be traced to several factors: resentment over the loss of superpower status, alarm over the growth of crime, and dissatisfaction with the growing gap between the upper and lower economic classes in Russia. In the minds of the ultranationalists and their supporters, these problems can be traced either to Western schemes or to the actions of Russian leaders acting in the interests of the West.

However, ultranationalists are not on the verge of taking charge in Moscow. The vote for the ultranationalists in the December 1993 election was at least in part a protest against the dislocation caused by the erratic reform policies of Yeltsin and Yegor Gaidar. Moreover, while the election resulted in ultranationalist and traditionalist parties gaining close to 40 percent of the seats in the Duma, centrists—who support continued reform but at a slower pace—gained a sufficient number of seats to ensure that reform will be continued, albeit at a slower pace and under more direct control by the government.

Combined with the fact that advocates of a foreign policy based on Russia's vital interests who are not ultranationalists gained the upper hand in the executive branch, this indicates that while Russia will be more independent of the West on security matters, it will not necessarily be reactionary or confrontational. There is, to be sure, support for a stronger Russia in international affairs, but not necessarily support for an aggressive foreign policy that risks confrontation with another major power.

The ultranationalists will, however, be able to influence both Russian policies in the near abroad and, indirectly, the activities of other Soviet successor states in the region. The ultranationalists are sure to create trouble wherever there are Russian populations living under the control of other ethnic groups—both inside and outside Russia itself. This, in itself, will likely cause the Russian government to make national security decisions in an environment that is highly emotional and confrontational.

Moreover, the ultranationalist groups will try to portray U.S. international actions as inherently anti-Russian. Thus relations between Washington and Moscow will be conducted in an environment in which ultranationalist forces seek to use U.S. actions to attack the legitimacy of the Russian regime in power.

The United States has sought to counter the specter of ultranationalism by supporting reform efforts designed to improve the material well-being of the average Russian and enhance the likelihood that Russia will play a positive role in international affairs. However, because of the prolonged deterioration of the Russian economy and the ability of ultranationalists to take political advantage of that deterioration, U.S. policy makers increasingly must consider how their actions toward Russian domestic matters and

international issues of interest to Russia will be perceived by the average Russian—whether that perception seems reasonable or not.

[Editor's note: The 1995 Russian elections saw an increase in support for pro-Communist groups, with these groups gaining seats in the Duma. The June 1996 presidential election takes on particular significance for Russian reform efforts in light of reformist losses in the 1995 state Duma election.]

UKRAINIAN STABILITY

The fact that Ukraine's internal differences over economic and international policies corresponds to an east-west ethnic and geographic division within the country presents the possibility of domestic instability. Labor problems in eastern Ukraine and the political battles between Crimean officials and the government in Kiev may foreshadow increased turmoil. Of the two, the Crimea problem has the greatest potential for creating international repercussions.

The elected government in Crimea is now actively seeking to loosen its ties to Kiev. While it is unclear as to how much autonomy the Crimeans are willing to settle for, many politically active Crimeans demand nothing less than reunification with Russia, or independence. Crimean appeals for Russian support have resulted in the dispute becoming international in nature, with both Kiev and Moscow reacting to the provocations of local Crimean officials. Anti-Ukraine Crimeans—with the support of Russian ultranationalists and even many moderate Russian political elements—have engaged in activities that have threatened to bring Russia and Ukraine into military conflict. For example, throughout the spring of 1994, Russian and Ukrainian leaders exchanged a series of low-key threats based primarily on reports of troop movements around the Crimea. Many of these reports proved to be false provocations originating from local political factions.

The leaderships of both countries appear to be trying to prevent increased tension over the Crimea. However, political conflicts between Crimean Russians and Ukrainians may continue to occur quite often—resulting in bellicose charges and countercharges, illegal seizures of property, and threatened troop deployments by Kiev and Moscow.

The situation is complicated by the fact that neither the Russian nor the Ukrainian government can afford politically to be seen as giving in to the other. Russia's leadership must be seen by its citizens to fully support the rights of ethnic Russians abroad, especially in the Crimea, which many Russians view as rightfully a part of their country. Ukraine's leadership, on the other hand, cannot afford to accept any agreements regarding the Crimea that convey the impression that Kiev is ceding part of its territory to Russia—the country that has historically dominated Ukraine and now looms as Kiev's most serious military threat. While the outcome of the Ukrainian parliamentary and presidential elections of 1994 may allow the political leaders of the two countries to discuss the problem in a spirit of good faith, domestic political pressures on both groups of leaders will remain.

The problem is further aggravated by the dispute over the Black Sea Fleet, which is supported by extensive facilities located on the Crimean peninsula. Russia is determined to maintain access to these facilities to support the part of the fleet that will go to Moscow. Specifically, Russia wants exclusive access to the facilities in Sevastopol, and is attempting to get Kiev to base its portion of the fleet in Odessa, which is not located on the peninsula. While Kiev has been willing to let Russia have the majority of the fleet's ships, and even recognizes Russia's need for an extensive support system, acceptance of Russia's exclusive access to support facilities in the Crimea is probably more of a concession than Kiev is willing to make, in light of its current efforts to assert control over the Crimea.

Because the leaders of Russia, Ukraine, and Belarus were interested in disbanding the central Soviet government as quickly as possible when they established the CIS in December 1991, they ignored many such contentious issues that would eventually have to be addressed. Agreements by the commonwealth signers to recognize each other's borders may have been politically expedient, but the capricious manner in which some of these borders were established are now being challenged by ethnic groups that are disadvantaged by the results. The Crimea will no doubt remain a problem for a long time, primarily because the leaders of both Russia and Kiev lack the political confidence and public support to offer the concessions that are necessary to resolve the situation.

For its part, the international community has tended to view the Crimea problem as an internal Ukrainian issue, and Russia as an external troublemaker seeking to take land that belongs to another nation. This position has tended to limit the West's potential to contribute constructively to the resolution of the problem. The West's view of the situation suggests that it should support Kiev; yet it cannot afford to antagonize Russia on an issue of such importance. Consequently, the West has relegated itself to the sidelines.

Nevertheless, the international community may have to play a role in the Crimea problem if a peaceful solution is to be achieved. The possibility of Russia and Ukraine accepting international arbitration would be greater if the problem were redefined as an international issue resulting from the inadequately prepared and hastily signed CIS agreement. Such arbitration might be welcomed by the political leaders involved, although not by Russian ultranationalists, who would likely interpret it as Western encroachment into Moscow's historic sphere of influence.

THE FUTURE OF ECONOMIC REFORMS

The status of economic reforms varies throughout the region, but in no state can the economy be considered strong. During 1992 and 1993 Yeltsin alternated between enacting radical economic reform measures advocated by the West and watering down those measures in order to limit public and political opposition. The result is that neither the market system envisioned by advocates of "shock therapy" nor the centrally managed reform approach advocated by economic moderates has materialized. The inflation rate in Russia reflects the results of the government's seesaw policies. During 1992 and 1993 the monthly rate was never lower than the July 1992 rate of 7.1 percent, and it reached a high of 31.1 percent two months later. (In January 1992 the rate hit 296 percent when the government lifted price controls, but this figure was an anomaly.)

The problem was aggravated by the fact that Russian legislatures during this time failed to create the legal basis for an investment-friendly environment. Moreover, there has been little progress in converting the vast military industrial complex to the production of consumer goods—a problem of major importance, since the most effective production elements of Russia are in the military industrial sector.

The Ukrainian economy is in even worse condition. Virtually no effort has been made by the Ukrainian government—or the governments of the other Soviet successor states, for that matter—to convert from a command to a market economy. Consequently, Ukraine has a small and unstable market sector and a huge, unproductive, and outdated state-controlled sector.

The dismal economic performances of the two largest states of the region have resulted in growing dissatisfaction with the political leadership of both countries, to the point that a further downturn in their economies could provoke major political unrest and a downfall of the leadership. Payment of wages routinely lags for months in Russia and Ukraine—in August 1994 Russia reported that wage arrears amounted to 3.5 trillion rubles and were increasing by 15 percent a month, resulting in numerous regional strikes and public protests. In mid-1994 Russian opposition groups called repeatedly for universal strikes in the transportation and oil industries in hopes that they would cause the downfall of the Yeltsin government.

As a result, some political leaders in the region have started to pay increased attention to the social consequences of their economic reform policies. Since at least the beginning of 1993, the Russian government has devoted increased attention to alleviation of economic hardship and prevention of social unrest. Unfortunately, these measures have not proven very fruitful.

Nevertheless, economic reform measures continue to be enacted. During 1994 the government made great and much-needed strides in controlling government deficits and inflation. In February 1994 the inflation rate dropped to 9.9 percent from 22 percent the month before, and remained in the single digits for several months.

In addition, Prime Minister Viktor Chernomyrdin successfully resisted pressure from the uniformed military and military-industrial leaders to approve a 1994 military budget of almost 90 trillion rubles, rather than the 40 trillion cap favored by the government, which may reduce defense orders by 80 percent. Moreover, in July 1994, Chernomyrdin started the long-awaited bankruptcy program for unprofitable state-supported industries.

In an effort to minimize social fallout from such reforms, the government has increased its control over the reform process, in an effort to balance the dislocations caused by market reforms with compensatory social programs. It has also increased efforts to reduce economic crime—including that by growing organized crime organizations—the prevalence of which tends to undermine public support for reform.

Ukraine and the other successor states, on the other hand, have yet to take major measures to reform their economies. A major reason for this appears to be that these countries have historically been more dependent on Russia than vice versa. To some extent, most had grown accustomed to this dependence, and were genuinely unprepared for what came next when the carpet of Russian support was pulled out from under their feet. In the fall of 1994 the newly elected president (Kuchma) and parliament passed a series of reform measures, but it is too soon to assess their success.

This economic relationship between Russia and the rest of the CIS is becoming more evident to the political leadership of the region and may well lead the non-Russian states, including Ukraine, to seek closer economic ties with Russia. As the dominant partner in any such economic relationship, Moscow will be able to choose and mold these economic ties on the basis of the advantages they offer to Russia.

The United States has been a strong supporter of economic reform in the region. Moreover, while the United States has advocated an aggressive approach to market reform, it recognizes that success requires that states themselves take the initiative. Washington's policy has been that U.S. support must follow the initiation of reform by individual states. Consequently, even in Russia, which has undertaken the greatest reform efforts to date, U.S. support has been provided in a series of stages corresponding to the reforms undertaken by Moscow.

U.S. bilateral economic support activities have been concentrated on the more rapidly reforming regions of Russia, in order to develop the fundamental building blocks of a market system and to provide models at the local level. Initial efforts involved primarily technical assistance programs. In fiscal 1994 Congress increased assistance to $2.5 billion.

In fiscal 1995 U.S. activities shifted to support for trade and investment. In order to lay the groundwork for this stage, Vice President Al Gore has met with Prime Minister Chernomyrdin in a series of meetings since 1993. The United States hopes that as a result of these efforts, capital flowing from the U.S. private sector will play a larger role in the economic renewal of Russia.

At the same time, the United States is actively pressing the international business community and international financial institutions to assist Russia's efforts to move to a market economy. The urgency of such international support increased after the Russian parliamentary elections of December 1993, which reflected the growing disillusion of the Russian people with the reform efforts. It is primarily through international channels—particularly the International Monetary Fund (IMF)—that meaningful financial and long-term technical support can be provided to Russia and the other newly established states of the region.

The IMF has been designated by the United States and the other Western industrial nations as the main agent for steering Russia and the other Soviet successor states through the reform process. The IMF provides loans to states only after they agree to undertake macroeconomic policy changes and establish economic performance targets. The IMF turned its attention to the former Soviet Union in 1991, inviting the Soviet republics to enter into a "special association" with the IMF and World Bank shortly after the failed August 1991 coup attempt in Moscow. Russia became a member of the IMF in June 1992; it has the ninth-largest IMF quota (which determines countries' voting and borrowing rights), ranking behind only the G-7 countries and Saudi Arabia. As of May 1994, Russia's quota allows it to borrow approximately $4.1 billion annually—if it meets its IMF budgetary and macroeconomic reform targets, which so far have posed major problems.

In April 1993 the G-7 deputies announced a $43 billion aid package to Russia. Because of Russia's problems with meeting IMF performance targets, the G-7 countries also agreed to create a new loan facility within the IMF—the Systemic Transformation Facility (STF)—which is intended to address criticisms that the rigorous conditionality of the IMF does not permit it to be sufficiently responsive to the needs of Russia and the other former Soviet republics. As of April 1994, Russia had received $3 billion in loans under the STF.

RUSSIA'S CHALLENGE ON THE CFE FLANK AGREEMENTS

The CFE Treaty signed by members of NATO and the Warsaw Pact in 1990 called, among other things, for limits on the number of forces that could be deployed on the northern and southern flanks of the former Soviet Union. These limits were to be achieved by November 1993.

[Editor's note: The CFE Treaty review conference, held in May 1996, sought to resolve the ongoing issue of flank limits.]

Since 1992, Russia has sought to have the flank limits revised upward to account for its assessments of new security threats to Russia in the wake of the Soviet Union's demise. Russia believes that increased turmoil in regions like the Transcaucasus and the possibility of a "Muslim threat" from the south requires it to have more forces deployed on its southern flank. On September 5, 1994, Minister of Defense Pavel Grachev emphasized this point by stating that the limits were against Russia's "vital interests."

Currently, agreements call for the Russian military to have no more than 580 armored personal carriers, 700 tanks, and 1,280 artillery pieces in its northern and southern flanks by the deadline in 1995. The agreement does, however, allow the Russians to transfer unlimited numbers of armored personnel carriers to internal security forces (as opposed to the Russian army) in the flank regions, as long as "such organizations refrain from the acquisition of combat capabilities in excess of those necessary for meeting internal security requirements." Moreover, the treaty offers Russia the possibility of addressing its flank concerns without breaking the limits through storage rules, temporary deployments, nonlimited equipment, and other means.

Since 1992 a Russian military buildup in the southern flank region has occurred, with the transfer of troops and weapons previously stationed in the Baltic states and East Germany. In 1994 Russian deployments in the flank regions exceeded the November 1995 limits by approximately 2,000 armored personnel carriers, 400 tanks, and 500 artillery pieces.

The flank limits were negotiated at the behest of Turkey and the nordic NATO countries out of concern that force reductions in Central Europe would be redeployed on the flanks and create an increased threat to those countries. They remain concerned and oppose Russia's request to revise the limits upward. There is also concern that if the CFE flank limits are revised, further revisions are bound to follow until the treaty is of little or no value. In addition, some suspect that Russia is really seeking revisions in the flank agreement in order to enhance its military capability to impose its will in the near abroad.

GREATER MIDDLE EAST

JED SNYDER, PHEBE MARR, AND PATRICK L. CLAWSON

This discussion covers developments in the Greater Middle East from Marrakesh to Bangladesh—North Africa, the Levant, the Persian Gulf, Central Asia, and South Asia. The region is not a cohesive whole; in particular, U.S. policy issues in South Asia often differ from those in the rest of the region. Nevertheless, there are some important common threads from the point of view of U.S. security interests.

DEFINING TRENDS

The political-military landscape of the Greater Middle East region has undergone a far-reaching transformation since 1990. Three major events have had a direct impact upon the region: the retreat of Moscow from its previous role as a major power broker; the initiation of an Arab-Israeli peace process at Madrid in October 1991; and the victory of the Western coalition in the Gulf War. In their wake, traditional strategic relationships have begun to shift. A new and more fluid balance of power is emerging in the region as the unifying notion of pan-Arabism gives way to national interests, the Arab-Israeli conflict ebbs, and new states emerge on the rim of the former Soviet Union.

These and related currents present fresh challenges for governments in the region, as well as for the United States and the West. Population pressures, reduced export revenues, urban environmental problems, and growing economic and social needs are taxing government capacities. Where the challenge is not met, messianic religious movements that espouse antisecular and anti-Western themes are gaining popular favor and threaten to become a destabilizing force. Islamic revivalism is the most pronounced of these, but extremist movements also include Arab nationalists and Hindu revivalists in India. In Turkey, Iraq, and some of the newly established states of the former Soviet Union, ethnic separatism has emerged to threaten the foundations of the nation-state. Even more portentous have been decisions by some governments in the region to acquire weapons of mass destruction (WMD); particularly worrisome is the situation in South Asia, where the nuclear forces of India and Pakistan have developed effective delivery systems.

EMERGING SECURITY CONCERNS ARE ENCOURAGING PROLIFERATION IN THE MIDDLE EAST REGION

Weapons of Mass Destruction

In the post–Cold War Greater Middle East, the decline of regional deterrence previously provided

---

This essay has been edited and is reprinted from Strategic Assessment 1995: U.S. Security Challenges in Transition, *ed. Patrick Clawson (Washington, D.C.: Institute for National Strategic Studies, 1995), 67–82, by permission of National Defense University Press.*

by superpower security guarantees has caused many nations to turn toward doctrines of greater self-reliance in security. The 1991 Gulf War may have deepened, rather than ameliorated, regional security concerns, and the result has been an increase in regional defense budgets and arms purchases. The Middle East has, of course, seen arms races before, but what is new and disturbing in the current rearmament cycle is the escalatory danger of weapons of mass destruction acquisition. States that depended on security guarantees by superpower allies and are now compelled to rely on themselves are likely to regard WMD acquisition as an urgent priority.

Increasingly, Middle Eastern political and defense elites are coming to see WMD as uniquely suited to filling the emerging security vacuum. WMD acquisition in the Middle East has been encouraged by many factors:

- The search for deterrence and for affordable alternatives to conventional arms.

- The increased availability of nuclear technology, fissile material, WMD infrastructure, and delivery systems.

- The example of regional NPT signatories (particularly Iraq) developing covert nuclear programs without incurring sanctions, at least initially.

- The political impact of chemical weapons use during the Iran-Iraq War.

- The probable growth of the Israeli nuclear stockpile and the modernization of its delivery capability.

- Fears of the emergence of another rogue regime that could threaten moderate governments.

- Insecurities generated by the seemingly permanent state of hostility among Iran, Iraq, and the Gulf Cooperation Council (GCC) states.

- Doubts about the willingness—and, given U.S. force structure cuts, the ability—of the United States to intervene again in the region on a massive scale.

- The attraction of WMD for radical regimes seeking instruments of revolution.

- A desire by regional states to increase their political-military clout, gain international prestige, divide coalitions, or intimidate neighbors.

In virtually every case where WMD programs have been initiated, the financial burdens have been greater than anticipated. Some governments, particularly Iraq's, have made the investment eagerly, even though this has involved sacrificing their populations' standard of living to some extent.

In the final analysis, the acquisition of an indigenous capability is not likely to bring long-term savings over reliance on sophisticated conventional arms, since building and sustaining the necessary infrastructure is expensive. On the other hand, acquiring biological, chemical, and even nuclear arms and their delivery systems from outside suppliers may indeed be regarded as a bargain by states looking for a relatively inexpensive force multiplier.

While nuclear weapons acquisition has been a clear priority for some Middle East states, other countries have pursued chemical and biological weapons development with as much fervor as nuclear weapons. While little officially confirmed data exists on production or possession of chemical weapons outside of the United States, Russia, and Iraq, at least eight governments in the region—Syria, Libya, Iran, Egypt, Israel, Saudi Arabia, India, and Pakistan—are suspected of pursuing chemical weapons. Chemical weapons have been used by both Iraq and Iran during the Iran-Iraq war, and by Iraq against its own population.

Despite initial optimistic assessments of damage to Iraq's WMD infrastructure (particularly the nuclear component), it now seems clear that little of that capability was destroyed during the Gulf War. In addition, efforts to locate and destroy mobile missiles were wholly unsuccessful, and relatively little of the deeply buried bunker system that houses Iraq's weapons and their command-and-control support was found or targeted. This was a function of both poor tactical intelligence and the unavailability of munitions for deep penetration strikes.

Iran's WMD ambitions are the subject of wide speculation. Economists point to the fragile state of the Iranian economy and question whether sufficient resources can be committed to a nuclear program, as distinct from a chemical weapons program. On the other hand, given a tight resource constraint, Iran might find the pursuit of nuclear weapons to be an attractive alternative to a higher cost acquisition of large numbers of modern conventional weapons.

Missile Proliferation

Surface-to-surface missiles (SSMs) have already been employed in several regional conflicts, notably by both parties during the Iran-Iraq war, by Iraq during the 1991 Gulf War, and during the Yemen civil war. SSMs are the platform of choice for WMD weapons, as they can carry nuclear, biological, or chemical payloads with minor modification to the missile's configuration. Longer-range ballistic missiles, like the Chinese CSS II purchased by Saudi Arabia, are likely to prove most attractive. India, Pakistan, and Israel already have longer-range systems under development. But even shorter-range and generally less-sophisticated missiles such as Soviet-built Scuds are valued as deterrents in the Middle East because distances between urban centers are relatively short. Missiles such as Scuds can also be effective weapons of terror against an opponent who lacks a retaliatory capability or is politically constrained. Iraq's use of Scuds against Israel during the Gulf War is an example.

The lack of precision guidance on most of the earlier generation of weapons that make up the bulk of current Middle Eastern missile inventories means these missiles are ineffective for use against dispersed targets, such as military units. However, they are effective against concentrated targets, such as air bases, port facilities, above-ground command-control facilities, and headquarters.

The acquisition of SSMs by a number of Middle Eastern states attests to the diffusion of low as well as high technology weapons throughout the region. The regional arms race casts doubt on the efficacy of supply-based strategies of denial pursued by the Western industrialized powers. Indeed, some Western countries continue to supply dual use technologies to the Middle East, while SSMs are sold by Russia, China, and North Korea.

AFTER REMARKABLE PROGRESS, THE ARAB-ISRAELI PEACE PROCESS TURNS TO ISRAELI-SYRIAN NEGOTIATIONS

Three events—the October 1991 Madrid peace conference; the September 13, 1993, signing of the Declaration of Principles between the Palestine Liberation Organization (PLO) and Israel; and the July 1994 Jordanian-Israeli accord—may mark the beginning of the end of the Arab-Israeli confrontation. Progress has also been made in the multilateral talks, which involve the industrial states and a number of Middle East states, though not Syria or Lebanon. Several proposals, including for confidence-building measures, are being discussed in the Arms Control and Regional Security (ACRS) talks.

In the bilateral talks, attention has now turned to Syria, but it is by no means clear if a Syrian-Israeli peace accord can be reached before the June 1996 deadline for the next Israeli election. On the Syrian side, the most common interpretation is that President Hafez al-Asad is genuinely interested in a deal but is proceeding cautiously. He wants to recover the Golan, but as a member of the small Alawite minority, Asad must be sensitive to charges from Syria's Sunni majority that he has sold out the Muslim cause in Palestine.

Any Israeli-Syrian agreement will require compromises that each side will be reluctant to make. Both sides regard the Golan Heights as militarily valuable territory, which provides an intelligence listening post, dominates Israeli territory six hundred feet below, and provides easy access to Damascus, which is only thirty miles away. Most analysts expect an Israeli-Syrian agreement patterned on the Camp David accord: Israeli withdrawal and full diplomatic relations between Syria and Israel, with both phased in over a period of years. This would be accompanied by a multinational peace force separating the two sides.

On the Palestinian-Israeli and Jordanian-Israeli fronts, the key issue in the peace process will be implementation of the September 13, 1993, accord and the May 4, 1994, Cairo Agreement. The transition from fighting to governing is proving difficult for the PLO and for the activists in the Israeli-occupied territories. Life in the Palestinian-administered zone is not improving as quickly as the population hoped, in part because aid flows have been delayed by ongoing disagreement between donors and the PLO. The new authority will face continuing challenges in negotiations over the extension of its zone to the rest of the West Bank and over the territories' final status.

Security policy is a politically charged issue. Some Palestinians are determined to continue attacks on Israelis, while some Israeli settlers are determined to stop the Palestinians from exerting authority over the West Bank. Palestinians and Israelis will be watching each other closely to determine how vigorously such lawbreakers are pursued by the other side. The Palestinian security forces, most of which are drawn from the ranks of the PLO, will be under pressure to perform police tasks for which many members are not trained. The Palestinian leaders are under domestic political pressure not to pursue too vigorously terrorists from Hamas, which at least in Gaza has strong popular support. On the Israeli side, public opinion about the peace process will be strongly affected by terrorist episodes, and the government could come under pressure to suspend negotiations with the PLO in the event of more terrorist episodes like the October 1994 Jerusalem shootings and the death of a soldier.

The expectation of 1993–94 that the improvement in Israeli-Arab relations would transform the region into a zone of prosperity has given way to more realistic expectations. Mistrust will not disappear overnight. Nor will protectionist governments in the region quickly agree to open up their economies. Ten years after Camp David removed all formal barriers to Israeli-Egyptian trade, Israel sells less than $10 million a year in the Egyptian market. There will of course be some economic benefits from the peace—for example, investors will be more willing to risk their funds in the region now that it is seen as less volatile—but the benefits are unlikely to have a discernable short-term effect on most national economies. The Palestinians are an exception. They are well positioned to serve as a bridge between Israel and the Arab world, and their economy is already highly dependent on trade.

THE ISLAMIC REVIVAL IS A GROWING CHALLENGE TO REGIONAL REGIMES

Following the overthrow of the Iranian shah in 1979, a politically oriented Islamic revival has gained strength in Iran, Egypt, Sudan, Algeria, and Lebanon. This revival rejects most Western models of modernization and secularism, seeks to establish governments based on traditional Islamic law, and in its most militant form works for the overthrow of governments tied to Western interests. Such movements are increasing in influence, intensity, and reach.

One must be careful, however, to distinguish extremists who practice violence from mainstream revival movements and parties that work openly for the gradual Islamization of their societies. In much of the Middle East, mainstream Muslim movements that work openly for gradual Islamization have put down deep roots and are unlikely to be easily displaced. In Egypt, the Muslim Brotherhood operates a network of grass roots institutions—including schools, clinics, banks, and charitable foundations—that constitutes a semialternative government. Mainstream Islamic parties, when allowed to run in open elections, do well but usually do not have a majority. In Jordan's 1993 election, Islamic candidates secured one-fifth of parliament's seats, down from 40 percent in 1989; in Pakistan, the same year, they got 4 percent, down from 8 percent in 1990.

Nor are revival movements in the Greater Middle East limited to Islamic populations. The Bharativa Janata Party has arisen in India to challenge India's tradition of secular rule. Israel has both religious parties that seek to make Israeli government and society conform to religious law, and outlawed extremist movements such as Kach. But Islamic movements, because of their breadth and intensity, present the greatest challenge to U.S. security interests in the region.

While the Islamic revival does not constitute a regionwide, monolithic movement, cross-border cooperation among individuals and groups—particularly among extremist organizations such as the Sunni Hamas in the West Bank and Gaza and the Shi'ite Hizballah in Lebanon—is growing. Increasingly important factors in providing linkage among extremist factions are the return to their homelands of Muslims who fought against the USSR in Afghanistan and the training and support given to extremist groups by Iran and Sudan.

However, Islamic movements exhibit several weaknesses that inhibit their effectiveness. First, movements have displayed a tendency to splinter. The mainstream Muslim Brotherhood in Egypt, with a membership estimated at two million, has produced numerous extremist offshoots, such as the Jihad, which assassinated Sadat, and the Gama'at, which is currently conducting a guerilla war against the government. Algeria's Islamic Salvation Front (FIS) has virtually disintegrated into numerous, highly localized groups. Islamic movements lack a unifying, charismatic leader to give them coherence and direction. As a result, they are unlikely to forge a coordinated regionwide threat to Western interests.

Second, Islamic groups that have taken power have been unable to create stable governing institutions. After fifteen years of rule in Iran, the clergy have neither overcome divisions in their own ranks nor adequately addressed social and economic problems. In Sudan, a bitter civil war continues as the north tries to press Islamic law on the non-Islamic south.

Despite these disabilities, violence-prone Islamic movements in a number of countries still have the capacity to destabilize regimes and to raise the political and economic costs of containing them.

Most threatening in the short term are militant extremists who pursue their aims through violence and terrorism. Such groups have increased in size, militancy, and sustainability in recent years. The increased reach and sophistication of Islamic terrorist groups are illustrated by the bombings of the World Trade Center in New York and of Jewish targets in Buenos Aires and London.

While extremist movements will probably increase their activities, they are unlikely to unseat any regimes in the near term, except possibly in Algeria. Should the Algerian government fall, reverberations would be felt throughout the region. Extremist movements will continue to challenge the legitimacy of existing governments, draining support from mainstream movements, which have been put on the defensive lately by growing extremism in their own ranks and increased repression from governments. In Tunisia, for example, all Islamic activists are in jail or have been exiled; in Egypt, the government has begun cracking down on the Muslim Brotherhood, as well as the radical extremists, but violence continues. In Gaza, radical militants in Hamas threaten the peace process.

However, demographic pressures, failed economic programs, and disillusionment with the quality of governance in many Middle Eastern states ensure that pressure for political change will continue to build. Where governments are reluctant to recognize moderate Islamic groups, domestic politics is likely to become increasingly polarized, to the detriment of existing secular regimes and the benefit of extremists.

REGIONAL GOVERNMENTS FACE CHALLENGES TO THEIR CONTINUANCE IN OFFICE

In addition to the Islamic revival, governments confront mounting challenges to the status quo in a number of key states. Many regimes, under pressure for poor past performance, face rising expectations and declining resources. A better-informed public and burgeoning civic groups are demanding greater participation in government and less authoritarian rule. Leadership changes in several countries may hasten the process of transition. Challenges to existing regimes are likely to keep the area volatile and unpredictable.

A New Generation of Leadership Is Inevitable in Many States

Many political systems in the region face challenges to their continuity from leadership succession. There are few well-established mechanisms for leadership change, and even where such processes exist, it is not clear that they will work well.

A number of the monarchies and one-party states on which the West relies for support have aging or ill leaders, some of whom are likely to be replaced within the next five years. King Hussein of Jordan is fifty-nine and has recently been hospitalized for cancer; King Fahd of Saudi Arabia is seventy-three; King Hassan II of Morocco is sixty-five; and President Asad of Syria is sixty-four and suffers from heart trouble. In some cases (Jordan, Saudi Arabia), the lines of succession have been delineated. In others (Egypt, Syria), change could produce a struggle for power that may weaken the regime. The demise of King Hussein could adversely affect the peace process. King Fahd's successor might be less accommodating to the United States. In almost all cases, leadership is likely to be assumed by a younger generation, often educated at home and with less exposure to the West. This could lead to greater independence in foreign policy and more reluctance to cooperate with the West.

Where leadership changes intersect with imploding political and social forces, a change of leadership could have profound implications for a state's foreign and domestic policy. In Algeria, a regime change, should it occur, is likely to be accompanied by domestic upheaval with the potential for the disintegration of the state. In Iraq, Saddam Hussein's removal could occasion serious instability, renewed ethnic and sectarian violence, the flight of refugees, and political or military intervention by its neighbors. Iran could experience a replacement of its clerical leadership, unable to satisfy economic demands or overcome diplomatic isolation.

Some of these changes (Iran, Iraq) could be favorable to U.S. interests in the longer term. The regime in Iraq could be replaced by one that is less repressive and more willing to abide by international norms. A change in Iran might put an end to that nation's support for anti-Western policies and international terrorism. However, leadership changes in key regional states now supporting U.S. objectives—Egypt, Saudi Arabia, Jordan, and Pakistan—are a more worrisome prospect.

Resource Pressures

The greatest natural resource of the Middle East is its oil wealth. The region has about 75 percent of the world's oil reserves and in 1994 produced about 25 percent of the world's oil. The economic fortunes of the region are closely linked to the state of the world oil market, which the oil-producing states are no longer able to influence to any great extent; the effects of the Organization of Petroleum Exporting Countries on markets are generally limited in size and in duration. The paradox is that the lower the price of oil, the more dependent the world becomes on Middle East oil, because it is by far the cheapest to produce. Therefore, low oil prices increase the importance of the Middle East to the economy of the United States and its allies.

Both the Middle East and South Asia face population pressures. In particular, finding employment for those joining the labor force is a serious problem in many countries at a time when unemployment is high and job creation is constrained by low economic growth. The most likely scenario is rising youth unemployment, which may translate into political unrest and add to pressures on weak and ineffective governments. Recruits for Islamic movements are often drawn from this pool of unemployed youth.

Middle East economies have done poorly in the last decade. For the region as a whole, per capita Gross National Product fell an average of 2.3 percent annually from 1980 through 1992, a cumulative 25 percent drop. Three factors explain this fall in income. First, 1994 oil prices, while fluctuating, average about a fifth of the 1980 level, when adjusted for inflation. Second, population has doubled since the 1973 oil price rise. Third, governments in most countries have fed unrealistic popular expectations about their ability to continue high expenditures and low taxation.

Economic problems are felt most keenly in the poorest countries of the region. Income disparities remain glaring: the most populous Arab country, Egypt, has a per capita income that is 3 percent that of the richest, the United Arab Emirates. On the other hand, the Western-oriented poor Arab states —Egypt, Jordan, Morocco, Tunisia—have all had relatively good economic growth in 1993 and 1994, thanks to better economic policies and continuing debt relief.

The oil-producing nations will not be able to achieve the level of per capita income that they enjoyed during the oil boom of 1973–85. After postponing painful adjustment as long as possible while continuing with inappropriately large state-sector investments, Algeria and Iran have run into serious external debt problems. Both have been forced to cut spending, endangering social stability and, in Iran's case, curtailing military ambitions. Saudi Arabia is borrowing heavily abroad to finance budget deficits. It has taken some measures to reduce the deficit, including stretching out arms purchases from the United States. However, continuing expenditure reductions and new taxes will be needed in order to avoid unsustainable foreign debt in the long run. In the meantime, Saudi Arabia has ample resources and borrowing capacity to continue its current policy path.

Israel provides a contrast to this trend. Israel's per capita GNP is about $12,000, 75 percent above the Saudi level. Furthermore, Israel's economy is growing at 3–4 percent per annum on a per capita basis. Much of the reason for this is that economic policies have helped correct the chronic budget deficits and overregulation that caused triple-digit inflation and stagnant output in the early 1980s. In addition, progress in the peace process is likely to give a boost to investment. After absorbing close to one million immigrants in 1989–94, Israel's unemployment rate has been brought below 7 percent. In short, Israel's economic lead over Arab states is likely to widen.

Allocation of scarce water resources, especially from rivers flowing across state boundaries, is a source of tension. The Middle East has the least water per capita in the world—1,070 cubic meters per capita per annum, compared with the world average of 7,700. At the same time, it has the highest water consumption per capita in the developing world, at 1,000 cubic meters per capita per annum—about twice the developing country average of 510. Frictions between states over water allocation, such as occurred among Turkey, Syria, and Iraq in the 1970s, can contribute to domestic as well as regional instability. Water scarcity contributes to increasing food imports, which put additional pressure on scarce funds.

The outlook for India is more optimistic. Thanks to an opening of the economy to market forces, India's per capita GNP grew 3.1 percent per annum from 1980 to 1992. Western and southern India seem poised on the edge of an East-Asian-style economic miracle. The less educated north, however, is still bound by rigid statist policies and inadequate investment in education and risks stagnation. The poor performance of the Hindu heartland could feed pressures from political-religious revival movements as well as tensions with the more prosperous regions. However, India's overall economic growth will make it increasingly attractive for U.S. investment and trade, although from an admittedly low base. (U.S. trade with India was $6 billion each year from 1989 through 1993, or less than one percent of total U.S. trade and about 15 percent of Indian trade). In the 1990s India's economic boom is not, however, likely to change the general U.S. perception that India is not central to U.S. interests.

Difficult Circumstances and Poor Governance May Produce Some Failed States

The most extreme manifestation of government collapse is the failed state, the regional exemplar of which is Lebanon, where a civil war allowed local militias and extended families to dominate politics while the governments of neighboring Syria and Israel extended their influence into the country. Such states provide a favorable environment for radical movements and terrorist activities.

There is a risk of additional failed states in the region. Extremist movements already seek to overthrow the existing governments in Algeria and, to a lesser extent, in Egypt. In Algeria, state disintegration could occur. Elsewhere, dissident ethnic or sectarian groups desire secession from existing states. The Sudanese government faces continuing civil war with non-Muslims in the south. Both Turkey and Iraq face challenges from Kurds seeking to change the distribution of power within these states. (A U.S. military mission, Provide Comfort 2, is currently engaged in protecting the Iraqi Kurds in territory now under their control.) Tensions have increased between Sunnis and Shi'ites in Iraq, and between Berbers and Arabs in Algeria.

In Central Asia and the Caucasus, eight new states face the daunting task of creating nations from ethnically diverse populations. Of the five predominantly Sunni Muslim Central Asian states, four are headed by former senior officials of the Soviet Communist Party, while one (Kyrgyzstan) is run by an individual who professes admiration for the democratic process. The anticipated collapse of these societies has not occurred in large part because of the continuing hold on central political authority by semi-rehabilitated Soviet officials, whose expertise in central management is valued by populations seeking to prevent the implosion of fragile economies and ethnically divided societies. In addition, Soviet rule tended to have a strong secularizing effect, blunting the influence of religious forces. In the Caucasus region (Georgia, Armenia, Azerbaijan), only one of the original post-Soviet governments (in Yerevan) has remained in power. Georgia and Azerbaijan are torn by ethnic violence. In Georgia, Abkhazian and south Ossetian separatists refuse to acknowledge the authority of the Georgian government in Tblisi. In Azerbaijan, the continued fighting over the predominantly Armenian enclave of Nagorno-Karabakh has heightened tensions between Armenia and Azerbaijan. In the North Caucasus, Russia has intervened militarily against the breakaway government of Chechnya, which declared its independence from Russia in 1991.

REGIONAL FRAGMENTATION MAKES THE ESTABLISHMENT OF A STABLE SECURITY FRAMEWORK UNLIKELY

The removal of Cold War constraints has encouraged the fragmentation of the Middle East into regional subgroups, a trend that will intensify. The Maghreb, the Levant, the Persian Gulf states, South Asia, the Caucasus, and Central Asia are each likely to follow separate paths.

The emerging regional blocs are primarily driven by economics, and cooperation within and among regional groups for security purposes is likely to be limited at best. Competition for scarce resources, the absence of a common security threat, domestic tensions, and pressure on the region's governments all serve to focus the attention of regional states on their own national interests, rather than security cooperation. The Arab Maghreb Union is unlikely to survive if Algeria collapses, while the eastern Mediterranean states still have tremendous problems to overcome in the Arab-Israeli peace process before security cooperation can become a reality. However, multilateral peace talks are moving the region toward more cooperation. As a result, the Levant may become one of the more promising areas for building future regional cooperation in economics, water control, arms control, and conflict resolution.

The collapse of the six-plus-two formula designed to unite Egypt and Syria with the Gulf Corporation Council (GCC) states as a deterrent mechanism in the Gulf is emblematic of the difficulties of establishing a stable framework for regional security cooperation. The region is returning to a checkerboard pattern of balancing power, while looking to the United States as the defense of last resort. This may increase feelings of insecurity in the near term, particularly on the part of key U.S. partners. Turkey, rejected for membership in the European Union and increasingly alienated from Europe over Bosnia, feels cut adrift. Pakistan faces a dramatic change in its relationship with the United States after the Afghanistan war, and remains bitter over the Pressler Amendment (which prohibits U.S. assistance to Pakistan, to punish Islamabad for its nuclear weapons program).

U.S. SECURITY INTERESTS

ENSURING THE FREE FLOW OF OIL AT REASONABLE PRICES

The United States wants to ensure that Persian Gulf oil flows without supply disruptions that could inflict considerable cost on the U.S. economy. The United States also wants the price of oil to be relatively stable at a level that does not throw the world into recession. Finally, the United States seeks to prevent any restraints on free shipping of oil along the sea lines of communication to the United States or its allies.

PRESERVING AND PROTECTING THE STATE OF ISRAEL

From the date of Israel's founding, the United States has been committed to protecting the territorial integrity of that state from the threat of aggression. The context for this commitment is changing as the Arab-Israeli peace process progresses and redefines the extent of Israel proper (as opposed to the occupied territories), and as the Arab rejectionist community is reduced. Israel's pursuit of the peace process is dependent upon U.S. guarantees of its security, including the annual appropriation of significant levels of military and economic assistance.

MAINTAINING A REGIONAL BALANCE FAVORABLE TO U.S. INTERESTS

Maintaining local military and political balances of power favorable to U.S. friends and allies can help prevent the outbreak of major regional conflicts that could entangle U.S. forces, and will also provide some leverage in containing transnational threats, such as massive refugee flows.

One way of achieving this goal is to prevent the emergence of a hostile regional hegemon in any subregion of the area. Any domination of the Persian Gulf by one state, especially a hostile state like Iraq or Iran, would threaten vital U.S. interests, because that state would be in a position to manipulate oil prices and to use its enhanced oil revenues to develop weapons of mass destruction—even if high oil prices could only be sustained for a few years until alternatives were developed. The domination of the Arab Fertile Crescent (Iraq, Jordan, Syria, Lebanon) by one state could endanger the Arab-Israeli peace process. The domination of North Africa by a radical Muslim regime could produce large-scale emigration to Western Europe and threaten a key U.S. ally, Egypt.

CONTROLLING WMD SPREAD

The spread of WMD and the technologies to support them is inimical to U.S. security interests. With the exception of the Israeli program, the United States has not condoned the acquisition of nuclear weapons by any Middle Eastern state and has universally condemned the spread of biological and chemical arms. In pursuing a policy of nonproliferation, Washington will also have to balance worries over the destabilizing effect of uncontrolled WMD spread with sensitivity to the security concerns of Middle East countries, whose leadership is increasingly convinced that weapons of mass destruction enhance security.

CONTAINING RADICAL MOVEMENTS AND FOSTERING HUMAN RIGHTS AND DEMOCRACY

The United States has a security interest in countering extremist movements—whether religious or secular—that can destabilize states that currently support U.S. goals in the region. At the same time, the United States has an interest in fostering democracy and supporting adherence to internationally accepted standards of human rights. However, the Greater Middle East has little tradition of Western-style democracy, except in India. Experiments in democracy could be short-lived, as was the case in Algeria, if elections are held before the establishment of a solid foundation of civic institutions and respect for human and minority rights.

The United States faces a delicate task in keeping these two interests—containing radicalism and supporting democracy—in balance. Pressure on friendly regimes to improve their records on human rights and to move toward democratic processes must be handled with sensitivity, lest it contribute to destabilizing fragile governments on which the United States relies. On the other hand, turning a blind eye to the domestic abuses of such governments can leave the United States open to charges of supporting repressive regimes, thereby reducing its credibility in the region.

PROMOTING STABILITY IN PERIPHERAL AREAS

The destabilization of the Caucasus republics of the former USSR could spill over into Turkey, a NATO ally. Increased Russian control over the Caucasus or Central Asia could become a point of friction between Russia and the United States, undermining a key U.S. global interest. The United States therefore has an interest in helping to defuse tensions among outside powers interested in exercising influence in these regions, and supporting the stability of the newly independent states.

KEY U.S. SECURITY POLICY ISSUES

MAINTAINING A PROACTIVE U.S. POLICY TOWARD REGIONAL PROLIFERATION

In the past, the WMD threat was not regarded by U.S. policy makers as a primary regional security concern, either in the Levant or in South Asia. Overriding Cold War global security issues took precedence, making Washington reluctant to pressure Pakistan or Israel on their nuclear programs. More recently, however, both the Bush and Clinton administrations have proposed ambitious regional nonproliferation proposals for the Greater Middle East.

The states in the region have not reacted enthusiastically to arms control initiatives. Although the use of chemical arms in the Iran-Iraq war and the fear that chemical or even nuclear arms would be used in the 1991 Gulf War refocused concern on the issue of controlling WMD, formidable obstacles remain to achieving arms control measures. They include

- Arab insistence that Israel sign the Nuclear Nonproliferation Treaty (NPT) and bring its program under the scrutiny of the International Atomic Energy Agency.

- A conventional arms race—with the United States as the main arms exporter—that discourages WMD arms control.

- Outstanding bilateral disputes that have hobbled progress on nonproliferation, such as Pakistan's insistence on the repeal of the Pressler Amendment.

The Greater Middle East does not lend itself easily to regionwide proposals, because of the distinct identities of the component subregions. Further, U.S. nonproliferation policy must be balanced against overall U.S. interests. Clearly, U.S. interests are not affected equally by Israel's and Iran's acquisition of nuclear weapons.

Another issue is whether continued reliance on global mechanisms such as the NPT is appropriate. How should Washington respond, for example, if India and Pakistan were to create a new regional nonproliferation regime? Could Washington accommodate such an initiative with its public insistence on NPT adherence, which both parties have rejected?

Finally, Washington must balance its commitment to curbing regional arms proliferation with continued support for conventional arms transfers to key Middle Eastern allies, some of which exacerbate security concerns among states that do not have such relationships with the United States.

PROVIDING RESOURCES FOR THE PEACE PROCESS

Recent successes in the Arab-Israeli peace process offer the prospect for the first time of transforming the security environment of the Middle East. In the 1970s and 1980s, the Arab-Israel front had one of the world's highest concentrations of advanced weaponry. If the peace process broadens to include a Syrian-Israeli accord and deepens with a final status agreement between Israelis and Palestinians, the Levant states are likely to move towards smaller militaries with older weapons. Furthermore, security cooperation patterns could change, as Israel ceases to be a pariah. However, even under the best of circumstances, changes will come slowly. One short-term difference, however, could be a change in Israeli attitudes towards U.S. arms sales to Arab states, as indicated by the end of Israeli objections to Jordanian purchases of weapons systems like the F-16.

In the event of an accord between Israel and Syria, the United States may be asked to provide the main component for a new multinational force on the Golan Heights in addition to the 1,200 U.N. forces now stationed there. The new force could be similar to the multilateral forces and observers now in the Sinai Peninsula, which include 1,000 U.S. soldiers. Such a force might be asked to monitor a demilitarized zone, a broader weapons control zone, or restrictions on military operations. It may also establish listening posts that provide intelligence to each side on the other's movements. The force is unlikely to be asked to enforce the peace agreement. Since both sides keep substantial armored forces nearby, the Golan would pose a difficult military challenge for any international force charged with repelling an attack.

In one important way, an Israeli-Syrian agreement is likely to differ from Camp David: there is not much prospect of U.S. security assistance to Syria. However, in the aftermath of any accord with Syria that requires redeploying forces off the Golan, Israel will want to modernize its military equipment. Further, while Israel may be more at peace with its immediate neighbors, Tel Aviv worries about dangers from more distant adversaries like Iran and Iraq. To meet such needs, Israel may therefore request additional security assistance from the United States beyond the existing $1.8 billion a year.

Any demands for more U.S. forces and more U.S. money after an Israeli-Syrian agreement could bring a reexamination of the $1.2 billion per annum in military aid Egypt now receives. Cairo will argue that a strong Egyptian force is useful for the United States in the event of instability in the Persian Gulf. Further, Egypt's domestic unrest makes this an awkward time to reduce the size of the armed forces, because of both their internal security role and the employment they provide for Egyptian youth.

RESPONDING TO RESURGENT ISLAM

The growing Islamic revival raises important questions. Is Islam's resurgence a by-product of a search for spiritual meaning by alienated publics, or is it a politically motivated attempt to remove Western influence from the region? Will such movements make room for secular influences and peaceful dissent, or do they wish to establish an all-embracing ideology and authoritarian regimes? Western analysts are divided on these issues. Some view resurgent Islam as an ideological, xenophobic challenge to the Christian West, with confrontation and conflict the inevitable outcome. Many base this view on the fact that in its most extreme form, resurgent Islam seeks to overthrow moderate regimes in the Middle East, endorses anti-Western strategies, and advocates Islamic supremacy.

The countervailing assessment is that Islamic groups are not necessarily or primarily anti-Western in orientation. Rather, much of their animosity is directed toward ineffectual governance at home. While the social practices that many Islamic groups wish to see enforced—strict dress codes for women, harsh penalties for theft, and so on—are not congruent with Western values, they do not pose a threat to Western security interests. Saudi Arabia, whose government enforces the strictest interpretation of Islamic law in the Middle East, has been a political-military partner of the United States for over half a century.

Two schools of thought have also emerged concerning appropriate strategies to deal with Islamic movements. One, led by a number of secular Middle East states such as Tunisia, Algeria, Syria, and Iraq that have been ruled by a single party or the military, sees little distinction between mainstream and militant movements, and has dealt harshly with both. In essence, such governments have drawn a line between religion and state, and refused participation by the former in the latter. Tunisia, for example, does not permit religious parties to run for election, and has thoroughly cowed a previously active Islamic movement. But Tunisia has also countered Islamic activists by vigorous, ameliorative economic and social actions. Algeria abruptly halted moves to open its political system when Islamic movements appeared on the verge of electoral victory. The result has been an isolated and discredited government struggling to gain control in an underground civil war against a number of Islamic groups.

A second school of thought advocates opening the political door to mainstream but not extremist Islamic groups. Political participation, in this view, will compel movements to become more pragmatic, and will tend to separate moderates from militants. Such an approach requires a conducive political environment and shrewd handling. Jordan, where Islamic forces received 42 percent of the vote in 1989 and three cabinet seats, has tried this strategy, thus far successfully. The Egyptian government, under enormous pressure from Islamic groups, is at a crossroads, but is wary of making Algeria's mistake of opening the system too widely and too quickly.

Policy analysts are at odds over the utility of a dialogue with Islamic movements. Algeria is on the cutting edge of this policy debate. The United States has favored a political solution and a dialogue with FIS elements that favor peaceful change. The French, on the other hand, have been more reluc-tant to talk to Islamic activists. However, the Algerian and French governments have been moving toward a more flexible position on dealing with moderates in the FIS, while still steering clear of terrorists who target foreigners.

MAINTAINING DUAL CONTAINMENT AND THE REGIONAL BALANCE OF POWER

Enunciated by the current administration, the policy of "dual containment" identifies both Iran and Iraq as hostile states and rejects the previous policy of tilting toward one to contain the other as the need arises. Instead, the United States, with help from its European allies, will strive to prevent either from achieving Gulf hegemony or attacking its neighbors. In Iraq, the policy officially demands fulfillment of all U.N. Security Council resolutions instituted after the Gulf War, which is interpreted by many as tantamount to seeking a regime replacement. The United States relies on drastic import and oil export restrictions and no-fly zones in the north and south of the country as instruments to that end. In Iran, a change of regime behavior on six key points is sought, among them cessation of terrorism, overt opposition to the peace process, and attempts to destabilize neighboring states. To this end, the United States seeks to deny credit and military technology to Iran.

Dual containment has generated debate on several grounds. Some argue that the oil export embargo on Iraq has penalized its people without producing a regime change, while measures taken to protect the Kurds in the north could result in Iraq's fragmentation. This would dramatically upset the Gulf balance of power in favor of Iran. Hence, these critics argue for less severe measures that would allow some economic recuperation and assure Iraq's territorial integrity.

Supporters of the policy point to Saddam's October 1994 military posturing on Kuwait's border as evidence of the need to continue, and perhaps to intensify, containment of the Baghdad regime. They cite success in compelling Saddam Hussein to submit to international inspection of WMD facilities and to recognize Kuwait and its borders. Moreover, his regime has been gravely weakened by rampant inflation, drastically lowered living standards, and a shrinking power base, making future Iraqi aggression less likely. The question is whether more of the same will produce his overthrow or whether his security apparatus will enable him to hold out longer than the West is willing to maintain sanctions.

In regard to Iran, some have argued that Tehran's objectionable behavior might better be modified by less restrictive economic measures that would open the country to Western influence and strengthen pragmatic elements. They favor dialogue, normalization of relations, and Iran's gradual integration into a regional security framework. However, there is not much evidence that those who determine policy in Tehran are interested in discussions with the United States or that Iran would be an acceptable regional partner until its behavior changed. Also, a nettling issue is how to prevent Iran from using increased access to credit to finance additional military expenditures. Another is the question of what instruments of deterrence against renewed aggressive behavior could be used should a more conciliatory policy fail. Advocates of the current policy point to some success in curtailing Iran's military expenditures through constraints on credit: Iran's annual military purchases have declined from $2 billion in 1989–91 to $800 million in 1993–94.

Also at issue is whether the United States will be willing to shoulder the burden of dual containment as it draws down its forces. The Gulf is already the most heavily armed region in the less developed world, and the arms race there is becoming ever more lethal and burdensome to the countries involved.

The October 1994 Gulf crisis demonstrated the growing expense of the policy to the U.S. and the Arab Gulf states. The cost of sending U.S. troops and equipment to the Gulf to compel a withdrawal of Iraqi troops from Kuwait's border may reach one billion dollars. The crisis brought home the need to contain Iraq more effectively and at lower cost. The most critical issue connected with dual containment, however, is how long it can be maintained.

In the Gulf, the United States must rely for support on the weakest Gulf element in the triad of powers—Saudi Arabia and its GCC partners. While economically well off, these states lack the manpower to defend themselves. The GCC states combined have about one-fifth of the population of Iran and Iraq and about one-fourth the men under arms.

Protection of the GCC is based on a four-tier strategy. The first tier consists of the military forces each GCC state can contribute. These forces are limited. Saudi Arabia possesses a reasonably effective air force and air defense system, but no other GCC state has indigenous air, ground, or naval assets that could do more than act as a tripwire in a military assault by Iran or Iraq. However, in the wake of the Gulf War, GCC forces are improving their equipment, training, doctrine, and joint coordination.

The second tier consists of integrated defense mechanisms constructed by the GCC that can act as a force multiplier. These are also minimal. The GCC joint force, the Peninsula Shield, consists of about ten thousand men, which may be doubled in the next few years. The GCC plans greater progress toward integrated command and control as well as joint operations; however, progress has been slow.

The third tier is U.S. and allied capacity to defend the GCC, which depends on prepositioned stocks in the region, local willingness to host such forces, and U.S. lift capacity. All have improved greatly in the wake of the Gulf War, although the U.S. military drawdown in the Europe may weaken this tier. Governments may also be less willing to host U.S. forces as domestic dissent in the Gulf rises and as local voices, including Islamic militants, demand more government accountability.

The fourth tier is the wider base of support for the United States in the Middle East, particularly from Turkey, Israel, and Egypt. These countries are important for

- Logistic support (Turkish air facilities are essential to Provide Comfort, the mission to protect the Kurds in northern Iraq).

- Intelligence, particularly of incipient terrorism and sabotage.

- The contribution of local forces to any military conflict, which is necessary to broaden the coalition and secure its regional acceptability.

- Political support.

Regional states may be less willing to support robust containment of Iraq and Iran than the United States, for example, because Iraq and Iran are still their neighbors with whom they must still do business on many bilateral issues. Turkey and Egypt are more willing to remove sanctions from Iraq than is the United States.

There has also been serious erosion of support for dual containment among European countries. Russia, France, and Italy are clearly preparing to do business with Baghdad after sanctions and are anxious to see the export restrictions lifted once Iraq has fulfilled the provisions of U.N. Security Council resolution 687 concerning WMD and Kuwait. However, they are prepared to support limitations on Iraq's rearmament. Many states have not agreed to the credit restrictions the United States would like to see imposed on Iran. In 1994, seventeen states agreed to $9 billion of debt rescheduling for Iran.

Iraq's threat to Kuwait in October 1994 highlighted these uncertainties, revealing fissures in the international coalition and differences on how to deal with Iraq. These vulnerabilities will make it a challenge for the United States to be able to continue the strict containment measures now applied to Iran and Iraq through the next two to five years.

SEEKING STABILITY IN SOUTH ASIA

India and Pakistan, both de facto nuclear weapons states, have been unable to resolve territorial disputes—or even to sustain a negotiating process—on issues that have created strong nationalist feelings in both countries. For example, there seems little prospect that the issue of Kashmir can be settled to the satisfaction of both sides. Escalation of the Kashmir crisis has, in turn, poisoned the environment for progress in discussions between New Delhi and Islamabad on controlling the spread of WMD. Ironically, this inability to improve their external relationship comes at a time when both countries are enjoying improved prospects for economic growth and political stability at home.

The U.S. relationship with both nations is at a crossroads. India is eager to rehabilitate its bilateral ties with the United States, which deteriorated during the Cold War. Pakistan is anxious to improve its security links with the United States, but its efforts are frustrated by Washington's overriding concern with Islamabad's nuclear program. The Pressler Amendment has brought to a halt nearly all U.S. assistance to Pakistan, yet the government of Benazir Bhutto believes that its security dependence on the United States is likely to increase.

A key policy question for Washington is whether India and Pakistan can be persuaded that the *perception* of nuclear capability—acknowledged possession of fissile material, a scientific infrastructure, technical proficiency, and means of delivery—is a sufficient deterrent against attack and that actually arming is unnecessary and destabilizing.

Virtually all Indo-Pakistani disputes are affected to some degree by the nuclear question, which has in turn inflamed tensions between New Delhi and Islamabad and increased the cost of precipitous political action. Further, the state of bilateral relations between the United States and these two states depends to a large degree on reaching a settlement of the regional nuclear issue.

CHAPTER 19

THE CHANGING NATURE OF WARFARE

THE MILITARY TECHNICAL REVOLUTION

MICHAEL J. MAZARR
With JEFFREY SHAFFER AND BENJAMIN EDERINGTON

The military technical revolution has the potential fundamentally to reshape the nature of warfare. Basic principles of strategy since the time of Machiavelli— the confusion and chance inherent in military operations, the concentration of forces to achieve a decisive victory at a critical location—may lose their relevance in the face of emerging technologies and doctrines.

MILITARY OPERATIONS FOR THE FUTURE

Figure 1 summarizes the kinds of military operations that are likely to occur and for which we must begin planning today. Within each type of operation, a host of specific tasks or missions could be conducted, ranging from air interdiction to amphibious assaults to civil affairs to air traffic control. Any specific crisis might require a combination of one or more of these operations, either simultaneously or in phases, and each operation would need to be backed up by a number of supporting functions, such as strategic lift or space communications.

As the figure suggests, these operations can be reduced to two basic types. Combined-arms operations involve those missions for which modern technologies and doctrines were developed—large-scale, mechanized warfare of the sort that was expected in Western Europe and that, to a degree, was fought in Desert Storm. But most common, both today and in the future, is the second type of military operation— a response to tensions or outright conflicts involving irregular, infantry-based forces. Such crises, which exist today in Bosnia, Somalia, Angola, Cambodia, and a dozen other countries around the world, may demand a U.S. response.

One topic of this discussion is the best role for military technical revolution (MTR) technologies and doctrines in these types of military operations. In larger-scale, combined-arms warfare, there is little doubt that the MTR has a role to play. For irregular operations, the initial question is whether the MTR can make a significant contribution and, if so, what it is; a subsidiary issue is the extent to which military operations here can be considered a "lesser-included case" of more major war.

These two types of military operations are also helpful in emphasizing the seamless transition required between combat and operations short of war. Strong connections exist between forward presence and regional contingency operations, on the one hand, and peacekeeping and peace enforcement, on the other. In both cases, while engaging in the mission short of war (forward presence or peacekeeping), U.S. forces must be ready to move into combat operations (regional war or peace enforcement) rapidly and effectively.

SETTING PRIORITIES

U.S. military planners cannot give equal emphasis to all possible contingencies. They possess neither the resources nor the force structure to build comprehensive capabilities for reconstitution, regional conflict, peacekeeping, and forward presence all at once. U.S. defense policy has always attempted to make some prioritization of potential missions (Figure 2). This is, then, the first major issue approached by this study: Of the types of military operations cited above, which should dominate U.S. military planning?

A close analysis of the nature of various contingencies faced by U.S. forces and the U.S. interests at stake in them suggests that *U.S. military forces ought to be designed and their development prioritized with primary emphasis on regional conflicts*, with a corresponding effort to make MTR technologies more relevant to irregular operations.

This is true for several reasons. First, our examination of deterrent and forward presence missions uniformly suggests that those capabilities best suited to *winning* a conflict are also best at *deterring* it. In short, what wins deters; forces that can convince a potential aggressor that it might lose a conflict do the best job of encouraging that aggressor not to go to war, provided that the state believes that the United States is able and willing to act. MTR technologies are uniquely designed to convey the impression of a U.S. willingness and ability to engage in such conflicts because they hold a promise that the United States can win—at relatively lower cost, with somewhat less collateral damage, and with a greater de-

This essay has been edited and is reprinted from The Military-Technical Revolution: A Structural Framework *(Washington, D.C.: Center for Strategic and International Studies, March 1993), 15–28, by permission of the Center for Strategic and International Studies.*

Figure 1
Future Military Operations: A Typology

COMBINED-ARMS OPERATIONS (traditional, large-scale, mechanized operations)

RECONSTITUTION
If Russia becomes hostile once again and poses a threat to Western Europe, the United States is currently bound by treaty to respond. This task encompasses homeland defense, to the degree that it is a relevant or necessary task today. Unlike other contingencies, it would require a large-scale buildup of U.S. forces and the preparation for a war of truly global potential.

REGIONAL CONFLICT
If North Korea strikes south, the United States is committed to provide at least some level of assistance in the context of an international effort. If Iraq attacks Kuwait again, the world coalition will undoubtedly respond once more. If a Libyan/Algerian coalition threatens sea-lanes in the Mediterranean, NATO and the world will use force to ensure safe transit. Some of these conflicts might not draw the United States in directly but would call for U.S. resupply of one or more participants or for a concerted effort at conflict limitation.

FORWARD PRESENCE AND DETERRENCE
For some years to come, the United States will remain involved in political alliances that require forward deployment of troops, or visits and exercises by mobile U.S. forces, to signal a commitment. Regional crises could also create the sudden, unexpected need for deterrent signals displaying credible capabilities with combined arms.

IRREGULAR OPERATIONS (infantry-based operations employing unconventional forces and primarily low-technology weapons)

PEACE ENFORCEMENT
Various shades of tasks more demanding than peacekeeping can be imagined. The Somalian deployment would fit in this category, as would outright counterinsurgency operations in, for example, Peru. Drug enforcement operations also fall under this category, as would limited precision strikes in support of "counterproliferation."

PEACEKEEPING AND HUMANITARIAN RELIEF
This is already under way in a host of countries and regions, from Cambodia to the Middle East to Angola. It includes the operations short of war in the irregular category.

---

gree of strategic flexibility. Deterrent missions are, in this sense, a lesser-included case of war-fighting missions; if U.S. forces are designed to win regional wars, they will also be designed to deter them. Yet, historically, conventional deterrence generally does not work very well. Differing national perceptions, the subjective nature of rationality and decision making, the difficulty in extending and communicating deterrent signals, and a host of other factors make deterrence one of the most difficult challenges in foreign policy. Nonetheless, to the extent that it can be successful, deterrence can best be accomplished with U.S. military forces designed to win the conflict whose outbreak the United States is attempting to prevent.

Second, the maintenance of a military capable of winning large-scale regional conflicts is the best way to keep alive the core of a military capable of responding to a revived global threat. A professional, highly trained military with the human and industrial capital necessary to remain ready for regional wars will be better able to gear up for a larger conflict than a military designed to fight lower-intensity wars. This may still be far from sufficient to fulfill the

reconstitution mission. But one thing is clear: so long as a careful defense industrial policy is developed to complement regular military planning, preparing for regional conflict would do a better job of preserving the foundations of reconstitution than any other affordable military policy.

Third, the United States will certainly be involved in conflicts of lesser intensity—peacekeeping, peace enforcement, and the like, which we term "irregular operations." However, large portions of the U.S. military should not be tailored specifically for such conflicts. For one thing, they usually pose a far less significant threat to U.S. interests than do regional conflicts. An Iranian or Iraqi attack on Persian Gulf oil fields, or even a North Korean strike south, would endanger fundamental U.S. and world interests and place U.S. prestige firmly on the line. Unless the United States itself chooses otherwise and invests some irregular operation with vast symbolic importance, as we did for a time in Vietnam, few lesser-intensity conflicts will claim such standing.

Another factor recommending against designing military forces exclusively for irregular operations is

Figure 2
Priorities in Military Missions

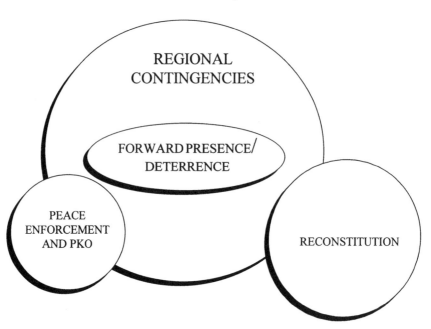

REGIONAL
CONTINGENCIES

FORWARD PRESENCE/
DETERRENCE

PEACE
ENFORCEMENT
AND PKO

RECONSTITUTION

that of flexibility. Forces designed for combined-arms operations have some relevance for irregular operations; the reverse is not the case. As in Somalia, troops trained for large-scale, mechanized warfare can perform low-intensity missions with some degree of success. The same would not be true of peacekeeping troops thrust into a major regional contingency.

Nonetheless, in the years ahead the U.S. military may operate in far more irregular than combined-arms environments, and it therefore makes sense to build as much irregular capability into future weapons and forces as possible. This is especially true because if the MTR succeeds, potential adversaries, aware that they cannot win at the combined-arms level, may resort to more insidious irregular operations to frustrate U.S. aims. The goal will be to modify MTR technologies, doctrines, and force structures in ways that do not detract from their combined-arms war-fighting and deterrent missions but that add greatly to their capabilities in irregular operations. A prominent example is special-operations forces, which can perform a wide variety of missions in lesser-intensity warfare. In a broader sense, however, little research exists on how this might be done. Clearly more work is needed on how to make MTR capabilities more relevant to irregular operations.

CRITERIA FOR MILITARY FORCES

Political and economic constraints will require U.S. leaders to conduct their wars in a particular fashion, with new and sometimes very stringent rules

of engagement. The criteria spelled out below will be used as a yardstick of sorts for measuring the effectiveness of the military forces.

- *Construct a force out of much lower budgets—as low as $220 billion (in 1993 dollars) by 1997.* This condition has two elements. One deals with force structure: U.S. planners must assume that they will possess no more, and possibly less, than the force levels envisioned by former Secretary of Defense Les Aspin in papers he released before the November 1992 election (in the range of fifteen active and reserve army divisions, twelve navy aircraft carriers, and eighteen active and reserve air force wings). The second element concerns procurement: current and prospective defense budgets will not support significant purchases of big-ticket weapons systems.

- *Fight in a nuclear, chemical, and biological (NBC) world.* Given the risks of NBC proliferation, U.S. forces should have a capability for avoidance, defense, and active suppression of such weapons—if possible, conventional arms. This requirement is not new, but it will become increasingly relevant in the coming years.

- *Tend to the U.S. image.* In general, future military operations will demand an emphasis on low U.S. and allied casualties and low collateral damage in the target country. When the U.S. interests at stake in a crisis or war are less than obvious to the public, the promise of a less destructive operation will allow U.S.

leaders to wield their military instrument more effectively.

This will not require that the United States suffer no casualties or that it cause no collateral damage. This criterion, like the criteria that follow, will vary in relevance or importance given the nature of the conflict and the U.S. interests at stake. Nonetheless, even in major regional engagements and certainly in peacekeeping or other unconventional missions, the American and world publics will expect relatively clean operations, cheap in terms of U.S. lives lost—especially to friendly fire, given the bad publicity it generates—and the damage done to the local society.

The doctrine of overwhelming force, as articulated by Chairman of the Joint Chiefs of Staff Colin Powell during and after the Persian Gulf War, is another way of accomplishing this goal. By putting into place forces with the capability of rapidly and decisively defeating the enemy, U.S. leaders can minimize U.S. casualties, collateral damage, and the length of public commitment required to prosecute the war.

- *Fight a "CNN" war.* U.S. forces must be capable of responding to media demands for instantaneous information, and of using the rapid transmission of data to its advantage. This magnifies the importance of tending to image considerations, the first criterion, especially in terms of the friendly fire problem. But it also suggests the need for greater information dominance and for some thought about how modern, real-time news reporting can be used to U.S. advantage in future military operations.

- *Shape multilateral operations.* Because nearly all military operations will be coalition enterprises, the United States must determine its best contribution to coalition warfare or multilateral operations short of war and must design its military forces with this task in mind. U.S. leaders must determine what capabilities they will contribute to international operations, and what sort of influence in the operation they hope to gain by their participation. An important element of this criterion is for the United States to build competence among potential coalition partners.

- *Conduct overseas presence with far fewer overseas bases.* As the U.S. foreign basing structure declines, overseas presence missions must become more self-sustaining. To do so, they will need to rely on innovative forms of strategic mobility (such as the use of prepositioned equipment and supplies) and on regular visits by air or naval forces or on rapid deployment forces.

- *Maintain readiness.* A major priority for the U.S. military establishment in the years ahead will be to avoid the typical result of the end of a war: the slashing of military readiness, training, education, and the like, which produces a large but "hollow" force of low morale and effectiveness. This mandates that operations and maintenance budgets not be cut or diluted by missions unrelated to readiness, investment in new training technologies, and a reconsideration of the role of the National Guard and Reserve in contingency operations.

- *Preserve some level of defense industrial base.* Vigorous debates are under way about the degree to which the United States must preserve a defense industrial base and the best ways of doing so. Nonetheless, the basic task remains valid. U.S. leaders have always demanded, and even in an interdependent world will continue to demand, the ability to produce certain especially critical defense products indigenously. This requirement will affect debates about weapons and force structure; in analyses of U.S. attack submarine requirements, for example, the impact of competing plans on U.S. shipbuilding industries has weighed heavily.

The preceding analysis has established the general context for U.S. military planning in the years ahead, the period in which MTR doctrines, technologies, and force structures will be debated and acquired. It will be a challenging period, full of new headaches and unconventional operations, one that does not offer an immediate threat to justify military budgets and provide a focus for military planning. This uncertainty will greatly exacerbate the problem of choosing among competing technologies and weapons systems. With so many missions to be considered, many of them new or at least still unfamiliar, no choices will be easy.

THE MTR CONCEPT

Revolutions in military affairs are not a new phenomenon. Throughout history, advances in technology and strategy have revolutionized the way wars are fought. Each revolution, however, is different. Some favor the offense, some the defense; some stem from the introduction of a new weapon, others from a novel idea about how wars can be fought.

Our first task, therefore, is to define and understand the current revolution in military affairs. This section lays out the rationale for and the constituent elements of today's MTR; it discusses the theories, capabilities, technologies, and doctrines that hold the potential to change completely the way wars are fought.

Our presumption is that, in the time frame of this report (the next fifteen years), only the United States has the capability to achieve the MTR. Other states may acquire pieces of the whole—precision weapons, for example, or innovative force structures—but only the U.S. military will be able to integrate all the elements of the MTR into a cohesive whole. The question of what specific aspects of it other nations might obtain, when they might do so, and what implications that would hold for U.S. forces is an important one.

This assumption adds urgency to possibly the most basic question about the MTR: why the United States needs such capabilities at all. Unlike many past military efforts, the MTR cannot be justified on an assessment of the threats to the United States and its interests. With the collapse of the Soviet Union and the concert of interests among major powers, this is a largely threatless moment globally, yet a highly unstable and dangerous world at the regional level. Existing U.S. forces can deal with those nations and trends that currently endanger U.S. interests; they did so, for example, in the Persian Gulf War.

The case for the MTR will not, therefore, rest as much on needs as on comparative advantages. Three stand out. First, the MTR will increase the combat effectiveness of U.S. forces, dramatically increasing the speed and decisiveness with which they can win conflicts or conduct operations short of war. If such capabilities can be obtained with current and prospective defense budgets, then it certainly makes sense to develop them. Second, the MTR helps hedge against the rise of a new global threat, representing a capability, a way of conducting war, that no challenger will be able to match in the foreseeable future. And third, MTR technologies will help U.S. defense planners deal with the constraints, both budgetary and political, on military policy in the years ahead. The MTR allows militaries to do more with less, and to conduct military operations at less cost.

What Is Revolutionary

Before considering the elements of the MTR, it is necessary to decide what is truly revolutionary in a military sense. Do the advances offered by new technologies and doctrines warrant the term? What is the difference between a revolutionary advance and one that is merely evolutionary?

To some degree this distinction is a semantic one. If a given set of technologies and doctrines provides an enormous military advantage, then in one sense it hardly matters what terms one uses to describe them. The capabilities will convey a great military advantage and are therefore desirable. Nonetheless, for our purposes it will still be helpful to have some specific notion of how a revolutionary advance might be defined. Such a definition would facilitate the choices by pointing toward some technologies, doctrines, and force structures that are revolutionary, whereas others are merely evolutionary or incremental in capability.

Various advances in military technology or doctrine are commonly understood to be revolutionary. The invention of gunpowder or nuclear weapons, the advent of mechanization, and other developments completely reshaped the nature of warfare. At certain times, new capabilities have made offensive warfare, on either a strategic or tactical scale, nearly impossible because of the costs involved; other shifts in military thought have helped render the battlefield fluid again. Sometimes revolutions counteract each other; often technology and doctrine pull in different directions.

Throughout history, revolutions in military affairs have generally shared several aspects in common, and it is those commonalities that point us to the central nature of an MTR. In one sense, an MTR can be defined as *a fundamental advance in technology, doctrine, or organization that renders existing methods of conducting warfare obsolete.* Advances in firepower made uncovered infantry operations much less effective; mechanized warfare did the same for nonmotorized infantry warfare. Guerrilla warfare rendered many conventional tactics ineffective for a particular class of wars.

An advance is also revolutionary when it *exercises a critical effect on some fundamental aspect of strategy.* If we think of classical military strategy as the fundamental concept found in Napoleon, Clausewitz, Jomini, Mahan, and dozens of others—that victory comes from concentration of one's forces at a critical point to win a decisive battle—then past military revolutions modified that strategy in basic ways. The new firepower characteristic of World War I transferred the advantage in concentration of force to the defense, rendering large-scale offensives extremely difficult and costly. World War II's mechanized warfare made maneuver, concentration, and a decisive battle possible once again, an effect later dissipated by the nuclear revolution and guerrilla warfare.

Finally, *a true revolution in military affairs is achieved by a combination of technology, organization, and doctrine.* One without the other more often constitutes an evolution. It was only when mechanized forces were combined with appropriate doctrines and force structures, for example, that their revolutionary aspects became apparent.

This brief survey of terms points beyond arguments about whether new technologies, doctrines, and organizations *currently* represent an evolutionary or a revolutionary step. By the criteria outlined above, advanced technologies and innovations in doctrine and organization clearly have the *potential* to revolutionize warfare. Like all dramatic advances in the implements and theories of war, however, the MTR also holds the potential to be squandered, to be so disrupted by pork barrel politics, interservice squabbling, and poor Department of Defense (DOD) decisions that its full effects never become evident. New technologies and doctrines offer exciting opportunities, but there are also persistent challenges to their implementation.

Elements of the MTR

The various technologies, doctrines, and force structures that collectively are known as the MTR

Figure 3
Elements of the MTR

INTEGRATING FRAMEWORK

Doctrine

Organization

ENABLING CAPABILITIES

Information dominance

Command and control

Simulation and training

Agility

EXECUTING CAPABILITIES (STRIKE SYSTEMS)

Smart weapons

Major platforms

Exotic weapons

have several key elements. As we will see below, it is the combination of these various elements that is particularly effective, and in this sense the MTR is an integrative process rather than a divisible set of weapons systems and ideas. Nonetheless, it is possible to lay out the individual aspects of the MTR. The elements, displayed in Figure 3, are divided into three broad categories: integrating frameworks, enabling capabilities, and executing capabilities.

Significantly, *each element includes both offensive and defensive aspects.* It is nearly as important to understand an opponent's doctrine, for example, as it is to develop one's own. It may be even more useful to deny an enemy the effective use of information than to guarantee it for one's own forces. And although smart weapons can aid U.S. forces, defending against an enemy's missiles and warheads, with active or passive measures, is a crucial task.

Critical to each of the categories listed below will be the quality of military personnel. More than ever before in peacetime, the United States will need a well-educated, highly motivated military capable of understanding the concepts of the MTR and motivated enough to put them into practice. Personnel policies are needed that offer sufficient benefits, challenges, and opportunities to attract the quality of personnel necessary.

At the level of ideas, of integrating theories and structures, the framework of the MTR has two critical components. One is *doctrine.* The new capabilities and technologies characteristic of the MTR must be employed in a fashion that maximizes their advantages. To do so, to match means against military ends effectively, requires a sound doctrine. Past revolutions have witnessed doctrinal as well as technological advances: for example, in World War II the new fleets of armored and motorized vehicles were em-

ployed in mechanized blitzkrieg warfare; the expansion of guerrilla wars required new doctrines for counterinsurgency operations; and the nuclear revolution gave rise to a whole new field of doctrine—nuclear strategy.

In an ideal world, doctrine would be developed first and inform all other decisions, dictating what kinds of military forces need to be deployed and what equipment they require. Of course, the process is interactive; only by knowing what technologies will be available, both now and in the future, can the authors of doctrine know what their forces might be capable of and devise tactics to take advantage of those capabilities.

It may be too early to tell exactly what operational concepts will characterize this MTR. Even flexible, deep-strike notions such as AirLand Battle and Follow-On Forces Attack may give way to much more radical ways of approaching warfare. The traditionally sharp distinction between battles and wars, between tactical and strategic operations, is becoming blurred, with military doctrines relying on simultaneous attacks across an entire enemy nation to paralyze its military efforts.

The other aspect of the MTR's framework is *organization.* The structure of all defense-related organizations, from combat units to DOD offices, must evolve in ways supportive of MTR technologies and doctrines. From an operational standpoint, organizational issues show up most clearly in force structure. It could be, for example, that the sorts of ground units best suited to implement the MTR are small, independent, all-arms combat teams using stealthy vehicles and precision munitions. Naval forces might make increasing use of stealth, both by making surface ships smaller and harder to find and by using submarines for a broader range of missions. The air force might extend the mix of aircraft down to the squadron level. Or the military as a whole might adopt much more radical force structures than those, combining ships, aircraft, and ground units into innovative packages. Within the Department of Defense, much must change as well. The current acquisition, strategy, and doctrine systems fragment MTR capabilities into anachronistic understandings of mission areas.

Falling within the broad category of enabling capabilities is the third element of the MTR, *information dominance.* This element includes such technologies as high-tech sensors, radar, high-resolution photography, motion detectors, thermal and infrared detectors, and night vision equipment. In the future, such sensors might become much more powerful and pervasive, creating a vast array of information constantly flowing back to real-time intelligence fusion centers. Working as an integrated network, these sensors provide an unprecedented amount of information about the battlefield. Once the information is gathered, it must be coordinated and disseminated, a task that calls for tough, lightweight computers and software linked into an integrated network.

Denying information to the enemy can be just as important as acquiring it. If opposing forces are deprived of nearly all important information about the war, their operations will be confused and ineffective, much as happened to Iraqi units in the Persian Gulf War. Information denial can be done passively, through the use of stealth, concealment, and hard-to-detect electronic signals, or it can be done more thoroughly through active means: the use of electronic warfare to jam enemy communications, employing smart weapons that home on enemy radars or radios, concentrating early attacks on enemy command and communications nodes (as in the Gulf War), and, more radically, using such advanced techniques as electromagnetic pulse weapons to wreck the enemy's electronic systems and computer viruses to incapacitate its software.

Once the enemy has been located and U.S. commanders have made decisions about their moves, the next step is to orchestrate the response of U.S. forces. This requires effective use of the fourth element of the MTR: *command and control.* Using advanced computers, communication networks, radios, and other technologies linked together into coherent command-and-control grids, the modern joint commander can be in constant and instant contact with every subordinate element of the force. Certain surveillance systems, such as AEGIS radar ships and aircraft such as the joint surveillance target attack radar system (JSTARS) and the airborne warning and control system (AWACS), also perform command-and-control functions, serving as battle management platforms for theater commanders. There is also an important denial aspect to command and control, achieved by many of the same technologies.

The fifth element of the MTR, *simulation and training,* works to match the human abilities of the process with its technological capabilities. High-technology simulation systems are producing a revolution in training even as MTR systems are creating a revolution on the battlefield. Modern computers can re-create a firefight, battle, or theater of operations in simulation laboratories, allowing troops to understand the concepts and flow of modern war without actually experiencing it. In this sense, along with doctrine, simulation and training provide soldiers with a *vision* of and confidence in what they will be attempting to accomplish on the battlefield.

But simulation technologies can do much more than prepare troops for war. They can save money by reducing the need for huge exercises or live-fire drills. They can provide a realistic test bed for new doctrines and organizations, a means of playing one idea against another and slowly winnowing away the ineffective ones *before* a war begins rather than after. And, perhaps most dramatic of all, simulators will eventually allow the military to test new weapons before they are deployed or even built.

The sixth element, *agility,* includes those capabilities, systems, and technologies designed to get a force into the field and sustain it there, tasks traditionally known as mobility and sustainment. It comprises things that can make those tasks easier—smaller and more reliable vehicles, directed-energy weapons that do not rely on ammunition, and so on—as well as the platforms (sealift ships or transport aircraft) that actually do the job.

The seventh element of the MTR, and of itself the broad category of executing capabilities, is *strike systems.* This element or category encompasses any weapon or class of weapons designed to reach out to the enemy and do some harm. It consists of three primary subcategories: smart weapons, major platforms, and exotic weapons.

Smart weapons include a host of guided, precision, and self-activated weapons that range from missiles (the guided Tomahawk, Hellfire and Maverick, the army's tactical missile system [ATACMS] and multiple-launch rocket system [MLRS] and the navy and air force's advanced cruise missiles) to individual warheads (the Copperhead guided artillery shell, laser-guided bombs, cluster munitions, and others) to smart antiarmor mines. This subcategory also encompasses an ability to defend against enemy smart weapons. The proliferation of cruise and tactical ballistic missiles, from small battlefield versions to large, long-range systems, magnifies the importance of new missile defenses. These might increasingly employ a new generation of systems, such as lasers and hypervelocity missiles. Finally, here too we find an element of denial; advances in smart weapons should allow U.S. and allied forces to deny the use of the air and sea to enemy forces.

The second component of MTR strike systems is major military platforms. New and advanced planes, ships, tanks, and other combat platforms are changing the way wars are fought. Stealth will play a major role in all these systems: already stealthy aircraft such as the F-117 fighter have proven stunningly effective, and the day of stealthy ships and ground vehicles is not far off. Major combat systems will benefit from a host of other technological advances in the years ahead, ranging from more reliable, smaller, lighter engines to light yet strong armor plating. It is important to remember as well that smart weapons are useless unless they can get to the target: one of the factors limiting the use of precision weapons in the Persian Gulf War was a shortage of platforms with the requisite electronics and designator systems to use them. Upgrade to major platforms should focus in this area.

Increasingly, MTR strike systems can encompass a third category—exotic weapons. Nonlethal technologies, such as warheads designed to cause temporary blindness or disorientation, can help render an opponent unable to fight without actually killing its soldiers. Space-age weapons, such as laser beams and directed energy weapons, might revolutionize the way in which firepower is delivered on the battlefield.

A Holistic Approach

Each element of the MTR is important, and any one alone would have a significant impact on warfare. Stealthy F-117 fighters, for example, played a major role in the Persian Gulf War, as did JSTARS surveillance aircraft and precision warheads. What is special about the next generation of technologies, however, and what might render it an MTR, is the way in which those technologies work together, the synergistic or holistic effect of the range of MTR technologies operating alongside more traditional conventional weapons. It is the *combination* of unprecedented advances in information dominance, command and control, major military systems, smart weapons, well-trained and motivated personnel, and effective organizations and doctrines, all working together across service lines, that makes the coming era in crisis management and warfare potentially so different from the past.

The military technical revolution calls for a complete rethinking of the ways in which wars are divided into various, discrete mission components and parsed out among various services, branches, and weapons systems. The MTR is about integration, synergy, and flexibility. All of this, of course, runs against service parochialism; it recommends an increasingly joint force—and a force whose jointness extends lower in the chain of command than ever before, which can avoid artificially joint operations even as it pursues a useful coordination of service efforts. This is not to suggest that the four services should be merged, only that they must work together more closely and effectively than ever before to bring the MTR to fruition.

Stealthy aircraft, for example, would lose much of their effectiveness if they did not have precision weapons to deliver when they reached their targets. Even with precision weapons, if they were not adequately targeted before their missions and controlled during them, the same aircraft would be only marginally more effective than existing ones. Without motivated, talented pilots, those aircraft would be useless. Only these various capabilities working together will have a truly revolutionary effect.

This is especially true of the interplay between technology, doctrine, and organization. Without a coherent joint doctrine to guide their employment and an effective organization to focus their effects on the battlefield, even the most advanced technologies will not reach their full potential. Before any technologies are integrated with one another, trends in doctrine, organization, and technology must be examined and reconciled. In a sense, decisions on doctrine therefore become a precondition and guidance for integrating the research and development of new technologies.

To a great extent, therefore, the use of traditional mission areas as an analytic tool is counterproductive to the MTR. It encourages thought in precisely the kind of reductive categories and boxes that the MTR is designed to overcome. We must think of the MTR in terms of the broad capabilities we wish to acquire, rather than in terms of specific missions such as close air support or amphibious assaults. It could be that the MTR could achieve the same goals as those missions without using the same weapons.

Put another way, what the MTR is truly after is the unraveling of specific systems and technologies from past constraints of their organizational context, and their recombination into a more coherent and mutually supportive whole. Today U.S. military doctrine prescribes the use of various technologies in ways that may not respond to the evolution of technology or the unique abilities of those particular systems. A full application of the ideas of the MTR would involve taking those cutting-edge technologies and reshaping them into new kinds of forces. The goal is flexible, all-arms task forces that represent the seamless combination and application of all elements of the MTR. Such forces may look very different from traditional armored or mechanized divisions or brigades, naval task forces, or air wings.

Operational Implications

If the full potential of MTR technologies and doctrines is realized, the implications for warfare will be profound. Such a change could justifiably—although not indisputably—be termed revolutionary. This section summarizes a few of the MTR's most profound implications for combat.

It is important to recognize at the outset that many aspects of war will not change even if the MTR occurs. Most of the determinants of success in war, from courage and willpower to small-unit initiative and cool decision making under fire, have little if anything to do with technology. War is at base a human affair, not a technological or scientific phenomenon; its human aspects will always predominate. High-quality military personnel are therefore the bedrock of all military activity. Nonetheless, the technologies, doctrines, and organizations of the MTR will exercise an important effect on the conduct of war; together they can help U.S. and allied forces maximize the performance of their troops while destroying the effectiveness and morale of enemy forces.

In the most basic sense, the MTR will partly *lift the fog of battle* that has bedeviled military operations since the beginning of organized warfare. It is the uncertainty, the lack of clear information about the enemy and one's own forces, that hinders the effectiveness of military operations. In many ways it is the fundamental fact of war, that introduces a major element of chance and risk into the enterprise.

MTR technologies will allow greater progress than ever before in giving a commander accurate, real-time information about the battlefield and the command and control architecture to act on that information (Figure 4). It is possible that modern sensors may someday provide a detailed picture of a theater, down to the location of individual tanks and squads of soldiers. Information-processing centers will gather this vast amount of information, synthesize it, and display it in a useful fashion. And fully integrated, joint, real-time command and control technologies will enable the commander to respond to the ebb and flow of a battle on a moment-to-moment basis.

The potential comparison with previous wars is stark. In the nineteenth century, messages to distant

Figure 4
Progress of the MTR

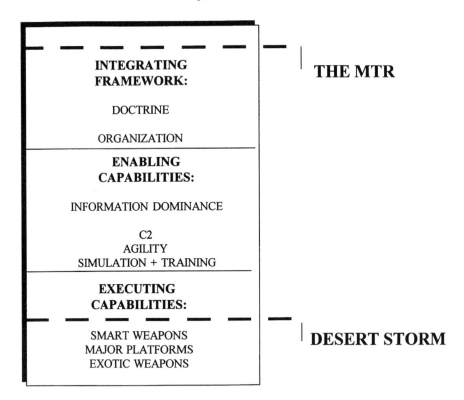

INTEGRATING
FRAMEWORK:

DOCTRINE

ORGANIZATION

ENABLING
CAPABILITIES:

INFORMATION DOMINANCE

C2
AGILITY
SIMULATION + TRAINING

EXECUTING
CAPABILITIES:

SMART WEAPONS
MAJOR PLATFORMS
EXOTIC WEAPONS

THE MTR

DESERT STORM

military units had to be carried across the sea by sailing ships. Commanders had little reliable information about the enemy, and once they did get information and decided to act, their command-and-control systems were slow and ponderous. In World War II, the connection between surveillance of the enemy, information synthesis and analysis, ordering a friendly unit into action, and the engagement of the enemy was a tenuous one; often it would take hours or days for the full chain to be complete, and even then mistakes were common. As late as the Persian Gulf War, U.S. intelligence about the number and location of Iraqi troops in the Kuwaiti theater was far from perfect, damage assessment was a slow process involving as much art as science, and coalition units occasionally found themselves misplaced on a confused battlefield.

By reducing the surveillance-synthesis-assessment-command-strike loop to a matter of minutes, the MTR has the potential to create a reliable process for managing—and, more than that, for controlling—a battle from one moment to the next. This is not to say that systems will not fail, command centers will not be destroyed, or mistakes will not be made—the friction of war will persist. Any human endeavor will be imperfect, and in the end the MTR represents merely a further step in a long-standing trend of improved surveillance and command and control. But that step is a gigantic one, which many military

experts view as revolutionary. It will render old ways of conducting battles obsolete; forces with the ability to manage a battle with such a degree of detail and speed will overwhelm adversaries without such a capability. A hint of this effect was present in the Persian Gulf War.

Given these facts, it is apparent that enemy countermeasures that threatened the sanctity of this information loop would be of deadly importance to U.S. forces. Electronic warfare, missiles designed to bring down flying command posts, special forces targeted against command centers or communications down-link stations, and perhaps especially antisatellite weapons could, together or individually, blind U.S. forces and ruin the effects of the MTR. Careful attention must be given to defeating such countermeasures and if that fails, to dealing with their effects. The MTR information loop, for example, should never depend on single, vulnerable sites for data collection or relay; enough redundancy must exist to guard against single-site failure.

A related but distinct aspect of the MTR is its implications for another fundamental tenet of military strategy: the notion of *concentration of force*. The MTR will allow firepower to be concentrated without the gathering of military forces themselves and indeed may make such concentrations dangerous. Long-range strike systems, ranging from fighter-bombers to tactical missiles, when combined with the sort of surveillance and command systems discussed above, will allow a commander to orchestrate near-instantaneous fire down on every important target on the battlefield. The strike systems themselves can be widely dispersed—aircraft at distant air bases or on aircraft carriers at sea, ATACMS and MLRS missile launchers sprinkled around the battlefield in small detachments, attack submarines loitering offshore firing sea-launched cruise missiles. When an enemy tank unit or command center is located, the combination of a real-time sensing and command network and the great precision of the MTR weapons will give a U.S. commander the ability to call down a rapid strike without ever having to concentrate friendly military units opposite the enemy unit.

As the MTR improves the military information loop and allows flexibility in the concentration of military effect without massing forces, it will strikingly accelerate the *tempo of war*. The pace of military operations will increase to an unprecedented degree, placing great stress on information and command and carrying major implications for other aspects of military policy. An accelerated tempo of operations will compress warning time and require much more rapid decision making. It will affect deterrence: forces capable of reacting more rapidly will be able to send more effective deterrent signals. And at some point, the frightening speed of MTR operations might increase the pressures for the conventional equivalent of a nuclear launch-on-warning policy in crises.

Technologies and doctrines representative of the MTR will also have a profound effect on *the balance between destructiveness and lethality*. The trend in warfare over at least the last two hundred years has been dominated by the increasing destructiveness of warfare and weapons. Greater lethality was achieved through the application of overwhelming firepower. This trend began in the Napoleonic war, intensified through the Civil War and World War I and II, and culminated in the development and use of nuclear weapons. The advent of precision weapons represents a break in this trend as it allows greater degrees of lethality to be achieved without corresponding increases in destructiveness, both as collateral damage to civilians and as the requirement to annihilate an enemy's forces in detail. This fact carries dramatic implications for the use of force as an instrument of a U.S. foreign policy.

If the MTR offers dramatic advances in the operational conduct of battles, it may have an even greater impact on the *definition of a theater of war*. For centuries, battlefields have been neatly divided into front lines of contact (the tactical arena), the battle zone (operational), and rear areas (strategic). Service responsibilities have largely been divided on the basis of the definition of these zones. Since the advent of mechanization and air forces, the tactical and operational spheres have been steadily expanding. These lines have now been blurred to such a degree that the distinction has become largely academic.

The same MTR information and strike systems that can so effectively and precisely destroy tanks can also be used to pinpoint attacks on the enemy's infrastructure. By striking throughout enemy territory in the initial stages of the war and attacking modern communications nodes, power sources, and the other building blocks of a technological society, MTR systems could thrust the enemy into darkness and, by delivering a devastating shock to the enemy nation, bring all significant military operations to a sudden halt.

Coalition attacks in the Persian Gulf War represented the first true test of such a strategy. It worked surprisingly well, in part because of Iraq's somewhat rudimentary social infrastructure; against a fully developed country, many more attacks would be required and the effect might be less complete. Moreover, the debate between proponents of close and deep MTR battles—between those who would concentrate attacks on the enemy's military forces and those who advocate operations throughout its entire country—has just begun. But in the long run, the MTR clearly holds the potential to blur, or permanently erase, the distinction between tactical, theater, and strategic war. In the future, a telephone switching center in a nation's heartland might be as likely a target on the first day of the war as a tank on the front lines. And insofar as this prospect already exists for developing nations considering a war against the United States, MTR systems augment deterrence immeasurably.

With the advent of the capabilities outlined above, the U.S. military may increasingly search for *systemic weaknesses* in its adversaries. Advances in information technology and simulation may allow U.S. forces to identify relatively small target sets that can cripple an adversary's will or ability to fight. This approach requires viewing an opponent as a system of interlinked pieces: if those pieces can be unhinged at critical points, then the entire system may collapse. This target set will likely be different for each adversary and operation to fit U.S. and coalition political objectives. Dictatorships, for example, may be more vulnerable to such focused attacks than a more dispersed society.

Together, these consequences will exercise a devastating *psychological effect* on opposing forces. Much of war is psychology, morale, and motivation—the intangible aspects of combat. As hinted at in the Persian Gulf War, the MTR's combination of information dominance, precision attack, and decisive tactics can destroy the will, and in a practical sense the ability, of an enemy to fight without destroying all of its equipment or killing most of its troops. The MTR may allow military forces to implement Sun Tzu's famous dictum: "supreme excellence" in war, he wrote, is not "to fight and conquer in all your battles," but rather lies in "breaking the enemy's resistance without fighting."

Finally, the MTR holds powerful implications for the traditional military principle of security, which deals with enhancing one's own freedom of action by reducing vulnerability to hostile acts, influence, or surprise. The survival of information dominance and command-and-control capabilities is paramount under an MTR regime. Satellite systems should be survivable and replaceable, command and control nodes dispersed and redundant. The current preference for theater-based intelligence assets, command centers, and battle management platforms may have to be reexamined if potential opponents devote greater resources to weapons designed specifically to attack such high-value systems. One solution may be synthesis and command stations in the continental United States (with prudent redundancies) that can be linked in real time to theater forces.

CYBERWAR IS COMING!

JOHN ARQUILLA AND DAVID RONFELDT

Suppose that war looked like this: small numbers of light, highly mobile forces defeat and compel the surrender of large masses of heavily armed, dug-in enemy forces, with little loss of life on either side. The mobile forces can do this because they are well prepared, make room for maneuver, concentrate their firepower rapidly in unexpected places, and have superior command, control, and information systems that are decentralized to allow tactical initiatives, yet provide central commanders with unparalleled intelligence and "topsight" for strategic purposes.

EMERGENT MODES OF CONFLICT

Warfare is no longer primarily a function of who puts the most capital, labor, and technology on the battlefield, but of who has the best information about the battlefield. What distinguishes the victors is their grasp of information, not only from the mundane standpoint of knowing how to find the enemy while keeping it in the dark but also in doctrinal and organizational terms. The analogy is rather like a chess game, where you see the entire board but your opponent sees only his own pieces; you can win even if he is allowed to start with additional powerful pieces.

We might appear to be extrapolating from the U.S. victory in the Persian Gulf War against Iraq. But our vision is inspired more by the example of the Mongols of the thirteenth century. Their "hordes" were almost always outnumbered by their opponents, yet they conquered, and held for over a century, the largest continental empire ever seen. The key to Mongol success was their absolute dominance of battlefield information. They struck when and where they deemed appropriate, and their "arrow riders" kept field commanders, often separated by hundreds of miles, in daily communication. Even the Great Khan, sometimes thousands of miles away, was aware of developments in the field within days of their occurrence.

Absent the galvanizing threat that used to be posed by the former Soviet Union, domestic political pressures will encourage the United States to make do with a smaller military in the future. The type of war-fighting capability that we envision, which is inspired by the Mongol example, but drawn mainly from our analysis of the information revolution, may allow America to protect itself and its far-flung friends and interests, regardless of the size and strength of its potential future adversaries.

THE ADVANCE OF TECHNOLOGY AND KNOW-HOW

Throughout history, military doctrine, organization, and strategy have continually undergone profound changes, owing in part to technological breakthroughs. The Greek phalanx, the combination of gun and sail, the *levée en masse*, the blitzkrieg, the Strategic Air Command—history is filled with examples in which new weapon, propulsion, communication, and transportation technologies provided a basis for advantageous shifts in doctrine, organization, and strategy that enabled innovators to avoid exhausting attritional battles and pursue instead a form of "decisive" warfare.[1]

Today a variety of new technologies are again taking hold, and further innovations are on the way. The most enticing include nonnuclear high-explosives; precision-guided munitions; stealth designs for aircraft, tanks, and ships; radio-electronic combat (REC) systems; new electronics for intelligence gathering, interference, and deception; new information and communications systems that improve command, control, communication, and intelligence (C3I) functions; and futuristic designs for space-

This essay has been edited and is reprinted from Comparative Strategy 2 *(April-June 1993): 141–65, by permission of Taylor & Francis, Inc. All rights reserved.*

based weapons and for automated and robotic warfare. In addition, virtual reality systems are being developed for simulation and training. Many of these advances enter into a current notion of a military technology revolution (MTR).[2]

The future of war—specifically, the U.S. ability to anticipate and wage war—will be shaped in part by how these technological advances are assessed and adopted. Yet, as military historians frequently warn, technology permeates war but does not govern it. It is not technology per se, but rather the organization of technology, broadly defined, that is important. Russell Weigley describes the situation this way:

The technology of war does not consist only of instruments intended primarily for the waging of war. A society's ability to wage war depends on every facet of its technology: its roads, its transport vehicles, its agriculture, its industry, and its methods of organizing its technology. As Van Creveld puts it, "Behind military hardware there is hardware in general, and behind that there is technology as a certain kind of know-how, as a way of looking at the world and coping with its problems."[3]

The technological shift that matches this broad view is the information revolution. This is what will bring the next major shift in the nature of conflict and warfare.

EFFECTS OF THE INFORMATION REVOLUTION

The information revolution reflects the advance of computerized information and communications technologies and related innovations in organization and management theory. Sea changes are occurring in how information is collected, stored, processed, communicated, and presented and in how organizations are designed to take advantage of increased information.[4] Information is becoming a strategic resource that may prove as valuable and influential in the postindustrial era as capital and labor have been in the industrial age.

Advanced information and communications systems, properly applied, can improve the efficiency of many kinds of activities. But improved efficiency is not the only, or even the best, possible effect. The new technology is also having a transforming effect, for it disrupts old ways of thinking and operating, provides capabilities to do things differently, and suggests how some things may be done better if done differently:

The consequences of new technology can be usefully thought of as first-level, or efficiency, effects and second-level, or social system, effects. The history of previous technologies demonstrates that early in the life of a new technology, people are likely to emphasize the efficiency effects and underestimate or overlook potential social system effects. Advances in networking technologies now make it possible to think of people, as well as databases and processors, as resources on a network.

Many organizations today are installing electronic networks for first-level efficiency reasons. Executives now be-ginning to deploy electronic mail and other network applications can realize efficiency gains such as reduced elapsed time for transactions. If we look beyond efficiency at behavioral and organizational changes, we'll see where the second-level leverage is likely to be. These technologies can change how people spend their time and what and who they know and care about. The full range of payoffs, and the dilemmas, will come from how the technologies affect how people can think and work together—the second-level effects.[5]

The information revolution, in both its technological and nontechnological aspects, sets in motion forces that challenge the design of many institutions. It disrupts and erodes the hierarchies around which institutions are normally designed. It diffuses and redistributes power, often to the benefit of what may be considered weaker, smaller actors. It crosses borders, and redraws the boundaries of offices and responsibilities. It expands the spatial and temporal horizons that actors should take into account. Thus it generally compels closed systems to open up. But while this may make life difficult, especially for large, bureaucratic, aging institutions, the institutional form per se is not becoming obsolete. Institutions of all types remain essential to the organization of society. The responsive, capable institutions will adapt their structures and processes to the information age. Many will evolve from traditional hierarchical forms to new, flexible, networklike models of organization. Success will depend on learning to interlace hierarchical and network principles.[6]

Meanwhile, the very changes that trouble institutions, such as the erosion of hierarchy, favor the rise of multiorganizational networks. Indeed, the information revolution is strengthening the importance of all forms of networks, such as social networks and communications networks. The network form is very different from the institutional form. While institutions (large ones, in particular) are traditionally built around hierarchies and aim to act on their own, multiorganizational networks consist of (often small) organizations or parts of institutions that have linked together to act jointly. The information revolution favors the growth of such networks by making it possible for diverse, dispersed actors to communicate, consult, coordinate, and operate together across greater distances and on the basis of more and better information than ever before.[7] These points bear directly on the future of the military, and of conflict and warfare more generally.

BOTH NETWAR AND CYBERWAR ARE LIKELY

The thesis of this thinkpiece is that the information revolution will cause shifts, both in how societies may come into conflict and how their armed forces may wage war. We offer a distinction between what we call *netwar*—societal-level ideational conflicts waged in part through internetted modes of communication—and *cyberwar* at the military level. These terms are admittedly novel, and better ones may yet be devised.[8] But for now they help illuminate a useful distinction and identify the breadth of ways in which the information revolution may alter the nature of conflict short of war, as well as the context and the conduct of warfare.[9]

While both netwar and cyberwar revolve around information and communications matters, at a deeper level they are forms of war about *knowledge,* about who knows what, when, where, and why, and about how secure a society or a military is regarding its knowledge of itself and its adversaries.[10]

EXPLAINING NETWAR

Netwar refers to information-related conflict at a grand level between nations or societies. It means trying to disrupt, damage, or modify what a target population knows or thinks it knows about itself and the world around it. A netwar may focus on public or elite opinion, or both. It may involve public diplomacy measures, propaganda and psychological campaigns, political and cultural subversion, deception of or interference with local media, infiltration of computer networks and databases, and efforts to promote dissident or opposition movements across computer networks. Thus, designing a strategy for netwar may mean grouping together from a new perspective a number of measures that have been used before but were viewed separately.

In other words, netwar represents a new entry on the spectrum of conflict that spans economic, political, and social, as well as military forms of "war." In contrast to economic wars that target the production and distribution of goods, and political wars that aim at the leadership and institutions of a government, netwars would be distinguished by their targeting of information and communications. Like other forms on this spectrum, netwars would be largely nonmilitary, but they could have dimensions that overlap into military war. For example, an economic war may involve trade restrictions, the dumping of goods, the illicit penetration and subversion of businesses and markets in a target country, and the theft of technology, none of which need involve the armed forces. Yet an economic war may also come to include an armed blockade or strategic bombing of economic assets, meaning it has also become a military war. In like manner, a netwar that leads to targeting an enemy's military C3I capabilities turns, at least in part, into what we mean by cyberwar.

Netwar will take various forms, depending on the actors. Some may occur between the governments of rival nation-states. In some respects, the U.S. and Cuban governments are already engaged in a netwar. This is manifested in the activities of Radio and TV Marti on the U.S. side, and on Castro's side by the activities of pro-Cuban support networks around the world.

Other kinds of netwar may arise between governments and nonstate actors. For example, netwar may be waged by governments against illicit groups and organizations involved in terrorism, proliferation of weapons of mass destruction, or drug smuggling. Or, to the contrary, it may be waged against the policies of specific governments by advocacy groups and movements, involving, for example, environmental, human-rights, or religious issues. The nonstate actors may or may not be associated with nations, and in some cases they may be organized into vast transnational networks and coalitions.

Another kind of netwar may occur between rival nonstate actors, with governments maneuvering on the sidelines to prevent collateral damage to national interests and perhaps to support one side or another. This is the most speculative kind of netwar, but the elements for it have already appeared, especially among advocacy movements around the world. Some movements are increasingly organizing into cross-border networks and coalitions, identifying more with the development of civil society (even global civil society) than with nation-states, and using advanced information and communications technologies to strengthen their activities. This may well turn out to be the next great frontier for ideological conflict, and netwar may be a prime characteristic.

Most netwars will probably be nonviolent, but in the worst cases one could combine the possibilities into some mean low-intensity conflict scenarios. Martin Van Creveld does this when he worries that "in the future, war will not be waged by armies but by groups whom today we call terrorists, guerrillas, bandits and robbers, but who will undoubtedly hit on more formal titles to describe themselves."[11] In his view, war between states will diminish, and the state may become obsolete as a major form of societal organization. Our views coincide with many of Van Creveld's, though we do not believe that the state is even potentially obsolete. Rather, it will be transformed by these developments.

Some netwars will involve military issues. Possible issue areas include nuclear proliferation, drug smuggling, and antiterrorism because of the potential threats they pose to international order and national security interests. Moreover, broader societal trends (e.g., the redefinition of security concepts, the new roles of advocacy groups, the blurring of traditional boundaries between what is military and what is nonmilitary, between what is public and what is private, and between what pertains to the state and what pertains to society) may engage the interests of at least some military offices in some netwar-related activities.

Netwars are not real wars, traditionally defined. But netwar might be developed into an instrument for trying, early on, to prevent a real war from arising. Deterrence in a chaotic world may become as much a function of one's cyber posture and presence as of one's force posture and presence.

EXPLAINING CYBERWAR

Cyberwar refers to conducting, and preparing to conduct, military operations according to information-related principles. It means disrupting, if not destroying, information and communications systems, broadly defined to include even military culture, on which an adversary relies in order to know itself: who it is, where it is, what it can do when, why it is fighting, which threats to counter first, and so forth. It means trying to know everything about an adversary while keeping the adversary from knowing much about oneself. It means turning the "balance of information and knowledge" in one's favor, especially if the balance of forces is not. It means using knowledge so that less capital and labor may have to be expended.

To give but a few examples, this form of warfare may involve diverse technologies, notably for C3I; for intelligence collection, processing, and distribution; for tactical communications, positioning, and identification-friend-or-foe (IFF); and for "smart" weapons systems. It may also involve electronically blinding, jamming, deceiving, overloading, and intruding into an adversary's information and communications circuits. Yet cyberwar is not simply a set of measures based on technology. And it should not be confused with past meanings of computerized, automated, robotic, or electronic warfare.

Cyberwar may have broad ramifications for military organization and doctrine. As noted, the literature on the information revolution calls for organizational innovations, so that different parts of an institution function like interconnected networks rather than separate hierarchies. Thus cyberwar may imply some institutional redesign for a military in both intra- and interservice areas. Moving to networked structures may require some decentralization of command and control, which may well be resisted in light of earlier views that the new technology would provide greater central control of military operations. But decentralization is only part of the picture: the new technology may also provide greater "topsight," a central understanding of the big picture that enhances the management of complexity.[12] Many treatments of organizational redesign laud decentralization; yet decentralization alone is not the key issue. The pairing of decentralization with topsight brings the real gains.

Cyberwar may also imply developing new doctrines about the kinds of forces needed, where and how to deploy them, and what and how to strike on the enemy's side. How and where to position what kinds of computers and related sensors, networks, databases, and so forth, may become as important as the question once was for the deployment of bombers and their support functions. Cyberwar may also have implications for integrating the political and psychological with the military aspects of warfare.

In sum, cyberwar may raise broad issues of military organization and doctrine, as well as strategy, tactics, and weapons design. It may be applicable in low- and high-intensity conflicts, in conventional and nonconventional environments, and for defensive or offensive purposes.

As an innovation in warfare, we anticipate that cyberwar may be to the twenty-first century what blitzkrieg was to the twentieth century. Yet, for now, we also believe that the concept is too speculative for precise definition. At a minimum, it represents an extension of the traditional importance of obtaining information in war: having superior C3I and trying to locate, read, surprise, and deceive the enemy before he does the same to you. That remains important no matter what overall strategy is pursued. In this sense, the concept means that information-related factors are more important than ever owing to new technologies, but it does not indicate a break with tradition. Indeed, it resembles Thomas Rona's concept of an "information war" that is "intertwined with, and superimposed on, other military operations."[13] Our concept is broader than Rona's, which focused on countermeasures to degrade an enemy's weapons systems while protecting one's own; yet we believe that this approach to defining cyberwar will ultimately prove too limiting.

In a deeper sense, cyberwar signifies a transformation in the nature of war. This, we believe, will prove to be the better approach to defining cyberwar. Our position is at odds with a view that uses the terms "hyperwar" and "cyberwar" to claim that the key implication of the MTR is the automated battlefield, that future wars will be fought mainly by "brilliant" weapons, robots, and autonomous computers, that man will be subordinate to the machine, and that combat will be unusually fast and laden with standoff attacks.[14] This view errs in its understanding of the effects of the information revolution, and our own view differs on every point. Cyberwar is about organization as much as technology. It implies new man-machine interfaces that amplify man's capabilities, not a separation of man and machine. In some situations, combat may be waged fast and from afar, but in many other situations, it may be slow and close in. New combinations of far and close and fast and slow may be the norm, not one extreme or the other.

The postmodern battlefield stands to be fundamentally altered by the information technology revolution, at both the strategic and tactical levels. The increasing breadth and depth of this battlefield and the ever-improving accuracy and destructiveness of even conventional munitions have heightened the importance of C3I matters to the point where dominance in this aspect alone may now yield consistent war-winning advantages to able practitioners. Yet cyberwar is a much broader idea than attacking an enemy's C3I systems while improving and defending one's own. In Clausewitz's sense, it is characterized by the effort to turn knowledge into capability.

Indeed, even though its full design and implementation require advanced technology, cyberwar is not reliant upon advanced technology per se. The continued development of advanced information and communications technologies is crucial for U.S. military capabilities. But cyberwar, whether waged by the United States or other actors, does not necessarily require the presence of advanced technology. The organizational and psychological dimensions may be as important as the technical. Cyberwar may actually be waged with low technology under some circumstances.

INFORMATION-RELATED FACTORS IN MILITARY HISTORY

Our contention is that netwar and cyberwar represent new (and related) modes of conflict that will be increasingly important in the future. The information revolution implies—indeed, it ensures—that a sea change is occurring in the nature of conflict and warfare. Yet both new modes have many historical antecedents; efforts have been made in the direction of conducting warfare from cyberlike perspectives in the past. Information, communications, and control are enduring concerns of warfighters. There is much historical evidence, tactical and strategic, that attempting to pierce the "fog of war" and envelop one's foe in it has played a continuing role.[15]

In the Second Punic War of the third century B.C., Carthaginian forces under the command of Hannibal routinely stationed observers with mirrors on hilltops, keeping their leader apprised of Roman movements, while the latter remained ignorant of his. Better communications contributed significantly to the ability of Hannibal's forces to win a string of victories over a sixteen-year period. In the most dramatic example of the use of superior information, Hannibal's relatively small forces were able to rise literally from the fog of war at Lake Trasimene to destroy a Roman army more than twice its size.[16]

Another famous, more recent example, occurred during the Napoleonic Wars. The British Royal Navy's undisputed command of the Mediterranean Sea, won at the Battle of the Nile in 1798, cut the strategic sea communications of Bonaparte's expeditionary force in North Africa, leading to its disastrous defeat. The invaders were stranded in Egypt without supplies or their commander, after Napoleon's flight, where they remained until the British came to take them prisoner.

A few years later in the same conflict, Lord Cochrane's lone British frigate was able to put French forces into total confusion along virtually the entire Mediterranean coast of occupied Spain and much of France. The French relied for their communications on a semaphore system to alert their troops to trouble and to tell coastal vessels when they could safely sail. Cochrane raided these signaling stations, then struck spectacularly, often in conjunction with Spanish guerrilla forces, while French communications were disrupted.[17]

Story upon story could be drawn from military history to illuminate the significance of information and communications factors. But this is meant to be only a brief discussion to posit the concept of cyberwar. Better we turn directly to an early example, a virtual model of this upcoming mode of warfare.

THE MONGOLS: AN EARLY EXAMPLE OF CYBERWAR

Efforts to strike at an enemy's communications and ensure the safety of one's own are found, to varying degrees, throughout history. The Mongol way of warfare, which reached its zenith in the twelfth and thirteenth centuries, may be the closest that anyone has come to waging pure cyberwar (or netwar, for that matter). Examining Mongol military praxis should, therefore, be instructive in developing the foundations for waging war in a like manner in the modern world. The Mongol example also reinforces the point that cyberwar does not depend on high technology, but rather on how one thinks about conflict and strategic interaction.

At the military level, Mongol doctrine relied for success almost entirely on learning exactly where their enemies were, while keeping their own whereabouts a secret until they attacked. This enabled them, despite a chronic inferiority in numbers, to overthrow the finest, largest armies of imperial China, Islam, and Christendom. The simplest way to illustrate their advantage is to suggest an analogy with chess: war against the Mongols resembled playing against an opponent who can hide the disposition of his pieces, but who can see the placement of both his and yours. Under such conditions, the player with knowledge of both sides' deployments could be expected to triumph with many fewer pieces. Moreover, the addition of even significant forces to the semiblinded side would generate no requirement for a similar increase on the "sighted" side. (Thus the similarity is not so much to chess as to its cousin, *kriegspiel*, in which both players start "blind" to their opponent's position. In our analogy, one player can see through the barrier that is normally placed between the boards of the players.)

So it was with the Mongols. In one of their greatest campaigns, against the mighty Muslim empire of Khwarizm (located approximately on the territory of today's Iran, Iraq, and portions of the central Asian republics of the former Soviet Union), a Mongol army of some 125,000 toppled a foe whose standing armies amounted to nearly half a million troops, with a similar number of reserves. How could this happen? The answer is that the Mongols identified the linear, forward dispositions of their foes and avoided them. Instead, they worked around the defenders, making a point of waylaying messengers moving between the capital and the front.

Muhammad Ali Shah, the ruler of Khwarizm, took the silence from the front as a good sign, until one day a messenger, having narrowly escaped a Mongol patrol, made his way to the capital, Samarkand. Muhammad inquired about the news from his army and was told that the frontier was holding. The messenger went on to add, however, that he had observed a large Mongol army but a day's march from the capital. The shah fled and his capital fell swiftly. This news, when given to the frontier armies, led to a general capitulation. Muhammad ended his days in hiding on the island of Abeshkum in the Caspian Sea, where he contracted and died from pleurisy.

The campaign against Khwarizm is typical of the Mongol strategic approach of first blinding an opponent, then striking at his heart (i.e., going for checkmate). Battles were infrequently fought, as they were often unnecessary for achieving war aims. There were times, however, when confrontations could not be avoided. When this happened, the Mongols relied heavily on coordinated operations designed to break down the plans and controls of their opponents.

Against the Polish-Prussian coalition forces at the battle of Liegnitz, for example, the Mongols engaged and defeated an army some four times their size. Their success was based on keeping a clear picture of the defending coalition's order of battle, while confusing the opponents as to their own whereabouts. Thus portions of the Western army chased after small detachments that were simple lures and ended up in the clutches of the Mongol main force. The Poles and Prussians were defeated piecemeal. Indeed, the Mongols were so sure of their information that they repeatedly used a river crossing during the battle in the intervals *between* its use by the Poles and Prussians.[18]

What about Mongol advantages in mobility and firepower? Certainly, their ability to move a division some 80 miles per day was superior to other armies, and their horn bows did outrange those of their enemies by 50–100 yards, on average. But neither of these factors could offset their foes' advantages in fortification technology, and the body armor of Western forces gave them distinct advantages over the Mongols in close combat. Thus Mongol tactical operations were often significantly stymied by defended cities,[19] and close engagements were exceedingly hard fought, with the Mongols suffering heavily. Indeed, the ferocity and effectiveness of the Prusso-Polish forces at Liegnitz, especially their cavalry, may have deterred the Mongols from continuing their invasion of Europe.[20] At the battle of Hims, the Mamelukes showed that the forces of Islam could also defeat the Mongols tactically. What neither Islam nor Christendom could do consistently, however, was outwit the Mongols strategically.

Clearly, the key to Mongol success was superior command, control, communication, and intelligence. Scouts and messengers always took along three or four extra horses, tethered, so that they could switch mounts and keep riding when one grew tired. This gave the Mongol horsemen, in relative terms, something approximating an ability to provide real-time intelligence, almost as from a satellite, on the enemy's order of battle and intentions. At the same time, this steppe-version of the pony express (the Khan called them "arrow riders") enabled field generals to keep the high command, often thousands of miles from the theater of war, informed as to all developments within four or five days of their occurrence. For communication between field forces, the Mongols also employed a sophisticated semaphore system that allowed for swift tactical shifts as circumstances demanded. Organizationally, the Mongols emphasized decentralized command in the field, unlike their foes who were generally required to wait for orders from their capitals. Yet by developing a communication system that kept their leadership apprised at all times, the Mongols enjoyed topsight as well as decentralization. The Khan "advanced his armies on a wide front, controlling them with a highly developed system of communication"; that was the secret of his success.[21]

In strategic terms, the Mongols aimed first to disrupt an enemy's communications, then to strike at his heart. Unlike Clausewitz, they put little store in the need to destroy enemy forces before advancing. Also, Mongol campaigns were in no way "linear." They struck where they wished, when circumstances were deemed favorable. That their Christian and Muslim foes seldom emulated the Mongols' organizational and communication techniques is to their great discredit. When, finally, the Mamelukes defeated the Mongols' attempted invasion of Egypt, it was because they kept track of Mongol movements and were led in the field by their king, Kilawan, who exercised rapid, effective control of his forces in the fluid battle situations that ensued. Also, the Mamelukes, employing carrier pigeons, had developed faster strategic communications than even the Mongols' arrow riders, allowing them to mass troops in time to defend effectively.[22]

As much as they form a paradigm for cyberwar, the Mongols also were adept at netwar. Early in their campaigns, they used terror tactics to weaken resistance. At the outset of any invasion, they broadcast that any city that resisted would be razed and its inhabitants slaughtered. Surrender, on the other hand, would result simply in coming under Mongol suzerainty; this entailed some initial rape and pillage, but thereafter settled into a distracted sort of occupation. As a result, peaceful surrenders were plentiful. In later campaigns, when the Mongols learned that both Christians and Muslims saw them as the dark forces of Gog and Magog, heralding the "end of times," they deliberately cultivated this image. They renamed themselves Tartars, as though they were the minions of "tartarum," the biblical nether world. Later, when it was clear that the world was not ending, the Mongols willingly adopted both Christianity and Islam, whichever eased the burden of captivity for particular peoples. This utilitarian approach to religion impeded the formation of opposing coalitions.

Some analysts have argued that the Mongols represent an early experiment with blitzkrieg.[23] In our view, however, the differences between cyberwar and blitzkrieg are significant, and the Mongols reflect the former more than the latter.

BLITZKRIEG, PEOPLE'S WAR, AND BEYOND

The relative importance of war against an enemy's command, control, and communications increased with the advent of mechanized warfare. In World War II, the German blitzkrieg doctrine—in some ways a forerunner of cyberwar—made the disruption of enemy communications and control an explicit goal at both the tactical and strategic levels. For example, the availability of radios in all of its tanks provided Germany with a tactical-force multiplier in its long war with the Soviet Union, whose tanks, though more numerous and better built, provided radios only for commanders.[24]

At the strategic level, the destruction of the Soviets' central communications and control site, by capturing Moscow, was a key element of the planning for Operation Barbarossa. But when an opportunity arose during the campaign to win large material gains in the Ukraine, Hitler diverted General Heinz Guderian's panzers away from their approach to Moscow, and it was never taken. There would be no "lightning" victory for the Germans, who soon found themselves on the weaker side of a massive attritional struggle, doomed to defeat.[25]

Following World War II, information and communication technologies improved greatly in the major industrialized nations, and the important wars with lessons for cyberwar were between these nations and the underdeveloped ones of the Third World. A comparison of two key conflicts illuminates the growing importance and applicability of cyberwar principles: the people's war waged by North Vietnam and the Viet Cong in the 1960s and 1970s, and the recent, more conventional conflict between the American-led coalition and Iraq.

Both wars represent turning points. In the case of Vietnam, the enemy may have applied cyber principles more effectively than did the United States, not only in military areas but also where cyberwar cuts into the political and societal dimensions of conflict. In the case of the war against Iraq, the United States did superior work applying cyberwar principles (they were not called that at the time, of course) against an enemy whose organization, doctrine, strategy, and tactics were from a different era.

In the Vietnam War, the United States appeared to have advantages up and down the chain of command and control, from the construction of quantitative indicators and computerized models and databases for analyzing the course of the war in Washington, through field radios for calling in prompt airstrikes, reinforcements, and rescue operations. But the thrall of computerization and quantitative techniques led analysts to overlook the softer, subtler aspects of the war where the enemy was winning. The excellence of U.S. communications capabilities encouraged inappropriate intrusion from above into battles and campaigns best planned and waged within the theater.

While U.S. forces had superior tactical communications, the guerrillas' strategic communications were largely unaffected. Meanwhile, the North Vietnamese and Viet Cong operated on Mao Zedong's doctrine that "command must be centralized for strategical purposes and decentralized for tactical purposes"[26] a classic combination of topsight and decentralization. The United States, on the other hand, appears to have allowed the timely availability of vast quantities of information at high levels to seduce leadership into maintaining central tactical as well as strategic control, and into believing that they had topsight when they did not.

The Vietnam example illustrates our point that good communications, though they provide necessary conditions, are insufficient to enable one to fight a cyberwar. For this endeavor, a doctrinal view of the overarching importance and value of maintaining one's own communications, while disabling the adversary's, is requisite. This entails the development of tactics and operational strategies that discard the basic tenets of both set-piece and even traditional maneuver war-fighting theories. Neither the grinding attritional approach of Ulysses S. Grant nor the explosive thrusts of Guderian will suffice. Instead, radically different models must be considered that focus upon the objective of systemically disorganizing the enemy.

To some extent, the recent American experience in the Persian Gulf War suggests that an increasing sensitivity to cyber principles is taking hold. First, it was made quite clear by President George Bush that he had no intention of micromanaging tactical or even operationally strategic actions. This is, in itself, a stark contrast to the classic image of President Lyndon Johnson poring over maps of North Vietnam, selecting each of the targets to be hit by Operation Rolling Thunder.

The military operations brought significant cyber elements into play, often utilizing them as "force multipliers."[27] The Apache helicopter strike against Iraqi air defense controls at the war's outset is but one, albeit very important, example. Also, the allied coalition had good knowledge of Iraqi dispositions, while the latter were forced to fight virtually blind. Along these lines, a further example of the force-multiplying effect of command of information is provided by the ability of a relatively small (less than 20,000 troops) Marine force afloat to draw away from the landward front and tie down roughly 125,000 Iraqi defenders.

A significant effort also was made to employ netwar principles in the Gulf War. The construction of an international consensus against the Iraqi aggression, backed by the deployment of large, mechanized forces, was intended to persuade Saddam Hussein to retreat. His intransigent behavior suggests that his vision of war was that of a prior generation.

An Implication: Institutions versus Networks

From a traditional standpoint, a military is an institution that fields armed forces. The form that all institutions normally take is the hierarchy, and militaries, in particular, depend heavily on hierarchy. Yet the information revolution is bound to erode hierarchies and redraw the boundaries around which institutions and their offices are normally built. Moreover, the information revolution favors organizational network designs. These points were made in the first section of this essay.

This second section leads to related insights, based on a quick review of history. The Mongols, a classic example of an ancient force that fought according to cyberwar principles, were organized more like a network than a hierarchy. More recently, a relatively minor military power that defeated a great modern power—the combined forces of North Vietnam and the Viet Cong—operated in many respects more like a network than an institution; it even extended political-support networks abroad. In both cases, the Mongols and the Vietnamese, their defeated opponents were large institutions whose forces were designed to fight set-piece attritional battles.

To this may be added a further set of observations drawn from current events. Most adversaries that the United States and its allies face in the realm of low-intensity conflict, such as international terrorists, guerrilla insurgents, drug smuggling cartels, ethnic factions, as well as racial and tribal gangs, are all organized like networks (although their leadership may be quite hierarchical). Perhaps a reason that military (and police) institutions have difficulty engaging in low-intensity conflicts is that they are not meant to be fought by institutions.

The lesson: institutions can be defeated by networks, and it may take networks to counter networks. The future may belong to whoever masters the network form.

ISSUES FOR THE FUTURE

The implications of a revolutionary technology are often not widely perceived at first. That was true of the tank, the machine gun, and the telephone. For example, with their newly developed, rapid-firing *mitrailleuse,* the French enjoyed a tremendous potential firepower advantage over the Prussians in 1870. Unfortunately, this early version of the machine gun looked more like a fieldpiece instead of a rifle, and it was deployed behind the front with the artillery. Thus the weapon that would dominate World War I a generation later had almost no effect on the Franco-Prussian conflict. People try to fit new technology into established ways of doing things; it is expected to prove itself in terms of existing standards of efficiency and effectiveness.

It may take time to realize that inserting new technology into old ways may create some new inefficiencies, even as some activities become more efficient. It may take still more time to realize that the activity itself, in both its operational and organizational dimensions, should be restructured, even transformed, in order to realize the full potential of the technology.[28] This pattern is documented in the early histories of the telephone and the electric motor and is being repeated with computer applications in the business world.

Why should anything different be expected for cyberwar? New information technology applications have begun to transform the business world both operationally and organizationally. The government world is, for the most part, moving slowly in adopting the information technology revolution. One might expect the military world to lag behind both the business and government worlds, partly because of its greater dependence on hierarchical traditions. But in fact parts of the U.S. military are showing a keen interest in applying the information revolution. As this unfolds, a constant, but often halting, contentious interplay between operational and organizational innovations should be expected.

GROWING AWARENESS OF THE INFORMATION REVOLUTION

An awareness is spreading in some U.S. military circles that the information revolution may transform the nature of warfare. One hears that the MTR implies a period of reevaluation and experimentation not unlike the one in the 1920s and 1930s that resulted in Germany's breakthrough formulation of the blitzkrieg doctrine. New questions are being asked about how to apply the new technology in innovative ways. For example, one set of arguments holds that the MTR may increasingly enable armed forces to stand off and destroy enemy targets with high-precision weapons fired from great distances, including from outer space. But another set holds that the information revolution may drive conflict and warfare toward the low-intensity end of the scale, giving rise to new forms of close-in combat. Clearly, military analysts and strategists are just beginning to identify the questions and call for the required thinking.

The military, like much of the business world, is in a stage of installing pieces of the new technology to make specific operations more effective. Indeed, techniques that we presume would be essential to cyberwar may be used to improve the cost-effectiveness of many military operations, no matter what overall strategy is being pursued (even if cyberwar remains unformulated). For example, improved surveillance and intelligence-gathering capabilities that help identify timely opportunities for surprise (to some extent, a purpose of the new Joint Targeting Network [JTN]) can be of service to a traditional attritional warfare strategy. Also, new capabilities for informing the members of a unit in real time about where their comrades are located and what each is doing, as in recent experiments with intervehicular information systems (IVIS), may improve the ability to concentrate force as a unit, and maintain that concentration throughout an operation. The list of new techniques that could be mentioned is long and growing.

We favor inquiring methodically into how the information revolution may provide specific new technical capabilities for warfare, regardless of the doctrine and strategy used. We also favor analyzing what kinds of operational and organizational innovations should be considered in light of such capabilities. And we recognize that it is quite another thing to try to leap ahead and propose that cyberwar may be a major part of the answer. But this thinkpiece is not meant to be so methodical; it is meant to be speculative and suggestive, in order to call attention to the possibility of cyberwar as a topic that merits further discussion and research.

INDICATIONS AND ASPECTS OF CYBERWAR

New theoretical ground needs to be broken regarding the information and communications dimensions of war and the role of "knowledge" in conflict environments. Cyberwar is not merely a new set of operational techniques. It is emerging as a new mode of warfare that will call for new approaches to plans and strategies, and new forms of doctrine and organization.

What would a cyberwar look like? Are there different types? What may be the distinctive attributes of cyberwar as a doctrine? Where does cyberwar fit in the history of warfare, and why would it represent a radical shift? What are the requirements and options for preparing for and conducting a cyberwar? Will it enable power to be projected in new ways? What are the roles of organizational and technological factors, and what other factors (e.g., psychological) should be considered? How could the concept enable one to think better, or at least differently in a useful way, about factors, such as C3I, REC (radio-electronic combat systems), and psywar, that are important but not ordinarily considered together? What measures of effectiveness (MOE) should be used? These kinds of questions, some of which are touched on in this essay, call for examination.

Paradigm Shift

We anticipate that cyberwar, like war in Clausewitz's view, may be a "chameleon." It will be adaptable to varying contexts; it will not represent or impose a single, structured approach. Cyberwar may be fought offensively and defensively, at the strategic or tactical levels. It will span the gamut of intensity, from conflicts waged by heavy mechanized forces across wide theaters, to counterinsurgencies where "the mobility of the boot" may be the prime means of maneuver.

Consider briefly the context of blitzkrieg. This doctrine for offensive operations, based on the close coordination of mobile armored forces and airpower, was designed for relatively open terrain and good weather. Its primary asset was speed; swift breakthroughs were sought, and swift follow-ups required to prevent effective defensive ripostes.

The blitzkrieg is predicated upon the assumption that the opponent's army is a large and complex machine that is geared to fighting along a well-established defensive line. In the machine's rear lies a vulnerable network, which comprises numerous lines of communication, along which supplies as well as information move, and key nodal points at which the various lines intersect. Destruction of this central nervous system is tantamount to destruction of the army. The principal aim of a blitzkrieg is therefore to effect a strategic penetration. The attacker attempts to pierce the defender's front and then to drive deep into the defender's rear, severing his lines of communication and destroying key junctures in the network.[29]

By comparison, cyberwar takes a different view of what constitutes the "battlefield." Cyberwar depends less on geographic terrain than on the nature of the electronic "cyberspace," which should be open to domination through advanced technology applications.[30] Cyberwar benefits from an open radio-electronic spectrum and good atmospheric and other conditions for utilizing that spectrum. Cyberwar may require speedy flows of information and communications, but not necessarily a speedy or heavily armed offense like blitzkrieg. If the opponent is blinded, it can do little against even a slow-moving adversary. How, when, and where to position battlefield computers and related sensors, communications networks, databases, and REC devices may become as important in future wars as the same questions were for tanks or bomber fleets and their supporting equipment in World War II.

Cyberwar may imply a new view, not only of what constitutes "attack," but also of "defeat." Throughout the era of modern nation-states, beginning about the sixteenth century, attrition has been the main mode of warfare. An enemy's armed forces had to be defeated before objectives could be taken. This lasted for centuries until the grotesque, massive slaughters of World War I led to a search for relief from wars of exhaustion. This in turn led to the development of blitzkrieg, which circumvented the more brutish aspects of attritional war. Yet this maneuver-oriented doctrine still required the destruction of the enemy's forces as the prerequisite to achieving war aims: attritional war had simply been "put on wheels."

Cyberwar may also imply (although we are not sure at this point) that victory can be attained without the need to destroy an opposing force. The Mongol defeat of Khwarizm is the best example of the almost total circumvention and virtual dismemberment of an enemy's forces. It is possible to see in cyberwar an approach to conflict that allows for decisive campaigning without a succession of bloody battles. Cyberwar may thus be developed as a postindustrial doctrine that differs from the industrial-age traditions of attritional warfare. It may even seek to avoid attritional conflict.[31] In the best circumstances, wars may be won by striking at the strategic heart of an opponent's cyber structures, his systems of knowledge, information, and communications.

It is hard to think of any kind of warfare as humane, but a fully articulated cyberwar doctrine might allow the development of a capability to use force not only in ways that minimize the costs to oneself, but that also allow victory to be achieved without the need to maximize the destruction of the enemy. If for no other reason, this potential of cyberwar to lessen war's cruelty demands its careful study and elaboration.

Organizational and Related Strategic Considerations

At the strategic level, cyberwar may imply Mao's military ideal of combining strategic centralization and tactical decentralization. The interplay between these effects is one of the more complex facets of the information revolution. Our preliminary view is that the benefits of decentralization may be enhanced if, to balance the possible loss of centralization, the high command gains *topsight*, the term mentioned earlier that we currently favor to describe the view of the overall conflict. This term carries with it an implication that temptations to micromanage will be resisted.

The new technology tends to produce a deluge of information that must be taken in, filtered, and integrated in real time. Informational overload and bottlenecking has long been a vulnerability of centralized, hierarchical structures for command and control.[32] Waging cyberwar may require major innovations in organizational design, in particular a shift from hierarchies to networks. The traditional reliance on hierarchical designs may have to be adapted to network-oriented models to allow greater flexibility, lateral connectivity, and teamwork across institutional boundaries. The traditional emphasis on command and control, a key strength of hierarchy, may have to give way to an emphasis on consultation and coordination, the crucial building blocks of network designs. This may raise transitional concerns about how to maintain institutional traditions, as various parts become networked with other parts (if not with other, outside institutions) in ways that may go "against the grain" of existing hierarchies.

The information revolution has already raised issues for inter- and intraservice linkages, and in the case of coalition warfare, for intermilitary linkages. Cyberwar doctrine may require such linkages. It may call for particularly close communication, consultation, and coordination between officers in charge of strategy, plans, and operations, and those in charge of C3I, not to mention units in the field.

Operational and tactical command in cyberwar may be exceptionally demanding. There may be little of the traditional chain of command to evaluate every move and issue each new order. Commanders, from corps to company levels, may be required to operate with great latitude. But if they are allowed to act more autonomously than ever, they may also have to act more as a part of integrated joint operations. Topsight may have to be distributed to facilitate this. Also, the types and composition of units may undergo striking changes. Instead of divisions, brigades, and battalions, cyberwar may require the creation of combined-arms task forces from each of the services, something akin to the current Marine Air-Ground Task Force.

There are many historical examples of innovative tinkering with units during wartime, going back to the creation of the Roman maniple as a counter to the phalanx. In modern times, World War II brought the rise of many types of units never before seen. For example, the U.S. Army began using combat commands or teams comprised of artillery-armor-infantry mixes. The German equivalent was the *kampfgruppe*. These kinds of units could often fulfill missions for which larger bodies, even corps, had

previously failed. The U.S. Navy was also an innovator in this area, creating the task force as its basic operating unit in the Pacific war. Our point here is that what have often been viewed as makeshift wartime organizational adjustments should now be viewed as a peacetime goal of our standing forces, to be achieved before the onset of the next war.

Force Size Considerations

A cyberwar doctrine and accompanying organizational and operational changes may allow for reductions in the overall size of the U.S. armed forces. But if the history of earlier sea changes in the nature of war fighting is any guide, long-term prospects for significant reductions are problematic. All revolutions in warfare have created advantages that became subject to fairly rapid "wasting," since successful innovations were quickly copied.[33]

If both sides to a future conflict possess substantial cyberwar capabilities, the intensity and complexity of that war may well require more rather than fewer forces. The better-trained, more skillful practitioner may prevail, but it is likely that "big battalions" will still be necessary, especially as the relative cyberwar-fighting proficiency of combatants nears parity. In any case, whether future U.S. forces are larger or smaller, they will surely be configured quite differently.

Operational and Tactical Considerations

Cyberwar may also have radical implications at the operational and tactical levels. Traditionally, military operations have been divisible into categories of "holding and hitting." Part of a force is used to tie down an opponent, freeing other assets for flank and other forms of maneuvering attacks.[34] Tactically, two key aspects of war fighting have been fire and movement. Covering fire allows maneuver, with maneuver units then firing to allow fellow units to move. Fire creates maneuver potential. Tactical advance is viewed as a sort of leapfrogging affair.

Cyberwar may give rise to different, if not opposite, principles. Superior knowledge and control of information are likely to allow for "hitting without holding," strategically, and for tactical maneuvers that create optimal conditions for subsequent fire.

Nuclear Considerations

What of nuclear weapons and cyberwar? Future wars that may involve the United States will probably be nonnuclear, for two reasons. First, the dismantling of the former Soviet Union is likely to persist, with further arms reductions making nuclear war highly unlikely. Second, the United States is ill-advised to make nuclear threats against nonnuclear powers.

Besides the lack of central threat and the normative inhibitions against using nuclear forces for coercive purposes, there is also a practical reason for eschewing them in this context: bullying could drive an opponent into the arms of a nuclear protector, or spur proliferation by the threatened party. However, even a successful proliferator will prefer to keep conflicts conventional, as the United States will continue to maintain overwhelming counterforce and countervalue advantages over all nascent nuclear adversaries. Therefore the likelihood that future wars, even major ones, will be nonnuclear adds all the more reason to make an effort to optimize our capabilities for conventional and unconventional wars by developing a cyberwar doctrine.

In the body of strategic and operational thought surrounding war with weapons of mass destruction, an antecedent of cyberwar is provided. Nuclear counterforce strategies were very much aimed at destroying key communications centers of the opponent, thereby making it impossible for him to command and control far-flung nuclear weapons. The "decapitation" of an opponent's leadership was an inherently cyber principle. The dilemmas of mutual deterrence forced this insight into war-fighting to remain in a suspended state for some decades.

Before leaving nuclear issues, we would note an exception in the case of naval warfare. Because the United States enjoys an overwhelming maritime preeminence, it is logical that our potential adversaries may seek ways to diminish or extinguish it. Nuclear weapons may thus grow attractive to opponents whose navies are small, if the pursuit of their aims requires nullifying our sealift capabilities. A century ago, the French *jeune école,* by developing swift vessels capable of launching a brand new weapon, the torpedo, sought to counter the Royal Navy's power in international affairs. Today latter-day navalists of continental or minor powers may be driven to seek their own new weapons.[35]

Fortunately, the U.S. Navy has been following a path that elevates the information and communication dimensions of war to high importance. For, at sea, to be located is to become immediately vulnerable to destruction. In fact, naval war may already be arriving at a doctrine that looks a lot like cyberwar. There may be deep historical reasons for this, in that our naval examples, even from the Napoleonic period, have a strong cyber character.

Suggested Next Steps for Research

Our ideas here are preliminary and tentative and leave many issues to be sorted out for analysis. Yet we are convinced that these are exciting times for rethinking the theory and practice of warfare, and that cyberwar should be one of the subjects of that rethinking. This is based on our assumption that technological and related organizational innovations will continue moving in revolutionary directions.

We suggest case studies to clarify what ought to be taken into account in developing a cyberwar perspective. As noted earlier, these case studies should include the Vietnam and Persian Gulf conflicts. Combined with other materials (e.g., literature reviews, interviews) about the potential effects of the information revolution, such studies may help to identify the theoretical and operational principles

for developing a framework that serves not only for analysis, but potentially also for the formulation of a doctrine that may apply from strategic to tactical levels, and to high- and low-intensity levels of conflict. Such studies may also help distinguish between the technological and the non-technological underpinnings of cyberwar.

We suggest analytical exercises to identify what cyberwar, and the different modalities of cyberwar, may look like in the early twenty-first century when the new technologies should be more advanced, reliable, and internetted than at present. These exercises should consider opponents that the United States may face in high- and low-intensity conflicts. The list might include armed forces of the former Soviet Union, North Korea, Iraq, Iran, and Cuba. Cyberwar against a country's command structure may have a special potency when the country is headed by a dictator whose base of national support is narrow.[36] Nonstate actors should also be considered opponents, including some millennialist, terrorist, and criminal (e.g., drug smuggling) organizations that cut across national boundaries. We expect that both cyberwar and netwar may be uniquely suited to fighting nonstate actors.

Moreover, we suggest that the exercises consider some potentially unusual opponents and countermeasures. The revolutionary forces of the future may consist increasingly of widespread multiorganizational networks that have no particular national identity, claim to arise from civil society, and include aggressive groups and individuals who are keenly adept at using advanced technology for communications, as well as munitions. How will we deal with that? Can cyberwar (not to mention netwar) be developed as an appropriate, effective response? Do formal institutions have so much difficulty combating informal networks, as noted earlier, that the United States may want to design new kinds of military units and capabilities for engaging in network warfare?

All of the foregoing may lead to requirements for new kinds of net assessments regarding U.S. cyberwar capabilities relative to those of our potential opponents. How much of an advantage does the United States have at present? How long will the advantage persist? Such assessments should compare not only the capabilities of all parties to wage or withstand a cyberwar, but also their abilities to learn, identify, and work around an opponent's vulnerabilities.

Finally, despite the inherently futuristic tone of this thinkpiece, two dangers are developing in the world that may be countered through the skillful application of netwar and cyberwar techniques. The first comes from the proliferation of weapons of mass destruction. While the specifics of acquisition and timetables for development of credible, secure arsenals are open to debate, American opposition to proliferation is unquestioned; effective action must be taken now to forestall or prevent it.

The prospects for proliferation in the post–Cold War era create a highly appropriate issue area for the application of netwar techniques, since suasion will be much preferred to the use of preventive force in dealing with most nation-state actors (including Germany and Japan, should either ever desire its own nuclear weapons).[37] A netwar designed to dissuade potential proliferators from acquiring such weapons might consist of a "full court press" along the many networks of communication that link us to them, including diplomatic, academic, commercial, journalistic, and private avenues of interconnection. The ideational aspect of the netwar would concentrate on convincing potential proliferators that they have no need for such weapons. Obtaining them would create new enemies and new risks to their survival, while the benefits would be minuscule and fleeting.

The second danger likely to arise in the post–Cold War world is to regional security. American defense spending is likely to continue decreasing for at least the next decade. U.S. forces will be drawn down, and overseas deployments curtailed. The number of air wings and carrier battle groups will decrease. Each of these developments spells a lessened American capability to effect successful deterrence against conventional aggression. From South Korea to the South Asian subcontinent, from the Persian Gulf to the Balkans and across the territory of the former Soviet satellites to the Baltic Sea, American forward presence will vary between modest and nonexistent. Indeed, when we consider the likely rise of age-old ideological, religious, ethnic, and territorial rivalries, we see a world in which regional deterrence is going to be a problematic practice.

If regional wars are likely, and if American forces will be fewer and farther away from most regions than in the past, then a cyberwar doctrine may help to compensate for problems of distance and small-force size. If we are correct about the implications of cyberwar, that traditional force requirements against opponents varying in size and strength no longer hold, then the United States ought to be able to hurl back aggressors when it chooses, even with relatively small forces. General Colin Powell summarizes the essence of this notion succinctly, on the basis of his analysis of the Gulf War:

A downsized force and a shrinking defense budget result in an increased reliance on technology, which must provide the force multiplier required to ensure a viable military deterrent. . . . Battlefield information systems became the ally of the warrior. They did much more than provide a service. Personal computers were force multipliers.[38]

While a cyberwar doctrine should provide us with robust war-fighting capabilities against the largest regional aggressors, we must recognize that the small size and (perhaps) unusual look of our forces may have less of an "intimidation effect" on future adversaries, thereby vitiating crisis and deterrence stability. There are two ways to mitigate this emergent dilemma. First, applying netwar techniques in regions that bear upon our interests may provide early warning signals and an opportunity to dissuade a potential aggressor as soon as we become aware of his intentions. The second means of shoring up regional deterrence consists of signaling our resolve tacitly. This may involve the deployment or "show" of military force quite early in a crisis and could even include the exemplary use of our military capabilities.[39] Indeed, if this sort of signaling was aimed at targets suggested by cyberwar doctrine, such as critical communication nodes, the aggressor's capabilities for offensive action might come close to being nil from the outset.

What might a cyberwar against a regional aggressor look like? In most cases, it may well follow a "Pusan-Inchon" pattern.[40] First, the aggressor's "knockout blow" would have to be blunted. Then, American forces would counterattack. The burden of preventing a complete overrun at the outset of a war would surely fall heavily upon the U.S. Air Force and its ability to knock out the attacker's communications and logistics. The details will vary across regions, as some attackers may be more vulnerable to strategic paralysis than others. For example, future Iraqi aggression against the Arabian peninsula would depend on its ability to use a few roads and two bridges across the Tigris River. On the other hand, North Korea has many avenues of advance to the south.

The forces needed to roll back aggression would likely be modest in size. Since the invader will have been blinded by the time U.S. ground forces arrive, the latter will be able to strike where and when they wish. On the Arabian peninsula, for example, even an invading army of a million men would not be able to hold out against an American cyberwar, particularly if a defensive lodgement had been maintained. The attacker, not knowing where the Americans might strike, would have to disperse his forces over a theater measured in many hundreds of kilometers in each direction. American airpower would blind him, and destroy his forces attempting to maneuver. Then, counterattacking forces would strike where least expected, destroying the invader's very ability to fight as a cohesive force. As the Mongols defeated an army some ten times their size in the campaign against Khwarizm, so modern cyberwarriors should be able routinely to defeat much larger forces in the field. Of course, details will vary by region. Again, the Korean example would be a bit more complicated, although the lack of strategic depth on that peninsula is more than offset by robust South Korean defensive capabilities.

It seems clear that a cyberwar doctrine will give its able practitioner the capability to defeat conventional regional aggression between nation-states decisively, at low cost in blood and treasure. Will it fare as well against unconventional adversaries? This is a crucial question, as many, notably Van Creveld, have argued that war is being transformed by nonstate actors, and by smaller states that must ever think of new ways to fight and defeat their betters.[41] Thus crises will likely be characterized by large, well-armed irregular forces, taking maximum advantage of familiar terrain, motivated by religious, ethnic, or tribal zeal. Finally, they may move easily within and between the "membranes" of fractionated states.

Cyberwar may not provide a panacea for all conflicts of this type, but it does create a new, useful framework for coping with them. For example, in the former Yugoslavia, where all of the above factors have manifested themselves, the U.S. Army's Air-Land Battle, or even Operation Desert Storm, should not be used as models for analysis. These frames of reference lead to thinking that an entire field army (400,000–500,000 troops) is the appropriate tool for decisive war fighting in this environment. Instead, an intervention could easily follow cyberwar's Pusan-Inchon approach to regional conflict. For example, indigenous defenders in Bosnia and other areas of the former Yugoslavia could be armed so that they could prevent any sort of overrun (the campaign's "Pusan"). Next, a small combined-arms American task force, including no more than a division of ground troops, might strike opportunistically where and when it chose (the "Inchon").[42] Enemy forces would be easily locatable from the air, from radio intercepts, and by unmanned ground sensors, especially if they try to move or fight. The fact that the aggressors are dispersed makes them easier to defeat in detail. If they concentrate, they fall prey to tremendous American firepower.

The Balkan crisis may prove to be a framing event for future unconventional conflicts. It may also provide an important case for developing cyberwar doctrine in this type of setting. We note, however, that our assessment does not imply support for intervention in this case.

While the advent of cyberwar enables us to feel more comfortable about the prospects for maintaining regional security in an era likely to be characterized by American force drawdowns and withdrawals, there is another concern associated with this sort of war-fighting capability. Should the United States seek out coalition partners when it fights future regional wars? It seems obvious that we should, since both international and domestic political problems are mitigated by the vision of a group of nations marching arm in arm, if not in step, against an aggressor. However, we should be concerned about trying to incorporate other nations' armed forces into a cyberwar campaign. Aside from difficulties with integration, the United States should not be in any hurry to share a new approach, particularly with allies who may have been recruited on an ad hoc basis. It is one thing to take a long-standing ally like Britain into our confidence; Syria is quite another matter. Perhaps this new tension can be resolved by having our allies defend the lodgements, the "Pusans," while we engage in the "Inchons." It is ironic, though, that our ability to fight and win wars in accordance with the principles of the information revolution may require us to withhold our newfound insights, even from our friends and allies.

ACKNOWLEDGMENTS

The authors thank Carl Builder, Gordon McCormick, Jonathan Pollack, Ken Watman, and Dean Wilkening for their comments on earlier drafts. This essay does not represent the views of RAND, its management, or any of its sponsors.

NOTES

1. See Hans Delbruck, *History of the Art of War,* 3 vols. (Westport, Conn.: Greenwood Press, 1985). Delbruck describes warfare as a dual phenomenon: it may be waged with either "exhaustion" or "annihilation" in mind.

2. This notion borrows from an earlier Soviet notion of a scientific technology revolution (STR).

3. Russell F. Weigley, "War and the Paradox of Technology," *International Security* (Fall 1989): 192–202, quoting Martin Van Creveld, *Technology and War: From 2000 B.C. to the Present* (New York: Free Press, 1989).

4. See Daniel Bell, "The Social Framework of the Information Society," in *The Micro Electronics Revolution: The Complete Guide to the New Technology and Its Impact on Society,* ed. Tom Forester (Cambridge, Mass.: MIT Press, 1980); James Beninger, *The Control Revolution* (Cambridge, Mass.: Harvard University Press, 1986); Alvin Toffler, *Powershift: Knowledge, Wealth, and Violence at the Edge of the 21st Century* (New York: Bantam Books, 1990).

5. Lee Sproull and Sara Kiesler, *Connections: New Ways of Working in the Networked Organization* (Cambridge, Mass.: MIT Press, 1991), 15–16.

6. The literature on these points is vast. Recent additions include Steve Bankes and Carl Builder, *The Etiology of European Change* (Santa Monica, Calif.: RAND, 1991); Thomas W. Malone and John F. Rockart, "Computers, Networks and the Corporation," *Scientific American* (September 1991): 128–36; David Ronfeldt, *Cyberocracy, Cyberspace, and Cyberology: Political Effects of the Information Revolution* (Santa Monica, Calif.: RAND, 1991); Lee Sproull and Sara Kielser, "Computers, Networks and Work," *Scientific American* (September 1991): 116–23; Sproull and Kiesler, *Connections;* Toffler, *Powershift.*

7. David Ronfeldt, "Institutions, Markets, and Networks," in preparation.

8. Terms with "cyber" used as the prefix—for example, cyberspace—are currently in vogue among some visionaries and technologists who are seeking names for new concepts related to the information revolution. The prefix is from the Greek root *kybernan,* meaning to steer or govern, and a related word *kybernetes,* meaning pilot, governor, or helmsman. The prefix was introduced by Norbert Wiener in the 1940s in his classic works creating the field of "cybernetics" (which is related to *cybernétique,* an older French word meaning the art of government). Some readers may object to our additions to the lexicon, but we prefer them to alternative terms like "information warfare," which has been used in some circles to refer to warfare that focuses on C3I capabilities. In our view, a case exists for using the prefix in that it bridges the fields of information and governance better than any other available prefix or term. Indeed, *kybernan,* the root of "cyber," is also the root of the word *govern* and its extensions. Perhaps rendering the term in German would help. A likely term would be *leitenkrieg,* which translates loosely as "control warfare" (our thanks to Denise Quigley for suggesting this term).

9. We are indebted to Carl Builder for observing that the information revolution may have as much impact on the *context* as on the *conduct* of warfare, and that an analyst ought to identify how the context may change before he or she declares how a military's conduct should change.

10. The difficult term is *information*. Defining it remains a key problem of the information revolution. While no current definition is satisfactory, as a rule many analysts subscribe to a hierarchy with data at the bottom, information in the middle, and knowledge at the top (some would add wisdom above that). Like many analysts, we often use the term *information* (or *information-related*) to refer collectively to the hierarchy, but sometimes we use the term to mean something more than data, but less than knowledge. Finally, one spreading view holds that new information amounts to "any difference that makes a difference."

11. Martin Van Creveld, *The Transformation of War* (New York: Free Press, 1991), 197.

12. The importance of topsight is identified by David Gelernter, *Mirror Worlds, Or the Day Software Puts the Universe in a Shoebox . . . How It Will Happen and What It Will Mean* (New York: Oxford University Press, 1991), 52: "If you're a software designer and you can't master and subdue monumental complexity, you're dead; your machines don't work. They run for a while and then sputter to a halt, or they never run at all. Hence, 'managing complexity' must be your goal. Or, we can describe exactly the same goal in a more positive light. We can call it *the pursuit of topsight*. Topsight—an understanding of the big picture—is an essential goal of every software builder. It's also the most precious intellectual commodity known to man."

13. Thomas P. Rona, *Weapon Systems and Information War* (Seattle, Wash.: Boeing Aerospace Co., July 1976), 2.

14. Eric H. Arnett, "Welcome to Hyperwar," *Bulletin of the Atomic Scientists* 48, no. 7 (1992): 14–21.

15. Martin Van Creveld puts it this way: "From Plato to NATO, the history of command in war consists essentially of an endless quest for certainty" (*Command in War* [Cambridge, Mass.: Harvard University Press, 1985], 264).

16. See Brian Caven, *The Punic Wars* (New York: St. Martin's Press, 1980).

17. Cochrane's methods are described in some detail in Bernard Brodie, *A Guide to Naval Strategy* (Princeton, N.J.: Princeton University Press, 1944); and Ian Grimble, *The Sea Wolf: The Life of Admiral Cochrane* (London: Blond & Briggs, 1978).

18. The discussion of Mongol military doctrine is based principally on James Chambers, *The Devil's Horsemen* (New York: Atheneum, 1985). Jeremiah Curtin, in *The Mongols* (Boston: Little, Brown, 1908), translated the original Mongol sagas, rendering them with eloquence and coherence. Harold Lamb's *Genghis Khan* (New York: Macmillan, 1927) remains an important exposition of Genghis Khan's approach to strategy.

19. Perhaps this is why the Mongols slaughtered besieged forces (and civilian supporters) who resisted their attacks. As word of this brutality spread, fewer cities resisted (a gruesome example of netwar).

20. Domestic political strife within the Mongol empire also played a part in halting operations.

21. Chambers, *The Devil's Horsemen*, 43.

22. Kilawan also showed sensitivity to the importance of command and control at the tactical level. At the outset of the battle of Hims, for example, he sent one of his officers, feigning desertion, over to the Mongol commander, Mangku-Temur. When close enough, the Mameluke officer struck Temur in the face with his sword. At the same moment the Mamelukes attacked. The Mongol staff officers, tending to Temur, were thus distracted during the crucial, opening phase of the battle, which contributed to their defeat. See Chambers, *The Devil's Horsemen*, 160–62.

23. See Sir Basil H. Liddell Hart's *Great Captains Unveiled* (New York: Putnam's, 1931), wherein his early formulation of armored maneuver warfare mentions the Mongols as a possible model for blitzkrieg.

24. See the memoirs of Heinz Guderian, *Panzer Leader* (New York: Ballantine Books, 1972); and F. W. von Mellenthin, *Panzer Battles* (New York: Ballantine Books, 1976). These works are replete with examples of how radio communication allowed German armor to concentrate fire until a target was destroyed, then shift to a new target. In particular, fire would be initially concentrated on enemy tanks flying command pennants, as the Germans were aware of the radio deficiencies of their foes. Though the Russians were heavily victimized by communication inferiority, even France, with its superior numbers of heavier armed tanks, suffered in 1940 because, while all armor had radios, only command vehicles could transmit. The French also suffered because they deployed their tanks evenly along the front instead of counterconcentrating them. Finally, it is interesting to note that Guderian began his career as a communications officer.

25. R. H. S. Stolfi contends that the German "right turn" into the Ukraine fatally compromised Hitler's only chance of winning a war with the Soviet Union by striking at the heart of its strategic communications (*Hitler's Panzers East: World War II Reinterpreted* [Tulsa: Oklahoma Press, 1992]). Liddell Hart, in *Great Captains Unveiled*, 157–70, refers to the debate over whether to attack Moscow directly or to destroy Soviet field armies, as the "battle of the theories," which was won by the "proponents of military orthodoxy."

26. Mao bases his theoretical point about guerrilla warfare on his experience in fighting the Japanese, who, as the Americans would in Vietnam, focused primarily on the disruption of tactical communications. See Mao Zedong, trans. Samuel Griffith, *On Guerrilla Warfare* (New York: Praeger Books, 1961). Mao's point is echoed in an analysis of the same conflict by Milton E. Miles, *A Different Kind of War* (New York: Doubleday, 1968). Lawrence's analysis of the Desert Revolt is also confirmatory. See Thomas E. Lawrence, *Seven Pillars of Wisdom* (New York: Doubleday, 1938).

27. Colin L. Powell, "Information-Age Warrior," *Byte* (July 1992): 370.

28. See the earlier quotation from Sproull and Kiesler, *Connections*, 15–16.

29. Barry R. Posen, *The Sources of Military Doctrine* (Ithaca, N.Y.: Cornell University Press, 1984).

30. This is another new term that some visionaries and practitioners have begun using. For example, see Michael Bendikt, ed., *Cyberspace: First Steps* (Cambridge, Mass.:

MIT Press, 1991). It comes from the seminal "cyberpunk" science-fiction novel by William Gibson, *Necromancer* (New York: Ace Books, 1984). It is the most encompassing of the terms being tried out for naming the new realm of electronic knowledge, information, and communications— parts of which exist in the hardware and software at specific sites, other parts in the transmissions flowing through cables or through air and space. General Powell, in "Information-Age Warriors," nods in this direction by referring to "battlespace" as including the "infosphere."

31. Chris Bellamy grapples with some of these issues in his analysis of future land warfare, *The Future of Land Warfare* (London: Helm, 1987).

32. Note that the acclaimed U.S. intelligence in Desert Storm rarely got to the division commanders; for them, every major encounter with the enemy's forces reportedly was a surprise. See Peter Grier, "The Data Weapon," *Government Executive* (June 1992): 20–23.

33. See Kenneth N. Waltz, *Theory of International Politics* (New York: Random House, 1979). Waltz considers this phenomenon of "imitation" a major factor in the process of "internal balancing" with which all nations are continually occupied. If a military innovation is thought to work, all will soon follow the innovator. A good example of this is the abrupt and complete shift of the world's navies from wooden to metal hulls in the wake of the naval experience with ironclads in the American Civil War.

34. A classic example is the 1944 battle for Normandy. Field Marshal Montgomery's forces tied down the German Seventh Army, allowing General Patton's Third Army to engage in a broad end run of the German defenses.

35. The authors are grateful to Gordon McCormick for his insights on this topic. Also on this point, see Eric H. Arnett, *Gunboat Diplomacy and the Bomb: Nuclear Proliferation and the U.S. Navy* (New York: Praeger, 1989).

36. This last point is inspired by the thinking of RAND colleague Ken Watman.

37. There is a class of proliferator toward which our reluctance to employ forceful measures will be diminished. Iraq, Iran, North Korea, Libya, and Cuba are some of the nations whose threatened acquisition of weapons of mass destruction may justify intervention. The notion that the United States should adopt a doctrine of "selective preventive force" against "outlaw" states is discussed in John Arquilla, "Nuclear Proliferation: Implications for Conventional Deterrence," in *American Grand Strategy in the Post–Cold War World*, ed. John Arquilla and Preston Niblack (Santa Monica, Calif.: RAND, 1992).

38. Powell, "Information-Age Warriors," 370.

39. John Arquilla discusses this in detail in "Louder than Words: Tacit Communication in International Crises," *Political Communication* 9 (1992): 155–72.

40. This notion is drawn from the Korean War, where U.S. forces began their involvement by preventing the overrun of the Korean peninsula in the opening months of the war. The Pusan perimeter held a portion of South Korea free, serving as a magnet for North Korean forces. The amphibious counterattack at Inchon, far from the battlefronts, threw the invaders into complete disarray.

41. Van Creveld, *The Transformation of War.*

42. See George Kenny and Michael J. Dugan, "Operation Balkan Storm: Here's a Plan," *New York Times*, 29 November 1992. The authors call for a "Balkan Storm" without employing *any* American ground forces. We disagree with this approach, rooted as it is in theories of "limited liability" and "airpower exceptionalism." Nonetheless, they do identify many of the key types of aerial cyberwar tactics that might be employed, even if their omission of an American ground component would seriously dilute any gains achieved.

THE COMING MILITARY REVOLUTION

JAMES R. FITZSIMONDS

There seems to be growing consensus that rapidly evolving technologies will result in a profound change in the character of warfare in the coming decades—likely culminating in what has come to be known as a Revolution in Military Affairs or RMA.[1] Operation Desert Storm served to highlight some of the remarkable capabilities that technology has brought to the high-intensity battlefield since World War II. Advanced sensors and communications now provide much greater information about the enemy as well as a higher degree of operational control over our own forces. Stealth and precision-guided warheads have reduced significantly the number of platforms and amount of ordnance necessary to destroy individual targets. Conventional weapon lethality has increased, while attrition and collateral damage have been significantly reduced. These developments portend perhaps an entirely new regime of high-technology warfare in the early twenty-first century.

All of the military services generally accept the idea that we are in a period of profound change, but none has yet formally articulated what will specific-

This essay has been edited and is reprinted from Parameters 25 *(Summer 1995): 30–36, by permission of* Parameters. *Copyright © 1995 by James R. FitzSimonds.*

ally characterize the possible "end states" of this on-going RMA. In other words, looking back from a vantage point fifty years in the future, what qualities of military capability would cause us to conclude that a military revolution has indeed occurred in the intervening decades? Although this theoretical bridge has not been crossed, both service doctrine and the application of advanced technology to military systems have begun to focus on one battlefield goal that may indeed have revolutionary implications: *tempo of operations.*[2]

It is commonly accepted that future information technologies will allow the commander to know a lot more about the battlefield—to have greater situational awareness of both his own and enemy forces. However, real combat leverage derives not simply from knowing more, but from *knowing more faster—and from having the ability to act on that information very rapidly.* The idea that higher relative tempo equates to increased military leverage is not new. What *is* new is that emerging information technologies now hold out the real prospect of increasing maneuver and strike tempo by orders of magnitude compared with past capabilities. Future command cycles may be reduced from weeks or days down to hours or minutes. Geographic massing of forces and fires may give way to temporal massing for simultaneous attacks against an enemy's tactical, operational, and strategic targets. The ability to identify and destroy a significant portion of an enemy's critical system vulnerabilities faster than he can move, hide, or react may lead to a new theory of victory: that of forcing the enemy's recognition of defeat not through sequential attrition, but rather by inducing massive systemic shock on his operating and control systems.[3] Indeed, Jeffrey Cooper suggests that a conceptual end state of the RMA may be the reduction of a protracted war to a "*coup de main* executed in a single main-force engagement."[4]

Achievement of this capability against the full range of our future enemies would undoubtedly signify a new regime of warfare—and the culmination of a military revolution. It is a compelling vision that is well suited to our national strategy of forward engagement, and to our national values, which favor short, decisive conflicts, with minimal cost and risk. At the very least, such high-tempo operations would virtually eliminate another nation's ability to project significant power across its own border. At best, this ability may help us to achieve the goal of universal strategic leverage—compelling any adversary to accede to our will, be that unconditional surrender or some lesser requirement. Moreover, an enemy's belief in our ability to execute this type of operation should provide a high level of nonnuclear strategic deterrence. In essence, the achievement of this end state will allow us to make the wholesale trade of force quantity for force quality in our twenty-first-century military.

Yet while this military goal of strategic leverage through vastly increased operational tempo is undoubtedly enticing, there may be significant costs and risks associated with it that have not been fully explored. As we continue to move down this path toward a new regime of warfare, it is time that we begin asking questions about the feasibility of achieving this goal, and, more important, about how well this end state will truly serve our national interests.

CHALLENGES OF THE REVOLUTION

Inflicting "massive systemic shock" on the enemy has conceptual utility down to the tactical level of military operations. However, the real essence of the military revolution—of this new regime of warfare—derives from our ability to forestall an enemy's effective reaction to our operations, his mobilization of additional forces, or his escalation of the conflict. Pursuit of "shock" warfare will, by necessity, be characterized by parallel strikes against critical targets across all levels of warfare—from tactical units up through the national decision-making process. In this new regime, all warfare becomes strategic warfare.[5]

Despite predictions of what will happen in the coming decades, the prospect of executing high-tempo strategic warfare depends upon our finding solutions to a number of critical problems.

CAN WE KNOW ENOUGH ABOUT OUR ENEMY?

Inducing massive systemic shock depends upon the rapid destruction of that set of critical vulnerabilities upon which the enemy's key military, political, and economic systems depend. The concept seems as theoretically sound today as it did when first postulated during World War I—yet it has never been successfully demonstrated in wartime. Although the technical problems of precision strike may have been solved, we nevertheless need to know a lot more about how national systems operate than we have been able to discern in the past. Advanced computer modeling and simulation will undoubtedly offer us significantly greater insight, but collapsing the enemy's will may depend more on our ability to understand more about individual human values of a very different culture than the physical operation of systems. Target sets will vary greatly in both number and type with each adversary, and even then will be constantly changing over time. Despite our best analytical efforts, the effectiveness of our conclusions can never be tested outside of war, and thus confidence in our ultimate success will never be more than a probability based upon assumption.[6]

CAN WE BECOME FAST ENOUGH?

Revolutionary leverage emanates not just from identifying critical targets, but from doing so very rapidly—faster than the enemy can move, hide, or adjust. The number of targets per hour that must be struck to "shock" an enemy system will undoubtedly vary with the adversary and our objectives, but an action cycle approaching real time—target identification-to-destruction in hours if not minutes—has emerged as the conceptual goal.[7] For a large, highly complex adversary this will doubtless require the synergy of an integrated reconnaissance-strike system to achieve near simultaneous identification and targeting of thousands of critical vulnerabilities.[8] Far more than the single sensor-to-shooter links demonstrated to date, such a system will have to integrate large numbers of theater sensors and weapons in real time—a data fusion problem of tremendous proportions, and one perhaps requiring as yet unforeseen breakthroughs in automatic target recognition technology and artificial intelligence. Moreover, our quest for speed must not result in an information and control system so centralized, standardized, and rigid that it offers critical vulnerabilities for enemy exploitation.

HOW GOOD CAN WE AFFORD TO BE?

Although the cost of microprocessing continues to drop, it is not evident that this trend will extend to commensurate reductions in the price of targeting data and precision-guided munitions (indeed, we need them to be cheap, but not so cheap that everyone in the world can acquire this capability). Unsophisticated and inexpensive countertargeting techniques may always keep offensive forces on the wrong side of the cost/exchange ratio, rendering it much less expensive for an adversary to deny timely information than for us to gather it. Whether we can achieve a revolutionary effect with information before a clever adversary makes that information too costly may be the most critical future technical challenge. To be sure, ambiguity in targeting data can be overcome by a willingness to expend large numbers of smart munitions. However, a key aspect of this RMA end state is that of moving beyond attrition warfare to the discrete application of force—and achieving economy by substituting quality for quantity. An added cost consideration is that not only must our arsenal of smart weapons be large enough to deal with the contingency at hand, but we must have enough left over so that we have not "demodernized" ourselves relative to our *next* opponent.[9]

Beyond the issues of technical capability and cost, the most daunting challenge will likely be that of the profound organizational change needed to exploit fully revolutionary advances in information processing. The most critical drag on high-tempo system performance is the cognitive limit of the human mind, the rate at which an individual can assimilate information and act. An information-intensive battle space may work to our advantage only if humans can be largely removed from the command loop. The need for speed will likely force today's hierarchical command structures to become very flat, with automated analysis and decision making largely replacing time-consuming and error-prone human deliberation. More profoundly, technical limitations of communications and data fusion may mean that humans will have to forgo a traditional "picture" of the battle space. The question then becomes whether future U.S. military commanders can accept a continuing reduction in their real-time battle information as the price of an increasing pace of activity. In a broader sense, the issue is whether we as a military can readily adapt not only to revolutionary changes in command relationships, but to changes in specialties, basic skills, and perhaps even professional values that are dictated by new technologies.[10]

BEING CAREFUL WHAT WE ASK FOR

If our faith in technology is rewarded and we can achieve this end state, then the issue becomes whether our nation can accommodate the strategic consequences of a continuously accelerating tempo of military operations. Indeed, nonnuclear strategic warfare may confront us with many of the same dilemmas of nuclear stalemate that we are seeking to leave behind.

CAN WARFARE BECOME TOO FAST?

As the world's military leader, the United States is now setting the pace in force capabilities and military measures of effectiveness. Other nations will undoubtedly follow our lead in acquiring integrated systems of advanced sensors and smart weapons. The result will be a competitive race for command cycle dominance not only in strike and maneuver, but in information superiority. This future battlefield in which all warfare is strategic could lead to a mutual perception that any relative delay in initiating military operations will invariably result in rapid and catastrophic national defeat.[11] The issue is whether our deliberate political process can accommodate a military system that is dependent upon strategic decisions of war and peace being made within hours or even minutes. Indeed, our future national security may come to depend upon our political willingness to initiate preemptive military strikes, an option that this nation has historically conceded to foreign "aggressors."

WILL WE BE BACKED INTO THE KINDS OF WARS THAT WE DON'T WANT?

Unable to replicate our high-technology conventional forces, future adversaries may try to exploit our different cultural values by attempting to counter our nonnuclear strategic capability with weapons of mass destruction.[12] An oft-repeated lesson of the Gulf War by a retired Indian Army chief of staff—"Don't fight the Americans without nuclear weapons"—may be indicative of a growing attitude about the need for RMA "deterrence."[13] Likewise, the Russian military doctrine of 1993 eliminated the traditional Soviet "no first use" pledge for nuclear weapons, implicitly because of the "nuclear effects" demonstrated by the U.S. conventional arsenal in the 1991 war.[14] Thus our achievement of nonnuclear strategic leverage may, at some level of perceived capability, elicit the type of dirty warfare that we are explicitly seeking to avoid.[15]

CAN OUR NATION BECOME PSYCHOLOGICALLY DEPENDENT UPON LIGHTNING VICTORY?

A major justification for our pursuit of a highly compressed war is the growing conviction within the military that the American public lacks the will to fight and win a protracted conflict.[16] Although this is a useful position to justify trading force quantity for quality, such an argument, if repeated long enough, can become a self-fulfilling prophecy. Certainly doctrinal statements of America's lack of resolve are not lost on potential adversaries who may hope to attain future strategic victory (or at least avoid strategic defeat) simply by outlasting our attempted *coup de main*. The question then becomes whether—having expended our high-tech arsenal to insufficient effect—this nation can suddenly reverse a psychological conviction that it lacks the will to fight on, even if our "vital" interests are at stake.

WILL OUR STRATEGIC NATIONAL INTERESTS BECOME SLAVED TO OUR MILITARY CAPABILITY?

A limited high-tech arsenal offering only one or two strategic engagements may become unusable—always being saved for the potentially more vital problem just over the horizon—or used too late in an enemy's mobilization and force deployment to have the desired effect. Conversely, if this capability lives up to the promise of near infinite leverage at minimal cost, it will be useful everywhere. Thus the argument that our vital national interests are "those interests for which the United States is willing to fight" becomes truly circular; since we can fight for anything, everything becomes a vital interest that must be fought for.[17] How then do we come to decide when *not* to intervene, and to justify our nonintervention? This need to define our national interests in terms of our national values may be the toughest challenge of all.

CONCLUSION: MILITARY MEANS AND STRATEGIC ENDS

The course of history should leave little doubt that the ongoing pace of technological change will culminate at some point in another military revolution. By definition, our failure to innovate and adapt successfully to this new regime of warfare will have potentially catastrophic consequences on some future battlefield. Our military will be facing some significant changes in the coming decades. We must be careful not to deter ourselves from profound innovation because of what might appear to be serious problems or challenges.

Nevertheless, the characteristics of the future battlefield are not predestined, but rather will depend upon specific choices that we and other nations will be making from an expanding array of technological, operational, and organizational options. Our pursuit of an increasing tempo of combat operations is not necessarily a bad choice, but at present it is being driven more by opportunity than necessity.[18] What is important for us to remember is that the ultimate value of any innovation is measured by its success on the battlefield relative to the enemy, and many seemingly brilliant conceptions have failed miserably in that test. More important, as the German blitzkrieg revealed, the "goodness" of a military capability is ultimately determined by its contribution to the nation's strategic goals and the success of the strategic outcome. That is indeed the criterion by which our exploitation of the ongoing military revolution must be measured.

NOTES

1. For recent discussions of the RMA, see, for example, Paul Bracken, "The Military after Next," *Washington Quarterly* (Autumn 1993); Jeffrey Cooper, *Another View of the Revolution in Military Affairs* (Carlisle Barracks, Pa.: U.S. Army War College, Strategic Studies Institute, 15 July 1994); James R. FitzSimonds and Jan M. van Tol, "Revolutions in Military Affairs," *Joint Force Quarterly* (Spring 1994); and Andrew F. Krepinevich Jr., "Keeping Pace with the Military Technical Revolution," *Issues in Science and Technology* (Summer 1994).

2. General Gordon R. Sullivan has called tempo the "key" to battle command ("A New Force for a New Century," *Army* [May 1994]). The importance of battlefield tempo is central to all service doctrine. See, for example, *Force XXI Operations*; TRADOC Pamphlet 525-5, 1 August 1994, 3-3 and 3-9; *Basic Aerospace Doctrine of the United States Air Force*, Air Force Manual 1-1, vol. 2 (Washington, D.C.: GPO, March 1992), 149; *Naval Warfare*, Naval Doctrine Publication 1, 18 March 1994, 35. Decisive action based upon nearly perfect, real-time knowledge is a formal goal of the DOD's *Defense Science and Technology Strategy* (Washington, D.C.: September 1994) and programs such as the Integrated Airborne Reconnaissance Strategy of the Defense Airborne Reconnaissance Office (DARO) and the Advanced Research Projects Agency's (ARPA) War Breaker.

3. See *Force XXI Operations*, 3-21; and Cooper, *Another View*, 30.

4. Cooper, *Another View*, 30.

5. The idea that increasing battlefield tempo will serve to merge the traditional levels of warfare has been noted by other analysts of the RMA. See Michael J. Mazarr, *The Military Technical Revolution: A Structural Framework* (Washington, D.C.: Center for Strategic and International Studies, March 1993), 27; and Douglas A. MacGregor, "Future Battle: The Merging Levels of War," *Parameters* 22 (Winter 1992–93): 42.

6. It is significant to note that the Air Force's *Gulf War Air Power Survey* questioned whether the problem of attaining strategic leverage by attacks on critical systems is

even amenable to a technological solution. Eliot A. Cohen, director, *Operations, and Effects and Effectiveness,* Gulf War Air Power Survey, vol. 2 (Washington, D.C.: GPO, 1993), 370.

7. There is, as observers have pointed out, a critical difference between striking a target a day for a thousand days and striking one thousand targets in a day. The specific rate of attack necessary to "shock" an enemy system has never been clearly articulated. The first of the five future joint war-fighting capabilities most needed by the U.S. combatant commands is to "maintain near perfect real-time knowledge of the enemy and communicate that to all forces in near-real time" (*Defense Science and Technology Strategy*, 3). How near to real time we must be able to strike all enemy targets is not delineated. General Gordon Sullivan predicts a future decision cycle marked by action in "an hour or less" ("War in the Information Age," *Military Review* [April 1994]: 47).

8. The number of critical targets that encompass a nation's strategic vulnerabilities continues to be a matter of speculation and probably cannot be confirmed outside of wartime. Target estimates for even the same country vary by orders of magnitude.

9. A sobering lesson is offered by the "demoderniza-tion" of the German blitzkrieg on the Eastern Front in World War II. See Omer Bartov, *Hitler's Army* (New York: Oxford University Press, 1992).

10. For example, the decreasing differentiation be-tween military and civilian information technologies could make victory in a future war dependent upon "soldiers" like computer counterhacker Clifford Stoll in his self-described "uniform" of "grubby shirt, faded jeans, long hair, and cheap sneakers." Clifford Stoll, *The Cuckoo's Egg* (New York: Doubleday, 1989), 4.

11. The army's Force XXI doctrine states that we must expect enemy preemptive strikes as a means to thwart our own high-tempo operations ("Force XXI Operations," 3–19).

12. There are those who maintain that any future RMA will not be a true revolution in warfare unless it specifically solves existing problems with weapons of mass destruction, terrorism, attrition warfare, and the like. The position of this essay is that an RMA creates a new regime of warfare that may or may not offer solutions to existing military problems.

13. Patrick J. Garrity, *Why the Gulf War Still Matters: Foreign Perspectives on the War and the Future of Interna-tional Security* (Los Alamos, N. Mex.: Los Alamos National Laboratory, Center for National Security Studies, July 1993), xiv.

14. The initial 1992 draft of the doctrine stated explic-itly that conventional attack could elicit a nuclear response. See Charles Dick, "The Military Doctrine of the Russian Federation," *Jane's Intelligence Review,* Special Report no. 1 (January 1994).

15. For a broader treatment of this issue, and the ulti-mate "disutility" of individual weapons, see Thomas J. Welch, "Technology Change and Security," *Washington Quarterly* (Spring 1990).

16. Navy doctrine, for example, states that "rapid con-clusion of hostilities is a key goal" because "protracted war can cause high casualties and unwanted political and eco-nomic consequences." (*Naval Warfare,* 35). The air force believes that we are entering an era in which "the American people will have low tolerance for prolonged combat oper-ations and mounting casualties" (*The Air Force and U.S. National Security: Global Reach–Global Power* [Washing-ton, D.C.: GPO, June 1990]).

17. For this definition of "vital" interests, see John H. Dalton, Admiral Jeremy M. Boorda, and General Carl E. Mundy Jr., "Forward . . . From the Sea," Naval Institute *Proceedings* (Washington, D.C.: GPO, December 1994), 46.

18. No high-technology threat at present requires an immediate U.S. response. Moreover, the idea that we must acquire new capabilities to reduce both casualties and risk in future military action may stem more from folklore than fact. See Benjamin C. Schwarz, *Casualties, Public Opinion, and U.S. Military Intervention: Implications for U.S. Re-gional Deterrence Strategies* (Santa Monica, Calif.: RAND, 1994). Eliot Cohen is probably right in concluding that military officers are far more sensitive to casualties than is the American public ("What to Do about National De-fense," *Commentary* [November 1994], 22).

CHAPTER 20

SOME FINAL THOUGHTS

THE FUTURE OF AMERICAN DEFENSE POLICY

PETER L. HAYS, BRENDA J. VALLANCE, AND ALAN R. VAN TASSEL

"What is the appropriate defense policy for today's national security challenges?" This is a question that many analysts, security specialists, and academics are struggling to answer. Indeed, the end of the Cold War requires us to reexamine past defense policy and question its applicability to today's security environment. This book provides students with a framework for examining defense policy by, first, establishing the process by which policy is made and, second, outlining the current debates and challenges to existing policy.

In this final chapter, we review the major elements of the book and reemphasize the use of the defense policy process model as an organizing principle and analytical tool. We then briefly discuss the future of American defense policy, a difficult task given the variety of inputs and actors in the policy-making process. However, given the long lead-times for defense acquisition, the difficulty of restructuring military forces, and the slow-moving nature of large bureaucracies, we must envision policies useful for the future if we are to man, train, organize, equip, deploy, and use our forces appropriately.

THE DEFENSE POLICY PROCESS MODEL

As we noted in Chapter 1, defense policy can be defined as a plan or course of action, the military component of U.S. national security, a political process, and a field of study. Throughout this book, we have used our defense policy process model to examine more closely the first three of these definitions. This model, pictured below, illustrates not only the dynamics of defense policy as a political process, but also furthers our understanding of this complicated subject by illustrating the lenses and images through which policy actors interpret events and take actions. It is this model that best explains daily defense decision making.

In the book's first chapter, we also discussed the realist paradigm used by many political scientists to describe defense policy making. That paradigm, however, is most useful in explaining crisis decisions and, in contrast to our model, it fails to capture the multiple inputs, actors, and political processes that broadly influence the making and implementation of American defense policy. This book, therefore, was

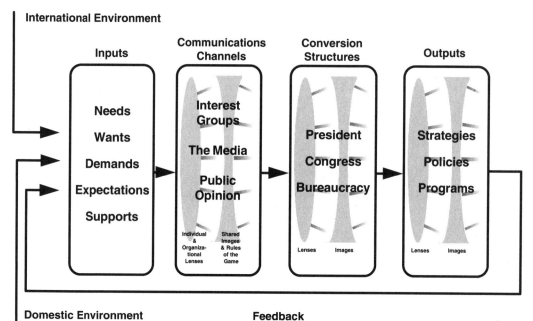

Defense Policy Process Model

organized around the defense policy process as captured by our model. Each part dealt with one of the steps in the model in order to explain this dynamic process and illustrate the debates over defense policy issues.

A BRIEF REVIEW

Part I examined the inputs to the defense policy process and served as the launching point for debate over the appropriate uses and limits of military power. In our changing international system, is military power still a useful instrument for protecting a state's national interests? With the end of the Cold War, are there new, more restrictive limits on this instrument of policy? Before answering these questions, the student must first decide the nature of the international system in which U.S. defense policy must operate. This is an area of great debate, and we included Donald Snow's article as the interpretation that best explains this environment and the challenges our nation faces.

Inputs to the defense policy-making process also come from the domestic environment. As Peterson and Sebenius noted, the domestic agenda increasingly draws attention away from international security issues. What is the proper balance between the international and domestic environments? How can we properly address problems of social degeneration and economic growth while also maintaining influence within the international system? Without unlimited resources, can we maintain a military presence throughout the world while also achieving social and economic stability at home?

Having introduced these debates over the environment in which defense policy exists and that serve as multiple and competing inputs into the policy process, Part II, "The Actors Who Influence American Defense Policy," examined how these inputs are aggregated, organized, and represented by communications channels in order for government institutions or conversion structures to make and implement policy. The media, interest groups, and public opinion all serve as important communications channels. In a society in which the people are sovereign, the reelection imperative drives elected officials to be responsive to the population's needs, wants, demands, and expectations.

Elected government officials, the president and Congress, possess both formal and informal powers that they may use to influence the defense policy process. We included a reading by Richard Neustadt on the president's power to persuade as an example of an important informal power. Elected officials, however, are not the only actors responsible for defense policy making and implementation. The intelligence community, the Office of the Secretary of Defense, and the military services also play a significant role.

As illustrated by the defense policy process model, individuals possess divergent views of the world which influence their approach to policy. Organizations also diverge in their attempts to pursue differing organizational interests. Yet the shared images that are a vital part of American strategic and political culture provide a basis for the compromise and consensus building necessary for defense policy to be made or implemented.

In Part III, "The Formulation of American Defense Policy," we examined the interaction between the communications channels and conversion structures. This interaction highlights the dynamics of the defense policy process and demonstrates the consensus building, bargaining, and compromise that characterize it. By comparing the formal decision-making models with actual case studies of defense issues, students should gain a better appreciation of how the political process shapes decisions.

This process also is affected by the perceptions of individuals and organizations involved in the policy process. How we interpret actions, how we communicate our intent, and the assumptions we make about others' actions and intentions all influence decision making. Individuals and groups responsible for making decisions also are responsive to stress, pressures from group members, and the dynamics of the decision-making environment.

Part IV, "American Defense Policies," examined the outputs of the defense policy process and discussed the six broad areas of strategy, nuclear policy, conventional policy, special operations/low intensity conflict (SOLIC) and operations other than war, arms control and proliferation, and civil–military relations. The readings in this section included the most current statements of national security and defense policy, such as the Joint Chiefs of Staff's national military strategy. Reflecting on the earlier parts of this book, the student should recognize and understand the controversy surrounding these statements. Given the environment discussed in Part I—in which debate centered on international versus domestic priorities, the nature of the international system, and the United States' role in that system—it should come as no surprise that such official statements engender debate over several issues, such as whether the United States should "engage" itself in world affairs, as the Clinton administration states in its national security strategy.

Just as overall U.S. strategy is enveloped in controversy, so too is the policy associated with force structure and organization. The essays selected for this part raise a number of questions currently being debated in defense policy circles. What is the role of nuclear weapons in the post–Cold War environment? How should the services arm and man themselves to address conventional threats appropriately? As warfare moves toward the lower end of the spectrum of conflict, are we prepared to commit forces to such nontraditional missions as humanitarian assistance and disaster relief? Perhaps one of the most significant issues facing the U.S. military is whether it should be used for "peacekeeping" missions, such as those in Haiti and Bosnia. These missions, and others that likely will arise in the future, raise the specter of placing U.S. forces under the authority of a U.N.-appointed commander. Are our forces trained and equipped for such a variety of missions, and are we as a nation prepared to see our troops fight under a U.N. flag and be directed by a multinational staff?

Clearly, we face a variety of problems when discussing nuclear and conventional policy, and there also are a number of challenges when discussing arms control and weapons proliferation. Have we laid the appropriate groundwork for limiting nuclear weapons in the future? During the Cold War, the existence of two rival superpowers whose interests caused them to counter each other's actions throughout the world served as a form of control over other states' intentions. Now that this control mechanism is gone, we face a world in which power rivalries among states are increasingly acted out through the proliferation of weapons of mass destruction. How can we limit the danger of these weapons when both supply and demand have created a thriving weapons market? If this threat is truly credible, how should the United States arm itself in order to counter this danger?

In the final chapter of this part, we examined U.S. civil–military relations within the context of many of the issues discussed above. What is the role of the professional officer in the political process? As an expert in his or her field, should the military officer have an input to the political process, or should he or she remain outside of this process? As the United States broadens its definition of national security by including nontraditional roles and missions, are we involving the military in areas outside of its competence? Are we running the risk of politicizing our officer corps at the expense of combat performance? Worse yet, could our officer corps gain too much influence in defense policy making, effectively militarizing such policy? The readings in this chapter examined these issues.

Finally, in Part V we turned to "The Future of American Defense Policy." The first two chapters of this part discuss regional threats and technological changes affecting defense policy. In discussing these issues, we are emphasizing the iterative nature of defense policy. In other words, the defense policy process results in outputs in the form of strategy, policy, and program decisions. These decisions may in turn result in technological innovations (e.g., incorporating "stealthy" technology into new aircraft or testing a new ballistic missile defense system) and changes in regional power balances (e.g., cutting U.S. forces overseas or selling advanced fighters to other countries), both of which affect the international and domestic environments. Thus feedback from these decisions serves as another input into the defense policy process.

The readings in Chapter 18 examined regional threats and challenges. This decade has been marked by tremendous changes in the international system, and clearly there will be many more changes before the decade is over. The readings in this chapter help frame the idea that our defense policy must be responsive to a rapidly changing international environment, but these circumstances make long-range planning and weapon systems acquisition particularly difficult.

Technology also plays an important part in shaping both the domestic and international environments. Technological advances may present opportunities to improve our military capabilities significantly, realign our force structure, and make once formidable threats inadequate. In the hands of potential enemies, however, technology presents threats that must be defeated. The readings in this section examined the technological advances associated with the revolution in military affairs. Will we be able to incorporate the developments in communications and advanced weaponry associated with this revolution, and what is the proper method of incorporating such technology into our force structure? What will the impact of such technologies be on our military forces? What changes will need to be made in force structure, command and control, and training to integrate such technology?

THE FUTURE OF AMERICAN DEFENSE POLICY

In this last section of *American Defense Policy,* we turn briefly to the defense policy developments and trends highlighted in the preceding chapters. The discussion that follows focuses on three areas that provide a foundation for our defense policy process model: the domestic environment, the international environment, and technological developments. These developments and trends will play a significant role in shaping America's defense policy for the near-term future.[1]

The most prominent feature of the domestic political landscape is the primacy of the domestic agenda. This was the dominant message of the 1992 presidential election, and the 1994 congressional elections pointed to new areas for emphasis within domestic politics. Clearly, both elections reinforced the primacy of domestic issues over foreign policy concerns. The familiar litany of domestic political woes afflicting the American body politic will continue to dominate our political discussions and in most cases will crowd out other concerns. Moreover, a combination of factors such as the continuing afterglow of the Gulf War, the limited threats to U.S. vital interests worldwide, and the belief that the U.S. military has already been downsized and restructured enough have created a higher level of satisfaction with American defense policy than with many of the other issues that currently seem more pressing. Thus for the foreseeable future there seem to be few political incentives to raise defense policy issues in general, and this is particularly true in relation to the politically complex and potentially divisive fundamental defense policy choices America faces today. Where defense policy concerns do emerge into the political limelight, they are most likely to be in the context of "hot button" domestic issues. Americans will continue to debate second-order issues such as gays in the military, women in combat, or U.S. military support for U.N. peacekeeping operations rather than address more fundamental and important questions concerning American defense policy for the post–Cold War world. These basic themes will in all likelihood dominate our domestic political agenda for some time—the situation will be one of "benign neglect" for American defense policy, with business as usual in most quarters and many fundamental questions left unexamined.

A related set of important domestic policy issues has to do with the state of U.S. civil–military relations. As several contributors to this volume pointed out, it is widely believed that we are today witnessing the most strained civil–military relations since President Harry Truman fired General Douglas MacArthur. While much of the argument and evidence presented by the alarmists is compelling, the trends need to be carefully evaluated to determine whether we can expect troubled civil–military relations to continue over the long term. In our judgment, we have already passed the point of greatest stress, in both perception and reality. Moreover, on balance, the alarmists have overstated their position. Much of their argument is centered on the personalities of Presidents George Bush and Bill Clinton interacting with the Gulf War–emboldened chairman of the Joint Chiefs of Staff, General Colin Powell, during the period from approximately 1991 to 1993. In contrast, we have recently seen a modest growth in President Clinton's stature vis-à-vis the military that is largely a function of the extremely low-key approach of Powell's successor, General John Shalikashvili. This turnaround illustrates just to what extent civil–military relations depend on individual personalities. Thus while several of the underlying, systemic sources of conflict remain, we believe that these tensions are likely to continue to subside in the near term. Indeed, it may be that the warnings issued by Colonel Charles Dunlap and others have already had more of a salutary effect than they could have hoped for.

The final, and perhaps most important, defense policy theme that emerges from the domestic environment is the lack of consensus on an appropriate U.S. national security strategy for the post–Cold War era. There is not yet an overarching American strategy for dealing with the changed international environment comparable to the containment and deterrence strategies that guided us through the Cold War. Containment was directed at the threat of expansion from the Soviet Union and would seem to be an inappropriate conceptual approach for different types of expanding threats such as instability or proliferation. Deterrence, as several of the articles above point out, also may be a less useful strategy for the United States now than it was during the Cold War. In the absence of such an overarching strategy, we have seen a profusion of strategic concepts and lists of criteria. The lack of such a strategy is most apparent in relation to a U.S. intervention policy for the post–Cold War world.[2] We do not envision the emergence of a consensus on an overarching strategic theme for U.S. defense policy anytime soon. There is too little incentive to vet this issue domestically, little agreement on the current and future shape of the international environment, and widely divergent views on what does or should constitute the components or objectives of U.S. national security. In the absence of such a strategy, we are likely to see a continuation of the often unsatisfying case-by-case approach to defense policy issues we have seen thus far during the 1990s. Thus while we might wish for more vision and consistency in our defense policy, we must also keep in mind that this desire for a comprehensive U.S. strategy for the post–Cold War world may itself be an inappropriate vestige of the Cold War and Cold War–type thinking.

When turning to the international environment, the situation is more confused, and fewer trends and themes clearly stand out. Despite the primacy of the domestic agenda, the international environment has and will continue to shape American defense policy and policy in general. Three broad and interrelated issues emerge when considering the impact of the international environment on American defense policy: what role America should play in the world, America's position in the international system, and the shape of the world system.

Perhaps the most logical approach to examining the international environment would be first to focus on what America's role should be in the world. America is a very powerful, if not the most powerful, actor in the international system and has some ability to help shape this system to its liking. Unfortunately, questions about what role the United States should play and what international structures it should attempt to build for the post–Cold War world are extremely difficult to address, for several reasons. First, this *a priori* approach depends greatly on the interrelated but unresolved issues of the nature of America's position in the international system, as well as the nature of the international environment itself. Questions about what we should do cannot be divorced from the issues of what we can do and the environment in which such actions would take place. More important, as discussed earlier, there are few political incentives to raise such difficult issues. America does not face the security threats or crises that would compel us to examine such fundamental questions in detail. One important development, however, has been the recent reawakening of the idealistic/utopian component of American strategic culture, as reflected in the debates over U.S. intervention in Somalia, Haiti, and Bosnia. It is also interesting to see how this issue contributes to a role-reversal between the Democrats and Republicans over intervention and the use of force. Nonetheless, to date these debates have generated far more heat than light, and we believe that our current lack of *a priori* thinking about what America's role should be in the international system will continue and will shape related policy issues.

America's position in the world system is another crucial issue for defense policy, but here the problem is not so much a lack of thinking as it is the widely divergent views on this subject. Some analysts emphasize the military dimension of state power and highlight America's victories in the Cold War and the Gulf War; they see the United States as the lone superpower and a unipolar structure in the international system. Other commentators focus on America's relative economic decline and internal decay when emphasizing that the United States is just one actor in a multipolar and increasingly interdependent system. Part of the problem in assessing the character of the international system today is that the transformation of the international system following the end of the Cold War seems to have no precedent—it is difficult to find another example of a systemic transformation without an accompanying major war. Moreover, the situation for the United States is in many ways the obverse of that at the end of the Second World War: at that point in time we were preeminent economically but faced a very significant military challenge from the Soviet Union. Such debates and questions directly influence many defense policy issues. For example, the threats perceived by and the interests of a moderately powerful state in a multipolar system are likely to be quite different from those faced by a lone superpower in a unipolar system. More specifically, a lone superpower has the luxury and perhaps also the responsibility to intervene unilaterally in certain situations, whereas a less powerful actor is far more dependent upon building and using coalitions. The emphasis on coalitions in the Clinton administration's national security strategy provides evidence of its view of America's position in the world. The continuing debate over America's position in the world system makes it difficult for us to draw out any more comprehensive themes in this area.

The final issue pertaining to the international environment is where the world system seems to be heading. Here, once again, there is a great deal of debate. Ideas run the gamut from Francis Fukuyama's benign "end of history" due to a worldwide convergence on the ideals of liberal democracy to Samuel Huntington's "clash of civilizations" or even to visions of world anarchy driven by ecological Armageddon.[3] The concept we found most useful for analyzing American defense policy in the context of a changing international environment is Donald Snow's two-tiered world discussed in Chapter 3. The most important result of the two-tiered system is what Snow terms the "interest-threat mismatch." What this means is that in contrast to the Cold War, circumstances today are such that the United States must carefully choose when and where to intervene because it has practically no vital interests at stake in the second-tier regions of the world where almost all threats to peace are found. This type of thinking clearly has greatly influenced the current emphasis on lists of criteria for intervention and the use of force. It is also directly related to our current focus

on an "exit strategy" for extracting the NATO peacekeepers from Bosnia after a one-year deployment.[4] We believe that the world of tiers and the interest-threat mismatch will continue into the foreseeable future and will be the most significant international factor shaping American defense policy during this time.

Before closing, we also must look briefly at some of the most important trends and developments in technology. The increasingly relentless pace of technology fundamentally shapes nearly all human developments, and American defense policy is particularly sensitive to such trends. The revolution in military affairs (RMA) and information warfare (IW) are two broad concepts that will be important determinants of future options.

As the discussions in Chapter 19 pointed out, an RMA is upon us. The changing nature of warfare has major implications for the American military in many respects: most notably, how it should prepare to fight, how it should be organized, and the types of weapons systems it needs in the future. The U.S. military's current emphasis on thinking about the RMA augurs well for keeping the United States at the forefront of this revolution. Some of the most interesting specific issues lie at the intersection of the RMA and nontraditional uses of force. The RMA seems to hold great potential for improving the efficacy of U.S. forces in nontraditional roles. For example, nonlethal technologies such as sticky foam to immobilize opponents, specialized units rehearsed for specific missions using virtual reality, and continuing improvements in sensors and information distribution systems could radically alter the ways in which the United States performs future peacekeeping operations. Along these lines, the U.S. military should carefully consider making high-technology assets such as power projection, intelligence, and specialized units its unique contribution to future coalition warfare, relying on its partners for the bulk of manpower requirements. Before getting too far afield in analyzing future technological trends, however, we must reemphasize that even in relation to the RMA, the key issue, as in all other areas, is the political process through which policy choices are made, rather than the technology itself. In this context, it is unclear how well Americans outside of the military understand or appreciate the RMA and how much support this concept will enjoy.

IW is a cutting-edge concept derived from the RMA. IW is concerned with how today's revolutionary means of collecting, analyzing, fusing, distributing, and controlling information radically changes the nature of warfare. For most analysts, the RMA focuses on changes in military hardware, while IW looks more broadly at the "software" required to achieve the greatest military effectiveness. IW is the buzzword of the day in the Pentagon and as such it runs the danger of becoming a fad. Some concentrated focus on IW seems highly prudent, but it is far too early to assess the staying power of IW as an item of emphasis in defense circles. It will be interesting to see how well IW fares following the departure of one of its chief proponents, Vice Chairman of the Joint Chiefs of Staff Admiral William Owens.

The other major point to be made in relation to IW is that the United States must be careful not to repeat the mistake many accused it of making in relation to nuclear weapons during the Cold War. That is, the United States should not go so far down the road of thinking about and preparing for IW that it is less prepared for the more likely form of conflict: low-tech, non-state warfare in the second tier. Brilliant info warriors capable of elegantly crashing enemy computer nets will be of little use in situations where the protagonists are using stones and machetes. Even in cases where second-tier states do obtain high-tech weapons, IW may still be of limited use because second-tier states are unlikely to have developed all the information architectures usually associated with high-tech weapons in first-tier states.

In closing, we return to our defense policy process model. We believe that this model will retain its utility for analyzing the making and implementation of American defense policy in the future. We hope that our description of the operation of this model and the many examples contained in this book will be useful to those who will be involved in future American defense policy. Much wisdom will be required of them as they grapple with the challenges of the post–Cold War world.

NOTES

1. The end of the Cold War has produced a spate of works that discuss the shape of the world and America's place in the international system. Three works that we found particularly useful when beginning to analyze Amer-ican defense policy for the post–Cold War world are Alvin Toffler and Heidi Toffler, *War and Anti-War: Survival at the Dawn of the 21st Century* (Boston: Little, Brown, 1993); Richard Szafranski, "When Waves Collide: Future Conflict," *Joint Forces Quarterly* (Spring 1995): 77–84; and Eliot A. Cohen, "What to Do about National Defense," *Commentary* 98 (November 1994): 21–32.

2. For an in-depth discussion of this issue see Arnold Kanter and Linton F. Brooks, eds., *U.S. Intervention Policy for the Post–Cold War World: New Challenges and New Responses* (New York: W. W. Norton, 1994).

3. Discussion of these broad interpretations of where the world is heading can be found in Francis Fukuyama, "The End of History?" *National Interest* 16 (Summer 1989): 3–18; Samuel P. Huntington, "The Clash of Civilizations?" *Foreign Affairs* 72 (Summer 1993): 22–49; and Robert D. Kaplan, "The Coming Anarchy," *Atlantic Monthly* (February 1994): 44–75.

4. The roots of the current emphasis on lists of criteria for the use of force and intervention can be traced to the six major tests for the use of U.S. forces in combat introduced by former Secretary of Defense Caspar Weinberger in a presentation to the National Press Club on 28 November 1984. Weinberger also discusses his six tests in some detail in "U.S. Defense Strategy," *Foreign Affairs* 64 (Spring 1986): 675–97. For his part, current Secretary of Defense William J. Perry has revised and updated these rules into eight "Criteria for the Use of Force." See U.S. Department of Defense, *Annual Report to the President and the Congress* (Washington, D.C.: GPO, February 1995), 16–17. The current U.S. emphasis on devising exit strategies prior to any intervention is closely associated with Clinton administration national security adviser Anthony Lake. See, for example, William J. Clinton, *A National Security Strategy of Engagement and Enlargement* (Washington, D.C.: GPO, February 1995), 12–13.

ABOUT THE CONTRIBUTORS

GORDON ADAMS focuses on military research as a member of the Council on Economic Priorities. He graduated magna cum laude from Stanford University and received his Ph.D. from Columbia University. He has written several books and articles on defense spending, including *The Iron Triangle* and, most recently, *The Role of Defense Budgets in Civil–Military Relations*.

CHARLES T. ALLAN, Lieutenant Colonel, U.S. Air Force, is currently serving as commander, 41st Electronic Combat Squadron at Davis Monthan Air Force Base, Arizona. A 1976 distinguished graduate from the U.S. Air Force Academy, he was also a distinguished graduate from Air Command and Staff College and a 1993 Air Force National Defense Fellow at the Center for Strategic and International Studies.

GRAHAM T. ALLISON is the Douglas Dillon Professor of Government at Harvard University's Kennedy School of Government. Dr. Allison received his Ph.D. from Harvard and was dean of the Kennedy School from 1977 to 1989. Dr. Allison also has served in the public sector and most recently was assistant secretary of defense for policy and plans in the Clinton administration. Published extensively, he is the author of *Rethinking America's Security: Beyond Cold War to New World Order* (with Gregory Treverton) and the contributing editor of *Cooperative Denuclearization: From Pledges to Deeds*.

GENEVIEVE ANTON is a military affairs reporter for the *Colorado Springs Gazette Telegraph*. In 1995 she received the Gerald R. Ford Prize for distinguished reporting on national defense. Ms. Anton graduated with distinction in public policy studies from Duke University.

JOHN ARQUILLA is an assistant professor of national security affairs at the Naval Postgraduate School. He has worked as a consultant for the RAND Corporation and served as an analyst for U.S. Central Command, the Joint Staff, and the intelligence community. Dr. Arquilla earned his Ph.D. from Stanford University and is the author of *The Strategic Implications of Information Dominance*.

ROBERT J. ART is the Herter Professor of International Relations and chair of the Department of Politics at Brandeis University. He received his

Ph.D. from Harvard University and worked as a research fellow for Harvard's Center for International Affairs. He is the author or editor of numerous books and articles, including *From Containment to Détente: American Foreign Policy, 1945–1978* and *International Politics: Enduring Concepts and Contemporary Issues* (with Robert Jervis).

CHARLES L. BARRY, Lieutenant Colonel, U.S. Army, is a senior military fellow at the National Defense University's Institute for National Strategic Studies. Colonel Barry holds an M.P.A. from Western Kentucky University and is a graduate of the Army's Command and General Staff College, the Army War College Defense Strategy Course, and the National Security Manager's Course at the Industrial College of the Armed Forces. He is the author of *The Search for Peace in Europe* and *Security Architecture for Europe* and most recently *Reforging the Trans-Atlantic Relationship*.

JEREMY M. BOORDA, Admiral, U.S. Navy, served as the chief of naval operations in Washington, D.C. Admiral Boorda received his master's degree from the Naval War College. His previous assignments included positions as commander of NATO forces in Southern Europe and as the chief of naval personnel. Admiral Boorda passed away in 1996.

JAN S. BREEMER is an associate professor of national security affairs at the Naval Postgraduate School. He holds a Ph.D. from the University of Southern California and has published extensively on both historical and contemporary maritime strategy issues, including a recent monograph on "The Burden of Trafalgar: Decisive Battle and Naval Strategic Expectations on the Eve of the First World War." Prior to his current position, Dr. Breemer was a Secretary of the Navy Senior Research Fellow at the Naval War College.

JAMES H. BRUSSTAR is a specialist in Russian security policies, decision-making procedures, and constitutional development at the National Defense University's Institute for National Strategic Studies. He is the author of *Russian Security Policies* and *The Loyalty of the Russian Military*.

CARL H. BUILDER is a senior member of the RAND Corporation's staff, specializing in strategy formulation and analysis. He graduated from the University of California, Los Angeles with an M.A. Mr. Builder has worked for various government agencies, including the Air Quality Management District for Los Angeles, the Nuclear Regulatory Commission, the U.S. Army, and the U.S. Air Force. He is the author of several books, including *The Icarus Syndrome.*

PATRICK L. CLAWSON is an economist and Middle East analyst for the Institute for National Strategic Studies at the National Defense University. He is the author of *Iran's Strategic Intentions and Capabilities, Iran's Challenge to the West,* and *Economic Consequences of Peace for Israel, Palestinians, Jordan.*

WILLIAM J. CLINTON is the forty-second president of the United States. He was a Rhodes Scholar and received a law degree from Yale University. Before being elected to his current office, President Clinton served as the governor of Arkansas.

ELIOT A. COHEN is a professor of strategic studies at the Paul H. Nitze School of Advanced International Studies, Johns Hopkins University. He received his Ph.D. from Harvard University. From 1991 to 1993 he directed the Department of Defense study that resulted in the five-volume *Gulf War Air Power Survey.*

JOHN H. DALTON is the seventieth secretary of the navy. He graduated with distinction from the United States Naval Academy in 1964. Previously, Secretary Dalton ran the San Antonio, Texas, office of Stephans, Inc., an investment banking firm. He also was involved with the Clinton-Gore and Carter-Mondale campaigns.

VINCENT DAVIS was awarded a Ph.D. from Princeton University and is currently director of the Patterson School of Diplomacy and International Commerce at the University of Kentucky. He served in the U.S. Naval Reserve where he advanced to the rank of captain. He wrote *Henry Kissinger and Bureaucratic Politics: A Personal Appraisal* and was a contributing editor to *Reorganizing America's Defense: Leadership in War and Peace* (with Robert Art and Samuel Huntington).

CHARLES J. DUNLAP JR., Colonel, U.S. Air Force, is the staff judge advocate for U.S. Strategic Command. During his previous assignment as the deputy staff judge advocate for U.S. Central Command, he deployed to Africa in support of Operation Provide Relief in Somalia. He is the author of numerous articles on legal and national security affairs. Colonel Dunlap holds a J.D. from the Villanova University School of Law and is a distinguished graduate from the National War College.

JAMES R. FITZSIMONDS, Captain, U.S. Navy, is a naval intelligence officer assigned to the Net Assessment Directorate of the Office of the Secretary of Defense. He served as deputy chief of staff for intelligence for the USS *America* Battle Group during Operation Desert Storm. Captain FitzSimonds is a distinguished graduate of the Industrial College of the Armed Forces.

RONALD R. FOGLEMAN, General, U.S. Air Force, is chief of staff of the air force. A 1963 graduate of the U.S. Air Force Academy, the general earned a master's degree from Duke University and is a graduate of the U.S. Army War College. A command pilot with over 6,300 flying hours, General Fogleman served as commander in chief of the U.S. Transportation Command prior to his present position.

JOHN H. GARRISON, Brigadier General, U.S. Air Force, currently is the chief of intelligence for Air Combat Command. He has served in various positions, including defense and air attaché to the People's Republic of China. From 1972 to 1975 General Garrison was a member of the U.S. Air Force Academy's Department of Political Science, teaching courses in U.S. politics, international relations, and public administration.

RICHARD C. HALLORAN is a special projects corespondent for the *Washington Post,* specializing in East Asian affairs. He completed the graduate studies program at Columbia University and was a Ford Foundation Fellow at the East Asian Institute. He has served in East Asia in both civil and military functions. As a U.S. Army paratrooper, he saw action in Korea and Vietnam.

MORTON H. HALPERIN is an independent defense consultant. Most recently, he was director of the Center for National Security Studies. He also is a consultant to the RAND Corporation. He holds a Ph.D. from Yale University and has written numerous books, including *Sino-Soviet Relations and Arms Control* and *Freedom vs. National Security* (with Daniel Hoffman).

OLE R. HOLSTI completed his Ph.D. at Stanford University and currently is the George V. Allen Professor of Political Science at Duke University. He serves as a member of the advisory board for the University Press of America and is the author of *American Leadership in World Affairs: The Breakdown of Consensus* (with James Rosenau).

SAMUEL P. HUNTINGTON received his Ph.D. from Harvard University where he now serves as the Albert J. Weatherhead III University Professor and director of the John M. Olin Institute for Strategic Studies. He served on the National Security Council from 1977 to 1978 and is the author of many works, including *Political Order in Changing Societies, The Soldier and the State: The Theory and Politics of Civil–Military Relations,* and *The Common Defense: Strategy Programs in National Politics.*

LINDA S. JAMISON is director of Government Relations at the Center for Strategic and International Studies. She earned an M.A. from American University in Washington, D.C., and served as a policy analyst for the House of Representatives.

IRVING L. JANIS is an adjunct professor of psychology at the University of California, Berkeley. He has a Ph.D. from Columbia University and served as a fellow for the American Psychological Association. He also served in the U.S. Army's Research Branch during the Second World War. Dr. Janis is the author of numerous books, including *Groupthink, Air War and Emotional Stress: Psychological Studies of Bombing and Civilian Defense,* and *Psychology and the Prevention of Nuclear War* (with R. White).

ROBERT JERVIS is the Adlai E. Stevenson Professor of International Relations at Columbia University. He earned a Ph.D. from the University of California, Berkeley, and received fellowships from the Council of Foreign Relations and the Guggenheim Foundation. Dr. Jervis's many works include *The Meaning of Nuclear Revolution: Statecraft and the Prospect of Armageddon* and *International Politics: Enduring Concepts and Contemporary Issues* (with Robert Art).

DOUGLAS V. JOHNSON, Lieutenant Colonel, U.S. Army Retired, is an associate research professor of national security affairs at the U.S. Army War College's Strategic Studies Institute. A 1963 graduate of the U.S. Military Academy, he was awarded a Ph.D. from Temple University. Colonel Johnson's career included two tours in Vietnam and teaching positions at West Point and the army's senior service schools. He has been published extensively—his works include *The Impact of Media upon National Security Decision Making*—and helped revise army doctrine and field manuals.

KERRY M. KARTCHNER is currently the U.S. Arms Control and Disarmament Agency representative to the Joint Compliance and Inspection Commission in Geneva, Switzerland. Dr. Kartchner previously served as an assistant professor of national security affairs at the Naval Postgraduate School. He is the author of *Negotiating START: Strategic Arms Reduction Talks and the Quest for Strategic Stability.* His Ph.D. in international relations is from the University of Southern California.

CATHERINE McARDLE KELLEHER is the secretary of defense representative to Europe and the defense adviser to the U.S. Mission at NATO. Prior to being appointed to these positions, Dr. Kelleher served as a professor of public policy and director of the Center for International Security Studies at the University of Maryland, College Park. She received her Ph.D. from the Massachusetts Institute of Technology and was a Fulbright Fellow, a

Ford Foreign Area Fellow, and received a fellowship at the Institute for War and Peace Studies, Columbia University. She has authored a number of books, including *Germany, Nuclear Weapons, and Alliance Relations* and *Evolving European Defense Policies* (with Gale Mattox).

NICK KOTZ is a writer for the *Washington Post.* He served in the U.S. Marine Corps Reserve from 1956 to 1958. A Pulitzer Prize winner, his work has appeared in *Look, Harper's, Nation, Progressive, Washington Monthly,* and other publications. He is the author of *Wild Blue Yonder: Money, Politics and the B-1 Bomber.*

JEFFREY A. LARSEN, Lieutenant Colonel, U.S. Air Force, is a senior associate professor of national security studies and founding director of the Institute for National Security Studies at the U.S. Air Force Academy. The author of numerous reports and monographs on national security topics, Colonel Larsen is also a contributing coeditor of *Arms Control: Toward the 21st Century.* He holds a Ph.D. in politics from Princeton University.

WILLIAM H. LEWIS is a professor of international relations and political science at George Washington University in Washington, D.C. He served as director of the university's Security Policy Studies Program, as well as a senior fellow of the Institute for National Strategic Studies at the National Defense University. Dr. Lewis is coauthor of *Riding the Tiger: The Middle East Challenge after the Cold War* (with Phebe Marr).

JAMES M. LINDSAY is a professor of political science at the University of Iowa. Dr. Lindsay received his Ph.D. from Yale University and is the author of *Congress and the Politics of U.S. Foreign Policy* and *Congress and Nuclear Weapons.*

PHEBE MARR is a specialist on Middle East security issues, with an emphasis on the Persian Gulf. Dr. Marr advised the Joint Staff, Office of the Secretary of Defense, and the White House on Iraq during Desert Shield and Desert Storm. She is the author of *The Modern History of Iraq.*

DAVE McCURDY is currently president of the University of Oklahoma. A seven-term Democratic U.S. representative from Oklahoma, he served as chairman of the House Permanent Select Committee on Intelligence.

MICHAEL J. MAZARR is the editor of the *Washington Quarterly* and the director of the New Millennium Project at the Center for Strategic and International Studies. Dr. Mazarr holds a Ph.D. from the University of Maryland School of Public Affairs. He also is an adjunct professor in the National Security Program at Georgetown University.

STEVEN METZ is an associate research professor of national security affairs at the Strategic Studies Institute, U.S. Army War College. He was awarded a Ph.D. from Johns Hopkins University and is well published in military and political science journals. His latest works include *From Theory to Policy, America's Civil–Military Relations: New Issues, Enduring Problems* and *Armies and Democracy in the New Africa: Lessons from Nigeria and South Africa.*

MARC DEAN MILLOT is a senior social scientist in the RAND Corporation's Washington, D.C., office. He also is an attorney and a member of the Virginia state bar. Mr. Millot did his graduate work at the Fletcher School of Law and Diplomacy and is the author of numerous RAND reports, including *"The Day After . . ." Study: Nuclear Proliferation in the Post–Cold War World* and *The Future U.S. Military Presence in Europe: Managing USEUCOM's Command Structure after the Cold War.*

ROGER C. MOLANDER is a consultant on international nuclear security issues. He was a member of the U.S. National Security Council Staff in the Nixon, Ford, and Carter administrations.

RONALD N. MONTAPERTO is a fellow at the National Defense University's Institute for National Strategic Studies specializing in East Asian security affairs and focusing on Chinese and Japanese foreign and national security policies. Currently, he is defining strategies and policies for managing future U.S. interests in the Asia Pacific region. His *Red Guard: The Political Biography of Dai Hsiao-ai* was nominated for a national book award.

JAMES W. MORRISON is a specialist on NATO and Europe for the National Defense University's Institute for National Strategic Studies. His areas of emphasis include Russia, Ukraine, and Eurasia. He is the author of *Vladimir Zhirinovskiy: An Assessment of a Russian Ultra-Nationalist.*

CARL E. MUNDY JR., General, U.S. Marine Corps Retired, served as commandant of the Marine Corps. He was awarded a master's degree from the Naval War College.

EDMUND S. MUSKIE was a former U.S. secretary of state and Democratic senator from Maine. He also was the Democratic Party's candidate for vice president in 1968. Mr. Muskie received a law degree from Cornell University and served in the U.S. Naval Reserve from 1942 to 1945, where he earned three battle stars for service on an escort destroyer. Mr. Muskie passed away in 1996.

CHARLES R. NELSON, Lieutenant Colonel, U.S. Air Force, is currently serving as Chief of Quality Control, 96th Air Base Wing, Eglin Air Force Base, Florida. Colonel Nelson holds an M.S. in industrial engineering and engineering management from the University of Tennessee and a Ph.D. in public administration from the University of Alabama. He is a graduate of the Program Managers Course at the Defense Systems Management College and Air Command and Staff College. He is the author of numerous publications in the areas of engineering, acquisition, and public policy.

RICHARD E. NEUSTADT is the Douglas Dillon Professor of Government, Emeritus, at Harvard University's John F. Kennedy School of Government. Dr. Neustadt received his Ph.D. from Harvard and has worked at the U.S. Atomic Energy Commission and at the U.S. Department of State, was a consultant for the RAND Corporation, and acted as an adviser to Presidents John F. Kennedy and Lyndon B. Johnson. He has written and contributed to many works, including *Thinking in Time: The Uses of History for Decision-Makers* (with Ernest May).

SAM NUNN is serving as a Democratic senator from Georgia and is a member of the Armed Services, Governmental Affairs, and Small Business Committees. He served as the chairman of the Senate Armed Services Committee for seven years and is currently the committee's ranking minority member.

PETER G. PETERSON is chairman of the Blackstone Group, a private investment bank. He also currently chairs the Council on Foreign Relations and the Institute for International Economics. He was secretary of commerce during the Nixon administration.

GREGORY J. RATTRAY, Major, U.S. Air Force, is a doctoral candidate at the Fletcher School of Law and Diplomacy, Tufts University, and a research associate at the Institute for Foreign Policy Analysis in Cambridge, Massachusetts. Previously, he was the deputy director of the U.S. Air Force Institute for National Security Studies. He is a coeditor of *Arms Control: Toward the 21st Century.*

DONALD B. RICE was secretary of the U.S. Air Force during the Bush administration. Dr. Rice received his Ph.D. from Purdue University. He has served as chief executive officer of the RAND Corporation and is currently president of Teledyne, a technology-based manufacturing company.

DAVID RONFELDT is a senior social scientist at the RAND Corporation. Dr. Ronfeldt received his Ph.D. from Stanford University and is the author of *Cyberocracy Is Coming* and *Beware the Hubris-Nemesis Complex.*

PAULA L. SCALINGI is a professional staff member for the U.S. House of Representatives Permanent Select Committee on Intelligence. She most recently served as a strategic affairs specialist with the U.S. Arms Control and Disarmament Agency.

JAMES SCHLESINGER is a counselor at the Center for Strategic and International Studies, senior adviser to Lehman Brothers, and chairman of Mitre Corporation. His distinguished government career includes service as secretary of defense, secretary of energy, chairman of the Atomic Energy Commission, and director of central intelligence. Mr. Schlesinger is the author of *America at Century's End.*

BRENT C. SCOWCROFT, Lieutenant General, U.S. Air Force Retired, served as special assistant to the president for national security affairs in the Ford and Bush administrations. He also was chairman of the Department of Political Science at the U.S. Air Force Academy from 1962 to 1964. General Scowcroft is currently president of the Forum for International Policy.

JAMES K. SEBENIUS is an associate professor at Harvard University's John F. Kennedy School of Government. He also is a special adviser to the Blackstone Group.

SARAH B. SEWALL currently serves as deputy assistant secretary of defense for peacekeeping and peace enforcement policy. She holds an M. Phil. from Oxford University, where she studied as a Rhodes Scholar. Prior to being appointed to her current post, Ms. Sewall worked as senior foreign policy adviser to Senator George Mitchell and served as a defense analyst at several private research organizations.

JOHN M. SHALIKASHVILI, General, U.S. Army, is serving as chairman of the Joint Chiefs of Staff. General Shalikashvili received his master's degree from George Washington University and graduated from the Naval Command and Staff College and the U.S. Army War College. Prior to his present position, the general served as commander in chief of the U.S. European Command and as NATO's supreme allied commander, Europe.

JEFFREY SIMON is a senior fellow for the Institute for National Strategic Studies at the National Defense University. Dr. Simon holds a Ph.D. from the University of Washington. Prior to serving at the National Defense University, he was chief of the National Military Strategy Branch and a Soviet threat analyst at the Strategic Studies Institute, U.S. Army War College. Dr. Simon also taught at Georgetown University and held research positions at System Planning Corporation, RAND, and the American Enterprise Institute. His writings include *European Security Policy after the Revolutions of 1989, NATO: The Challenge of Change,* and *Central European Civil–Military Relations and NATO Expansion.*

IKE SKELTON is a Democratic U.S. representative from Missouri. First elected in 1977, Representative Skelton has served on the House Committee on National Security and its Military Procurement and Military Personnel Subcommittees.

DONALD M. SNOW is a professor of political science and international studies at the University of Alabama. He has served as a visiting professor at the Air Command and Staff College, as well as lecturing at all of the military's senior service schools and the U.S. Military Academy. Dr. Snow was awarded a Ph.D. from Indiana University and served as a Secretary of the Navy Senior Research Fellow. He is the author of many works, including *The Necessary Peace: Nuclear Weapons and Superpower Relations* and *The Eagle's Talons: War, Politics, and the American Experience* (with Dennis Drew).

JED SNYDER is the leader of research and analysis for the Middle East/Persian Gulf, South Asia, and the southern regions of the former Soviet Union at the National Defense University's Institute for National Strategic Studies. He currently is directing a new project on the proliferation of weapons of mass destruction and is the author of *Defending the Fringe: NATO, the Mediterranean and the Persian Gulf.*

CARL W. STINER, General, U.S. Army Retired, is the former commander in chief of U.S. Special Operations Command. He graduated from the Army War College and was operational commander of all forces for Operation Just Cause in Panama.

JEFF THOMAS is a general assignment and business journalist for the *Colorado Springs Gazette Telegraph.* In 1994 Mr. Thomas was named journalist of the year by the Colorado Chapter of the Society of Professional Journalists.

JOHN G. TOWER was a Republican U.S. senator from Texas and chairman of the Senate Armed Services Committee. He received his postgraduate degree from the London School of Economics and Politics, where he also served as a research fellow. Senator Tower passed away in 1991.

SHEILA E. WIDNALL is currently serving as the secretary of the U.S. Air Force. She holds a Ph.D. from the Massachusetts Institute of Technology. Secretary Widnall has been a professor of aeronautics and astronautics at MIT for twenty-eight years, and she became an associate provost at the university in 1992. She has also served on many boards, panels, and committees in government, academia, and industry.

HEATHER WILSON is president of Keystone International, Inc., in Albuquerque, New Mexico. A 1982 distinguished graduate from the U.S. Air Force Academy, she was director for defense policy and arms control on the National Security Council Staff during the Bush administration.

PETER A. WILSON is a consultant on international security affairs. He served on the Policy Planning Staff in the U.S. Department of State during the Carter administration.

ABOUT THE EDITORS

PETER L. HAYS, Lieutenant Colonel, U.S. Air Force, is an assistant professor and director of the U.S. Air Force Institute for National Security Studies located at the U.S. Air Force Academy. He holds a Ph.D. in international relations from the Fletcher School of Law and Diplomacy at Tufts University and a master's degree in defense and strategic studies from the University of Southern California. A 1979 honor graduate of the U.S. Air Force Academy, he is a command pilot with over three thousand hours of flying time, primarily in the C-141 Starlifter. He has focused his studies and research on U.S. military space policy by developing an Air Force Academy course on space policy, serving as a research assistant for the Office of Science and Technology Policy and the National Space Council, and writing a dissertation on U.S. military space doctrine.

BRENDA J. VALLANCE, Lieutenant Colonel, U.S. Air Force, is a senior associate professor and deputy department head, Department of Political Science, U.S. Air Force Academy. She holds a Ph.D. in political science from the University of California, Los Angeles, and a master's degree in Soviet Studies from the University of Oklahoma. She was a UCLA/RAND graduate fellow in the Center for Soviet Studies. She has served as an intelligence officer in numerous assignments. Most recently, she served at Headquarters U.S. Air Force, where she was responsible for intelligence support to weapon system acquisitions. She has written on democratization in the Russian military.

ALAN R. VAN TASSEL, Major, U.S. Air Force, is deputy director of the U.S. Air Force Institute for National Security Studies (INSS) located at the U.S. Air Force Academy. He holds a Ph.D. in government and politics from the University of Maryland and a master's degree in political science from Wichita State University. Before his assignment to the INSS, he was an associate professor and director of comparative politics and area studies in the Department of Political Science at the U.S. Air Force Academy. Prior to that, he was a launch control officer for intercontinental ballistic missiles. Major Van Tassel also has worked as a research assistant at the Office of the Secretary of Defense, U.S. Space Command, and the Air Staff.

INDEX